This module contains four sections that help students take the management theories, approaches, and ideas that they've learned in the book and apply them to real management situations.

## Diversity

Have your students practice managing a changing workforce. These interactive exercises put students in the challenging role of a manager making decisions related to age, gender, or ethnic diversity.

## Passport: Managing in a Global Environment

Make globalization come alive for your students. This multimedia module illustrates the globalization challenges that managers face. There are three to four global case scenarios at the ends of Parts Two through Six, spanning thirteen different countries. Students will find a map and click a desired country to get information about that country (video and written information is provided). Using this information, students make decisions about the most appropriate ways to handle the managerial problems described in the case scenarios.

## Ethics

Help students understand the ethical challenges they'll face as managers. In these interactive exercises, students are put in the role of a manager making decisions about current ethical issues.

## PRactical Interactive Skills Modules (PRISM)

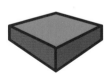

Let students manage. This module consists of 12 interactive decision-tree style comprehensive exercises that provide students with an opportunity to try out different management skills and learn why certain approaches are better than others.

# Go To
# www.prenhall.com/rolls

# Management

#### ninth edition

## Stephen P. Robbins

*San Diego State University*

## Mary Coulter

*Missouri State University*

PEARSON

Prentice
Hall

**Upper Saddle River, NJ 07458**

Library of Congress Cataloging-in Publication Data

Robbins, Stephen P.
    Management / Stephen P. Robbins, Mary Coulter. -- 9th ed.
        p. cm.
    Includes bibliographical references and index.
    ISBN 0-13-225773-4
    1. Management.  I. Coulter, Mary K.  II. Title.

HD31.R5647 2007
658--dc22

2006049824

Senior Acquisitions Editor: Michael Ablassmeir
VP/Editorial Director: Jeff Shelstad
Product Development Manager: Ashley Santora
Assistant Editor: Denise Vaughn
Product Development Manager, Media: Nancy Welcher
Marketing Manager: Anne Howard
Marketing Assistant: Susan Osterlitz
Associate Director, Production Editorial: Judy Leale
Permissions Coordinator: Charles Morris
Associate Director, Manufacturing: Vinnie Scelta
Manufacturing Buyer: Diane Peirano
Design/Composition Manager: Christy Mahon
Composition Liaison: Nancy Thompson
Art Director: Steve Frim
Interior Design: Steve Frim
Cover Design: Steve Frim
Illustration (Interior): Bruce Kilmer
Director, Image Resource Center: Melinda Patelli
Manager, Rights and Permissions: Zina Arabia
Manager: Visual Research: Beth Brenzel
Image Permission Coordinator: Annette Linder
Photo Researcher: Melinda Alexander
Composition: BookMasters, Inc.
Printer/Binder: Quebecor World Color/Versailles
Typeface 10.5/12 New Baskerville

Credits and acknowledgments borrowed from other sources and reproduced, with permission, in this textbook appear on the appropriate page within text.

Pearson Education LTD.
Pearson Education Singapore, Pte. Ltd
Pearson Education, Canada, Ltd
Pearson Education–Japan

Pearson Education Australia PTY, Limited
Pearson Education North Asia Ltd
Pearson Educación de Mexico, S.A. de C.V.
Pearson Education Malaysia, Pte. Ltd.

10 9 8 7 6 5 4 3 2 1
0-13-225773-4

For my whole gang: Laura, Dana, Jenny, Jim, Mallory, Judi, David, Mom, and Lad —SPR

For my mom and dad, Marion and Mildred Maaks . . . you are the best! Thanks for everything! —MC

# About the Authors

**Stephen P. Robbins** (Ph.D., University of Arizona) is professor emeritus of management at San Diego State University and the world's best-selling author of textbooks in both management and organizational behavior. His books are used at more than a thousand U.S. colleges and universities, have been translated into 16 languages, and have adapted editions for Canada, Australia, South Africa, and India. Dr. Robbins is also the author of the best-selling *The Truth About Managing People* (Financial Times/Prentice Hall, 2002) and *Decide & Conquer* (Financial Times/Prentice Hall, 2004).

In his "other life," Dr. Robbins actively participates in masters' track competition. Since turning 50 in 1993, he's won 14 national championships, 11 world titles, and set numerous U.S. and world age-group records at 60, 100, 200, and 400 meters. In 2005, Dr. Robbins was elected into the USA Masters' Track & Field Hall of Fame.

**Mary Coulter** received her Ph.D. in Management from the University of Arkansas in Fayetteville. Before completing her graduate work, she held different jobs including high school teacher, legal assistant, and government program planner. She has taught at Drury University, the University of Arkansas, Trinity University, and since 1983, at Missouri State University. Dr. Coulter's research interests have focused on competitive strategies for not-for-profit arts organizations and the use of new media in the educational process. Her research on these and other topics has appeared in such journals as *International Journal of Business Disciplines, Journal of Business Strategies, Journal of Business Research, Journal of Nonprofit and Public Sector Marketing,* and *Case Research Journal.* In addition to *Management,* Dr. Coulter has published other books with Prentice Hall including *Strategic Management in Action,* now in its third edition, and *Entrepreneurship in Action,* which is in its second edition. When she's not busy teaching or writing, she enjoys puttering around in her flower gardens, playing the piano, reading all different types of books, and enjoying many different activities with husband Ron and daughters Sarah and Katie.

# Brief Contents

# Contents

# Preface

This book is the number-one selling basic management textbook in the United States and the world! It has been translated into Spanish, Russian, Dutch, Thai, Bahasa Indonesian, Czech, and Chinese, and reprinted in English in the Philippines and China, with special adapted editions for Canada, Australia, and India. If there's such a thing as a "global" management textbook, this book probably has earned that distinction.

There's no doubt that the world managers confront has changed, is changing, and will continue to change. The dynamic nature of today's organizations means both rewards *and* challenges for those individuals who will be managing those organizations. Management is a dynamic discipline and a textbook on the subject should reflect those changes to help prepare you to manage under those conditions. Thus, we've written this ninth edition of *Management* to provide you with the best possible understanding of what it means to be a manager confronting these changes.

## Hallmark Features

We want students to "put on their management hat" and see what being a manager is about. Adopters continually praise this book for its strong applications orientation. This book doesn't just describe management theories. In addition to including explanatory examples throughout the chapters (which most other textbooks do), we go out and talk with real managers and bring their experiences to our readers. No other textbook has so successfully blended management theory with management practice. We're confident that the ninth edition will continue to make management concepts meaningful and to excite readers about the possibilities for careers in management. We'd like to describe some of the features we have retained in this edition.

# "A Manager's Dilemma" and "Managers Respond to a Manager's Dilemma"

Each chapter opens with a dilemma that a real-life manager is facing. These managers come from a wide variety of companies—including (among others) UPS, Nike, Ubisoft, the National Football League, Bank of Nova Scotia, and MTV—and eight of the chapter openers are global in nature. Each dilemma ends with the statement "What would you do?" encouraging students to "put on their management hat" and to think about what they actually would do in this situation. Then,

## A Manager's Dilemma

Cash flow. Revenue sharing. Double-digit growth. Leverage. Metrics. That's the language that Kim Williams speaks. As senior vice president of finance for the National Football League (NFL), she may not use the language of play-action pass, pitch sweep, reverse, or quarterback draw in her job, but it's certain that the 32 teams that make up the NFL do. Now she wants them to communicate with—and understand—her language.[1]

The NFL is the organization that oversees professional football, the United States' most popular spectator sport. In its role as a trade association for the member teams, the NFL's primary business units are NFL Properties, which generates billions of dollars through merchandising and licensing deals and NFL Enterprises, which negotiates national broadcasting rights for the teams. Its other subsidiaries include NFL Charities and NFL Films. And in 2003, the league launched its own television channel, the NFL Network, a round-the-clock football network, which football junkies consider a godsend. And, then, of course, there's the Super Bowl—the NFL's extremely popular championship game, which draws in millions of viewers and even millions more dollars. With the average going rate for a 30-second commercial shown during the Super Bowl in the millions (in 2006, it was $2.5 million), the NFL has scored a winner. With the exception of the "wardrobe malfunction" scandal during the 2004 Super Bowl, this annual event highlights the competitive strength of the NFL.

The NFL is considered financially the best-run professional league. Kim says, "One of the underlying strengths of the NFL is that we are a trade association, meaning that the [32 team] clubs are independent entities. So there is a lot of discussion, financially, legally, and from a community standpoint, about what rights are maintained nationally." And as the chief financial officer of the NFL, Kim must communicate regularly with the owners regarding all financial issues.

Put yourself in Kim's shoes. What can she do to improve the effectiveness of her communications with team owners about sometimes complicated and sensitive financial matters?

**What would you do?**

at the end of the chapter, we give students a real-life dose of management as real, practicing managers provide a short discussion of what they'd do if they were faced with the opening dilemma, drawing on the management concepts and tools presented in the chapter.

## Managers Respond to a Manager's Dilemma

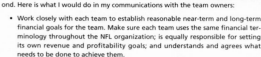

### Faith Tsao, CFA
Director of Traditional External Investments, Atlantic Trust Private Wealth Management, Boston, MA

First, I would not be too concerned about communicating with team owners using football language. Team owners are business people first and football fans second. Here is what I would do in my communications with the team owners:

- Work closely with each team to establish reasonable near-term and long-term financial goals for the team. Make sure each team uses the same financial terminology throughout the NFL organization; is equally responsible for setting its own revenue and profitability goals; and understands and agrees what needs to be done to achieve them.
- Share the big picture. Football team owners understand the importance of teamwork. Specify what collaborative efforts are needed among teams to achieve organizational goals.
- Communicate frequently. Since football is a contact sport, face-to-face communications will work best with team owners. I would organize nationwide conferences every quarter to share progress, ask for feedback, and modify plans when needed.

### James W. Buhler
CFO, Clement Publishing Group, Concordville, PA

Kim should make sure that she and all 32 owners have a crystal clear understanding of all the financial terms and language that they will discuss. One way to do this is to develop a list of standard terms and distribute it to all the owners. It will be a lot easier for her to communicate if all involved parties are using a common language base.

The next step for Kim to undertake is to break down these complicated financial matters to their simplest forms. Because Kim has many years of complex accounting experience behind her, she must remember that her audience may or may not be as financially astute as she is in every situation. By breaking down complex financial matters to their simplest forms, it will allow more of the owners to possess a greater understanding of the communicated message.

Kim should also hold follow-up communications with the owners to make sure that the message she was trying to communicate was received clearly and that all involved parties understood it.

---

## Managers speak out

**Ted V. Schaefer**
**Partner**
**PricewaterhouseCoopers**
**Denver, CO**

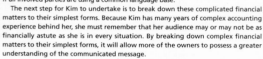

*Describe your job.*

I am a partner in PricewaterhouseCoopers' Denver office, and I work in the System & Process Assurance group. I provide our clients with internal control and process improvement services.

*Why are controls important to your organization?*

Controls are critical to the quality delivery of PricewaterhouseCoopers' audit, tax, and advisory services. We have many professional, regulatory, and internal controls that help to ensure that we meet our goals. Controls provide staff with a clear road map to follow for client service delivery, human resources, career development, client independence, code of conduct, and regulatory and professional rules. Our industry is based on controls that provide staff with the ability to carry out their jobs in an orderly fashion.

*What control issues do you think are particularly important to managers today?*

Continuing business scandals have raised the bar for strong internal controls. The government took a major step in regulating internal control through the enactment of Sarbanes-Oxley, which requires public companies to implement an effective internal control structure that must be externally audited. However, even if Sarbanes-Oxley wasn't law, internal controls are just good business for several reasons. Controls allow companies to manage regulatory compliance and financial and operational activities to meet business goals. They also provide for an orderly environment so management can focus their time on strategic issues. Companies with poor controls are constantly putting out fires, taking away from more important activities. Companies need to align controls with the goals of the organization and ensure they provide a cost benefit.

*What skills do you think managers need to be effective?*

Due to the fast-paced business environment, managers must be lifelong learners to maintain their edge. Soft skills like communication, creativity, and the ability to motivate and challenge employees are equally important for success. Knowing when employees need help or when to stay out of their way is a skill necessary to manage people. It is important to be a good mentor and provide career-enhancing opportunities to employees, so they can continue to grow and advance in their careers.

## "Managers Speak Out"

In selected chapters, you'll find this theme box in which real managers are interviewed and answer a broad range of questions. Some of these managers include the CEO of a large global media company and the finance director of a video game and entertainment retailer based in Germany. The managers profiled in these boxes provide a diverse perspective of managerial philosophies and reinforce that this textbook truly links management theory and practice.

## "Becoming a Manager"

To reinforce our already strong applications orientation and to further encourage students to "put on their management hat," we retained and updated this box theme in every chapter. The "Becoming a Manager" boxes provide suggestions for students on things they can do right now to help them prepare to be managers.

### becoming a Manager

✓ Learn as much as you can about other countries.

✓ Familiarize yourself with current global political, economic, and cultural issues.

✓ If given the opportunity, try to have your class projects or reports (in this class and other classes) cover global issues or global companies.

✓ Talk to professors or students who may be from other countries and ask them what the business world is like in their country.

✓ If you have the opportunity, travel to other countries.

✓ Go see a foreign film.

✓ Go to the Self-Assessment Library found on www.prenhall.com/rolls and complete S.A.L. #III.B.5—Am I Well-Suited for a Career as a Global Manager?

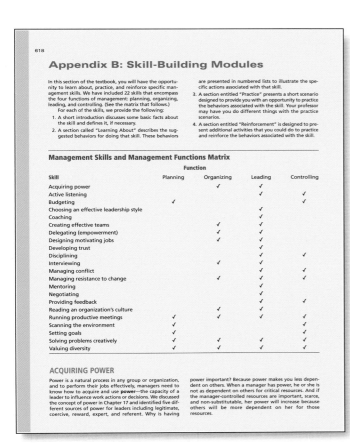

## Skills Modules

Management students need to learn *how to do* management tasks as well as to learn *about* management. Today, the "hows" of being a manager have become just as important as the "whats." To reflect the importance placed on skills, we retained our in-book Skills Modules. The 22 key skills found in the Skill-Building Modules following the Managing Entrepreneurial Ventures appendix encompass the four management functions and provide an excellent way for students to "put on their management hat."

## Writing Style

This revision continues both authors' commitment to presenting management concepts in a lively and conversational style. Our goal is to present chapter material in a way that's interesting and relevant without oversimplifying the discussion. We think you'll find our writing style and numerous examples make our book very readable.

# New to This Edition

We are very excited about the innovations incorporated into *Management 9e!* This is truly a textbook for students in today's changing world. We think one of the reasons this book is the market leader is that it has developed a reputation for continually introducing new content. Some of our new topics include:

- Anticapitalism backlash (Chapters 2 and 4)
- Global outsourcing (Chapters 2 and 4)
- Born globals (Chapter 4)
- Global political risk categories (Chapter 4)
- CAFTA (Chapter 4)
- Social investing funds (Chapter 5)
- Global Reporting Initiative (Chapter 5)
- ISO 14001 (Chapter 5)
- Social entrepreneurship (Chapter 5)
- Cultural differences in decision making (Chapter 6)
- Framing issues (Chapter 7)
- Business models (Chapter 8)
- Corporate reputations ( Chapter 8)
- Strategic flexibility (Chapter 8)
- Strategic leadership (Chapter 8)
- Rolling forecasts (Chapter 9)
- Early warning indicators (Chapter 9)
- Keeping employees connected (Chapter 10)
- Global structural issues (Chapter 10)
- Blogs/wikis/Web conferencing (Chapter 11)
- Impact of demographic trends on human resource management (Chapter 12)
- Workplace romances (Chapter 12)

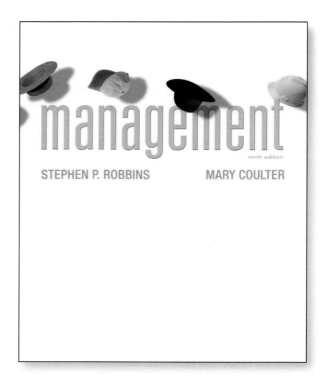

- Controlling HR costs (Chapter 12)
- Global organizational development (Chapter 13)
- Employee stress in different countries (Chapter 13)
- Workplace misbehavior (Chapter 14)
- Impression management (Chapter 14)
- Managing generational differences (Chapter 14)
- Managing negative behaviors in the workplace (Chapter 14)
- Managing global teams (Chapter 15)
- Understanding social networks (Chapter 15)
- Distributed workforce (Chapter 16)
- Workplace privacy (Chapter 18)

**Continuing Case** Sit back, grab a latté, and get ready to discover the challenges of managing a global company . . . Starbucks! At the end of each of the six parts in the book, you'll find a continuing comprehensive case that follows the challenges managers at Starbucks face. These continuing cases, which follow this one company, provide students another opportunity to "put on their management hat" by looking at the big picture issues from a broad perspective and allowing them to see the linkages among the four functions of management.

**Integrative Topics** In addition to this new material, we chose to highlight seven integrative topics in 9e. These topics are **globalization, diversity, ethics, customer service, innovation, IT, and leadership.**

# Exhibit P.1 Integrative Topics

| Chapter | Globalization and Cross-Cultural Differences | Diversity | Ethics | Customer Service | Innovation | IT | Leadership |
|---|---|---|---|---|---|---|---|
| 1 | | | 7, 15 | 15-16 | 16-17 | | 10 |
| 2 | 40-41 | 43-44 | 41-42, 47 | 48-49 | 27, 46-47, 50 | 45-46 | |
| 3 | 78 | 67, 72 | 69-70; 80-82, 86 | 70-71, 74 | 60-61, 69 | | 67-68 |
| 4 | 90-109 | | 102, 111 | | 107-109 | 100 | 103 |
| 5 | 132-135 | | 127, 128-143, 147 | | 122-125, 142-143 | | 126-128, 135-136, 140, 141, 143 |
| 6 | | 172 | 167, 180 | | 159 | 170 | 170-171, 175 |
| 7 | | | 197, 203-204 | | 199-201 | | 185, 188 |
| 8 | 212, 217-219, 226-227 | | 213, 234 | 210-211, 228-229 | 217-219, 221-224 226-227, 229-230 | 216, 228 | 227 |
| 9 | 240 | | 240, 258-259 | | 243, 254-256 | | |
| 10 | 284-285 | | 268, 288-289 | | 275, 283-284 | 283 | 270, 271, 272 |
| 11 | 301 | 300 | 308, 318 | 312-313 | 311-312 | 307-310, 311 | 310-314 |
| 12 | 324 | 342-343 | 333, 352 | | | 340 | 336, 342-347 |
| 13 | 373 | 368 | 370, 379-380 | | 372-376 | | 371-372 |
| 14 | 391, 402 | | 412, 419-420 | 392 | 401 | | 396, 403, 404-405, 409, 414-415 |
| 15 | 440, 442-444 | 428 | 431, 447-448 | | | 433 | 440-442 |
| 16 | 468-469 | 470-471 | 476, 483 | | | | 476-479 |
| 17 | 510-511 | | 506, 508, 509, 518 | | | | 486-514 |
| 18 | 546-547 | 536 | 544, 553-555, 559 | 551-553 | 544-545 | 543-544 | |
| 19 | 565, 566 | | 572, 584 | 568-573, 576-581 | 566-567, 575-576, 580-581 | 570, 572 | 571-572 |
| Part-Ending | 150-151, 152, 260-261, 382-383, 520-521, 586-587 | | 150, 152-153, 260, 382, 520, 586 | 587-588 | 54-55, 261-263, 385 | | 151-152, 522-523 |
| App. A | 592-593 | | 594 | | 591-592, 595-598, 606-607 | 611 | 609-610 |

**"Managing IT"**   In this new box theme, we introduce students to the important role of information technology in the manager's job. From looking at how IT is changing the manager's job to IT's role in company strategy to IT's impact on organizational design, students will see how managing IT is another "hat" that managers need to wear.

**"Focus on Leadership"**   How important is leadership to organizations? Extremely important! Being a successful leader is another of the "hats" that managers need to wear. That's why we added a new box feature focusing on leadership. In this feature we look at those leadership issues that affect the way managers manage such as the role of national culture in leadership, the moral dimensions of leadership, the way leaders frame issues, and the challenges of leading in today's nontraditional organizations.

**Management: By the Numbers**   Did you know that 76 percent of American employees like the work they do but their manager's habits make the workplace less enjoyable? Or that more than half of employees surveyed said that a disagreeable boss was the top reason they leave their job? Want to know more? Check out our new feature called "Management: By the Numbers." Here you'll find interesting tidbits of information and statistics about managers, employees, and organizations. They're a fun way to generate classroom discussion or even to use them to do your own in-class polls.

# HOW DO YOU GET YOUR STUDENTS TO THINK LIKE MANAGERS?

## Robbins OnLine Learning System (R.O.L.L.S.)

A three-part online experience, seamlessly integrated with the book, allowing your students to be more successful in the classroom and beyond.

### Part I: Understand the Concepts

The Q&A section further explains theories that are presented in the book and provides immediate extra help for things that aren't clear.

*Once students understand the material, they move on to . . .*

### Part II: Understand Yourself

Robbin's Self-Assessment Library (S.A.L.) helps students to learn more about themselves—their attitudes, feelings, and aptitudes in regard to a wide range of personal skills, abilities, and interests.

*Equipped with self-awareness, students now get to work . . .*

### Part III: Put On Your Management Hat

Four modules: Diversity, Passport, Ethics, and PRISM help students to apply the concepts they've learned in the text to realistic management situations, and then receive feedback about their choices.

**Go to
www.prenhall.com/rolls**

## Understand the Concepts

"It's 11:30 P.M. I'm sure my management instructor is asleep and office hours aren't for two more days. I can't get my friend on IM—she's probably out having fun. I need some help understanding this path-goal leadership theory we talked about in class today. What do I do now?"

**Q&A** is a 24/7 tutorial for students. The questions from each chapter that students ask most frequently are answered by the authors— in both written and video format. It's like having an instructor standing over their shoulder at the times students need it the most.

Q & A

How can I best prepare if I want to work globally? Q & A 4.3 will give you some suggestions.

### MANAGING IN A GLOBAL ENVIRONMENT

Assume for a moment that you're a manager going to work for a branch of a global organization in a foreign country. You know that your environment will differ from the one at home, but how? What should you be looking for? ( Go to www.prenhall.com/rolls)

Any manager who finds himself or herself in a foreign country faces new challenges. In this section, we'll look at some challenges and offer guidelines for responding. Although our discussion is presented through the eyes of a U.S. manager, our analytical framework could be used by any manager regardless of national origin who has to manage in a foreign environment.

## Understand Yourself

"I wonder if I'm any good at leading teams? I think I'd be good at it because people seem to look to me to make decisions and to help keep our class team projects on target. Let me find out . . ."

**S.A.L.** The Self-Assessment Library (S.A.L.) helps students create a skills portfolio. It is an interactive library of 51 behavioral questionnaires that helps students discover things about themselves, their attitudes, and their personal strengths and weaknesses. Learning more about themselves gives students interesting insights into how they might behave as a manager and motivates them to learn more about management theories and practices that can help them better understand what it takes to be a successful manager.

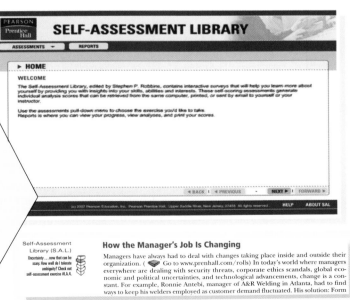

Self-Assessment
Library (S.A.L.)

Uncertainty . . . now that can be scary. How well do I tolerate ambiguity? Check out self-assessment exercise R.A.4.

### How the Manager's Job Is Changing

Managers have always had to deal with changes taking place inside and outside their organization. ( Go to www.prenhall.com/rolls) In today's world where managers everywhere are dealing with security threats, corporate ethics scandals, global economic and political uncertainties, and technological advancements, change is a constant. For example, Ronnie Antebi, manager of A&R Welding in Atlanta, had to find ways to keep his welders employed as customer demand fluctuated. His solution: Form

❝A surf shop in Costa Rica sounds like a winner. But what will the locals think? Will I fit in and get along with the people? And I sure don't want to do anything to harm the coast's natural beauty. What should I do? Should I open one? Do I have the management skills to make this work? ❞

This module contains four sections that help students take the management theories, approaches, and ideas that they've learned in the book and apply them to real management situations.

## Diversity Have your
students practice managing a changing workforce. These interactive exercises put students in the challenging role of a manager making decisions related to age, gender, or ethnic diversity.

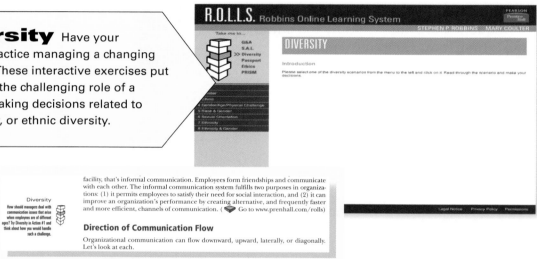

## Passport: Managing in a Global Environment

Make globalization come alive for your students. This multimedia module illustrates the globalization challenges that managers face. There are three to four global case scenarios at the ends of Parts Two through Six, spanning thirteen different countries. Students will find a map and click a desired country to get information about that country (video and written information is provided). Using this information, students make decisions about the most appropriate ways to handle the managerial problems described in the case scenarios.

# Ethics
Help students understand the ethical challenges they'll face as managers. In these interactive exercises, students are put in the role of a manager making decisions about current ethical issues.

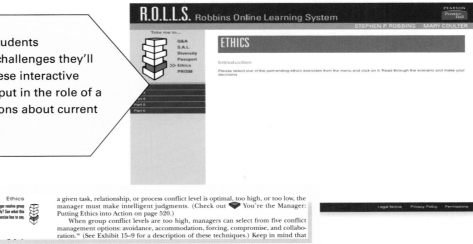

**Ethics**

Can a manager resolve group conflict ethically? See what this Ethics exercise has to say.

a given task, relationship, or process conflict level is optimal, too high, or too low, the manager must make intelligent judgments. (Check out You're the Manager: Putting Ethics into Action on page 520.)

When group conflict levels are too high, managers can select from five conflict management options: avoidance, accommodation, forcing, compromise, and collaboration.[90] (See Exhibit 15–9 for a description of these techniques.) Keep in mind that

# PRactical Interactive Skills Modules (PRISM)
Let students manage. This module consists of 12 interactive decision-tree style comprehensive exercises that provide students with an opportunity to try out different management skills and learn why certain approaches are better than others.

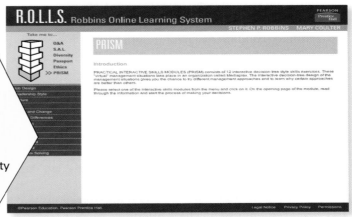

**PRISM**

Want to see how skilled you are at assessing cross-cultural differences? Go to PRISM #6 and give it a try in our virtual company, Mediaplex.

The GLOBE project gives managers additional information to help them identify and manage cultural differences. It extended Hofstede's work—not replaced it. In fact, the GLOBE project confirms that Hofstede's five dimensions are still valid. But it also adds some cultural dimensions and provides us with an updated description of national culture characteristics. ( Go to www.prenhall.com/rolls)

**Global Management in Today's World**

# IN-TEXT LEARNING AIDS

A good textbook should teach as well as present ideas. To that end, we've tried to make this book an effective learning tool. We'd like to point out some specific pedagogical features that we designed to help readers better assimilate the material presented.

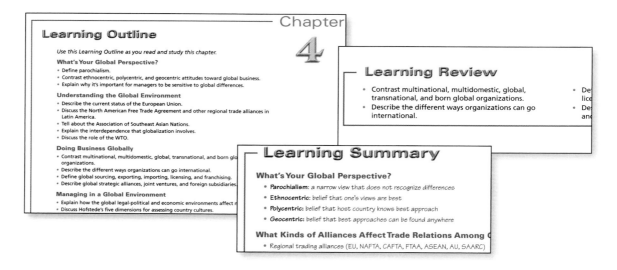

## Learning Outline, Learning Review, and Learning Summary

While most textbooks have learning objectives and a chapter summary, there's no clear link between these and the chapter material. Here's a solution. The chapter-opening "Learning Outline" combines a chapter outline and the learning objectives, so students can see what material they're going to be covering in the chapter. Then, at the end of each major chapter section, students will find a "Learning Review" where they can review the material they just read. Finally, at the end of the chapter, the "Learning Summary" summarizes the important chapter material. This approach helps students focus their attention on the major issues within each chapter.

## Thinking About Management Issues

At the end of every chapter you'll find questions that are designed to get you to think about management issues. These questions require you to demonstrate that you not only know the key facts but also can apply those facts in dealing with more complex issues.

## Working Together: Team-Based Exercise

The pervasiveness of teamwork in organizations led us to design a team-based exercise at the end of every chapter that explores and builds on concepts or theories presented in the chapter.

## Thinking Critically About Ethics

Being able to think critically about issues is important for managers. In the body of each chapter, you'll find a "Thinking Critically About Ethics" box. This learning aid provides material that stresses the ethical values in managerial decisions.

## Ethical Dilemma Exercise

Highly publicized ethics scandals of recent years have reemphasized the importance of managerial and organizational ethics. In addition to our "Thinking Critically About Ethics" boxes found in each chapter, we've added end-of-chapter ethics exercises that introduce students to current and real ethical dilemmas faced by managers.

## Case Application and Questions

Each chapter includes a case application and questions for analysis. A case is simply a description of a real-life situation. By reading and analyzing the case and answering the questions at the end of the case, you can see if you understand and can apply the management concepts discussed in the chapter. Six of these chapter case applications are about global companies.

## Key Terms

Every chapter highlights a number of key terms you'll need to know. These terms are highlighted in bold print when they first appear. Then, to make finding and studying these terms easier, just look for them on the lower right-hand pages throughout a chapter.

# SUPPLEMENTS

The ninth edition supplements package has been designed to help you understand all the wonderful tools that are available and how best to integrate the media, technology, and test questions for your classroom needs.

- ## Instructor's Manual

- ## Test Item File

    The completely revamped, reviewed, and accuracy-checked Test Item File includes new multiple-choice, true/false, scenario-based, discussion, and comprehensive essay questions. The Test Item File is available in print and in electronic formats through the Instructor Resource Center.

- ## Instructor's Resource CD-ROM

    Contains the electronic testing software, PowerPoints, Instructor's Manual, and Test Item File.

- ## Test Gen Test Generating Software

- ## Study Guide

- ## R.O.L.L.S. (Robbins OnLine Learning System) Web Site (www.prenhall.com/rolls)

    Features (1) Q&A, (2) Self-Assessment Library (S.A.L.), (3) Diversity, (4) Passport, (5) Ethics, and (6) PRISM (Practical Interactive Skills Modules). The R.O.L.L.S. Web site has been completely revised and is now easier to navigate.

- ## Companion Website (www.prenhall.com/robbins)

    Featuring an interactive study guide for students.

- ## OneKey *Online Resources*

    OneKey gives you access to the best teaching and learning resources all in one place. OneKey for Robbins/Coulter *Management,* Ninth Edition, is all your students need for anywhere–anytime access to your course materials.
    - OneKey is all you need to plan and administer your course.
    - All your instructor resources are in one place to simplify your course preparation.
    - OneKey for convenience, simplicity, and success . . . for you and your students.

    For more information, visit www.prenhall.com/robbins.

- ## Online Courses

    WebCT, Course Compass, and Blackboard contents are available with this text.

- ## VangoNotes in MP3 Format

    Students can study on the go with VangoNotes, chapter reviews in downloadable MP3 format that offer brief audio segments for each chapter:
    - Big Ideas: the vital ideas in each chapter
    - Practice Test: lets students know if they need to keep studying
    - Key Terms: audio "flashcards" that review key concepts and terms
    - Rapid Review: a quick drill session—helpful right before tests

    Students can learn more at www.vangonotes.com.

# NEW VIDEO PACKAGE

Prentice Hall is committed to providing you with the most up-to-date principles of management video library! These videos are tied to the most pertinent topics in management today—highlighting cutting-edge companies, not-for-profits, and entrepreneurial enterprises.

Our goal is to provide you with video segments that highlight relevant issues in the news, illustrating how people lead, manage, and work effectively. Following are the descriptions of some of the exciting segments included in *Management* 9e's video library.

**JetBlue.** CEO David Neeleman refers to JetBlue as a service company, not an airline. Launched in February 2000 with a $130 million investment from Weston Presidio Capital, Chase Capital, and George Soros, JetBlue turned a profit within the first six months. Accustomed to the cutthroat environment of low-cost carriers, Neeleman based his business model on doing more with fewer employees, buying brand-new planes that cost less to maintain, leather seats that "cost twice as much but last twice as long," and providing 24 channels of free live satellite TV at every seat.

**American Apparel.** One look at American Apparel and anyone can see it's not your average garment factory. Nestled among the sewing machines are happy workers enjoying an afternoon massage. In the distance you can hear the roar of a crowd. No, they're not  grumbling about wages or staging a walkout. It's actually a pep rally led by American Apparel's fearless and somewhat eccentric leader, Dov. At this T-shirt manufacturer, every employee's well-being is valued—whether you're a product designer or moving boxes in the warehouse. All this attention to people makes it possible for American Apparel to be innovative and risk taking. And, it allows it to make some of best shirts on the planet.

**Army Boot Camp.** One glimpse into army boot camp and it's not too hard to find adjectives to describe its culture. Discipline reigns supreme. Boot camp is designed to slowly break down the recruits until they submit to the highly structured and controlled world of the military. It sounds like torture and yet high-ranking officers assert that this rigorous orientation is essential in order for recruits to graduate from basic training ready to serve.

**Patagonia.** Yvon Chouinard founded Patagonia more than 20 years ago, making climbing gear by hand for his friends. In addition to its commitment to customers—"serious users who rely on the product in extreme conditions"—the firm also is responsible to its employees, providing a family-friendly workplace, and to the environment, donating millions of dollars to grassroots environmentalist groups in the United States and abroad.

**Massachusetts General Hospital.** All you have to do is catch one episode of ER to know that a hospital is a hectic place. In the high-stakes world of medicine, a simple error can mean life or death. At Boston's renowned Massachusetts General Hospital, they're trying to change all that. Through the use of a wireless network, barcode scanners, desktop stations, and an intranet database of patient information, Mass General and its affiliates are able to have all the patient info electronically at their fingertips. No more handwritten charts, insurance nightmares, or medicine mix-ups. You even can have your medical records zapped directly to a new doctor when it matters most—in an emergency.

**Ernst & Young.** Work's a drag, but that's life in the big city. At Ernst & Young, life just got a little bit better for its 160,000 employees around the world. By putting "people first," Ernst and Young has been able to improve the lives of its employees both on the job and off. Providing flexible work schedules allows Ernst & Young's employees to spend a little more time in the business of life without sacrificing service to their clients.

**Fired for Being Fat.** The Borgata Hotel, Casino, and Spa in Atlantic City, New Jersey, threatens to suspend or fire cocktail servers and bartenders if they put on too much weight. A former female employee describes what it was like to work in an environment in which her body size was constantly monitored. Is this kind of company policy legal and what does it say about the values of the organization?

**Dr. Martens.** Dr. Martens makes shoes that say something about the wearer. Whether they're old or young, fans of the 40-year-old firm are proud to own distinctive footwear that speaks to the rebellious spirit in them and proclaims them as out of the ordinary. Dr. Martens' management feels a strong responsibility to its workforce and believes that developing employees is good for individuals *and* for the firm. Listen as Howard Johnstone, group administration director and company secretary, discusses values, attitudes, and motivation at this popular footwear company.

**Surfer Girl Makes Comeback.** Bethany Hamilton was well on her way to becoming a professional surfer when tragedy struck. While waiting to catch a wave one Halloween morning, a shark attacked Bethany and bit off her entire left arm. After this traumatic event, Bethany's attitude helped her heal both emotionally and physically, and it propelled her back into the water where she still competes as surfer.

**Bullies on the Job.** Every school has its share of bullies, but it turns out some of the kids grow up to be bullies at work too. About one out of every six people experiences psychological abuse in the workplace. Gary Namie, the author of a book called *The Bully at Work,* explains the phenomenon and provides some advice on how to confront the problem.

**WNBA.** Ever hear the old expression, "There are no small parts, just small actors?" Spend a day with the WNBA's Connecticut Sun and you'll be a believer. In basketball and business alike, it's a team game—whether you're making that 3-point shot at the buzzer, icing down an ankle at halftime, or arranging travel. On this team, everyone shines.

**Body Glove.** This well-known maker of wetsuits has expanded to other products ranging from cell phone covers to resort hotels. How did it get there? Interviews with Scott Daley (vice president of marketing) and Russ Lesser (president) explain how the company came up with its product ideas, where it found the materials used in many of its products, and how services (like diving cruises) fit into the whole picture.

# ACKNOWLEDGMENTS

Every author relies on the comments of reviewers, and ours were particularly helpful. We want to thank the following people for their insightful and helpful comments and suggestions for the ninth edition of *Management:*

Jenell Bramlage, University of Northwestern Ohio

Mary Ann Edwards, College of Mount St. Joseph

Bruce Fischer, Elmhurst College

William Laing, Anderson College

James Mazza, Middlesex Community College

Clint Relyea, University of Arkansas

Eva Smith, Spartanburg Technical College

Carolyn Waits, Cincinnati State University

In addition, we would like to thank the reviewers of previous editions. Their contributions are appreciated.

## Eighth Edition

Louis Firenze, Northwood University

Les Ledger, Central Texas College

Henry C. Bohleke, San Juan College

Henry Jackson, Delaware County Community College

Michele Fritz, DeAnza College

Barbara Foltz, Clemson University

Wendy Wysocki, Monroe Community College

Corey Moore, Angelo State University

Jacqueline H. Bull, Immaculata University

Kathleen Jones, University of North Dakota

Phillip Flamm, Angelo State University

James C. Hayton, Utah State University

Clint Relyea, Arkansas State University

James Salvucci, Curry College

Bobbie Chan, Open University of Hong Kong

William H. Kirchman, Fayetteville Technical Community College

Ellis L. Langston, Texas Tech University

Susan D. Looney, Delaware Technical and Community College

Patrick Rogers, North Carolina A&T University

Rhonda Palladi, Georgia State University

Michelle Reavis, University of Alabama Huntsville

Don C. Mosley, Jr., University of South Alabama

Marvin Karlins, University of South Florida

Allen D. Engle, Sr., Eastern Kentucky University

Wei He, Indiana State University

Jay Christensen-Szalanski, University of Iowa

Robert W. Hanna, California State University, Northridge

Charles Stubbart, Southern Illinois University

Sandy J. Miles, Murray State University

James F. Cashman, The University of Alabama

H. Gregg Hamby, University of Houston

Frank Hamilton, University of South Florida

Dena M. Stephenson, Calhoun Community College

Tan Eng, Ngee Ann Polytechnic

## Seventh Edition

W.L. Loh, Mohawk Valley Community College

Lavelle Mills, West Texas A&M University

Elliot M. Ser, Barry University

Anne C. Cowden, California State University, Sacramento

Russell Kent, Georgia Southern University

Roy Cook, Fort Lewis College

Judson C. Faurer, Metro State College

Phyllis G. Holland, Valdosta State College

Diane L. Ferry, University of Delaware

Aline Arnold, Eastern Illinois University

Janice Feldbauer, Austin Community College

Donald Conlon, University of Delaware

Gary L. Whaley, Norfolk State University

James Spee, The Claremont Graduate School

Joseph F. Michlitsch, Southern Illinois University-Edwardsville

John L. Kmetz, University of Delaware

Suhail Abboushi, Duquesne State

Philip M. VanAuken, Baylor University

Augustus B. Colangelo, Penn State

Dale M. Feinauer, University of Wisconsin, Oshkosh

**Sixth Edition**

Daniel Cochran, Mississippi State University

Ram Subramanian, Grand Valley State University

Gary Kohut, University of North Carolina at Charlotte

Thomas Deckleman, Owens Community College

Victor Preisser, Golden Gate University

Robb Bay, Community College of Southern Nevada

Claudia Daumer, California State University – Chico

Anne M. O'Leary-Kelly, Texas A&M University

Frank Tomassi, Johnson & Wales University

James McElroy, Iowa State University

Ernest Bourgeois, Castleton State College

Sharon Clinebell, University of N. Colorado

Thomas Clark, Xavier University

**Fifth Edition**

June Freund, Pittsburgh State University

James Robinson, The College of New Jersey

Rick Moron, University of California, Berkeley

Bill Walsh, University of Illinois

Andy Kein, Keller Graduate School of Management

Daivd Kennedy, Berkeley School of Business

Jim Jones, University of Nebraska, Omaha

Rick Castaldi, San Francisco State University

**Fourth Edition**

Isaiah O. Ugboro, North Carolina A&T State University

Emilia S. Westney, Texas Tech University

Shelia Pechinski, University of Maine

Tracy Huneycutt Sigler, Western Washington University

Thomas G. Thompson, University of Maryland, University College

Gary M. Lande, Montana State University

Charles V. Goodman, Texas A&M University

Bobbie Williams, Georgia Southern University

Joseph Atallah, Devry Institute of Technology

Roger R. Stanton, California State University

Regardless of how good a manuscript is that we turn in, it's only a few computer files until our team at Prentice Hall swings into action. This team of editors, production experts, technology whizzes, designers, marketing specialists, and sales representatives turn those digital characters into a bound textbook and see that it gets into faculty and students' hands. Our thanks to the folks making this book "go" include Michael Ablassmeir, Anne Howard, Judy Leale, Denise Vaughn, Melissa Yu, Elisa Adams, Melinda Alexander, Steve Frim, Charles Morris, Diane Peirano, and Jeff Shelstad. In addition, we would like to thank Carol Harvey of Assumption College and June Allard of Worcester State College, who are diversity experts and authors of *Understanding and Managing Diversity: Readings, Cases, and Exercises, Third Edition* (Prentice Hall, 2005), for taking our ideas for the interactive diversity exercises on R.O.L.L.S. and making them the outstanding feature they are. Also, we want to thank Marian Wood for developing and writing the wonderful end-of-chapter ethics exercises and interactive ethics exercises on R.O.L.L.S.

A special THANK YOU! goes to Anita Looney who coordinated the responses from our "real-life" managers. We also appreciate and thank all of those managers who so graciously gave of their time to either be part of the "Managers Speak Out" feature or the "Managers Respond to a Manager's Dilemma" feature. Without their contributions, our belief in showing managers as real people would be hard to do.

Finally, Steve would like to thank his wife Laura for her encouragement and support. Mary would like to acknowledge and thank her extremely understanding and supportive husband, Ron, and their beautiful and talented daughters, Sarah and Katie.

# Chapter 1

## Learning Outline

*Use this Learning Outline as you read and study this chapter.*

### Who Are Managers?

- Explain how managers differ from nonmanagerial employees.
- Describe how to classify managers in organizations.

### What Is Management?

- Define management.
- Explain why efficiency and effectiveness are important to management.

### What Do Managers Do?

- Describe the four functions of management.
- Explain Mintzberg's managerial roles.
- Describe Katz's three managerial skills and how the importance of these skills changes depending on managerial level.
- Discuss the changes that are impacting managers' jobs.
- Explain why customer service and innovation are important to the manager's job.

### What Is an Organization?

- Describe the characteristics of an organization.
- Explain how the concept of an organization is changing.

### Why Study Management?

- Explain the universality of management concept.
- Discuss why an understanding of management is important.
- Describe the rewards and challenges of being a manager.

# Introduction to Management and Organizations

## A Manager's Dilemma

"The one error that people make early on in their careers is that they're very selective about opportunities, so they avoid some, prefer others. I always accepted all opportunities that presented themselves because from each one you can learn something, and they serve as a platform for future endeavors." This philosophy has guided Jovita Carranza in her career at United Parcel Service (UPS) from her first job in 1976 as a part-time night-shift clerk at the Los Angeles hub to her current position as vice president of air operations, where she manages the world's largest package distribution facility in Louisville, Kentucky.[1] This $1.1 billion facility serves as the hub of UPS's international air operation, and it is massive—4 million square feet, covering a size of more than 80 football fields, containing 17,000 conveyors that can handle 304,000 packages an hour, and housing computers that process nearly 1 million transactions a minute. And, it's all Jovita's responsibility. In this position, she manages half of the more than 25,000 employees in Louisville and every aspect of the hub's operation from technology and engineering to security and human resources.

Although she's a woman (and an Hispanic woman, at that) in a male-dominated industry, Jovita's determination, drive, innovation, and leadership have helped her succeed. But she is the first to acknowledge the important role her team plays. She has surrounded herself with capable, skilled employees who are loyal to the company and committed to results. She says, "I have total reliance on the coordination of my team. . . . I can rely on my staff to stay on top of what they have responsibility for . . . and it's that trust factor that keeps you driven." However, Jovita doesn't just interact with her direct-reporting team. She remembers her early days of loading packages and realizes how important it is for her to also personally visit with frontline workers. "I value the input of the staff and the frontline workers. One of my [approaches] is to sit back and listen and observe. You learn more by not speaking. . . ."

Jovita's goals for the hub include continuing to find ways to be efficient and to contain costs and continually developing her employees' abilities. Put yourself in her shoes. What skills will be most important for Jovita to encourage her first-line supervisors to develop to help reach these goals?

## What would you do?

Jovita Carranza is a good example of what today's successful managers are like and the skills they must have in dealing with the problems and challenges of managing in the twenty-first century. These managers may not be who or what you might expect! They may be under the age of 18 or over age 80. They run large corporations as well as entrepreneurial start-ups. They're found in government departments, hospitals, small businesses, not-for-profit agencies, museums, schools, and even such nontraditional organizations as political campaigns and consumer cooperatives. Managers can also be found doing managerial work in every country around the globe. Too, some managers are top-level managers while others are first-line managers; today, they are just as likely to be women as they are men. Although women are well represented in the lower and middle levels of management, the number of women in top executive positions remains low. Data collected by Catalyst, a nonprofit research group, found that women hold 50.3 percent of all management and professional positions; however, only 1.4 percent of Fortune 500 CEOs are women.[2] Many organizations, though, including Southwest Airlines, PepsiCo, Nordstrom, Avon, Kraft Foods, Xerox, and Pfizer, have taken significant steps to attract and promote female executives. No matter where managers are found or what gender they are, the fact is that managers have exciting and challenging jobs. And organizations need managers more than ever in these uncertain, complex, and chaotic times. Managers do matter! How do we know that managers matter to organizations? The Gallup Organization, which has polled millions of employees and tens of thousands of managers, has found that the single most important variable in employee productivity and loyalty isn't pay or benefits or workplace environment; it's the quality of the relationship between employees and their direct supervisors.[3] In addition, Watson Wyatt Worldwide, a global consulting firm, found in its WorkUSA 2004/2005 study that the way a company manages its people can significantly affect its financial performance.[4] We can conclude from these reports that it pays to manage people right.

This book is about the important managerial work that Jovita Carranza and the millions of other managers like her do. It recognizes the reality facing today's managers—that the world has changed and thus is redefining how work is done in organizations and the relationships between workers and managers. In workplaces of all types—offices, restaurants, retail stores, factories, and the like—new technologies and new ways of organizing work are altering old approaches. Today's successful managers must blend tried-and-true management methods with new approaches. In this chapter, we introduce you to managers and management by looking at who managers are, what management is, what managers do, and what an organization is. Finally, we'll wrap up the chapter by discussing why it's important to study management.

## WHO ARE MANAGERS?

It used to be fairly simple to define who managers were: They were the organizational members who told others what to do and how to do it. It was easy to differentiate *managers* from *nonmanagerial employees*; the latter term described those organizational members who worked directly on a job or task and had no one reporting to them. But it isn't quite that simple anymore. The changing nature of organizations and work has, in many organizations, blurred the distinction between managers and nonmanagerial employees. Many traditional nonmanagerial jobs now include managerial activities.[5] (  Go to www.prenhall.com/rolls) For example, managerial responsibilities are

Q & A
Did you ever wonder why managers are needed in organizations? Go to Q & A 1.1 and find out.

We have integrated many exercises from the **R**obbins **O**nline **L**earning **S**ystem (R.O.L.L.S.), found on ***www.prenhall.com/rolls***, throughout this text. These exercises are called out by a color that is keyed to a particular section of the R.O.L.L.S. Web site. When you see the color bar, go to ***www.prenhall.com/rolls*** to find an exercise that relates to the topic being discussed.

### Understand the Concepts

**Q & A** When you see this ⬥ click on Q & A, your 24/7 educational assistant. These video clips and written material presented by your authors address questions that we have found students frequently ask.

### Understand Yourself

**S.A.L. (Self-Assessment Library)** When you see this ⬥ click on S.A.L. and complete the suggested self-assessment exercise. These exercises will help you discover things about yourself, your attitudes, and your personal strengths and weaknesses.

### Put On Your Management Hat

**Diversity**—When you see this ⬥ click on Diversity to find an exercise that puts you in the role of a manager making a decision about diversity.

**Passport**—When you see this ⬥ click on Passport to find information about thirteen different countries. You'll use this information to complete the Passport case scenarios found at the end of Parts Two–Six.

**Ethics**—When you see this ⬥ click on Ethics to find an interactive exercise that puts you in the role of a manager making decisions about ethical issues.

**PRISM**—When you see this ⬥ click on PRISM (PRactical Interactive Skills Modules). These interactive decision-tree style exercises provide you with an opportunity to tyr out different management skills and to learn why certain approaches are better than others.

---

shared by managers and team members at General Cable Corporation's facility in Moose Jaw, Saskatchewan, Canada. Most of the employees at Moose Jaw are cross-trained and multiskilled. Within a single shift, an employee can be a team leader, equipment operator, maintenance technician, quality inspector, or improvement planner.[6]

How *do* we define who managers are? A **manager** is someone who coordinates and oversees the work of other people so that organizational goals can be accomplished. A manager's job is not about *personal* achievement—it's about helping *others* do their work. That may mean coordinating the work of a departmental group, or it might mean supervising a single person. It could involve coordinating the work activities of a team composed of people from several different departments or even people outside the organization, such as temporary employees or employees who work for the organization's suppliers. Keep in mind, also, that managers may have other work duties not related to coordinating the work of others. For example, an insurance claims supervisor may also process claims in addition to coordinating the work activities of other claims clerks.

Is there some way to classify managers in organizations? In traditionally structured organizations (which are said to be shaped like a pyramid because there are more

**manager**
Someone who coordinates and oversees the work of other people so that organizational goals can be accomplished.

# Managers *speak out*

**Marjorie Scardino, CEO**
**Pearson PLC**
**London, England**

*Describe your job.*

I am the CEO of a media company that publishes books, newspapers and magazines, and educational materials—both textbooks and online programs. We're all about "education" in the broadest sense of the word: education for a five-year-old learning to read, a CEO understanding the way his or her industry is heading, an investor picking a stock, or a college student studying a course like the one you're in now. The company has total sales of about $7,045M (in U.K. numbers, that's $7 billion and $45 million), employs some 30,000 people, has headquarters in London and New York, and makes about 70 percent of its sales in the United States.

My job has three main parts:

1. *Strategy.* It's my responsibility to figure out what the company should do to become more valuable and to produce returns for shareholders, as well as to add something to the world. To do this, we have to look at our assets and our markets and the relevant economic, political, and social trends and decide on the most promising combination of those factors. Then, we have to create a plan for shaping the business into that combination and making sure that our products, sales, and operations are all consistent with that plan.

2. *Execution.* No matter how good our strategy, we won't get very far if we can't carry out our plan. That involves innovative product design, ingenious market-ing strategy, irresistible sales skills, and efficient and engaging customer service. It involves judicious attention to the costs of conceiving, making, selling, and delivering our products, and keeping the right balance between growth and costs. It involves making the pursuit of the plan a process that we can measure and monitor and constantly adjust. It involves knowing when to take a risk.

3. *Culture and people.* Finally, and possibly most importantly, my job is to set the tone for a company environment and way of behaving in which we can all be most productive and to exemplify that culture myself. The ingredients in culture include everything from pay and benefits to communicating with each other to how we deal with outsiders and how we treat each other inside. A company's culture is important in determining whether we can attract and keep the best people and whether, when situations are confusing, our employees know how they must behave.

*Why are managers important to organizations?*

Managers set the goals, the agenda, the measures of achievement, and the standards of behavior. In the most successful organizations, they do all that by setting an example, inspiring and orchestrating in a democratic rather than an autocratic way.

*What skills do managers need to be effective in today's environment?*

The ability to see the bigger picture, concentration, parallel thinking, ability to see connections, listening, sense of humor, risk taking, humility, and generosity.

**Q & A**

Does this pyramidal shape describe all organizations? Q & A 1.2 explains.

employees at lower organizational levels than at upper organizational levels), managers are often described as first-line, middle, or top. These managers may have a variety of titles (see Exhibit 1–1). ( ▼ Go to www.prenhall.com/rolls) **First-line managers**, the lowest level of management, manage the work of nonmanagerial employees who typically are involved with producing the organization's products or servicing the organization's customers. First-line managers often have the title of *supervisor*, but they may also be called *shift managers, district managers, department managers, office managers,* or even *foreperson.* **Middle managers** include all levels of management between the first level and the top level of the organization. These managers manage the work of first-line

Exhibit 1–1

**Managerial Levels**

Top Managers
Middle Managers
First-Line Managers
Nonmanagerial Employees

managers and may have titles such as *regional manager, project leader, plant manager,* or *division manager.* At or near the upper levels of the organizational structure are the **top managers**, who are responsible for making organization-wide decisions and establishing the plans and goals that affect the entire organization. These individuals typically have titles such as *executive vice president, president, managing director, chief operating officer, chief executive officer,* or *chairperson.* In the opening case, Jovita Carranza is a top-level manager. She holds the title of vice president. Marjorie Scardino, profiled in "Managers Speak Out," is also a top-level manager. Both are involved in creating and implementing broad and comprehensive changes that affect the entire organization.

Not all organizations get work done by using this traditional pyramidal form, however. Some organizations, for example, are more loosely configured with work being done by ever-changing teams of employees who move from one project to another as work demands arise. Although it's not as easy to tell who the managers are in these organizations, we do know that someone must fulfill that role—that is, there must be someone who coordinates and oversees the work of others, even if that "someone" changes as work tasks or projects change.

## Learning Review

- Explain how managers differ from nonmanagerial employees.
- Describe how to classify managers in organizations.

## WHAT IS MANAGEMENT?

Simply speaking, management is what managers do. But that simple statement doesn't tell us much, does it? A better explanation is that **management** involves coordinating and overseeing the work activities of others so that their activities are completed efficiently and effectively. We already know that coordinating and overseeing the work of others is what distinguishes a managerial position from a nonmanagerial one. However, this doesn't mean that managers can do what they want anytime, anywhere, or in any way. Instead, management involves ensuring that work activities are completed efficiently and effectively by the people responsible for doing them, or at least that's what managers aspire to do.

### *thinking critically about* **Ethics**

How far should a manager go to achieve efficiency or effectiveness? Suppose that you're the catering manager at a local country club and you're asked by the club manager to lie about information on the number of attendees at the events your work group has catered. Suppose that by lying you'll save an employee's job. Is that okay? What about saving five employees' jobs? Is lying always wrong, or might it be acceptable under certain circumstances? What, if any, would those circumstances be? What about simply misrepresenting information that you have? Is that always wrong, or might it be acceptable under certain circumstances? When does "misrepresenting" become "lying"?

**first-line managers**
Managers at the lowest level of the organization that manage the work of nonmanagerial employees.

**middle managers**
Managers between the first level and the top level of the organization who manage the work of first-line managers.

**top managers**
Managers at or near the upper levels of the organization structure who are responsible for making organization-wide decisions and establishing the goals and plans that affect the entire organization.

**management**
Coordinating and overseeing the work activities of others so that their activities are completed efficiently and effectively.

Exhibit 1–2

**Efficiency and Effectiveness in Management**

Efficiency (Means)

Resource Usage

Low Waste

Effectiveness (Ends)

Goal Attainment

High Attainment

Management Strives for:
Low Resource Waste (high efficiency)
High Goal Attainment (high effectiveness)

**Efficiency** refers to getting the most output from the least amount of inputs. Because managers deal with scarce inputs—including resources such as people, money, and equipment—they're concerned with the efficient use of those resources. For instance, at the HON Company plant in Cedartown, Georgia, where employees make and assemble steel and wooden office furniture, efficient manufacturing techniques were implemented by doing things such as cutting inventory levels, decreasing the amount of time to manufacture products, and lowering product reject rates. These efficient work practices paid off as the plant not only reduced costs by over $7 million in one year, but also was named one of *Industry Week's* best plants for 2005.[7] Efficiency is often referred to as "doing things right"—that is, not wasting resources. However, it's not enough just to be efficient. Management is also concerned with being effective, completing activities so that organizational goals are attained. **Effectiveness** is often described as "doing the right things"—that is, doing those work activities that will help the organization reach its goals. For instance, at the HON Company, goals included meeting customers' increasingly stringent needs, executing world-class manufacturing strategies, and making employee jobs easier and safer. Through various work methods and programs, these goals were pursued *and* achieved. Whereas efficiency is concerned with the *means* of getting things done, effectiveness is concerned with the *ends*, or attainment of organizational goals (see Exhibit 1–2). Management is concerned, then, not only with getting activities completed and meeting organizational goals (effectiveness) but also with doing so as efficiently as possible. In successful organizations, high efficiency and high effectiveness typically go hand in hand. (  Go to www.prenhall.com/rolls) Poor management is most often due to both inefficiency and ineffectiveness or to effectiveness achieved through inefficiency.

Q & A

Want to know more about efficiency and effectiveness? Check out Q & A 1.3 for additional information.

## Learning Review

- Define management.
- Explain why efficiency and effectiveness are important to management.

## WHAT DO MANAGERS DO?

Describing what managers do isn't easy or simple. Just as no two organizations are alike, no two managers' jobs are alike. Despite this fact, management researchers have, after many years of study, developed three specific categorization schemes to describe what managers do: functions, roles, and skills. In this section, we'll examine each of these approaches and take a look at how the manager's job is changing.

### Management Functions

According to the functions approach, managers perform certain activities as they efficiently and effectively coordinate the work of others. What are these activities or functions? In the early part of the twentieth century, Henri Fayol, a French industrialist,

Exhibit 1–3

**Management Functions**

| Planning | Organizing | Leading | Controlling |
|---|---|---|---|

*Lead to →*

| Defining goals, establishing strategy, and developing plans to coordinate activities | Determining what needs to be done, how it will be done, and who is to do it | Motivating, leading, and any other actions involved in dealing with people | Monitoring activities to ensure that they are accomplished as planned | Achieving the organization's stated purposes |
|---|---|---|---|---|

first proposed that all managers perform five functions: planning, organizing, commanding, coordinating, and controlling.[8] In the mid-1950s, a management textbook first used the functions of planning, organizing, staffing, directing, and controlling as a framework. Today, most management textbooks (including this one) are still organized around the basic management functions, which now include planning, organizing, leading, and controlling (see Exhibit 1–3). Let's briefly look at each function.

If you have no particular destination in mind, then you can take any road. However, if you have someplace in particular you want to go, you've got to plan the best way to get there. Because organizations exist to achieve some particular purpose, someone must clearly define that purpose and the means for its achievement. Management is that someone. As managers engage in **planning**, they define goals, establish strategies for achieving those goals, and develop plans to integrate and coordinate activities.

Managers are also responsible for arranging and structuring work to accomplish the organization's goals. We call this function **organizing**. When managers organize, they determine what tasks are to be done, who is to do them, how the tasks are to be grouped, who reports to whom, and where decisions are to be made.

Every organization includes people, and a manager's job is to work with and through people to accomplish organizational goals. This is the **leading** function. When managers motivate subordinates, help resolve work group conflicts, influence individuals or teams as they work, select the most effective communication channel, or deal in any way with employee behavior issues, they are leading.

The final management function is **controlling**. After the goals and plans are set (planning), the tasks and structural arrangements determined (organizing), and the people hired, trained, and motivated (leading), there has to be some evaluation of whether things are going as planned. To ensure that goals are being met and that work is being completed as it should be, managers must monitor and evaluate performance. Actual performance must be compared with the previously set goals. If there are significant deviations, it's management's job to get work performance back on track. This process of monitoring, comparing, and correcting is what we mean by the controlling function.

Just how well does the functions approach describe what managers do? Do managers always plan, organize, lead, and then control? In reality, what a manager does may not always happen in this sequence. But that doesn't negate the importance of these functions. Regardless of the order in which they're performed, the fact is that managers do plan, organize, lead, and control as they manage. To illustrate, look back at the opening case. How was Jovita Carranza involved in planning, organizing, leading, and controlling? Planning can be seen in her goals for the Louisville hub of finding ways to be efficient and contain costs and to continually develop her employees' abilities. An example of organizing can be seen in the way in which Jovita has surrounded herself with people who can be trusted to stay on top of what they're responsible for. Leading can be seen in the way Jovita gets input from the staff and frontline workers

**efficiency**
Doing things right, or getting the most output from the least amount of inputs.

**effectiveness**
Doing the right things, or completing activities so that organizational goals are attained.

**planning**
Management function that involves defining goals, establishing strategies for achieving those goals, and developing plans to integrate and coordinate activities.

**organizing**
Management function that involves arranging and structuring work to accomplish the organization's goals.

**leading**
Management function that involves working with and through people to accomplish organizational goals.

**controlling**
Management function that involves monitoring, comparing, and correcting work performance.

## *focus on* Leadership

### The Real World: Do Organizations Need Managers or Leaders or Both?

How important are managers to organizations? How important are leaders? In today's dynamic environment, organizations need both strong leadership *and* strong management for optimal effectiveness. Leaders are needed to challenge the status quo, to create visions of the future, and to inspire organizational members to want to achieve those visions. Managers are needed to formulate detailed plans, to create appropriate and sufficient organizational structures for doing the organization's work, to oversee day-to-day operations, and to implement appropriate evaluation systems to ensure that work is being done as planned. Can they be one and the same? Ideally, yes! It's important for managers to be able to lead—after all, it is one of the four functions of management. A 2004 survey by the American Management Association showed that managers at all levels were devoting more time to leading than in the past. Let's look at an example of an organization that has recognized the important leadership role that managers, especially first-line managers, play.

BP, the world's largest integrated oil and energy corporation with business dealings on every continent, has created a training program for its frontline managers, who supervise 70 percent to 80 percent of the company's more than 100,000 worldwide employees. Their decisions, in aggregate, made an enormous difference in BP's turnover, costs, quality, safety, innovation, and environmental performance. They were also the people usually called upon to prevent small problems from becoming full-scale operational disasters. Yet BP didn't have a comprehensive training program for them. But that's no longer the case. Since early in the twenty-first century, BP has invested significant resources in developing its frontline managers. One of the initial changes was to call this group "first-level leaders," a title deliberately chosen to emphasize the managers' significance to BP. These first-level leaders now go through a comprehensive training program that covers supervisory essentials; the context of BP's overall strategy and its implications for all parts of the organization; and thorough training on developing better communication skills, management and leadership skills, and work team dynamics. How successful has the program been? BP says that the managers who have been through the training are consistently ranked higher in performance than those who haven't. Other BP executives say that the program has helped make the organization more collaborative and capable. What can we learn from this example? Organizations need both strong leadership *and* strong management for optimal effectiveness.

*Sources:* A. Priestland and R. Hanig, "Developing First-Level Leaders," *Harvard Business Review,* June 2005, pp. 113–120; and "AMA 2004 Importance of Leadership Survey," www.amanet.org/research, Copyright © 2004, American Management Association, New York, NY 10019.

and acknowledges the important role her team plays. Controlling can be seen as Jovita focuses on results and looks for ways to be more efficient.

The continued popularity of the functions approach to describe what managers do is a tribute to its clarity and simplicity. But some have argued that this approach isn't appropriate or relevant.[9] So let's look at another perspective.

## Management Roles

Henry Mintzberg, a prominent management researcher, studied actual managers at work. He concluded that what managers do can best be described by looking at 10 different but highly interrelated management roles they use at work.[10] The term **management roles** refers to specific categories of managerial behavior. (Think of the different roles you play—student, employee, student group member, volunteer, sibling, and so forth—and the different behaviors you're expected to play in these roles.) As shown in Exhibit 1–4, Mintzberg's 10 management roles are grouped around interpersonal relationships, the transfer of information, and decision making.

The **interpersonal roles** are roles that involve people (subordinates and persons outside the organization) and other duties that are ceremonial and symbolic in nature. The three interpersonal roles include figurehead, leader, and liaison. The **informational roles** involve collecting, receiving, and disseminating information. The three informational roles are monitor, disseminator, and spokesperson. Finally, the **decisional roles** entail making decisions or choices. The four decisional roles are entrepreneur, disturbance handler, resource allocator, and negotiator.

As managers perform these different roles, Mintzberg concluded that their actual work activities involved interacting with others, with the organization itself, and with

Exhibit 1–4

**Mintzberg's Managerial Roles**

| Role | Description | Examples of Identifiable Activities |
|------|-------------|-------------------------------------|
| **Interpersonal** | | |
| Figurehead | Symbolic head; obliged to perform a number of routine duties of a legal or social nature | Greeting visitors; signing legal documents |
| Leader | Responsible for the motivation of subordinates; responsible for staffing, training, and associated duties | Performing virtually all activities that involve subordinates |
| Liaison | Maintains self-developed network of outside contacts and informers who provide favors and information | Acknowledging mail; doing external board work; performing other activities that involve outsiders |
| **Informational** | | |
| Monitor | Seeks and receives wide variety of internal and external information to develop thorough understanding of organization and environment | Reading periodicals and reports; maintaining personal contacts |
| Disseminator | Transmits information received from outsiders or from subordinates to members of the organization | Holding informational meetings; making phone calls to relay information |
| Spokesperson | Transmits information to outsiders on organization's plans, policies, actions, results, etc. | Holding board meetings; giving information to the media |
| **Decisional** | | |
| Entrepreneur | Searches organization and its environment for opportunities and initiates "improvement projects" to bring about changes | Organizing strategy and review sessions to develop new programs |
| Disturbance handler | Responsible for corrective action when organization faces important, unexpected disturbances | Organizing strategy and review sessions that involve disturbances and crises |
| Resource allocator | Responsible for the allocation of organizational resources of all kinds—making or approving all significant organizational decisions | Scheduling; requesting authorization; performing any activity that involves budgeting and the programming of subordinates' work |
| Negotiator | Responsible for representing the organization at major negotiations | Participating in union contract negotiations |

*Source:* H. Mintzberg, *The Nature of Managerial Work* (New York: Harper & Row, 1973), pp. 93–94. Copyright © 1973 by Henry Mintzberg. Reprinted by permission of Harper & Row, Publishers, Inc.

the context outside the organization. He also proposed that as managers perform these roles, their activities include reflection (thoughtful thinking) and action (practical doing).[11] When managers reflect, they're thinking, pondering, and contemplating. When managers act, they're doing something; they're performing; they're actively engaged. We can see both reflection and action in our chapter opener. Reflection is shown in the way Jovita interacts with her staff by listening and observing. Action is shown by the personal visits Jovita has with frontline workers.

A number of follow-up studies have tested the validity of Mintzberg's role categories in different types of organizations and at different levels within given organizations.[12] The evi-

**management roles**
Specific categories of managerial behavior.

**interpersonal roles**
Managerial roles that involve people and other duties that are ceremonial and symbolic in nature.

**informational roles**
Managerial roles that involve collecting, receiving, and disseminating information.

**decisional roles**
Managerial roles that revolve around making choices.

dence generally supports the idea that managers—regardless of the type of organization or level in the organization—perform similar roles. However, the emphasis that managers give to the various roles seems to change with their organizational level.[13] At higher levels of the organization, the roles of disseminator, figurehead, negotiator, liaison, and spokesperson are more important; the leader role (as Mintzberg defined it) is more important for lower-level managers than it is for either middle- or top-level managers.

So which approach is correct—functions or roles? Each describes what managers do. However, the functions approach still represents the most useful way of describing the manager's job. "The classical functions provide clear and discrete methods of classifying the thousands of activities that managers carry out and the techniques they use in terms of the functions they perform for the achievement of goals."[14] However, our decision to use the management functions to describe what managers do doesn't mean that Mintzberg's role categories are invalid. His approach did offer important insights into managers' work. Many of his roles align well with one or more of the functions. For instance, resource allocation is part of planning, as is the entrepreneurial role, and all three of the interpersonal roles are part of the leading function. Although most of the other roles fit into one or more of the four functions, not all do. The difference can be explained by the fact that all managers do some work that isn't purely managerial.[15]

## Management Skills

A manager's job is varied and complex. Managers need certain skills to perform the duties and activities associated with being a manager. What types of skills does a manager need? Research by Robert L. Katz concluded that managers needed three essential skills.[16] **Technical skills** are the job-specific knowledge and techniques needed to proficiently perform specific tasks. These skills tend to be more important for lower-level managers because they typically are managing employees who are using tools and techniques to produce the organization's products or service the organization's customers. Because of the importance of these skills at lower organizational levels, employees with excellent technical skills often get promoted to first-line manager on the basis of those skills. For example, Mark Ryan of Verizon Communications manages almost 100 technicians who service half a million of the company's customers. Before becoming a manager, however, Ryan was a telephone lineman. He says, "The technical side of the business is important, but managing people and rewarding and recognizing the people who do an outstanding job is how we (Verizon) are going to succeed."[17] Ryan is a manager who's used his technical skills, but also recognizes the importance of **human skills**, which involve the ability to work well with other people both individually and in a group. Because managers deal directly with people, these skills are essential and equally important at all levels of management. Managers with good human skills are able to get the best out of their people. They know how to communicate, motivate, lead, and inspire enthusiasm and trust. (  Go to www.prenhall.com/rolls) Finally, **conceptual skills** are the skills managers use to think and to conceptualize about abstract and complex situations. Using these skills, managers must see the organization as a whole, understand the relationships among various subunits, and visualize how the organization fits into its broader environment. These skills are most important at the top management levels. Exhibit 1–5 shows the relationship of these skills and the levels of management.

Exhibit 1–5

**Skills Needed at Different Managerial Levels**

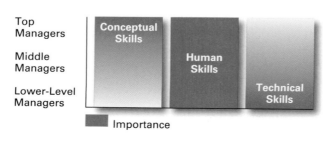

Other important managerial skills were identified in a survey of practicing managers by the American Management Association. These skills—described in Exhibit 1–6—included conceptual, communication, effectiveness, and interpersonal.[18]

In today's demanding and dynamic workplace, employees who want to be valuable assets to an organization must be willing to constantly upgrade their skills and take on extra work outside their own specific job area. There's no doubt that skills will continue

Exhibit 1–6

**Managerial Skills**

**Conceptual Skills**

- Ability to use information to solve business problems
- Identification of opportunities for innovation
- Recognizing problem areas and implementing solutions
- Selecting critical information from masses of data
- Understanding of business uses of technology
- Understanding of organization's business model

**Communication Skills**

- Ability to transform ideas into words and actions
- Credibility among colleagues, peers, and subordinates
- Listening and asking questions
- Presentation skills; spoken format
- Presentation skills; written and/or graphic formats

**Effectiveness Skills**

- Contributing to corporate mission/departmental objectives
- Customer focus
- Multitasking: working at multiple tasks in parallel
- Negotiating skills
- Project management
- Reviewing operations and implementing improvements
- Setting and maintaining performance standards internally and externally
- Setting priorities for attention and activity
- Time management

**Interpersonal Skills**

- Coaching and mentoring skills
- Diversity skills: working with diverse people and cultures
- Networking within the organization
- Networking outside the organization
- Working in teams; cooperation and commitment

Source: Based on American Management Association Survey of Managerial Skills and Competencies, March/April 2000, found on AMA Web site, www.amanet.org, October 30, 2002.

**technical skills**
Job-specific knowledge and techniques needed to proficiently perform specific tasks.

**human skills**
The ability to work well with other people individually and in a group.

**conceptual skills**
The ability to think and to conceptualize about abstract and complex situations.

*Jada and Brett Holcomb have built a successful business around their jewelry cart in an Atlanta mall. To reach $300,000 in annual revenues, the Holcombs have relied on their technical and conceptual skills, especially when it comes to planning. Brett explains how planning avoids one pitfall of the vending cart business: "One critical mistake a lot of people make is that they try to go into a [shopping] center for Christmas, the highest-cost leasing month, with an unproven product. . . . It's not always the case that just because it's the holidays you make a lot of money." The Holcombs' future plans include staying in the mall but moving into the wholesaling end of the business as well.*

to be an important way of describing what a manager does. In fact, understanding and developing management skills are so important that we've incorporated a condensed skills feature in the text. At the end of this book and on our R.O.L.L.S. Web site (*www.prenhall.com/rolls*), you'll find material on skill building, including our interactive skills exercises. The 22 skills we've chosen to feature in these skill-building modules reflect a broad crosssection of managerial activities that we and most experts believe are important elements of the four management functions. A matrix showing the relationship between these skills and the management functions is shown in Exhibit 1–7. Note that many of the skills are important to multiple functions. As you study the functions in more depth in later chapters of the book, you'll have the opportunity to practice some of the key skills that are part of doing what a manager does. Although no skill-building exercise can make you an instant expert in a certain area, these modules can provide you an introductory understanding of some of the skills you'll need to master in order to be an effective manager.

Exhibit 1–7

**Management Skills and Management Functions Matrix**

| Skill | Function | | | |
|---|---|---|---|---|
| | Planning | Organizing | Leading | Controlling |
| Acquiring power | | ✓ | ✓ | |
| Active listening | | | ✓ | ✓ |
| Budgeting | ✓ | | | ✓ |
| Choosing an effective leadership style | | | ✓ | |
| Coaching | | | ✓ | |
| Creating effective teams | | ✓ | ✓ | |
| Delegating (empowerment) | | ✓ | ✓ | |
| Designing motivating jobs | | ✓ | ✓ | |
| Developing trust | | | ✓ | |
| Disciplining | | | ✓ | ✓ |
| Interviewing | | ✓ | ✓ | |
| Managing conflict | | | ✓ | ✓ |
| Managing resistance to change | | ✓ | ✓ | ✓ |
| Mentoring | | | ✓ | |
| Negotiating | | | ✓ | |
| Providing feedback | | | ✓ | ✓ |
| Reading an organization's culture | | ✓ | ✓ | |
| Running productive meetings | ✓ | ✓ | ✓ | ✓ |
| Scanning the environment | ✓ | | | ✓ |
| Setting goals | ✓ | | | ✓ |
| Solving problems creatively | ✓ | ✓ | ✓ | ✓ |
| Valuing diversity | ✓ | ✓ | ✓ | ✓ |

## How the Manager's Job Is Changing

Managers have always had to deal with changes taking place inside and outside their organization. ( 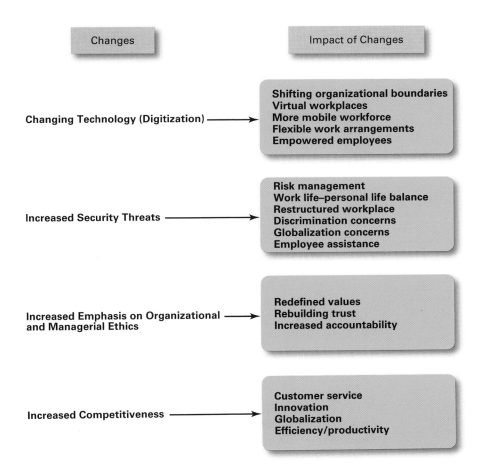 Go to www.prenhall.com/rolls) In today's world where managers everywhere are dealing with security threats, corporate ethics scandals, global economic and political uncertainties, and technological advancements, change is a constant. For example, Ronnie Antebi, manager of A&R Welding in Atlanta, had to find ways to keep his welders employed as customer demand fluctuated. His solution: Form special crews of welders who are sent out of state when local demand falls.[19] Or consider the management challenges faced by Paul Raines, Home Depot's southern division manager, who coordinated the efforts of employees after Hurricane Katrina hit New Orleans, Biloxi, Gulfport, and other Gulf Coast communities. "At the company's hurricane center in Atlanta, staff from different divisions—maintenance, HR (human resources), logistics—worked 18 hours a day to cut through logjams and get things where they needed to be." The company's preparations before, during, and after Katrina paid off when, a day after the storm, all but 10 of the company's 33 stores in Katrina's path had reopened.[20] Although most managers are not likely to have to manage under such demanding circumstances, the fact is that *how* managers manage is changing. Exhibit 1–8 illustrates some of the most important changes facing managers. Throughout the rest of this book, we'll be discussing these changes and their impact on the way managers plan, organize, lead, and control. We want to highlight two of these changes: the increasing importance of both customers and innovation.

IMPORTANCE OF CUSTOMERS TO THE MANAGER'S JOB.   Every workday, John Chambers, CEO of Cisco Systems, listens to 15 to 20 voice mails that have been forwarded to him from dissatisfied Cisco customers. He says, "E-mail would be more efficient, but I want

Exhibit 1–8

**Changes Impacting the
Manager's Job**

| Changes | | Impact of Changes |
|---|---|---|
| Changing Technology (Digitization) → | | Shifting organizational boundaries<br>Virtual workplaces<br>More mobile workforce<br>Flexible work arrangements<br>Empowered employees |
| Increased Security Threats → | | Risk management<br>Work life–personal life balance<br>Restructured workplace<br>Discrimination concerns<br>Globalization concerns<br>Employee assistance |
| Increased Emphasis on Organizational and Managerial Ethics → | | Redefined values<br>Rebuilding trust<br>Increased accountability |
| Increased Competitiveness → | | Customer service<br>Innovation<br>Globalization<br>Efficiency/productivity |

In the wake of devastating Hurricane Katrina, Paul Raines (right), the southern division manager of Home Depot, worked from a hotel in Baton Rouge to coordinate shipments of supplies to the stricken area so that emergency relief workers, and eventually its customers, would have needed materials to help in recovery and rebuilding efforts.

to hear the emotion, I want to hear the frustration, I want to hear the caller's level of comfort with the strategy we're employing. I can't get that through e-mail."[21] Here's a manager who recognizes the importance of customers. Every organization needs customers. Without customers, most organizations would cease to exist. Yet, focusing on the customer has long been thought to be the responsibility of marketing types. "Let the marketers worry about the customers" is how many managers felt. We're discovering, however, that employee attitudes and behaviors play a big role in customer satisfaction. For instance, an analysis of a Qantas Airways passenger survey confirms this. Passengers were asked to rate their "essential needs" in air travel. Almost every factor listed by passengers was directly influenced by the actions of Qantas's employees—from prompt baggage delivery, to courteous and efficient cabin crews, to assistance with connections, to quick and friendly check-ins.[22] Today, the majority of employees in developed countries work in service jobs. For instance, some 80 percent of the U.S. labor force is employed in service industries. In Australia, 70 percent work in service industries. In the United Kingdom, Germany, and Japan, the figures are 80 percent, 64 percent, and 70 percent, respectively.[23] Examples of these service jobs include technical support representatives, fast-food counter workers, sales clerks, teachers, waitpersons, nurses, computer repair technicians, front desk clerks, consultants, purchasing agents, credit representatives, financial planners, and bank tellers. Managers everywhere are beginning to understand that delivering consistent high-quality service is essential for success and survival in today's competitive environment and that employees are an important part of that equation.[24] The implication is clear—they must create a customer responsive organization where employees are friendly and courteous, accessible, knowledgeable, prompt in responding to customer needs, and willing to do what's necessary to please the customer.[25] We'll examine customer service management and its importance to planning, organizing, leading, and controlling in several chapters.

IMPORTANCE OF INNOVATION TO THE MANAGER'S JOB.   Nothing is more risky than not innovating.[26] Innovation means doing things differently, exploring new territory, and taking risks. And innovation isn't just for high-tech and technologically advanced organizations. Examples of successful innovation can be found in organizations you might not expect. For instance, for over 25 years, CSX Transportation (the railroad company) had transported Tropicana's orange juice products from the processing plants to market.[27] Mistrust between the two organizations had built up over the years, and the relationship was often adversarial, which affected the way employees in both organizations did their jobs. One day a CSX rail inspector proposed the idea of inspecting the rail cars on the Tropicana property rather than bringing them all the way to the CSX rail yard many miles away, as had been done for years. The back-and-forth transport of rail cars simply for inspection was costly and time-consuming.

*Charles Schwab was recalled to his old job as CEO in order to reverse the decline of the personal finance company that bears his name. One of his priorities was rebuilding customer relationships: "We lost the emotional connection with our client. We did a long series of things that antagonized our client relationship—raising fees and rates in a bunch of areas, impersonal marketing. We lost one of the great sources of our growth in the past, our happy customers referring new customers to us." After more than a year of restructuring, "We're real happy where we're at now."*

Granted, the idea wasn't a technological breakthrough, but it was innovative—a way of doing things differently. It was also valuable for both parties. What role did managers play? Someone had to create and maintain an environment in which employees felt free to innovate, and someone had to act on the idea. That someone was the managers. In today's world, organizational managers—at all levels and in all areas—need to encourage their employees to be on the lookout for new ideas and new approaches, not just in the products or services the organization provides, but in everything that's done. Take, for example, Eric Taverna, store manager of Best Buy store 484 in Manchester, Connecticut, who clearly understands the importance of getting employees to think and act innovatively, a task made particularly challenging because the average Best Buy store is often staffed by young adults in their first or second jobs. "The complexity of the products demands a high level of training, but the many distractions that tempt college-aged employees keep the turnover potential high." However, Taverna tackled the problems at his store by getting his employees to suggest new ideas and approaches. One of those suggested approaches—a "team close," in which employees scheduled to work at the store's closing time closed the store together and walked out together as a team—has had a remarkable impact on employee attitudes and commitment.[28] We'll examine innovation and its importance to planning, organizing, leading, and controlling in several chapters.

## Learning Review

- Describe the four functions of management.
- Explain Mintzberg's managerial roles.
- Describe Katz's three managerial skills and how the importance of these skills changes depending on managerial level.

- Discuss the changes that are impacting managers' jobs.
- Explain why customer service and innovation are important to the manager's job.

## WHAT IS AN ORGANIZATION?

Managers work in organizations. But what is an **organization**? An organization is a deliberate arrangement of people to accomplish some specific purpose. Your college or university is an organization; so are fraternities and sororities, government departments,

**organization**
A deliberate arrangement of people to accomplish some specific purpose.

Exhibit 1–9

**Characteristics of Organizations**

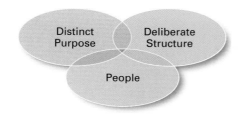

churches, Amazon.com, your neighborhood video store, the United Way, the Colorado Rockies baseball team, and the Mayo Clinic. These are all organizations because they have three common characteristics, as shown in Exhibit 1–9.

First, each organization has a distinct purpose. This purpose is typically expressed in terms of a goal or set of goals that the organization hopes to accomplish. Second, each organization is composed of people. One person working alone is not an organization, and it takes people to perform the work that's necessary for the organization to achieve its goals. Third, all organizations develop some deliberate structure so that their members can do their work. That structure may be open and flexible, with no clear and precise job duties or strict adherence to explicit job arrangements—in other words, it may be a simple network of loose relationships. Or the structure may be more traditional, with clearly defined rules, regulations, and job descriptions and some members identified as "bosses" who have authority over other members. But no matter what type of structural arrangement an organization uses, it does require some deliberate structure so members' work relationships are clarified.

Although these three characteristics are important to our definition of what an organization is, the nature of an organization is changing. It's no longer appropriate to assume that all organizations are going to be structured like Procter & Gamble, ExxonMobil, or Ford Motor, with clearly identifiable divisions, departments, and work units. Instead, today's organizations may be structured more like Google, which chose a flatter, networked structure over a hierarchical structure with layers of management and decisions made in narrow business functional areas. At Google, most big projects, of which there are hundreds going on at the same time, are tackled by small, tightly focused employee teams that set up in an instant and complete work just as quickly.[29] Like Google, contemporary organizations tend to rely more on flexible work arrangements, employee work teams, open communication systems, and supplier alliances. Just how is the concept of an organization changing? Exhibit 1–10 lists some differences between traditional organizations and contemporary organizations. As these lists show, today's organizations are becoming more open, flexible, and responsive to changes.[30]

Why are organizations changing? Because the world around them has changed and continues to change. Societal, economic, global, and technological changes have

Exhibit 1–10

**The Changing Organization**

| Traditional Organization | Contemporary Organization |
|---|---|
| • Stable | • Dynamic |
| • Inflexible | • Flexible |
| • Job-focused | • Skills-focused |
| • Work is defined by job positions | • Work is defined in terms of tasks to be done |
| • Individual-oriented | • Team-oriented |
| • Permanent jobs | • Temporary jobs |
| • Command-oriented | • Involvement-oriented |
| • Managers always make decisions | • Employees participate in decision making |
| • Rule-oriented | • Customer-oriented |
| • Relatively homogeneous workforce | • Diverse workforce |
| • Workdays defined as 9 to 5 | • Workdays have no time boundaries |
| • Hierarchical relationships | • Lateral and networked relationships |
| • Work at organizational facility during specific hours | • Work anywhere, anytime |

created an environment in which successful organizations (those that consistently attain their goals) must embrace new ways of getting work done. As we stated earlier, even though the concept of organizations may be changing, managers and management continue to be important to organizations.

## Learning Review

- Describe the characteristics of an organization.

- Explain how the concept of an organization is changing.

## WHY STUDY MANAGEMENT?

Q & A

Can't you just learn management "on the job?" Q & A 1.4 explains.

You may be wondering why you need to study management. ( Go to www.prenhall.com/rolls) If you're an accounting major, a marketing major, or any major other than management, you may not understand how studying management is going to help you in your career. We can explain the value of studying management by looking at the universality of management, the reality of work, and the rewards and challenges of being a manager.

### The Universality of Management

Just how universal is the need for management in organizations? We can say with absolute certainty that management is needed in all types and sizes of organizations, at all organizational levels and in all organizational work areas, and in all organizations, no matter what country they're located in. This is known as the **universality of management**

## Managing your Career

### Career Opportunities in Management

Merck plans to cut about 11 percent of its workforce. Unisys reduces its workforce by 10 percent. Pfizer Japan Inc. is cutting its workforce by 5 percent. Kodak plans to eliminate up to 25,000 jobs. Are management jobs disappearing? You might think so based on news reports showing widespread layoffs. The truth is: The future looks bright! Business administration and management continues to be one of the top 10 most popular college majors, and there are likely to be jobs waiting for those graduates.

Some 6 million individuals in the United States are employed as managers. The U.S. Bureau of Labor Statistics estimates 10 percent to 20 percent growth in all executive, administrative, and managerial jobs through

the year 2012. These jobs, however, may not be in the organizations or fields that you'd expect. The demand for managers in traditional, *Fortune* 500 organizations and particularly in the area of traditional manufacturing is not going to be as strong as the demand for managers in small and medium-sized organizations in the services field, particularly information and health care services. So keep in mind that a good place to land a management position can be a smaller-sized organization.

*Sources: Occupational Outlook Handbook, 2004-05 Edition*, U.S. Department of Labor, Bureau of Labor Statistics, available online at www.bls.gov/oco, December 12, 2005; and M. Ballinger and E. White, "Matters of Degree," *Wall Street Journal*, January 4, 2005, p. B4.

**universality of management**
The reality that management is needed in all types and sizes of organizations, at all organizational levels, in all organizational areas, and in organizations in all countries around the globe.

(see Exhibit 1–11). Managers in all these situations will plan, organize, lead, and control. However, this is not to say that management is done the same way. What a supervisor in a software applications testing facility at Microsoft does versus what the CEO of Microsoft does is a matter of degree and emphasis, not of function. Because both are managers, both will plan, organize, lead, and control, but how they do so will differ.

Because management is universally needed in all organizations, we have a vested interest in improving the way organizations are managed. Why? We interact with organizations every single day. Does it frustrate you when you have to spend 2 hours in a department of motor vehicles office to get your driver's license renewed? Are you irritated when none of the salespeople in a retail store seems interested in helping you? Do you get annoyed when you call an airline three times and their sales representatives quote you three different prices for the same trip? These are all examples of problems created by poor management. Organizations that are well managed—and we'll share many examples of these throughout the text—develop a loyal customer base, grow, and prosper. Those that are poorly managed find themselves losing customers and revenues. By studying management, you'll be able to recognize poor management and work to get it corrected. In addition, you'll be able to recognize good management and encourage it, whether it's in an organization with which you're simply interacting or whether it's in an organization in which you're employed.

## The Reality of Work

Another reason for studying management is the reality that for most of you, once you graduate from college and begin your career, you will either manage or be managed. For those who plan to be managers, an understanding of the management process forms the foundation upon which to build your management skills. For those of you who don't see yourself managing, you're still likely to have to work with managers. Also, assuming that you will have to work for a living and recognizing that you are very likely to work in an organization, you'll probably have some managerial responsibilities even if you're not a manager. Our experience tells us that you can gain a great deal of insight into the way your boss behaves and how organizations function by studying management. Our point is that you don't have to aspire to be a manager to gain something valuable from a course in management.

## Rewards and Challenges of Being a Manager

We can't leave our discussion of the value of studying management without looking at the rewards and challenges of being a manager (see Exhibit 1-12). What *does* it mean to be a manager in today's dynamic workplace?

Exhibit 1–12

**Rewards and Challenges of Being a Manager**

| Rewards | Challenges |
|---|---|
| • Create a work environment in which organizational members can work to the best of their ability<br>• Have opportunities to think creatively and use imagination<br>• Help others find meaning and fulfillment in work<br>• Support, coach, and nurture others<br>• Work with a variety of people<br>• Receive recognition and status in organization and community<br>• Play a role in influencing organizational outcomes<br>• Receive appropriate compensation in form of salaries, bonuses, and stock options<br>• Good managers are needed by organizations | • Do hard work<br>• May have duties that are more clerical than managerial<br>• Have to deal with a variety of personalities<br>• Often have to make do with limited resources<br>• Motivate workers in chaotic and uncertain situations<br>• Successfully blend knowledge, skills, ambitions, and experiences of a diverse work group<br>• Success depends on others' work performance |

Self-Assessment Library (S.A.L.)

Not everyone is motivated to be a manager. Are you? Self-Assessment exercise #III.B.4 will help you answer that question.

First, there are many challenges. (  Go to www.prenhall.com/rolls) It can be a tough and often thankless job. In addition, a portion of a manager's job (especially at lower organizational levels) may entail duties that are often more clerical (such as compiling and filing reports, dealing with bureaucratic procedures, or doing paperwork) than managerial.[31] Managers often may have to deal with a variety of personalities and often have to make do with limited resources. It can be a challenge to motivate workers in the face of uncertainty and chaos. Managers may find it difficult to effectively blend the knowledge, skills, ambitions, and experiences of a diverse work group. Finally, as a manager, you're not in full control of your destiny. Your success typically is dependent upon others' work performance.

## *becoming* a Manager

✓ Keep up with current business news.

✓ Read books about good and bad examples of managing.

✓ Remember that one of the things good managers do is discover what is unique about each person and capitalize on it.

✓ Keep in mind the simple advice of the late Peter Drucker, who has been called the most influential management thinker of the twentieth century: Management is about people.

✓ Work on your "soft" skills—work ethic, communications, information gathering, and people skills. These are what employers cite as the most important factors for getting jobs.

✓ Observe managers and how they handle people and situations.

✓ Talk to actual managers about their experiences—good and bad.

✓ Get experience in managing by taking on leadership roles in student organizations.

✓ Start thinking about whether you'd enjoy being a manager.

✓  Go to www.prenhall.com/rolls and complete any of these exercises from the Self-Assessment Library found on R.O.L.L.S.: S.A.L. #I.A.4—How Well Do I Handle Ambiguity?, S.A.L. #I.C.6—How Confident Am I in My Abilities to Succeed?, S.A.L. #I.C.7—What's My Attitude Toward Achievement?, S.A.L. #I.E.1—What's My Emotional Intelligence Score?, and S.A.L. #III.B.4—How Motivated Am I to Manage?

Self-Assessment Library (S.A.L.)

Yet, despite these challenges, being a manager *can be* very rewarding. You're responsible for creating a work environment in which organizational members can do their work to the best of their ability and help the organization achieve its goals. In addition, as a manager, you often have the opportunity to think creatively and use your imagination. You help others find meaning and fulfillment in their work. You get to support, coach, and nurture others and help them make good decisions. You'll get to meet and work with a variety of people—both inside and outside the organization. Other rewards of being a manager may include receiving recognition and status in your organization and in the community, playing a role in influencing organizational outcomes, and receiving attractive compensation in the form of salaries, bonuses, and stock options. Finally, organizations need good managers. Nothing great ever happens alone! It's through the combined efforts of motivated and passionate people working together that organizations accomplish their goals. As a manager, you can be assured that your efforts, skills, and abilities are needed.

## Learning Review

- Explain the universality of management concept.
- Discuss why an understanding of management is important.

- Describe the rewards and challenges of being a manager.

# Managers Respond to a Manager's Dilemma

## Cynthia Brewer
Staff Development Manager, Sears Holding Corporation, Chicago, IL

Jovita evidently understands how important her first-line people are to the overall success of her facility. In fact, it appears that she makes an effort to get out and interact with the frontline workers despite the important responsibilities that she probably has as a vice president. I think that the first-line supervisors are going to be dealing with the issues and problems that undoubtedly arise daily when managing an operation the size of this hub facility. So it is important that these supervisors have appropriate skills for dealing with these challenges. Thus, I think the most important skills that Jovita would first need to encourage her first-line supervisors to develop would be interpersonal and communication skills.

Since they directly manage the package handlers, they'll need good human skills if they're going to get the best out of their people in a fast-paced work environment with set deadlines for when the packages have to be loaded in order to meet delivery schedules. That's why I also think it's important that Jovita's first-line supervisors have some technical skills—they need to be able to jump in and help out if work gets backed up. They also need to be able to answer questions that may come up as packages are routed and loaded. Finally, I think these supervisors also may need some conceptual skills to help them recognize problem areas and how best to attack those problems.

# Learning Summary

## Who Are Managers?

Managers coordinate and oversee the work of other people so that organizational goals can be accomplished

- Top managers
- Middle managers
- First-line managers

## What Is Management?

Coordinating and overseeing the work activities of others so that their activities are completed efficiently and effectively

- Efficiency—getting the most output from the least amount of input; doing things right
- Effectiveness—doing those work activities that help the organization reach its goals; doing the right things

## What Do Managers Do?

### Functions

- Planning—defining goals, establishing strategies, and developing plans
- Organizing—arranging and structuring work
- Leading—working with and through people
- Controlling—evaluating whether things are going as planned

### Roles

- Interpersonal—figurehead, leader, liaison
- Informational—monitor, disseminator, spokesperson
- Decisional—entrepreneur, disturbance handler, resource allocator, negotiator

### Skills

- Technical, human, conceptual
- Importance of these skills varies depending on managerial level

### How the manager's job is changing

- Changes impacting manager's job—changing technology, increased security threats, increased emphasis on ethics, increased competitiveness
- Importance of customers
- Importance of innovation

## What Is an Organization?

Deliberate arrangement of people to accomplish some specific purpose;

organizations are changing because the world around them is changing

## Why Study Management?

- Universality of management—universal need for management
- Reality of work—either manage or be managed
- Challenges and rewards of being a manager

## Management: By the Numbers

- Ninety-one percent of senior executives surveyed by *CFO* magazine say that workforce effectiveness/productivity is one of the top three factors in their company's overall performance.
- In an OfficeTeam survey of almost 1,000 respondents who were asked if they would like to be boss, 71 percent said no.
- Seventy-six percent of American employees like the work they do, but their manager's habits make the workplace less enjoyable, according to a survey by Sirota Survey Intelligence.
- Fourteen percent of workers surveyed by the Conference Board said that they are very satisfied with their job, but 40 percent of workers feel disconnected from their employers.
- More than half the employees surveyed by VitalSmarts.survey said that a disagreeable boss was their top reason to leave their job.

- A Gallup poll said that 77 percent of "engaged" workers (employees who work with passion and have a deep connection to their company) strongly agreed that their supervisors played a crucial role in their well-being and workplace commitment. Only 23 percent of the "not-engaged" workers and 4 percent of the "actively disengaged" workers strongly agreed.

*Sources:* J. Yang and R. W. Ahrens, "USA Today Snapshots," *USA Today,* January 25, 2006, p. 1B; J. Krueger and E. Killhan, "At Work, Feeling Good Matters," *Gallup Management Journal,* December 8, 2005, gmj.gallup.com; "Bring It On, Boss," *Springfield News Leader,* November 15, 2005, p. 1F; L. Kroll, "No Employee Left Behind," *Forbes,* October 3, 2005, p. 60; "Survey Says," *CFO I.T.,* Fall 2005, p. 56; J. MacIntyre, "Bosses and Bureaucracy," *Springfield Business Journal,* August 1–7, 2005, p. 29; P. Panchak, "Wanted: Inspired Leaders, Engaged Employees," *Industry Week,* May 2005, p. 7; and "The Stat," *Business Week,* March 28, 2005, p. 14.

## Thinking About Management Issues

1. Is your course instructor a manager? Discuss in terms of managerial functions, managerial roles, and skills.

2. "The manager's most basic responsibility is to focus people toward performance of work activities to achieve desired outcomes." What's your interpretation of this statement? Do you agree with this statement? Why or why not?

3. Why do you think the skills of job candidates have become so important to employers? What are the implications for (a) managers in general, and (b) you, personally?

4. Is there one best "style" of management? Why or why not?

5. What characteristics of new organizations appeal to you? Why? Which do not? Why?

6. In today's environment, which is more important to organizations—efficiency or effectiveness? Explain your choice.

7. Can you think of situations where management doesn't matter to organizations? Explain.

8. "Management was, is, and always will be the same thing: the art of getting things done." Do you agree? Why or why not?

## Working Together: Team-Based Exercise

By this time in your life, each of you has had to work with individuals in managerial positions (or maybe *you* were the manager), either through work experiences or through other organizational experiences (social, hobby/interest, religious, and so forth). What do you think makes some managers better than others? Are there certain characteristics that distinguish good managers? Form small groups (three or four people per group) with other class members. Discuss your experiences with managers—good and bad. Draw up a list of the characteristics of those individuals you felt were good managers. For each item, indicate which management function you think it falls under. As a group, be prepared to share your list with the class and to explain your choice of management function.

# Case Application

## Managing the Virus Hunters

Imagine what life would be like if your product were never finished, if your work were never done, if your market shifted 30 times a day. The computer-virus hunters at Symantec Corp. don't have to imagine. That's the reality of their daily work life. At the company's Response Lab in Santa Monica, California, described as the "dirtiest of all our networks at Symantec," software analysts collect viruses and other suspicious code and try to figure out how they work so security updates can be provided to the company's customers. By the door to the lab, there's even a hazardous materials box marked "Danger" where they put all the disks, tapes, and hard drives with the nasty viruses that need to be carefully and completely disposed of. Symantec's situation may seem unique, but the company, which makes content and network security software for both consumers and businesses, reflects the realities facing many organizations today: quickly shifting customer expectations and continuously emerging global competitors that have drastically shortened product life cycles. Managing talented people in such an environment can be quite challenging as well.

Vincent Weafer, a native of Ireland, has been the leader of Symantec's virus-hunting team since 1999. Back then, he said, "There were less than two dozen people, and . . . nothing really happened. We'd see maybe five new viruses a day, and they would spread in a matter of months, not minutes." Now, Symantec's virus hunters around the world deal with some 20,000 virus samples each month, not all of which are unique, stand-alone viruses. To make the hunters' jobs even more interesting, computer attacks are increasingly being spread by criminals wanting to steal information, whether corporate data or personal user account information that can be used in fraud. Dealing with these critical and time-sensitive issues requires special talents. The response-center team is a diverse group whose members weren't easy to find. Says Weaver, "It's not as if colleges are creating thousands of anti-malware or security experts every year that we can hire. If you find them in any part of the world, you just go after them." The response-center team's makeup reflects that. For instance, one senior researcher is from Hungary; another is from Iceland; and another works out of her home in Melbourne, Florida. But they all share something in common: They're all motivated by solving problems.

The launch of the Blaster-B worm in August 2003 changed the company's approach to dealing with viruses. The domino effect of Blaster-B and other viruses spawned by it meant the frontline software analysts were working around the clock for almost 2 weeks. The "employee burnout" potential made the company realize that its virus-hunting team would now have to be much deeper talent-wise. Now, the response center's team numbers in the hundreds and managers can rotate people from the front lines, where they're responsible for responding to new security threats that crop up, into groups where they can help with new-product development. Others write internal research papers. Still others are assigned to develop new tools that will help their colleagues battle the next wave of threats. There's even an individual who tries to

*Vincent Weafer, leader of Symantec's virus chasers, in the company's Response Lab.*

figure out what makes the virus writers tick—and the day never ends for these virus hunters. When Santa Monica's team finishes its day, colleagues in Tokyo take over. When the Japanese team finishes its day, it hands off to Dublin, who then hands back to Santa Monica for the new day. It's a frenetic, chaotic, challenging work environment that spans the entire globe. But Weafer says his goals are to "try to take the chaos out, to make the exciting boring," to have a predictable and well-defined process for dealing with the virus threats, and to spread work evenly to the company's facilities around the world. It's a managerial challenge that Weafer has embraced.

### DISCUSSION QUESTIONS

1. Keeping professionals excited about work that is routine and standardized *and* chaotic is a major challenge for Vincent Weafer. How could he use technical, human, and conceptual skills to maintain an environment that encourages innovation and professionalism among the virus hunters?

2. What management roles would Vincent be playing as he (a) had weekly security briefing conference calls with coworkers around the globe, (b) assessed the feasibility of adding a new network security consulting service, or (c) kept employees focused on the company's commitments to customers?

3. Go to Symantec's Web site (**www.symantec.com**) and look up information about the company. What can you tell about its emphasis on customer service and innovation? In what ways does the organization support its employees in servicing customers and in being innovative?

4. What could other managers learn from Vincent Weafer and Symantec's approach?

*Sources:* Information from company Web site, www.symantec.com, December 14, 2005; N. Rothbaum, "The Virtual Battlefield," *Smart Money*, January 2006, pp. 76–80; S. H. Wildstrom, "Viruses Get Smarter—and Greedy," *Business Week Online*, November 22, 2005; and S. Kirsner, "Sweating in the Hot Zone," *Fast Company*, October 2005, pp. 60–65.

# Learning Outline

*Use this Learning Outline as you read and study this chapter.*

### Historical Background of Management

- Explain why studying management history is important.
- Describe some early evidences of management practice.

### Scientific Management

- Describe the important contributions made by Frederick W. Taylor and Frank and Lillian Gilbreth.
- Explain how today's managers use scientific management.

### General Administrative Theory

- Discuss Fayol's contributions to management theory.
- Describe Max Weber's contribution to management theory.
- Explain how today's managers use general administrative theories of management.

### Quantitative Approach

- Explain what the quantitative approach has contributed to the field of management.
- Discuss how today's managers use the quantitative approach.

### Toward Understanding Organizational Behavior

- Describe the contributions of the early advocates of OB.
- Explain the contributions of the Hawthorne Studies to the field of management.
- Discuss how today's managers use the behavioral approach.

### The Systems Approach

- Describe an organization using the systems approach.
- Discuss how the systems approach helps us understand management.

### The Contingency Approach

- Explain how the contingency approach differs from the early theories of management.
- Discuss how the contingency approach helps us understand management.

### Current Trends and Issues

- Explain why we need to look at the current trends and issues facing managers.
- Describe the current trends and issues facing managers.

# Management Yesterday and Today

## A Manager's Dilemma

"Deliver more based on less." That's the product design approach that John R. Hoke III now wants his designers to use as they create new footwear.[1] As the vice president of global footwear design for Nike, Hoke leads an international team of global footwear designers responsible for dreaming up, creating, and commercializing hundreds of footwear styles each year. This new approach to sustainable design came from a corporate-wide mission called "Nike Considered," which has been described as "an entirely new perspective, where innovation meets conservation." (See a description of Nike Considered at www.nike.com.nikebiz/nikeconsidered.)

Hoke's team of designers isn't afraid to push the design envelope. They're the ones who created the radically new cushioning systems used in Nike Air and Nike Shox. They're also the ones who designed the distinctive barefoot running sneakers called "Nike Free." Now Hoke is pushing his team to look at nature as a guide and to "take out what is not necessary" when designing new products. So how has Hoke encouraged his team to be innovative as they "consider" sustainable design? One thing he does is send teams on "design inspiration trips." For instance, designers have gone to the zoo to observe and sketch animals' feet. Designers also draw inspiration from an annual trip to the Detroit car show, where they study lines, silhouettes, styling, function, and color schemes of the automobiles. Another source of inspiration came from a study of origami. As part of this learning experience, Hoke brought in an Israeli origami artist for three days to instruct the designers on paper folding. Says Hoke, "The ideas that have come from that session are phenomenal. It forced us to look deeper at flexibility and how geometry works." Another lesson involved building an ergonomic chair out of cardboard; participants had to focus on bending and folding to hold the chair together instead of using traditional glue. Hoke then made that assignment more interesting by having the chairs judged based on whether they could hold people during a contest of musical chairs.

Although being innovative is the norm with Hoke's design team, innovation also will be critically important throughout the rest of the company if it is to continue to be an industry leader. Put yourself in Hoke's position. What advice could he give other company managers who wanted to encourage innovative thinking?

## What would you do?

ike's push to come up with something innovative for the marketplace isn't all that unusual today. Many organizations, large and small, have made similar commitments to pursuing innovation with all its challenges and rewards. Why? Global competition and general competitive pressures reflect today's reality: innovate or lose. Although John Hoke was innovative in how he inspired his employees to think in new ways about shoe design, he recognized that it's not always easy to implement new ideas. In fact, the history of management is filled with evolutions and revolutions in implementing new ideas.

Looking at management history can help us understand today's management theory and practice. It can help us see what did and did not work. In this chapter, we'll introduce you to the origins of many contemporary management concepts and show how they have evolved to reflect the changing needs of organizations and society as a whole. We'll also introduce important trends and issues that managers currently face, in order to link the past with the future and to demonstrate that the field of management is still evolving. (  Go to www.prenhall.com/rolls)

**Q & A**

Can looking at management history help me be a better manager? Go to Q & A 2.1 to find out.

## HISTORICAL BACKGROUND OF MANAGEMENT

Organized endeavors directed by people responsible for planning, organizing, leading, and controlling activities have existed for thousands of years. The Egyptian pyramids and the Great Wall of China, for instance, are tangible evidence that projects of tremendous scope, employing tens of thousands of people, were completed in ancient times. The pyramids are a particularly interesting example. The construction of a single pyramid occupied more than 100,000 workers for 20 years.[2] Who told each worker what to do? Who ensured that there would be enough stones at the site to keep workers busy? The answer to such questions is *managers*. Regardless of what these individuals were called, someone had to plan what was to be done, organize people and materials to do it, lead and direct the workers, and impose some controls to ensure that everything was done as planned.

Another example of early management can be seen during the 1400s in the city of Venice, a major economic and trade center. The Venetians developed an early form of business enterprise and engaged in many activities common to today's organizations. For instance, at the arsenal of Venice, warships were floated along the canals and at each stop, materials and riggings were added to the ship. Doesn't that sound a lot like a car "floating" along an automobile assembly line and components being added to it? In addition to this assembly line, the Venetians also used warehouse and inventory systems to keep track of materials, human resource management functions to manage the labor force, and an accounting system to keep track of revenues and costs.[3]

As these examples demonstrate, organizations and managers have been around for thousands of years. However, two historical events are especially significant to the study of management.

First, in 1776, Adam Smith published *The Wealth of Nations*, in which he argued the economic advantages that organizations and society would gain from the **division of labor (or job specialization)**—the breakdown of jobs into narrow and repetitive tasks. Using the pin industry as an example, Smith claimed that 10 individuals, each doing a specialized task, could produce about 48,000 pins a day among them. However, if each person worked alone, performing each task separately, it would be quite an accomplishment to produce even 10 pins a day! Smith concluded that division of labor increased productivity by increasing each worker's skill and dexterity, by saving time lost in changing tasks, and by creating labor-saving inventions and machinery. The continued popularity of division of labor—for example, specific tasks performed by members of a hospital surgery team, specific meal preparation tasks done by workers in restaurant kitchens, or specific positions played by players on a football team—is undoubtedly due to the economic advantages cited by Adam Smith.

The second important event, which started in the late eighteenth century, is the **industrial revolution**. During this time, machine power was substituted for human power, making it more economical to manufacture goods in factories rather than at home. These large efficient factories needed managers to forecast demand, ensure that enough material was on hand to make products, assign tasks to people, direct daily activities, and so forth. The need for formal theories to guide managers in running these large organizations had arrived. However, it wasn't until the early 1900s that the first steps toward developing such theories were taken.

In the next sections we present the six major approaches to management: scientific management, general administrative, quantitative, organizational behavior, systems, and contingency (see Exhibit 2–1). Keep in mind that each approach is concerned with the same "animal"; the differences reflect the backgrounds and interests of the writer. A relevant analogy is the classic story of the blind men and the elephant, in which each man declares the elephant to be like the part he is feeling: The first man touches the side and declares that the elephant is like a wall; the second touches the trunk and says the elephant is like a snake; the third feels one of the elephant's tusks and believes the elephant to be like a spear; the fourth grabs a leg and says an elephant is like a tree; and the fifth touches the elephant's tail and concludes that the animal is like a rope. Each is encountering the same elephant, but what each observes depends on where he stands. Similarly, each of the six perspectives is correct and contributes to our overall understanding of management. However, each is also a limited view of a larger animal. We'll begin our journey into management's past by looking at the first major theory of management—scientific management.

Exhibit 2–1 **Development of Major Management Theories**

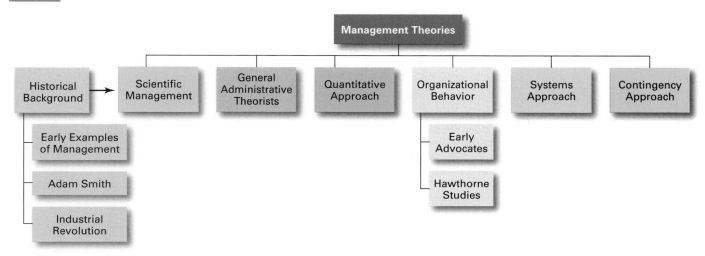

**division of labor (or job specialization)**
The breakdown of jobs into narrow and repetitive tasks.

**industrial revolution**
The substitution of machine power for human power, which made it more economical to manufacture goods in factories rather than at home.

## Learning Review

- Explain why studying management history is important.

- Describe some early evidences of management practice.

## SCIENTIFIC MANAGEMENT

If you had to pinpoint the year modern management theory was born, 1911 might be a logical choice. That was the year Frederick Winslow Taylor's *Principles of Scientific Management* was published. Its contents became widely accepted by managers around the world. The book described the theory of **scientific management**: the use of scientific methods to define the "one best way" for a job to be done.

### Important Contributions

Frederick W. Taylor and Frank and Lillian Gilbreth made important contributions to scientific management theory. Let's look at what they did.

**Frederick W. Taylor**   Taylor worked at the Midvale and Bethlehem Steel Companies in Pennsylvania. As a mechanical engineer with a Quaker and Puritan background, he was continually appalled by workers' inefficiencies. Employees used vastly different techniques to do the same job. They were inclined to "take it easy" on the job, and Taylor believed that worker output was only about one-third of what was possible. Virtually no work standards existed. Workers were placed in jobs with little or no concern for matching their abilities and aptitudes with the tasks they were required to do. Taylor set out to correct the situation by applying the scientific method to shop-floor jobs. He spent more than two decades passionately pursuing the "one best way" for such jobs to be done.

Taylor's experiences at Midvale led him to define clear guidelines for improving production efficiency. He argued that these four principles of management (see Exhibit 2–2) would result in prosperity for both workers and managers.[4] How did these scientific principles really work? Let's look at an example.

Probably the best-known example of Taylor's scientific management efforts was the pig iron experiment. Workers loaded "pigs" of iron (each weighing 92 pounds) onto railcars. Their daily average output was 12.5 tons. However, Taylor believed that by scientifically analyzing the job to determine the "one best way" to load pig iron, output could be increased to 47 or 48 tons per day. After scientifically applying different

*Frederick W. Taylor (1856–1915) was the father of scientific management. Working at Midvale Steel Company, Taylor witnessed many inefficiencies. He sought to create a mental revolution among both workers and managers by defining clear guidelines for improving production efficiency.*

Exhibit 2–2

**Taylor's Four Principles of Management**

> 1. Develop a science for each element of an individual's work, which will replace the old rule-of-thumb method.
>
> 2. Scientifically select and then train, teach, and develop the worker.
>
> 3. Heartily cooperate with the workers so as to ensure that all work is done in accordance with the principles of the science that has been developed.
>
> 4. Divide work and responsibility almost equally between management and workers. Management takes over all work for which it is better fitted than the workers.

Q & A

Frederick Taylor sounds like a pretty strict manager. Was he? Q & A 2.2 explains.

combinations of procedures, techniques, and tools, Taylor succeeded in getting that level of productivity. How? He put the right person on the job with the correct tools and equipment, had the worker follow his instructions exactly, and motivated the worker with an economic incentive of a significantly higher daily wage. ( Go to www.prenhall.com/rolls) Using similar approaches for other jobs, Taylor was able to define the "one best way" for doing each job. Overall, Taylor achieved consistent productivity improvements in the range of 200 percent or more. For his groundbreaking studies of manual work using scientific principles, Taylor became known as the "father" of scientific management. His ideas spread in the United States, France, Germany, Russia, and Japan, and inspired others to study and develop methods of scientific management. His most prominent followers were Frank and Lillian Gilbreth.

**Frank and Lillian Gilbreth** A construction contractor by trade, Frank Gilbreth gave up that career to study scientific management after hearing Taylor speak at a professional meeting. Frank and his wife Lillian, a psychologist, studied work to eliminate inefficient hand-and-body motions. The Gilbreths also experimented with the design and use of the proper tools and equipment for optimizing work performance.[5]

Frank is probably best known for his experiments in bricklaying. By carefully analyzing the bricklayer's job, he reduced the number of motions in laying exterior brick from 18 to about 5, and on laying interior brick the motions were reduced from 18 to 2. Using Gilbreth's techniques, a bricklayer was more productive and less fatigued at the end of the day.

The Gilbreths were among the first researchers to use motion pictures to study hand-and-body motions. They invented a device called a microchronometer that recorded a worker's motions and the amount of time spent doing each motion. Wasted motions missed by the naked eye could be identified and eliminated. The

*Frank and Lillian Gilbreth, parents of 12 children, ran their household using scientific management principles and techniques. Two of their children wrote a book,* Cheaper by the Dozen, *which described life with the two masters of efficiency.*

**scientific management**
Using the scientific method to determine the "one best way" for a job to be done.

Gilbreths also devised a classification scheme to label 17 basic hand motions (such as search, grasp, hold), which they called **therbligs** (Gilbreth spelled backward with the *th* transposed). This scheme allowed the Gilbreths a more precise way of analyzing a worker's exact hand movements.

## How Do Today's Managers Use Scientific Management?

The guidelines that Taylor and others devised for improving production efficiency are still used in organizations today.[6] For instance, when an employee is sorting a stack of papers and the papers are all aligned except they're upside down, is it more efficient to turn each paper right-side up as it's sorted or to turn the whole stack right-side up? When managers analyze the basic work tasks that must be performed, use time-and-motion study to eliminate wasted motions, hire the best qualified workers for a job, and design incentive systems based on output, they're using the principles of scientific management. (         Go to www.prenhall.com/rolls) But current management practice isn't restricted to scientific management. In fact, we can see ideas from the next major approach—general administrative theory—being used as well.

**Q & A**
How is scientific management a "management" theory if it was focused on improving laborers' jobs? See Q & A 2.3 for an explanation.

## Learning Review

- Describe the important contributions made by Frederick W. Taylor and Frank and Lillian Gilbreth.

- Explain how today's managers use scientific management.

## GENERAL ADMINISTRATIVE THEORY

Another group of writers looked at the subject of management from the perspective of the entire organization. This approach, known as **general administrative theory**, described what managers do and what constituted good management practice. Let's look at some important contributions of this perspective.

### Important Contributions

The two most prominent theorists behind the general administrative approach were Henri Fayol and Max Weber.

**Henri Fayol** We introduced Fayol in Chapter 1 because he identified five functions of managers: planning, organizing, commanding, coordinating, and controlling. Because his ideas were important, let's look closer at what he had to say.[7]

Fayol wrote during the same time period as Taylor. While Taylor was concerned with first-line managers and the scientific method, Fayol's attention was directed toward the activities of *all* managers. He wrote from personal experience as he was the managing director of a large French coal-mining firm.

Fayol described the practice of management as something distinct from accounting, finance, production, distribution, and other typical business functions. His belief that management was an activity common to all business endeavors, government, and even in the home led him to develop 14 **principles of management**—fundamental rules of management that could be taught in schools and applied in all organizational situations. These principles are shown in Exhibit 2–3. (         Go to www.prenhall.com/rolls)

**Q & A**
Why is Taylor considered the "father of management" when Fayol was the one who actually studied managers? Check out Q & A 2.4.

**Max Weber** Weber (pronounced VAY-ber) was a German sociologist who studied organizations. Writing in the early 1900s, he developed a theory of authority structures and relations.[8] Weber described an ideal type of organization he called a **bureaucracy**—a form of organization characterized by division of labor, a clearly defined hierarchy, detailed rules and regulations, and impersonal relationships.

Exhibit 2–3

**Fayol's 14 Principles of Management**

1. *Division of work.* Specialization increases output by making employees more efficient.
2. *Authority.* Managers must be able to give orders and authority gives them this right.
3. *Discipline.* Employees must obey and respect the rules that govern the organization.
4. *Unity of command.* Every employee should receive orders from only one superior.
5. *Unity of direction.* The organization should have a single plan of action to guide managers and workers.
6. *Subordination of individual interests to the general interest.* The interests of any one employee or group of employees should not take precedence over the interests of the organization as a whole.
7. *Remuneration.* Workers must be paid a fair wage for their services.
8. *Centralization.* This term refers to the degree to which subordinates are involved in decision making.
9. *Scalar chain.* The line of authority from top management to the lowest ranks is the scalar chain.
10. *Order.* People and materials should be in the right place at the right time.
11. *Equity.* Managers should be kind and fair to their subordinates.
12. *Stability of tenure of personnel.* Management should provide orderly personnel planning and ensure that replacements are available to fill vacancies.
13. *Initiative.* Employees who are allowed to originate and carry out plans will exert high levels of effort.
14. *Esprit de corps.* Promoting team spirit will build harmony and unity within the organization.

Weber recognized that this "ideal bureaucracy" didn't exist in reality. Instead he intended it as a basis for theorizing about how work could be done in large groups. His theory became the model structural design for many of today's large organizations. The features of Weber's ideal bureaucratic structure are outlined in Exhibit 2–4.

Bureaucracy, as described by Weber, is a lot like scientific management in its ideology. Both emphasize rationality, predictability, impersonality, technical competence, and authoritarianism. Although Weber's writings were less practical than Taylor's, the fact that his "ideal type" still describes many contemporary organizations attests to the importance of his work.

## How Do Today's Managers Use General Administrative Theories?

Some of our current management ideas and practices can be directly traced to the contributions of general administrative theory. For instance, the functional view of the manager's job can be attributed to Fayol. In addition, his 14 principles serve as a frame of reference from which many current management concepts have evolved.

Weber's bureaucracy was an attempt to formulate an ideal prototype for organizations. Although many characteristics of Weber's bureaucracy are still evident in large organizations, his model isn't as popular today as it was in the twentieth century. Many

**therbligs**
A classification scheme for labeling 17 basic hand motions.

**general administrative theory**
A theory of management that focused on describing what managers do and what constitutes good management practice.

**principles of management**
Fundamental rules of management that could be taught in schools and applied in all organizational situations.

**bureaucracy**
A form of organization characterized by division of labor, a clearly defined hierarchy, detailed rules and regulations, and impersonal relationships.

Exhibit 2–4   **Weber's Ideal Bureaucracy**

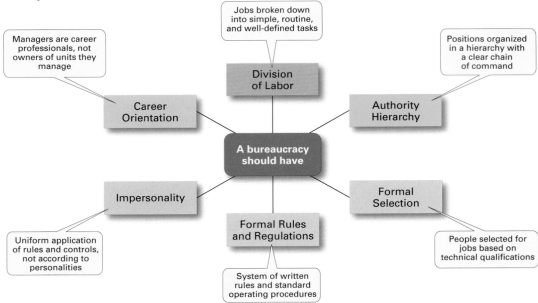

contemporary managers feel that bureaucracy's emphasis on strict division of labor, adherence to formal rules and regulations, and impersonal application of rules and controls hinders individual employees' creativity and the organization's ability to respond quickly to an increasingly dynamic environment. However, even in highly flexible organizations of creative professionals—such as Samsung, General Electric, or Cisco Systems—some bureaucratic mechanisms are necessary to ensure that resources are used efficiently and effectively.

## Learning Review

- Discuss Fayol's contributions to management theory.
- Describe Max Weber's contribution to management theory.
- Explain how today's managers use general administrative theories of management.

## QUANTITATIVE APPROACH TO MANAGEMENT

Although passengers bumping into each other when trying to find their seats on an airplane can be a mild annoyance for them, it's a bigger problem for airlines because of the backed-up lines it can create, slowing how quickly the plane can take off. Based on research in space–time geometry, America West Airlines innovated a unique boarding process called "reverse pyramid" that has saved at least 2 minutes in boarding time.[9] This is an example of the **quantitative approach**, which involves the use of quantitative techniques to improve decision making. This approach also has been called *operations research* or *management science*.

### Important Contributions

The quantitative approach evolved from the development of mathematical and statistical solutions to military problems during World War II. After the war was over, many of the techniques that had been used for military problems were applied to businesses.

One group of military officers, nicknamed the Whiz Kids, joined Ford Motor Company in the mid-1940s and immediately began using statistical methods and quantitative models to improve decision making. Two of these individuals whose names you might recognize are Robert McNamara (who went on to become president of Ford, U.S. Secretary of Defense, and head of the World Bank) and Charles "Tex" Thornton (who founded Litton Industries).

What exactly does the quantitative approach do? It involves applications of statistics, optimization models, information models, and computer simulations to management activities. Linear programming, for instance, is a technique that managers use to improve resource allocation decisions. Work scheduling can be more efficient as a result of critical-path scheduling analysis. The economic order quantity model helps managers determine optimum inventory levels. Each of these is an example of quantitative techniques being applied to improve managerial decision making.

## How Do Today's Managers Use the Quantitative Approach?

At Circuit City's 600-plus locations, everything from the clothes the floor salespeople wear to how long 0 percent financing should be offered has been studied by statisticians. They found, for instance, that flat commissions worked better than the product-based commissions that had been used for over 48 years. This and other findings led to company changes that in one year alone contributed an estimated $300 million in sales.

The quantitative approach contributes directly to management decision making in the areas of planning and control. For instance, when managers make budgeting, scheduling, quality control, and similar decisions, they typically rely on quantitative techniques. Specialized software has made the use of quantitative techniques somewhat less intimidating for managers, although they must still be able to interpret the results. We cover some of the more important quantitative techniques in Chapters 6, 9 and 18.

Despite its potential impact on managerial decision making, the quantitative approach hasn't influenced management practice as much as the next one we're going to discuss—organizational behavior—for a number of reasons. These include the fact that many managers are unfamiliar with and intimidated by the quantitative tools, behavioral problems are more widespread and visible, and it is easier for most students and managers to relate to real, day-to-day people problems than to quantitative models.

*After Marla (right) and Bonnie Schaefer, co-CEOs and chairs of the board, inherited Claire's Stores, Inc., a chain of jewelry and accessories outlets for teens and tweens, from their father, they quickly shifted the company's buying strategies. Profits have nearly doubled thanks to their relying on quantitative methods to guide their buyers, such as market research to track teen trends, instead of relying on the buyers' personal taste, as their father did. The sisters also studied the profit margins of Claire's many product lines and changed focus to sell more jewelry, that has higher margins.*

**quantitative approach**
The use of quantitative techniques to improve decision making.

# Learning Review

- Explain what the quantitative approach has contributed to the field of management.

- Discuss how today's managers use the quantitative approach.

## TOWARD UNDERSTANDING ORGANIZATIONAL BEHAVIOR

As we know, managers get things done by working with people. This explains why some writers have chosen to look at management by focusing on the organization's people. The field of study concerned with the actions (behavior) of people at work is called **organizational behavior (OB)**. Much of what currently makes up the field of human resource management, as well as contemporary views on motivation, leadership, trust, teamwork, and conflict management, has come out of organizational behavior research.

### Early Advocates

Although several individuals in the late 1800s and early 1900s recognized the importance of people to an organization's success, four stand out as early advocates of the OB approach: Robert Owen, Hugo Munsterberg, Mary Parker Follett, and Chester Barnard. Their contributions were varied and distinct, yet they all believed that people were the most important asset of the organization and should be managed accordingly. Their ideas provided the foundation for such management practices as employee selection procedures, employee motivation programs, employee work teams, and organization–environment management techniques. Exhibit 2–5 summarizes the most important ideas of these early advocates.

Exhibit 2–5   **Early Advocates of OB**

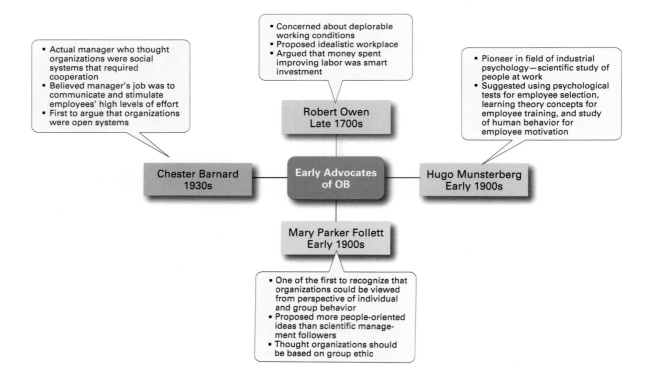

## The Hawthorne Studies

Without question, the most important contribution to the emergent OB field came out of the **Hawthorne Studies**, a series of studies conducted at the Western Electric Company Works in Cicero, Illinois. These studies, which started in 1924, were initially designed by Western Electric industrial engineers as a scientific management experiment. They wanted to examine the effect of various lighting levels on worker productivity. Like any good scientific experiment, control and experimental groups were set up with the experimental group being exposed to various lighting intensities, and the control group working under a constant intensity. If you were the industrial engineers in charge of this experiment, what would you have expected to happen? It's logical to think that individual output in the experimental group would be directly related to the intensity of the light. However, they found that as the level of light was increased in the experimental group, output for both groups increased. Then, much to the surprise of the engineers, as the light level was decreased in the experimental group, productivity continued to increase in both groups. In fact, a productivity decrease was observed in the experimental group *only* when the level of light was reduced to that of a moonlit night. What would explain these unexpected results? The engineers weren't sure, but they concluded that lighting intensity was not directly related to group productivity, and that something else must have contributed to the results. They weren't able to pinpoint what that "something else" was, though.

In 1927, the Western Electric engineers asked Harvard professor Elton Mayo and his associates to join the study as consultants. Thus began a relationship that would last through 1932 and encompass numerous experiments in the redesign of jobs, changes in workday and workweek length, introduction of rest periods, and individual versus group wage plans.[10] For example, one experiment was designed to evaluate the effect of a group piecework incentive pay system on group productivity. The results indicated that the incentive plan had less effect on a worker's output than did group pressure, acceptance, and security. The researchers concluded that social norms or group standards were the key determinants of individual work behavior.

Scholars generally agree that the Hawthorne Studies had a dramatic impact on management beliefs about the role of people in organizations. Mayo concluded that people's behavior and attitudes are closely related, that group factors significantly affect individual behavior, that group standards establish individual worker output, and that money is less a factor in determining output than are group standards, group attitudes, and security. These conclusions led to a new emphasis on the human behavior factor in the management of organizations.

Although critics attacked the research procedures, analyses of findings, and conclusions, it's of little importance from a historical perspective whether the Hawthorne studies were academically sound or their conclusions justified.[11] What *is* important is that they stimulated an interest in human behavior in organizations. (  Go to www.prenhall.com/rolls)

**Q & A**
The Hawthorne Studies were an important turning point in management theory. Q & A 2.5 explains why.

## How Do Today's Managers Use the Behavioral Approach?

The behavioral approach has largely shaped how today's organizations are managed. From the way that managers design jobs to the way that they work with employee teams to the way that they use open communication, we can see elements of the behavioral approach. Much of what the early OB advocates proposed and the conclusions from the Hawthorne Studies provided the foundation for our current theories of motivation, leadership, group behavior and development, and numerous other behavioral topics.

**organizational behavior (OB)**
The field of study concerned with the actions (behavior) of people at work.

**Hawthorne Studies**
A series of studies during the 1920s and 1930s that provided new insights into individual and group behavior.

# Learning Review

- Describe the contributions of the early advocates of OB.
- Explain the contributions of the Hawthorne Studies to the field of management.

- Discuss how today's managers use the behavioral approach.

## THE SYSTEMS APPROACH

During the 1960s, management researchers began to analyze organizations from a systems perspective, a concept taken from the physical sciences. A **system** is a set of inter-related and interdependent parts arranged in a manner that produces a unified whole. The two basic types of systems are closed and open. **Closed systems** are not influenced by and do not interact with their environment. In contrast, **open systems** dynamically interact with their environment. Today, when we describe organizations as systems, we mean open systems. Exhibit 2–6 shows a diagram of an organization from an open systems perspective. As you can see, an organization takes in inputs (resources) from the environment and transforms or processes these resources into outputs that are distributed into the environment. The organization is "open" to and interacts with its environment.

### The Systems Approach and Managers

How does the systems approach contribute to our understanding of management? Researchers envisioned an organization as being made up of "interdependent factors, including individuals, groups, attitudes, motives, formal structure, interactions, goals, status, and authority."[12] What this means is that as managers coordinate work activities in the various units of the organization, they ensure that all these interdependent units are working together so that the organization's goals can be achieved. For example, the systems approach would recognize that, no matter how efficient the production department might be, if the marketing department doesn't anticipate changes in customer tastes and work with the product development department in creating products customers want, the organization's overall performance will suffer.

In addition, the systems approach implies that decisions and actions taken in one organizational area will affect others and vice versa. For example, if the purchasing department doesn't acquire the right quantity and quality of inputs, the production department will not be able to do its job effectively.

Exhibit 2–6

**The Organization as an Open System**

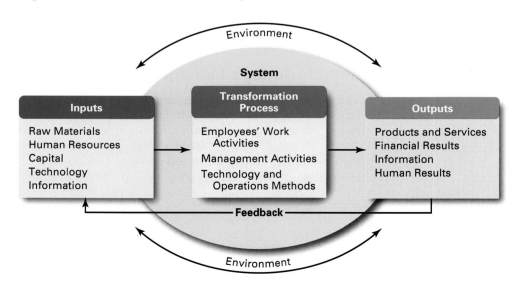

Finally, the systems approach recognizes that organizations are not self-contained. They rely on their environment for essential inputs and as outlets to absorb their outputs. No organization can survive for long if it ignores government regulations, supplier relations, or the varied external constituencies upon which it depends. (We'll cover these external forces in Chapter 3.)

How relevant is the systems approach to management? Quite relevant. Think, for example, of a day-shift manager at a local Wendy's restaurant who every day must coordinate the work of employees filling customer orders at the front counter and the drive-through windows, direct the delivery and unloading of food supplies, and address any customer concerns that arise. This manager "manages" all parts of the "system" so that the restaurant meets its daily sales goals. (  Go to www.prenhall.com/rolls)

**Q & A**
As a manager, why should I be concerned with understanding how my organization works as a system? Go to Q & A 2.6 to find out.

## Learning Review

- Describe an organization using the systems approach.
- Discuss how the systems approach helps us understand management.

## THE CONTINGENCY APPROACH

**Self Assessment Library (S.A.L.)**
I get it... organizations face changing situations. But I'm not too sure how well I'll adapt to all that change. Complete S.A.L. #III.C.1 to find out.

Early management theorists such as Taylor, Fayol, and Weber gave us principles of management that they generally assumed to be universally applicable. Later research found exceptions to many of their principles. For example, division of labor is valuable and widely used, but jobs can become *too* specialized. Bureaucracy is desirable in many situations, but in other circumstances, other structural designs are *more* effective. Management is not (and cannot be) based on simplistic principles to be applied in all situations. Different and changing situations require managers to use different approaches and techniques. The **contingency approach** (sometimes called the *situational approach*) says that organizations are different, face different situations (contingencies), and require different ways of managing. (  Go to www.prenhall.com/rolls)

### The Contingency Approach and Managers

The contingency approach can be described as "if, then." *If* this is the way my situation is, *then* this is the best way for me to manage. It's intuitively logical because organizations and even units within the same organization are diverse—in size, goals, work activities, and the like. It would be surprising to find universally applicable management rules that would work in *all* situations. But, of course, it's one thing to say that the way to manage "depends on the situation" and another to say what the situation is. Management researchers have been working to identify these situational or "what" variables. Exhibit 2–7 describes four popular contingency variables. The list is by no means comprehensive—more than 100 different "what" variables have been identified—but it represents those most widely used and gives you an idea of what we mean by the term *contingency variable.* As you can see, the contingency variables can have a significant impact on managers. The primary value of the contingency approach is that it stresses there are no simplistic or universal rules for managers to follow. (  Go to www.prenhall.com/rolls)

**Q & A**
Saying "it all depends" seems like I'll never have any guidance on the best way to manage people or situations. True? Q & A 2.7 and 2.8 tell you why the contingency approach is valuable to managers.

---

**system**
A set of interrelated and interdependent parts arranged in a manner that produces a unified whole.

**closed systems**
Systems that are not influenced by and do not interact with their environment.

**open systems**
Systems that interact with their environment.

**contingency approach**
Management approach that says that organizations are different, face different situations (contingencies), and require different ways of managing.

Exhibit 2–7

**Popular Contingency Variables**

**Organization Size.** As size increases, so do the problems of coordination. For instance, the type of organization structure appropriate for an organization of 50,000 employees is likely to be inefficient for an organization of 50 employees.

**Routineness of Task Technology.** To achieve its purpose, an organization uses technology. Routine technologies require organizational structures, leadership styles, and control systems that differ from those required by customized or nonroutine technologies.

**Environmental Uncertainty.** The degree of uncertainty caused by environmental changes influences the management process. What works best in a stable and predictable environment may be totally inappropriate in a rapidly changing and unpredictable environment.

**Individual Differences.** Individuals differ in terms of their desire for growth, autonomy, tolerance of ambiguity, and expectations. These and other individual differences are particularly important when managers select motivation techniques, leadership styles, and job designs.

## Learning Review

- Explain how the contingency approach differs from the early theories of management.

- Discuss how the contingency approach is appropriate for studying management.

## CURRENT TRENDS AND ISSUES

What current management concepts and practices are shaping "tomorrow's history"? In this section, we'll attempt to answer that question by introducing several trends and issues that we believe are changing the way managers do their jobs. We introduced you to two important trends in Chapter 1—customer service management and innovation. In this chapter, we'll examine others including globalization, ethics, workforce diversity, entrepreneurship, e-business, knowledge management and learning organizations, and quality management. Throughout the text we focus more closely on these issues in various boxes, examples, and exercises included in each chapter.

### Globalization

Managers are no longer constrained by national borders. BMW builds cars in South Carolina. McDonald's sells hamburgers in China. Toyota makes cars in Kentucky. Australia's leading real-estate company, Lend Lease Corporation, built the Bluewater shopping complex in Kent, England, and contracted with Coca-Cola to build bottling plants in Southeast Asia. Danish toy maker Lego Group opened factories and a distribution center in the Czech Republic. Swiss company ABB Ltd. constructed power-generating plants in Malaysia, South Korea, China, and Indonesia. As these examples illustrate, the world has definitely become a global village, leading to important changes in the manager's job.

WORKING WITH PEOPLE FROM DIFFERENT CULTURES. Even in your own country, you're likely to find yourself working with bosses, peers, and other employees who were born or raised in different cultures. What motivates you may not motivate them. Or your style of communication may be direct and open, but they may find this approach uncomfortable and threatening. To work effectively with a group of diverse people, you'll need to understand how their culture, geography, and religion have shaped their values, attitudes, and beliefs and adjust your management style accordingly.

COPING WITH ANTICAPITALIST BACKLASH. Capitalism's emphasis on profits, efficiency, and growth may be generally accepted in the United States, Australia, and Hong Kong, but that emphasis is not nearly as popular in places like France, the Middle East, or the Scandinavian countries. Managers at global companies like Coca-Cola, McDonald's, or

*Textile workers in Italy are facing some of the challenges of globalization as inexpensive imports from Asia force the Italian clothing industry to cut jobs. But Italy's 120,000-member textile union, Filtea, is taking a controversial stand. The union leadership believes that the best way to protect Italian workers and their jobs is not to impose protective duties or quotas or to strike, but rather to press for better working conditions, tax breaks for corporate research, and ultimately better Italian products that will be more competitive through streamlined manufacturing processes.*

Procter & Gamble have come to realize that economic values aren't universally transferable. Management practices need to be modified to reflect the values of the different countries in which an organization operates.

MOVEMENT OF JOBS TO COUNTRIES WITH LOW-COST LABOR.    Globalization means businesses can hire, source, and sell wherever they want. It's increasingly difficult for managers in economically advanced nations, where minimum wages are typically $6 or more an hour, to compete against companies who rely on workers from developing nations where labor is available for 30 cents an hour. It's not by chance that a good portion of Americans wear clothes made in China, work on computers whose parts came from Thailand, and watch movies filmed in Canada. In a global economy, jobs tend to flow to places where lower costs provide businesses with a comparative advantage. This "outsourcing" of jobs, however, has taken a new and unexpected turn, especially for those who think that the movement of jobs to countries with low-cost labor only affects factory workers and call-center operators. A number of low-cost countries are now graduating "large numbers of well-educated young people fully qualified to work in an information-based economy."[13] In 2005, there were 3.3 million college graduates in China and 3.1 million in India (all of whom are English-speaking) and only 1.3 million in the United States.[14] Why is this important? Because the service-intensive economy of the United States is especially vulnerable to potential outflows of information-based jobs. The implication for managers is that they must be prepared to deal with the difficult task of balancing the interests of their organization as it looks for ways to keep costs low and remain competitive with their responsibilities to the communities within which they operate.

SUMMARY.    Yes, globalization can be controversial, as these issues show. Regardless of these controversies, managers in organizations of all sizes and types around the world have to confront the challenges of operating in a global market.[15] Globalization is such an important topic that we devote one chapter to it (Chapter 4) and integrate discussion of its impact on the various management functions throughout the text. A number of our chapter-opening manager dilemmas, end-of-chapter cases, and chapter examples feature global managers and organizations. To reinforce the importance of your need to "think globally," we've included on our R.O.L.L.S. Web site *www.prenhall.com/rolls* background data on several countries and opportunities for you to use this country information as you analyze a number of case scenarios at the end of Parts Two through Six.

## Ethics

Bernie Ebbers of WorldCom—sentenced to 25 years for fraud relating to his role in an $11 billion accounting scandal. Former Enron CEO Jeff Skilling—charged with 35 counts including insider trading, fraud, conspiracy, and lying on financial statements. John Rigas of Adelphia Communications—sentenced to 15 years on charges of fraud and conspiracy. Former Tyco executives Dennis Kozlowski and Mark Swartz—sentenced to 8⅓ to 25 years in prison and ordered to pay more than $239 million in restitution and fines for looting nearly $600 million from their company.[16] The sad reality is that after these executives committed these crimes, their companies lay in ruins and the jobs and retirement savings of thousands of their employees had vanished.

During the early years of this decade, it seemed as if every day brought to light another case of corporate lying, misrepresentation, and financial manipulation. What happened to managerial ethics? Ethical behavior seemed to have been forgotten or ignored as these managers put their self-interest ahead of others who might be affected by their decisions. Take, for example, the "Enron Three"—former chairman Ken Lay (Ken Lay died July 6, 2006, in Aspen, Colorado, while awaiting sentencing on fraud conviction.), former CEO Jeff Skilling, and former CFO Andy Fastow. Each behaved as if the laws and accounting rules didn't apply to him. They were greedy and manipulative, and conspired to deceive their board of directors, employees, stockholders, and others about Enron's worsening financial condition. Because of these managers' highly unethical actions, thousands of Enron employees lost their jobs and the company stock set aside in their retirement savings became worthless. Although Enron seemed to be the most publicized example in this corporate ethics crisis, executives at a number of other companies also were engaging in similar kinds of unethical actions.

What would you have done had you been a manager in these organizations? How would you have reacted? One thing we know is that ethical issues aren't simple or easy. Make one decision and someone will be affected; make another, and someone else is likely to be affected. In today's changing workplace, managers need an approach to deal with the complexities and uncertainties associated with the ethical dilemmas that arise. We propose a process as outlined in Exhibit 2–8. What does this process entail? First, managers need to make sure they understand the ethical dilemma they're facing. They need to step back and think about what issue (or issues) is at stake. Next, it's important to identify the stakeholders that would be affected by the decision. What individuals or groups are likely to be impacted by my decision? Third, managers should identify the factors that are important to the decision. These include personal, organizational, and possibly external factors. We'll cover these factors in detail in Chapter 5. Next, managers should identify and evaluate possible courses of action, keeping in mind that each alternative will impact affected stakeholders differently. Then, it's time to make a decision and act. As today's managers manage, they can use this process to help them assess those ethical dilemmas they face and to develop appropriate courses of action.

Although most managers continue to behave ethically, these highly publicized abuses highlight a need to "upgrade" ethical standards, a need that's being addressed at two levels. First, ethics education is being widely emphasized in college curriculums. Second, organizations themselves are taking a more active role in creating and using codes of ethics, providing ethics training programs, and hiring ethics officers. We want to prepare you to deal with the ethics dilemmas you're likely to face. Therefore, we've included a "Thinking Critically About Ethics" box and an end-of-chapter ethics exercise in almost every chapter. In addition, we've included five comprehensive integrative and interactive ethics scenarios that you'll find on our R.O.L.L.S. Web site *www.prenhall.com/rolls*. You'll have numerous opportunities to experience what it's like to deal with ethical issues and dilemmas!

---

Exhibit 2–8

**A Process for Addressing Ethical Dilemmas**

> Step 1: What is the ethical dilemma?
>
> Step 2: Who are the affected stakeholders?
>
> Step 3: What personal, organizational, and external factors are important to my decision?
>
> Step 4: What are possible alternatives?
>
> Step 5: Make a decision and act on it.

# Workforce Diversity

One of the most important issues currently facing managers is coordinating work efforts of diverse organizational members in accomplishing organizational goals. Today's organizations are characterized by **workforce diversity**—a workforce that's heterogeneous in terms of gender, race, ethnicity, age, and other characteristics that reflect differences. ( ◆ Go to www.prenhall.com/rolls)

How diverse is the U.S. workforce? A report called *Workforce 2020* stated that the U.S. labor force will continue to reflect increasing ethnic diversity, although at a slower pace.[17] Between 1994 and 2005, minorities accounted for slightly more than one-half of net new entrants to the U.S. workforce. From 2005 to 2020, the fastest growth in the U.S. labor force will be Asian and Hispanic workers. In fact, Hispanics have now surpassed African Americans as the largest minority group in the United States.[18] Another significant demographic force affecting workforce diversity during the next decade will be the aging of the population, especially as the first wave of baby boomers (a population group encompassing individuals born between the years 1946 and 1964) turns 60. However, the impact may not be what you might expect. New research suggests that the boomers will have the ability—and the desire—to work productively and innovatively well beyond today's normal retirement age.[19] What impact might this trend have on the U.S. workplace? Many of these individuals may choose to continue working, either full-time or part-time, especially because medical research is showing that work can actually help an individual stay mentally and physically fit. Yet, for some other older workers who might otherwise have chosen to retire, the weak performance of the stock market and its effect on their retirement investment accounts have forced them to continue working. For whatever reason older workers may decide to continue working, many corporations also have begun to recognize the extensive experience and knowledge that mature employees bring to the workplace. To slow the "brain drain," more companies are "looking to keep older workers by investing in training programs and flexible work schedules...."[20] Although 61.5 million boomers currently make up 42 percent of the U.S. workforce, Generation Y (which is typically described as individuals born between 1977–1989) has been the fastest-growing segment of the workforce, growing from 14 to 21 percent during 2000–2004.[21] Eventually, there will be some 70 million of these Gen Y'ers, and their workplace attitudes are likely to create significant challenges for managers in the increasingly multigenerational workplaces. We'll study the challenges of managing generational differences in more detail in Chapter 14. (Turn to the back of the book and check out the Skills Module on Valuing Diversity.)

But workforce diversity isn't just an issue for U.S. managers. It's a concern for managers in Canada, Australia, South Africa, Japan, Europe, and other countries. For instance, Japanese managers from Hitachi, Matsushita, Sony, and other Japanese multinationals manage Chinese employees in Dalian. The European Union trade agreement, which opened up borders throughout much of western and now eastern Europe, has increased workforce diversity in organizations that operate in countries such as Spain, Germany, Italy, and France. Even in these and other economically developed nations, managers are finding that they need to effectively manage diversity as the level of immigration increases in Italy, the number of women entering the workforce rises in Japan, and the population ages in Germany.[22]

Does the fact that workforce diversity is an issue today mean that organizations weren't diverse before? No. They were, but diverse individuals made up a small percentage of the workforce, and organizations, for the most part, ignored the issue. Before the early 1980s, people took a "melting pot" approach to differences.

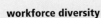

**workforce diversity**
A workforce that's heterogeneous in terms of gender, race, ethnicity, age, and other characteristics that reflect differences.

We assumed that people who were "different" would want to assimilate. But we now recognize that employees don't set aside their cultural values and lifestyle preferences when they come to work. The challenge for managers, therefore, is to make their organizations more accommodating to diverse groups of people by addressing different lifestyles, family needs, and work styles. The melting pot assumption has been replaced by the recognition and celebration of differences.[23] Smart managers recognize that diversity can be an asset because it brings a broad range of viewpoints and problem-solving skills to a company, and additionally helps organizations better understand a diverse customer base. Many companies such as Altria, Citigroup, PepsiCo, and Turner Broadcasting have strong diversity programs.[24] For example, in the Frito Lay division of PepsiCo, the Hispanic employee affinity group provided input in the development of a line of guacamole-flavored potato chips, which has become a $100 million product.[25] We'll highlight many diversity-related issues and how companies are responding to those issues throughout this text in our "Managing Workforce Diversity" boxes. In addition, you'll find interactive diversity exercises on our R.O.L.L.S. Web site *www.prenhall.com/rolls.*

## Entrepreneurship

Entrepreneurship is an important global activity.[26] But what exactly is **entrepreneurship**? It's the process of starting new businesses, generally in response to opportunities. Three important themes are implied in this definition of entrepreneurship. First is the pursuit of opportunities. Entrepreneurship is about pursuing environmental trends and changes that no one else has seen or paid attention to. For example, Jeff Bezos, founder of Amazon.com, was a successful programmer at an investment firm on Wall Street in the mid-1990s. However, statistics on the explosive growth in the use of the Internet (at that time, it was growing about 2,300 percent a month) kept nagging at him. He decided to quit his job and pursue what he felt were going to be enormous online retailing opportunities. Today, you can buy books, music, cars, furniture, jewelry, and numerous other items on Amazon.

The second important theme in entrepreneurship is innovation. Entrepreneurship involves changing, revolutionizing, transforming, or introducing new products or services or new ways of doing business. Dineh Mohajer is a good example. As a fashion-conscious young woman, she hated the brilliant and bright nail polishes for sale in stores because the bright colors clashed with her trendy pastel-colored clothing. She wanted pastel nail colors that would match what she was wearing. When she couldn't find the right shade of nail polish to match her strappy blue sandals, Mohajer decided to mix her own. When her friends raved over her homemade colors, she decided to

*Working part-time at an auto-body shop while pursuing his master's degree, engineering student Joe Born wondered whether an industrial paint buffer could smooth out the scratches that had ruined one of his favorite music CDs. The idea worked like a charm, and after receiving a patent on it, Born spent 4 years perfecting SkipDr, an inexpensive disc-repair kit that he marketed successfully to Best Buy, Radio Shack, and Wal-Mart. Born's new company, Digital Innovations, how sells 50 different products to clean and repair CDs, DVDs, video games, and office equipment and is worth about $25 million.*

## *managing* IT

### How IT Is Changing the Manager's Job

IT (that's an abbreviation for "information technology")[27] is changing many things in today's world. On campuses—the "world" you're most familiar with now—students are downloading professors' lectures to their iPods and other MP3 players. Laptops in classrooms are now a common sight. Some experts say that this anytime-anywhere access for students has tangible benefits. Says one IT consultant, "To compete globally, we're going to have to produce a nation of problem-solvers and analytical thinkers, and we're going to have to do it using twenty-first–century tools." But IT isn't just drastically changing the educational world; it's having a major impact on businesses and how managers do their job.

At the Springfield, Missouri, branch of Kansas City–based UMB Bank, employees gather daily in a sales huddle and listen to managers dole out a mix of praise and exhortation. Although a daily employee meeting like this may not seem like a big deal, it's an indicator of the massive changes taking place at this almost-century-old organization. Mediocre performance throughout the bank's branches in seven midwestern states led to new management being brought in to "shake things up." One of the changes made by the new management team was the implementation of electronic management scorecards designed to track company performance, set business-unit goals, stimulate new ideas, and motivate managers and employees to do better. The sales huddles are a way for managers to connect personally with employees and keep them focused on meeting the quantitative benchmarks of the scorecards.

Electronic scorecards are just one example of ways that managers are using IT to manage their organizations more efficiently and effectively. As managers plan, organize, lead, and control, they can look to IT as a tool to help them collect and use information. Throughout the book in these "Managing IT" boxes, we'll describe many other ways that managers are using IT in their jobs.

---

take samples of her nail polish to exclusive stores in Los Angeles. They were an instant hit! Today, the Hard Candy line features over 150 cosmetic products—all the result of Mohajer's innovative ideas.

The final important theme in entrepreneurship is growth. Entrepreneurs pursue growth. They are not content for their organizations to stay small. Entrepreneurs work very hard to pursue growth as they continually look for trends and to innovate new products and new approaches.

We think an understanding of entrepreneurship is important and have included an all-inclusive appendix on entrepreneurship after Chapter 19. In addition, we feature entrepreneurs in many of our chapter-opening manager dilemmas, end-of-chapter cases, and chapter examples. (  Go to www.prenhall.com/rolls)

**Self-Assessment Library (S.A.L.)**

I think being an entrepreneur might be fun. I wonder if I have what it takes to be one. S.A.L. #I.E.4 will help you see.

## Managing in an E-Business World

Do you use e-mail to communicate? Can you find an advertisement that doesn't have a Web address in it somewhere? Today's managers function in an e-business world. In fact, as a student, your learning may increasingly be taking place in an electronic environment. Although some critics questioned the viability of Internet-based companies (dot-coms) after many went out of business in the early part of this decade, e-business is here to stay. E-business offers many advantages to organizations—small to large, profit or not-for-profit, global and domestic, and in all industries.[28]

**E-business (electronic business)** is a comprehensive term describing the way an organization does its work by using electronic (Internet-based) linkages with its key constituencies (employees, managers, customers, clients, suppliers, and partners) in order to efficiently and effectively achieve its goals. It includes **e-commerce**, which is essentially the sales and marketing aspect of e-business.[29] Firms such as Dell (computers) and

---

**entrepreneurship**
The process of starting new businesses, generally in response to opportunities.

**e-business (electronic business)**
The way an organization does its work by using electronic (Internet-based) linkages with its key constituencies in order to efficiently and effectively achieve its goals

**e-commerce (electronic commerce)**
The sales and marketing of e-business.

Exhibit 2–9

**Categories of E-Business
Involvement**

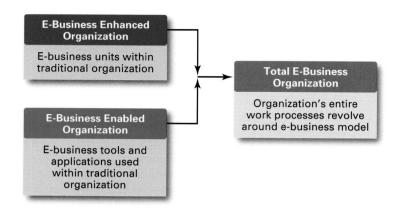

Varsitybooks (textbooks) are engaged in e-commerce because they sell items over the Internet.

Not every organization is, or needs to be, a total e-business. Exhibit 2–9 illustrates three types of e-business.[30] The first type is an e-business *enhanced* organization, a traditional organization that sets up e-business capabilities, usually e-commerce, while maintaining its traditional structure. Many *Fortune* 500–type organizations have evolved into e-businesses using this approach. They use the Internet to *enhance* (not to replace) their traditional ways of doing business. For instance, the Internet division of Sears Holding, a traditional bricks-and-mortar retailer with thousands of physical stores worldwide, is intended to expand, not replace, the company's main source of revenue.

Another category of e-business is an e-business *enabled* organization that uses the Internet to perform its traditional business functions better, but not to sell anything. In other words, the Internet *enables* organizational members to do their work more efficiently and effectively. Numerous organizations use electronic linkages to communicate with employees, customers, or suppliers and to support them with information. For instance, Levi Strauss uses its Web site to interact with customers, providing them the latest information about the company and its products, but not to sell the jeans. It also uses an **intranet**, a Web-based internal communication system accessible only by organizational employees.

The last category of e-business involvement is when an organization becomes a total e-business. Organizations such as Amazon.com, Google, Yahoo!, Blue Nile, and eBay are total e-business organizations. Their whole existence is based around the Internet. An interesting management aspect of total e-businesses is that they can operate their business with a relatively small number of employees. Google, for example, had over $6.1 billion in sales in 2005 with a little more than 5,600 employees; Amazon.com had over $8.5 billion in sales in 2005 with around 9,000 employees.

## Knowledge Management and Learning Organizations

Do you have space for one 30-foot shelf filled from top to bottom with books? That would be your (and every other person's) share if all the new information produced in a single year alone were divided equally worldwide.[31] Today's managers confront an environment in which knowledge creation and change take place at an unprecedented rate. As a result, many past management approaches and principles—created for a world that was more stable and predictable—no longer apply.

Organizations in the twenty-first century must be able to learn and respond quickly. These organizations will be led by managers who can effectively challenge conventional wisdom, manage the organization's knowledge base, and make needed changes. These organizations will need to be **learning organizations**—that is, ones that

Exhibit 2–10

**Learning Organization
Versus Traditional
Organization**

|  | Traditional Organization | Learning Organization |
|---|---|---|
| Attitude toward change | If it's working, don't change it. | If you aren't changing, it won't be working for long. |
| Attitude toward new ideas | If it wasn't invented here, reject it. | If it was invented or reinvented here, reject it. |
| Who's responsible for innovation? | Traditional areas such as R&D | Everyone in organization |
| Main fear | Making mistakes | Not learning; not adapting |
| Competitive advantage | Products and service | Ability to learn, knowledge and expertise |
| Manager's job | Control others | Enable others |

have developed the capacity to continuously learn, adapt, and change. Exhibit 2–10 clarifies how a learning organization is different from a traditional organization.

Part of a manager's responsibility is to create learning capabilities throughout the organization—from lowest level to highest level and in all areas. How? An important step is understanding the value of knowledge as an important resource, just like cash, raw materials, or office equipment. To illustrate the value of knowledge, think about how you register for college classes. Do you talk to others who have had a certain professor? Do you listen to their experiences with this individual and make your decision based on what they have to say (their knowledge about the situation)? If you do, you're tapping into the value of knowledge. But in an organization, just recognizing the value of accumulated knowledge or wisdom isn't enough. Managers must deliberately manage that base of knowledge. **Knowledge management** involves cultivating a learning culture where organizational members systematically gather knowledge and share it with others in the organization so as to achieve better performance.[32] For instance, accountants and consultants at Ernst & Young, a professional-services firm, document best practices they have developed, unusual problems they have dealt with, and other work information. This "knowledge" is then shared with all employees through computer-based applications and through COIN (community of interest) teams that meet regularly throughout the company. Many

## thinking critically about **Ethics**

Information is power—those who have information have power. Because information gives them power, it's human nature to want to keep that information, not share it. Knowledge hoarding is a business habit that's hard to break. In fact, it's an attitude that still characterizes many businesses. In a learning organization, however, we're asking people to share information.

Getting people to share information may turn out to be one of the key challenges facing managers. Is it ethical to ask people to share information that they've worked hard to obtain? What if performance evaluations are based on how well individuals do their jobs, and how well they do their jobs is dependent on the special knowledge that they have? Is it ethical to ask them to share that information? What ethical implications are inherent in creating an organizational environment that promotes knowledge sharing?

**intranet**
A Web-based internal communication system accessible only by organizational employees.

**learning organization**
An organization that has developed the capacity to continuously learn, adapt, and change.

**knowledge management**
Cultivating a learning culture where organizational members systematically gather knowledge and share it with others in the organization so as to achieve better performance.

Chapter

3

# Learning Outline

*Use this Learning Outline as you read and study this chapter.*

### The Manager: Omnipotent or Symbolic
- Contrast the actions of managers according to the omnipotent and symbolic views.
- Explain the parameters of managerial discretion.

### The Organization's Culture
- Describe the seven dimensions of organizational culture.
- Discuss the impact of a strong culture on organizations and managers.
- Explain the source of an organization's culture.
- Describe how culture is transmitted to employees.
- Describe how culture affects managers.

### Current Organizational Culture Issues Facing Managers
- Describe the characteristics of an ethical culture, an innovative culture, and a customer-responsive culture.
- Explain why workplace spirituality seems to be an important concern.
- Describe the characteristics of a spiritual organization.

### The Environment
- Describe the components of the specific and general environments.
- Discuss the two dimensions of environmental uncertainty.
- Identify the most common organizational stakeholders.
- Explain the four steps in managing external stakeholder relationships.

# Organizational Culture and Environment: The Constraints

## A Manager's Dilemma

Yves Guillemot is CEO of France-based Ubisoft, a leading international developer, publisher, and distributor of interactive entertainment products or what most people know better as . . . video games.[1] The company's *Myst, Prince of Persia,* and *Tom Clancy's Splinter Cell* games are among some of the most popular and most critically acclaimed titles on the market. However, instead of building fancy studios in Southern California like Electronic Arts, the biggest U.S. video-game company and a competitor, Yves has opened numerous low-cost game studios in some 20 countries around the world including Australia, Canada, China, Germany, Morocco, and Romania, among others. Says Yves, "For me, it has never been about making cheap games. What I wanted to do was find a way to make the highest-quality games at the most competitive cost." Doing that, however, required having a strong pipeline of computer science students to fill the jobs. Managing all that young creative talent has been, and will continue to be, critical to the company's success as well.

Yves uses the same managerial approach in operating each of his company's widespread design studios, where a collaborative environment is essential. One way he achieves this in each location is by having a team of 80 to 90 employees, including managers, who work together in a single "war room" to create a game's core technology. But that collaboration isn't limited to just one location—it extends between studios. For example, during the development of the *Prince of Persia* game, the core software came from a studio in the French Alps, while the top programmer in Canada was on loan from Ubisoft Shanghai. By the way, that game turned out to be an award winner! However, such cross-border collaboration doesn't always work that well. In one instance, the Shanghai studio was assigned to develop a racing game before Yves realized that no one there knew how to drive. But even that drawback can have a bright side—sometimes that lack of knowledge or experience means that designers are more open to trying risky new ideas.

Put yourself in Yves's position. As his company continues to grow and add employees around the globe, how can he ensure that Ubisoft's culture will be transmitted to these employees?

## What would you do?

Yves Guillemot recognizes how important organizational culture is to his organization. He has formed a culture where employees enjoy being with each other and supporting each other. He also recognizes the challenges facing his organization in trying to manage its internal culture, especially as the organization grows. But how much actual impact does a manager like Yves have on an organization's success or failure? In the following section, we explore this important question.

## THE MANAGER: OMNIPOTENT OR SYMBOLIC?

The dominant view in management theory and society in general is that managers are directly responsible for an organization's success or failure. We'll call this perspective the **omnipotent view of management**. In contrast, some observers have argued that much of an organization's success or failure is due to external forces outside managers' control. This perspective has been labeled the **symbolic view of management**. Let's look more closely at each of these perspectives so we can try to clarify just how much credit or blame managers should receive for their organization's performance.

### The Omnipotent View

In Chapter 1, we discussed the importance of managers to organizations. This view reflects a dominant assumption in management theory: The quality of an organization's managers determines the quality of the organization itself. It's assumed that differences in an organization's performance are due to the decisions and actions of its managers. Good managers anticipate change, exploit opportunities, correct poor performance, and lead their organizations toward their goals, which may be changed if necessary. When profits are up, managers take the credit and reward themselves with bonuses, stock options, and the like. When profits are down, top managers are often fired in the belief that "new blood" will bring improved results. For instance, Sears Holdings Corp. (the retailer created when Kmart Holding purchased Sears in March 2005) demoted CEO Alan J. Lacy (whose experience and skills were finance) so that a leader with more experience in marketing and promoting brands could help the organization be more responsive to customers.[2]

The view of managers as omnipotent is consistent with the stereotypical picture of the take-charge business executive who can overcome any obstacle in carrying out the organization's goals. (  Go to www.prenhall.com/rolls) This omnipotent view, of course, isn't limited to business organizations. We can also use it to help explain the high turnover among college and professional sports coaches, who can be considered the "managers" of their teams. Coaches who lose more games than they win are fired and replaced by new coaches who, it is hoped, will correct the inadequate performance.

In the omnipotent view, when organizations perform poorly, someone has to be held accountable regardless of the reasons, and in our society, that "someone" is the manager. Of course, when things go well, we need someone to praise. So managers also get the credit—even if they had little to do with achieving positive outcomes.

### The Symbolic View

Fleetwood Enterprises of Riverside, California, is the number-one U.S. maker of recreational vehicles and the number-three maker of manufactured housing. In a period of about 6 weeks from late August 2005, the company's stock price rose 29 percent. Also, Joanne Foist, director of marketing services, confirmed that FEMA (Federal Emergency Management Agency) had bought much of the company's retail stock after Hurricanes Katrina and Rita.[3] Were these outcomes the result of managers' decisions and actions, or was it beyond their control? The symbolic view would suggest the latter.

The symbolic view says that a manager's ability to affect outcomes is influenced and constrained by external factors.[4] In this view, it's unreasonable to expect managers

**Q & A**

Omnipotent . . . now that's an unusual way to describe managers. How can they be considered omnipotent? Go to Q & A 3.1 for an example.

Exhibit 3–1

**Parameters of Managerial Discretion**

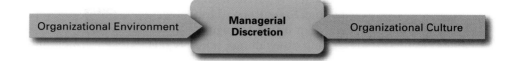

to significantly affect an organization's performance. Instead, an organization's results are influenced by factors managers don't control such as the economy, customers, governmental policies, competitors' actions, industry conditions, control over proprietary technology, and decisions made by previous managers.

The "symbolic" view is based on the belief that managers symbolize control and influence.[5] How? By creating meaning out of randomness, confusion, and ambiguity or by trying to innovate and adapt. Because their effect on organizational outcomes is limited, a manager's actions often involve developing plans, making decisions, and engaging in other managerial activities, which they do for the benefit of stockholders, customers, employees, and the public. However, the actual part that managers play in organizational success or failure is minimal.

## Reality Suggests a Synthesis

Q & A

Organizations succeed. Organizations fail. Are the managers responsible? Q & A 3.2 can help explain what role managers play in organizational success and failure.

In reality, managers are neither helpless nor all powerful. ( ◆ Go to www.prenhall.com/rolls) Internal and external constraints that restrict a manager's decision options exist within every organization. Internal constraints come from the organization's culture and external constraints come from the organization's environment.

Exhibit 3–1 shows managers as operating within the constraints imposed by the organization's culture and environment. Yet, despite these constraints, managers are not powerless. They can still influence an organization's performance. In the remainder of this chapter, we'll discuss organizational culture and environment as constraints. However, as we'll see in other chapters, these constraints don't mean that a manager's hands are tied. As Yves Guillemot in our chapter-opening dilemma recognized, managers can and do influence their culture and environment.

## Learning Review

- Contrast the actions of managers according to the omnipotent and symbolic views.

- Explain the parameters of managerial discretion.

## THE ORGANIZATION'S CULTURE

We know that every person has a unique personality—traits and characteristics that influence the way we act and interact with others. When we describe someone as warm, open, relaxed, shy, or aggressive, we're describing personality traits. An organization, too, has a personality, which we call its *culture*.

## What Is Organizational Culture?

Payless Shoe Source, headquartered in Topeka, Kansas, understands what organizational culture is. As the world's largest footwear retailer, it's quite vulnerable to competitive attacks by the dynamic duo of retailing—Wal-Mart and Target. To be prepared, Payless's

---

**omnipotent view of management**
The view that managers are directly responsible for an organization's success or failure.

**symbolic view of management**
The view that much of an organization's success or failure is due to external forces outside managers' control.

managers knew the company's culture would have to be more aggressive, creative, and risk taking. To reinforce these values, at an annual sales meeting all the district managers were sent out on a scavenger hunt into the community to find certain "treasures" including, among other things, a hook-and-ladder fire truck (which one team actually did find and bring back), hospital scrubs, and a FedEx truck. Teams also had to photograph themselves next to certain items while carrying rubber chickens. And all this had to be accomplished within 2 hours. Why? To prove to the managers that they could work together to come up with creative solutions even under pressure-packed conditions. Although a single scavenger hunt couldn't, by itself, bring about such a culture, it was a step toward the type of thinking that would be crucial if Payless was to continue growing.[6]

**Q & A**

Do all organizations have a culture? See Q & A 3.3.

What is **organizational culture**? It's the shared values, principles, traditions, and ways of doing things that influence the way organizational members act. ( 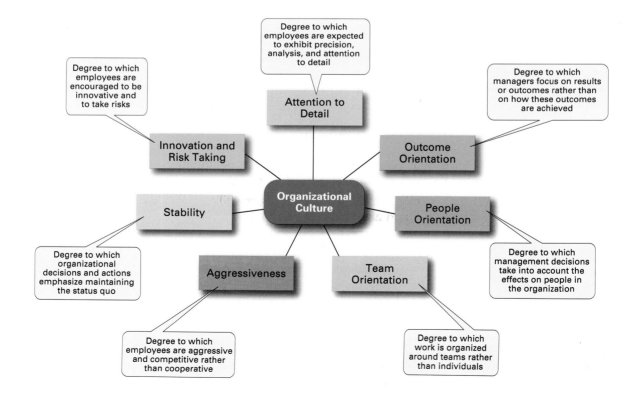 Go to www.prenhall.com/rolls) In most organizations, these important shared values and practices have evolved over time and determine, in large degree, what employees perceive about their organizational experiences and how they behave in the organization.[7] The organizational culture—the "way we do things around here"—influences what employees can do and how they view, define, analyze, and resolve problems and issues. ( Go to www.prenhall.com/rolls)

**Q & A**

It seems from this definition that an organization's culture is something that wouldn't change very often. Correct? Q & A 3.4 explains.

Our definition of culture implies three things. First, culture is a *perception.* Individuals perceive the organizational culture on the basis of what they see, hear, or experience within the organization. Second, even though individuals may have different backgrounds or work at different organizational levels, they tend to describe the organization's culture in similar terms. That's the *shared* aspect of culture. Finally, organizational culture is *descriptive.* It's concerned with how members perceive the organization, not with whether they like it. It describes rather than evaluates.

Research suggests that there are seven dimensions that capture the essence of an organization's culture.[8] These dimensions are described in Exhibit 3–2. Each dimension ranges from low to high, which simply is a way of saying that it's not very typical of the cul-

Exhibit 3–2 **Dimensions of Organizational Culture**

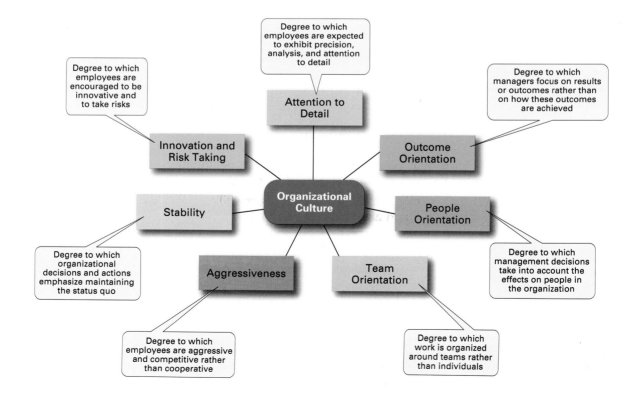

Exhibit 3–3

**Contrasting
Organizational Cultures**

**Organization A**

This organization is a manufacturing firm. Managers are expected to fully document all decisions, and "good managers" are those who can provide detailed data to support their recommendations. Creative decisions that incur significant change or risk are not encouraged. Because managers of failed projects are openly criticized and penalized, managers try not to implement ideas that deviate much from the status quo. One lower-level manager quoted an often-used phrase in the company: "If it ain't broke, don't fix it."

Employees are required to follow extensive rules and regulations in this firm. Managers supervise employees closely to ensure that there are no deviations. Management is concerned with high productivity, regardless of the impact on employee morale or turnover.

Work activities are designed around individuals. There are distinct departments and lines of authority, and employees are expected to minimize formal contact with other employees outside their functional area or line of command. Performance evaluations and rewards emphasize individual effort, although seniority tends to be the primary factor in the determination of pay raises and promotions.

**Organization B**

This organization is also a manufacturing firm. Here, however, management encourages and rewards risk taking and change. Decisions based on intuition are valued as much as those that are well rationalized. Management prides itself on its history of experimenting with new technologies and its success in regularly introducing innovative products. Managers or employees who have a good idea are encouraged to "run with it," and failures are treated as "learning experiences." The company prides itself on being market driven and rapidly responsive to the changing needs of its customers.

There are few rules and regulations for employees to follow, and supervision is loose because management believes that its employees are hardworking and trustworthy. Management is concerned with high productivity but believes that this comes through treating its people right. The company is proud of its reputation as being a good place to work.

Job activities are designed around work teams, and team members are encouraged to interact with people across functions and authority levels. Employees talk positively about the competition between teams. Individuals and teams have goals, and bonuses are based on achievement of outcomes. Employees are given considerable autonomy in choosing the means by which the goals are attained.

**Q & A**

Since an organization's culture isn't really something that you can physically see, how do I know what it's like? Check out Q & A 3.5 for some tips on how to describe an organization's culture.

ture (low) or is very typical of the culture (high). Appraising an organization on these seven dimensions gives a composite picture of the organization's culture. (  Go to www.prenhall.com/rolls) In many organizations, one of these cultural dimensions often is emphasized more than the others and essentially shapes the organization's personality and the way organizational members work. For instance, at Sony Corporation the focus is product innovation. The company "lives and breathes" new product development (outcome orientation), and employees' work decisions, behaviors, and actions support that goal. In contrast, Southwest Airlines has made its employees a central part of its culture (people orientation). Exhibit 3–3 describes how the dimensions can be combined to create significantly different organizations.

## Strong Versus Weak Cultures

Although all organizations have cultures, not all cultures have an equal impact on employees' behaviors and actions. **Strong cultures**—cultures in which the key values are deeply held and widely shared—have a greater influence on employees than do weak cultures. The more employees accept the organization's key values and the greater their commitment to those values, the stronger the culture is. ( Go to www.prenhall.com/rolls) Exhibit 3–4 contrasts strong and weak organizational cultures.

**Q & A**

Okay . . . a strong culture would also have to be a very stable one. Couldn't that stability be a problem? See Q & A 3.6.

**organizational culture**
The shared values, principles, traditions, and ways of doing things that influence the way organizational members act.

**strong cultures**
Organizational cultures in which the key values are intensely held and widely shared.

Exhibit 3–4

**Strong Versus Weak Organizational Cultures**

| Strong Cultures | Weak Cultures |
| --- | --- |
| Values widely shared | Values limited to a few people—usually top management |
| Culture conveys consistent messages about what's important | Culture sends contradictory messages about what's important |
| Most employees can tell stories about company history/heroes | Employees have little knowledge of company history or heroes |
| Employees strongly identify with culture | Employees have little identification with culture |
| Strong connection between shared values and behaviors | Little connection between shared values and behaviors |

Whether an organization's culture is strong, weak, or somewhere in between depends on factors such as the size of the organization, how long it has been around, how much turnover there has been among employees, and the intensity with which the culture was originated. Although strong cultures may be more likely in smaller organizations that have low employee turnover and clear, well-defined values that have shaped and guided the organization for a period of time, *most* organizations have moderate to strong cultures; that is, there is relatively high agreement on what's important, what defines "good" employee behavior, what it takes to get ahead, and so forth.

What impact does a strong culture have on an organization? One study found that employees in organizations with strong cultures were more committed to their organization than were employees in organizations with weak cultures. The organizations with strong cultures also used their recruitment efforts and socialization practices to build employee commitment.[9] And an increasing body of evidence suggests that strong cultures are associated with high organizational performance.[10] It's easy to understand why a strong culture enhances performance. After all, when values are clear and widely accepted, employees know what they're supposed to do and what's expected of them so they can act quickly to take care of problems, thus preventing any potential performance decline. However, the drawback is that the same strong culture also might prevent employees from trying new approaches, especially during periods of rapid change.[11]   ( 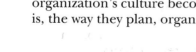 Go to www.prenhall.com/rolls)

**Q & A**
How can an organization have a strong culture *and* be able to adapt during rapid change? Go to Q & A 3.7 for an explanation.

What are the implications of a strong culture for the way managers manage? As an organization's culture becomes stronger, it increasingly affects what managers do; that is, the way they plan, organize, lead, and control.[12]

*Olive Garden, the chain of family-oriented Italian restaurants, has a strong culture in which the 70,000 employees are considered family members, and mutual respect and high standards are important company values.*

## The Source of Culture

An organization's current customs, traditions, and general way of doing things are largely due to what it has done before and how successful it has been with those endeavors. The original source of an organization's culture usually reflects the vision or mission of the organization's founders. Their focus might be aggressiveness or it might be treating employees as family. The founders establish the early culture by projecting an image of what the organization should be. They're not constrained by previous customs or approaches. And the small size of most new organizations helps the founders instill their vision in all organizational members.

For example, Yvon Chouinard, the founder of the outdoor gear company Patagonia, Inc., was an avid "extreme adventurer." He approached the business in a laid-back, casual manner and hired employees not on the basis of any specific business skills but because he had climbed, fished, or surfed with them. Employees were friends, and work was treated as something fun to do. In a speech Chouinard gave a few years go, he is said to have uttered the line, "Let my people go surfing!" Although the company (now called "Lost Arrow") has more than 900 employees and revenues of around $250 million (2004), its culture still reflects Chouinard's values and philosophy. To keep employees happy, it offers child-care and yoga classes at work and donates 1 percent of its sales to green causes. And if the surf is good, employees are free to go enjoy it![13]

The impact of a founder on an organization's culture isn't unique to the United States. At Hyundai Corporation, the giant Korean conglomerate, the culture reflects the fierce, competitive style of its founder, Chung Ju Yung. Other well-known contemporary examples of founders from the United States and other countries who have had an enormous impact on their organization's culture include Bill Gates at Microsoft, Herb Kelleher at Southwest Airlines, Fred Smith at Federal Express, Sam Walton at Wal-Mart, Akio Morita at Sony, Ingvar Kamprad at IKEA, and Richard Branson at the Virgin Group.

## How an Organization's Culture Continues

Once a culture is in place, certain organizational practices help maintain it. For instance, during the employee selection process, managers typically judge job candidates not only on the job requirements, but also on how well they might fit into the organization. At the same time, job candidates find out information about the organization and determine whether they are comfortable with what they see. (  Go to www.prenhall.com/rolls)

The actions of top executives also have a major impact on the organization's culture. Aylwin B. Lewis, promoted in September 2005 to CEO of Sears Holding Corporation, addressed a group of Kmart managers at a dinner meeting by shouting, "Our worst stores are dungeons! Well, who wants to work in a dungeon? Who wants to shop in a dungeon? Who wants to walk into an environment that is so dull and lifeless that it is sucking the air out of your body?" Lewis knew that he had to convey the importance of changing the company's inward-looking culture and becoming more customer-focused if the merged Kmart–Sears were to have any hope of surviving in the tough retail environment. Rather than being insulted and demoralized, the managers responded by hooting loudly and giving him a standing ovation.[15] Through what they say and how they behave, top-level managers establish norms that filter down through the organization. This can have a positive effect on employees' willingness to take risks or to provide exceptional customer service, for instance. IBM's CEO Sam Palmisano wanted employees to value teamwork so he chose to take several million dollars from his yearly bonus and give it to his top executives based on their teamwork. He said, "If you say you're about a team, you have to be a team. You've got to walk the talk, right?"[16] It also can have the opposite effect if top managers' behavior is self-serving, as we saw in the corporate ethics scandals.

**PRISM**

When it's time to look for a job, wouldn't you like to be able to determine how comfortable you'd be in various organizational cultures? Develop your skill at "reading" an organization's culture by completing PRISM #3.

*managing your* **Career**

### Find a Culture That Fits

Richard D'Ambrosio thought he had found the perfect job at an accounting firm. It had all the outward appearances of a good workplace—employee recognition awards and managers with "politically correct" answers to work–life questions. Yet, as soon as he signed on, he found himself in a culture that prized working long hours just for the sake of working long hours and where junior accountants were expected to be at the beck and call of the partners. If it was your wedding anniversary, too bad. If it was a holiday, too bad. It only took a few months before he quit. How can you avoid the same problem? How can you find a culture that fits?[14] Here are some suggestions.

First, *figure out what suits you.* For instance, do you like working in teams or on your own? Do you like to go out after work with colleagues or go straight home? Are you comfortable in a more formal or a more casual environment? Then, narrow your job search to those kinds of employers.

Once you've gotten through the initial job screening process and begin interviewing, the real detective work begins. It involves more than investigating the "official" information provided by the employer. *Try to uncover the values that drive the organization.* Ask questions such as the proudest accomplishments or how it responded to past emergencies and crises. Ask, "If I have an idea, how do I make it happen?" Ask if you can talk to someone who's on the "fast track" to promotions and find out what they're doing and why they're being rewarded. Ask how you'll be evaluated—after all, if you're going to be in the game, shouldn't you know how the score is kept? Also, look for nonverbal clues. What do people have at their desks—family pictures or only work stuff? Are office doors closed or open? Are there doors? How does the physical climate feel? Is it relaxed and casual or more formal? Do people seem to be helping each other as they work? Are the bathrooms dirty, which might indicate a low value placed on anything to do with employees. Look at the material symbols and who seems to have access to them. And finally, during your investigation, do *pay particular attention to the specific department or unit where you'd work.* After all, this would be where you'd spend the majority of your working hours. Can you see yourself being happy there?

---

Finally, an organization must help employees adapt to its culture through a process called **socialization**, a process which has many benefits. Socialization helps new employees learn the organization's way of doing things. For instance, all new employees at Starbucks, the global specialty coffee retailer, go through 24 hours of training. Classes are offered on everything necessary to turn new employees into brewing consultants (baristas). They learn the Starbucks philosophy, the company jargon, and even how to help customers make decisions about beans, grinding, and espresso machines. The result is employees who understand Starbucks' culture and are enthusiastic and knowledgeable with customers.[17] Another benefit of socialization is that it minimizes the chance that new employees, who are unfamiliar with the organization's culture, might disrupt the beliefs and customs that are in place.

**Self-Assessment Library (S.A.L.)**

What will be the "right" culture for you? Complete S.A.L. #III.B.1 and find out.

Exhibit 3–5 summarizes how an organization's culture is established and maintained. (  Go to www.prenhall.com/rolls) The original culture is derived from the founder's philosophy. This, in turn, strongly influences the criteria used in hiring. The actions of the current top managers set the general expectations as to what is acceptable behavior and what is not. Socialization processes, if successful, will match new employees' values to those of the organization during the selection process and provide support during that critical time when employees have joined the organization and are learning the ropes.

## How Employees Learn Culture

Culture is transmitted to employees in a number of ways. The most significant are stories, rituals, material symbols, and language.

**Stories** Organizational "stories" typically contain a narrative of significant events or people, including such things as the organization's founders, rule breaking, reactions to past mistakes, and so forth.[18] For instance, managers at Nike feel that stories told about the company's past help shape the future. Whenever possible, corporate "story-

Exhibit 3–5  **How an Organization's Culture Is Established and Maintained**

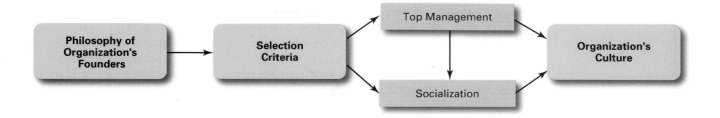

tellers" (senior executives) explain the company's heritage and tell stories that celebrate people getting things done. When they tell the story of how co-founder Bill Bowerman (now deceased) went to his workshop and poured rubber into his wife's waffle iron to create a better running shoe, they're celebrating and promoting Nike's spirit of innovation. These company stories provide examples that people can learn from.[19] At the 3M Company, the product-innovation stories are legendary. There's the story about the 3M scientist who spilled chemicals on her tennis shoe and came up with Scotchgard. Then, there's the story about Art Fry, a researcher, who wanted a better way to mark the pages of his church hymnal and invented the Post-It Note. These stories reflect what made 3M great and what it will take to continue that success.[20] To help employees learn the culture, organizational stories anchor the present in the past, provide explanations and legitimacy for current practices, exemplify what is important to the organization, and provide compelling pictures of an organization's goals.[21]

**Rituals**  The "Passing of the Pillars" is an important ritual at Boston Scientific's facility near Minneapolis. When someone has a challenging and tough project or assignment, they're "awarded" a small two-foot-high plaster-of-Paris pillar to show that they've got support from all their colleagues. Corporate rituals are repetitive sequences of activities

*The corporate culture of Keefe, Bruyette & Woods Inc., a research, trading, and consulting firm in the financial industry, now includes as one of its "stories" a memorial to its 67 employees who were killed in the collapse of the World Trade Center on September 11, 2001. This painting of the U.S. flag, which hangs in the company's midtown New York City offices, is made up of the names of all those who died. The company also paid $40 million to the families of employees who died that day.*

**socialization**
The process that helps employees adapt to the organization's culture.

that express and reinforce the values of the organization, what goals are most important, and which people are important.[22] One of the best-known corporate rituals is Mary Kay Cosmetics' annual awards ceremony for its sales representatives. Looking like a cross between a circus and a Miss America pageant, the ceremony takes place in a large auditorium, on a stage in front of a large, cheering audience, with all the participants dressed in glamorous evening clothes. Salespeople are rewarded for their success in achieving sales goals with an array of flashy gifts including gold and diamond pins, furs, and pink Cadillacs. This "show" acts as a motivator by publicly acknowledging outstanding sales performance. In addition, the ritual aspect reinforces late founder Mary Kay's determination and optimism, which enabled her to overcome personal hardships, start her own company, and achieve material success. It conveys to her salespeople that reaching their sales goals is important and through hard work and encouragement, they too can achieve success. Your second author had the experience of being on a flight out of Dallas one year with a planeload of Mary Kay sales representatives headed home from the annual awards meeting. Their contagious enthusiasm and excitement made it obvious that this annual "ritual" played a significant role in establishing desired levels of motivation and behavioral expectations, which, after all, is what an organization's culture should do.

**Material Symbols**　When you walk into different businesses, do you get a "feel" for what type of work environment it is—formal, casual, fun, serious, and so forth? These feelings demonstrate the power of material symbols in creating an organization's personality. The layout of an organization's facilities, how employees dress, the types of automobiles provided to top executives, and the availability of corporate aircraft are examples of material symbols. Others include the size of offices, the elegance of furnishings, executive "perks" (extra benefits provided to managers such as health club memberships, use of company-owned resort facilities, and so forth), employee fitness centers or on-site dining facilities, and reserved parking spaces for certain employees. At WorldNow, a provider of Internet technology to local media companies, an important material symbol is an old dented drill that the founders purchased for $2 at a thrift store. The drill symbolizes the company's culture of "drilling down to solve problems." When an employee is presented with the drill in recognition of outstanding work, he or she is expected to personalize the drill in some way and devise a new rule for caring for it. One employee installed a Bart Simpson trigger; another made the drill wireless by adding an antenna. The company's "icon" carries on the culture even as the organization evolves and changes.[23]

Material symbols convey to employees who is important, the degree of equality desired by top management, and the kinds of behavior (for example, risk taking, conservative, authoritarian, participative, individualistic, and so forth) that are expected and appropriate.

**Language**　Many organizations and units within organizations use language as a way to identify and unite members of a culture. By learning this language, members attest to their acceptance of the culture and their willingness to help preserve it. For instance, Microsoft employees have their own unique vocabulary: *work judo* (the art of deflecting a work assignment to someone else without making it appear that you're avoiding it); *eating your own dog food* (a strategy of using your own software programs or products in the early stages as a way of testing it even if the process is disagreeable); *flat food* (goodies from the vending machine that can be slipped under the door to a colleague who's working feverishly on deadline); *facemail* (actually talking to someone face-to-face, which is considered a technologically backward means of communicating); *death march* (the countdown to shipping a new product), and so on.[24]

Over time, organizations often develop unique terms to describe equipment, key personnel, suppliers, customers, processes, or products related to its business. New employees are frequently overwhelmed with acronyms and jargon that, after a short period of time, become a natural part of their language. Once learned, this language acts as a common denominator that bonds members.

## How Culture Affects Managers

Houston-based Apache Corp. has become one of the best performers in the independent oil drilling business because it has fashioned a culture that values quick decision making and risk taking. Potential hires are judged on how much initiative they've shown in getting projects done at other companies. And company employees are handsomely rewarded if they meet profit and production goals.[25] Because an organization's culture constrains what they can and cannot do, it is particularly relevant to managers. These constraints are rarely explicit. They're not written down. It's unlikely that they'll even be spoken. But they're there, and all managers quickly learn what to do and not to do in their organization.  (  Go to www.prenhall.com/rolls.) For instance, you won't find the following values written down anywhere, but each comes from a real organization.

**Q & A**
What happens when a manager just doesn't "fit" in with the organization's culture? Go to Q & A 3.8 to find out.

- Look busy even if you're not.
- If you take risks and fail around here, you'll pay dearly for it.
- Before you make a decision, run it by your boss so that he or she is never surprised.
- We make our product only as good as the competition forces us to.
- What made us successful in the past will make us successful in the future.
- If you want to get to the top here, you have to be a team player.

The link between values such as these and managerial behavior is fairly straightforward. (Check out Passport Scenario 1 on page 150.) Take, for example, a so-called "ready-aim-fire" culture. In such an organization, managers will study proposed projects first and analyze them endlessly before committing to them. However, in a "ready-fire-aim" culture, managers take action and then analyze what has been done. Or, say an

## managing workforce Diversity

### Creating an Inclusive Workplace Culture

We know from our discussion in Chapter 2 that managing a diverse workforce is an important issue facing today's managers. As the composition of the workforce changes, managers must take a long hard look at their organizational culture to see if the shared meaning and beliefs that were appropriate for a more homogeneous workforce will support diverse views. How can managers create a workplace culture that advocates and encourages diversity?[26]

Diversity efforts by organizations are no longer driven by federal mandate. Instead, organizations have recognized that inclusive workplaces are good for business. Among other things, diversity contributes to more creative solutions to problems and enhances employee morale. Creating a workplace culture that supports and encourages the inclusion of all diverse individuals and views is a major organizational effort. Managers throughout the organization must value diversity and show that they do by their decisions and actions. An organization that truly wants to promote inclusiveness must shape its culture to allow diversity to flourish. One way to do this is for managers to assimilate diverse perspectives while performing the managerial functions. For example, at the Marriott Marquis Hotel in New York's Times Square, managers are taught in required diversity training classes that the best way to cope with diversity-related conflict is to focus narrowly on performance and never to define problems in terms of gender, culture, race, or disability. At Prudential, the annual planning process includes key diversity performance goals that are measured and tied to managers' compensation.

Beyond the day-to-day managerial activities, organizations should consider developing ways to reinforce employee behaviors that exemplify inclusiveness. Some suggestions include encouraging individuals to value and defend diverse views, creating traditions and ceremonies that celebrate diversity, rewarding appropriate "heroes" and "heroines" who accept and promote inclusiveness, and communicating formally and informally about employees who champion diversity issues.

Developing an organizational culture that supports diversity and inclusiveness may be challenging but offers high potential benefits. Organizations that allow diversity to prosper and thrive see cultural or environmental changes not as constraints, but as opportunities to bring out the best in all of its members.

Exhibit 3–6

**Managerial Decisions Affected by Culture**

---

**Planning**

- The degree of risk that plans should contain
- Whether plans should be developed by individuals or teams
- The degree of environmental scanning in which management will engage

**Organizing**

- How much autonomy should be designed into employees' jobs
- Whether tasks should be done by individuals or in teams
- The degree to which department managers interact with each other

**Leading**

- The degree to which managers are concerned with increasing employee job satisfaction
- What leadership styles are appropriate
- Whether all disagreements—even constructive ones—should be eliminated

**Controlling**

- Whether to impose external controls or to allow employees to control their own actions
- What criteria should be emphasized in employee performance evaluations
- What repercussions will occur from exceeding one's budget

---

organization's culture supports the belief that profits can be increased by cost cutting and that the company's best interests are served by achieving slow but steady increases in quarterly earnings. Managers are unlikely to pursue programs that are innovative, risky, long term, or expansionary. For organizations that value and encourage workforce diversity, the organizational culture and thus managers' decisions and actions will be supportive of diversity efforts. (See the "Managing Workforce Diversity" box for more information on creating an inclusive workplace.) In an organization whose culture conveys a basic distrust of employees, managers are more likely to use an authoritarian leadership style than a democratic one. Why? The culture establishes for managers what is appropriate and expected behavior. At St. Luke's advertising agency in London, for example, a culture shaped by the value placed on freedom of expression, a lack of coercion and fear, and a determination to make work fun influences the way employees work and the way that managers plan, organize, lead, and control. The organization's culture is reinforced even by the office environment, which is open, versatile, and creative.[27]

As shown in Exhibit 3–6, a manager's decisions are influenced by the culture in which he or she operates. An organization's culture, especially a strong one, constrains a manager's decision-making options in all four management functions.

## Learning Review

- Describe the seven dimensions of organizational culture.
- Discuss the impact of a strong culture on organizations and managers.

- Explain the source of an organization's culture.
- Describe how culture is transmitted to employees.
- Describe how culture affects managers.

# CURRENT ORGANIZATIONAL CULTURE ISSUES FACING MANAGERS

Nordstrom, the specialty retail chain, is renowned for its attention to customers. Nike's innovations in running shoe technology are legendary. Tom's of Maine is known for its commitment to doing things ethically and spiritually. How have these organizations achieved such reputations? Their organizational cultures have played a crucial role. Let's look at four current cultural issues managers should consider: creating an ethical culture, creating an innovative culture, creating a customer-responsive culture, and nurturing workplace spirituality.

## Creating an Ethical Culture

Andrew Fastow, former chief financial officer of Enron Corporation (who was convicted in 2004 and sentenced to 10 years in prison for wire and securities fraud) had a Lucite cube on his desk that laid out the company's values. It included the following inscription: "When Enron says it's going to rip your face off, it will rip your face off."[28] Other Enron employees described a culture in which personal ambition was valued over teamwork, youth over wisdom, and earnings growth at any cost.[29]

The content and strength of an organization's culture influences its ethical climate and ethical behavior of its members.[30] A strong organizational culture will exert more influence on employees than a weak one. If the culture is strong and supports high ethical standards, it should have a very powerful and positive influence on employee behavior. For example, Alfred P. West, founder and CEO of financial services firm SEI Investments Company, spends a lot of time emphasizing to employees his vision for the company—an open culture of integrity, ownership, and accountability. He says, "We tell our employees a lot about where the company is going. We overcommunicate the vision and strategy and continually reinforce the culture."[31]

An organizational culture most likely to shape high ethical standards is one that's high in risk tolerance, low to moderate in aggressiveness, and focused on means as well as outcomes. Managers in such a culture are supported for taking risks and innovating, are discouraged from engaging in uncontrolled competition, and will pay attention to *how* goals are achieved as well as to *what* goals are achieved.

What can managers do to create a more ethical culture? Exhibit 3–7 outlines some suggestions.

## Creating an Innovative Culture

You may not recognize IDEO's name, but you've probably used a number of its products. IDEO is a product design firm. It takes the product ideas that corporations bring it and turns those ideas into reality. Some of its creations range from the first commercial mouse (for Apple Computer) to the first standup toothpaste tube (for Procter & Gamble) to the handheld personal organizer (for Palm). It's critical that IDEO's culture support creativity and innovation.[32] *Cirque du Soleil*®, the Montreal-based creator of circus theatre, is another innovative organization. Its managers state that the

**Exhibit 3–7**

**Suggestions for Managers: Creating a More Ethical Culture**

- Be a *visible role model*.
- Communicate *ethical expectations*.
- Provide *ethics training*.
- Visibly *reward ethical acts and punish unethical ones*.
- Provide *protective mechanisms* so employees can discuss ethical dilemmas and report unethical behavior without fear.

*Cirque du Soleil® is innovative not only in its unique circus performances, but also in its culture. Job applicants can find the following statement on the company's Web site: "At Cirque, it's not every employee who walks around balancing balls on their nose . . . but you never know! Joining our team of almost 3,000 employees means working in a relaxed environment, where social and cultural action is one of our everyday ambitions."*

organization's culture is based on involvement, communication, creativity, and diversity, which they see as keys to innovation.[33] Although these two companies are in industries where continual innovations are crucial to success (product design and entertainment), the fact is that successful organizations in all types of industries need cultures that support innovation.

What does an innovative culture look like? According to Swedish researcher Goran Ekvall, it would be characterized by the following:

- *Challenge and involvement:* How much employees are involved in, motivated by, and committed to the long-term goals and success of the organization.
- *Freedom:* The degree to which employees can independently define their work, exercise discretion, and take initiative in their day-to-day activities.
- *Trust and openness:* The degree to which employees are supportive and respectful to each other.
- *Idea time:* The amount of time individuals have to elaborate on new ideas before taking action.
- *Playfulness/humor:* How much spontaneity, fun, and ease there is in the workplace.
- *Conflict resolution:* The degree to which individuals make decisions and resolve issues based on the good of the organization versus personal interest.
- *Debates:* How much employees are allowed to express their opinions and put forth their ideas for consideration and review.
- *Risk taking:* How much managers tolerate uncertainty and ambiguity and whether employees are rewarded for taking risks.[34]

## Creating a Customer-Responsive Culture

Harrah's Entertainment, the world's largest gaming company, is fanatical about customer service and for good reason. Company research showed that customers who

*thinking critically about* **Ethics**

Do you think it's possible for a manager with high ethical standards to live by the values in an organizational culture that tolerates, or even encourages, unethical practices? How could a manager deal with such situations?

were satisfied with the service they received at a Harrah's casino increased their gaming expenditures by 10 percent and those who were extremely satisfied increased their gaming expenditures by 24 percent. When customer service translates into these types of results, of course managers would want to create a customer-responsive culture![35]

But what does a customer-responsive culture look like? Research shows that six characteristics are routinely present.[36] First is the type of employees themselves. Successful, service-oriented organizations hire employees who are outgoing and friendly. Second is few rigid rules, procedures, and regulations. Service employees need to have the freedom to meet changing customer-service requirements. Third is the widespread use of empowerment. Empowered employees have the decision discretion to do what's necessary to please the customer. Fourth are good listening skills. Employees in customer-responsive cultures have the ability to listen to and understand messages sent by the customer. Fifth is role clarity. Service employees act as links between the organization and its customers, which can create considerable ambiguity and conflict. This reduces employees' job satisfaction and can hinder employee service performance. Successful customer-responsive cultures reduce employee uncertainty about their role and the best way to perform their jobs. (  Go to www.prenhall.com/rolls) Finally, customer-responsive cultures have employees who are conscientious in their desire to please the customer. They're willing to take the initiative, even when it's outside their normal job requirements, to satisfy a customer's needs. Based on these characteristics, what can managers do to make their cultures more customer-responsive? Exhibit 3–8 lists some suggestions.

**Self-Assessment Library (S.A.L.)**

Can you see how important it would be to know whether job and family responsibilities conflict? Do you want to see how you'd rate on that? Check out S.A.L. #111.B.3 to see.

## Spirituality and Organizational Culture

What do Southwest Airlines, Ben & Jerry's, Timberland, HomeBanc Mortgage, Hewlett-Packard, and Tom's of Maine have in common? They're among a growing number of organizations that have embraced workplace spirituality. What is **workplace spirituality**? It's a culture where organizational values promote a sense of purpose through meaningful work that takes place in the context of community.[37] Organizations with a spiritual culture recognize that people have a mind and a spirit, seek to find meaning and purpose in their work, and desire to connect with other human beings and be part of a community.

Workplace spirituality seems to be important now for a number of reasons. Employees are looking for ways to counterbalance the stresses and pressures of a turbulent pace of life. Contemporary lifestyles—single-parent families, geographic mobility,

**Exhibit 3–8**

**Suggestions for Managers: Creating a More Customer-Responsive Culture**

- Hire service-contact people with the personality and attitudes consistent with customer service—friendliness, enthusiasm, attentiveness, patience, concern about others, and listening skills.
- Train customer service people continuously by focusing on improving product knowledge, active listening, showing patience, and displaying emotions.
- Socialize new service-contact people to the organization's goals and values.
- Design customer-service jobs so that employees have as much control as necessary to satisfy customers.
- Empower service-contact employees with the discretion to make day-to-day decisions on job-related activities.
- As the leader, convey a customer-focused vision and demonstrate through decisions and actions the commitment to customers.

**workplace spirituality**
A culture where organizational values promote a sense of purpose through meaningful work that takes place in the context of community.

the temporary nature of jobs, new technologies that create distance between people—underscore the lack of community that many people feel. People are looking for involvement and connection. In addition, aging baby boomers are reaching mid-life and looking for something meaningful in their lives, something beyond the job. Others desire to integrate their personal life values with their professional lives. For others, formalized religion hasn't worked and they continue to look for anchors to replace a lack of faith and to fill a growing sense of emptiness. What type of organizational culture can meet such demands? What differentiates spiritual organizations from their nonspiritual counterparts? Although research on this question is preliminary, spiritual organizations tend to have five cultural characteristics.[38]

**Strong Sense of Purpose** Spiritual organizations build their cultures around a meaningful purpose. Although profits are important, they're not the primary values of the organization. Southwest Airlines, for example, is strongly committed to providing the lowest airfares, on-time service, and a pleasant experience for customers. Tom's of Maine strives to sell personal care products that are made from natural ingredients and are environmentally friendly. Timberland's slogan is "Boots, Brand, Belief," which embodies the company's intent to use its "resources, energy, and profits as a publicly traded footwear-and-apparel company to combat social ills, help the environment, and improve conditions for laborers around the globe . . . and to create a more productive, efficient, loyal, and committed employee base."[39]

**Focus on Individual Development** Spiritual organizations recognize the worth and value of individuals. They aren't just providing jobs; they seek to create cultures in which employees can continually grow and learn.

**Trust and Openness** Spiritual organizations are characterized by mutual trust, honesty, and openness. Managers aren't afraid to admit mistakes, and they tend to be extremely upfront with employees, customers, and suppliers. The president of Wetherill Associates, a highly successful auto parts distributor, says, "We don't tell lies here, and everyone knows it. We are specific and honest about quality and suitability of the product for our customers' needs, even if we know they might not be able to detect any problems."[40]

**Employee Empowerment** The high-trust climate in spiritual organizations, when combined with the desire to promote learning and growth, leads to managers empowering employees to make most work-related decisions. Managers trust employees to make thoughtful and conscientious decisions. For instance, at Southwest Airlines, employees—including flight attendants, baggage handlers, gate agents, and customer service representatives—are encouraged to take whatever action they deem necessary to meet customer needs or help fellow workers, even if it means going against company policies.

**Toleration of Employee Expression** The final characteristic that differentiates spiritually based organizations is that they don't stifle employee emotions. They allow people to be themselves—to express their moods and feelings without guilt or fear of reprimand.

Although a number of organizations have created cultures that promote spirituality, critics of the spirituality movement in organizations have focused on two issues. First is the question of legitimacy. Do organizations have the right to impose spiritual values on their employees? Second is the question of economics—that is, are spirituality and profits compatible?

As far as the first question, an emphasis on spirituality clearly has the potential to make some employees uneasy. Critics might argue that secular institutions, especially businesses, have no business imposing spiritual values on employees. This criticism is probably valid when spirituality is defined as bringing religion and God into the workplace.[41] However, the criticism is less valid when the goal of a more spiritual organization is helping employees find meaning in their work. If the concerns about today's lifestyles and pressures discussed earlier truly characterize a growing number of workers, then maybe it is time for organizations to help employees find meaning and purpose in their work and to use the workplace to create a sense of community.

The issue of whether spirituality and profits are compatible is certainly relevant for business managers and investors. The evidence, although limited, suggests that the two may be compatible. A study by a major consulting firm found that companies that introduced spiritually based techniques improved productivity and significantly reduced turnover.[42] Another study found that organizations that provided their employees with opportunities for spiritual development outperformed those that didn't.[43] Other studies also report that spirituality in organizations was positively related to creativity, employee satisfaction, team performance, and organizational commitment.[44]

## Learning Review

- Describe the characteristics of an ethical culture, an innovative culture, and a customer-responsive culture.
- Explain why workplace spirituality seems to be an important concern.

- Describe the characteristics of a spiritual organization.

## THE ENVIRONMENT

In Chapter 2, our discussion of an organization as an open system explained that an organization interacts with its environment as it takes in inputs and distributes outputs. Anyone who questions the impact the external environment has on managing should consider the following:

- The bottled water industry has seen a tremendous increase in sales since the mid-1990s. Although Europe still leads the world in bottled water consumption (34 percent share), bottled water consumption in the United States has surpassed that of milk, coffee, and beer.
- Approximately 41 million people (with 150,000 more added each day) now use Skype, a program that allows them to make free calls over the Internet.
- Japanese consumers can get toilet paper, eggs, and popcorn (among other products) and charge cell phone batteries from vending machines, which accounts for some $56 billion of revenue annually, an amount nearly twice the U.S. total.[45]

As these examples show, there are forces in the environment that play a major role in shaping managers' actions. In this section, we'll identify some of the critical environmental forces that affect managers and show how they constrain managerial discretion.

### Defining the External Environment

The term **external environment** refers to those factors and forces outside the organization that affect the organization's performance. As shown in Exhibit 3–9, it includes two components: the specific environment and the general environment.

**external environment**
Those factors and forces outside the organization that affect the organization's performance.

Exhibit 3–9

**The External Environment**

**The Specific Environment** The **specific environment** includes those external forces that have a direct impact on managers' decisions and actions and are directly relevant to the achievement of the organization's goals. Each organization's specific environment is unique and changes with conditions. For instance, Timex and Rolex both make watches, but their specific environments differ because they operate in distinctly different market niches. The main forces that make up the specific environment are customers, suppliers, competitors, and pressure groups.

CUSTOMERS  Organizations exist to meet the needs of customers. It's the customer who consumes or uses the organization's output. This is true even for governmental organizations and other not-for-profits.

Customers obviously represent potential uncertainty to an organization. Their tastes can change or they can become dissatisfied with the organization's products or service. Of course, some organizations face more uncertainty as a result of their customers than do others. For example, what comes to mind when you think of Club Med? Club Med's image was traditionally one of carefree singles having fun in the sun at exotic locales. Club Med found, however, that as their target customers married and had children, these same individuals were looking for family-oriented vacation resorts where they could bring the kids. Although Club Med responded to the changing demands of its customers by offering different types of vacation experiences, including family-oriented ones, the company found that changing its image wasn't easy.

SUPPLIERS  When you think of an organization's suppliers, you typically think in terms of organizations that provide materials and equipment. For Walt Disney World resorts in Florida, that includes organizations that sell soft drinks, computers, food, flowers and other nursery stock, concrete, and paper products. But the term *suppliers* also includes providers of financial and labor inputs. Stockholders, banks, insurance companies, pension funds, and other similar organizations are needed to ensure a continuous supply of capital. Labor unions, colleges and universities, occupational associations, trade schools, and local labor markets are sources of employees. When the sources of employees dry up, it can constrain managers' decisions and actions. For example, a lack of qualified nurses, a serious problem plaguing the health care industry, impacts health care providers' ability to meet demand and keep service levels high.

Managers seek to ensure a steady flow of needed inputs at the lowest price available. Because these inputs represent uncertainties—that is, their unavailability or

*When the Internet search engine Google decided to accept heavy censorship of its Chinese site in compliance with Communist Party requirements, its founders said the widely criticized compromise would allow Internet access to a fifth of the world's population as "a great way of improving the world." Among those who disagreed with Google were these members of Students for a Free Tibet.*

delay can significantly reduce the organization's effectiveness—managers typically go to great efforts to ensure a steady reliable flow. The application of e-business techniques is changing the way that organizations deal with suppliers. For example, Toyota Motor Corporation established electronic linkages with suppliers to ensure that it has the right materials at the right time and in the right place. Although these linkages might help managers manage uncertainty, they certainly don't eliminate it.

COMPETITORS    All organizations have one or more competitors. Even though it's a monopoly, the U.S. Postal Service competes with FedEx, UPS, and other forms of communication such as the telephone, e-mail, and fax. Nike competes against adidas-Salomon, Fila, and New Balance, among others. Coca-Cola competes against Pepsi and other soft-drink companies. Not-for-profit organizations such as the Metropolitan Museum of Art, the International Committee of the Red Cross, and Girl Scouts USA also compete for dollars, volunteers, and customers.

Managers cannot afford to ignore the competition. When they do, they suffer. For instance, until the 1980s, the three major broadcast networks—ABC, CBS, and NBC—virtually controlled what you watched on television. Now, with digital cable, satellite, DVD players, and the Web, customers have a much broader choice of what to watch. As technology continues to change and improve, the number of viewing options will provide even more competition for the broadcast networks. The Internet is also having an impact on determining an organization's competitors because it has virtually eliminated the geographic boundaries. Using online marketing, a small maple syrup maker in Vermont can compete with the likes of Pillsbury, Quaker Oats, and Smuckers.

These examples illustrate that competitors—in terms of pricing, new products developed, services offered, and the like—represent an environmental force that managers must monitor and to which they must be prepared to respond.

PRESSURE GROUPS    Managers must recognize the special-interest groups that attempt to influence the actions of organizations. For instance, PETA's (People for the Ethical Treatment of Animals) pressure on McDonald's Corporation over its handling of animals during the slaughter process led McDonald's to stop buying beef from one of its suppliers until it met its standards for processing cattle. And it would be an unusual week if we didn't read about environmental or human rights activists picketing, boycotting, or

**specific environment**
Those external forces that have a direct impact on managers' decisions and actions and are directly relevant to the achievement of the organization's goals.

threatening some organization in order to get managers to change some decision or action.

As social and political attitudes change, so too does the power of pressure groups. For example, through their persistent efforts, groups such as MADD (Mothers Against Drunk Driving) and SADD (Students Against Destructive Decisions) have managed to make changes in the alcoholic beverage and restaurant and bar industries and raised public awareness about the problem of drunk drivers.

**The General Environment** The **general environment** includes the broad economic, political/legal, sociocultural, demographic, technological, and global conditions that affect the organization. Although these external factors don't affect organizations to the extent that changes in the specific environment do, managers must consider them as they plan, organize, lead, and control.

ECONOMIC CONDITIONS    Interest rates, inflation, changes in disposable income, stock market fluctuations, and the stage of the general business cycle are some economic factors that can affect management practices in an organization. For example, many specialty retailers such as Ikea, Gap, and Williams-Sonoma are acutely aware of the impact consumer disposable income has on their sales. When consumers' incomes fall or when their confidence about job security declines, they will postpone purchasing anything that isn't a necessity. Even charitable organizations such as the United Way or the Salvation Army feel the impact of economic factors. During economic downturns, not only does the demand for their services increase, but their contributions typically decrease also.

POLITICAL/LEGAL CONDITIONS    Federal, state, and local laws, as well as global and other country laws and regulations, influence what organizations can and cannot do. Some federal legislation has significant implications. For example, the Americans with Disabilities Act of 1990 (ADA) was designed to make jobs and facilities more accessible to people with disabilities, whether as a customer or as an employee. Exhibit 3–10 lists other significant legislation affecting businesses.

Organizations spend a great deal of time and money to meet governmental regulations, but the effects go beyond time and money. They also reduce managerial discretion by limiting available choices. Consider the decision to dismiss an employee.[46] Historically, employees were free to quit an organization at any time and employers had the right to fire an employee at any time with or without cause. Laws and court decisions, however, have limited what employers may do. Employers are expected to deal with employees by following the principles of good faith and fair dealing. Employees who feel they've been wrongfully discharged often take their case to court where juries decide what is "fair." This trend has made it more difficult for managers to fire poor performers or to dismiss employees for inappropriate off-duty conduct.

Other aspects of the political/legal sector are political conditions and the general stability of a country where an organization operates and the attitudes that elected governmental officials hold toward business. In the United States, for example, organizations have generally operated in a stable political environment. However, since management is a global activity, managers should be aware of major political changes in countries in which they operate because these political conditions can influence decisions and actions.[47]

SOCIOCULTURAL CONDITIONS    Rocco Papalia, senior vice president of research and development at Frito Lay, the snack-food unit of PepsiCo Inc., is overseeing a move to make its snacks healthier. The company's natural and organic snack line is one of the outcomes. Why is Frito Lay looking at such products? Because health officials and consumers are increasingly concerned about the dangers of obesity and poor diet.[48] Managers must adapt their practices to the changing expectations of the society in which they operate. As societal values, customs, and tastes change, managers also must change. For instance, as workers have begun seeking more balanced lives, organizations have had to adjust by offering family leave policies, flexible work hours, and even on-site child-care facilities. Other sociocultural trends in the United States include an increasing fear of violence and

Exhibit 3–10

**Selected U.S. Legislation Affecting Business**

| Legislation | Purpose |
|---|---|
| Occupational Safety and Health Act of 1970 | Requires employer to provide a working environment free from hazards to health. |
| Consumer Product Safety Act of 1972 | Sets standards on selected products, requires warning labels, and orders product recalls. |
| Equal Employment Opportunity Act of 1972 | Forbids discrimination in all areas of employer–employee relations. |
| Worker Adjustment and Retraining Notification Act of 1988 | Requires employers with 100 or more employees to provide 60 days' notice before a facility closing or mass layoff. |
| Americans with Disabilities Act of 1990 | Prohibits employers from discriminating against individuals with physical or mental disabilities or the chronically ill; also requires organizations to reasonably accommodate these individuals. |
| Civil Rights Act of 1991 | Reaffirms and tightens prohibition of discrimination; permits individuals to sue for punitive damages in cases of intentional discrimination. |
| Family and Medical Leave Act of 1993 | Grants 12 weeks of unpaid leave each year to employees for the birth or adoption of a child or the care of a spouse, child, or parent with a serious health condition; covers organizations with 50 or more employees. |
| Child Safety Protection Act of 1994 | Provides for labelling requirements on certain toys that contain parts or packaging that could harm children and requires manufacturers of such toys to report any serious accidents or deaths of children to the Consumer Product Safety Commission. |
| U.S. Economic Espionage Act of 1996 | Makes theft or misappropriation of trade secrets a federal crime. |
| Electronic Signatures in Global and National Commerce Act of 2000 | Gives online contracts (those signed by computer) the same legal force as equivalent paper contracts. |
| Sarbanes–Oxley Act of 2002 | Holds businesses to higher standards of disclosure and corporate governance. |
| Fair and Accurate Credit Transactions Act of 2003 | Requires employers to "destroy" personal information about employees before disposing of it, if they got the information from a credit report. |

crime; more acceptance of gambling and gaming activities; more emphasis on religion and spiritual activities; pursuit of healthy lifestyles; pursuit of happiness; increasing use of surveillance; and increasing dependence on technology. Each of these trends may pose a potential constraint to managers' decisions and actions. If an organization does business in other countries, managers need to be familiar with those country's values and cultures and manage in ways that recognize and embrace those specific sociocultural aspects.

DEMOGRAPHIC CONDITIONS    The demographic conditions encompass trends in the physical characteristics of a population such as gender, age, level of education, geographic location, income, family composition, and so forth. Changes in these characteristics may constrain how managers plan, organize, lead, and control.

**general environment**
Broad external conditions that may affect the organization.

*A recent survey found that salary, power, and prestige, which motivated many baby boomers' careers, ranked nearly last in a list of things Gen Xers expected from their jobs. They prefer positive relationships, interesting work, and ongoing opportunities to learn. What will appeal to and motivate Gen Yers, like those pictured here?*

In the United States, population researchers have labeled specific age cohorts. These include the Depression group (born 1912–1921), the World War II group (born 1922–1927), the postwar group (born 1928–1945), baby boomers (born 1946–1964), Generation X (born 1965–1977), and Generation Y (born 1978–1994). Although each of these groups has its own unique characteristics, Gen Y is of particular interest because they're learning, working, shopping, and playing in fundamentally different ways that are likely to impact managers and organizations.

TECHNOLOGICAL   In terms of the general environment, the most rapid changes have occurred in technology. We live in a time of continuous technological change. For instance, the human genetic code has been cracked. Just think of the implications of such knowledge! Information gadgets are getting smaller and more powerful. We have automated offices, electronic meetings, robotic manufacturing, lasers, integrated circuits, faster and more powerful microprocessors, synthetic fuels, and entirely new models of doing business in an electronic age. Companies that capitalize on technology such as General Electric, eBay, and Google prosper. In addition, many successful retailers such as Wal-Mart and Limited Brands use sophisticated information systems to keep on top of current sales trends. Other organizations such as Prime Trucking Inc. and Amazon.com use information as a competitive advantage and have adopted technologically advanced systems to stay ahead of their competitors. Similarly, hospitals, universities, airports, police departments, and even military organizations that adapt to major technological advances have a competitive edge over those that do not. The whole area of technology is radically changing the fundamental ways that organizations are structured and the way that managers manage. We highlight many of these changes in our "Managing Information Technology" boxes found in several chapters throughout the book.

GLOBAL   By the end of this decade, Nigeria will have a larger population than Russia. Ethiopia will have more people than Germany, and Morocco will be more populous than Canada.[49] Do these facts surprise you? They shouldn't. They simply reflect what we said in Chapter 2—that globalization is one of the major factors affecting managers and organizations. Managers of both large and small organizations are challenged by an increasing number of global competitors and markets as part of the external environment. We'll cover this component of the external environment in detail in the next chapter.

## How the Environment Affects Managers

**PRISM**

How good would you be at scanning the environment? Do PRISM #3 and see what's involved.

Knowing *what* the various components of the environment are is important to managers. However, understanding *how* the environment affects managers is equally as important. ( ⬙ Go to www.prenhall.com/rolls) And there are two ways the environment affects managers—first, through the degree of environmental uncertainty that is present, and second, through the various stakeholder relationships that exist between the organization and its external constituencies.

**Assessing Environmental Uncertainty**  Not all environments are the same. They differ by what we call their **environmental uncertainty**, which is the degree of change and complexity in the organization's environment (see Exhibit 3–11).

The first of these dimensions is the degree of change. If the components in an organization's environment change frequently, we call it a *dynamic* environment. If change is minimal, we call it a *stable* one. A stable environment might be one in which there are no new competitors, few technological breakthroughs by current competitors, little activity by pressure groups to influence the organization, and so forth. For instance, Zippo Manufacturing, best known for its Zippo lighters, faces a relatively stable environment. There are few competitors and little technological change. Probably the main environmental concern for the company is the declining trend in tobacco smokers, although the company's lighters have other uses and global markets remain attractive.

In contrast, the recorded music industry faces a highly uncertain and unpredictable environment. Digital formats and music-downloading sites like iTunes have turned the industry upside down. Although music companies traditionally earned revenues by selling physical commodities such as LP records, cassettes, and CDs, changing digital technology represents chaos and uncertainty. This environment can definitely be described as dynamic.

What about rapid change that's predictable? Is that considered dynamic? Department stores provide a good example. They typically make one-quarter to one-third of their sales in December. The drop-off from December to January is significant. However, because the change is predictable, we don't consider the environment to be dynamic. When we talk about degree of change, we mean change that is unpredictable. If change can be accurately anticipated, it's not an uncertainty that managers must confront.

Exhibit 3–11

**Environmental Uncertainty Matrix**

| | **Degree of Change** | |
|---|---|---|
| | **Stable** | **Dynamic** |
| **Simple** | **Cell 1**<br>Stable and predictable environment<br>Few components in environment<br>Components are somewhat similar and remain basically the same<br>Minimal need for sophisticated knowledge of components | **Cell 2**<br>Dynamic and unpredictable environment<br>Few components in environment<br>Components are somewhat similar but are in continual process of change<br>Minimal need for sophisticated knowledge of components |
| **Complex** | **Cell 3**<br>Stable and predictable environment<br>Many components in environment<br>Components are not similar to one another and remain basically the same<br>High need for sophisticated knowledge of components | **Cell 4**<br>Dynamic and unpredictable environment<br>Many components in environment<br>Components are not similar to one another and are in continual process of change<br>High need for sophisticated knowledge of components |

*(Degree of Complexity — vertical axis label)*

**environmental uncertainty**
The degree of change and complexity in an organization's environment.

The other dimension of uncertainty describes the degree of **environmental complexity**. The degree of complexity refers to the number of components in an organization's environment and the extent of the knowledge that the organization has about those components. For example, Hasbro Toy Company, the second largest toy manufacturer (behind Mattel) has simplified its environment by acquiring many of its competitors such as Tiger Electronics, Wizards of the Coast, Kenner Toys, Parker Brothers, and Tonka Toys. When an organization has to deal with fewer competitors, customers, suppliers, government agencies, and so forth, the less complex—and less uncertain—its environment is.

Complexity is also measured in terms of the knowledge an organization needs about its environment. For instance, managers at the online brokerage E*Trade must know a great deal about their Internet service provider's operations if they want to ensure that their Web site is available, reliable, and secure for their stock-trading customers. On the other hand, managers of college bookstores have a minimal need for sophisticated knowledge about their suppliers.

How does the concept of environmental uncertainty influence managers? Looking again at Exhibit 3–11, each of the four cells represents different combinations of degree of complexity and degree of change. Cell 1 (an environment that is stable and simple) represents the lowest level of environmental uncertainty. Cell 4 (an environment that is dynamic and complex) is the highest. Not surprisingly, managers have the greatest influence on organizational outcomes in cell 1 and least in cell 4.

Because uncertainty is a threat to an organization's effectiveness, managers try to minimize it. Given a choice, managers would prefer to operate in environments such as those in cell 1. However, they rarely control that choice. In addition, most industries today are facing more dynamic change, making their environments more uncertain.

**Managing Stakeholder Relationships** What has made VH1 *the* cable channel for music-loving baby boomers? One reason is that the company realizes the importance of building relationships with its various stakeholders: the viewers, the music celebrities, advertisers, the affiliate TV stations, public service groups, and others. The nature of stakeholder relationships is another way in which the environment influences managers. The more obvious and secure these relationships become, the more influence managers will have over organizational outcomes.

Who are **stakeholders**? We define them as any constituencies in the organization's environment that are affected by the organization's decisions and actions. These groups have a stake in or are significantly influenced by what the organization does. (Check out You're the Manager: Putting Ethics into Action on page 150.) In turn, these groups can influence the organization. For example, think of the groups that might be affected by the decisions and actions of Starbucks—coffee bean farmers, employees, specialty coffee competitors, local communities, and so forth. Some of these stakeholders also may impact decisions and actions of Starbucks' managers. The

*Ginger Graham is CEO of Amylin Pharmaceuticals Inc., which produces two new drugs to treat diabetes. Among the stakeholders affected by Graham's management decisions are drugstore chains, doctors, hospitals, clinics, the company's employees and stockholders, the rest of the pharmaceutical industry, and diabetics and their families.*

idea that organizations have stakeholders is now widely accepted by both management academics and practicing managers.[50]

Q & A

Knowing your stakeholders seems to be important. How will you know who's in your organization's environment? See Q & A 3.9.

With what types of stakeholders might an organization have to deal? Exhibit 3–12 identifies some of the most common. (  Go to www.prenhall.com/rolls) Note that these stakeholders do include internal and external groups. Why? Because both can affect what an organization does and how it operates. However, we're primarily interested in the external groups and their impact on managers' discretion in planning, organizing, leading, and controlling. This doesn't mean that the internal stakeholders aren't important, but we explain these relationships, primarily with employees, throughout the rest of the book.

Why is stakeholder relationship management important? Why should managers even care about managing stakeholder relationships?[51] One reason is that it can lead to organizational outcomes such as improved predictability of environmental changes, more successful innovations, greater degree of trust among stakeholders, and greater organizational flexibility to reduce the impact of change. But, does it affect organizational performance? The answer is yes! Management researchers who have looked at this issue are finding that managers of high-performing companies tend to consider the interests of all major stakeholder groups as they make decisions.[52]

Another reason given for managing external stakeholder relationships is that it's the "right" thing to do. What does this mean? It means that an organization depends on these external groups as sources of inputs (resources) and as outlets for outputs (goods and services), and managers should consider their interests as they make decisions and take actions. We'll address this issue in more detail in Chapter 5 as we look at the concepts of managerial ethics and corporate social responsibility.

How can these relationships be managed? (Check out Passport Scenario 2 on page 150.) There are four steps. First, identify who the organization's stakeholders are. Which of the various groups might be impacted by decisions that managers make and which groups might influence those decisions? Those groups that are likely to be influenced by and to influence organizational decisions are the organization's stakeholders. Second, determine what particular interests or concerns these stakeholders might have—product quality, financial issues, safe working conditions, environmental protection, and so forth. Next, decide how critical each stakeholder is to the organization's decisions and actions. In other words, how critical is it to consider this stakeholder's

Exhibit 3–12

**Organizational Stakeholders**

---

**environmental complexity**
The number of components in an organization's environment and the extent of the organization's knowledge about those components.

**stakeholders**
Any constituencies in the organization's environment that are affected by the organization's decisions and actions.

## *becoming* a Manager

√ When you read current business or general news stories, see if omnipotent or symbolic views of management are being described.

√ Notice aspects of organizational culture as you interact with different organizations.

√ Read books about different organizations and entrepreneurs to better understand how an organization culture forms and how it's maintained.

√ Start thinking about the type of organizational culture in which you're going to be most comfortable.

√ If you belong to a student organization, evaluate its culture. What is the culture like? How do new members learn the culture? How is the culture maintained?

√ When you evaluate companies for class assignments (in this class and others), get in the habit of looking at the stakeholders that might be impacted by these companies' decisions and actions.

√ Practice defining the general and specific environments of different organizations and notice how they're similar and different.

Self-Assessment
Library (S.A.L.)

√  Go to www.prenhall.com/rolls and complete any of these exercises from the Self-Assessment Library: S.A.L. #III.B.1—What's the Right Organizational Culture for Me?, S.A.L. #III.B.3—Am I Experiencing Work/Family Conflict?, or S.A.L. #III.C.1—How Well Do I Respond to Turbulent Change?

concerns as you plan, organize, lead, and control? The very idea of a stakeholder—a group that has a "stake" in what the organization does—means that it is important. But some stakeholders are more critical to the organization's decisions and actions than others. For instance, a critical stakeholder of a publicly supported state university would be the state legislature because it controls how much budget money the university gets each year. On the other hand, the university's computer hardware and software suppliers are important but not critical. Once managers have determined these things, the final step is to determine how to manage the external stakeholder relationships. This decision depends on how critical the external stakeholder is to the organization and how uncertain the environment is.[53] The more critical the stakeholder and the more uncertain the environment, the more that managers need to rely on establishing explicit stakeholder partnerships rather than just acknowledging their existence.

## Learning Review

- Describe the components of the specific and general environments.
- Discuss the two dimensions of environmental uncertainty.

- Identify the most common organizational stakeholders.
- Explain the four steps in managing external stakeholder relationships.

# Managers Respond to a Manager's Dilemma

## Debbie Galonsky

Corporate Accounts Manager, Graphic Systems, Agfa
Corporation, Ridgefield Park, NJ

Team-based cultures are the most difficult environments to maintain. That's why it is imperative that compensation, recognition, and the work environment are all developed with the team in mind. For Yves to maintain his team culture and ensure its success, the following practices should be in place:

1. Bonuses need to be rewarded to a *team* for outstanding accomplishments, not to an individual.
2. To promote camaraderie within the teams, additional bonus incentives need to be given for the best cross-functional performance.
3. Give recognition for a job well done as a team or teams, not for individual accomplishments.
4. Team members need to be responsible for each other's performance, and the team should address individual performance—not the managers.
5. When the goal of an organization is to compete and succeed as a unified force, the disciplines and actions are all based on combined success. A profitable year at Ubisoft is a profitable for *all* employees; everyone is equally committed and rewarded as a team.

## Robert Roliardi

President, Pearson Digital Learning, Scottsdale, AZ

As Yves Guillemot has discovered, it is a small world! I am reading this dilemma while on a flight from our headquarters in Scottsdale, AZ, to Mumbai, India, where I will visit two development sites we have there. To make such a far-flung enterprise truly work effectively, remote sites must understand the mission of the organization. They need to see how the work they do fits into the larger picture. In our case, the purpose of my trip is to show them that the president of the company values what they are doing. We produced a video to show them who they are working with in our corporate offices. The video demonstrates how students use the software that they helped build and how students learn more effectively due to their efforts. This is something that Yves might try with his employees around the world.

I think it's also important to invest in tools that help make the work process more efficient, such as sophisticated project management software and top-quality video conferencing equipment. But it is also important to take cultural sensitivities into account when using such tools to communicate across the organization.

Finally, no matter where people "sit" in the organization, everyone needs to understand the mission, realize how their work fits in so as to insure success, and understand how their contributions are valued.

# Learning Summary

## How Much Control Do Managers Have?

- **Omnipotent view:** managers are directly responsible for success or failure
- **Symbolic view:** success or failure is due to external forces outside manager's control

## What Is Organizational Culture?

- Shared values, principles, traditions, and ways of doing things; influences the way organizational members act
- Seven dimensions include: attention to detail, outcome orientation, people orientation, team orientation, aggressiveness, stability, and innovation/risk-taking

## What Do We Know About Culture?

- Strong cultures (values are deeply held and widely shared) have greater influence than weak cultures
- Original source of culture is organization's founder(s); continues through what managers say and how they behave, and through socialization
- Employees learn culture through stories, rituals, material symbols, and language

## What Kinds of Cultures Can Managers Create?

- Ethical
- Innovative
- Customer-responsive

## What Effect Does Culture Have on Managers?

Constrains the way managers plan, organize, lead, and control

## What Influence Does the Environment Have on Managers?

- External environment
  - Specific (customers, suppliers, competitors, pressure groups)
  - General (economic, political/legal, sociocultural, demographic, technological, and global)
- Environmental uncertainty
  - **Degree of change:** Do changes happen frequently or seldom?
  - **Degree of complexity:** Are there many or few environmental components?
- Stakeholder relationships
  - All the different constituencies in the organization's environment that have a stake in or are affected by the organization
  - Includes external and internal groups such as customers, competitors, governments, suppliers, and so forth
  - Managers manage these stakeholder relationships by knowing who stakeholders are and how critical they are

# Management: By the Numbers

- In a study of more than 2,000 respondents, nearly 80 percent believe that lack of respect and courtesy is a serious problem in the workplace and 60 percent believe that the problem is getting worse.
- A poll of nearly 800 U.S. employees showed that 10 percent reported witnessing incivility (lack of regard for one another) within their workplace. Some 20 percent said they were personal, direct targets of workplace incivility.
- A survey of 1,000 respondents by KRC Research showed 61 percent believed that businesses or workplaces could benefit from more spirituality.
- Research shows that one of the primary reasons organizational newcomers leave is inadequate socialization.
- A 5-year ongoing survey by Sirota Consulting of some 1.2 million employees at 52 *Fortune* 1000 companies found that employees who had been with their employer an average of 6 months had an overall job satisfaction rating of 80 out of 100 but the rating for employees who had been with their employer between 1 and 5 years was 69 out of 100.
- A study of more than 400 senior financial officers found that the pressure exerted by market stakeholders (investors, customers, suppliers, banks) is the strongest influence in terms of convincing managers to enforce the rules and guidelines found in their company's codes of ethics.
- A recent survey of HR professionals by the Society for Human Resource Management found that

78 percent said that diversity practices helped reduce costs and 74 percent said it improved the financial bottom line. However, only 38 percent of all organizations have a method of measuring the impact of diversity practices.
- A survey of close to 2,100 U.S. workers by Hudson Highland Group found that 31 percent have witnessed co-workers engaging in ethical misconduct. Only half (52 percent) of those who have witnessed such acts have actually reported it to someone in authority. However, 78 percent state that their organizations clearly communicate what they consider to be unethical and ethical workplace behavior.

*Sources:* "Nearly One-Third of Workers Witness Ethical Misconduct, But Only Half Report It, Reveals Hudson Survey," *HR Powerhouse,* www.hrpowerhouse.com, January 21, 2006; "Diversity Is Important to the Bottom Line," *HR Powerhouse,* www.hrpowerhouse.com, January 21, 2006; C. M. Pearson and C. L. Porath, "On the Nature, Consequences, and Remedies of Workplace Incivility: No Time for 'Nice'? Think Again," *Academy of Management Executive,* February 2005, pp. 7–18; J. M. Stevens, H. K. Steensma, D. A. Harrison, and P. L. Cochran, "Symbolic or Substantive Document? The Influence of Ethics Codes on Financial Executives' Decisions," *Strategic Management Journal,* January 2005, pp. 181–195; D. Sirota, L. A. Mischkind, and M. I. Meltzer, *The Enthusiastic Employee: How Companies Profit by Giving Workers What They Want* (Wharton School Publishing, 2005); D. G. Allen, "Do Organizational Socialization Tactics Influence Newcomer Embeddedness and Turnover," *Academy of Management Conference Proceedings Best Paper,* August 2004; and D. Haralson and S. Parker, "USA Today Snapshots," *USA Today,* October 29, 2003, p. 1B.

# Thinking About Management Issues

1. Refer to Exhibit 3–3. How would a first-line manager's job differ in these two organizations? How about a top-level manager's job?

2. Describe an effective culture for (a) a relatively stable environment and (b) a dynamic environment. Explain your choices.

3. Classrooms have cultures. Describe your classroom culture using the seven dimensions of organizational culture. Does the culture constrain your instructor? How?

4. Can culture be a liability to an organization? Explain.

5. Why is it important for managers to understand the external forces that are acting on them and their organization?

6. "Businesses are built on relationships." What do you think this statement means? What are the implications for managing the external environment?

7. What would be the drawbacks to managing stakeholder relationships?

# Working Together: Team-Based Exercise

Although all organizations face environmental constraints, the forces in their specific and general environments differ. Get into a small group with three to four other class members and choose one organization from two different industries. Describe the specific and general external factors for each organization. How are your descriptions different for the two organizations? How are they similar?

Now, using the same two organizations, see if you can identify the important stakeholders for these organizations. Also indicate whether these stakeholders are critical for the organization and why they are or are not. As a group, be prepared to share your information with the class and to explain your choices.

## Ethical Dilemma Exercise

Managing relations with a variety of stakeholder groups is a challenge in any situation—but it's even more difficult when the culture tolerates or encourages ethically questionable behavior. This is what happened at Computer Associates International, a business software company in New York. When Computer Associates reported year after year of impressive sales growth, the stock price soared and investors cheered. During one quarter, however, the company failed to meet Wall Street's earnings expectations, and the stock price plummeted more than 40 percent in a single day as investors fled.

Because CEO Sanjay Kumar and a few top executives wanted to please investors by keeping up the appearance of continued growth, they began booking software sales *before* the contracts were signed. They also told salespeople to change or remove dates on some contracts to clear the way for backdating those deals. Then the *New York Times* printed an article about accounting irregularities at Computer Associates—touching off a lengthy federal investigation that eventually led to Kumar and four former executives pleading guilty to securities fraud.[54]

Imagine this is your second day at work as a manager supervising a team of financial analysts in a major technology corporation. Your boss, the chief financial officer, calls you in and asks you to have your team find "creative" ways of improving sales figures. Look back at the framework in Exhibit 3–8 and think about the potential consequences as you decide which of the following options you will choose, and why.

**Option A:** Call a meeting of your analyst team and present the boss's request as a hypothetical challenge designed to sharpen their skills. Present the results to your boss without telling the team.

**Option B:** Work by yourself to dream up a few outlandish, impractical ideas so you can avoid being seen as someone who is not committed to your company's success.

**Option C:** Privately discuss the situation with the human resources manager who hired you (or another manager you trust) and explain why you are concerned about your boss's request.

## Case Application

### A Perfect Response to an Imperfect Storm

Twelve days. That's how long it took for Mississippi Power to restore electric power to the heavily damaged areas of southern Mississippi after Hurricane Katrina slammed into the Mississippi Gulf Coast on August 29, 2005, with 145-mph winds and pounding rain. That's remarkable, given the devastation that news photos and television newscasts so graphically displayed. It's something that even the federal and state governments could not accomplish. How bad was the damage company employees dealt with? One hundred percent of the company's customers were without power. Sixty-five percent of its transmission and distribution facilities were destroyed. And yet, this organization of 1,250 employees did what it had to do, despite the horrible circumstances and despite the fact that more than half of its employees suffered substantial damage to their own homes. It speaks volumes about the cultural climate that the managers of Mississippi Power had created.

As a corporate subsidiary of utility holding company Southern Company, Mississippi Power provides electric services to more than 190,000 customers in the Magnolia State. When Hurricane Katrina turned toward Mississippi, managers at Mississippi Power swung into action with a swift and ambitious disaster plan. After Katrina's landfall, Mississippi Power's management team responded "with a style designed for speed and flexibility, for getting things done amid confusion and chaos." David Ratcliffe, senior executive of Southern Company said, "I could not be prouder of our response." What factors led to the company's ability to respond as efficiently and effectively as it did?

One key element is the company's can-do organizational culture, which is evidenced by the important values inscribed on employees' identification tags: "Unquestionable Trust, Superior Performance, Total Commitment." Because the values were visible daily, employees knew their importance. They knew what was expected of them, in a disaster response or in just doing their everyday work. In addition, through employee training and managerial example, the organization had "steeped its culture" in Stephen Covey's book, *The 7 Habits of Highly Effective People*. (The company's training building—the Covey Center—flooded during the storm.) These ingrained habits—be proactive; begin with the end in mind; put first

*Mississippi Power utility workers responded quickly to areas devastated by Katrina.*

things first; think win/win; seek first to understand, then to be understood; synergize; and sharpen the saw—also guided employee decisions and actions.

Another important element in the company's successful post-storm response was the clear lines of responsibility of the 20 "storm directors," who had clear responsibility and authority for whatever task they had been assigned. These directors had the power to do what needed to be done backed by unquestionable trust from their bosses. Said one, "I don't have to ask permission."

Finally, the company's decentralized decision-making approach contributed to the way in which employees were able to accomplish what they did. The old approach of responding to a disaster with top–down decision making had been replaced by decision making being pushed further down to the electrical substation level, a distribution point that serves some 5,000 people. Crews working to restore power reported to these substations and had a simple mission—get the power back on. "Even out-of-state line crews, hired on contract and working unsupervised, were empowered to engineer their own solutions." What the crews often did to "get the power back on" was quite innovative and entrepreneurial. For instance, one crew "stripped a generator off an ice machine to get a substation working." Mississippi Power's president Anthony Topazi said, " . . . This structure made things happen faster than we expected. People were getting more done."

All in all, employees at Mississippi Power, working in difficult, treacherous, and often dangerous situations, did what they had to do. They got the job done. In recognition of the company's outstanding efforts to restore power in the wake of Hurricane Katrina, Mississippi Power was honored with an "Emergency Response Award" by the Edison Electric Institute in January 2006. It's an award that all the company's employees can be proud of.

## Discussion Questions

1. Using Exhibit 3–2, describe the culture at Mississippi Power. Why do you think this type of culture might be important to an electric power company? On the other hand, what might be the drawbacks of such a culture?

2. Describe how you think new employees at Mississippi Power "learn" the culture.

3. What stakeholders might be important to Mississippi Power? What concerns might each of these stakeholders have? Would these stakeholders change if there was a disaster to which the company had to respond?

4. What could other organizations learn from Mississippi Power about the importance of organizational culture?

*Sources:* Company Web site, www.southernco.com/mspower; Edison Electric Institute, "EEI Honors Mississippi Power with *'Emergency Response Award' for Hurricane Recovery Efforts,*" PR Newswire, www.prnewswire.com, January 11, 2006; S. Lewis, "Contractors to the Rescue," *Transmission & Distribution World,* tdworld.com/mag/power_contractors_rescue/index.html, December 1, 2005; D. Cauchon, "The Little Company That Could," *USA Today,* October 10, 2005, pp 1B+; and S. Covey, *The 7 Habits of Highly Effective People* (New York: Free Press, 1989).

# Learning Outline

*Use this Learning Outline as you read and study this chapter.*

### What's Your Global Perspective?

- Define parochialism.
- Contrast ethnocentric, polycentric, and geocentric attitudes toward global business.
- Explain why it's important for managers to be sensitive to global differences.

### Understanding the Global Environment

- Describe the current status of the European Union.
- Discuss the North American Free Trade Agreement and other regional trade alliances in Latin America.
- Tell about the Association of Southeast Asian Nations.
- Explain the interdependence that globalization involves.
- Discuss the role of the WTO.

### Doing Business Globally

- Contrast multinational, multidomestic, global, transnational, and born global organizations.
- Describe the different ways organizations can go international.
- Define global sourcing, exporting, importing, licensing, and franchising.
- Describe global strategic alliances, joint ventures, and foreign subsidiaries.

### Managing in a Global Environment

- Explain how the global legal-political and economic environments affect managers.
- Discuss Hofstede's five dimensions for assessing country cultures.
- Explain the nine GLOBE dimensions for assessing country cultures.
- Discuss the challenges of doing business globally in today's world.

# Managing in a Global Environment

## A Manager's Dilemma

Zara, the European clothing retailer, has been described at various times as having more style than GAP, faster growth than Target, and logistical expertise that rivals Wal-Mart's.[1] Although the company isn't yet a household name in North America, Zara's managers have positioned the company for continued global success. And that success is based on a simple rule—in fashion, nothing is as important as getting products to market quickly.

Using PDA technology, Zara's store managers around the world send customer feedback and observations on cuts, fabrics, and even new products to in-house design teams. After reviewing the ideas, these teams at headquarters in La Coruna, Spain, decide what to make. Designers draw up the ideas on their computers and send them over the company's intranet to its nearby factories. Within days, the cutting, dyeing, sewing, and assembling commence. In three weeks, the clothes will be in stores from Barcelona to Berlin to Beirut. That time frame isn't just a *bit* faster than rivals—it's over six times faster. Zara has a twice-a-week delivery schedule that restocks old styles and brings in new designs. The company's just-in-time production (an idea borrowed from the automobile industry) gives it a competitive edge in terms of speed and flexibility. An important piece of this incredible operation is a warehouse run by Lorena Alba, Zara's managing director of logistics.

Lorena runs the 4-story, 5-million-square-foot building (about the size of 90 football fields) with clockwork efficiency. To her, the warehouse isn't a place to store clothes, but a place to move them. The warehouse is connected to its factories through a maze of tunnels with rails, along which cables carry merchandise bundles "addressed" with a metal bar so they end up exactly where they're supposed to. In the warehouse, each of Zara's stores has its own "staging" area where its specific merchandise is packed. From there, the merchandise is sent to a loading dock and packed on a truck with other shipments in order of delivery.

As Zara continues to open new stores worldwide, Lorena will have to work closely with suppliers and in-store personnel from different cultures. Put yourself in her shoes. How should she deal with the cross-cultural problems that come up?

**what would you do?**

The Zara example illustrates that the global marketplace presents opportunities and challenges for managers. With the entire world as a market and national borders becoming increasingly irrelevant, the potential for organizations, such as Zara, to grow expands dramatically. A study of U.S. manufacturing firms found that companies that operated in multiple countries had twice the sales growth and significantly higher profitability than strictly domestic firms.[2] The global opportunities are there for managers to exploit. ( ◆ Go to www.prenhall.com/rolls)

However, as our opening dilemma also implies, even large successful organizations with talented managers face challenges in managing in the global environment. New competitors can suddenly appear at any time from anyplace on the globe. And, most importantly, managers must deal with cultural, economic, and political differences. Because U.S. workers are concerned over outsourcing of jobs to other countries and because 9/11 remains part of our collective social consciousness, these differences continue to be significant, creating increased challenges for managers in global organizations. Managers who don't closely monitor changes in their global environment or who don't take the specific characteristics of their location into consideration as they plan, organize, lead, and control are likely to find limited global success. In this chapter, we're going to discuss the issues managers have to face in managing in a global environment. ( ◆ Go to www.prenhall.com/rolls)

**Self-Assessment Library (S.A.L.)**

Do you think you'd be a good global manager? Go to S.A.L. #III.B.5 and find out.

**Q & A**

See Q & A 4.1 to find out why it's important to know about managing globally.

## WHO OWNS WHAT?

One way to see how global the manager's environment has become is to consider the country of ownership origin for some familiar products and companies. You might be surprised to find that many products you thought were made by U.S. companies aren't! Take the following quiz[3] and then check your answers at the end of the chapter on page 113.

1. Ben and Jerry's Ice Cream is owned by a company based in:
   a. Mexico   b. Saudi Arabia   c. United Kingdom   d. United States

2. Bic pens are made by a company based in:
   a. Japan   b. United Kingdom   c. United States   d. France

3. Rajah spices are products of a company based in:
   a. Brazil   b. Switzerland   c. United States   d. India

4. RCA television sets are produced by a company based in:
   a. France   b. United States   c. Malaysia   d. Taiwan

5. Skippy brand peanut butter is a product of a company based in:
   a. United States   b. Canada   c. Venezuela   d. United Kingdom

6. The owner of Godiva chocolate is based in:
   a. United States   b. Switzerland   c. France   d. Sweden

7. The company that produces Boboli Pizza Crust is based in:
   a. United States   b. Mexico   c. Italy   d. Spain

8. The parent company of Braun electric shavers is located in:
   a. Switzerland   b. Germany   c. United States   d. Japan

9. IBM personal computers are products of a company with controlling ownership in:
   a. China   b. United States   c. Canada   d. France

10. Eckerd Drugstores are owned by a company based in:
    a. United States   b. Canada   c. France   d. Russia

11. Lean Cuisine frozen meals are products of a company based in:
    a. Germany   b. United States   c. Switzerland   d. Brazil

12. Dr. Pepper and 7-Up are products of a company based in:
    a. United States   b. Japan   c. Canada   d. United Kingdom

13. The company that markets Lipton Tea is based in:
    a. China   b. United Kingdom   c. Japan   d. United States

14. Häagen-Daz ice cream is a product of a company based in:
    a. Germany   b. France   c. United States   d. Switzerland

15. Wella hair care products are marketed by a company based in:
    a. United States   b. Switzerland   c. France   d. Germany

How well did you score? Were you aware of how many products we use every day that are made by companies *not* based in the United States? Most of us don't fully understand or appreciate the truly global nature of today's marketplace. And as you can see, these companies represent a broad cross-section of products, markets, and industries.

## WHAT'S YOUR GLOBAL PERSPECTIVE?

It's not unusual for Germans, Italians, or Indonesians to speak three or four languages. More than half of all primary school children in China now learn English and the number of English speakers in India and China—500 million—now exceeds the total number of mother-tongue English speakers elsewhere in the world. On the other hand, most U.S. children study only English in school—only 24,000 are studying Chinese. And only 22 percent of the population in the United States speaks a language other than English.[4] Americans tend to think of English as the only international business language and don't see a need to study other languages. A major research report commissioned by the British Council says that the competitiveness of both Britain and the United States is being undermined by only speaking English. Once everyone speaks English, competitive advantage can only be maintained by having something else—other skills, such as speaking several languages.[5]

Monolingualism is one sign that a nation suffers from **parochialism**, which is viewing the world solely through one's own eyes and perspectives.[6] People with a parochial attitude do not recognize that others have different ways of living and working. Parochialism is a significant obstacle for managers working in a global business world.

**parochialism**
Viewing the world solely through your own perspectives, leading to an inability to recognize differences between people.

**Exhibit 4–1**

**Key Information About
Three Global Attitudes**

|  | Ethnocentric | Polycentric | Geocentric |
|---|---|---|---|
| Orientation | **Home Country** | **Host Country** | **World** |
| Advantages | • Simpler structure<br>• More tightly controlled | • Extensive knowledge of foreign market and workplace<br>• More support from host government<br>• Committed local managers with high morale | • Forces understanding of global issues<br>• Balanced local and global objectives<br>• Best people and work approaches used regardless of origin |
| Drawbacks | • More ineffective management<br>• Inflexibility<br>• Social and political backlash | • Duplication of work<br>• Reduced efficiency<br>• Difficult to maintain global objectives because of intense focus on local traditions | • Difficult to achieve<br>• Managers must have both local and global knowledge |

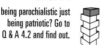

**Q & A**

Isn't being parochialistic just
being patriotic? Go to
Q & A 4.2 and find out.

If managers fall into the trap of ignoring others' values and customs and rigidly applying an attitude of "ours is better than theirs" to foreign cultures, they'll find it difficult to compete with other organizations around the world that *are* seeking to understand foreign customs and market differences. (    Go to www.prenhall.com/rolls) This type of narrow, restricted attitude is one approach that managers might take, but it's not the only one.[7] Exhibit 4-1 summarizes the key points about three possible global attitudes. Let's look at each more closely.

An **ethnocentric attitude** is the parochialistic belief that the best work approaches and practices are those of the *home* country (the country in which the company's headquarters are located). Managers with an ethnocentric attitude believe that people in foreign countries do not have the needed skills, expertise, knowledge, or experience to make the best business decisions as people in the home country do. They wouldn't trust foreign employees with key decisions or technology.

A **polycentric attitude** is the view that the managers in the *host* country (the foreign country in which the organization is doing business) know the best work approaches and practices for running their business. Managers with a polycentric attitude view every foreign operation as different and hard to understand. Thus, these managers are likely to leave their foreign facilities alone and let foreign employees figure out how best to do things.

The last type of global attitude that managers might have is a **geocentric attitude**, which is a *world-oriented* view that focuses on using the best approaches and people

*Thomas O. Binford, retired from Stanford University, arrived in Bangalore several years ago with a few suitcases and his retirement fund and is now about to sign the first business customer for his new company, Read-Ink Technologies. Read-Ink specializes in advanced handwriting recognition software that will read scanned forms and records. Like many entrepreneurs, Binford was drawn to Bangalore by its low labor costs and its huge pool of recent engineering graduates with expertise in specialized new technologies.*

**Exhibit 4–2**

**Examples of Cross-Cultural Blunders**

- You're in Shanghai on business. Walking down the street one day, you pass a Chinese colleague. He asks you. "Have you eaten yet?" You answer, "No, not yet." He rushes off, looking embarrassed and uncomfortable. The phrase, "Have you eaten yet?" is a common greeting—just like "Hi, how are you?" in the United States. It's the Chinese way of saying "Is your belly full today?" or "Is life treating you well?"

- A U.S. manager transferred to Saudi Arabia successfully obtained a signature on a million-dollar contract from a Saudi manufacturer. The manufacturer's representative had arrived at the meeting several hours late, but the U.S. executive considered this tardiness unimportant. The American was certainly surprised and frustrated to learn later that the Saudi had no intention of abiding by the contract. He had signed it only to be polite after showing up late for the appointment.

- A U.S. executive visiting Germany for the first time was invited to the home of his largest customer. He decided to be a good guest and brought the hostess a bouquet of a dozen red roses. He later learned that in Germany it is bad luck to present an even number of flowers and that red roses are symbolic of a strong romantic interest.

- A U.S. executive based in Peru was viewed by Peruvian managers as cold and unworthy of trust because in face-to-face discussions he kept backing away. He didn't understand that in Peru and other Latin-American countries, the custom is to stand quite close to the person with whom you are speaking.

- The "thumbs up" gesture is considered offensive in the Middle East, rude in Australia, and a sign of "OK" in France.

- It's rude to cross your arms while facing someone in Turkey.

*Source:* See D. A. Ricks, M. Y. C. Fu, and J. S. Arpas, *International Business Blunders* (Columbus, OH: Grid, 1974); A. Bennett, "American Culture is Often a Puzzle for Foreign Managers in the U.S." *Wall Street Journal*, February 12, 1986, p. 29; C.F. Valentine, "Blunders Abroad," *Nation's Business*, March 1989, p. 54; R. E. Axtell (ed.), *Do's and Taboos around the World*, 3rd ed. (New York: John Wiley & Sons, 1993); B. Pachter, "When in Japan, Don't Cross Your Legs," *Business Ethics*, March–April 1996, p. 50; and V. Frazee, "Keeping Up on Chinese Culture," *Global Workforce*, October 1996, pp. 16–17.

from around the globe. Managers with this type of attitude believe that it's important to have a global view both at the organization's headquarters in the home country *and* in the various foreign work facilities. For instance, the CEO of Home Décor (a disguised name), a fast-growing manufacturer of household accessories, is a Chinese immigrant who describes the company's strategy as "combining Chinese costs with Japanese quality, European design, and American marketing."[8] Using the geocentric view, major issues and decisions are viewed globally by looking for the best approaches and people regardless of origin.

Successful global management requires enhanced sensitivity to differences in national customs and practices. Management practices that work in Chicago might not be appropriate in Bangkok or Berlin. In Exhibit 4-2, read some examples of the cultural blunders that can happen when managers ignore foreign values and customs and rigidly apply their own. Later in this chapter and throughout the rest of the book, you'll see how a geocentric attitude toward managing requires eliminating parochial attitudes and carefully developing an understanding of cultural differences between countries.

## Learning Review

- Define parochialism.
- Contrast ethnocentric, polycentric, and geocentric attitudes toward global business.

- Explain why it's important for managers to be sensitive to global differences.

**ethnocentric attitude**
The parochialistic belief that the best work approaches and practices are those of the home country.

**polycentric attitude**
The view that the managers in the host country know the best work approaches and practices for running their business.

**geocentric attitude**
A world-oriented view that focuses on using the best approaches and people from around the globe.

# UNDERSTANDING THE GLOBAL ENVIRONMENT

As we discussed in Chapter 2, management is no longer constrained by national borders. Managers in all sizes and types of organizations are faced with the opportunities and challenges of managing in a global environment. What is the global environment like? One important feature is global trade, which, if you remember history class, isn't new. Countries and organizations have been trading with each other for centuries. Trade is central to human health, prosperity, and social welfare.[9] Examples of global trade abound, as we saw in the chapter-opening quiz. When trade is allowed to flow freely, countries benefit from economic growth and productivity gains because they specialize in producing the goods they're best at and importing goods that are more efficiently produced elsewhere. Global trade is being shaped by two forces: regional trading alliances and the agreements negotiated through the World Trade Organization.

## Regional Trading Alliances

Not so long ago, global competition was best described in terms of country against country—the United States versus Japan, France versus Germany, Mexico versus Canada. Now, global competition has been reshaped by the creation of regional trading agreements including the European Union (EU), North American Free Trade Agreement (NAFTA), the Association of Southeast Asian Nations (ASEAN), and others.

**The European Union** The signing of the Maastricht Treaty (named for the Dutch town where the treaty was signed) in February 1992 created the **European Union (EU)**, a unified economic and trade entity with 12 original members—Belgium, Denmark, France, Greece, Ireland, Italy, Luxembourg, the Netherlands, Portugal, Spain, the United Kingdom, and Germany. The primary motivation for the joining of these European nations was to reassert their economic position against the strength of the United States and Japan. Working in separate countries with barriers against one another, European industries couldn't develop the efficiency of American and Japanese businesses. Three other countries—Austria, Finland, and Sweden—joined the group in 1995 (see Exhibit 4-3). In 2004, the EU added 10 new members—Cyprus, Malta, the Czech Republic, Estonia, Hungary, Latvia, Lithuania, Poland, Slovakia, and Slovenia. Four other countries (Bulgaria, Croatia, Romania, and Turkey) have applied

**Exhibit 4–3**

**European Union Countries**

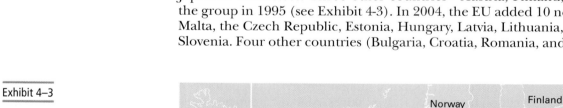

for membership and Bulgaria and Romania are expected to join in 2007.[10] The economic power represented by the EU is considerable. The current EU membership covers a population base of 450 million people and the European Commission (the Brussels-based executive body of the EU) reports that unification has boosted gross domestic product and added 2.5 million jobs since 1993.[11]

Before the creation of the EU, each nation had border controls, taxes, and subsidies; nationalistic policies; and protected industries. Now, as a single market, there are no barriers to travel, employment, investment, and trade. The EU took an enormous step toward full unification when 12 countries became part of the Economic and Monetary Union, the formal system responsible for the development of the **euro**, a single European currency. Nine additional countries will adopt the euro before 2010.[12]

The EU was dealt a blow during May 2005 when voters in France and the Netherlands rejected the planned new European Union constitution.[13] Despite this setback, the EU will continue to evolve and assert its economic power in one of the world's richest markets. European businesses will continue to play an important role in the global economy. For instance, Unilever PLC of the United Kingdom is a powerful force in consumer products (look back at the "Who Owns What" quiz), DaimlerChrysler AG of Germany is a solid competitor in automobiles, and Nokia of Finland is a dominant player in cell phones.

**North American Free Trade Agreement (NAFTA)**  When agreements in key issues covered by the **North American Free Trade Agreement (NAFTA)** were reached by the Mexican, Canadian, and U.S. governments on August 12, 1992, a vast economic bloc was created. Between 1994, when NAFTA went into effect, and 2003 (the most recent year for complete statistics), exports to Canada increased 62 percent and exports to Mexico increased 106 percent.[14] Canada continues to be the top U.S. trading partner with Mexico following at number three. (China is second.) Eliminating the barriers to free trade (tariffs, import licensing requirements, customs user fees) has resulted in a strengthening of the economic power of all three countries.

Other Latin American nations are moving to become part of free-trade blocs. Colombia, Mexico, and Venezuela led the way when all three signed an economic pact in 1994 eliminating import duties and tariffs. The U.S.–Central America Free Trade Agreement (CAFTA), approved in an extremely narrow vote by the U.S. House of Representatives in late July 2005, promotes trade liberalization between the United States and five Central American countries: Costa Rica, El Salvador, Guatemala, Honduras, and Nicaragua. However, only El Salvador is ready to join. The other four countries have yet to change laws to be in line with the agreement.[15] The United States also signed a trade deal with Colombia that is said to be the largest Washington has negotiated with a Latin American country since signing NAFTA.[16] Also, negotiators from 34 countries in the Western Hemisphere continue work on a Free Trade Area of the Americas (FTAA) agreement, which was to have been operational no later than 2005. However, at a November 2005 summit, the leaders of these 34 nations failed to reach any agreement, leaving the future of the FTAA still up in the air.[17] Already in existence is another free-trade bloc of eight South American countries known as the Southern Cone Common Market or Mercosur, which was formed in 1991. However, it's facing serious problems as many of those participating countries look to become part of the larger, and potentially more powerful, FTAA.[18]

**Association of Southeast Asian Nations (ASEAN)**  The **ASEAN** is a trading alliance of 10 Southeast Asian nations (see Exhibit 4-4). The ASEAN region has a population of about 500 million with a combined gross domestic product of US$737 billion.[19]

---

**European Union (EU)**
A union of 25 European nations created as a unified economic and trade entity.

**euro**
A single common European currency.

**North American Free Trade Agreement (NAFTA)**
An agreement among the Mexican, Canadian, and U.S. governments in which barriers to trade have been eliminated.

**Association of Southeast Asian Nations (ASEAN)**
A trading alliance of 10 Southeast Asian nations.

Exhibit 4–4

**ASEAN Members**

Source: Based on J. McClenahen and T. Clark, "ASEAN at Work," *IW*, May 19, 1997, p. 42.

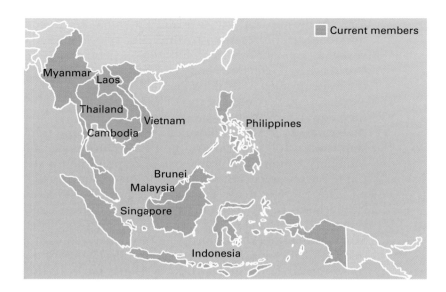

During the years ahead, the Southeast Asian region promises to be one of the fastest growing economic regions of the world and will be an increasingly important regional economic and political alliance whose impact eventually could rival that of both NAFTA and the EU.

**Other Trade Alliances** Other regions around the world continue to develop regional trading alliances. For instance, the 53-nation African Union (AU) came into existence in July 2002, with the vision of building an integrated, prosperous and peaceful Africa.[20] Members of this alliance plan to create an economic development plan and to work to achieve greater unity among Africa's nations. Like members of other trade alliances, these countries hope to gain economic, social, cultural, and trade benefits from their association.

Also, the South Asian Association for Regional Cooperation (SAARC) composed of seven nations (India, Pakistan, Sri Lanka, Bangladesh, Bhutan, Nepal, and the Maldives) started eliminating tariffs on January 1, 2006.[21] Its aim, like all the other regional trading alliances, is to allow for the free flow of goods and services.

## The World Trade Organization

Global growth and trade among nations doesn't just happen on its own. Systems and mechanisms are needed so that efficient and effective trading relationships can develop. Indeed, one of the realities of globalization is that countries are interdependent—that is, what happens in one can impact others, good or bad. For example, the severe Asian financial crisis in the late 1990s had the potential to totally disrupt economic growth around the globe and bring on worldwide recession. But it didn't. Why? Because there were mechanisms in place to prevent that from happening—mechanisms that encouraged global trade and averted the potential crisis. One of the most important of these mechanisms is the multilateral trading system called the **World Trade Organization (WTO)**.[22]

The WTO was formed in 1995 and evolved from the General Agreement on Tariffs and Trade (GATT), an agreement in effect since the end of World War II. Today, the WTO is the only *global* organization dealing with the rules of trade among nations. Its membership consists of 149 member countries and 32 observer governments (which have a specific time frame within which they must apply to become members). At its core are the various trade agreements, negotiated and ratified by the vast majority of the world's trading nations. The goal of the WTO is to help businesses (importers and exporters) conduct their business. Although a number of vocal critics have staged highly visible and public protests lambasting the WTO and claiming that it destroys jobs and the natural environment, the WTO appears to play an important role in monitoring and promoting global trade.

## Learning Review

- Describe the current status of the European Union.
- Discuss the North American Free Trade Agreement and other regional trade alliances in Latin America.
- Tell about the Association of Southeast Asian Nations.

- Explain the interdependence that globalization involves.
- Discuss the role of the WTO.

## DOING BUSINESS GLOBALLY

At 2 P.M. on a Saturday afternoon north of Moscow, a hypermarket operated by French retail group Auchan is jam-packed with Russian shoppers. McDonald's Corporation says it's on track to continue expanding aggressively in China even though it already has more than 700 locations and opened its first drive-through in Dongguan, Guangdong Province, in December 2005. Fabian Gomez, an audit partner for the Mexican branch of Deloitte Touche Tohmatsu, a global accounting and business-services organization, says, "A lot of our business is serving Mexican subsidiaries of international companies and the executives usually come from other places." And two Asian automakers—Toyota of Japan and Kia from South Korea—are investing in new manufacturing plants in two states (Indiana and Georgia) that U.S. carmakers exited.[23] As you can see from these examples, organizations in different industries *and* from different countries are pursuing global opportunities. But how do organizations do business globally? That's what we want to look at in this section.

### Different Types of International Organizations

Organizations doing business globally aren't anything new. DuPont started doing business in China in 1863. H.J. Heinz Company was manufacturing food products in the United Kingdom in 1905. Ford Motor Company set up its first overseas sales branch in France in 1908. By the 1920s, other companies, including Fiat, Unilever, and Royal Dutch/Shell, had gone international. But it wasn't until the mid-1960s that international companies became quite common. Today, there are very few companies that don't have some type of international dealings. However, in spite of the fact that doing business internationally is so widespread, there's no one generally accepted approach to describing the different types of international companies—they're called different things by different authors. However, we're going to use the terms *multinational, multidomestic, global,* and *transnational* to describe the various types of international organizations.[24] A **multinational corporation (MNC)** is a broad term usually used to refer to any and all types of international companies that maintain operations in multiple countries.

A **multidomestic corporation** is an MNC that decentralizes management and other decisions to the local country. This type of organization doesn't attempt to replicate its domestic successes by managing foreign operations from its home country. Instead, local employees typically are hired to manage the business and marketing strategies are tailored to that country's unique characteristics. This type of globalization reflects the polycentric attitude. For example, Switzerland-based Nestlé can be described as a multidomestic corporation. With operations in almost every country on the globe, its managers match the company's products to its consumers. In parts of Europe, Nestlé sells products

---

**World Trade Organization (WTO)**
A global organization of 149 countries that deals with the rules of trade among nations.

**multinational corporations (MNCs)**
A broad term that refers to any and all types of international companies that maintain operations in multiple countries.

**multidomestic corporation**
An international company that decentralizes management and other decisions to the local country.

that are not available in the United States or Latin America. Another example of a multidomestic is Frito-Lay, a division of PepsiCo, which markets a Dorito chip in the British market that differs in both taste and texture from the U.S. and Canadian version. Many consumer companies manage their global businesses using this approach because they must adapt their products and services to meet the needs of the local markets.

Then, there's the type of MNC called a **global company** that centralizes its management and other decisions in the home country. These companies treat the world market as an integrated whole and focus on the need for global efficiency. Although these companies may have considerable global holdings, management decisions with company-wide implications are made from headquarters in the home country. This approach to globalization reflects the ethnocentric attitude. Some examples of companies that can be considered global companies include Sony, Deutsche Bank AG, and Merrill Lynch.

Other companies are going international by eliminating structural divisions that impose artificial geographical barriers. This type of MNC is often called a **transnational or borderless organization** and reflects a geocentric attitude.[25] For example, IBM dropped its organizational structure based on country and reorganized into industry groups. Spain's Telefonica eliminated the geographic divisions between Madrid headquarters and its widespread phone companies. The company will be organized, instead, along business lines such as Internet services, cellular phones, and media operations. Managers choose this form of international organization to increase efficiency and effectiveness in a competitive global marketplace.[26]

Our classification of different types of international organizations tends to describe large international businesses. However, there are an increasingly large number of businesses called **born globals** that choose to go global from inception.[27] These companies (also known as *international new ventures* or *INVs*) commit resources upfront (material, people, financing) to doing business in more than one country and are likely to continue to play an increasingly important role in international business.

## How Organizations Go International

When organizations do go international, they often use different approaches depending on whether they're just starting or whether they've been doing business internationally for awhile (see Exhibit 4-5). During the initial stages of going international, managers look at ways to get into a global market without having to invest a lot of capital. At this stage, companies may start with **global sourcing** (also called *global outsourcing*), which is purchasing materials or labor from around the world wherever it is cheapest. The goal: Take advantage of lower costs in order to be more competitive. For instance, Massachusetts General Hospital uses radiologists in India to interpret CT

Exhibit 4–5

**How Organizations Go Global**

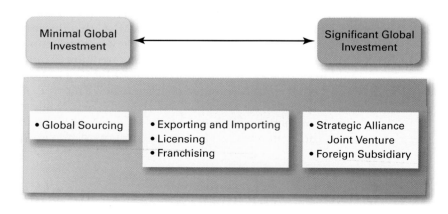

scans.[28] Although global sourcing is often the first step to going international, many organizations continue to use this approach even as they become more international because of the competitive advantages it offers. Beyond global sourcing, however, each successive stage of becoming more international requires more investment and thus entails more risk for the organization.

Next, managers may go international by **exporting** the organization's products to other countries—that is, making products domestically and selling them abroad. In addition, an organization might choose **importing**, which involves acquiring products made abroad and selling them domestically. Both exporting and importing are steps toward being a full-blown international business and still usually involve minimal investment and minimal risk. Many organizations, especially small businesses, may choose to continue with exporting and importing as the way they do business internationally. For instance, Haribhai's Spice Emporium, a small business (revenues around US$7 million) in Durban, South Africa, exports spices and rice to customers all over Africa, Europe, and the United States. However, other organizations have built multi-million-dollar businesses by importing or exporting. That's what specialty retailer Pier 1 Imports has done—importing products from more than 40 countries for sale in its more than 1,100 North American stores.

Finally, in the early stages of doing business internationally, managers can use licensing or franchising, which are similar approaches involving an organization's giving another organization the right to use its brand name, technology, or product specifications in return for a lump sum payment or a fee usually based on sales. The only difference is that **licensing** is primarily used by manufacturing organizations that make or sell another company's products and **franchising** is primarily used by service organizations that want to use another company's name and operating methods. For example, Thai consumers can enjoy Bob's Big Boy hamburgers, Filipinos can dine on Shakey's Pizza, and Malaysians can consume Schlotzsky's deli sandwiches—all because of franchises in these countries. Anheuser-Busch licensed the right to brew and market Budweiser beer to other brewers, such as Labatt in Canada, Modelo in Mexico, and Kirin in Japan.

Typically once an organization has been doing business internationally for awhile and has gained experience in international markets, managers may decide to make more of a direct investment. One way they can do this is through **strategic alliances**, which are partnerships between an organization and a foreign company partner or partners in which both share resources and knowledge in developing new products or building production facilities. The partners also share the risks and rewards of this alliance. For example, IBM of the United States, Toshiba of Japan, and Siemens of Germany formed a partnership to develop new generations of computer chips. A specific type of strategic alliance in which the partners agree to form a separate, independent organization for some business purpose is called a **joint venture**. For example, Hewlett-Packard has had numerous joint ventures with various suppliers around the globe to develop different components for its computer equipment. These partnerships provide a fast, inexpensive way for companies to compete globally rather than doing it on their own.

---

**global company**
An international company that centralizes management and other decisions in the home country.

**transnational or borderless organization**
A type of international company in which artificial geographical barriers are eliminated.

**born global**
An international company that chooses to go global from inception.

**global sourcing**
Purchasing materials or labor from around the world wherever it is cheapest.

**exporting**
Making products domestically and selling them abroad.

**importing**
Acquiring products made abroad and selling them domestically.

**licensing**
An organization gives another organization the right to make or sell its products using its technology or product specifications.

**franchising**
An organization gives another organization the right to use its name and operating methods.

**strategic alliances**
Partnerships between an organization and a foreign company partner(s) in which both share resources and knowledge in developing new products or building production facilities.

**joint venture**
A specific type of strategic alliance in which the partners agree to form a separate, independent organization for some business purpose.

*managing* **IT**

## IT in a Global World

Managers around the globe are tapping into the power of information technology.[29] For example, when it found that e-mail was extremely inefficient for employee collaboration, Dresdner Kleinwort Wasserstein, a London-based financial services firm, moved to using **wikis** (a type of web site that allows anyone visiting it to add, remove, or otherwise edit the content) and **blogs** (an online journal that usually focuses on a particular subject) as a way for many of its 1,500 employees to create, edit, comment on, and revise projects in real time. The payoff: e-mail volume down 75 percent, meeting times slashed, and team members more productive. South Korean company Samsung Electronics uses online links with suppliers and retailers to help improve demand forecasts, which has resulted in cutting days of inventory from 80 days to about 2 weeks. Both examples—and there are many others—illustrate how important IT can be to global organizations.

As global managers look to exploit the benefits of IT, might their geographic location have an impact? It might be interesting to look at Internet usage statistics. The following table summarizes these statistics for the various world regions. Are you surprised at the results? Although we can't conclude or even assume that organizations in those countries with the highest Internet usage rate will be more likely to use IT, it does raise some issues about where innovations and ideas on how best to manage IT efficiently and effectively may come from in the future.

### World Internet Usage and Population Statistics

| World Regions | Population (2006 Est.) | Population % of World | Internet Usage, Latest Data | % Population (Penetration) | Usage % of World | Usage Growth 2000–2005 |
|---|---|---|---|---|---|---|
| Africa | 915,210,928 | 14.1% | 23,649,000 | 2.5% | 2.2% | 403.7% |
| Asia | 3,667,774,066 | 56.4% | 364,270,713 | 9.9% | 35.7% | 218.7% |
| Europe | 807,289,020 | 12.4% | 291,600,898 | 35.9% | 28.5% | 176.1% |
| Middle East | 190,084,161 | 2.9% | 18,203,500 | 9.6% | 1.8% | 454.2% |
| North America | 331,473,276 | 5.1% | 227,303,680 | 68.1% | 22.2% | 108.9% |
| Latin America/Caribbean | 553,908,632 | 8.5% | 79,962,809 | 14.3% | 7.8% | 337.4% |
| Oceania/Australia | 33,956,977 | 0.5% | 17,872,707 | 52.9% | 1.8% | 132.2% |
| World Total | 6,499,697,060 | 100.0% | 1,022,863,307 | 15.7% | 100.0% | 182.0% |

*Notes:* (1) Internet Usage and World Population Statistics were updated for March 31, 2006. (2) CLICK on each world region for detailed regional information. (3) Demographic (Population) numbers are based on data contained in the world-gazetteer Web site. (4) Internet usage information comes from data published by Nielsen//NetRatings, by the International Telecommunications Union, by local NICs, and other other reliable sources. (5) For definitions, disclaimer, and navigation help, see the Site Surfing Guide. (6) Information from this site may be cited, giving due credit and establishing an active link back to www.internetworldstats.com. © Copyright 2006, Miniwatts Marketing Group. All rights reserved.

Or, managers may choose to make a direct investment in a foreign country by setting up a **foreign subsidiary** as a separate and independent production facility or office. This subsidiary can be managed as a multidomestic (local control) or as a global organization (centralized control). As you can probably guess, this arrangement involves the greatest commitment of resources and poses the greatest amount of risk. For instance, United Plastics Group of Westmont, Illinois, built three injection-molding facilities in Suzhou, China, and plans to build at least two more. However, Chuck Villa, the company's executive vice president for business development, says that level of investment is necessary because "it fulfills our mission of being a global supplier to our global accounts."[30]

## Learning Review

- Contrast multinational, multidomestic, global, transnational, and born global organizations.
- Describe the different ways organizations can go international.
- Define global sourcing, exporting, importing, licensing, and franchising.
- Describe global strategic alliances, joint ventures, and foreign subsidiaries.

*Fast-food giant KFC is like many big franchise firms opening more new outlets overseas. Along the way the company is making appropriate changes in its menu offerings, such as substituting juice and fruit for Coke and fries. This Shanghai promotion features new egg tarts.*

## MANAGING IN A GLOBAL ENVIRONMENT

**Q & A**

How can I best prepare if I want to work globally? Q & A 4.3 will give you some suggestions.

Assume for a moment that you're a manager going to work for a branch of a global organization in a foreign country. You know that your environment will differ from the one at home, but how? What should you be looking for? ( 　 Go to www.prenhall.com/rolls)

Any manager who finds himself or herself in a foreign country faces new challenges. In this section, we'll look at some challenges and offer guidelines for responding. Although our discussion is presented through the eyes of a U.S. manager, our analytical framework could be used by any manager regardless of national origin who has to manage in a foreign environment.

### The Legal-Political Environment

U.S. managers are accustomed to stable legal and political systems. Changes are slow, and legal and political procedures are well established. Elections are held at regular intervals. Even changes in political parties after an election do not produce radical or quick transformations. The stability of laws governing the actions of individuals and institutions allows for accurate predictions. The same can't be said for all countries. Managers in a global organization must stay informed of the specific laws in countries where they do business.

Also, some countries have a history of unstable governments. Deutsche Banks' analysis of global political risk categorizes countries into different stability categories: maximum, high, moderate, low, and failed states. Some of the countries high on the stability list included Australia, Germany, Japan, Spain, and the United States. Some of the countries low on the list included Afghanistan, Bosnia and Herzegovina, Mozambique, Nigeria, and North Korea.[31] Managers of businesses in countries with lower stability levels face dramatically greater uncertainty as a result of that instability. In addition, political interference is a fact of life in some regions, especially in some Asian countries. For instance, many large businesses have postponed doing business in China because the government controls what organizations do and how they do it. As Chinese consumers gain more power, however, that attitude is likely to change.

**wikis**
Server software that allows users to freely create and edit Web-page content using any Web browser.

**blogs**
Web logs or online diaries.

**foreign subsidiary**
Directly investing in a foreign country by setting up a separate and independent production facility or office.

*thinking critically about* **Ethics**

Foreign countries often have lax product-labeling laws. As a product manager for a U.S. pharmaceutical company, you're responsible for the profitability of a new drug whose side effects can be serious, although not fatal. Adding this information to the label or even putting an informational insert into the package will add to the product's cost, threatening profitability margins. What will you do? Why? What factors will influence your decision?

The legal-political environment doesn't have to be unstable to be a concern to managers. Just the fact that a country's legal-political system differs from that of the United States is important. Managers must recognize these differences if they hope to understand the constraints under which they operate and the opportunities that exist.

## The Economic Environment

The global manager must be aware of economic issues when doing business in other countries. One of the first is understanding the country's type of economic system. The two major types are a market economy and a command economy. A **market economy** is one in which resources are primarily owned and controlled by the private sector. A **command economy** is one in which economic decisions are planned by a central government. In actuality, no economy is purely market or command. For instance, the United States and United Kingdom are two countries at the market end of the spectrum but they do have minimal governmental control. The economies of Vietnam and North Korea, however, would be more command-based. Then, there's China, a country that's more command-based, but is moving toward being more market-based. Why would managers need to know about a country's economic system? Because it has the potential to constrain decisions and actions. Other economic issues a manager might need to understand include currency exchange rates, inflation rates, and diverse tax policies.

A global firm's profits can vary dramatically depending on the strength of its home currency and the currencies of the countries in which it operates. For instance, China's revaluation of the yuan in the summer of 2005 was cheered by General Motors even though a stronger yuan could raise the costs of Chinese-made parts that GM buys. Why would GM be happy about higher costs? Because a rising Chinese yuan could also lead to a stronger Japanese yen, which could hurt rival Toyota Motor Corporation.[32] Any revaluation of a nation's currency can affect managers' decisions and the level of a company's profits.

Inflation means that prices for products and services are going up. But it also affects interest rates, exchange rates, the cost of living, and the general confidence in a country's political and economic system. In most developing countries, consumer prices are rising more slowly than they were in the late 1990s, although inflation rates can, and do, vary widely.[33] The *World Factbook* shows country inflation rates ranging from a negative 3.6 percent (Nauru) to a whopping positive 246 percent (Zimbabwe).[34] Managers need to monitor inflation trends so they can make good decisions and anticipate any possible changes in a country's monetary policies.

Finally, diverse tax policies are a major worry for a global manager. Some host countries are more restrictive than the organization's home country. Others are far more lenient. About the only certainty is that tax rules differ from country to country. Managers need exact information on the various tax rules in countries in which they operate to minimize their business's overall tax obligation.

## The Cultural Environment

A large global oil company found that employee productivity in one of its Mexican plants was off 20 percent and sent a U.S. manager to find out why. After talking to several employees, the manager discovered that the company used to have a monthly fiesta in the parking lot for all the employees and their families. Another U.S. manager had canceled the fiestas, saying they were a waste of time and money. The message employees were getting was that the company didn't care about their families anymore. When the fiestas were reinstated, productivity and employee morale soared.

At Hewlett-Packard, a cross-global team of U.S. and French engineers were assigned to work together on a software project. The U.S. engineers sent long, detailed e-mails to their counterparts in France. The French engineers viewed the lengthy e-mails as patronizing and replied with quick, concise e-mails. This made the U.S. engineers think that the French were hiding something from them. The situation spiraled out of control and negatively affected output until team members went through cultural training.[37]

As we know from Chapter 3, organizations have different cultures. Countries have cultures too. **National culture** is the values and attitudes shared by individuals from a specific country that shape their behavior and their beliefs about what is important.[36]

Which is more important to a manager—national culture or organizational culture? For example, is an IBM facility in Germany more likely to reflect German culture or IBM's corporate culture? Research indicates that national culture has a greater effect on employees than does their organization's culture.[37] German employees at an IBM facility in Munich will be influenced more by German culture than by IBM's

## *focus on* **Leadership**

### Leading Here Is Not Like Leading There: The Role of National Culture in Effective Leadership

Is leadership culturally bound?[37] This is a question that international organizations struggle with, and it is one that both Hoftstede's research and the GLOBE studies have attempted to answer. In fact, the GLOBE project has been called the "most ambitious study of global leadership."

On the one hand, it is believed that leaders must adapt their styles to different national cultures. What works in the United States, for instance, isn't likely to work in Germany or China. Instead, leaders need to adapt their approach to the cultural environment. And both Hofstede and the GLOBE studies would say that there are cultural differences that leaders must take into consideration as they manage.

However, the GLOBE studies did identify 22 leader behaviors that were *universally* deemed to be desirable and 8 leader behaviors that are *universally* undesirable. These are shown in the table on the right.

So what conclusion can we reach about the role of national culture in effective leadership? It's fair to say that although there are differences among countries in terms of effective cross-cultural leadership, there are also similarities. The key for global leaders is to develop a global mind-set and to show cultural adaptability and flexibility.

#### Cultural Views of Leadership Effectiveness

The following is a partial list of leadership attributes with the corresponding primary leadership dimension in parentheses.

**Universal Facilitators of Leadership Effectiveness**

- Being trustworthy, just, and honest (integrity)
- Having foresight and planning ahead (charismatic–visionary)
- Being positive, dynamic, encouraging, motivating, and building confidence (charismatic–inspirational)
- Being communicative, informed, a coordinator, and team integrator (team builder)

**Universal Impediments to Leadership Effectiveness**

- Being a loner and asocial (self-protective)
- Being noncooperative and irritable (malevolent)
- Being dictatorial (autocratic)

**Culturally Contingent Endorsement of Leader Attributes**

- Being individualistic (autonomous)
- Being status conscious (status conscious)
- Being a risk taker (charismatic, self-sacrificial)

*Source:* M. Javidan, P. W. Dorfman, M. S. deLuque, and R. J. House, "In the Eye of the Beholder: Cross-Cultural Lessons in Leadership from Project GLOBE," *Academy of Management Perspective*, February 2006, p. 75.

---

**market economy**
An economic system in which resources are primarily owned and controlled by the private sector.

**command economy**
An economic system in which all economic decisions are planned by a central government.

**national culture**
The values and attitudes shared by individuals from a specific country that shape their behavior and beliefs about what is important.

National culture influences many aspects of competing abroad. India now graduates about 350,000 engineering students each year; the United States, 70,000. Organizations that need employees with engineering skills in order to be competitive are going to have to understand national cultures, such as that of India.

culture. This means that as influential as organizational culture may be on managerial practice, national culture is even more influential.

Legal, political, and economic differences among countries are fairly obvious. The Japanese manager who works in the United States or his or her American counterpart in Japan can get information about laws or tax policies without too much difficulty. Getting information about a country's cultural differences isn't quite that easy! (  Go to www.prenhall.com/rolls) The primary reason is that it's hard for natives to explain their country's unique cultural characteristics to someone else. For instance, if you were born and raised in the United States, how would you characterize U.S. culture? In other words, what are Americans like? Think about it for a moment and see how many of the characteristics in Exhibit 4-6 you identified.

**Q & A**

Global information isn't easy to get, but Q & A 4.4 provides some clues on where to look.

**Q & A**

See Q & A 4.5 to see why Hofstede's cultural dimensions are so useful.

**Hofstede's Framework for Assessing Cultures** One of the most widely referenced approaches to helping managers better understand differences between national cultures was developed by Geert Hofstede. (  Go to www.prenhall.com/rolls) His

Exhibit 4–6

**What Are Americans Like?**

- Americans are *very informal*. They tend to treat people alike even when there are great differences in age or social standing.

- Americans are *direct*. They don't talk around things. To some foreigners, this may appear as abrupt or even rude behavior.

- Americans are *competitive*. Some foreigners may find Americans assertive or overbearing.

- Americans are *achievers*. They like to keep score, whether at work or at play. They emphasize accomplishments.

- Americans are *independent and individualistic*. They place a high value on freedom and believe that individuals can shape and control their own destiny.

- Americans are *questioners*. They ask a lot of questions, even of someone they have just met. Many of these questions may seem pointless ("How ya' doin'?") or personal ("What kind of work do you do?").

- Americans *dislike silence*. They would rather talk about the weather than deal with silence in a conversation.

- Americans *value punctuality*. They keep appointment calendars and live according to schedules and clocks.

- Americans *value cleanliness*. They often seem obsessed with bathing, eliminating body odors, and wearing clean clothes.

*Sources:* Based on M. Ernest (ed.), *Predeparture Orientation Handbook: For Foreign Students and Scholars Planning to Study in the United States* (Washington, DC: U.S. Information Agency, Bureau of Cultural Affairs, 1984), pp. 103–05; A. Bennett, "American Culture Is Often a Puzzle for Foreign Managers in the U.S.," *Wall Street Journal*, February 12, 1986, p. 29; "Don't Think Our Way's the Only Way," *The Pryor Report*, February 1988, p. 9; and B. J. Wattenberg, "The Attitudes behind American Exceptionalism," *U.S. News & World Report*, August 7, 1989, p. 25.

research found that managers and employees vary on five dimensions of national culture, which are as follows:

- *Individualism versus collectivism:* Individualism is the degree to which people in a country prefer to act as individuals rather than as members of groups. In an individualistic society, people are supposed to look after their own interests and those of their immediate family and do so because of the large amount of freedom that an individualistic society allows its citizens. The opposite is collectivism, which is characterized by a social framework in which people prefer to act as members of groups and expect others in groups of which they are a part (such as a family or an organization) to look after them and to protect them.

- *Power distance:* Hofstede used the term *power distance* as a measure of the extent to which a society accepts the fact that power in institutions and organizations is distributed unequally. A high power distance society accepts wide differences in power in organizations. Employees show a great deal of respect for those in authority. Titles, rank, and status carry a lot of weight. In contrast, a low power distance society plays down inequalities as much as possible. Superiors still have authority, but employees are not afraid of or in awe of the boss.

- *Uncertainty avoidance:* Uncertainty avoidance describes the degree to which people tolerate risk and prefer structured over unstructured situations. People in low uncertainty avoidance societies are relatively comfortable with risks. They're also relatively tolerant of behavior and opinions that differ from their own because they don't feel threatened by them. On the other hand, people in a society that's high in uncertainty avoidance feel threatened by uncertainty and ambiguity and experience high levels of anxiety, which manifests itself in nervousness, high stress, and aggressiveness.

- *Achievement versus nurturing:* The fourth cultural dimension, like individualism and collectivism, is a dichotomy. Achievement is the degree to which values such as assertiveness, the acquisition of money and material goods, and competition prevail. Nurturing is a national cultural attribute that emphasizes relationships and concern for others.[39]

- *Long-term and short-term orientation:* This cultural attribute looks at a country's orientation toward life and work. People in cultures with long-term orientation look to the future and value thrift and persistence. Also, in these cultures, leisure time is not so important and it is believed that the most important events in life will occur in the future. A short-term orientation values the past and present and emphasizes respect for tradition and fulfilling social obligations. Leisure time is important and it is believed that the most important events in life occurred in the past or in the present.

Although we don't have the space to review Hofstede's entire results for all the countries studied, we provide 12 examples of the first four variables in Exhibit 4-7. The long-term orientation variable isn't included in this table because scores for some of the countries weren't reported. However, the top five countries with higher long-term orientation (LTO) scores are China, Hong Kong, Taiwan, Japan, and South Korea. Countries such as Sweden, Germany, Australia, United States, United Kingdom, and Canada had lower LTO scores, which reflect a more short-term orientation.[40]

**The GLOBE Framework for Assessing Cultures** Although Hofstede's cultural dimensions have been the main framework for differentiating among national cultures, much of the data on which it's based is somewhat outdated. Since the time of Hofstede's original studies, there have been a number of changes in the global environment, suggesting the need for an updated assessment of cultural dimensions, which the GLOBE project provides.[41]

cadmium, mercury, and certain flame retardants in most electrical and electronic products.[42] Doing business globally today isn't easy! Managers face serious challenges—challenges arising from the openness associated with globalization and from significant cultural differences.

The push to go global has been widespread. Advocates praise the economic and social benefits that come from globalization. Yet, that very globalization has created challenges because of the openness that's necessary for it to work. The uproar over the proposed acquisition of certain U.S. ports by a Dubai company illustrates the concerns and fears (real or perceived) that having an open economy and open borders provokes.[43] What challenges has openness created? One is the increased threat of terrorism by a truly global terror network. Globalization is meant to open up trade and to break down the geographical barriers separating countries. Yet, opening up means just that—being open to the bad as well as the good. From the Philippines and the United Kingdom to Israel and Pakistan, organizations and employees face the risk of terrorist attacks. Another challenge from openness is the economic interdependence of trading countries. If one country's economy falters, it potentially could have a domino effect on other countries with which it does business. So far, however, that has not happened. The world economy has proved to be quite resilient. And there are mechanisms in place, such as the World Trade Organization, to isolate and address potential problems.

But it's not just simply the challenges from openness managers must be prepared to face. The far more serious challenges for managers reflect intense underlying and fundamental cultural differences—differences that encompass traditions, history, religious beliefs, and deep-seated values. Managing in such an environment will be extremely complicated.  (   Go to www.prenhall.com/rolls) Although globalization has long been praised for its economic benefits, there are those who think that globalization is simply a euphemism for "Americanization"—that is, the way U.S. cultural values and U.S. business philosophy are said to be slowly taking over the world.[44] At its best, proponents of Americanization hope others will see how progressive, efficient, industrious, and free U.S. society and businesses are and want to emulate that way of doing things. However, critics claim that this attitude of the "almighty American dollar wanting to spread the American way to every single country" has created many problems.[45] Although history is filled with clashes between civilizations, what's unique about our time period is the speed and ease with which misunderstandings and disagreements can erupt and escalate. The Internet, television and other media, and global air travel have brought the good and the bad of American entertainment, prod-

## becoming a Manager

✓ Learn as much as you can about other countries.

✓ Familiarize yourself with current global political, economic, and cultural issues.

✓ If given the opportunity, try to have your class projects or reports (in this class and other classes) cover global issues or global companies.

✓ Talk to professors or students who may be from other countries and ask them what the business world is like in their country.

✓ If you have the opportunity, travel to other countries.

✓ Go see a foreign film.

✓  Go to the Self-Assessment Library found on www.prenhall.com/rolls and complete S.A.L. #III.B.5—Am I Well-Suited for a Career as a Global Manager?

Self-Assessment Library (S.A.L.)

ucts, and behaviors to every corner of the globe. For those who don't like what Americans do, say, or believe, it can lead to resentment, dislike, distrust, and even outright hatred.

Successfully managing in today's global environment will require incredible sensitivity and understanding. Managers from any country will need to be aware of how their decisions and actions will be viewed, not only by those who may agree, but more importantly, by those who may disagree. They will need to adjust their leadership styles and management approaches to accommodate these diverse views. Yet, as always, they will need to do this while still being as efficient and effective as possible in reaching the organization's goals.

## Learning Review

- Explain how the global legal-political and economic environments affect managers.
- Discuss Hofstede's five dimensions for assessing country cultures.
- Explain the nine GLOBE dimensions for assessing country cultures.
- Discuss the challenges of doing business globally in today's world.

## Managers Respond to a Manager's Dilemma

### Ronald Heimler

President, Walter Heimler Company, New York, NY; Adjunct Professor, LIM College and Long Island University, New York, NY; Lecturer, California State University—Pomona, CA

In the fashion industry (that Lorena is in) and the fashion jewelry industry (that I'm engaged in), speed to market is critical to reduce risk and to meet customers' demands for instant gratification. Zara responded to immediate retail fashion demands by using information technology and focusing on input from employees and customers. However, with the rapid global expansion of the company, cross-cultural challenges can arise. As a proactive manager, Lorena should "Think globally and act locally."

One thing she may consider is having teams in the warehouse made up of employees familiar with different locales and cultures. That way, these teams could share information about specific cultural contexts of various regions through Zara's intranet. With this information, Zara could adapt its supply and logistics capabilities to fit the unique markets they're in. Additionally, the teams could utilize their cultural perspective to interpret sales information from each locale and assimilate these factors into the design and manufacturing processes.

# Learning Summary

## What's Your Global Perspective?

- **Parochialism**: *a narrow view that does not recognize differences*
- **Ethnocentric**: *belief that one's views are best*
- **Polycentric**: *belief that host country knows best approach*
- **Geocentric**: *belief that best approaches can be found anywhere*

## What Kinds of Alliances Affect Trade Relations Among Countries?

- *Regional trading alliances (EU, NAFTA, CAFTA, FTAA, ASEAN, AU, SAARC)*
- *World Trade Organization*

## How Do Companies Do Business Globally?

### Types of international organizations

- **Multinational corporation (MNC)**: *any and all types of international companies that maintain operations in multiple countries*
- **Multidomestic corporation**: *an MNC that decentralizes management and other decisions to the local country*
- **Global company**: *an MNC that centralizes management and other decisions in the home country*
- **Transnational or borderless**: *an MNC that eliminates artificial geographical barriers*
- **Born globals**: *businesses that choose to go global from inception*

### How organizations go international

- *Minimal investment: global sourcing*
- *Medium investment: exporting-importing; licensing; franchising*
- *Significant investment: strategic alliance—joint venture; foreign subsidiary*

## What Are the Challenges of Doing Business Globally?

- *Legal-political environment (laws and regulations, stability of government)*
- *Economic environment (market/command economy, currency exchange rates, inflation rates, tax policies)*
- *Cultural environment (national culture characteristics)*
  - *Hofstede's framework (individualism-collectivism; power distance; uncertainty avoidance; achievement-nurturing; long- or short-term orientation)*
  - *GLOBE framework (assertiveness, future orientation, gender differentiation, uncertainty avoidance, power distance, individualism-collectivism, in-group collectivism, performance orientation, human orientation)*
  - *Extended Hofstede's work*

# Management: By the Numbers

- In a survey of almost 1,500 executives, Spanish was cited as the second most useful language in business after English. Chinese came in third, followed by French, German, Japanese, and Italian.
- Only 24 percent of a sample of financial executives around the world said that they rated the risks of globalization high; however, 41 percent rated the risks of globalization as moderate.
- A poll by Harris Interactive showed that 58 percent of Americans say they are very satisfied with their lives. Other results from this poll showing how satisfied individuals are with their lives: Danes—64 percent; Germany—21 percent; and Italians—16 percent.
- A poll by Korn/Ferry International found that 9 out of 10 executive recruiters believe that job candidates who speak only one language will be less and less marketable in the years ahead.

*Sources: J. Yang and K. Gelles, "USA Today Snapshots," USA Today, February 8, 2006, p. 1B; J. MacIntyre, "Danes, Americans Rank Most Satisfied with Life," Springfield Business Journal, September 5–11, 2005, p. 26; J. Yang and A. Lewis, "USA Today Snapshots," USA Today, June 20, 2005, p. 1B; and A. Fisher, "Offshoring Could Boost Your Career," Fortune, January 24, 2005, p. 36.*

# Thinking About Management Issues

1. What are the managerial implications of a borderless organization?

2. Can the GLOBE framework presented in this chapter be used to guide managers in a Thai hospital or a government agency in Venezuela? Explain.

3. Compare the advantages and drawbacks of the various approaches to going global.

4. What challenges might confront a Mexican manager transferred to the United States to manage a manu-facturing plant in Tucson, Arizona? Will these be the same for a U.S. manager transferred to Guadalajara? Explain.

5. In what ways do you think global factors have changed the way organizations select and train managers? What impact might the Internet have on this? Explain.

6. How might a continued war on terrorism impact U.S. managers and companies doing business globally?

# Working Together: Team-Based Exercise

Moving to a foreign country isn't easy, no matter how many times you've done it or how receptive you are to new experiences. Successful global organizations are able to identify the best candidates for global assignments, and one of the ways they do this is through individual assessments prior to assigning people to global facilities. Form groups of three to five individuals. Your newly formed team, the Global Assignment Task Force, has been given the responsibility for developing a global aptitude assessment form for Zara (the company described at the beginning of the chapter). Because Zara is expanding its global operations significantly, it wants to make sure that it's sending the best possible people to the various global locations. Your team's assignment is to come up with a rough draft of a form to assess people's global aptitude. Think about the characteristics, skills, and attitudes that you think a successful global employee would need. Your team's draft should be at least one-half page but not longer than one page. Be prepared to present your ideas to your classmates and professor.

# Ethical Dilemma Exercise

Companies can enter global markets in a number of ways. Montreal-based Cirque du Soleil, known for its lavish circus performances, licenses its brand to a clothing manufacturer that creates women's fashions to sell in boutiques worldwide. New Balance, headquartered in Boston, has strategic alliances with overseas suppliers to make and distribute its sneakers internationally. Either approach to global business may lead to ethical dilemmas. For example, should firms let customers know when a product is made under license or by a partner? Should they be able to restrict how licensees or partners use proprietary processes? And should partners be allowed to compete against partners in the global marketplace?

Consider New Balance's experience in China. More than half of the company's shoes are manufactured by local suppliers in China and sold through retailers in the United States and other countries. Eyeing fast-growing profit opportunities in China, the company contracted with a long-time local supplier, Howard Chang, to make and sell basic New Balance sneakers within China. Only a few years later, however, New Balance became concerned that selling so many basic sneakers might hurt its image in China. Although the company told Chang to cut production and then notified him that his contract was being terminated, Chang " . . . continued to sell and was actively trying to sell product outside the country," says New Balance's vice president for intellectual property.

Chang fought back in Chinese courts, citing an older document he said allowed him to make New Balance sneakers until the end of the contract. A company formerly seen as a strategic partner had become one of New Balance's global competitors.[46]

Imagine you're a manager reporting to New Balance's vice president for international sales. You just found out that several Japanese discount stores are selling basic sneakers made by Chang and bearing the New Balance brand at the bargain-basement price of $25 per pair. Although you want to protect your company's name and reputation, you cannot stop Chang from selling shoes he produced before New Balance terminated his contract. Review Exhibit 4-5 as you decide which of the following options to choose.

**Option A:** Tell the Japanese stores to stop selling the basic sneakers because New Balance considers them counterfeits and doesn't want consumers to be deceived.

**Option B:** Alert Japanese consumers to the deception by placing ads in newspapers and magazines saying that New Balance considers the basic sneakers to be counterfeit.

**Option C:** Offer to buy the remaining stock of basic sneakers from the Japanese stores so you can keep them off the market.

Case Application

Chapter

5

# Learning Outline

*Use this Learning Outline as you read and study this chapter.*

### What Is Social Responsibility?

- Contrast the classical and socioeconomic views of social responsibility.
- Discuss the role that stakeholders play in the four stages of social responsibility.
- Differentiate between social obligation, social responsiveness, and social responsibility.

### Social Responsibility and Economic Performance

- Explain what research studies have shown about the relationship between an organization's social involvement and its economic performance.
- Define social screening.
- Explain what conclusion can be reached regarding social responsibility and economic performance.

### The Greening of Management

- Describe how organizations can go green.
- Relate the approaches to being green to the concepts of social obligation, social responsiveness, and social responsibility.

### Values-Based Management

- Discuss what purposes shared values serve.
- Describe the relationship of values-based management to ethics.

### Managerial Ethics

- Discuss the factors that affect ethical and unethical behavior.
- Discuss the six determinants of issue intensity.
- Tell what codes of ethics are and how their effectiveness can be improved.
- Describe the important roles managers play in encouraging ethical behavior.

### Social Responsibility and Ethics Issues in Today's World

- Explain why ethical leadership is important.
- Discuss how managers and organizations can protect employees who raise ethical issues or concerns.
- Explain what role social entrepreneurs play.
- Describe social impact management.

# Social Responsibility and Managerial Ethics

## A Manager's Dilemma

Fred P. Keller, president, chairman, and CEO of Cascade Engineering, founded his company in 1973 on the belief that a business could be profitable *and* socially and environmentally responsible. His company emphasizes sustainable business practices that invest equally in three things: social, environmental, and financial capital. Fred says, "I like the idea that business is for a purpose, and the purpose isn't just maximizing dollar return."[1]

Fred's company manufactures plastic injected molded products for the automotive and home and office industries including door panels, fenders, decorative trim, residential air conditioning components, waste collection carts, and numerous other industrial and consumer items. One of Cascade's manufacturing "claims to fame" is a 9,000-ton injection molding press, one of the largest in North America, which is used to produce high-tech waste containers for the nation's leading waste haulers. More than 1,200 people worldwide work for Cascade, most of them at company headquarters in Grand Rapids, Michigan.

One of the important cornerstones of Fred's approach to doing business is Cascade Engineering's Business Conduct Policies, newly adopted in September 2005. As stated in the introduction to the policies, "These documents cover the legal and ethical principles that should guide you in your work as a member of the Cascade team." The policies go on to state: "Consistent with our overall commitment to honesty and integrity, we will focus on producing a quality product and providing excellent service; conduct our affairs as a responsible corporate citizen at all times; comply with all state, federal, and local laws and regulations; and provide all of our employees with a (emphasis as shown in actual document) **challenging and rewarding work experience,** along with **a safe and healthy work environment."**

The company's socially responsible and sustainable approach to doing business has brought it a number of awards. In 2005, Cascade received an Employer Recognition Award—Women in the Workplace by the Women's Resource Center; a Consumer's Energy Partner Award; and an Environmental Stewardship Award by the Society of Plastics Engineers Environmental Division. And in 2004, Cascade was number eight on the list of 25 Best Small to Medium Companies to Work for in America.

Put yourself in Fred's position. From a long-term perspective, would it make more sense to be less socially responsible and more focused on profits?

### What would you do?

At stage 3, managers expand their responsibilities to other stakeholders in the specific environment, primarily customers and suppliers. Socially responsible actions for these stakeholders might include fair prices, high-quality products and services, safe products, good supplier relations, and similar actions. Their philosophy is that they can meet their responsibilities to stockholders only by meeting the needs of these other stakeholders.

Finally, at stage 4, which characterizes the highest socioeconomic commitment, managers feel they have a responsibility to society as a whole. They view their business as a public entity and therefore feel it's important to advance the public good. The acceptance of such responsibility means that managers actively promote social justice, preserve the environment, and support social and cultural activities. They do these things even if such actions may negatively affect profits.

## Arguments For and Against Social Responsibility

Another way to decide whether organizations should be socially responsible is to look at the arguments for and against social responsibility. Exhibit 5–2 outlines the major points that have been presented.[8]

Exhibit 5–2

**Arguments For and Against Social Responsibility**

| For | Against |
| --- | --- |
| **Public expectations**<br>Public opinion now supports businesses pursuing economic and social goals. | **Violation of profit maximization**<br>Business is being socially responsible only when it pursues its economic interests. |
| **Long-run profits**<br>Socially responsible companies tend to have more secure long-run profits. | **Dilution of purpose**<br>Pursuing social goals dilutes business's primary purpose—economic productivity. |
| **Ethical obligation**<br>Businesses should be socially responsible because responsible actions are the right thing to do. | **Costs**<br>Many socially responsible actions do not cover their costs and someone must pay those costs. |
| **Public image**<br>Businesses can create a favorable public image by pursuing social goals. | **Too much power**<br>Businesses have a lot of power already and if they pursue social goals they will have even more. |
| **Better environment**<br>Business involvement can help solve difficult social problems. | **Lack of skills**<br>Business leaders lack the necessary skills to address social issues. |
| **Discouragement of further governmental regulation**<br>By becoming socially responsible, businesses can expect less government regulation. | **Lack of accountability**<br>There are no direct lines of accountability for social actions |
| **Balance of responsibility and power**<br>Businesses have a lot of power and an equally large amount of responsibility is needed to balance against that power. | |
| **Stockholder interests**<br>Social responsibility will improve a business's stock price in the long run. | |
| **Possession of resources**<br>Businesses have the resources to support public and charitable projects that need assistance. | |
| **Superiority of prevention over cures**<br>Businesses should address social problems before they become serious and costly to correct. | |

Q & A

Really now... how could someone argue against a business being socially responsible? Q & A 5.2 provides some insight.

How much and what type of social responsibility businesses should engage in continues to be a topic of interest and heated debate. ( ◆ Go to www.prenhall.com/rolls) But if we decide that organizations *should* be socially responsible, what does that mean? Now is a good time to define what we mean by the term *social responsibility*.

## From Obligations to Responsiveness to Responsibility

Few concepts have been described in as many different ways as *social responsibility*. For instance, it's been called "profit making only," "going beyond profit making," "voluntary activities," and "concern for the broader social system."[9] We can understand social responsibility better if we first compare it to two similar concepts: social obligation and social responsiveness.[10] **Social obligation** is when a firm engages in social actions because of its obligation to meet certain economic and legal responsibilities. The organization does only what it's obligated to do, which indicates it's following the classical view of social responsibility. In contrast to social obligation, however, both social responsiveness and social responsibility go beyond merely meeting basic economic and legal standards.

**Social responsiveness** is when a firm engages in social actions in response to some popular social need. Managers in a socially responsive organization are guided by social norms and make practical decisions about the societal actions in which they engage.[11] For instance, managers at American Express Company identified three themes—community service, cultural heritage, and economic independence—to guide in deciding which worldwide projects and organizations to support. By making these choices, managers were "responding" to what they felt were important social needs.[12]

A socially *responsible* organization views things a little differently, and goes beyond what it's obligated to do or chooses to do because of some popular social need, to do what it can to help improve society because it's the right thing to do. We define **social responsibility** as a business's intention, beyond its legal and economic obligations, to do the right things and act in ways that are good for society.[13] Note that this definition assumes that a business obeys laws and pursues economic interests, but it also emphasizes that businesses have to differentiate between right and wrong.

Social responsibility adds an ethical imperative to do those things that make society better and not to do those that could make it worse. As Exhibit 5–3 shows, social responsibility requires business to determine what is right or wrong and to engage in ethical business activities. A socially responsible organization does what is right because it feels it has a responsibility to act that way. For example, when Aspen Skiing Company completed one of the first certified "green" (environmentally sustainable) buildings in the United States, CEO Pat O'Donnell said, in response to reporters' questions about whether the decision made economic sense, "We did

Exhibit 5–3

**Social Responsibility Versus Social Responsiveness**

|  | Social Responsibility | Social Responsiveness |
|---|---|---|
| Major consideration | Ethical | Pragmatic |
| Focus | Ends | Means |
| Emphasis | Obligation | Responses |
| Decision framework | Long term | Medium and short term |

*Source:* Adapted from S. L. Wartick and P. L. Cochran, "The Evolution of the Corporate Social Performance Model," *Academy of Management Review*, October 1985, p. 766.

**social obligation**
When a firm engages in social actions because of its obligation to meet certain economic and legal responsibilities.

**social responsiveness**
When a firm engages in social actions in response to some popular social need.

**social responsibility**
A business's intention, beyond its legal and economic obligations, to do the right things and act in ways that are good for society.

this because it was the right thing to do. It cost us hundreds of thousands of dollars more, but management and ownership agreed that this is part of our guiding principles and part of our values-based business."[14] That's the attitude of a socially responsible manager and organization.

How should we view an organization's social actions? In the United States, a company that meets pollution control standards established by the federal government or that does not discriminate against employees over the age of 40 in promotion decisions is meeting its social obligation and nothing more because there are laws mandating these actions. However, when it provides on-site child-care facilities for employees, packages products in 100 percent recycled paper, or announces that it will not purchase, process, or sell any tuna caught with dolphins, it is being socially responsive. Why? Working parents and environmentalists have voiced these social concerns and demanded such actions.

Many companies in the United States and around the world practice social responsiveness. For example, during March 2006, Wal-Mart Stores—recognizing that "hunger is a serious issue that has a lasting impact on not only children and our elderly, but on our entire nation"—sponsored a program to help the cause. Customers donated money to Second Harvest Network by purchasing puzzle pieces and Wal-Mart and Sam's Club matched the first $5 million raised. As part of this program, Wal-Mart ran advertisements in large newspapers showing the word H_NGER and the tag line, "The problem can't be solved without You."[15]

**Q & A**

It seems to me that social responsiveness is focused on social issues that are popular right now. Right? Go to Q & A 5.3 and see.

Advocates believe that social responsiveness replaces philosophical talk with practical market-oriented action. They see it as a more tangible and achievable goal than social responsibility.[16] (  Go to www.prenhall.com/rolls) Rather than assessing what's good for society in the long term and making moral judgments, managers in a socially responsive organization identify the prevailing social norms and then change their social involvement to respond to changing societal conditions. For instance, environmental stewardship seems to be an important social norm at present and many companies are looking at ways to be environmentally responsible. Alcoa of Australia developed a novel way to recycle the used linings of aluminum smelting pots, and Japanese auto parts manufacturer Denso generates its own electricity and steam at many of its facilities. Other organizations are addressing other popular social issues. For instance, media companies such as Prentice Hall, McGraw-Hill, the *New York Times,* and the *Washington Post* are involved in efforts to increase literacy. ( Go to www.prenhall.com/rolls) These are examples of socially responsive actions for today.

**Q & A**

Would YOU work for a company whose products might be harmful if misused? Q & A 5.4 addresses this dilemma.

## Learning Review

- Contrast the classical and socioeconomic views of social responsibility.
- Discuss the role that stakeholders play in the four stages of social responsibility.

- Differentiate between social obligation, social responsiveness, and social responsibility.

## SOCIAL INVOLVEMENT AND ECONOMIC PERFORMANCE

In this section, we want to look at the question: Does being socially involved help or hurt a company's economic performance? A number of research studies have tried to answer this question.[17]

Although the majority of these studies showed a positive relationship between social involvement and economic performance, no general conclusions can be made because the studies didn't use standardized measures of "social responsibility" and "economic performance."[18] Because many of the studies determined a company's social actions by analyzing the content of annual reports, news articles, or "reputation" indexes, these criteria certainly might be questionable as reliable measures of a firm's social responsibility. And although measures of economic performance (such as net income, return on equity, or per share stock prices) are more objective, they are generally used to indicate only short-term economic performance. It may well be that the impact of social responsibility on a firm's profits—positive or negative—takes a number of years to appear. If there's a time lag, studies that use short-term financial measures are not likely to show valid results. Another issue is causation. If, for example, evidence showed that social involvement and economic performance were positively related, this wouldn't necessarily mean that social involvement *caused* higher economic performance. It very well could be the opposite. That is, it might mean that high profits afforded companies the luxury of being socially involved.[19] We shouldn't take these methodological concerns lightly. In fact, one study found that if the flawed empirical analyses in these studies were "corrected," social responsibility had a neutral impact on a company's financial performance.[20] Another study found that participating in social issues not related to the organization's primary stakeholders was negatively associated with shareholder value.[21] However, that's not the final word! A more recent and methodologically rigorous re-analysis of several of these studies concluded that managers can afford to be (and should be) socially responsible.[22]

Another way to look at the issue of social responsibility and economic performance is by evaluating socially responsible mutual stock funds. These mutual funds provide a way for individual investors to support socially responsible companies. (For a list of such funds, go to www.socialfunds.com.) Typically, these funds use some type of **social screening** or applying social criteria to investment decisions. For instance, these funds usually will not invest in companies that are involved in liquor, gambling, tobacco, nuclear power, weapons, price fixing, fraud, or in companies that have poor product safety, employee relations, and environmental track records. Although some people may think that these social funds are fine "for people more interested in saving spotted owls than saving for retirement," that just isn't the case.[23] Since the mid-2000s, the assets of these social-investing funds have grown to more than $2 trillion—about 11 percent of assets under professional management in the United States.[24] (See Exhibit 5–4 for the 10-year trend in social investing.) How have these funds performed overall? Morningstar, a mutual fund tracking organization, reports that 37 percent of the social funds it follows earned 4- or 5-star ratings, compared with only 32 percent of all mutual funds. Also, since 2002, those social funds that invested in large company

*Starbucks buys about 11.5 million pounds of fair-trade coffee each year in an effort to ensure that when consumers pay for their frappucinos and lattes, the farmers who grow the coffee beans receive a fair return on their labor. Although some fair-trade products are more expensive than normal and others fail to filter profits back to the growers, Starbucks' CAFÉ (Coffee and Farmer Equity) program works to ensure quality while protecting the environment and maintaining equitable relationships with the growers.*

**social screening**
Applying social criteria (screens) to investment decisions.

Exhibit 5–4

**10-Year Trend in Social Investing**

| (In Billions) | 1995 | 1997 | 1999 | 2001 | 2003 | 2005 |
|---|---|---|---|---|---|---|
| Social Screening[1] | $162 | $529 | $1,497 | $2,010 | $2,143 | $1,685 |
| Shareholder Advocacy | $473 | $736 | $922 | $897 | $448 | $703 |
| Screening and Shareholder[2] | N/A | ($84) | ($265) | ($592) | ($441) | ($117) |
| Community Investing | $4 | $4 | $5 | $8 | $14 | $20 |
| Total | $639 | $1,185 | $2,159 | $2,323 | $2,164 | $2,290 |

1. Social Screening includes mutual funds and separate accounts. Since 2003, SRI mutual fund assets have increased (see Section II) while separate account assets have declined (see Section III) as single issue screening has waned and shareholder advocacy increased on the part of institutional investors.

2. Assets involved in Screening and Shareholder Advocacy are subtracted to avoid double counting. Tracking Screening and Shareholder Advocacy only began in 1997, so there is no datum for 1995.

*Source:* Courtesy of social Investment Forum Foundation.

stocks had a 4.8 percent annualized return, which was better than the overall large company mutual funds category, which was up only 4.5 percent.[25]

What conclusion can we draw? The most meaningful is that there is little evidence to say that a company's social actions hurt its long-term economic performance. Given political and societal pressures on business to be socially involved, managers would be wise to take social goals into consideration as they plan, organize, lead, and control. In fact, some large investment banks wanting to avoid potential problems with their investment portfolios have added socially responsible investing teams to their research departments. Their reasoning: When a company acts socially irresponsible, it creates significant business risks.[26]

## Learning Review

- Explain what research studies have shown about the relationship between an organization's social involvement and its economic performance.
- Define social screening.

- Explain what conclusion can be reached regarding social responsibility and economic performance.

## THE GREENING OF MANAGEMENT

In January 2006, natural food grocer Whole Foods Market announced that it would rely on wind energy for all of its electricity needs, making it the largest corporate user of renewable energy in the United States. At U.K.–based Scottish Power, the importance of energy and environmental goals is obvious, as each division has a senior manager who's accountable for complying with those goals. Tokyo-based Ricoh hires rubber-gloved workers to sort through company trash to analyze what might be reused or recycled. And company employees have two garbage cans—one for recycling and one for waste. If a recyclable item is found in a waste bin, it's placed back on the offender's desk for proper removal.[27] Until the late 1960s, few people (and organizations) paid attention to the environmental consequences of their decisions and actions.[28] Although there were some groups concerned with conserving natural resources, about the only popular reference to saving the environment you would have seen was the ubiquitous printed request "Please Do Not Litter." A number of highly publicized environmental disasters (Exxon *Valdez* oil spill, mercury poisoning in Japan, and Three Mile Island and Chernobyl nuclear power plant accidents) brought about a new spirit of environmentalism among individuals, groups, and organizations. Increasingly, managers began to confront questions about an organization's impact on the natural environment. This recognition of the close link between an organization's decisions and activities and its impact on the natural environment is referred to as the **greening of management**. Let's look at some green issues managers may have to address.

## Global Environmental Problems

Americans spend more on trash bags to throw away waste than 90 other countries spend on all consumed products. The average mass-produced water bottle contains small amounts of a heavy toxic metal known to cause cancer. The rubber soles on a pair of shoes are loaded with lead that can last decades after the shoes are thrown away. The Business Roundtable, an organization that represents some of the United States' largest companies and has long challenged the science behind global warming, appeared to significantly change its stance when it announced it was asking all members to measure their current levels of greenhouse-gas emissions and then pledge to reduce them by a specific amount over time. Scientists fear that if the current rate of global warming and habitat destruction continues, half of the plant and animal species will be gone by the end of the twenty-first century.[29] Do we have your attention yet? Managers must be informed about green issues. To do so, however, requires first understanding the nature of global environmental problems—and the list is long.

Some of the more serious problems include natural resource depletion, global climate change, pollution (air, water, and soil), industrial accidents, and toxic wastes. How did these problems occur? Much of the blame can be placed on industrial activities in developed (economically affluent) countries over the last half-century.[30] Various reports have shown that affluent societies account for more than 75 percent of the world's energy and resource consumption and create most of the industrial, toxic, and consumer waste.[31] An equally unsettling picture is that as the world population continues to grow and as emerging countries become more market oriented and affluent, global environmental problems can be expected to worsen.[32] However, many managers and organizations around the world have embraced their responsibility to respect and protect the natural environment. What role *can* organizations play in addressing global environmental problems? In other words, how can they go green?

## How Organizations Go Green

Managers and organizations can do many things to protect and preserve the natural environment.[33] Some do no more than what is required by law—that is, they fulfill their social obligation. However, others have made radical changes to make their products and production processes cleaner. For instance, carpet-maker Shaw Industries of Dalton, Georgia, transforms its carpet and wood manufacturing waste into energy. Paris-based TOTAL, SA, one of the world's largest integrated oil companies, is cleaning up and greening up by implementing tough new rules on oil tanker safety and working with groups such as Global Witness and Greenpeace. UPS, the world's largest package delivery company, has done numerous things—from retrofitting its aircraft with advanced technology and fuel-efficient engines to developing a powerful computer network to efficiently dispatch its fleet of brown trucks and using alternative fuel to run them. And there are many more examples of organizations committed to being green. Although these examples are interesting, they don't tell us much about how organizations go green. One model of environmental responsibility

**greening of management**
The recognition of the close link between an organization's decisions and activities and its impact on the natural environment.

Exhibit 5–5

**Approaches to Being Green**

*Source:* Based on R. E. Freeman, J. Pierce, and R. Dodd, *Shades of Green: Business Ethics and the Environment* (New York: Oxford University Press, 1995).

Low ────────── Environmental Sensitivity ────────── High

| Legal Approach (Light Green) | Market Approach | Stakeholder Approach | Activist Approach (Dark Green) |

uses the term *shades of green* to describe the different approaches that organizations may take.[34] (See Exhibit 5–5.)

The first approach is the *legal* (or *light green*) *approach*—that is, simply doing what is required legally. Under this approach, organizations exhibit little environmental sensitivity. They obey laws, rules, and regulations willingly and without legal challenge and may even try to use the law to their own advantage, but that's the extent of their being green. For example, many durable product manufacturers have taken the legal approach and comply with the relevant environmental laws and regulations, but go no further. This approach is a good illustration of social obligation—these organizations simply follow the legal requirements to prevent pollution and protect the environment.

As an organization becomes more sensitive to environmental issues, it may adopt the *market approach*, where organizations respond to the environmental preferences of their customers. Whatever customers demand in terms of environmentally friendly products will be what the organization provides. For example, DuPont developed a new type of herbicide that helped farmers around the world reduce their annual use of chemicals by more than 45 million pounds. By developing this product, the company was responding to the demands of its customers (farmers) who wanted to minimize the use of chemicals on their crops.

Under the next approach, the *stakeholder approach*, the organization works to meet the environmental demands of multiple stakeholders such as employees, suppliers, or the community. For instance, Hewlett-Packard has several corporate environmental programs in place for its supply chain (suppliers), product design and product recycling (customers and society), and work operations (employees and community). Both the market approach and the stakeholder approach are good illustrations of social responsiveness.

Finally, if an organization pursues an *activist* (also called a *dark green*) *approach*, it looks for ways to respect and preserve the earth and its natural resources. The activist approach exhibits the highest degree of environmental sensitivity and is a good illustration of social responsibility. For example, Ecover (EDC nv), a Belgian company that produces cleaning products from natural soaps and renewable raw materials, operates a near-zero-emissions factory. This ecological factory is an environmentally sound

*In one recent year, U.S. consumers threw away 65 million personal computers and 130 million cell phones. Millions of unused televisions and computers sit in homes because their owners don't know how to dispose of them properly. To try to deal with possible health risks of dumping old electronics full of mercury, cadmium, and lead into landfills, many states are considering different forms of legislation on electronic waste. Among the companies that supported a recent new law mandating manufacturer participation in electronic waste recycling programs were Hewlett-Packard and Amazon.com.*

engineering marvel with a huge grass roof that keeps the factory cool in summer and warm in winter and a water treatment system that runs on wind and solar energy. The company chose to build this type of facility because of its deep commitment to protecting and preserving the environment.

## Evaluating the Greening of Management

As organizations become "greener," we find more and more of them issuing detailed reports on their environmental performance, many of them through the guidelines developed by the Global Reporting Initiative (GRI). Founded in 1997, the GRI is an independent entity that develops and disseminates globally applicable Sustainability Reporting Guidelines. Using the G3 (third generation) guidelines, almost 800 organizations around the globe are voluntarily reporting their efforts in promoting environmental sustainability. These reports, which can be found in the database on the GRI Web site, describe the numerous "green" actions these organizations are pursuing (www.globalreporting.org).

Another way that organizations can show their commitment to being green is through adopting the ISO 14001 standards. The nongovernmental ISO (International Organization for Standardization) is the world's largest developer of standards. Although ISO has developed more than 15,000 international standards, it's probably best known for its ISO 9000 (quality management) and ISO 14000 (environmental management) standards. Organizations that want to become ISO 14000 compliant must develop a total environmental management system for meeting environmental challenges. This means that the organization must minimize the effects of its activities on the environment and continually improve its environmental performance. If the organization can meet these standards, they can state that they are ISO 14001 compliant. Although these standards are voluntary, over 760,000 organizations in 154 countries have implemented ISO 9000 and ISO 14000. In addition to its environmental management standards, the ISO is developing an international standard to be released in 2008 that will provide guidelines for social responsibility. This voluntary standard, which will be known as ISO 26000, will not include requirements, so organizations will not be able to become "certified" if they meet the standards. However, ISO believes that organizations that meet these guidelines will demonstrate they are behaving in a socially responsible way that meets the "generalized requirements of society."[35]

The final way to evaluate a company's "green" actions is by the list of the 100 Most Sustainable Corporations in the World, a project that was launched in 2005 as a collaboration between the Canadian-based media company Corporate Knights and the research firm Innovest Strategic Value Advisers (www.global100.org). To be named as one of the 100 most sustainable corporations in the world, a company must have displayed an ability to effectively manage environmental and social factors. The companies that comprise the Global 100 are announced each year at the renowned World Economic Forum in Davos, Switzerland. Some of the companies on the 2006 list included ABB Limited (Switzerland), Cadbury Schweppes PLC (Great Britain), NTT Docomo Inc. (Japan), Enbridge Inc. (Canada), Group Danone (France), Insurance Australia Group (Australia), and Intel Corporation (United States).[36]

## Learning Review

- Describe how organizations can go green.
- Relate the approaches to being green to the concepts of social obligation, social responsiveness, and social responsibility.

## VALUES-BASED MANAGEMENT

Q & A
Why the big fuss about values? Check out Q & A 5.5 for an explanation.

"Make it better." From this simple statement, employees at Timberland know what actions and behaviors are expected and valued, that is, to find ways to make it better—whether it's creating quality products for customers, performing community service activities, designing employee training programs, or figuring out how to make the company's packaging more environmentally friendly. As CEO Jeffery Swartz says on the company's Web site, "Everything we do at Timberland grows out of our relentless pursuit to find a way to make it better." Timberland is an example of a company that practices values-based management. **Values-based management** is an approach to managing in which managers are guided by the organization's shared values in their management practices. An organization's values reflect what it stands for and what it believes in. As we discussed in Chapter 3, the shared organizational values form the organization's culture and serve many purposes.[37] ( ⬛ Go to www.prenhall.com/rolls)

### Purposes of Shared Values

Exhibit 5–6 shows the four purposes of shared values. One purpose that shared values serve is to guide managerial decisions and actions.[38] For instance, at Tom's of Maine, a manufacturer of all-natural personal care products, the corporate Statement of Beliefs guides managers as they plan, organize, lead, and control. One of the eight beliefs states, "We believe that different people bring different gifts and perspectives to the team and that a strong team is founded on a variety of gifts."[39] This statement expresses to managers the value of diversity—diversity of opinions, diversity of abilities—and serves as a guide for managing teams of people.

Another purpose of shared values is to shape employee behavior and communicate what the organization expects of its members. For example, Nortel Networks has six core values: customers are the driving force, people are our strength, quality is in every aspect, innovation fuels our future, accountability brings clarity, and integrity underpins everything.[40] As employees do their jobs, they know what behaviors are expected of them because the shared values are clear as far as things such as how to treat customers (customers are the driving force), how to do their work (quality is in every aspect), or how to negotiate with suppliers (being honest in dealings).

Shared corporate values also influence marketing efforts. For example, we previously mentioned Avon's commitment to educating women about breast cancer. Its managers decided to support this program after the company asked women what their number-one health concern is and breast cancer was the answer. How does Avon's commitment to women's health influence its marketing efforts? The company's global sales force of some 4.9 million independent representatives educates women about the disease by bringing brochures on their sales visits. The director of the Breast Cancer Awareness Crusade said, "All of the interaction that happens with an Avon rep on something as important as breast cancer should improve customer relations and make for easier sales." Avon has found a way to link its business to an important social concern and to improve its marketing efforts all at the same time.

Exhibit 5–6    **Purposes of Shared Values**

## *thinking critically about* **Ethics**

In an effort to be (or at least appear to be) socially responsible, many organizations donate money to philanthropic and charitable causes. In addition, many organizations ask their employees to make individual donations to these causes. Suppose you're the manager of a work team, and you know that several of your employees can't afford to pledge money right now because of various personal and financial problems. You've also been told by your supervisor that the CEO has been known to check the list of individual contributors to see who is and is not supporting these very important causes. What would you do? What ethical guidelines might you suggest for individual and organizational contributions to philanthropic and charitable causes?

**Passport**

How are a company's values stressed to global employees in distant locations? Do this Passport scenario and find out!

Finally, shared values are a way to build team spirit in organizations. When employees embrace the stated corporate values, they develop a deeper personal commitment to their work and feel obligated to take responsibility for their actions. Because the shared values influence the way work is done, employees are more enthused about working together as a team to support the values they believe in. When IBM decided to take a look at its core values, it invited all 300,000-plus employees to engage in an open "values jam" using the company's intranet. And tens of thousands of employees did. The open and candid exchange resulted in the identification of three values that would drive employee actions: dedication to every client's success; innovation that matters; and trust and personal responsibility in all relationships.[41] Through stated company values, IBM'ers—as well as employees at companies such as Tom's of Maine, Avon, and Timberland—know what is expected of them on the job. The shared corporate values not only guide the way they work, but they also serve to unite them in a common quest. (Check out  ◆  Passport Scenario 1 on page 150.)

## The Bottom Line on Shared Corporate Values

An organization's managers are responsible for creating an environment that encourages employees to embrace the desired corporate values as they do their jobs. A survey on corporate values by the American Management Association showed that managers at a number of organizations have committed to a set of core values and are holding their employees accountable to them.[42] Almost 86 percent of the respondents said the corporate values of their organization were specifically written or stated. (A listing of these stated values is provided in Exhibit 5–7.) However, this survey also showed that these organizations didn't just state their values—64 percent said that their corporate values were linked to performance evaluations and compensation.

In another survey of global corporations in 30 countries, the most significant finding was that a large number of companies are making their values explicit.[43] More than 89 percent of those companies surveyed said they had a written corporate values statement. Other findings of interest: Most of the companies believed that their values influenced relationships and reputation; the top-performing companies consciously connected values and the way employees did their work; and the top managers were important to reinforcing the importance of the values throughout the organization. Just how do shared values affect behavior? To see the impact, all you have to do is look at Xerox, where CEO Anne Mulcahy acknowledged that corporate values "helped save Xerox during the worst crisis in our history and that living our values has been one of Xerox's five performance objectives for the past several years." The company's stated

**values-based management**
An approach to managing in which managers are guided by the organization's shared values in their management practices.

Exhibit 5–7

**Survey of Stated Values of Organizations**

| Core Value | Percentage of Respondents That Stated Core Value |
| --- | --- |
| Customer satisfaction | 77% |
| Ethics/integrity | 76% |
| Accountability | 61% |
| Respect for others | 59% |
| Open communication | 51% |
| Profitability | 49% |
| Teamwork | 47% |
| Innovation/change | 47% |
| Continuous learning | 43% |
| Positive work environment | 42% |
| Diversity | 41% |
| Community service | 38% |
| Trust | 37% |
| Social responsibility | 33% |
| Security/safety | 33% |
| Empowerment | 32% |
| Employee job satisfaction | 31% |
| Have fun | 24% |

*Source:* "AMA Corporate Values Survey," www.amanet.org, October 30, 2002.

values—which include customer satisfaction, quality and excellence, premium return on assets, use of technology for market leadership, valuing employees, and corporate citizenship—are ". . . far from words on a piece of paper. They are accompanied by specific objectives and hard measures," said Mulcahy.[44]

As all these examples of values-based management show, an organization's values should be reflected in the decisions and actions of employees. In the next section, we're going to look at managerial ethics and the things that influence whether employees choose to behave ethically or unethically.

## Learning Review

- Discuss what purposes shared values serve.
- Describe the relationship of values-based management to ethics.

## MANAGERIAL ETHICS

Two weeks after firing seven top managers for failing to meet company standards, Wal-Mart, the world's biggest retailer, issued an extensive new ethics policy to employees. Takafumi Horie, founder of the Tokyo-based Internet company Livedoor Inc., was charged in February 2006 with securities violations. Former WorldCom CEO Bernie Ebbers was sentenced in July 2005 to 25 years for fraud, conspiracy, and false filings. In late 2005, the Gemological Institute of America, which grades diamonds for independent dealers and large retailers, fired four employees and made changes to top management after an internal investigation showed that lab workers took bribes to inflate the quality of diamonds in grading reports.[45] When you hear about such unscrupulous behaviors—especially considering the fairly recent, high-profile financial wrongdoings at Enron, WorldCom, Parmalat, Royal Ahold NV, Tyco International, and Imclone, among others—you may conclude that global businesses have no ethics. Although that is by no means true, what *is* true is that managers—at all levels, in all areas, in all sizes, and in all kinds of organizations—will face ethical

*As worries about bird flu mount around the world, the U.S. poultry industry faces a difficult ethical situation. Most of the 10 billion chickens produced each year in the United States are raised in "factory farms," in which the chickens are confined to cages and don't go outside. The poultry industry feels that raising birds in indoor facilities could be their strongest protection against accidental transmission of disease from wild birds. But it has struggled to find a way to get the word out to consumers. The indoor confinement of farm chickens has long been an issue with animal rights groups such as People for the Ethical Treatment of Animals (PETA).*

**Q & A**

Still don't think you'll face ethical dilemmas when you manage? Go to Q & A 5.6 for some advice.

issues and dilemmas. ( ⬗ Go to www.prenhall.com/rolls and check out Q & A 5.6) For instance, is it ethical for a sales representative to offer a bribe to a purchasing agent as an inducement to buy? Would it make any difference if the bribe came out of the sales rep's commission? Is it ethical for someone to use a company car for private use? How about using company e-mail for personal correspondence or using the company phone to make personal phone calls? What if you managed an employee who worked all weekend on an emergency situation and who you let take off 2 days later by telling him to mark it down as "sick days" because your company had a clear policy that overtime would not be compensated for any reason?[46] Would that be okay? How would you handle these situations? As managers plan, organize, lead, and control, they must consider ethical dimensions.

What do we mean by ethics? The term **ethics** refers to principles, values, and beliefs that define what is right and wrong behavior.[47] In this section, we examine the ethical dimensions of managerial decisions. Many decisions that managers make require them to consider who may be affected—in terms of the result as well as the process.[48] To better understand the issues involved in managerial ethics, we'll look at the factors that influence a person's ethics and offer some suggestions for what organizations can do to improve the ethical behavior of employees.

## Factors That Affect Employee Ethics

Whether a person acts ethically or unethically when faced with an ethical dilemma is the result of complex interactions between the stage of moral development and several moderating variables including individual characteristics, the organization's structural design, the organization's culture, and the intensity of the ethical issue (see Exhibit 5–8). People

Exhibit 5–8

**Factors That Affect Ethical and Unethical Behavior**

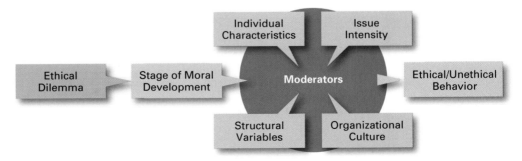

**ethics**
Principles, values, and beliefs that define what is right and wrong behavior.

Exhibit 5–9

**Stages of Moral Development**

*Source:* Based on L. Kohlberg, "Moral Stages and Moralization: The Cognitive-Development Approach," in T. Lickona (ed.), *Moral Development and Behavior: Theory, Research, and Social Issues* (New York: Holt, Rinehart & Winston, 1976), pp. 34–35.

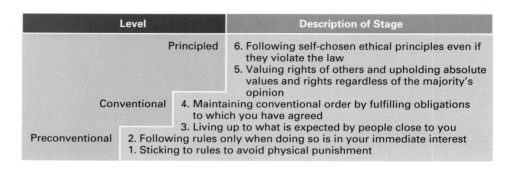

| Level | | Description of Stage |
|---|---|---|
| | Principled | 6. Following self-chosen ethical principles even if they violate the law |
| | | 5. Valuing rights of others and upholding absolute values and rights regardless of the majority's opinion |
| Conventional | | 4. Maintaining conventional order by fulfilling obligations to which you have agreed |
| | | 3. Living up to what is expected by people close to you |
| Preconventional | | 2. Following rules only when doing so is in your immediate interest |
| | | 1. Sticking to rules to avoid physical punishment |

who lack a strong moral sense are much less likely to do the wrong things if they're constrained by rules, policies, job descriptions, or strong cultural norms that disapprove of such behaviors. Conversely, intensely moral individuals can be corrupted by an organizational structure and culture that permits or encourages unethical practices. Let's look more closely at the factors that influence whether individuals will behave ethically or unethically.

**Stage of Moral Development** Research confirms the existence of three levels of moral development, each composed of two stages.[49] At each successive stage, an individual's moral judgment becomes less and less dependent on outside influences. The three levels and six stages are described in Exhibit 5–9.

The first level is labeled *preconventional*. At this level, a person's choice between right or wrong is based on personal consequences involved, such as physical punishment, reward, or exchange of favors. Ethical reasoning at the *conventional* level indicates that moral values reside in maintaining expected standards and living up to the expectations of others. At the *principled* level, individuals make a clear effort to define moral principles apart from the authority of the groups to which they belong or society in general.

We can draw some conclusions from research on the levels and stages of moral development.[50] First, people proceed through the six stages sequentially. They move up the moral ladder, stage by stage. Second, there is no guarantee of continued moral development. An individual's moral development can stop at any stage. Third, the majority of adults are at stage 4. They are limited to obeying the rules and will be inclined to behave ethically, although for different reasons. For instance, a manager at stage 3 is likely to make decisions that will receive peer approval; a manager at stage 4 will try to be a "good corporate citizen" by making decisions that respect the organization's rules and procedures; and a stage 5 manager is likely to challenge organizational practices that he or she believes to be wrong.

**Individual Characteristics** Every person joins an organization with a relatively entrenched set of **values**. Our values—developed at a young age from parents, teachers, friends, and others—represent basic convictions about what is right and wrong. (  Go to www.prenhall.com/rolls) Thus, managers in the same organization often possess very different personal values.[51] Although *values* and *stage of moral development* may seem similar, they're not. Values are broad and cover a wide range of issues; the stage of moral development specifically is a measure of independence from outside influences.

Two personality variables also have been found to influence an individual's actions according to his or her beliefs about what is right or wrong: ego strength and locus of control. **Ego strength** is a personality measure of the strength of a person's convictions. People who score high on ego strength are likely to resist impulses to act unethically and instead follow their convictions. That is, individuals high in ego strength are more likely to do what they think is right. We would expect employees with high ego strength to be more consistent in their moral judgments and actions than those with low ego strength.

**Self-Assessment Library (S.A.L.)**

Do you know what things are important to you? S.A.L #I.B.1 will help you discover what you value.

**Locus of control** is a personality attribute that measures the degree to which people believe they control their own fate. People with an *internal* locus of control believe that they control their own destinies; those with an *external* locus believe that what happens to them is due to luck or chance. How does this influence a person's decision to act ethically or unethically? Externals are less likely to take personal responsibility for the consequences of their behavior and are more likely to rely on external forces. Internals, on the other hand, are more likely to take responsibility for consequences and rely on their own internal standards of right and wrong to guide their behavior.[52] Also, employees with an internal locus of control are likely to be more consistent in their moral judgments and actions than those with an external locus of control.

**Structural Variables**  An organization's structural design influences whether employees behave ethically. Some structures provide strong guidance, whereas others create ambiguity and uncertainty. Structural designs that minimize ambiguity and uncertainty through formal rules and regulations and those that continuously remind employees of what is ethical are more likely to encourage ethical behavior. Other organizational mechanisms that influence ethics include the use of goals, performance appraisal systems, and reward allocation procedures.

Although many organizations use work goals to guide and motivate employees, research has shown that the use of goals can create some unexpected problems, especially as it relates to unethical behavior. People who didn't meet set goals were more likely to engage in unethical behavior, even when they did or did not have economic incentives to do so. The researchers concluded that "goal setting can lead to unethical behavior."[53] Examples of such behaviors abound—from companies shipping unfinished products just to reach sales goals or "managing earnings" to meet financial analysts' expectations, to schools excluding certain groups of students when reporting standardized test scores to make their "pass" rate look better.[54]

The organization's performance appraisal systems also can influence ethical behavior. Some systems focus exclusively on outcomes, whereas others evaluate means as well as ends. When employees are evaluated only on outcomes, they may be pressured to do whatever is necessary to look good on the outcome variables, and not be concerned with how they got those results. Research suggests that success may serve to excuse unethical behaviors.[55] Just think of the impact of this type of thinking. The danger is that if managers take a more lenient view of unethical behaviors for successful employees, other employees will model their behavior on what they see.

Closely associated with the organization's appraisal system is the way rewards are allocated. (  Go to www.prenhall.com/rolls) The more that rewards or punishment depend on specific goal outcomes, the more pressure there is on employees to do whatever they must to reach those goals, perhaps compromising their ethical standards. Although these structural factors are important influences on employees, they're not the most important. What *is* the most important?

Research continues to show that the behavior of managers is the single most important influence on an individual's decision to act ethically or unethically.[56] People look to see what those in authority are doing and use that as a benchmark for acceptable practices and expectations.

**Organization's Culture**  The content and strength of an organization's culture also influence ethical behavior.[57] (  Go to www.prenhall.com/rolls) An organizational

---

**values**
Basic convictions about what is right and wrong.
**ego strength**
A personality measure of the strength of a person's convictions.

**locus of control**
A personality attribute that measures the degree to which people believe they control their own fate.

culture most likely to encourage high ethical standards is one that's high in risk tolerance, control, and conflict tolerance. Employees in such a culture are encouraged to be
aggressive and innovative, are aware that unethical practices will be discovered, and feel
free to openly challenge expectations they consider to be unrealistic or personally
undesirable.

**Q & A**

Does an organization's culture also
affect the way employees view
social responsibility issues?
Q & A 5.7 discusses this.

As we discussed in Chapter 3, a strong culture will exert more influence on
employees than a weak one. If the culture is strong and supports high ethical standards, it has a very powerful and positive influence on their decision to act ethically or
unethically. ( Go to www.prenhall.com/rolls) The Boeing Company, for example,
has a strong culture that has long stressed ethical dealings with customers, employees,
the community, and stockholders. To reinforce the importance of ethical behaviors,
the company developed a series of serious and thought-provoking posters (see some
examples below) designed to get employees to recognize that their individual decisions and actions are important to the way the organization is viewed.

**Issue Intensity** A student who would never consider breaking into an instructor's office to steal an accounting exam doesn't think twice about asking a friend
who took the same course from the same instructor last semester what questions
were on the exam. Similarly, a manager might think nothing about taking home a
few office supplies yet be highly concerned about the possible embezzlement of
company funds.

These examples illustrate the final factor that affects a manager's ethical behavior:
the intensity of the ethical issue itself.[58] As Exhibit 5–10 shows, six characteristics determine issue intensity: greatness of harm, consensus of wrong, probability of harm,
immediacy of consequences, proximity to victim(s), and concentration of effect.[59]
These six factors determine how important an ethical issue is to an individual.
According to these factors, the larger the number of people harmed, the more agreement that the action is wrong, the greater the likelihood that the action will cause
harm, the more immediately that the consequences of the action will be felt, the closer
the person feels to the victim(s), and the more concentrated the effect of the action on
the victim(s), the greater the issue intensity. The more important an ethical issue is—
that is, more intense—the more we should expect employees to behave ethically.

## Ethics in an International Context

Are ethical standards universal? Hardly! Social and cultural differences among
countries are important factors that determine ethical and unethical behavior.

*The Boeing Company's
imaginative poster series
reinforces the core values of
integrity and ethical
behavior for its employees.*

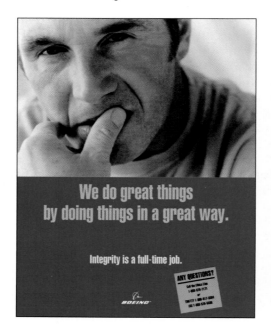

Exhibit 5–10    **Determinants of Issue Intensity**

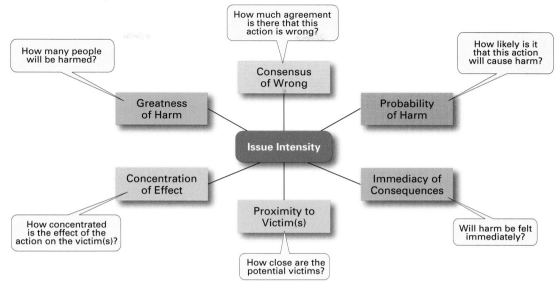

**Q & A**

Suppose that a manager is sent by his company to work in another country. Won't there be ethical issues to deal with there? Check out Q & A 5.8 for more information.

(  Go to www.prenhall.com/rolls) For example, the manager of a Mexican firm bribes several high-ranking government officials in Mexico City to secure a profitable government contract. Such a practice would be seen as unethical, if not illegal, in the United States, but is acceptable business practice in Mexico.

Should Coca-Cola employees in Saudi Arabia adhere to U.S. ethical standards, or should they follow local standards of acceptable behavior? If Airbus (a European company) pays a "broker's fee" to a middleman to get a major contract with a Middle Eastern airline, should the Boeing Company be restricted from doing the same because such practices are considered improper in the United States?

In the case of payments to influence foreign officials or politicians, there is a law to guide U.S. managers. The Foreign Corrupt Practices Act makes it illegal for U.S. firms to knowingly corrupt a foreign official. However, even this law doesn't always reduce ethical dilemmas to black and white. In some countries, government bureaucrats are paid ridiculously low salaries because custom dictates that they receive small payments from those they serve. Payoffs to these bureaucrats "grease the machinery" of government and ensure that things get done. The Foreign Corrupt Practices Act does not expressly prohibit small payoffs to foreign government employees whose duties are primarily administrative or clerical *when* such payoffs are an accepted part of doing business in that country. In 2004, 18 violations of this law were investigated, more than double the 7 violations reported just 2 years earlier. The fines for breaking the law have also increased. For example, San Diego–based Titan Corporation paid a penalty of $28.5 million, more than 8 times the bribe they were accused of paying to an agent in Benin, a country in western Africa.[60]

It's important for individual managers working in foreign cultures to recognize the various social, cultural, and political-legal influences on what is appropriate and acceptable behavior.[61] And global organizations must clarify their ethical guidelines so that employees know what is expected of them while working in a foreign location, which adds another dimension to making ethical judgments.

At the 1999 World Economic Forum in Davos, Switzerland, the United Nations Secretary-General challenged world business leaders to "embrace and enact" The Global Compact, a document outlining principles for doing business globally in the areas of human rights, labor, the environment, and anticorruption.[62] (See Exhibit 5–11.) Today, hundreds of global businesses and international labor organizations have incorporated these guidelines into their business activities. The goal: a more sustainable and inclusive global economy. Organizations making this commitment are doing so because they believe that the world business community can play a significant role in improving economic and social conditions. In addition, the Organization for Economic

Exhibit 5–11

**The Global Compact**

**Human Rights**

Principle 1:    Support and respect the protection of international human rights within their sphere of influence.

Principle 2:    Make sure business corporations are not complicit in human rights abuses.

**Labor Standards**

Principle 3:    Freedom of association and the effective recognition of the right to collective bargaining.

Principle 4:    The elimination of all forms of forced and compulsory labor.

Principle 5:    The effective abolition of child labor.

Principle 6:    The elimination of discrimination in respect of employment and occupation.

**Environment**

Principle 7:    Support a precautionary approach to environmental challenges.

Principle 8:    Undertake initiatives to promote greater environmental responsibility.

Principle 9:    Encourage the development and diffusion of environmentally friendly technologies.

Principle 10:   Businesses should work against corruption in all its forms, including extortion and bribery.

*Source:* Courtesy of Global Compact.

Co-Operation and Development (OECD) also provides guidance and assistance to global managers (www.oecd.org). The OECD, a group of 30 member countries that share a commitment to democratic government and the market economy, developed an Anti-Bribery Convention (or set of rules and guidelines) in 1997 to combat corruption in cross-border business deals. In the 36 countries that have ratified it (the 30 OECD members and 6 nonmembers), significant gains have been made in fighting corruption because bribing a foreign public official is outlawed and a crime.[63]

## Improving Ethical Behavior

Managers can do a number of things if they're serious about reducing unethical behaviors in their organization. They can hire individuals with high ethical standards, establish codes of ethics and decision rules, lead by example, delineate job goals and performance appraisal mechanisms, provide ethics training, conduct social audits, and provide support to individuals facing ethical dilemmas. (  Go to www.prenhall.com/rolls) Taken individually, these actions will probably not have much impact. But when all or most of them are implemented as part of a comprehensive ethics program, they have the potential to significantly improve an organization's ethical climate. The key term here, however, is *potential*. There are no guarantees that a well-designed ethics program will lead to the desired outcome. Sometimes corporate ethics programs can be little more than public relations gestures, having minimal influence on managers and employees. For instance, retailer Sears had a long history of encouraging ethical business practices through its corporate Office of Ethics and Business Practices. However, the company's ethics programs didn't stop managers from illegally trying to collect payments from bankrupt charge account holders or from routinely deceiving automotive service center customers into thinking they needed unnecessary repairs. Even Enron's 2000 annual report outlined values that most would consider ethical—communication, respect, integrity, and excellence—yet the way top managers behaved didn't reflect those values at all.[64]

**Employee Selection**    Given that individuals are at different stages of moral development and possess different personal value systems and personalities, the selection process—interviews, tests, background checks, and so forth—could be used to eliminate

Self-Assessment Library (S.A.L.)

How ethical do you think you are? Complete S.A.L. #I.D.3 and find out.

ethically questionable applicants. The selection process should be viewed as an opportunity to learn about an individual's level of moral development, personal values, ego strength, and locus of control.[65] But it isn't easy! Even under the best circumstances, individuals with questionable standards of right and wrong will be hired. However, this shouldn't be a problem if other ethics controls are in place.

**Codes of Ethics and Decision Rules** George David, CEO and chairman of Hartford, Connecticut-based United Technologies Corporation, believes in the power of a code of ethics. The company has a detailed 16-page code of ethics, including 35 standards of conduct. Employees know the behavioral expectations, especially when it comes to ethics.[66] However, that's not the way it is in all organizations.

Ambiguity about what is and is not ethical can be a problem for employees. A **code of ethics**, a formal statement of an organization's primary values and the ethical rules it expects employees to follow, is a popular choice for reducing that ambiguity. Research shows that 97 percent of organizations with more than 10,000 employees have a written code of ethics. Even in smaller organizations, nearly 93 percent have one.[67] And, codes of ethics are becoming more popular globally. Research by the Institute for Global Ethics says that shared values such as honesty, fairness, respect, responsibility, and caring are pretty much universally embraced worldwide.[68] In addition, a survey of business organizations in 22 countries found that 78 percent have formally stated ethics standards and codes of ethics.[69]

What should a code of ethics look like? It's been suggested that codes should be specific enough to show employees the spirit in which they're supposed to do things yet loose enough to allow for freedom of judgment.[70] A survey of companies' codes of ethics found their content tended to fall into three categories: (1) Be a dependable organizational citizen; (2) don't do anything unlawful or improper that will harm the organization; and (3) be good to customers.[71] Exhibit 5–12 lists the variables included in each of these clusters.

How well do codes of ethics work? In reality, they're not always effective in encouraging ethical behavior in organizations. A survey of employees in U.S. businesses with ethics codes found that 75 percent of those surveyed had observed ethical or legal violations in the previous 12 months including such things as deceptive sales practices, unsafe working conditions, sexual harassment, conflicts of interest, and environmental violations.[72] And even Enron had an extremely detailed, 60-page ethics code![73] Does this mean that codes of ethics shouldn't be developed? No. However, in doing so, managers could use these suggestions. First, the organization's leaders play an absolutely essential role as they set the tone for being ethical both by modeling appropriate behavior and by rewarding those who act ethically on the job. Next, all levels of management should continually reaffirm the importance of the ethics code and the organization's commitment to it and consistently discipline those who break it. When managers consider the code of ethics to be important, regularly affirm its content, and publicly reprimand rule breakers, ethics codes can supply a strong foundation for an effective corporate ethics program. Also, as ethics codes are developed or improved, managers should consider the organization's stakeholders—customers, employees, investors, suppliers, communities—but especially, the employees. An ethics code should not be created solely by senior managers. Then, the ethics code should be communicated and regularly reinforced to employees.[74] Finally, an organization's code of ethics might be designed around the 12 questions listed in Exhibit 5–13 (on page 137) that can be used as decision rules in guiding managers as they handle ethical dilemmas in decision making.[75]

PRISM

Being trustworthy seems to be important for leaders. You can practice your skills at developing trust by completing PRISM #4.

**Top Management's Leadership** As we've seen throughout this section, doing business ethically requires a commitment from top managers. Why? Because it's the top managers who uphold the shared values and set the cultural tone. ( Go to

**code of ethics**
A formal statement of an organization's primary values and the ethical rules it expects its employees to follow.

Exhibit 5–12

**Clusters of Variables
Found in 83 Corporate
Codes of Business Ethics**

### Cluster 1. Be a Dependable Organizational Citizen

1. Comply with safety, health, and security regulations.
2. Demonstrate courtesy, respect, honesty, and fairness.
3. Illegal drugs and alcohol at work are prohibited.
4. Manage personal finances well.
5. Exhibit good attendance and punctuality.
6. Follow directives of supervisors.
7. Do not use abusive language.
8. Dress in business attire.
9. Firearms at work are prohibited.

### Cluster 2. Do Not Do Anything Unlawful or Improper That Will Harm the Organization

1. Conduct business in compliance with all laws.
2. Payments for unlawful purposes are prohibited.
3. Bribes are prohibited.
4. Avoid outside activities that impair duties.
5. Maintain confidentiality of records.
6. Comply with all antitrust and trade regulations.
7. Comply with all accounting rules and controls.
8. Do not use company property for personal benefit.
9. Employees are personally accountable for company funds.
10. Do not propagate false or misleading information.
11. Make decisions without regard for personal gain.

### Cluster 3. Be Good to Customers

1. Convey true claims in product advertisements.
2. Perform assigned duties to the best of your ability.
3. Provide products and services of the highest quality.

*Source:* F. R. David, "An Empirical Study of Codes of Business Ethics: A Strategic Perspective," paper presented at the 48th Annual Academy of Management Conference, Anaheim, California, August 1988.

www.prenhall.com/rolls) They're role models in terms of both words and actions, though what they *do* is far more important than what they *say*. If top managers, for example, take company resources for their personal use, inflate their expense accounts, or give favored treatment to friends, they imply that such behavior is acceptable for all employees.

Top managers also set the cultural tone by their reward and punishment practices. The choices of who and what are rewarded with pay increases and promotions send a strong signal to employees. As we said earlier, when an employee is rewarded for achieving impressive results in an ethically questionable manner, it indicates to others that those ways are acceptable. When wrongdoing is uncovered, managers who want to emphasize their commitment to doing business ethically must punish the offender and publicize the fact by making the outcome visible to everyone in the organization. This practice sends a message that doing wrong has a price and it's not in employees' best interests to act unethically!

**Job Goals and Performance Appraisal** Employees in three Internal Revenue Service offices were found in the bathrooms flushing tax returns and other related documents down the toilets. When questioned, they openly admitted doing it, but

**Exhibit 5–13**

**Twelve Questions for Examining the Ethics of a Business Decision**

1. Have you defined the problem accurately?
2. How would you define the problem if you stood on the other side of the fence?
3. How did this situation occur in the first place?
4. To whom and to what do you give your loyalty as a person and as a member of the corporation?
5. What is your intention in making this decision?
6. How does this intention compare with the probable results?
7. Whom could your decision or action injure?
8. Can you discuss the problem with the affected parties before you make the decision?
9. Are you confident that your position will be as valid over a long period of time as it seems now?
10. Could you disclose without qualm your decision or action to your boss, your chief executive officer, the board of directors, your family, society as a whole?
11. What is the symbolic potential of your action if understood? If misunderstood?
12. Under what conditions would you allow exceptions to your stand?

*Source:* Reprinted by permission of *Harvard Business Review.* An exhibit from "Ethics Without the Sermon," by L. L. Nash. November–December 1981, p. 81. Copyright © 1981 by the President and Fellows of Harvard College. All rights reserved.

offered an interesting explanation for their behavior. The employees' supervisors had been putting increasing pressure on them to complete more work in less time. If the piles of tax returns weren't processed and moved off their desks more quickly, they were told that their performance reviews and salary raises would be adversely affected. Frustrated by few resources and an overworked computer system, the employees decided to "flush away" the paperwork on their desks. Although these employees knew what they did was wrong, it illustrates the power of unrealistic goals and performance appraisals on behavior.[76] Under the stress of unrealistic goals, otherwise ethical employees may feel they have no choice but do whatever is necessary to meet those goals.

Whether an individual achieves his or her goals is usually a key issue in performance appraisal. Keep in mind, though, that if performance appraisals focus only on economic goals, ends will begin to justify means. If an organization wants its employees to uphold high ethical standards, the performance appraisal process should include this dimension. For example, a manager's annual review of employees might include a point-by-point evaluation of how their decisions measured up against the company's code of ethics as well as how well goals were met.

Q & A

Can people really be taught to be ethical? Q & A 5.9 discusses this important issue.

**Ethics Training** More and more organizations are setting up seminars, workshops, and similar ethics training programs to encourage ethical behavior. (  Go to www.prenhall.com/rolls) The National Business Ethics Survey conducted by the Ethics Resource Center found that some 69 percent of U.S. companies provide some form of ethics training.[77] But these training programs aren't without controversy. The primary debate is whether you can actually teach ethics. Critics stress that the effort is pointless because people establish their individual value systems when they're young. Others might question the value of such programs especially when considering that the survey of business ethics described previously reported that even in the 69 percent of companies with ethics training, more than half of the employees (52 percent) said that they had observed misconduct in their workplace that year. And of those individuals who observed unethical behavior, only 55 percent reported it to management.[78] Proponents note, however, that several studies have found that values can be learned after early childhood. In addition, they cite evidence that shows that teaching ethical problem solving can make an actual difference in ethical behaviors[79]; that training has increased individuals' level of moral development[80]; and that, if it does nothing else, ethics training increases awareness of ethical issues in business.[81]

How do you teach ethics? Let's look at how it's done at global defense contractor Lockheed Martin Corporation.[82] As one of the pioneers in the case-based approach to ethics training, Lockheed's employees take annual ethics training courses delivered by their managers. The main focus of these short courses is Lockheed-specific case situations "chosen for their relevance to department or job-specific issues." In each organizational department, employee teams review and discuss the cases and then apply an "Ethics Meter" to "rate whether the real-life decisions were ethical, unethical, or somewhere in between." For example, one of the possible ratings on the Ethics Meter, "On Thin Ice," is explained as "bordering on unethical and should raise a red flag." After the teams have applied their ratings, managers lead discussions about the ratings and examine "which of Lockheed's core ethics principles were applied or ignored in the cases." In addition to its ethics training, Lockheed has a widely used written code of ethics, an ethics helpline that employees can call for guidance on ethical issues, and ethics officers based in the company's various business units.

Ethics training sessions can provide a number of benefits.[83] They reinforce the organization's standards of conduct. They're a reminder that top managers want employees to consider ethical issues in making decisions. They clarify what practices are and are not acceptable. Finally, when employees discuss common concerns among themselves, they get reassurance they're not alone in facing ethical dilemmas, which can strengthen their confidence when they have to take unpopular but ethically correct stances.

**Independent Social Audits** An important element of deterring unethical behavior is the fear of being caught. Independent social audits, which evaluate decisions and management practices in terms of the organization's code of ethics, increase the likelihood of detection. These social audits can be routine evaluations, performed on a regular basis just as financial audits are, or they can occur randomly with no prior announcement. An effective ethical program should probably have both. To maintain integrity, auditors should be responsible to the company's board of directors and present their findings directly to the board. This arrangement gives the auditors clout and lessens the opportunity for retaliation from those being audited. With the passage of the Sarbanes–Oxley Act, which holds businesses to more rigorous standards of financial disclosure and corporate governance, many organizations find the idea of independent social audits appealing. As the publisher of *Business Ethics* magazine stated, "The debate has shifted from *whether* to be ethical to *how* to be ethical."[84]

**Formal Protective Mechanisms** Our last recommendation is for organizations to provide formal mechanisms to protect employees who face ethical dilemmas so they can do what's right without fear of reprimand. (  Go to www.prenhall.com/rolls) An organization might designate ethical counselors. When employees face an ethics dilemma, they could go to these advisers for guidance. As a sounding board, the ethical counselor would let employees openly verbalize their ethical problem, the problem's cause, and their own options. After the options are clear, the adviser might take on the role of advocate who champions the ethically "right" alternatives. Other organizations have appointed ethics officers who design, direct, and modify the organization's ethics programs as needed.[85] The Ethics and Compliance Officer Association reports its total membership at over 1,200 (including more than half of the *Fortune* 100 companies) and covering several countries including among others, the United States, Germany, India, Japan, and Canada.[86] Another protective mechanism an organization might create is a special appeals process that employees could use to raise ethical issues. We'll discuss these protective mechanisms more thoroughly in the next section.[87]

Q & A
How can employees be loyal and committed to the organization if we're encouraging them to point out ethical wrongdoing? Go to Q & A 5.10 for some insights.

# Learning Review

- Discuss the factors that affect ethical and unethical behavior.
- Discuss the six determinants of issue intensity.

- Tell what codes of ethics are and how their effectiveness can be improved.
- Describe the important roles managers play in encouraging ethical behavior.

# SOCIAL RESPONSIBILITY AND ETHICS ISSUES IN TODAY'S WORLD

Today's managers face serious challenges in being socially responsible and ethical. There are three current issues we're going to examine: how to manage ethical lapses and social irresponsibility, social entrepreneurship, and social impact management.

## Managing Ethical Lapses and Social Irresponsibility

News headlines continue to report stories of irresponsible and ethically questionable practices at large public companies: the CEO of RadioShack—who admitted that he "clearly misstated my academic record" after claiming that he had two bachelor's degrees from a small college when the college said he had not graduated at all—resigned a short while after his lie was discovered (see the Case Application on page 148); at Red Robin Gourmet Burgers, which prided itself on a culture of "unbridled acts," the CEO "retired" after an audit turned up over $1 million of expenses that were "inconsistent with Company policies or that lacked sufficient documentation"; Marsh & McLennan, the insurance brokerage company, agreed to pay $850 million to the government to settle allegations of price-fixing and collusion; and at Toronto-based Hollinger, the ex-CEO was caught on a security camera toting off several cartons of files from his former office after facing charges that he looted the company of tens of millions of dollars.[88] Then, of course, we can't forget the past list of U.S. companies plagued by financial scandals including, among others, Adelphia Communications, Arthur Andersen, Dynegy, Enron, ImClone, Qwest, and WorldCom. What's going on? Have ethics and social responsibility been ignored by businesses?

Recent surveys found that between 31 percent and 52 percent of U.S. workers have witnessed co-workers acting unethically.[89] Another survey of employees showed that workplace pressures were leading more of them to consider acting unethically or illegally on the job—56 percent of those surveyed felt pressured to act unethically or illegally on the job, with 48 percent saying they had actually committed such activities.[90] Here's a sampling of these types of unethical business activities reported:

- Cut corners on quality control (16 percent)
- Covered up incidents (14 percent)
- Abused or lied about sick days (11 percent)
- Lied to or deceived customers (9 percent)
- Put inappropriate pressure on others (7 percent)
- Falsified numbers or reports (6 percent)
- Lied to or deceived superiors on serious matters (5 percent)
- Withheld important information (5 percent)
- Misused or stole company property (4 percent)
- Took credit for someone's work or idea (4 percent)
- Engaged in copyright or software infringement (3 percent)

Unfortunately, it's not just at work that we see these behaviors. Irresponsible and unethical behaviors are prevalent across our society. Studies conducted by the Center for Academic Integrity showed that 26 percent of college and university business majors admitted to "serious cheating" on exams and 54 percent admitted to cheating on written assignments. But business students weren't the worst cheaters—that distinction belonged to journalism majors, of whom 27 percent said they had cheated.[91] And a survey by Students in Free Enterprise (SIFE) found that only 19 percent of students would report a classmate who cheated.[92] What does this say about what managers and organizations may have to deal with in the future? It's not too far-fetched to say that organizations may have difficulty upholding high ethical standards when their future employees—these students—so readily accept unethical behavior.

Given these realities, what can managers do? Two actions seem to be particularly important: ethical leadership and protection for those who report wrongdoing.

**Ethical Leadership**    Not long after Herb Baum took over as CEO of Dial Corporation, he got a call from Reuben Mark, the CEO of competitor Colgate-Palmolive, who told him he had a copy of Dial's strategic marketing plan that had come from a former Dial salesperson who recently had joined Colgate-Palmolive. Mark told Baum that he had not looked at it, didn't intend to look at it, and was returning it. In addition, he himself was going to deal appropriately with the new salesperson.[94] As this example illustrates, managers must provide ethical leadership. As we said earlier, what managers do has a strong influence on employees' decisions to behave ethically or not. When managers cheat, lie, steal, manipulate, take advantage of situations or people, or treat others unfairly, what kinds of signals are they sending to employees (or other stakeholders)? Probably not the ones they want to send. What can managers do to provide ethical leadership?

The best thing managers can do is be a *good role model*. Be ethical and honest. Unfortunately, in a national poll, only 31 percent of the public believes that U.S. firms operate honestly.[95] And in another survey, only 54 percent of employees said they believe most corporate executives are honest and ethical.[96] Yet, employees crave honesty more than any other quality of leadership. In a survey of employees who were given a list of 28 attributes, respondents said honesty was, by far, the most important, followed by integrity/morals/ethics.[97] What does it mean to be honest? It means telling the truth—not hiding or manipulating information. Even bad news is more tolerable when people know they're being told the truth. Because workplace honesty can't be regulated or legislated, it has to be encouraged by leaders who themselves are honest and willing to admit their failures.[98]

**Passport**

Being an ethical leader is difficult enough, but add in trying to be one when faced with different global cultures and it becomes even more challenging! How would you handle the situation in this Passport scenario?

Other things ethical leaders should do include *sharing their values*—that is, regularly communicating to employees what they believe about ethics and values; *stressing important shared values* through visible organizational culture manifestations such as symbols, stories, ceremonies, and slogans; and *using the reward system* to hold everyone accountable to the values, which means paying attention to what employee behaviors are rewarded and which are punished. (Check out  Passport Scenario 2 on page 150.)

**Protecting Employees Who Raise Ethical Issues**    What would you do if you saw other employees doing something illegal, immoral, or unethical? Although the highly publicized corporate financial scandals have made all of us more aware of the devastation that corporate wrongdoing can cause, would you have stepped forward? Many of us may be reluctant because of the perceived risks. However, it's important that managers assure employees who raise ethical concerns or issues to others inside or outside the organization that they will not face personal or career risks. These individuals,

*Ethical leadership starts with being a good role model. When Reuben Mark, CEO of Colgate-Palmolive, found himself unexpectedly in possession of proprietary information about competitor Dial Corporation, he returned it, unread and unopened, to Dial's CEO.*

## focus on **Leadership**

### Providing Moral Leadership

How important are ethics to leadership? Vitally important! Yet despite its importance, the topic of leadership and ethics has received surprisingly little attention.[93] Only recently have ethics and leadership researchers begun to consider the ethical implications in leadership. Why now? One reason may be the growing interest in ethics through the field of management. For instance, former Cendant Corporation chairman Walter Forbes is being tried a third time on charges he participated in a massive fraud that cost the company and investors more than $3 billion. In Japan, the company behind a well-known food brand falsified information on its labels. Even nonprofit organizations aren't immune from unethical decisions. In early 2006, the former board president of Memphis' Influence 1 Foundation pled guilty to bilking the group for more than $100,000 to prop up his failing private business. Undoubtedly, the unethical

practices by some executives have increased the public's concerns about ethical standards in business.

Leadership is not value free. Providing moral leadership involves addressing the *means* that a leader uses in trying to achieve goals as well as the content of those goals. For instance, George David, chairman and CEO of United Technologies Corporation, is very clear about his role in providing moral leadership. In a meeting of his company's board of directors at the New York Public Library, he said, "What you see is what you get. The library is among the most truly open institutions in the world and UTC aspires to be held to the same kind of standards and expectations. We must have a spotless, perfect record. Period." The company's 16-page code of ethics provides guidance—that is, the *means*—for employees. As a recent study concluded, ethical leadership is more than being ethical; it's reinforcing ethics through organizational mechanisms such as communication and the reward system.

often called **whistle-blowers**, can be a key part of any company's ethics program because they're willing to step forward and expose unethical behavior, no matter the cost professionally or personally. For example, Bunnatine (Bunny) Greenhouse came forward before members of Congress to testify about billions in federal contracts awarded to a Halliburton subsidiary.[99] David Windhauser, the former controller for Trane, complained to his supervisor that managers were fraudulently recording expenses on financial statements. Theresa Hagman, a former Washington Mutual vice president, reported that construction loans were being improperly funded and underwritten.[100] However, the most recognized whistle-blower in recent memory is probably Sherron Watkins, a vice president at Enron, who wrote a letter to then chairman Ken Lay where she clearly outlined her concerns about the company's accounting practices. Her statement, "I am incredibly nervous that we will implode in a wave of accounting scandals," couldn't have been more prophetic.[101] She and two other whistle-blowers (Coleen Rowley, who blew the whistle on her employer, the FBI, and Cynthia Cooper, who blew the whistle on WorldCom) were named *Time* magazine's persons of the year in 2002.[102] Despite the accolades given to these women, research has shown that most observers of wrongdoing don't report it.[103] That's the attitude managers have to address. What can they do to protect employees so they're willing to step up if they see bad things occurring?

Many companies have set up toll-free ethics hotlines and are encouraging whistle-blowers to come forward. For instance, Dell Computer has an ethics hotline that employees can call anonymously to report infractions that the company will then investigate. At Charlotte-based Duke Energy, employees can call a toll-free ethics hotline run by an outside organization and leave their name or remain anonymous. Wal-Mart encourages employees to report unethical behaviors to superiors or to use the company's ethics hotline.[104] In addition, managers need to encourage a culture where bad news can be heard and acted on before it's too late. Michael Josephson, founder of the Josephson Institute of Ethics (www.josephsoninstitute.org) says, "It is absolutely and unequivocally important to establish a culture where it is possible for employees to complain and protest and to get heard."[105] Even if some whistle-blowers do have a personal agenda they're pursuing, it's imperative that a whistle-blower's information be

**whistle-blower**
Individual who raises ethical concerns or issues to others
inside or outside the organization.

taken seriously. Finally, there is some legal protection. Under the Sarbanes–Oxley Act, whistle-blowers in the United States who report suspected corporate violations of laws now have broad protection from reprisals and retaliation. And there's a stiff penalty for a manager who retaliates—a 10-year jail sentence.[106] Unfortunately, despite this protection, hundreds of employees who have stepped forward and revealed wrongdoings at their companies have been fired or let go from their jobs.[107] At the present time, it's not a perfect solution. There are still risks to whistle-blowers, but it is a step in the right direction to protect employees who raise ethical issues.

## Social Entrepreneurship

The social problems are many and viable solutions are few. But there are numerous people and organizations working to solve these problems. For instance, Teresa Fritschi, James Potemkin, and Raquel Marchenese share a common bond even though they don't know each other. Each sells unique handmade items made by artisans from different parts of the globe—Scotland, Mexico, Guatemala, Pakistan, Peru. But each also shares a passionate belief in fair trade and acts on this belief by paying their supplier artisans more for their works. Fair trade proponents seek to "give businesses or solo artists in poor or marginalized parts of the world a higher price for what they create and a more direct route into lucrative markets in America, Europe, and Asia."[108] Each is also an example of a **social entrepreneur**, an individual or organization who seeks out opportunities to improve society by using practical, innovative, and sustainable approaches.[109] "What business entrepreneurs are to the economy, social entrepreneurs are to social change."[110] Social entrepreneurs want to make the world a better place and have a driving passion to make that happen. For example, the International Senior Lawyers Project is a nonprofit group that matches experienced U.S. attorneys with needs in developing countries. They have taught black attorneys in South Africa how to practice business law and have provided assistance to public defenders in Bulgaria.[111] Also, social entrepreneurs use creativity and ingenuity to solve problems. For instance, Seattle-based PATH (which stands for Program for Appropriate Technology in Health) is an international nonprofit organization that uses low-cost technology to provide needed health care solutions for poor, developing countries. By collaborating with public groups and for-profit businesses, PATH has developed simple life-saving solutions, such as clean birthing kits and disposable vaccination syringes that can't be reused. One of their most promising projects is the medical "lab on a card." Because many poor countries in the developing world lack medical labs with expensive equipment, this inexpensive credit-card-sized test kit will let health workers in poor countries diagnose diseases and illnesses within minutes.[112] PATH's innovative approaches to solving global medical problems led them to be named by the Schwab Foundation for Social Entrepreneurship as an

## *becoming* a Manager

√ Try to clarify your own personal views on how much social responsibility you think an organization should have.

√ Research different companies' codes of ethics.

√ Think about the organizational values that will be important to you.

√ When faced with an ethical dilemma, use the 12 questions in Exhibit 5–13 to help you make a decision.

√ Work through the Thinking Critically About Ethics dilemmas found in each chapter.

√ 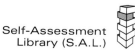 Go to www.prenhall.com/rolls and complete S.A.L. #I.D.3—How Do My Ethics Rate?

Self-Assessment
Library (S.A.L.)

Outstanding Social Entrepreneur and to be selected as one of the winners in the 2006 *Fast Company* Social Capitalist Awards.

What can managers and organizations learn from these social entrepreneurs? Although many organizations have committed to doing business ethically and responsibly, perhaps there is more they can do, as these social entrepreneurs show. Maybe, as in the case of PATH, it's simply a matter of business organizations collaborating with public groups or nonprofit organizations to address a social issue. Or maybe, as in the case of the Senior Lawyers Project, it's providing expertise where needed. Or, it may involve endorsing and nurturing individuals who passionately and unwaveringly believe they have an idea that could make the world a better place and simply need the organizational support to pursue it.

## Social Impact Management

As stakeholders continue to pressure organizations to respond to societal issues, managers are expected to be responsible in the way they do business. Some experts have suggested that managers address their social responsibilities from the perspective of the impacts they have on society. This has been called **social impact management**, which can be defined as an approach to managing in which managers examine the social impacts of their decisions and actions. This concept developed by associates at the Aspen Institute, an international not-for-profit organization dedicated to informed dialogue and inquiry on issues of global concern, attempts to get businesspeople to understand the interdependency between business needs and wider societal concerns. For instance, in the marketing area, social impact management would address the cultural impacts of advertising messages or the impacts of product development, design, and pricing on customers; in the human resource management area, it would address issues such as employee rights and participation, work/life balance, and workplace equity and diversity; in the finance area, it would involve issues such as differential access to capital, the changing nature and role of shareholders, or the impacts of money flows across international borders. Thus, as managers plan, organize, lead, and control, they would ask, "How does this work when we think about the social context within which business operates?"[113] At the least, if managers think about managing social impacts, just as they manage risk or strategy, they will be more aware of whether they're being responsible in their decisions and actions.

Doing the right thing—that is, managing responsibly and ethically—isn't always easy. However, because society's expectations of its institutions are regularly changing, managers must continually monitor those expectations. What is acceptable today may be a poor guide for the future.

## Learning Review

- Explain why ethical leadership is important.
- Discuss how managers and organizations can protect employees who raise ethical issues or concerns.

- Explain what role social entrepreneurs play.
- Describe social impact management.

**social entrepreneur**
An individual or organization who seeks out opportunities to improve society by using practical, innovative, and sustainable approaches.

**social impact management**
An approach to managing in which managers examine the social impacts of their decisions and actions.

- Establish codes of ethics
- Set job goals and use for appraisal
- Independent social audits

### How Should Managers Manage Social Responsibility and Ethics in Today's World?

- Provide ethical leadership
- Protect employees who raise ethical issues
- Encourage and support social entrepreneurs
- Examine social impacts of decisions and actions (social impact management)

## Management: By the Numbers

As you can tell from reading this chapter, business ethics and social responsibility are favorite polling topics. Here are some additional survey results to consider:

- Sixty-four percent of respondents to a survey of a cross-section of industries by the U.S. Chamber of Commerce and Boston College's Center for Corporate Citizenship believed that integrating community, social, and ethical concerns into the management of their business benefits their bottom lines. A majority (81 percent) of these respondents also believed that corporate citizenship should be a priority.
- Eighty-six percent of the respondents to a survey by Deloitte & Touche said that volunteering can have a positive impact on their careers and 78 percent saw volunteering as an opportunity to develop business skills.
- Eighty-one percent of the global companies surveyed by Booz Allen Hamilton and the Aspen Institute believed that their management practices encouraged ethical behavior among staff. Another finding from this same survey: Seventy-seven percent said that CEO support in reinforcing values is one of the most effective practices for reinforcing the company's ability to act on its values.
- A survey of over 1,300 companies found that only 9 percent said that employee compensation was tied to corporate responsibility performance.
- The National Business Ethics Survey conducted by the Ethics Resource Center found that 65 percent of senior managers said that ethics training was "very useful" to them. However, only 48 percent of nonmanagers agreed.

- In a poll of teens ages 13 to 18 conducted by JA Worldwide and Deloitte & Touche, 69 percent believe that people who practice good business ethics are more successful than those who don't. However, only 12 percent of teens believe that business leaders of today are ethical.
- In a recent poll of 2,000 adults by Opinion Research for LRN, 72 percent said they would prefer to buy products and services from a company with ethical business practices and higher prices rather than from a company with questionable business practices and lower prices.
- A recent survey of 2,450 workers by Careerbuilder.com found that at least once in the past year, 43 percent said they called in sick when they felt well.
- Twenty-nine percent of teens polled by Junior Achievement and Deloitte& Touche USA said that one has to bend the rules to succeed in business.

*Sources:* H. B. Herring, "A Company's Ethics Do Concern Shoppers (or So They Say)," *New York Times Online,* www.nytimes.com, January 29, 2006; "Next Cheat Sheet: Survey Finding," *Fast Company,* December 2005, p. 45; J. Yang and A. Lewis, "Teens Respect Good Business Ethics," *USA Today Snapshots,* December 12, 2005, p. 1B; J. Yang and F. Pompa, "Teens' Opinions of Business Leaders Drop," *USA Today Snapshots,* December 7, 2005, p. 1B; "A Kinder, Gentler Corporation," *Industry Week,* November 2005, p. 14; M. Weinstein, "Survey Says Ethics Training Works," *Training,* November 2005, p. 15; "Readers Report," *Business Week,* September 12, 2005, pp. 18–20; R. Van Lee, L. Fabish, and N. McGaw, "The Value of Corporate Values," *Strategy & Business,* Summer 2005, pp. 52–65; "The Stat," *Business Week,* September 20, 2004, p. 16; and S. Caminiti, "Social Stewardship," *Fortune,* May 17, 2004, pp. 163–168.

## Thinking About Management Issues

1. What does social responsibility mean to you personally? Do *you* think business organizations should be socially responsible? Explain.

2. Do you think values-based management is just a "do-gooder" ploy? Explain your answer.

3. Internet file sharing programs are popular among college students. These programs work by allowing nonorganizational users to access any local network where desired files are located. Because these types of file sharing programs tend to clog bandwidth, local users' ability to access and use a local network is

reduced. What ethical and social responsibilities does a university have in this situation? To whom do they have a responsibility? What guidelines might you suggest for university decision makers?

4. What are some problems that could be associated with employee whistle-blowing for (a) the whistle-blower and (b) the organization?

5. Describe the characteristics and behaviors of someone you consider to be an ethical person. How could the types of decisions and actions this person engages in be encouraged in a workplace?

# Working Together: Team-Based Exercise

You have obviously faced many ethical dilemmas already in your life—at school, in social settings, and even at work. Form groups of three to five individuals. Appoint a spokesperson to present your group's findings to the class. Each member of the group is to think of some unethical behaviors he or she has observed in organizations. The incidents could be something experienced as an employee, customer, client, or an action observed informally.

Once everyone has identified some examples of ethically questionable behaviors, the group should identify three important criteria that could be used to determine whether a particular action is ethical. Think carefully about these criteria. They should differentiate between ethical and unethical behavior. Write your choices down. Use these criteria to assess the examples of unethical behavior described by group members.

When asked by your instructor, the spokesperson should be ready to describe several of the incidents of unethical behavior witnessed by group members, your criteria for differentiating between ethical and unethical behavior, and how you used these criteria for assessing these incidents.

# Ethical Dilemma Exercise

Is ecotourism compatible with profitability? According to the Worldwatch Institute, ecotourism is "responsible travel to sites where the environment is conserved and where the welfare of local peoples is promoted." Today ecotourism is booming as more tourists flock to environmentally fragile destinations for glimpses of rare wildlife and unspoiled vistas. This presents managers at companies like Lindblad Expeditions, a cruise line that brings tourists to the Galapagos Islands and other areas of natural beauty, with a dilemma: How can the firm increase ecotourism without upsetting the delicate ecological balance that attracts visitors to places like the Galapagos?

To minimize the environmental impact of its cruises, Lindblad takes steps such as serving meals on reusable rather than disposable plates; providing biodegradable shampoo for use on board; and recycling trash from kitchens and guest cabins. "Dark green" doesn't mean "spartan," however: After travelers to the Galapagos return from activities such as day hikes to beaches or mountains, they are pampered with spa services and gourmet food. Sven Lindblad, the company's president, stresses that environmental sensitivity is "not philanthropy" because "you're not going to have a good business in a degraded place. Guests aren't going to want to go to a degraded place." In fact, after each Galapagos cruise, Lindblad's crews describe the conservation measures underway and invite travelers to contribute. And they do: Lindblad raises more than $500,000 annually for environmental initiatives in the islands.[114]

Imagine you're taking over as Lindblad's marketing manager. You need to keep the company's Galapagos cruises full for reasons of profitability, yet you also want to support and highlight the company's "dark green" policies. Review Exhibit 5-5 as you consider which of the following options you will choose in this situation, and why.

**Option A:** Encourage contributions and repeat business by giving Lindblad cruise passengers who donate $250 or more a credit, in the amount donated, that can be redeemed on a future Lindblad cruise.

**Option B:** Strengthen Lindblad's "dark green" environmentalism with a policy requiring employees to devote 1 vacation day each year to working on Galapagos conservation projects.

**Option C:** Advertise to inform travelers about the environmentally unsound practices of conventional cruise lines compared with Lindblad's "dark green" Galapagos cruises.

# Case Application

### You've Got Questions . . .

At Texas-based RadioShack Corporation, whose brand-positioning slogan reads, "You've Got Questions, We've Got Answers," the events of early February 2006 surely had the company's board of directors and top executives wondering whether the questions they had about former CEO David Edmondson would ever be answered to their satisfaction. The problems began when the company's hometown newspaper, *The Fort Worth Star-Telegram*, ran a story by reporter Heather Landy that the "unaccredited bible college from which Mr. Edmondson claimed two degrees said he had not graduated." The paper also reported that its investigation showed that on two occasions, Mr. Edmondson had been charged with (but not convicted of) driving while intoxicated. In addition, the paper reported that shortly after being named CEO, he was arrested on a third DWI charge. "It was this last incident, scheduled to go to trial in April 2006, that had made the *Star-Telegram* sufficiently skeptical to begin checking out the local CEO."

*Former RadioShack Corporation CEO David Edmondson.*

Mr. Edmondson joined RadioShack in 1994, worked his way up the corporate ladder, and had been a senior executive since 1998. He served 2 years as senior vice president before being named as the company's president and chief operating officer in 2000. When RadioShack's board of directors announced in January 2005 that CEO Len Roberts was transitioning out of the CEO position but would remain as the executive chairman of the board, it also announced that it had selected David Edmondson as the new CEO. This CEO transition had been a planned succession given that the two men had worked side-by-side for 10 years in revitalizing the company. Roberts had "always believed that one of the most important jobs of a CEO was to select, groom and mentor a successor," and he felt he had done that with the hiring of Edmondson. As the company's Web site stated, "From the first time he met Edmondson, Roberts instinctively knew that Edmondson had the potential to one day become the company's CEO." And he mentored Edmondson, grooming him to take over the top spot someday.

When Roberts stepped down, Edmondson was named RadioShack's new CEO. During his 13 months'

tenure in this position, the company struggled with flat sales and a lagging stock price. Three days after the newspaper story ran, Edmondson offered two apologies in a conference call with investors: one for the performance of the company and one for having lied about his educational background. He then announced a turnaround plan for the company that included the closing of 400 to 700 of the company's 7,000 stores and dropping slow-moving products from its stores' inventory. He also reiterated that he was going to stay on as CEO. The stock market reacted with RadioShack's share price falling to a 3-year low. In a later phone news conference that same day, Mr. Edmondson replied to a question about whether the company had fired other employees for submitting false resumes by stating, "I would not want to comment on that." He also refused to comment as to whether his conduct violated the company's ethics code. At this point in time, RadioShack's board was still supporting its CEO.

However, by February 21, just days after he told investors that he intended to stay as CEO, Edmondson resigned. Board chairman Roberts announced the resignation, stating that it was a "tough decision," but a mutual decision between the board and Mr. Edmondson. He said, "When our company's credibility becomes based on a single individual, it is time for a change. One of the most important things we have as a corporation is integrity and trust. We have to restore that back to the company."

Although the situation at RadioShack certainly seems to have nowhere to go but up, new questions have been raised about the severance package Edmondson received. According to a regulatory filing, he received a cash payout worth at least $1.03 million in addition to payments for accrued and unpaid vacation and salary. RadioShack did not state the total value of the severance package, which also included 4 months of insurance coverage and the right to exercise outstanding stock options and stock awards. Claire Babrowski, the company's chief operating officer, was named acting CEO while an outside search for a new CEO is conducted. In addition to these changes, an examination of the company's Web site, where the company's Code of Ethics can be found, showed the following stated in bold print on the front cover: "Revision 02.21.06." Would this ultimately be the answer to the ethical and corporate responsibility questions that were sure to follow?

### Discussion Questions

1. Evaluate this situation from the viewpoint of David Edmondson's ethical leadership. What could RadioShack have done differently?

2. What stakeholders might be impacted by this situation? What concerns might each stakeholder have had? Were any of the stakeholders' concerns in conflict with each other? Explain. What impact might this have had on employees?

3. Do you think the board's decision to fire Edmondson was "tough," as Len Roberts suggested? Why or why not? Why do you think Mr. Roberts would have described this decision as such?

Exhibit 6–1

**The Decision-Making Process**

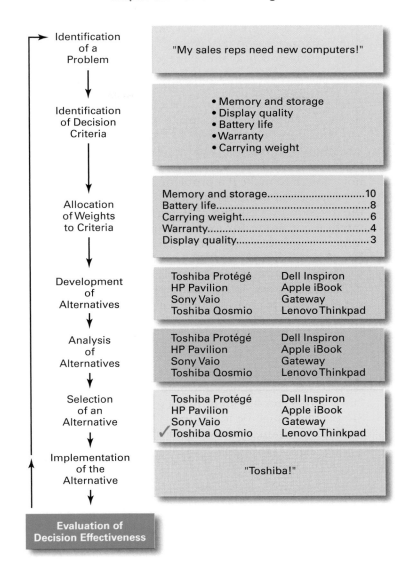

Identification of a Problem

"My sales reps need new computers!"

Identification of Decision Criteria

- Memory and storage
- Display quality
- Battery life
- Warranty
- Carrying weight

Allocation of Weights to Criteria

Memory and storage..................................10
Battery life...............................................8
Carrying weight.........................................6
Warranty..................................................4
Display quality..........................................3

Development of Alternatives

Toshiba Protégé       Dell Inspiron
HP Pavilion           Apple iBook
Sony Vaio             Gateway
Toshiba Qosmio        Lenovo Thinkpad

Analysis of Alternatives

Toshiba Protégé       Dell Inspiron
HP Pavilion           Apple iBook
Sony Vaio             Gateway
Toshiba Qosmio        Lenovo Thinkpad

Selection of an Alternative

Toshiba Protégé       Dell Inspiron
HP Pavilion           Apple iBook
Sony Vaio             Gateway
✓ Toshiba Qosmio      Lenovo Thinkpad

Implementation of the Alternative

"Toshiba!"

**Evaluation of Decision Effectiveness**

sales manager whose sales representatives need new laptops because their old ones are inadequate to do their jobs efficiently and effectively. For simplicity's sake, assume that Amanda has determined that it's not economical to simply add memory to the old computers and that it's the organization's policy that managers purchase new computers rather than lease them. Now we have a problem. There's a disparity between the sales reps' current computers and their need to have more efficient, effective ones to do their jobs properly. Amanda has a decision to make.

One thing our example doesn't tell us is how managers identify problems. In the real world, most problems don't come with neon signs flashing "problem." The sales reps' complaints that their computers are inadequate to do their jobs might be a clear signal to Amanda that something needs to be done, but few problems are that obvious. Managers also have to be cautious not to confuse problems with the symptoms of the problem. Is a 5 percent drop in sales a problem? Or are declining sales merely a symptom of the real problem, such as poor-quality products, high prices, or bad advertising? Also, keep in mind that problem identification is subjective. What one manager

**decision**
A choice from two or more alternatives.

**decision-making process**
A set of eight steps that include identifying a problem, selecting an alternative, and evaluating the decision's effectiveness.

**problem**
A discrepancy between an existing and a desired state of affairs.

considers a problem might not be considered a problem by another manager. In addition, a manager who mistakenly resolves the wrong problem perfectly is likely to perform just as poorly as the manager who doesn't identify the right problem and does nothing.

As you can see, effectively identifying problems isn't simple or trivial.[5] Managers can be better at it if they understand the three characteristics of problems: being aware of them, being under pressure to act, and having the resources needed to take action.[6]

Managers become aware of a problem by looking at actual conditions and at the conditions that are required or desired. If conditions aren't what they should be or what managers would like them to be, then a problem (discrepancy) exists. But that's not enough to make it a problem.

A problem without pressure to act is a problem that can be postponed. To trigger the decision process, the problem must put pressure on the manager to act. Pressure might come from, for example, deadlines, financial crises, competitor actions, customer complaints, expectations from the boss, organizational policies, or an upcoming performance evaluation.

Finally, managers aren't likely to see something as a problem if they believe they don't have the authority, information, or resources necessary to act on it. If managers recognize a problem and are under pressure to act but feel they have inadequate resources, they usually describe the situation as one in which unrealistic expectations are being placed on them.

## Step 2: Identifying Decision Criteria

Once a manager has identified a problem, the **decision criteria** important to resolving the problem must be identified. That is, managers must determine what's relevant in making a decision. Whether explicitly stated or not, every decision maker has criteria that guide his or her decisions. In our laptop purchase example, Amanda has to assess what factors are relevant to her decision. These might include criteria such as price, convenience, multimedia capability, memory and storage capabilities, display quality, battery life, expansion capability, warranty, and carrying weight. After careful consideration, she decides that memory and storage capabilities, display quality, battery life, warranty, and carrying weight are the relevant criteria in her decision.

**Q & A**

Not quite sure how decision makers allocate weights to decision criteria? Q & A 6.1 provides an answer.

## Step 3: Allocating Weights to the Criteria

If the relevant criteria aren't equally important, the decision maker must weight the items in order to give them the correct priority in the decision. How do you weight criteria? ( ⬦ Go to www.prenhall.com/rolls) A simple approach is to give the

*The choice of a new laptop computer relies on specific decision criteria like price, convenience, memory and storage capacity, display quality, battery life, warranty, and even carrying weight.*

Exhibit 6–2

**Criteria and Weights
for Computer
Replacement Decision**

| | |
|---|---|
| Memory and storage | 10 |
| Battery life | 8 |
| Carrying weight | 6 |
| Warranty | 4 |
| Display quality | 3 |

most important criterion a weight of 10 and then assign weights to the rest using that standard. Thus, a criterion with a weight of 10 would be twice as important as one given a 5. Of course, you could use 100 or 1,000 or any number you select as the highest weight.

Exhibit 6–2 lists the criteria and weights that Amanda developed for her computer replacement decision. As you can see, memory and storage capabilities are the most important criterion in her decision, and display quality is the least important.

## Step 4: Developing Alternatives

PRISM
Want to practice your skills at creative problem solving? Try PRISM #12.

The fourth step requires the decision maker to list viable alternatives that could resolve the problem. This is the step where a decision maker wants to be creative in coming up with possible alternatives. ( Go to www.prenhall.com/rolls) However, no attempt is made to evaluate the alternatives just yet, only to list them. Our sales manager, Amanda, identified eight laptops as possible choices including Toshiba Protégé S100, Dell Inspiron 700m, Toshiba QosmioG15-AV501, Apple iBook, Sony Vaio VGN-FS790, Gateway NX850X, HP Pavilion zd8000, and Lenovo Thinkpad R52.

## Step 5: Analyzing Alternatives

Once the alternatives have been identified, a decision maker must analyze each one. How? By evaluating it against the criteria established in steps 2 and 3. From this comparison, the strengths and weaknesses of each alternative become evident. Exhibit 6–3 shows the assessed values that Amanda gave each of her eight alternatives after she had talked to some computer experts and read the latest information from computer magazines and from the Web.

Keep in mind that the ratings given the eight computer models listed in Exhibit 6–3 are based on the personal assessment made by Amanda. Some assessments can be

Exhibit 6–3

**Assessed Values of Laptop
Computers Using Decision
Criteria**

| | Memory and Storage | Battery Life | Carrying Weight | Warranty | Display Quality |
|---|---|---|---|---|---|
| Toshiba Protégé S100 | 10 | 3 | 10 | 8 | 5 |
| Dell Inspiron 700m | 8 | 7 | 7 | 8 | 7 |
| HP Pavilion zd8000 | 8 | 5 | 7 | 10 | 10 |
| Apple iBook | 8 | 7 | 7 | 8 | 7 |
| Sony Vaio VGN-FS790 | 7 | 8 | 7 | 8 | 7 |
| Gateway NX850X | 8 | 3 | 6 | 10 | 8 |
| Toshiba QosmioG15-AV501 | 10 | 7 | 8 | 6 | 7 |
| Lenovo Thinkpad R52 | 4 | 10 | 4 | 8 | 10 |

**decision criteria**
Criteria that define what's relevant in a decision.

| | Memory and Storage | Battery Life | Carrying Weight | Warranty | Display Quality | Total |
|---|---|---|---|---|---|---|
| Toshiba Protégé S100 | 100 | 24 | 60 | 32 | 15 | 231 |
| Dell Inspiron 700m | 80 | 56 | 42 | 32 | 21 | 231 |
| HP Pavilion zd8000 | 80 | 40 | 42 | 40 | 30 | 232 |
| Apple iBook | 80 | 56 | 42 | 32 | 21 | 231 |
| Sony Vaio VGN-FS790 | 70 | 64 | 42 | 32 | 21 | 229 |
| Gateway NX850X | 80 | 24 | 36 | 40 | 24 | 204 |
| Toshiba QosmioG15-AV501 | 100 | 56 | 48 | 24 | 21 | 249 |
| Lenovo Thinkpad R52 | 40 | 80 | 24 | 32 | 30 | 206 |

done objectively. For instance, carrying weight is easy to determine by looking at descriptions online or in computer magazines. However, the assessment of display quality is more of a personal judgment. The point is that most decisions by managers involve judgments—the criteria chosen in step 2, the weights given to the criteria in step 3, and the evaluation of alternatives in step 5. This explains why two computer buyers with the same amount of money may look at two totally different sets of alternatives or even rate the same alternatives differently.

Exhibit 6–3 represents only an assessment of the eight alternatives against the decision criteria. It doesn't reflect the weighting done in step 3. If you multiply each alternative (Exhibit 6–3) by its weight (Exhibit 6–2), you get Exhibit 6–4. The sum of these scores represents an evaluation of each alternative against both the established criteria and weights. There are times when a decision maker might not have to do this step. If one alternative had scored 10 on every criterion, you wouldn't need to consider the weights because that alternative would already be the top choice. Similarly, if the weights were all equal, you could evaluate each alternative to determine the top choice merely by summing up the appropriate lines as shown in Exhibit 6–3. In this instance, for example, the score for the Toshiba Protégé would be 36 and the score for Gateway would be 35.

## Step 6: Selecting an Alternative

The sixth step is choosing the best alternative from among those considered. Once all the pertinent criteria in the decision have been weighted and viable alternatives analyzed, you merely choose the alternative that generated the highest total in step 5. In our example (Exhibit 6–4), Amanda would choose the Toshiba Qosmio because it scored highest (249 total) on the basis of the criteria identified, the weights given to the criteria, and her assessment of each laptop's ranking on the criteria. It's the "best" alternative.

## Step 7: Implementing the Alternative

**Q & A**

Putting a decision into action isn't as easy as it sounds. Q & A 6.2 explains.

Step 7 is concerned with putting the decision into action by conveying the decision to those affected by it and getting their commitment to it. (  Go to www.prenhall.com/rolls) We do know that if the people who must implement a decision participate in the process, they're more likely to enthusiastically support the outcome than if you just tell them what to do. Another thing managers also may need to do during the implementation process is to reassess the environment for any changes, especially if the decision is one that takes a longer period of time to implement. Do the criteria, alternatives, and choice still seem to be the best ones, or has the environment changed in such a way that we need to reevaluate? Parts Three through Five of this book describe how decisions are implemented by effective planning, organizing, and leading. ( Check out Passport Scenario 1 on page 260.)

**Passport**

How is decision making affected by different cultural environments? Try this global exercise and see!

## Step 8: Evaluating Decision Effectiveness

Q & A

What happens if your decision doesn't resolve the problem? What then? Q & A 6.3 has an answer.

The last step in the decision-making process involves evaluating the outcome or result of the decision to see if the problem has been resolved. (   Go to www.prenhall. com/rolls) How to evaluate results is detailed in Part Six of this book, where we look at the control function.

What if this evaluation showed the problem still existed? Then the manager would need to assess what went wrong. Was the problem incorrectly defined? Were errors made in the evaluation of the various alternatives? Was the right alternative selected but poorly implemented? The answers to questions like these might send the manager back to one of the earlier steps. It might even require starting the whole decision process over.

## Learning Review

• Define decision and decision-making process.

• Describe the eight steps in the decision-making process.

## THE MANAGER AS DECISION MAKER

Everyone in an organization makes decisions, but decision making is particularly important in a manager's job. As Exhibit 6–5 shows, decision making is part of all four managerial functions. In fact, that's why we say that decision making is the essence of management.[7] That's why managers—when they plan, organize, lead, and control—are called *decision makers.*

The fact that almost everything a manager does involves making decisions doesn't mean that decisions are always time-consuming, complex, or evident to an outside observer. Much of a manager's decision making is routine. Every day of the year you make a decision about when to eat dinner. It's no big deal. You've made the decision thousands of times before. It's a pretty simple decision and can usually be handled quickly. It's the type of decision you almost forget *is* a decision. Managers make dozens of these routine decisions every day, such as, for example, which employee will work what shift next week, what information should be included in a report, or how to resolve a customer's complaint. Keep in mind that even though a decision seems easy to make or has been faced by a manager a number of times before, it still is a decision.

Exhibit 6–5

**Decisions in the Management Functions**

| Planning | Leading |
|---|---|
| • What are the organization's long-term objectives? | • How do I handle employees who appear to be low in motivation? |
| • What strategies will best achieve those objectives? | • What is the most effective leadership style in a given situation? |
| • What should the organization's short-term objectives be? | • How will a specific change affect worker productivity? |
| • How difficult should individual goals be? | • When is the right time to stimulate conflict? |

| Organizing | Controlling |
|---|---|
| • How many employees should I have report directly to me? | • What activities in the organization need to be controlled? |
| • How much centralization should there be in the organization? | • How should those activities be controlled? |
| • How should jobs be designed? | • When is a performance deviation significant? |
| • When should the organization implement a different structure? | • What type of management information system should the organization have? |

*Faced with research indicating that General Motors was perceived as arrogant and cold, the company's director of Hispanic diversity marketing and sales, Sonia Maria Green, had to make decisions about how to humanize GM to improve sales. In addition to spending most of a year on the road talking to dealers about their Hispanic customers, she convinced the president of GM North America to appear in a Spanish-language television ad.*

We've made it pretty clear that managers make decisions, but we still don't know much about the manager as a decision maker and how decisions are actually made in organizations. How can we best describe the decision-making situation and the person who makes the decisions? We look at those issues in this section. We'll start by looking at three perspectives on how decisions are made.

## Making Decisions: Rationality, Bounded Rationality, and Intuition

When Hewlett-Packard (HP) acquired Compaq for $25 billion in 2002, the company did no research on how customers viewed Compaq products until months after then-CEO Carly Fiorina publicly announced the deal and privately warned her top management team that she didn't want to hear any dissent pertaining to the acquisition. By the time they discovered that customers perceived Compaq products as inferior—just the opposite of what customers felt about HP products—it was too late. HP's performance suffered and Fiorina eventually lost her job.[8]

We assume that managers' decision making is going to be **rational**. By that we mean that managers make consistent, value-maximizing choices within specified constraints.[9] After all, managers have all sorts of tools and techniques (see the "Managing IT" box on page 170) to help them be rational decision makers. But as the HP example illustrates, managers aren't always rational. What are the underlying assumptions of rationality, and how valid are those assumptions?

**Assumptions of Rationality**  A decision maker who was perfectly rational would be fully objective and logical. The problem would be clear and unambiguous and the decision maker would have a clear and specific goal and know all possible alternatives and consequences. Moreover, making decisions rationally would consistently lead to selecting the alternative that maximizes the likelihood of achieving that goal. Exhibit 6–6 summarizes the assumptions of rationality.

Exhibit 6–6

**Assumptions of Rationality**

- The problem is clear and unambiguous.
- A single, well-defined goal is to be achieved.
- All alternatives and consequences are known.
- Preferences are clear.
- Preferences are constant and stable.
- No time or cost constraints exist.
- Final choice will maximize payoff.

Lead to

Rational Decision Making

The assumptions of rationality apply to any decision—personal or managerial. However, because we're looking at managerial decision making, we need to add one additional assumption. Rational managerial decision making assumes that decisions are made in the best interests of the organization. That is, the decision maker is assumed to be maximizing the organization's interests, not his or her own interests.

How realistic are these assumptions? It's possible that managerial decision making can be rational if the following conditions are met: The manager is faced with a simple problem in which the goals are clear and the alternatives limited, in which the time pressures are minimal and the cost of seeking out and evaluating alternatives is low, for which the organizational culture supports innovation and risk taking, and in which the outcomes are relatively concrete and measurable.[10] Not surprisingly, most decisions that managers face don't meet these requirements. So, how are most decisions in organizations usually made? The concept of bounded rationality can help answer that question.

**Bounded Rationality** Despite the limits to perfect rationality, managers are expected to be rational when making decisions.[11] Managers understand that "good" decision makers are supposed to do certain things and exhibit good decision-making behaviors as they identify problems, consider alternatives, gather information, and act decisively but prudently. By doing so, they're showing others that they're competent and that their decisions are the result of intelligent deliberation. However, certain aspects of the decision-making process aren't realistic with respect to how managers actually make decisions. Managers tend to make decisions under assumptions of **bounded rationality**; that is, they make decisions rationally, but are limited (bounded) by their ability to process information.[12] Because they can't possibly analyze all information on all alternatives, managers **satisfice**, rather than maximize. That is, they accept solutions that are "good enough." (  Go to www.prenhall.com/rolls) They're being rational within the limits (bounds) of their ability to process information. Let's look at an example. Suppose that you're a finance major and upon graduation you want a job, preferably as a personal financial planner, with a minimum salary of $34,000 and within a hundred miles of your hometown. You accept a job offer as a business credit analyst—not exactly a personal financial planner but still in the finance field—at a bank 50 miles from home at a starting salary of $35,000. If you had done a more comprehensive job search, you would have discovered a job in personal financial planning at a trust company only 25 miles from your hometown and starting at a salary of $38,000. However, because the first job offer was satisfactory (or "good enough"), you behaved in a bounded rationality manner by accepting it. Yet, according to the assumptions of perfect rationality, you didn't maximize your decision by searching all possible alternatives and then choosing the best. (  Go to www.prenhall.com/rolls)

Most decisions that managers make don't fit the assumptions of perfect rationality and, instead, they make those decisions based on alternatives that are satisfactory. However, keep in mind that their decision making also may be strongly influenced by the organization's culture, internal politics, power considerations, and by a phenomenon called **escalation of commitment**, which is an increased commitment to a previous decision despite evidence that it may have been wrong.[13] For example, studies of the events leading up to the *Challenger* space shuttle disaster point to an escalation of commitment by decision makers to launch the shuttle on that day even though the decision was questioned by several individuals who believed that it was a bad one. Why would decision makers want to escalate commitment to a bad decision? Because they don't want to admit that their initial decision may have been flawed. Rather than search for new alternatives, they simply increase their commitment to the original solution.

**Q & A**

Satisficing seems like settling for second best. Is that true? Check out Q & A 6.4 to see.

**Q & A**

Probably one of the biggest decisions you've made is which college to attend. Would you say that you maximized or satisficed your choice? Q & A 6.5 provides some insights.

**rational decision making**
Decision-making behavior where choices are consistent and value-maximizing within specified constraints.

**bounded rationality**
Decision-making behavior that's rational, but limited (bounded) by an individual's ability to process information.

**satisficing**
Accepting solutions that are "good enough."

**escalation of commitment**
An increased commitment to a previous decision despite evidence that it may have been wrong.

**Role of Intuition**  When managers at stapler-maker Swingline saw the company's market share declining, they decided to use a logical scientific approach to help them address the issue. For 3 years, they exhaustively researched stapler users before deciding what new products to develop. However, at newcomer Accentra, Inc., founder Todd Moses used a more intuitive decision approach to come up with his line of unique PaperPro staplers. His stapler sold 1 million units in 6 months in a market that only sells 25 million units total annually—a pretty good result for a new product.[14]

Like Todd Moses, managers often use their intuition and it may actually help their decision making. What is **intuitive decision making**? It's making decisions on the basis of experience, feelings, and accumulated judgment. Researchers studying managers' use of intuitive decision making have identified five different aspects of intuition, which are described in Exhibit 6–7.[15]

Making a decision on intuition or "gut feeling" doesn't necessarily happen independently of rational analysis; rather, the two complement each other. A manager who has had experience with a similar type of problem or situation often can act quickly with what appears to be limited information. Such a manager doesn't rely on a systematic and thorough analysis of the problem or identification and evaluation of alternatives but instead uses his or her experience and judgment to make a decision. (       Go to www.prenhall.com/rolls)

How common is intuitive decision making? One survey of corporate executives found that almost half of them used intuition more than formal analysis to run their companies.[16] Many managers are using their intuition to make decisions—like those at the WB Network who decided to stop formally testing TV show pilots and instead to go with their own gut instincts in deciding what new programs to air.[17]

**Q & A**

Making a decision based on your gut feeling seems pretty risky. Is it? Check out Q & A 6.6 for an answer.

## Types of Problems and Decisions

Managers at eating establishments in Springfield, Missouri, make decisions weekly about purchasing food supplies and scheduling employee work shifts. It's something they've done numerous times. But now they're facing a different kind of decision—one they've never encountered: how to adapt to a newly enacted no-smoking ordinance. And this situation isn't all that unusual. Managers in all kinds of organizations will face different types of problems and decisions as they do their jobs. Depending on the nature of the problem, the manager can use different types of decisions.

Exhibit 6–7    **What Is Intuition?**

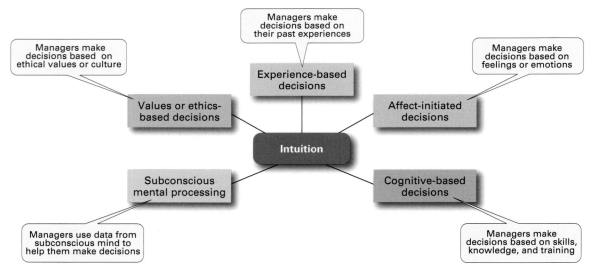

*Source:* Based on L. A. Burke and M. K. Miller, "Taking the Mystery Out of Intuitive Decision Making," *Academy of Management Executive*, October 1999, pp. 91–99.

*Intuition played a strong part in Barbara Choi's decision to locate her firm, a cosmetics and personal care products manufacturer, in Valley Springs Industrial Center in Los Angeles. In Chinese, the numbers of the building's address signify continued growth.*

**Structured Problems and Programmed Decisions** Some problems are straightforward. The goal of the decision maker is clear, the problem is familiar, and information about the problem is easily defined and complete. Examples of these types of problems might include a customer's returning a purchase to a store, a supplier's being late with an important delivery, a news team's response to a fast-breaking event, or a college's handling of a student wanting to drop a class. Such situations are called **structured problems**, which are straightforward, familiar, and easily defined. For instance, a server in a restaurant spills a drink on a customer's coat. The manager has an upset customer and something needs to be done. Because drinks are frequently spilled, there's probably some standardized routine for handling the problem. For example, the manager offers to have the coat cleaned at the restaurant's expense. This is what we call a **programmed decision**, a repetitive decision that can be handled by a routine approach. Because the problem is structured, the manager doesn't have to go to the trouble and expense of going through an involved decision process. The "develop-the-alternatives" stage of the decision-making process either doesn't exist or is given little attention. Why? Because once the structured problem is defined, the solution is usually self-evident or at least reduced to a few alternatives that are familiar and have proved successful in the past. The spilled drink on the customer's coat doesn't require the restaurant manager to identify and weight decision criteria or to develop a long list of possible solutions. Rather, the manager relies on a programmed decision, of which there are three types: procedure, rule, or policy.

A **procedure** is a series of interrelated sequential steps that a manager can use to respond to a structured problem. The only real difficulty is in identifying the problem. Once it's clear, so is the procedure. For instance, a purchasing manager receives a request from a warehouse manager for 15 PDA handhelds for the company's inventory clerks. The purchasing manager knows how to make this decision—that is, follow the established purchasing procedure.

A **rule** is an explicit statement that tells a manager what he or she can or cannot do. Rules are frequently used because they're simple to follow and ensure consistency. For example, rules about lateness and absenteeism permit supervisors to make disciplinary decisions rapidly and fairly.

---

**intuitive decision making**
Making decisions on the basis of experience, feelings, and accumulated judgment.

**structured problems**
Straightforward, familiar, and easily defined problems.

**programmed decision**
A repetitive decision that can be handled by a routine approach.

**procedure**
A series of interrelated sequential steps that can be used to respond to a well-structured problem.

**rule**
An explicit statement that tells managers what they can or cannot do.

**Q & A**

What good are guidelines if they only act as guides to decision making? Q & A 6.7 explains.

A third type of programmed decisions is a **policy**, which is a guideline for making a decision. In contrast to a rule, a policy establishes general parameters for the decision maker rather than specifically stating what should or should not be done. Policies typically contain an ambiguous term that leaves interpretation up to the decision maker. (  Go to www.prenhall.com/rolls) Here are some sample policy statements:

- The customer always comes first and should always be *satisfied*.
- We promote from within, *whenever possible*.
- Employee wages shall be *competitive* within community standards.

Notice that the terms *satisfied, whenever possible,* and *competitive* require interpretation. For instance, the policy of paying competitive wages doesn't tell a company's human resources manager the exact amount he or she should pay, but it does guide the decision he or she makes.

**Unstructured Problems and Nonprogrammed Decisions**  Not all problems managers face are structured and solvable by a programmed decision. Many organizational situations involve **unstructured problems**, which are problems that are new or unusual and for which information is ambiguous or incomplete. Whether to build a new manufacturing facility in China is an example of an unstructured problem. So too is the problem facing restaurant managers in Springfield when deciding how to modify their facilities and operations to comply with the city's new no-smoking ordinance. When problems are unstructured, managers must rely on nonprogrammed decision making in order to develop unique solutions. **Nonprogrammed decisions** are unique and nonrecurring and require custom-made solutions. When a manager confronts an unstructured problem, there is no cut-and-dried solution. It requires a custom-made response through nonprogrammed decision making.

**Integration**  Exhibit 6–8 describes the differences between programmed and nonprogrammed decisions. Because lower-level managers confront familiar and repetitive problems, they mostly rely on programmed decisions such as procedures, rules, and policies. The problems confronting managers usually become more unstructured as they move up the organizational hierarchy. Why? Because lower-level managers handle the routine decisions themselves and let upper-level managers deal with the decisions they find unusual or difficult. Similarly, higher-level managers delegate routine decisions to their subordinates so they can deal with more difficult issues.[18] (  Go to www.prenhall.com/rolls)

**Q & A**

Even though you've made many decisions in your life, you still may feel unprepared to make decisions as a manager. How important is experience to good decision making? How about creativity? See Q & A 6.8.

*Many people believe that China will become the next big market for powerful brand-name products, and Zong Qinghou, founder of China's Wahaha beverage group, plans to be ready. But brand names are a new concept in Chinese markets, and Zong prefers his own firsthand information to market research. He will face many nonprogrammed decisions as he tries to make his brand a success at home and eventually abroad.*

Exhibit 6–10

**Payoff Matrix**

| (in millions of dollars) Visa Marketing Strategy | MasterCard's Response | | |
|---|---|---|---|
| | CA$_1$ | CA$_2$ | CA$_3$ |
| S$_1$ | 13 | 14 | 11 |
| S$_2$ | 9 | 15 | 18 |
| S$_3$ | 24 | 21 | 15 |
| S$_4$ | 18 | 14 | 28 |

the minimum possible payoff); and the manager who desires to minimize his maximum "regret" will opt for a *minimax* choice. Let's look at these different choice approaches using an example.

A marketing manager at Visa International has determined four possible strategies (S$_1$, S$_2$, S$_3$, and S$_4$) for promoting the Visa card throughout the west coast region of the United States. The marketing manager also knows that major competitor MasterCard has three competitive actions (CA$_1$, CA$_2$, CA$_3$) it's using to promote its card in the same region. For this example, we'll assume that the Visa manager had no previous knowledge that would allow her to determine probabilities of success of any of the four strategies. She formulates the matrix shown in Exhibit 6–10 to show the various Visa strategies and the resulting profit depending on the competitive action used by MasterCard.

In this example, if our Visa manager is an optimist, she'll choose strategy 4 (S$_4$) because that could produce the largest possible gain: $28 million. Note that this choice maximizes the maximum possible gain (maximax choice).

If our manager is a pessimist, she'll assume that only the worst can occur. The worst outcome for each strategy is as follows: S$_1$ = $11 million; S$_2$ = $9 million; S$_3$ = $15 million; S$_4$ = $14 million. These are the most pessimistic outcomes from each strategy. Following the *maximin* choice, she would maximize the minimum payoff; in other words, she'd select S$_3$ ($15 million is the largest of the minimum payoffs).

In the third approach, managers recognize that once a decision is made, it will not necessarily result in the most profitable payoff. There may be a "regret" of profits given up—*regret* referring to the amount of money that could have been made had a different strategy been used. Managers calculate regret by subtracting all possible payoffs in each category from the maximum possible payoff for each given event, in this case for each competitive action. For our Visa manager, the highest payoff, given that MasterCard engages in CA$_1$, CA$_2$, or CA$_3$, is $24 million, $21 million, or $28 million, respectively (the highest number in each column). Subtracting the payoffs in Exhibit 6–10 from those figures produces the results shown in Exhibit 6–11.

The maximum regrets are S$_1$—$17 million; S$_2$—$15 million; S$_3$—$13 million; and S$_4$—$7 million. The *minimax* choice minimizes the maximum regret, so our Visa

Exhibit 6–11

**Regret Matrix**

| (in millions of dollars) Visa Marketing Strategy | MasterCard's Response | | |
|---|---|---|---|
| | CA$_1$ | CA$_2$ | CA$_3$ |
| S$_1$ | 11 | 7 | 17 |
| S$_2$ | 15 | 6 | 10 |
| S$_3$ | 0 | 0 | 13 |

**uncertainty**
A situation in which a decision maker has neither certainty nor reasonable probability estimates available.

## managing **IT**

### Making Better Decisions with IT

BudNet is the "crown jewel of the King of Beers." What is BudNet? It's Anheuser-Busch's powerful and sophisticated information system. Every night, data is collected from Anheuser-Busch (AB) distributors' computer servers. Each morning then, managers can see what brands are selling in which packages using which promotional materials and pricing discounts. According to dozens of analysts, beer-industry veterans, and distributor execs, Anheuser has made a deadly accurate science out of finding out what beer lovers are buying, as well as when, where, and why. All this information allows AB managers to continually adjust production and fine-tune marketing campaigns.

Most companies are drowning in data and don't know how to bring order to it or make sense out of it.[20] As this example shows, however, one of the primary uses for IT can be to help managers—and other employees—make better decisions by sorting through tons of data looking for trends, patterns, and other insights. As we saw in our discussion of bounded rationality, a person's ability to process such a massive amount of information would be severely limited. So managers use IT to help

them make sense of all this information so they can make better decisions.

Another way that IT can help managers make better decisions is by using software tools that help them analyze data. Consultants estimate that some 75 percent of individual managers rely on personal productivity tools, such as spreadsheets, which can be used to gather and report information to help them make decisions in their own local area of responsibility. However, when you have each manager using his or her own data collection tools, there are no linkages or collaboration. Thus, on the organization-wide level, there's the more sophisticated **business performance management** (or **BPM**, also sometimes called *corporate performance management*) software to help make decisions. BPM, which provides key performance indicators that help companies monitor efficiency of projects and employees, was initially believed to be the silver bullet that had the potential to help corporate managers control their organization's performance in an increasingly volatile world. Although it hasn't quite lived up to those lofty expectations, as BPM software improves, it increasingly will be a tool managers organization-wide use to help make better decisions.

---

manager would choose $S_4$. By making this choice, she'll never have a regret of profits given up of more than $7 million. This result contrasts, for example, with a regret of $15 million had she chosen $S_2$ and MasterCard had taken $CA_1$.

Although managers will try to quantify a decision when possible by using payoff and regret matrices, uncertainty often forces them to rely more on intuition, creativity, hunches, and "gut feel." Regardless of the decision situation, each manager has his or her own style of making decisions.

## Decision-Making Styles

William D. Perez's tenure as Nike's CEO lasted a short but turbulent 13 months. Analysts attributed his abrupt dismissal to a difference in decision-making approaches between him and Nike co-founder Phil Knight. Perez tended to rely more on data and facts when making decisions, while Knight highly valued, and had always used, his judgment and feelings to make decisions.[21] As this example clearly shows, managers have different styles when it comes to making decisions.

Suppose that you were a new manager at American Savings Bank in Honolulu or at the local YMCA. How would you make decisions? Managers' decision-making styles differ along two dimensions.[22] The first is an individual's *way of thinking*. Some of us are more rational and logical in the way we process information. A rational type looks at information in order and makes sure that it's logical and consistent before making a decision. Others tend to be creative and intuitive. Intuitive types don't have to process information in a certain order but are comfortable looking at it as whole.

The other dimension describes an individual's *tolerance for ambiguity*. Again, some of us have a low tolerance for ambiguity. These types need consistency and order in the way they structure information so that ambiguity is minimized. On the other hand, some of us can tolerate high levels of ambiguity and are able to process many thoughts at the same time. (  Go to www.prenhall.com/rolls) When we diagram these two dimensions, we get four decision-making styles: directive, analytic, conceptual, and behavioral (see Exhibit 6–12). Let's look more closely at each style.

Self-Assessment Library (S.A.L.)

Are you comfortable with uncertainty? Do S.A.L. #I.A.4 to see how well you handle ambiguity.

Exhibit 6–12

**Decision-Making Matrix**

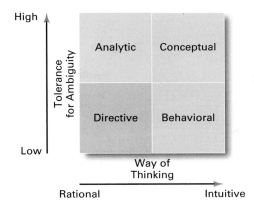

- *Directive style.* Decision makers using the **directive style** have low tolerance for ambiguity and are rational in their way of thinking. They're efficient and logical. Directive types make fast decisions and focus on the short run. Their efficiency and speed in making decisions often result in their making decisions with minimal information and assessing few alternatives.
- *Analytic style.* Decision makers with an **analytic style** have much greater tolerance for ambiguity than do directive types. They want more information before making a decision and consider more alternatives than a directive decision maker does. Analytic decision makers are characterized as careful decision makers with the ability to adapt or cope with unique situations.
- *Conceptual style.* Individuals with a **conceptual style** tend to be very broad in their outlook and look at many alternatives. They focus on the long run and are very good at finding creative solutions to problems.
- *Behavioral style.* Decision makers with a **behavioral style** work well with others. They're concerned about the achievements of those around them and are receptive to suggestions from others. They often use meetings to communicate, although they try to avoid conflict. Acceptance by others is important to this decision-making style.

Although these four decision-making styles are distinct, most managers have characteristics of more than one style. It's probably more realistic to think of a manager's dominant style and alternate styles. (  Go to www.prenhall.com/rolls) Look back at our chapter-opening dilemma, for example. As a customer service manager, what style(s) might Renee use? Although some managers will rely almost exclusively on their dominant style, others are more flexible and can shift their style depending on the situation.

Managers should also recognize that their employees may use different decision-making styles. (  Go to www.prenhall.com/rolls) Some employees may take their time, carefully weighing alternatives and considering riskier options (analytic style), while other employees may be more concerned about getting suggestions from others before making decisions (behavioral style). This doesn't make one approach better than the other. It just means that their decision-making styles are different. (  Go to www.prenhall.com/rolls) The "Managing Workforce Diversity" box addresses some of the issues associated with valuing diversity in decision making.

**Q & A**

What if a manager's decision-making style doesn't fit the cultural expectations in the organization? Then what? Q & A 6.9 provides an explanation.

**Q & A**

Do you think your approach to making decisions is better than the way your friends approach decision making? Sorry...there is no one best style of making decisions! See Q & A 6.10.

**Self-Assessment Library (S.A.L.)**

Don't know your decision-making style? Try S.A.L. #I.D.1 and find out!

The choice of an advertising agency is often made by those with a conceptual approach to decision making. Marketing executives from Virgin Atlantic Airways saw presentations from five ad agencies before choosing Crispin Porter & Bogusky, a small firm whose inventive proposal showed how efficiently the airline's $15 million ad budget could be spent. The marketing team from Virgin allowed 10 weeks to make a decision; it took 4 days. The winning team is pictured here with the paper airplanes that played a part in their pitch.

## Decision-Making Biases and Errors

When managers make decisions, not only do they use their own particular style, but many also use "rules of thumb" or **heuristics**, to simplify their decision making. Rules of thumb can be useful to decision makers because they help make sense of complex, uncertain, and ambiguous information.[24] Even though managers may use rules of thumb, that doesn't mean those rules are reliable. Why? Because they may lead to errors and biases in processing and evaluating information. Exhibit 6–13 identifies 12 common decision errors and biases that managers make. Let's take a quick look at each.[25]

When decision makers tend to think they know more than they do or hold unrealistically positive views of themselves and their performance, they're exhibiting the *overconfidence bias.* The *immediate gratification bias* describes decision makers who tend to want immediate rewards and to avoid immediate costs. For these individuals, decision

## managing workforce Diversity

### The Value of Diversity in Decision Making

Have you decided what your major is going to be? How did you decide? Do you feel your decision is a good one? Is there anything you could have done differently to make sure that your decision was the best one?[23]

Making good decisions is tough! Managers are continuously making decisions—for instance, developing new products, establishing weekly or monthly goals, implementing an advertising campaign, reassigning an employee to a different work group, resolving a customer's complaint, or purchasing new laptops for sales representatives. One important suggestion for making better decisions is to tap into the diversity of the work group. Drawing upon diverse employees can prove valuable to a manager's decision making. Why? Diverse employees can provide fresh perspectives on issues. They can offer differing interpretations on how a problem is defined and may be more open to trying new ideas. Diverse employees usually are more creative in generating alternatives and more flexible in resolving issues. And getting input from diverse sources increases the likelihood that creative and unique solutions will be generated.

Even though diversity in decision making can be valuable, there are drawbacks. The lack of a common perspective usually means that more time is spent discussing the issues. Communication may be a problem particularly if language barriers are present. In addition, seeking out diverse opinions can make the decision-making process more complex, confusing, and ambiguous. And with multiple perspectives on the decision, it may be difficult to reach a single agreement or to agree on specific actions. Although these drawbacks are valid concerns, the value of diversity in decision making outweighs the potential disadvantages.

Now, about that decision on a major: Did you ask others for their opinions? Did you seek out advice from professors, family members, friends, or co-workers? Getting diverse perspectives on an important decision like this could help you make the best decision! Managers also should consider the value to be gained from diversity in decision making.

Exhibit 6–13

**Common Decision-Making Errors and Biases**

choices that provide quick payoffs are more appealing than those in the future. The *anchoring effect* describes when decision makers fixate on initial information as a starting point and then, once set, fail to adequately adjust for subsequent information. First impressions, ideas, prices, and estimates carry unwarranted weight relative to information received later. When decision makers selectively organize and interpret events based on their biased perceptions, they're using the *selective perception bias*. This influences the information they pay attention to, the problems they identify, and the alternatives they develop. Decision makers who seek out information that reaffirms their past choices and discount information that contradicts past judgments exhibit the *confirmation bias*. These people tend to accept at face value information that confirms their preconceived views and are critical and skeptical of information that challenges these views. The *framing bias* is when decision makers select and highlight certain aspects of a situation while excluding others. By drawing attention to specific aspects of a situation and highlighting them, while at the same time downplaying or omitting other aspects, they distort what they see and create incorrect reference points. The *availability bias* is when decisions makers tend to remember events that are the most recent and vivid in their memory. The result? It distorts their ability to recall events in an objective manner and results in distorted judgments and probability estimates. When decision makers assess the likelihood of an event based on how closely it resembles other events or sets of events, that's the *representation bias*. Managers exhibiting this bias draw analogies and see identical situations where they don't exist. The *randomness bias* describes when decision makers try to create meaning out of random events. They do this because most decision makers have difficulty dealing with chance even though random events happen to everyone and there's nothing that can be done to predict them. The *sunk costs error* is when decision makers forget that current choices can't correct the past. They incorrectly fixate on past expenditures of time, money, or effort in assessing choices rather than on future consequences. Instead of ignoring sunk costs, they can't forget them. Decision makers who are quick to take credit for their successes and to blame failure on outside factors are exhibiting the *self-serving bias*. Finally, the *hindsight bias* is the tendency for decision makers to falsely believe that they would have accurately predicted the outcome of an event once that outcome is actually known.

**heuristics**
Rules of thumb that managers use to simplify decision making.

Exhibit 6–14    **Overview of Managerial Decision Making**

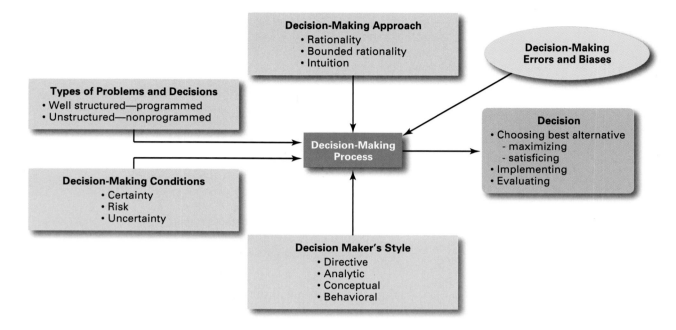

How can managers avoid the negative effects of these decision errors and biases? Mainly by being aware of them and then not using them! Beyond that, managers also should pay attention to "how" they make decisions and try to identify the heuristics they typically use and critically evaluate how appropriate those are. Finally, managers might want to ask those around them to help identify weaknesses in their decision-making style and try to improve on them.

## Summing Up Managerial Decision Making

How can we best sum up managerial decision making? Exhibit 6–14 provides an overview. Because it is in their best interests, managers *want* to make good decisions—that is, choose the "best" alternative, implement it, and determine whether it takes care of the problem, which is the reason the decision was needed in the first place. Their decision-making process is affected by four factors: the decision-making approach, the decision-making conditions, the type of problem, and their own style of decision making. In addition, certain decision-making errors and biases may impact the process. Each factor plays a role in determining how the manager makes a decision. So whether that decision involves addressing an employee's habitual tardiness, resolving a product quality problem, or determining whether to enter a new market, remember that it has been shaped by a number of factors.

## Learning Review

- Discuss the assumptions of rational decision making.
- Describe the concepts of bounded rationality, satisficing, and escalation of commitment.
- Explain intuitive decision making.
- Contrast programmed and nonprogrammed decisions.
- Contrast the three decision-making conditions.
- Explain maximax, maximin, and minimax decision choice approaches.

- Describe the four decision-making styles.
- Discuss the twelve decision-making biases managers may exhibit.
- Describe how managers can avoid the negative effects of decision errors and biases.
- Explain the managerial decision-making model.

## DECISION MAKING FOR TODAY'S WORLD

Per Carlsson, a product development manager at IKEA, spends his days creating Volvo-style kitchens at Yugo prices. His job is to take the "problems" identified by the company's product-strategy council (a group of globe-trotting senior managers that monitors consumer trends and establishes product priorities) and turn them into furniture that the entire world wants to buy. One "problem" recently identified by the council: the kitchen has replaced the living room as the social and entertaining center in the home. Customers are looking for kitchens that convey comfort and cleanliness while still allowing them to pursue their gourmet aspirations. Carlsson has to take this information and make things happen. There are a lot of decisions to make—programmed and nonprogrammed—and the fact that IKEA is a global company makes it even more challenging. Comfort in Asia means small, cozy appliances and spaces, while North American customers want oversized glassware and giant refrigerators. His ability to make good decisions quickly has significant implications for IKEA's success.[26]

Today's business world revolves around making decisions, often risky ones, usually with incomplete or inadequate information, and under intense time pressure. Most managers are making one decision after another, and as if that weren't challenging enough, more is at stake than ever before. Bad decisions can cost millions. What do managers need to do to make effective decisions in today's fast-moving world? Here are some guidelines.

- *Understand cultural differences.* Managers everywhere want to make good decisions. However, is there only one "best" way worldwide to make decisions? Or does the best way depend on the values, beliefs, attitudes, and behavioral patterns of the people involved?[27] The "Focus on Leadership" box addresses some of the issues involved in understanding cultural differences in decision making.

## *focus on* Leadership

### Cultural Differences in Leaders' Decision-Making Styles

In Chinese businesses, superstition plays a crucial role in managerial decision making. In the United States, managers perceive most situations as problems to be solved by making decisions. However, in Indonesian, Malay, and Thai cultures, managers see no need to change most situations but rather attempt to accept life as it is.[28] As these examples show, cultural differences can and do impact the way managers make decisions. What kinds of differences?

If we look at the decision-making process, cultural differences can be seen in five areas: identifying problems, searching for information, developing alternatives, making choices, and in implementing alternatives. Let's look briefly at each.

When *identifying problems*, managers might be from a culture that is focused on problem solving. Or their culture might be one of situation acceptance. When *searching for information*, managers might come from a culture that gathers facts or from a culture that is more intuitive in gathering ideas and possibilities. As a decision maker *develops alternatives*, is the culture a more future-oriented one where many new alternatives are encouraged? Or is it a culture that is more conservative and past-oriented, where alternatives are developed from historical patterns? Once alternatives have been developed and it's time to *make a choice*, is the culture

one where individual or group decision making is encouraged? Finally, during *implementation*, a manager might be from a culture that is quick or slow, innovative or disruptive, managed from the top or involves participation from all levels within the organization, and managed by an individual or a group.

Finally, findings from studies by Geert Hofstede and from GLOBE researchers (see Chapter 4) provide additional insights into cultural differences in decision making, especially with respect to how much risk and uncertainty decision makers are willing to accept and how much participation decision makers encourage. Not surprisingly, in high uncertainty avoidance countries (such as Austria, Denmark, and Germany), decision making is more formalized and analytical. In low uncertainty countries (such as Russia, Hungary, and Bolivia), decision making tends to be based more on intuition than on formal analysis. The amount of participation decision makers encourage and allow also varies by country. For instance, one study showed that German, Austrian, and Swiss managers were the most participative; Polish and Czech managers were the most autocratic; and U.S. and French managers were somewhere in between. However, this same study also found that Polish managers were likely to be participative on trivial matters, but not on important issues and that U.S. and Polish managers were likely to become more autocratic in conflict-producing situations.

- *Know when it's time to call it quits.* When it's evident that a decision isn't working, don't be afraid to pull the plug. For instance, Christopher McCormick, CEO of L.L.Bean, pulled the plug on building a new customer call center in Waterville, Maine—literally stopping the bulldozers in their tracks—after T-Mobile USA said it was building its own call center right next door. McCormick was afraid that the city did not have enough qualified workers to supply his company's and T-Mobile's needs. So McCormick decided to build 55 miles away in Bangor.[29] He knew when it was time to call it quits. However, as we said earlier, many decision makers block or distort negative information because they don't want to believe that their decision was bad. They become so attached to the decision that they refuse to recognize when it's time to move on. In today's dynamic environment, this type of thinking simply won't work.

- *Do use an effective decision-making process.* Experts say an effective decision-making process has these six characteristics: (1) It focuses on what's important; (2) It's logical and consistent; (3) It acknowledges both subjective and objective thinking and blends analytical with intuitive thinking; (4) It requires only as much information and analysis as is necessary to resolve a particular dilemma; (5) It encourages and guides the gathering of relevant information and informed opinion; and (6) It's straightforward, reliable, easy to use, and flexible.[30]

The remaining suggestions for making decisions in today's fast-moving world come from Karl Weick, an organizational psychologist, who has made a career of studying organizations and how people work. He says that the best way for managers to respond to unpredictability and uncertainty is by building an organization that expertly spots the unexpected when it crops up and then quickly adapts to the changed environment.[31] He calls these organizations *highly reliable organizations* (HROs) and says they share five habits. First, they're *not tricked by their success.* HROs are preoccupied with their failures. They're alert to the smallest deviations and react early and quickly to anything that doesn't fit with their expectations. He talks about Navy aviators who describe "leemers"—a gut feeling that something isn't

## *becoming* a Manager

✓ Pay close attention to decisions you make and how you make them.

✓ When you feel you haven't made a good decision, assess how you could have made a better decision. Which step of the decision-making process could you have improved?

✓ Work at developing good decision-making skills.

✓ Remember that the quality of your decisions is what ultimately will make you valuable to an organization.

✓ Read books about decision making.

✓ Ask people you admire for advice on how they make good decisions.

✓ Will these suggestions help you be a better decision maker? You'll have to decide!

 Self-Assessment Library (S.A.L.)

✓ 🔷 Complete these exercises from the Self-Assessment Library found on www.prenhall.com/rolls: S.A.L. #I.A.4—How Well Do I Handle Ambiguity?, S.A.L. #I.D.1—What's My Decision-Making Style?, and S.A.L. #III.C.1—How Well Do I Respond to Turbulent Change?

right. Typically, these leemers turn out to be accurate. Something, in fact, is wrong. Organizations need to create climates where people feel safe trusting their leemers. Another characteristic of HROs is that they *defer to the experts on the front line*. Frontline workers—those who interact day in and day out with customers, products, suppliers, and so forth—have firsthand knowledge of what can and cannot be done, what will and will not work. Get their input. Let them make decisions. Next, HROs *let unexpected circumstances provide the solution*. One of Weick's better-known works is his study of the Mann Gulch fire in Montana that killed 13 smoke jumpers in 1949. The event was a massive, tragic organizational failure. However, the reaction of the foreman illustrates how effective decision makers respond to unexpected circumstances. When the fire was nearly on top of his men, he invented the escape fire—a small fire that consumed all the brush around the team, leaving an area where the larger fire couldn't burn. His action was contrary to everything firefighters are taught (that is, you don't start fires—you extinguish them), but at the time it was the best decision. The fourth habit of HROs is that they *embrace complexity*. Because business is complex, these organizations recognize that it takes complexity to sense complexity. Rather than simplifying data, which we instinctively try to do when faced with complexity, these organizations aim for deeper understanding of the situation. They ask "why" and keep asking why as they probe more deeply into the causes of the problem and possible solutions. Finally, HROs *anticipate, but also anticipate their limits*. These organizations do try to anticipate as much as possible, but they recognize that they can't anticipate everything. As Weick says, they don't "think, then act." They think by acting. By actually doing things, you'll find out what works and what doesn't.

Making decisions in today's fast-moving world isn't easy. Successful managers will need good decision-making skills to effectively and efficiently plan, organize, lead, and control.

## Learning Review

- Explain how managers can make effective decisions in today's world.
- List the six characteristics of an effective decision-making process.

- Describe the five habits of highly reliable organizations.

# Managers Respond to a Manager's Dilemma

## Joan Verbonitz

Senior Consultant, CBI Group, Wilmington, DE

In order to evaluate the effectiveness of the phone system, Renee should remind herself of the primary reason for its development and implementation. The executives chose this system to provide increased and more convenient accessibility for their customers. Renee should start the evaluation by gathering and analyzing relevant data regarding the phone system itself. Are customers using the system? How many? How frequently? When are they calling? What time of day? What day of the week? From what area or region? Answering these types of questions will provide an understanding of the usage and effectiveness of the system, supported by quantitative data.

However, it is critical for Renee to also consider the most important evaluator of the phone system's effectiveness—the customer and his or her experience. Since management has received very few customer comments, Renee should proactively contact customers for their feedback. A series of questions should be developed for customers using the system to see if it accomplished what executives were aiming for—increased convenience and accessibility. Renee should also contact some customers who are not using the system. This will provide comprehensive insight as to why some customers aren't using the automated phone system. Some of the questions may be: Are they aware of the system? Is it too cumbersome? Too impersonal? All of these suggestions could help her evaluate the effectiveness of the phone system and provide a foundation for her recommendations.

## Karen V. Ellifritz, MBA, CPA

Assistant Controller, The Reybold Group, Bear, DE

I would begin by quantifying the results of the phone service initiative. The bank should look for a positive correlation between decreasing use of in-person customer support services and increasing use of the new automated system. To prevent self-serving bias from entering the equations, someone other than Renee should perform the analysis. Simple customer service metrics such as those listed below are commonly used to evaluate the success of innovative initiatives.

1. How many automated calls are completed each day without being redirected to a live rep? Is the amount increasing or decreasing? At what rate?
2. Are calls requesting to speak to a live customer service representative increasing or decreasing? At what rate?
3. Is ATM usage increasing or decreasing? At what rate?
4. How has the overall customer retention rate behaved since starting this program?
5. How do these figures compare with those of companies the bank uses as benchmarks?

But statistics are not enough. The bank's customers will eventually seek higher levels of service in less time and with less effort. Sometimes there are legitimate reasons for wanting these changes; sometimes not. Either way, Renee should be mindful that customer expectations for value evolve and change over time, and that she should **actively seek** customer feedback as another important evaluation tool.

# Learning Summary

## How Do Managers Make Decisions?

- Identifying problem (discrepancy) and decision criteria (what's relevant in making the decision)
- Allocating weights to those criteria
- Developing, analyzing, and selecting alternatives
- Implementing a chosen alternative and evaluating decision effectiveness

## How Are Decisions Made?

- **Rationality**: consistent, value-maximizing choices where the problem is clear and unambiguous, the decision maker's goal is clear and specific, and the decision maker knows all possible alternatives
- **Bounded rationality**: decisions are made rationally, but decision makers are limited by (bounded) their ability to process information so they end up satisficing; decision making may be strongly influenced by organization's culture, internal politics, power considerations, and escalation of commitment
- **Intuition**: making decisions on the basis of experience, feelings, and accumulated judgment

## What Types of Problems and Decisions Do Managers Face?

- Structured problems → programmed decisions: usually lower-level managers
  - Policies, procedures, rules
- Unstructured problems → nonprogrammed decisions: usually top-level managers

## Under What Conditions Do Managers Make Decisions?

- **Certainty**: outcome of every alternative is known
- **Risk**: can estimate likelihood of certain outcomes
- **Uncertainty**: outcomes are not certain and cannot make reasonable probability estimates

## How Will Decision-Making Style Affect a Manager's Decision Making?

1. **Directive**: low tolerance for ambiguity and rational way of thinking
2. **Analytic**: high tolerance for ambiguity and rational way of thinking
3. **Conceptual**: high tolerance for ambiguity and intuitive way of thinking
4. **Behavioral**: low tolerance for ambiguity and intuitive way of thinking

## What Biases and Errors Affect Decision Making?

- Overconfidence
- Anchoring effect
- Confirmation
- Sunk costs
- Representation
- Self-serving
- Immediate gratification
- Selective perception
- Framing
- Availability
- Randomness
- Hindsight

## What Do Managers Need to Know About Making Decisions in Today's World?

- Understand cultural differences
- Know when it's time to call it quits
- Use an effective decision-making process
- Develop highly reliable organizations

# Management: By the Numbers

- Fifty-nine percent of employees in a survey by Sirota Survey Intelligence say that a key obstacle in their job is that more attention is given to placing blame than solving problems.
- In a survey of managers, 77 percent said that the number of decisions they made during a typical workday had increased. Also, 43 percent said that the amount of time given to each decision had decreased.

- The value of RPS (rock, paper, scissors) as a decision tiebreaking tool is more recognized in Asia than in the United States.

*Sources:* J. MacIntyre, "Bosses and Bureaucracy," *Springfield Business Journal,* August 1–7, 2005, p. 29; J. Crick, "Hand Jive," *Fortune,* June 13, 2005, pp. 40–41; and "Hurry Up and Decide!" *Business Week,* May 14, 2001, p. 16.

# Thinking About Management Issues

1. Why is decision making often described as the essence of a manager's job?
2. How might an organization's culture influence the way managers make decisions?
3. All of us bring biases to the decisions we make. What would be the drawbacks of having biases? Could there be any advantages to having biases? Explain. What are the implications for managerial decision making?
4. Would you call yourself a systematic or intuitive thinker? What are the decision-making implications of these labels? What are the implications for choosing where you want to work?

5. "As managers use computers and software tools more often, they'll be able to make more rational decisions." Do you agree or disagree with this statement? Why?
6. How can managers blend the guidelines for making effective decisions in today's world with the rationality and bounded rationality models of decision making, or can they? Explain.
7. Is there a difference between wrong decisions and bad decisions? Why do good managers sometimes make wrong decisions? Bad decisions? How can managers improve their decision-making skills?

# Working Together: Team-Based Exercise

Being effective in decision making is something that managers obviously want. What is involved with being a good decision maker? Form groups of three to four students. Discuss your experiences making decisions—for example, buying a car or some other major purchase, choosing classes and professors, making summer or spring break plans, and so forth. Each of you should share times when you felt you made good decisions. Analyze what happened during that decision-making process that contributed to it being a good decision. Then consider some decisions that you felt were bad. What happened to make them bad? What common characteristics, if any, did you identify among the good decisions? The bad decisions? Come up with a bulleted list of practical suggestions for making good decisions. As a group, be prepared to share your list with the class.

# Ethical Dilemma Exercise

Decisions involving billions of dollars are rarely programmed and structured—especially when the decision alternatives entail potential conflicts of interest. This was the situation facing Jon Bauman, executive director of the $34 billion Illinois Teachers Retirement System. Bauman wondered whether any fees were flowing between the professional money managers who handle his system's retirement funds and the consultants that provide advice and sell investments. Digging deeper, he says he "was surprised by the overall levels of payments that were going on between consultants and money managers."

Bauman found that two of his money managers were paying to license stock market indexes from Wilshire Associates and Russell Investment Group so they could compare the pension fund's performance with that of the market. He also knew that Wilshire and Russell not only license benchmark indexes, but they also sell a variety of investments. But were the payments actually influencing the consultants' advice or the money managers' investments? Because the Illinois Teachers Retirement System pays an independent pension consultant to provide expert advice—and because all fees were now being disclosed—Bauman decided that the payments were not a problem: Just because there is a potential for conflict does not mean there is an actual conflict.[32] Such decisions will remain on the management agenda as the Labor Department and the Securities and Exchange Commission continue investigating pension consultant deals.

Imagine you're Bauman's assistant at the Illinois Teachers Retirement System. To get the latest payment information, you've sent a questionnaire to the money managers and investment consultants working with your fund. One consultant refused to disclose any fees received, saying that the payments aren't relevant to what his company does for your fund. Review Exhibit 6–8 as you consider which of the following options you will choose, and why.

**Option A:** You send an anonymous note about the consultant to the Securities and Exchange Commission.

**Option B:** You ask the consultant to sign a sworn statement affirming that any payments received are irrelevant to the services being provided to your fund.

**Option C:** You recommend to Bauman that the fund stop doing business with any consultant that refuses to disclose fees.

# Case Application

## Fast Company

What comes to mind when you think of NASCAR? Fast cars, roaring engines, the smell of gasoline, beer-guzzling spectators? That's the image that Brian France, chairman and CEO, wanted to change. But will those changes keep the company on the fast track or cause a spin out?

NASCAR (National Association for Stock Car Auto Racing) was founded in 1948 by Brian's grandfather, "Big Bill" France Sr., as a place for ex-moonshine runners to show off their driving skills. During the early years, "Big Bill" tirelessly promoted the sport with the help of race-track owners who wanted to make their stock car races official. The sport grew rapidly in the 1950s and 1960s. Racetrack owners responded by upgrading their facilities and building new paved tracks to replace the older dirt tracks. In 1971, NASCAR signed R.J. Reynolds Tobacco Company as a major sponsor and held the first Winston 500 race in Talladega, Alabama. The first televised race—the Daytona 500—aired on CBS in 1979. Cable sports network ESPN began airing races in 1981. NBC, Fox, and TNT paid the company $2.4 billion for the NASCAR circuit's broadcasting rights from 2000 to 2006. Not surprisingly, TV viewership soared—its ratings have increased by more than 50 percent since signing the networks deal. From 2007 to 2014, Disney's ABC and ESPN, Fox, TNT, and the Speed Channel have paid $4.4 billion for broadcasting rights. The untimely deaths of drivers Adam Petty in 2000 and Dale Earnhardt in 2001 only served to heighten the appeal of the sport as exciting and dangerous.

Today, NASCAR continues to be one of the fastest-growing spectator sports in the United States. Sales of NASCAR-branded products have increased more than 250 percent over the last decade. NASCAR runs about 90 races a year in 25 states through three racing circuits: Busch, Craftsman Truck, and the Nextel Cup Series (formerly the Winston Cup). The Nextel Cup, with big-name drivers like Jeff Gordon, Dale Earnhardt Jr., Kyle Petty, and Michael Waltrip, alone draws more than 7 million race fans each year. Despite the company's success—as a private company, its revenues are estimated at over $3 billion—Brian realized that changes were necessary. The company's top management team had a goal of making the sport grow in a way that invigorates hard-core fans and makes it attractive to people who might want to sample racing." And making those changes hasn't been easy. It meant making decisions that balanced what's made the company successful and adapting to change.

What were some of these changes? A major one dealt with car and driver safety requirements, especially after the death of Dale Earnhardt. But does making the sport "safer" make it less appealing to the fans who come to experience vicariously in the stands or on television the speed, the danger, and the excitement of going really, really fast in a crowd of cars? Other changes the company made included more late-afternoon and night races and the addition of a foreign automaker, Toyota, to the Craftsman Truck series. And it's implemented a change in the points system whereby drivers' series rankings and

Brian France, chairman and CEO of NASCAR.

earnings are determined—something that hadn't changed since 1975.

Also, Brian decided that NASCAR had to go after new fans. Kyle Petty, a racing legend, feels that decision only makes sense. He said, "If NASCAR feels like they have the Southern white male segment of the market wrapped up, then where are they going to go? They're going to have to go after a Hispanic market. They're going to have to go after a black market. They're going to have to go after an upscale market." NASCAR's ability to do so not only impacts whether it can attract new fans but also affects its ability to attract new corporate sponsors and advertisers, important contributors to the company's revenues.

## Discussion Questions

1. How do you think good decision making has contributed to the success of NASCAR?

2. A decision to go after a new market as Brian is doing is a major decision. How could he have used the decision-making process to help make this decision?

3. What criteria do you think would be most important to Brian as he makes decisions about the company's future?

4. Would you characterize the conditions surrounding NASCAR as conditions of certainty, risk, or uncertainty? Explain your choice.

5. What could Brian learn from the concept of highly reliable organizations to help him be a better decision maker?

Sources: B. O'Keefe and J. Schlosser, "America's Fastest-Growing Sport," Fortune, September 5, 2005, pp. 48–64; E. Smith, "NASCAR Courts Minorities," Wall Street Journal, March 3, 2005, pp. B1+; M. Benjamin, "Life in the Fast Lane," US News & World Report, November 22, 2004, pp. 64–66; T. Lowry, "The Prince of NASCAR," Business Week, www.businessweek.com, February 23, 2004; R. Underwood, "Joe Redneck, Meet Eustace Tilly," Fast Company, December 2003, p. 36; and C. Jenkins, "The Changing Face of NASCAR," USA Today, August 29, 2003, pp. 1E+.

# Learning Outline

*Use this Learning Outline as you read and study this chapter.*

### What Is Planning and Why Do Managers Plan?

- Define planning.
- Differentiate between formal and informal planning.
- Describe the purposes of planning.
- Discuss the conclusions from studies of the relationship between planning and performance.

### How Do Managers Plan?

- Define goals and plans.
- Describe the types of goals organizations might have.
- Explain why it's important to know an organization's stated and real goals.
- Describe each of the different types of plans.

### Establishing Goals and Developing Plans

- Discuss how traditional goal setting works.
- Explain the concept of the means–end chain.
- Describe the management by objectives (MBO) approach.
- Describe the characteristics of well-designed goals.
- Explain the steps in setting goals.
- Discuss the contingency factors that affect planning.
- Describe the approaches to planning.

### Contemporary Issues in Planning

- Explain the criticisms of planning and whether they're valid.
- Describe how managers can effectively plan in today's dynamic environment.

# Foundations of Planning

## A Manager's Dilemma

In war-torn economies of countries such as Afghanistan, Bosnia, and Herzegovina, microfinance has provided much-needed assistance to entrepreneurs and small businesses. *Microfinance* is the lending of small sums to poor people who would otherwise be shut out of access to capital. In the northeastern Bosnian village of Zivinice, Edina Bukvic is using microfinance to pursue a childhood dream of making wedding dresses like the ones she used to see in magazines.[1]

Edina's capital funding to start her business came from an initial $900 6-month loan at 36 percent interest from a nonprofit group called Mi-Bospo. Mi-Bospo is a part of Women's World Banking (WWB), a global nonprofit network of lenders and banks that work with women in Third World and developing countries. On Mi-Bospo's Web site, it states its purpose as "economically empowering the woman because an economically empowered woman can better influence social change and contribute to the better quality of life for her family." Without her much-needed loan, Edina probably would still be working nights in a restaurant that she and her husband own. But now she doesn't have to work nights or weekends and usually has her shop open from 10 A.M. to 2 P.M., giving her more time to spend with her two daughters. Edina says, "I love what I'm doing. I have more time for myself and my family now." And she is making more money as well, netting almost $10,000 a year.

With her loan, Edina started out making the wedding dresses herself, but now finds it easier to buy them. Her inventory of 40 dresses gives customers several choices. And paying a rental fee of only $100 is a lot less expensive for the brides-to-be as well. But Edina has plans for the future. She would like an even bigger business and wants to turn the restaurant they own into a large dress store with windows. She says, "It would be the only wedding dress shop in the Zivinice region." Edina has obtained another $7,000 2-year loan to buy 25 dresses from a wedding shop owner in western Bosnia who is selling out.

Put yourself in Edina's position. What types of plans might she need to guide her business as it grows?

## What would you do?

Like Edina Bukvic, managers in all organizations everywhere need to plan. In this chapter we present the basics of planning: what it is, why managers plan, and how they plan. Then we'll finish the chapter by looking at some contemporary issues in planning.

## WHAT IS PLANNING?

Harley-Davidson is known worldwide for its motorcycles—the Fat Boy, Electra Glide, Deuce, and Night Train are among its most popular models. However, demand for some of these popular models continues to exceed supply, forcing some customers to wait for delivery. In addition, company executives believe that the demand for its motorcycles will continue to grow in the range of 7 percent to 9 percent per year.[2] Although that may seem like a nice problem to have, what happens if customers get upset enough to buy from a competitor? Should the managers have planned better? Recognizing that this situation was creating problems, Harley executives now plan to continue expanding production capacity.

As we stated in Chapter 1, **planning** involves defining the organization's goals, establishing an overall strategy for achieving those goals, and developing plans for organizational work activities. It's concerned with both ends (what's to be done) and means (how it's to be done).

Planning can either be formal or informal. All managers plan, although that planning might be informal. In informal planning, nothing is written down, and there is little or no sharing of goals with others in the organization. Also, informal planning is general and lacks continuity. (  Go to www.prenhall.com/rolls) Although it's more common in smaller organizations, informal planning does exist in some large organizations as well. And, some small businesses may have detailed planning processes and formal plans.

When we use the term *planning* in this book, we do mean *formal* planning. In formal planning, specific goals covering a period of years are defined. These goals are written and shared with organizational members to reduce ambiguity and create a common understanding about what needs to be done. Finally, specific action plans exist for achieving these goals; that is, managers define how the goals will be reached. (  Go to www.prenhall.com/rolls)

*O'Reilly Auto Parts of Springfield, Missouri, has grown from a single store founded in 1957 to over 1,400 locations. Its management team, pictured here, intends to continue that pattern of growth with the best possible combination of price, quality, and service, and with pay and benefits to attract the right kind of employees. Achieving these goals will require a great deal of formal planning to provide direction, minimize waste and error, and set standards of performance.*

## WHY DO MANAGERS PLAN?

Setting goals, establishing strategies to achieve those goals, and developing a set of plans that integrate and coordinate activities seem pretty complicated. Given that fact, why should managers plan? What impact does planning have on performance?

### Purposes of Planning

We can identify at least four reasons why managers need to plan. First, planning *provides direction* to managers and nonmanagers alike. When employees know what their organization or work unit is trying to accomplish and what they must contribute to reach goals, they can coordinate their activities, cooperate with each other, and do what it takes to accomplish those goals. Without planning, departments and individuals might work at cross-purposes, preventing the organization from moving efficiently toward its goals.

Next, planning *reduces uncertainty* by forcing managers to look ahead, anticipate change, consider the impact of change, and develop appropriate responses. Even though planning can't eliminate change or uncertainty, managers plan in order to anticipate change and to develop the most effective response to it.

In addition, planning *minimizes waste and redundancy*. When work activities are coordinated around established plans, redundancy can be minimized. Furthermore, when means and ends are made clear through planning, inefficiencies become obvious and can be corrected or eliminated.

Finally, planning *establishes the goals or standards used in controlling*. If we're unsure of what we're trying to accomplish, how can we determine whether we've actually done so? When managers plan, they develop goals and plans. When they control, they see whether the plans have been carried out and the goals met. Without planning, there would be no way to control.

### Planning and Performance

Q & A
Can a manager do too much planning? See Q & A 7.2.

Is planning worthwhile? Do managers and organizations that plan outperform those that don't? Intuitively, you would expect the answer to be a resounding yes. Numerous studies have looked at the relationship between planning and performance.[3] Although most studies showed generally positive relationships, we can't say that organizations that formally plan *always* outperform those that don't plan. ( ◆ Go to www.prenhall.com/rolls) What *can* we conclude from these studies?

First, generally speaking, formal planning is associated with positive financial results such as higher profits, higher return on assets, and so forth. Second, it seems that doing a good job of planning and implementing those plans play a bigger part in high performance than does the extent and amount of planning done. Next, in those studies where formal planning didn't lead to higher performance, the external environment often was the culprit. Critical environmental forces such as governmental regulations and powerful labor unions often constrain managers' options and reduce the impact of planning on an organization's performance. Finally, the planning/performance relationship seems to be influenced by the planning time frame; that is, organizations seem to need at least four years of systematic formal planning before seeing any impact on performance.

**planning**
Defining the organization's goals, establishing an overall strategy for achieving those goals, and developing plans for organizational work activities.

## Learning Review

- Define planning.
- Differentiate between formal and informal planning.

- Describe the purposes of planning.
- Discuss the conclusions from studies of the relationship between planning and performance.

## HOW DO MANAGERS PLAN?

Planning is often called the primary management function because it establishes the basis for all the other things that managers do. Without planning, managers wouldn't know what to organize, lead, or control. In fact, without plans, there wouldn't *be* anything to organize, lead, or control! So how *do* managers plan? That's what we want to look at in this section.

### The Role of Goals and Plans in Planning

Planning involves two important elements: goals and plans. **Goals** are desired outcomes for individuals, groups, or entire organizations.[4] They're also called *objectives*, and we use the two terms interchangeably. They guide all management decisions and form the criterion against which actual work being done is measured. That's why they're often called the *foundation* of planning. And you have to know the desired target or outcome before you can establish plans for reaching it.

**Plans** are documents that outline how goals are going to be met. The plans usually include resource allocations, schedules, and other necessary actions to accomplish the goals. As managers plan, they're developing both goals and plans.

**Types of Goals**  At first glance, it might appear that organizations have a single objective—for business firms, the goal is to make a profit; for not-for-profit organizations, the goal is to meet the needs of some constituent group(s). In reality, all organizations have multiple goals. For instance, businesses also want to increase market share and keep employees enthused about working for the organization. A church provides a place for religious practices, but also assists economically disadvantaged individuals in its community and acts as a social gathering place for church members. As you can see, no single goal can be used to evaluate whether an organization is successful. (  Go to www.prenhall.com/rolls) If managers emphasize one goal, such as profit, other goals that must also be met to achieve long-term success are ignored. Also, as we discussed in Chapter 5, using a single objective such as profit can result in unethical practices because managers and employees will ignore other important parts of their jobs in order to look good on that one measure.[5]

**Q & A**

If businesses only have one goal, that must mean they don't need other goals, correct? Q & A 7.3 will explain why that's not true.

Goals are the outcomes we desire. At the Bronx Zoo, Patrick Thomas, curator of mammals, recently gazed into the eyes of Siberian tiger "Taurus" through a sheet of inch-thick glass "Our goal is to have animals engaged in normal behaviors," Thomas states. Thomas goes on to say of the tiger habitat, "You want the exhibit to inspire visitors to care about saving tigers." The goal of the 3-acre Tiger Mountain is particularly important; its six residents represent the mere 5,000 tigers left in the wild.

What types of goals do companies pursue? Most company's goals can be classified as either strategic or financial. Financial goals are related to the financial performance of the organization while strategic goals are related to other areas of an organization's performance. Examples of both financial and strategic goals from some well-known companies are shown in Exhibit 7–1. Some of these goals could apply to a not-for-profit organization as well. Note, too, that although survival isn't specifically mentioned as a goal, it's important to all organizations. An organization must survive if other goals are to be achieved.

Another way to describe goals is in terms of whether they're real or stated. Exhibit 7–1 is a list of **stated goals**—official statements of what an organization says, and what it wants its stakeholders to believe, its goals are. However, stated goals—which can be found in an organization's charter, annual report, public relations announcements, or in public statements made by managers—are often conflicting and excessively influenced by what society believes organizations should do. (◆ Go to www.prenhall.com/rolls)

**Q & A**

Stated goals make it sound like organizations don't want to tell people their real intentions, which seems deceitful. Check out Q & A 7.4 for a discussion.

Exhibit 7–1

**Stated Goals of Large Global Companies**

---

Execute strategic roadmap—"Plan to Win."
Grow the business profitably.
Identify and develop diverse talent.
Promote balanced, active lifestyles.
(McDonald's Corporation)

Continue to win market share globally.
Focus on higher-value products.
Reduce production costs.
Lower purchasing costs.
Integrate diversity.
Gain ISO 14001 certification for all factories.
(L'Oreal)

Respect the environment.
Respect and support family unity and national traditions.
Promote community welfare.
Continue implementing quality systems.
Continue to be a strong cash generator.
(Grupo Bimbo)

Control inventory.
Maintain industry's lowest inventory shrinkage rate.
Open 25–30 new locations in fiscal 2006.
Live by the code of ethics every day.
(Costco)

Expand selection of competitively priced products.
Manage inventory carefully.
Continue to improve store format every few years.
Operate 2,000 stores by the end of the decade.
Continue gaining market share.
(Target)

Roll out newly-designed environmentally friendly cup in 2006.
Open approximately 1,800 new stores globally in 2006.
Attain net revenue growth of approximately 20 percent in 2006.
Attain annual EPS growth of between 20 percent to 25 percent for the next 3 to 5 years.
(Starbucks)

*Source:* Information from company's *Annual Reports,* 2004–2005.

---

**goals**
Desired outcomes for individuals, groups, or entire organizations.

**plans**
Documents that outline how goals are going to be met.

**stated goals**
Official statements of what an organization says, and what it wants its various stakeholders to believe, its goals are.

## focus on Leadership

### Knowing What's Important: How Leaders Frame Issues

Antonio Villaraigosa, the first Latino mayor of Los Angeles in more than a century, blends the "idealism of the 1960s, when all things seemed possible, with the realism of the twenty-first century, when it's clearer what *is* possible." He has pledged to plant 1 million trees, to start building a subway to the ocean, and to take over the city's ineffective school system, in which almost 60 percent of Latinos and 50 percent of African Americans drop out.[9] Although he is guided by what's in his heart, gut, and head, he understands reality. What Villaraigosa does well is *frame* the issues in such a way that others can see it the way he sees it.

**Framing** is a way to use language to manage meaning. It's a way for leaders to influence how events are seen and understood. It involves selecting and highlighting one or more aspects of a subject while excluding others. Framing is similar to what a good photographer does. When a photographer aims a camera and focuses on a specific shot, she frames the photo. Others then see what she wants them to see. They see her point of view. That is precisely what leaders do when they frame an issue. They choose which aspects or portions of the subject they want others to focus on and which portions they want excluded.

Why is framing relevant to leaders today? Because in a complex and turbulent environment, what a leader chooses to say is important. Leaders can use language to influence followers' perceptions of the world, the meaning of events, beliefs about causes and consequences, and visions of the future. It's through framing that leaders determine whether people notice problems, how they understand and remember problems, and how they react to problems. It's a powerful tool by which leaders influence how others see and interpret reality.

The conflict in stated goals exists because organizations respond to a variety of stakeholders. And these stakeholders frequently evaluate the organization by different criteria. For example, when Bill Ford Jr., chairman of Ford Motor Company, announced the goal of making its vehicles more fuel efficient and more environmentally friendly as a way to best serve its customers and shareholders, environmentalists and Ford executives viewed it differently.[6] The company reached out to environmental groups by initiating discussions on fuel economy issues. It also released a report on the business impact of climate change in which it said, "We know that many of our stakeholders expect this report to spell out specific targets and milestones for improvements in the fleet fuel efficiency of our products. It will not do that. In our highly competitive industry, there continues to be too wide a range of possible futures for technologies, markets, and regulatory frameworks for our company to set unilateral targets on the in-use performance of our products. Nevertheless, Ford Motor Company is committed to doing its part." Environmentalists, although encouraged by the company's concern, continued to be wary of Ford's ultimate intent. In the same report, Ford states, "We develop, produce, and market vehicles for retail customers. Our viability as a business depends above all on offering products and services that customers will buy." And it seems that the U.S. market shows that few customers choose cars based on specific concerns about climate change. Even fewer are willing to pay the incremental cost of "green" automotive technologies or accept trade-offs of other attributes (safety, performance, features, styling). Ford executives are well aware of the need to produce vehicles that the public demands and that add dollars to the bottom line. Was the goal of being more environmentally friendly true and the goal of doing the best for its customers and ultimately its shareholders false? No. Both were true, but they did conflict.

Have you ever read an organization's goals as stated in its company literature? For instance, Claire's Stores' goal is "to continue expanding our brand strength and proven formula across North America, Europe, and Japan." Nike's goal is "to bring inspiration and innovation to every athlete." Canadian company EnCana's vision is "to be the world's high performance benchmark independent oil and gas company." Winnebago's goal is "to continually improve products and services to meet or exceed the expectations of our customers." And Deutsche Bank's goal is "to be the leading global provider of financial solutions for demanding clients creating exceptional value for our shareholders and people."[7] These types of statements are usually vague and more likely to represent management's public relations skills than being meaningful guides to what the organization is actually trying to accomplish. It shouldn't be surprising then to find that an organization's stated goals are often quite irrelevant to what actually goes on.[8] Such goals are substantially determined by what various stakeholders want to hear. If you want to know an organization's **real goals**— those goals that an organization actually pursues—observe what organizational members are doing. Actions define priorities. For example, universities that proclaim the goal of limiting class size, facilitating close student–faculty relations, and actively involving students in the learning process and then put them into lecture classes of 300 or more are pretty common. An awareness that real and stated goals differ is important for understanding what might otherwise seem to be management inconsistencies. ( Go to www.prenhall.com/rolls)

**Types of Plans** The most popular ways to describe organizational plans are by their breadth (strategic versus operational), time frame (short term versus long term), specificity (directional versus specific), and frequency of use (single-use versus standing). These planning classifications aren't independent. As Exhibit 7–2 illustrates, strategic plans are long term, directional, and single use. Operational plans are short term, specific, and standing. Let's describe each of these types of plans.

**Strategic plans** are plans that apply to the entire organization, establish the organization's overall goals, and seek to position the organization in terms of its environment. Plans that specify the details of how the overall goals are to be achieved are called **operational plans**. How do the two types of plans differ? Strategic plans tend to cover a longer time frame and a broader view of the organization. Strategic plans also include the formulation of goals whereas operational plans define ways to achieve the goals. Also, operational plans tend to cover shorter time periods—monthly, weekly, and day-to-day.

The difference in years between short term and long term has decreased considerably. Long-term used to mean anything over seven years. Try to imagine what you're likely to be doing in seven years and you can begin to appreciate how difficult it was for managers to establish plans that far in the future. As organizational environments have become more uncertain, the definition of *long term* has changed. We define **long-term plans** as those with a time frame beyond three years.[10] We define **short-term plans** as

Exhibit 7–2 **Types of Plans**

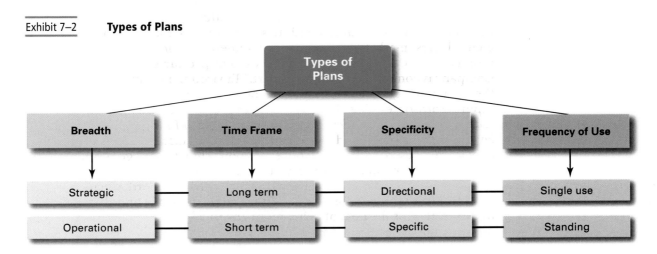

---

**framing**
A way to use language to manage meaning.

**real goals**
Goals that an organization actually pursues, as defined by the actions of its members.

**strategic plans**
Plans that apply to the entire organization, establish the organization's overall goals, and seek to position the organization in terms of its environment.

**operational plans**
Plans that specify the details of how the overall goals are to be achieved.

**long-term plans**
Plans with a time frame beyond 3 years.

**short-term plans**
Plans covering 1 year or less.

*When the founders of Blue Man Group, a 3-man band/performance troupe, decided they were ready to expand by hiring performers to do Blue Man shows around the country, they were eager to keep the acts consistent with their original vision. They finally realized they needed a specific plan to guide the 38 new performers they were bringing on board, so they locked themselves in an apartment and talked through their creative vision in great detail. The result? A 132-page operating manual that tells the story of the Blue Man show and allows it to be reproduced by others. Ironically, by writing the plan, though it is a somewhat unorthodox one, the founders were able to express artistic ideals that had been understood among them but never stated.*

those covering one year or less. The intermediate term is any time period in between. Although these time classifications are fairly common, an organization can designate any time frame it wants for planning purposes.

Intuitively, it would seem that specific plans would be preferable to directional, or loosely guided, plans. **Specific plans** are plans that are clearly defined and that leave no room for interpretation. They have clearly defined objectives. There's no ambiguity and no problem with misunderstanding. For example, a manager who seeks to increase his or her unit's work output by 8 percent over a given 12-month period might establish specific procedures, budget allocations, and schedules of activities to reach that goal. The drawbacks of specific plans are that they require clarity and a sense of predictability that often do not exist.

When uncertainty is high and managers must be flexible in order to respond to unexpected changes, directional plans are preferable. **Directional plans** are flexible plans that set out general guidelines. (Exhibit 7–3 illustrates how specific and directional plans differ.) They provide focus but don't lock managers into specific goals or courses of action. For example, Sylvia Rhone, president of Motown Records says she has a simple goal—to "sign great artists."[11] So instead of creating a specific plan to produce and market 10 albums from new artists this year, she might formulate a directional plan to use a network of people around the world to alert her to new and promising talent so she can increase the number of new artists she has under contract. Keep in mind, however, that the flexibility inherent in directional plans must be weighed against the loss of clarity provided by specific plans.

Some plans that managers develop are ongoing while others are used only once. A **single-use plan** is a one-time plan specifically designed to meet the needs of a unique situation. For instance, when Wal-Mart decided to drastically expand the number of its

Exhibit 7–3

**Specific Versus Directional Plans**

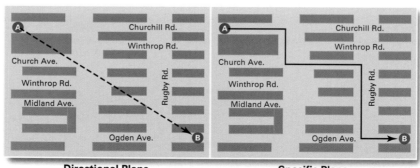

**Directional Plans**          **Specific Plans**

**Q & A**
Sometimes it seems like organizations have way too many rules and procedures. Why? Q & A 7.5 provides some answers.

stores in China, top-level executives formulated a single-use plan as a guide. In contrast, **standing plans** are ongoing plans that provide guidance for activities performed repeatedly. Standing plans include policies, rules, and procedures that we defined in Chapter 6. ( ◆ Go to www.prenhall.com/rolls) An example of a standing plan is the sexual harassment policy developed by the University of Arizona. It provides guidance to university administrators, faculty, and staff as they do their jobs.

## Learning Review

- Define goals and plans.
- Describe the types of goals organizations might have.

- Explain why it's important to know an organization's stated and real goals.
- Describe each of the different types of plans.

## ESTABLISHING GOALS AND DEVELOPING PLANS

Taylor Luttrell-Deeds has just been elected president of her business school's honorary fraternity. She wants the organization to be more actively involved in the business school than it has been in the past. Francisco Garza graduated from Tecnologico de Monterrey with a degree in marketing and computers three years ago and went to work for a regional consulting services firm. He recently was promoted to manager of an eight-person e-business development team and hopes to strengthen the team's financial contributions to the firm. What should Taylor and Francisco do now? The first thing is to establish goals. How? That's what we're going to look at in this section.

### Approaches to Establishing Goals

As we stated earlier, goals provide the direction for all management decisions and actions and form the criteria against which actual accomplishments are measured. Everything organizational members do should be oriented toward helping their work units and helping the organization achieve the goals. These goals can be established through a process of traditional goal setting or management by objectives.

In **traditional goal setting**, goals are set at the top of the organization and then broken into subgoals for each organizational level. For example, the president of a manufacturing business tells the vice president of production what he expects manufacturing costs to be for the coming year and tells the marketing vice president what level he expects sales to reach for the year. These goals then are passed down to the next organizational level and written to reflect the work responsibilities of that level, passed down to the next level, and so forth. Then, at some later point, performance is evaluated to determine whether the assigned goals have been achieved. This traditional perspective assumes that top managers know what's best because they see the "big picture." Thus, the goals that are established and passed down to each succeeding level serve to direct, guide, and, in some ways, constrain individual employees' work behaviors. Employees work to meet the goals that have been assigned in their areas of responsibility. Or that's the structured, logical way it's supposed to happen. But in reality, it doesn't always happen that easily. Translating corporate goals into departmental, team, and ultimately individual objectives is difficult and potentially expensive, particularly for large global corporations.[12] For instance, at Seagate Technology, the California-based computer hard-disk drive manufacturer, executive vice president and CFO Charles Pope led an effort to find a way to align employee goals with company goals.

---

**specific plans**
Plans that are clearly defined and that leave no room for interpretation.

**directional plans**
Plans that are flexible and that set out general guidelines.

**single-use plan**
A one-time plan specifically designed to meet the needs of a unique situation.

**standing plans**
Ongoing plans that provide guidance for activities performed repeatedly.

**traditional goal setting**
An approach to setting goals in which goals are set at the top level of the organization and then broken into subgoals for each level of the organization.

Exhibit 7–4

**The Downside of Traditional Goal Setting**

"We need to improve the company's performance."

"I want to see a significant improvement in this division's profits."

Top Management's Objective

"Increase profits regardless of the means."

Division Manager's Objective

"Don't worry about quality; just work fast."

Department Manager's Objective

Individual Employee's Objective

Q & A

So what can go wrong when goals are "passed down" from level to level in an organization? See Q & A 7.6.

Another problem with this traditional approach is that if top managers define the organization's goals in broad terms—achieving "sufficient" profits or increasing "market leadership"—these ambiguous goals have to be made more specific as they flow down through the organization. At each level, managers define the goals, applying their own interpretations and biases as they make them more specific. However, what often happens is that goals lose clarity and unity as they make their way down from the top of the organization to lower levels. Exhibit 7–4 illustrates what can happen in this situation. ( Go to www.prenhall.com/rolls) But this doesn't have to happen. For example, at Tijuana-based dj Orthopedics de Mexico, employee teams see the impact of their daily work output on company goals. Says human resource manager Joaquin Samaniego, "When people get a close connection with the result of their work, when they every day know what they are supposed to do and how they achieved the goals, that makes a strong connection with the company and their job."[13]

When the hierarchy of organizational goals *is* clearly defined, as it is at dj Orthopedics, it forms an integrated network of goals, or a **means–ends chain**. This means that higher-level goals (or ends) are linked to lower-level goals, which serve as the means for their accomplishment. In other words, the achievement of goals at lower levels becomes the means to reach the goals at the next level (ends). The accomplishment of goals at that level becomes the means to achieve the goals at the next level (ends), and so forth and so on, up through the different levels of the organization. That's how the traditional goal setting approach is supposed to work.

Instead of traditional goal setting, many organizations use **management by objectives (MBO)**, a process of setting mutually agreed-upon goals and using those goals to evaluate employee performance. In MBO, specific performance goals are jointly

The goal of Prairie Stone Pharmacy is to use automation to free workers from the routine aspects of their jobs, speeding work and saving costs, and more importantly, allowing its pharmacists to spend time on the actual practice of pharmacy, advising customers about the use and interaction of drugs.

**Exhibit 7–5**

**Steps in a Typical MBO Program**

1. The organization's *overall objectives and strategies* are formulated.
2. Major objectives are allocated among *divisional and departmental units.*
3. Unit managers *collaboratively set specific objectives* for their units with their managers.
4. Specific objectives are collaboratively set with *all department members.*
5. *Action plans,* defining how objectives are to be achieved, are specified and agreed upon by managers and employees.
6. The action plans are *implemented.*
7. Progress toward objectives is *periodically reviewed,* and *feedback is provided.*
8. Successful achievement of objectives is reinforced by *performance-based rewards.*

determined by employees and their managers, progress toward accomplishing these goals is periodically reviewed, and rewards are allocated on the basis of this progress. Rather than using goals only as controls to make sure employees are doing what they're supposed to be doing, MBO uses them to motivate employees as well.

MBO programs have four elements: goal specificity, participative decision making, an explicit time period, and performance feedback.[14] The appeal of MBO is that it focuses on employees working to accomplish goals they've had a hand in determining. Exhibit 7–5 lists the steps in a typical MBO program.

Does MBO work? Studies of actual MBO programs have shown that it can increase employee performance and organizational productivity. For example, one review of 70 MBO programs found productivity gains in 68 of them.[15] But how relevant are MBO approaches for today's organizations? If we view MBO as a way of setting goals, then research does show that goal setting can be a highly effective approach to motivating employees.[16] (We'll study goal-setting theory extensively in Chapter 16.) However, there are some challenges that managers who might want to use MBO need to address.

One problem is that MBO may not be as effective in times of dynamic environmental change. Under an MBO program, employees need some stability to work toward accomplishing the set goals. If new goals must be set every few weeks, there's no time for employees to work on accomplishing the goals and measuring that accomplishment. Another problem of MBO programs is that an overemphasis by an employee on accomplishing his or her goals without regard to others in the work unit can be counterproductive. A manager must work closely with all members of the work unit to assure that employees aren't working at cross-purposes. Finally, if MBO is viewed simply as an annual exercise in filling out paperwork, employees won't be motivated to accomplish the goals. (  Go to www.prenhall.com/rolls)

**Q & A**

An MBO approach sounds ideal. So what problems could there possibly be? Go to Q & A 7.7 to see.

**Characteristics of Well-Designed Goals** Goals are not all created equal. Some goals are better at stating desired outcomes than others are. How do you tell the difference? What makes a "well-designed" goal?[17] Exhibit 7–6 outlines the characteristics of well-designed goals.

A well-designed goal should be *written in terms of outcomes* rather than actions. The desired end result is the most important element of any goal and the goal should be

**Exhibit 7–6**

**Characteristics of Well-Designed Goals**

- Written in terms of outcomes rather than actions
- Measurable and quantifiable
- Clear as to a time frame
- Challenging yet attainable
- Written down
- Communicated to all necessary organizational members

**means–ends chain**
An integrated network of goals in which the accomplishment of goals at one level serves as the means for achieving the goals, or ends, at the next level.

**management by objectives (MBO)**
A process of setting mutually agreed-upon goals and using those goals to evaluate employee performance.

written to reflect this. Next, a goal should be *measurable and quantifiable.* It's much easier to determine if a goal has been met if it's measurable. For instance, suppose one of your goals is "to produce a high-quality product." What exactly do you mean by high quality? Because you can define quality in a number of ways, the goal should state specifically how you will measure whether the product is high quality. This means that even in areas where it may be difficult to quantify your intent, you should try to find some specific way or ways to measure whether that goal is accomplished. Otherwise, why have the goal if you can't measure whether it's been met? In addition to specifying a quantifiable measure of accomplishment, a well-designed goal should also be *clear as to a time frame.* Although open-ended goals may seem preferable because of their flexibility, in fact, goals without a time frame make an organization less flexible because you're never sure when the goal has been met or when you should call it quits because the goal will never be met regardless of how long you work at it. A well-designed goal will specify a time frame for meeting it. Next, a well-designed goal should be *challenging but attainable.* Goals that are too easy to accomplish are not motivating and neither are goals that are not attainable even with exceptional effort. Next, well-designed goals should be *written down.* Although actually writing down goals may seem

# Managers *speak out*

**Jerry Englert**

**Working Chairman,
Bank of Internet USA,
San Diego, CA**

*Describe your job.*

I am a working chairman of a high-tech Internet bank. My responsibilities give me the ultimate management control of all facets of the bank's operation and direction. Most of my time is spent on future projects and growth. My areas of direct involvement are strategic planning, business planning, technology, and corporate culture and team development. We are continuously looking at new technologies, market opportunities, and merger and acquisition opportunities

*How important are goals to what you do?*

Goals have many names in the business world. Here are just a few: Business plan. Strategic plan. Logistic plan. And the most important one, PROFITS.

I have seen many a business fail with defined goals. But, I have never seen one succeed without a realistic, attainable set of goals.

Goals serve as the corporate and personal scoreboard. Realistic goals are the scoreboard used to measure all facets of the business, including one's personal development.

For example, if an unattainable business plan is developed—one which predicts margins that are not obtainable, impossibly high revenue predictions, too low manufacturing costs, and other items that are not realistic—the managers who have the job of meeting these goals cannot win if the goals are unattainable. They have been given an impossible task. The result

of those bad goals ripples through the complete organization—top to bottom.

*What challenges do you think managers face when trying to build a plan?*

Here are some:

- Not making the effort to understand all the issues.
- Knowing the in and outs of the product, market, costs, and people involved when carrying out the assignment.
- Not getting the people who will execute the plan involved in the development of the plan. Good planners will have their team buy into the plan, so it becomes "our" plan. This is a major challenge, as it requires superb people skills and it can be the hardest ingredient to find in a good planner.
- Another difficult challenge a planner faces is not having a vision of the completed plan. Not looking forward enough. Not understanding that there will be competition and pricing pressure adjustments that need to be put in the plan. Not anticipating personnel changes. In other words, simply not properly anticipating the life cycle of the plan or the product or service within the plan.

*What skills do managers need to be effective in today's environment?*

Work ethic. Lead by example in the type and amount of effort put forth.

People skills.

Good manners.

Computer skills.

Consistency in actions and deeds.

too time-consuming, the process of writing the goals forces people to think them through. In addition, the written goals become visible and tangible evidence of the importance of working toward something. Finally, well-designed goals are *communicated to all organizational members* who need to know the goals. Why? Making people aware of the goals ensures that they're all "on the same page" and working in ways to ensure the accomplishment of the organizational goals.

**Steps in Goal Setting**  What steps should managers follow in setting goals? The goal-setting process consists of five steps.

1. *Review the organization's* **mission**, *the purpose of an organization.* These broad statements of what the organization's purpose is and what it hopes to accomplish provide an overall guide to what organizational members think is important. (We'll look more closely at organizational mission in Chapter 8.) It's important to review these statements before writing goals because the goals should reflect the intent of the company's mission.

2. *Evaluate available resources.* You don't want to set goals that are impossible to achieve given your available resources. Even though goals should be challenging, they should be realistic. After all, if the resources you have to work with won't allow you to achieve a goal no matter how hard you try or how much effort is exerted, that goal shouldn't be set. That would be like the person with a $50,000 annual income and no other financial resources setting a goal of building an investment portfolio worth $1 million in 3 years. No matter how hard he or she works at it, it's not going to happen.

3. *Determine the goals individually or with input from others.* These goals reflect desired outcomes and should be congruent with the organizational mission and goals in other organizational areas. These goals should be measurable, specific, and include a time frame for accomplishment.

4. *Write down the goals and communicate them to all who need to know.* We've already explained the benefit of writing down and communicating goals.

5. *Review results and whether goals are being met.* If goals aren't being met, make changes to the goals, as needed.

Once the goals have been established, written down, and communicated, a manager is ready to develop plans for pursuing the goals.

## Developing Plans

The process of developing plans is influenced by three contingency factors and by the planning approach followed.

**Contingency Factors in Planning**  Look back at our chapter-opening manager's dilemma. How will Edina know what types of plans to develop for guiding her business as it grows? Will strategic or operational plans be needed? How about specific or directional plans? In some situations, long-term plans make sense; in others, they do not. What are these situations? Three contingency factors affect planning: level in the organization, degree of environmental uncertainty, and length of future commitments.[18]

Exhibit 7–7 shows the relationship between a manager's level in the organization and the type of planning done. For the most part, lower-level managers mostly do operational planning while upper-level managers mostly do strategic planning.

**mission**
The purpose of an organization.

Exhibit 7–7

**Planning in the Hierarchy of Organizations**

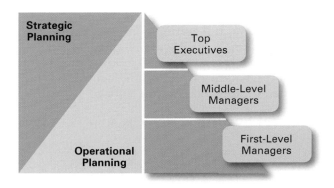

Self-Assessment
Library (S.A.L.)

How good are you at coping with
uncertainty? Do S.A.L. #I.A.4 and
find out!

The second contingency factor that affects planning is environmental uncertainty. When environmental uncertainty is high, plans should be specific, but flexible. Managers must be prepared to change or amend plans as they're implemented. (  Go to www.prenhall.com/rolls) At times, managers may even have to abandon their plans.[19] For example, at Continental Airlines, now-retired CEO Gordon M. Bethune and his management team established a specific goal of focusing on what customers wanted most—on-time flights—to help the company become more competitive in the highly uncertain airline industry. Because of the high level of uncertainty, the management team identified a destination, but not a flight plan, and changed plans as necessary to achieve that goal of on-time service. During periods of environmental uncertainty, it's important for managers to continue formal planning efforts because studies have shown that it takes at least four years of such efforts before any positive impact on organizational performance is seen.[20]

The last contingency factor affecting planning also is related to the time frame of plans. The more that current plans affect future commitments, the longer the time frame is for which managers should plan. This **commitment concept** means that plans should extend far enough to meet those commitments made when the plans were developed. Planning for too long or too short a time period is inefficient and ineffective. To see how important the commitment concept is to planning, just look at the data centers where companies' computers are housed. Many are finding that their "power-hungry computers" are creating significant problems. For instance, at Pomona Valley Medical Center the expansion from 30 servers to 70 servers generated so much heat that its data center's air-conditioning system was overwhelmed. At San Antonio–based Rackspace Ltd., which manages servers for clients, utility power needs have swelled from 3 to 8 megawatts, sending its electric bill soaring. And at the Department of Energy's National Energy Research Computing Center, providing adequate power for its supercomputer meant digging up a parking lot in order to knock a hole in a basement wall to install locomotive-sized power sources and air-conditioning units.[21] How does this illustrate the commitment concept? As organizations expand and update their computing technology, they're "committed" to whatever future expenses are generated by that plan. They have to live with the decision and plan for all its consequences, good and bad.

**Approaches to Planning** Federal, state, and local government officials are working together on a plan to boost populations of wild salmon in the northwestern United States. Managers in the Global Fleet Graphics division of the 3M Company are developing plans detailing innovative solutions for satisfying increasingly demanding customers and battling more aggressive competitors. Emilio Azcárraga Jean, chairman, president, and CEO of Grupo Televisa, the Mexican broadcasting company, gets input from many different people before setting company goals and then turns over the planning for achieving the goals to various executives. In each of these situations, planning is done a little differently. *How* an organization plans can best be understood by looking at *who* does the planning. (  Check out Passport Scenario 2 on page 260.)

Passport

How do managers plan and set
goals when they're dealing with
different global locations? Try this
global exercise and see!

## *thinking critically about* Ethics

As companies prepare plans to keep their businesses operating if a bird flu pandemic hits, thorny issues are arising. For instance, Procter & Gamble "asked its company doctors whether it should try to secure a private stash of the avian-influenza drug Tamiflu for its staff in Asia." The company's medical leader in southern Asia said, "How ethical would it be if we were holding supplies that the general public didn't have access to but badly needed?"[22] What do you think? Would it be unethical for a company to protect its own employees? Why or why not? What other alternatives might there be?

In the traditional approach, planning was done entirely by top-level managers who were often assisted by a **formal planning department**, a group of planning specialists whose sole responsibility was helping to write the various organizational plans. Under this approach, plans developed by top-level managers flowed down through other organizational levels, much like the traditional approach to goal setting. As they flowed down through the organization, plans were tailored to the particular needs of each level. Although this approach helped make managerial planning thorough, systematic, and coordinated, all too often the focus was on developing "the plan," a thick binder (or binders) full of meaningless information that was stuck away on a shelf and never used by anyone for guiding or coordinating work efforts. In fact, in a survey of managers about formal top–down organizational planning processes, over 75 percent said that their company's planning approach was unsatisfactory.[23] A common complaint was, "plans are documents that you prepare for the corporate planning staff and later forget." Although this traditional top–down approach to planning is still used by many organizations, it can be effective only if managers understand the importance of creating workable, usable documents that organizational members actually use, not documents that look impressive but are never used.

Another approach to planning is to involve more organizational members in the process. In this approach, plans aren't handed down from one level to the next, but instead are developed by organizational members at the various levels and in the various work units to meet their specific needs. For instance, at Dell's facility in Austin, Texas, employees from production, supply management, and channel management meet weekly to make plans based on current product demand and supply. In addition, work teams set their own daily schedules and track their progress against those schedules. If a team falls behind, team members develop "recovery" plans to try to get back on schedule.[24] When organizational members are more actively involved in planning, they see that the plans are more than just something written down on paper. They can actually see that the plans are used in directing and coordinating work.

## Learning Review

- Discuss how traditional goal setting works.
- Explain the concept of the means–end chain.
- Describe the management by objectives (MBO) approach.
- Describe the characteristics of well-designed goals.
- Explain the steps in setting goals.
- Discuss the contingency factors that affect planning.
- Describe the approaches to planning.

**commitment concept**
Plans should extend far enough to meet those commitments made today.

**formal planning department**
A group of planning specialists whose sole responsibility is helping to write organizational plans.

# CONTEMPORARY ISSUES IN PLANNING

We conclude this chapter by addressing two contemporary issues in planning. Specifically, we're going to look at criticisms of planning, and then at how managers can plan effectively in dynamic environments.

## Criticisms of Planning

Formalized organizational planning became popular in the 1960s and, for the most part, still is today. It makes sense for an organization to establish some direction. But critics have challenged some of the basic assumptions underlying planning. What arguments are directed at formal planning?

1. *Planning may create rigidity.*[25] Formal planning efforts can lock an organization into specific goals to be achieved within specific timetables. When these goals were set, the assumption may have been that the environment wouldn't change during the time period the goals covered. If that assumption is faulty, managers who follow a plan may face trouble. Rather than remaining flexible—and possibly throwing out the plan—managers who continue to do the things required to achieve the original goals may not be able to cope with the changed environment. Forcing a course of action when the environment is changing can be a recipe for disaster.

2. *Plans can't be developed for a dynamic environment.*[26] Most organizations today face dynamic environments. If a basic assumption of making plans—that the environment won't change—is faulty, then how can you make plans at all? Today's business environment is often chaotic, at best. By definition, that means random and unpredictable. Managing under those conditions requires flexibility, and that may mean not being tied to formal plans. ( Go to www.prenhall.com/rolls)

**Q & A**

Managers can't really expect to plan effectively when there's so much change taking place outside the organization, can they? Q & A 7.8 provides some answers.

3. *Formal plans can't replace intuition and creativity.*[27] Successful organizations are typically the result of someone's innovative vision. But visions have a tendency to become formalized as they evolve. Formal planning efforts typically involve a thorough investigation of the organization's capabilities and opportunities and a mechanical analysis that reduces the vision to some type of programmed routine. That approach can spell disaster for an organization. For example, the rapid growth of Apple Computer in the late 1970s and throughout the 1980s was attributed, in part, to the innovative and creative approaches of one of its co-founders, Steven Jobs. As the company grew, Jobs felt there was a need for more formalized management—something he was uncomfortable doing. He hired a CEO who ultimately ousted Jobs from his own company. With Jobs's departure came increased organizational formality, including detailed planning—the same things that Jobs despised so much because he felt that they hampered creativity. By the mid-1990s, Apple, once an industry leader, was struggling for survival. The situation became so bad that Jobs was brought back as CEO to get Apple back on track. The company's renewed focus on innovation led to the debut of the iMac in 1998, the iPod in 2001, a radically new look for the iMac in 2002, an online music store in 2003, and a video iPod in 2005.

4. *Planning focuses managers' attention on today's competition, not on tomorrow's survival.*[28] Formal planning has a tendency to focus on how to capitalize on existing business opportunities within an industry. It often doesn't allow managers to consider creating or reinventing an industry. Consequently, formal plans may result in costly blunders and high catch-up costs when other competitors take the lead. On the other hand, companies such as Intel, General Electric, Nokia, and Sony have found success forging into uncharted waters, creating new industries as they went.

Q & A

If you do a good job planning, then you never have to change those plans, do you? Wrong! See Q & A 7.9.

5. ***Formal planning reinforces success, which may lead to failure.***[29] Success breeds success. That's an American tradition. If it's not broken, don't fix it, right? ( ⬢ Go to www.prenhall.com/rolls) Well, maybe not! Success may, in fact, breed failure in an uncertain environment. It's hard to change or discard previously successful plans—to leave the comfort of what works for the anxiety of the unknown. Successful plans, however, may provide a false sense of security, generating more confidence in the formal plans than is warranted. Many managers will not face the unknown until they're forced to do so by environmental changes. By then, it may be too late.

6. ***Just planning isn't enough.*** It's not enough for managers just to plan. They have to start doing![30] When executives at the *Wall Street Journal* decided that they had to do something to respond to a prolonged slump in financial and technology advertising, they developed a plan for how best to accomplish that goal. And then they set about doing it. One of the first things they did was to make some design changes by adding more color to its pages, redesigning the typeface, and making other format changes. Another thing they did to bring in more readers was to launch a Saturday edition in September 2005. Next on the agenda: cutting down the size of the newspaper with the smaller format starting in January 2007.[31] As this example shows, just planning to do something doesn't get it done. Planning to have enough money so you can retire at age 35 isn't enough. You have to put that plan into motion and do it. Managers need to plan, but they also need to see that the plan is carried out.

How valid are these criticisms? Should managers forget about planning? No! Although the criticisms have merit when directed at rigid, inflexible planning, today's managers can be effective planners if they understand planning in dynamic uncertain environments.

## Effective Planning in Dynamic Environments

The external environment is continually changing. For instance, Wi-Fi, a wireless networking technology, is revolutionizing all kinds of industries from airlines to automobile manufacturing to consumer electronics. The power of the Internet also is being used by companies in new and unique ways including product design or logistics. Consumers continue to increase how much they spend on eating out instead of cooking at home. The euro is now the official currency of a number of countries in the European Union, and experts believe that China and India will transform the twenty-first century global economy.

*Few business environments are more dynamic or challenging than the online music industry. Van Toffler, president of MTV Networks Group, is planning new ways to satisfy customers and benefit recording artists, too. In addition to helping Madonna's new album reach the #1 spot on the charts with a tv movie, ring tones, and exclusive broadband content, Toffler's unit is also looking at ways to revive the "lost art" of album covers with inexpensive Flash animations. "If we do it right," he says, "people will want to spend time with this, not just buy a 99-cent single and leave."*

## becoming a Manager

✓ Practice setting goals for various aspects of your personal life such as academics, career preparation, family, and so forth.

✓ For goals that you've set, write out plans for achieving those goals.

✓ Be prepared to change your goals as circumstances change.

✓ Write a personal mission statement.

✓ If you're employed, talk to your manager(s) about the types of planning they do. Ask them for suggestions on how to be a better planner.

✓  Complete any of the following exercises from the Self-Assessment Library found on www.prenhall.com/rolls: S.A.L. #I.C.7—What's My Attitude Toward Achievement?, S.A.L. #I.C.5—What Are My Course Performance Goals?, S.A.L. #I.E.2—What Time of Day Am I Most Productive?, and S.A.L. #I.E.3—How Good Am I at Personal Planning?

Self-Assessment
Library (S.A.L.)

Self-Assessment
Library (S.A.L.)

Are you ready to cope with continual change? S.A.L. #III.C.1 can help you discover how well you'll adapt to change.

How can managers effectively plan when the external environment is continually changing? (  Go to www.prenhall.com/rolls) We have already discussed uncertain environments as one of the main contingency factors that affect the types of plans managers develop. Because dynamic environments are more the norm than the exception for today's managers, let's revisit how to plan in an uncertain environment.

In an uncertain environment, managers want to develop plans that are specific, but flexible. Although this may seem contradictory, it's not. To be useful, plans need some specificity, but the plans should not be cast in stone. Managers must recognize that planning is an ongoing process. The plans serve as a roadmap although the destination may be changing constantly due to dynamic market conditions. They should be willing to change directions if environmental conditions warrant. This flexibility is particularly important as plans are implemented. Managers must stay alert to environmental changes that could impact the effective implementation of plans and make changes as needed. Keep in mind, also, that's it important to continue formal planning efforts, even when the environment is highly uncertain, in order to see any effect on organizational performance. It's the persistence in planning efforts that contributes to significant performance improvement. Why? It seems that, as with most activities, managers "learn to plan" and the quality of their planning improves when they continue to do it.[32]

Finally, effective planning in dynamic environments means flattening the organizational hierarchy as the responsibility for establishing goals and developing plans is shoved to lower organizational levels because there's little time for goals and plans to flow down from the top. Managers must train their employees in setting goals and establishing plans and then trust that they will do so. And you need look no further than Bangalore, India, to find a company that effectively understands this. Just a short decade ago, Wipro Limited was "an anonymous conglomerate selling cooking oil and personal computers, mostly in India." Today, it is a $2.3 billion-a-year global company with most of its business (some 90 percent) coming from information technology services."[33] Accenture, EDS, IBM, and the big U.S. accounting firms know all too well the competitive threat Wipro represents. Not only are Wipro's employees cheap, but they're also knowledgeable and skilled. And they play an important role in the company's planning. Because the information services industry is continually changing, employees are taught to analyze situations and to define the scale and scope of a client's problems in order to offer the best solutions. They're the ones on the front line with the clients and it's their responsibility to establish what to do and how to do it. It's an approach that has positioned Wipro for success no matter how the industry changes.

## Learning Review

- Explain the criticisms of planning and whether they're valid.

- Describe how managers can effectively plan in today's dynamic environment.

# Managers Respond to a Manager's Dilemma

## Amanda Ferguson

Sales Representative, Eli Lilly and Company, Kirkwood, MO

Edina has been able to do some pretty impressive things already with her wedding shop. By using planning, she should be able to do even more. Before she looks at developing plans, I think she should set some goals for her business. What would she like to accomplish over the next 6 months? The next year? The next 2 years? Knowing what her goals are, she can then develop plans that will help her reach those goals. What types of plans might she need? I think she probably first needs to focus on short-term, specific, and operational plans because she wants to make sure that her business is successful before looking at planning for the long term. However, because she recently obtained a 2-year loan to purchase additional wedding dresses, any plans that she develops should extend far enough to ensure that she will be able to pay off her loan, hopefully early.

# Learning Summary

## What Is Planning and Why Is It Important?

**Planning:** defining organization's goals, establishing overall strategy, and developing plans

- Formal planning is important because it:
  1. provides direction
  2. reduces uncertainty
  3. minimizes waste and redundancy
  4. establishes the goals or standards used in controlling
  5. is associated with positive financial results
     - external environment impacts this relationship, as does
     - planning time frame

## How Do Managers Plan?

Two important elements: **goals** (desired outcomes); **plans** (documents outlining how goals will be met)

- Types of goals
  - strategic or financial
  - stated and real
- Types of plans
  - breadth: strategic or operational
  - time frame: short term or long term
  - specificity: directional or specific
  - frequency of use: single-use or standing

## How Do Managers Set Goals?

Traditional approach: top-down

- If hierarchy of goals is clearly defined, a means–end chain is formed
- If not clearly defined, goals lose clarity and unity

Management by objectives (MBO) approach: four elements

1. goal specificity
2. participative decision making
3. explicit time period
4. performance feedback

Characteristics of well-defined goals—stated in terms of outcomes, measurable and quantifiable, clear time frame, challenging but attainable, written down, communicated to all organizational members

## How Do Managers Develop Plans?

Influenced by:

- contingency factors
  - level in the organization
  - environmental uncertainty
  - commitment concept
- approaches
  - formal planning department
  - involving more organizational members in process

## What Contemporary Planning Issues Face Managers?

Criticisms of planning:

- creates rigidity
- can't be developed for dynamic environment
- can't replace intuition and creativity
- focuses on today, not tomorrow
- reinforces success, which can lead to failure
- planning isn't enough

Planning in dynamic environments

# Management: By the Numbers

- In a survey of information executives, 7 percent said they have no plan for disaster recovery.
- Of 1,000 Americans surveyed, 61 percent said Wi-Fi technology helps or will help them be more productive at home or in school.
- Seventy-five percent of managers surveyed said that their company's planning approach was unsatisfactory.
- In an American Management Association survey, 19 percent of executives said that planning was an important skill.

- In that same survey, 45 percent of the executives said that accomplishing difficult assignments without the necessary resources was a leadership challenge.

*Sources:* Wi-Fi Alliance, www.wi-fi.org/news/pressrelease, December 13, 2005; "Disaster Recovery Plan," *USA Today Snapshot*, November 13, 2005, p. 1B; and American Management Association, "2003 Survey on Leadership Challenges," www.amanet.org.

# Thinking About Management Issues

1. Will planning become more or less important to managers in the future? Why?

2. If planning is so crucial, why do some managers choose not to do it? What would you tell these managers?

3. Explain how planning involves making decisions today that will have an impact later.

4. How might planning in a not-for-profit organization such as the American Cancer Society differ from planning in a for-profit organization such as Coca-Cola?

5. What types of planning do you do in your personal life? Describe these plans in terms of being (a) strategic or operational, (b) short or long term, and (c) specific or directional.

# Working Together: Team-Based Exercise

People Power, a training company that markets its human resource programs to corporations around the globe, has had several requests to design a training program to teach employees how to use the Internet for researching information. This training program will then be marketed to potential corporate customers. Your team is spearheading this important project. There are three stages to the project: (1) researching corporate customer needs, (2) researching the Internet for specific information sources and techniques that could be used in the training module, and (3) designing and writing specific training module. The first thing your team has to do is identify at least three goals for each stage. As you proceed with this task, you don't need to come up with specifics about "how" to proceed with these activities; just think about "what" you want to accomplish in each stage.

Form small groups of three or four individuals, and complete your assigned work. Be sure that your goals are well designed. Be prepared to share your team's goals with the rest of the class.

# Ethical Dilemma Exercise

Should schools have fund-raising relationships with businesses? Although every school's goal is to provide quality education, administrators often face serious budget constraints. That's why many schools welcome money from fund-raisers sponsored by the neighborhood stores and restaurants or local branches of national chains like McDonald's. For example, when cell-phone manufacturer Motorola started a recycling program in which schools receive $3 for each old phone turned in, the 500 students at John L. Husmann Elementary School in Crystal Lake,

Illinois, were able to raise nearly $1,500 to buy audiovisual equipment. The principal couldn't have been more pleased to participate.

On the other hand, Professor Alex Molnar, who heads Arizona State University's Education Policy Studies Laboratory, doesn't see a huge economic benefit for schools that have fund-raising relationships with businesses. In his view, such arrangements arguably harm the community and the child. Professor Molnar observes that few school officials ask tough questions like: "How does this actually benefit the school? Might this be a distraction? Are we encouraging behavior and values that undermine what we are saying in the schools' curriculum?" Yet for many schools, the bottom line is that fund-raising relationships can be good for the bottom line of both sides. According to Carol Shepherd of the Apache Junction Unified School District in Arizona: "Maybe the businesses' motive is, in fact, commercial purpose. It is still providing some help for schools."[34]

Imagine you've been promoted into a management position in your local school district. Yesterday the parents

of one of the high school students suggested a fund-raising idea: their family business, a local supermarket, will donate 20 percent of the revenue from a special "shop for school night" to be held just before the junior–senior prom. Your district agrees and asks you to work out some of the details. Which of the following options will you recommend—and why?

**Option A:** Encourage a little competition by asking the supermarket to post the names of all the families that buy on "shop for school night," along with the amount spent.

**Option B:** Be sure the teachers send "shop for school night" flyers home with each student on the day of the fund-raiser, along with free bumper stickers featuring the store's logo.

**Option C:** Invite the family that operates the supermarket to present the donation at the official after-prom party in the school gym.

# Case Application

### Ready or Not . . .

For once, governments and public health officials appear to be more prepared than businesses do. They have spent billions preparing for a potential influenza pandemic by buying medicines, running disaster drills, and developing strategies for tighter border controls. On the other hand, a survey of global companies by London-based newsletter *Continuity Central* found that 72 percent have not even begun to get ready for a potential bird flu pandemic. Businesses in the United States seem to be particularly unprepared. In a survey by Deloitte & Touche of 100 U.S. executives, two-thirds said their companies had not yet prepared adequately for avian flu, and most had no one specifically in charge of such a plan. What these businesses might not realize is how they potentially will be affected. For instance, how will they continue to do their business if their workforce is ill or quarantined; if transportation, communication, utility services, or other necessary public infrastructure functions are not available or are only available in limited areas; or if financial services are curtailed? How will they earn revenues if the general public is sick or not able to venture out? It's a scenario with monumental implications for both the short term and the long term.

One company that has planned for any potential avian flu outbreak is Deutsche Bank. The steps it has taken include making sure employees in infected zones don't carry the disease to co-workers, moving others out of harm's way, communicating medical bulletins to far-flung offices, and preparing for the inevitable economic shocks

as mass illness slows trade and undermines both public services and private commerce. Kenny Seow, Deutsche Bank's business continuity manager in Singapore, says, "The moment that there is human-to-human infection, we would execute a set of measures."

Businesses in Southeast Asia seem to be better prepared for a possible flu disaster. For one thing, many of these companies had to deal with the SARS (sudden acute respiratory syndrome) outbreak in 2003—a frightening situation that brought commerce in Hong Kong, Singapore, and Beijing to a near standstill. A survey of 80 corporate executives at a seminar held by the American Chamber of Commerce in Hong Kong found that nearly every company had someone in charge of avian flu policy and 60 percent had clearly stated plans that could be put in place immediately. One of the most prepared companies is global bank HSBC, which has made preparations for employees to work from home and is also preparing to divide work among multiple sites. At Turner International Asia Pacific, a Time Warner unit in Hong Kong, they're working on a mechanized cart that could automatically load tape after tape into a satellite transmission system so it could keep stations like Cartoon Network on the air—a boon if children were homebound for months. And even FedEx says that it has developed contingency plans down to every district or market in Asia Pacific.

What now? What about those businesses that have not begun to prepare for a possible outbreak? As the Deloitte report on avian flu concluded, "In a world where the global supply chain and real-time inventories

*One of the most prepared companies for the potential bird flu pandemic is global bank HSBC.*

determine almost everything we do, down to the food available for purchase in our grocery stores, the importance of advanced planning cannot be overstated."

## Discussion Questions

1. What role do you think goals might play in a company's planning for any potential bird flu outbreak? List some goals that you think might be important.

2. What types of plans might companies need for this situation? (For instance, short term, long term or both?) Explain why you think these plans would be important.

3. How does this scenario reflect planning in a dynamic environment? What would managers need to do to make their planning effective in such an environment?

4. What could other businesses learn from Deutsche Bank's and HSBC's experiences?

5. Pick a company (any size, any kind, or any location) and describe how an influenza pandemic might affect it. Now, develop plans for this company to deal with such an outbreak.

*Sources:* M. Siegel, "Is Yesterday's Swine Flu Today's Bird Flu?" *USA Today,* March 22, 2006, p. 13A; M. Warner, "Preparing for the Avian Flu Threat in the U.S.," *New York Times Online,* www.nytimes.com, March 21, 2006; E. Rosenthal and K. Bradsher, "Is Business Ready for a Flu Pandemic?" *New York Times Online,* www.nytimes.com, March 16, 2006; "Avian Flu Pandemic Employer Preparedness: Deloitte Center for Health Solutions/ERIC Survey Resuts,"*Deloitte Human Capital IQ Newsletter,* www. deloitte.com/dtt/newsletter, January 2006; and J. Carey, "Avian Flu: Business Thinks the Unthinkable,"*Business Week,* November 28, 2005, pp. 36–39.

# Learning Outline

*Use this Learning Outline as you read and study this chapter.*

## The Importance of Strategic Management
- Define strategic management, strategy, and business model.
- Explain why strategic management is important.

## The Strategic Management Process
- List the six steps in the strategic management process.
- Describe what managers do during external and internal analyses.
- Explain the role of resources, capabilities, and core competencies.
- Define strengths, weaknesses, opportunities, and threats.

## Types of Organizational Strategies
- Describe the three major types of corporate strategies.
- Discuss the BCG matrix and how it's used.
- Describe the role of competitive advantage in business strategies.
- Explain Porter's five forces model.
- Describe Porter's three generic competitive strategies and the rule of three.

## Strategic Management in Today's Environment
- Explain why strategic flexibility is important.
- Describe e-business strategies.
- Explain what strategies organizations might use to become more customer oriented and to be more innovative.

# Strategic Management

## A Manager's Dilemma

"Our Brand Mission is to provide the world with technically advanced products engineered with our exclusive fabric construction, supreme moisture management, and proven innovation." And that's exactly what Kevin Plank's company, Under Armour, has been able to do.[1] The company's unique and innovative sweat-wicking undershirt launched the fastest-growing category of performance sportswear—premium synthetic compression garments that are worn under an athlete's uniform or equipment and that provide a snug, light fit, allowing the individual to remain drier. Under Armour dominates this product category with some 90 percent of the market, much to the dismay of the athletic sportswear industry giants—Nike, Adidas, and Reebok.

As special teams captain during the mid-1990s for the University of Maryland football team, Kevin hated having to repeatedly change the cotton T-shirt he wore under his jersey as it became wet and heavy during the course of a game. He knew there had to be a better alternative and set out to make it. After a year of fabric and product testing, Kevin introduced the first Under Armour compression product—a synthetic shirt worn like a second skin under a uniform or jersey. It was an immediate hit! The silky fabric was light and made athletes feel faster and fresher, giving them, according to Kevin, an important psychological edge.

Today, Under Armour has clothing and equipment for various sports, climates, and settings, including shirts, sweats, batting gloves, boxers, and other sports-specific products. Most of the company's products are still made with the moisture-wicking and heat-dispersing fabrics that have proven to be successful and that appeal to the primarily male athletes for whom they're designed.

But Kevin's company is now facing a new and especially important challenge. It's actively working to expand its products to women and children. Put yourself in Kevin's shoes. How could SWOT analysis help him as he takes Under Armour in this direction?

What would you do?

The importance of having good strategies can be seen by what Kevin Plank has accomplished with Under Armour. By designing effective strategies to attract customers, his company has taken on the big companies in the intensely competitive athletic wear industry. And as he considers expansion plans, strategic management will once again play an important role. An underlying theme in this chapter is that effective strategies result in high organizational performance.

## THE IMPORTANCE OF STRATEGIC MANAGEMENT

Colgate-Palmolive buys Tom's of Maine, the all-natural personal care brand, for $100 million. French cosmetics company L'Oreal buys The Body Shop for $1.1 billion. Dell, the world's largest maker of personal computers, doubles the size of its workforce in India and is building a manufacturing facility in the country. And recognizing that Web-based offerings would be vitally important to its future, Microsoft reaffirmed its focus on engineering new online products.[2] These are just a few of the business news stories from a single week and every one is about a company's strategies.

**Q & A**
Find out how strategic management is related to planning by going to Q & A 8.1.

Strategic management is very much a part of what managers do. Effective managers around the world recognize the role that strategic management plays in their organization's performance.  (  Go to www.prenhall.com/rolls) For instance, using well-designed strategies, Grupo Empresarial Antioqueño, Colombia's largest business, is preparing to go global by expanding into Central America, the Caribbean, Mexico, and the United States. Al Jazeera, the Arabic-language news network based in Qatar, is starting a new channel, Al Jazeera International, that will broadcast in English and is hiring employees from old-line news organizations such as the BBC, CNN, and Associated Press Television News. And based on demographic trends, Best Buy Co. has launched several new store concepts including one called "eq-life," which offers Pilates classes, massages, and health-related tech products for sale.[3] These companies illustrate the value of strategic management. In this section, we want to look at what strategic management is and why managers consider it important.

### What Is Strategic Management?

To begin to understand the basics of strategy and strategic management, you need look no further than at what's happened in the discount retail industry. The industry's two largest competitors—Wal-Mart and Kmart Corporation (which is now part of an entity called "Sears Holdings" after it purchased Sears, Roebuck in 2005)—have battled for market dominance since 1962, the year both companies were founded. The two chains have other striking similarities: store atmosphere, names, markets served, and organizational purpose. Yet, Wal-Mart's performance (financial and otherwise) has far surpassed that of Kmart. Wal-Mart is the world's largest and most successful retailer, and Kmart was the largest retailer ever to seek Chapter 11 bankruptcy protection (from which it emerged in May 2003). Why the difference in performance? Organizations vary in how well they perform because of differences in their strategies and competitive abilities.[4] Wal-Mart has excelled at strategic management, while Kmart has struggled to find the right combination.

**Strategic management** is what managers do to develop the organization's strategies. What are an organization's **strategies**? They're the decisions and actions that determine the long-run performance of an organization. Through strategic management, managers establish the game plan or roadmap—that is, the strategies—for how the organization will do whatever it's in business to do, how it will compete successfully, and how it will attract and satisfy its customers in order to achieve its goals.[5] It's an important task of managers and ultimately entails all of the basic management functions—planning, organizing, leading, and controlling. We'll discuss in detail how managers do strategic management at a later point in the chapter.

One term that's often used in conjunction with strategic management and strategies is **business model**, which is a strategic design for how a company intends to profit from its strategies, work processes, and work activities. A company's business model focuses on two things: (1) whether customers will value what the company is providing and (2) whether the company can make any money doing that.[6] For instance, Dell pioneered a new business model for selling computers to consumers directly on the Internet instead of selling its computers, like all the other computer manufacturers, through computer retailers. Did customers "value" that? Absolutely! Did Dell make money doing it that way? Absolutely! As managers think about strategies for their businesses, they need to give some thought to the economic viability of their business model.

## Why Is Strategic Management Important?

In the summer of 2002, a British television show spin-off called *American Idol* became an instant success for Fox Broadcasting Company and was one of the biggest shows in American television history. Now, even five seasons later, a large audience still seems to be tuning in (your second author admits to being a fan!). Says one industry executive, "*Idol* is part of American culture, like McDonald's or Starbucks. If the brand is carefully handled, there's no reason it can't last indefinitely."[7] The managers behind *Idol* seem to understand the importance of strategic management because they're developing and exploiting every aspect of the *Idol* business—the television show, the music, the concerts, and all the other associated licensed products.

Why is strategic management so important? One of the most significant reasons is that it can make a difference in how well an organization performs. The most basic questions about strategy look at why firms succeed or fail, and why, when faced with the same environmental conditions, their performance levels vary. (Remember our Wal-Mart and Kmart example.) Studies of the factors that contribute to organizational performance generally have shown a positive relationship between strategic planning and performance.[8] In other words, it appears that organizations that use strategic management do have higher levels of performance. And that makes it pretty important for managers!

Another reason strategic management is important has to do with the fact that organizations of all types and sizes face continually changing situations. These changes may be minor or significant, but it's still change with which managers must cope. That's where strategic management comes in. Using the strategic management process, managers examine relevant factors in deciding what actions to take, thus helping them better cope with uncertain environments.

Strategic management is also important because of the nature of organizations. They're composed of diverse divisions, departments, functions, and work activities—manufacturing, marketing, accounting, and so forth—that all need to be coordinated and focused on achieving the organization's goals. Strategic management does this. For example, Wal-Mart has over 1.8 million employees worldwide who work in various departments, functions, and store types. How does strategic management help in coordinating and focusing those employees? By clarifying and pinpointing what's important, and by providing the reasons for why they're doing what they're doing. (  Go to www.prenhall.com/rolls)

Finally, strategic management is important because it's involved in many of the decisions that managers make. As we saw in the earlier examples, most of the stories reported in the various business publications involve managers making strategic decisions. How widespread is the use of strategic management? One survey found that 69 percent of business owners used strategic plans, and among those owners, 89 percent

**Self-Assessment Library (S.A.L.)**

Do you like situations to be more structured or do you thrive on not knowing what's going to happen? Take S.A.L. #1.A.4 and find out how well you handle ambiguity.

---

**strategic management**
What managers do to develop the organization's strategies.

**strategies**
The decisions and actions that determine the long-run performance of an organization.

**business model**
A strategic design for how a company intends to profit from its strategies, processes, and activities.

*The strategic management philosophy at 37signals LLC, a small software maker in Chicago, is to stay competitive by never taking more than 3½ months to launch a new product. "This is a new model, not just for building a product but for running a company," says CEO Jason Fried (left), who's shown here with programmer David Heinemeier Hansson (right) and designer Ryan Singer (seated).*

responded that their plans were effective.[9] They stated, for example, that strategic planning gave them specific goals and provided their staff with a unified vision. Although a few management researchers have claimed that strategic planning is "dead," most continue to emphasize its importance.[10]

Today, strategic management has moved beyond for-profit business organizations to include governmental agencies, hospitals, and other not-for-profit organizations. For instance, when the U.S. Postal Service found itself in intense competitive battles with overnight package delivery companies, electronic mail services, and private mailing facilities, its CEO (the U.S. Postmaster General) used strategic management to help pinpoint important issues and to design appropriate strategic responses including the popular self-adhesive stamps and an electronic postmark used to certify e-mail messages. In fact, the USPS continues to use strategic management. Check out the organization's *Strategic Transformation Plan 2006–2010*, which can be found on its Web site.[11] Although strategic management in not-for-profits hasn't been as well researched as that in for-profit organizations, we know it's important for these organizations as well.

## Learning Review

- Define strategic management, strategy, and business model.
- Explain why strategic management is important.

## THE STRATEGIC MANAGEMENT PROCESS

The **strategic management process** (see Exhibit 8–1) is a six-step process that encompasses strategy planning, implementation, and evaluation. Although the first four steps describe the planning that must take place, implementation and evaluation are just as important. Even the best strategies can fail if management doesn't implement or evaluate them properly. Let's examine in detail the six steps.

### Step 1: Identifying the Organization's Current Mission, Goals, and Strategies

Q & A

Have you seen the mission statements of organizations you belong to? See what your authors have to say about written mission statements in Q & A 8.2.

Every organization needs a **mission**—a statement of the purpose of an organization. The mission answers the question: What is our reason for being in business? Defining the organization's mission forces managers to identify what it's in business to do. ( Go to www.prenhall.com/rolls) For instance, the mission of Avon is "To be the com-

Exhibit 8–1    **The Strategic Management Process**

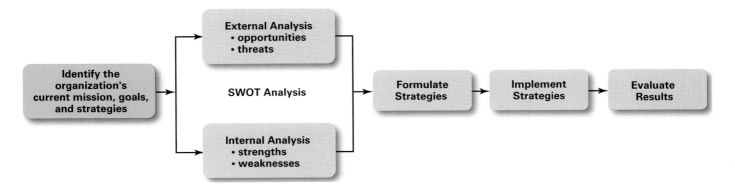

pany that best understands and satisfies the product, service, and self-fulfillment needs of women on a global level." The mission statement for the U.S. Federal Bureau of Prisons reads, "It is the mission of the Federal Bureau of Prisons to protect society by confining offenders in the controlled environments of prisons and community-based facilities that are safe, humane, cost-efficient, and appropriately secure, and that provide work and other self-improvement opportunities to assist offenders in becoming law-abiding citizens." The mission of eBay is "to build an online marketplace that enables practically anyone to trade practically anything almost anywhere in the world." The mission of the National Heart Foundation of Australia is to "reduce suffering and death from heart, stroke, and blood vessel disease in Australia." These statements provide clues to what these organizations see as their purpose. What should a mission statement include? See Exhibit 8–2 for a description of the typical components.

It's also important for managers to identify the goals currently in place and the strategies currently being used. As we explained in Chapter 7, goals are the foundation of planning and provide the measurable performance targets that employees are working to meet. Knowing the company's current goals gives managers a basis for assessing whether those goals need to be changed. For the same reasons, it's important for managers to know the organization's current strategies—to assess whether any need to be changed.

Exhibit 8–2

**Components of a Mission Statement**

| |
|---|
| *Customers:* Who are the firm's customers? |
| *Markets:* Where does the firm compete geographically? |
| *Concern for survival, growth, and profitability:* Is the firm committed to growth and financial stability? |
| *Philosophy:* What are the firm's basic beliefs, values, and ethical priorities? |
| *Concern for public image:* How responsive is the firm to societal and environmental concerns? |
| *Products or services:* What are the firm's major products or services? |
| *Technology:* Is the firm technologically current? |
| *Self-concept:* What are the firm's major competitive advantage and core competencies? |
| *Concern for employees:* Are employees a valuable asset of the firm? |
| *Source:* Based on F. David, *Strategic Management*, 11 ed. (Upper Saddle River, NJ: Prentice Hall, 2007), p. 70. |

**strategic management process**
A six-step process that encompasses strategic planning, implementation, and evaluation.

**mission**
A statement of the purpose of an organization.

## Step 2: Doing an External Analysis

Of the world's top 25 information-technology companies, 6 are based in the United States; 14 are based in Asia. One researcher says, "Traditional colleges and universities are doomed. Technology, lethargy, and astronomical costs will destroy the current model of higher education to create a $100-billion-a-year opportunity for businesses and investors." Web-enabled computers and other digital tools have accelerated the amount of electronic multitasking going in, particularly among "Gen M," the term being used to describe young teens and young adults who seem to be simultaneously talking on their cell phones, carrying on multiple IM (instant messaging) chats, watching TV, and doing homework.[12] What impact might such trends have for organizations? That's what an external analysis attempts to answer.

PRISM

Try your hand at scanning the environment. Go to PRISM #3 and see how our virtual organization Mediaplex deals with a new rival.

In Chapter 3, we described the external environment as an important constraint on a manager's actions. Analyzing that environment is a critical step in the strategic management process. (  Go to www.prenhall.com/rolls) Managers in every organization need to do an external analysis. They need to know, for instance, what the competition is doing, what pending legislation might affect the organization, or what the labor supply is like in locations where it operates. In analyzing the external environment, managers should examine both the specific and general environments to see what trends and changes are occurring. ( Go to www.prenhall.com/rolls) For example, managers in the movie theatre industry recognized that their industry was changing.[13] From changing technology (DVDs and flat-screen, surround-sound home entertainment systems) to changing demographics (a younger generation brought up with video games and other sophisticated visual technology) to changing customer needs (wanting more out of the movie-going experience while paying for less), these managers have looked for strategies to accommodate the trends. Their challenge is finding a way to reverse the decline in attendance by offering something that moviegoers can't get anywhere else—at home or through other entertainment options. These managers want to stay on top of changes in the external environment so they can develop appropriate strategies.

Q & A

Find out where you can get information on the external environment in Q & A 8.3.

After analyzing the environment, managers need to assess what they have learned in terms of opportunities that the organization can exploit, and threats that it must counteract or buffer against. **Opportunities** are positive trends in external environmental factors; **threats** are negative trends.

One last thing to understand about external analysis is that the same environment can present opportunities to one organization and pose threats to another in the same industry because of their different resources and capabilities. For example, Southwest Airlines has prospered in a turbulent industry (33 straight profitable years), while others such as United and Delta have struggled (each has declared bankruptcy at one point).

## Step 3: Doing an Internal Analysis

Now we move from looking outside the organization to looking inside. The internal analysis provides important information about an organization's specific resources and capabilities. An organization's **resources** are its assets—financial, physical, human, intangible—that are used by the organization to develop, manufacture, and deliver products or services to its customers. Its **capabilities** are its skills and abilities in doing the work activities needed in its business. The major value-creating capabilities and skills of the organization are known as its **core competencies**.[14] Both resources and core competencies can determine the organization's competitive weapons. ( Go to www.prenhall.com/rolls) For instance, Fujio Cho, Toyota Motor Corporation's chairman, called the company's Prius, "a giant leap into the future," but the highly popular car is simply one more example of the company's resources and core competencies in product research and design, manufacturing, marketing, and managing its human resources. Toyota is renowned worldwide for its effectiveness and efficiency. Experts who have studied the company point to its ability

Q & A

So why are core competencies so important? Find out in Q & A 8.4.

to nourish and preserve employee creativity and flexibility in a work environment that's fairly rigid and controlled.[15]

After doing the internal analysis, managers should be able to identify organizational strengths and weaknesses. Any activities the organization does well or any unique resources that it has are called **strengths**. **Weaknesses** are activities the organization doesn't do well or resources it needs but doesn't possess. This step forces managers to recognize that their organizations, no matter how large or successful, are constrained by the resources and capabilities they have.

Doing an internal analysis of an organization's financial and physical assets is fairly easy because information on those areas is readily available. However, evaluating an organization's intangible assets—things such as employees' skills, talents, and knowledge; databases and other IT assets; organizational culture; and so forth—is a bit more challenging. Organizational culture, specifically, is one crucial part of the internal analysis that's often overlooked.[16] It's crucial because strong and weak cultures do have different effects on strategy and the content of a culture has a major effect on strategies pursued. (  Go to www.prenhall.com/rolls) In a strong culture, almost all employees have a clear understanding of what the organization is about. This clarity makes it easy for managers to convey to new employees the organization's core competencies and strengths. For example, at Nordstrom's, which has a very strong culture of customer service and satisfaction, managers can instill cultural values in new employees in a much shorter time than they could if the company had a weak culture. The negative side of a strong culture, of course, is that it may be more difficult to change organizational strategies. Successful organizations with strong cultures may become prisoners of their own successes. Research has also shown that the kind of culture an organization has can promote or hinder its strategic actions. Firms with "strategically appropriate cultures" outperformed corporations with less appropriate cultures.[17] What is a strategically appropriate culture? It's one that supports the firm's chosen strategy. For instance, Avis, the number-two U.S. car rental company, has for a number of years stood on top of its category in an annual survey of brand loyalty. By creating a culture where employees obsess over every step of the rental car experience, Avis has built an unmatched record for customer loyalty.[18]

Another intangible asset that's important, but tricky to assess during an internal analysis, is corporate reputation. Does the fact that General Electric is ranked (once again) as America's "most admired corporation" make a difference? Does the fact that Johnson & Johnson sits atop the National Corporate Reputation Survey list (for the seventh consecutive year) mean anything? Does the fact that Coca-Cola has the world's most powerful global brand give it any edge? (See Exhibit 8–3 for some partial lists of

**Q & A**

An organization's culture is important to its strategy. Q & A 8.5 will explain why.

## thinking critically about Ethics

Many company Web sites have an "About Us" link that provides information about the company and its products or services—past, present, and oftentimes, future. This information is available for anyone to read, even competitors. In an intensely competitive industry where it's difficult for a company to survive, much less be successful, would it be wrong for managers to include misleading or even false information on its Web site? Why or why not? Suppose that the industry wasn't intensely competitive? Would you feel differently? Explain.

**opportunities**
Positive trends in external environmental factors.

**threats**
Negative trends in external environmental factors.

**resources**
An organization's assets that are used to develop, manufacture, and deliver products or services to its customers.

**capabilities**
An organization's skills and abilities in doing the work activities needed in its business.

**core competencies**
The organization's major value-creating skills and capabilities that determine its competitive weapons.

**strengths**
Any activities the organization does well or any unique resources that it has.

**weaknesses**
Activities the organization does not do well or resources it needs but does not possess.

Exhibit 8–3

**Corporate Rankings (partial lists)**

---

**Interbrand/*BusinessWeek* 100 Top Global Brands (2005)**

1. Coca-Cola
2. Microsoft
3. IBM
4. General Electric
5. Intel

**Harris Interactive/*Wall Street Journal* National Corporate Reputation (2005)**

1. Johnson & Johnson
2. Coca-Cola
3. Google
4. United Parcel Service
5. 3M Company

**Hay Group/*Fortune* America's Most Admired Companies (2006)**

1. General Electric
2. FedEx
3. Southwest Airlines
4. Procter & Gamble
5. Starbucks

**Great Place to Work Institute/*Fortune* 100 Best Companies to Work For (2006)**

1. Genentech
2. Wegman's Food Markets
3. Valero Energy
4. Griffin Hospital
5. W. L. Gore & Associates

*Sources:* "America's Most Admired Companies," *Fortune*, February 22, 2006, p. 65; "The 100 Best Companies to Work For," *Fortune*, January 11, 2006, p. 89; R. Alsop, "Ranking Corporate Reputations," *Wall Street Journal*, December 6, 2005, p. B1; and "The 100 Top Brands," *BusinessWeek*, August 1, 2005, p. 90.

---

corporate rankings.) Studies of reputation and corporate performance show that it can have a positive impact.[19] As one researcher said, " . . . a strong, well-managed reputation can and should be an asset for any organization."[20]

The combined external and internal analyses are called **SWOT analysis** because it's an analysis of the organization's *s*trengths, *w*eaknesses, *o*pportunities, and *t*hreats. After completing the SWOT analysis, managers are ready to formulate appropriate strategies—that is, strategies that (1) exploit an organization's strengths and external opportunities, (2) buffer or protect the organization from external threats, or (3) correct critical weaknesses. (  Go to www.prenhall.com/rolls)

**Q & A**
SWOT analysis **is** important to organizations. Why? See Q & A 8.6 for the answer!

**Self-Assessment Library (S.A.L.)**

Managers may have to get creative when formulating strategies. Could you be creative? Complete S.A.L. #I.A.5 and discover how creative you are.

## Step 4: Formulating Strategies

As managers formulate strategies, they have to consider the realities of the external environment and their available resources and capabilities and design strategies that will help the organization achieve its goals. What types of strategies do managers need to formulate? There are three main types: corporate, business, and functional, each of which we'll describe shortly. (  Go to www.prenhall.com/rolls)

## Step 5: Implementing Strategies

**Q & A**

Have you ever made plans and then didn't do what you had planned to do? See what you authors say about implementation in Q & A 8.7.

After strategies are formulated, they must be implemented. A strategy is only as good as its implementation. No matter how effectively an organization has planned its strategies, it can't succeed if the strategies aren't implemented properly. ( Go to www.prenhall.com/rolls) The rest of the chapters in this book address a number of issues related to strategy implementation. For instance, in Chapter 10, we discuss the strategy–structure relationship. In Chapter 12, we show that if new strategies are to succeed, they often require hiring new people with different skills, transferring some current employees to new positions, or laying off some employees. Also, because more organizations are using teams, the ability to build and manage effective teams is an important part of implementing strategy—a topic we cover in Chapter 15. Finally, top management leadership is a necessary ingredient in a successful strategy. So, too, is a motivated group of middle- and lower-level managers to carry out the organization's specific strategies. Chapters 16 and 17 discuss ways to motivate people and offer suggestions for improving leadership effectiveness.

## *managing your* **Career**

### Doing a Personal SWOT Analysis

A SWOT analysis can be a useful tool for examining your own skills, abilities, career preferences, and career opportunities. Doing a personal SWOT analysis involves taking a hard look at what your individual strengths and weaknesses are and then assessing the opportunities and threats of various career paths that might interest you.[21]

*Step 1: Assessing Personal Strengths and Weaknesses*
All of us have special skills, talents, and abilities. Each of us enjoys doing certain activities and not others. For example, some people hate sitting at a desk all day; others panic at the thought of having to interact with strangers. List the activities you enjoy and the things you're good at. Also, identify some things you don't enjoy and aren't so good at. It's important to recognize our weaknesses so that we can either try to correct them or stay away from careers in which those things would be important. List your important individual strengths and weaknesses and highlight those you think are particularly significant.

*Step 2: Identifying Career Opportunities and Threats*
We know from this chapter and Chapter 3 that different industries face different external opportunities and threats. It's important to identify these external factors for the simple reason that your initial job offers and future career advancement can be significantly influenced by the opportunities and threats. A company that's in an industry where there are significant negative

trends will offer few job openings or career advancement opportunities. On the other hand, job prospects will be bright in industries that have significant positive external trends. List two or three industries you have an interest in and critically evaluate the opportunities and threats facing those industries.

*Step 3: Outlining 5-Year Career Goals* Take your SWOT assessment and list four or five career goals that you would like to accomplish within 5 years of graduation. These goals might include things such as type of job you'd like to have, how many people you might be managing, or the type of salary you'd like to be making. Keep in mind that ideally you should try to match your individual strengths with industry opportunities.

*Step 4: Outlining a 5-Year Career Action Plan* Now it's time to get specific! Write a specific career action plan for accomplishing each of the career goals you identified in the previous step. State exactly what you will do, and by when, in order to meet each goal. If you think you'll need special assistance, state what it is and how you will get it. For example, your SWOT analysis may indicate that in order to achieve your desired career goal, you need to take more courses in management. Your career action plan should indicate when you will take those courses. Your specific career action plan will provide you with guidance for making decisions, just as an organization's plans provide direction to managers.

**SWOT analysis**
An analysis of the organization's strengths, weaknesses, opportunities, and threats.

_managing_ **IT**

### IT's Role in Company Strategy

How important is IT to a company's strategy? These two examples will illustrate just how important it can be! Harrah's Entertainment, the world's largest gaming company, is fanatical about customer service, and for good reason. Company research showed that customers who were satisfied with the service they received at a Harrah's casino increased their gaming expenditures by 10 percent, and those who were extremely satisfied increased their gaming expenditures by 24 percent. Harrah's was able to discover this important customer service–expenditures connection because of its incredibly sophisticated information system. But an organization's IT doesn't always have such a positive payoff. At Prada's $40 million Manhattan flagship store, store designers were hoping for a "radically new shopping experience" that combined cutting-edge architecture and twenty-first–century customer service. Or at least that was the

strategy. Prada invested almost one-fourth of the store's budget into IT, including wireless networks linked to an inventory database. As envisioned, sales staff would roam the store armed with PDAs so they could check whether items were in stock. Even the dressing rooms would have touch screens so customers could do the same. But, the strategy didn't work as planned. The equipment malfunctioned and the staff was overwhelmed with trying to cope with crowds and equipment that didn't work. It's no wonder the multimillion-dollar investment might not have been the best strategy.

Again, how important is IT to a company's strategy? Undoubtedly, when the IT system is working as it's supposed to, it's a wonderful asset and tool, as the Harrah's example shows. However, as Prada so painfully discovered, when the IT system isn't working as it's supposed to, it can create serious problems.[22]

## Step 6: Evaluating Results

Q & A

Changing strategy must be hard. Q & A 8.8 explains how often a company may need to change strategy.

The final step in the strategic management process is evaluating results. How effective have the strategies been? Have they helped the organization reach its goals? What adjustments, if any, are necessary? ( 📦 Go to www.prenhall.com/rolls) Since taking over as CEO of Xerox Corporation in 2001, Anne Mulcahy has made strategic adjustments to regain market share and improve her company's bottom line. For instance, the company cut jobs, sold assets, and reorganized management. She did this after assessing the results of previous strategies and determined that changes were needed. We discuss evaluation in our coverage of the control process in Chapter 18.

## Learning Review

- List the six steps in the strategic management process.
- Describe what managers do during external and internal analyses.

- Explain the role of resources, capabilities, and core competencies.
- Define strengths, weaknesses, opportunities, and threats.

## TYPES OF ORGANIZATIONAL STRATEGIES

As we said earlier, the three types of organizational strategies are corporate, business, and functional (see Exhibit 8–4). Top-level managers typically are responsible for corporate strategies; middle-level managers, for business or competitive strategies; and lower-level managers, for the functional strategies. Let's look more closely at each type.

## Corporate Strategy

As the world's largest supplier of vehicle interior parts—including seats, door handles, and instrument panels—Johnson Controls could have suffered the same fate as many other auto suppliers who have either filed for bankruptcy protection or lost consider-

Exhibit 8–4 **Types of Organizational Strategy**

able market value as their stock prices plummeted. But it chose to offset the problems of the auto industry by branching out into other businesses that make control systems for buildings and that sell car batteries to retail stores. The company's CEO had this to say about the company's corporate strategy: "We're really in a unique position with three very strong businesses that complement each other."[23]

**Corporate strategy** is a strategy that determines what businesses a company is in, should be in, or wants to be in, and what it wants to do with those businesses. It's based on the mission and goals of the organization and the roles that each business unit of the organization will play. Take PepsiCo, for instance. Its mission is to be a successful producer and marketer of beverage and packaged food products, and its strategy for pursuing that mission and various goals is through its different businesses including North American Soft Drinks, Frito-Lay, Gatorade, Tropicana Products, and PepsiCo International. At one time, PepsiCo had a restaurant division that included Taco Bell, Pizza Hut, and KFC, but because of intense competitive pressures in the restaurant industry and the division's inability to contribute to corporate growth, PepsiCo made a strategic decision to spin off that division as a separate and independent business entity, now known as YUM! Brands, Inc. What types of corporate strategies do organizations, such as PepsiCo, use?

There are three main types of corporate strategies: growth, stability, and renewal. To illustrate, Wal-Mart, Cadbury Schweppes, and General Motors are companies that seem to be going in different directions. Wal-Mart is rapidly expanding its operations and developing new business and retailing concepts. Cadbury's managers, on the other hand, are content to maintain the status quo and focus on the candy industry. Meanwhile, sluggish sales and an uncertain outlook in the automobile industry have prompted GM to take drastic measures in dealing with its problems. Each of these organizations is using a different type of corporate strategy. Let's look closer at each type.

**Growth** Even though it's the world's number-one retailer, Wal-Mart continues to grow internationally and in the United States. Because it plans to open 550 to 600 new stores in 2006, its corporate strategy is definitely growth! A **growth strategy** is used when an organization wants to grow and does so by expanding the number of products offered or markets served, either through its current business(es) or through new business(es). As a result of its growth strategy, the organization may increase sales revenues, number of employees, market share, or other quantitative measures. How can organizations grow? By using concentration, vertical integration, horizontal integration, or diversification.

Growth through concentration is achieved when an organization concentrates on its primary line of business and grows by increasing the number of products offered or

Steven Shore (on left in photo) and Barry Prevor (on right, in checkered shirt) of Steve & Barry's University Sportswear fuel their company's growth through low-cost operations. The two CEOs save money on everything from the low rent they pay in midsize malls hungry for tenants to hefty allowances for building the interiors of their stores, fees the chain's size allows them to negotiate. Buying direct from factories overseas and farming out steady instead of seasonal work also cuts expenses, as does favoring African factories to avoid expensive quotas and duties. Word-of-mouth advertising saves even more, and the company pays modest salaries, hiring mostly recent college grads. The company doubled the number of its retail outlets in 2005; its 10-year compounded sales growth rate is 70 percent.

markets served in this primary business; that is, the company chooses to grow by increasing its own business operations. For instance, Beckman Coulter, Inc., a Fullerton, California–based organization with annual revenues of close to $2.5 billion, has successfully used the concentration strategy to become one of the world's largest medical diagnostics and research equipment companies. Another example is Bose Corporation of Framingham, Massachusetts. The company's focus on developing innovative audio products have helped make it one of the world's leading manufacturers of speakers for home entertainment, automotive, and pro audio markets with sales of more than $1.8 billion. Looking back at our chapter-opening case, Kevin Plank has chosen a concentration growth strategy that will take his company into a new market—women and children.

A company also might choose to grow by vertical integration, either backward, forward, or both. In backward vertical integration, the organization attempts to gain control of its inputs by becoming its own supplier. For instance, French hospitality giant Accor, which owns Motel 6, Red Roof Inns, and numerous other lodging properties around the world, also owns a majority of Carlson Wagonlit Travel, one of the world's largest travel agencies and also operates several hospitality and food service companies. In forward vertical integration, the organization gains control of its outputs (products or services) by becoming its own distributor. For example, several manufacturers with strong brands—including Coach, Apple, LaCoste, and Lego—have opened select stores where customers can buy products. In other words, they've become their own distributor.

In horizontal integration, a company grows by combining with other organizations in the same industry—that is, its competitors. For instance, Vail Resorts Inc., the nation's largest ski area, grew by combining with other ski resorts in Colorado—Breckenridge, Keystone, Vail Mountain, Beaver Creek—and in California—Heavenly Valley. Horizontal integration has been used frequently in a number of industries in the last few years—for example, financial services, consumer products, airlines, department stores, and software, among others. Because combining with competitors might decrease the amount of competition in an industry, the U.S. Federal Trade Commission assesses the impact of such proposed growth actions and must approve them. Other countries have similar restrictions. For instance, managers at Oracle Corporation had to get approval from the European Commission, the "watchdog" for the European Union, before it could acquire rival business-software maker PeopleSoft.

Finally, an organization can grow through diversification, either related or unrelated. **Related diversification** is when a company grows by combining with firms in different, but related, industries. For example, American Standard Cos., based in Piscataway, New Jersey, is in a variety of businesses including bathroom fixtures, air conditioning and heating units, plumbing parts, and pneumatic brakes for trucks. The company's "strategic fit" in these diverse businesses is its exploitation of efficiency-oriented manufacturing techniques developed in its primary business—bathroom fixtures—and transferred to all its other businesses. **Unrelated diversification** is when a company grows by combining with firms in different and unrelated industries. For instance, Charoen Pokphand Group of Thailand has businesses in agriculture (vegetable seeds, animal feed, poultry breeding, and broiler farming), a brewery and motorcycle factory in China, telecommunication products, petrochemicals, shrimp farming, and numerous others. And Lancaster Colony Corporation of Columbus, Ohio, operates businesses that make salad dressing, car mats, and scented candles: businesses that are different *and* unrelated.

Many companies use a combination of these approaches to grow. For instance, McDonald's has grown using concentration by opening almost 32,000 outlets in more than 100 countries, of which about 30 percent are company owned. In addition, it has used horizontal integration by purchasing Boston Market, Chipotle Mexican Grill (which it spun off as a separate entity in 2006), and Donato's Pizza chains (which it sold in late 2003). It also has a minority stake in the U.K.-based sandwich shops Pret A Manger. McDonald's newest twist on its growth strategy is a move into the premium coffee market with its McCafe coffee shops.

**Stability** As U.S. sales of candy and chocolate continue to decline, Cadbury Schweppes—with almost half of its confectionary sales coming from chocolate—is maintaining things as they are. A **stability strategy** is a corporate strategy characterized by an absence of significant change in what the organization is currently doing. Examples of this strategy include continuing to serve the same clients by offering the same product or service, maintaining market share, and sustaining the organization's current business operations. The organization does not grow, but it doesn't fall behind, either.

Although it may seem strange that an organization might not want to grow, there are times when its resources and core competencies are stretched to their limits and expanding operations further might jeopardize its future success. When might managers decide that the stability strategy is the most appropriate choice? One situation might be that the industry is in a period of rapid upheaval with external forces drastically changing and making the future uncertain. At times like these, managers might decide that the prudent course of action is to sit tight and wait to see what happens.

Another situation when the stability strategy might be appropriate is if the industry is facing slow- or no-growth opportunities, like the candy and chocolate industry. In this instance, managers might decide to keep the organization operating at its current levels before making any strategic moves. This period of stability would allow them time to analyze their strategic options. The grocery industry is another one that's growing very slowly. This fact, plus the all-out assault of Wal-Mart into grocery retailing, for instance, led managers at grocery chain A&P to use a stability strategy.

Finally, owners and managers of small businesses often purposefully choose to follow a stability strategy. Why? They may feel that their business is successful enough just as it is, that it adequately meets their personal goals, and that they don't want the hassles of a growing business.

**Renewal** The popular business periodicals frequently report stories of organizations that aren't meeting their goals or whose performance is declining. For instance, Newell-Rubbermaid—which makes housewares, hardware, home furnishings, hair products, office products, and children's products—continued to struggle as 2005 sales were down 6 percent. To counteract its problems, the company's new CEO announced a global 3-year restructuring plan. Nokia, the world's number-one maker of cell phones, saw its

---

**related diversification**
When a company grows by combining with firms in different, but related, industries.

**unrelated diversification**
When a company grows by combining with firms in different and unrelated industries.

**stability strategy**
A corporate strategy characterized by an absence of significant change in what the organization is currently doing.

*J.C. Penney is attempting a renewal strategy under the leadership of CEO Mike Ullman III. The 103-year-old retail chain wants to leave behind its image as "your mother's store" and become a fashion destination for trend-conscious younger shoppers—"so when she walks into the store she says, 'This is my store; they get me,'" says Ullman. The turnaround will depend in large part on how successful the company is with its rollout of the a.n.a. brand, its largest launch ever of a proprietary brand.*

2005 net income drop by 1.5 percent. In response, it reorganized into four business units and discontinued production of a product line (TV decoder boxes). When an organization is in trouble, something needs to be done. Managers need to develop strategies that address organizational weaknesses that are leading to performance declines. These strategies are called **renewal strategies**. There are two main types of renewal strategies. A **retrenchment strategy** is a short-run renewal strategy used in situations when performance problems aren't as serious. There's no shortage of companies that have pursued a retrenchment strategy at some point. A partial list includes some big corporate names: Procter & Gamble, Unilever, Limited Brands, Heinz, Nokia, Reebok, IBM, Canon, Cemex, and Union Carbide, among others. When an organization is facing minor performance setbacks, a retrenchment strategy helps it stabilize operations, revitalize organizational resources and capabilities, and prepare to compete once again.

What happens if an organization's problems are more serious? What if the organization's profits aren't just declining, but instead there are no profits, just losses? General Motors reported a net loss in 2005 of $3.6 billion. And Kodak had a $1.3 billion loss for 2005. These types of situations call for a more drastic strategy. The **turnaround strategy** is a renewal strategy for times when the organization's performance problems are more critical.

For both renewal strategies, managers cut costs and restructure organizational operations. However, a turnaround strategy typically involves a more extensive use of these measures than does a retrenchment strategy. For instance, one of GM's more drastic measures in its turnaround strategy was making buyout offers to about 113,000 workers. GM hoped that at least 30,000 employees would accept the offer so it could get to 100 percent plant capacity by 2008 and avoid having to potentially file for bankruptcy.

**Corporate Portfolio Analysis**    When an organization's corporate strategy involves a number of businesses, managers can manage this collection, or portfolio, of businesses using a corporate portfolio matrix.[24] The first portfolio matrix—the **BCG matrix**—developed by the Boston Consulting Group, introduced the idea that an organization's various businesses could be evaluated and plotted using a 2 × 2 matrix (see Exhibit 8–5) to identify which ones offered high potential and which were a drain on organizational resources.[25] The horizontal axis represents market share, which was evaluated as either low or high; and the vertical axis indicates anticipated market growth, which also was evaluated as either low or high. Based on its evaluation, the business was placed in one of four categories:

- *Cash cows (low growth, high market share):* Businesses in this category generate large amounts of cash, but their prospects for future growth are limited.

**Exhibit 8–5**

**The BCG Matrix**

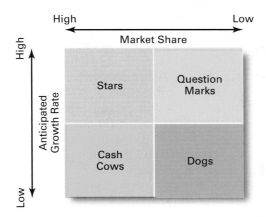

- *Stars (high growth, high market share):* These businesses are in a fast-growing market, and hold a dominant share of that market. Their contribution to cash flow depends on their need for resources.
- *Question marks (high growth, low market share):* These businesses are in an attractive industry but hold a small market share percentage.
- *Dogs (low growth, low market share):* Businesses in this category do not produce, or consume, much cash. However, they hold no promise for improved performance.

What are the strategic implications of the BCG matrix? Managers should "milk" cash cows for as much as they can, limit any new investment in them, and use the large amounts of cash generated to invest in stars and question marks with strong potential to improve market share. Heavy investment in stars will help take advantage of the market's growth and help maintain high market share. The stars, of course, will eventually develop into cash cows as their markets mature and sales growth slows. The hardest decision for managers is related to the question marks. After careful analysis, some will be sold off and others turned into stars. The dogs should be sold off or liquidated as they have low market share in markets with low growth potential.

A corporate portfolio matrix, such as the BCG matrix, can be a useful strategic management tool. It provides a framework for understanding diverse businesses and helps managers establish priorities for making resource allocation decisions.

## Business (or Competitive) Strategy

Now we move to the business level. A **business (or competitive) strategy** is a strategy focused on how an organization will compete in each of its businesses. For a small organization in only one line of business or a large organization that has not diversified into different products or markets, the competitive strategy simply describes how the company will compete in its primary or main market. For organizations in multiple businesses, however, each business will have its own competitive strategy that defines its competitive advantage, the products or services it will offer, the customers it wants to reach, and the like. For example, the French company LVMH-Moët Hennessy Louis Vuitton SA has different competitive strategies for its different businesses, which include Donna Karan fashions, Louis Vuitton leather goods, Guerlain perfume, TAG Heuer watches, Dom Perignon champagne, and other luxury products. Each business

**renewal strategy**
A corporate strategy designed to address organizational weakness that are leading to performance declines.

**retrenchment strategy**
A short-run renewal strategy.

**turnaround strategy**
A renewal strategy for situations in which the organization's performance problems are more serious.

**BCG matrix**
A strategy tool that guides resource allocation decisions on the basis of market share and growth rate of SBUs.

**business (or competitive) strategy**
An organizational strategy focused on how the organization will compete in each of its businesses.

has developed its own unique approach for competing. When an organization is in several different businesses, these single businesses that are independent and formulate their own strategies are often called **strategic business units** or SBUs.

**The Role of Competitive Advantage**   Michelin has mastered a complex technological process in making superior radial tires. Coca-Cola has created the world's most powerful brand using specialized marketing and merchandising capabilities. The Ritz-Carlton and Four Seasons hotels have a unique ability to deliver personalized customer service. Each of these companies has created a competitive advantage. Developing an effective business or competitive strategy requires an understanding of competitive advantage, a key concept in strategic management.[26] **Competitive advantage** is what sets an organization apart, that is, its distinctive edge. That distinctive edge can come from the organization's core competencies, which, as we know from earlier in the chapter, come from doing something that others cannot do or doing it better than others can do it. For example, Dell has developed a competitive advantage from its ability to create a direct-selling e-commerce channel that's highly responsive to customers. Southwest Airlines has a competitive advantage because of its skills at giving passengers what they want—convenient, inexpensive, and fun service. Competitive advantage also can come from organizational resources—the organization has something that its competitors do not have. For instance, Wal-Mart's state-of-the-art information system allows it to monitor and control inventories and supplier relations more efficiently than its competitors, which Wal-Mart has turned into a cost advantage. 3M Corporation's culture, which stresses risk taking and innovation, has given it a competitive advantage in developing and marketing products. Harley-Davidson, Nike, and Coca-Cola all have well-known global trademarks that set them apart from competitors and that they use to get premium prices for their products.

**Quality as a Competitive Advantage**   When W. K. Kellogg started manufacturing his cornflake cereal in 1906, his goal was to provide his customers with a high-quality, nutritious product that was enjoyable to eat. That emphasis on quality is still important today. Every Kellogg employee—working in areas from manufacturing to packaging to quality control—has a responsibility to maintain the high quality of Kellogg products.[27] If implemented properly, quality can be a way for an organization to create a sustainable competitive advantage.[28] That's why many organizations apply quality management concepts to their operations in an attempt to set themselves apart from competitors.

As we first discussed in Chapter 2, quality management focuses on customers and continuous improvement. To the degree that an organization can satisfy a customer's need for quality, it can differentiate itself from competitors and attract a loyal customer base. Moreover, constant improvement in the quality and reliability of an organization's products or services may result in a competitive advantage that can't be taken away.[29]

*At Luxottica's factory in Agordo, Italy, designer-brand eyeglass frames are carefully inspected for scratches or other imperfections before being shipped to stores all over the world. Quality has remained a top priority at the company as it has grown dramatically in the last several years. The focus begins in the design phase and extends all the way through production, 80 percent of which is still done in Italy in the heart of the mountainous areas where artisans have specialized in eyeglasses for generations.*

**Sustaining Competitive Advantage** Given the fact that every organization has resources and capabilities, what makes some organizations more successful than others? Why do some professional baseball teams consistently win championships or draw large crowds? Why do some organizations have consistent and continuous growth in revenues and profits? Why do some colleges, universities, or departments experience continually increasing enrollments? Why do some companies consistently appear at the top of lists ranking the "best," or the "most admired," or the "most profitable"? Although every organization has resources (assets) and capabilities (how work gets done) to do whatever it's in business to do, not every one is able to effectively exploit its resources and to develop the core competencies that can provide it with a competitive advantage. And it's not enough for an organization simply to create a competitive advantage; it must be able to sustain it—that is, to keep its edge despite competitors' actions or evolutionary changes in the industry. But that's not easy to do. Market instabilities, new technology, and other types of significant, but unpredictable, changes can challenge managers' attempts at creating a long-term, sustainable competitive advantage. However, by using strategic management, managers can better position their organizations to get a sustainable competitive advantage.

**Competitive Strategies** Many important ideas in strategic management have come from the work of Michael Porter.[30] One of his major contributions has been to explain how managers can create and sustain a competitive advantage that will give a company above-average profitability. An important element in doing this is an industry analysis.

Porter proposes that some industries are inherently more profitable (and, therefore, more attractive to enter and remain in) than others. For example, the software industry has high profit margins, and the grocery industry has notoriously low ones. But a company can still make a lot of money in a "dull" industry and lose money in a "glamorous" industry. The key is to exploit a competitive advantage.

In any industry, five competitive forces dictate the rules of competition. Together, these five forces (see Exhibit 8–6) determine industry attractiveness and profitability. Managers assess an industry's attractiveness using these five factors:

1. *Threat of new entrants.* How likely is it that new competitors will come into the industry?
2. *Threat of substitutes.* How likely is it that other industries' products can be substituted for our industry's products?
3. *Bargaining power of buyers.* How much bargaining power do buyers (customers) have?
4. *Bargaining power of suppliers.* How much bargaining power do suppliers have?
5. *Current rivalry.* How intense is the rivalry among current industry competitors?

Another thing Porter did was identify three generic competitive strategies managers can use. Once managers have assessed the five forces and determined any threats and opportunities, they're ready to select an appropriate competitive strategy—that is, one that fits the competitive strengths (resources and capabilities) of the organization and the industry it's in. According to Porter, no firm can be successful by trying to be all things to all people. He proposed that managers select a strategy that will give the organization a competitive advantage, which he says arises out of either having lower costs than all other industry competitors or by being significantly different from competitors. On that basis, managers can choose one of three strategies: cost leadership, differentiation, or focus. Which one they select depends on the organization's strengths and core competencies and its competitors' weaknesses.

**strategic business units**
The single businesses of an organization in several different businesses that are independent and formulate their own strategies.

**competitive advantage**
What sets an organization apart; its distinctive edge.

Exhibit 8–6

**Forces in the Industry Analysis**

*Source:* Based on M. E. Porter, *Competitive Strategy: Techniques for Analyzing Industries and Competitors* (New York: The Free Press, 1980).

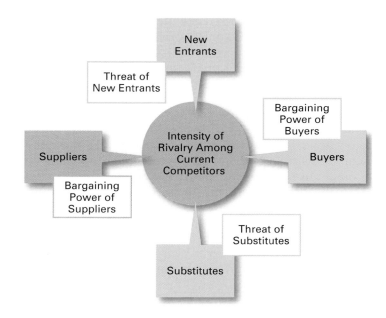

When an organization competes on the basis of having the lowest costs in its industry, it's following a **cost leadership strategy**. A low-cost leader aggressively searches out efficiencies in production, marketing, and other areas of operation. Overhead is kept to a minimum, and the firm does everything it can to cut costs. You won't find expensive art or interior décor at offices of low-cost leaders. For example, at Wal-Mart's headquarters in Bentonville, Arkansas, office furnishings are functional, not elaborate—maybe not what you'd expect for the world's largest retailer. Although low-cost leaders don't place a lot of emphasis on "frills," the product or service being sold must be perceived as comparable in quality to that offered by rivals or at least be acceptable to buyers. Examples of companies that have used the low-cost leader strategy include Wal-Mart, Hyundai, and Southwest Airlines.

A company that competes by offering unique products that are widely valued by customers is following a **differentiation strategy**. Sources of differentiation might be exceptionally high quality, extraordinary service, innovative design, technological capability, or an unusually positive brand image. The key to this competitive strategy is that whatever product or service attribute is chosen for differentiating must set the firm apart from its competitors and be significant enough to justify a price premium that exceeds the cost of differentiating.

Practically any successful consumer product or service can be identified as an example of the differentiation strategy: Nordstrom's (customer service); 3M Corporation (product quality and innovative design); Coach handbags (design and brand image); and Apple's iPod (product design).

These two competitive strategies are aimed at the broad marketplace—that is, at many different market segments. However, the final generic competitive strategy—the **focus strategy**—involves a cost advantage (cost focus) or a differentiation advantage (differentiation focus) in a narrow segment or niche. That is, managers select a market segment in an industry and attempt to exploit it rather than serve the broad market. Segments can be based on product variety, type of end buyer, distribution channel, or geographical location of buyers. For example, Hospitality Mints, a $20 million Boone, North Carolina, company, manufactures custom-wrapped mints for customers such as Arby's and Holiday Inn or for engaged couples wanting wedding favors. Although research suggests that the focus strategy may be the most effective choice for smaller businesses because they typically don't have the economies of scale or resources to successfully pursue one of the other two strategies, there are large organizations that successfully use the focus strategy. For example, Denmark's Bang & Olufsen, whose revenues are over $620 million, focuses on high-end audio equipment sales. Whether a focus strategy is feasible depends on the size of the segment and whether the organization can make money serving that segment.

*The Ortiz brothers, Nicolas, George, and Oliver, have earned almost $400 million in revenues in a country of only 3.5 million people by creating Iki, now the second-largest supermarket chain in Lithuania. Iki's 67 stores and 15 convenience outlets cater to the once-Communist country's long-unmet niche market for luxury goods like French cheese, American personal-care products, free-range chickens, and gourmet mushrooms. The brothers now plan to expand Iki to Latvia and Estonia.*

What happens if an organization is unable to develop a cost or differentiation advantage? Porter uses the term **stuck in the middle** to describe those organizations, which find it very difficult to achieve long-term success. Porter goes on to note that successful organizations frequently get into trouble by reaching beyond their competitive advantage and ending up stuck in the middle.

However, subsequent research has shown that organizations *can* successfully pursue a low cost and a differentiation advantage and achieve high performance.[31] However, it's not easy to pull off! To do so successfully means an organization must be strongly committed to keeping costs low *and* establishing solid sources of differentiation. For example, companies such as Anheuser-Busch, FedEx, Intel, and Coca-Cola differentiate their products while at the same time maintaining low-cost operations.

**The Rule of Three** Similar to Porter's generic competitive strategies is a concept called the "rule of three," which explains how, in many industries, three major players emerge to dominate the market.[32] For instance: fast food—McDonald's, Wendy's, Burger King. Credit cards—VISA, MasterCard, American Express. Full-service U.S. airlines: American, United, and Delta. Why three? Research on companies and industries seems to suggest that two companies tend to lead to monopolistic pricing or mutual destruction, while four encourages continual price wars. These three companies are usually highly efficient, "full-line generalists." Then, in addition to these three, other firms in the industry that want to be successful—the "super niche players"—specialize through either product or market segmentation. Then, there are the "ditch dwellers," organizations that aren't one of the highly efficient generalists or one of the highly focused niche players. Just as Porter pointed out with his stuck-in-the-middle strategy, the "rule of three" concept says that managers should avoid making strategic decisions that might cause their organizations to end up in the ditch!

Despite the research behind the rule of three, there are some limitations to the concept. First, there are notable industry exceptions—for instance, athletic footwear (only two major competitors remain—Nike and Adidas, which purchased Reebok in 2006); cruise lines (Carnival and Royal Caribbean); and soft drinks (Coca-Cola and

**cost leadership strategy**
A business or competitive strategy in which the organization competes on the basis of having the lowest costs in its industry.

**differentiation strategy**
A business or competitive strategy in which a company offers unique products that are widely valued by customers.

**focus strategy**
A business or competitive strategy in which a company pursues a cost or differentiation advantage in a narrow industry segment.

**stuck in the middle**
A situation where an organization hasn't been able to develop either a low-cost or a differentiation competitive advantage.

Pepsi). In addition, the rule of three seems to have limited applicability in many countries outside the United States. In the European Union, for example, a rule of four seems to have evolved.[33]

## Functional Strategy

**Functional strategies** are the strategies used by an organization's various functional departments to support the business or competitive strategy. For example, when R. R. Donnelley & Sons Company, a Chicago-based printer, wanted to become more competitive and invested in high-tech digital printing methods, its marketing department had to develop new sales plans and promotional pieces, the production department had to incorporate the digital equipment in the printing plants, and the human resources department had to update its employee selection and training programs. We don't cover specific functional strategies in this book because you'll cover them in other business courses you take.

## Learning Review

- Describe the three major types of corporate strategies.
- Discuss the BCG matrix and how it's used.
- Describe the role of competitive advantage in business strategies.

- Explain Porter's five forces model.
- Describe Porter's three generic competitive strategies and the rule of three.

## STRATEGIC MANAGEMENT IN TODAY'S ENVIRONMENT

There's no better example of the strategic challenges faced by managers in today's market environment than the recorded music industry. Global album sales tumbled 7.2 percent in 2005—the fifth drop in a row—and industry executives braced for more declines. However, digital track and digital album downloads were up 150 percent and 194 percent, respectively. Cell phone ring-tone sales doubled from the previous year, but challenges still remain. Rampant global piracy (according to the IFPI—an organization that represents the worldwide recording industry—one in three music discs sold worldwide is an illegal copy), economic uncertainty, and intense competition from other forms of entertainment have devastated the music industry. Its very nature continues to change, and managers are struggling to find strategies that will help their organizations succeed in such an environment.[34] But the music industry isn't the only industry dealing with such enormous strategic challenges. Managers in all kinds of organizations face increasingly intense global competition and high performance expectations by investors and customers. How have managers responded to these new realities? (  Go to www.prenhall.com/rolls) In this section we want to look at some current issues in strategy, including the need for strategic flexibility, and at how managers are designing strategies to emphasize e-business, customer service, and innovation.

### Strategic Flexibility

Jürgen Schrempp, former CEO of DaimlerChrysler stated, "My principle always was . . . move as fast as you can and [if] you indeed make mistakes, you have to correct them. It's much better to move fast, and make mistakes occasionally, than move too slowly."[35] You wouldn't think that smart individuals who are paid lots of money to manage organizations would make mistakes when it comes to strategic decisions. But even when managers "manage strategically" by following the strategic management process, there's no guarantee that the chosen strategies will lead to positive outcomes. Reading any of the current business periodicals would certainly support this assertion! But the key for managers is responding quickly when it's obvious that the strategy isn't working. In other words, they

### Strategic Leadership: It's All About Vision . . . and More

No matter how we characterize the upper-level manager's job, you can be certain that from their perspective at the top of the organization that it's like no other job in the organization. By definition, upper-level managers are ultimately responsible for every decision and action of every organizational employee. One important role they do play in strategic management is being an effective strategic leader.[36] What does it mean to be an effective strategic leader? It involves six important responsibilities.

First, an effective strategic leader *determines the organization's purpose or vision.* The responsibility for deciding what the organization is and what it can become is the responsibility of the top-level manager. Next, a strategic leader *exploits and maintains the core competencies.* Why is this an important responsibility? Because the core competencies can be important sources of competitive advantage. The third responsibility of an effective strategic leader is *developing the organiza-*

*tion's human capital.* An organization is nothing without its people. Strategic leaders understand this and invest in programs and activities that improve employees' skills, abilities, and knowledge. Next, an effective strategic leader *creates and sustains a strong organizational culture.* Success will depend on the ability of a firm's top managers to form a community of citizens rather than a band of employees working for a firm. An effective strategic leader establishes a culture—a community—that epitomizes the values that will make the organization successful. The fifth responsibility of an effective strategic leader is *emphasizing ethical decisions and practices.* What else needs to be said? Doing business ethically and responsibly is imperative and it starts at the top. Finally, an effective strategic leader *establishes appropriately balanced controls.* This simply means that strategic leaders must know what's going on and why and be willing to make changes as needed to insure the long-run success of the organization.

need **strategic flexibility**—that is, the ability to recognize major external environmental changes, to quickly commit resources, and to recognize when a strategic decision isn't working. Given the environment that managers face today—oftentimes, highly uncertain and changing—strategic flexibility seems absolutely necessary. Exhibit 8–7 provides some suggestions for developing strategic flexibility.

## New Directions in Organizational Strategies

ESPN.com gets more than 16 million unique users a month. 16 million! That's almost twice the population size of New York City. Its popular online business is just one of many business ventures that ESPN is in. Originally founded as a television channel, ESPN is now into original programming (ESPN develops its own shows and movies); radio (the largest U.S. sports-radio network); online (ESPN.com); publishing (*ESPN The Magazine*); wireless (Mobile ESPN); gaming (video games by exclusive licensee Electronic Arts); X games (annual extreme sports competition); ESPY awards (recognizing

Exhibit 8–7

**Creating Strategic Flexibility**

- Know what's happening with strategies currently being used by *monitoring and measuring results.*
- Encourage employees to *be open about disclosing and sharing negative information.*
- *Get new ideas and perspectives from outside* the organization.
- Have *multiple alternatives* when making strategic decisions.
- *Learn from mistakes.*

*Source:* Based on K. Shimizu and M. A. Hitt, "Strategic Flexibility: Organizational Preparedness to Reverse Ineffective Strategic Decisions," *Academy of Management Executive*, November 2004, pp. 44–59.

**functional strategies**
The strategies used by an organization's various functional departments to support the business or competitive strategy.

**strategic flexibility**
The ability to recognize major external environmental changes, to quickly commit resources, and to recognize when a strategic decision was a mistake.

top achievements in sports); ESPN Zones (sports-theme restaurants); and global (ESPN programming is available in 11 languages in more than 180 countries).[37] Company president George Bodenheimer runs one of the most successful and envied franchises in entertainment, and obviously understands how to successfully manage its various strategies in today's environment. What strategies are important for today's environment? We think there are three: e-business, customer service, and innovation.

**e-Business Strategies** As we discussed in Chapter 2, e-business offers many advantages to organizations, whether it's simply through e-commerce efforts or through being a total e-business.

There's no doubt that Internet technology has changed, and is changing, the way organizations do business. Using the Internet, companies have, for instance, (1) created knowledge bases that employees can tap into anytime, anywhere; (2) turned customers into collaborative partners who help design, test, and launch new products; (3) become virtually paperless in specific tasks such as purchasing and filing expense reports; (4) managed logistics in real time; and (5) changed the nature of numerous work tasks throughout the organization.

Managers can formulate e-business strategies that contribute to the development of a sustainable competitive advantage.[38] A cost leader can use e-business to reduce costs in a variety of ways. It might use online bidding and order processing to eliminate the need for sales calls and to decrease sales force expenses; it could use Web-based inventory control systems that reduce storage costs; or it might use online testing and evaluation of job applicants. For example, General Electric applied e-business techniques by initiating several Internet-based purchasing activities in order to reduce costs.

A differentiator needs to offer products or services that customers perceive and value as unique. How could e-business contribute? The differentiator might use Internet-based knowledge systems to shorten customer response times; provide rapid online responses to service requests; or automate purchasing and payment systems so that customers have detailed status reports and purchasing histories. Dell Computer is an excellent example of a company that has exploited the differentiation advantage made possible by e-business.

Finally, because the focuser targets a narrow market segment with customized products, it might provide chat rooms or discussion boards for customers to interact with others who have common interests; design niche Web sites that target specific groups with specific interests; or use Web sites to perform standardized office functions such as payroll or budgeting. One focuser that has capitalized on Internet technology is SalvageSale, a unique Web business that specializes in quick liquidation of commercial salvage goods. Its efficient use of e-business techniques allows it to keep costs low *and* appeal to a specific customer group, primarily insurance and transportation companies.

Research has shown that an important e-business strategy might be a clicks-and-bricks strategy. A clicks-and-bricks firm is one that uses both online (clicks) and traditional stand-alone locations (bricks).[39] For example, Walgreen's established an online site for ordering prescriptions, but some 90 percent of its customers who placed orders on the Web preferred to pick up their prescriptions at a nearby store rather than have them shipped to their home. So its "clicks-and-bricks" strategy works . . . and works well!

**Customer Service Strategies** Companies that emphasize customer service need strategies that cultivate that atmosphere from top to bottom. What kinds of strategies does that take? It takes giving customers what they want, communicating effectively with them, and providing employees with customer service training. Let's look first at the strategy of giving customers what they want.

New Balance Athletic Shoes does something that Nike and Reebok do not. It gives customers a truly unique product: shoes in varying widths. No other athletic shoe manufacturer has shoes for narrow or wide feet and in practically any size.[40] Also, look back at our chapter-opening dilemma at how Kevin Plank's Under Armour products were specifically designed with the customer in mind. It should come as no surprise that an important customer service strategy is giving customers what they want, a major aspect of an organization's overall marketing strategy.

_Google's strategy is to constantly innovate. Marissa Mayer, the company's director of consumer Web products, champions Google's philosophy that good ideas can come from anywhere. Her office is across from the engineering department's snack area, inviting visits from employees with new ideas to discuss. Three times a week Mayer has office hours reserved for hearing and critiquing new projects in progress. "I keep my ears open," she says. "I work at building a reputation for being receptive."_

Another important customer service strategy involves communication. Hot Topic is a popular retail specialist that's fanatical about customer feedback, which it gets in the form of shopper "report cards." The company's CEO, Betsy McLaughlin, pores over more than 1,000 of them each week.[41] Managers should know what's going on with customers. They need to find out what customers liked and didn't like about their purchase encounter—from their interactions with employees to their experience with the actual product or service. But communication isn't a one-way street. It's also important to let customers know what's going on with the organization that might affect future purchase decisions. Having an effective customer communication system is an important customer service strategy.

Finally, we've discussed previously the importance of an organization's culture in emphasizing customer service. This requires that employees be trained to provide exceptional customer service. For example, Singapore Airlines is well-known for its customer treatment. "On everything facing the customer, they do not scrimp," says an analyst based in Singapore.[42] Employees are expected to "get service right," leaving employees with no doubt about the expectations as far as how to treat customers. Singapore Airlines' service strategy is a good example of what managers must do if customer service is an important organizational goal and an important part of the company's culture.

**Innovation Strategies** When Procter & Gamble purchased the Iams pet-food business, it did what it always does—used its renowned research division to look for

## _becoming_ a Manager

✓ As you keep up with the current business news, pay attention to organizational strategies that managers are using. What types of strategies are the successful organizations using?

✓ Use SWOT analysis when you apply for jobs—after all, why would you want to work for some organization that has a lot of weaknesses or is facing significant threats?

✓ Talk to managers about strategy. Ask them how they know when it's time to try a different strategy.

✓ As described in the "Managing Your Career" box, do a personal SWOT analysis.

✓ Go to www.prenhall.com/rolls and complete any of the following exercises from the Self-Assessment Library: S.A.L. #I.A.4—How Well Do I Handle Ambiguity?, S.A.L. #I.A.5—How Creative Am I?, and S.A.L. #III.C.1—How Well Do I Respond to Turbulent Change?

Self-Assessment Library (S.A.L.)

Exhibit 8–8

**First-Mover Advantages—
Disadvantages**

| Advantages | Disadvantages |
|---|---|
| • Reputation for being innovative and industry leader<br>• Cost and learning benefits<br>• Control over scarce resources and keeping competitors from having access to them<br>• Opportunity to begin building customer relationships and customer loyalty | • Uncertainty over exact direction technology and market will go<br>• Risk of competitors imitating innovations<br>• Financial and strategic risks<br>• High development costs |

ways to transfer technology from its other divisions to make new products.[43] One of the outcomes of this cross-divisional combination: a new tartar-fighting ingredient from toothpaste that's included in all of its dry adult pet foods.

As this example shows, innovation strategies aren't necessarily focused on just the radical, breakthrough products. They can include the application of existing technology to new uses. And organizations of all kinds and sizes have successfully used both approaches. What types of innovation strategies do organizations need in today's environment? Those strategies should reflect their philosophy about innovation, which is shaped by two strategic decisions: innovation emphasis and innovation timing.

Managers must first decide where the emphasis of their innovation efforts will be. Is the organization going to focus on basic scientific research, product development, or process improvement? Basic scientific research requires the heaviest resource commitment because it involves the nuts-and-bolts activities and work of scientific research. In numerous industries (for instance, genetics engineering, cosmetics, information technology, or pharmaceuticals), an organization's expertise in basic research is the key to a sustainable competitive advantage. However, not every organization requires this extensive commitment to scientific research to achieve high performance levels. Instead, many depend on product development strategies. Although this strategy also requires a significant resource investment, it's not in the areas associated with scientific research. Instead, the organization takes existing technology and improves on it or applies it in new ways, just as Procter & Gamble did when it applied tartar-fighting knowledge to pet food products. Both of these first two strategic approaches to innovation (basic scientific research and product development) can help an organization achieve high levels of differentiation, which is a significant source of competitive advantage.

Finally, the last strategic approach to innovation emphasis is a focus on process development. Using this strategy, an organization looks for ways to improve and enhance its work processes. The organization innovates new and improved ways for employees to do their work in all organizational areas. This innovation strategy can lead to an organization's lowering costs, which, as we know, also can be a significant source of competitive advantage.

Once managers have determined the focus of their innovation efforts, they must decide their innovation timing strategy. Some organizations want to be the first with innovations whereas others are content to follow or mimic the innovations. An organization that's first to bring a product innovation to the market or to use a new process innovation is called a **first mover**. Being a first mover has certain strategic advantages and disadvantages, as shown in Exhibit 8–8. Some organizations pursue this route, hoping to develop a sustainable competitive advantage. Others have successfully developed a sustainable competitive advantage by being the followers in the industry. They let the first movers pioneer the innovations and then mimic their products or processes. Which approach managers choose depends on their organization's innovation philosophy and specific resources and capabilities.

## Learning Review

- Explain why strategic flexibility is important.
- Describe e-business strategies.

- Explain what strategies organizations might use to become more customer oriented and to be more innovative.

# Managers Respond to a Manager's Dilemma

## Shruti Bansal

Associate Vice President, Atlantic Trust,
Boston, MA

I think SWOT analysis is of extreme importance to Kevin and will give him a good starting point to strategically plan Under Armour's expansion to women and children's products. Here are some issues I would address before beginning any planning process:

- What is Under Armour recognized for: men's products or as a provider of sports clothing in general? Sometimes it is difficult to beat your own brand image.
- Who are the current manufacturers of products catering to women and children? What market share do they have?
- What barriers to entry—such as brand loyalty—exist in this industry? Are there any opportunities to collaborate with existing manufacturers?
- What additional costs are associated with launching new products? For example, are there any legal issues of making sure material for kids is nonflammable or hypoallergenic?
- What internal capabilities and resources can be utilized and shifted to the design and production of these new products? What new resources will be needed?
- Have we looked at the market demand for these two new groups?
- What difficulties did we encounter while launching Under Armour's men's products? Are those issues relevant to these new products?
- Should we pay more attention to colors, designs, overall look, and appeal since women and kids tend to be more fashion conscious?

**first mover**
An organization that's first to bring a product innovation
to the market or to use a new process innovation.

# Learning Summary

## What Is Strategic Management?

*What managers do to develop the organization's strategies*

- **Strategies**: the decisions and actions that determine the long-run performance of the organization
- **Business model**: a strategic design for how a company intends to profit from its strategies, work processes, and work activities

## What Does Strategic Management Involve?

### Step 1: Identify current mission, goals, strategies

### Step 2: Analyze the external environment for:
- **Opportunities**: positive trends
- **Threats**: negative trends

### Step 3: Analyze the organization's resources, capabilities, and core competencies:
- **Strengths**: activities the organization does well or unique resources it has
- **Weaknesses**: activities it doesn't do well or resources it needs, but lacks

  This is known as the **SWOT ANALYSIS**.

### Step 4: Select appropriate strategies to use
- Corporate strategies (what businesses a company is in, should be in, or wants to be in, and what it wants to do with those businesses)
  - Growth: concentration, vertical or horizontal integration, or diversification
  - Stability: stay the same
  - Renewal: retrenchment, turnaround
  - Analyze corporate portfolio of businesses using BCG matrix (cash cows, stars, question marks, dogs)
- Business or competitive strategies (how organization will compete in each business)
  - Determine competitive advantage (what sets organization apart; competitive edge) and then determine best competitive strategy
    - Porter's five forces model (threat of new entrants, threat of substitutes, bargaining power of buyers, bargaining power of suppliers, and threat of substitutes)
  - Cost leadership
  - Differentiation
  - Focus (cost or differentiation)
  - Stuck in the middle (can't develop cost or differentiation advantage)
- Functional strategies (strategies used by various functional areas to support competitive strategies)

### Step 5: Implement strategies (through organizing and leading)

### Step 6: Evaluate strategies (through controlling)

## What Current Strategy Challenges Do Managers Face?
- Must have strategic flexibility (ability to recognize major changes and to quickly respond to them)
- Important new strategies (e-business, customer service, and innovation)

## Management: By the Numbers

- In a recent Annual Reputation Quotient study by Harris Interactive, 71 percent of the respondents said that corporate America's reputation is "not good or is terrible."
- In a survey of workers by FranklinCovey, 48 percent said that their firm has a clear strategic direction. However, only 37 percent understood the reason for that direction.
- In this same survey, 44 percent of workers said their organization had clearly communicated its most important goals. However, a separate study by FranklinCovey showed that only 15 percent of workers could identify their organization's top three goals.
- According to a survey of 156 large companies, senior executives often make strategic decisions outside the formal planning process, without rigorous analysis or productive debate.

- In a study that looked at who puts their mission statements on the Web, only 23 of 100 mission statement sites identified were for-profit corporations. Educational institutions and not-for-profit associations made up 58 percent of the sites.
- In this same study, 55 percent of a *Fortune* 500 sample appeared to have no mission statement posted on the Web at all.

*Sources:* M. C. Mankins and R. Steele, "Stop Making Plans; Start Making Decisions," *Harvard Business Review,* January 2006, pp. 76–84; Harris Interactive, "Johnson & Johnson Ranks No. 1 in National Corporate Reputation Survey for Seventh Consecutive Year," www.harrisinteractive.com, December 7, 2005; "Clear as Mud," *Industry Week,* May 2004, p. 16; and C. K. Bart, "Exploring the Application of Mission Statements on the World Wide Web," *Internet Research: Electronic Networking Applications and Policy,* vol. 11 (4), 2001, pp. 360–368.

## Thinking About Management Issues

1. Perform a SWOT analysis on a local business you think you know well. What, if any, competitive advantage does this organization have?

2. How might the process of strategy formulation, implementation, and evaluation differ for (a) large businesses, (b) small businesses, (c) not-for-profit organizations, and (d) global businesses?

3. "The concept of competitive advantage is as important for not-for-profit organizations as it is for for-profit organizations." Do you agree or disagree with this statement? Explain, using examples to make your case.

4. Should ethical considerations be included in analyses of an organization's internal and external environments? Why or why not?

5. How could the Internet be helpful to managers as they follow the steps in the strategic management process?

6. Find examples of five different organizational mission statements. Using the mission statements, describe what types of corporate-level and business-level strategies each organization might use to fulfill that mission statement. Explain your rationale for choosing each strategy.

## Working Together: Team-Based Exercise

Examples of organizational strategies are found everywhere in business and general news periodicals. You should be able to recognize the different types of strategies from these news stories.

Form groups of three or four individuals. Using materials that your instructor provides you, find examples of five different organizational strategies. Determine whether the examples are corporate, business, or functional and explain why your group made that choice. Be prepared to share your examples with the class.

# Chapter 9

# Learning Outline

*Use this Learning Outline as you read and study this chapter.*

### Techniques for Assessing the Environment

- List the different approaches to assess the environment.
- Explain what competitor intelligence is and ways that managers can do it legally and ethically.
- Describe how managers can improve the effectiveness of forecasting.
- List the steps in the benchmarking process.

### Techniques for Allocating Resources

- List the four techniques for allocating resources.
- Describe the different types of budgets.
- Explain what a Gantt chart and a load chart do.
- Describe how PERT network analysis works.
- Understand how to compute a breakeven point.
- Describe how managers can use linear programming.

### Contemporary Planning Techniques

- Explain why flexibility is so important to today's planning techniques.
- Describe project management.
- List the steps in the project planning process.
- Discuss why scenario planning is an important planning tool.

# Planning Tools and Techniques

## A Manager's Dilemma

It's one of the most famous and popular zoos in the world. The San Diego Zoo is one of the departmental units of the Zoological Society of San Diego (as it's officially known). As the largest zoological membership association in the world, more than half a million members pay dues to both support and enjoy the Zoo's numerous and expansive wildlife exhibits. Paula Brock is the CFO of the Zoological Society, which operates the zoo.[1] When she took over that job in 2001, Brock immediately saw the need to link the nonprofit organization's strategy to its budgeting process. And the importance of doing so soon became quickly apparent.

When exotic Newcastle Disease—one of the most infectious bird diseases in the world—broke out in southern California in 2003, it could have been a complete disaster for the San Diego Zoo. Paula says, "We have one of the most valuable collections of birds in the world, if not *the* most valuable." Keeping the disease out of the zoo itself and its nearby wildlife sanctuary (Wild Animal Park) was absolutely critical. However, doing so would become an enormous unplanned and unbudgeted expense. Ultimately, the zoo, with $150 million in revenues, spent almost half a million dollars on quarantine measures. But all the preventive measures (such as sanitizing delivery truck tires, shutting bird exhibits to the public, changing and cleaning zookeeper uniforms daily, and so forth) worked. None of the zoo's birds caught the disease. In addition, Paula was also able to avoid damage to the zoo's budget by using monthly budget reforecasting procedures that she had introduced a year earlier. She said, "When we get a hit like this, we still have to find a way to make our bottom line. To keep your company on a path, it has to have some kind of map. The budgeting-and-planning process is that map. I cannot imagine an organization feeling in control if it didn't have that sort of discipline."

Paula's next task is to get the zoo's professional scientists and animal keepers to be involved with the budgeting process—without it turning into bureaucratic number crunching—by educating them about the importance of budgeting updates throughout the year. Put yourself in her position. How should she approach this task?

## What would you do?

In this chapter we'll discuss some basic planning tools and techniques that managers like Paula Brock or managers at any businesses—large or small—could use.(  Go to www.prenhall.com/rolls) We'll begin by looking at some techniques for assessing the environment. Then we'll review techniques for allocating resources. Finally, we'll discuss some contemporary planning techniques including project management and scenarios.

## TECHNIQUES FOR ASSESSING THE ENVIRONMENT

Leigh Knopf, former senior manager for strategic planning at the AICPA, says that many larger accounting firms have set up external analysis departments to "study the wider environment in which they, and their clients, operate." These organizations have recognized that, "What happens in India in today's environment may have an impact on an American accounting firm in North Dakota."[2] In our description of the strategic management process in Chapter 8, we discussed the importance of assessing the organization's environment. In this section, we review three techniques to help managers do that: environmental scanning, forecasting, and benchmarking.

### Environmental Scanning

How important is environmental scanning? Just ask Bill Gates, chairman and chief software architect of Microsoft. In December 2003, he was looking around on competitor Google's company Web site and found a help-wanted page with descriptions of all the open jobs. What piqued his interest was that many of these posted job qualifications were identical to Microsoft's job requirements. He began to wonder why Google—a Web search company—would be posting job openings for software engineers with backgrounds that "had nothing to do with Web searches and everything to do with Microsoft's core business of operating-system design, compiler optimization, and distributed-systems architecture." Gates e-mailed an urgent message to some of his top executives saying that Microsoft had better be on its toes because it sure looked like Google was preparing to move into being more of a software company.[3]

How can managers become aware of significant environmental changes such as a new law in Germany permitting shopping for "tourist items" on Sunday; the increased trend of counterfeit consumer products in South Africa; the precipitous decline in the working-age populations in Japan, Germany, Italy, and Russia; or the decrease in family size in Mexico? Managers in both small and large organizations use **environmental scanning**, which is the screening of large amounts of information to anticipate and interpret changes in the environment. Extensive environmental scanning is likely to reveal issues and concerns that could affect an organization's current or planned activities. (  Go to www.prenhall.com/rolls). Research has shown that companies that use environmental scanning have higher performance.[4] Organizations that don't keep on top of environmental changes are likely to experience the opposite. For instance, Tupperware, the food storage container company, enjoyed unprecedented success during the 1960s and 1970s selling its products at home-hostessed parties where housewives played games, socialized, and saw product demonstrations. However, as U.S. society changed—more women working full-time outside the home, an increasing divorce rate, and young adults waiting longer to marry—the popularity of Tupperware parties began to decline because no one had time to go to them. The company's North American market share fell from 60 percent to 40 percent while Rubbermaid, a competitor that marketed its plastic food storage containers in retail outlets, increased its market share from 5 percent to 40 percent. By the early 1990s, most American women had no desire to go to a Tupperware party or knew how to find Tupperware products. Yet, Tupperware's president, obviously clueless about the changed environment, predicted that before the end of the 1990s, the party concept would be popular once again, a prediction that didn't materialize. Tupperware now faces other strong competitors in addition to Rubbermaid including Pampered Chef, Williams-Sonoma, and Glad-Ware.[5] This example shows how a once-successful company can suffer by failing to recognize how the environment has changed.

**Competitor Intelligence** One of the fastest-growing areas of environmental scanning is **competitor intelligence**.[6] It's a process by which organizations gather information about their competitors and get answers to questions such as: Who are they? What are they doing? How will what they're doing affect us? Let's look at an example of how one organization used competitor intelligence in its planning. Dun & Bradstreet (D&B), a leading provider of business information, has an active business intelligence division. The division manager received a call from an assistant vice president for sales in one of the company's geographic territories. This person had been on a sales call with a major customer and the customer happened to mention in passing that another company had visited and made a major presentation about its services. What was interesting was that, although D&B had plenty of competitors, this particular company wasn't one of them. The manager gathered together a team that sifted through dozens of sources (research services, Internet, personal contacts, and other external sources) and quickly became convinced that there was something to this. Managers at D&B jumped into action to develop plans to counteract this competitive attack.[7]

Competitor intelligence experts suggest that 80 percent of what managers need to know about competitors can be found out from their own employees, suppliers, and customers.[8] Competitor intelligence doesn't have to involve spying. Advertisements, promotional materials, press releases, reports filed with government agencies, annual reports, want ads, newspaper reports, and industry studies are examples of readily accessible sources of information. Attending trade shows and debriefing the company's sales force can be other good sources of competitor information. Many firms regularly buy competitors' products and have their own engineers study them (through a process called *reverse engineering*) to learn about new technical innovations. In addition, the Internet has opened up vast sources of competitor intelligence as many corporate Web pages include new product information and other press releases. (  Go to www.prenhall.com/rolls)

*To avoid prosecution on charges that Boeing improperly received thousands of pages of proprietary information from Lockheed Martin Corp., its competitor in military rockets, the company recently negotiated a settlement with the Justice Department. This $615 million settlement is the biggest financial penalty ever imposed on a U.S. defense contractor for such ethical violations. Boeing has also lost existing contracts and has been barred from bidding on some Pentagon work.*

**Q & A**
You know that you can find pretty much anything on the Internet. What about competitor information? Q & A 9.1 discusses how managers might use the Internet.

**environmental scanning**
The screening of large amounts of information to anticipate and interpret changes in the environment.

**competitor intelligence**
Environmental scanning activity by which organizations gather information about competitors.

## *thinking critically about* **Ethics**

Here are some techniques that have been suggested for gathering competitor information: (1) Get copies of lawsuits and civil suits that may have been filed against competitors. These court proceedings are public records and can expose surprising details. (2) Call the Better Business Bureau and ask if competitors have had complaints filed against them because of fraudulent product claims or questionable business practices. (3) Pretend to be a journalist and call competitors to ask questions. (4) Get copies of your competitors' in-house newsletters and read them. (5) Buy a single share of competitors' stock so you get the annual report and other information the company sends out. (6) Send someone from your organization to apply for a job at a competitor and have that person ask specific questions. (7) Dig through a competitor's trash.

Which, if any, of these are unethical? Defend your choices. What ethical guidelines would you suggest for competitor intelligence activities?

The concerns about competitor intelligence pertain to the ways in which competitor information is gathered. For instance, at Procter & Gamble (P&G), executives hired competitive intelligence firms to gather information on its competitors in the hair-care business. At least one of these firms misrepresented themselves to competitor Unilever's employees, trespassed at Unilever's hair-care headquarters in Chicago, and went through trash dumpsters to gain information. When P&G's CEO found out, he immediately fired the individuals responsible and apologized to Unilever.[9] Competitor intelligence becomes illegal corporate spying when it involves the theft of proprietary materials or trade secrets by any means. The Economic Espionage Act passed by Congress in 1996 makes it a crime in the United States to engage in economic espionage or to steal a trade secret.[10] The difficult decisions about competitive intelligence arise because often there's a fine line between what's considered *legal and ethical* and what's considered *legal but unethical.* Although the top manager at one competitive intelligence firm contends that 99.9 percent of intelligence gathering is legal, there's no question that some people or companies will go to any lengths—many unethical—to get information about competitors.[11]

**Global Scanning** One type of environmental scanning that's particularly important is global scanning. Because world markets are complex and dynamic, managers have expanded the scope of their scanning efforts to gain vital information on global forces that might affect their organizations.[12] The value of global scanning to managers, of course, is largely dependent on the extent of the organization's global activities. For a company that has significant global interests, global scanning can be quite valuable. For instance, Sealed Air Corporation of Saddle Brook, New Jersey—you may be familiar with its most famous and popular product, Bubble Wrap—tracks global demographic changes. It found that as countries move from agriculture-based societies to industrial ones, the population tends to eat out more and favor prepackaged foods, which means more sales of its food packaging products.[13]

The sources that managers use for scanning the domestic environment are too limited for global scanning. Managers need to globalize their perspectives and information sources. For instance, they can subscribe to information clipping services that review world newspapers and business periodicals and provide summaries of desired information. Also, there are numerous electronic services that provide topic searches and automatic updates in global areas of special interest to managers.

## Forecasting

The second technique managers can use to assess the environment is forecasting. Forecasting is an important part of planning and managers need forecasts that will

**Q & A**

Where does the information to do forecasts come from? See Q & A 9.2.

allow them to predict future events effectively and in a timely manner. ( ◆ Go to www.prenhall.com/rolls) Environmental scanning establishes the basis for **forecasts**, which are predictions of outcomes. Virtually any component in the organization's environment can be forecasted. Let's look at how managers forecast and how effective forecasts are.

**Forecasting Techniques** Forecasting techniques fall into two categories: quantitative and qualitative. **Quantitative forecasting** applies a set of mathematical rules to a series of past data to predict outcomes. These techniques are preferred when managers have sufficient hard data that can be used. **Qualitative forecasting**, in contrast, uses the judgment and opinions of knowledgeable individuals to predict outcomes. Qualitative techniques typically are used when precise data are limited or hard to obtain. Exhibit 9–1 describes some popular forecasting techniques.

Today, many organizations collaborate on forecasts using Internet-based software known as CPFR®, which stands for collaborative planning, forecasting, and

**Exhibit 9–1**

**Forecasting Techniques**

| Technique | Description | Application |
|---|---|---|
| **Quantitative** | | |
| Time series analysis | Fits a trend line to a mathematical equation and projects into the future by means of this equation | Predicting next quarter's sales on the basis of 4 years of previous sales data |
| Regression models | Predicts one variable on the basis of known or assumed other variables | Seeking factors that will predict a certain level of sales (for example, price, advertising expenditures) |
| Econometric models | Uses a set of regression equations to simulate segments of the economy | Predicting change in car sales as a result of changes in tax laws |
| Economic indicators | Uses one or more economic indicators to predict a future state of the economy | Using change in GNP to predict discretionary income |
| Substitution effect | Uses a mathematical formula to predict how, when, and under what circumstances a new product or technology will replace an existing one | Predicting the effect of DVD players on the sale of VHS players |
| **Qualitative** | | |
| Jury of opinion | Combines and averages the opinions of experts | Polling the company's human resource managers to predict next year's college recruitment needs |
| Sales force composition | Combines estimates from field sales personnel of customers' expected purchases | Predicting next year's sales of industrial lasers |
| Customer evaluation | Combines estimates from established customers' purchases | Surveying major car dealers by a car manufacturer to determine types and quantities of products desired |

**forecasts**
Predictions of outcomes.

**quantitative forecasting**
Forecasting that applies a set of mathematical rules to a series of past data to predict outcomes.

**qualitative forecasting**
Forecasting that uses the judgment and opinions of knowledgeable individuals to predict outcomes.

replenishment.[14] CPFR offers a standardized way for retailers and manufacturers to use the Internet to exchange data. Each organization relies on its own data about past sales trends, promotion plans, and other factors to calculate a demand forecast for a particular product. If their respective forecasts differ by a certain amount (say 10 percent), the retailer and manufacturer use the Internet to exchange more data and written comments until they arrive at a single and more accurate forecast. This collaborative forecasting helps both organizations do a better job of planning.

**Forecasting Effectiveness**  The goal of forecasting is to provide managers with information that will facilitate decision making. Despite its importance to planning, managers have had mixed success with it.[15] For instance, prior to a holiday weekend at the Procter & Gamble factory in Lima, Ohio, managers were preparing to shut down the facility early so as not to have to pay employees for just sitting around and to give them some extra time off. The move seemed to make sense because an analysis of purchase orders and historical sales trends indicated that the factory had already produced enough cases of Liquid Tide detergent to meet laundry demand over the holiday. However, managers got a real surprise. One of the company's largest retail customers placed a sizable—and unforeseen—order. They had to reopen the plant, pay the workers overtime, and schedule emergency shipments to meet the retailer's request.[16] As this example shows, managers' forecasts aren't always accurate. And in a survey of financial managers in organizations in the United States, United Kingdom, France, and Germany, 84 percent of the respondents said their financial forecasts were inaccurate by 5 percent or more; 54 percent of the respondents reported inaccuracy of 10 percent or more.[17] But it is important to try to make forecasting as effective as possible since research shows that a company's forecasting ability can be a distinctive competence.[18] How can managers make their forecasting more effective? ( ⬧ Go to www.prenhall.com/rolls)[19]

**Q & A**

Why forecast if most forecasts are wrong? Q & A 9.3 explains.

First, it's important to understand that forecasting techniques are most accurate when the environment is not rapidly changing. The more dynamic the environment, the more likely managers are to forecast ineffectively. Also, forecasting is relatively ineffective in predicting nonseasonal events such as recessions, unusual occurrences, discontinued operations, and the actions or reactions of competitors. Next, use simple forecasting methods. They tend to do as well as, and often better than, complex methods that may mistakenly confuse random data for meaningful information. For instance, at St. Louis–based Emerson Electric, chairman emeritus Chuck Knight found that forecasts developed as part of the company's planning process were indicating that the competition wasn't just domestic anymore, but global. He didn't use any complex mathematical techniques to come to this conclusion but instead relied on the information already collected as part of his company's planning process. Next, look at involving more people in the process. At *Fortune* 100 companies, it's not unusual to have 1,000 to 5,000 managers providing forecasting input. These businesses are finding that the more people are involved in the process, the more they can improve the reliability of the outcomes.[20] Next, compare every forecast with "no change." A no-change forecast is accurate approximately half the time. Next, use *rolling* forecasts that look 12 to 18 months ahead, instead of using a single, static forecast. These types of forecasts can help managers spot trends better and help their organizations be more adaptive in changing environments.[21] It's also important to not rely on a single forecasting method. Make forecasts with several models and average them, especially when making longer-range forecasts. Next, don't assume that you can accurately identify turning points in a trend. What is typically perceived as a significant turning point often turns out to be simply a random event. And, finally, remember that forecasting *is* a managerial skill and as such can be practiced and improved. Forecasting software has made the task somewhat less mathematically challenging, although the "number crunching" is only a small part of the activity. Interpreting the forecast and incorporating that information into planning decisions is the challenge facing managers.

# Benchmarking

Suppose that you're a talented pianist or gymnast. To make yourself better, you want to learn from the best so you watch outstanding musicians or athletes for motions and techniques they use as they perform. That's what is involved in the final technique for assessing the environment we're going to discuss—**benchmarking**, the search for the best practices among competitors or noncompetitors that lead to their superior performance.[22] Does benchmarking work? Studies show that users have achieved 69 percent faster growth and 45 percent greater productivity.[23]

**Q & A**

If you're "stealing" someone else's approach, isn't benchmarking unethical? Go to Q & A 9.4 for an answer.

The basic idea behind benchmarking is that managers can improve performance by analyzing and then copying the methods of the leaders in various fields. ( ◆ Go to www.prenhall.com/rolls) Today, organizations such as Nissan, Payless Shoe Source, the U.S. military, General Mills, United Airlines, and Volvo Construction Equipment have used benchmarking as a tool in their quest for performance improvement. In fact, some companies have chosen some pretty unusual benchmarking partners! United Airlines, for example, studied NASCAR pit crews, who can change a race-car tire in under 15 seconds, to see how they could make gate turnarounds even faster. IBM studied Las Vegas casinos for ways to discourage employee theft. Many hospitals have benchmarked their admissions processes against Marriott Hotels. And Giordano Holdings Ltd., a Hong Kong–based manufacturer and retailer of mass-market casual wear, borrowed its "good quality, good value" concept from Marks & Spencer, used Limited Brands to benchmark its point-of-sales computerized information system, and modeled its simplified product offerings on McDonald's menu.[24]

What does benchmarking involve? Exhibit 9–2 illustrates the four steps typically used in benchmarking.

## Learning Review

- List the different approaches to assess the environment.
- Explain what competitor intelligence is and ways that managers can do it legally and ethically.

- Describe how managers can improve the effectiveness of forecasting.
- List the steps in the benchmarking process.

Exhibit 9–2

**Steps in Benchmarking**

*Source:* Based on Y. K. Shetty, "Aiming High: Competitive Benchmarking for Superior Performance," *Long Range Planning*, February 1993, p. 42.

**benchmarking**
The search for the best practices among competitors or noncompetitors that lead to their superior performance.

*Wipro, Ltd., a business-process outsourcing company in Bangalore, India, actively benchmarks Toyota's smoothly run manufacturing processes, looking for ways to operate its own labor-intensive business more efficiently. P. V. Priya (center in photo), medical claims supervisor for Wipro, starts each day in a stand-up meeting with her team in the "War Zone," where she congratulates them on work done and asks for suggestions about how to improve team performance.*

**Self-Assessment Library (S.A.L.)**

If you're like other students, how you spend your time (a valuable resource) is important to you. Are you spending your valuable time wisely? Do S.A.L. #I.E.2 and find out!

**Q & A**

How can a budget be variable and be a way to "plan" expenditures? That seems contradictory. Q & A 9.5 explains.

Exhibit 9–3

**Types of Budgets**

*Source:* Based on R. S. Russell and B. W. Taylor III, *Production and Operations Management* (Upper Saddle River, NJ: Prentice Hall, 1995), p. 287.

## TECHNIQUES FOR ALLOCATING RESOURCES

As we know from Chapter 7, once an organization's goals have been established, an important aspect of planning is determining how those goals are going to be accomplished. Before managers can organize and lead in order to implement the goals, they must have **resources**, which are the assets of the organization (financial, physical, human, and intangible). How can managers allocate these resources effectively and efficiently so that organizational goals are met? That's what we want to look at in this section. Although managers can choose from a number of techniques for allocating resources (many of which are covered in courses on accounting, finance, human resources, and operations management), we'll discuss four techniques here: budgeting, scheduling, breakeven analysis, and linear programming. ( Go to www.prenhall.com/rolls)

### Budgeting

Most of us have had some experience, as limited as it might be, with budgets. We probably learned at a very early age that unless we allocated our "revenues" carefully, our weekly allowance was spent on "expenses" before the week was half over.

A **budget** is a numerical plan for allocating resources to specific activities. Managers typically prepare budgets for revenues, expenses, and large capital expenditures such as equipment. It's not unusual, though, for budgets to be used for improving time, space, and use of material resources. These types of budgets substitute nondollar numbers for dollar amounts. Such items as person-hours, capacity utilization, or units of production can be budgeted for daily, weekly, or monthly activities. Exhibit 9–3 describes the different types of budgets that managers might use. ( Go to www.prenhall.com/rolls)

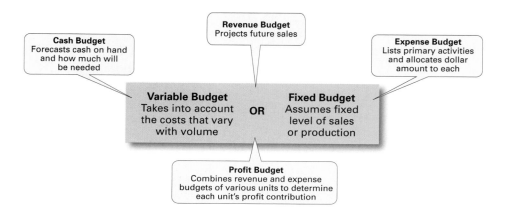

*Richard Hayne, founder and CEO of Urban Outfitters, sees his chain's budgeting process as "two sides of the brain working together." Budget controls at headquarters are tight, but the two brand presidents, who make quarterly plans determined by the budget and by fashion forecasts, have enough flexibility to change direction within a week based on what items are selling well. Despite daily monitoring, Urban Outfitters' individual merchandise buyers also have wide latitude; they can take markdowns when they need to instead of waiting for decisions from headquarters. "If you take the markdown when you need it," says the company's chief financial officer, "you have a better chance of selling it."*

Why are budgets so popular? Probably because they're applicable to a wide variety of organizations and work activities within organizations. We live in a world in which almost everything is expressed in monetary units. Dollars, rupees, pesos, euros, yuan, yen, and the like are used as a common measuring unit within a country. It seems only logical, then, that monetary budgets would be a useful tool for allocating resources and guiding work in such diverse departments as manufacturing and information systems or at various levels in an organization. Budgets are one planning technique that most managers, regardless of organizational level, use. It's an important managerial activity because it forces financial discipline and structure throughout the organization. (Look back at our chapter-opening dilemma on the role that budgeting played at the San Diego Zoo.) However, many managers don't like preparing budgets because they feel the process is time-consuming, inflexible, inefficient, and ineffective.[25] How can the budgeting process be improved? Exhibit 9–4 provides some suggestions. Organizations such as Texas Instruments, IKEA, Hendrick Motorsports, Volvo, and Svenska Handelsbanken have incorporated several of these suggestions as they revamped their budgeting processes. (See the Budgeting Skills Module on page 621 for an explanation of the mechanics of the budgeting process.)

## Scheduling

Ann is a manager at an Express store in San Francisco. Every week, she determines employees' work hours and the store area where each employee will be working. If you

---

**Exhibit 9–4**

**Suggestions for Improving Budgeting**

- Collaborate and communicate.
- Be flexible.
- Goals should drive budgets—budgets should not determine goals.
- Coordinate budgeting throughout the organization.
- Use budgeting/planning software when appropriate.
- Remember that budgets are tools.
- Remember that profits result from smart management, not because you budgeted for them.

---

**resources**
The assets of the organization including financial, physical, human, and intangible.

**budget**
A numerical plan for allocating resources to specific activities.

observed any group of supervisors or department managers for a few days, you would see them doing much the same—allocating resources by detailing what activities have to be done, the order in which they are to be completed, who is to do each, and when they are to be completed. These managers are **scheduling**. In this section, we'll review some useful scheduling devices including Gantt charts, load charts, and PERT network analysis.

**Gantt Charts**  The **Gantt chart** was developed during the early 1900s by Henry Gantt, an associate of Frederick Taylor, the scientific management expert. The idea behind a Gantt chart is simple. It's essentially a bar graph with time on the horizontal axis and the activities to be scheduled on the vertical axis. The bars show output, both planned and actual, over a period of time. The Gantt chart visually shows when tasks are supposed to be done and compares that with the actual progress on each. It's a simple but important device that lets managers detail easily what has yet to be done to complete a job or project and to assess whether an activity is ahead of, behind, or on schedule.

Exhibit 9–5 depicts a simplified Gantt chart for book production developed by a manager in a publishing company. Time is expressed in months across the top of the chart. The major work activities are listed down the left side. Planning involves deciding what activities need to be done to get the book finished, the order in which those activities need to be completed, and the time that should be allocated to each activity. Where a box sits within a time frame reflects its planned sequence. The shading represents actual progress. The chart also serves as a control tool because the manager can see deviations from the plan. In this example, both the design of the cover and the printing of first pages are running behind schedule. Cover design is about three weeks behind (note that there has been no actual progress—shown by the blue color line—as of the reporting date), and galley proof printing is about two weeks behind schedule (note that as of the report date, actual progress—shown by the red color line—is about six weeks, out of a goal of completing in two months). Given this information, the manager might need to take some action to either make up for the two lost weeks or to ensure that no further delays will occur. At this point, the manager can expect that the book will be published at least two weeks later than planned if no action is taken.

**Load Charts**  A **load chart** is a modified Gantt chart. Instead of listing activities on the vertical axis, load charts list either entire departments or specific resources. This arrangement allows managers to plan and control capacity utilization. In other words, load charts schedule capacity by work areas.

For example, Exhibit 9–6 shows a load chart for six production editors at the same publishing company. Each editor supervises the production and design of several books. By reviewing a load chart, the executive editor, who supervises the six production editors, can see who is free to take on a new book. If everyone is fully scheduled, the executive editor might decide not to accept any new projects, to accept new projects and delay others, to make the editors work overtime, or to employ more production

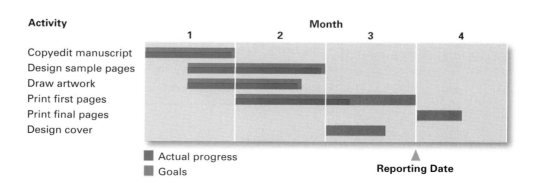

Exhibit 9–5

**A Gantt Chart**

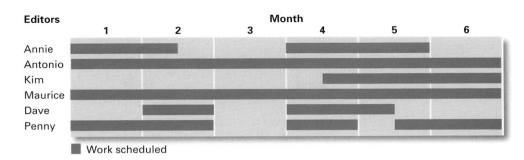

Exhibit 9–6

**A Load Chart**

editors. In Exhibit 9–6 only Antonio and Maurice are completely scheduled for the next six months. The other editors have some unassigned time and might be able to accept new projects or be available to help other editors who get behind.

**PERT Network Analysis** Gantt and load charts are useful as long as the activities being scheduled are few in number and independent of each other. But what if a manager had to plan a large project such as a departmental reorganization, the implementation of a cost-reduction program, or the development of a new product that required coordinating inputs from marketing, manufacturing, and product design? Such projects require coordinating hundreds and even thousands of activities, some of which must be done simultaneously and some of which can't begin until preceding activities have been completed. If you're constructing a building, you obviously can't start putting up the walls until the foundation is laid. How can managers schedule such a complex project? The Program Evaluation and Review Technique (PERT) is highly appropriate for such projects.

A **PERT network** is a flowchart diagram that depicts the sequence of activities needed to complete a project and the time or costs associated with each activity. With a PERT network, a manager must think through what has to be done, determine which events depend on one another, and identify potential trouble spots. PERT also makes it easy to compare the effects alternative actions might have on scheduling and costs. Thus, PERT allows managers to monitor a project's progress, identify possible bottlenecks, and shift resources as necessary to keep the project on schedule.

To understand how to construct a PERT network, you need to know four terms. **Events** are end points that represent the completion of major activities. **Activities** represent the time or resources required to progress from one event to another. **Slack time** is the amount of time an individual activity can be delayed without delaying the whole project. The **critical path** is the longest or most time-consuming sequence of events and activities in a PERT network. Any delay in completing events on this path would delay completion of the entire project. In other words, activities on the critical path have zero slack time.

Developing a PERT network requires that a manager identify all key activities needed to complete a project, rank them in order of occurrence, and estimate each activity's completion time. Exhibit 9–7 explains the steps in this process.

Most PERT projects are complicated and include numerous activities. Such complicated computations can be done with specialized PERT software. However, let's

**scheduling**
Detailing what activities have to be done, the order in which they are to be completed, who is to do each, and when they are to be completed.

**Gantt chart**
A scheduling chart developed by Henry Gantt that shows actual and planned output over a period of time.

**load chart**
A modified Gantt chart that schedules capacity by entire departments or specific resources.

**PERT network**
A flowchart diagram showing the sequence of activities needed to complete a project and the time or cost associated with each.

**events**
End points that represent the completion of major activities in a PERT network.

**activities**
The time or resources needed to progress from one event to another in a PERT network.

**slack time**
The amount of time an individual activity can be delayed without delaying the whole project.

**critical path**
The longest sequence of activities in a PERT network.

Exhibit 9–7

**Steps in Developing a PERT Network**

1. *Identify every significant activity that must be achieved for a project to be completed.* The accomplishment of each activity results in a set of events or outcomes.

2. *Determine the order in which these events must be completed.*

3. *Diagram the flow of activities from start to finish, identifying each activity and its relationship to all other activities.* Use circles to indicate events and arrows to represent activities. This results in a flowchart diagram called a PERT network.

4. *Compute a time estimate for completing each activity.* This is done with a weighted average that uses an *optimistic* time estimate ($t_o$) of how long the activity would take under ideal conditions, a *most likely* estimate ($t_m$) of the time the activity normally should take, and a *pessimistic* estimate ($t_p$) that represents the time that an activity should take under the worst possible conditions. The formula for calculating the expected time ($t_e$) is then

$$t_e = \frac{t_o + 4t_m + t_p}{6}$$

5. *Using the network diagram that contains time estimates for each activity, determine a schedule for the start and finish dates of each activity and for the entire project.* Any delays that occur along the critical path require the most attention because they can delay the whole project.

work through a simple example. Assume that you're the superintendent at a construction company and have been assigned to oversee the construction of an office building. Because time really is money in your business, you must determine how long it will take to get the building completed. You've determined the specific activities and events. Exhibit 9–8 outlines the major events in the construction project and your estimate of the expected time to complete each. Exhibit 9–9 shows the actual PERT network based on the data in Exhibit 9–8. You've also calculated the length of time that each path of activities will take:

A-B-C-D-I-J-K (44 weeks)
A-B-C-D-G-H-J-K (50 weeks)
A-B-C-E-G-H-J-K (47 weeks)
A-B-C-F-G-H-J-K (47 weeks)

Your PERT network shows that if everything goes as planned, the total project completion time will be 50 weeks. This is calculated by tracing the project's critical path (the longest sequence of activities)—A-B-C-D-G-H-J-K—and adding up the times. You know that any delay in completing the events on this path would delay the completion of the entire project. Taking six weeks instead of four to put in the floor covering and paneling (event I) would have no effect on the final completion date. Why?

Exhibit 9–8

**Events and Activities in Constructing an Office Building**

| Event | Description | Expected Time (in weeks) | Preceding Event |
|---|---|---|---|
| A | Approve design and get permits. | 10 | None |
| B | Dig subterranean garage. | 6 | A |
| C | Erect frame and siding. | 14 | B |
| D | Construct floor. | 6 | C |
| E | Install windows. | 3 | C |
| F | Put on roof. | 3 | C |
| G | Install internal wiring. | 5 | D, E, F |
| H | Install elevator. | 5 | G |
| I | Put in floor covering and paneling. | 4 | D |
| J | Put in doors and interior decorative trim. | 3 | I, H |
| K | Turn over to building management group. | 1 | J |

**Exhibit 9–9**

**A PERT Network for Constructing an Office Building**

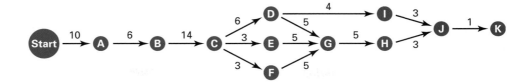

Because that event isn't on the critical path. However, taking seven weeks instead of six to dig the subterranean garage (event B) would likely delay the total project. A manager who needed to get back on schedule or to cut the 50-week completion time would want to concentrate on those activities along the critical path that could be completed faster. How might the manager do this? He or she could look to see if any of the other activities *not* on the critical path had slack time in which resources could be transferred to activities that *were* on the critical path.

## Breakeven Analysis

Managers at Glory Foods want to know how many units of their new seasoned canned vegetables must be sold in order to break even—that is, the point at which total revenue is just sufficient to cover total costs. **Breakeven analysis** is a widely used resource allocation technique to help managers determine breakeven point.[26]

Breakeven analysis is a simple calculation, yet it's valuable to managers because it points out the relationship between revenues, costs, and profits. To compute breakeven point *(BE)*, a manager needs to know the unit price of the product being sold *(P)*, the variable cost per unit *(VC)*, and total fixed costs *(TFC)*. An organization breaks even when its total revenue is just enough to equal its total costs. But total cost has two parts: fixed and variable. *Fixed costs* are expenses that do not change regardless of volume. Examples include insurance premiums, rent, and property taxes. *Variable costs* change in proportion to output and include raw materials, labor costs, and energy costs.

Breakeven point can be computed graphically or by using the following formula:

$$BE = \frac{TFC}{P - VC}$$

This formula tells us that (1) total revenue will equal total cost when we sell enough units at a price that covers all variable unit costs and (2) the difference between price and variable costs, when multiplied by the number of units sold, equals the fixed costs. Let's work through an example.

Assume that Randy's Photocopying Service charges $0.10 per photocopy. If fixed costs are $27,000 a year and variable costs are $0.04 per copy, Randy can compute his breakeven point as follows: $27,000 ÷ ($0.10 – $0.04) = 450,000 copies, or when annual revenues are $45,000 (450,000 copies × $0.10). This same relationship is shown graphically in Exhibit 9–10.

As a planning tool, breakeven analysis could help Randy set his sales goal. For example, he could determine his profit goal and then calculate what sales level is needed to reach that goal. Breakeven analysis could also tell Randy how much volume has to increase to break even if he's currently operating at a loss or how much volume he can afford to lose and still break even.

**breakeven analysis**
A technique for identifying the point at which total revenue is just sufficient to cover total costs.

Exhibit 9–10

**Breakeven Analysis**

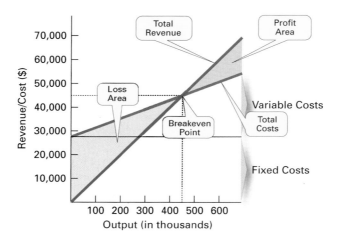

## Linear Programming

Maria Sanchez manages a manufacturing plant that produces two kinds of cinnamon-scented home fragrance products: wax candles and a woodchip potpourri sold in bags. Business is good and she can sell all of the products she can produce. This is her problem: Given that the bags of potpourri and the wax candles are manufactured in the same facility, how many of each product should she produce to maximize profits? Maria can use **linear programming** to solve her resource allocation problem.

Although linear programming can be used here, it can't be applied to all resource allocation problems because it requires that there be limited resources, that the goal be outcome optimization, that there be alternative ways of combining resources to produce a number of output mixes, and that there be a linear relationship between variables (a change in one variable must be accompanied by an exactly proportional change in the other).[27] For Maria's business, that last condition would be met if it took exactly twice the amount of raw materials and hours of labor to produce two of a given home fragrance product as it took to produce one.

What kinds of problems can be solved with linear programming? Some applications include selecting transportation routes that minimize shipping costs, allocating a limited advertising budget among various product brands, making the optimal assignment of people among projects, and determining how much of each product to make with a limited number of resources. Let's return to Maria's problem and see how linear programming could help her solve it. Fortunately, her problem is relatively simple,

*Circuit City used a quantitative technique called multivariable testing to try to find out what in-store factors contributed to higher sales. Testing different combinations of 15 ideas generated by store-level employees in 16 randomly selected stores, the company was able to study dozens of variables simultaneously on the selling floor. After looking at weekly tallies of data on sales and net margins at each store, managers were surprised to discover that methods it had long relied on had no effect on revenues, and that paying salespeople flat commissions worked better to raise revenue than either paying product-based commissions or hiring more employees.*

Exhibit 9–11

**Production Data for Cinnamon-Scented Products**

| | Number of Hours Required (per unit) | | |
| Department | Potpourri Bags | Scented Candles | Monthly Production Capacity (in hours) |
| --- | --- | --- | --- |
| Manufacturing | 2 | 4 | 1,200 |
| Assembly | 2 | 2 | 900 |
| Profit per unit | $10 | $18 | |

Q & A

Where do managers get information to do linear programming? See Q & A 9.6 for the answer.

so we can solve it rather quickly. For complex linear programming problems, managers can use computer software programs designed specifically to help develop optimizing solutions. ( ◆ Go to www.prenhall.com/rolls)

First, we need to establish some facts about Maria's business. She has computed the profit margins on her home fragrance products at $10 for a bag of potpourri and $18 for a scented candle. These numbers establish the basis for Maria to be able to express her *objective function* as maximum profit = $10P + $18S, where P is the number of bags of potpourri produced and S is the number of scented candles produced. The objective function is simply a mathematical equation that can predict the outcome of all proposed alternatives. In addition, Maria knows how much time each fragrance product must spend in production and the monthly production capacity (1,200 hours in manufacturing and 900 hours in assembly) for manufacturing and assembly (see Exhibit 9–11). The production capacity numbers act as *constraints* on her overall capacity. Now Maria can establish her constraint equations:

$$2P + 4S \le 1,200$$
$$2P + 2S \le 900$$

Of course, Maria can also state that: $P \ge 0$ and $S \ge 0$, because neither fragrance product can be produced in a volume less than zero.

Maria has graphed her solution in Exhibit 9–12. The shaded area represents the options that don't exceed the capacity of either department. What does this mean? Well, let's look first at the manufacturing constraint line BE. We know that total manufacturing capacity is 1,200 hours, so if Maria decides to produce all potpourri bags, the maximum she can produce is 600 (1,200 hours ÷ 2 hours required to produce a bag of potpourri). If she decides to produce all scented candles, the maximum she can produce is 300 (1,200 hours ÷ 4 hours required to produce a scented candle). The other constraint Maria faces is that of assembly, shown by line DF. If Maria decides to produce all potpourri bags, the maximum she can assemble is 450 (900 hours

Exhibit 9–12

**Graphical Solution to Linear Programming Problem**

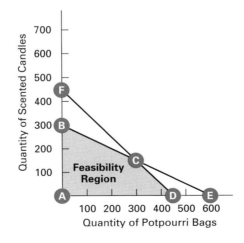

**linear programming**
A mathematical technique that solves resource allocation problems.

production capacity ÷ 2 hours required to assemble). Likewise, if Maria decides to produce all scented candles, the maximum she can assemble is also 450 because the scented candles also take 2 hours to assemble. The constraints imposed by these capacity limits establish Maria's *feasibility region*. Her optimal resource allocation will be defined at one of the corners within this feasibility region. Point C provides the maximum profits within the constraints stated. How do we know? At point A, profits would be 0 (no production of either potpourri bags or scented candles). At point B, profits would be $5,400 (300 scented candles × $18 profit and 0 potpourri bags produced = $5,400). At point D, profits would be $4,500 (450 potpourri bags produced × $10 profit and 0 scented candles produced = $4,500). At point C, however, profits would be $5,700 (150 scented candles produced × $18 profit and 300 potpourri bags produced × $10 profit = $5,700).

## Learning Review

- List the four techniques for allocating resources.
- Describe the different types of budgets.
- Explain what a Gantt chart and a load chart do.
- Describe how PERT network analysis works.

- Understand how to compute a breakeven point.
- Describe how managers can use linear programming.

## CONTEMPORARY PLANNING TECHNIQUES

Wi-fi applications. Bird flu pandemic. Directional audio technology. Chemical/biological attacks. Deflation/inflation worries. Category 4 or 5 hurricanes. Changing competition. Today's managers face the challenges of planning in an environment that's both dynamic and complex. Two planning techniques that are appropriate for this type of environment are project management and scenarios. Both techniques emphasize *flexibility*, something that's important to making planning more effective and efficient in this type of organizational environment.

## Managers *speak out*

**Jochen Braun**

**Finance Director—Germany, Austria, and Switzerland; GameStop Deutschland GmbH; Memmingen, Germany**

*Describe your job.*

I am the Finance Director with GameStop Germany, Austria, and Switzerland. My daily job is to supervise a group of people and to make sure that we are delivering compliant and accurate financial statements to our headquarters in Dallas, Texas. I am also responsible for financial forecasting and budgeting, insurance coverage, and legal.

*What types of planning do you do in your job? What planning tools or techniques do you use in helping you plan?*

I have to plan for the company's financial future. Here, I use bottom-up planning techniques verified by top-down techniques.

Personally, I also plan my time by using time management techniques like prioritization and delegation.

*What advice would you give to someone who wants to be an effective planner?*

Be precise where necessary and appraise where possible. Do not try to plan for 100 percent accuracy, because you will fail. Also, always keep your overall goal in mind, otherwise you will get lost in the details.

*What skills do managers need to be effective in today's environment?*

Managers, and therefore leaders, need not only be precise and consistent, fair and predictable, but also straightforward in their decisions especially when it comes to uncomfortable situations. We live in a world of rapid change in our ever-more globalized world. Therefore, one very important skill a manager needs to have is being able to quickly adapt to these changes in many different ways, while always considering the human resources affected by the change.

# Project Management

Different types of organizations, from manufacturers such as DaimlerChrysler and Boeing to software design firms such as Plumtree and Microsoft, use projects. A **project** is a one-time-only set of activities that has a definite beginning and ending point in time.[28] Projects vary in size and scope—from Boston's "big dig" downtown traffic tunnel to a sorority's holiday formal. **Project management** is the task of getting a project's activities done on time, within budget, and according to specifications.[29] ( ◆ Go to www.prenhall.com/rolls)

More and more organizations are using project management because the approach fits well with the need for flexibility and rapid response to perceived market opportunities. When organizations undertake projects that are unique, have specific deadlines, contain complex interrelated tasks requiring specialized skills, and are temporary in nature, these projects often do not fit into the standardized planning procedures that guide an organization's other routine work activities. Instead, managers use project management techniques to effectively and efficiently accomplish the project's goals. What does the project management process involve?

**Project Management Process** In the typical project, work is done by a project team whose members are assigned from their respective work areas to the project and who report to a project manager. The project manager coordinates the project's activities with other departments. When the project team accomplishes its goals, it disbands and members move on to other projects or back to their permanent work area.

The essential features of the project planning process are shown in Exhibit 9–13. The process begins by clearly defining the project's goals. This step is necessary because the manager and the team members need to know what's expected. All activities in the project and the resources needed to do them must then be identified. What materials and labor are needed to complete the project? This step may be time-consuming and complex, particularly if the project is unique and the managers have no history or experience with similar projects. Once the activities have been identified, the sequence of completion needs to be determined. What activities must be completed before others can begin? Which can be done simultaneously? This step often uses flowchart diagrams such as a Gantt chart, a load chart, or a PERT network. ( ◆ Go to www.prenhall.com/rolls) Next, the project activities need to be scheduled. Time estimates for each activity are done and these estimates are used to develop an overall project schedule and completion date. Then the project schedule is compared to the goals, and any necessary adjustments are made. If the project completion time is too long, the manager might assign more resources to critical activities so they can be completed faster.

Today, the project management process can take place online as a number of Web-based software packages are available. These packages cover aspects from project accounting and estimating to project scheduling and bug and defect tracking.[30]

Exhibit 9–13    **Project Planning Process**

*Source:* Based on R. S. Russell and B. W. Taylor III, *Production and Operations Management* (Upper Saddle River, NJ: Prentice Hall, 1995), p. 287.

**project**
A one-time-only set of activities that has a definite beginning and ending point in time.

**project management**
The task of getting a project's activities done on time, within budget, and according to specifications.

## *becoming* a Manager

✓ Get in the habit of reading general news and business periodicals. Pay attention to events, trends, and changes.

✓ Practice competitor intelligence by using published sources about different companies when writing papers for class assignments.

✓ Take classes to learn about linear programming and forecasting techniques.

✓ Practice budgeting by applying it to your personal life.

✓ Try different scheduling tools when faced with class projects that need to be planned and managed.

✓  Complete any of these exercises from the Self-Assessment Library found on www.prenhall.com/rolls: S.A.L. #I.E.2—What Time of Day Am I Most Productive?, S.A.L. #I.E.3—How Good Am I at Personal Planning?, or S.A.L. #II.C.1—How Well Do I Respond to Turbulent Change?

Self-Assessment
Library (S.A.L. )

**The Role of the Project Manager**  The temporary nature of projects makes managing them different from, say, overseeing a production line or preparing a weekly tally of costs on an ongoing basis. The one-shot nature of the work makes project managers the organizational equivalent of a hired gunman. There's a job to be done. It has to be defined—in detail—and the project manager is responsible for how it's done. At J.B. Hunt Transportation Services, Phil Kindy, head of project management, trains project managers on both technical and interpersonal skills so that they know how to run a project effectively.[31]

Even with the availability of sophisticated computerized and online scheduling programs and other project management tools, the role of project manager remains difficult because he or she is managing people who typically are still assigned to their permanent work areas. The only real influence project managers have is their communication skills and their power of persuasion. To make matters worse, team members seldom work on just one project. They're usually assigned to two or three at any given time. So project managers end up competing with each other to focus a worker's attention on his or her particular project.

## Scenario Planning

During the 1990s, business was so good at Colgate-Palmolive that CEO Reuben Mark worried about what "might go wrong." He installed an "early-warning system to flag problems before they blew up into company-wrecking crises." For instance, a red-flag report alerted Mark "that officials in Baddi, India, had questions about how a plant treated wastewater." Mark's response was to quickly assign an engineering team to check it out and prevent potential problems.[32]

We already know how important it is that today's managers do what Reuben Mark was doing—monitor and assess the external environment for trends and changes. As they assess the environment, issues and concerns that could affect their organization's current or planned operations are likely to be revealed. All of these won't be equally important, so it's usually necessary to focus on a limited set that are most important and to develop scenarios based on each.

A **scenario** is a consistent view of what the future is likely to be. Developing scenarios also can be described as *contingency planning*; that is, if this is what happens, then these are the actions we need to take. If, for instance, environmental scanning reveals increasing interest by the U.S. Congress for raising the national minimum wage, managers at Subway could create

*Many companies learned planning lessons, large and small, from the devastation of Hurricane Katrina, which hit New Orleans in August 2005. At GAP, relief efforts included the donation by employees of some of their paid time off to the company's 1,300 affected workers, as well as housing and clothing allowances and a 30-day payroll extension given by the company. But as Paul Pressler, CEO, noted, "One of the challenges has been getting money to our employees. Many live paycheck to paycheck. One thing we're going to do is encourage more employees to set up direct deposit—a small tactic, but a lesson we learned from Katrina."*

multiple scenarios to assess the possible consequences of such an action. What would be the implications for its labor costs if the minimum wage was raised to $8 an hour? How about $9 an hour? What effect would these changes have on the chain's bottom line? How might competitors respond? Different assumptions lead to different outcomes. The intent of scenario planning is not to try to predict the future but to reduce uncertainty by playing out potential situations under different specified conditions.[33] Subway could, for example, develop a set of scenarios ranging from optimistic to pessimistic in terms of the minimum wage issue. It would then be prepared to implement new strategies to get and keep a competitive advantage. An expert in scenario planning said, "Just the process of doing scenarios causes executives to rethink and clarify the essence of the business environment in ways they almost certainly have never done before."[34]

Although scenario planning is useful in anticipating events that *can be* anticipated, it's difficult to forecast random events—the major surprises and aberrations that can't be foreseen. For instance, an outbreak of deadly and devastating tornadoes in southwest Missouri on March 12, 2006, was a scenario that could be anticipated. The disaster recovery planning that took place after the storms was effective because this type of scenario had been experienced in the past. A response had already been planned and people knew what to do. But the planning challenge comes from those totally random and unexpected events. For instance, the 9/11 terrorist attacks in New York and Washington, D.C., were random, unexpected, and a total shock to many organizations. Scenario planning was of little use because no one could have envisioned this scenario. As difficult as it may be for managers to anticipate and deal with these random events, they're not totally vulnerable to the consequences. (  Go to www.prenhall.com/rolls) Exhibit 9–14 lists some suggestions for preparing for unexpected events. One suggestion that has been identified by risk experts as particularly important is to have an early warning system in place. (A similar idea is the tsunami warning systems in the Pacific and in Alaska, which alert officials to potentially dangerous tsunamis and give them time to take

**Q & A**

If environments are so chaotic and unpredictable, why even plan? Q & A 9.9 will explain.

Exhibit 9–14

**Preparing for Unexpected Events**

- Identify potential unexpected events.
- Determine if any of these events would have early indicators.
- Set up an information-gathering system to identify early indicators.
- Have appropriate responses (plans) in place if these unexpected events occur.

*Source:* S. Caudron, "Frontview Mirror," *Business Finance,* December 1999, pp. 24–30.

**scenario**
A consistent view of what the future is likely to be.

action.) Early warning indicators for organizations can give managers advance notice of potential problems and changes—such as it did Reuben Mark at Colgate-Palmolive—so they, too, can take action.

Planning tools and techniques can help managers prepare confidently for the future. ( ⬗ Go to www.prenhall.com/rolls) But they should remember that all the tools we've described in this chapter are just that—tools. They will never replace the manager's skills and capabilities in using the information gained to develop effective and efficient plans.

## Learning Review

- Explain why flexibility is so important to today's planning techniques.
- Describe project management.

- List the steps in the project planning process.
- Discuss why scenario planning is an important planning tool.

# Managers Respond to a Manager's Dilemma

### Bob Bagga

CEO, BizExchange Inc., Seattle, WA

Paula needs to get buy-in from her people. She already has one success under her belt and has proven what budgeting has done for the organization when the Exotic Newcastle Disease broke out. Because she had a budgeting and planning process in place, she was able to avoid this potential disaster and without financial impact to the bottom line. My recommendations are as follows:

- Review the budgeting process she already has in place with the scientists and animal keepers.

- Use the Exotic Newcastle Disease as an example and show how the planning, budgeting, and reforecast evolved and adapted to the crisis when it arose.

- Clearly show the results and benefits of this process. Get buy-in!

- Encourage feedback and open dialogue from the scientists and animal keepers to understand what changes may be needed or special circumstances which may apply to their specific departments.

- Through this dialogue, engage the scientists and have them share what this would look like in their departments. Have them take ownership of implementing this process.

- Show them the benefits of the budgeting and planning process drawing from previous experiences the scientists and animal keepers may have had. Show them, or better yet have them reach the conclusions of how those experiences would have turned out differently if they did have the budgeting and planning process in place.

- Have them take ownership of the budget. Since I am not familiar with how much autonomy the scientists and animal keepers have right now, I assume that, if implemented properly, the budgeting and planning process will allow for more autonomy, creativity, and innovation on their part. Perhaps they will be able to try new ideas and innovate.

- Hold them accountable to their budgets, and tie in pay for performance on budget such as quarterly and/or annual bonuses upon meeting or exceeding targets.

# Learning Summary

## What Techniques Can Managers Use to Assess the Environment?

**Environmental scanning**: screening large amounts of information to anticipate and interpret changes in the environment

- **Competitor intelligence**: collecting data about competitors
- **Global scanning**: gathering information on global environmental forces

**Forecasting**: trying to predict outcomes; a managerial skill that can be practiced and improved

- Quantitative and qualitative forecasting
- Most accurate when environment is not changing rapidly, more people are involved in the process, rolling forecasts are used, more than one type of forecast is used

**Benchmarking**: searching for the best practices of other companies that lead to their superior performance

## What Techniques Can Managers Use to Allocate Resources?

**Budget**: numerical plan for allocating resources to specific activities

- Variable or fixed
- Cash, revenue, expense, and profit

**Scheduling**: allocating resources by detailing what activities have to be done in what order, by whom, and by when

- Gantt chart: shows actual and planned output over a period of time
- Load chart: modified Gantt chart that schedules capacity by departments or specific resources
- PERT network analysis: a flowchart that shows the sequence of activities needed to complete a project and the time or cost associated with each

**Breakeven analysis**: techniques used to determine point where revenue just equals costs

**Linear programming**: mathematical technique that determines how best to allocate limited resources for optimal outcomes

## What Are the Newest Planning Techniques?

**Project management**: techniques used to get project activities done on time, within budget, and according to specifications

**Scenario planning**: developing plans based on various possible future scenarios

# Management: By the Numbers

- Of 1,000 U.S. and European firms surveyed by Fuld & Co., almost half said they had an organized competitor intelligence program. Forty-five percent of the U.S. companies that did not have one said they planned to do so within a year.
- Ninety-seven percent of global corporate strategists surveyed say that their companies have no early warning systems in place for being alerted to critical environmental changes.
- Fifty-nine percent of respondents to a survey said that competitive intelligence was an integral part of their strategic planning process.

- In this same survey, however, 71 percent said they didn't have the means, understanding, or interest to use competitive intelligence properly.
- Also, 20 percent of these same respondents said that company executives did not recognize the value of competitive intelligence.

*Sources:* Outward Insights, "Ostriches and Eagles: Competitive Intelligence Usage and Understanding in U.S. Companies," www.outwardinsights.com, February 2005; L. Fuld, "Be Prepared," *Harvard Business Review,* November 2003, pp. 20–21; and K. Girard, "Snooping on a Shoestring," *Business 2.0,* May 2003, pp. 64–66.

# Thinking About Management Issues

1. "It's a waste of time and other resources to develop a set of sophisticated scenarios for situations that may never occur." Do you agree or disagree? Support your position.

2. Do intuition and creativity have any relevance in quantitative planning tools and techniques? Explain.

3. The *Wall Street Journal* and other business periodicals often carry reports of companies that have not met their sales or profit forecasts. What are some reasons a company might not meet its forecast? What suggestions could you make for improving the effectiveness of forecasting?

4. In what ways is managing a project different from managing a department or other structured work area? In what ways are they the same?

5. "People can use statistics to prove whatever it is they want to prove." What do you think? What are the implications for managers and how they plan?

6. Predicting the future is very difficult, but that hasn't stopped companies from trying. How could managers make it less difficult? Or can they even do so? Explain.

7. What might be some early warning signs of (a) a new competitor coming into your market; (b) an employee work stoppage; or (c) a new technology that could change demand for your product?

# Working Together: Team-Based Exercise

Benchmarking can be an important tool and source of information for managers. It also can be useful to students. Form small groups of three to four students. In your small group, discuss study habits that each of you has found to be effective from your years of being in school. As a group, come up with a bulleted list of at least eight suggestions in the time period allotted by your instructor. When the instructor calls time, each group should combine with one other group and share your ideas, again in the time allotted by your instructor. In this larger group, be sure to ask questions about suggestions that each respective small group had. Each small group should make sure that it understands the suggestions of the other small group it's working with. When the instructor calls time, each small group will then present and explain the study habit suggestions of the *other* small group it was working with. After all groups have presented, the class will come up with what it feels are the "best" study habits of all the ideas presented.

# Ethical Dilemma Exercise

Managers at all levels rely on forecasts for planning, especially when predicting revenues and profits. In turn, financial analysts and investors rely on management's forecasts when assessing a company's investment potential; bankers use the forecasts to determine whether a company can repay its loans. Unfortunately, this can lead to a situation "where the need to meet the analysts' expectations becomes the sole focal point of management's work ethics," observes Mitchell Pally of the Long Island Association, a New York business group.

Consider what happened at HealthSouth, a company that met many ambitious growth forecasts as it developed into a multibillion-dollar chain of clinics and surgical centers. Once its acquisitions slowed, however, the firm had difficulty living up to lofty forecasts. Founder Richard Scrushy, who was then CEO, repeatedly said the firm would meet forecasts. Yet HealthSouth often announced lower than expected results, in part because of changes in government regulations. The stock price fell and Scrushy reportedly pushed his executives to find ways of avoiding disappointing results. After government investigators began looking more closely at the company's financials, 11 former company managers ultimately pleaded guilty to accounting fraud. Scrushy was acquitted on these charges, although he was later indicted on bribery charges and paid $1.5 million to settle a lawsuit over losses in the firm's retirement plan stemming from the low stock price. In the end, HealthSouth announced that it actually lost money during 2 years that were originally touted as profitable.[35]

Imagine you're the financial manager of a HealthSouth clinic preparing revenue forecasts for the coming quarter. Too high a number will set unrealistic expectations for senior managers, analysts, investors, and bankers to use in decision making; too low a number will make you and your facility look bad to upper management. Review Exhibit 9–1 as you think about this ethical challenge and decide which of the following options to choose—and why.

**Option A:** Use quantitative techniques to arrive at a preliminary estimate of future revenue. Ask for input from your facility's managers, and submit the most realistic figure you can.

**Option B:** Benchmark your desired results against competitors' forecasts. Then use the jury of opinion technique to involve your staff in forecasting revenue and ask them to share responsibility by signing the forecast along with you.

**Option C:** Talk with your boss about the estimates submitted by other HealthSouth facilities, and then use quantitative techniques to arrive at a forecast in a similar range.

## Case Application

### A New Pitch for an Old Classic

Andrew E. Friedman is a new breed of manager in America's favorite pastime—the classic game of baseball. As the general manager of the Tampa Bay Devil Rays (his formal title is executive vice president of baseball operations), Friedman is responsible for overseeing and directing the team's overall baseball operations. And he's doing it his way—by relying on financial models and data mining to help improve the team's performance and valuation. For the 2006 season, *Sports Illustrated* has ranked the team 24th overall out of the 30 MLB (Major League Baseball) teams. Its payroll of $35 million puts it at the bottom of the league in terms of players' salaries. However, Friedman uses his own numbers approach to assess the value of his team and to help it realize its maximum potential.

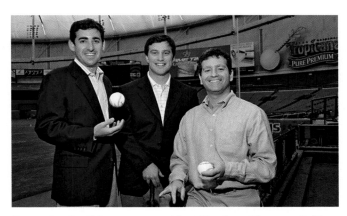

*Tampa Bay Devil Rays team president Matthew Silverman (left) with general manager Andrew Friedman (center), and owner Stuart Sternberg.*

With a degree in management and finance from Tulane University in New Orleans, Friedman understands the language of business. He spent 5 years on Wall Street before joining the Devil Rays organization as director of baseball development. Having played on Tulane's baseball team until an injury sidelined him, Friedman is no stranger to the game. However, in baseball, quantitative, statistics-based methods of player talent assessment, team valuation, and contract negotiations are not the usual approach to doing business. That's why Friedman isn't concerned about having the lowest payroll of any major league team because his assessment—based upon a valuation technique used on Wall Street—places the real value of the Devil Rays' payroll at closer to $50 million.

Friedman also uses a quantitative approach to trading players. He says, "I am purely market driven. I love players I think that I can get for less than they are worth. It's positive arbitrage, the valuation asymmetry in the game." He and team owner Stuart Sternberg and team president Matt Silverman recently put their philosophy of quantitative, statistics-based talent assessment into action as they made their first big trade, "exchanging their all-star closer Danys Baez, for two untested starting pitchers from the Los Angeles Dodgers, Edwin Jackson and Chuck Tiffany." The trio is betting that the two prospects will blossom into top-rated starting pitchers—"perhaps the most elusive and highly valued commodity in baseball today." Despite the emphasis on stats and quantitative analysis, the Devil Rays management team understands that it "cannot be a substitute for old-fashioned scouting and talent assessment, an area it also wants to strengthen."

Although there may be a new pitch to an old classic, computers, Blackberrys, and economic models can't, and will probably never, provide all the answers. However, the tools and techniques hopefully may help the organization achieve, as its owner says, its maximum potential.

### Discussion Questions

1. What other planning tools and techniques might be useful to Andrew Friedman as he oversees and directs the team's operations? Be specific.

2. In baseball, where the traditional approach to assessing player potential and performance has involved watching the individual play in different settings (scouting the player) and where most of the team management would not have a business background, how might you overcome the doubts of "traditionalists" about the benefits of using quantitative tools and techniques?

3. What are some ways that Friedman might evaluate whether his quantitative tools are working? Be specific.

*Sources:* Information from team Web site, tampabay.devilrays.mlb.com, April 7, 2006; S. Kirchhoff, "Batter Up! Sports Economics Hits Field," *USA Today,* July 27, 2006, pp. 1B+; L. Thomas, Jr., "Case Study: Fix a Baseball Team," *New York Times Online,* www.nytimes.com, April 2, 2006; and A. Tillin, "Paul Podesta: The Stats Wonk Who Runs a Pro Sports Team," *Business 2.0,* November 2004, p. 103.

# Part Three

## You're the Manager: Putting Ethics into Action

*As a manager, you'll often face decisions involving ethical questions. How can you learn to identify an ethical dilemma, keep stakeholders in mind, think through the alternatives, and foresee the consequences of your decisions? This unique interactive feature, positioned at the end of Parts 2, 3, 4, 5, and 6, casts you in the role of a manager dealing with hypothetical yet realistic ethical issues. To begin, read the following preview paragraph. Then log onto www.prenhall.com/rolls Web site to consider the decisions you would make in the role of manager.*

What ethical complications might managers of a health care company have to confront when pursuing healthy profits? Consider what happened at HealthSouth, which owns a chain of surgical centers and clinics across the United States. Feeling pressure to keep profits growing as quickly and steadily as they had forecast in reports to Wall Street analysts, senior managers used accounting tricks that made earnings appear higher—yet the company was actually losing money. After the accounting problems were uncovered, a new management team was hired to bring order to HealthSouth's finances, reevaluate the company's situation, and develop a new strategy for profitability. In this hypothetical scenario, you play the role of a financial manager at a HealthSouth clinic. You've been implementing an impressive new cost-cutting plan—with unintended consequences for your staff. How far can or should you go to keep costs at or below forecast levels? Log onto www.prenhall.com/rolls to put ethics into action!

## Passport

### Scenario 1

As Luke Castillo, the quality control manager for Deere & Company's farm tractor division, waits for his flight from Chicago to São Paulo to depart, he jots down some notes about his meeting tomorrow with Ricardo Espinoza, manager of Deere's Brazilian plant. In his job, Luke travels a couple of weeks each month to the company's various manufacturing plants in the United States, Canada, Argentina, Brazil, and Mexico to assist them with quality control issues. Product quality is important in this industry and Luke is well versed in quality management techniques, having attended a number of quality certification programs and holding quality management positions in two other organizations. He's been in this particular position with Deere for 3 years and loves the challenge of getting the company's employees involved in resolving difficult product quality problems, although there are times when the job is more challenging. The current trip to the Brazilian plant is likely to be one of those times!

Deere's Brazilian facility, located outside São Paulo, is managed by Ricardo Espinoza. Ricardo is new to the plant manager's position, although he has worked at the plant for 15 years. He started out on the assembly line and steadily moved up to positions with more responsibility. He is respected by his peers and by his regional manager. One of Ricardo's main goals for his plant is to improve the quality of the tractors made there and he has asked for Luke's assistance. But Ricardo knows it will not be an easy task to implement a quality improvement program. Many of the plant's employees have worked there all their lives and are pretty set in their ways.

Employee involvement in planning and implementing this program will be essential to its success. What issues might Luke and Ricardo face as they prepare to introduce a quality improvement program in the plant? What will work best with Deere's Brazilian employees? How should Luke and Ricardo approach this project?

*To answer these questions, you'll have to do some research on the countries. Go to the R.O.L.L.S. Web site and click on "Passport." When the map appears, click on the countries you need to research. You'll find background information on the country and general information about the country's economy, population, and workforce. In addition, you'll find specific information on the country's culture and the unique qualities associated with doing business there.*

### Scenario 2

Yoko Sato is the merchandising manager for Toys"R"Us International in Tokyo, a position she has held for 5 years. After graduating from the University of Washington with a degree in marketing management, Yoko worked for a toy importer in Los Angeles for 8 years—a job that provided numerous opportunities to learn about the toy business. When a new position with mega-retailer Toys"R"Us opened up back home in Japan, Yoko applied for the job and got it. Her educational training and years of work experience with the toy import industry were the deciding factors in her getting the job.

As merchandising manager for Japan, Yoko must ensure that all Toys"R"Us International stores located there have the correct mix of products they need, when they need them, and where they need them. She relies on several planning tools to get the product mix right. If she makes a bad decision, the stores either run out of popular selling toys or have a surplus of unsold toys. By doing a good job of planning, Yoko hopes to avoid those outcomes.

Tomorrow Yoko is meeting with a new toy importer, Wu Sihai, from Nanjing, China, to discuss a possible business deal. She has not done business with Wu before but is looking forward to discussing the possibilities. Keeping in mind that setting goals and planning are extremely important to Yoko's job performance, will there be any differences in how Yoko and Wu view the role of goal setting and planning? Explain. What might Yoko need to do to emphasize how important goals and planning are and yet still establish a business relationship with Wu?

*To answer these questions, you'll have to do some research on the countries. Go to the R.O.L.L.S. Web site and click on "Passport." When the map appears, click on the countries you need to research. You'll find background information on the country and general information about the country's economy, population, and workforce. In addition, you'll find specific information on the country's culture and the unique qualities associated with doing business there.*

## Scenario 3

Tomasso Perelli, vice president of global operations for Benito Sportswear in Turin, Italy, is responsible for the efficient and cost-effective manufacturing of the company's fashions. Although the company has a fairly limited product line, its sportswear is known for its durability and trendy style. Customers have come to expect quality and fun products from Benito Sportswear and so far have been willing to pay the higher price for Benito's products. Over the past 2 weeks, however, Benito's customer service department has alerted Tomasso to some inventory and quality control problems with some products coming out of the manufacturing plant in China. This is an important issue that can't wait, and Tomasso is preparing notes for a conference call with Li Kou, the plant manager, about the best way to address the problems. What should Tomasso know about the Chinese culture in order to have a productive conversation with Mr. Li? What might work best with the company's Chinese employees?

Once the production problems at the Chinese plant have been addressed, Tomasso must turn his attention to launching a new manufacturing facility. One of the locations the company is considering is Latin America. But before making that decision, Tomasso wants to make sure that the Latin American culture will be suitable for the fast-paced demands of the fashion industry. Goals, plans, and forecasts are important tools for succeeding in this industry. Given this, what issues might Tomasso and Benito Sportswear face in opening a manufacturing plant in a Latin American country?

*To answer these questions, you'll have to do some research on the countries. Go to the R.O.L.L.S. Web site and click on "Passport." When the map appears, click on the countries you need to research. You'll find background information on the country and general information about the country's economy, population, and workforce. In addition, you'll find specific information on the country's culture and the unique qualities associated with doing business there.*

# Continuing Case

## Starbucks—Planning

One thing that all managers do is plan. The planning they do may be extensive or it may be limited. It might be for the next week or month or it might be for the next couple of years. It might cover a work group or it might cover an entire division. No matter what type or extent of planning a manager does, the important thing is that planning takes place. Without planning, there would be nothing for managers to organize, lead, or control. Based on the numerous accomplishments that Starbucks has achieved through the efforts of its employees, managers, no doubt, have done their planning.

## Company Goals

As of April 2006, Starbucks had 11,377 stores in 37 countries. During the 30 weeks that ended April 30, the company opened 755 new stores in the United States and 381 new stores overseas. However, that's a far cry from where the company wants and intends to be someday. CEO Jim Donald says Starbucks' long-term goal is 15,000 U.S. stores and 30,000 stores globally. For 2006, the company's goal is to open approximately 1,800 new stores globally and to reach about $7.6 billion in revenues. Goals for the next 3 to 5 years include attaining total net revenue growth of 20 percent and earnings per share growth between 20 to 25 percent.

In addition to its financial and other growth goals, Starbucks has an even "glitzier" goal. It wants to have a hand in helping define society's pop culture menu. Although this goal takes Starbucks beyond its coffee roots, it seems to fit well with the unconventional approach to business that Howard Schultz has followed from the beginning.

## Company Strategies

Starbucks has been called the most dynamic retail brand conceived over the last 2 decades. It has been able to rise above the commodity nature of its product and become a global brand leader by reinventing the coffee experience. Millions of times each week, a customer receives a drink from a Starbucks barista. It's a reflection of the success that Howard Schultz has had in creating something that never really existed in the United States—café life. And in so doing, he created a cultural phenomenon. Starbucks is changing what we eat and drink. It's altering where we work and play. It's shaping how we spend time and money. No one is more surprised by this cultural impact than Howard Schultz. He says, "It amazes all of us how we've become part of popular culture. Our customers have given us permission to extend the experience."

Starbucks has found a way to appeal to practically every customer demographic as its customers cover a broad base. It's not just the affluent or the urban professionals and it's not just the intellectuals or the creative types who frequent Starbucks. You'll find soccer moms, construction workers, bank tellers, and clerical assistants at Starbucks. And despite the high price of its products, customers pay it because they think it's worth it. What they get for that price is some of the finest coffee available commercially, custom preparation, and, of course, that Starbucks ambiance—the music, the comfy chairs, the aromas, the hissing steam from the espresso machine—all invoking that warm feeling of community and connection that Schultz experienced on his first business trip to Italy and knew instinctively could work elsewhere.

There's no hiding the fact that Starbucks' broad strategy is to grow into a global empire. Howard Schultz says, "We are in the second inning of a 9-inning game. We are just beginning to tap into all sorts of new markets, new customers, and new products." But any growth that Starbucks pursues is done so with great care and planning. CEO Jim Donald says that all company growth is governed by whether quality can be maintained. If there is any uncertainty about quality, a new strategy won't fly, no matter how good it might seem. Starbucks has designed its growth strategies to exploit the customer connections it has so carefully nurtured and the brand equity it has so masterfully built. And company executives have taken the company in new directions even while continuing to grow store numbers and locations and increasing same-store sales.

As the world's number-one specialty coffee retailer, Starbucks sells coffee drinks, food items, coffee beans, and coffee-related accessories and equipment. In addition, Starbucks sells whole bean coffees through a specialty sales group and grocery stores. Starbucks has grown beyond coffee into related businesses such as coffee-flavored ice cream and ready-to-drink coffee beverages. These Starbucks-branded products have been developed with other companies. For instance, its Frappuccino® and DoubleShot™ coffee drinks were developed with Pepsi-Cola. Its Starbucks Ice Cream was developed with Dreyer's. In early 2006, Starbucks launched its ready-to-drink coffee drink, Starbucks Iced Coffee, through a joint venture with Pepsi-Cola. The company extended its success at brand extensions to selected global markets when it launched a fresh Starbucks-branded premium ready-to-drink chilled coffee called Starbucks Discoveries™ in convenience stores in Taiwan and Japan. This product was enthusiastically embraced by customers immediately. In addition, Starbucks markets a selection of premium tea products since its acquisition of Tazo, LLC.

Starbucks has also pursued other strategic initiatives to enhance its core business. For instance, in November 2001, the company launched the Starbucks prepaid card. Since that time, more than 77 million prepaid cards have been activated and loaded with more than $1 billion. The director of Starbucks global card services says, "We've been pleasantly surprised by the card business, by how fast it's grown in percentage of tender, and how people use the card. It offers so many opportunities to grow from there. It's one of our fastest-growing channels." Industry experts say that part of the reason for its success is its dual use—as gift cards and for customer loyalty. Also important to its success, however, is the fact that the company has made it easy to purchase, reload, and use. The company is on the leading edge in finding innovative ways to get the prepaid cards into potential customers' hands such as parent–student cards, gift-card malls, and business gifts and incentives.

Having conquered the coffee business, one of the company's most interesting brand extensions has been music. Selling music at Starbucks began when a store manager made tapes for his store. These tapes proved to be so popular that the company began licensing music compilation CDs for sale. Initially, Howard Schultz had to be persuaded about this product and recalls, "I began to understand that our customers looked to Starbucks as kind of editor. It was like . . . we trust you. Help us choose." And if you think about it, music has always been part of the café or coffeehouse experience. In addition to selling its private-label CDs, the company launched the HearMusic Café in Santa Monica, California, in March 2004. At these stores, customers burn their own compilation CDs. After sampling selections, if they choose to buy, customers can walk up to a music "bar" and order a custom CD with any variation of songs and have it delivered to their table when it's completed. Based on the success Starbucks has had with music, it decided to selectively link the Starbucks brand with certain kinds of movies, the first being *Akeelah and the Bee*. The president of Starbucks Entertainment division says, "Movies are a very important part of our entertainment strategy. The thought was to start with music, build some success, establish credibility, and then move into films." Eventually, the company wants to be a destination not just for java but also for music, movies, books, and more.

*A customer selects songs for burning to a CD as another orders coffee at the Starbucks' HearMusic cafe in Santa Monica, California.*

Not everything that Starbucks touches turns to gold. One of its big flops was a magazine called *Joe* launched by the company and *Time*. It lasted three issues before being called off. A carbonated coffee beverage product called *Mazagran*, developed with Pepsi-Cola, never made it to market. Too, Starbucks decided to close its Torrefazione Italia cafés when they didn't meet the goals set for them.

What about the core industry Starbucks is in? How is it doing? The hot drinks market continues to sizzle. It's forecasted to increase 10.9 percent between now and 2010. In addition, the 2006 National Coffee Drinking Trends report of the National Coffee Association of the United States says that coffee tied soft drinks in daily market penetration for the first time since 1990. And Starbucks wants to remain at the forefront of the industry. Some 24 percent of Starbucks customers visit 16 times per month—a number that no other fast-food chain even comes close to.

There's no doubt that Howard Schultz has built and continues to build Starbucks to be big. Growth has been funded through cash flow, not by selling stock or by using debt financing. Some of the new ideas to be implemented include an aggressive roll-out of drive-through windows, which now number more than 1,000 U.S. locations and 35 Canadian sites; a co-branded Web site between Yahoo! and Starbucks where online daters can arrange to meet and drink free coffee; a partnership between Starbucks and Kellogg that created a hot breakfast product; and two new banana-based blended drinks.

## Discussion Questions

1. Starbucks has some pretty specific goals it wants to achieve. Given this, do you think managers would be more likely to make rational decisions, bounded rationality decisions, or intuitive decisions? Explain.

2. Give examples of decisions that Starbucks managers might make under conditions of certainty. Under conditions of risk. Under conditions of uncertainty.

3. Make a list of Starbucks' goals. Describe what type of goal each is. Then, describe how that stated goal might affect how the following employees do their jobs: (a) a part-time store employee—a barista—in Omaha; (b) a quality assurance technician at the company's roasting plant in Carson City, Nevada; (c) a regional sales manager; (d) the senior vice president of new markets; and (e) the CEO.

4. Discuss the types of growth strategies that Starbucks has used. Be specific.

5. Evaluate the growth strategies Starbucks is using. What do you think it will take for these strategies to be successful?

6. What competitive advantage(s) do you think Starbucks has? What will it have to do to maintain that (those) competitive advantage(s)?

7. Do you think the Starbucks brand can become too saturated—that is, extended to too many different products? Why or why not?

8. What companies might be good benchmarks for Starbucks? Why? What companies might want to benchmark Starbucks? Why?

9. Describe how the following Starbucks managers might use forecasting, budgeting, and scheduling (be specific): (a) a retail store manager; (b) a regional marketing manager; (c) the manager of global trends; and (d) the CEO.

10. Describe Howard Schultz as a strategic leader.

11. Is Starbucks "living" its mission? Explain. (You can find the company mission on its Web site, www.starbucks.com, or in the continuing case found at the end of Part 2.

12. Do a brief SWOT analysis of Starbucks.

# Chapter
# 10

## Learning Outline

*Use this Learning Outline as you read and study this chapter.*

### Defining Organizational Structure

- Discuss the traditional and contemporary views of work specialization, chain of command, and span of control.
- Describe each of the five forms of departmentalization.
- Explain cross-functional teams.
- Differentiate authority, responsibility, and unity of command.
- Tell what factors influence the amount of centralization and decentralization.
- Explain how formalization is used in organizational design.

### Organizational Design Decisions

- Contrast mechanistic and organic organizations.
- Explain the relationship between strategy and structure.
- Tell how organizational size affects organizational design.
- Discuss Woodward's findings on the relationship of technology and structure.
- Explain how environmental uncertainty affects organizational design.

### Common Organizational Designs

- Contrast the three traditional organizational designs.
- Explain team, matrix, and project structures.
- Describe the design of virtual and network organizations.
- Discuss the organizational design challenges facing managers today.

## Chapter 10

# Organizational Structure and Design

## A Manager's Dilemma

Can your boss ever be your good buddy? Or more importantly, *should* your boss ever be your good buddy? It's a question that Penny Baker, CEO and founder of National Bankcard Systems (NBS), found out the hard way that he had to answer. Founded in 1997, NBS provides merchant services such as credit card acceptance, electronic check acceptance, electronic benefit transfer, debit card, gift card, ATM, and other electronic payment methods.[1]

One of the attractive qualities of a small business is the fact that they tend to be less formal than large businesses, which often have elaborate and rigid hierarchies. When Penny—an outgoing, friendly type of guy who is described as "the opposite of stuffy"—founded his company, he wanted it to be as friendly as possible. He hired his close friends for key organizational positions and often socialized with his employees on a regular basis, going out for happy hour or dinner several times a week. As the company thrived and succeeded, it grew to 75 employees and over $5 million in sales in just 3 years. That's when Penny began to sense that his laid-back, "huggy, touchy" management style was no longer acceptable. Many of the company's employees, all of whom were fun drinking buddies or dinner companions, became a little too complacent at work, acting as if they had earned some kind of special job consideration and protection, just because they socialized with the boss. Even some of Penny's longtime friends were slacking off on the job. He says, "I figured if I hired my buddies, they'd work their butts off for me. But I don't want people to feel like I owe them anything because we're friends." Eventually, he had to fire two of them. However, the "last straw came one night at happy hour when one of his salespeople—the brother of a college pal—got drunk and proclaimed that he could do a better job than Baker and was starting a rival business." That was Penny's clue that he had to do something.

Put yourself in Penny's shoes. How should he structure his organization so that he can be a "nice boss who encourages employees to have fun, but keeps them at arm's length by behaving in a more businesslike manner"?

**What would you do?**

Penny Baker is struggling, like managers do, with organizational structure and design decisions. His desire to make his organization more businesslike while still retaining the camaraderie and informality he feels are important is a tough challenge. Although his approach might not be right for others, it does illustrate the importance of designing an organizational structure that helps accomplish organizational goals. In this chapter, we'll present information about designing appropriate organizational structures. We'll look at the various elements of organizational structure and what contingency factors influence the design. We'll look at some traditional and contemporary organizational designs. And finally we'll describe the organizational design challenges facing managers—like Penny Baker—today.

## DEFINING ORGANIZATIONAL STRUCTURE

Six miles south of McAlester, Oklahoma, employees in a vast factory complex make products that must be perfect. These people "are so good at what that do and have been doing it for so long that they have a 100 percent market share."[2] What do they make? Bombs for the U.S. military. And doing so requires a work environment that's an interesting mix of the mundane, structured, and disciplined, coupled with high levels of risk and emotion, but the work gets done efficiently and effectively. Work also gets done efficiently and effectively at the Canadian Customs and Revenue Agency. Its workforce is more spread out and they rely on shared workspaces, mobile computing, and virtual private networks to get work done.[3] Both of these examples reflect the importance of organizing and organizational structure to get an organization's work done, even though both organizations approach it differently.

No other topic in management has undergone as much change in the past few years as that of organizing and organizational structure. Traditional approaches to organizing work are being reevaluated as managers search out structural designs that will best support and facilitate employees' doing the organization's work—designs that can achieve efficiency but also have the flexibility that's necessary for success in today's dynamic environment. Recall from Chapter 1 that **organizing** is arranging and structuring work to accomplish the organization's goals. It's the process through which managers design an organization's structure. That process is important and serves many purposes, as shown in Exhibit 10–1. The challenge for managers is to design an organizational structure that allows employees to effectively and efficiently do their work. (  Go to www.prenhall.com/rolls)

Just what is **organizational structure**? It's the formal arrangement of jobs within an organization. When managers develop or change the structure, they're engaged in **organizational design**, a process that involves decisions about six key elements: work specialization, departmentalization, chain of command, span of control, centralization and decentralization, and formalization.[4]

**Q & A**

Even lower-level managers do some organizing activities. Q & A 10.1 explains.

**Exhibit 10–1**

**Purposes of Organizing**

- Divides work to be done into specific jobs and departments.
- Assigns tasks and responsibilities associated with individual jobs.
- Coordinates diverse organizational tasks.
- Clusters jobs into units.
- Establishes relationships among individuals, groups, and departments.
- Establishes formal lines of authority.
- Allocates and deploys organizational resources.

# Work Specialization

Remember our discussion of Adam Smith in Chapter 2, who first identified division of labor and concluded that it contributed to increased employee productivity. Early in the twentieth century, Henry Ford applied this concept in an assembly line where every Ford worker was assigned a specific, repetitive task.

Today we use the term **work specialization** to describe dividing work activities in an organization into separate job tasks. The essence of work specialization is that an entire work activity is not done by one individual, but instead is broken down into tasks with each task completed by a different person. Individual employees "specialize" in doing part of an activity rather than the entire activity. For instance, at the Wilson Sporting Goods factory in Ada, Ohio, workers make every football used in the National Football League and most of those used in college and high school football games. To meet daily output goals—between 3,000 and 5,000 footballs depending on the time of the year—the workers specialize in job tasks such as molding, stitching and sewing, lacing, and so forth.[5] ( 　　　 Go to www.prenhall.com/rolls)

During the first half of the twentieth century, managers viewed work specialization as an unending source of increased productivity, and, for a time, it was! Because it wasn't widely used, when work specialization *was* implemented, employee productivity rose. By the 1960s, however, it had become evident that a good thing could be carried too far. The point had been reached in some jobs where human diseconomies from work specialization—boredom, fatigue, stress, poor quality, increased absenteeism, and higher turnover—more than offset the economic advantages.

**Today's View** Most managers today see work specialization as an important organizing mechanism but not as a source of ever-increasing productivity. They recognize the efficiencies it creates in certain types of jobs, but they also recognize the problems it creates when it's carried to extremes. McDonald's, for example, uses high work specialization to efficiently make and sell its products, and most employees in health care organizations are specialized. However, other organizations, such as Avery-Dennison, Hallmark, American Express, and Ford Australia have broadened the scope of employees' jobs and reduced work specialization.

Q & A
What about employees who work as part of a team? Can their work be specialized? See Q & A 10.2

*Work specialization might make the job of answering phone calls all day monotonous to some, but not to Graciela Barreña (in front in picture), who works for the Argentine call center Indicom, in Buenos Aires. Her 6-hour shift follows a pattern, with pager messages and calls about highway toll cards arriving in the early morning, and responses to free raffles and other toll-free calling services her employer offers filling much of the rest of the day. In between, Barreña provides customer service for a cheese factory and a diaper manufacturer.*

**organizing**
Arranging and structuring work to accomplish the organization's goals.

**organizational structure**
The formal arrangement of jobs within an organization.

**organizational design**
Developing or changing an organization's structure.

**work specialization**
Dividing work activities into separate job tasks.

## *thinking critically about* **Ethics**

Changes in technology have reduced the long-term value of many employees' skills. A factory or office worker used to be able to learn one job and be reasonably sure that the skills to do that job would be sufficient for most of his or her work years. That's no longer the case. What ethical obligation do organizations have to assist workers whose skills have become obsolete? What about employees? Do they have an obligation to keep their skills from becoming obsolete? What ethical guidelines might you suggest for dealing with employee skill obsolescence?

## Departmentalization

Does your college have a department of student services? A financial aid or student housing office? Are you taking this course through a management or business administration department? After work activities have been divided up through work specialization into separate job tasks, common job tasks need to be grouped back together so the work can be done in a coordinated, integrated way. The basis by which jobs are grouped together is called **departmentalization**. Every organization will have its own specific way of classifying and grouping jobs. Exhibit 10–2 shows the five common forms of departmentalization.

**Functional departmentalization** groups jobs by functions performed. This approach can be used in all types of organizations, although the functions change to reflect the organization's purpose and work. **Product departmentalization** groups jobs by product line. For instance, Avon Products has three main product lines: beauty (which includes cosmetics, fragrances, skin care, and toiletries); beauty plus (which includes fashion jewelry, watches, apparel, and accessories); and beyond beauty (which includes home products and gift and decorative products). **Geographical departmentalization** groups jobs on the basis of geographical region such as southern, midwestern, or northwestern regions or maybe North American, European, Latin American, and Asian–Pacific regions. **Process departmentalization** groups jobs on the basis of product or customer flow. In this approach, work activities follow a natural processing flow of products or even of customers. Finally **customer departmentalization** groups jobs on the basis of specific and unique customers who have common needs or problems that can best be met by having specialists for each. For instance, Merrill Lynch is organized around three customer groups: wealthy individuals, institutional investors, and small corporations.

Large organizations often combine most or all of these forms of departmentalization. For example, a major Japanese electronics firm organizes each of its divisions along functional lines, its manufacturing units around processes, its sales units around seven geographic regions, and its sales regions into four customer groupings.

**Today's View**  Two popular trends today in departmentalization are the increasing use of customer departmentalization and the use of cross-functional teams. Customer departmentalization helps managers better monitor customers' needs and respond to changes in those needs. For example, L.L.Bean is organized around seven customer groups. Many other organizations are using this type of structure as well, as it allows them to better understand their customers and to respond faster to their needs. Second, managers are using **cross-functional teams**, which are work teams composed of individuals from various functional specialties. For instance, at Ford's material planning and logistics division, a cross-functional team with employees from the company's finance, purchasing, engineering, and quality control areas and with representatives

**departmentalization**
The basis by which jobs are grouped together.
**functional departmentalization**
Grouping jobs by functions performed.
**product departmentalization**
Grouping jobs by product line.

**geographical departmentalization**
Grouping jobs on the basis of geographical region.
**process departmentalization**
Grouping jobs on the basis of product or customer flow.

**customer departmentalization**
Grouping jobs on the basis of specific and unique customers who have common needs.
**cross-functional teams**
Work teams composed of individuals from various functional specialties.

Exhibit 10–2    **The Five Common Forms of Departmentalization**

**Functional Departmentalization**

+   Efficiencies from putting together similar specialties and
    people with common skills, knowledge, and orientations
+   Coordination within functional area
+   In-depth specialization
−   Poor communication across functional areas
−   Limited view of organizational goals

**Geographical Departmentalization**

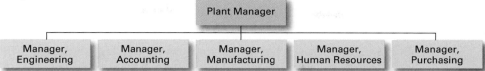

+   More effective and efficient handling of specific regional
    issues that arise
+   Serve needs of unique geographic markets better
−   Duplication of functions
−   Can feel isolated from other organizational areas

**Product Departmentalization**
Source: Bombardier Annual Report

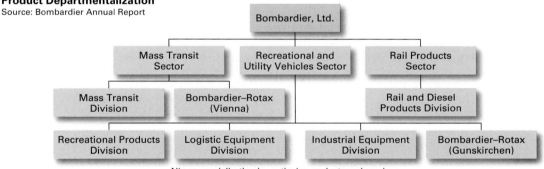

+   Allows specialization in particular products and services
+   Managers can become experts in their industry
+   Closer to customers
−   Duplication of functions
−   Limited view of organizational goals

**Process Departmentalization**

+   More efficient flow of work activities
−   Can only be used with certain types of products

**Customer Departmentalization**

+   Customers' needs and problems can be met by specialists
−   Duplication of functions
−   Limited view of organizational goals

from the company's outside logistics suppliers has made several work improvement ideas.[6] We'll discuss the use of cross-functional teams more fully in Chapter 15.

## Chain of Command

For many years, the chain-of-command concept was a cornerstone of organizational design. As you'll see, it has far less importance today. But managers still need to consider its implications when deciding how best to structure their organizations. The **chain of command** is the line of authority extending from upper organizational levels to the lowest levels, which clarifies who reports to whom. It helps employees answer questions such as "Who do I go to if I have a problem?" or "To whom am I responsible?"

Q & A

When you're a manager, do you have both authority and power? Do you have to be a manager to have both authority and power? Check out Q & A 10.3 for the answer.

You can't discuss the chain of command without discussing three other concepts: authority, responsibility, and unity of command. **Authority** refers to the rights inherent in a managerial position to tell people what to do and to expect them to do it.[7] An organization's managers, who are in the chain of command, are granted a certain degree of authority to do their job of coordinating and overseeing the work of other people. (　　Go to www.prenhall.com/rolls) As managers assign work to employees, those employees assume an obligation to perform any assigned duties. This obligation or expectation to perform is known as **responsibility**. Finally, the **unity of command** principle (one of Fayol's 14 principles of management) helps preserve the concept of a continuous line of authority. It states that a person should report to only one manager. Without unity of command, conflicting demands and priorities from multiple bosses can create problems. It did for Damian Birkel, a merchandising manager in the Fuller Brands division of CPAC, Inc., who found himself reporting to two bosses—one in charge of the department-store business and the other in charge of discount chains. Birkel tried to minimize the conflict by making a combined to-do list that he would update and change as work tasks changed.[8]

**Today's View** Early management theorists (Fayol, Weber, Taylor, and others) were enamored with the concepts of chain of command, authority, responsibility, and unity of command. However, times change and so have the basic tenets of organizational design. However, it's been hard for some organizations to give up the control that a formal chain of command represents. Take, for instance, General Motors. Here's a company having serious problems, part of which can be attributed to its "cumbersome and unresponsive" bureaucratic chain of command. One example—the company's marketing to the Cuban–Hispanic population in Miami. One ad created at headquarters in Detroit used the word "breakthrough," which doesn't even have a direct Spanish translation. Another ad showed a "woman in a Mexican dress standing in front of the Alamo as GM Saturns raced around her." And when GM dealers in Miami suggested back in the late 1990s, before the company's Escalade became so popular, that the company should build a luxury SUV, executives in Detroit shot down the idea, saying it would never sell. Is it any wonder that the company has no top-selling vehicle in car-crazy Miami?[9]

In addition, concepts such as chain of command, authority, and so forth are considerably less relevant today because of things like information technology (see the Managing IT box on page 283). Employees throughout the organization can access information that used to be available only to top managers in a matter of a few seconds. Also, with computers, employees communicate with anyone else anywhere in the organization without going through formal channels—that is, the chain of command. Moreover, as more organizations use self-managed and cross-functional teams and as new organizational designs with multiple bosses are implemented, these traditional concepts are less relevant.

## Span of Control

How many employees can a manager efficiently and effectively manage? The traditional view was that managers could not—and should not—directly supervise more

Exhibit 10–3

**Contrasting Spans of Control**

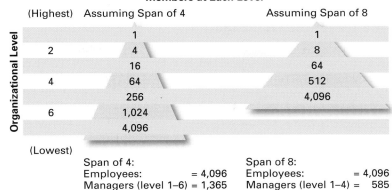

**Members at Each Level**

| (Highest) | Assuming Span of 4 | Assuming Span of 8 |
|---|---|---|
| | 1 | 1 |
| 2 | 4 | 8 |
| | 16 | 64 |
| 4 | 64 | 512 |
| | 256 | 4,096 |
| 6 | 1,024 | |
| | 4,096 | |

Organizational Level

(Lowest)

Span of 4:
Employees:                = 4,096
Managers (level 1–6) = 1,365

Span of 8:
Employees:                = 4,096
Managers (level 1–4) =   585

than five or six subordinates. This question of **span of control** is important because, to a large degree, it determines the number of levels and managers an organization has. All things being equal, the wider or larger the span, the more efficient the organization. An example can show why.

Assume that we have two organizations, both of which have approximately 4,100 employees. As Exhibit 10–3 shows, if one organization has a uniform span of 4 and the other a span of 8, the wider span will have 2 fewer levels and approximately 800 fewer managers. If the average manager made $42,000 a year, the organization with the wider span would save over $33 million a year in management salaries alone! Obviously, wider spans are more efficient in terms of cost. However, at some point, wider spans reduce effectiveness. When the span becomes too large, employee performance suffers because managers no longer have the time to provide the necessary leadership and support. (  Go to www.prenhall.com/rolls)

**Today's View** The contemporary view of span of control recognizes that many factors influence the appropriate number of employees that a manager can efficiently *and* effectively manage. These factors include the skills and abilities of the manager and the employees, and the characteristics of the work being done. For instance, the more training and experience employees have, the less direct supervision they'll need. Therefore, managers with well-trained and experienced employees can function quite well with a wider span. Other contingency variables that determine the appropriate span include similarity of employee tasks, the complexity of those tasks, the physical proximity of subordinates, the degree to which standardized procedures are in place, the sophistication of the organization's information system, the strength of the organization's culture, and the preferred style of the manager.[10]

The trend in recent years has been toward larger spans of control, which are consistent with managers' efforts to reduce costs, speed up decision making, increase flexibility, get closer to customers, and empower employees. (  Go to www.prenhall.com/rolls) However, to ensure that performance doesn't suffer because of these wider spans, organizations are investing heavily in employee training. Managers recognize that they can handle a wider span when employees know their jobs well or can turn to co-workers if they have questions.

**Q & A**
How does a manager know how many people he or she can effectively supervise? See Q & A 10.4.

**Q & A**
With larger spans of control being more popular, employees may rely more on office politics. Why? Q & A 10.5 explains.

**chain of command**
The line of authority extending from upper organizational levels to the lowest levels, which clarifies who reports to whom.

**authority**
The rights inherent in a managerial position to tell people what to do and to expect them to do it.

**responsibility**
The obligation to perform any assigned duties.

**unity of command**
The management principle that each person should report to only one manager.

**span of control**
The number of employees a manager can efficiently and effectively manage.

## *focus on* **Leadership**

### When There's No One There: The Challenges of Online Leadership

How do you lead people who are physically separated from you and with whom your interactions are basically reduced to written digital communications?[11] Although most leadership research has looked at face-to-face and verbal situations, the reality is that today's managers and their employees are increasingly being linked by networks rather than geographical proximity. Obvious examples include leaders who regularly use e-mail to communicate with their staff, managers overseeing virtual projects or work teams, and managers whose telecommuting employees are linked to the office by computer. What little research has been done in online leadership suggests there are three challenges: communication, performance management, and trust.

In a virtual setting, leaders may need to learn new communication skills to be effective. They have to carefully choose the words, structure, tone, and style of their digital communications. In addition, leaders must be alert to expressions of emotion as they learn to "read between the lines" in the messages they receive from employees.

Another challenge of online leadership is managing performance. It's important to define performance and facilitate and encourage it with online employees. It's important to ensure that your online employees understand the goals and their responsibilities. There should be no surprises or uncertainties about performance expectations.

Finally, trust is a big issue in online leadership. In an online setting, there are numerous opportunities to violate trust. It's important that leaders convey an attitude of trust in all their interactions with online employees.

## Centralization and Decentralization

In some organizations, top managers make all the decisions and lower-level managers and employees simply carry out their orders. At the other extreme are organizations in which decision making is pushed down to the managers who are closest to the action. The former organizations are centralized, and the latter are decentralized.

**Centralization** describes the degree to which decision making is concentrated at upper levels of the organization. If top managers make the organization's key decisions with little or no input from below, then the organization is centralized. In contrast, the more that lower-level employees provide input or actually make decisions, the more **decentralization** there is. Keep in mind that the concept of centralization-decentralization is relative, not absolute—that is, an organization is never completely centralized or decentralized. Few organizations could function effectively if all decisions were made by only a select group of top managers; nor could they function if all decisions were delegated to employees at the lowest levels. (  Go to www.prenhall.com/rolls)

What determines whether an organization will tend to be more centralized or decentralized? Exhibit 10–4 lists some of the factors that have been identified as influencing the amount of centralization or decentralization an organization uses.[12]

PRISM

Have you ever delegated work to someone else? Practice your delegation skills by completing PRISM #10.

Exhibit 10–4

**Factors That Influence the Amount of Centralization and Decentralization**

| More Centralization | More Decentralization |
|---|---|
| • Environment is stable. | • Environment is complex, uncertain. |
| • Lower-level managers are not as capable or experienced at making decisions as upper-level managers. | • Lower-level managers are capable and experienced at making decisions. |
| • Lower-level managers do not want to have a say in decisions. | • Lower-level managers want a voice in decisions. |
| • Decisions are relatively minor. | • Decisions are significant. |
| • Organization is facing a crisis or the risk of company failure. | • Corporate culture is open to allowing managers to have a say in what happens. |
| • Company is large. | • Company is geographically dispersed. |
| • Effective implementation of company strategies depends on managers retaining say over what happens. | • Effective implementation of company strategies depends on managers having involvement and flexibility to make decisions. |

**Today's View** As organizations have had to become more flexible and responsive, there's been a distinct trend toward decentralizing decision making. In large companies, especially, lower-level managers are "closer to the action" and typically have more detailed knowledge about problems and how best to solve them than do top managers. For instance, at Terex Corporation, CEO Ron Defeo, a big proponent of decentralized management tells his managers, "You gotta run the company you're given." And they have! The company generated revenues of $6.4 billion in 2005 with a little over 15,000 employees worldwide and a corporate headquarters staff of just 66 people.[13] Another example can be seen at Honeywell Pacific, which moved from a hierarchical management structure to one that is much flatter and team-based. Before the change, nearly all decisions were made at headquarters, but authority was pushed down to individual plant and brand managers. The results have been increased revenues and a more intimate knowledge of the company's major customers.[14] Likewise, the Bank of Montreal's some 1,100 branches were organized into 236 "communities"—a group of branches within a limited geographical area. Each community is led by an area manager, who typically works within a 20-minute drive of the other branches. This area manager can respond faster and more intelligently to problems in his or her community than could some senior executive in Toronto. As the company continues its southward expansion into the United States, it continues to use decentralization to successfully manage its various businesses.[15]

Another term for increased decentralization is **employee empowerment**, which is giving employees more authority (power) to make decisions. (  Go to www.prenhall.com/rolls) We'll address empowerment more thoroughly in our discussion of leadership in Chapter 17.

**Self-Assessment Library (S.A.L.)**

How good do you think you are delegating? Check out S.A.L. # III.A.2 and see!

## Formalization

**Formalization** refers to how standardized an organization's jobs are and the extent to which employee behavior is guided by rules and procedures. If a job is highly formalized, then the person doing that job has little discretion over what is to be done, when it's to be done, and how he or she does it. Employees can be expected to handle the same input in exactly the same way, resulting in consistent and uniform output. In highly formalized organizations, there are explicit job descriptions, numerous organizational rules, and

*Koch Industries, led by Charles Koch, recently acquired the timber and paper company Georgia-Pacific to become the largest privately held company in the world. Koch relies on a combination of centralized and decentralized management methods, empowering employees to act like owners of the company assets they're responsible for and to negotiate the share of overhead costs each unit charges against its profits. Regional managers have wide discretion over hiring decisions and over setting business strategy. Environmental compliance, however, is centralized at headquarters, after the company was assessed a $30 million fine for oil spills in 2000.*

**centralization**
The degree to which decision making is concentrated at upper levels of the organization.

**decentralization**
The degree to which lower-level employees provide input or actually make decisions.

**employee empowerment**
Giving employees more authority (power) to make decisions.

**formalization**
How standardized an organization's jobs are and the extent to which employee behavior is guided by rules and procedures.

Q & A

In today's environment, why would organizations want or need to have high levels of formalization? Go to Q & A 10.6 and see.

clearly defined procedures covering work processes. (  Go to www.prenhall.com/rolls) On the other hand, where formalization is low, job behaviors are relatively unstructured and employees have a great deal of freedom in how they do their work.

The degree of formalization varies widely between organizations and even within organizations. For instance, at a newspaper publisher, news reporters often have a great deal of discretion in their jobs. They may pick their news topic, find their own stories, research them the way they want, and write them up, usually within minimal guidelines. On the other hand, compositors who lay out the newspaper pages don't have that type of freedom. They have constraints—both time and space—that standardize how they do their work.

**Today's View** Although some formalization is important and necessary for consistency and control, many of today's organizations seem to be less reliant on strict rules and standardization to guide and regulate employee behavior. For instance, consider the following situation:

> It is 2:37 P.M. and a customer at a branch of a large national drugstore chain is trying to drop off a roll of film for same-day developing. Store policy states that film must be dropped off by 2:00 P.M. for this service. The clerk knows that rules like this are supposed to be followed. At the same time, he wants to be accommodating to the customer, and he knows that the film could, in fact, be processed that day. He decides to accept the film and, in so doing, to violates the policy. He just hopes that his manager does not find out.[16]

Has this employee done something wrong? He did "break" the rule. But by breaking the rule, he actually brought in revenue and provided the customer good service: so good, in fact, that the customer may be satisfied enough to come back in the future.

Considering the fact that there are numerous situations like these where rules may be too restrictive, many organizations have allowed employees some latitude, giving them sufficient autonomy to make those decisions that they feel are best under the circumstances. It doesn't mean that all organizational rules are thrown out the window because there *will* be rules that are important for employees to follow—and these rules should be explained so employees understand why it's important to adhere to them. But for other rules, employees may be given some leeway in application.[17]

## Learning Review

- Discuss the traditional and contemporary views of work specialization, chain of command, and span of control.
- Describe each of the five forms of departmentalization.
- Explain cross-functional teams.

- Differentiate authority, responsibility, and unity of command.
- Tell what factors influence the amount of centralization and decentralization.
- Explain how formalization is used in organizational design.

## ORGANIZATIONAL DESIGN DECISIONS

Organizations don't, and won't, have identical structures. A company with 30 employees isn't going to look like one with 30,000 employees. But even organizations of comparable size don't necessarily have similar structures. What works for one organization may not work for another. How do managers decide what organizational design to use? That decision depends upon certain contingency factors. In this section, we'll look at two generic models of organizational design and then at the contingency factors that favor each.

Exhibit 10–5

**Mechanistic Versus
Organic Organization**

| Mechanistic | Organic |
|---|---|
| • High specialization | • Cross-functional teams |
| • Rigid departmentalization | • Cross-hierarchical teams |
| • Clear chain of command | • Free flow of information |
| • Narrow spans of control | • Wide spans of control |
| • Centralization | • Decentralization |
| • High formalization | • Low formalization |

## Mechanistic and Organic Organizations

Exhibit 10–5 describes two organizational forms.[18] A **mechanistic organization** is a rigid and tightly controlled structure. It's characterized by high specialization, rigid departmentalization, narrow spans of control, high formalization, a limited information network (mostly downward communication), and little participation in decision making by lower-level employees.

Mechanistic organizational structures tend to be efficiency machines and rely heavily on rules, regulations, standardized tasks, and similar controls. This organizational design tries to minimize the impact of differing personalities, judgments, and ambiguity because these human traits are seen as inefficient and inconsistent. Although there's no totally mechanistic organization, almost all large corporations and governmental agencies have some of these mechanistic characteristics.

In direct contrast to the mechanistic form of organization is the **organic organization**, which is as highly adaptive and flexible a structure as the mechanistic organization is rigid and stable. Rather than having standardized jobs and regulations, the organic organization is flexible, meaning jobs can change rapidly as needs require. Organic organizations may have specialized jobs, but those jobs are not standardized. Employees are highly trained and empowered to handle diverse job activities and problems, and these organizations frequently use employee teams. Employees in organic type organizations require minimal formal rules and little direct supervision. Their high levels of skills and training and the support provided by other team members make formalization and tight managerial controls unnecessary. For example, a much-needed organizational restructuring at GlaxoSmithKline, the London-based pharmaceutical company, made it more of an organic structure. Before the restructuring, research at Glaxo was hampered by a slow-moving bureaucracy. Decisions about which drugs to fund were made by a committee of research and development executives far removed from the research labs—a time-consuming process not at all appropriate for a company dependent on scientific breakthroughs. Now, lab scientists set the priorities and allocate the resources. The change has "helped produce an entrepreneurial environment akin to a smaller, biotechnology outfit."[19]

When is a mechanistic structure preferable and when is an organic one more appropriate? Let's look at the main contingency factors that influence the decision. ( Go to www.prenhall.com/rolls)

**Q & A**

How does a manager know whether to use a more mechanistic or a more organic structure? Q & A 10.7 provides some clues.

## Contingency Factors

Pete Rahn, director of the Missouri Department of Transportation, told state lawmakers during his annual State of Transportation speech that they would see 866 projects totaling $7.3 billion in the next 5 years. He said, "We dream big, and we deliver big. Gone is the indecisive bureaucracy. Arrived is the more nimble organization that gets things done."[20] Top managers of most organizations typically put a great deal of thought into designing an appropriate structure. What that appropriate structure is depends on four contingency variables: the organization's strategy, size, technology, and degree of environmental uncertainty. ( Go to www.prenhall.com/rolls)

**Q & A**

A contingency approach to organizational design—what's that all about? Check out Q & A 10.8 for the answer.

**mechanistic organization**
An organizational design that's rigid and tightly controlled.

**organic organization**
An organizational design that's highly adaptive and flexible.

**Strategy and Structure** An organization's structure should help it achieve its goals. Because goals are an important part of the organization's strategies, it's only logical that strategy and structure should be closely linked. More specifically, if managers significantly change the organization's strategy, the structure should change to support the new strategy; that is, structure should "follow" strategy.

Alfred Chandler initially researched the strategy–structure relationship.[21] He studied several large U.S. companies and concluded that changes in corporate strategy led to changes in an organization's structure. He found that these organizations usually began with a single product or product line that required only a simple or loose form of organization. However, as these organizations grew, their strategies became more ambitious and elaborate and the structure changed to support the chosen strategy.

Most current strategy frameworks tend to focus on three dimensions: (1) innovation, which reflects the organization's pursuit of meaningful and unique innovations; (2) cost minimization, which reflects the organization's pursuit of tightly controlled costs; and (3) imitation, which reflects an organization's seeking to minimize risk and maximize profit opportunities by copying the market leaders. What structural design works best with each?[22] Innovators need the flexibility and free-flowing information of the organic structure, whereas cost minimizers seek the efficiency, stability, and tight controls of the mechanistic structure. Imitators might use structural characteristics of both—the mechanistic structure to maintain tight controls and low costs or the organic structure to mimic the industry's innovative directions.

**Size and Structure** There's considerable evidence that an organization's size significantly affects its structure.[23] For instance, large organizations—those with 2,000 or more employees—tend to have more specialization, departmentalization, centralization, and rules and regulations than do small organizations. However, the relationship isn't linear. It seems that as an organization grows past a certain size, size has less influence on structure. Why? Essentially, once an organization has around 2,000 employees, it's already fairly mechanistic. Adding 500 employees to a firm with 2,000 employees won't have much of a structural impact. On the other hand, adding 500 employees to an organization that has only 300 members is likely to result in a shift toward a more mechanistic structure.

**Technology and Structure** Every organization uses some form of technology to convert its inputs into outputs. For instance, workers at Whirlpool's Manaus, Brazil, facility build microwave ovens and air conditioners on a standardized assembly line. Employees at FedEx Kinko's Office and Print Services produce custom design and print jobs for individual customers. And employees at Bayer's facility in Karachi, Pakistan, make pharmaceutical products using a continuous-flow production line.

The initial interest in technology as a determinant of structure can be traced to the work of a British scholar, Joan Woodward, who studied several small manufacturing

3M has surged ahead of its competitors in sales of products based on applications of nanotechnology. At the same time, R&D spending as a percentage of sales is at a record low, which means the company's research efforts are paying off as never before. The reason? Larry Wendling, vice president of the central R&D lab, reorganized the company's researchers around emerging technologies like nanotechnology, setting lower priorities on old technologies like adhesives. A $1 billion research budget is also a factor, but Wendling credits the reorganization. "The best way to transfer ideas," he says, "is to transfer people."

**Exhibit 10–6**

**Woodward's Findings on Technology, Structure, and Effectiveness**

|  | Unit Production | Mass Production | Process Production |
|---|---|---|---|
| Structural characteristics | Low vertical differentiation | Moderate vertical differentiation | High vertical differentiation |
|  | Low horizontal differentiation | High horizontal differentiation | Low horizontal differentiation |
|  | Low formalization | High formalization | Low formalization |
| Most effective structure | Organic | Mechanistic | Organic |

firms in southern England to determine the extent to which structural design elements were related to organizational success.[24] Woodward was unable to find any consistent pattern until she segmented the firms into three categories based on the size of their production runs. The three categories, representing three distinct technologies, had increasing levels of complexity and sophistication. The first category, **unit production**, described the production of items in units or small batches. The second category, **mass production**, described large-batch manufacturing. Finally, the third and most technically complex group, **process production**, included continuous-process production. A summary of her findings is shown in Exhibit 10–6.

Since Woodward's initial work, numerous studies have been done on the technology–structure relationship. These studies generally demonstrate that organizations adapt their structures to their technology.[25] The processes or methods that transform an organization's inputs into outputs differ by their degree of routineness. In general, the more routine the technology, the more mechanistic the structure can be. Organizations with more nonroutine technology are more likely to have organic structures.[26]

**Environmental Uncertainty and Structure** In Chapter 3 we introduced the organization's environment and the amount of uncertainty in that environment as constraints on managerial discretion. Why should an organization's structure be affected by its environment? Because of environmental uncertainty! Some organizations face relatively stable and simple environments; others face dynamic and complex environments. Because uncertainty threatens an organization's effectiveness, managers will try to minimize it. One way to reduce environmental uncertainty is through adjustments in the organization's structure.[27] The greater the uncertainty, the more an organization needs the flexibility offered by an organic design. For example, due to the uncertain nature of the oil industry, those companies need to be flexible. Soon after being named CEO of Royal Dutch Shell PLC, Jeroen van der Veer streamlined the corporate structure to counteract some of the volatility in the oil industry. One thing he did was to eliminate the company's cumbersome, overly analytical process of making deals with OPEC countries and other major oil producers.[28] On the other hand, in stable, simple environments, mechanistic designs tend to be most effective.

**Today's View** The evidence on the environment–structure relationship helps to explain why so many managers today are restructuring their organizations to be lean, fast, and flexible. Global competition, accelerated product innovation by competitors, and increased demands from customers for high quality and faster deliveries are examples of dynamic environmental forces. Mechanistic organizations are not equipped to respond to rapid environmental change and environmental uncertainty. As a result, we're seeing organizations become more organic. (  Go to www.prenhall.com/rolls)

Q & A
What impact does information technology have on structural design? See Q & A 10.9.

---

**unit production**
The production of items in units or small batches.

**mass production**
The production of items in large batches.

**process production**
The production of items in continuous processes.

## Learning Review

- Contrast mechanistic and organic organizations.
- Explain the relationship between strategy and structure.
- Tell how organizational size affects organizational design.

- Discuss Woodward's findings on the relationship of technology and structure.
- Explain how environmental uncertainty affects organizational design.

## COMMON ORGANIZATIONAL DESIGNS

What organizational designs do Ford, Toshiba, Nestlé, Procter & Gamble, and eBay have? In making organizational design decisions, managers have some common structural designs from which to choose. We'll first look at some traditional organizational designs and then at some more contemporary designs.

### Traditional Organizational Designs

In designing a structure to support the efficient and effective accomplishment of organizational goals, managers may choose to use more traditional organizational designs. These designs—simple structure, functional structure, and divisional structure—tend to be more mechanistic. Exhibit 10–7 summarizes the strengths and weaknesses of each of these designs.

**Simple Structure**  Most organizations start as entrepreneurial ventures with a simple structure consisting of owners and employees. A **simple structure** is an organizational design with low departmentalization, wide spans of control, authority centralized in a single person, and little formalization.[29] This structure is most commonly used by small businesses in which the owner and manager are one and the same.

Most organizations do not remain simple structures, especially as they grow and add employees. As the number of employees increases, the structure tends to become more specialized and formalized. Rules and regulations are introduced, work becomes specialized, departments are created, levels of management are added, and the organization becomes increasingly bureaucratic. (You can review Weber's concept of bureaucracy in Chapter 2.) ( Go to www.prenhall.com/rolls) At this point, a manager might choose to organize using a functional structure or a divisional structure.

**Q & A**

Bureaucracies have such a negative image. Do organizations even use bureaucratic elements today? Go to Q & A 10.10 for an explanation.

Exhibit 10–7

**Strengths and Weaknesses of Traditional Organizational Designs**

---

**Simple Structure**

- Strengths: Fast; flexible; inexpensive to maintain; clear accountability.
- Weaknesses: Not appropriate as organization grows; reliance on one person is risky.

**Functional Structure**

- Strengths: Cost-saving advantages from specialization (economies of scale, minimal duplication of people and equipment) and employees are grouped with others who have similar tasks.
- Weaknesses: Pursuit of functional goals can cause managers to lose sight of what's best for overall organization; functional specialists become insulated and have little understanding of what other units are doing.

**Divisional Structure**

- Strengths: Focuses on results—division managers are responsible for what happens to their products and services.
- Weaknesses: Duplication of activities and resources increases costs and reduces efficiency.

**Functional Structure** A **functional structure** is an organizational design that groups similar or related occupational specialties together. It's functional departmentalization applied to the entire organization. For instance, Revlon, Inc., is organized around the functions of manufacturing, marketing, finance, human resources, and product research and development.

**Divisional Structure** The **divisional structure** is an organizational structure made up of separate business units or divisions.[30] In this structural design, each unit or division has limited autonomy, with a division manager responsible for performance and who has strategic and operational authority over his or her unit. In divisional structures, however, the parent corporation typically acts as an external overseer to coordinate and control the various divisions, and often provides support services such as financial and legal. Take Wal-Mart, for example. Its divisions include Wal-Mart Stores, International, Specialty Stores, Sam's Clubs, and Wal-Mart Distribution Centers. Limited Brands is another example of an organization with a divisional structure. Its segments include Apparel (Express, Limited, Henri Bendel), Intimate Brands (Victoria's Secret, Bath and Body Works, and White Barn Candle Company), and Support Businesses (Limited Creative Services, Limited Real Estate, Limited Technology Services, Mast Industries, and others).

## Contemporary Organizational Designs

Managers in contemporary organizations are finding that these traditional hierarchical designs often aren't appropriate for the increasingly dynamic and complex environments they face. In response to marketplace demands for being lean, flexible, and innovative, managers are finding creative ways to structure and organize work and to make their organizations more responsive to the needs of customers, employees, and other organizational constituents.[31] We want to introduce you to some of the newer concepts in organizational design. (See Exhibit 10–8 for a summary of these designs.)

**Q & A**

If an organization is structured around teams, that means it won't need departments, right? Find out the answer in Q & A 10.11.

**Team Structures** Larry Page and Sergey Brin, co-founders of Google, have created a corporate structure that "tackles most big projects in small, tightly focused teams."[32] In a **team structure**, the entire organization is made up of work teams that perform the organization's work.[33] (  Go to www.prenhall.com/rolls) Needless to say, employee empowerment is crucial in a team structure because there is no line of managerial authority from top to bottom. Rather, employee teams are free to design work in the way they think is best. However, the teams are also held responsible for all work and performance results in their respective areas. Let's look at another example of an organization that is organized around teams.

Whole Foods Market, Inc., the largest natural-foods grocer in the United States, uses a team structure.[34] Each of the company's almost 200 stores is organized around self-managed teams, each with a designated team leader. The team leaders in each store are a team; the store leaders in each region are a team; and the company's 11 regional directors are a team.

In large organizations, the team structure complements what is typically a functional or divisional structure. This allows the organization to have the efficiency of a bureaucracy while providing the flexibility that teams provide. For instance, companies such as Amazon, Louis Vuitton, Motorola, and Xerox extensively use employee teams to improve productivity in various functional areas. At companies such as

---

**simple structure**
An organizational design with low departmentalization, wide spans of control, centralized authority, and little formalization.

**functional structure**
An organizational design that groups similar or related occupational specialties together.

**divisional structure**
An organizational structure made up of separate, semi-autonomous units or divisions.

**team structure**
An organizational structure in which the entire organization is made up of work groups or teams.

Exhibit 10–8

**Contemporary Organizational Designs**

**Team Structure**

- What it is:    A structure in which the entire organization is made up of work groups or teams.

- Advantages:    Employees are more involved and empowered. Reduced barriers among functional areas.

- Disadvantages:    No clear chain of command. Pressure on teams to perform.

**Matrix-Project Structure**

- What it is:    Matrix is a structure that assigns specialists from different functional areas to work on projects but who return to their areas when the project is completed. Project is a structure in which employees continuously work on projects. As one project is completed, employees move on to the next project.

- Advantages:    Fluid and flexible design that can respond to environmental changes. Faster decision making.

- Disadvantages:    Complexity of assigning people to projects. Task and personality conflicts.

**Boundaryless Structure**

- What it is:    A structure that is not defined by or limited to artificial horizontal, vertical, or external boundaries; includes *virtual and network* types of organizations.

- Advantages:    Highly flexible and responsive. Draws on talent wherever it's found.

- Disadvantages:    Lack of control. Communication difficulties.

Boeing, Avery-Dennison, Baxter International, and Hewlett-Packard, cross-functional teams are used to design new products and coordinate major projects.

**Matrix and Project Structures**    Other popular contemporary designs are the matrix and project structures. The **matrix structure** is an organizational structure that assigns specialists from different functional departments to work on one or more projects being led by project managers. Exhibit 10–9 shows an example of the matrix structure used in a consumer products firm. Along the top are the familiar organizational functions.

*Acxiom Corporation of Little Rock, Arkansas, needed an organizational design that would facilitate staying at the cutting edge of its field (data mining). So the company abandoned its old hierarchical structure and adopted a streamlined culture that focuses on teams, like the Global Data Development team, shown here, which meets twice each month. Lee Parrish, leader of another Acxiom team, compared the firm's team structure to the hierarchy at his previous employer: "You had a job title. . . . Here, you have a role. Instead of a lot of wasted motion, you can reach out to people and spend your time working on proactive solutions to problems."*

Exhibit 10–9    **An Example of a Matrix Organization**

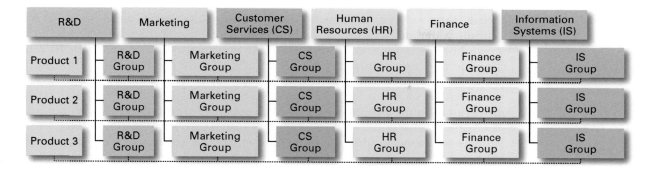

The specific products the firm has currently are listed along the left-hand side. Each product is managed by an individual who staffs his or her product team with people from each of the functional departments. The addition of this vertical dimension to the traditional horizontal functional departments, in effect, "weaves together" elements of functional and product departmentalization creating a matrix arrangement. (  Go to www.prenhall.com/rolls) How does a matrix structure work in reality?

**Q & A**

This matrix structure looks (and sounds) pretty confusing. It can't really work in real life, can it? See Q & A 10.12.

One unique aspect of this design is that it creates a *dual chain of command*, which violates the classical organizing principle of unity of command. Employees in a matrix organization have two managers: their functional area manager and their product or project manager, who share authority. The project managers have authority over the functional members who are part of their project team in areas related to the project's goals. However, decisions such as promotions, salary recommendations, and annual reviews typically remain the functional manager's responsibility. To work effectively, project and functional managers have to communicate regularly, coordinate work demands on employees, and resolve conflicts together. One company that uses a matrix organizational structure is Skanska, the United Kingdom's leading ground-engineering business. Employees from the company's proposals, operations, and commercial areas are assigned to the various engineering projects taking place in different geographic locations.[35]

Although the matrix structure is an effective structural design choice for some organizations, many are using a more "advanced" type of **project structure**, in which employees continuously work on projects. Unlike the matrix structure, a project structure has no formal departments that employees return to at the completion of a project. Instead, employees take their specific skills, abilities, and experiences to other projects. In addition, all work in project structures is performed by teams of employees who become part of a project team because they have the appropriate work skills and abilities. For instance, at IDEO, a design firm, project teams form, disband, and form again as the work requires. Employees "join" project teams because they bring needed skills and abilities to that project. Once the project is completed, however, they move on to the next one.[36]

Project structures tend to be fluid and flexible organizational designs. There's no departmentalization or rigid organizational hierarchy to slow down decision making or taking actions. In this type of structure, managers serve as facilitators, mentors, and coaches. They "serve" the project teams by eliminating or minimizing organizational obstacles and by ensuring that the teams have the resources they need to effectively and efficiently complete their work.

**The Boundaryless Organization** Another approach to contemporary organizational design is the concept of a **boundaryless organization**, an organization whose

---

**matrix structure**
An organizational structure that assigns specialists from different functional departments to work on one or more projects.

**project structure**
An organizational structure in which employees continuously work on projects.

**boundaryless organization**
An organization whose design is not defined by, or limited to, the horizontal, vertical, and horizontal boundaries imposed by a predefined structure.

**Q & A**

If having some type of structure is so important, how can a boundaryless organization work? Q & A 10.13 provides an explanation.

design is not defined by, or limited to, the horizontal, vertical, or external boundaries imposed by a predefined structure.[37] Former GE chairman Jack Welch coined the term because he wanted to eliminate vertical and horizontal boundaries within GE and break down external barriers between the company and its customers and suppliers. Although the idea of eliminating boundaries may seem odd, many of today's most successful organizations are finding that they can operate most effectively by remaining flexible and *unstructured*: that the ideal structure for them is *not* having a rigid, bounded, and predefined structure.[38] ( Go to www.prenhall.com/rolls)

What do we mean by "boundaries"? There are two types: *internal* boundaries—the horizontal boundaries imposed by work specialization and departmentalization and the vertical boundaries that separate employees into organizational levels and hierarchies; and *external* boundaries—the boundaries that separate the organization from its customers, suppliers, and other stakeholders. To minimize or eliminate these boundaries, managers might use virtual or network structural designs.

A **virtual organization** is an organization that consists of a small core of full-time employees and that hires outside specialists temporarily as needed to work on projects.[39] An example of a virtual organization is StrawberryFrog, an international advertising agency based in Amsterdam and New York. There's only a small administrative staff—StrawberryFrog has just 100 people in its two main offices. However, it also has an international network of about 100 freelancers who are assigned to work for clients. By relying on this web of freelancers around the globe, the company enjoys a network of talent without all the unnecessary overhead and structural complexity.[40] The inspiration for this structural approach comes from the film industry. If you look at the film industry, people are essentially "free agents" who move from project to project applying their skills—directing, talent search, costuming, makeup, set design—as needed.

Another structural option for managers wanting to minimize or eliminate organizational boundaries is a **network organization**, which is an organization that uses its own employees to do some work activities and networks of outside suppliers to provide other needed product components or work processes.[41] This organizational form also is sometimes called a modular organization, especially in manufacturing organizations.[42] This structural approach allows organizations to concentrate on what they do best by contracting out other activities to companies that can do those activities best. Many companies are using such an approach for certain organizational work activities. Nike, for instance, is essentially a product development and marketing company that contracts with outside organizations to manufacture its athletic footwear. Sweden's Ericsson contracts its manufacturing and even some of its research and development to more cost-effective contractors in New Delhi, Singapore, California, and other global locations.[43] And at Penske Truck Leasing, dozens of business processes such as securing permits and titles, entering data from drivers' logs, and processing data for tax filings and accounting have been outsourced to Mexico and India.[44]

*Trend Micro Inc., a maker of antivirus software, is a virtual organization with financial headquarters in Tokyo, product development people in Taiwan, and sales offices in Silicon Valley (the better to serve the huge U.S. market). Its computer-virus response center is in Manila, and its smaller labs are scattered around the world from Munich to Tokyo. Says CEO Steve Chang, "With the Internet, viruses became global. To fight them, we had to become a global company." Trend Micro has responded to virus threats in as little as 30 minutes.*

## Today's Organizational Design Challenges

As managers look for organizational designs that will best support and facilitate employees doing their work efficiently and effectively in today's dynamic environment, there are certain challenges with which they must contend. These include keeping employees connected, building a learning organization, and managing global structural issues.

**Keeping Employees Connected** Many organizational design concepts were developed during the twentieth century, when work tasks were fairly predictable and constant, most jobs were full-time and continued indefinitely, and work was done at an employer's place of business under a manager's supervision.[45] That's not what it's like in many organizations today, as you saw in our preceding discussion of virtual and network organizations. A major structural design challenge for managers is finding a way to keep widely dispersed and mobile employees connected to the organization. The Managing IT box describes ways that information technology is helping keep employees connected. In addition, the Focus on Leadership box on page 272 looks at how leaders deal with workers who "aren't there." We'll also cover information in Chapter 16 on motivating these employees.

**Building a Learning Organization** We first introduced the concept of a learning organization in Chapter 2 as we looked at some of the current issues facing managers. The concept of a learning organization doesn't involve a specific organizational design per se but instead describes an organizational mind-set or philosophy that has design implications. (  Go to www.prenhall.com/rolls)

**Q & A**
How is a learning organization different from other organizations? Go to Q & A 10.14 and find out.

---

### *managing* IT

#### IT's Impact on Organizational Design: The Good and the Bad

It's fair to say that the world of work will never be like it was 10 years ago. IT has opened up new possibilities for employees to do their work in locations as remote as Patagonia or in the middle of downtown Seattle. Although organizations have always had employees who had to travel to distant corporate locations to take care of business, these employees no longer have to find the nearest pay phone or wait to get back to "the office" to see what problems have cropped up. Instead, mobile computing and communication have given organizations and employees ways to stay connected and to be more productive.[46] Let's look at some of the technologies that are changing the way work is done.

- Handheld devices that have e-mail, calendars, and contacts can be used anywhere there's a wireless network. And these devices can even be used to log into corporate databases and company intranets.

- Employees can videoconference using broadband networks and Webcams.

- Many companies are giving employees key fobs with constantly changing encryption codes that allow them to log onto the corporate network to access e-mail and company data from any computer hooked up to the Internet.

- Cell phones switch seamlessly between cellular networks and corporate wi-fi connections.

The biggest issue in doing your work anywhere, anytime is security. Companies need to protect their important and sensitive information. However, software and other disabling devices have minimized security issues considerably. Even insurance providers are more comfortable giving their mobile employees access to information. For instance, Health Net Inc. gave BlackBerrys to many of its managers so they can tap into customer records from anywhere. As one tech company CEO said, "Companies now can start thinking about innovative apps (applications) they can create and deliver to their workers anywhere."

---

**virtual organization**
An organization that consists of a small core of full-time employees and that hires outside specialists temporarily as needed to work on projects.

**network organization**
An organization that uses its own employees to do some work activities and networks of outside suppliers to provide other needed product components or work processes.

## *becoming* a Manager

✓ If you belong to a student organization or are employed, notice how various activities and events are organized through the use of work specialization, chain of command, authority, responsibility, and so forth.

✓ As you read current business periodicals, note what types of organizational structures businesses use and whether or not they're effective.

✓ Talk to managers about how they organize work and what they have found to be effective.

✓ Because delegating is part of decentralizing and is an important management skill, complete the Skill-Building Module on Delegating. Then practice delegating in various situations.

✓ Look for examples of **organizational charts** (a visual drawing of an organization's structure) and use it to try to determine what structural design the organization is using.

✓  Complete the following exercises from the Self-Assessment Library found on www.prenhall.com/rolls: S.A.L. #III.A.1—What Type of Organization Structure Do I Prefer?, S.A.L. #III.B.2—How Willing Am I to Delegate?, S.A.L. #II.C.3—How Good Am I at Playing Politics?, and S.A.L. #I.A.4—How Well Do I Handle Ambiguity?

Self-Assessment
Library (S.A.L.)

Q & A
What is a learning organization
really like?
Q & A 10.15 discusses this.

What is a **learning organization**? It's an organization that has developed the capacity to continuously learn, adapt, and change.[47] In a learning organization, employees continually acquire and share new knowledge and are willing to apply that knowledge in making decisions or performing their work. Some organizational theorists even go so far as to say that an organization's ability to do this—that is, to learn and to apply that learning—may be the only sustainable source of competitive advantage.[48] ( Go to www.prenhall.com/rolls) What structural aspects does a learning organization need?

First, it's critical for members in a learning organization to share information and collaborate on work activities throughout the entire organization—across different functional specialties and even at different organizational levels. To do this requires minimal structural and physical barriers. In such a boundaryless environment, employees can work together and collaborate in doing the organization's work the best way they can and learn from each other. Finally, because of this need to collaborate, teams also tend to be an important feature of a learning organization's structural design. Employees work in teams that are empowered to make decisions about doing whatever work needs to be done or resolving issues. With empowered employees and teams, there's little need for "bosses" to direct and control. Instead, managers serve as facilitators, supporters, and advocates.

**Managing Global Structural Issues** Are there global differences in organizational structures? Are Australian organizations structured like those in the United States? Are German organizations structured like those in France or Mexico? Given the global nature of today's business environment, this is an issue with which managers need to be familiar. Researchers have concluded that the structures and strategies of organizations worldwide are similar, "while the behavior within them is maintaining its cultural uniqueness."[49] What does this mean for designing effective and efficient structures? When designing or changing structure, managers may need to think about the cultural implications of certain design elements. For instance, one study showed that formalization—rules and bureaucratic mechanisms—may be more important in less economically developed countries and less important in more economically developed countries where employees may have higher levels of professional education and skills.[50] Other structural design elements may be affected by cultural differences as well.

**A Final Thought** No matter what structural design managers choose for their organizations, the design should help employees do their work in the best—most efficient and effective—way they can. The structure should aid and facilitate organizational members as they carry out the organization's work. After all, the structure is simply a means to an end. (  Go to www.prenhall.com/rolls)

Self-Assessment Library (S.A.L.)

Now that you've seen what organizing and organizational structures are all about, what type of structure do you think you'd prefer? Try S.A.L #III.A.1 and see!

# Learning Review

- Contrast the three traditional organizational designs.
- Explain team, matrix, and project structures.

- Describe the design of virtual and network organizations.
- Discuss the organizational design challenges facing managers today.

**organizational chart**
A visual drawing of an organization's structure.

**learning organization**
An organization that has developed the capacity to continuously learn, adapt, and change.

# Managers Respond to a Manager's Dilemma

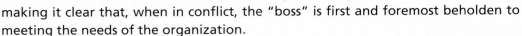

## Ann Kelly

Partner, Lake Partners Strategy Consultants,
Seattle, WA

It is extremely difficult to be both a great boss and a great friend. There will always come a point where a trade-off needs to be made between the relationships. The key is making it clear that, when in conflict, the "boss" is first and foremost beholden to meeting the needs of the organization.

In Penny's case, he needs to formally set the standard for the firm's culture from the top down through a combination of organizational structure and policy development:

- Hire or appoint a COO who is not a long-time friend who has the authority to evaluate, hire, and fire Penny's former direct reports. This preserves Penny's ability to serve as "fun, firm culture czar" while removing the boss/friend conflict.
- Put in place a "Professional Conduct" policy for defining appropriate and inappropriate behavior in the workplace.
- Put in place a merit-based "Performance Review" process that makes clear the metrics (including "contribution to firm culture") on which each professional will be evaluated on a regular basis.
- Introduce both of these at an all-hands meeting that includes a shared vision for a success-driven company that is also a fun place to work.

Informally, Penny needs to better "check" inappropriate behavior immediately when he sees it.

## John J. Staley, Jr.

VP of Marketing and Sales, Staley Electric Supply,
Conshohocken, PA

Penny needs to place a buffer between himself and his employees. He needs to create an organizational structure that provides accountability. He can do this by hiring or promoting somebody to the position of manager. Employees would report to the manager, and the manager would review employee performance. The only time employees should report to Penny should be in cases of a problem with the manager. That way, Penny can spend his time focusing on moving the company forward, and he can still be friendly with the employees if he wishes.

# Learning Summary

## What Do Managers Do When They Organize?

**Organizing**: arranging and structuring work to accomplish the organization's goals; that is, creating the organization's structure

**Organizational structure**: the formal arrangement of jobs within an organization

**Organizational design**: changing or developing an organization's structure

## What Are the Six Elements of Organizational Structure?

- **Work specialization**: dividing work activities into separate job tasks
  - Increased efficiency versus human diseconomies
- **Departmentalization**: grouping like jobs back together
  - Functional, product, geographical, process, and customer
- **Chain of command**: line of authority from top to bottom of organization clarifying who reports to whom
  - **Authority**: rights inherent in managerial position to tell others what to do and to expect them to do it
  - **Responsibility**: obligation to perform assigned duties
  - **Unity of command**: idea that each person should report to only one manager
- **Span of control**: number of employees that a manager manages
  - Depends on skills and abilities of manager and employees and work characteristics
- **Centralization-decentralization**: where decision making is concentrated
  - **Employee empowerment**: giving employees more authority (power) to make decisions
- **Formalization**: extent to which employees' jobs are standardized and controlled

## What Are the Factors That Affect the Type of Organizational Structure Managers Design?

Organizations are either more **mechanistic** or **organic**, depending on

1. **Strategy**
   - As strategy changes, structure changes to support strategy
   - Innovation strategy requires more organic design; cost minimization strategy requires more mechanistic design; imitator strategy could use either design
2. **Size**
   - Large organizations tend to be more mechanistic
   - However, past a certain point (around 2,000 employees), size has less influence on structure
3. **Technology**
   - Woodward's production technologies: unit production—organic; mass production—mechanistic; and process production—organic
4. **Degree of environmental uncertainty**
   - More uncertainty, more organic structure

## What Are the Common Types of Organizational Designs?

### Traditional

- Simple
- Functional
- Divisional

### Contemporary

- Team
- Matrix
- Project
- Boundaryless
  - Virtual
  - Network
  - Modular

> **What Design Challenges Do Managers Face Today?**
> - Keeping employees connected
> - Building a learning organization
> - Global structural issues

## Management: By the Numbers

- Sixty percent of respondents to a survey of professional, managerial, and technical knowledge workers in companies with more than 1,000 employees said that work is often duplicated because people are unaware of each other's work.
- In this same survey, 51 percent of the respondents said that wrong decisions were regularly made because employee knowledge wasn't effectively tapped.
- According to a survey by Sirota Survey Intelligence, 62 percent of the respondents said a key obstacle in performing their job was excessive bureaucracy.

- A survey of telecommuters (individuals who work at home but are linked to the office by computer) from 20 countries found that 46 percent of the women and 52 percent of the men said that telecommuting made them feel more productive.

*Sources:* D. Stead, "The Big Picture: Slippers and Stubble," *Business Week,* April 3, 2006, p. 13; J. Macintyre, "Bosses and Bureaucracy," *Springfield Business Journal,* August 1–7, 2005, p. 29; and D. Gilmour, "How to Fix Knowledge Management," *Harvard Business Review,* October 2003, pp. 16–17.

## Thinking About Management Issues

1. Can an organization's structure be changed quickly? Why or why not? Should it be changed quickly? Explain.

2. Would you rather work in a mechanistic or an organic organization? Why?

3. What types of skills would a manager need to effectively work in a project structure? In a boundaryless organization? In a learning organization?

4. The boundaryless organization has the potential to create a major shift in the way we work. Do you agree or disagree? Explain.

5. With the availability of advanced information technology that allows an organization's work to be done anywhere at any time, is organizing still an important managerial function? Why or why not?

## Working Together: Team-Based Exercise

In relatively decentralized organizations, managers must delegate (assign or turn over) authority to another person to carry out specific duties. Read through the Skills Module on Delegating found on pages 625-626. Form groups of three or four students. Your instructor will assign groups to either "effective delegating" or "ineffective delegating." Come up with a role-playing situation illustrating what your group was assigned (effective or ineffective delegating) that you will present in class. Be prepared to explain how your situation was an example of effective or ineffective delegating.

## Ethical Dilemma Exercise

Can a manager act unethically by simply following orders within the chain of command? In one survey of human resources managers, 52 percent of the respondents felt some pressure to bend ethical rules, often because of orders from above or to achieve ambitious goals. At WorldCom and Enron, this happened in the finance and accounting departments—but managers in any department may feel pressure to act unethically. One manager in human resources, on the job just a few weeks, began to suspect that his new employer was using illegal immigrant workers. He checked into the situation until his boss ordered him to stop, saying the company feared being "short-handed" if the workers were terminated. The manager remained uneasy, however, and he quickly left for a job with a different company.

Another example: The human resources manager of a small nonprofit organization was shocked when she found out that management had faked the paperwork so some employees would be unable to collect overtime pay. She was just as outraged when she received orders to enroll a newly hired executive in the retirement plan, violating the usual waiting period for eligibility. When she expressed her objections, the organization's lawyer responded: "You will do what you're told." What is a manager's ethical responsibility in such situations?[51]

Imagine you're a manager in the human resources department of the electronics retailer RadioShack. You were hired a few months after former CEO David Edmondson admitted he had lied on his résumé—showing two college degrees he had not earned—and resigned (see the Chapter 5 Case Application). Today the executive vice president called you about hiring her preferred candidate for the position of merchandising manager. You haven't yet verified the candidate's credentials, but the executive vice president insists that this candidate should be hired immediately. Review this chapter's material on chain of command as you decide what to do next—and why.

**Option A:** Say that you'll hire the candidate on probation so the job offer can be rescinded if you determine that the credentials have been inflated or faked.

**Option B:** Draft an official policy memo requiring pre-employment verification of candidates' credentials and ask the CEO to sign it right away.

**Option C:** Firmly but politely refuse, saying you must take the time to thoroughly verify the credentials of the chosen candidate before hiring.

## Case Application

### Fixing What's Broken: H-P's Structural Challenge

Best known for its printers, cameras, calculators, and computers, Hewlett-Packard Company (H-P) has had its share of organizing challenges over the years. Carly Fiorina, who was named CEO of H-P in 1999—a move that made news headlines because H-P was now one of the first major U.S. corporations to be headed by a woman—continued the company's strategy of growing by acquiring businesses. Her most controversial acquisition was the $25 billion purchase of rival Compaq Computers—a decision that was the beginning of the end for Fiorina. The combined companies experienced many problems—financial, cultural, and structural—resulting in poor performance. Her differences with the company's board of directors over the direction H-P was going finally led to her firing in early February 2005. By the end of March 2005, Mark Hurd, CEO of NCR, had been selected by the board as the new CEO of H-P.

A few weeks after arriving at H-P, Hurd began hearing complaints about the company's sales force. At a retreat "with 25 top corporate customers, several of them told Mr. Hurd they didn't know whom to call at H-P because of the company's confusing management layers." He also heard the same complaints inside the organization. The company's head of corporate technology told Mr. Hurd that "it once took her three months to get approval to hire 100 sales specialists." Another executive said that "his team of 700 salespeople typically spent 33 percent to 36 percent of their time with customers. The rest of the time was spent negotiating internal H-P bureaucracy." Even the sales reps said that they didn't get to spend time with customers because they were "often burdened with administrative tasks." Getting a price quote or a sample product to a customer became a time-consuming ordeal. It didn't take Hurd long to realize that there was a "fundamental problem" that he had to address.

Delving into H-P's sales structure, Hurd found 11 layers of management between him and customers—way too many, he decided. And the company's sales structure was highly inefficient. For instance, in Europe, H-P had four people from different departments working to close a sales deal while competitors typically only had three people. "That meant H-P was slower to cut a deal and lost many bids." And the final issue Hurd uncovered: Of the 17,000 people working in corporate sales, less than 60 percent of them directly sold to customers. The rest were support staff or in management. It was a situation that Hurd knew had to be changed if the organization was going to again become an industry leader.

Mr. Hurd's first move was to fire underperformers and eliminate three layers of sales management. Then, he eliminated one sales group entirely and merged those individuals into other sales groups. Now, many sales reps are assigned to only one top customer so those customers always know whom to contact. Top H-P executives now say that they can make speedier decisions with the new sales structure. And salespeople are spending more than 40 percent of their time with customers, as compared to around 30 percent a year earlier.

### Discussion Questions

1. Describe the structural problems H-P had.

2. How did Mark Hurd decide to address his company's structural problems? What do you think of his changes? How do you think the company's customers responded to these changes? How about the company's executives and sales force?

3. Would a more mechanistic or a more organic organization be appropriate for H-P? Why?

4. What role do you think organizational structure plays in an organization's efficiency and effectiveness? Explain.

*Sources:* P. W. Tam, "System Reboot," *Wall Street Journal*, April 3, 2006, pp. A1+; A. Lashinsky, "Can HP Win Doing It the Hurd Way?" *Fortune*, April 3, 2006, p. 65; P. Burrows, "H-P Says Goodbye to Drama," *BusinessWeek*, September 12, 2005, pp. 83–86; A. Lashinsky, "Mark Hurd Takes His First Swing at H-P," *Fortune*, August 8, 2005, p. 24; P. Burrows and B. Elgin, "The Un-Carly Unveils His Game Plan," *BusinessWeek*, June 27, 2005, p. 36; and A. Lashinsky, "Take a Look at H-P," *Fortune*, June 13, 2005, pp. 117–120.

*Hewlett-Packard CEO Mark Hurd.*

# Learning Outline

*Use this Learning Outline as you read and study this chapter.*

## Understanding Communication

- Explain why effective communication is important for managers.
- Define communication.
- Differentiate between interpersonal and organizational communication.
- Discuss the functions of communication.

## Interpersonal Communication

- Explain all the components of the communication process.
- List the communication methods managers might use.
- Describe nonverbal communication and how it takes place.
- Explain the barriers to effective interpersonal communication and how to overcome them.

## Organizational Communication

- Contrast formal and informal communication.
- Explain how communication can flow in an organization.
- Describe the three common communication networks.
- Discuss how managers should handle the grapevine.

## Understanding Information Technology

- Describe how technology affects managerial communication.
- Define e-mail, instant messaging, blogs and wikis, voice mail, fax, EDI, teleconferencing, videoconferencing, Web conferencing, intranet, and extranet.
- Explain how information technology affects organizations.

## Communication Issues in Today's Organizations

- Discuss the challenges of managing communication in an Internet world.
- Explain how organizations can manage knowledge.
- Describe why communicating with customers is an important managerial issue.
- Explain how political correctness is affecting communication.

# Communication and Information Technology

## A Manager's Dilemma

Cash flow. Revenue sharing. Double-digit growth. Leverage. Metrics. That's the language that Kim Williams speaks. As senior vice president of finance for the National Football League (NFL), she may not use the language of play-action pass, pitch sweep, reverse, or quarterback draw in her job, but it's certain that the 32 teams that make up the NFL do. Now she wants them to communicate with—and understand—her language.[1]

The NFL is the organization that oversees professional football, the United States' most popular spectator sport. In its role as a trade association for the member teams, the NFL's primary business units are NFL Properties, which generates billions of dollars through merchandising and licensing deals and NFL Enterprises, which negotiates national broadcasting rights for the teams. Its other subsidiaries include NFL Charities and NFL Films. And in 2003, the league launched its own television channel, the NFL Network, a round-the-clock football network, which football junkies consider a godsend. And, then, of course, there's the Super Bowl—the NFL's extremely popular championship game, which draws in millions of viewers and even millions more dollars. With the average going rate for a 30-second commercial shown during the Super Bowl in the millions (in 2006, it was $2.5 million), the NFL has scored a winner. With the exception of the "wardrobe malfunction" scandal during the 2004 Super Bowl, this annual event highlights the competitive strength of the NFL.

The NFL is considered financially the best-run professional league. Kim says, "One of the underlying strengths of the NFL is that we are a trade association, meaning that the [32 team] clubs are independent entities. So there is a lot of discussion, financially, legally, and from a community standpoint, about what rights are maintained nationally." And as the chief financial officer of the NFL, Kim must communicate regularly with the owners regarding all financial issues.

Put yourself in Kim's shoes. What can she do to improve the effectiveness of her communications with team owners about sometimes complicated and sensitive financial matters?

**What would you do?**

K im Williams recognizes the importance of effective communication. Communication between managers and employees provides the information necessary to get work done effectively and efficiently in organizations. As such, there's no doubt that communication is fundamentally linked to managerial performance.[2] In this chapter, we'll present basic concepts in managerial communication. We'll explain the interpersonal communication process, methods of communicating, barriers to effective communication, and ways to overcome those barriers. We'll also look at organizational communication issues including communication flow and communication networks. Also, because managerial communication is so greatly influenced by information technology, we'll look at it. Finally, we'll discuss several contemporary communication issues facing managers.

## UNDERSTANDING COMMUNICATION

Unlike the character Bill Murray plays in *Groundhog Day*, Neal L. Patterson, CEO of Cerner Corporation, a health care software development company based in Kansas City, probably wishes he *could* do over one day. Upset with the fact that employees didn't seem to be putting in enough hours, he sent an angry and emotional e-mail to about 400 company managers that said, in part:

> We are getting less than 40 hours of work from a large number of our K.C.–based EMPLOYEES. The parking lot is sparsely used at 8 A.M.; likewise at 5 P.M. As managers, you either do not know what your EMPLOYEES are doing, or you do not CARE. You have created expectations on the work effort, which allowed this to happen inside Cerner, creating a very unhealthy environment. In either case, you have a problem and you will fix it or I will replace you . . . I will hold you accountable. You have allowed things to get to this state. You have 2 weeks. Tick, tock.[3]

Although the e-mail was meant only for the company's managers, it was leaked and posted on a Yahoo! discussion site. The tone of the e-mail surprised industry analysts, investors, and of course, Cerner's managers and employees. The company's stock price dropped 22 percent over the next 3 days. Patterson apologized to his employees and acknowledged, "I lit a match and started a firestorm." This is a good example of why it's important for managers to understand the impact of communication.

The importance of effective communication for managers can't be overemphasized for one specific reason: Everything a manager does involves communicating. Not *some* things, but everything! A manager can't make a decision without information. That information has to be communicated. Once a decision is made, communication must again take place. Otherwise, no one would know that a decision was made. The best idea, the most creative suggestion, the best plan, or the most effective job redesign can't take shape without communication. Managers need effective communication skills. ( Go to www.prenhall.com/rolls) We aren't suggesting that good communication skills alone make a successful manager. We can say, however, that ineffective communication skills can lead to a continuous stream of problems for the manager.

**Q & A**

It sounds like managers must communicate a lot. Is it ever okay for them to distort information that they're communicating? Check out Q & A 11.1 for a discussion of the ethics of doing so.

### What Is Communication?

**Communication** is the transfer and understanding of meaning. The first thing to note about this definition is the emphasis on the *transfer* of meaning. This means that if no information or ideas have been conveyed, communication hasn't taken place. The speaker who isn't heard or the writer who isn't read hasn't communicated. More importantly, however, communication involves the *understanding* of meaning. For communication to be successful, the meaning must be imparted and understood. A letter written in Portuguese addressed to a person who doesn't read Portuguese can't be considered communication until it's translated into a language the person does read and understand. Perfect communication, if such a thing existed, would be when a transmitted thought or idea was received and understood by the receiver exactly as it was envisioned by the sender.

Another point to keep in mind is that *good* communication is often erroneously defined by the communicator as *agreement* with the message instead of clearly understanding the message.[4] If someone disagrees with us, many of us assume that the person just didn't fully understand our position. In other words, many of us define good communication as having someone accept our views. But I can clearly understand what you mean and just *not* agree with what you say. In fact, many times when a conflict has gone on a long time, people will say it's because the parties aren't communicating effectively. That assumption reflects the tendency to think that effective communication equals agreement. (  Go to www.prenhall.com/rolls)

**Q & A**
What is "perfect" communication?
Q & A 11.2 explains.

The final point we want to make about communication is that it encompasses both **interpersonal communication**—communication between two or more people—and **organizational communication**—all the patterns, networks, and systems of communication within an organization. Both these types of communication are important to managers in organizations.

## Functions of Communication

Rajesh Subramaniam, president of FedEx Canada, was awarded the 2006 Excellence in Communication Leadership (EXCEL) Award by the International Association of Business Communicators (IABC). According to the IABC chair, "Rajesh recognizes the communication challenges unique to the structure of the FedEx operation with 85 percent of employees, primarily on-road couriers, without regular intranet or e-mail access. He ensured that systems were in place so that these frontline employees were kept informed and engaged in their organization. Rajesh makes communication a key component of his business decision making and understands the value and importance of communication in achieving business success."[5]

*Good communication is characterized by an understanding of the sender's meaning, not necessarily by agreement between the parties. At Parkland Memorial Hospital in Dallas, which delivers more babies than any other hospital in the country, 50 faculty members, 40 midwives, and 100 nurses communicate around the clock, and not just in person as they do at the nurse's station shown here. The charge nurses wear walkie-talkies to ensure that communication is ongoing no matter where they are.*

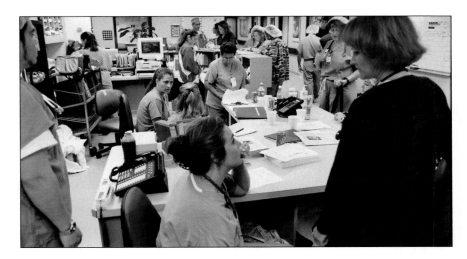

**communication**
The transfer and understanding of meaning.

**interpersonal communication**
Communication between two or more people.

**organizational communication**
All the patterns, networks, and systems of communication within an organization.

Why is communication important to managers and organizations? It serves four major functions: control, motivation, emotional expression, and information.[6]

Communication acts to *control* employee behavior in several ways. As we know from Chapter 10, organizations have authority hierarchies and formal guidelines that employees are expected to follow. For instance, when employees are required to communicate any job-related grievance first to their immediate manager, to follow their job description, or to comply with company policies, communication is being used to control. But informal communication also controls behavior. When work groups tease a member who's working too hard or producing too much (making the rest of the group look bad), they're informally controlling the member's behavior.

Communication encourages *motivation* by clarifying to employees what is to be done, how well they're doing, and what can be done to improve performance if it's not up to par. As employees set specific goals, work toward those goals, and receive feedback on progress toward goals, communication is required.

For many employees, their work group is a primary source of social interaction. The communication that takes place within the group is a fundamental mechanism by which members share frustrations and feelings of satisfaction. Communication, therefore, provides a release for *emotional expression* of feelings and for fulfillment of social needs.

Finally, individuals and groups need information to get things done in organizations. Communication provides that *information*.

No one of these four functions is more important than the others. For groups to work effectively, they need to maintain some form of control over members, motivate members to perform, provide a means for emotional expression, and make decisions. You can assume that almost every communication interaction that takes place in a group or organization is fulfilling one or more of these four functions.

## Learning Review

- Explain why effective communication is important for managers.
- Define communication.

- Differentiate between interpersonal and organizational communication.
- Discuss the functions of communication.

## INTERPERSONAL COMMUNICATION

Before communication can take place, a purpose, expressed as a **message** to be conveyed, must exist. It passes between a source (the sender) and a receiver. The message is converted to symbolic form (called **encoding**) and passed by way of some medium (**channel**) to the receiver, who retranslates the sender's message (called **decoding**). The result is the transfer of meaning from one person to another.[7]

Exhibit 11–1 illustrates the seven elements of the **communication process**: the communication source, the message, encoding, the channel, decoding, the receiver, and feedback. In addition, note that the entire process is susceptible to **noise**—disturbances that interfere with the transmission, receipt, or feedback of a message. Typical examples

Exhibit 11–1

**The Interpersonal Communication Process**

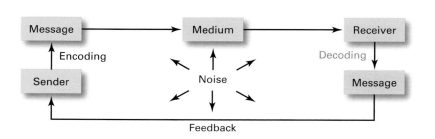

of noise include illegible print, phone static, inattention by the receiver, or background sounds of machinery or co-workers. Remember that anything that interferes with understanding can be noise, and noise can create distortion at any point in the communication process. Let's look at how distortions can happen with the sender, the message, the channel, the receiver, and the feedback loop.

A *sender* initiates a message by *encoding* a thought. Four conditions influence the effectiveness of that encoded message: the skills, attitudes, and knowledge of the sender, and the social-cultural system. How? We'll use ourselves, as your textbook authors, as an example. If we don't have the requisite skills, our message won't reach you, the reader, in the form desired. Our success in communicating to you depends on our writing skills. In addition, any preexisting ideas (attitudes) that we may have about numerous topics will affect how we communicate. For instance, our attitudes about managerial ethics or the importance of managers to organizations influences our writing. Next, the amount of knowledge we have about a subject affects the message(s) we are transferring. We can't communicate what we don't know; if our knowledge is too extensive, it's possible that our writing won't be understood by the readers. Finally, the social-cultural system in which we live influences us as communication senders. Our beliefs and values (all part of culture) act to influence what and how we communicate. Think back to our chapter-opening manager's dilemma and how Kim Williams wants to be an effective communicator. As she encodes her ideas into messages when communicating with team owners, she'll need to reflect on her skill, attitudes, knowledge, and the social-cultural system in order to reduce any possible noise.

The *message* itself can distort the communication process, regardless of the kinds of supporting tools or technologies used to convey it. A message is the actual physical product encoded by the source. It can be a written document, an oral speech, and even gestures and facial expressions we use. The message is affected by the symbols used to transfer meaning (words, pictures, numbers, and so forth), the content of the message itself, and the decisions that the sender makes in selecting and arranging both the symbols and the content. Noise can distort the communication process in any of these areas.

The *channel* chosen to communicate the message also has the potential to be affected by noise. Whether it's a face-to-face conversation, an e-mail message, or a company-wide memorandum, distortions can, and do, occur. Managers need to recognize that certain channels are more appropriate for certain messages. (Think back to how Cerner's CEO chose to communicate his frustration with his managers by e-mail and whether that was an appropriate choice.) Obviously, if the office is on fire, a memo to convey the fact is inappropriate! And if something is important, such as an employee's performance appraisal, a manager might want to use multiple channels—perhaps an oral review followed by a written letter summarizing the points. This decreases the potential for distortion.

The *receiver* is the individual to whom the message is directed. Before the message can be received, however, the symbols in it must be translated into a form that the receiver can understand. This is the *decoding* of the message. Just as the sender was limited by his or her skills, attitudes, knowledge, and social-cultural system, so is the receiver. And just as the sender must be skillful in writing or speaking, the receiver must be skillful in reading or listening. A person's knowledge influences his or her ability to receive. Moreover, the receiver's attitudes and social-cultural background can distort the message.

The final link in the communication process is a *feedback loop*. Feedback returns the message to the sender and provides a check on whether the receiver understood the message. Because feedback can be transmitted along the same types of channels as the original message, it faces the same potential for distortion.

**message**
A purpose to be conveyed.

**encoding**
Converting a message into symbols.

**channel**
The medium a message travels along.

**decoding**
Retranslating a sender's message.

**communication process**
The seven elements involved in transferring meaning from one person to another.

**noise**
Any disturbances that interfere with the transmission, receipt, or feedback of a message.

*Communication channels have multiplied with the spread of technologies like wi-fi. At the 141 warehouse-type stores operated by BJ's Wholesale Club, for instance, managers have saved time and money by switching to wi-fi for their internal communications. The devices mean that managers like John Barrows can talk to customers, suppliers, or even the boss without having to hike across the aisles to the store's front-office telephone.*

**Q & A**
Written communication can be more effective since you have something in writing, right?
Go to Q & A 11.3 and find out!

## Methods of Communicating Interpersonally

You need to communicate to your employees the organization's new policy on sexual harassment; you want to compliment one of your workers on the extra hours she's put in to help your team complete a customer's order; you must tell one of your employees about changes to his job; or you would like to get employees' feedback on your proposed budget for next year. In each of these instances, how would you communicate this information? Managers have a wide variety of communication methods from which to choose. (◆ Go to www.prenhall.com/rolls) These include face-to-face, telephone, group meetings, formal presentations, memos, traditional mail, fax machines, employee publications, bulletin boards, other company publications, audio- and videotapes, hotlines, e-mail, computer conferencing, voice mail, teleconferences, and videoconferences. All of these communication channels include oral or written symbols, or both. How do you know which to use? Managers can use 12 questions to help them evaluate the various communication methods.[8]

1. *Feedback.* How quickly can the receiver respond to the message?
2. *Complexity capacity.* Can the method effectively process complex messages?
3. *Breadth potential.* How many different messages can be transmitted using this method?
4. *Confidentiality.* Can communicators be reasonably sure their messages are received only by those intended?
5. *Encoding ease.* Can the sender easily and quickly use this channel?
6. *Decoding ease.* Can the receiver easily and quickly decode messages?
7. *Time–space constraint.* Do senders and receivers need to communicate at the same time and in the same space?
8. *Cost.* How much does it cost to use this method?
9. *Interpersonal warmth.* How well does this method convey interpersonal warmth?
10. *Formality.* Does this method have the needed amount of formality?
11. *Scanability.* Does this method allow the message to be easily browsed or scanned for relevant information?
12. *Time of consumption.* Does the sender or receiver exercise the most control over when the message is dealt with?

Exhibit 11–2 provides a comparison of the various communication methods on these 12 criteria. Which method a manager ultimately chooses should reflect the

Exhibit 11–2    **Comparison of Communication Methods**

| | | | | | | | Criteria | | | | | |
|---|---|---|---|---|---|---|---|---|---|---|---|---|
| Channel | Feedback Potential | Complexity Capacity | Breadth Potential | Confiden-tiality | Encoding Ease | Time-Decoding Ease | Space Constraint | Cost | Personal Warmth | Formality | Scanability | Consumption Time |
| Face-to-face | 1 | 1 | 1 | 1 | 1 | 1 | 1 | 2 | 1 | 4 | 4 | S/R |
| Telephone | 1 | 4 | 2 | 2 | 1 | 1 | 3 | 3 | 2 | 4 | 4 | S/R |
| Group meetings | 2 | 2 | 2 | 4 | 2 | 2 | 1 | 1 | 2 | 3 | 4 | S/R |
| Formal presentations | 4 | 2 | 2 | 4 | 3 | 2 | 1 | 1 | 3 | 3 | 5 | Sender |
| Memos | 4 | 4 | 2 | 3 | 4 | 3 | 5 | 3 | 5 | 2 | 1 | Receiver |
| Postal mail | 5 | 3 | 3 | 2 | 4 | 3 | 5 | 3 | 4 | 1 | 1 | Receiver |
| Fax | 3 | 4 | 2 | 4 | 3 | 3 | 5 | 3 | 3 | 3 | 1 | Receiver |
| Publications | 5 | 4 | 2 | 5 | 5 | 3 | 5 | 2 | 4 | 1 | 1 | Receiver |
| Bulletin boards | 4 | 5 | 1 | 5 | 3 | 2 | 2 | 4 | 5 | 3 | 1 | Receiver |
| Audio/videotapes | 4 | 4 | 3 | 5 | 4 | 2 | 3 | 2 | 3 | 3 | 5 | Receiver |
| Hot lines | 2 | 5 | 2 | 2 | 3 | 1 | 4 | 2 | 3 | 3 | 4 | Receiver |
| E-mail | 3 | 4 | 1 | 2 | 3 | 2 | 4 | 2 | 4 | 3 | 4 | Receiver |
| Computer conference | 1 | 2 | 2 | 4 | 3 | 2 | 3 | 2 | 3 | 3 | 4 | S/R |
| Voice mail | 2 | 4 | 2 | 1 | 2 | 1 | 5 | 3 | 2 | 4 | 4 | Receiver |
| Teleconference | 2 | 3 | 2 | 5 | 2 | 2 | 2 | 2 | 3 | 3 | 5 | S/R |
| Videoconference | 3 | 3 | 2 | 4 | 2 | 2 | 2 | 1 | 2 | 3 | 5 | S/R |

*Note:* Ratings are on a 1–5 scale where 1 = high and 5 = low. Consumption time refers to the reception of communication. S/R means the sender and receiver share control.

*Source:* P. G. Clampitt, *Communicating for Managerial Effectiveness* (Newbury Park, CA: Sage Publications, 1991), p. 136.

Self-Assessment
Library (S.A.L.)
Do you know what your face-to-
face communication style is?
Try S.A.L #II.A.1 and see.

needs of the sender, the attributes of the message, the attributes of the channel, and the needs of the receiver. For instance, if you need to communicate to an employee the changes being made in her job, face-to-face communication would be a better choice than a memo because you want to be able to address immediately any questions and concerns that she might have. (  Go to www.prenhall.com/rolls)

We can't leave the topic of interpersonal communication methods without looking at the role of **nonverbal communication**— that is, communication transmitted without words. Some of the most meaningful communications are neither spoken nor written. A loud siren or a red light at an intersection tells you something without words. When a college instructor is teaching a class, she doesn't need words to tell her that her students are bored when their eyes are glassed over or they begin to read the school newspaper in the middle of class. Similarly, when students start putting their papers, notebooks, and book away, the message is clear: Class time is about over. The size of a person's office or the clothes he or she wears also convey messages to others. These are all forms of nonverbal communication. The best-known types of nonverbal communication are body language and verbal intonation.

**Body language** refers to gestures, facial expressions, and other body movements that convey meaning. A person frowning "says" something different from one who's smiling. Hand motions, facial expressions, and other gestures can communicate emotions or temperaments such as aggression, fear, shyness, arrogance, joy, and anger. Knowing the meaning behind someone's body moves and learning how to put forth your best body language can help you personally and professionally.[9]

**Verbal intonation** refers to the emphasis someone gives to words or phrases that conveys meaning. To illustrate how intonations can change the meaning of a message, consider the student who asks the instructor a question. The instructor replies, "What do you mean by that?" The student's reaction will vary, depending on the tone of the instructor's response. A soft, smooth vocal tone conveys interest and creates a different meaning from one that is abrasive and puts a strong emphasis on saying the last word. Most of us would view the first intonation as coming from someone sincerely interested in clarifying the student's concern, whereas the second suggests that the person is defensive or aggressive.

The fact that every oral communication also has a nonverbal message can't be overemphasized. Why? Because the nonverbal component usually carries the greatest impact. It's not *what* you said, but *how* you said it. People respond to *how* something is said as well as *what* is said. Managers should remember this as they communicate. (  Go to www.prenhall.com/rolls)

Q & A
Don't employees look at what
managers say rather than at what
they do? What do you think?
Q & A 11.4 discusses this.

## Barriers to Effective Interpersonal Communication

In our discussion of the interpersonal communication process, we noted the continual potential for distortion. What causes distortion? In addition to the general distortions identified in the communication process, managers face other barriers to effective communication. (  Go to www.prenhall.com/rolls)

Q & A
Don't you find it difficult to
communicate with someone who is
constantly on a cell phone,
computer, or Blackberry? Go to
Q & A 11.5 for some advice.

**Filtering** Filtering is the deliberate manipulation of information to make it appear more favorable to the receiver. For example, when a person tells his or her manager what the manager wants to hear, that individual is filtering information. Does this happen much in organizations? Yes, it does! As information is communicated up through organizational levels, it's condensed and synthesized by senders so those on top don't become overloaded with information. Those doing the condensing filter communications through their personal interests and perceptions of what is important. (  Go to www.prenhall.com/rolls)

Q & A
Do managers "selectively" hear or
see information? Q & A 11.10
explains.

*Filtering, or shaping information to make it look good to the receiver, might not always be intentional. For John Seral, vice president and chief information officer for GE Aviation and GE Energy, the problem was that when the CEO asked how the quarter was looking, he got a different answer depending on whom he asked. Seral solved the problem by building a continuously updated database of the company's most important financial information that gives not just the CEO but also 300 company managers instant access to sales and operating figures on their PCs and BlackBerrys. Instead of dozens of analysts compiling the information, the new systems require only six.*

The extent of filtering tends to be a function of the number of vertical levels in the organization and the organizational culture. The more vertical levels there are in an organization, the more opportunities there are for filtering. As organizations use more collaborative, cooperative work arrangements, information filtering may become less of a problem. In addition, the ever-increasing use of e-mail to communicate in organizations reduces filtering because communication is more direct. Finally, the organizational culture encourages or discourages filtering by the type of behavior it rewards. The more that organizational rewards emphasize style and appearance, the more managers will be motivated to filter communications in their favor.

**Emotions**  How a receiver feels when a message is received influences how he or she interprets it. You'll often interpret the same message differently, depending on whether you're happy or upset. Extreme emotions are most likely to hinder effective communication. In such instances, we often disregard our rational and objective thinking processes and substitute emotional judgments. It's best to avoid reacting to a message when you're upset because you're not likely to be thinking clearly.

**Information Overload**  A marketing manager goes on a weeklong sales trip to Spain where he doesn't have access to his e-mail and is faced with 1,000 messages on his return. It's not possible to fully read and respond to each and every one of those messages without facing **information overload**—when the information we have to work with exceeds our processing capacity. Today's typical executive frequently complains of information overload. Statistics show that the average business e-mail user devotes 107 minutes a day to e-mail—about 25 percent of the workday. Other statistics show that employees send and receive an average of 204 e-mail messages every day.[10] The demands of keeping up with e-mail, phone calls, faxes, meetings, and professional reading create an onslaught of data that is nearly impossible to process and assimilate. What happens when individuals have more information than they can sort and use? They tend to select out, ignore, pass over, or forget information. Or, they may put off further processing until the overload situation is over. Regardless, the result is lost information and less effective communication. (  Go to www.prenhall.com/rolls)

**Q & A**
Is it possible for managers to over-communicate? Check out Q & A 11.7 for an answer.

**Defensiveness**  When people feel that they're being threatened, they tend to react in ways that reduce their ability to achieve mutual understanding. That is, they become defensive—engaging in behaviors such as verbally attacking others, making

---

**nonverbal communication**
Communication transmitted without words.

**body language**
Gestures, facial configurations, and other movements of the body that convey meaning.

**verbal intonation**
An emphasis given to words or phrases that conveys meaning.

**filtering**
The deliberate manipulation of information to make it appear more favorable to the receiver.

**information overload**
The information we have to work with exceeds our processing capacity.

## _managing workforce_ **Diversity**

### The Communication Styles of Men and Women

"You don't understand what I'm saying, and you never listen!" "You're making a big deal out of nothing." Have you heard or said these statements or ones like them to friends of the opposite sex? Most of us probably have! Research shows that men and women tend to have different communication styles.[11] Let's look closer at these differing styles and the problems that can arise, and try to suggest ways to minimize the barriers.

Deborah Tannen has studied the ways that men and women communicate and reports some interesting differences. The essence of her research is that men use talk to emphasize status, while women use it to create connection. She states that communication between the sexes can be a continual balancing act of juggling our conflicting needs for intimacy, which suggests closeness and commonality, and independence, which emphasizes separateness and differences. It's no wonder, then, that communication problems arise! Women speak and hear a language of connection and intimacy. Men hear and speak a language of status and independence. For many men, conversations are merely a way to preserve independence and maintain status in a hierarchical social order. Yet for many women, conversations are negotiations for closeness and seeking out support and confirmation. Let's look at a few examples of what Tannen has described.

Men frequently complain that women talk on and on about their problems. Women, however, criticize men for not listening. What's happening is that when a man hears a women talking about a problem, he frequently asserts his desire for independence and control by offering solutions. Many women, in contrast, view conversing about a problem as a way to promote closeness. The woman talks about a problem to gain support and connection, not to get the male's advice.

Here's another example: Men are often more direct than women in conversation. A man might say, "I think you're wrong on that point." A woman might say, "Have you looked at the marketing department's research report on that issue?" The implication in the woman's comment is that the report will point out the error. Men frequently misread women's indirectness as "covert" or "sneaky," but women aren't as concerned as men with the status and one-upmanship that directness often creates.

Finally, men often criticize women for seeming to apologize all the time. Men tend to see the phrase "I'm sorry" as a sign of weakness because they interpret the phrase to mean the woman is accepting blame, when he may know she's not to blame. The woman also knows she's not at fault. Yet she's typically using "I'm sorry" to express regret: "I know you must feel bad about this and I do, too."

Because effective communication between the sexes is important in _all_ organizations, how can we manage these differences in communication styles? To keep gender differences from becoming persistent barriers to effective communication requires acceptance, understanding, and a commitment to communicate adaptively with each other. Both men and women need to acknowledge that there are differences in communication styles, that one style isn't better than the other, and that it takes real effort to "talk" with each other successfully.

---

sarcastic remarks, being overly judgmental, and questioning others' motives.[12] When individuals interpret another's message as threatening, they often respond in ways that hinder effective communication.

**Language** Words mean different things to different people. Age, education, and cultural background are three of the more obvious variables that influence the language a person uses and the definitions he or she gives to words. Author/journalist William F. Buckley Jr. and rap artist Nelly both speak English, but the language each uses is vastly different.

In an organization, employees typically come from diverse backgrounds and have different patterns of speech. Even employees who work for the same organization but in different departments often have different **jargon**—specialized terminology or technical language that members of a group use to communicate among themselves. (  Go to www.prenhall.com/rolls)

Keep in mind that although we may speak the same language, our use of that language is far from uniform. Senders tend to assume that the words and phrases they use mean the same to the receiver as they do to them. This, of course, is incorrect and creates communication barriers. Knowing how each of us modifies the language would help minimize those barriers.

Q & A

Think of groups you belong to. Does that group use special jargon? Does it make the group more effective? Q & A 11.8 looks at jargon and group performance.

**National Culture** For technological and cultural reasons, Chinese people "hate" voice mail. It's a reality that people doing business in China must accept.[13] As this shows, communication differences can arise from national culture as well as different languages that individuals use. Interpersonal communication isn't the same around the world. For example, let's compare countries that place a high value on individualism (such as the United States) with countries where the emphasis is on collectivism (such as Japan).[14]

In the United States, communication tends to be oriented to the individual and clearly spelled out. U.S. managers rely heavily on memoranda, announcements, position papers, and other formal forms of communication to state their positions on issues. U.S. supervisors may hoard information in an attempt to make themselves look good and as a way of persuading their employees to accept decisions and plans. And for their own protection, lower-level employees often engage in this practice as well.

In collectivist countries, such as Japan, there's more interaction for its own sake and a more informal manner of interpersonal contact. The Japanese manager engages in extensive verbal consultation with subordinates over an issue first and draws up a formal document later to outline the agreement that was made. The Japanese value decisions by consensus, and open communication is an inherent part of the work setting. Also, face-to-face communication is encouraged.

Cultural differences can affect the way a manager chooses to communicate. And these differences undoubtedly can be a barrier to effective communication if not recognized and taken into consideration.

## Overcoming the Barriers

On average, an individual must hear new information seven times before he or she truly understands.[15] In light of this fact and the barriers to communication, what can managers do to overcome these barriers and be more effective communicators? The following suggestions should help make your interpersonal communication more effective.

**Use Feedback** Many communication problems can be directly attributed to misunderstanding and inaccuracies. These problems are less likely to occur if the manager uses the feedback loop in the communication process, either verbally or nonverbally.

If a manager asks an employee, "Did you understand what I said?" the response represents feedback. Good feedback means getting more than yes-and-no answers. The manager can ask a set of questions about a message to determine whether the message was received and understood as intended. Better yet, the manager can ask the receiver to restate the message in his or her own words. If the manager hears what was intended, understanding and accuracy should improve. Feedback includes subtler methods than directly asking questions or having the receiver summarize the message. General comments can give a manager a sense of the receiver's reaction to a message. ( Go to www.prenhall.com/rolls)

Of course, feedback doesn't have to be conveyed in words. Actions *can* speak louder than words. A sales manager sends an e-mail to his or her staff describing a new monthly sales report that all sales representatives will need to complete. If some of them don't turn in the new report, the sales manager has received feedback. This feedback suggests that the sales manager needs to clarify further the initial communication. Similarly, when you're talking to someone, you watch their eyes and look for nonverbal clues to tell whether they're getting your message or not.

**Simplify Language** Because language can be a barrier, managers should choose words and structure their messages in ways that will make those messages clear and understandable to the receiver. The manager needs to consider the audience to whom

**jargon**
Specialized terminology or technical language that members of a group use to communicate among themselves.

the message is directed so that the language can be tailored to the receivers. Remember, effective communication is achieved when a message is both received and *understood*. Understanding is improved by using language with which the audience is familiar. This means, for example, that a hospital administrator should always try to communicate in clear, easily understood terms and that the language used in messages to the surgical staff should be purposefully different from that used with office employees. Jargon can facilitate understanding when it's used within a group of those who know what it means, but it can cause many problems when used outside that group. For instance, look back at our chapter-opening dilemma and consider the jargon that Kim Williams uses in her job and profession and how it differs from the jargon that the team owners are more familiar with.

Self-Assessment
Library (S.A.L.)

How good do you think your
listening skills are?
Try S.A.L #II.A.2 and see!

**Listen Actively** When someone talks, we hear, but too often we don't listen. Listening is an active search for meaning, whereas hearing is passive. In listening, two people are engaged in thinking: the sender *and* the receiver.

Many of us are poor listeners. ( Go to www.prenhall.com/rolls) Why? Because it's difficult, and most of us would rather do the talking. Listening, in fact, is often more tiring than talking. It demands intellectual effort. Unlike hearing, **active listening**, which is listening for full meaning without making premature judgments or interpretations, demands total concentration. The average person normally speaks at a rate of about 125 to 200 words per minute. However, the average listener can comprehend up to 400 words per minute.[16] The difference obviously leaves lots of idle time for the brain and opportunities for the mind to wander.

Active listening is enhanced by developing empathy with the sender—that is, by placing yourself in the sender's position. Because senders differ in attitudes, interests, needs, and expectations, empathy makes it easier to understand the actual content of a message. An empathetic listener reserves judgment on the message's content and carefully listens to what is being said. The goal is to improve your ability to receive the full meaning of a communication without its being distorted by premature judgments or interpretations. Other specific behaviors that active listeners demonstrate are listed in Exhibit 11–3. ( Go to www.prenhall.com/rolls)

PRISM

Active listening seems like a lot of
work. And it takes some skill to do!
Try your hand at active listening by
completing PRISM #11.

**Constrain Emotions** It would be naïve to assume that managers always communicate in a rational manner. We know that emotions can severely cloud and distort the transference of meaning. A manager who is emotionally upset over an issue is more likely to misconstrue incoming messages and fail to communicate his or her outgoing messages clearly and accurately. What can the manager do? The simplest answer is to refrain from communicating until he or she has regained composure.

Exhibit 11–3

**Active Listening Behaviors**

*Source:* Based on P. L. Hunsaker, *Training in Management Skills* (Upper Saddle River, NJ: Prentice Hall, 2001).

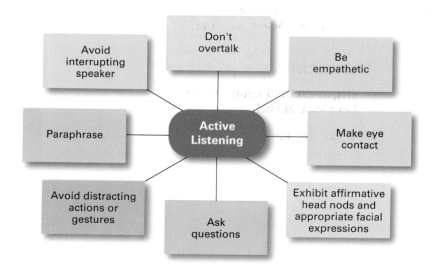

**Watch Nonverbal Cues**  If actions speak louder than words, then it's important to watch your actions to make sure they align with and reinforce the words that go along with them. The effective communicator watches his or her nonverbal cues to ensure that they convey the desired message.

## Learning Review

- Explain all the components of the communication process.
- List the communication methods managers might use.
- Discuss the criteria that help managers evaluate the various communication methods.

- Describe nonverbal communication and how it takes place.
- Explain the barriers to effective interpersonal communication.
- Discuss the ways to overcome the barriers.
- List the active listening behaviors.

## ORGANIZATIONAL COMMUNICATION

An understanding of managerial communication isn't possible without looking at the fundamentals of organizational communication. In this section, we look at several important aspects of organizational communication including formal versus informal communication, the flow patterns of communication, and formal and informal communication networks.

### Formal Versus Informal Communication

Communication within an organization is often described as formal or informal. **Formal communication** refers to communication that follows the official chain of command or is part of the communication required to do one's job. For example, when a manager asks an employee to complete a task, he or she is communicating formally. So is the employee who brings a problem to the attention of his or her manager. Any communication that takes place within prescribed organizational work arrangements would be classified as formal.

**Informal communication** is organizational communication that is not defined by the organization's structural hierarchy. When employees talk with each other in the lunchroom, as they pass in hallways, or as they're working out at the company exercise facility, that's informal communication. Employees form friendships and communicate with each other. The informal communication system fulfills two purposes in organizations: (1) it permits employees to satisfy their need for social interaction, and (2) it can improve an organization's performance by creating alternative, and frequently faster and more efficient, channels of communication. (  Go to www.prenhall.com/rolls)

### Direction of Communication Flow

Organizational communication can flow downward, upward, laterally, or diagonally. Let's look at each.

**Downward**  Every morning and often several times a day, managers at UPS package delivery facilities gather workers for mandatory meetings that last precisely three minutes. During those 180 seconds, managers relay company announcements and go over local information like traffic conditions or customer complaints. Then, each meeting

**active listening**
Listening for full meaning without making premature judgments or interpretations.

**formal communication**
Communication that follows the official chain of command or is required to do one's job.

**informal communication**
Communication that is not defined by the organization's structural hierarchy.

ends with a safety tip. The three-minute meetings have proved so successful that many of the company's office workers are using the idea.[17] Any communication that flows downward from a manager to employees is **downward communication**. Downward communication is used to inform, direct, coordinate, and evaluate employees. When managers assign goals to their employees, they're using downward communication. Managers are also using downward communication by providing employees with job descriptions, informing them of organizational policies and procedures, pointing out problems that need attention, or evaluating their performance. Downward communication can take place through any of the communication methods we described earlier.

**Upward Communication** Managers rely on their employees for information. Reports are given to managers to inform them of progress toward goals and any current problems. **Upward communication** is communication that flows upward from employees to managers. It keeps managers aware of how employees feel about their jobs, their co-workers, and the organization in general. Managers also rely on upward communication for ideas on how things can be improved. Some examples of upward communication include performance reports prepared by employees, suggestion boxes, employee attitude surveys, grievance procedures, manager–employee discussions, and informal group sessions in which employees have the opportunity to identify and discuss problems with their manager or even representatives of top-level management.

The extent of upward communication depends on the organizational culture. If managers have created a climate of trust and respect and use participative decision making or empowerment, there will be considerable upward communication as employees provide input to decisions. For example, FedEx CIO Robert Carter holds town-hall meetings with his staff about every six weeks and sits down once a month with a small group of randomly selected employees to talk over issues and concerns. He has created an environment where employees want to share information and has found these communication encounters to be prime opportunities for finding out what's going on with his employees.[18] In a more highly structured and authoritarian environment, upward communication still takes place, but will be limited both in style and content.

**Lateral Communication** Communication that takes place among employees on the same organizational level is called **lateral communication**. In today's often chaotic and rapidly changing environment, horizontal communications are frequently needed to save time and facilitate coordination. Cross-functional teams, for instance, rely heavily on this form of communication interaction. However, it can create conflicts if employees don't keep their managers informed about decisions they've made or actions they've taken.

*W.L. Gore & Associates, the maker of Gore-Tex® fabric, has successfully applied technology to new products ranging from spacesuits to surgical stents, but new CEO Terri Kelly believes it must do a better job of communicating and exchanging ideas internally in order to fight off low-cost competitors from abroad. She plans to visit as many Gore plants and offices as she can to do her part. "You're only a leader if you can get that followership," she believes.*

**Diagonal Communication** **Diagonal communication** is communication that cuts across both work areas *and* organizational levels. When an analyst in the credit department communicates directly with a regional marketing manager—note the different department and different organizational level—about a customer problem, that's diagonal communication. In the interest of efficiency and speed, diagonal communication can be beneficial. And the increased use of e-mail facilitates diagonal communication. In many organizations, any employee can communicate by e-mail with any other employee, regardless of organizational work area or level, even with upper-level managers. In many organizations, the CEOs have adopted an "open inbox" e-mail policy. For example, William H. Swanson, head of defense contractor Raytheon Company, figures that he has received and answered more than 150,000 employee e-mails. And Henry McKinnell Jr., CEO of Pfizer, says that the approximately 75 internal e-mails he receives every day are "an avenue of communication I don't otherwise have."[19] However, just as with lateral communication, diagonal communication has the potential to create problems if employees don't keep their managers informed.

## Organizational Communication Networks

The vertical and horizontal flows of organizational communication can be combined into a variety of patterns called **communication networks**. Exhibit 11–4 illustrates three common communication networks.

**Types of Communication Networks** In the *chain* network, communication flows according to the formal chain of command, both downward and upward. The *wheel* network represents communication flowing between a clearly identifiable and strong leader and others in a work group or team. The leader serves as the hub through whom all communication passes. Finally, in the *all-channel* network, communication flows freely among all members of a work team.

As a manager, which network should you use? The answer depends on your goal. Exhibit 11–4 also summarizes the effectiveness of the various networks according to four criteria: speed, accuracy, the probability that a leader will emerge, and the importance of member satisfaction. One observation is immediately apparent: No single network is best for all situations. If you're concerned with high member satisfaction, the all-channel network is best; if having a strong and identifiable leader is important, the wheel facilitates this; and if accuracy is most important, the chain and wheel networks work best.

**Exhibit 11–4**

**Three Common Organizational Communication Networks and How They Rate on Effectiveness Criteria**

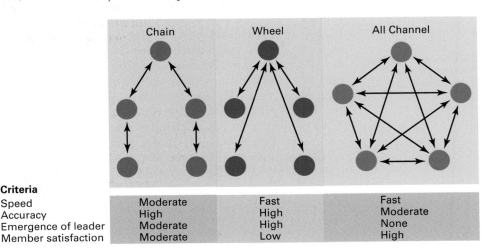

| Criteria | Chain | Wheel | All Channel |
|---|---|---|---|
| Speed | Moderate | Fast | Fast |
| Accuracy | High | High | Moderate |
| Emergence of leader | Moderate | High | None |
| Member satisfaction | Moderate | Low | High |

**downward communication**
Communication that flows downward from a manager to employees.

**upward communication**
Communication that flows upward from employees to managers.

**lateral communication**
Communication that takes place among any employees on the same organizational level.

**diagonal communication**
Communication that cuts across work areas and organizational levels.

**communication networks**
The variety of patterns of vertical and horizontal flows of organizational communication.

*It looks like graffiti, but it's really informal communication at work. Dozens of whiteboards dot the hallways and common areas of Google's Mountain View headquarters in California. Some of the boards are used by product teams swapping ideas, while the two largest are filled with cartoons and jokes. "It's collaborative art," says the company's director of communications and a frequent contributor. "When new hires see the boards, they get a quick, comprehensive snapshot of our personality."*

**The Grapevine** We can't leave our discussion of communication networks without discussing the **grapevine**—the informal organizational communication network. The grapevine is active in almost every organization. Is it an important source of information? You bet! One survey reported that 63 percent of employees say that they hear about important matters first through rumors or gossip on the grapevine.[20]

What are the implications for managers? Certainly, the grapevine is an important part of any group or organization communication network and well worth understanding.[21] It identifies for managers those bewildering issues that employees consider important and anxiety producing. It acts as both a filter and a feedback mechanism, picking up on the issues employees consider relevant. More importantly, from a managerial point of view, it *is* possible to analyze what is happening on the grapevine—what information is being passed, how information seems to flow, and what individuals seem to be key conduits of information. By being aware of the grapevine's flow and patterns, managers can stay on top of issues that concern employees and, in turn, can use the grapevine to disseminate important information. Because the grapevine can't be eliminated, managers should "manage" it as an important information network.

Rumors that flow along the grapevine also can never be eliminated entirely. What managers can do, however, is minimize the negative consequences of rumors by limiting their range and impact. How? By communicating openly, fully, and honestly with employees, particularly in situations where employees may not like proposed or actual managerial decisions or actions. (  Go to www.prenhall.com/rolls) Open and honest communication with employees can impact the organization in various ways. A study by Watson Wyatt Worldwide concluded that effective communication "connects employees to the business, reinforces the organization's vision, fosters process improvement, facilitates change, and drives business results by changing employee behavior." For those companies that communicated effectively, total returns to shareholders were 57 percent higher over a 5-year period than for companies with less effective communication. And the study also showed that companies that were highly effective communicators were 20 percent more likely to report lower turnover rates.[22]

**Q & A**

Can managers use the grapevine to be more effective at their jobs? Q & A 11.9 has the answer!

## Learning Review

- Contrast formal and informal communication.
- Explain how communication can flow in an organization.
- Describe the three common communication networks.
- Discuss how managers should handle the grapevine.

# UNDERSTANDING INFORMATION TECHNOLOGY

Technology is changing the way we live and work. Take the following four examples: Japanese employees, managers, housewives, and teens use wireless interactive Web phones to send e-mail, surf the Web, swap photos, and play computer games. At DreamWorks Animation, a sophisticated videoconferencing system allows animators in three different locations to edit films collaboratively. Nearly 8,000 employees at Ford Motor stopped using their landlines and now use cell phones exclusively. A recent survey of employees showed that 93 percent of those polled use the Internet at work.[23]

The world of communication isn't what it used to be! Managers are challenged to keep their organizations functioning smoothly while continually improving work operations *and* staying competitive even though both the organization and the environment are changing rapidly. Although changing technology has been a significant source of the environmental uncertainty facing organizations, these same technological advances have enabled managers to coordinate the work efforts of employees in ways that can lead to increased efficiency and effectiveness. Information technology now touches every aspect of almost every company's business. The implications for the ways managers communicate are profound.

## How Technology Affects Managerial Communication

Technology, and more specifically information technology, has radically changed the way organizational members communicate. For example, it has significantly improved a manager's ability to monitor individual or team performance, has allowed employees to have more complete information to make faster decisions, and has provided employees more opportunities to collaborate and share information. In addition, information technology has made it possible for people in organizations to be fully accessible, any time, regardless of where they are. Employees don't have to be at their desk with their computer on to communicate with others in the organization. Two developments in information technology seem to be most significant for managerial communication: networked computer systems and wireless capabilities.

**Networked Computer Systems** In a networked computer system, an organization links its computers creating an organizational network. Organizational members can then communicate with each other and tap into information whether they're down the hall, across town, or halfway across the world. Although we won't get into the mechanics of how a network system works, we will address some of its communication applications including e-mail, instant messaging, blogs and wikis, voice mail, fax, electronic data interchange, teleconferencing and videoconferencing, and intranets and extranets.

**E-mail** is the instantaneous transmission of written messages on linked computers. Messages wait at the receiver's computer and are read at the receiver's convenience. E-mail is fast and cheap and can be used to send the same message to numerous people at the same time. It's a quick and convenient way for organizational members to share information and communicate.

Some organizational members who find e-mail slow and cumbersome are using **instant messaging (IM)**. This interactive real-time communication takes place among computer users who are logged onto the network at the same time. IM first became popular among teens and pre-teens who wanted to communicate online with their friends. Now, it's moving to the workplace. With IM, there's no waiting for a colleague to read e-mail. Whatever information back-and-forth needs to be communicated can be done so instantaneously.

---

**grapevine**
The informal organizational communication network.

**e-mail**
The instantaneous transmission of written messages on computers that are linked together.

**instant messaging (IM)**
Interactive real-time communication that takes place among computer users logged on the computer network at the same time.

## _thinking critically about_ **Ethics**

According to a survey by Websense, 58 percent of employees spend time at nonwork-related Web sites. Another survey by Salary.com and AOL found that personal Internet surfing was the top method of goofing off at work. And, funny stories, jokes, and pictures make their way from one employee's e-mail inbox to another, to another, and so forth. An elf bowling game sent by e-mail was a favorite diversion during the holiday season.

Although these may seem like fun and harmless activities, it's estimated that such technological distractions cost businesses over $54 billion annually. Although there's a high dollar cost associated with using the Internet at work for other than business reasons, is there a psychological benefit to be gained by letting employees do something to relieve the stress of pressure-packed jobs? What are the ethical issues associated with widely available Internet access at work for both employees and for organizations?[24]

Blogs and wikis are other online communication media that managers and employees are using. A **blog**, short for Web log, is an online journal that usually focuses on a particular subject. There are millions of blogs—well over 34 million of them, as indexed by Internet search engine Technorati.[25] Some bloggers are corporate employees who may post official or semiofficial blogs about their work. Another relatively new online communication medium is a **wiki**, which is a type of Web site that allows anyone visiting it to add, remove, or otherwise edit the content. The term comes from _wiki wiki,_ which, in the native language of Hawaii, is commonly used as an adjective for quick or fast.[26] As a communication medium, a wiki easily and conveniently allows employees to collaborate on reports, projects, or other creative work.

A **voice-mail** system digitizes a spoken message, transmits it over the network, and stores the message for the receiver to retrieve later.[27] Voice mail allows information to be transmitted even though a receiver may not be physically present to take the information. Receivers can choose to save the message for future use, delete it, or route it to other parties.

**Fax** machines allow the transmission of documents containing both text and graphics over ordinary telephone lines. A sending fax machine scans and digitizes the document. A receiving fax machine reads the scanned information and reproduces it in hard-copy form. Information that is best viewed in printed form can be easily and quickly shared by organizational members.

**Electronic data interchange (EDI)** is a way for organizations to exchange standard business transaction documents, such as invoices or purchase orders, using direct computer-to-computer networks. Organizations often use EDI with vendors, suppliers, and customers because it saves time and money. How? Information on transactions is transmitted from one organization's computer system to another through a telecommunications network. The printing and handling of paper documents at one organization are eliminated as is the inputting of data at the other organization.

Meetings—one-on-one, team, divisional, or organization-wide—have always been a way to share information. The limitations of technology used to dictate that meetings take place among people in the same physical location, but that's no longer the case. **Teleconferencing** allows a group of people to confer simultaneously using telephone or e-mail group communications software. If meeting participants can see each other over video screens, the simultaneous conference is called **videoconferencing**. Work groups, large and small, that might be in different locations can use these communication network tools to collaborate and share information. After 9/11 and during the SARS virus outbreak in 2003, several companies used videoconferencing to communicate with customers and employees. Another alternative for sharing information or collaborating is **Web conferencing**, which is holding group meetings or live presentations over the Internet. For instance, Amer Sports of Helsinki (parent company of Wilson Sporting Goods) uses Web conferencing so employees in Chicago, Finland, Australia, Canada, and Japan can work on projects together.[28]

Networked computer systems have allowed the development of organizational intranets and extranets. An **intranet** is an organizational communication network that uses Internet technology and is accessible only by employees. Many organizations use intranets as ways for employees to share information and collaborate on documents and projects from different locations. For example, Buckman Laboratories, a manufacturer of specialty chemicals based in Memphis, Tennessee, uses an intranet so employees can easily find information about products, markets, and customers. Employees contribute information to and get information from this knowledge network, known as K'Netix®. An **extranet** is an organizational communication network that uses Internet technology and allows authorized users inside the organization to communicate with certain outsiders such as customers or vendors. For instance, Harley-Davidson has developed an extranet that allows faster and more convenient communications with dealers. ( Go to www.prenhall.com/rolls)

**Q & A**
With all these fun distractions, how do you keep people from "goofing off" at work? See Q & A 11.6 for some suggestions.

**Wireless Capabilities** At Seattle-based Starbucks Corporation, district managers have been outfitted with mobile technology, allowing them to spend more time in the company's stores. Anne Saunders, executive vice president of Starbucks, says, "These are the most important people in the company. Each has between 8 to 10 stores that he or she services. And while their primary job is outside of the office—and in those stores—they still need to be connected."[29] As this example shows, wireless communication technology has the ability to improve work for managers and employees. Wireless communication depends on signals sent through air or space without the need for wired connections by using microwave signals, satellites, radio waves and radio antennas, or infrared light rays. Even wireless Internet access is available through "wi-fi hot spots," which are locations where users gain access. The number of these hot spots continues to grow—in 2006, there were over 112,000. The top three "hot spot" cities at that time were Seoul, Tokyo, and London; the top three "hot spot" countries were the United States, the United Kingdom, and South Korea.[30] Because more than 21 million U.S. workers are on the move on any given day, smartphones, notebook computers, and other pocket communication devices have spawned a whole new way for managers to keep in touch. And the number of these mobile communication users keeps increasing.[31] Employees don't have to be at their desks with their phones or computers wired in and turned on to communicate with others in the organization. As technology continues to improve in this area, we'll see more and more organizational members using wireless communication as a way to collaborate and share information.

## How Information Technology Affects Organizations

Employees—working in teams or as individuals—need information to make decisions and to do their work. After describing the communications capabilities managers have at their disposal, it's clear that technology *can* significantly affect the way that organizational members communicate, share information, and do their work.

Communication and the exchange of information among organizational members are no longer constrained by geography or time. Collaborative work efforts

**blog**
An online journal that usually focuses on a particular subject.

**wiki**
A type of Web site that allows anyone visiting it to add, remove, or otherwise edit the content.

**voice mail**
A communication system that digitizes a spoken message, transmits it over a network, and stores the message on disk for the receiver to retrieve later.

**fax**
Communication through machines that allow the transmission of documents containing both text and graphics over ordinary telephone lines.

**electronic data interchange (EDI)**
A way for organizations to exchange standard business transaction documents using direct computer-to-computer networks.

**teleconferencing**
Communication system that allows a group of people to confer simultaneously using telephone or e-mail group communications software.

**videoconferencing**
A simultaneous communication conference where participants can see each other.

**Web conferencing**
Holding group meetings or live presentations over the Internet.

**intranet**
An organizational communication network that uses Internet technology and is accessible only by organizational employees.

**extranet**
An organizational communication network that uses Internet technology and allows authorized users inside the organization to communicate with certain outsiders.

*Technology need not always reduce face-to-face communication. To make contact easier between employees at its call center and in its information systems department, ASB, a New Zealand bank, adopted an open layout encompassing five areas on three different floors. There's a landscaped park area in the center, a café, a minigolf green, a TV room, and a barbecue area, all of which help bring people together. Since moving into the new design, bank managers have noted that the volume of interdepartmental e-mails has dropped, indicating that people are communicating in person more frequently.*

among widely dispersed individuals and teams, sharing of information, and integration of decisions and work throughout an entire organization have the potential to increase organizational efficiency and effectiveness. Although the economic benefits of information technology are obvious, managers must not forget to address the psychological drawbacks.[32] For instance, what is the psychological cost of an employee always being accessible? Will there be increased pressure for employees to "check in" even during their off hours? How important is it for employees to separate their work lives and their personal lives? Though there are no easy answers to these questions, these are issues that managers will have to face. (We've addressed many of those issues in our "Managing IT" boxes throughout the book.) In the next section, we're going to look at other important communication issues that managers in today's organizations face.

## Learning Review

- Describe how technology affects managerial communication.
- Define e-mail, instant messaging, blogs and wikis, voice mail, fax, EDI, teleconferencing,

videoconferencing, Web conferencing, intranet, and extranet.
- Explain how information technology affects organizations.

## COMMUNICATION ISSUES IN TODAY'S ORGANIZATIONS

"Pulse lunches." That's what managers at Citibank's offices throughout Malaysia used to address pressing problems with declining customer loyalty and staff morale and increased employee turnover. By connecting with employees and listening to their concerns—that is, taking their "pulse"—during informal lunch settings, managers were able to make changes that boosted both customer loyalty and employee morale by over 50 percent and reduced employee turnover to nearly zero.[33]

Being an effective communicator in today's organizations means being connected—most importantly to employees and customers, but actually to any of the organization's stakeholders. In this section, we want to examine four communication issues that are of particular significance to today's managers including managing communication in an Internet world, managing the organization's knowledge resources, communicating with customers, and using politically correct communication.

## Managing Communication in an Internet World

At eBay's headquarters, CEO Meg Whitman banned wireless devices from Monday staff meetings. She said, "There was a little grumbling from the top execs who regularly attend the meetings. [However], personal interaction is much more important than instantly answering e-mails."[34]

Managers are learning, the hard way sometimes, that all this new technology has created special communication challenges. The two main ones are (1) legal and security issues and (2) lack of personal interaction.

Chevron paid $2.2 million to settle a sexual-harassment lawsuit stemming from inappropriate jokes being sent by employees over company e-mail. U.K. firm Norwich Union had to pay £450,000 in an out-of-court settlement after an employee sent an e-mail stating that their competitor Western Provident Association was in financial difficulties.

Although e-mail is a quick and easy way to communicate, managers need to be aware of potential legal problems from inappropriate e-mail usage. Electronic information is potentially admissible in court. For instance, during the Enron trial, prosecutors entered into evidence e-mails and other documents they say showed that the defendants defrauded investors. Says one expert, "Today, e-mail and instant messaging are the electronic equivalent of DNA evidence."[35] But e-mail's legal problems aren't the only issue facing managers. Security concerns are another. Managers need to ensure that confidential information is kept confidential. Employee e-mails and blogs should not communicate—inadvertently or purposely—proprietary information. Corporate computer and e-mail systems should be protected against hackers (people who try to gain unauthorized access to computer systems) and spam (electronic junk mail). These are serious issues that managers and organizations must address if the benefits that communication technology offers are to be realized.

Another communication challenge posed by the Internet age we live and work in is the lack of personal interaction. Even when two people are communicating face-to-face, understanding is not always achieved. However, when communication takes place in a virtual environment, it can be *really* hard to achieve understanding and collaborate on getting work done. Some companies have gone so far as to ban e-mail on certain days of the week. Others have simply encouraged employees to collaborate more in-person. Yet, there are situations and times when personal interaction isn't physically possible—your colleagues work across the continent or even across the globe. In those instances, real-time collaboration software (such as private workplace wikis, blogs, instant messengers, and other types of groupware) may be a better communication choice than sending an e-mail and waiting for a response.[36]

## Managing the Organization's Knowledge Resources

Kara Johnson is a materials expert at product design firm Ideo. To make finding the right materials easier, she's building a master library of samples linked to a database that explains their properties and manufacturing processes.[37] What Johnson is doing is managing knowledge and making it easier for others at Ideo to learn and benefit from her knowledge. That's what today's managers need to do with the organization's knowledge resources—make it easy for employees to communicate and share their knowledge so they can learn from each other ways to do their jobs more effectively and efficiently. One way organizations can do this is to build online information databases that employees can access. For example, William Wrigley Jr. Co. recently launched an interactive Web site that allows sales agents to access marketing data and other product information. The sales agents can question company experts about products or search an online knowledge bank. In its first year, Wrigley estimates that the site has cut research time of the sales force by 15,000 hours and made them more efficient and effective.[38] This is one example of how managers can use communication tools to manage this valuable organizational resource called knowledge.

*Tampa Bay head coach John Gruden is among the NFL coaches who have begun to move their strategizing and play making into the digital age. Although he still prefers an outdated Mac program for diagramming plays, Gruden has come a long way. He started out as a computerphobic assistant coach for the San Francisco 49ers where he learned how to use SuperPaint 1.0, still his favorite tool, and later began using Microsoft Word for keeping notes about players, strategy, and coaching techniques. His files are only a couple of mouse clicks away, and with them he can recall every play he has ever called. Add to that an Avid video workstation that can break game tapes down into catalogs by type of play and you have the technological basis for the painstaking preparation that can help a team be successful.*

In addition to online information databases for sharing knowledge, some knowledge management experts suggest that organizations create **communities of practice**, which are "groups of people who share a concern, a set of problems, or a passion about a topic, and who deepen their knowledge and expertise in that area by interacting on an ongoing basis."[39] The keys to this concept are that the group must actually meet in some fashion on a regular basis and use its information exchanges to improve in some way. For example, repair technicians at Xerox tell "war stories" to communicate their experiences and to help others solve difficult problems with repairing machines.[40] This isn't to say that communities of practice don't face challenges. They do. For instance, in large global organizations, keeping communities of practice going takes additional effort. To make these communities of practice work, it's important to maintain strong human interactions through communication. Interactive Web sites, e-mail, and videoconferencing are essential communication tools. In addition, these groups face the same communication problems that individuals face—filtering, emotions, defensiveness, over-documentation, and so forth. However, groups can resolve these issues by focusing on the same suggestions we discussed earlier: using feedback, simplifying language, listening actively, constraining emotions, and watching for nonverbal cues.

## The Role of Communication in Customer Service

You've been a customer many times; in fact, you probably find yourself in a customer service encounter several times a day. So what does this have to do with communication? As it turns out, a lot! *What* communication takes place and *how* it takes place can have a significant impact on a customer's satisfaction with the service and the likelihood of being a repeat customer. Managers in service organizations need to make sure that employees who interact with customers are communicating appropriately and effectively with those customers. How? By first recognizing the three components in any service delivery process: the customer, the service organization, and the individual service provider.[41] Each plays a role in whether communication is working. Obviously, managers don't have a lot of control over what or how the customer communicates, but they can influence the other two.

An organization with a strong service culture already values taking care of customers—finding out what their needs are, meeting those needs, and following up to make sure that their needs were met satisfactorily. Each of these activities involves communication, whether face-to-face, by phone or e-mail, or through other channels. In addition, communication is part of the specific customer service strategies the organization pursues. One strategy that many service organizations use is personalization. For instance, at Ritz-Carlton Hotels, customers are provided with more than a clean bed and room.

Customers who have stayed at a location previously and indicated that certain items are important to them—such as extra pillows, hot chocolate, or a certain brand of shampoo—will find those items waiting in their room at arrival. The hotel's database allows service to be personalized to customers' expectations. In addition, all employees are asked to communicate information related to service provision. For instance, if a room attendant overhears guests talking about celebrating an anniversary, he or she is supposed to relay the information so something special can be done.[42] Communication plays an important role in the hotel's customer personalization strategy.

Communication also is important to the individual service provider or contact employee. The quality of the interpersonal interaction between the customer and that contact employee does influence customer satisfaction.[43] That's especially true when the service encounter isn't up to expectations. People on the front line involved with those critical service encounters are often the first to hear about or notice service failures or breakdowns. They must decide *how* and *what* to communicate during these instances. Their ability to listen actively and communicate appropriately with the customer goes a long way in whether or not the situation is resolved to the customer's satisfaction or spirals out of control. Another important communication concern for the individual service provider is making sure that he or she has the information needed to deal with customers efficiently and effectively. If the service provider doesn't personally have the information, there should be some way to get the information easily and promptly.[44]

## "Politically Correct" Communication

Sears tells its employees to use phrases such as "person with a disability" instead of "disabled person" when writing or speaking about people with disabilities. They also suggest that when talking with a customer in a wheelchair for more than a few minutes, employees place themselves at the customer's eye level by sitting down to make a more comfortable atmosphere for everyone.[45] These suggestions, provided in an employee brochure that discusses assisting customers with disabilities, reflect the importance of politically correct communication. How you communicate with someone who isn't

*becoming* a Manager

✓ Practice being a good communicator—as a sender and a listener.

✓ When preparing to communicate, think about the most appropriate channel for your communication and why it may or may not be the most appropriate.

✓ Pay attention to your and other's nonverbal communication. Learn to notice the cues.

✓ Complete the Skill-Building Module on Active Listening found on page 620.

Self-Assessment Library (S.A.L.)

✓ 🢒 Complete the following exercises from the Self-Assessment Library found on www.prenhall.com/rolls: S.A.L. #II.A.1—What's My Face-to-Face Communication Style?, S.A.L. #II.A.2—How Good Are My Listening Skills?, and S.A.L. #II.A.3—How Good Am I at Giving Performance Feedback?

**communities of practice**
Groups of people who share a concern, a set of problems, or a passion about a topic, and who deepen their knowledge and expertise in that area by interacting on an ongoing basis.

like you, what terms you use in addressing a female customer, or what words you use to describe a colleague who is wheelchair-bound can mean the difference between losing a client, an employee, a lawsuit, a harassment claim, or a job.[46]

Most of us are acutely aware of how our vocabulary has been modified to reflect political correctness. For instance, most of us refrain from using words like *handicapped, blind,* and *elderly* and use instead terms like *physically challenged, visually impaired,* or *senior.* We must be sensitive to others' feelings. Certain words can and do stereotype, intimidate, and insult individuals. With an increasingly diverse workforce, we must be sensitive to how words might offend others. Although it's complicating our vocabulary and making it more difficult for people to communicate, it is something managers can't ignore.

Words are the primary means by which people communicate. When we eliminate words from use because they're politically incorrect, we reduce our options for conveying messages in the clearest and most accurate form. For the most part, the larger the vocabulary used by a sender and a receiver, the greater the opportunity to accurately transmit messages. By removing certain words from our vocabulary, we make it harder to communicate accurately. When we further replace these words with new ones whose meanings are less well understand, we've reduced the likelihood that our messages will be received as we had intended them.

We must be sensitive to how our choice of words might offend others, but we need to acknowledge that politically correct language restricts communication clarity. Nothing suggests that this increased communication ambiguity is likely to be reduced anytime soon. This is just another communication challenge for managers.

## Learning Review

- Discuss the challenges of managing communication in an Internet world.
- Explain how organizations can manage knowledge.
- Describe why communicating with customers is an important managerial issue.
- Explain how political correctness is affecting communication.

# Managers Respond to a Manager's Dilemma

### Faith Tsao, CFA

Director of Traditional External Investments,
Atlantic Trust Private Wealth Management,
Boston, MA

First, I would not be too concerned about communicating with team owners using football language. Team owners are business people first and football fans second. Here is what I would do in my communications with the team owners:

- Work closely with each team to establish reasonable near-term and long-term financial goals for the team. Make sure each team uses the same financial terminology throughout the NFL organization; is equally responsible for setting its own revenue and profitability goals; and understands and agrees what needs to be done to achieve them.
- Share the big picture. Football team owners understand the importance of teamwork. Specify what collaborative efforts are needed among teams to achieve organizational goals.
- Communicate frequently. Since football is a contact sport, face-to-face communications will work best with team owners. I would organize nationwide conferences every quarter to share progress, ask for feedback, and modify plans when needed.

### James W. Buhler

CFO, Clement Publishing Group, Concordville, PA

Kim should make sure that she and all 32 owners have a crystal clear understanding of all the financial terms and language that they will discuss. One way to do this is to develop a list of standard terms and distribute it to all the owners. It will be a lot easier for her to communicate if all involved parties are using a common language base.

The next step for Kim to undertake is to break down these complicated financial matters to their simplest forms. Because Kim has many years of complex accounting experience behind her, she must remember that her audience may or may not be as financially astute as she is in every situation. By breaking down complex financial matters to their simplest forms, it will allow more of the owners to possess a greater understanding of the communicated message.

Kim should also hold follow-up communications with the owners to make sure that the message she was trying to communicate was received clearly and that all involved parties understood it.

# Learning Summary

## What Is Communication?

- The transfer and understanding of meaning
- Effective communication is when a transmitted thought or idea is received and understood by the receiver as it was intended by the sender; it doesn't mean agreement with the transmitted thought or idea
- Communication encompasses both interpersonal and organizational

## What Are the Functions of Communication?

1. Acts to control behavior
2. Encourages motivation
3. Provides a release to emotional expression of feelings and for fulfillment of social needs
4. Provides information

## What Does the Interpersonal Communication Process Involve?

- A communication source or sender
- Message
- Encoding
- The channel
- Decoding
- Receiver
- Feedback

Noise (any interfering disturbances) can occur at any point in the process

## How Can Managers Communicate Interpersonally?

- Variety of communication methods from which to choose
- Effectiveness and efficiency of each method varies
- **Nonverbal communication** (communication transmitted without words) also plays a role
  - Body language
  - Verbal intonation

## Why Does Communication Break Down?

- Filtering
- Emotions
- Information overload
- Selective perception
- Defensiveness
- Language
- Jargon
- National culture

## How Can Managers Overcome the Barriers to Communication?

Provide good feedback, simplify language, listen actively, constrain emotions, and watch nonverbal cues

## How Does Communication Flow in Organizations?

**Formal communication** is communication that follows official chain of command and is needed to do one's job

**Informal communication** is communication that is not defined by organization's structural hierarchy

- Flow
  - Downward—used to inform, direct, coordinate, and evaluate employees
  - Upward—used by employees to inform managers

- Lateral—used by employees on the same organizational level
- Diagonal—cuts across both work areas and organizational levels
- Networks
  - Chain
  - Wheel
  - All channel
  - *Grapevine*—the informal organizational communication network

## How Does Information Technology Affect an Organization?

Allows greater sharing of information and ease of information

Can also lead to information overload

- Networked systems
- Wireless systems

## What Are Today's Major Communication Issues?

- Managing communication in an Internet world
  - Legal and security issues
  - Lack of personal interaction
- Managing the organization's knowledge resources
- Managing customer-service communication
- Politically correct communication

# Management: By the Numbers

- Fewer than half of 335 U.S. companies with global operations surveyed by Watson Wyatt said they are doing an effective job communicating with their global employees.
- In a survey of 2,800 employees and employers, 46 percent of employees and 59 percent of employers said that information employees get from the grapevine about things going on at work often turns out to be wrong.
- In this same survey, 83 percent of *employers* said employees hear about major changes at work through their managers, while only 17 percent of them said employees hear about major changes through the grapevine. On the other hand, 46 percent of the *employees* said they hear about major changes through the grapevine and 53 percent through their managers.

- Seventy-six percent of companies said they are concerned about outgoing e-mail containing confidential memos.
- According to research, two-thirds of all employees feel that management isn't listening to them.
- According to a workplace etiquette survey, 32 percent of employees surveyed say that loud talkers are one of their biggest pet peeves at work.

*Sources:* J. MacIntyre, "Pet Peeves," *Springfield Business Journal,* April 3–9, 2006, p. 64; "Effective Communication: A Leading Indicator of Financial Performance—2005/2006 Communication ROI Study," Watson Wyatt Worldwide, Washington, DC; M. Weinstein, "Hey, I'm Talking Here," *Training,* December 2005, p. 9; J. Swartz, "More Firms Keep an Eye on Outgoing E-Mail," *USA Today,* July 14, 2004, p. 1B; "Grapevine Growing Wrong Information," *USA Today,* October 15, 2003, p. 1A; and "Hear It Through the Grapevine?" *USA Today,* October 14, 2003, p. 1A.

# Thinking About Management Issues

1. Why isn't effective communication synonymous with *agreement*?

2. Which do you think is more important for the manager: speaking accurately or listening actively? Why?

3. "Ineffective communication is the fault of the sender." Do you agree or disagree with this statement? Discuss.

4. How might managers use the grapevine for their benefit?

5. Is information technology helping managers be more effective and efficient? Explain your answer.

## Working Together: Team-Based Exercise

Form groups of five or six individuals. Each group should choose one person to remain in the room while the other members of each group leave the room. Your instructor will give you instructions on what happens next.

After the exercise is over, each group should discuss where communication errors (both in sending and receiv-ing information) occurred. You should also discuss what you learned about managerial communication from this exercise. Be prepared to share your important ideas with the class.

## Ethical Dilemma Exercise

More and more organizational members are initiating messages through corporate blogs. Officially known as Web logs, these are Web sites where an individual can post comments and express opinions or ideas. Because anyone can visit the site and read the messages, compa-nies have become concerned about messages that include sensitive data, criticize managers or competitors, use inflammatory language, or contain misrepresentations. Companies also worry about the reactions of stakehold-ers who disagree with or are offended by blog postings. Now companies such as Sun Microsystems have devel-oped blog policies for employees to follow (see www.sun.com/aboutsun/media/blogs/policy.html).

But what happens when a CEO sets up a blog? Jonathan Schwartz, CEO of Sun Microsystems, blogs about new technologies, management issues, and more (see blogs.sun.com/jonathan). Alan Meckler, the CEO of Jupiter-media, originally started his blog as "a diary of the ups and downs of trying to do something monumental"—to create a new industry-wide technology conference. This event put Jupitermedia squarely in competition with another well-established industry event. In early blog entries, Meckler talked bluntly about the competing conference's manage-ment. Based on legal advice (and negative feedback from a few conference exhibitors), he softened his tone in later entries. Although Meckler still blogs, he says, "I'm not stir-ring the pot anymore, which isn't my nature."[46]

What is the most ethical way to deal with a corporate blog, especially one by a senior manager? Imagine that you're Jupitermedia's public relations director. The CEO has just posted a blog message saying your conference was more financially successful than the competing con-ference. Because neither company releases profitability details, you know this statement can't be verified. You don't want Jupitermedia to look bad; you also know that your CEO likes to express himself. Review Exhibit 11–1 as you think about the ethical challenge posed by this blog communication and decide which of the following options to choose, and why.

**Option A:** Meet with the CEO, explain your concerns, and suggest that he post a message stating honestly that he changed his message on the advice of the public relations department.

**Option B:** Leave the message but issue a press release reminding the public that the CEO's blog contains personal thoughts and does not represent the official views of Jupitermedia.

**Option C:** Contact your company's lawyers and ask them to force your CEO to remove this message from his blog before any conference exhibitors complain.

## Case Application

### Communication Lesson

This is a story about a hallway conversation that cost $200,000 and 4 months of unnecessary effort. Talk about a communication blunder.

Voyant, a tech company based in Colorado, makes teleconferencing technology that allows users to call var-ious people at once and invite them to join a conference call. The company was acquired by videoconferencing provider Polycom in 2004. Prior to that acquisition, a chance meeting in a headquarters hallway between company CEO Bill Ernstrom and his chief engineer led to the decision to have its engineers add streaming media to the company's flagship product. Now, Ernstrom wishes he had never had that conversation, especially after a product manager who had learned of the project pro-duced a marketing report that showed most customers

had little interest in streaming anything. That incident underscored a communication challenge that had been ignored for too long: Top engineers weren't listening to the product managers—and vice versa. Ernstrom says, "We got a long way down the road, built the code, got the engineers excited. Then we found out that we'd sell about 10 units."

The communication barriers experienced by Voyant aren't all that unusual in high-tech organizations. The cul-tural and language gap between computer "geeks" and the more market/business-oriented colleagues happens time and time again. In these types of organizations, the early stages of a new project belong to the engineers. It's crucial to get the technology right, but what they produce is "often elegant technology that has no market, is too complicated, or doesn't match customers' expectations."

*Bill Ernstrom (center) and managers Jeremy DuPont (right) and Warren Baxley (left) of Voyant Technologies.*

Ernstrom's challenge was to get the two competing groups to collaborate. His solution involved structural and communications changes.

The first structural change Ernstrom made was to hire managers to lead each of the company's four product lines. But this change alone wasn't enough as the engineers felt that these individuals knew little about the company's culture and even less about technology. To improve the situation, Ernstrom decided that another new position was needed—a chief product officer. The person he hired, John Guillaume, had a strong telecommunications background in both engineering and marketing. Guillaume's first move was to raise the profile of the four product managers by giving them visible tasks, such as writing product definitions and presenting marketing research. Then, Guillaume took a riskier step and asked two of the star engineers to lead product groups,

which they did reluctantly. With the structural changes in place, Ernstrom was ready to try some changes in communication.

Among these changes is that now when an employee has an idea for a new product, he or she submits a proposal through the company intranet. A team of engineers and product managers and the executive team assess the proposal. There's a lot more interaction between the "geeks" and the "suits." If the proposal is given the go-ahead, managers determine what content will be delivered at what time and the engineers get bonuses for meeting those goals.

By themselves, these changes might have accomplished little, but together they've done a lot to close the gap. Ernstrom firmly believes that the company's customers are happier than ever. As one engineer put it, "We're building stuff that people use."

## Discussion Questions

1. What barriers to communication were evident at Voyant? What other communication barriers likely existed? Explain.

2. What suggestions presented in the chapter might Voyant's employees have used to overcome communication barriers?

3. Why were the structural changes important to the success of the communication changes?

4. Why do you think Ernstrom believes that the company's customers are happier than ever before? What role do you think communication plays?

*Sources:* Information on company from Hoover's Online, www.hoovers.com, April 14, 2006; and S. Clifford, "How to Get the Geeks and the Suits to Play Nice," *Business 2.0,* May 2002, pp. 92–93.

# Learning Outline

*Use this Learning Outline as you read and study this chapter.*

### Why Human Resource Management Is Important; The Human Resource Management Process

- Explain how an organization's human resources can be a significant source of competitive advantage.
- List the eight activities necessary for staffing the organization and sustaining high employee performance.
- Discuss the environmental factors that most directly affect the HRM process.

### Human Resource Planning; Recruitment/Decruitment; Selection; Orientation; Training

- Contrast job analysis, job description, and job specification.
- Discuss the major sources of potential job candidates.
- Describe the different selection devices and which work best for different jobs.
- Tell what a realistic job preview is and why it's important.
- Explain why orientation is so important.
- Describe the different types of training and how that training can be provided.

### Employee Performance Management; Compensation and Benefits; Career Development

- Describe the different performance appraisal methods.
- Discuss the factors that influence employee compensation and benefits.
- Describe skill-based and variable pay systems.
- Describe career development for today's employees.

### Current Issues in Human Resource Management

- Explain how managers can manage downsizing.
- Discuss how managers can manage workforce diversity.
- Explain what sexual harassment is and what managers need to know about it.
- Describe how organizations are dealing with work–family life balance issues.
- Discuss how organizations are controlling HR costs.

# Human Resource Management

## A Manager's Dilemma

Toronto-based Bank of Nova Scotia (also called "Scotiabank"), Canada's third-largest bank, provides retail, corporate, and investment banking services worldwide. Scotiabank has more than 950 domestic branches and 775 offices in about 45 countries including, among others, China, Vietnam, Malaysia, Egypt, United Kingdom, El Salvador, Mexico, Chile, and the United States. At the end of 2005, the bank had total assets of almost $266 billion and had exceeded all key financial goals for the year. Net income was up 10 percent over 2004 while earnings per share increased 11.7 percent. Although Scotiabank has more than 50,000 employees, President and CEO Rick Waugh worries that too many will be leaving within the next 5 to 10 years. He expects that about half of the bank's senior managers—vice presidents and those at higher levels—will retire during that time.[1]

Managing human resources so that an organization has the right people in the right place at the right time is often thought to be a key role of human resource management. Waugh thinks that isn't enough, however. As he told attendees at a Conference Board of Canada National Leadership Summit, "Responsibility for leadership development must begin at the very top. HR can and does play an important role facilitating the process, but it must be owned and executed by current leaders."

Waugh also wants to make sure that Scotiabank taps the full potential of its workforce. For instance, although women represent about 50 percent of Scotiabank's management-level employees, they have much less representation at the executive level. Waugh will be working with senior managers to make sure that more qualified women get opportunities in senior management.

Put yourself in Rick's shoes. What can he do to make sure that Scotiabank will (1) have a high-quality workforce and (2) have enough people to fill important management roles as others retire?

What would you do?

A s Rick Waugh clearly understands, the quality of an organization, to a large degree, is dependent upon the quality of people it hires and keeps. And like many of today's managers, he is facing a major human resource management (HRM) challenge. He wants to ensure that his company has a high-quality workforce and enough people to fill important management roles. Getting and keeping competent employees are critical to the success of every organization, whether the organization is just starting or has been in business for years. If an organization doesn't take its HRM responsibilities seriously, performance and goal accomplishment may suffer. Therefore, part of every manager's job in the organizing function is human resource management. ( ◆ Go to www.prenhall.com/rolls)

**Q & A**

How does organizing involve human resource management? Go to Q & A 12.1 and find out.

## WHY HUMAN RESOURCE MANAGEMENT IS IMPORTANT

"Our people are our most important asset." Many organizations say this, or something close to it, to acknowledge the important role that employees play in organizational success. These organizations also recognize that *all* managers must engage in some human resource management activities—even if there is a separate HRM department. These managers interview job candidates, orient new employees, and evaluate their employees' work performance.

*Can* HRM be an important strategic tool? *Can* it help establish an organization's sustainable competitive advantage? The answers to these questions seem to be yes. Various studies have concluded that an organization's human resources can be a significant source of competitive advantage.[2] And that's true for organizations around the world, not just U.S. firms. The Human Capital Index, a comprehensive study of over 2,000 firms in North America, Europe and the Asia–Pacific region conducted by consulting firm Watson Wyatt Worldwide concluded that people-oriented HR gives an organization an edge by creating superior shareholder value.[3]

Achieving competitive success through people requires a fundamental change in how managers think about their employees and how they view the work relationship. It involves working with and through people and seeing them as partners, not just as costs to be minimized or avoided. That's what people-oriented organizations such as Southwest Airlines, The Container Store, and Timberland do. In addition to being an important part of organizational strategy and contributing to competitive advantage, an organization's HRM practices have been found to have a significant impact on organizational performance.[4] For instance, one study reported that significantly

*The Container Store is one organization that proves good human resource management can be a competitive advantage. With a corporate culture that strives to match employees' skills to the right job, focuses on talent rather than titles, and values "great" people as measurably more productive than merely "good" ones, this retailer of storage and organizing products has been on Fortune's list of 100 best companies to work for several years in a row. According to the company's Web site, "Customer service is The Container Store's core competency, so hiring people who are self-motivated and team-oriented with a passion for customer service is key."*

Exhibit 12–1

**Examples of High-Performance Work Practices**

- Self-managed teams
- Decentralized decision making
- Training programs to develop knowledge, skills, and abilities
- Flexible job assignments
- Open communication
- Performance-based compensation
- Staffing based on person–job and person–organization fit

*Source:* Based on W. R. Evans and W. D. Davis, "High-Performance Work Systems and Organizational Performance: The Mediating Role of Internal Social Structure," *Journal of Management,* October 2005, p. 760.

improving an organization's HRM practices could increase its market value by as much as 30 percent.[5] Another study that tracked average annual shareholder returns of the publicly traded companies on *Fortune's* list of 100 best companies to work for found that these companies significantly beat the S&P 500 over 10-year, 5-year, 3-year, and 1-year periods.[6] The term used to describe the practices that lead to such results is **high-performance work practices**. High-performance work practices (some examples are listed in Exhibit 12–1) lead to both high individual and high organizational performance. The common thread in these practices seems to be a commitment to improving the knowledge, skills, and abilities of an organization's employees, increasing their motivation, reducing loafing on the job, and enhancing the retention of quality employees while encouraging low performers to leave.

Even if an organization chooses not to implement high-performance work practices, there are certain HRM activities that must be completed in order to ensure that the organization has qualified people to perform the work that needs to be done—activities that comprise the human resource management process.

## THE HUMAN RESOURCE MANAGEMENT PROCESS

Q & A

Is human resource management different from personnel management? Q & A 12.2 explains.

Exhibit 12–2 introduces the key components of an organization's **human resource management process**, which consists of eight activities necessary for staffing the organization and sustaining high employee performance. (  Go to www.prenhall.com/rolls) The first three activities ensure that competent employees are identified and selected; the next two involve providing employees with up-to-date knowledge and skills; and the final three ensure that the organization retains competent and high-performing employees.

Note in Exhibit 12–2 that the entire HRM process is influenced by the external environment. We discussed environmental constraints on managers in Chapter 3, but let's briefly review those factors that most directly influence the HRM process—employee labor unions, governmental laws and regulations, and demographic trends.

Q & A

Labor unions … don't they just keep employees unmotivated and unhappy? Not necessarily. See what Q & A 12.3 says.

**Employee Labor Unions** A **labor union** is an organization that represents workers and seeks to protect their interests through collective bargaining. (  Go to www.prenhall.com/rolls) In unionized organizations, many HRM decisions are regulated by the terms of collective agreements, which usually define such things as recruitment sources; criteria for hiring, promotions, and layoffs; training eligibility; and disciplinary practices. About 12.5 percent of the workforce in the United States is

---

**high-performance work practices**
Work practices that lead to both high individual and high organizational performance.

**human resource management process**
Activities necessary for staffing the organization and sustaining high employee performance.

**labor union**
An organization that represents workers and seeks to protect their interests through collective bargaining.

Exhibit 12–2    **Human Resource Management Process**

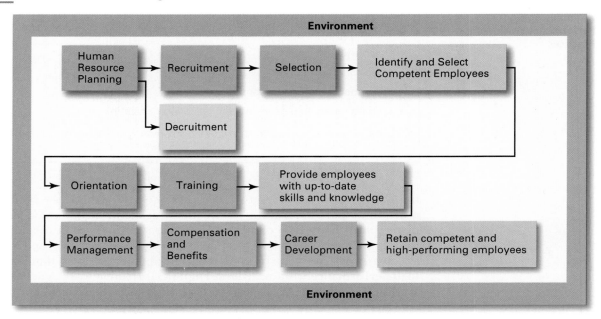

unionized, but the percentage is higher in other countries. For instance (and all these numbers are approximate), in Japan, 19.6 percent of the labor force belongs to a union; in Germany, 27 percent; in Australia, 22.7 percent; in Canada, 30 percent; and in Mexico, 19 percent.[7] Although labor unions can affect an organization's HRM practices, no environmental constraint can match the influence of governmental laws and regulations, especially in North America.

**Governmental Laws and Regulations** HRM practices are governed by a country's laws, which vary from country to country. Within countries, there are state or provincial and local regulations that also impact specific practices. In the United States, the federal government has enacted a number of laws and regulations that influence the HRM process (see Exhibit 12–3). For example, decisions regarding who will be hired, for instance, or which employees will be chosen for a training program must be made without regard to race, sex, religion, age, color, national origin, or disability. Exceptions can occur only when special circumstances exist. For instance, a community fire department can deny employment to a firefighter applicant who is confined to a wheelchair; but if that same individual is applying for a desk job, such as a dispatcher, the disability cannot be used as a reason to deny employment. The issues, however, are rarely that clear-cut. For example, employment laws protect most employees whose religious beliefs require a specific style of dress—robes, long shirts, long hair, and the like. However, if the specific style of dress may be hazardous or unsafe in the work setting (e.g., when operating machinery), a company could refuse to hire a person who won't adopt a safer dress code.[8] (  Go to www.prenhall.com/rolls)

Trying to balance the "shoulds and should-nots" of many of these laws often falls within the realm of **affirmative action**. Through affirmative action programs, an organization actively seeks to enhance the status of members from protected groups.

U.S. managers are not completely free to choose whom they hire, promote, or fire. Although laws and regulations have helped reduce employment discrimination and unfair employment practices, they have, at the same time, reduced managers' discretion over human resource decisions. (  Go to www.prenhall.com/rolls) Because an increasing number of workplace lawsuits are targeting supervisors, as well as their organizations, managers need to be aware of what they can and cannot do by law.[9] Also, it's important that managers in other countries be familiar with the specific laws and regulations that apply there.

**Q & A**

The only thing all these laws and regulations seem to do is "tie managers' hands." You'll find a discussion of this in Q & A 12.4.

**Q & A**

All these rules and regulations are focused on the negatives … don't do this, you can't do this, and so forth. Are there any benefits? See Q & A 12.5.

Exhibit 12–3

**Major U.S. Federal Laws and Regulations Related to HRM**

| Year | Law or Regulation | Description |
|------|-------------------|-------------|
| 1963 | Equal Pay Act | Prohibits pay differences based on sex for equal work |
| 1964 | Civil Rights Act, Title VII (amended in 1972) | Prohibits discrimination based on race, color, religion, national origin, or sex |
| 1967 | Age Discrimination in Employment Act | Prohibits age discrimination against employees between 40 and 65 years of age |
| 1973 | Vocational Rehabilitation Act | Prohibits discrimination on the basis of physical or mental disabilities |
| 1974 | Privacy Act | Gives employees the legal right to examine personnel files and letters of reference concerning them |
| 1978 | Mandatory Retirement Act | Prohibits the forced retirement of most employees before the age of 70; upper limit on age was removed in 1986 |
| 1986 | Immigration Reform and Control Act | Prohibits unlawful employment of aliens and unfair immigration-related employment practices |
| 1988 | Worker Adjustment and Retraining Notification Act | Requires employers with 100 or more employees to provide 60 days notice before a facility closing or mass layoff |
| 1990 | Americans with Disabilities Act | Prohibits employers from discriminating against individuals with physical or mental disabilities or the chronically ill; also requires organizations to reasonably accommodate these individuals |
| 1991 | Civil Rights Act of 1991 | Reaffirms and tightens prohibition of discrimination; permits individuals to sue for punitive damages in cases of intentional discrimination |
| 1993 | Family and Medical Leave Act of 1993 | Permits employees in organizations with 50 or more workers to take up to 12 weeks of unpaid leave each year for family or medical reasons |
| 1996 | Health Insurance Portability and Accountability Act of 1996 | Allows portability of employees' health insurance from one employer to another |
| 2003 | Fair and Accurate Credit Transactions Act | Employers must destroy personal information about employees before discarding it if they received the information from the credit report. |
| 2004 | FairPay Overtime Initiative | Strengthens overtime pay protections for many workers. |

**Demographic Trends** The statistics are clear: By 2010, more than half of all workers in the United States will be over age 40; tens of millions of baby boomers will start turning 60 in 2006; more than 40 percent of the U.S. labor force will reach the traditional retirement age by the end of this decade; Hispanics are the largest ethnic group in the United States; and Gen Y is the fastest-growing segment of the workforce—from 14 percent to 21 percent in 2006.[10] These and other demographic trends already have begun to impact HRM practices and will continue to be important in the future.

## Learning Review

- Explain how an organization's human resources can be a significant source of competitive advantage.
- List the eight activities necessary for staffing the organization and sustaining high employee performance.
- Discuss the environmental factors that most directly affect the HRM process.

**affirmative action**
Programs that enhance the organizational status of members of protected groups.

# HUMAN RESOURCE PLANNING

Some 40 percent of the manufacturing workforce is expected to retire in the next 10 years according to the National Association of Manufacturers.[11] Aware of these predictions, managers at firms like Deere & Company have plans in place to ensure they have enough qualified technicians to fulfill their HR needs.[12]

**Human resource planning** is the process by which managers ensure that they have the right number and kinds of capable people in the right places and at the right times. Through planning, organizations can avoid sudden talent shortages and surpluses.[13] HR planning consists of two steps: (1) assessing current human resources and (2) meeting future HR needs.

## Current Assessment

Managers begin HR planning by reviewing the organization's current human resource status, usually through a *human resource inventory*. Such an inventory is created from forms filled out by employees with information such as name, education, training, prior employment, languages spoken, special capabilities, and specialized skills. The availability of sophisticated databases makes getting and keeping this information quite easy. For example, Stephanie Cox, Schlumberger's director of personnel for North and South America, uses a company planning program called PeopleMatch to help pinpoint managerial talent. Suppose that she needs a manager for Brazil. She types in the qualifications: someone who is mobile, can speak Portuguese, and is a "high potential" employee. Using the planning program, 31 names of possible candidates pop up within a minute.[14]

Another part of the current assessment is the **job analysis**, which is an assessment that defines jobs and the behaviors necessary to perform them. For instance, what are the duties of a level 3 accountant who works for Kodak? What minimal knowledge, skills, and abilities are necessary to be able to adequately perform this job? How do these requirements compare with those for a level 2 accountant or for an accounting manager? Information for a job analysis can be gathered by directly observing or filming individuals on the job, interviewing employees individually or in a group, having employees complete a structured questionnaire, having job "experts" (usually managers) identify a job's specific characteristics, or having employees record their daily activities in a diary or notebook.

With information from the job analysis, managers develop or revise job descriptions and job specifications. A **job description** is a written statement that describes a job—typically, job content, environment, and conditions of employment. A **job specification** states the minimum qualifications that a person must possess to perform a given job successfully. It identifies the knowledge, skills, and attitudes needed to do the job effectively. Both the job description and specification are important documents when managers begin recruiting and selecting.

## Meeting Future Human Resource Needs

Future human resource needs are determined by the organization's mission, goals and strategies. Demand for employees is a result of demand for the organization's products or services. For instance, at Corning Inc. the company's expansion into some markets in developing countries was being slowed by the lack of capable employees in manufacturing. To continue its strategic growth, therefore, it needs more employees with those skills and now has to plan how to meet those needs.[15]

Once managers have assessed both current capabilities and future needs, they can estimate areas in which the organization will be understaffed or overstaffed. With this information, managers are ready to proceed to the next step in the HRM process.

# RECRUITMENT AND DECRUITMENT

Once managers know their current HR status and their future needs, they can begin to do something about any shortages or excesses. If one or more vacancies exist, they can use the information gathered through job analysis to guide them in **recruitment**—that is, locating, identifying, and attracting capable applicants.[16] On the other hand, if HR planning shows a surplus of employees, management may want to reduce the organization's workforce through **decruitment**.[17]

## Recruitment

How do organizations find employees? At a job fair, a Southwest Airlines recruitment team distributed air sickness bags printed with the slogan "Sick of your job?"[18] Although a little more conservative in its recruiting approach, accounting firm PricewaterhouseCoopers recognized that attracting tomorrow's accountants, mostly Gen Y, meant using recruitment tools that appealed to them—in this case, an interactive Flash-animated Web site.[19] As these examples illustrate, potential job candidates can be found by using several sources, which are explained in Exhibit 12–4.[20]

Online recruiting has become a popular choice for organizations and applicants. For instance, Federated Department Stores has a Web site called Retailology that is designed to attract both entry-level and experienced applicants. The site has proved so successful that the company expanded it. Applicants can now self-select interview times after submitting their résumés and passing the first round of screening.[21]

Although online recruiting allows organizations to identify applicants cheaply and quickly, the quality of those applicants may not be as good as other sources. What recruiting sources do produce superior candidates? The majority of research has found that employee referrals generally produce the best candidates.[22] Why? First, applicants referred by current employees are prescreened by these employees. Because the recommenders know both the job and the person being recommended, they tend to refer applicants who are well qualified. Also, because current employees often feel their reputation is at stake, they tend to refer others only when they're reasonably confident that the person will not make them look bad.

Exhibit 12–4

**Major Sources of Potential Job Candidates**

| Source | Advantages | Disadvantages |
|---|---|---|
| Internet | Reaches large numbers of people; can get immediate feedback | Generates many unqualified candidates |
| Employee referrals | Knowledge about the organization provided by current employee; can generate strong candidates because a good referral reflects on the recommender | May not increase the diversity and mix of employees |
| Company Web site | Wide distribution; can be targeted to specific groups | Generates many unqualified candidates |
| College recruiting | Large centralized body of candidates | Limited to entry-level positions |
| Professional recruiting organizations | Good knowledge of industry challenges and requirements | Little commitment to specific organization |

**human resource planning**
Ensuring that the organization has the right number and kinds of capable people in the right places and at the right times.

**job analysis**
An assessment that defines jobs and the behaviors necessary to perform them.

**job description**
A written statement that describes a job.

**job specification**
A statement of the minimum qualifications that a person must possess to perform a given job successfully.

**recruitment**
Locating, identifying, and attracting capable applicants.

**decruitment**
Reducing an organization's workforce.

*PriceWaterhouseCoopers, the nation's largest accounting firm, has developed a Web site designed for recruiting a very specific group of people—the under-22 college market. Found at www.pwcglobal.com/lookhere, the interactive site with Flash animations includes videos of young interns and associates talking about their jobs and offers career advice and tips. The firm, recently voted the "ideal employer" by more than 9,000 business undergraduates, is committed to recruiting in the college market and chose the Web as its medium for the campaign because it is "radio, TV, newspaper, entertainment, and information all rolled up into one."*

## Decruitment

The other approach to controlling labor supply is decruitment, which is not a pleasant task for any manager. The decruitment options are shown in Exhibit 12–5. Obviously people can be fired, but other choices may be more beneficial to the organization. Keep in mind that, regardless of the method used to reduce the number of employees in the organization, there is no easy way to do it, even when absolutely necessary.

## SELECTION

Once the recruiting effort has developed a pool of candidates, the next step in the HRM process is to determine who is best qualified for the job. This step is called **selection** or screening job applicants to ensure that the most appropriate candidates are hired. Hiring errors can have far-reaching implications. For instance, one of the drivers at Fresh Direct, an online grocer that delivers food to masses of apartment-dwelling New Yorkers, was charged with, and later pled guilty to, stalking and harassing female customers.[23] And at cell-phone company T-Mobile, lousy customer service led to its being ranked last in the J.D. Power customer-satisfaction surveys. The company's senior vice president of customer service launched a total overhaul. The first

Exhibit 12–5

**Decruitment Options**

| Option | Description |
| --- | --- |
| Firing | Permanent involuntary termination |
| Layoffs | Temporary involuntary termination; may last only a few days or extend to years |
| Attrition | Not filling openings created by voluntary resignations or normal retirements |
| Transfers | Moving employees either laterally or downward; usually does not reduce costs but can reduce intraorganizational supply–demand imbalances |
| Reduced workweeks | Having employees work fewer hours per week, share jobs, or perform their jobs on a part-time basis |
| Early retirements | Providing incentives to older and more senior employees for retiring before their normal retirement date |
| Job sharing | Having employees share one full-time position |

step: revamping the company's hiring practices to increase the odds of hiring employees who would be good at customer service.[24]

## What Is Selection?

Selection is an exercise in prediction. It seeks to predict which applicants will be successful if hired. In filling a sales position, for example, the selection process should be able to predict which applicants will generate a high volume of sales; for a position as a network administrator, it should predict which applicants will be able to effectively oversee and manage the organization's computer network.

Any selection decision can result in four possible outcomes. As shown in Exhibit 12–6, two outcomes would be correct, and two would indicate errors.

A decision is correct when the applicant was predicted to be successful and proved to be successful on the job, or when the applicant was predicted to be unsuccessful and would perform accordingly if hired. In the first case, we have successfully accepted; in the second case, we have successfully rejected.

Problems arise when errors are made in rejecting candidates who would have performed successfully on the job (reject errors) or in accepting those who ultimately perform poorly (accept errors). These problems can be significant. Given today's HR laws and regulations, reject errors can cost more than the additional screening needed to find acceptable candidates. Why? Because they can expose the organization to charges of discrimination, especially if applicants from protected groups are disproportionately rejected. On the other hand, the costs of accept errors include the cost of training the employee, the profits lost because of the employee's incompetence, the cost of severance, and the subsequent costs of further recruiting and screening. The major emphasis of any selection activity should be reducing the probability of reject errors or accept errors while increasing the probability of making correct decisions. How do managers do this? By using selection procedures that are both valid and reliable.

## Validity and Reliability

Any selection device that a manager uses should demonstrate **validity**, a proven relationship between the selection device and some relevant criterion. For example, laws prohibit managers from using a test score as a selection device unless there is clear evidence that, once on the job, individuals with high scores on this test outperform individuals with low test scores. The burden is on managers to support that any selection device they use to differentiate applicants is related to job performance.

Exhibit 12–6

**Selection Decision Outcomes**

| | Selection Decision | |
|---|---|---|
| | **Accept** | **Reject** |
| **Successful** | Correct decision | Reject error |
| **Unsuccessful** | Accept error | Correct decision |

*Later Job Performance*

---

**selection**
Screening job applicants to ensure that the most appropriate candidates are hired.

**validity**
The proven relationship that exists between a selection device and some relevant job criterion.

In addition to being valid, a selection device must also demonstrate **reliability**, which indicates whether the device measures the same thing consistently. For example, if a test is reliable, any single individual's score should remain fairly consistent over time, assuming that the characteristics being measured are also stable. No selection device can be effective if it's low in reliability. Using such a device would be like weighing yourself every day on an erratic scale. If the scale is unreliable—randomly fluctuating, say 10 to 15 pounds every time you step on it—the results don't mean much. To be effective predictors, selection devices must possess an acceptable level of consistency.

## Types of Selection Devices

Managers can use a number of selection devices to reduce accept and reject errors. The best-known devices include application forms, written and performance-simulation tests, interviews, background investigations, and in some cases, physical exams. Let's briefly review each of these devices. (See Exhibit 12–7 for a list of the strengths and weaknesses of each.)[25]

**Application Forms** Almost all organizations require job candidates to fill out an application. The application might be a form on which the person gives his or her name, address, and telephone number. Or it might be a comprehensive personal history profile, detailing the person's activities, skills, and accomplishments.

**Written Tests** Typical written tests include tests of intelligence, aptitude, ability, and interest. Today, personality, behavioral, and aptitude assessment tests are popular among businesses. When properly designed, tests can reduce the likelihood of poor selection decisions. However, managers need to be careful regarding their use because legal challenges against such tests have been successful when they're not job related or when they elicit information concerning sex, age, or other areas protected by equal employment opportunity laws.[26] For instance, Ford Motor settled a $10 million class-action lawsuit that alleged bias in tests used for admission to an apprenticeship program.[27]

**Performance-Simulation Tests** What better way is there to find out whether an applicant for a technical writing position at Matsushita can write technical manuals than by having him or her do it? Performance-simulation tests are made up of actual job behaviors. The best-known of these are work sampling and assessment centers.

**Work sampling** is a type of job tryout in which applicants perform a task or set of tasks that are central to it. Applicants demonstrate that they have the necessary skills and abilities by actually doing the tasks. This type of test is appropriate for jobs where work is routine or standardized.

**Assessment centers** are used to evaluate managerial potential through job simulation activities.[28] Such activities might include mock interviews, in-basket problem-solving exercises, group discussions, and business decision games. For instance, when Greg Schober, an operations manager at a car plant, applied for that job, he had to perform an in-basket exercise in which he had to sift through a pile of memos to determine the day's priorities. Schober found the experience worthwhile and very true to real life in a manufacturing environment.[29]

**Interviews** The interview, like the application form, is an almost universal selection device.[30] Not many of us have ever gotten a job without one or more interviews. Because there are so many variables that can impact interviewer judgment, the interview may not be the most useful selection device.[31] (  Go to www.prenhall.com/rolls) However, managers can make interviews more valid and reliable by following the suggestions listed in Exhibit 12–8 on page 332.

Another important factor in interviewing is the legality of certain questions. Employment law attorneys warn managers to be extremely cautious in the types of questions they ask candidates. Exhibit 12–9 on page 332 lists some examples of typical interview questions that managers can and cannot ask. (  Go to www.prenhall.com/rolls)

Q & A

Why do organizations use interviews as selection tools when there's so many limitations to them? Go to Q & A 12.6 and find out.

Q & A

What questions can be legally asked during an interview? Q & A 12.7 provides some guidance.

Exhibit 12–7

**Selection Devices**

**Application Forms**

**Strengths:**

- Relevant biographical data and facts that can be verified have been shown to be valid performance measures for some jobs.
- When items on the form have been weighted to reflect job relatedness, this device has proved to be a valid predictor for diverse groups.

**Weaknesses:**

- Usually only a couple of items on the form prove to be valid predictors of job performance and then only for a specific job.
- Weighted-item applications are difficult and expensive to create and maintain.

**Written Tests**

**Strengths:**

- Tests of intellectual ability, spatial and mechanical ability, perceptual accuracy, and motor ability are moderately valid predictors for many semiskilled and unskilled lower-level jobs in industrial organizations.
- Intelligence tests are reasonably good predictors for supervisory positions.

**Weaknesses:**

- Intelligence and other tested characteristics can be somewhat removed from actual job performance, thus reducing their validity.

**Performance-Simulation Tests**

**Strengths:**

- Based on job analysis data and easily meet the requirement of job relatedness.
- Have proven to be valid predictors of job performance.

**Weaknesses:**

- Expensive to create and administer.

**Interviews**

**Strengths:**

- Must be structured and well organized to be effective predictors.
- Interviewers must use common questioning to be effective predictors.

**Weaknesses:**

- Interviewers must be aware of legality of certain questions.
- Subject to potential biases, especially if interviews are not well structured and standardized.

**Background Investigations**

**Strengths:**

- Verifications of background data are valuable sources of information.

**Weaknesses:**

- Reference checks are essentially worthless as a selection tool.

**Physical Examinations**

**Strengths:**

- Has some validity for jobs with certain physical requirements.
- Done primarily for insurance purposes.

**Weaknesses:**

- Must be sure that physical requirements are job related and do not discriminate.

---

**reliability**
The ability of a selection device to measure the same thing consistently.

**work sampling**
A type of job tryout in which applicants perform a task or set of tasks that are central to it.

**assessment centers**
Evaluating managerial potential through job simulation activities.

Exhibit 12–8

**Suggestions for
Interviewing**

1. Structure a *fixed set of questions* for all applicants.
2. Have *detailed information about the job* for which applicants are interviewing.
3. *Minimize any prior knowledge* of applicants' background, experience, interests, test scores, or other characteristics.
4. *Ask behavioral questions* that require applicants to give detailed accounts of actual job behaviors.
5. Use a *standardized evaluation form.*
6. *Take notes* during the interview.
7. *Avoid short interviews* that encourage premature decision making.

*Source:* Based on D. A. DeCenzo and S. P. Robbins, *Human Resource Management,* 7th ed. (New York: Wiley, 2002), p. 200.

| Can't Ask | Can Ask |
|---|---|
| • What's your birth date? or How old are you? <br> • What's your marital status? or Do you plan to have a family? <br> • What's your native language? <br> • Have you ever been arrested? | • Are you over 18? <br> • Would you relocate? <br> • Are you authorized to work in the United States? <br> • Have you ever been convicted of [fill in the blank]?— The crime must be reasonably related to the performance of the job. |

*Note:* Managers should be aware that there are numerous other "can and can't ask" questions. Be sure to always check with your HR department for specific guidance.

**Background Investigations**  If managers at Lucent Technologies had done a thorough background check, they might have discovered that the individual who eventually became director of recruitment (who is no longer with the company) was imprisoned for stealing money from student funds while a principal at a California high school and had lied about earning at doctorate at Stanford.[32]

Background investigations are of two types: verifications of application data and reference checks. The first type has proved to be a valuable source of selection information. For instance, managers at Krause Gentle Corporation, which operates more than 400 convenience stores in 13 states, perform background checks and drug and personality testing on new full-time hires. The result has been positive—lower employee turnover, which saves the company the headaches and additional costs of continually hiring.[33] On the other hand, reference checks are essentially worthless as a selection tool because applicants' references tend to be almost universally positive. After all, a person isn't going to ask someone to write a reference if that person is likely to write a negative one.

**Physical Examination**  This device would be useful only for a small number of jobs that have certain physical requirements. Instead, the physical examination is mostly used for insurance purposes as organizations want to be sure that new hires will not submit insurance claims for injuries or illnesses they had before being hired.

## What Works Best and When?

Many selection devices are of limited value in making selection decisions, and managers should use those that effectively predict for a given job. Exhibit 12–10 summarizes the validity of these devices for particular jobs.

One thing managers need to carefully watch is how they portray the organization and the work an applicant will be doing. If they expose applicants only to the positive characteristics, they're likely to have a workforce that is dissatisfied and prone to high turnover.[34]

Exhibit 12–10

**Quality of Selection
Devices as Predictors**

| | Position | | | |
| Selection Device | Senior Management | Middle and Lower Management | Complex Nonmanagerial | Routine Work |
| --- | --- | --- | --- | --- |
| Application form | 2 | 2 | 2 | 2 |
| Written tests | 1 | 1 | 2 | 3 |
| Work samples | — | — | 4 | 4 |
| Assessment center | 5 | 5 | — | — |
| Interviews | 4 | 3 | 2 | 2 |
| Verification of application data | 3 | 3 | 3 | 3 |
| Reference checks | 1 | 1 | 1 | 1 |
| Physical exam | 1 | 1 | 1 | 2 |

*Note:* Validity is measured on a scale from 5 (highest) to a 1 (lowest). A dash means "not applicable."

During the hiring process, every job applicant develops a set of expectations about the company and about the job. When the information an applicant receives is excessively inflated, a number of potentially negative things happen. First, mismatched applicants are less likely to withdraw from the selection process. Second, because inflated information builds unrealistic expectations, new employees are likely to become quickly dissatisfied and to leave the organization. Third, new hires are prone to become disillusioned and less committed to the organization when they face the unexpected harsh realities of the job. In many cases, these individuals may feel that they were misled during the hiring process and may become problem employees.

To increase job satisfaction among employees and reduce turnover, you should consider a **realistic job preview (RJP)**, which includes both positive and negative information about the job and the company. For instance, in addition to the positive comments typically expressed during an interview, the job applicant might be told that there are limited opportunities to talk to co-workers during work hours, that promotional advancement is slim, or that work hours fluctuate so erratically that employees may be required to work during what are usually off hours (nights and weekends). Research indicates that applicants who have been given a realistic job preview hold lower and more realistic job expectations for the jobs they will be performing and are better able to cope with the frustrating elements of the job than are applicants who have been given only inflated information.

## thinking critically about Ethics

What you say online *can* come back to haunt you. Organizations are using Google, MySpace, and Facebook to check out applicants and current employees. In fact, some organizations see Google as a way to get "around discrimination laws, inasmuch as employers can find out all manner of information—some of it for a nominal fee—that is legally off-limits in interviews: your age, your marital status, fraternity pranks, stuff you wrote in college, political affiliations and so forth." And for those individuals who like to rant and rave about employers, there might be later consequences. That's why one individual, a senior at the University of Massachusetts, pulled his Facebook profile.[35] What do you think of what these companies are doing? What positives and negatives are there to such behavior? What are the ethical implications? What guidelines might you suggest for an organization's selection process?

**realistic job preview (RJP)**
A preview of a job that provides both positive and negative information about the job and the company.

## ORIENTATION

Did you participate in some type of organized introduction to college life when you started school? If so, you may have been told about your school's rules and the procedures for activities such as applying for financial aid, cashing a check, or registering for classes; and you were probably introduced to some of the college administrators. A person starting a new job needs the same type of introduction to his or her job and the organization. This introduction is called **orientation**.

There are two types of orientation. *Work unit orientation* familiarizes the employee with the goals of the work unit, clarifies how his or her job contributes to the unit's goals, and includes an introduction to his or her new co-workers. *Organization orientation* informs the new employee about the company's goals, history, philosophy, procedures, and rules. It should also include relevant human resource policies and maybe even a tour of the facilities.

Many organizations, particularly large ones, have formal orientation programs. Others may use a more informal orientation program in which, for instance, the manager assigns the new employee to a senior member of the work group who introduces the new employee to immediate co-workers and shows him or her locations of the copy room, coffee machine, restrooms, cafeteria, and the like. And then there are intense orientation programs like those at Randstad, a staffing company based in Atlanta. The company's 16-week program covers everything from the culture of the company to on-the-job training. The company executive in charge of curriculum development says, "It's a very defined process. It's not just about what new hires have to learn and do, but also about what managers have to do."[36]

Managers have an obligation to make the integration of the new employee into the organization as smooth and as free of anxiety as possible. They need to openly discuss employee beliefs regarding mutual obligations of the organization and the employee.[37] It's in the best interests of the organization and the new employee to get the person up and running in the job as soon as possible. Successful orientation, whether formal or informal, results in an outsider-insider transition that makes the new member feel comfortable and fairly well adjusted, lowers the likelihood of poor work performance, and reduces the probability of a surprise resignation by the new employee only a week or two into the job.

## EMPLOYEE TRAINING

Q & A
Why is training so important? See what Q & A 12.8 says.

Everything that employees at Ruth's Chris Steak House restaurants need to know can be found on sets of 4 by 8 ½ inch cards. Whether it's a recipe for caramelized banana cream pie or how to acknowledge customers, it's on the cards. And because the cards for all jobs are readily available, employees know the behaviors and skills it takes to get promoted. It's a unique approach to employee training, but it seems to work. Since the card system was implemented, employee turnover has decreased, something that's not easy to accomplish in the restaurant industry.[38]

Employee training is an important HRM activity. (  Go to www.prenhall.com/rolls) As job demands change, employee skills have to change. It's been estimated that U.S. business firms spend over $51 billion annually on formal employee training.[39] Managers, of course, are responsible for deciding what type of training employees need, when they need it, and what form that training should take.

### Types of Training

Ranked as one of the top two training organizations in the United States for 3 years in a row, IBM obviously takes employee training seriously. It uses different types of training ranging from sales to technical to leadership development. The company's chief learning officer, Ted Hoff, says, "Research has shown that workers learn approximately 80 percent of the skills they acquire on the job and around 20 percent

*Infosys Technologies, India's fast-growing software company, has created Infosys University, one of the largest training centers in the world, to train the 15,000 new employees the company hires each year. The $120 million campus-like facility bans alcohol and offers only single-sex dorms, but there are three movie theaters, a pool and gym, and dozens of instructors as well as online courses to teach recruits everything from technical skills and team building to interpersonal communication and corporate etiquette. Says CEO Nandan Nikekani, "Companies haven't been investing enough in people. Rather than train them, they let them go. Our people are our capital. The more we invest in them, the more they can be effective."*

through formal courses."[40] And the company makes it easy for employees to get training material and apply it to their work with an on-demand e-learning system.

When organizations invest in employee training, what are they offering? Exhibit 12–11 describes the major types of training that organizations provide. Some of the most popular types of training that organizations provide include sexual harassment, safety, management skills and development, and supervisory skills.[41] For many organizations, employee interpersonal skills training—communication, conflict resolution, team building, customer service, and so forth—is a high priority. For example, Shannon Washbrook, director of training and development for Vancouver-based Boston Pizza International, says, "Our people know the Boston Pizza concept; they have all the hard skills. It's the soft skills they lack." To address that, Washbrook launched Boston Pizza College, a training initiative that uses hands-on, scenario-based learning about many interpersonal skills topics.[42]

## Training Methods

Employee training can be delivered in traditional ways including on-the-job training, job rotation, mentoring and coaching, experiential exercises, workbooks and manuals, or classroom lectures. But many organizations are relying more on technology-based training methods because of their accessibility, cost, and ability to deliver information.

**Exhibit 12–11**

**Types of Training**

| Type | Includes |
| --- | --- |
| General | Communication skills, computer systems application and programming, customer service, executive development, management skills and development, personal growth, sales, supervisory skills, and technological skills and knowledge |
| Specific | Basic life/work skills, creativity, customer education, diversity/cultural awareness, remedial writing, managing change, leadership, product knowledge, public speaking/presentation skills, safety, ethics, sexual harassment, team building, wellness, and others |

*Source:* Based on "2005 Industry Report—Types of Training," *Training,* December 2005, p. 22.

**orientation**
Introducing a new employee to his or her job and the organization.

## *focus on* **Leadership**

### How to Find and Train Effective Leaders

Organizations around the globe spend billions of dollars, yen, and euros on leadership training and development.[43] These efforts take many forms—from $50,000 leadership programs offered by universities such as Harvard to sailing experiences at the Outward Bound School. Although much of the money spent on training may provide doubtful benefits, our review suggests that there are some things managers can do to get the maximum effect from leadership training.

First, let's recognize the obvious. Some people don't have what it takes to be a leader. For instance, evidence indicates that leadership training is more likely to be successful with individuals who are good self-monitors—that is, individuals who have the ability to adjust their behavior as the situation changes. In addition, organizations may find that individuals with higher levels of a trait called "motivation to lead" are more receptive to leadership development opportunities.

For those individuals who are likely to benefit from leadership training, research is showing that people *can* be trained to be better leaders. What kinds of things can individuals learn that might be related to being a more effective leader? Skills such as trust building and mentoring can be taught. And leaders can be taught to evaluate situations, how to modify situations to make them fit better with their style of leadership, and how to assess which leader behaviors might be most effective in given situations. At Lockheed Martin, for instance, future leaders are assigned an executive coach who works with them on developing and enhancing their leadership skills and knowledge. The program has been quite effective in training individuals to be better leaders.

Exhibit 12–12 provides a description of the various traditional and technology-based training methods that managers might use. Of all these training methods, experts believe that organizations will increasingly rely on e-learning applications to deliver important information and to develop employees' skills.

## Learning Review

- Contrast job analysis, job description, and job specification.
- Discuss the major sources of potential job candidates.
- Describe the different selection devices and which work best for different jobs.

- Tell what a realistic job preview is and why it's important.
- Explain why orientation is so important.
- Describe the different types of training and how that training can be provided.

---

**Exhibit 12–12**

**Employee Training Methods**

### Traditional Training Methods

- *On-the-job*—Employees learn how to do tasks simply by performing them, usually after an initial introduction to the task.
- *Job rotation*—Employees work at different jobs in a particular area, getting exposure to a variety of tasks.
- *Mentoring and coaching*—Employees work with an experienced worker who provides information, support, and encouragement; also called an apprentice in certain industries.
- *Experiential exercises*—Employees participate in role playing, simulations, or other face-to-face types of training.
- *Workbooks/manuals*—Employees refer to training workbooks and manuals for information.
- *Classroom lectures*—Employees attend lectures designed to convey specific information.

### Technology-Based Training Methods

- *CD-ROM/DVD/videotapes/audiotapes*—Employees listen to or watch selected media that convey information or demonstrate certain techniques.
- *Videoconferencing/teleconferencing/satellite TV*—Employees listen to or participate as information is conveyed or techniques demonstrated.
- *E-learning*—Internet-based learning where employees participate in multimedia simulations or other interactive modules.

# EMPLOYEE PERFORMANCE MANAGEMENT

Managers need to know whether their employees are performing their jobs efficiently and effectively or whether there is need for improvement. ( Go to www. prenhall.com/rolls) This is what a **performance management system** does—establishes performance standards that are used to evaluate employee performance. Let's look at some different methods of doing performance appraisal.

## Performance Appraisal Methods

Managers can choose from seven different performance appraisal methods. The advantages and disadvantages of each are shown in Exhibit 12–13.

**Written Essays** In a **written essay**, an evaluator appraises an employee's performance through a written description of an employee's strengths and weaknesses, past performance, and potential. In addition, the evaluator makes suggestions for improvement.

**Critical Incidents** Using **critical incidents**, an evaluator appraises an employee's performance by focusing on critical behaviors that separate effective from ineffective job performance. The appraiser writes down anecdotes that describe what an employee did that was especially effective or ineffective. The key here is that only specific behaviors, not vaguely defined personality traits, are cited.

**Graphic Rating Scales** One of the most popular performance appraisal methods is **graphic rating scales**. This method lists a set of performance factors such as quantity and quality of work, job knowledge, cooperation, loyalty, attendance, honesty, and initiative. The evaluator goes down the list and rates the employee on each factor using an incremental scale. For instance, a factor such as job knowledge might be rated from 1 ("poorly informed about work duties") to 5 ("has complete mastery of all phases of the job").

**Behaviorally Anchored Rating Scales** Another popular approach is **behaviorally anchored rating scales (BARS)**, which combine elements from the critical incident and graphic rating scale approaches. The appraiser rates an employee according to items along a numerical scale, but the items are examples of actual job behaviors rather than general descriptions or traits.

**Exhibit 12–13**

**Advantages and Disadvantages of Performance Appraisal Methods**

| Method | Advantage | Disadvantage |
|---|---|---|
| Written essays | Simple to use | More a measure of evaluator's writing ability than of employee's actual performance |
| Critical incidents | Rich examples; behaviorally based | Time-consuming; lack quantification |
| Graphic rating scales | Provide quantitative data; less time-consuming than others | Do not provide depth of job behavior assessed |
| BARS | Focus on specific and measurable job behaviors | Time-consuming; difficult to develop |
| Multiperson comparisons | Compares employees with one another | Unwieldy with large number of employees; legal concerns |
| MBO | Focuses on end goals; results oriented | Time-consuming |
| 360-degree appraisals | Thorough | Time-consuming |

**performance management system**
Establishes performance standards that are used to evaluate employee performance.

**written essay**
Appraising performance through a written description.

**critical incidents**
Appraising performance by focusing on the critical job behaviors.

**graphic rating scales**
Appraising performance using a rating scale on a set of performance factors.

**behaviorally anchored rating scales (BARS)**
Appraising performance using a rating scale on examples of actual job behavior.

*New Web-enabled software allows employers to track employee performance with greater precision than they have in the past. These British Airways reps are among those whose work time and personal time can be carefully documented by the software, which also tracks reps' handling of ticket sales and customer complaints, so managers can reward those whose performance is exemplary. Says Steven Pruneau, the manager in charge of the evaluation project, "We knew how many hours our planes were on the ground or in the air . . . but we didn't have a fraction of that kind of information about the productivity of our other assets—our human capital."*

**Multiperson Comparisons** **Multiperson comparisons** compare one person's performance with that of others.[44] Made popular by former General Electric CEO Jack Welch, managers were required to rate employees as top performers (20 percent), middle performers (70 percent), or bottom performers (10 percent). It was believed that by using this type of "rank and yank" appraisal, the company would rid itself of slackers and thus be more productive. However, critics of such systems say that they unfairly penalize groups made up of star performers and hinder risk-taking and collaboration.[45] For instance, Sprint used forced rankings for a year and discontinued the program because it found more effective ways to differentiate performance.[46] Are forced rankings a good idea or a bad idea? Research has shown that in companies that used forced rankings and fired the bottom 5 percent to10 percent of employees, productivity increased an impressive 16 percent over the first couple of years. But then in subsequent years, productivity gains dropped off considerably.[47] So, companies are questioning the wisdom of strict forced ranking. Even GE has been looking at ways to make its system more flexible and has encouraged its managers to use more common sense in assigning rankings.[48]

**Objectives** We previously introduced management by objectives (MBO) in Chapter 7. MBO is also a mechanism for appraising performance. In fact, it's often used for assessing managers and professional employees.[49] With MBO, employees are evaluated by how well they accomplish specific goals that have been established by them and their manager.

**360-Degree Feedback** One method that utilizes feedback from supervisors, employees, and co-workers is **360-degree feedback**. In other words, this appraisal utilizes information from the full circle of people with whom the manager interacts. Some 60 percent of HR professionals have said that their companies are using or were planning to use 360-degree feedback.[50] Companies such as Alcoa, DuPont, Levi Strauss, UPS, and W.L. Gore & Associates have used this approach. Users warn that it's not appropriate for determining pay, promotions, or terminations, but can be effective for career coaching and helping a manager recognize his or her strengths and weaknesses.

## COMPENSATION AND BENEFITS

Executives at Discovery Communications Inc. had an employee morale problem on their hands. Many of the company's top performers were making the same salaries as the poorer performers and the company's compensation program didn't allow for giving raises to people who stayed in the same position. The only way for managers to reward the top performers was to give them a bonus or promote them to another position. Executives were discovering that not only was that unfair, but it was also counterproductive, so they overhauled the program.[51]

Most of us expect to receive appropriate compensation from our employer. Developing an effective and appropriate compensation system is an important part of the HRM process.[52] Why? Because it can help attract and retain competent and talented individuals who help the organization accomplish its mission and goals. In addition, an organization's compensation system has been shown to have an impact on its strategic performance.[53] (  Go to www.prenhall.com/rolls)

Managers must develop a compensation system that reflects the changing nature of work and the workplace in order to keep people motivated. Organizational compensation can include many different types of rewards and benefits such as base wages and salaries, wage and salary add-ons, incentive payments, and other benefits and services. Some organizations offer employees some unusual, but popular, benefits. For instance, at Timberland, employees receive a $3,000 subsidy to buy a hybrid automobile. At Worthington Industries, onsite haircuts are just $4. And at J. M. Smucker, employees get 100 percent tuition reimbursement, with no limits.[54]

How do managers determine who gets paid $9 an hour and who gets $350,000 a year? Several factors influence the differences in compensation and benefit packages for different employees. Exhibit 12–14 summarizes these factors, which are both job-based and business- or industry-based. Many organizations, however, are choosing to use alternative approaches to determining compensation: skill-based pay and variable pay.

**Skill-based pay** systems reward employees for the job skills and competencies they can demonstrate. Under this type of pay system, an employee's job title doesn't define his or her pay category; skills do.[55] Research shows that these types of pay systems seem to be more successful in manufacturing organizations than in service organizations

**Q & A**

In an organization, who decides what the compensation system is going to include? Q & A 12.9 discusses this.

---

**Exhibit 12–14**

**Factors That Influence Compensation and Benefits**

*Sources:* Based on R. I. Henderson, *Compensation Management,* 6th ed. (Upper Saddle River, NJ: Prentice Hall, 1994), pp. 3–24; and A. Murray, "Mom, Apple Pie, and Small Business," *Wall Street Journal,* August 15, 1994, p. A1.

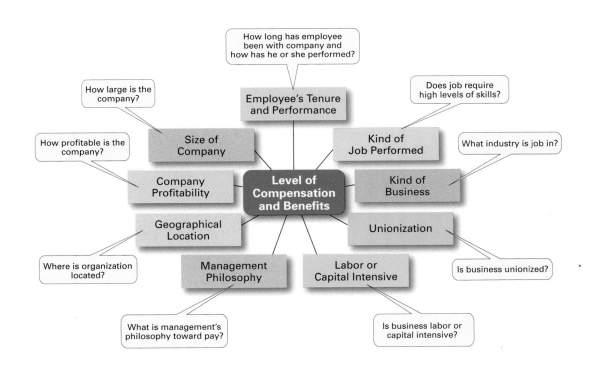

---

**multiperson comparisons**
Appraising performance by comparing it with others' performance.

**360-degree feedback**
Appraising performance by using feedback from supervisors, employees, and co-workers.

**skill-based pay**
A pay system that rewards employees for the job skills they can demonstrate.

and organizations pursuing technical innovations.[56] On the other hand, many organizations are using **variable pay** systems, in which an individual's compensation is contingent on performance—78 percent of U.S. organizations use variable pay plans, and 81 percent of Canadian and Taiwanese organizations do.[57] In Chapter 16, we'll discuss variable pay systems further as they relate to employee motivation.

Although many factors influence the design of an organization's compensation system, flexibility is a key consideration. The traditional approach to paying people reflected a more stable time when an employee's pay was largely determined by seniority and job level. Given the dynamic environments that many organizations face, the trend is to make pay systems more flexible and to reduce the number of pay levels. However, whatever approach managers take, they must establish a fair, equitable, and motivating compensation system that allows the organization to recruit and keep a talented and productive workforce.

## CAREER DEVELOPMENT

The term *career* has several meanings. In popular usage, it can mean advancement ("she is on a management career track"), a profession ("he has chosen a career in accounting"), or a lifelong sequence of jobs (his career has included 12 jobs in 6 organizations"). For our purposes, we define a **career** as the sequence of positions held by a person during his or her lifetime.[59] Using this definition, it's apparent that we all have, or will have, a career. Moreover, the concept is as relevant to unskilled laborers as it is to software designers or physicians. But career development isn't what it used to be![60]

### The Way It Was

Although career development has been an important topic in management courses for years, we've witnessed some dramatic changes in the concept. Career development programs were typically designed to help employees advance their work lives within a specific organization. The focus of such programs was to provide employees the information, assessment, and training needed to help them realize their career goals. Career development was also a way for organizations to attract and retain highly talented people. This approach has all but disappeared in today's workplace. Widespread organizational changes have led to uncertainty as far as the concept of a traditional organizational career. Downsizing, restructuring, and other organizational adjustments have brought us to one significant conclusion about career development: The individual—not the organization—is responsible for designing, guiding, and developing his or her own career.[61] ( Go to www.prenhall.com/rolls)

Q & A

The thought of being responsible for your own career may be scary. Why is this "the way it is" now?
See Q & A 12.10.

## *managing* IT

### HR and IT

HR has gone digital.[58] Using software that automates many of the basic HR processes associated with recruiting, selecting, orienting, training, appraising performance, and storing and retrieving employee information, HR departments have cut costs and optimized service. One of the main areas where IT has had a significant impact is in training.

In a survey by the American Society for Training and Development, 95 percent of the responding companies reported using some form of e-learning. Using technology to deliver needed knowledge, skills, and attitudes

has had many benefits. As one researcher said, "The ultimate purpose of e-learning is not to reduce the cost of training, but to improve the way your organization does business." And in many instances, it seems to do that! For example, when Hewlett-Packard looked at how its customer service was affected by a blend of e-learning and other instructional methods, rather than just classroom training, it found that "sales representatives were able to answer questions more quickly and accurately, enhancing customer- service provider relations." Unilever found that after e-learning training for sales employees, sales increased by several million dollars.

Exhibit 12–15

**What Do College Grads Want from Their Jobs?**

| Top Factors for U.S. Students | Top Factors for U.K. Students |
| --- | --- |
| • Work–life balance<br>• Annual base salary<br>• Job stability and security<br>• Recognition for a job done well<br>• Increasingly challenging tasks<br>• Rotational programs | • International career opportunities<br>• Flexible working hours<br>• Variety of assignments<br>• Paid overtime |

*Sources:* Based on S. Shellenbarger, "Avoiding the Next Enron: Today's Crop of Soon-to-Be Grads Seeks Job Security," *Wall Street Journal Online,* February 16, 2006; "MBAs Eye Financial Services and Management Consulting," *HRMarketer.com,* June 7, 2005; and J. Boone, "Students Set Tighter Terms for Work," *FinancialTimes.com,* May 21, 2005.

## You and Your Career Today

Self-Assessment
Library (S.A.L)

Are you satisfied with the job you have now? Do S.A.L. #I.B.3 and find out.

This idea of increased personal responsibility for one's career has been described as a *boundaryless career.*[62] The challenge is that there are few hard-and-fast rules to guide you.[63] (  Go to www.prenhall.com/rolls)

One of the first decisions you have to make is career choice. The optimum choice is one that offers the best match between what you want out of life and your interests, abilities, and market opportunities. Good career choices should result in a series of positions that give you an opportunity to be a good performer, make you want to maintain your commitment to your career, lead to highly satisfying work, and give you the proper balance between work and personal life. A good career match, then, is one in which you are able to develop a positive self-concept, to do work that you think is important, and to lead the kind of life you desire.[64] Exhibit 12–15 describes the factors college graduates are looking for in their jobs. As you look at this list, think about what's important to you.

Q & A

Do you want to look good during an interview? Q & A 12.11 has some suggestions.

Once you've identified a career choice, it's time to initiate the job search. We aren't going to get into the specifics of job hunting, writing a resume, or interviewing successfully, although those things are important. ( Go to www.prenhall.com/rolls) Let's fast-forward through all that and assume that your job search was successful. It's time to go to work! How do you survive and excel in your career? Exhibit 12–16 lists some suggestions for a successful management career.[65] By taking an active role in managing your career, your work life can be more exciting, enjoyable, satisfying, and rewarding.

Exhibit 12–16

**Some Suggestions for a Successful Management Career**

Develop a Network
Continue Upgrading Your Skills
Consider Lateral Career Moves
Stay Mobile
Support Your Boss
Find a Mentor
Don't Stay Too Long in Your First Job
Stay Visible
Gain Control of Organizational Resources
Learn the Power Structure
Present the Right Image
Do Good Work
Select Your First Job Judiciously

---

**variable pay**
A pay system in which an individual's compensation is contingent on performance.

**career**
A sequence of positions held by a person during his or her lifetime.

## Learning Review

- Describe the different performance appraisal methods.
- Discuss the factors that influence employee compensation and benefits.

- Describe skill-based and variable pay systems.
- Describe career development for today's employees.

## CURRENT ISSUES IN HUMAN RESOURCE MANAGEMENT

We'll conclude this chapter by looking at some contemporary HR issues facing today's managers. These include managing downsizing, workforce diversity, sexual harassment, work–life balance, and controlling HR costs.

### Managing Downsizing

**Downsizing** is the planned elimination of jobs in an organization. When an organization has too many employees—which can happen when it's faced with declining market share, grown too aggressively, or been poorly managed—one option for improving profits is by eliminating some of those excess workers. Well-known companies around the world such as Boeing, Volkswagen, McDonald's, Dell, General Motors, Unisys, Siemens, Merck, Washington Mutual, and many others have downsized.[66] How can managers best manage a downsized workplace? Expect disruptions in the workplace and in employees' personal lives. Stress, frustration, anxiety, and anger are typical reactions of both individuals being laid off and the job survivors. But, managers can lessen the trauma.[67]

Open and honest communication is critical. Individuals who are being let go need to be informed as soon as possible. Survivors need to know the company's new goals and expectations, how their jobs might change, and what the future holds. Managers who have been through downsizing point out the importance of communicating openly and as soon as information is available.

In providing assistance to employees being downsized, many organizations offer some form of severance pay or benefits for a specified period of time. Managers want to be sure they're following any laws that might affect the length of time pay and benefits must be offered and the types of pay and benefits that must be provided. In addition, many organizations provide job search assistance.

Finally, studies find that downsizing is as stressful for the survivors as it is for the victims. Survivors often fear being the next to lose their jobs. Or they find their job responsibilities have increased in order to get all the work completed. To help survivors cope, managers might want to provide counselors for employees to talk to, hold group discussions, and communicate to them how important they are.

### Managing Workforce Diversity

We've discussed the changing makeup of the workforce in several places throughout the book and provided insights in our "Managing Workforce Diversity" boxes in several chapters. In this section we want to discuss how workforce diversity is directly affected by basic HRM activities.

**Recruitment** To improve workforce diversity, managers need to widen their recruiting net. For example, the popular practice of relying on employee referrals as a source of job applicants tends to produce candidates who are similar to current employees. Some organizations, such as Exabyte, of Boulder, Colorado, used this to their advantage in recruiting diverse employees. The company's positive experience with a hearing-impaired employee led to hiring other hearing-impaired employees through employee referrals, but not every organization is able to do this. So managers may have to look for job applicants in places where they might not have looked in the past. To increase diversity, managers are turning to nontraditional recruitment sources such as women's job networks, over-50 clubs, urban job banks, disabled people's training centers, ethnic newspapers, and gay rights organizations. This type of outreach should enable the organization to broaden its pool of diverse applicants.

**Selection** Once a diverse set of applicants exists, efforts must be made to ensure that the selection process does not discriminate. Moreover, applicants need to be made comfortable with the organization's culture and be made aware of management's desire to accommodate their needs. For instance, because a small percentage of women apply for Microsoft's technical jobs, the company makes every effort to hire a high percentage of female applicants and strives to make sure that these women have a successful experience once they're on the job.[68]

**Orientation and Training** The outsider-insider transition is often more challenging for women and minorities than for white males. Many organizations provide special workshops to raise diversity awareness issues. For example, at a Kraft manufacturing facility in Missouri, managers developed an ambitious diversity program reflecting the increased value the organization had placed on incorporating diverse perspectives. One thing they did was to reward "diversity champions," individual employees who supported and promoted the benefits of diversity. They also added diversity goals to employee evaluations, encouraged nontraditional promotions, sponsored six ethnic meal days annually, and trained over half of the plant's employees in diversity issues.[69]

Some organizations are aggressively pursuing diversity efforts. For instance, after a gender bias lawsuit cost it $72.5 million, Boeing agreed to change its hiring, pay, promotion, and complaint investigation processes. Abercrombie and Fitch agreed to hire a vice president of diversity and hire up to 25 diversity recruiters after it paid $40 million to settle a class-action lawsuit that accused it of promoting whites at the expense of minorities. Home Depot has aggressively recruited older workers because of the expertise, skills, and attitudes they bring to the workplace.[70]

*Wal-Mart recently backed up its promise to increase employee diversity and prevent discrimination by publicly releasing the information it files each year with the EEOC. The 2005 report showed that minorities account for 32 percent of the company's 1.34 million U.S. employees (some of whom are shown here at a store opening in Decatur, Georgia), and women account for 60 percent. The percentages vary by organizational level. Women, for instance, make up 39 percent of officers and managers but 75 percent of sales workers.*

**downsizing**
The planned elimination of jobs in an organization.

## Sexual Harassment

Sexual harassment is a serious issue in both public and private sector organizations. During 2005, more than 12,600 complaints were filed with the Equal Employment Opportunity Commission (EEOC). Although most complaints are filed by women, the percentage of charges filed by males has risen every year but two since 1992.[71] The costs of sexual harassment are high. Almost all *Fortune* 500 companies in the United States have had complaints lodged by employees, and at least a third of them have been sued.[72] Settlements in these cases are costly for the companies in terms of litigation— the average is over $15 million.[73] In addition, it's estimated that sexual harassment costs a "typical *Fortune* 500 company $6.7 million per year in absenteeism, low productivity, and turnover."[74]

Sexual harassment isn't a problem just in the United States; it's a global issue. For instance, data collected by the European Commission found that between 30 to 50 percent of female employees in European Union countries had experienced some form of sexual harassment.[75] And sexual harassment charges have been filed against employers in other countries such as Japan, Australia, New Zealand, and Mexico.[76]

Even though discussions of sexual harassment cases often focus on the large awards granted by a court, there are other concerns for employers. Sexual harassment creates an unpleasant work environment and undermines workers' ability to perform their job. ( Go to www.prenhall.com/rolls)

**Sexual harassment** is defined as any unwanted action or activity of a sexual nature that explicitly or implicitly affects an individual's employment, performance, or work environment. It can occur between members of the opposite sex or of the same sex.

**Q & A**

What if you wanted to ask out someone you work with? Is that okay or does it create too many problems? See Q & A 12.12 and see.

Many problems associated with sexual harassment involve determining exactly what constitutes this illegal behavior. The EEOC defines sexual harassment as "unwelcome sexual advances, requests for sexual favors, and other verbal or physical conduct of a sexual nature . . . when submission to or rejection of this conduct explicitly or implicitly affects an individual's employment, unreasonably interferes with an individual's work performance, or creates an intimidating, hostile or offensive work environment."[77] For many organizations, it's the offensive or hostile environment issue that is problematic. Managers must be aware of what constitutes such an environment. Another thing that managers must understand is that the victim doesn't necessarily have to be the person harassed but could be anyone affected by the offensive conduct.[78] The key is being attuned to what makes fellow employees uncomfortable—and if we don't know, we should ask.[79]

What can an organization do to protect itself against sexual harassment claims?[80] The courts want to know two things: First, did the organization know about, or should it have known about, the alleged behavior? And second, what did managers do to stop it? With the number and dollar amounts of the awards against organizations increasing, there is a greater need to educate all employees on sexual harassment matters and have mechanisms available to monitor employees. In addition, organizations need to ensure that no retaliatory actions—such as cutting back hours, assigning back-to-back work shifts without a rest break—are taken against a person who has filed harassment charges, especially in light of a recent U.S. Supreme Court ruling that broadened what retaliation is.[81] One final area of interest we want to discuss in terms of sexual harassment is workplace romances.

**Workplace Romances** If you're employed, have you ever dated someone at work? If not, have you ever been attracted to someone in your workplace and thought about pursuing a relationship? Such situations are more common than you might think—40 percent of employees surveyed by the *Wall Street Journal* said that they have had an office romance. And another survey found that 54 percent of single men and 40 percent of single women said they would be open to dating a co-worker.[82] The environment in today's organizations with mixed-gender work teams and working long hours is undoubtedly contributing to this situation. "People realize they're going to be at work such long hours, it's almost inevitable that this takes place," said one survey director. But a workplace romance is something that can potentially become a really big problem for organizations.[83] In addition to the potential conflicts and retaliation between co-workers who decide to stop dating or to end a romantic relationship, the more serious problems stem from the potential for sexual harassment accusations, especially when it's between supervisor and subordinate. The standard used by judicial courts has been that workplace sexual conduct is prohibited sexual harassment *if* it is unwelcome. If it's welcome, it still may be inappropriate, but usually is not unlawful. However, a new ruling by the California Supreme Court concerning specifically a supervisor–subordinate relationship that got out of hand is worth noting. That ruling said the "completely consensual workplace romances can create a hostile work environment for others in the workplace."[84]

What should organizations do about workplace romances? The best bet is to have some type of policy regarding workplace dating among co-workers, particularly in terms of educating employees about the potential for sexual harassment. However, because possible liability is more serious when it comes to supervisor–subordinate relationships, organizations need to be more proactive in these situations in terms of discouraging such relationships and perhaps even requiring supervisors to report any such relationships to the HR department. At some point, the organization may even want to consider banning such relationships, although an outright ban may be difficult to put into practice.

## Work–Family Life Balance

What kinds of work–family life balance issues might come up that affect an employee's job performance? Here are some examples:

- Is it OK for someone to bring his baby to work because of an emergency crisis with normal child-care arrangements?
- Is it OK to expect an employee to work 60 or more hours a week?
- Should an employee be given the day off to watch a child perform in a school event?

*becoming* a Manager

✓ Using the Internet, research different companies that interest you and check out what they say about careers or their people.

✓ Make sure that your résumé provides specific information to describe your work skills and experience rather than meaningless phrases such as "results-oriented."

✓ If you're working, note what types of HRM activities your managers do. What do they do that seems to be effective? Ineffective? What can you learn from this?

✓ Do career research in your chosen career by finding out what it's going to take to be successful in that career.

✓ Complete the Skill-Building Modules on Interviewing found on pages 629-630 and Valuing Diversity found on pages 641-642.

Self-Assessment Library (S.A.L.)

✓ Complete the following exercises from the Self-Assessment Library found on www.prenhall.com/rolls: S.A.L. #III.A.3—How Good Am I at Giving Feedback?, S.A.L. #I.B.3—How Satisfied Am I with My Job?, S.A.L. #III.B.3—Am I Experiencing Work–Family Conflict?, and S.A.L. #I.B.4—What Are My Attitudes Toward Workplace Diversity?

**sexual harassment**
Any unwanted action or activity of a sexual nature that explicitly or implicitly affects an individual's employment, performance, or work environment.

Self-Assessment
Library (S.A.L.)

Are you experiencing conflicts
between work and family?
S.A.L. #III.B.3 can help you answer
that question.

In the 1980s, organizations began to recognize that employees don't leave their families and personal lives behind when they walk into work. An organization hires an individual who has a personal life outside the office, personal problems, and family commitments. Although managers can't be sympathetic with every detail of an employee's family life, we *are* seeing organizations more attuned to the fact that employees have sick children, elderly parents who need special care, and other family issues that may require special arrangements. In response, many organizations took actions to make their workplaces more family-friendly by offering **family-friendly benefits**, which accommodate employees' needs for work–family life balance. They introduced programs such as on-site child care, summer day camps, flextime, job sharing, time off for school functions, telecommuting, and part-time employment. Work–family life conflicts are as relevant to male workers with children and women without children as they are for female employees with children. Heavy workloads and increased travel demands, for instance, have made it hard for many employees to satisfactorily juggle both work and personal responsibilities. ( Go to www.prenhall.com/rolls) A *Fortune* survey found that 84 percent of male executives surveyed said that "they'd like job options that let them realize their professional aspirations while having more time for things outside work." Also, 87 percent of these executives believed that any company that restructured top-level management jobs in ways that would both increase productivity and make more time available for life outside the office would have a competitive advantage in attracting talented employees.[85] Younger employees, particularly, put a higher priority on family and a lower priority on jobs and are looking for organizations that give them more work flexibility.[86]

Today's progressive workplaces accommodate the varied needs of a diverse workforce. This includes providing a wide range of scheduling options and benefits that allow employees more flexibility at work and that allow them to better balance or integrate their work and personal lives. Despite these organizational efforts, work–family life programs have room for improvement. One survey showed that over 31 percent of college-educated male workers spend 50 or more hours a week at work (up from 22 percent in 1980) and that about 40 percent of American adults get less than 7 hours of sleep on weekdays (up from 34 percent in 2001).[87] What about women? Another survey showed that the percentage of American women working 40 hours or more per week had increased. By the way, this same survey showed that the percentage of European women working 40 hours or more had actually declined.[88] Other workplace surveys still show high levels of employee stress stemming from work–family life conflicts. And large groups of women and minority workers remain unemployed or underemployed because of family responsibilities and bias in the workplace.[89] So what can managers do?

Research on work–family life balance has provided some new insights. For instance, we're beginning to see evidence that there are positive outcomes when individuals are able to combine work and family roles.[90] As one study participant noted, "I think being a mother and having patience and watching someone else grow has made me a better

*Gary Newman and Dana Walden have both been president of 20th Century Fox Television for several years. They don't share the job; in a unique arrangement, they both perform it in a partnership that requires trust, communication, and coordination. "If one of us has to step up and make a decision," says Newman, "we do it and move on, and worry about straightening it out between us the next day." The arrangement allows both presidents to lead fuller lives outside the office as well, and if one of them has to skip a day for personal or family reasons, the other is always there.*

manager. I am better able to be patient with other people and let them grow and develop in a way that is good for them."[91] In addition, individuals who have family-friendly workplace support appear to be more satisfied on the job.[92] This seems to strengthen the notion that organizations benefit by creating a workplace in which employee work–family life balance is possible. And the benefits show up in financial results as well. Research has shown a significant, positive relationship between work–family initiatives and an organization's stock price.[93] However, managers need to understand that people do differ in their preferences for work–family life scheduling options and benefits.[94] Some people prefer organizational initiatives that better *segment* work from their personal lives. Others prefer programs that facilitate *integration*. For instance, flextime schedules segment because they allow employees to schedule work hours that are less likely to conflict with personal responsibilities. On the other hand, on-site child care integrates by blurring the boundaries between work and family responsibilities. People who prefer segmentation are more likely to be satisfied and committed to their jobs when offered options such as flextime, job sharing, and part-time hours. People who prefer integration are more likely to respond positively to options such as on-site child care, gym facilities, and company-sponsored family picnics.

## Controlling HR Costs

Employees at Aetna can earn financial incentives up to $345 a year for participating in weight-management and fitness classes. Some 80 percent of employees at Fairview Health Services in Minneapolis participate in a comprehensive health-management program. Employees of King County in Seattle get health insurance discounts if they do not smoke, are not overweight, and do not speed when driving. At Alaska Airlines, employees must abide by a no-smoking policy, and new hires must submit to a urine test to prove they're tobacco-free.[95] All of these are examples of how companies are trying to control skyrocketing employee health care costs. Since 2002, health care costs have risen an average of 15 percent a year.[96] And smokers cost companies even more—about 25 percent more for health care than nonsmokers do.[97] Is it any wonder that organizations are looking for ways to control their health care costs? How? First, many organizations are providing opportunities for employees to lead healthy lifestyles. From financial incentives to company-sponsored health and wellness programs, the goal is to stave off rising health care costs. About 41 percent of companies use some type of positive incentives aimed at encouraging healthy behavior, up from 34 percent in 1996.[98] In the case of smokers, however, some companies have taken a more aggressive stance by increasing the amount smokers pay for health insurance or by firing them if they refuse to stop smoking.

The other area where organizations are looking to control costs is employee pension plans. Corporate pensions have been around since the nineteenth century.[99] However, the days when companies could afford to give employees a broad-based pension that provided them with guaranteed retirement income have changed. Pension commitments have become such an enormous burden that companies can no longer afford them. In fact, the corporate pension system has been described as fundamentally broken.[100] It's not just the struggling companies that have eliminated employee pension plans. Lots of reasonably sound companies—for instance, NCR, Lockheed Martin, and Motorola—no longer provide pensions. Even IBM, which closed its pension plan to new hires in December 2004, told employees that their pension benefits would be frozen starting in 2008.[101] Obviously, the pension issue is one that directly affects HR decisions. On the one hand, organizations want to attract talented, capable employees by offering them desirable benefits such as pensions. But on the other hand, organizations have to balance that with the costs of providing such benefits.

**family-friendly benefits**
Benefits that accommodate employees' needs for work-life balance.

## Learning Review

- Explain how managers can manage downsizing.
- Discuss how managers can manage workforce diversity.
- Explain what sexual harassment is and what managers need to know about it.

- Describe how organizations are dealing with work–family life balance issues.
- Discuss how organizations are controlling HR costs.

# Managers Respond to a Manager's Dilemma

## Debra Barnhart

Director, Medical Management Support,
St. John's Health System, Springfield, MO

Rick Waugh is a forward-thinking leader. He recognizes that his organization's future successes are highly dependent on the company's workforce and is willing to invest in ensuring a smooth transition. A comprehensive strong human resource management program is essential to maintaining a highly qualified workforce and recruiting persons with the skill sets needed in an ever-changing business environment. Rick might begin with a current assessment, evaluation, and changes to the key components of Scotiabank's human resource management program including the following:

- Process for recruitment and selection
- Performance evaluation and feedback system
- Learning opportunities for employees
- Educational development opportunities for mid-level managers
- Internal communication programs
- Recognition, compensation, and incentive programs
- Internship opportunities as a recruitment strategy
- Assessment of employee satisfaction and factors contributing to turnover

Rick also understands the role senior managers play in leadership development and the role mid-level managers serve as an important source of senior management. He will want to develop a structured leadership transition program for mid-level managers. The program may include the identification of mid-level managers with skill sets and competencies for future senior leadership roles for "management development" positions; offering a company-sponsored degree program in management for mid-level managers in association with a local university; ongoing communication training; and job rotations.

# Karen S. Stewart

Human Resources Manager, The Philadelphia Coca-Cola
Bottling Company, Philadelphia, PA

**W**ith 50 percent of the senior managers of Scotiabank in a position to retire in 5 to 10 years, Rick needs to move quickly to ensure the next generation of leaders is ready and that valuable knowledge is not lost. While I agree that responsibility for leadership development must begin at the top of the organization, it is critical that human resourses' expertise be represented at the senior level. A strategic plan would include the following:

Working in partnership with human resourses, the company needs to embark on a global succession planning process. This process should identify:

- High-potential employees (those with the potential to move higher in the organization) according to a readiness scale (ready now; ready in 1–2 years; ready in 3–5 years; etc.)

- High-performing employees (those who excel in a specialty critical to the organization but unlikely to advance beyond that role)

Once high potentials have been identified, the next step is to escalate their development through the design of leadership initiatives. Individualized Development Plans (IDPs) can include classroom learning, rotational leadership opportunities, and strategically designed action learning projects. Initiatives designed to retain high performers are needed as well.

In order to increase representation of women at the senior-most levels, it will be important to ensure that women are well represented in the selection of candidates for the leadership initiatives. In addition, there should be a strong base of programs and benefits in place to provide for their support.

Lastly, I would design a process to pair "high potentials" on projects with potentially retiring senior leaders. These leaders have valuable knowledge and experience that will be lost to the organization when they leave if steps are not taken to arrange for the transfer of that knowledge.

Rick is in a great position. He is aware of the challenges and, with clear focus and commitment, has the time to put the strategies in place to take his organization to the next level of excellence.

# Learning Summary

## Why Is HRM Important?

- An important strategic tool that helps organization establish sustainable competitive advantage
- High performance work practices (lead to high individual and organizational performance)

## How Does the External Environment Affect HRM?

- Labor unions
- Governmental laws and regulations (especially affirmative action)
- Demographic trends

## How Do Organizations Assess Their HR Needs?

- Current assessment
  - Human resource inventory
  - Job analysis: job description and job specification
- Meeting future needs (balance supply and demand by recruiting/decruiting)

## How Do Organizations Identify and Select Competent Employees?

Identify: recruitment process

Select: predict which candidates will be good or not so good using valid and reliable selection tools

- Application forms
- Performance-simulation tests
- Background investigation
- Realistic job preview
- Written tests
- Interviews
- Physical examination

## How Do Organizations Help Employees Adapt and Stay Up-to-Date?

Orientation: Introduction of a new employee to his or her job and the organization

Training: What types of training do employees need? What methods will be used to train?

## How Do Managers Know Whether Employees Are Performing Jobs Well?

Performance management system establishes performance standards that are used to evaluate employee performance

- Written essays
- Graphic rating scales
- Multiperson comparison
- 360-degree feedback
- Critical incidents
- BARS
- MBO

## How Do Managers Attract New Employees and Reward Current Employees?

Compensation and benefits packages

- Skill-based pay
- Variable pay

## How Are Careers Managed?

Organizational responsibility: information, assessment, and training

Individual responsibility: actively manage your own career

## What HR Issues Currently Face Managers?

- Managing downsizing
- Managing workforce diversity (recruiting, selecting, and orienting/training)
- Sexual harassment
- Work–family life balance
- Controlling HR costs

# Management: By the Numbers

- Sixty-eight percent of adults surveyed negatively rate the job being done by unions.
- Fifty-eight percent of HR executives surveyed felt referrals were the method that helped them find their best job applicants.
- A company that does background checks found that 56 percent of résumés contained falsehoods of some kind.
- A survey of workers found that 21 percent had overheard age-related ridicule at work; 30 percent had overheard racial slurs; 28 percent had overheard ethnic slurs; and 20 percent had overheard ridicule concerning sexual orientation.
- At least 3 in 10 employers use personality tests in hiring.
- Eighty-five percent of executives say that their career is related to the area of their college degree.
- A survey found that 34 percent of employees check in with the office so frequently while on vacation that they come back just as, or more, stressed than when they left.
- Seventy-two percent of companies do not have a policy about employees dating.
- Sixty-seven percent of HR professionals fear that co-workers' romantic break-ups might cause conflicts and retaliation; 77 percent fear that these romances might lead to sexual harassment allegations.

- A survey of employed adults found that 36 percent believed that openly dating a co-worker could jeopardize job security or advancement opportunities; 34 percent said that it wouldn't; and 30 percent were neutral.
- In a survey of college students, 62 percent said they had been sexually harassed in some way.
- Nearly 1 out of every 6 employees in the United States said they were discriminated against at work during the last year.
- In a survey of over 10,000 U.S. workers, 60 percent think that tenure determines pay where they work; 35 percent believe performance is the deciding factor.

*Sources:* A. Murphy Paul and P. Sackett, "Testing, Testing," *Time,* April 3, 2006, p. 89; M. Villano, "Served As King of England, Said the Résumé," *New York Times Online,* March 19, 2006; J. Yang and S. Ward, "Workers Split on Office Romance," *USA Today,* February 14, 2006, p. 1B; "2006 Workplace Romance Survey: Cupid in the Cubicles," *Society for Human Resource Management,* February 14, 2006; J. Yang and B. Laird, "HR Executives' Hiring Preference," *USA Today,* February 9, 2006, p. 1B; S. Jayson, "Workplace Romance No Longer Gets the Kiss-Off," *USA Today,* February 9, 2006, p. 9D; S. Koehler, "Much Sexual Harassment Unreported," *Springfield News-Leader,* January 26, 2006, pp. 1B+; J. MacIntyre, "Unions Versus Corporations," *Springfield Business Journal,* December 5–11, 2005, p. 45; H. Yen, The Associated Press, "One in Six Polled Report Discrimination," *Springfield News-Leader,* December 9, 2005, p. 5B; A. Fisher, "Helping Employees Stay Healthy," *Fortune,* August 8, 2005, p. 114; J. MacIntyre, "Ridicule," *Springfield Business Journal,* August 1–7, 2005, p. 29; and "The Stat," *Business Week,* July 4, 2005, p. 12.

# Thinking About Management Issues

1. How does HRM affect all managers?

2. Should an employer have the right to choose employees without governmental interference? Support your conclusion.

3. Some critics claim that corporate HR departments have outlived their usefulness and are not there to help employees, but to keep the organization from legal problems. What do you think? What benefits are there to having a formal HRM process? What drawbacks?

4. Studies show that women's salaries still lag behind men's and even with equal opportunity laws and regulations women are paid about 76 percent of what men are paid. How would you design a compensation system that would address this issue?

5. What drawbacks, if any, do you see in implementing flexible benefits? (Consider this question from the perspective of both the organization and the employee.)

6. What are the benefits and drawbacks of realistic job previews? (Consider this question from the perspective of both the organization and the employee.)

7. What, in your view, constitutes sexual harassment? Describe how companies can minimize sexual harassment in the workplace.

8. Go the Society for Human Resource Management Web site (www.shrm.org) and find the HR News section. Pick one of the news stories to read. Write a summary of the information. At the end of your summary, discuss the implications of the topic for managers.

# Chapter

# 13

## Learning Outline

*Use this Learning Outline as you read and study this chapter.*

### Forces for Change; Two Views of the Change Process

- Discuss the external and internal forces for change.
- Contrast the calm waters and white-water rapids metaphors of change.
- Explain Lewin's 3-step model of the change process.
- Discuss the environment that managers face today.

### Managing Organizational Change

- Define organizational change.
- Contrast using internal and external change agents.
- Describe how managers might change structure, technology, and people.
- Explain why people resist change and how resistance might be managed.

### Contemporary Issues in Managing Change

- Explain why changing organizational culture is so difficult and how managers can do it.
- Describe employee stress and how managers can help employees deal with stress.
- Discuss what it takes to make change happen successfully.

### Stimulating Innovation

- Explain why innovation isn't just creativity.
- Explain the systems view of innovation.
- Describe the structural, cultural, and human resource variables that are necessary for innovation.
- Explain what idea champions are and why they're important to innovation.

# Managing Change and Innovation

## A Manager's Dilemma

Anyone who's ever prepared a meal likely would recognize OXO International's household tools by the familiar trademark handle—"thick, black, and made of a nonslip rubber called Santoprene with small flexible ridges (or 'fins' in OXO lingo) that allow for a firm grip."[1] Every product OXO makes, no matter how ordinary, is designed to be pleasing and clever. The company's mission statement says, "OXO International is dedicated to providing innovative consumer products that make everyday living easier." But that's not as easy as it sounds!

Alex Lee, OXO's president, is responsible for and guides the company's design process, and OXO is one of the most respected design shops around. Many of its products have received design awards from professional organizations. In fact, several products have been chosen as part of the permanent collections at the Modern Museum of Art and the Cooper–Hewitt National Design Museum, both of which are in New York. OXO's design approach is based on the concepts and principles of universal design, which in its simplest terms means designing products to be usable by as many people as possible. (One bit of interesting company history: The name was chosen because "OXO" always reads "OXO" whether it's horizontal, vertical, upside down, or backwards—a good example of universal design!)

Alex's view of innovation is that people learn the most when something goes wrong. He doesn't want his employees to stop making mistakes because then you kill creativity. And design mistakes have happened! For instance, a new toilet brush wouldn't fit one-third of toilets. And a bagel slicer wouldn't work with Chicago bagels, which are smaller than New York–sized bagels.

With a small workforce (the company has only 41 employees, or "OXOnians," as they call themselves), getting *everyone* to be creative and innovative is absolutely essential. Put yourself in Alex's shoes. How can he ensure that creativity and innovation continue to thrive in his organization?

**What would you do?**

The managerial challenges facing Alex Lee in encouraging creativity and innovation among all his employees are certainly not unique. Big companies and small businesses, universities and colleges, state and city governments, and even the military are forced to be innovative. Although innovation has always been a part of the manager's job, it has become even more important in recent years. We'll describe why innovation is important and how managers can manage innovation in this chapter. Because innovation is often closely tied to an organization's change efforts, we'll start by looking at change and how managers manage change.

## FORCES FOR CHANGE

Jim Zawacki, chairman of GR Spring & Stamping Inc., a metal stampings and products supplier in Grand Rapids, Michigan, is like many managers today who are taking steps to make their workplaces more efficient and flexible. Why? In Zawacki's case, it's the threat of losing manufacturing jobs to low-wage nations like China.[2] Zawacki is doing what managers everywhere must do—change!

If it weren't for change, the manager's job would be relatively easy. Planning would be simple because tomorrow would be no different from today. The issue of effective organizational design would also be resolved because the environment would not be uncertain and there would be no need to adapt. Similarly, decision making would be dramatically streamlined because the outcome of each alternative could be predicted with almost certain accuracy. It would, indeed, simplify the manager's job if, for example, competitors did not introduce new products or services, if customers didn't demand new and improved products, if governmental regulations were never modified, or if employees' needs never changed. But that's not the way it is. Change is an organizational reality.[3] And managing change is an integral part of every manager's job. What brings about the need to change? In Chapter 3, we pointed out the external and internal forces that constrain managers. These same forces also bring about the need for change. Let's briefly look at these factors.

### External Forces

The external forces that create the need for change come from various sources. In recent years, the *marketplace* has affected firms such as Yahoo! as competition from Google, Ask.com, About, and InfoSpace intensified. These companies constantly adapt to changing consumer desires as they develop new search capabilities.

*Governmental laws and regulations* are a frequent impetus for change. For example, the Sarbanes–Oxley Act required U.S. companies to change the way they disclose financial information and enact corporate governance.

*Technology* also creates the need for change. For example, technological improvements in diagnostic equipment have created significant economies of scale for hospitals and medical centers. Assembly-line technology in other industries is changing dramatically as organizations replace human labor with robots. In the greeting card industry, e-mail and the Internet have changed the way people exchange greeting cards.

The fluctuation in *labor markets* also forces managers to make changes. Organizations that need certain kinds of employees must change their human resource management activities to attract and retain skilled employees in the areas of greatest need. For instance, health care organizations facing severe nursing shortages have had to change the way they schedule work hours.

*Economic changes*, of course, affect almost all organizations. For instance, global economic pressures force organizations to become more cost efficient. But even in a strong economy, uncertainties about interest rates, federal budget deficits, and currency exchange rates create conditions that may force organizations to change.

*Profound changes taking place in the Chinese economy are creating labor shortages at hundreds of factories, as seen in the many public job postings at this location in Shenzhen, China. Managers around the world must expect that wages in China may go up as the middle class continues to grow, which will have an impact on the price of manufacturing goods. Some international companies are already considering moving to lower-wage countries such as Vietnam.*

## Internal Forces

Internal forces also create the need for change. These internal forces tend to originate from the internal operations of the organization or from the impact of external changes.

A redefinition or modification of an organization's *strategy* often introduces a host of changes. For instance, when Steve Bennett took over as CEO of troubled Intuit Inc. (Quicken, QuickBooks, and TurboTax are its best known products), he found a company still being run as haphazardly as a start-up venture. "The operation was a mess. It was losing money. Its technology was outdated. Execution was grindingly slow, and nothing was documented."[4] By orchestrating a series of well-planned and dramatic strategic changes, he turned it into a profitable company with extremely committed employees.

In addition, an organization's *workforce* is rarely static. Its composition changes in terms of age, education, ethnic background, sex, and so forth. Take, for instance, an organization where a large number of experienced executives, because of financial reasons, decide to continue working instead of retiring. There might be a need to restructure jobs in order to retain and motivate younger managers because promotions may be harder to come by. Also, the compensation and benefits system might need to be adapted to reflect the needs of this older workforce.

The introduction of new *equipment* represents another internal force for change. Employees may have their jobs redesigned, need to undergo training on how to operate the new equipment, or be required to establish new interaction patterns within their work group.

Finally, *employee attitudes* such as job dissatisfaction may lead to increased absenteeism, more voluntary resignations, and even labor strikes. Such events often lead to changes in management policies and practices.

## TWO VIEWS OF THE CHANGE PROCESS

We can use two very different metaphors to describe the change process.[5] One metaphor envisions the organization as a large ship crossing a calm sea. The ship's captain and crew know exactly where they're going because they've made the trip many times in the past. Change comes in the form of an occasional storm, a brief distraction in an otherwise calm and predictable trip. In the calm waters metaphor, change is seen as an occasional disruption in the normal flow of events. In the other metaphor, the organization is seen as a small raft navigating a raging river with uninterrupted white-water rapids. Aboard the raft are half-a-dozen people who have never worked together, who are totally unfamiliar with the river, who are unsure of their eventual destination, and who, as if things weren't bad enough, are traveling at night. In the white-water rapids metaphor, change is an expected and natural state, and managing change is a continual process. These two metaphors present very different approaches to understanding and responding to change. Let's take a closer look at each one.

## The Calm Waters Metaphor

Up until the late 1980s, the calm waters metaphor was fairly descriptive of the situation that managers faced. It's best illustrated by Kurt Lewin's 3-step change process.[6] (See Exhibit 13–1.)

According to Lewin, successful change can be planned and requires *unfreezing* the status quo, *changing* to a new state, and *refreezing* to make the change permanent. The status quo is considered an equilibrium state. To move out of this equilibrium, unfreezing is necessary. Unfreezing can be thought of as preparing for the needed change. It can be done by increasing the *driving forces,* which are forces pushing for change; by decreasing the *restraining forces,* which are forces that resist change; or by combining the two approaches.

Once unfreezing is done, the change itself can be implemented. However, merely introducing change doesn't ensure that the change will take hold. The new situation needs to be *refrozen* so that it can be sustained over time. Unless this last step is done, there's a strong chance that the change will be short lived as employees revert back to the old equilibrium state—that is, the old ways of doing things. The objective of refreezing, then, is to stabilize the new situation by reinforcing the new behaviors.

Note how Lewin's 3-step process treats change simply as a move away from the organization's current equilibrium state. ( 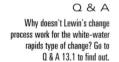 Go to www.prenhall.com/rolls) It's a calm waters scenario where an occasional disruption (a "storm") means changing to deal with the disruption. Once the disruption has been dealt with, however, things can go back to business as usual. However, this type of calm waters environment isn't what most managers face today.

*Q & A*
*Why doesn't Lewin's change process work for the white-water rapids type of change? Go to Q & A 13.1 to find out.*

## White-Water Rapids Metaphor

Susan Whiting is CEO of Nielsen Media, the company best known for its television ratings, which are frequently used to determine how much advertisers pay for TV commercials. The media research business isn't what it used to be, however, as the Internet, video on demand, cell phones, iPods, digital video recorders, and other changing technologies have made data collection much more challenging. Whiting says, "If you look at a typical week I have, it's a combination of trying to lead a company in change in an industry in change."[7] That's a pretty accurate description of what change is like in our second change metaphor—white-water rapids.

Exhibit 13–1

**The Change Process**

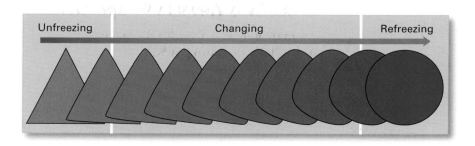

Unfreezing    Changing    Refreezing

The white-water rapids metaphor is consistent with our discussion of uncertain and dynamic environments in Chapters 3 and 8. It's also consistent with a world that's increasingly dominated by information, ideas, and knowledge.[8]

To get a feeling for what managing change might be like when you have to continually maneuver in uninterrupted and uncertain rapids, consider attending a college that had the following rules: Courses vary in length. When you sign up, you don't know how long a course will run. It might go for 2 weeks or 30 weeks. Furthermore, the instructor can end a course any time he or she wants, with no prior warning. If that isn't bad enough, the length of the class changes each time it meets: Sometimes the class lasts 20 minutes; other times it runs for 3 hours. And the time of the next class meeting is set by the instructor during this class. There's one more thing. All exams are unannounced, so you have to be ready for a test at any time. To succeed in this type of environment, you'd have to be incredibly flexible and able to respond quickly to changing conditions. Students who were overly structured, "slow" to respond, or uncomfortable with change would not be able to adapt and survive.

Increasingly, managers are coming to accept that their job is much like what a student would face in such a college. The stability and predictability of the calm waters metaphor do not exist. Disruptions in the status quo are not occasional and temporary, and they are not followed by a return to calm waters. Many managers never get out of the rapids. Like Susan Whiting, described earlier, they face constant change.

Is the white-water rapids metaphor an exaggeration? Probably not! Although you'd expect this type of chaotic and dynamic environment in high-tech industries, even organizations in non–high-tech industries are faced with constant change. Take the case of Swedish home appliance company Electrolux. Although you might think that the home appliances industry couldn't be all that difficult—after all, most households need the products, which are fairly uncomplicated—that impression would be wrong. Electrolux's chief executive Hans Straberg has had several challenges to confront.[9] First, there's the challenge of trying to come up with products that will appeal to a wide range of global customers. Then, there's the challenge of cheaper products from Asia and Eastern Europe flooding the market. In addition, Electrolux faces intense competition in the United States, where it gets 40 percent of its sales. Because approximately 80 percent of the workforce in Sweden belongs to a labor union, companies certainly face expectations as far as how they treat their employees. However, Straberg recognized that his company was going to have to change if it was going to survive and prosper. One thing he did was to shift production to lower-cost facilities in Asia and Eastern Europe. Then, to better grasp what today's consumers are thinking, the company held in-depth interviews with 160,000 customers from around the world. Using this information, a group of Electrolux employees gathered in Stockholm for a weeklong brainstorming session to search for insights on what hot new products to pursue. Finally, to make the new product development process speedier, Straberg eliminated the structural divisions between departments. Designers, engineers, and marketers now have to work together to come up with ideas. These changes were essential for Electrolux to survive the white-water rapids environment in which it operated.

## Putting the Two Views in Perspective

**Self-Assessment Library (S.A.L.)**

How well do you handle turbulent change? Do S.A.L. #III.C.1 and find out!

Does *every* manager face a world of constant and chaotic change? No, but the number who don't is dwindling. ( Go to www.prenhall.com/rolls) Managers in such businesses as computer software, telecommunications, pharmaceuticals, and women's apparel have long confronted a world of white-water rapids. These managers used to envy their counterparts in industries such as banking, utilities, oil exploration, publishing, and air transportation where the environment was historically more stable and predictable. However, those days of stability and predictability are long gone!

*For a company in the midst of white-water rapids, look no further than Levi Strauss & Co., the venerable maker of jeans and jackets. Robert Hanson, president of the U.S. brand, and designer Caroline Calvin returned from assignment in Europe with a mission to get the company back on track. Trying to increase lagging sales when department stores are consolidating and the denim market has numerous competitors will require creating and implementing changes throughout the firm. For example, here's how Hanson described the character of the new designs Levi's will unveil: "It has a bold, confident stature that doesn't say, 'Levi's is back.' It says, 'Levi's is leading.'"*

**Q & A**

If change is continual and constant, how can managers ever hope to manage it effectively?
See Q & A 13.2.

Today, any organization that treats change as the occasional disturbance in an otherwise calm and stable world runs a great risk. Too much is changing too fast for an organization or its managers to be complacent. It's no longer business as usual. And managers must be ready to efficiently and effectively manage the changes facing their organization or their work area. ( Go to www.prenhall.com/rolls) How? That's what we'll discuss next.

## Learning Review

- Discuss the external and internal forces for change.
- Contrast the calm waters and white-water rapids metaphors of change.

- Explain Lewin's 3-step model of the change process.
- Discuss the environment that managers face today.

## MANAGING ORGANIZATIONAL CHANGE

Managers at Hallmark, the world's largest greeting card company, know that as cultural values and people's lifestyles change, so do the types of greeting cards customers are looking for. Some of the emerging and evolving consumer trends they identified included *"present perfect"* (slowing down, living in the present, savoring the moment); *"truthiness"* (what people care about—what may have happened or what people want to see happen); and *"new and novel . . . now"* (people are drawn more and more to the new or novel and want it now).[10] To accommodate these trends, Hallmark's managers will look at changing the company's products, advertising, and perhaps even their human resource practices.

### What Is Organizational Change?

Most managers, at one point or another, will have to make changes in some aspects of their workplace. We classify these changes as **organizational change**—which is any alteration of people, structure, or technology. Organizational changes often need someone to act as a catalyst and assume the responsibility for managing the change process—that is, a **change agent**. Who can be change agents?

We assume that changes are initiated and coordinated by a manager within the organization. However, the change agent could be a nonmanager—for example, a change specialist from the HR department or even an outside consultant whose expertise is in change implementation. For major system-wide changes, an organization often hires outside consultants to provide advice and assistance. Because they're from the outside, they offer an objective perspective that insiders may lack. However, outside consultants are usually at a disadvantage because they have a limited understanding of the organization's history, culture, operating procedures, and people. Outside consultants also are likely to initiate more drastic change than insiders would (which can be either a benefit or a disadvantage) because they don't have to live with the repercussions after the change is implemented. In contrast, internal managers who act as change agents may be more thoughtful, but possibly overcautious, because they must live with the consequences of their decisions.

As change agents, managers are motivated to initiate change because they are committed to improving their organization's performance. Initiating change involves identifying what types of changes might be needed and putting the change process in motion. But that's not all there is to managing organizational change. Managers must manage employee resistance to change. What types of organizational change might managers need to make, and how do managers deal with resistance to change?

## Types of Change

What *can* a manager change? There are three types: structure, technology, and people (see Exhibit 13–2). Changing *structure* includes any change in structural variables such as reporting relationships, coordination mechanisms, employee empowerment, or job redesign. Changing *technology* encompasses modifications in the way work is performed or the methods and equipment that are used. Changing *people* refers to changes in attitudes, expectations, perceptions, and behavior of individuals or groups.

**Changing Structure** Managers' organizing responsibilities include such activities as designing the organization's structure, allocating authority, and determining how formalized the organization will be. Once those structural decisions have been made, however, they aren't final. Changing conditions or changing strategies bring about the need to make structural changes.

Exhibit 13–2

**Three Categories of Change**

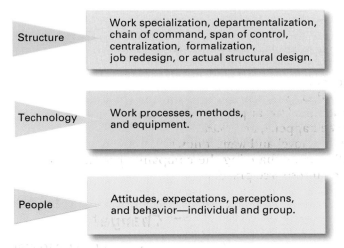

Structure → Work specialization, departmentalization, chain of command, span of control, centralization, formalization, job redesign, or actual structural design.

Technology → Work processes, methods, and equipment.

People → Attitudes, expectations, perceptions, and behavior—individual and group.

**organizational change**
Any alteration of people, structure, or technology in an organization.

**change agent**
Someone who acts as a catalyst and assumes the responsibility for managing the change process.

What options does the manger have for changing structure? The same ones we introduced in our discussion of structure and design in Chapter 10. A few examples should make this clearer. Because an organization's structure is defined in terms of work specialization, departmentalization, chain of command, span of control, centralization and decentralization, and formalization, managers can alter one or more of these *structural components*. For instance, departmental responsibilities could be combined, organizational levels eliminated, or spans of control widened to make the organization flatter and less bureaucratic. More rules and procedures could be implemented to increase standardization. Or an increase in decentralization could be used to make decision making faster.

Another option would be to make major changes in the actual *structural design*. For instance, when Hewlett-Packard acquired Compaq Computer, several structural changes were made as product divisions were dropped, merged, or expanded. Or structural design changes might include a shift from a functional to a product structure or the creation of a project structure design. Avery-Dennis Corporation, for example, revamped its traditional functional structure to a new design that arranges work around cross-functional teams.

**Changing Technology**  Managers can also change the technology used to convert inputs into outputs. Most early management studies—such as the work of Taylor and the Gilbreths—dealt with changing technology. If you recall, scientific management sought to implement changes that would increase production efficiency based on time-and-motion studies. Today, technological changes usually involve the introduction of new equipment, tools, or methods; automation; or computerization.

Competitive factors or new innovations within an industry often require managers to introduce *new equipment, tools,* or *operating methods*. For example, coal-mining companies in New South Wales updated operational methods, installed more efficient coal-handling equipment, and made changes in work practices to be more productive. Even the U.S. Army applied sophisticated technology to its operations, including such advancements as 3-dimensional shootout training devices and high-speed data links among troops on the battlefield.[11]

*Automation* is a technological change that replaces certain tasks done by people with tasks done by machines. It began in the Industrial Revolution and continues today as one of a manager's options for structural change. Automation has been introduced (and sometimes resisted) in organizations such as the U.S. Postal Service, where automatic mail sorters are used, or in automobile assembly lines, where robots are programmed to do jobs that blue-collar workers used to perform.

*When Dr. George Saleh switched his medical practice to a digital paperless system, the initial results were chaotic as he and his staff learned to work with the new software, entering patient information on a screen with drop-down menus, for instance, instead of on a clipboard. After a few months, however, Saleh found himself seeing the same number of patients in less time, reducing his secretarial expenses, and being reimbursed by insurance companies in days instead of months. He can access his patient records from home or from the hospital, search his patient database to find out who is taking which drug, and spend time asking patients important questions about partner abuse or sexual dysfunction. The new system "has made me a better doctor," says Saleh. "It has changed the way I work every day."*

Probably the most visible technological changes in recent years, though, have come through managers' efforts to expand *computerization*. Most organizations have sophisticated information systems. For instance, grocery stores and other retailers use scanners linked to computers that provide instant inventory information. Also, it's very uncommon for an office to not be computerized. At BP p.l.c., employees had to learn how to deal with the personal visibility and accountability brought about by the implementation of an enterprise-wide information system. The integrative nature of this system meant that what any employee did on his or her computer automatically affected other computer systems on the internal network.[12] And the Benetton Group SpA uses computers to link its manufacturing plants outside Treviso, Italy, with the company's various sales outlets and a highly automated warehouse.[13]

**Changing People** Changing people—that is, changing attitudes, expectations, perceptions, and behaviors—isn't easy. Yet, for almost 40 years, academic researchers and actual managers have been interested in finding ways for individuals and groups within organizations to work together more effectively. The term **organizational development (OD)**, though occasionally referring to all types of change, essentially focuses on techniques or programs to change people and the nature and quality of interpersonal work relationships.[14] The most popular OD techniques are described in Exhibit 13–3. The common thread in these techniques is that each seeks to bring about changes in the organization's people. For example, executives at Scotiabank, Canada's second-largest bank, knew that the success of a new customer sales and service strategy depended on changing employee attitudes and behaviors. Managers used different OD techniques during the strategic change including team building, survey feedback, and intergroup development. One indicator of how well these techniques worked in

Exhibit 13–3    **Organizational Development Techniques**

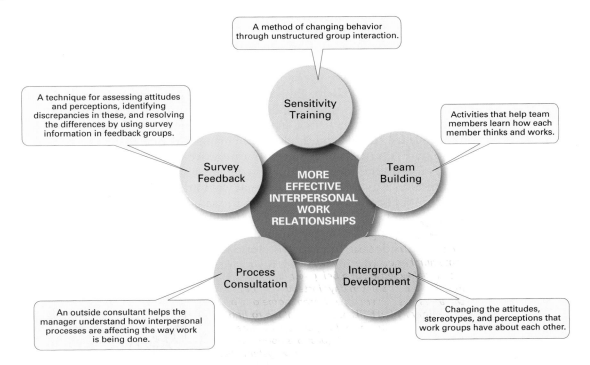

**organizational development (OD)**
Techniques or programs to change people and the nature and quality of interpersonal work relationships.

getting people to change was that every branch in Canada implemented the new strategy on or ahead of schedule.[15]

**Global OD**   Much of what we know about OD practices has come from North American research. However, managers need to recognize that although there may be some similarities in the types of OD techniques used, some techniques that work for U.S. organizations may not be appropriate for organizations or organizational divisions based in other countries.[16] For instance, a study of OD interventions showed that "multirater (survey) feedback as practiced in the United States is not embraced in Taiwan" because the cultural value of "saving face is simply more powerful than the value of receiving feedback from subordinates."[17] What's the lesson for managers? Before using the same techniques to implement behavioral changes, especially across different countries, managers need to be sure that they've taken into account cultural characteristics and whether the techniques "make sense for the local culture."

## Managing Resistance to Change

**Q & A**

Change is important, so why do people fight it? Q & A 13.3 explains.

**Passport**

How would you get global employees to accept needed changes? Try this Passport exercise and see what you would do.

"When David Russo, chief people officer at SAS Institute, gives a speech about how to win employee loyalty, it doesn't take long for someone in the audience to raise their hand and explain why that can't be done."[18] Change can be a threat to people in an organization. ( ⬛ Go to www.prenhall.com/rolls) Organizations can build up inertia that motivates people to resist changing their status quo, even though change might be beneficial. Why do people resist change and what can be done to minimize their resistance? ( ◆ Check out Passport Scenario 2 on page 382.)

**Why People Resist Change**   It's often said that most people hate any change that doesn't jingle in their pockets. This resistance to change is well documented.[19] Why *do* people resist change? An individual is likely to resist change for the following reasons: uncertainty, habit, concern over personal loss, and the belief that the change is not in the organization's best interest.[20]

Change replaces the known with ambiguity and uncertainty. No matter how much you may dislike attending college, at least you know what's expected of you. When you leave college for the world of full-time employment, you'll trade the known for the unknown. Employees in organizations are faced with similar uncertainty. For example, when quality control methods based on sophisticated statistical models are introduced into manufacturing plants, many quality control inspectors have to learn the new methods. Some inspectors may fear that they will be unable to do so and may, therefore, develop a negative attitude toward the change or behave poorly if required to use them.

Another cause of resistance is that we do things out of habit. Every day, when you go to school or work you probably go the same way, whether walking, driving, or using mass transit. If you're like most people, you find a single approach and use it regularly. As human beings, we're creatures of habit. Life is complex enough—we don't want to have to consider the full range of options for the hundreds of decisions we make every day. To cope with this complexity, we rely on habits or programmed responses. But when confronted with change, our tendency to respond in our accustomed ways becomes a source of resistance.

The third cause of resistance is the fear of losing something already possessed. Change threatens the investment you've already made in the status quo. The more that people have invested in the current system, the more they resist change. Why? They fear the loss of status, money, authority, friendships, personal convenience, or other economic benefits that they value. This helps explain why older workers tend to resist change more than younger workers. Older employees have generally invested more in the current system and thus have more to lose by changing.

A final cause of resistance is a person's belief that the change is incompatible with the goals and interests of the organization. For instance, an employee who believes that a proposed new job procedure will reduce product quality or productivity can be expected to resist the change. If the employee expresses his or her resistance positively, this actually can be beneficial to the organization.

**Techniques for Reducing Resistance** When managers see resistance to change as dysfunctional, they can use any of seven actions to deal with the resistance.[21] These seven actions described in Exhibit 13–4 include education and communication, participation, facilitation and support, negotiation, manipulation and cooptation, selecting people who accept change, and coercion. Depending on the type and source of the resistance, managers might choose to use any of these. (  Go to www.prenhall.com/rolls)

PRISM

Do you think you have the skills to manage people's resistance to change? Try out PRISM #5.

Exhibit 13–4

**Managerial Actions to Reduce Resistance to Change**

---

**Education and Communication**

- Communicate with employees to help them see the logic of change.
- Educate employees through one-on-one discussions, memos, group meetings, or reports.
- Appropriate if source of resistance is either poor communication or misinformation.
- Must be mutual trust and credibility between managers and employees.

**Participation**

- Allows those who oppose a change to participate in the decision.
- Assumes that they have expertise to make meaningful contributions.
- Involvement can reduce resistance, obtain commitment to seeing change succeed, and increase quality of change decision.

**Facilitation and Support**

- Provide supportive efforts such as employee counseling or therapy, new skills training, or short, paid leave of absence.
- Can be time-consuming and expensive.

**Negotiation**

- Exchange something of value to reduce resistance.
- May be necessary when resistance comes from a powerful source.
- Potentially high costs and likelihood of having to negotiate with other resisters.

**Manipulation and Co-optation**

- Manipulation is covert attempts to influence such as twisting or distorting facts, withholding damaging information, or creating false rumors.
- Co-optation is a form of manipulation and participation.
- Inexpensive and easy ways to gain support of resisters.
- Can fail miserably if targets feel they've been tricked.

**Selecting People Who Accept Change**

- Ability to easily accept and adapt to change is related to personality.
- Select people who are open to experience, take a positive attitude toward change, are willing to take risks, and are flexible in their behavior.

**Coercion**

- Using direct threats or force.
- Inexpensive and easy way to get support.
- May be illegal. Even legal coercion can be perceived as bullying.

## *managing your* **Career**

### Reinvent Yourself

Face it. The only constant thing about change is that it is constant. These days you don't have the luxury of dealing with change only once in awhile. No, the workplace seems to change almost continuously. How can you reinvent yourself to deal with the demands of a constantly changing workplace?[22]

Being prepared isn't a credo just for the Boy Scouts; it should be your motto for dealing with a workplace that is constantly changing. Being prepared means taking the initiative and being responsible for your own personal career development. Rather than depending on your organization to provide you with career development and training opportunities, do it yourself. Take advantage of continuing education or graduate courses at local colleges. Sign up for workshops and seminars

that can help you enhance your skills. Upgrading your skills to keep them current is one of the most important things you can do to reinvent yourself.

It's also important for you to be a positive force when faced with workplace changes. We don't mean that you should routinely accept any change that's being implemented. If you think that a proposed change won't work, speak up. Voice your concerns in a constructive manner. Being constructive may mean suggesting an alternative. However, if you feel that the change is beneficial, support it wholeheartedly and enthusiastically.

The changes that organizations make in response to a dynamic environment can be overwhelming and stressful. However, you can take advantage of these changes by reinventing yourself.

## Learning Review

- Define organizational change.
- Contrast using internal and external change agents.
- Describe how managers might change structure, technology, and people.

- Explain why people resist change and how resistance might be managed.

## CONTEMPORARY ISSUES IN MANAGING CHANGE

Today's change issues—changing organizational cultures, handling employee stress, and making change happen successfully—are critical concerns for managers. What can managers do to change an organization's culture when that culture no longer supports the organization's mission? What can managers do to handle the stress created by today's dynamic and uncertain environment? And how can managers successfully manage the challenges of introducing and implementing change? These are the topics we'll be looking at in this section.

### Changing Organizational Culture

When W. James McNerney, Jr., took over as CEO of 3M Company, he brought managerial approaches from his old employer, General Electric. But he soon discovered that what was routine at GE was unheard of at 3M. For instance, he was the only one who showed up at meetings without a tie. His blunt, matter-of-fact, and probing style of asking questions caught many 3M managers off guard. McNerney soon realized that he would first need to address the cultural issues before tackling any needed organizational changes.[23] The fact that an organization's culture is made up of relatively stable and permanent characteristics (see Chapter 3) tends to make it very resistant to change.[24] A culture takes a long time to form, and once established it tends to become entrenched. Strong cultures are particularly resistant to change because employees have become so committed to them. For instance, it didn't take long for Lou Gerstner, who was CEO of IBM from 1993 to 2002, to discover the power of a strong culture. Gerstner, the first outsider to lead IBM, needed to overhaul the ailing, tradition-bound

*General Electric was an early adopter of the Six Sigma methodology, which emphasizes strict quality-control measures and performance rankings. Recently the company, led by CEO Jeff Immelt, has begun what might signal a major culture change, from controlling quality to managing innovation and risk. Evaluations of its top 5,000 managers are now based on hard-to-define "growth traits" like "external focus" and "imagination and courage."*

company if it was going to regain its role as the dominant player in the computer industry. However, accomplishing that in an organization that prided itself on its long-standing culture was Gerstner's biggest challenge. He said, "I came to see in my decade at IBM that culture isn't just one aspect of the game—it *is* the game."[25] If, over time, a certain culture becomes inappropriate to an organization and a handicap to management, there might be little a manager can do to change it, especially in the short run. Even under the most favorable conditions, cultural changes have to be viewed in years, not weeks or even months.

**Q & A**

Why would an organization ever need to change its culture? Check out Q & A 13.4 and see.

**Understanding the Situational Factors** What favorable conditions might facilitate cultural change? ( Go to www.prenhall.com/rolls) The evidence suggests that cultural change is most likely to take place when most or all of the following conditions exist:

- *A dramatic crisis occurs.* This can be the shock that weakens the status quo and makes people start thinking about the relevance of the current culture. Examples are an unexpected financial setback, the loss of a major customer, or a dramatic technological innovation by a competitor.

- *Leadership changes hands.* New top leadership, who can provide an alternative set of key values, may be perceived as being more capable of responding to the crisis than the old leaders were. Top leadership includes the organization's chief executive but might include all senior managers.

- *The organization is young and small.* The younger the organization, the less entrenched its culture. Similarly, it's easier for managers to communicate new values in a small organization than in a large one.

- *The culture is weak.* The more widely held the values and the higher the agreement among members on those values, the more difficult it will be to change. Conversely, weak cultures are more receptive to change than are strong ones.[26]

These situational factors help to explain why companies such as IBM and 3M faced challenges in reshaping their cultures. For the most part, employees liked the old ways of doing things and didn't see the company's problems as critical.

**How Can Cultural Change Be Accomplished?** If conditions are right, how do managers change culture? No single action is likely to have the impact necessary to change something that's so ingrained and highly valued. Managers need to have a strategy for managing cultural change, as described in Exhibit 13–5.

As you can see, these suggestions focus on specific actions that managers can take to change the culture. Following these suggestions, however, is no guarantee that a

**Exhibit 13–5**

**Strategies for Managing Cultural Change**

- *Set the tone through management behavior*; top managers, particularly, need to be positive role models.
- Create *new stories, symbols, and rituals* to replace those currently in use.
- Select, promote, and support employees who *adopt the new values*.
- *Redesign socialization processes* to align with the new values.
- To encourage acceptance of the new values, *change the reward system*.
- Replace unwritten norms with *clearly specified expectations*.
- *Shake up current subcultures* through job transfers, job rotation, and/or terminations.
- Work to get consensus through *employee participation* and creating a climate with a high level of trust.

manager's cultural change efforts will succeed. Organizational members don't quickly let go of values that they understand and that have worked well for them in the past. Managers must be patient. Change, if it comes, will be slow. And managers must stay alert to protect against any return to old, familiar practices and traditions.

## Handling Employee Stress

Self-Assessment Library (S.A.L.)

Are you stressed out? Do S.A.L. #III.C.2 and see how stressful your life is.

As a student, you've probably experienced stress when finishing class assignments and projects, taking exams, or finding ways to pay rising college costs, which may mean juggling a job and school. ( Go to www.prenhall.com/rolls) Then, there's the stress associated with getting a decent job after graduation. But even after you've landed that job, your stress isn't likely to stop. For many employees, organizational change creates stress. A dynamic and uncertain environment characterized by time pressures, increasing workloads, mergers, and restructuring has created a large number of employees who are overworked and stressed.[27] In fact, depending on which survey you look at, the number of employees experiencing job stress in the United States ranges anywhere from 40 percent to 80 percent.[28] However, workplace stress isn't just an American problem. Global studies show the following: Some 50 percent of workers surveyed from 16 European countries reported that stress and job responsibility have risen significantly over a 5-year period; 35 percent of Canadian workers surveyed said they are under high job stress; in Australia, cases of occupational stress jumped 21 percent in a 1-year period; over 57 percent of Japanese employees suffer from work-related stress; some 83 percent of call-center workers in India suffer from sleeping disorders; and a study of stress in China showed that as that country undergoes massive economic and

## *managing workforce* **Diversity**

### The Paradox of Diversity

When organizations bring diverse individuals in and socialize them into the culture, a paradox is created.[29] Managers want these new employees to accept the organization's core cultural values. Otherwise, the employees may have a difficult time fitting in or being accepted. At the same time, managers want to openly acknowledge, embrace, and support the diverse perspectives and ideas that these employees bring to the workplace.

Strong organizational cultures put considerable pressure on employees to conform, and the range of

acceptable values and behaviors is limited. Therein lies the paradox. Organizations hire diverse individuals because of their unique strengths, yet their diverse behaviors and strengths are likely to diminish in strong cultures as people attempt to fit in.

A manager's challenge in this paradox of diversity is to balance two conflicting goals: to encourage employees to accept the organization's dominant values and to encourage employees to accept differences. When changes are made in the organization's culture, managers need to remember the importance of keeping diversity alive.

social changes, managers are experiencing more stress.[30] In this section, we review what stress is, what causes it, how to identify it, and what managers can do to reduce it.

**What Is Stress?** **Stress** is the adverse reaction people have to excessive pressure placed on them from extraordinary demands, constraints, or opportunities.[31] Stress is not always bad. Although it's often discussed in a negative context, stress does have a positive value, particularly when it offers a potential gain. For instance, functional stress allows an athlete, stage performer, or employee to perform at his or her highest level in crucial situations. (  Go to www.prenhall.com/rolls)

Q & A
Is stress always bad? Can it ever be a good thing? Q & A 13.5 explains.

However, stress is more often associated with constraints and demands. A constraint prevents you from doing what you desire; demands refer to the loss of something desired. When you take a test at school or have your annual performance review at work, you feel stress because you confront opportunity, constraints, and demands. A good performance review may lead to a promotion, greater responsibilities, and a higher salary. But a poor review may keep you from getting the promotion. An extremely poor review might lead to your being fired.

Just because the conditions are right for stress to surface, however, doesn't always mean it will. Two conditions are necessary for *potential* stress to become *actual* stress.[32] First, there must be uncertainty over the outcome, and second, the outcome must be important.

**Causes of Stress** As shown in Exhibit 13–6, stress can be caused by personal factors and by job-related factors. Clearly, change of any kind—personal or job-related—has the potential to cause stress as it can involve demands, constraints, or opportunities. Because organizational changes are frequently created in a climate of uncertainty and around issues that are important to employees, it's not surprising that change is a major stressor.

**Symptoms of Stress** What signs indicate that an employee's stress level might be too high? Stress is shown in a number of ways. For instance, an employee who is experiencing high stress may become depressed, accident prone, or argumentative; may have difficulty making routine decisions; may be easily distracted; and so on. As Exhibit 13–7 shows, stress symptoms can be grouped under three general categories: physical, psychological, and behavioral. All of these can significantly affect an employee's work. (  Go to www.prenhall.com/rolls)

Self-Assessment Library (S.A.L.)
Too much stress can lead to burnout. Are you there? Try S.A.L. #III.C.3 and see.

In Japan, there's a stress phenomenon called karoshi (pronounced kah-roe-she), which is translated literally as "death from overwork." During the late 1980s, "several high-ranking Japanese executives still in their prime years suddenly died without any previous sign of illness."[33] As public concern increased, even the Japanese Ministry of Labour got involved, and it now publishes statistics on the number of karoshi deaths. As Japanese multinational companies expand operations to China, Korea, and Taiwan, it's feared that the karoshi culture may follow.

Exhibit 13–6

**Causes of Stress**

**stress**
The adverse reaction people have to excessive pressure placed on them from extraordinary demands, constraints, or opportunities.

Exhibit 13–7

**Symptoms of Stress**

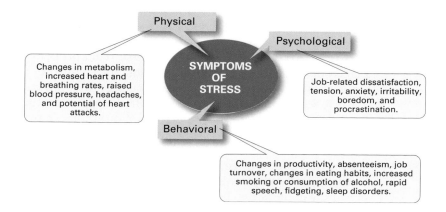

**Reducing Stress** As we mentioned earlier, not all stress is dysfunctional. Because stress can never be totally eliminated from a person's life, either off the job or on, managers are concerned with reducing the stress that leads to dysfunctional work behavior. How? Through controlling certain organizational factors to reduce job-related stress and, to a more limited extent, offering help for personal stress.

Things that managers can do in terms of job-related factors begin with employee selection. Managers need to make sure that an employee's abilities match the job requirements. When employees are in over their heads, their stress levels typically will be high. A realistic job preview during the selection process can minimize stress by reducing ambiguity over job expectations. Improved organizational communications will keep ambiguity-induced stress to a minimum. Similarly, a performance planning program such as MBO will clarify job responsibilities, provide clear performance goals, and reduce ambiguity through feedback. Job redesign is also a way to reduce stress. If stress can be traced to boredom or to work overload, jobs should be redesigned to increase challenge or to reduce the workload. Redesigns that increase opportunities for employees to participate in decisions and to gain social support have also been found to lessen stress.[34]

Stress from an employee's personal life raises two problems. First, it's difficult for the manager to control directly. Second, there are ethical considerations. Specifically, does the manager have the right to intrude—even in the most subtle ways—in an employee's personal life? If a manager believes it's ethical and the employee is receptive, there are a few approaches the manager can consider. Employee *counseling* can provide stress relief. Employees often want to talk to someone about their problems, and the organization—through its managers, in-house human resource counselors, or free or low-cost outside professional help—can meet that need. Companies such as Citicorp, AT&T, and Johnson & Johnson provide extensive counseling services for their employees. A *time management program* can help employees whose personal lives suffer from a lack of planning to sort

*thinking critically about* **Ethics**

One in five companies offers some form of stress management program.[35] Although these programs are available, many employees may choose not to participate. Why? Many employees are reluctant to ask for help, especially if a major source of that stress is job insecurity. After all, there's still a stigma associated with stress. Employees don't want to be perceived as being unable to handle the demands of their job. Although they may need stress management now more than ever, few employees want to admit that they're stressed. What can be done about this paradox? Do organizations even *have* an ethical responsibility to help employees deal with stress?

out their priorities.[36] Still another approach is organizationally sponsored *wellness programs*. For example, Wellmark Blue Cross Blue Shield of Des Moines, Iowa, offers employees an on-site health and fitness facility that is open 6 days a week. At Cianbro, a general contracting company located in the northeastern United States, employees are provided a wellness program that's been tailored to the unique demands of the construction environment.[37] And at software firm Analytical Graphics, employees can take advantage of yoga or Pilates classes to alleviate stress.[38]

## Making Change Happen Successfully

Organizational change isn't necessary only when strategies change or crises occur; it's an ongoing daily challenge facing managers in the United States *and* around the globe. In a global study of organizational changes in over 2,000 organizations in Europe, Japan, the United States, and the United Kingdom, 82 percent of the respondents had implemented major information systems changes, 74 percent had created horizontal sharing of services and information, 65 percent had implemented flexible human resource practices, and 62 percent had decentralized operational decisions.[39] Each of these major changes entailed numerous other changes in structure, technology, and people. When changes are needed, who makes them happen? Who manages them? Although you may think that it's just top-level managers, actually managers at *all* organizational levels are involved in the change process.

Even with the involvement of all levels of managers in change efforts, change processes don't always work the way they should. In fact, a global study of organizational change concluded that, "Hundreds of managers from scores of U.S. and European companies [are] satisfied with their operating prowess . . . [but] dissatisfied with their ability to implement change."[40] What can be done to address this shortcoming? How can managers make change happen successfully? Managers can increase the likelihood of making change happen successfully by (1) focusing on making the organization ready for change, (2) understanding their own role in the process, and (3) increasing the role of individual employees. Let's look at each of these suggestions.

In an industry where growth is slowing and competitors are becoming stronger, United Parcel Service (UPS) prospers. How? By embracing change! Managers spent a decade creating new worldwide logistics businesses because they anticipated slowing domestic shipping demand. They continue change efforts in order to exploit new opportunities.[41] UPS is what we call a change-capable organization. What does it take to be a change-capable organization? Exhibit 13–8 summarizes the characteristics.

**Exhibit 13–8**

**Characteristics of Change-Capable Organizations**

---

- *Link the present and the future*. Think of work as more than an extension of the past; think about future opportunities and issues and factor them into today's decisions.

- *Make learning a way of life*. Change-friendly organizations excel at knowledge sharing and management.

- *Actively support and encourage day-to-day improvements and changes*. Successful change can come from the small changes as well as the big ones.

- *Ensure diverse teams*. Diversity ensures that things won't be done like they've always been done.

- *Encourage mavericks*. Since their ideas and approaches are outside the mainstream, mavericks can help bring about radical change.

- *Shelter breakthroughs*. Change-friendly organizations have found ways to protect those breakthrough ideas.

- *Integrate technology*. Use technology to implement changes.

- *Build and deepen trust*. People are more likely to support changes when the organization's culture is trusting and managers have credibility and integrity.

*Source:* Based on P. A. McLagan, "The Change-Capable Organization," *T&D*, January 2003, pp. 50–59.

## focus on **Leadership**

**Championing Change: Leaders As Change Agents**

A survey by the American Management Association looked at reasons why leadership is more important than ever, and the "increasingly competitive business environment" was overwhelmingly cited as the top reason.[42] Surviving in such an environment requires managers to be change leaders. As a change leader, María Aramburuzabala de Garza, vice chairman of Grupo Modelo, understands this well. Although her company controls 60 percent of the Mexican beer market, she still champions whatever changes are necessary to strengthen Grupo Modelo's competitive position in an increasingly competitive environment.

What *can* a change leader, like María, do to champion change and ensure that change happens successfully?

Here are some suggestions:

- Create a simple, compelling statement of the need for change.
- Communicate constantly and honestly throughout the process.
- Get as much employee participation as possible.
- Respect employees' apprehension about the change but encourage them to be flexible.
- Remove those who resist but only after all possible attempts have been made to get their commitment to the change.
- Aim for short-term change successes because large-scale change can be a long time coming.
- Set a positive example.

The second component of making change happen successfully is for managers to recognize their own important role in the process. Managers can, and do, act as change agents. But their role in the change process includes more than being catalysts for change. They also must be change leaders. When organizational members resist change, it's the manager's responsibility to lead the change effort. But even when there's no resistance to the change, someone has to assume leadership. That someone is the organization's managers.

The final aspect of making change happen successfully revolves around getting all organizational members involved. Successful organizational change is not a one-person job. Individual employees are a powerful resource in identifying and addressing change issues. "If you develop a program for change and simply hand it to your people, saying, 'Here, implement this,' it's unlikely to work. But when people help to build something, they will support it and make it work."[43] Managers need to encourage employees to be change agents—to look for those day-to-day improvements and changes that individuals and teams can make. For instance, a study of organizational change found that 77 percent of changes at the work group level were reactions to a specific, current problem or to a suggestion from someone outside the work group; and 68 percent of those changes occurred in the course of employees' day-to-day work.[44]

## Learning Review

- Explain why changing organizational culture is so difficult and how managers can do it.
- Describe employee stress and how managers can help employees deal with stress.

- Discuss what it takes to make change happen successfully.

## STIMULATING INNOVATION

**Q & A**
Is innovation really that important? Go to Q & A 13.6 to find out.

"The way you will thrive in this environment is by innovating—innovating in technologies, innovating in strategies, innovating in business models."[45] That's the message IBM CEO Sam Palmisano gave an audience of executives at an innovation-themed leadership conference held in Rome recently. And how true it is! Success in business today demands innovation. Such is the stark reality facing today's managers. ( ◆ Go to

*Some of the most exciting innovations that companies produce are those from which even more innovation can spring. Google's interactive mapping technology has been embraced by users who have combined it with everything from real estate listings to sites listing the locations of local poker games.*

www.prenhall.com/rolls) In the dynamic, chaotic world of global competition, organizations must create new products and services and adopt state-of-the-art technology if they're going to compete successfully.[46] General Electric, for instance, has long been known for its innovations. From light bulbs to electric washing machines to 4D ultrasound imaging, GE has been on the forefront of many industry innovations. However, the company isn't resting on its past successes. It continues to be on the cutting edge in innovating products and processes.

What companies come to mind when you think of successful innovators? Maybe Sony Corporation, with its MiniDisks, PlayStations, Aibo robot pets, Cyber-Shot digital cameras and MiniDV Handycam camcorders. Maybe 3M Corporation, with its Post-It notes, Scotchgard protective coatings, and cellophane tape. Maybe Toyota, with its continual advancements in product and manufacturing process designs. (See Exhibit 13–9 for a list of companies that respondents from around the world named as most innovative in a *BusinessWeek* survey.) What's the secret to the success of these innovator champions? What, if anything, can other managers do to make their organizations more innovative? In the following pages, we'll try to answer those questions as we discuss the factors behind innovation.

Exhibit 13–9    **Innovative Companies Around the World**

| Apple and Google reign worldwide. But respondents from different regions often favored local companies.* | **ASIA-PACIFIC** | | **EUROPE** | | **NORTH AMERICA** | |
|---|---|---|---|---|---|---|
| | **1** Apple | **9** Nokia | **1** Apple | **9** GE | **1** Apple | **9** IBM |
| | **2** Google | **10** Infosys | **2** Google | **10** eBay | **2** Google | **10** Dell |
| | **3** 3M | **11** Virgin | **3** Nokia | **11** IKEA | **3** P&G | **11** Wal-Mart |
| | **4** Samsung | **12** P&G | **4** Microsoft | **12** RyanAir | **4** 3M | **12** IDEO |
| | **5** Microsoft | **13** Dell | **5** 3M | **13** Sony | **5** Toyota | **13** Target |
| | **6** IBM | **14** Sony | **6** Toyota | **14** Intel | **6** GE | **14** Samsung |
| | **7** GE | **15** Intel | **7** Virgin | **15** Porsche | **7** Starbucks | **15** Southwest |
| | **8** Toyota | | **8** BMW | | **8** Microsoft | |

Data: Boston Consulting Group * We broke ties by comparing 10-year annualized total shareholder returns. In ties between a public and a private company, the public company was favored.

*Source:* "A Global Pulse of Innovation," *BusinessWeek*, April 24, 2006, p. 74.

Exhibit 13–10

**Systems View of Innovation**

*Source:* Adapted from R. W. Woodman, J. E. Sawyer, and R. W. Griffin, "Toward a Theory of Organizational Creativity," *Academy of Management Review,* April 1993, p. 309.

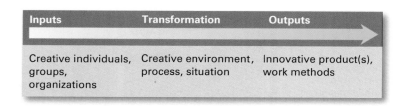

## Creativity Versus Innovation

**Creativity** refers to the ability to combine ideas in a unique way or to make unusual associations between ideas.[47] An organization that stimulates creativity develops unique ways to work or novel solutions to problems. But creativity by itself isn't enough. The outcomes of the creative process need to be turned into useful products or work methods, which is defined as **innovation**. Thus, the innovative organization is characterized by its ability to channel creativity into useful outcomes. When managers talk about changing an organization to make it more creative, they usually mean they want to stimulate and nurture innovation. Sony, 3M, and Toyota are aptly described as innovative because they take novel ideas and turn them into profitable products and work methods.

## Stimulating and Nurturing Innovation

Q & A
How do you get people to be creative and innovative? Q & A 13.7 discusses this.

Using the systems model we introduced in Chapter 2, we can better understand how organizations become more innovative.[48] (See Exhibit 13–10.) We see from this model that getting the desired outputs (innovative products and work methods) involves transforming inputs. Inputs include creative people and groups within the organization. But having creative people isn't enough. It takes the right environment for the innovation process to take hold and prosper as the inputs are transformed. (  Go to www.prenhall.com/rolls) What does this "right" environment—that is, an environment that stimulates innovation—look like? We've identified three sets of variables that have been found to stimulate innovation: the organization's structure, culture, and human resource practices (see Exhibit 13–11).

Exhibit 13–11

**Innovation Variables**

**Structural Variables**  Research into the effect of structural variables on innovation shows five things.[49] First, organic structures positively influence innovation. Because this type of organization is low in formalization, centralization, and work specialization, organic structures facilitate the flexibility, adaptability, and cross-fertilization necessary in innovation. Second, the easy availability of plentiful resources provides a key building block for innovation. With an abundance of resources, managers can afford to purchase innovations, can afford the cost of instituting innovations, and can absorb failures. Third, frequent interunit communication helps break down barriers to innovation.[50] Cross-functional teams, task forces, and other such organizational designs facilitate interaction across departmental lines and are widely used in innovative organizations. Fourth, innovative organizations try to minimize extreme time pressures on creative activities despite the demands of white-water-rapids-type environments. Although time pressures may spur people to work harder and may make them feel more creative, studies show that it actually causes them to be less creative.[51] Finally, studies have shown that when an organization's structure provided explicit support for creativity from work and nonwork sources, an employee's creative performance was enhanced. What kinds of support were found to be beneficial? Things like encouragement, open communication, readiness to listen, and useful feedback.[52] 3M, for instance, is highly decentralized, has many of the characteristics of small, organic organizations, and supports its employees in their creative activities. The company also has the "deep pockets" needed to support its policy of allowing scientists and engineers to use a portion of their time on projects of their own choosing.[53]

**Cultural Variables**  "Throw the bunny" is part of the lingo used by a project team at toy company Mattel. It refers to a juggling lesson where team members tried to learn to juggle two balls and a stuffed bunny. Most people easily learn to juggle two balls but can't let go of that third object. Creativity, like juggling, is learning to let go—that is, to "throw the bunny." And for Mattel, having a culture where people are encouraged to "throw the bunny" is important to its continued product innovations.[54]

Innovative organizations tend to have similar cultures.[55] They encourage experimentation; reward both successes and failures; and celebrate mistakes. An innovative organization is likely to have the following characteristics.

- *Acceptance of ambiguity.* Too much emphasis on objectivity and specificity constrains creativity. (  Go to www.prenhall.com/rolls)
- *Tolerance of the impractical.* Individuals who offer impractical, even foolish, answers to what-if questions are not stifled. What at first seems impractical might lead to innovative solutions.
- *Low external controls.* Rules, regulations, policies, and similar organizational controls are kept to a minimum.
- *Tolerance of risk.* Employees are encouraged to experiment without fear of consequences should they fail. Mistakes are treated as learning opportunities. For instance, remember the philosophy of our manager Alex Lee in our chapter-opening case—people learn the most when something goes wrong, so he doesn't want his employees to stop making mistakes.
- *Tolerance of conflict.* Diversity of opinions is encouraged. Harmony and agreement between individuals or units are *not* assumed to be evidence of high performance.
- *Focus on ends rather than means.* Goals are made clear, and individuals are encouraged to consider alternative routes toward meeting the goals. Focusing on ends suggests that there might be several right answers to any given problem.
- *Open-system focus.* Managers closely monitor the environment and respond to changes as they occur. For example, at Starbucks, product development depends on "inspiration field trips to view customers and trends." Michelle

---

**creativity**
The ability to combine ideas in a unique way or to make unusual associations between ideas.

**innovation**
Taking creative ideas and turning them into useful products or work methods.

## *becoming* a Manager

√ Pay attention to how you handle change. Figure out why you resist certain changes and not others.

√ Practice using different approaches to managing resistance to change at work or in your personal life.

√ Read material that's been written about how to be a more creative person.

√ Find ways to be innovative and creative as you complete class projects or work projects.

√  Complete the following exercises from the Self-Assessment Library found on www.prenhall.com/rolls: SAL #I.A.4—How Well Do I Handle Ambiguity?, S.A.L. #I.A.5—How Creative Am I?, S.A.L. #III.C.1—How Well Do I Respond to Turbulent Change?, S.A.L. #III.C.2—How Stressful Is My Life?, and S.A.L. #III.C.3—Am I Burned Out?

Self-Assessment Library (S.A.L.)

Gass, the company's senior vice president for category management, "took her team to Paris, Düsseldorf, and London to visit local Starbucks and other restaurants to get a better sense of local cultures, behaviors, and fashions." She says, "You come back just full of different ideas and different ways to think about things than you would had you read about it in a magazine or e-mail."[56]

- *Positive feedback.* Managers provide positive feedback, encouragement, and support so employees feel that their creative ideas receive attention. For instance, at Research in Motion, Mike Lazaridis, president and co-CEO says, "I think we have a culture of innovation here, and [engineers] have absolute access to me. I live a life that tries to promote innovation."[57]

**Human Resource Variables** In this category, we find that innovative organizations actively promote the training and development of their members so their knowledge remains current; offer their employees high job security to reduce the fear of getting fired for making mistakes; and encourage individuals to become **idea champions**, actively and enthusiastically supporting new ideas, building support, overcoming resistance, and ensuring that innovations are implemented. (  Go to www.prenhall.com/rolls) Research finds that idea champions have common personality characteristics: extremely high self-confidence, persistence, energy, and a tendency toward risk taking. They also display characteristics associated with dynamic leadership. They inspire and energize others with their vision of the potential of an innovation and through their strong personal conviction in their mission. They're also good at gaining the commitment of others to support their mission. In addition, idea champions have jobs that provide considerable decision-making discretion. This autonomy helps them introduce and implement innovations in organizations.[58] For instance, *Spirit* and *Opportunity*, two golf-cart-sized exploration rovers exploring the surface of Mars, never would have been built had it not been for an idea champion by the name of Donna L. Shirley. As head of Mars exploration in the 1990s at NASA's Jet Propulsion Laboratory in Pasadena, California, Shirley had been working since the early 1980s on the idea of putting roving vehicles on Mars. Despite ongoing funding and management support problems, she continued to champion the idea until it was approved in the early 1990s. The images and data being transmitted back to earth by these rovers have been invaluable to NASA scientists, none of which would have been possible without that idea champion.[59]

Self-Assessment Library (S.A.L.)

Do you think you're creative? Check out S.A.L. #I.A.5 and see!

## Learning Review

- Explain why innovation isn't just creativity.
- Explain the systems view of innovation.
- Describe the structural, cultural, and human resource variables that are necessary for innovation.

- Explain what idea champions are and why they're important to innovation.

# Managers Respond to a Manager's Dilemma

## James F. Kahn

Associate Vice President—Investments, Wachovia Securities, Jenkintown, PA

While creativity and innovation are critical components of a successful organization, they are not the final goal. These attributes serve as a driver for success, and this success must be measurable. Here are some things Alex might do:

Set specific measurable goals with benchmarks and time frames to be met. What actions are necessary in order to achieve these goals? This is where the creativity and innovation are critical. Are the existing systems in place sufficient to increase product or market share? Are new systems necessary? What happens if interim and final goals are met? What if goals are not met? Can rewards and/or recognition be used to encourage participation in this effort?

Most importantly, when all of the moving parts are recognized, communicate all of the goals, needs, and expectations to team members involved in the project so everyone is on the same page. Ongoing monitoring and feedback with team members will help assure long-term success.

## Steve Meredith

Store Director, Toys"R"Us, Williston, VT

The recent successes of OXO, as highlighted by its design awards and recognition, indicate that the basic innovation variables have been in place and are currently stimulating successful innovation. In my effort to continue this success, I would be very vigilant with regard to the human resources variables. It is within this category that the structural and cultural variables are either championed or lost. As with most managerial endeavors, the best plans cannot become a reality without the human resource commitment.

It is the people within any organization that determine whether a company's mission statement is transformed into practice. I would be very focused on celebrating the workforce. Constant recognition through spontaneous personal accolades coupled with specific, periodic commendations for behaviors that champion innovation would do much to create a work environment that embraces the innovative and creative behavior of employees necessary for OXO to continue to prosper.

**idea champion**
Individuals who actively and enthusiastically support new ideas, build support, overcome resistance, and ensure that innovations are implemented.

# Learning Summary

## What Factors Create the Need for Change?

- **External factors**: marketplace, governmental laws and regulations, technology, labor markets, economic changes
- **Internal factors**: strategy, workforce, equipment, employee attitudes

## Is Change Episodic or Ongoing?

Calm waters metaphor suggests that change is episodic and can be planned and managed using:

- Lewin's 3-step change model (unfreezing, changing, refreezing)

White-water rapids metaphor suggests that change is ongoing, so planning and managing change must be also

## How Do Managers Manage Organizational Change?

- Types of **organizational change** include structure, technology, or people
  - Changes in structure could be structural components or structural design
  - Changes in technology could be equipment/tools/operating methods; automation; or computerization
  - Changing people—**organizational development** is used to change people; that is, their attitudes, expectations, perceptions, and behaviors
- **Change agents** may be needed to act as a catalyst and to manage the change process
  - May be manager or nonmanager
  - May be internal or external
- Resistance to change comes from uncertainty, habit, concern over personal loss, and belief that change isn't in organization's best interests
- Managers can manage resistance by using education and communication, participation, facilitation and support, negotiation, manipulation and co-optation, selecting people who accept change, and coercion

## What Current Change Issues Are Managers Facing?

- Changing organizational culture is difficult, so conditions have to be favorable before managers can do it
- Handling employee stress, which organizational change often creates
  - **Stress** involves excessive pressure coming from extraordinary demands, constraints, or opportunities
  - Stress is a global problem, but isn't always bad
  - Potential stress becomes actual stress when there's uncertainty over an important outcome
  - Stress can come from job-related and personal factors
  - Stress symptoms include physical, psychological, and behavioral
  - There are ways for managers to reduce job-related stress and to offer help for personal stress
- Make change happen successfully by making the organization ready for change, being a change leader, and increasing the role of others in change

## How Can Managers Manage Innovation?

Innovation and creativity are not the same. **Creativity** is combining ideas in a unique way or making unusual associations between ideas. **Innovation** is turning the outcomes of the creative process into useful products or work methods.

- Input-process-output perspective of innovation
- Factors that affect innovation
  1. **Structural variables**: organic-type structure, plentiful resources, frequent interunit communication, minimal time pressures, support for creative work from work and nonwork sources
  2. **Cultural variables**: accept ambiguity, tolerate the impractical, keep controls to a minimum, tolerate risks and conflict, focus on goals, monitor the environment, and provide positive feedback
  3. **Human resource variables**: training and development, high job security, and creative people (*idea champions*)

# Management: By the Numbers

- Innovation in products, services, and business models was named as the single factor contributing most to the accelerating pace of change in the global business environment today.
- Fifty-four percent of workers polled said that opportunities to innovate are missed because the right people do not work together.
- In a poll of Chinese and U.S./Canadian managers, Chinese managers said that creativity or innovation was the second most respected leadership quality; for the U.S./Canadian managers, creativity or innovation ranked last on the list.
- Eighty-six percent of global business leaders surveyed said that speed, flexibility, and adaptability were a top priority for their companies.

- Thirty-four percent of workers polled said their jobs are more difficult with more stress; 31 percent said their jobs are more difficult with longer hours.
- Twenty percent of American adults surveyed said that they think most creatively in their cars.

*Sources:* "An Executive Take on the Top Business Trends: A McKinsey Global Survey," *The McKinsey Quarterly Online,* April 2006; D. Beucke, "The Big Picture: All Talk?" *BusinessWeek,* March 6, 2006, p. 13; S. Armour, "Financial Stress Hinders Job Performance," *USA Today,* October 5, 2005, p. 8B; "On the Road to Invention," *Fast Company,* February 2005, p. 16; "We Need to Be Flexible," *Springfield News-Leader,* January 6, 2005, p. 1F; and D. Gilmour, "How to Fix Knowledge Management," *Harvard Business Review,* October 2003, p. 17.

# Thinking About Management Issues

1. Can a low-level employee be a change agent? Explain your answer.

2. Innovation requires allowing people to make mistakes. However, being wrong too many times can be fatal. Do you agree? Why or why not? What are the implications for nurturing innovation?

3. How are opportunities, constraints, and demands related to stress? Give an example of each.

4. Planned change is often thought to be the best approach to take in organizations. Can unplanned change ever be effective? Explain.

5. Organizations typically have limits to how much change they can absorb. As a manager, what signs would you look for that might suggest that your organization has exceeded its capacity to change?

# Working Together: Team-Based Exercise

Stress is something that all of us face, and college students, particularly, may have extremely stressful lives. How do you recognize when you're under a lot of stress? What do you do to deal with that stress?

Form teams of three or four students. Each person in the group should describe how he or she knows when he or she is under a lot of stress. What symptoms does each person show? Make a list of these symptoms and categorize them using Exhibit 13–7. Then, each person should also describe things that he or she has found to be particularly effective in dealing with stress. Make a list of these stress-handling techniques. Out of that list, identify your top three stress reducers and be prepared to share these with the class.

# Ethical Dilemma Exercise

What is the most ethical way to deal with change that will take away some employees' jobs or completely alter the work environment? Managers at the Boots chain, which operates 1,400 drugstores and employs 60,000 people in the United Kingdom, faced this issue not long ago. They had just formulated a long-term plan to cut costs and increase efficiency by replacing a group of older distribution facilities with a new automated warehouse. Closing the facilities would take years and save the company millions of dollars—but it would also mean displacing more than 2,000 workers. The challenge was to manage the change in a sensitive way and minimize resistance while maintaining high productivity.

To reduce the stress on its workforce, Boots announced the change 3 years in advance and emphasized that the employees affected by the closures would be offered other jobs in the company. To increase participation and support, the company also held talks with the main union representing employees. Going further, management praised employee performance and kept on communicating about the progress toward constructing the new warehouse and closing individual facilities. Productivity has not suffered so far, although the combination of changing structure and technology will probably add some stress and encounter a degree of internal resistance. This is just the beginning, notes a senior executive: "Boots is changing very fast, probably faster than any other large U.K. retailer."[60]

Imagine you're the manager of a Boots store. During a staff meeting, one of your employees suggests that the store remain open 1 hour later on Thursday nights. This would increase sales and help your store compete with a drugstore 2 blocks away. Although you like the idea, your assistant manager—an outstanding employee—raises a number of objections and keeps complaining even after the meeting ends. Review Exhibit 13–4 as you decide which of the following actions to take next, and why.

**Option A:** Ask your assistant manager to plan a trial run so you can see whether keeping the store open later will pay off.

**Option B:** Ask whether your assistant manager will publicly support the idea if he doesn't have to work on Thursday evenings.

**Option C:** Ask your assistant manager to find out what happened when other stores tried extended evening hours.

## Case Application

### The "FedEx" of Junk Removal

Eighteen thousand expired cans of sardines. Fifty garden gnomes. A mechanical bull. An antique silver set (worth a lot of money). That's just some of the weird stuff that 1-800-Got-Junk? customers have asked the uniformed people in the freshly scrubbed blue trucks to haul away. Company founder and CEO Brian Scudamore discovered there was a lucrative niche between "trash cans and those big green bins dropped off by" the giant waste haulers. But even in such an uncomplicated business as hauling people's junk, Scudamore must be concerned with managing change and managing innovation.

1-800-Got-Junk? is based in Vancouver, British Columbia, with a corporate staff of about 170 individuals. "With a vision of creating the 'FedEx' of junk removal," says Scudamore, "I dropped out of university with just 1 year left to become a full-time JUNKMAN! Yes, my father, a liver transplant surgeon, was not impressed to say the least." However, in 2005, the company had over 247 franchises and system-wide revenues were over $66 million. Not surprisingly, Scudamore's father is a little more understanding these days about his son's business! Since 1997, the company has grown exponentially. In fact, the company made the list of *Entrepreneur* magazine's 100 fastest-growing franchises in 2005 and 2006.

Hauling junk would be, to most people's minds at least, a pretty simple business. However, the company Scudamore founded is a "curious hybrid." It's been described as a blend of "old economy and new economy."

The company's product—hauling away trash—has been done for hundreds, if not thousands, of years. But 1-800-Got-Junk? also relies heavily on up-to-date information technology and has the kind of organizational culture that most people associate with high-tech start-ups. The company uses its 1-800-Got-Junk? call center to do the booking and dispatching for all their franchise partners. The franchise partners also use the company's proprietary intranet and customer-relationship management site—dubbed JunkNet—to access schedules, customer information, real-time reports, and so forth. Scudamore's philosophy was that this approach allowed franchise partners to "work on the business" instead of "work in the business." On any given day, all a franchisee has to do is open up JunkNet to see the day's schedule. If a new job comes in during a workday, the program automatically sends an alert to the franchisee. Needless to say, the company's franchisees tend to be quite tech-savvy. In fact, some of them have installed GPS devices in their trucks to help find the most efficient routes on a job. Others use online navigation sites. With the price of gas continuing to increase, this type of capability is important.

1-800-Got-Junk? also has a culture that would rival any high-tech start-up. The head office is known as The Junktion. Grizzly, Scudamore's dog, comes to the office every day and helps employees relieve stress by playing catch anytime, anywhere. Each morning at exactly 10:55, all employees at the Junktion meet for a 5-minute huddle, where they share good news, announcements, metrics, and problems they're encountering. Visitors to the Junktion have to join the group huddle also. One of the most conspicuous features of the Junktion—"the first thing one sees upon entering—is the Vision Wall," which contains the "fruits of Scudamore's brainstorms." Other members of the executive team have visions for the company's future as well. Periodically they'll "wander through the offices of Genome Sciences Centre, the tenant occupying the space above them, to visualize a future when Got-Junk has expanded so sufficiently" that it will take over that office space. Company franchisees are also encouraged to take initiative and be creative. For instance, the Toronto franchise, which has 12 trucks, sometimes gets a blue truck motorcade going down Yonge Street through the heart of the city as a way to be noticed and publicize their services.

*1-800-Got-Junk founder and CEO Brain Scudamore.*

## Discussion Questions

1. Do you think 1-800-Got-Junk? faces more of a calm waters or white-water rapids environment? Explain. What external and internal forces might create the need for the company to change?

2. Do you think 1-800-Got-Junk? would be a change-capable organization? Use Exhibit 13–8 to help you answer this question.

3. Using information from Exhibit 13–11, how could Brian Scudamore stimulate and nurture innovation at the Junktion and with company franchisees?

4. What could other organizations learn about change and innovation from 1-800-Got-Junk?

*Sources:* Information from press kit on company's Web site, www. 1800gotjunk.com; "Fastest-Growing Franchises 2006 Rankings," *Entrepreneur,* www.entrepreneur.com, April 29, 2006; J. Hainsworth, The Associated Press, "Canadian Company Finds Treasures in People's Trash," *Springfield News-Leader,* April 24, 2006, p. 5B; and J. Martin, "Cash from Trash," *Fortune,* November 2003, pp. 52–56.

# Part Four

## You're the Manager: Putting Ethics into Action

*As a manager, you'll often face decisions involving ethical questions. How can you learn to identify an ethical dilemma, keep stakeholders in mind, think through the alternatives, and foresee the consequences of your decisions? This unique interactive feature, positioned at the end of Parts 2, 3, 4, 5, and 6, casts you in the role of a manager dealing with hypothetical, yet realistic ethical issues. To begin, read the following preview paragraph. Then log onto www.prenhall.com/rolls to consider the decisions you would make in the role of manager.*

General Electric has long been known for the quality of its products and its management. One reason the company continues to be so highly regarded—and so profitable—is its careful attention to human resources management. In this hypothetical scenario, you play the role of a General Electric executive who must appraise subordinates' performance using a multiperson ranking system. How will you deal ethically with those you rank among the lowest performers? Log onto www.prenhall.com/rolls to put ethics into action!

## Passport

### Scenario 1

Patrick Hollis is the Corporate Director of Strategic Planning for Grupo Bimbo, SA, Mexico's largest commercial baking company and one of the top baking companies in the world. He transferred from the London office to the headquarters in Mexico City nine months ago. In Patrick's previous position as Director of Strategic Planning for the European division, he had developed an annual strategic planning procedure that the European managers had used quite successfully. One of his first goals in his new corporate position was implementing this strategic planning procedure throughout the organization. But the initiative had not gone as smoothly as he had hoped, and it needed to be dealt with.

Patrick had a number of other critical strategic projects that his boss, the CEO, had assigned him so he had delegated the assignment of finding out what had happened with the strategic planning initiative to two of his team members, Maria Mendez and Satoshi Okuda. He had also asked Maria and Satoshi to come up with some recommendations for addressing the problem.

Maria, a native of Mexico, received her MBA from the Universidad de Monterrey (University of Monterrey) and had worked in strategic planning at Grupo Bimbo for two years. Satoshi had recently joined the company after completing his studies at Chiba University. Patrick had thought that the unique global perspective of these team members would be beneficial to uncovering the problems associated with the implementation of the corporate strategic planning process. However, after two weeks, the two hadn't made any progress and, in fact, had expressed to others in the department that they were uncomfortable with being delegated such an important task. What role might cross-cultural differences in delegating tasks play here? How can Patrick get Maria and Satoshi to proceed with this important assignment?

*To answer these questions, you'll have to do some research on the countries. Go www.prenhall.com/rolls and click on Passport. When the map appears, click on the countries you need to research. You'll find background information on the country and general information about the*
*country's economy, population, and workforce. In addition, you'll find specific information on the country's culture and the unique qualities associated with doing business there.*

### Scenario 2

After studying the idea for some time, Scott Estes, manager of global marketing research for Reebok International (now a division of the number two sporting-goods maker, adidas Salomon AG of Herzogenaurach, Germany) is convinced that the athletic footwear and apparel company would benefit greatly from a customer-based, interactive Web site. Considering that communicating via the Internet is second nature to most teens and young adults and that these age groups are the prime target market for athletic footwear and apparel, Scott believes that good marketing research feedback and information could be obtained from such a site.

Scott manages a great team of marketing research experts—Kerstin Muller from Germany, Antony Liow from Singapore, and Marta Ochoa from Brazil have several years of industry and marketing research experience among them. It's a great resource and knowledge base that Scott relies on as each team member brings a different perspective to the department's marketing research tasks. However, when Scott presented the idea of an interactive customer research Web site at last week's meeting, his globally diverse marketing research team wasn't sold on the idea. However, Scott wants to implement the idea. How can he get his team behind the change? Keeping in mind any cross-cultural differences, what will Scott need to do to overcome their resistance to this new idea? If you were Scott, what would you do?

*To answer these questions, you'll have to do some research on the countries. Go to www.prenhall.com/rolls and click on Passport. When the map appears, click on the countries you need to research. You'll find background information on the country and general information about the country's economy, population, and workforce. In addition, you'll find specific information on the country's culture and the unique qualities associated with doing business there.*

## Scenario 3

Paul Souza is an HR consultant with the São Paulo office of Ernst & Young. One of his major clients, Brazilian aircraft manufacturer Embraer, is studying the feasibility of opening production facilities in France (where unemployment is running about 10 percent) and in South Africa (where unemployment stands at about 25 percent). However, before committing millions of dollars to build these facilities, Embraer's managers want to ensure that they would be able to staff these facilities with individuals who would understand the importance of stringent and rigorous production standards and quality controls. Thus, they have asked Paul to provide an overview of the cultural characteristics and work ethic of the population of these two countries. In addition, they want some information about managerial approaches and practices that are commonly used. Pretend that you are Paul Souza. Do some research on country cultures and managerial practices common to these two proposed locations. Write up a report for your clients summarizing your research.

*To answer these questions, you'll have to do some research on the countries. Go to www.prenhall.com/rolls and click on Passport. When the map appears, click on the countries you need to research. You'll find background information on the country and general information about the country's economy, population, and workforce. In addition, you'll find specific information on the country's culture and the unique qualities associated with doing business there.*

# Continuing Case

## Starbucks—Organizing

Organizing is an important task of managers. Once the organization's goals and plans are in place, the organizing function sets in motion the process of seeing that those goals and plans are pursued. When managers organize, they're defining what work needs to get done and creating a structure that enables work activities to be completed efficiently and effectively by organizational members hired to do that work. As Starbucks continues its global expansion and pursues innovative strategic initiatives, managers must deal with the realities of continually organizing and reorganizing its work efforts.

## Structuring Starbucks

Like many start-up businesses, Starbucks' original founders organized their company around a simple structure based on each person's unique strengths: Zev Siegl became the retail expert; Jerry Baldwin took over the administrative functions; and Gordon Bowker was the dreamer who called himself "the magic, mystery, and romance man" and recognized from the start that a visit to Starbucks could "evoke a brief escape to a distant world." As Starbucks grew to the point where Jerry recognized that he needed to hire professional and experienced managers, Howard Schultz (now Starbucks' chairman) joined the company, bringing his skills in sales, marketing, and merchandising. When the original owners eventually sold the company to Schultz, he was able to take the company on the path to becoming what it is today and what it hopes to be in the future.

As Starbucks has expanded, its organizational structure has changed to accommodate that growth. However, the company prides itself on its "lean" corporate structure. Howard Schultz is chairman and chief global strategist and Jim Donald is president and CEO. Schultz has focused on hiring a team of executives from companies like Wal-Mart, Dell, and PepsiCo. He says, "I wanted to bring in people who had experience working at $10 billion companies." These senior corporate officers include the following: president of Starbucks Coffee U.S. and president of Starbucks Coffee International, 4 executive vice presidents, and 29 senior vice presidents. These positions range from senior vice president of finance, to senior vice president of coffee and global procurement, to senior vice president of corporate social responsibility. (A complete list of upper-level managers can be found in the company's annual report on its Web site.)

Although the executive team provides the all-important strategic direction, the "real" work of Starbucks gets done at the company's support center, zone offices, retail stores, and roasting plants. The support center provides support to and assists all other aspects of corporate operations in the areas of accounting, finance, information technology, and sales and supply chain management.

The zone offices oversee the regional operations of the retail stores and provide support in human resource management, facilities management, account management, financial management, and sales management. The essential link between the zone offices and each retail store is the district manager, each of whom oversees 8 to 10 stores apiece, which is down from the dozen or so stores they used to oversee. Since district managers need to be out working with the stores, most use mobile technology that allows them to spend more time in the stores and still remain connected to their own office. A company executive says, "These are the most important people in the company. And while their primary job is outside the office and in those stores, they still need to be connected."

In the retail stores, hourly employees (baristas) service customers under the direction of assistant store managers and store managers. These managers are responsible for the day-to-day operations of each Starbucks location. One of the organizational challenges for many store managers has been the company's decision to add more drive-through windows to retail stores, which appears to be a smart strategic move since the average annual volume at a store with a drive-through window is about 30 percent higher than a store without one. However, a drive-through window often takes up to 4 people to operate: one to take orders, one to operate the cash register, one to work the espresso machine, and a "floater" who can fill in where needed. And these people have to work rapidly

# Chapter 14

## Learning Outline

*Use this Learning Outline as you read and study this chapter.*

### Why Look at Individual Behavior?

- Explain why the concept of an organization as an iceberg is important to understanding organizational behavior.
- Describe the focus and the goals of organizational behavior.
- Define the six important employee behaviors that managers want to explain, predict, and influence.

### Attitudes

- Describe the three components of an attitude.
- Discuss the three job-related attitudes.
- Describe the impact job satisfaction has on employee behavior.
- Explain how individuals reconcile inconsistencies between attitudes and behavior.

### Personality

- Contrast the MBTI® and the Big Five Model of personality.
- Describe the five personality traits that have proved to be the most powerful in explaining individual behavior in organizations.
- Explain how emotions and emotional intelligence impact behavior.

### Perception

- Explain how an understanding of perception can help managers better understand individual behavior.
- Describe the key elements of attribution theory.
- Discuss how the fundamental attribution error and self-serving bias can distort attributions.
- Name three shortcuts used in judging others.

### Learning

- Explain how operant conditioning helps managers understand, predict, and influence behavior.
- Describe the implications of social learning theory for managing people at work.
- Discuss how managers can shape behavior.

### Contemporary OB Issues

- Describe the challenges managers face in managing Gen Y workers.
- Explain what managers can do to deal with workplace misbehavior.

# Foundations of Behavior

## A Manager's Dilemma

Naguib Sawiris is known as a risk taker who makes decisions quickly.[1] He's the chairman and CEO of Orascom Telecom Holding, a telecommunications company he incorporated as part of the Orascom group of companies in 1998. Since that time, Orascom Telecom has grown to be among the largest and most diversified telecommunications players in the world by taking advantage of huge market opportunities in the Middle East, Africa, and South Asia. In 2005, the company more than doubled its subscriber base to over 25 million users and is on target to double that again in 2006.

Orascom Telecom goes into markets where populations are large but telephone service and use historically are low, usually around 2 to 3 percent. And this Cairo-based mobile phone provider frequently chooses to operate in "difficult and primitive target areas" including, among others, Algeria, Tunisia, Pakistan, Congo, Zimbabwe, Bangladesh, and now Iraq. Orascom Telecom has invested $160 million in the first mobile phone service provider in Iraq. This provider, Iraqna, "operates in the volatile central provinces of Baghdad, Anbar, and Diyala. Its employees have been kidnapped and its outlets have been attacked." Mr. Sawiris says, "The only major difference between doing business in Iraq and any other place in the world is having to negotiate with kidnappers. We know that calm will come one day and Iraq will be a second Saudi Arabia. In the mobile telecom business, we invest where the service is needed and we can build value." Meanwhile, however, Orascom Telecom's annual security costs run about $30 million.

Mr. Sawiris states on his company's Web site, "We do not fear difficult missions, and we spare neither money nor resources to build and develop each target area and to find the best working environment for our employees in them!" Potential employees who will function best in the types of environments in which Orascom operates also need to be risk takers who can make decisions quickly.

Put yourself in Mr. Sawiris' position. How can he make sure that his company hires employees with these attitudes and personality?

**What would you do?**

Naguib Sawaris' desire to attract and retain employees with the right attitude and personality is something most managers want—they want people who show up and work hard, get along with co-workers and customers, and have good attitudes and exhibit good work behaviors. But as you're probably already aware, people don't always behave like that "ideal" employee. People differ in their behaviors and even the same person can behave one way one day and a completely different way another day. For instance, haven't you seen family members, friends, or co-workers behave in ways that prompted you to wonder: Why did they do that? As the chapter-opening case implies, effective managers need to understand and use the concepts of behavior in managing.

## WHY LOOK AT INDIVIDUAL BEHAVIOR?

The material in this and the next three chapters draws heavily on the field of study that's known as *organizational behavior (OB)*. Although it's concerned with the subject of **behavior**—that is, how people act—**organizational behavior** is concerned more specifically with studying how people act at work.

One of the challenges in understanding organizational behavior is that it addresses issues that aren't obvious. Like an iceberg, OB has a small visible dimension and a much larger hidden portion (see Exhibit 14–1). What we see when we look at organizations are their visible aspects: strategies, goals, policies and procedures, structure, technology, formal authority relationships, and chain of command. But under the surface are other elements that managers need to understand—elements that also influence how employees behave at work. As we'll show, OB provides managers with considerable insights into these important, but hidden, aspects of the organization. ( 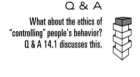 Go to www.prenhall.com/rolls) For instance, Tony Levitan, founder and former CEO of EGreetings (now a part of AG Interactive), found out the hard way about the power of behavioral elements. When he tried to "clean-up" the company's online greeting-card site for a potential partnership with Hallmark, his employees rebelled. He soon realized that he shouldn't have unilaterally made such a major decision without getting input from his staff, and reversed the move.[2]

**Q & A**
What about the ethics of "controlling" people's behavior? Q & A 14.1 discusses this.

### Focus of Organizational Behavior

Organizational behavior focuses on two major areas. First, OB looks at *individual behavior*. Based predominantly on contributions from psychologists, this area includes

Exhibit 14–1

**The Organization as an Iceberg**

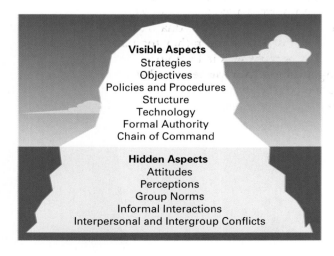

Visible Aspects
Strategies
Objectives
Policies and Procedures
Structure
Technology
Formal Authority
Chain of Command

Hidden Aspects
Attitudes
Perceptions
Group Norms
Informal Interactions
Interpersonal and Intergroup Conflicts

such topics as attitudes, personality, perception, learning, and motivation. Second, OB is concerned with *group behavior*, which includes norms, roles, team building, leadership, and conflict. Our knowledge about groups comes basically from the work of sociologists and social psychologists. Unfortunately, the behavior of a group of employees can't be understood by merely summing up the actions of the individuals in the group because individuals in a group setting behave differently from individuals acting alone. Think about yourself and your group of closest friends. Have you done things with your group of friends that you wouldn't ever do on your own? Most of us have. Because employees in an organization are both individuals and members of groups, we need to study them at two levels. In this chapter, we'll provide the foundation for understanding individual behavior. Then, in the next chapter, we'll introduce the basic concepts related to understanding group behavior.

## Goals of Organizational Behavior

**Q & A**
Don't people behave the way they do because that's what they want to do? So how can managers control employee behavior? See Q & A 14.2 for an answer.

The goals of OB are to *explain, predict,* and *influence* behavior. Why do managers need to be able to do these? Simply, in order to manage their employees' behavior. We know that a manager's success depends on getting things done through people. To do this, the manager needs to be able to *explain* why employees engage in some behaviors rather than others, *predict* how employees will respond to various actions the manager might take, and *influence* how employees behave. ( ⬤ Go to www.prenhall.com/rolls)

What employee behaviors are we specifically concerned with explaining, predicting, and influencing? Six important ones have been identified: employee productivity, absenteeism, turnover, organizational citizenship behavior (OCB), job satisfaction, and workplace misbehavior. **Employee productivity** is a performance measure of both efficiency and effectiveness. Managers want to know what factors will influence the efficiency and effectiveness of employees. **Absenteeism** is the failure to report to work. It's difficult for work to get done if employees don't show up. Studies have shown that unscheduled absences cost companies around $660 per employee per year.[3] Although absenteeism can never be totally eliminated, excessive levels will have a direct and immediate impact on the organization's functioning. **Turnover** is the voluntary and involuntary permanent withdrawal from an organization. It can be a problem because of increased recruiting, selection, and training costs and work disruptions. Just like absenteeism, managers can never eliminate turnover, but it is something they want to minimize, especially among high-performing and difficult-to-replace employees. **Organizational citizenship behavior** is discretionary behavior that's not part of an employee's formal job requirements, but which promotes the effective functioning of the organization.[4] Examples of good OCB include helping others on one's work team, volunteering for extended job activities, avoiding unnecessary conflicts, and making constructive statements about one's work group and the organization. Organizations need individuals who will do more than their usual job duties and the evidence indicates that organizations that have such employees outperform those that don't.[5] However, there are some drawbacks to OCB as employees may experience work overload, stress, and work–family conflicts.[6] **Job satisfaction** refers to an individual's general attitude toward his or her job. Although job satisfaction is an attitude rather than a behavior, it's an outcome that concerns many managers because satisfied employees are more likely to show up for work and stay with an organization. **Workplace misbehavior** is any intentional employee behavior that has negative consequences for the organization or individuals within the organization. Workplace misbehavior shows up in organizations in four ways: deviance, aggression,

---

**behavior**
How people act.

**organizational behavior**
The study of how people act at work.

**employee productivity**
A performance measure of both efficiency and effectiveness.

**absenteeism**
The failure to report to work.

**turnover**
The voluntary and involuntary permanent withdrawal from an organization.

**organizational citizenship behavior**
Discretionary behavior that is not part of an employee's formal job requirements, but that promotes the effective functioning of the organization.

**job satisfaction**
An employee's general attitude toward his or her job.

**workplace misbehavior**
Any form of intentional behavior that has negative consequences for the organization or individuals within the organization.

antisocial behavior, and violence.[7] Such behaviors can range from playing loud music just to irritate co-workers to verbally abusing a customer to sabotaging work, all of which can create havoc in any organization. In the following pages, we'll address how an understanding of four individual psychological factors—employee attitudes, personality, perception, and learning—can help us predict and explain these employee behaviors.

## Learning Review

- Explain why the concept of an organization as an iceberg is important to understanding organizational behavior.
- Describe the focus and goals of organizational behavior.

- Define the six important employee behaviors that managers want to explain, predict, and influence.

## ATTITUDES

**Attitudes** are evaluative statements—either favorable or unfavorable—concerning objects, people, or events. They reflect how an individual feels about something. When a person says, "I like my job," he or she is expressing an attitude about work.

An attitude is made up of three components: cognition, affect, and behavior.[8] The **cognitive component** of an attitude refers to the beliefs, opinions, knowledge, or information held by a person. The belief that "discrimination is wrong" illustrates a cognition. The **affective component** of an attitude is the emotional or feeling part of an attitude. Using our example, this component would be reflected by the statement, "I don't like Pat because he discriminates against minorities." Finally, affect can lead to behavioral outcomes. The **behavioral component** of an attitude refers to an intention to behave in a certain way toward someone or something. To continue our example, I might choose to avoid Pat because of my feelings about him. Understanding that attitudes are made up of three components—cognition, affect, and behavior—helps show their complexity. But for the sake of clarity, keep in mind that the term *attitude* usually refers only to the affective component.

Naturally, managers aren't interested in every attitude an employee has, but are especially interested in job-related attitudes. (  Go to www.prenhall.com/rolls) The three most widely known are job satisfaction, job involvement, and organizational commitment, which have been popular topics for organizational researchers.[9]

Q & A
Why should managers care about employees' attitudes? Q & A 14.3 explains.

*Among the winners of Canada's 2005 Best Managed Companies award is Lammle's Western Wear & Tack, based in Calgary. Winners of the prestigious award have key attributes in common, among them several that contribute to employees' job satisfaction: fostering a culture of teamwork, hiring the right people, setting challenging goals, and rewarding employees.*

# Job Satisfaction

As we know from our earlier definition, job satisfaction refers to a person's general attitude toward his or her job. (  Go to www.prenhall.com/rolls) A person with a high level of job satisfaction has a positive attitude toward his or her job, while a person who is dissatisfied has a negative attitude. When people speak of employee attitudes, they usually are referring to job satisfaction. Let's look at some findings about job satisfaction.

Are most people satisfied with their jobs? (  Go to www.prenhall.com/rolls) Studies of U.S. workers over the past 30 years generally indicate that the majority of workers were satisfied with their jobs. However, since the 1990s, the number of workers who say they're satisfied with their jobs has been declining. A Conference Board study in 1995 found that some 60 percent of Americans were satisfied with their jobs. By 2005, that percentage was down to 50 percent.[10] Although job satisfaction tends to increase as income increases, only 55 percent of individuals earning more than $50,000 are satisfied with their jobs. For individuals earning less than $15,000, about 45 percent of workers say they are satisfied with their jobs.[11] Does the fact that those with higher incomes have slightly higher levels of job satisfaction mean that money can buy happiness? Not necessarily. While it's possible that higher pay alone translates into higher job satisfaction, an alternative explanation is that higher pay reflects different types of jobs. Higher-paying jobs generally require more advanced skills, give jobholders greater responsibilities, are more stimulating and provide more challenges, and allow workers more control. It's more likely that the reports of higher satisfaction among higher-income levels reflect the greater challenge and freedom they have in their jobs rather than the pay itself.

**Global Job Satisfaction** What about employee job satisfaction levels in other countries? Although surveys of European workers, like U.S. workers, indicate generally lower levels of job satisfaction, there are some regional variations.[12] For instance, 68 percent of Scandinavian workers report that they are satisfied with their jobs, as do 61 percent of workers in France. But only 53 percent of Swiss and Italian workers, and 50 percent of German workers, report being satisfied with their jobs.[13] On the other hand, 60 percent of Canadian workers report being satisfied with their jobs as do 61 percent of employees from the Asia–Pacific region.[14]

What effect does job satisfaction have on employee behavior—that is, on productivity, absenteeism, and turnover? (  Go to www.prenhall.com/rolls)

**Satisfaction and Productivity** As a result of the Hawthorne Studies (discussed in Chapter 2), managers generalized that if their employees were satisfied with their jobs, then that satisfaction would translate to working hard. So, for a good part of the twentieth century, managers believed that happy workers were productive workers. Because it's not been that easy to determine whether job satisfaction caused job productivity or vice versa, some management researchers felt that belief was generally wrong. However, we can say with some certainty that the correlation between satisfaction and productivity is fairly strong.[15] And when satisfaction and productivity information is gathered for the organization as a whole, we find that organizations with more satisfied employees tend to be more effective than organizations with fewer satisfied employees.[16]

**Satisfaction and Absenteeism** Although research shows that satisfied employees have lower levels of absenteeism than do dissatisfied employees, the correlation isn't

---

**attitudes**
Evaluative statements—favorable or unfavorable—concerning objects, people, or events.

**cognitive component**
That part of an attitude that's made up of the beliefs, opinions, knowledge, or information held by a person.

**affective component**
That part of an attitude that's the emotional or feeling part.

**behavioral component**
That part of an attitude that refers to an intention to behave in a certain way.

For example, a recruiter for R&S Services Company who visits college campuses, identifies qualified job candidates, and sells them on the advantages of R&S as a good place to work would experience conflict if he personally believed that R&S had poor working conditions and few opportunities for promotion. This recruiter could, over time, find his attitudes toward R&S becoming more positive. He might actually convince himself by continually articulating the merits of working for the company. Another alternative is that the recruiter could become openly negative about R&S and the opportunities within the company for prospective applicants. The original enthusiasm that the recruiter might have shown would dwindle and probably be replaced by outright cynicism toward the company. Finally, the recruiter might acknowledge that R&S is an undesirable place to work, but as a professional recruiter, realize that his obligation is to present the positive aspects of working for the company. He might further rationalize that no workplace is perfect and that his job is not to present both sides of the issue but to present a favorable picture of the company.

## Cognitive Dissonance Theory

Q & A

Cognitive dissonance... now that's a strange-sounding thing. What is it? Go to Q & A 14.6 for an explanation.

Can we assume from this consistency principle that an individual's behavior can always be predicted if we know his or her attitude on a subject? The answer, unfortunately, is more complex than merely "yes" or "no." The reason is cognitive dissonance theory. ( ◆ Go to www.prenhall.com/rolls)

Cognitive dissonance theory sought to explain the relationship between attitudes and behavior.[31] **Cognitive dissonance** is any incompatibility or inconsistency between attitudes or between behavior and attitudes. The theory argued that any form of inconsistency is uncomfortable and that individuals will try to reduce the dissonance and, thus, the discomfort. In other words, individuals seek stability with a minimum of dissonance.

Of course, no one can completely avoid dissonance. You know that cheating on your tax return is wrong, but you "fudge" the numbers a bit every year and hope that you won't be audited. Or you tell your children to floss their teeth every day, but don't do it yourself. In each of these instances, there's an inconsistency between attitude and behavior. How do people cope with cognitive dissonance? The theory proposed that the desire to reduce dissonance is determined by the *importance* of the factors creating the dissonance, the degree of *influence* the individual believes he or she has over those factors, and the *rewards* that may be involved in dissonance.

If the factors creating the dissonance are relatively unimportant, the pressure to correct the inconsistency will be low. For instance, say that a corporate manager—Mrs. Sanchez—believes strongly that no company should treat assembly-line employees unfairly or inhumanely. Unfortunately, because of job requirements Mrs. Sanchez is placed in the position of having to make decisions that would trade off her company's profitability against her attitudes on compassionate treatment of employees. She knows that running an efficient manufacturing facility is in her company's best interest. What will she do? Clearly, Mrs. Sanchez will be experiencing a high degree of cognitive dissonance. Because of the *importance* of the issue to Mrs. Sanchez, we can't expect her to ignore the inconsistency, but there are things she can do to deal with her discomfort. She can change her behavior by using her authority to order that employees be treated fairly and humanely. Or she can reduce dissonance by concluding that the dissonant behavior isn't so important after all ("I've got to have a job, and in my role as a corporate decision maker, I often have to place the good of my company above that of society"). A third alternative would be for Mrs. Sanchez to change her attitude ("There's nothing wrong with the way our employees are treated. After all, they do have a job"). Still another choice would be for her to identify compatible factors that outweigh the dissonant ones ("The benefits to society from our giving people jobs more than offset the cost to society of not always treating employees compassionately").

The degree of *influence* that individuals believe they have over the factors also will affect their reaction to the dissonance. If they perceive the dissonance to be uncontrollable—something about which they have no choice—they're not likely to be receptive to attitude change or feel a need to do so. If, for example, the dissonance-producing behavior was required as a result of a manager's order, the pressure to reduce dissonance would be less than if the behavior had been performed voluntarily. Although dissonance would exist, it could be rationalized and justified by the need to follow the manager's orders—that is, the individual has no choice and control.

Finally, *rewards* also influence the degree to which individuals are motivated to reduce dissonance. Coupling high dissonance with high rewards tends to reduce the discomfort inherent in the dissonance, by motivating the individual to believe that there is consistency.

These moderating factors suggest that, just because individuals experience dissonance, doesn't mean they'll try to reduce it. If the issues contributing to the dissonance are of minimal importance, if an individual perceives that the dissonance is externally imposed and is substantially uncontrollable by him or her, or if rewards are significant enough to offset the dissonance, the individual will not be pressured to reduce the dissonance.

What are the behavioral implications of cognitive dissonance theory? It can help predict how likely individuals are to change their attitudes and behaviors. For example, if job demands require individuals to say or do things that contradict their personal attitudes, they'll tend to modify their attitude in order to make it compatible with the belief (cognition) of what they have said or done. In addition, the greater the dissonance—moderated by importance, influence, and reward factors—the greater the pressure to reduce it.

## Attitude Surveys

Many organizations regularly survey their employees about their attitudes.[32] Exhibit 14–2 shows what an attitude survey might look like. Typically, **attitude surveys** consist of a set of statements or questions that ask employees how they feel about their jobs, work groups, supervisors, or the organization.

Managers can get valuable feedback on how employees perceive their working conditions by using attitude surveys on a regular basis. It can help them see that policies and practices they view as objective and fair may be seen as inequitable by employees in general or by certain groups of employees. The regular use of attitude surveys, therefore, can alert managers to potential problems and employees' intentions early enough to do something about them.[33] For instance, managers at the Tennessee Valley

*Employees at Eaton Corp., a manufacturer in Cleveland, complete an employee survey every year to help their company measure manager effectiveness and improve operations. "The responses from our employees really do drive [management] actions," says the company's vice president for human resources. "The responses are as much a component of our business strategies as financial and succession planning."*

**cognitive dissonance**
Any incompatibility or inconsistency between attitudes or between behavior and attitudes.

**attitude surveys**
Surveys that ask employees how they feel about their jobs, work groups, supervisors, or the organization.

Exhibit 14–2

**Sample Attitude Survey**

Please answer each of the following statements using the following rating scale:
5 = Strongly agree
4 = Agree
3 = Undecided
2 = Disagree
1 = Strongly disagree

| Statement | Rating |
|---|---|
| 1. This company is a pretty good place to work. | ____ |
| 2. I can get ahead in this company if I make the effort. | ____ |
| 3. This company's wage rates are competitive with those of other companies. | ____ |
| 4. Employee promotion decisions are handled fairly. | ____ |
| 5. I understand the various fringe benefits the company offers. | ____ |
| 6. My job makes the best use of my abilities. | ____ |
| 7. My workload is challenging but not burdensome. | ____ |
| 8. I have trust and confidence in my boss. | ____ |
| 9. I feel free to tell my boss what I think. | ____ |
| 10. I know what my boss expects of me. | ____ |

*Source:* Based on T. Lammers, "The Essential Employee Survey," *Inc.*, December 1992, pp. 159–161.

Authority, the largest U.S. government–run energy company, used a "Cultural Health Index" to measure employee attitudes. They found that business units that scored high on the attitude surveys were also the ones whose performance was high. For underperforming business units, early signs of potential trouble had shown up in the attitude surveys.[34]

## Implications for Managers

**Diversity**

Diversity is one area where people can have fairly intense feelings. How would you handle such a situation? Try Diversity in Action #3.

Managers should be interested in employees' attitudes because they influence behavior. ( Go to www.prenhall.com/rolls) Satisfied and committed employees, for instance, have lower rates of turnover and absenteeism. Given that managers want to keep resignations and absences down—especially among their more productive employees—they'll want to do the things that will generate positive job attitudes.

The findings about the satisfaction–productivity relationships also have important implications for managers. Just simply trying to make employees happy on the assumption that their being happy will lead to high productivity is probably misdirected. Managers who follow this strategy might end up with a content, but unproductive, group of employees. Instead, managers should focus on those factors conducive to high levels of employee job satisfaction: mentally challenging work, equitable rewards, supportive working conditions, and supportive colleagues.[35] These factors are likely to help employees be more productive.

**Q & A**

As a manager, why should I know about cognitive dissonance? Q & A 14.7 discusses why.

Finally, managers should also recognize that employees will try to reduce dissonance. ( Go to www.prenhall.com/rolls) If employees are required to do things that appear inconsistent to them or that are at odds with their attitudes, managers should remember that pressure to reduce the dissonance is minimized when the employee perceives that the dissonance is externally imposed and uncontrollable. The pressure is also decreased if rewards are significant enough to offset the dissonance. So the manager might point to external forces such as competitors, customers, or other factors when explaining the need to perform some work activity the individual may have some dissonance about. Or the manager can provide rewards that an individual desires in order to decrease his or her attempts to eliminate the dissonance.

# Learning Review

- Describe the three components of an attitude.
- Discuss the three job-related attitudes.
- Describe the impact job satisfaction has on employee behavior.

- Explain how individuals reconcile inconsistencies between attitudes and behavior.

## PERSONALITY

**Self-Assessment Library (S.A.L.)**

How would you describe your personality? Try S.A.L. #I.A.1 and see.

**Q & A**

Seeing how different people's personalities are is fun, but how will this help you be a better manager? Find out in Q & A 14.8.

"Let's face it, dating is a drag. There was a time when we thought the computer was going to make it all better... But most of us learned the hard way that finding someone who shares our love of film noir and obscure garage bands does not a perfect match make."[36] Now, however, Chemistry.com, an affiliate of online dating site Match.com, is trying to do something about making the whole dating process better. How? With in-depth personality assessment and profiling as a way to bring compatible singles together using scientific methods rather than relying on those online dating profiles that usually don't come close to portraying reality.

Personality. We all have one. Some of us are quiet and passive; others are loud and aggressive. When we describe people using terms such as *quiet, passive, loud, aggressive, ambitious, extroverted, loyal, tense,* or *sociable,* we're describing their personalities. An individual's **personality** is a unique combination of emotional, thought, and behavioral patterns that affect how a person reacts and interacts with others. (    Go to www.prenhall.com/rolls) Personality is most often described in terms of measurable traits that a person exhibits. We're interested in looking at personality because, just like attitudes, it too affects how and why people behave the way they do. (    Go to www.prenhall.com/rolls)

There are hundreds of personality traits. Over the years, researchers have attempted to focus specifically on which traits could be used to describe personality. Two approaches to classifying personality traits have received the most attention: the Myers-Briggs Type Indicator (MBTI®) and the Big Five Model.

*Despite taking a tough line on spending and focusing a major part of her efforts on the unglamorous issue of upgrading the city's water pipes, Shirley Franklin enjoys a 75 percent approval rating in her job as mayor of Atlanta, Georgia. Her no-nonsense approach to rooting out corruption and restoring trust in the government springs from role models like Coretta Scott King, along with what Franklin calls "the sheer will to get something done." She says of herself, "I have a tremendous ability to stay focused . . . and I'm willing to do whatever it takes that is legal . . . ethical, and moral to get there." It's obvious that Franklin's skills and personality have helped her get to where she is.*

**personality**
The unique combination of emotional, thought, and behavioral patterns that affect how a person reacts and interacts with others.

## MBTI®

One of the most popular approaches to classifying personality traits is a general personality assessment called the MBTI®. The MBTI® consists of more than a hundred questions asking people how they usually act or feel in different situations.[37] ( ⬥ Go to www.prenhall.com/rolls) The way you respond to these questions puts you at one end or another of four dimensions:

1. *Social interaction: Extrovert or Introvert (E or I).* An extrovert is someone who is outgoing, dominant, and often aggressive and who wants to change the world. Extroverts need a work environment that's varied and action oriented, that lets them be with others, and that gives them a variety of experiences. An individual who's shy and withdrawn and focuses on understanding the world is described as an introvert. Introverts prefer a work environment that is quiet and concentrated, that lets them be alone, and that gives them a chance to explore in depth a limited set of experiences.

2. *Preference for gathering data: Sensing or Intuitive (S or N).* Sensing types dislike new problems unless there are standard ways to solve them; they like an established routine, have a high need for closure, show patience with routine details, and tend to be good at precise work. On the other hand, intuitive types are individuals who like solving new problems, dislike doing the same thing over and over again, jump to conclusions, are impatient with routine details, and dislike taking time for precision.

3. *Preference for decision making: Feeling or Thinking (F or T).* Individuals who are feeling types are aware of other people and their feelings, like harmony, need occasional praise, dislike telling people unpleasant things, tend to be sympathetic, and relate well to most people. Thinking types are unemotional and uninterested in people's feelings, like analysis and putting things into logical order, are able to reprimand people and fire them when necessary, may seem hard-hearted, and tend to relate well only to other thinking types.

4. *Style of making decisions: Perceptive or Judgmental (P or J).* Perceptive types are curious, spontaneous, flexible, adaptable, and tolerant. They focus on starting a task, postpone decisions, and want to find out all about the task before starting it. Judgmental types are decisive, good planners, purposeful, and exacting. They focus on completing a task, make decisions quickly, and want only the information necessary to get a task done.

   Combining these preferences provides descriptions of 16 personality types. Exhibit 14–3 summarizes a few of them.

More than two million people a year take the MBTI® in the United States alone. Organizations that have used it include Apple Computer, AT&T, Citigroup, GE, and 3M, plus many hospitals, educational institutions, and even the U.S. Armed Forces. It may be somewhat surprising given its popularity, but there's no hard evidence that the MBTI® is a valid measure of personality. However, that doesn't seem to deter its widespread use in a variety of organizations.

How could the MBTI® help managers? Proponents of the assessment believe that it's important to know these personality types because they influence the way people interact and solve problems. For instance, if your boss is an intuitive type and you're a sensing type, you'll gather information in different ways. An intuitive type prefers gut reactions, whereas a sensor prefers facts. To work well with your boss, you would have to present more than just facts about a situation and bring out how you feel about it. Also, the MBTI® has been used to help managers select employees who are well matched to certain types of jobs.

## The Big Five Model

Although the MBTI® is popular, it lacks research evidence to support its validity. The same can't be said about the Big Five Model. In recent years, research has shown that

Exhibit 14–3

**Examples of MBTI®
Personality Types**

| Type | Description |
|---|---|
| INFJ (introvert, intuitive, feeling, judgmental) | Quietly forceful, conscientious, and concerned for others. Such people succeed by perseverance, originality, and the desire to do whatever is needed or wanted. They are often highly respected for their uncompromising principles. |
| ESTP (extrovert, sensing, thinking, perceptive) | Blunt and sometimes insensitive. Such people are matter-of-fact and do not worry or hurry. They enjoy whatever comes along. They work best with real things that can be assembled or disassembled. |
| ISFP (introvert, sensing, feeling, perceptive) | Sensitive, kind, modest, shy, and quietly friendly. Such people strongly dislike disagreements and will avoid them. They are loyal followers and quite often are relaxed about getting things done. |
| ENTJ (extrovert, intuitive, thinking, judgmental) | Warm, friendly, candid, and decisive; also usually skilled in anything that requires reasoning and intelligent talk, but may sometimes overestimate what they are capable of doing. |

*Source:* Based on I. Briggs-Myers, *Introduction to Type* (Palo Alto, CA: Consulting Psychologists Press, 1980), pp. 7–8.

five basic personality dimensions underlie all others and encompass most of the significant variation in human personality.[38] The five personality traits in the **Big Five Model** are:

1. *Extraversion.* The degree to which someone is sociable, talkative, and assertive.
2. *Agreeableness.* The degree to which someone is good-natured, cooperative, and trusting.
3. *Conscientiousness.* The degree to which someone is responsible, dependable, persistent, and achievement oriented.
4. *Emotional stability.* The degree to which someone is calm, enthusiastic, and secure (positive) or tense, nervous, depressed, and insecure (negative).
5. *Openness to experience.* The degree to which someone is imaginative, artistically sensitive, and intellectual.

The Big Five provide more than just a personality framework. Research has shown that important relationships exist between these personality dimensions and job performance. For example, one study examined five categories of occupations: *professionals* (such as engineers, architects, and attorneys), *police, managers, salespeople,* and *semiskilled and skilled employees.*[39] Job performance was defined in terms of employee performance ratings, training competence, and personnel data such as salary level. The results of the study showed that conscientiousness predicted job performance for all five occupational groups. Predictions for the other personality dimensions depended on the situation and on the occupational group. For example, extraversion predicted performance in managerial and sales positions—occupations in which high social interaction is necessary. Openness to experience was found to be important in predicting training competency. Ironically, emotional security wasn't positively related to job performance. Although you might expect calm and secure workers to perform better than nervous ones, that wasn't the case. This might reflect

**Big-Five Model**
Five-factor model of personality.

*Dr. Paul Farmer, shown here at work in Africa, is the founder of Partners In Health, a highly respected system for delivering public health services to the poor of Haiti, Peru, Russia, Mexico, Guatemala, Rwanda, and its headquarters city of Boston. "What set him apart as a young man," says Ophelia Dahl, president of Partners In Health, who has known Farmer for years, "was his ability to envision things that no one else could. A lot of young people go to places like Haiti and see the desperate conditions, but . . . Paul saw an opportunity, drew up a plan, and saw it through." Farmer's conscientiousness is characteristic of someone with an internal locus of control.*

that it's more likely that emotionally stable workers often keep their jobs while emotionally unstable workers often do not. Given that all the people who participated in the study were employed, the variance on that dimension was small and insignificant.

## Additional Personality Insights

In addition to the Big Five Model, personality researchers have identified five other personality traits that have proved to be the most powerful in explaining individual behavior in organizations. These are *locus of control, Machiavellianism, self-esteem, self-monitoring,* and *risk propensity.*

1. *Locus of control.* Some people believe that they control their own fate. Others see themselves as pawns, believing that what happens to them in their lives is due to luck or chance. The **locus of control** in the first case is *internal*; these people believe that they control their own destiny. The locus of control in the second case is *external*; these people believe that their lives are controlled by outside forces.[40] Research evidence indicates that employees who rate high on externality are less satisfied with their jobs, more alienated from the work setting, and less involved in their jobs than are those who rate high on internality.[41] A manager might also expect externals to blame a poor performance evaluation on their boss's prejudice, their co-workers, or other events outside their control; internals would explain the same evaluation in terms of their own actions.

2. *Machiavellianism.* The second characteristic is called **Machiavellianism** (Mach) named after Niccolo Machiavelli, who wrote in the sixteenth century on how to gain and manipulate power. An individual who is high in Machiavellianism is pragmatic, maintains emotional distance, and believes that ends can justify means.[42] "If it works, use it" or "I'm prepared to do whatever I have to do to get ahead" are consistent with a high Mach perspective. Do high Machs make good employees? That depends on the type of job and whether you consider ethical factors in evaluating performance. In jobs that require bargaining skills (such as a purchasing manager) or that have substantial rewards for winning (such as a salesperson working on commission), high Machs can be productive. In jobs in which ends do not justify the means or that lack absolute measures of performance, it's difficult to predict the performance of high Machs. (  Go to www.prenhall.com/rolls)

3. *Self-esteem.* People differ in the degree to which they like or dislike themselves. This trait is called **self-esteem**.[43] The research on self-esteem (SE) offers some interesting insights into organizational behavior. For example, self-esteem is directly related to expectations for success. High SEs believe that they possess

Self-Assessment
Library (S.A.L.)

Are you a high mach?
Do S.A.L. #II.C.1 and see.

the ability they need in order to succeed at work. Individuals with high SEs take more risks in job selection and are more likely to choose unconventional jobs than are people with low SEs. (  Go to www.prenhall.com/rolls)

The most common finding on self-esteem is that low SEs are more susceptible to external influence than are high SEs. Low SEs are dependent on receiving positive evaluations from others. As a result, they're more likely to seek approval from others and are more prone to conform to the beliefs and behaviors of those they respect than are high SEs. In managerial positions, low SEs will tend to be concerned with pleasing others and, therefore, will be less likely to take unpopular stands than are high SEs.

Not surprisingly, self-esteem has also been found to be related to job satisfaction. A number of studies confirm that high SEs are more satisfied with their jobs than are low SEs.

4. *Self-monitoring.* Another personality trait that has received increasing attention is called **self-monitoring**.[44] It refers to an individual's ability to adjust his or her behavior to external, situational factors. Individuals high in self-monitoring show considerable adaptability in adjusting their behavior. They're highly sensitive to external cues and can behave differently in different situations. High self-monitors are capable of presenting striking contradictions between their public persona and their private selves. Low self-monitors can't adjust their behavior. They tend to display their true dispositions and attitudes in every situation, and there's high behavioral consistency between who they are and what they do.

Research indicates that high self-monitors pay closer attention to the behavior of others and are more flexible than are low self-monitors.[45] In addition, high self-monitoring managers tend to be more mobile in their careers, receive more promotions (both internal and cross-organizational), and are more likely to occupy central positions in an organization.[46] We might also hypothesize that high self-monitors will be successful in managerial positions that require them to play multiple, and even contradictory, roles. The high self-monitor is capable of putting on different "faces" for different audiences. And research shows that high self-monitors tend to engage in **impression management**, which is when individuals attempt to control the impression others form of them.[47] (  Go to www.prenhall.com/rolls)

5. *Risk taking.* People differ in their willingness to take chances. Differences in the propensity to assume or to avoid risk have been shown to affect how long it takes managers to make a decision and how much information they require before making their choice. For instance, in one study, a group of managers worked on simulated exercises that required them to make hiring decisions.[48] High risk-taking managers took less time to make decisions and used less information in making their choices than did low-risk taking managers. Interestingly, the decision accuracy was the same for the two groups. To maximize organizational effectiveness, managers should try to align employee risk-taking propensity with specific job demands. (Look back at our chapter-opening case.) For instance, high risk-taking propensity may lead to effective performance for a commodities trader in a brokerage firm because this type of job demands rapid decision making. On the other hand, high risk-taking propensity might prove a major obstacle to accountants auditing financial statements.

---

**locus of control**
The degree to which people believe they control their own fate.

**Machiavellianism**
The degree to which people are pragmatic, maintain emotional distance, and believe that ends justify means.

**self-esteem**
An individual's degree of like or dislike for himself or herself.

**self-monitoring**
An individual's ability to adjust his or her behavior to external situational factors.

**impression management**
When individuals attempt to control the impression others form of them.

*Michael O'Leary is not afraid to take risks. As CEO of Ryanair, the most profitable airline in Europe, he's so focused on keeping down the costs of running his airline that he's even removed the planes' seat-back pockets, to eliminate the cost of cleaning them and to reduce the weight of the planes. Revenues recently rose an astonishing 20 percent, even though O'Leary charges passengers for baggage check-in and snacks. He's sold ad space on the exteriors of his planes, is considering in-flight gambling to boost profits, and is looking for ways to capture part of the fees earned by airport parking lots and concession stands. The ultimate goal of all his cost-cutting and innovative revenue streams is to someday allow passengers to fly for free. On Ryanair, a quarter of them already do.*

## Personality Types in Different Cultures

Do personality frameworks, like the Big Five Model, transfer across cultures? Are dimensions like locus of control relevant in all cultures? Let's try to answer these questions.

The five personality factors studied in the Big Five Model appear in almost all cross-cultural studies.[49] This includes a wide variety of diverse cultures such as China, Israel, Germany, Japan, Spain, Nigeria, Norway, Pakistan, and the United States. Differences are found in the emphasis on dimensions. Chinese, for example, use the category of conscientiousness more often and use the category of agreeableness less often than do Americans. But there is a surprisingly high amount of agreement, especially among individuals from developed countries. As a case in point, a comprehensive review of studies covering people from the European Community found that conscientiousness was a valid predictor of performance across jobs and occupational groups.[50] This is exactly what U.S. studies have found.

We know that there are certainly no common personality types for a given country. You can, for instance, find high risk takers and low risk takers in almost any culture. Yet a country's culture influences the *dominant* personality characteristics of its people. We can see this effect of national culture by looking at one of the personality traits we just discussed: locus of control.

National cultures differ in terms of the degree to which people believe they control their environment. For instance, North Americans believe that they can dominate their environment; other societies, such as those in Middle Eastern countries, believe that life is essentially predetermined. Notice how closely this distinction parallels the concept of internal and external locus of control. On the basis of this particular cultural characteristic, we should expect a larger proportion of internals in the U.S. and Canadian workforces than in the workforces of Saudi Arabia or Iran.

As we have seen throughout this section, personality traits influence employees' behavior. For global managers, understanding how personality traits differ takes on added significance when looking at it from the perspective of national culture.[51]

## Emotions and Emotional Intelligence

"Trying to sell wedding gowns to anxious brides-to-be" can be quite a stressful experience for the salesperson, needless to say. To help its employees stay "cheery," David's Bridal, a chain of over 260 stores, relied on research into joyful emotions. Now, when

## *focus on* **Leadership**

### Know Thyself

"He who knows others is wise; he who knows himself is enlightened."
—Chinese philosopher, Lao-Tzu (640 BC–531 BC)

Studies have indicated that emotional intelligence (EI)—more than intelligence, expertise, or any other single factor—is the best predictor of who will emerge as a leader.[52] Intelligence and technical abilities are "threshold capabilities"—necessary, but not sufficient requirements for leadership. It's having EI that allows an individual to become a star performer. For instance, Meg Whitman, CEO of eBay, is a leader with high emotional intelligence. She is described as self-confident, trustworthy, culturally sensitive, a high achiever, and expert at building teams and leading change. Without EI, a person can have outstanding training, a highly analytical mind, a long-term vision, and an endless supply of creative ideas, but still not make a great leader. One of the components of EI—self-awareness—is particularly important. Self-aware leaders tend to be the best performers because they are able to change their behavior and adapt to changes in the organizational environment.

The self-assessment exercises included in the Self-Assessment Library on www.prenhall.com/rolls can help you become "enlightened." Will you become a "great" leader by knowing yourself and your skills, abilities, and interests?

"faced with an indecisive bride," salespeople have been taught emotional coping techniques and know how to focus on "things that bring them joy."[53]

We can't leave the topic of personality without looking at another important behavioral aspect—emotions, especially since how we respond emotionally and how we deal with our emotions can be functions of our personality. **Emotions** are intense feelings that are directed at someone or something. They're object specific; that is, emotions are reactions to an object.[54] For instance, when a work colleague criticizes you for the way you spoke to a client, you might become angry at him. That is, you show emotion (anger) toward a specific object (your colleague). Since employees bring an emotional component with them to work every day, managers need to understand the role that emotions play in employee behavior.[55]

How many emotions are there? Although you could probably name several dozen, research has identified six universal emotions: anger, fear, sadness, happiness, disgust, and surprise.[56] Do these six basic emotions surface in the workplace? Absolutely! I get *angry* after receiving a poor performance appraisal. I *fear* that I could be laid off as a result of a company cutback. I'm *sad* about one of my co-workers leaving to take a new job in another city. I'm *happy* after being selected as employee-of-the-month. I'm *disgusted* with the way my supervisor treats women on our team. And I'm *surprised* to find out that management plans a complete restructuring of the company's retirement program.

People respond differently to identical emotion-provoking stimuli. In some cases, this can be attributed to the individual's personality because people vary in their inherent ability to express emotions. For instance, you undoubtedly know people who almost never show their feelings. They rarely get angry. They never show rage. In contrast, you probably also know people who seem to be on an emotional roller coaster. When they're happy, they're ecstatic. When they're sad, they're deeply depressed. And two people can be in the exact same situation—one showing excitement and joy, the other remaining calm and collected.

However, at other times how people respond is a result of job requirements. Jobs make different demands in terms of what types and how much emotion needs to be displayed. For instance, air traffic controllers and trial judges are expected to be calm and controlled, even in stressful situations. On the other hand, the effectiveness of public-address announcers at sporting events and lawyers can depend on their ability to alter their emotional intensity as the need arises.

**emotions**
Intense feelings that are directed at someone or something.

One area of emotions research that's offered interesting insights into personality is **emotional intelligence (EI)**, which is the ability to notice and to manage emotional cues and information.[57] It's composed of five dimensions:

| | |
|---|---|
| *Self-awareness:* | Being aware of what you're feeling |
| *Self-management:* | Being able to manage your emotions and impulses |
| *Self-motivation:* | Being able to persist in the face of setbacks and failures |
| *Empathy:* | Being aware of how others are feeling |
| *Social skills:* | Being able to handle the emotions of others |

EI has been shown to be positively related to job performance at all levels. For instance, one study looked at the characteristics of Lucent Technologies' engineers who were rated as stars by their peers. The researchers concluded that stars were better at relating to others. That is, it was EI, not academic intelligence, that characterized high performers. A study of Air Force recruiters generated similar findings. Top-performing recruiters exhibited high levels of EI. Despite these findings, EI has been a controversial topic in OB. Supporters of the concept say that EI has intuitive appeal and predicts behavior that's important.[58] Critics say that EI is vague, can't be measured, and has questionable validity.[59] What can we conclude from these results? One thing is for sure—EI is here to stay. Also, EI appears to be especially relevant to success in jobs that demand a high degree of social interaction. (  Go to www.prenhall.com/rolls)

Self-Assessment Library (S.A.L.)

How would you score on emotional intelligence? Go to S.A.L. #I.E.1 and find out!

## Implications for Managers

The major value in understanding personality differences probably lies in employee selection. Managers are likely to have higher-performing and more-satisfied employees if consideration is given to matching personalities with jobs. The best-documented personality–job fit theory has been developed by psychologist John Holland.[60] His theory states that an employee's satisfaction with his or her job, as well as his or her likelihood of leaving that job, depends on the degree to which the individual's personality matches the occupational environment. Holland identified six basic personality types. Exhibit 14–4 describes each of the six types, their personality characteristics, and sample occupations.

**Exhibit 14–4**

**Holland's Typology of Personality and Sample Occupations**

| Type | Personality Characteristics | Sample Occupations |
|---|---|---|
| *Realistic.* Prefers physical activities that require skill, strength, and coordination. | Shy, genuine, persistent, stable, conforming, practical | Mechanic, drill press operator, assembly-line worker, farmer |
| *Investigative.* Prefers activities involving thinking, organizing, and understanding. | Analytical, original, curious, independent | Biologist, economist, mathematician, news reporter |
| *Social.* Prefers activities that involve helping and developing others. | Sociable, friendly, cooperative, understanding | Social worker, teacher, counselor clinical psychologist |
| *Conventional.* Prefers rule-regulated, orderly, and unambiguous activities. | Conforming, efficient, practical, unimaginative, inflexible | Accountant, corporate manager, bank teller, file clerk |
| *Enterprising.* Prefers verbal activities in which there are opportunities to influence others and attain power. | Self-confident, ambitious, energetic, domineering | Lawyer, real estate agent, public relations specialist, small business manager |
| *Artistic.* Prefers ambiguous and unsystematic activities that allow creative expression. | Imaginative, disorderly, idealistic, emotional, impractical | Painter, musician, writer, interior decorator |

*Source:* Based on J. L. Holland, *Making Vocational Choices: A Theory of Vocational Personalities and Work Environments* (Odessa, FL: Psychological Assessment Resources, 1997).

Holland's theory proposes that satisfaction is highest and turnover lowest when personality and occupation are compatible. Social individuals should be in "people" type jobs, and so forth. A realistic person in a realistic job will be more satisfied than a realistic person in an investigative job. The key points of this theory are that (1) there do appear to be intrinsic differences in personality among individuals; (2) there are different types of jobs; and (3) people in job environments compatible with their personality types should be more satisfied and less likely to resign voluntarily than should people in incongruent jobs. In addition, personality concepts are particularly important in service settings since a worker's emotional state influences customer service, which influences whether a customer is satisfied enough to come back.[61]

In addition, there are other benefits to a manager's understanding of personality. By recognizing that people approach problem solving, decision making, and job interactions differently, a manager can better understand why, for instance, an employee is uncomfortable with making quick decisions or why another employee insists on gathering as much information as possible before addressing a problem. Or, for instance, managers can expect that individuals with an external locus of control may be less satisfied with their jobs than internals and also that they may be less willing to accept responsibility for their actions. Also, managers need to recognize that personality traits, especially conscientiousness, play a role in driving employee motivation.[62]

Finally, being a successful manager and accomplishing goals means working well with others both inside and outside the organization. In order to work effectively together, you need to understand each other. This understanding comes, at least in part, from recognizing the ways in which people differ from each other—that is, from an appreciation of personality traits and emotions.

## Learning Review

- Contrast the MBTI® and the Big Five Model of personality.
- Describe the five personality traits that have proved to be the most powerful in explaining individual behavior in organizations.

- Tell how emotions and emotional intelligence impact behavior.

## PERCEPTION

**Q & A**

If people perceive things differently how can a manager ever decide the best way to manage? Q & A 14.9 explains.

Nadia Aman, Mirza Baig, M. Yusuf Mohamed, and Ammar Barhouty have three things in common. They're all young, Muslim, and work for the U.S. federal government. Since 9/11, their lives have changed—mostly due to stereotypes that co-workers and the public have of Muslims.[63] Stereotyping shapes how we make judgments about others and is one of the ways that perception influences employee behavior.

**Perception** is a process by which individuals give meaning to their environment by organizing and interpreting their sensory impressions. Research on perception consistently demonstrates that individuals may look at the same thing yet perceive it differently. ( ◆ Go to www.prenhall.com/rolls) One manager, for instance, can interpret the fact that her assistant regularly takes several days to make important decisions as evidence that the assistant is slow, disorganized, and afraid to make decisions. Another manager with the same assistant might interpret the same tendency as evidence that the assistant is thoughtful, thorough, and deliberate. The first manager would probably evaluate her assistant negatively; the second manager would probably evaluate the person positively. The point is that none of us sees reality. We interpret what we see and call it reality. And, of course, as the example shows, we behave according to our perceptions.

---

**emotional intelligence (EI)**
The ability to notice and to manage emotional cues and information.

**perception**
The process of organizing and interpreting sensory impressions in order to give meaning to the environment.

*Costco started out much like other warehouse clubs, carrying cut-rate groceries and office supplies in bulk packages amid a spartan environment. But CEO Jim Sinegal has been slowly and steadily changing customers' perceptions of the store by upgrading the merchandise and adopting a "treasure hunt" strategy to raise customers' expectations of what they'll find on any given trip to the store. Right next to crates of toilet paper and stacks of tires you might find a 42-inch plasma TV, a Lalique crystal vase, fresh lobster, wine and champagne, or even a diamond ring. Says one well-heeled shopper, "I find better deals here on high-end stuff than I do at Neiman Marcus or Saks. You don't get the box, but so what?"*

## Factors That Influence Perception

How do we explain the fact that people can perceive the same thing differently? A number of factors act to shape and sometimes distort perception. These factors can reside in the *perceiver*; in the object, or *target*, being perceived; or in the context of the *situation* in which the perception occurs.

**The Perceiver** When an individual looks at a target and attempts to interpret what he or she sees, the individual's personal characteristics will heavily influence the interpretation. These personal characteristics include attitudes, personality, motives, interests, experiences, and expectations.

**The Target** The characteristics of the target being observed can also affect what's perceived. Loud people are more likely than quiet people to be noticed in a group. So, too, are extremely attractive or unattractive individuals. Because targets aren't looked at in isolation, the relationship of a target to its background also influences perception, as does our tendency to group close things and similar things together. You can experience these tendencies by looking at the visual perception examples shown in Exhibit 14–5. Notice how what you see changes as you look differently at each one.

**The Situation** The context in which we see objects or events is also important. The time at which an object or event is seen can influence attention, as can location, light, heat, color, and any number of other situational factors.

Exhibit 14–5

**Perception Challenges: What Do You See?**

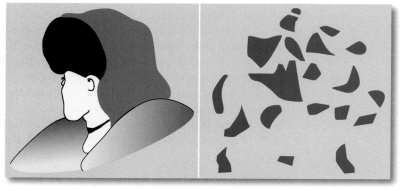

Old woman or young woman?          A knight on a horse?

## Attribution Theory

Much of the research on perception is directed at inanimate objects. Managers, though, are more concerned with people. Our discussion of perception, therefore, should focus on how we perceive people.

Our perceptions of people differ from our perception of inanimate objects because we make inferences about the behaviors of people that we don't make about objects. Objects don't have beliefs, motives, or intentions; people do. The result is that when we observe an individual's behavior, we try to explain why they behave in certain ways. Our perception and judgment of a person's actions, therefore, will be significantly influenced by the assumptions we make about the person.

**Attribution theory** was developed to explain how we judge people differently depending on what meaning we attribute to a given behavior.[64] Basically, the theory suggests that when we observe an individual's behavior, we attempt to determine whether it was internally or externally caused. Internally caused behaviors are those that are believed to be under the personal control of the individual. Externally caused behavior results from outside factors; that is, the person is forced into the behavior by the situation. That determination, however, depends on three factors: distinctiveness, consensus, and consistency.

*Distinctiveness* refers to whether an individual displays different behaviors in different situations. Is the employee who arrived late today the same person that some employees are complaining is a "goof-off"? What we want to know is whether this behavior is unusual. If it's unusual, the observer is likely to attribute the behavior to external forces, something beyond the control of the person. However, if the behavior isn't unusual, or distinctive, it will probably be judged as internal.

If everyone who's faced with a similar situation responds in the same way, we can say the behavior shows *consensus*. A tardy employee's behavior would meet this criterion if all employees who took the same route to work were also late. From an attribution perspective, if consensus is high, you're likely to give an external attribution to the employee's tardiness; that is, some outside factor—maybe road construction or a traffic accident—caused the behavior. However, if other employees who come the same way to work made it on time, you would conclude that the cause of the late behavior was internal.

Finally, an observer looks for *consistency* in a person's actions. Does the person engage in the behaviors regularly and consistently? Does the person respond the same way over time? Coming in 10 minutes late for work isn't perceived in the same way if, for one employee, it represents an unusual case (she hasn't been late in months), while for another employee, it's part of a routine pattern (she's late two or three times every week). The more consistent the behavior, the more the observer is inclined to attribute it to internal causes. (  Go to www.prenhall.com/rolls)

**Q & A**
Do managers really use attribution theory? Check out Q & A 14.10 and see.

Exhibit 14–6 summarizes the key elements of attribution theory. It would tell us, for instance, that if an employee—let's call him Mr. Liu—generally performs at or about the same level on other related tasks as he does on his current task (low distinctiveness), if other employees frequently perform differently (better or worse) than Mr. Liu does on that current task (low consensus), and if Mr. Liu's performance on this current task is consistent over time (high consistency), his manager or anyone else who is judging Mr. Liu's work is likely to hold him primarily responsible for his task performance (internal attribution).

One of the most interesting findings drawn from attribution theory is that there are errors or biases that distort attributions. For instance, there's substantial evidence that when we make judgments about the behavior of other people, we have a tendency to *under*estimate the influence of external factors and to *over*estimate the influence of

**attribution theory**
A theory that explains how we judge people differently depending on the meaning we attribute to a given behavior.

Exhibit 14–6

**Attribution Theory**

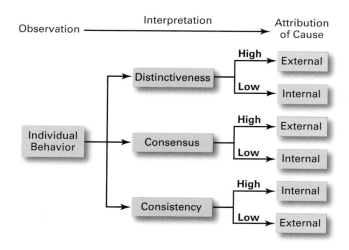

**Q & A**

So why is knowing about the fundamental attribution error important? See Q & A 14.11 for an answer.

internal or personal factors.[65] This tendency is called the **fundamental attribution error** and can explain why a sales manager may be prone to attribute the poor performance of her sales representative to laziness rather than to the innovative product line introduced by a competitor. ( ▰ Go to www.prenhall.com/rolls) There's also a tendency, called the **self-serving bias**, in which individuals attribute their own successes to internal factors such as ability or effort while putting the blame for personal failure on external factors such as luck. This suggests that feedback provided to employees in performance reviews is likely to be predictably distorted by them depending on whether it's positive or negative.

Are these errors or biases that distort attributions universal across different cultures? The evidence is mixed, but most suggests that there are cultural differences.[66] For instance, a study of Korean managers found that, contrary to the self-serving bias, they tended to accept responsibility for group failure "because I was not a capable leader" instead of attributing it to group members.[67] Attribution theory was developed largely based on experiments with Americans and Western Europeans. But the Korean study suggests caution in making attribution theory predictions in non-Western societies, especially in countries with strong collectivist traditions.

## Shortcuts Frequently Used in Judging Others

Perceiving and interpreting what others do is a lot of work so we use a number of shortcuts to make the task more manageable. These techniques are valuable as they let us make accurate perceptions rapidly and provide valid data for making predictions. However, they aren't perfect. They can and do get us into trouble. An understanding of these shortcuts can be helpful for recognizing when they can result in significant distortions.

It's easy to judge others if we assume that they're similar to us. In **assumed similarity**, or the "like me" effect, the observer's perception of others is influenced more by the observer's own characteristics than by those of the person observed. For example, if you want challenges and responsibility in your job, you'll assume that others want the same. People who assume that others are like them can, of course, be right, but most of the time they're wrong.

When we judge someone on the basis of our perception of a group he or she is part of, we're using the shortcut called **stereotyping**. For instance, "Married people are more stable employees than single persons" and "Union people expect something for nothing" are examples of stereotyping. To the degree that a stereotype is based on fact, it may produce accurate judgments. However, many stereotypes have no foundation in fact and thus distort judgment.[68]

When we form a general impression about a person on the basis of a single characteristic, such as intelligence, sociability, or appearance, we're being influenced by the **halo effect**. This effect frequently occurs when students evaluate their classroom instructor. Students may isolate a single trait such as enthusiasm and allow their entire evaluation to be slanted by the perception of this one trait. An instructor may be quiet, assured, knowledgeable, and highly qualified, but if his classroom teaching style lacks enthusiasm, he might be rated lower on a number of other characteristics.

## Implications for Managers

Managers need to recognize that their employees react to perceptions, not to reality. So whether a manager's appraisal of an employee is actually objective and unbiased or whether the organization's wage levels are among the highest in the community is less relevant than what employees perceive them to be. If individuals perceive appraisals to be biased or wage levels low, they'll behave as if those conditions actually exist. Employees organize and interpret what they see, so there is always the potential for perceptual distortion.

The message to managers should be clear: Pay close attention to how employees perceive both their jobs and management actions. Remember, the valuable employee who quits because of an inaccurate perception is just as great a loss to an organization as the valuable employee who quits for a valid reason.

## Learning Review

- Explain how an understanding of perception can help managers better understand individual behavior.
- Describe the key elements of attribution theory.
- Discuss how the fundamental attribution error and self-serving bias can distort attributions.
- Name three shortcuts used in judging others.

## LEARNING

The last individual behavior concept we're going to introduce is learning. It's included for the obvious reason that almost all complex behavior is learned. If we want to explain, predict, and influence behavior, we need to understand how people learn.

What is learning? The definition used by psychologists is considerably broader than the average person's view that "it's what we do in school." We define **learning** as any relatively permanent change in behavior that occurs as a result of experience. In actuality, each of us is constantly learning from our experiences. How do people learn, then? We're going to look at two learning theories relevant to understanding how and why individual behavior occurs: operant conditioning and social learning. Then, we'll discuss how managers can use learning principles to shape employees' behaviors.

### Operant Conditioning

**Operant conditioning** argues that behavior is a function of its consequences. People learn to behave to get something they want or to avoid something they don't want. Operant behavior describes voluntary or learned behavior in contrast to reflexive or unlearned behavior. The tendency to repeat learned behavior is influenced by the reinforcement or lack of reinforcement that happens as a result of the behavior. Reinforcement, therefore, strengthens a behavior and increases the likelihood that it will be repeated.

---

**fundamental attribution error**
The tendency to underestimate the influence of external factors and overestimate the influence of internal factors when judging other's behavior.

**self-serving bias**
The tendency for individuals to attribute their own successes to internal factors while putting the blame for failures on external factors.

**assumed similarity**
The belief that others are like oneself.

**stereotyping**
Judging a person on the basis of one's perception of a group to which he or she belongs

**halo effect**
A general impression of an individual based on a single characteristic.

**learning**
Any relatively permanent change in behavior that occurs as a result of experience.

**operant conditioning**
A type of learning in which desired voluntary behavior leads to a reward or prevents a punishment.

Building on earlier work in the field, B. F. Skinner's research widely expanded our knowledge of operant conditioning.[69] Even his most outspoken critics admit that his operant concepts work.

Behavior is assumed to be determined from without—that is, *learned*—rather than from within—reflexive or unlearned. Skinner argued that creating pleasing and desirable consequences to follow some specific behavior would increase the frequency of that behavior. People will most likely engage in desired behaviors if they are positively reinforced for doing so; and rewards are most effective if they immediately follow the desired response. In addition, behavior that isn't rewarded or is punished is less likely to be repeated.

You see examples of operant conditioning everywhere. Any situation in which it's either explicitly stated or implicitly suggested that reinforcement (rewards) is contingent on some action on your part is an example of operant conditioning. Your instructor says that if you want a high grade in this course, you must perform well on tests by giving correct answers. A salesperson working on commission knows that earning a sizable income is contingent upon generating high sales in his or her territory. Of course, the linkage between behavior and reinforcement can also work to teach the individual to behave in ways that work against the best interests of the organization. Assume that your boss tells you that if you'll work overtime during the next 3-week busy season, you'll be compensated for it at the next performance appraisal. Then, when performance appraisal time comes, you are given no positive reinforcements (such as being praised for pitching in and helping out when needed). What will you do the next time your boss asks you to work overtime? You'll probably refuse. Your behavior can be explained by operant conditioning: If a behavior isn't positively reinforced, the probability that the behavior will be repeated declines.

## *managing your* **Career**

### Learning to Get Along with Difficult People

We've all been around people who are, to put it nicely, difficult to get along with. These people might be chronic complainers, they might be meddlers who think they know everything about everyone else's job and don't hesitate to tell you so, or they might exhibit any number of other unpleasant interpersonal characteristics. They can make your job as a manager extremely hard and your workday very stressful if you don't know how to deal with them. Being around difficult people tends to bring out the worst in all of us. What can you do? How do you learn to get along with these difficult people?[70]

Getting along with difficult people takes a little bit of patience, planning, and preparation. What you need is an approach that helps you diffuse a lot of the negative aspects of dealing with these individuals. For instance, it helps to write down a detailed description of the person's behavior. Describe what this person does that bothers you. Then, try to understand that behavior. Put yourself in that person's shoes and attempt to see things from his or her perspective. Doing these things initially might help you better understand, predict, and influence behavior.

Unfortunately, trying to understand the person usually isn't enough for getting along. You'll also need some specific strategies for coping with different types of difficult personalities. Here are some of the most common types of difficult people you'll meet and some strategies for dealing with them.

*The Hostile, Aggressive Types*  With this type, you need to stand up for yourself; give them time to run down; don't worry about being polite; just jump in if you need to; get their attention carefully; get them to sit down; speak from your own point of view; avoid a head-on fight; and be ready to be friendly.

*The Complainers*  With the complainers you need to listen attentively; acknowledge their concerns; be prepared to interrupt their litany of complaints; don't agree, but do acknowledge what they're saying; state facts without comment or apology; and switch them to problem solving.

*The Silent or Nonresponsive Types*  With this type, you need to ask open-ended questions; use the friendly, silent stare; don't fill the silent pauses for them in conversations; comment on what's happening; and help break the tension by making them feel more at ease.

*The Know-It-All Experts*  The keys to dealing with this type are be on top of things; listen and acknowledge their comments; question firmly, but don't confront; avoid being a counterexpert; and work with them to channel their energy in positive directions.

## Social Learning

Some 60 percent of the Radio City Rockettes have danced in prior seasons. The veterans help newcomers with "Rockette style"—where to place their hands, how to hold their hands, how to keep up stamina, and so forth.[71]

As the Rockettes are well aware, individuals also can learn by observing what happens to other people and just by being told about something as well as by direct experiences. So, for example, much of what we have learned comes from watching others (models)—parents, teachers, peers, television and movie actors, managers, and so forth. (  Go to www.prenhall.com/rolls) This view that we can learn both through observation and direct experience is called **social learning theory**.

The influence of others is central to the social learning viewpoint. The amount of influence that these models will have on an individual is determined by four processes:

1. *Attentional processes.* People learn from a model only when they recognize and pay attention to its critical features. We tend to be most influenced by models who are attractive, repeatedly available, thought to be important, or are seen as similar to us.

2. *Retention processes.* A model's influence will depend on how well the individual remembers the model's action, even after the model is no longer readily available.

3. *Motor reproduction processes.* After a person has seen a new behavior by observing the model, the watching must become doing. This process then demonstrates that the individual can actually do the modeled activities.

4. *Reinforcement processes.* Individuals will be motivated to exhibit the modeled behavior if positive incentives or rewards are provided. Behaviors that are reinforced will be given more attention, learned better, and performed more often.

## Shaping: A Managerial Tool

Because learning takes place on the job as well as prior to it, managers are concerned with how they can teach employees to behave in ways that most benefit the organization. Thus, managers will often attempt to "mold" individuals by guiding their learning in graduated steps. This process is called **shaping behavior**.

Consider the situation in which an employee's behavior is significantly different from that sought by his or her manager. If the manager reinforced the individual only when he or she showed desirable responses, there might be very little reinforcement taking place. In such a case, shaping offers a logical approach toward achieving the desired behavior.

We shape behavior by systematically reinforcing each successive step that moves the individual closer to the desired behavior. If an employee who has chronically been a half-hour late for work comes in only 20 minutes late, we can reinforce the improvement. Reinforcement would increase as an employee gets closer to the desired behavior.

There are four ways to shape behavior: positive reinforcement, negative reinforcement, punishment, or extinction. When a behavior is followed by something pleasant, such as when a manager praises an employee for a job well done, it's called *positive reinforcement*. Positive reinforcement will increase the likelihood of the desired behavior being repeated. Rewarding a response with the elimination or withdrawal of something unpleasant is called *negative reinforcement*. A manager who says "I won't dock your pay if you start getting to work on time" is using negative reinforcement. The desired behavior (getting to work on time) is being encouraged by the withdrawal of something

---

**social learning theory**
A learning theory that says people learn through observation and direct experience.

**shaping behavior**
Systematically reinforcing each successive step to move an individual closer to the desired behavior.

## *thinking critically about* **Ethics**

Is shaping behavior a form of manipulative control? Animal trainers use rewards to get dogs, porpoises, and whales to perform extraordinary stunts. Behavioral psychologists put rats through thousands of experiments by manipulating their food supply. Trainers and researchers shape the behavior of animals by controlling consequences. Such learning techniques may be appropriate for animals performing in zoos, circuses, or laboratories, but are they appropriate for managing the behavior of people at work?

Suppose an employee does something the organization judges to be wrong but that was motivated by a manager's control of rewards. Say, for instance, an employee inflates the numbers on a sales report because bonuses are based on sales volume. Is that employee any less responsible for his or her actions than if such rewards had not been involved? Explain your position.

**Q & A**

Both negative reinforcement and punishment focus on something negative. So how are they different? Go to Q & A 14.12 to find out.

unpleasant (the employee's pay being docked). On the other hand, *punishment* penalizes undesirable behavior and will eliminate it. Suspending an employee for two days without pay for habitually coming to work late is an example of punishment. (  Go to www.prenhall.com/rolls) Finally, eliminating any reinforcement that's maintaining a behavior is called *extinction*. When a behavior isn't reinforced, gradually it disappears. In meetings, managers who wish to discourage employees from continually asking irrelevant or distracting questions can eliminate this behavior by ignoring those employees when they raise their hands to speak. Soon this behavior should disappear.

Both positive and negative reinforcement result in learning. They strengthen a desired behavior and increase the probability that the desired behavior will be repeated. Both punishment and extinction also result in learning; however, they weaken an undesired behavior and tend to decrease its frequency.

### Implications for Managers

Employees are going to learn on the job. The only issue is whether managers are going to manage their learning through the rewards they allocate and the examples

## *becoming* a Manager

√ Begin paying attention to the behaviors of those around you. Try to use what you've learned about attitudes, personality, perception, and learning to explain how and why they're behaving the ways they do.

√ Write down some of your own attitudes and try to identify the cognitive, affective, and behavioral components of those attitudes.

√ Take different personality tests so you have a good feel for your own unique personality.

√ A lot of business people think that how you treat service workers says a lot about your character and attitudes. How would you be evaluated on the "waiter rule"?

√ Notice when you're using shortcuts in judging others and how these shortcuts either helped or hindered your behavior.

√ Pay attention to how you shape the behaviors of those around you.

√  There are a number of Self-Assessments from www.prenhall.com/rolls that are relevant to this chapter. Complete the ones that have been listed throughout the chapter.

Self-Assessment
Library (S.A.L.)
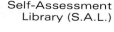

they set, or allow it to occur haphazardly. If marginal employees are rewarded with pay raises and promotions, they will have little reason to change their behavior. In fact, productive employees, seeing that marginal performance gets rewarded, might change their behavior. If managers want behavior A, but reward behavior B, they shouldn't be surprised to find employees' learning to engage in behavior B. Similarly, managers should expect that employees will look to them as models. Managers who are consistently late to work, take 2 hours for lunch, or help themselves to company office supplies for personal use should expect employees to read the message they are sending and model their behavior accordingly.

## Learning Review

- Explain how operant conditioning helps managers understand, predict, and influence behavior.
- Describe the implications of social learning theory for managing people at work.
- Discuss how managers can shape behavior.

## CONTEMPORARY OB ISSUES

By this point, you're probably well aware of why managers need to understand the concepts of behavior—that is, how and why employees behave the way they do. But we want to conclude by looking at two contemporary OB issues that are having a major influence on managers' jobs today. One issue is managing generational differences in the workplace and the other is the challenge of managing negative behavior in the workplace.

### Managing Generational Differences in the Workplace

They're young, smart, brash. They wear flip-flops to the office or listen to iPods at their desk. They want to work, but they don't want work to be their life. This is Generation Y, a force of as many as 70 million, and the first wave is just now embarking on their careers—taking their place in an increasingly multigenerational workplace.[72] As you can see, one of the more challenging issues that managers will have to face in the next few years is how to successfully integrate Generation Y (Gen Y) employees into the workplace.

**Just Who Is Gen Y?** There's no consensus about the exact time span that Gen Y comprises, but most definitions include those individuals born after 1978. But one

*Anna Stassen has had a typical life for a Gen Y'er. "In high school I did everything—student council, golf, volleyball, theater, choir. . . . In the past 2 years, I've run a marathon, gone skydiving, been to surf camp, learned how to shoot a handgun. Once I finish one thing, I check it off my list and look for the next thing." About her bosses at ad agency Fallon Worldwide, she says, "I don't have time to be intimidated. It's not that I'm disrespectful; it's just a waste of energy to be fearful."*

Exhibit 14–7

**Gen Y Workers**

*Source:* Bruce Tulgan of Rainmaker Thinking. Used with permission.

**Gen Y Workers**

**High Expectations of Self**
They aim to work faster and better than other workers.

**High Expectations of Employers**
They want fair and direct managers who are highly engaged in their professional development.

**Ongoing Learning**
They seek out creative challenges and view colleagues as vast resources from whom to gain knowledge.

**Immediate Responsibility**
They want to make an important impact on Day 1.

**Goal-Oriented**
They want small goals with tight deadlines so they can build up ownership of tasks.

thing is for sure—they're bringing new attitudes with them to the workplace. As the children of the baby boomers, Gen Ys have grown up with an amazing array of experiences and opportunities. And they want their work life to provide that as well, as shown in Exhibit 14–7. For instance, Stella Kenyi, who is passionately interested in international development, was sent by her employer, the National Rural Electric Cooperative Association, to Yai, Sudan, to survey energy use.[73] At Best Buy's corporate offices, Beth Trippie, a senior scheduling specialist, feels that as long as the results are there, why should it matter how it gets done. She says, "I'm constantly playing video games, on a call, doing work, and the thing is, all of it gets done, and it gets done well."[74] Dan Ross, an associate consultant at Covance, "asked his future supervisors for more feedback and communication." Now he tries to do the same for the young staffers that he supervises.[75] And Katie Patterson, an assistant account executive in Atlanta says, "We are willing and not afraid to challenge the status quo. An environment where creativity and independent thinking are looked upon as a positive is appealing to people my age. We're very independent and tech savvy."[76]

**Dealing with the Managerial Challenges** Managing Gen Y workers presents some unique challenges for managers. Conflicts and resentment can arise over issues including appearance, technology, and management style.

How flexible must an organization be in terms of what "appropriate" office attire is? Much of what "appropriate" office attire is depends on the type of work being done and the size of the organization. There are many organizations where jeans, t-shirts, and flip-flops are acceptable. However, in other settings, employees are expected to dress a little more conventionally. But even in those more conservative organizations, one possible solution to accommodate the more casual attire preferred by Gen Y is to be more flexible in what's acceptable. For instance, the guideline might be that when the person is not interacting with someone outside the organization, more casual wear can be worn.

What about technology? This is a generation that has lived much of their lives with ATMs, DVDs, cell phones, e-mail, instant messaging, laptops, and the Internet. When they don't have information they need, they just simply enter a few keystrokes to get it. Having grown up with technology, Gen Ys tend to be totally comfortable with it. They're quite content to meet virtually to solve important problems, while bewildered baby boomers expect important problems to be solved with an in-person meeting.

Baby boomers complain about Gen Y's inability to focus on one task, while Gen Ys see nothing wrong with multitasking. Again, flexibility—from both—may be the key here.

Finally, what about managing Gen Ys? Like the old car advertisement that used to say "this isn't your father's car," we can say that "this isn't your father's or mother's way of managing." Gen Y employees want bosses who are:

- Open minded
- Experts in their field, even if they aren't tech-savvy
- Organized
- Teachers, trainers, and mentors
- Not authoritarian or paternalistic
- Respectful of their generation
- Understanding of their need for work–life balance
- Providing constant feedback
- Communicating in a vivid and compelling way
- Providing stimulating and novel learning experiences[77]

Gen Y employees have a lot to offer organizations in terms of their knowledge, passion, and abilities. Managers, however, have to recognize and understand the behaviors of this group in order to create an environment in which work can be accomplished efficiently, effectively, and without disruptive conflict.

## Managing Negative Behavior in the Workplace

Jerry notices the oil is low in his forklift, but continues to drive it until it overheats and can't be used. After enduring 11 months of repeated insults and mistreatment from her supervisor, Maria quits her job. An office clerk slams her keyboard and then shouts profanity when her computer freezes up. Rudeness, hostility, aggression, and other forms of workplace negativity have become all too common in today's organizations. In a survey of U.S. employees, 10 percent said they witnessed rudeness daily within their workplaces and 20 percent said that they personally were direct targets of incivility at work at least once a week. In a survey of Canadian workers, 25 percent reported seeing incivility daily and 50 percent said they were the direct targets at least once per week.[78] And it's been estimated that negativity costs the U.S. economy some $300 billion a year.[79] What can managers do to manage negative behavior in the workplace?

The main thing is to recognize that it's there. Pretending that negative behavior doesn't exist or ignoring such misbehaviors will only confuse employees about what is expected and acceptable behavior. Although there's some debate among researchers about the preventive or responsive actions to negative behaviors, in reality, both are needed.[80] Preventing negative behaviors by carefully screening potential employees for certain personality traits and responding immediately and decisively to unacceptable negative behaviors can go a long way toward managing negative workplace behavior. But it's also important to pay attention to employee attitudes since negativity will show up there as well. As we said earlier, when employees are dissatisfied with their jobs, they *will* respond somehow.

## Learning Review

- Describe the challenges managers face in managing Gen Y workers.

- Explain what managers can do to deal with workplace misbehavior.

# Managers Respond to a Manager's Dilemma

## Cynthia Brewer

Staff Development Manager, Sears Holding Corporation, Chicago, IL

As the leader of a growing company pursuing opportunities in locations that are, as he describes them, "difficult and primitive," Mr. Sawiris definitely needs employees that have the appropriate attitudes and personality for that type of environment. The first thing I think he needs to do is identify individuals who are currently working for him who have been successful in these types of environments. What types of personalities do they have? What attitudes appear to have contributed to their work success? With this information, he can hopefully pinpoint what attitudes and personalities are likely to be important for hiring employees for his growing company.

Another thing I think Mr. Sawiris needs to do is reward employees who exhibit expected and appropriate attitudes. For instance, if employees step up in situations and quickly make decisions when needed or when they show a willingness to be risk-takers, reward them. Other employees will quickly learn what is expected and important.

Finally, and this has nothing to do with personality or attitudes, I think Mr. Sawiris needs to be very clear about what type of work and work environments his employees will face. That way, employees who feel they can't work under those conditions would be discouraged from applying.

# Learning Summary

## Why Study Organizational Behavior?

Organizational behavior: studying how people act at work

- Iceberg concept: OB has a small visible aspect and a much larger hidden portion
- Focuses on individual behavior and group behavior
- Goals of OB: explain, predict, and influence six important employee behaviors

  1. Employee productivity        4. Organizational citizenship behavior

  2. Absenteeism                      5. Job satisfaction

  3. Turnover                            6. Workplace misbehavior

- Four individual psychological factors (attitudes, personality, perception, learning)

## How Do Attitudes Affect Employee Behavior?

Attitude: evaluative statements (favorable or unfavorable) concerning objects, people, or events; include cognitive, affective, and behavioral components

Job-related attitudes are:

- Job satisfaction (general attitude toward job)
  - Findings about job satisfaction—United States and global
  - Satisfaction–productivity link
  - Satisfaction–absenteeism link
  - Satisfaction–turnover link
  - Job satisfaction–customer satisfaction link
  - Satisfaction–workplace misbehavior link
- Job involvement (level of identification with and commitment to job)
- Organizational commitment (level of identification with and commitment to organization)—perceived organizational support (does organization value employee contribution)

People seek consistency among their attitudes and between attitudes and behavior

- Cognitive dissonance theory
  - Desire to reduce dissonance is determined by importance of factors creating dissonance, degree of influence over these factors, and rewards involved in dissonance

Attitude surveys give managers feedback on employee attitudes

## How Does Personality Affect Employee Behavior?

Personality: a unique combination of emotional, thought, and behavioral patterns that affect how a person reacts and interacts with others

Classifying personality traits:

- MBTI®—widely used
  - Social interaction—extrovert (E) or introvert (I)
  - Preference for gathering data—sensing (S) or intuitive (N)
  - Preference for decision making—feeling (F) or thinking (T)
  - Style of making decisions—perceptive (P) or judgmental (J)
- Big-Five Model: five basic personality dimensions that underlie all others—extraversion, agreeableness, conscientiousness, emotional stability, and openness to experience
- Other personality traits—most powerful in explaining individual behavior in organizations
  - locus of control, Machiavellianism, self-esteem, self-monitoring, and risk taking

Emotions (intense feelings directed at someone or something) also are affected by personality

- Six universal emotions (anger, fear, sadness, happiness, disgust, and surprise)
- Emotional intelligence: the ability to notice and to manage emotional cues and information
  - Self-awareness, self-management, self-motivation, empathy, and social skills

### How Does Perception Affect Employee Behavior?

Perception: process by which individuals give meaning to their environment

- Factors that influence perception—perceiver, target, and situation
- Attribution theory
  - To what do we "attribute" this person's behavior: internally caused or externally caused?
  - Depends on three factors: distinctiveness, consensus, and consistency
  - Attributions are distorted by fundamental attribution error and self-serving bias
- Shortcuts used in judging others
  - Assumed similarity, stereotyping, and halo effect

### How Does Learning Affect Employee Behavior?

Learning: any relatively permanent change in behavior occurring as a result of experience

Two learning theories:

- Operant conditioning (behavior is function of consequences)
- Social learning (learning occurs through observation and direct experience)

Managers can "shape" behavior using positive reinforcement, negative reinforcement, punishment, and extinction

### What Important OB Issues Are Facing Managers Today?

- Managing generational differences, especially Gen Y
- Managing negative behavior in the workplace

# Management: By the Numbers

- Emotional intelligence studies of over 100,000 senior executives, managers, and line employees on six continents show that CEOs have the lowest level of emotional intelligence.
- More than half of employees surveyed by VitalSmarts say that a disagreeable boss was the main reason they left a job.
- Sixty-eight percent of employees who said the amount of work they had was just right were satisfied with their jobs; 60 percent of employees who said the amount of work they had was too much were satisfied with their jobs; however, only 37 percent of employees who said their amount of work was much too little were satisfied with their jobs.
- Forty percent of employees surveyed by the Conference Board said they felt disconnected from their employers; 25 percent of these employees were showing up just to collect a paycheck.
- Forty-six percent of more than 4,500 respondents from 42 countries said that mentoring or coaching had a great impact on their career success.
- Eighty-nine percent of *Fortune* 100 companies use the MBTI® in hiring and promoting.

- Nineteen percent of office workers say they tell lies at the office at least once a week; 5 percent have been caught in a lie.
- Twenty-four percent of hiring managers say they have fired an employee for being dishonest.
- HR executives who were asked about reasons for unscheduled employee absences at work said that 14 percent were due to an "entitlement mentality."
- Sixty-four percent of workers in a recent survey said they felt a strong sense of commitment to their organizations, up from 58 percent in 2002.

*Sources:* J. Yang and K. Simmons, "Personal Illness Tops Absentee List," *USA Today Snapshots,* May 1, 2006, p. 1B; L. T. Cullen, "SATS for J-O-B-S," *Time,* April 30, 2006, p. 89; J. MacIntyre, "Liar, Liar," *Springfield Business Journal,* April 3–9, 2006, p. 64; J. Yang and K. Gelles, "Mentoring's Impact," *USA Today Snapshots,* March 22, 2006, p. 1B; "Overworked Employees Are Happy Employees," *Training,* January 2006, p. 9; T. Bradberry and J. Greaves, "Heartless Bosses?" *Harvard Business Review,* December 2005, p. 24; "Bring It On, Boss," *Springfield News-Leader,* November 15, 2005, p. 1F; "Positivity Is Working," *Springfield News-Leader,* June 23, 2005, p. 1F; and P. Panchak, "Wanted: Inspired Leaders, Engaged Employees," *Industry Week,* May 2005, p. 7.

# Thinking About Management Issues

1. How, if at all, does the importance of knowledge of OB differ based on a manager's level in the organization? Be specific.

2. "A growing number of companies are now convinced that people's ability to understand and to manage their emotions improves their performance, their collaboration with peers, and their interaction with customers." What are the implications of this statement for managers?

3. What behavioral predictions might you make if you knew that an employee had (a) an external locus of control, (b) a low Mach score, (c) low self-esteem, or (d) high self-monitoring tendencies?

4. "Managers should never use discipline with a problem employee." Do you agree or disagree? Discuss.

5. A Gallup Organization survey shows that most workers rate having a caring boss even higher than they value money or fringe benefits. How should managers interpret this information? What are the implications?

6. Does a job's prestige (as assessed by others outside the organization) increase an employee's job satisfaction? Research data is beginning to show that it does. What do you think? What are the implications for organizations?

7. Suppose that you're responsible for managing a group whose members are much older than you are. What challenges might you face and how will you address those challenges?

# Working Together: Team-Based Exercise

When we use shortcuts to judge others, are the consequences always negative? Form teams of three to four students. Your instructor will assign each class team either to "yes, the consequences are always negative" or to "no, the consequences aren't always negative." After these assignments are made, your group should discuss this question. Come up with evidence and examples to support your group's argument. Be prepared to debate your group's position in class.

# Ethical Dilemma Exercise

Can too much communication create an ethical dilemma? Companies that demonstrate support by keeping employees fully informed seek to build trust in management, avoid misperceptions, and encourage positive attitudes. After the Dutch company Royal Ahold bought and merged two U.S. supermarket chains, Giant Food Stores and Stop & Shop, both employee morale and market share dropped. Top executives initially held meetings to allow employees "to vent their frustration to people high up in the company," remembers the head of the local supermarket union. A second round of meetings, held a few months later, paved the way for improvements by focusing specifically on problem-solving and employee motivation. "Communication is a key to building a successful organization," explained a company spokesperson, "and that was the purpose of the meetings we held."

Another example is Avon Products, where information technology managers and employees worried that their jobs would be moved to another country or an outside supplier—until management met the issue head-on. "Avon told us in October that they had looked at outsourcing but didn't feel it met their requirements," states one technology manager. "As a result, I don't think anybody feels right now that the company has any plans to outsource [information technology]." However, will employees maintain their positive attitudes and perceptions if they receive too many or too frequent communications about possible outsourcing or potential lay-off plans? How much communication is appropriate to avoid putting additional stress on employees and provoking negative attitudes and perceptions?[81]

Imagine that you're the vice president of information technology for Avon. To save money, you are again exploring the idea of outsourcing some tasks currently handled by your department. Even though outsourcing didn't make sense in previous years, this time could be different. You've just begun to ask suppliers for proposals; a final decision will not be made for 6 months or more. What should you communicate to your staff and when should you communicate it? Review the section on goals of organizational behavior as you consider this ethical challenge and decide which of the following options to choose, and why.

**Option A:** Talk with your employees now, so they are prepared for the possibility that some jobs will be eliminated if you eventually decide that outsourcing is the right approach.

**Option B:** Say nothing to your employees until a decision has been reached to outsource some or all

of the department's tasks within a definite time period.

**Option C:** Mention the possibility of outsourcing only to the managers who report directly to you but have them say nothing to avoid upsetting the entire department.

## Case Application

### Washington Mutual, Inc.

Its core values are fair, caring, human, dynamic, and driven. Those words speak volumes about Seattle-based Washington Mutual. Yet they're quite fitting given how the company views its customers and employees.

In business since 1889, WaMu (as it's known) is a financial services retailer, providing a variety of financial products and services to individual consumers and to small and medium-sized businesses. Its key markets are in California, Florida, Oregon, Texas, and Washington. Also, WaMu is increasing its presence in key cities including Atlanta, Chicago, Denver, Las Vegas, Phoenix, and Tampa. And CEO Kerry Killinger isn't finished yet. He wants to reinvent how people think about banking. His goal is to have WaMu thought of in the same category as Wal-Mart, Southwest Airlines, Best Buy, and Target. Killinger says, "In every retailing industry, there are category killers who figure out how to have a very low cost structure and pass those advantages on to customers, day in and day out, with better pricing. I think we have a shot at doing that in this segment." WaMu is extremely customer focused. As the largest thrift institution in the United States, WaMu serves more than 10 million customers. And that means taking care of those customers.

With the company's push to keep costs low, you might think that employees (or as they call themselves,

"Wamulians") would not rank high on the list of priorities. Yet, that impression would be wrong. Killinger knows how important his employees are to the success of the company. In fact, the company was named by *Fortune* magazine as one of the 100 best companies to work for in 2006. With more than 60,000 employees, WaMu's managers tend to see a lot of behaviors—good and not so good. To become the financial powerhouse it wants to be, those employee behaviors must be channeled in an appropriate direction. And the company has done this by focusing on its culture and hiring for attitude.

WaMu's culture is simple: Everyone should be treated with dignity and respect. The company has created a work environment in which *everyone* has the opportunity to thrive, have fun, and succeed. As mentioned earlier, customer service is a high priority. "People don't want conversations with uptight bankers; they want a friendly smile, fast service, and our respect." And the company recognizes that it's not just the frontline employees—the tellers—who service customers. Every WaMu employee has customers, whether they're external or internal. Even for those employees whose only contact is with other employees, the expectations are the same: outstanding service. Another important priority is innovation. The design of WaMu's new Occasio™ retail branches was so innovative that it actually took out a U.S. patent on the concept. The word "occasio" is Latin for favorable opportunity, and that's what WaMu has done with the design of these branches—created a favorable opportunity to interact with customers through an open, welcoming space, rather than an institutional design.

With the company's continued growth, it's important to maintain that customer service and innovative culture. They do this by hiring for attitude—a philosophy first espoused by former Southwest Airlines' CEO Herb Kelleher, who said, "We draft great attitudes. If you don't have a good attitude, we don't want you, no matter how skilled you are. We can change skill level through training. We can't change attitude." WaMu adheres to that philosophy. Employees can be taught the mechanics of financial services, but to be successful, they must have the right attitude—fair, caring, human, dynamic, and driven.

*Washington Mutual's Occasio concept.*

## Discussion Questions

1. What type of personality characteristics might fit best into WaMu's customer service and innovative culture?

2. Design an employee attitude survey that WaMu's managers might use. If you want, check out information on the company's Web site, www.wamu.com.

3. WaMu was named by *Fortune* magazine in 2006 as one of the 100 best companies to work for. What predictions, if any, could you make about job satisfaction at WaMu? How might job satisfaction affect work outcomes at WaMu?

4. The company's core values include fair, caring, human, dynamic, and driven. How does the company exhibit these values?

*Sources:* Information from company Web site, www.wamu.com, and 2005 Annual Report; R. Levering and M. Moskowitz, "And the Winners Are . . . ," *Fortune*, January 11, 2006, pp. 89–113; T. Mucha, "How to Crack New Markets," *Business 2.0*, July 2003, p. 45; L. Tischler, "Bank of (Middle) America," *Fast Company*, March 2003, pp. 104–109; and G. Anders, "7 Lessons from WaMu's Playbook," *Fast Company*, January 2002, p. 102.

# Learning Outline

*Use this Learning Outline as you read and study this chapter.*

### Understanding Groups

- Define the different types of groups.
- Describe the five stages of group development.

### Explaining Work Group Behavior

- Explain the major components that determine group performance and satisfaction.
- Discuss how roles, norms, conformity, status systems, group size, and group cohesiveness influence group behavior.
- Explain how group norms can both help and hurt an organization.
- Define groupthink and social loafing.
- Describe the relationships between group cohesiveness and productivity.
- Discuss how conflict management influences group behavior.
- Tell the advantages and disadvantages of group decision making.

### Turning Groups into Effective Teams

- Compare groups and teams.
- Explain why teams have become so popular in organizations.
- Describe the four most common types of teams.
- List the characteristics of effective teams.

### Current Challenges in Managing Teams

- Discuss the challenges of managing global teams.
- Explain the role of informal (social) networks in managing teams.

# Understanding Groups and Teams

## A Manager's Dilemma

With around 80 percent of the computer processor market, Intel, a $38 billion company, is "by far the foremost semiconductor maker in the world." Its technological capabilities and foresight are known the world over. For instance, "researchers at a panda preserve in China use an Intel® architecture-based wireless computing network to chronicle the animals' activities and share data. A Russian bus manufacturer uses Intel-based servers to shorten vehicle development cycles and boost product quality." One of the company's premier research and development labs, located in Haifa, Israel, has employed engineers for more than 30 years.[1] The technology behind the highly successful Centrino chips for laptops came out of this lab, as did the newest common processors for servers, PCs, and laptops. Dadi Perlmutter, an Intel senior vice president, leads this chip design group.

Dadi describes his group as having a strong culture of debate and confrontation. Sometimes too much. However, it's that group atmosphere that actually helped Centrino get off the ground and become the more than $5 billion business it is. During the initial design stages, the focus, as always, was on processor chip speed or frequency, but fast chips consumed more power, which meant shorter battery life. And when designing a product to be used by wireless computers, that wasn't a good thing at all! One of Dadi's engineers came to him and suggested that by giving up half the frequency, they could cut power consumption by half as well. Such a suggestion probably wouldn't have survived long at the home office because it involved challenging accepted practices. However, here in a location where the group was not bound by such cultural constraints, it led to the development of a winning product.

Another benefit of having design groups thousands of miles away from headquarters in Santa Clara, California (28 percent of the company's more than 7,000 R&D employees are located in more than 20 countries outside the United States), is that these locations don't suffer from bureaucratic inertia of constant meetings and committees. Dadi says, "Groups far from the center of power have to work harder to stay in the loop."

Put yourself in Dadi's shoes. What can he do to maintain his team's effectiveness at challenging the status quo when new designers join his group?

**What would you do?**

You've probably already had a lot of experience working in groups—class project teams, maybe an athletic team, a fund-raising committee, or even a sales team at work. Work teams are one of the realities—and challenges—of managing in today's dynamic global environment. Thousands of organizations have made the move to restructure work around teams rather than individuals. Why? What do these teams look like? And, like the challenge facing Dadi Perlmutter, how can managers build effective teams? These are some of the questions we'll be answering in this chapter. First, however, let's begin by developing our understanding of group behavior.

## UNDERSTANDING GROUPS

Each person in the group had his or her assigned role: The Spotter, The Back Spotter, The Gorilla, and The Big Player. For over 10 years, this group—former MIT students who were members of a secret Black Jack Club—used their extraordinary mathematical abilities, expert training, teamwork, and interpersonal skills to take millions of dollars from some of the major casinos in the United States.[2]

Although most groups aren't formed for such dishonest purposes, the success of this group at its task was impressive. Managers would like their employees to be successful at their tasks also. How can they do so? As we discussed in the previous chapter, managers need to understand the behavior of individuals in organizations. But because most organizational work is done by individuals who are part of a work group, it's important for managers also to understand group behavior. And the behavior of a group is not merely the sum total of the behaviors of all the individuals in the group. Why? Because individuals act differently in groups than they do when they are alone. Therefore, if we want to fully understand organizational behavior, we need to study groups.

### What Is a Group?

A **group** is defined as two or more interacting ~~and interdependent~~ individuals who come together to achieve specific goals. Groups can either be formal or informal. *Formal groups* are work groups defined by the organization's structure that have designated work assignments and specific tasks. In formal groups, appropriate behaviors are established by and directed toward organizational goals. Exhibit 15–1 provides some examples of different types of formal groups in today's organizations. ( Go to www.prenhall.com/rolls)

In contrast, *informal groups* are social. These groups occur naturally in the workplace in response to the need for social contact. For example, three employees from different departments who regularly eat lunch together are an informal group. Informal groups tend to form around friendships and common interests.

Diversity

What challenges do managers face in managing diverse groups? Try Diversity in Action #3 and see.

Exhibit 15–1

**Examples of Formal Groups**

- *Command Groups:* Groups that are determined by the organization chart and composed of individuals who report directly to a given manager.
- *Task Groups:* Groups composed of individuals brought together to complete a specific job task; their existence is often temporary because once the task is completed, the group disbands.
- *Cross-Functional Teams:* Groups that bring together the knowledge and skills of individuals from various work areas or groups whose members have been trained to do each others' jobs.
- *Self-Managed Teams:* Groups that are essentially independent and in addition to their own tasks, take on traditional managerial responsibilities such as hiring, planning and scheduling, and performance evaluations.

Exhibit 15–2

**Stages of Group Development**

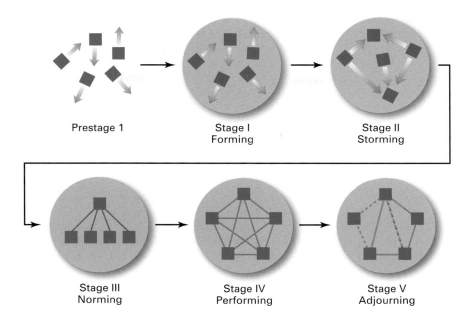

Prestage 1

Stage I
Forming

Stage II
Storming

Stage III
Norming

Stage IV
Performing

Stage V
Adjourning

## Stages of Group Development

Group development is a dynamic process. Most groups are in a continual state of change. Even though groups probably never reach complete stability, research shows they go through five stages.[3] As shown in Exhibit 15–2, these five stages are *forming, storming, norming, performing,* and *adjourning*.

The first stage, **forming**, has two phases. The first occurs as people join the group. People join a formal group because of some work assignment. In the case of an informal group, people join for some other desired benefit—such as status, self-esteem, affiliation, power, or security.

Once the group's membership is in place, the second phase begins: the task of defining the group's purpose, structure, and leadership. This phase is characterized by a great deal of uncertainty as members "test the waters" to determine what types of behaviors are acceptable. This stage is complete when members begin to think of themselves as part of a group.

The **storming** stage is appropriately named because it's a stage of intragroup conflict. Members accept the existence of the group but resist the control that the group imposes on individuality. Further, there is conflict over who will control the group. When this stage is complete, there will be a relatively clear hierarchy of leadership within the group and agreement on the group's direction.

The third stage is one in which close relationships develop and the group becomes cohesive. There's now a strong sense of group identity and camaraderie. This **norming** stage is complete when the group structure solidifies and the group has assimilated a common set of expectations (or norms) regarding member behavior. (  Go to www.prenhall.com/rolls)

The fourth stage is **performing**. The group structure at this point is in place and accepted by group members. Group members' energies have moved from getting to know and understand each other to performing the task at hand.

Q & A
Do groups limit how hard group members work? Q & A 15.1 explains.

---

**group**
Two or more interacting and interdependent individuals who come together to achieve specific goals.

**forming**
The first stage of group development in which people join the group and then define the group's purpose, structure, and leadership.

**storming**
The second stage of group development, which is characterized by intragroup conflict.

**norming**
The third stage of group development, which is characterized by close relationships and cohesiveness.

**performing**
The fourth stage of group development when the group is fully functional.

*Self-managing teams at Toyo Ink in Australia are in the performing stage. There are no more time clocks because team members are responsible for the amount of work they do, and they will soon also be in charge of planning and organizing their own vacation times. Information sharing is more efficient, and communication with management has increased as well.*

Performing is the last stage of development for permanent work groups. However, temporary groups—such as project teams, task forces, and similar groups that have a limited task to perform—have a fifth stage, **adjourning**. In this stage, the group prepares to disband. High levels of task performance are no longer the group's top priority as attention is directed at wrapping up activities. Reactions of group members vary at this stage. Some are upbeat, thrilled about the group's accomplishments. Others may be sad over the loss of camaraderie and friendships gained during the work group's life.

Many of you have probably experienced these stages as you've worked on a group project for a class. Group members are selected or assigned and then meet for the first time. There's a "feeling out" period to assess what the group is going to do and how it's going to be done. This is usually rapidly followed by a battle for control: Who's going to be in charge? Once this issue is resolved and a "hierarchy" agreed on, the group identifies specific aspects of the task, who's going to do them, and dates by which the assigned work needs to be completed. General expectations are established and accepted by each member. These decisions form the foundation for what you hope will be a coordinated group effort culminating in a project well done. Once the project is complete and turned in, the group breaks up. Of course, some groups don't get much beyond the forming or storming stages; these groups typically have serious interpersonal conflicts, turn in disappointing work, and get lower grades.

Should you automatically assume from the preceding discussion that a group becomes more effective as it progresses through the first four stages? Some researchers argue that the effectiveness of work groups increases at advanced stages, but it's not that simple.[4] That assumption may be generally true, but what makes a group effective is a complex issue. Under some conditions, high levels of conflict are conducive to high levels of group performance. There might be situations in which groups in Stage II (storming) outperform those in Stages III (norming) or IV (performing). Similarly, groups don't always proceed sequentially from one stage to the next. Sometimes, in fact, several stages may be going on simultaneously, as when groups are storming and performing at the same time. Groups even occasionally regress to previous stages. Therefore, don't always assume that all groups precisely follow this developmental process or that Stage IV (performing) is always the most preferable. It's better to think of this model as a general framework that underscores the fact that groups are dynamic entities. It can help you better understand the problems and issues that are most likely to surface during a group's duration. (  Go to www.prenhall.com/rolls)

**Diversity**

What if group members are different ages? Does this affect the group's development? Diversity in Action #1 looks at this.

## ⌐ **Learning Review**

* Define the different types of groups.

* Describe the five stages of group development.

Exhibit 15–3

**Group Behavior Model**

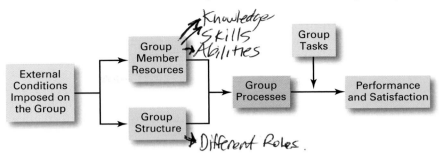

## EXPLAINING WORK GROUP BEHAVIOR

Many people consider them the most successful "team" of our times. Who is it? None other than . . . The Beatles. "The Beatles were great artists and entertainers, but in many respects they were four ordinary guys who, as a team, found a way to achieve extraordinary artistic and financial success and have a great time together while doing it. Every business team can learn from their story."[5]

Why *are* some groups more successful than others? Why do some groups achieve high levels of performance and high levels of member satisfaction and others do not? The answers are complex, but include variables such as the abilities of the group's members, the size of the group, the level of conflict, and the internal pressures on members to conform to the group's norms. Exhibit 15–3 presents the major components that determine group performance and satisfaction.[6] Let's look at each.

### External Conditions Imposed on the Group

To understand behavior of work groups, you need to recognize they're part of a larger organization. For instance, a quality control team at a Kraft Foods plant in Suttontown, Australia, is part of Kraft Foods Australia and must live within the rules and policies handed down from headquarters in Melbourne. As a part of a larger organizational system, a work group is influenced by external conditions imposed on it from outside. These external conditions include the organization's strategy, authority relationships, formal rules and regulations, availability of organizational resources, employee selection criteria, the organization's performance management system and culture, and general physical layout of the group's work space. For instance, some groups will have modern, high-quality tools and equipment to do their jobs while other groups aren't as fortunate. Or the organization might be pursuing a strategy of lowering costs or improving quality, which will affect what a group does and how it does it.

### Group Member Resources

A group's performance potential depends to a large extent on the individual resources its members bring to the group. These include members' knowledge, abilities, skills, and personality characteristics.

Part of a group's performance can be predicted by looking at the knowledge, abilities, and skills of its individual members. (Look back at our chapter-opening Manager's Dilemma and think about the knowledge and skills each member of the Intel R&D lab team likely brings to the group.) We do occasionally hear about an athletic team composed of mediocre players who, because of excellent coaching, determination,

**adjourning**
The final stage of group development for temporary groups during which group members are concerned with wrapping up activities rather than task performance.

and precision teamwork, beat a far more talented group of players. Such examples make the news precisely because they are unusual. Group performance isn't merely the summation of its individual members' knowledge and abilities. However, their knowledge and abilities do set parameters on what members can do and how effectively they will perform in a group. In addition, interpersonal skills—especially conflict management and resolution, collaborative problem solving, and communication—consistently emerge as important for high performance by work groups.[7] For instance, group members need to be able to recognize the type and source of conflict confronting the group and to implement an appropriate conflict-resolution strategy; to identify situations requiring participative group problem solving and to utilize the proper degree and type of participation; and to listen nonevaluatively and to appropriately use active listening techniques.

What about the relationship between personality traits and group attitudes and behaviors? Research has shown that attributes that tend to be viewed as positive in our culture (such as sociability, self-reliance, and independence) tend to be positively related to group productivity and morale. In contrast, negative personality characteristics such as authoritarianism, dominance, and unconventionality tend to be negatively related to productivity and morale.[8] These personality traits affect group performance by strongly influencing how the individual will interact with other group members.

## Group Structure

Work groups aren't unorganized crowds. They have an internal structure that shapes members' behavior and makes it possible to explain, predict, and influence a large

## managing workforce **Diversity**

### The Challenge of Managing Diverse Teams

Understanding and managing teams composed of people who are similar can be difficult! Add in diverse members and managing teams can be even more of a challenge. However, the benefits to be gained from the diverse perspectives, skills, and abilities often more than offset the extra effort.[9] How can you meet the challenge of coordinating a diverse work team? It's important to stress four critical interpersonal behaviors: understanding, empathy, tolerance, and communication.

You know that people aren't the same, yet they need to be treated fairly and equitably. And differences (cultural, physical, or other) can cause people to behave in different ways. Team leaders need to understand and accept these differences. Each and every team member should be encouraged to do the same.

Empathy is closely related to understanding. As a team leader, you should try to understand others' perspectives. Put yourself in their place and encourage team members to empathize as well. For instance, suppose an Asian woman joins a team of Caucasian and Hispanic men. They can make her feel more welcome and comfortable by identifying with how she might feel. Is she excited or disappointed about her new work assignment? Has she had any experiences working with male colleagues? How has her cultural experiences shaped her

attitudes toward men? By putting themselves in her position, the existing team members can enhance their ability to work together as an effective group.

Tolerance is another important interpersonal behavior in managing diverse teams. Just because you understand that people are different and you empathize with them doesn't mean that it's any easier to accept different perspectives or behaviors. But it's important in dealing with diverse ages, gender, and cultural backgrounds to be tolerant—to allow team members the freedom to be themselves. Part of being tolerant is being open-minded about different values, attitudes, and behaviors.

Finally, open communication is important to managing a diverse team. Diversity problems may intensify if people are afraid or unwilling to openly discuss issues that concern them. And communication within a diverse team needs to be two-way. If a person wants to know whether a certain behavior is offensive to someone else, it's best to ask. Likewise, a person who is offended by a certain behavior of someone else should explain his or her concerns and ask that person to stop. As long as these communication exchanges are handled in a non-threatening, low-key, and friendly manner, they generally will have a positive outcome. Finally, it helps to have an atmosphere within the team that supports and celebrates diversity.

portion of individual behavior within the group as well as the performance of the group itself. This structure defines member roles, norms, conformity, status systems, group size, group cohesiveness, and formal leadership positions. Let's look at the first six of these. We'll look at the seventh—leadership—in Chapter 17.

**Roles**  We introduced the concept of roles in Chapter 1 when we discussed what managers do. (Remember Mintzberg's managerial roles.) Of course, managers aren't the only individuals in an organization who play various roles. The concept of roles applies to all employees in organizations and to their life outside the organization as well. ( Go to www.prenhall.com/rolls)

**Q & A**
Saying that we "act out" roles in different situations, doesn't that mean people are just a bunch of phonies? Go to Q & A 15.2 and find out.

A **role** refers to behavior patterns expected of someone occupying a given position in a social unit. In a group, individuals are expected to do certain things because of their position (role) in the group. These roles tend to be oriented toward either task accomplishment or toward maintaining group member satisfaction.[10] Think about groups that you've been in and the roles that you played. Were you continually trying to keep the group focused on getting its work done? If so, you were filling a task accomplishment role. Or were you more concerned that group members had the opportunity to offer ideas and that they were satisfied with the experience? If so, you were performing a group member satisfaction role. Both roles are important to the ability of a group to function effectively and efficiently.

A general problem that arises in understanding role behavior is that individuals play multiple roles, adjusting their roles to the group to which they belong at the time. They read their job descriptions, get suggestions from their manager, and watch what their co-workers do. When that individual is confronted by different role expectations, he or she experiences *role conflict*. Employees often face role conflicts. For instance, a new college instructor's colleagues want him to give very few high grades in order to maintain the department's reputation for having tough standards, but students want him to give high grades to enhance their grade point averages. To the degree that the instructor wants to satisfy the expectations of both his colleagues and his students, he faces role conflict. ( Go to www.prenhall.com/rolls)

**Q & A**
Why do managers need to know about group roles and group norms? See Q & A 15.3.

**Norms**  All groups have **norms**—standards or expectations that are accepted and shared by a group's members. Norms dictate factors such as work output levels, absenteeism, promptness, and the amount of socializing allowed on the job. ( Go to www.prenhall.com/rolls)

**Q & A**
What if a group's norms are dysfunctional? What then? Check out Q & A 15.4 for some advice.

The eight-man support team that rode with seven-time Tour de France winner Lance Armstrong is "the muscle behind it; it is the brawn," says Armstrong (rider No. 1, at the left in the photo). With physical skills and stamina honed to perfection by endless practice and unyielding discipline, the team sets the pace of the contest, shields Armstrong from wind, protects him from crashes, and even supplies him with snacks and fluids. The so-called Blue Train is considered a large factor in Armstrong's success. "The key is the huge form of his team," said the sports director of a competing team. "They won't crack."

**role**
Behavior patterns expected of someone occupying a given position in a social unit.

**norms**
Standards or expectations that are accepted and shared by a group's members.

Norms, for example, dictate the "arrival ritual" among office assistants at Coleman Trust Company. The workday begins at 8 A.M. Most employees typically arrive a few minutes earlier and hang up their coats and put their purses and other personal items on their chair or desk so everyone knows they're "at work." They then go to the company cafeteria to get coffee and chat. Any employee who violates this norm by starting work sharply at 8 A.M. is teased and pressured to encourage behavior that conforms to the group's standard.

Although a group has its own unique set of norms, common organizational norms focus on effort and performance, dress, and loyalty. Probably the most widespread norms are related to levels of effort and performance. Work groups typically provide their members with explicit cues on how hard to work, what level of output to have, when to look busy, when it's acceptable to goof off, and the like. These norms are very powerful in influencing an individual employee's performance. They're so powerful that performance predictions that are based solely on an employee's ability and level of personal motivation often prove to be wrong. And dress norms frequently dictate the kind of clothing that should be worn to work. Of course, what's acceptable dress in one organization may be very different from what's acceptable in another. Finally, loyalty norms will influence whether individuals work late, work on weekends, or move to locations they might not prefer to live. (  Go to www.prenhall.com/rolls)

**Q & A**

Think about groups that you've been in. How did you learn the norms? Q & A 15.5 discusses how this happens.

One negative aspect of norms is that being part of a group can increase an individual's antisocial actions. If the norms of the group are such that it tolerates deviant behavior, someone who normally wouldn't engage in such behavior might be more likely to do so. For instance, one recent study suggests that those working in a group were more likely to lie, cheat, and steal than were individuals working alone.[11] Why? Because groups provide anonymity, thus giving individuals—who might otherwise be afraid of getting caught—a false sense of security.

**Conformity**  Because individuals want to be accepted by groups to which they belong, they're susceptible to conformity pressures. The impact that group pressures for conformity can have on an individual member's judgment and attitudes was demonstrated in research by Solomon Asch.[12] In his conformity experiments, groups of seven or eight people were asked to compare two cards held up by the experimenter. One card had three lines of different lengths and the other had one line, which was equal in length to one of the three lines on the other card (see Exhibit 15–4). Each group member was to announce aloud which of the three lines matched the single line. Asch wanted to know what would happen if members began to give incorrect answers. Would pressures to conform cause individuals to align with the others? The experiment was "fixed" so that all but one of the members (the unsuspecting subject) had been told ahead of time to start giving obviously incorrect answers after one or two rounds of these matching exercises. Over many experiments and trials, the unsuspecting subject conformed over a third of the time; that is, the person gave answers he or she knew were wrong but were consistent with the replies of other group members.

**Q & A**

If a group member doesn't adhere to the norms, what happens to them? See Q & A 15.6.

Are these conclusions still valid after all these years? Research does suggest that levels of conformity have declined since Asch's studies. However, this doesn't mean that managers should ignore conformity since it can still be a powerful force in groups.[13] (  Go to www.prenhall.com/rolls) As group members, we often want to

Exhibit 15–4

**Examples of Cards Used in the Asch Study**

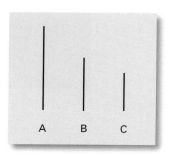

be considered one of the group and to avoid being visibly different. We find it more pleasant to be in agreement than to be disruptive, even if disruption may be necessary to improve the effectiveness of the group's decisions. So we conform. But conformity can go too far, especially when an individual's opinion of objective data differs significantly from that of others in the group. When this happens, the group often exerts extensive pressure on the individual to align his or her opinion to conform to others' opinions, a phenomenon known as **groupthink**. Fortunately, groupthink doesn't appear in all groups. It seems to occur most often when there is a clear group identity, where members hold a positive image of their group that they want to protect, and when the group perceives a collective threat to this positive image.[14]

**Status Systems** Status is a prestige grading, position, or rank within a group. As far back as researchers have been able to trace groups, they have found status hierarchies. Status systems are an important factor in understanding behavior. It's a significant motivator and has behavioral consequences when individuals see a disparity between what they perceive their status to be and what others perceive it to be.

Status in a group may be informally conferred by characteristics such as education, age, skill, or experience. Anything can have status value if others in the group evaluate it that way. Of course, just because status is informal doesn't mean that it's unimportant or that it's hard to determine who has it or who does not. Group members have no problem placing people into status categories, and they usually agree about who has high, middle, or low status.

Status is also formally conferred, and it's important for employees to believe that the organization's formal status system is congruent—that is, there's consistency and equity between the perceived ranking of an individual and the status symbols he or she is given by the organization. For instance, status incongruence would occur when a supervisor earns less than his or her subordinates, a desirable office is occupied by a person in a low-ranking position, or paid country club memberships are provided to division managers but not to vice presidents. Employees expect the "things" an individual receives to be congruent with his or her status. When they're not, employees are likely to question the authority of their managers. Also, the motivational potential of promotions declines, and the general pattern of order and consistency in the organization is disturbed.

**Group Size** At Amazon, work teams have considerable autonomy to innovate and to investigate their ideas. And according to Jeff Bezos, founder and CEO, teams should be

## thinking critically about Ethics

You've been hired as a summer intern in the events planning department of a public relations firm in Dallas. After working there about a month, you conclude that the attitude in the office is "anything goes." Employees know that supervisors won't discipline them for ignoring company rules. For example, employees have to turn in expense reports, but the process is a joke; nobody submits receipts to verify reimbursement, and nothing is ever said. In fact, when you tried to turn in your receipts with your expense report, you were told, "Nobody else turns in receipts and you don't really need to, either." You know that no expense check has ever been denied because of failure to turn in a receipt, even though the employee handbook says that receipts are required. Also, your co-workers use company phones for personal long-distance calls even though that is prohibited by the employee handbook. And one permanent employee told you to "help yourself" to any paper, pens, or pencils you might need here or at home. What are the norms of this group? Suppose that you were the supervisor in this area. How would you go about changing the norms?

---

**groupthink**
When a group exerts extensive pressure on an individual to align his or her opinion with others' opinions.

**status**
A prestige grading, position, or rank within a group.

*Managers should think carefully about what size group would be most effective and efficient. That decision will depend on what the group is expected to accomplish. A small group, like the one pictured here, would be best for getting things done.*

no larger than who can be fed with two pizzas. This "two-pizza" philosophy usually limits these groups to five to seven people, depending, of course, on team member appetites.[15]

Does the size of a group affect the group's overall behavior? Yes, but the effect depends on which outcomes you're focusing on.[16] The evidence indicates, for instance, that small groups are faster at completing tasks than are larger ones. However, if the group is engaged in problem solving, large groups consistently get better results than smaller ones. Translating these findings into specific numbers is a bit more difficult, but we can offer some guidelines. Large groups—those with a dozen or more members—are good for getting diverse input. Thus, if the goal of the group is to find facts, a larger group should be more effective. On the other hand, smaller groups are better at doing something productive with those facts. Groups of approximately seven members tend to be more effective for taking action.

One important finding related to group size is **social loafing**, which is the tendency for an individual to expend less effort when working collectively than when working individually.[17] It directly challenges the logic that the group's productivity should at least equal the sum of the productivity of each group member. What causes this social loafing effect? It may be due to a belief that others in the group are not carrying their fair share. If you see others as lazy or inept, you can reestablish equity by reducing your effort. Another explanation is the dispersion of responsibility. Because the results of the group can't be attributed to any one person, the relationship between an individual's input and the group's output is unclear. In such situations, individuals may be tempted to become "free riders" and coast on the group's efforts. In other words, efficiency will decline when individuals think that their contribution can't be measured.

The implications of social loafing for managers are significant. When managers use groups to enhance morale and teamwork, they must have a way to identify individual efforts. If this isn't done, the potential losses in productivity from using groups must be weighed against any possible gains in employee satisfaction.[18]

**Group Cohesiveness** Intuitively, it makes sense that groups in which there's a lot of internal disagreement and lack of cooperation are less effective in completing their tasks than are groups in which members generally agree, cooperate, and like each other. Research in this area has focused on **group cohesiveness**, or the degree to which members are attracted to a group and share the group's goals. Cohesiveness is important because it has been found to be related to a group's productivity.[19]

Research has generally shown that highly cohesive groups are more effective than are less cohesive ones.[20] However, this relationship between cohesiveness and effectiveness is a little more complex than that. (  Go to www.prenhall.com/rolls) A key moderating variable is the degree to which the group's attitude aligns with its goals or with the goals of the organization.[21] (See Exhibit 15–5.) The more cohesive the group,

**Q & A**

It seems like a cohesive group could "gang up" on the manager, so should managers encourage cohesive groups? Q & A 15.7 explains.

Exhibit 15–5

**The Relationship Between Cohesiveness and Productivity**

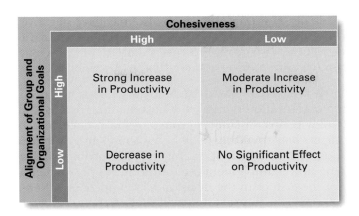

the more its members will follow its goals. If the goals are desirable (for instance, high output, quality work, cooperation with individuals outside the group), a cohesive group is more productive than a less cohesive group. But if cohesiveness is high and attitudes are unfavorable, productivity decreases. If cohesiveness is low and goals are supported, productivity increases but not as much as when both cohesiveness and support are high. When cohesiveness is low and goals are not supported, there's no significant effect on productivity.

## Group Processes

The next component in our group behavior model concerns the processes that go on within a work group—the communication patterns used by members to exchange information, group decision processes, power dynamics, conflict interactions, and the like. Why are these processes important to understanding work group behavior? Because in groups, one and one don't necessarily add up to two. Every group begins with a potential defined by its constraints, resources, and structure. Then you add in the positive and negative process factors created within the group itself. An example of a positive process factor is the synergy of four people on a marketing research team who are able to generate far more ideas as a group than the members could produce

*managing* **IT**

### IT and Groups

Like individuals, work groups need information to do their work. With work groups often being not just steps away, but continents away from each other, it's important to have a way for group members to communicate and collaborate. That's where IT comes in. Technology has enabled greater online communication and collaboration within groups of all types.[22]

The idea of technologically aided collaboration actually originated in the development of online search engines. The Internet itself was initially intended as a way for groups of scientists and researchers to share information. Then, as more and more information was put "on the Web," users relied on a variety of search engines to help them find that information. Now, we see many examples of collaborative technologies such as wiki pages, blogs, and even online multiplayer virtual reality games.

Today, online collaborative tools have enabled work groups more efficient and effective ways to get work done. For instance, engineers at Toyota use collaborative communication tools to share process improvements and innovations. They have developed a "widely disseminated, collectively owned pool of common knowledge, which drives innovation at a speed few other corporate systems can match." And there's no disputing the successes Toyota has achieved. Managers everywhere should look to the power of IT to help work groups improve the way work gets done.

**social loafing**
The tendency for individuals to expend less effort when working collectively than when working individually.

**group cohesiveness**
The degree to which group members are attracted to one another and share the group's goals.

individually. However, the group also may have negative process factors such as social loafing, high levels of conflict, or poor communication, which may hinder group effectiveness. Two group processes that are of particular importance to managers are group decision making and conflict management.

**Group Decision Making**  Many organizational decisions are made by groups. It's a rare organization that doesn't at some time use committees, task forces, review panels, study teams, or similar groups to make decisions. In addition, studies show that managers may spend up to 30 hours a week in group meetings.[23] Undoubtedly, a large portion of that time is spent formulating problems, developing solutions, and determining how to implement the solutions. It's possible, in fact, for groups to be assigned any of the 8 steps in the decision-making process. (Refer to Chapter 6 for a review of these steps.) In this section, we'll look at the advantages and disadvantages of group decision making, discuss when groups would be preferred, and present some techniques for improving group decision making.

What advantages do group decisions have over individual decisions?

1. *Generate more complete information and knowledge.* A group brings a diversity of experience and perspectives to the decision process that an individual cannot.
2. *Generate more diverse alternatives.* Because groups have a greater amount and diversity of information, they can identify more diverse alternatives than an individual.
3. *Increase acceptance of a solution.* Group members are reluctant to fight or undermine a decision they have helped develop.
4. *Increase legitimacy.* Decisions made by groups may be perceived as being more legitimate than decisions made unilaterally by one person.

If groups are so good at making decisions, how did the phrase "A camel is a horse put together by a committee" become so popular? The answer, of course, is that group decisions also have disadvantages.

1. *Time consuming.* Groups almost always take more time to reach a solution than it would take an individual.
2. *Minority domination.* The inequality of group members creates the opportunity for one or more members to dominate others. A dominant and vocal minority frequently can have an excessive influence on the final decision.

*Google's Web site explains that the company looks for exceptional people, and one of the skills they need is the ability to work as a team member. "We work in small teams, which we believe promotes spontaneity, creativity, and speed," the company says, "and team achievements are highly valued."*

Exhibit 15–6

**Group Versus Individual Decision Making**

| Criteria of Effectiveness | Groups | Individuals |
|---|---|---|
| Accuracy | √ | |
| Speed | | √ |
| Creativity | √ | |
| Degree of acceptance | √ | |
| Efficiency | | √ |

3. **Pressures to conform.** As we know from our earlier discussion, there are pressures to conform in groups. Groupthink undermines critical thinking in the group and eventually harms the quality of the final decision.[24]
4. **Ambiguous responsibility.** Group members share responsibility, but the responsibility of any single member is diluted.

Determining whether groups are effective at making decisions depends on the criteria you use to assess effectiveness.[25] Exhibit 15–6 summarizes when groups or individuals are most effective.

Keep in mind, however, that the effectiveness of group decision making is also influenced by the size of the group. Although a larger group provides greater opportunity for diverse representation, it also requires more coordination and more time for members to contribute their ideas. So groups probably should not be too large. Evidence indicates, in fact, that groups of five, and to a lesser extent, seven, are the most effective for making decisions.[26] Having an odd number in the group helps avoid decision deadlocks. Also, these groups are large enough for members to shift roles and withdraw from unfavorable positions but still small enough for quieter members to participate actively in discussions.

What techniques can managers use to help groups make more creative decisions? Exhibit 15–7 describes three possible techniques.

**Conflict Management** Another important group process is how a group manages conflict. As a group performs its assigned tasks, disagreements inevitably arise. When we use the term **conflict**, we're referring to *perceived* incompatible differences resulting in some form of interference or opposition. Whether the differences are real is irrelevant. If people in a group perceive that differences exist, then there is conflict.

Over the years, three different views have evolved regarding conflict.[27] One view argues that conflict must be avoided—that it indicates a problem within the group.

Exhibit 15–7

**Techniques for Making More Creative Group Decisions**

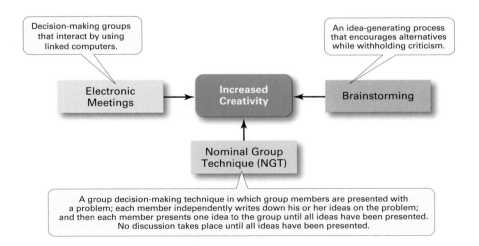

**conflict**
Perceived incompatible differences that result in interference or opposition.

**Q & A**

Wouldn't all conflict in an organization be bad? After all, have you ever had any positive experiences with personal conflicts? Go to Q & A 15.8 and find out.

**Q & A**

How will you know when a group conflict is no longer functional and that it's time to do something about it? Check out Q & A 15.9.

We call this the **traditional view of conflict**. ( Go to www.prenhall.com/rolls) A second view, the **human relations view of conflict**, argues that conflict is a natural and inevitable outcome in any group and need not be negative but, rather, has potential to be a positive force in contributing to a group's performance. The third and most recent perspective proposes that not only can conflict be a positive force in a group but also that some conflict is *absolutely necessary* for a group to perform effectively. This third approach is called the **interactionist view of conflict**.

The interactionist view doesn't suggest that all conflicts are good. Some conflicts are seen as supporting the goals of the work group and improving its performance; these are **functional conflicts** of a constructive nature. Other conflicts are destructive and prevent a group from achieving its goals. These are **dysfunctional conflicts**. Exhibit 15–8 illustrates the challenge facing managers. ( Go to www.prenhall.com/rolls)

What differentiates functional from dysfunctional conflict? Research indicates that you need to look at the *type* of conflict.[28] Three types have been identified: task, relationship, and process.

**Task conflict** relates to the content and goals of the work. **Relationship conflict** focuses on interpersonal relationships. **Process conflict** refers to how the work gets done. Studies demonstrate that relationship conflicts are almost always dysfunctional. Why? It appears that the friction and interpersonal hostilities inherent in relationship conflicts increase personality clashes and decrease mutual understanding, thereby hindering the completion of organizational tasks. On the other hand, low levels of process conflict and low-to-moderate levels of task conflict are functional. For process conflict to be productive, it must be minimal. Intense arguments about who should do what become dysfunctional when they create uncertainty about task roles, increase the time to complete tasks, and lead to members working at cross-purposes. A low-to-moderate level of task conflict consistently leads to a positive effect on group performance because it stimulates discussion of ideas that help groups be more innovative.[29] Because we don't yet have a sophisticated measuring instrument for assessing whether

Exhibit 15–8

**Conflict and Group Performance**

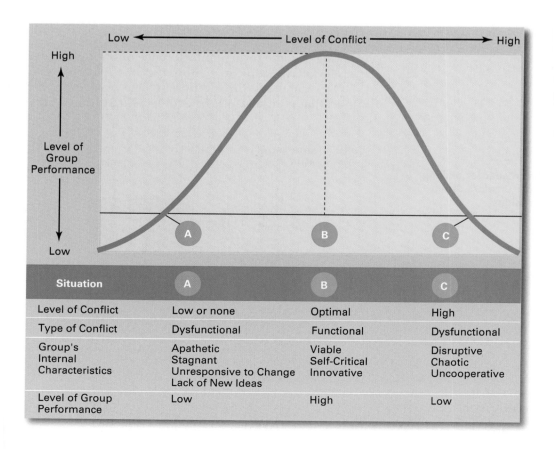

| Situation | A | B | C |
|---|---|---|---|
| Level of Conflict | Low or none | Optimal | High |
| Type of Conflict | Dysfunctional | Functional | Dysfunctional |
| Group's Internal Characteristics | Apathetic Stagnant Unresponsive to Change Lack of New Ideas | Viable Self-Critical Innovative | Disruptive Chaotic Uncooperative |
| Level of Group Performance | Low | High | Low |

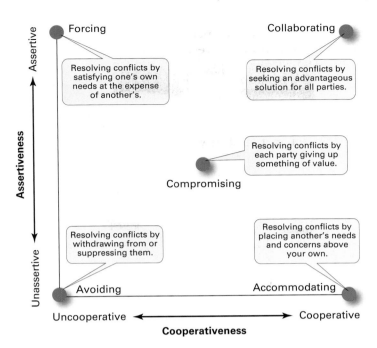

Exhibit 15–9

**Conflict-Management Techniques**

*Source:* Adapted from K. W. Thomas, "Conflict and Negotiation Processes in Organizations," in M. D. Dunnette and L. M. Hough (eds.), *Handbook of Industrial and Organizational Psychology*, vol. 3, 2d ed. (Palo Alto, CA: Consulting Psychologists Press, 1992), p. 668. With permission.

**Ethics**

Can a manager resolve group conflict ethically? See what this Ethics exercise has to say.

**Q & A**

What affects the choice of how you'll resolve conflicts: the situation or your personal style? See Q & A 15.10.

a given task, relationship, or process conflict level is optimal, too high, or too low, the manager must make intelligent judgments. (Check out ▼ You're the Manager: Putting Ethics into Action on page 520.)

When group conflict levels are too high, managers can select from five conflict management options: avoidance, accommodation, forcing, compromise, and collaboration.[30] (See Exhibit 15–9 for a description of these techniques.) Keep in mind that no one option is ideal for every situation. Which approach to use depends upon the circumstances. (▼ Go to www.prenhall.com/rolls)

## Group Tasks

At Hackensack University Medical Center in New Jersey, daily reviews of each patient in each nursing unit are conducted in MDRs (multidisciplinary rounds) by teams of nurses, case managers, social workers, and an in-hospital doctor. These teams perform tasks such as prescribing drugs or even recommending a patient be discharged. Employee teams at Lockheed Martin Maritime Systems' New York facility custom build complex products such as ground-based radar systems using continuous quality improvement techniques. The seven people who make up the Skinny Improv group in Springfield, Missouri, perform their unique brand of comedy every weekend in a downtown venue.[31] Each of these groups has a different type of task to accomplish as a group.

The impact that group processes have on group performance and member satisfaction is modified by the task the group is doing. More specifically, the *complexity* and *interdependence* of tasks influence the group's effectiveness.[32]

Tasks can be generalized as either simple or complex. Simple tasks are routine and standardized. Complex tasks are ones that tend to be novel or nonroutine. We

**traditional view of conflict**
The view that all conflict is bad and must be avoided.

**human relations view of conflict**
The view that conflict is a natural and inevitable outcome in any group.

**interactionist view of conflict**
The view that some conflict is necessary for a group to perform effectively.

**functional conflicts**
Conflicts that support a group's goals and improve its performance.

**dysfunctional conflicts**
Conflicts that prevent a group from achieving its goals.

**task conflict**
Conflict over content and goals of the work.

**relationship conflict**
Conflict based on interpersonal relationships.

**process conflict**
Conflict over how work gets done.

*Volkswagen put together a team of 23 employees from the United States and Europe, with expertise in engineering, marketing, design, and sales, to find out how to make more appealing cars for the U.S. market by devoting 2 years to living in and experiencing the American culture. The team began the assignment by visiting 24 U.S. cities in 24 days—attending a rodeo and a drag race, witnessing spring break in Florida, shadowing customers to observe how they used their cars, and sampling every mode of transportation including rental cars (a different model each week) and red-eye flights. One surprise for the team was that unlike Europeans, who simply drive, Americans view their cars as a second home, spending hours driving from place to place while eating, listening to music, and talking on the phone. Said one team member of the experience, "It was about living the customer's life and putting ourselves in their place."*

would hypothesize that the more complex the task, the more the group will benefit from discussion among group members about alternative work methods. If the task is simple, group members don't need to discuss such alternatives. They can rely on standard operating procedures. Similarly, if there's a high degree of interdependence among the tasks that group members must perform, they'll need to interact more. Effective communication and controlled conflict should, therefore, be most relevant to group performance when tasks are complex and interdependent.

## Learning Review

- Explain the major components that determine group performance and satisfaction.
- Discuss how roles, norms, conformity, status systems, group size, and group cohesiveness influence group behavior.
- Explain how group norms can both help and hurt an organization.

- Define groupthink and social loafing.
- Describe the relationship between group cohesiveness and productivity.
- Discuss how conflict management influences group behavior.
- Tell the advantages and disadvantages of group decision making.

## TURNING GROUPS INTO EFFECTIVE TEAMS

More than 25 years ago when companies like W.L. Gore, Volvo, and Kraft Foods introduced teams into their production processes, it made news because no one else was doing it. Today, it's just the opposite—the organization that *doesn't* use teams would be newsworthy. It's estimated that some 80 percent of *Fortune* 500 companies have half or more of their employees on teams. More than 70 percent of U.S. manufacturers use work teams.[33] And the popularity of teams is likely to continue. Why? Research evidence suggests that teams typically outperform individuals when the tasks being done require multiple skills, judgment, and experience.[34] As organizations have restructured to become more competitive, they're relying on teams as a way to use employee talents better. Managers have found that teams are more flexible and responsive to changing events than are traditional departments or other permanent work groups. Teams have the ability to quickly assemble, deploy, refocus, and disband. (  Go to www.prenhall.com/rolls) In this section, we'll discuss what a work team is, the different types of teams that organizations might use, and how to develop and manage work teams.

**Q & A**

Don't most people in North America prefer working on their own … you know the "rugged individualist" type? Q & A 15.11 looks at this.

| Work Group | Team |
| --- | --- |
| • Strong, clearly focused leader | • Shared leadership roles |
| • Individual accountability | • Individual and mutual accountability |
| • The group's purpose is the same as the broader organizational mission | • Specific team purpose that the team itself delivers |
| • Individual work products | • Collective work products |
| • Runs efficient meetings | • Encourages open-ended discussion and active problem-solving meetings |
| • Measures its effectiveness indirectly by its influence on others (such as financial performance of the business) | • Measures performance directly by assessing collective work products |
| • Discusses, decides, and delegates together | • Discusses, decides, and does real work |

## What Is a Team?

Most of you are already familiar with teams especially if, for no other reason, you've watched or participated in organized sports events. A sports team has many of the same characteristics as a work team, but work *teams* are different from work *groups* and have their own unique traits (see Exhibit 15–10). Work groups interact primarily to share information and to make decisions to help each member do his or her job more efficiently and effectively. These groups have no need or opportunity to engage in collective work that requires joint effort. On the other hand, **work teams** are groups whose members work intensely on a specific, common goal using their positive synergy, individual and mutual accountability, and complementary skills.

## Types of Teams

Teams can do a variety of things. They can design products, provide services, negotiate deals, coordinate projects, offer advice, and make decisions.[35] For instance, at Rockwell Automation's facility in North Carolina, teams are used in work process optimization projects. At Arkansas-based Acxiom Corporation, a team of human resource professionals planned and implemented a cultural change that was focused more on customer service. And every summer weekend at any NASCAR race, you can see work teams in action during drivers' pit stops.[36] The four most common types of teams you're likely to find in an organization include problem-solving teams, self-managed work teams, cross-functional teams, and virtual teams.

If we look back to when work teams were becoming popular, most were what we call **problem-solving teams**, which are teams from the same department or functional area who are involved in efforts to improve work activities or to solve specific problems. In problem-solving teams, members share ideas or offer suggestions on how work processes and methods can be improved. However, these teams are rarely given the authority to unilaterally implement any of their suggested actions.

Although problem-solving teams were on the right track, they didn't go far enough in getting employees involved in work-related decisions and processes. This led to the development of another type of team that could not only solve problems but also implement solutions and take full responsibility for outcomes. These teams are called **self-managed work teams**, a formal group of employees who operate without a manager and are responsible for a complete work process or segment. The self-managed team is responsible for getting the work done *and* for managing themselves. This usually includes planning and scheduling of work, assigning tasks to members, collective

*and interdependently*

**work teams**
Groups whose members work intensely on a specific, common goal using their positive synergy, individual and mutual accountability, and complementary skills.

**problem-solving team**
A team from the same department or functional area that's involved in efforts to improve work activities or to solve specific problems.

**self-managed work team**
A type of work team that operates without a manager and is responsible for a complete work process or segment.

control over the pace of work, making operating decisions, and taking action on problems. For instance, teams at Corning have no shift supervisors and work closely with other manufacturing divisions to solve production-line problems and coordinate deadlines and deliveries. The teams have the authority to make and implement decisions, finish projects, and address problems.[37] Other organizations such as Xerox, Boeing, PepsiCo, Hewlett-Packard, and Industrial Light & Magic use self-managed teams. It's estimated that about 30 percent of U.S. employers now use this form of team; and among large firms, the number is probably closer to 50 percent.[38] How effective are self-managed teams? Most organizations that use them find them to be successful and plan to expand their use in the coming years.[39]

The third type of team we want to discuss is the **cross-functional team**, which we introduced in Chapter 10 and defined as a work team composed of individuals from various specialties. Many organizations use cross-functional teams. For example, at the AMS Operations Hillend factory in Fife, Scotland, cross-functional teams manufacture printed circuit boards that are used in military applications.[40] The concept of cross-functional teams is even being applied in health care. For instance, at Suburban Hospital in Bethesda, Maryland, intensive care unit (ICU) teams composed of a doctor trained in intensive care medicine, a pharmacist, a social worker, a nutritionist, the chief ICU nurse, a respiratory therapist, and a chaplain meet daily with every patient's bedside nurse to discuss and debate the best course of treatment. The hospital credits this team care approach with reducing errors, shortening the amount of time patients spent in ICU, and improving communication between families and the medical staff.[41] ( Go to www.prenhall.com/rolls)

The final type of team we want to discuss is the **virtual team**. Virtual teams are teams that use technology to link physically dispersed members in order to achieve a common goal. For instance, StrawberryFrog, a small advertising agency with just 100 people in its two main offices in Amsterdam and New York, also relies on a global network of more than 100 freelancers from 22 countries. These freelancers and their skills are brought in as needed on various projects. By relying on virtual teams, StrawberryFrog is able to exploit a network of talent without unnecessary overhead and complex work arrangements.[42] In a virtual team, members collaborate online with tools such as wide-area networks, videoconferencing, fax, e-mail, or Web sites where the team can hold online conferences.[43] Virtual teams can do all the things that other teams can—share information, make decisions, and complete tasks; however, they miss the normal give-and-take of face-to-face discussions. Because of this omission, virtual teams tend to be more task-oriented especially if the team members have never personally met.

**Q & A**

Is a self-directed team different from a cross-functional team? Q & A 15.12 explains.

## Creating Effective Teams

Teams are not automatic productivity enhancers. They can also be disappointments. How can managers create effective teams? ( Go to www.prenhall.com/rolls)

Research on teams provides insights into the characteristics associated with effective teams.[44] Let's look closer at these characteristics as listed in Exhibit 15–11.

**PRISM**

Start developing your skills at coaching and creating effective teams by completing PRISM #9.

**Clear Goals**   High-performance teams have a clear understanding of the goal to be achieved. Members are committed to the team's goals, know what they're expected to accomplish, and understand how they will work together to achieve these goals.

**Relevant Skills**   Effective teams are composed of competent individuals who have the necessary technical and interpersonal skills to achieve the desired goals while working well together. This last point is important since not everyone who is technically competent has the interpersonal skills to work well as a team member.

**Mutual Trust**   Effective teams are characterized by high mutual trust among members. That is, members believe in each other's ability, character, and integrity. But as you probably know from personal relationships, trust is fragile. Maintaining this trust requires careful attention by managers. ( Go to www.prenhall.com/rolls)

**Self-Assessment Library (S.A.L.)**

Do people see you as trustworthy? S.A.L. #II.B.4 will show you.

Exhibit 15–11

**Characteristics of Effective Teams**

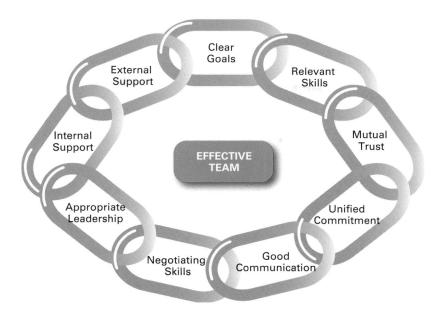

**Unified Commitment** Unified commitment is characterized by dedication to the team's goals and a willingness to expend extraordinary amounts of energy to achieve them. Members of an effective team exhibit intense loyalty and dedication to the team and are willing to do whatever it takes to help their team succeed.

**Good Communication** Not surprisingly, effective teams are characterized by good communication. Members convey messages, verbally and nonverbally, among each other in ways that are readily and clearly understood. Also, feedback helps guide team members and correct misunderstandings. Like a couple who has been together for many years, members on high-performing teams are able to quickly and efficiently share ideas and feelings. (  Go to www.prenhall.com/rolls)

Self-Assessment Library (S.A.L.)

How good are your listening skills? Complete S.A.L. #II.A.2 and find out!

**Negotiating Skills** Effective teams are continually making adjustments as to who does what. This flexibility requires team members to possess negotiating skills. Since problems and relationships are regularly changing in teams, members need to be able to confront and reconcile differences.

*All the work that employees do at Whole Foods Markets is based around teamwork. Characteristics of effective teams, like job skills, commitment, trust, communication, and effective training and support, are important for making this kind of structure successful and contributing to the rapid growth of the organic-food retailer.*

**cross-functional team**
A work team composed of individuals from various specialties.

**virtual team**
A type of work team that uses technology to link physically dispersed members in order to achieve a common goal.

## becoming a Manager

✓ Use any opportunities that come up to work in a group. Note things such as stages of group development, roles, norms, social loafing, and so forth.

✓ When confronted with conflicts, pay attention to how you manage or resolve them.

✓ In group projects, try different techniques for improving the group's creativity.

✓ When you see a successful team, try to assess what makes it successful.

✓  There are a number of Self-Assessments from www.prenhall.com/rolls that are relevant to this chapter. Complete the ones that have been listed throughout the chapter.

**Self-Assessment Library (S.A.L.)**

**Self-Assessment Library (S.A.L.)**

S.A.L. #II.B.6 will show you how good you are at building and leading a team. Take it and see how you rate.

**Appropriate Leadership** Effective leaders can motivate a team to follow them through the most difficult situations. How? By clarifying goals, demonstrating that change is possible by overcoming inertia, increasing the self-confidence of team members, and helping members to more fully realize their potential. Increasingly, effective team leaders act as coaches and facilitators. They help guide and support the team, but don't control it. ( 🔷 Go to www.prenhall.com/rolls)

**Internal and External Support** The final condition necessary for an effective team is a supportive climate. Internally, the team should have a sound infrastructure, which means having proper training, a clear and reasonable measurement system that team members can use to evaluate their overall performance, an incentive program that recognizes and rewards team activities, and a supportive human resource system. The right infrastructure should support members and reinforce behaviors that lead to high levels of performance. Externally, managers should provide the team with the resources needed to get the job done.

## Learning Review

- Compare groups and teams.
- Explain why teams have become so popular in organizations.

- Describe the four most common types of teams.
- List the characteristics of effective teams.

## CURRENT CHALLENGES IN MANAGING TEAMS

Few trends have influenced how work gets done in organizations as much as the massive move to introduce teams into the workplace. The shift from working alone to working on teams requires employees to cooperate with others, share information, confront differences, and sublimate personal interests for the greater good of the team. Like Dadi Perlmutter, the manager highlighted in our chapter opener, managers can build effective teams by understanding their behavior. However, managers also face some current challenges in managing teams, primarily those associated with managing global teams and with understanding organizational social networks.

### Managing Global Teams

**PASSPORT**

Creating an effective global team can't be too easy. See what it's like by trying out this Passport Scenario.

Two characteristics of today's organizations are obvious: (1) they're global; and (2) work is increasingly done by groups or teams. This means that any manager is likely, at some point in time, to have to manage a global team. What do we know about managing global teams? We know there are both drawbacks and benefits in using global teams (see Exhibit 15–12). ( 🔷 Check out Passport Scenario 1 on page 520.)

Exhibit 15–12

**Drawbacks and Benefits of Global Teams**

Source: Based on N. Adler, *International Dimensions in Organizational Behavior*, 4th ed. (Cincinnati, OH: Southwestern, 2002), pp. 141–147.

| Drawbacks | Benefits |
| --- | --- |
| • Dislike team members | • Greater diversity of ideas |
| • Mistrust team members | • Limited groupthink |
| • Stereotyping | • Increased attention on understanding others' ideas, perspectives, etc. |
| • Communication problems | |
| • Stress and tension | |

And using our group behavior model as a framework, we can see some of the issues associated with managing global teams.

**Group Member Resources in Global Teams** In global organizations, understanding the relationship between group performance and group member resources is more challenging because of the unique cultural characteristics represented by members of a global team. In addition to recognizing team members' abilities, skills, knowledge, and personality, managers need to be familiar with and clearly understand the cultural characteristics of the groups and the group members they manage.[45] For instance, is the global team from a culture in which uncertainty avoidance is high? If so, members will not be comfortable dealing with unpredictable and ambiguous tasks. Also, as managers work with global teams, they need to be aware of the potential for stereotyping, which has been shown to be a problem with global teams.[46]

**Group Structure** Some of the structural areas where we see differences in managing global teams include conformity, status, social loafing, and cohesiveness.

Are conformity findings generalizable across cultures? Research suggests that Asch's findings are culture-bound.[47] For instance, as might be expected, conformity to social norms tends to be higher in collectivist cultures than in individualistic cultures. Despite this, however, groupthink tends to be less of a problem in global teams because members are less likely to feel pressured to conform to the ideas, conclusions, and decisions of the group.[48]

How about status? Do cultural differences affect status? Yes! The importance of status varies between cultures. The French, for example, are extremely status conscious. Also, countries differ on the criteria that confer status. For instance, status for Latin Americans and Asians tends to come from family position and formal roles held in organizations. In contrast, although status is important in countries like the United States and Australia, it tends to be less "in your face." And it tends to be given based on accomplishments rather than on titles and family history. Managers should be sure to understand who and what holds status when interacting with people from a culture different from their own. An American manager who doesn't understand that office size isn't a measure of a Japanese executive's position or who fails to grasp the importance the British place on family genealogy and social class is likely to unintentionally offend others and lessen his or her interpersonal effectiveness.

What about social loafing? The phenomenon has a Western bias. It's consistent with individualistic cultures, like the United States and Canada, which are dominated by self-interest. It's not consistent with collectivistic societies, in which individuals are motivated by in-group goals. For instance, in studies comparing employees from the United States with employees from the People's Republic of China and Israel (both collectivistic societies), the Chinese and Israelis showed no propensity to engage in social loafing. In fact, they actually performed better in a group than when working alone.[49]

Cohesiveness is another group structural element where managers may face special challenges. In a cohesive group, members are unified and "act as one." There's a great deal of camaraderie and group identity is high. In global teams, however, cohesiveness is often more difficult to achieve because of higher levels of mistrust, miscommunication, and stress.[50]

**Group Processes** The processes global teams use to do their work can be particularly challenging for managers. For one thing, communication problems often arise because not all team members may be fluent in the team's working language. This can lead to inaccuracies, misunderstandings, and inefficiencies.[51] However, research has also shown that a multicultural global team is better able to capitalize on the diversity of ideas represented if a wide range of information is used.[52]

Managing conflict in global teams, especially when those teams are virtual teams, isn't easy. Conflict in multicultural teams can interfere with how information is used by the team. However, research shows that in collectivistic cultures, a collaborative conflict management style can be most effective.[53]

**Manager's Role** Despite the challenges associated with managing global teams, there are things managers can do to provide the group with an environment in which efficiency and effectiveness are enhanced.[54] First, because communication skills are vital, managers should focus on developing those skills. Also, as we've said earlier, managers must consider cultural differences when deciding what type of global team to use. For instance, evidence suggests that self-managed teams have not fared well in Mexico largely due to that culture's low tolerance of ambiguity and uncertainty and employees' strong respect for hierarchical authority.[55] Finally, it's vital that managers be sensitive to the unique differences of each member of the global team. But, it's also important that team members be sensitive to each other as well.

## Understanding Social Networks

We can't leave this chapter on group behavior without looking at the patterns of informal connections among individuals within groups—that is, at the **social network structure**.[56] What actually happens *within* groups? How *do* group members relate to each other and how does work get done?

Managers need to understand the social networks and social relationships of work groups. Why? Because a team's informal social relationships can help or hinder its effectiveness. For instance, research on social networks has shown that when people need help getting a job done, they'll choose a friendly colleague over someone who may be more capable.[57] Another recent review of team studies showed that teams with high levels of interpersonal interconnectedness actually attained their goals better and were more committed to staying together.[58] Organizations are recognizing the practical benefits of knowing the social networks within teams. For instance, when Ken Loughridge, an IT manager with MWH Global, was transferred from Cheshire, England, to New Zealand, he had a "map" of the informal relationships and connections among company IT employees. This map had been created a few months earlier using the results of a survey that asked employees who they "consulted most frequently, who they turned to for expertise, and who either boosted or drained their energy levels." Not only did this map help Loughridge identify well-connected technical experts, but it also helped him minimize potential problems when a key manager in the Asia region left the company because he knew who this person's closest contacts were. Loughridge said, "It's as if you took the top off an ant hill and could see where there's a hive of activity. It really helped me understand who the players were."[59]

## Learning Review

- Discuss the challenges of managing global teams.

- Explain the role of informal (social) networks in managing teams.

# Managers Respond to a Manager's Dilemma

## Matthew Leavy

Executive Vice President, International and
Professional Group, Pearson Higher Education,
Upper Saddle River, NJ

**D**adi has nurtured and maintained "a strong culture of debate and confrontation," and his challenge is to preserve and enhance that culture as new people join his team. Part of this challenge is to avoid the temptation to create a new orthodoxy around those approaches that have worked in the past. There are several tactics that Dadi can employ to achieve these goals:

1. Hire well. He should look for designers that have a track record of challenging the status quo and are willing to disagree, even in the interview. He should also look for diverse experiences and background as he brings new designers in— people who are likely to have a different mental framework for looking at issues.

2. Integrate new hires with the cultural leaders of the team. He should seek opportunities for having new hires work closely with established team members who exemplify the cultural values Dadi is trying to preserve.

3. Manage by storytelling. A team culture can be preserved and extended by communicating the stories of past successes and the values that led to those successes.

## Dave Blodgett

Director of IT and On Demand Services, Cybershift, Inc.,
Parsippany, NJ

**D**adi is working from a good starting position: His team already challenges the status quo. His challenge lies with nurturing and perpetuating this desirable culture, which in itself can be a difficult task. There are many elements that can erode team culture, most notably influence by other teams or individuals. The scenario states that design groups located at company headquarters suffer from "bureaucratic inertia." As a result, Dadi should make a conscious effort to limit the influence of those teams on his own. The geographic separation of Dadi's team from the core of the organization represents a slight advantage on this front.

Dadi should work to develop a method of filtering undesirable outside influences (while not completely isolating his team from the rest of the company) and promoting the desirable trait of creative, out-of-the-box thinking. New hires should be assimilated into the culture through orientation and education programs, and senior resources should be encouraged to promote this way of thinking. Positive reinforcement and clear communication of team culture will be Dadi's most effective tool for ensuring its continued success.

**social network structure**
The patterns of informal connections among individuals within a group.

# Learning Summary

## How Do Groups Develop in Organizations?

**Group:** two or more interacting and interdependent individuals who come together to achieve specific goals

- Formal groups—defined by the organization; include command, task, cross-functional, and self-managed
- Informal groups—occur naturally because of friendships and common interests
- Groups develop through five stages: forming, storming, norming, performing, and for temporary groups, adjourning

## What Factors Affect Group Behavior?

- External conditions: available resources, rules and regulations, culture, etc.
- Group member resources: individual members' knowledge, skills, abilities, and personalities
- Group structure
  - **Roles**—expected behavior patterns of a person occupying some position in a social unit; watch for role conflict
  - **Norms**—acceptable standards or expectations shared by group members; common norms focus on effort and performance, dress, and loyalty
  - Conformity—pressures placed on individuals to adhere to the group's opinions and decisions; Asch's conformity experiments
    - **Groupthink**—extensive and excessive pressure on group members to align their opinions
  - **Status**—prestige grading, position, or rank within a group; status system needs to be congruent
  - Group size; large groups are better for getting diverse input and more facts while smaller groups are better at doing something productive with those facts
    - **Social loafing**—the tendency for individuals to expend less effort when working collectively than when working individually
  - **Group cohesiveness**—degree to which members are attracted to a group and share its goals; highly cohesive groups are more effective but a key moderating variable is how the group's attitude aligns with goals
- Group processes
  - Decision making—advantages and disadvantages of group decision making
  - Conflict management
    - Three views of conflict: **traditional**, **human relations** view, and **interactionist** view
    - **Functional** versus **dysfunctional conflicts**
    - Three types of conflict: **Task** (low to moderate levels are functional), **relationship** (always dysfunctional), and **process** (low levels are functional)
  - Group tasks—complexity and interdependence of tasks

## How Can Groups Become Effective Teams?

- **Work teams**—members work intensely on a specific, common goal using their positive synergy, individual and mutual accountability, and complementary skills; they are different from work groups
- Types of teams
  - **Problem-solving**—teams from same department involved in efforts to improve work activities or to solve specific problems
  - **Self-managed**—teams that operate without a manager and are responsible for complete work process or segment
  - **Cross-functional**—team composed of individuals from various specialties
  - **Virtual team**—teams that use technology to link physically dispersed members to achieve a common goal
- Creating effective teams: clear goals, relevant skills, mutual trust, unified commitment, good communication, negotiating skills, appropriate leadership, and internal and external support

## What Current Challenges Do Managers Face in Managing Teams?

- Managing global teams
- Understanding social networks
  - **Social network structure**—patterns of informal connections among individuals within groups

# Management: By the Numbers

- In 2004, 70 percent of production workers were part of self-managed or empowered work teams. However, that figure has dropped. In 2000, more than 85 percent of production workers belonged to these types of teams.
- The average number of production workers per team has stayed around 10 to 12.
- The top three problems employees face in working on teams are poor sharing of information,

unclear or inappropriate expectations, and unclear lines of accountability or control.
- In a survey of actual work groups, 33 percent of female respondents wanted more face-to-face meetings, compared to only 27 percent of male respondents.

*Sources:* T. Purdum, "Teaming, Take 2," *Industry Week,* May 2005, pp. 41–43; and L. G. Boiney, "Gender Impacts Virtual Work Teams," *The Graziadio Business Report,* Fall 2001, Pepperdine University.

# Thinking About Management Issues

1. Think of a group to which you belong (or have belonged). Trace its development through the stages of group development shown in Exhibit 15–2. How closely did its development parallel the group development model? How might the group development model been used to improve the group's effectiveness?

2. How do you think scientific management theorists would react to the increased reliance on teams in organizations? How would behavioral science theorists react?

3. How do you explain the popularity of work teams in the United States when its culture places such high value on individualism and individual effort?

4. Why might a manager want to stimulate conflict in a group or team? How could conflict be stimulated?

5. Do you think that everyone should be expected to be a team player, given the trends we're seeing in the use of teams? Discuss.

# Working Together: Team-Based Exercise

What happens when groups are presented with a task that must be completed within a certain time frame? Does the group exhibit characteristics of the stages of group development? Can the group behavior model

(Exhibit 15–3) explain what happens in the group? Your instructor will divide the class into groups and give you instructions about what to do next.

# Ethical Dilemma Exercise

How can managers from competing companies deal with the ethical issues that arise when they participate in task groups making decisions that affect the overall industry? Industry-wide standards for product performance are often developed by committees of representatives drawn from a number of companies. The idea is to minimize noncompatibility problems (for products such as cell phones) or meet government-imposed requirements (such as water conservation rules) by adopting a single set of specifications. However, committee members may face role conflict because their decisions have consequences for their companies as well as the entire industry.

For example, consider the issues facing committees working on standards for Bluetooth wireless technology, used for data transfer between electronic devices. The original standard was backed by the Bluetooth Special Interest Group (BSIG), consisting of representatives from Ericsson, Intel, Motorola, and other companies. Later, the UWB Forum (including representatives of a company spun off from Motorola) and the WiMedia Alliance (including representatives from Motorola rival Intel)

tried but failed to agree on a new, speedier Bluetooth standard. The BSIG eventually adopted the WiMedia Alliance's specifications as standard. Yet UWB's standard was the first to be used in consumer products, even though WiMedia's standard was supported by a larger number of companies—including many in the BSIG. What are the implications for the industry's competitive situation?[60]

Imagine you're an Intel engineer on the BSIG committee considering higher-speed Bluetooth transmission standards. Although the UWB and the WiMedia Alliance are proposing different standards, everyone agrees on the merits of enabling faster transmission of large files between devices such as video cameras and televisions. If your committee adopts the UWB's specifications, you suspect Intel will need a lot of time and money to comply. If your committee adopts the WiMedia Alliance's specifications—which you believe are superior—you suspect Motorola will have difficulty getting ready. Review this chapter's section on work group behavior as you decide which of the following options to choose.

**Option A:** Vote to adopt the UWB's standard. Otherwise, your company could be perceived as being biased against your competitor, Motorola.

**Option B:** Vote to adopt the WiMedia Alliance's standard with an immediate implementation deadline, because consumers will benefit the most.

**Option C:** Vote to adopt the WiMedia Alliance's standard with a flexible implementation deadline, to allow all companies time to prepare.

# Case Application

### Designing Superior Design Teams

It's now the world's largest and most profitable consumer electronics company. No, it's not Sony. It's Samsung Electronics, and in 2005, it knocked off Sony as the world's most valuable consumer electronics brand, according to the most recent valuable global brands survey done by the Interbrand Consulting Group. Its clever product designs have won over consumers and won numerous awards.

Samsung Group was founded as a trucking company in the 1930s and in the 1960s became one of several *chaebol* (large conglomerates) "shaped by the Korean government and protected from foreign competition by import duties and other government-sponsored regulations." The electronics division, Samsung Electronics, is by far the largest and most global of the Samsung businesses.

Although Samsung Electronics is sitting on top now, Kim Byung Cheol, a senior executive, is worried about his company's future. Why? Because Samsung "still has not mastered one crucial factor: originality." Much of Samsung's success in electronics can be traced to its ability to mimic and enhance others' inventions, but it has never been the design innovator. Mr. Kim says, "We are at a pivotal moment for the company. If we don't become an innovator, we could end up like one of those Japanese companies, mired in difficulties." However, analysts say that if any company can change itself, it's Samsung.

*A Samsung team.*

One of the first things the company is doing is investing $40 billion in research and development over the next 5 years, double the amount it spent in the previous 5 years. And accordingly, it is doubling its number of product and design researchers, going from 13,900 to 32,000. Samsung's extensive commitment to changing its R&D capabilities is showcased in its newest facility—the Digital Research Center, which is located in its research and development center in Suwon, a city just south of Seoul. The Digital Research Center has office and laboratory space for 9,000 researchers, although only around 5,000 have been hired. Samsung is making it a global endeavor; 150 of these researchers are from foreign countries, including China, the United States, and India. However, R&D isn't the only area where Samsung is focusing its efforts. Product design continues to be an important component of its future strategies, as well.

At the company's design center just a few blocks away from headquarters, in Seoul, the geographical distance isn't the only evidence of separation. Here, designers work in small teams with three to five members coming from various specialty areas and levels of seniority. Even though Korean culture has loosened up somewhat, respect for elders and a reluctance to speak out of turn are still the norm. But here at Samsung's design center, there's no dress code and team members work as equals. Everyone—even the younger staffers who often have their hair dyed green or pink—is encouraged to speak up and challenge their superiors. But the departure from corporate tradition has helped Samsung emerge as an innovative design leader. With innovative design and innovative products, Samsung Electronics is positioning itself to continue its successful global brands strategy.

### Discussion Questions

1. Using Exhibit 15–3, describe Samsung's approach to managing its design teams.

2. Suppose Samsung decided to use work teams at its new Digital Research Center. Describe the types of issues managers might face in managing these teams. What could they do to ensure that these teams experience the kinds of successes that the design teams have?

3. It's your chance to be creative! Think of a team-building exercise that would help these work teams achieve one of the characteristics of an effective team (see Exhibit 15.11). Describe the characteristic you chose and then describe the exercise you'd use to help a team develop or enhance that characteristic.

4. What could other managers learn about managing teams from Samsung's successes?

*Sources:* M. Fackler, "Raising the Bar at Samsung," *New York Times Online,* www.nytimes.com, April 25, 2006; B. Breen, "The Seoul of Design," *Fast Company,* December 2005, pp. 90–97; E. Ramstad, "Standing Firm," *Wall Street Journal,* March 16, 2005, pp. A1+; and D. Rocks and M. Ihlwan, "Samsung Design," *BusinessWeek,* December 6, 2004, pp. 88–96.

# Learning Outline

*Use this Learning Outline as you read and study this chapter.*

**What Is Motivation?**

- Define motivation.
- Explain the energy, direction, and persistence aspects of motivation.

**Early Theories of Motivation**

- Describe Maslow's hierarchy of needs and how it can be used to motivate.
- Discuss how Theory X and Theory Y managers approach motivation.
- Describe Herzberg's motivation-hygiene theory.
- Explain Herzberg's views of satisfaction and dissatisfaction.

**Contemporary Theories of Motivation**

- Describe the three needs McClelland proposed as being present in work settings.
- Explain how goal-setting and reinforcement theories explain employee motivation.
- Describe the job characteristics model as a way to design motivating jobs.
- Discuss the motivation implications of equity theory.
- Contrast distributive justice and procedural justice.
- Explain the three key linkages in expectancy theory and their role in motivation.

**Current Issues in Motivation**

- Describe the cross-cultural challenges of motivation.
- Discuss the challenges managers face in motivating unique groups of workers.
- Describe open-book management, employee recognition, pay-for-performance, and stock option programs.

# Motivating Employees

## A Manager's Dilemma

Trying to prove something can cause people to reach above and beyond what they thought they could. And Tom Despres can attest to the truth of that.[1] He manages a Storage Technology (StorageTek) manufacturing plant in Ponce, Puerto Rico. The company's CEO was considering moving production to China, where costs would be lower, but he gave Tom and his employees a chance to prove themselves . . . and they set out to do so.

When Tom was first named president and director of the Puerto Rican plant, he continued what his predecessor had started in terms of emphasizing training, technology, and results. Although many manufacturers often struggle with getting employees to accept changes in their work processes, the employees at StorageTek's largest plant "fully embraced" total quality management, Six Sigma, agile manufacturing, and other established process improvement methods. They did things like separate high-volume products from high-mix products and reconfigure the production floor. Such improvements allowed the plant to increase volume in one area alone by 33 percent with the same number of employees. The payoff: Employees decreased costs by $2.5 million in 2004. Then there was the incident that happened New Year's Eve, 2004. In Puerto Rico, the celebrations often include gunfire, which, not surprisingly, can be a little dangerous. Sometime a little after 6 P.M., Tom called the plant to make sure the employees were shutting down so everyone could get home before the gunfire started. However, an order for 13 of the company's larger storage systems had come in earlier that day from a valued customer, and the employees had only 11 of the systems ready to ship. And they weren't going anywhere until those 2 remaining units were finished. Tom says, "I just couldn't believe it. The employees weren't willing to turn down the customer's request."

Put yourself in Tom's position. Not only does he have motivated, passionate employees, but their efforts also led to the facility's being named one of *Industry Week's* Best Plants for 2005. What should Tom do to ensure that his employees continue to put forth their best efforts when giving them more money isn't really an option if they're going to keep costs down?

Motivating and rewarding employees is one of the most important, and one of the most challenging, activities that managers do. Successful managers, like Tom Despres, understand that what motivates each employee personally may have little or no effect on others. Just because *you're* motivated by being part of a cohesive work team, don't assume everyone is. Or just because *you're* motivated by challenging work doesn't mean that everyone is. Effective managers who want their employees to put forth maximum effort recognize that they need to know how and why employees are motivated and to tailor their motivational practices to satisfy the needs and wants of those employees.

## WHAT IS MOTIVATION?

As the president of Ajilon, a staffing firm based in New Jersey, Neil Lebovits had some serious employee problems.[2] Turnover was high and morale was low. The severity of the situation hit home when he hosted an after-work party and only 5 out of 50 employees bothered to show up. Lebovits wanted to improve employees' spirits, but like many managers, he didn't have the resources to give out big raises. So he tried some different things that wouldn't cost a lot of money. He started in-house training programs on various topics in which employees had expressed interest. He initiated monthly conference calls with every employee to discuss management decisions point by point. He set up an e-mail address where employees could propose ideas and responded to every single one. And he gave every employee 3 "YDOs" or Your Days Off a year with no questions asked. After implementing these changes, staff morale skyrocketed. Company employees even sent notes to Lebovits, enthusing about how they felt reenergized.

Neil Lebovits is a good motivator. Like Neil, all managers need to be able to motivate their employees and that requires understanding what motivation is. To understand what motivation is, let's begin by pointing out what motivation is not. Why? Because many people incorrectly view motivation as a personal trait—that is, a trait that some people have and others don't. Although, in reality, a manager might describe a certain employee as unmotivated, our knowledge of motivation tells us that we can't label people that way. What we *do* know is that motivation is the result of an interaction between a person and a situation. Individuals differ in motivational drive and their overall motivation varies from situation to situation. For instance, your level of motivation probably differs between the various classes you take each term. As we study the concept of motivation, keep in mind that the level of motivation varies both between individuals and within individuals at different times and in different situations. (  Go to www.prenhall.com/rolls)

**Motivation** refers to the process by which a person's efforts are energized, directed, and sustained toward attaining a goal.[3] Although, generally speaking, motivation involves any effort exerted toward a goal, we're most interested in organizational goals because our focus is on work-related behavior. Three key elements are important to this definition: energy, direction, and persistence.[4]

The *energy* element is a measure of intensity or drive. A motivated person puts forth effort and works hard. However, the quality of the effort must be considered as well as its intensity. High levels of effort don't necessarily lead to favorable job performance unless the effort is channeled in a *direction* that benefits the organization. Effort that's directed toward, and consistent with, organizational goals is the kind of effort we want from employees. Finally, motivation includes a *persistence* dimension. We want employees to persist in putting forth effort to achieve those goals.

Motivating high levels of employee performance is an important organizational concern and managers keep looking for answers. For instance, a recent Gallup poll found that a large majority of U.S. employees—some 73 percent—are not engaged with their work. As the researchers stated, "These employees are essentially 'checked out.'"

They're sleepwalking through their workday, putting time, but not energy or passion, into their work."[5] It's no wonder then that both practicing managers and academic researchers want to understand and explain employee motivation. In this chapter, we're going to first look at some early motivation theories and then at several contemporary theories. We'll finish by looking at some current motivation issues and some practical suggestions managers can use in motivating employees.

## Learning Review

- Define motivation.

- Explain the energy, direction, and persistence aspects of motivation.

## EARLY THEORIES OF MOTIVATION

We begin by looking at three early theories of motivation that, although questionable in terms of validity, are probably the most widely known approaches to employee motivation. These three theories are *Maslow's hierarchy of needs*, *McGregor's Theories X and Y*, and *Herzberg's two-factor theory*. Although more valid explanations of motivation have been developed, you should know these early theories because (1) they represent the foundation from which contemporary motivation theories were developed, and (2) practicing managers continue to use these theories to explain employee motivation.

### Maslow's Hierarchy of Needs Theory

**Q & A**
How does Maslow's hierarchy of needs explain motivation? See Q & A 16.1.

When Lincoln Hershberger's team was honored for best exemplifying one of his company's (video-game company Electronic Arts or EA) important values at the end of a fiscal quarter, it wasn't the trophy or shaking the CEO's hand that most excited him. It was getting one of the six desirable parking spaces in the front row of the first floor of the indoor parking lot for 3 months. And he isn't alone in coveting those parking spots—many employees at EA are motivated to win the privilege of parking in those spots.[6] EA's managers obviously understand employee needs and their impact on motivation. The first motivation theory we're going to look at addresses employee needs. ( Go to www.prenhall.com/rolls)

The best-known theory of motivation is probably Abraham Maslow's **hierarchy of needs theory**.[7] Maslow was a psychologist who proposed that within every person is a hierarchy of five needs:

1. **Physiological needs**: Food, drink, shelter, sex, and other physical requirements.
2. **Safety needs**: Security and protection from physical and emotional harm, as well as assurance that physical needs will continue to be met.
3. **Social needs**: Affection, belongingness, acceptance, and friendship.
4. **Esteem needs**: Internal esteem factors such as self-respect, autonomy, and achievement and external esteem factors such as status, recognition, and attention.
5. **Self-actualization needs**: Growth, achieving one's potential, and self-fulfillment; the drive to become what one is capable of becoming.

---

**motivation**
The process by which a person's efforts are energized, directed, and sustained toward attaining a goal.

**hierarchy of needs theory**
Maslow's theory that there is a hierarchy of five human needs.

**physiological needs**
A person's needs for food, drink, shelter, sexual satisfaction, and other physical needs.

**safety needs**
A person's needs for security and protection from physical and emotional harm.

**social needs**
A person's needs for affection, belongingness, acceptance, and friendship.

**esteem needs**
A person's needs for internal factors such as self-respect, autonomy, and achievement, and external factors such as status, recognition, and attention.

**self-actualization needs**
A person's need to become what he or she is capable of becoming.

Exhibit 16–1

**Maslow's Hierarchy of Needs**

Self-
Actualization

Esteem

Social

Safety

Physiological

Maslow argued that each level in the needs hierarchy must be substantially satis-fied before the next is activated and that once a need is substantially satisfied, the next need becomes dominant. That is, an individual moves up the needs hierarchy from one level to the next (see Exhibit 16–1).

How does Maslow's theory explain motivation? The theory proposed that, although no need is ever fully satisfied, a substantially satisfied need no longer moti-vates an individual to satisfy that need. Therefore, if you want to motivate someone, you need to understand what need level that person is on in the hierarchy and focus on satisfying needs at or above that level. Managers who used Maslow's hierarchy in motivating employees attempted to change their organizations and management practices so that employees' needs could be satisfied.

In addition, Maslow separated the five needs into higher and lower levels. Physiological and safety needs were considered *lower-order needs*; social, esteem, and self-actualization were considered *higher-order needs*. The difference was that higher-order needs are satisfied internally while lower-order needs are predominantly satis-fied externally. (  Go to www.prenhall.com/rolls)

Maslow's need theory received wide recognition during the 1960s and 1970s, espe-cially among practicing managers, probably because it was intuitively logical and easy to understand. However, Maslow provided no empirical support for his theory, and several studies that sought to validate it could not.[8]

## McGregor's Theory X and Theory Y

Douglas McGregor is best known for proposing two sets of assumptions about human nature: Theory X and Theory Y.[9] Very simply, **Theory X** is a negative view of people that assumes workers have little ambition, dislike work, want to avoid responsibility, and need to be closely controlled to work effectively. **Theory Y** is a positive view that assumes workers can exercise self-direction, accept and actually seek out responsibil-ity, and consider work to be a natural activity. McGregor believed that Theory Y assumptions best captured the true nature of workers and should guide management practice. (  Go to www.prenhall.com/rolls)

What did McGregor's analysis imply about motivation? The answer is best expressed in the framework presented by Maslow. Theory X assumed that lower-order needs dominated individuals, and Theory Y assumed that higher-order needs domi-nated. McGregor himself held to the belief that the assumptions of Theory Y were more valid than those of Theory X. Therefore, he proposed that participation in deci-sion making, responsible and challenging jobs, and good group relations would maxi-mize employee motivation. (  Go to www.prenhall.com/rolls)

Unfortunately, there's no evidence to confirm that either set of assumptions is valid or that being a Theory Y manager makes employees more motivated. For instance, Jen-Hsun Huang, founder of Nvidia Corporation, an innovative and success-ful microchip manufacturer, has been known to use both reassuring hugs and tough love in motivating employees. But he has little tolerance for screw-ups. "In one leg-endary meeting, he's said to have ripped into a project team for its tendency to repeat

Self-Assessment
Library (S.A.L.)

What are your dominant needs? Do
S.A.L. #I.C.2 and find out.

Self-Assessment
Library (S.A.L.)

How do you view people?
S.A.L. #I.C.4 can tell you.

Q & A

Can a Theory X manager ever be an
effective manager? Go to
Q & A 16.2 for the answer.

Exhibit 16–2

**Herzberg's Motivation-
Hygiene Theory**

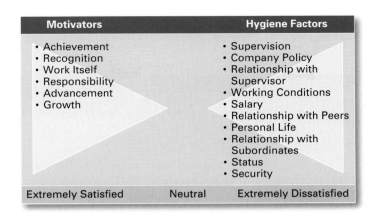

mistakes. 'Do you suck?' he asked the stunned employees. 'Because if you suck, just get up and say you suck.'" His message, delivered in classic Theory X style, was that if you need help, ask for it.[10]

## Herzberg's Two-Factor Theory

Frederick Herzberg's **two-factor theory** (also called *motivation-hygiene theory*) proposes that intrinsic factors are related to job satisfaction, while extrinsic factors are associated with job dissatisfaction.[11] Believing that individuals' attitudes toward work determined success or failure, Herzberg asked people for detailed descriptions of situations in which they felt exceptionally good or bad about their jobs. These findings are shown in Exhibit 16–2.

Herzberg concluded from his analysis that the replies people gave when they felt good about their jobs were significantly different from the replies they gave when they felt badly. Certain characteristics were consistently related to job satisfaction (factors on the left side of the exhibit), and others to job dissatisfaction (factors on the right side). Those factors associated with job satisfaction were intrinsic and included things such as achievement, recognition, and responsibility. When people felt good about their work, they tended to attribute these characteristics to themselves. On the other hand, when they were dissatisfied, they tended to cite extrinsic factors such as company policy and administration, supervision, interpersonal relationships, and working conditions.

In addition, Herzberg believed that the data suggested that the opposite of satisfaction was not dissatisfaction, as traditionally had been believed. Removing dissatisfying characteristics from a job would not necessarily make that job more satisfying (or motivating). As shown in Exhibit 16–3, Herzberg proposed that a dual continuum existed: The opposite of "satisfaction" is "no satisfaction," and the opposite of "dissatisfaction" is "no dissatisfaction."

According to Herzberg, the factors that led to job satisfaction were separate and distinct from those that led to job dissatisfaction. Therefore, managers who sought to eliminate factors that created job dissatisfaction could bring about workplace harmony but not necessarily motivation. The extrinsic factors that create job dissatisfaction were called **hygiene factors**. When these factors are adequate, people won't be dissatisfied, but they won't be satisfied (or motivated) either. To motivate people on their jobs, Herzberg suggested emphasizing **motivators**, the intrinsic factors that increase job satisfaction.

---

**Theory X**
The assumption that employees dislike work, are lazy, avoid responsibility, and must be coerced to perform.

**Theory Y**
The assumption that employees are creative, enjoy work, seek responsibility, and can exercise self-direction.

**two-factor theory**
The motivation theory that intrinsic factors are related to job satisfaction and motivation, whereas extrinsic factors are associated with job dissatisfaction.

**hygiene factors**
Factors that eliminate job dissatisfaction, but don't motivate.

**motivators**
Factors that increase job satisfaction and motivation.

Exhibit 16–3

**Contrasting Views of Satisfaction–Dissatisfaction**

**Traditional View**

| Satisfied | Dissatisfied |
|---|---|

**Herzberg's View**

| Motivators | | Hygiene Factors | |
|---|---|---|---|
| Satisfaction | No Satisfaction | No Dissatisfaction | Dissatisfaction |

Herzberg's theory enjoyed wide popularity from the mid-1960s to the early 1980s, despite criticisms of his procedures and methodology. Although some critics said his theory was too simplistic, it has had a strong influence on how we currently design jobs.

## Learning Review

- Describe Maslow's hierarchy of needs and how it can be used to motivate.
- Discuss how Theory X and Theory Y managers approach motivation.

- Describe Herzberg's motivation-hygiene theory.
- Explain Herzberg's views of satisfaction and dissatisfaction.

## CONTEMPORARY THEORIES OF MOTIVATION

The theories and approaches we're going to look at in this section represent current explanations of employee motivation. Although these theories may not be as well known as those we just discussed, they are supported by research.[12] What are these contemporary motivation approaches? We're going to look at six: three-needs theory, goal-setting theory, reinforcement theory, designing motivating jobs, equity theory, and expectancy theory.

### Three-Needs Theory

David McClelland and others have proposed the **three-needs theory**, which says there are three acquired (not innate) needs that are major motives in work.[13] These three needs include the **need for achievement (nAch)**, which is the drive to excel, to achieve in relation to a set of standards, and to strive to succeed; the **need for power (nPow)**, which is the need to make others behave in a way that they would not have behaved otherwise; and the **need for affiliation (nAff)**, which is the desire for friendly and close interpersonal relationships. Of these three needs, the need for achievement has been researched the most. What does this research show?

People with a high need for achievement are striving for personal achievement rather than for the trappings and rewards of success. They have a desire to do something better or more efficiently than it's been done before.[14] They prefer jobs that offer personal responsibility for finding solutions to problems, in which they can receive rapid and unambiguous feedback on their performance in order to tell whether they're improving, and in which they can set moderately challenging goals. High achievers aren't gamblers; they don't like succeeding by chance. They're motivated by and prefer the challenge of working at a problem and accepting personal responsibility for success or failure. (  Go to www.prenhall.com/rolls) An important point is that high achievers avoid what they perceive to be very easy or very difficult tasks. Also, a high need to achieve doesn't necessarily lead to being a good manager, especially in large organizations. A high nAch pharmaceutical sales

Q & A

Are most employees high achievers? See Q & A 16.4.

representative for Pfizer doesn't necessarily make a good sales manager and good managers in large organizations such as Verizon, Wal-Mart, or Microsoft don't necessarily have a high need to achieve. The reason high achievers don't necessarily make good managers is probably because high achievers focus on their *own* accomplishments while good managers emphasize helping *others* accomplish their goals.[15] We also know that employees can be trained to stimulate their achievement need. Trainers have been effective in teaching individuals to think in terms of accomplishments, winning, and success, and then helping them learn to act in a high achievement way by seeking out situations in which they have personal responsibility, feedback, and moderate risks.[16] (  Go to www.prenhall.com/rolls)

**Q & A**
How do managers motivate high achievers? See Q & A 16.4.

The other two needs in this theory haven't been researched as extensively as the need for achievement. However, we do know that the needs for affiliation and power are closely related to managerial success.[17] The best managers tend to be high in the need for power and low in the need for affiliation.

How do you determine your levels of these needs? All three are typically measured using a projective test (known as the *Thematic Apperception Test* or *TAT*), in which respondents react to a set of pictures. Each picture is briefly shown to a person who writes a story based on the picture. (See Exhibit 16–4 for some examples of these pictures.) Trained interpreters then determine the individual's levels of nAch, nPow, and nAff from the stories written.

Exhibit 16–4    **Examples of Pictures Used for Assessing Levels of nAch, nAff, and nPow**

nAch:  Indicated by someone in the story wanting to perform or do something better.
nAff:   Indicated by someone in the story wanting to be with someone else and enjoy mutual friendship.
nPow:  Indicated by someone in the story desiring to have an impact or make an impression on others in the story.

**three-needs theory**
The motivation theory that says three acquired (not innate) needs—achievement, power, and affiliation—are major motives in work.

**need for achievement (nAch)**
The drive to excel, to achieve in relation to a set of standards, and to strive to succeed.

**need for power (nPow)**
The need to make others behave in a way that they would not have behaved otherwise.

**need for affiliation (nAff)**
The desire for friendly and close interpersonal relationships.

## Goal-Setting Theory

At Wyeth's research division, executive vice president Robert Ruffolo established challenging new product quotas for the company's scientists in an attempt to bring more efficiency to the innovation process. He made bonuses contingent on meeting those goals.[18] Before a big assignment or major class project presentation, has a teacher ever encouraged you to "Just do your best"? What does that vague statement, "do your best" mean? Would your performance on a class project have been higher had that teacher said you needed to score a 93 percent to keep your A in the class? Would you have done better in high school English had your parents said, "You want to try to get 85 percent or higher on all your work in English class" rather than telling you to do your best? Research on goal-setting theory addresses these issues, and the findings, as you'll see, are impressive in terms of the effect that goal specificity, challenge, and feedback have on performance.[19] (  Go to www.prenhall.com/rolls)

Self-Assessment Library (S.A.L.)

Have you set goals for yourself in this class you're taking? S.A.L. #I.C.5 can help.

There is substantial research support for **goal-setting theory**, which says that specific goals increase performance and that difficult goals, when accepted, result in higher performance than do easy goals. What does goal-setting theory tell us?

First, intention to work toward a goal is a major source of job motivation. Studies on goal setting have demonstrated that specific and challenging goals are superior motivating forces.[20] Specific hard goals produce a higher level of output than does the generalized goal of "do your best." The specificity of the goal itself acts as an internal stimulus. For instance, when a sales representative commits to making 8 sales calls daily, this intention gives him a specific goal to try to attain. We can say that, all things being equal, the sales representative with a specific goal will outperform someone else operating with no goals or the generalized goal of "do your best."

Is it a contradiction that goal-setting theory says that motivation is maximized by *difficult* goals, whereas achievement motivation (from three-needs theory) is stimulated by *moderately challenging* goals? No, and our explanation is twofold.[21] First, goal-setting theory deals with people in general; the conclusions on achievement motivation are based on people who have a high nAch. Given that no more than 10 to 20 percent of North Americans are naturally high achievers (a proportion that's likely lower in underdeveloped countries), difficult goals are still recommended for the majority of employees. Second, the conclusions of goal-setting theory apply to those who accept and are committed to the goals. Difficult goals will lead to higher performance *only* if they are accepted.

Next, what about participating in setting goals? Will employees try harder if they have the opportunity to participate in the setting of goals? (  Go to www.prenhall.com/rolls) We can't say that having employees participate in the goal-setting process is

Q & A

Who sets the goals in goal-setting theory? Go to Q & A 16.5 for an answer.

*Mark Cuban, who made a fortune selling his company Broadcast.com to Yahoo! and who owns the NBA Dallas Mavericks, appears to believe in the idea that people are motivated by having difficult goals. When all his ticket reps made their sales quotas, he rewarded them by saying, "Good. That's what you're supposed to do."*

*always* desirable. In some cases, participatively set goals elicited superior performance; in other cases, individuals performed best when their manager assigned goals. However, participation is probably preferable to assigning goals when you expect resistance to accepting difficult challenges.[22]

Finally, we know that people will do better if they get feedback on how well they're progressing toward their goals because feedback helps identify discrepancies between what they have done and what they want to do; that is, feedback acts to guide behavior. But all feedback isn't equally effective. Self-generated feedback—where the employee is able to monitor his or her own progress—has been shown to be a more powerful motivator than externally generated feedback.[23]

Are there any contingencies in goal-setting theory, or we can we just assume that difficult and specific goals always lead to higher performance? In addition to feedback, three other factors have been found to influence the goals–performance relationship. These are (1) goal commitment, (2) adequate self-efficacy, and (3) national culture.

First, goal-setting theory presupposes that an individual is committed to the goal—that is, is determined not to decrease or abandon the goal. Commitment is most likely to occur when goals are made public, when the individual has an internal locus of control, and when the goals are self-set rather than assigned.[24]

Next, **self-efficacy** refers to an individual's belief that he or she is capable of performing a task.[25] The higher your self-efficacy, the more confidence you have in your ability to succeed in a task. So, in difficult situations, we find that people with low self-efficacy are likely to reduce their effort or give up altogether, whereas those with high self-efficacy will try harder to master the challenge.[26] In addition, individuals with high self-efficacy seem to respond to negative feedback with increased effort and motivation, whereas those with low self-efficacy are likely to reduce their effort when given negative feedback.[27]

Finally, goal-setting theory is culture bound. It's well adapted to countries like the United States and Canada because its main ideas align reasonably well with North American cultures. It assumes that subordinates will be reasonably independent (not too high a score on power distance), that managers and employees will seek challenging goals (low in uncertainty avoidance), and that performance is considered important by both managers and subordinates (high in assertiveness). So don't expect goal setting to necessarily lead to higher employee performance in countries such as Portugal or Chile, where the country's cultural characteristics aren't like this.

Exhibit 16–5 summarizes the relationships among goals, motivation, and performance. Our overall conclusion from goal-setting theory is that intentions—as

**Exhibit 16–5**

**Goal-Setting Theory**

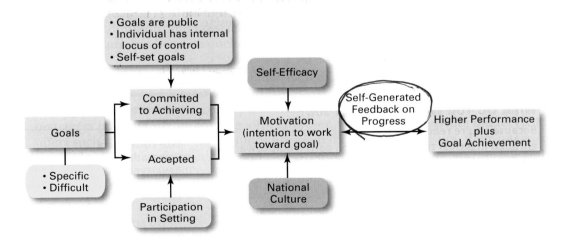

**goal-setting theory**
The proposition that specific goals increase performance and that difficult goals, when accepted, result in higher performance than do easy goals.

**self-efficacy**
An individual's belief that he or she is capable of performing a task.

4. *Expand jobs vertically.* Vertical expansion (job enrichment) gives employees responsibilities and controls that were formerly reserved for managers. It partially closes the gap between the "doing" and the "controlling" aspects of the job and increases employee autonomy.

5. *Open feedback channels.* Feedback lets employees know how well they're performing their jobs and whether their performance is improving, deteriorating, or remaining constant. Ideally, employees should receive performance feedback directly as they do their jobs rather than from managers on an occasional basis. For example, frequent fliers at Continental Airlines bestow Pride in Performance certificates to employees who have been helpful. Employees can then redeem the coupons for valuable merchandise.[39]

## Equity Theory

Do you ever wonder what kind of grade the person sitting next to you in class makes on a test or on a major class assignment? Most of us do! Being human, we tend to compare ourselves with others. (  Go to www.prenhall.com/rolls) If someone offered you $50,000 a year on your first job after graduating from college, you'd probably jump at the offer and report to work enthusiastic, ready to tackle whatever needed to be done, and certainly satisfied with your pay. How would you react, though, if you found out a month into the job that a co-worker—another recent graduate, your age, with comparable grades from a comparable school, and with comparable work experience—was getting $55,000 a year? You'd probably be upset! Even though in absolute terms, $50,000 is a lot of money for a new graduate to make (and you know it!), that suddenly isn't the issue. You see the issue now as what you believe is *fair*—what is *equitable*. The term *equity* is related to the concept of fairness and equitable treatment compared with others who behave in similar ways. There's considerable evidence that employees compare themselves to others and that inequities influence the degree of effort that employees exert.[40] (  Go to www.prenhall.com/rolls)

**Equity theory**, developed by J. Stacey Adams, proposes that employees compare what they get from a job situation (outcomes) in relation to what they put into it (inputs) and then compare their inputs–outcomes ratio with the inputs–outcomes ratios of relevant others (see Exhibit 16–8). If an employee perceives her ratio to be equitable in comparison to those of relevant others—in other words, she perceives that her situation is fair—then justice prevails. However, if the ratio is inequitable, she views herself as underrewarded or overrewarded. When inequities occur, employees attempt to do something about it. What will employees do when they perceive an inequity?

Equity theory proposes that employees might (1) distort either their own or others' inputs or outcomes, (2) behave in some way to induce others to change their inputs or outcomes, (3) behave in some way to change their own inputs or outcomes, (4) choose a different comparison person, or (5) quit their job. These types of employee reactions have generally proved to be correct.[41] A review of the research

Exhibit 16–8

**Equity Theory**

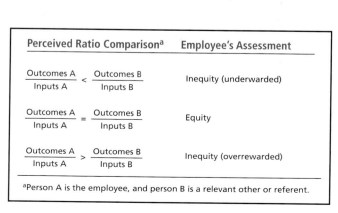

| Perceived Ratio Comparison[a] | | Employee's Assessment |
|---|---|---|
| $\dfrac{\text{Outcomes A}}{\text{Inputs A}} < \dfrac{\text{Outcomes B}}{\text{Inputs B}}$ | | Inequity (underrewarded) |
| $\dfrac{\text{Outcomes A}}{\text{Inputs A}} = \dfrac{\text{Outcomes B}}{\text{Inputs B}}$ | | Equity |
| $\dfrac{\text{Outcomes A}}{\text{Inputs A}} > \dfrac{\text{Outcomes B}}{\text{Inputs B}}$ | | Inequity (overrewarded) |

[a]Person A is the employee, and person B is a relevant other or referent.

consistently confirms the equity thesis: Employee motivation is influenced significantly by relative rewards as well as by absolute rewards. Whenever employees perceive inequity, they'll act to correct the situation.[42] The result might be lower or higher productivity, improved or reduced quality of output, increased absenteeism, or voluntary resignation.

Who are these "others" against whom people compare themselves? The **referent**—the other persons, systems, or selves individuals compare themselves against in order to assess equity—is an important variable in equity theory.[43] These three referent categories are each important. The "persons" category includes other individuals with similar jobs in the same organization but also includes friends, neighbors, or professional associates. On the basis of what they hear at work or read about in newspapers or trade journals, employees compare their pay with that of others. The "system" category includes organizational pay policies and procedures and the administration of the system. Whatever precedents have been established by the organization regarding pay allocation are major elements of this category. The "self" category refers to inputs–outcomes ratios that are unique to the individual. It reflects past personal experiences and contacts and is influenced by criteria such as past jobs or family commitments. The choice of referents is related to the information available about the referents as well as to their perceived relevance.

Historically, equity theory focused on **distributive justice**, which is the perceived fairness of the amount and allocation of rewards among individuals. Recent equity research has focused on looking at issues of **procedural justice**, which is the perceived fairness of the process used to determine the distribution of rewards. This research shows that distributive justice has a greater influence on employee satisfaction than procedural justice, while procedural justice tends to affect an employee's organizational commitment, trust in his or her boss, and intention to quit.[44] What are the implications of these findings for managers? They should consider openly sharing information on how allocation decisions are made, follow consistent and unbiased procedures, and engage in similar practices to increase the perception of procedural justice. By increasing the perception of procedural justice, employees are likely to view their bosses and the organization as positive even if they're dissatisfied with pay, promotions, and other personal outcomes.

In conclusion, equity theory shows that, for most employees, motivation is influenced significantly by relative rewards as well as by absolute rewards, but some key issues are still unclear.[45] For instance, how do employees define inputs and outcomes? How do they combine and weigh their inputs and outcomes to arrive at totals? When and how do the factors change over time? And how do people choose referents? Despite these limitations, equity theory is backed by an impressive amount of research and offers important insights into employee motivation.

## Expectancy Theory

The most comprehensive explanation of employee motivation to date is Victor Vroom's **expectancy theory**.[46] Although the theory has its critics,[47] most research evidence supports it.[48]

Expectancy theory states that an individual tends to act in a certain way based on the expectation that the act will be followed by a given outcome and on

---

**equity theory**
The theory that an employee compares his or her job's input-outcomes ratio with that of relevant others and then corrects any inequity.

**referents**
The persons, systems, or selves against which individuals compare themselves to assess equity.

**distributive justice**
Perceived fairness of the amount and allocation of rewards among individuals.

**procedural justice**
Perceived fairness of the process used to determine the distribution of rewards.

**expectancy theory**
The theory that an individual tends to act in a certain way based on the expectation that the act will be followed by a given outcome and on the attractiveness of that outcome to the individual.

Exhibit 16–9

**Simplified Expectancy Model**

Individual Effort → **A** → Individual Performance → **B** → Organizational Rewards → **C** → Individual Goals

**A** = Effort–performance linkage
**B** = Performance–reward linkage
**C** = Attractiveness of reward

the attractiveness of that outcome to the individual. It includes three variables or relationships (see Exhibit 16–9):

1. *Expectancy* or *effort–performance linkage* is the probability perceived by the individual that exerting a given amount of effort will lead to a certain level of performance.

2. *Instrumentality* or *performance–reward linkage* is the degree to which the individual believes that performing at a particular level is instrumental in attaining the desired outcome.

3. *Valence* or *attractiveness of reward* is the importance that the individual places on the potential outcome or reward that can be achieved on the job. Valence considers both the goals and needs of the individual. (  Go to www.prenhall.com/rolls)

**Self-Assessment Library (S.A.L.)**
What rewards do you value most? S.A.L. #I.C.3 can show you.

This explanation of motivation might sound complicated, but it really isn't. It can be summed up in the questions: How hard do I have to work to achieve a certain level of performance, and can I actually achieve that level? What reward will performing at that level of performance get me? How attractive is the reward to me, and does it help me achieve my own personal goals? Whether you are motivated to put forth effort (that is, to work hard) at any given time depends on your goals and your perception of whether a certain level of performance is necessary to attain those goals. Let's look at an example. Many years ago, your second author had a student who went to work for IBM as a sales representative. Her favorite work "reward" was having an IBM corporate jet fly into Springfield, Missouri, to pick up her best customers and her and take them for a weekend of golfing at some fun location. But to get that particular "reward," she had to achieve at a certain level of performance, which involved exceeding her sales goals by *x* percentage. How hard she was willing to work (that is, how motivated she was to put forth effort) was dependent on the level of performance that had to be met and the likelihood that if she achieved at that level of performance she would receive that reward. Because she "valued" that reward (it was highly attractive to her personally), she always worked hard to exceed her sales goals. The performance–reward linkage was clear because her hard work and performance achievements were always rewarded by the company with the reward she valued (access to the corporate jet).

The key to expectancy theory is understanding an individual's goal and the linkage between effort and performance, between performance and rewards, and finally, between rewards and individual goal satisfaction. It emphasizes payoffs, or rewards. As a result, we have to believe that the rewards an organization is offering align with what the individual wants. Expectancy theory recognizes that there is no universal principle for explaining what motivates individuals and thus stresses that managers understand why employees view certain outcomes as attractive or unattractive. After all, we want to reward individuals with those things they value positively. Also, expectancy theory emphasizes expected behaviors. Do employees know what is expected of them and how they'll be evaluated? Finally, the theory is concerned with perceptions. Reality is irrelevant. An individual's own perceptions of performance, reward, and goal outcomes, not the outcomes themselves, will determine his or her motivation (level of effort). (  Go to www.prenhall.com/rolls)

**Q & A**
You could use expectancy theory to explain why someone you know lacks motivation. See Q & A 16.9 for how.

## Integrating Contemporary Theories of Motivation

We've looked at six contemporary motivation theories. You might be tempted to view them independently, but that would be a mistake. Many of the ideas underlying the theories are complementary, and you'll better understand how to motivate people if you see how the theories fit together.[49] Exhibit 16–10 presents a model that integrates much of what we know about motivation. Its basic foundation is the expectancy model shown in Exhibit 16–9. Let's work through the model, starting on the left.

The individual effort box has an arrow leading into it. This arrow flows from the individual's goals. Consistent with goal-setting theory, this goals–effort link is meant to illustrate that goals direct behavior. Expectancy theory predicts that an employee will exert a high level of effort if he or she perceives that there is a strong relationship between effort and performance, performance and rewards, and rewards and satisfaction of personal goals. Each of these relationships is, in turn, influenced by certain factors. You can see from the model that the level of individual performance is determined not only by the level of individual effort but also by the individual's ability to perform and by whether the organization has a fair and objective performance evaluation system. The performance–reward relationship will be strong if the individual perceives that it is performance (rather than seniority, personal favorites, or some other criterion) that is rewarded. The final link in expectancy theory is the rewards–goal relationship. Need theories come into play at this point. Motivation would be high to the degree that the rewards an individual received for his or her high performance satisfied the dominant needs consistent with his or her individual goals.

A closer look at the model also shows that it considers the achievement–need, reinforcement, equity, and JCM theories. The high achiever isn't motivated by the

Exhibit 16–10

**Integrating Contemporary Theories of Motivation**

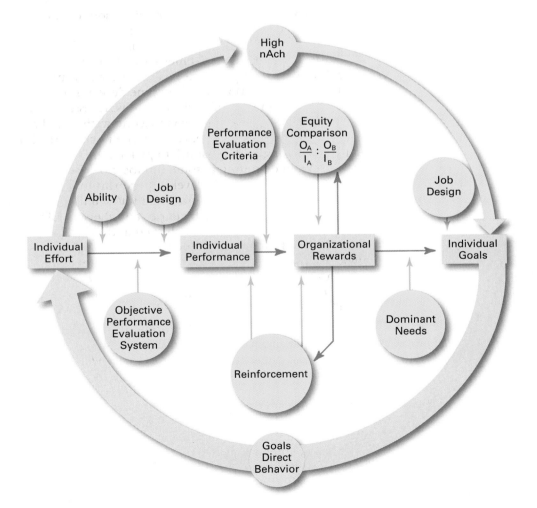

organization's assessment of his or her performance or organizational rewards; hence, the jump from effort to individual goals for those with a high nAch. Remember that high achievers are internally driven as long as the jobs they're doing provide them with personal responsibility, feedback, and moderate risks. They're not concerned with the effort–performance, performance–reward, or rewards–goals linkages.

Reinforcement theory is seen in the model by recognizing that the organization's rewards reinforce the individual's performance. If managers have designed a reward system that is seen by employees as "paying off" for good performance, the rewards will reinforce and encourage continued good performance. Rewards also play a key part in equity theory. Individuals will compare the rewards (outcomes) they have received from the inputs or efforts they made with the inputs–outcomes ratio of relevant others. If inequities exist, the effort expended may be influenced.

Finally, the JCM is seen in this integrative model. Task characteristics (job design) influence job motivation at two places. First, jobs that are designed around the five job dimensions are likely to lead to higher actual job performance because the individual's motivation will be stimulated by the job itself—that is, they will increase the linkage between effort and performance. Second, jobs that are designed around the five job dimensions also increase an employee's control over key elements in his or her work. Therefore, jobs that offer autonomy, feedback, and similar task characteristics help to satisfy the individual goals of employees who desire greater control over their work.

## Learning Review

- Describe the three needs McClelland proposed as being present in work settings.
- Explain how goal-setting and reinforcement theories explain employee motivation.
- Describe the job characteristics model as a way to design motivating jobs.

- Discuss the motivation implications of equity theory.
- Contrast distributive justice and procedural justice.
- Explain the three key linkages in expectancy theory and their role in motivation.

## CURRENT ISSUES IN MOTIVATION

Understanding and predicting employee motivation is one of the most popular areas in management research. We've introduced you to several motivation theories. However, even current studies of employee motivation are influenced by some significant workplace issues—cross-cultural challenges, motivating unique groups of workers, and designing appropriate rewards programs. Let's take a closer look at each of these issues.

### Cross-Cultural Challenges

In today's global business environment, managers can't automatically assume that motivational programs that work in one geographic location are going to work in others. Most current motivation theories were developed in the United States by Americans and about Americans.[50] Maybe the most blatant pro-American characteristic in these theories is the strong emphasis on individualism and achievement cultural characteristics. For instance, both goal-setting and expectancy theories emphasize goal accomplishment as well as rational and individual thought. Let's look at the motivation theories to see if there's any cross-cultural transferability.

Maslow's need hierarchy argues that people start at the physiological level and then move progressively up the hierarchy in order. This hierarchy, if it has any application at all, aligns with American culture. In countries like Japan, Greece, and

*It can be difficult or even misleading to apply Western theories of motivation to employees like Rina Masuda of Sharp Corp. Masuda uses a soldering iron to quickly and delicately repair tiny computer chips, a task so extraordinarily precise that she is among only a few thousand of all Japan's workers honored with the title of "super technician," or supaa ginosha. These workers receive certificates and pins, but seldom money. "The soldering I do by hand is far superior to anything the machines can do," says Masuda, her pride expressing the common view that recognition and honor are enough.*

Mexico, where uncertainty avoidance characteristics are strong, security needs would be on top of the need hierarchy. Countries that score high on nurturing characteristics—Denmark, Sweden, Norway, the Netherlands, and Finland—would have social needs on top.[51] We would predict, for instance, that group work will be more motivating when the country's culture scores high on the nurturing criterion.

Another motivation concept that clearly has an American bias is the achievement need. The view that a high achievement need acts as an internal motivator presupposes two cultural characteristics—a willingness to accept a moderate degree of risk (which excludes countries with strong uncertainty avoidance characteristics) and a concern with performance (which applies almost singularly to countries with strong achievement characteristics). This combination is found in Anglo-American countries like the United States, Canada, and Great Britain.[52] On the other hand, these characteristics are relatively absent in countries such as Chile and Portugal.

Equity theory has a relatively strong following in the United States. That's not surprising given that U.S.–style reward systems are based on the assumption that workers are highly sensitive to equity in reward allocations. In the United States, equity is meant to closely link pay to performance. However, recent evidence suggests that in collectivist cultures, especially in the former socialist countries of Central and Eastern Europe, employees expect rewards to reflect their individual needs as well as their performance.[53] Moreover, consistent with a legacy of communism and centrally planned economies, employees exhibited a greater "entitlement" attitude—that is, they expected outcomes to be greater than their inputs.[54] These findings suggest that U.S.–style pay practices may need to be modified, especially in Russia and other former communist countries, in order to be perceived as fair by employees.

Despite these cross-cultural differences in motivation, don't assume there are no cross-cultural consistencies, because there are some. For instance, the desire for interesting work seems important to almost all workers, regardless of their national culture. In a study of seven countries, employees in Belgium, Britain, Israel, and the United States ranked "interesting work" number one among 11 work goals. It was ranked either second or third in Japan, the Netherlands, and Germany.[55] Similarly, in a study comparing job-preference outcomes among graduate students in the United States, Canada, Australia, and Singapore, growth, achievement, and responsibility were rated the top three and had identical rankings.[56] Both studies suggest some universality to the importance of intrinsic factors identified by Herzberg in his two-factor theory. Another recent study examining workplace motivation trends in Japan also seems to indicate that Herzberg's model is applicable to Japanese employees.[57]

## Motivating Unique Groups of Workers

Motivating employees has never been easy! Employees come into organizations with very different needs, personalities, skills, abilities, interests, and aptitudes. They have different expectations of their employers and different views of what they think their employer has a right to expect of them. And they vary widely in what they want from their jobs. For instance, some employees get more satisfaction out of their personal interests and pursuits and only want a weekly paycheck—nothing more. They're not interested in making their work more challenging or interesting or in "winning" performance contests. Others derive a great deal of satisfaction in their jobs and are motivated to exert high levels of effort. Given these differences, how can managers do an effective job of motivating the unique groups of employees found in today's workforce? One thing managers must do is understand the motivational requirements of these groups including diverse employees, professionals, contingent workers, and low-skilled minimum-wage employees.

**Motivating a Diverse Workforce** To maximize motivation among today's workforce, managers need to think in terms of *flexibility*. For instance, studies tell us that men place more importance on having autonomy in their jobs than do women. In contrast, the opportunity to learn, convenient and flexible work hours, and good interpersonal relations are more important to women.[58] Having the opportunity to be independent and to be exposed to different experiences is important to Gen Y employees whereas older workers may be more interested in highly structured work opportunities.[59] Managers need to recognize that what motivates a single mother with two dependent children who's working full-time to support her family may be very different from the needs of a single part-time employee or an older employee who is working only to supplement his or her retirement income. A diverse array of rewards is needed to motivate employees with such diverse needs. Many of the work–family life balance programs (see Chapter 12) that organizations have implemented are a response to the varied needs of a diverse workforce. In addition, many organizations have developed flexible work arrangements that recognize different needs. For instance, a **compressed workweek** is a workweek where employees work longer hours per day but fewer days per week. The most common arrangement is four 10-hour days (a 4-40 program). However, organizations could design whatever schedules they wanted to fit employees' needs. Another alternative is **flexible work hours** (also known as **flextime**), which is a scheduling system in which employees are required to work a specific number of hours a week but are free to vary those hours within certain limits. In a flextime schedule, there are certain common core hours when all employees are required to be on the job, but starting, ending, and lunch-hour times are flexible. Flextime is not as popular as it used to be.[60] Some 56 percent of employers offered flextime to workers in 2005 as compared to 64 percent in 2002.[61]

In Great Britain, McDonald's is experimenting with an unusual program—dubbed the Family Contract—to reduce absenteeism and turnover at some of its restaurants. Under this Family Contract, employees from the same immediate family can fill in for one another for any work shift without having to clear it first with their manager.[62] This type of job scheduling, which can be effective in motivating a diverse workforce, is called **job sharing**—the practice of having two or more people split a full-time job. Although something like McDonald's Family Contract may be appropriate for a low-skilled job, other organizations might offer job sharing to professionals who want to work but don't want the demands and hassles of a full-time position. For instance, at global accounting firm Ernst & Young, employees in many of the company's locations— Bermuda, New Zealand, and South Africa, for instance—can choose from a variety of flexible work arrangements including job sharing.

Another alternative made possible by information technology is **telecommuting**. Here, employees work at home and are linked to the workplace by computer and modem. It's estimated that some 12 percent (and maybe even as high as 15 percent) of the U.S. workforce is part of this "distributed workforce."[63] For example, around 40 percent of IBM's workforce has no physical office space. The number is even higher for Sun Microsystems, where nearly 50 percent of employees work off-site. And in 2003, Agilent Technologies closed 48 U.S. sales offices and told its employees to work remotely, which some 70 percent now do.[64] Because many jobs can be done at off-site locations, this approach might be close to the ideal job for many people as there is no commuting, the hours are flexible, there's freedom to dress as you please, and there are little or no interruptions from colleagues. However, keep in mind that not all employees embrace the idea of telecommuting. Some workers relish the informal interactions at work that satisfy their social needs as well as being a source of new ideas. ( ▱ Go to www.prenhall.com/rolls)

Q & A
Motivating someone who's not even physically there has to be tough. Q & A 16.10 explains how a manager could do so.

Do flexible work arrangements motivate employees? Although such arrangements might seem highly motivational, both positive and negative relationships have been found. For instance, a recent study looking at the impact of telecommuting on job satisfaction found that job satisfaction initially increased as the extent of telecommuting increased, but as the number of hours spent telecommuting increased, job satisfaction started to level off, decreased slightly, and then stabilized.[65]

**Motivating Professionals** In contrast to a generation ago, the typical employee today is more likely to be a professional with a college degree than a blue-collar factory worker. What special concerns should managers be aware of when trying to motivate a team of engineers at Intel's India Development Center, software designers at SAS Institute in North Carolina, or a group of consultants at Accenture in Singapore?

## managing workforce Diversity

### Developing Employee Potential: The Bottom Line of Diversity

One of a manager's more important goals is helping employees develop their potential.[66] This is particularly important in managing talented diverse employees who can bring new perspectives and ideas to the business but who may find that the workplace environment is not as conducive as it could be to accepting and embracing these different perspectives. For instance, managers at Lucent Technologies' distinguished Bell Labs, which was acquired by France-based Alcatel in April 2006, have worked hard to develop an environment in which the ideas of diverse employees are encouraged openly. What can managers do to ensure that their diverse employees have the opportunity to develop their potential? One thing they can do is make sure that there are diverse role models in leadership positions so that others see that there are opportunities to grow and advance. Giving motivated, talented, hard-working, and enthusiastic diverse employees opportunities to excel in decision-making roles can be a powerful motivator to other diverse employees to work hard to develop their own potential. A mentoring program in which diverse employees are given the opportunity to work closely with organizational leaders can be a powerful tool. At Silicon Graphics, for instance, new employees become part of a mentoring group called "Horizons." Through this mentoring group, diverse employees have the opportunity to observe and learn from key company decision makers.

Another way for managers to develop the potential of their diverse employees is to offer developmental work assignments that provide a variety of learning experiences in different organizational areas. DaimlerChrysler, for example, started its Corporate University, which offers a comprehensive series of learning opportunities for all employees. The company's director of diversity and work/family says that employees who are provided the opportunity to learn new processes and new technology are more likely to excel at their work and to stay with the company. These types of developmental opportunities are particularly important for diverse employees because it empowers them with tools that are critical to professional development.

**compressed workweek**
A workweek where employees work longer hours per day but fewer days per week.

**flexible work hours (flextime)**
A scheduling system in which employees are required to work a certain number of hours per week, but are free, within limits, to vary the hours of work.

**job sharing**
The practice of having two or more people split a full-time job.

**telecommuting**
A job approach where employees work at home and are linked to the workplace by computer and modem.

*Before she quit her high-level corporate job to found the Center for Workforce Excellence, which she runs from her home, Trudy Bourgeois worked 80 hours a week and was often away from home. When her daughter said, "Mommy, I don't want to be like you when I grow up," Bourgeois said, "I concluded that my life was out of control. I was defined by my job. I WAS the rat race." Experiences like hers have led many employers to adopt flexible work arrangements to attract and retain professionals.*

Professionals are typically different from nonprofessionals.[67] They have a strong and long-term commitment to their field of expertise. Their loyalty is more often to their profession than to their employer. To keep current in their field, they need to regularly update their knowledge, and because of their commitment to their profession they rarely define their workweek as 8 A.M. to 5 P.M., five days a week.

What motivates professionals? Money and promotions typically are low on their priority list. Why? They tend to be well paid and enjoy what they do. In contrast, job challenge tends to be ranked high. They like to tackle problems and find solutions. Their chief reward in their job is the work itself. Professionals also value support. They want others to think that what they are working on is important. That may be true for all employees, but professionals tend to be focused on their work as their central life interest, whereas nonprofessionals typically have other interests outside of work that can compensate for needs not met on the job.

**Motivating Contingent Workers** As full-time jobs have been eliminated through downsizing and other organizational restructurings, the number of openings for part-time, contract, and other forms of temporary work have increased. Contingent workers don't have the security or stability that permanent employees have, and they don't identify with the organization or display the commitment that other employees do. Temporary workers also typically get little or no benefits such as health care or pensions.[68]

There's no simple solution for motivating contingent employees. For that small set of individuals who prefer the freedom of their temporary status—for instance, some students, working mothers, retirees—the lack of stability may not be an issue. In addition, temporariness might be preferred by highly compensated physicians, engineers, accountants, or financial planners who don't want the demands of a full-time job. But these are the exceptions. For the most part, temporary employees are not temporary by choice.

What will motivate involuntarily temporary employees? An obvious answer is the opportunity to become a permanent employee. In cases in which permanent employees are selected from a pool of temps, the temps will often work hard in hopes of becoming permanent. A less obvious answer is the opportunity for training. The ability of a temporary employee to find a new job is largely dependent on his or her skills. If the employee sees that the job he or she is doing can help develop marketable skills, then motivation is increased. From an equity standpoint, you should also consider the repercussions of mixing permanent and temporary workers when pay differentials are significant. When temps work alongside permanent employees who earn more, and get benefits, too, for doing the same job, the performance of temps is likely to suffer. Separating such employees or perhaps minimizing interdependence between them might help managers decrease potential problems.[69]

**Motivating Low-Skilled, Minimum-Wage Employees** Suppose that in your first managerial position after graduating, you're responsible for managing a work

**Q & A**

Have you had a minimum-wage service job? Could that job have been enriched? Q & A 16.11 has some suggestions.

group of low-skilled, minimum-wage employees. Offering more pay to these employees for high levels of performance is out of the question: Your company just can't afford it. In addition, these employees have limited education and skills. What are your motivational options at this point? ( Go to www.prenhall.com/rolls)

One trap we often fall into is thinking that people are motivated only by money. Although money is important as a motivator, it's not the only reward that people seek and that managers can use. In motivating minimum-wage employees, managers might look at employee recognition programs, which we'll describe later in this chapter. And many managers also recognize the power of praise. However, you need to be sure that these "pats on the back" are sincere and given for the right reasons.

## Designing Appropriate Rewards Programs

Blue Cross of California, one of the nation's largest health insurers, pays bonuses to doctors serving its health maintenance organization members based on patient satisfaction and other quality standards. FedEx's drivers are motivated by a pay system that rewards them for timeliness and how much they deliver.[70] Employee rewards programs play a powerful role in motivating appropriate employee behavior. In this section, we want to look at how managers can design appropriate rewards programs by using open-book management, employee recognition programs, pay-for-performance programs, and stock option programs.

**Open-Book Management**  Within 24 hours after managers of the Heavy Duty Division of Springfield Remanufacturing Company (SRC) gather to discuss a multipage financial document, every plant employee will have seen the same information. If the employees can meet shipment goals, they'll all share in a large year-end bonus.[71] Many organizations of various sizes involve their employees in workplace decisions by opening up the financial statements (the "books"). They share that information so that employees will be motivated to make better decisions about their work and better able to understand the implications of what they do, how they do it, and the ultimate impact on the bottom line. ( Go to www.prenhall.com/rolls) This approach is called **open-book management**.[72] Who's using it? More than 3,500 organizations, including SRC, Allstate Insurance, Amoco Canada, Rhino Foods, and Sprint's Government Systems division.[73]

**Q & A**

How would letting employees see the financial statements motivate them? Q & A 16.12 explains.

The goal of open-book management is to get employees to think like an owner by seeing the impact their decisions and actions have on financial results. Because most employees don't have the knowledge or background to understand the financials, they have to be taught how to read and understand the organization's financial statements. Once employees have this knowledge, however, managers need to share the numbers regularly with them. By sharing this information, employees begin to see the link between their efforts, level of performance, and operational results.

**Employee Recognition Programs**  **Employee recognition programs** consist of personal attention and expressing interest, approval, and appreciation for a job well done.[74] They can take numerous forms. For instance, Nichols Foods, a British manufacturer, has a comprehensive recognition program.[75] The main hallway in the production department is hung with "bragging boards" on which the accomplishments of employee teams are noted. Monthly awards are presented to people who have been nominated by peers for extraordinary effort on the job. Monthly award winners are eligible for further recognition at an off-site meeting for all employees. In contrast, most

---

**open-book management**
A motivational approach in which an organization's financial statements (the "books") are shared with all employees.

**employee recognition programs**
Personal attention and expressing interest, approval, and appreciation for a job well done.

*Open-book management is growing as a means of motivating employees by sharing with them important information about the way their company works. Sabre Holdings, the travel company that operates the Travelocity Web site and a well-known airline reservation system, recently used a board game called Zodiak as a simulation to teach employees about income statements, balance sheets, and return on equity. After playing the game for a fictional fiscal year, during which they refinanced debt, brought out a new product, watched competitors hire away their employees, were sued, and boosted earnings, the four members of each "owner" team came away with a better understanding of Sabre Holding's business and some rudimentary financial skills.*

managers use a far more informal approach. For example, when Julia Stewart, currently the president and CEO of IHOP International, was president of Applebee's Restaurants, she would frequently leave sealed notes on the chairs of employees after everyone had gone home.[76] These notes explained how critical Stewart thought the person's work was or how much she appreciated the completion of a project. Stewart also relied heavily on voice-mail messages left after office hours to tell employees how appreciative she was for a job well done. Recognition doesn't have to come only from managers. Some 35 percent of companies encourage co-workers to recognize peers for outstanding work efforts.[77] For instance, managers at Yum Brands Inc. (the Kentucky-based parent of food chains Taco Bell, KFC, and Pizza Hut) were looking for ways to reduce employee turnover. They found a successful customer service program involving peer recognition at KFC restaurants in Australia. Workers there spontaneously rewarded fellow workers with "Champs cards," an acronym for attributes such as cleanliness, hospitality, and accuracy. Yum implemented the program in other restaurants around the world and credits the peer recognition with reducing hourly employee turnover from 181 percent to 109 percent.[78]

A recent survey of organizations found that 84 percent had some type of program to recognize worker achievements.[79] And do employees think these programs are important? You bet! A survey of a wide variety of employees asked what they considered the most powerful workplace motivator. Their response? Recognition, recognition, and more recognition![80]

Consistent with reinforcement theory, rewarding a behavior with recognition immediately following that behavior is likely to encourage its repetition. And recognition can take many forms. You can personally congratulate an employee in private for a good job. You can send a handwritten note or e-mail message acknowledging something positive that the employee has done. For employees with a strong need for social acceptance, you can publicly recognize accomplishments. To enhance group cohesiveness and motivation, you can celebrate team successes. For instance, you can do something as simple as throw a pizza party to celebrate a team's accomplishments. Some of these things may seem simple, but they can go a long way in showing employees they're valued.

**Pay-for-Performance**   At Dallas-based la Madeleine Bakery, Café & Bistro, top performing restaurant managers will get raises in 2006 ranging from 3 to 5 percent; average performers will get between 2 to 3 percent; and poor performers will get 1.5 percent or less. The company is part of a broader trend of companies linking pay to workers' performance.[81] **Pay-for-performance programs** are variable compensation plans that pay employees on the basis of some performance measure.[82] Piece-rate pay plans, wage incentive plans, profit sharing, and lump-sum bonuses are examples. What differentiates these forms of pay from more traditional compensation plans is that instead of paying a person for time on the job, pay is adjusted to reflect some performance measure. (  Go to www.prenhall.com/rolls) These performance measures might include such things as individual productivity, team or work group productivity, departmental productivity, or the overall organization's profit performance.

**Q & A**

Pay-for-performance sounds so logical. Why isn't every organization doing that? See Q & A 16.13.

Pay-for-performance is probably most compatible with expectancy theory. Specifically, individuals should perceive a strong relationship between their performance and the rewards they receive for motivation to be maximized. If rewards are allocated only on nonperformance factors—such as seniority, job title, or across-the-board pay raises—then employees are likely to reduce their efforts. From a motivation perspective, making some or all of an employee's pay conditional on some performance measure focuses his or her attention and effort toward that measure, then reinforces the continuation of the effort with a reward. If the employee, team, or organization's performance declines, so does the reward. Thus, there's an incentive to keep efforts and motivation strong. (  Go to www.prenhall.com/rolls)

**Q & A**

What if performance isn't easily measured? How would you use pay-for-performance then? Go to Q & A 16.14 and find out.

Pay-for-performance programs are popular. In 2005, some 78 percent of large U.S. companies had some form of variable pay plan.[83] These types of pay plans have also been tried in other countries such as Canada and Japan. About 30 percent of Canadian companies and 22 percent of Japanese companies have company-wide pay-for-performance plans.[84] However, one Japanese company, Fujitsu, dropped its performance-based program after 8 years because it proved to be "flawed and a poor fit with Japanese culture."[85] Management found that some employees set goals as low as possible for fear of falling short. Others set extremely short-term goals. As a result, Fujitsu executives felt that ambitious projects that could produce hit products were being avoided.

Do pay-for-performance programs work? For the most part, studies seem to indicate that they do. For instance, one study found that companies that used pay-for-performance programs performed better financially than those that did not.[86] Another study showed that pay-for-performance programs with outcome-based incentives had a positive impact on sales, customer satisfaction, and profits.[87] If the organization uses work teams, managers should consider group-based performance incentives that will reinforce team effort and commitment. But whether these programs are individual based or team based, managers need to ensure that they're specific about the relationship between an individual's pay and his or her expected level of appropriate performance. Employees must clearly understand exactly how performance—theirs and the organization's—translates into dollars on their paychecks.[88] The sometimes tenuous link between pay and performance is nowhere more evident than in the final type of rewards program we're going to look at—employee stock options.

**Stock Option Programs** A recent study by The Corporate Library found that between 2001 and 2005, CEOs at 11 of the largest U.S. companies received a total of $865 million in pay even though their companies suffered a loss of $640 billion in shareholder value.[89] Not included as part of this group was Henry R. Silverman, Cendant Corporation's CEO, who got a bonus in 2005 of over $12 million even though the company's total stock return fell 21 percent. Nor was Scott McNealy, CEO of Sun Microsystems, who averaged $13.3 million a year in compensation even though his company's stock had a 6-year annualized return of minus 31.5 percent.[90] Such executive bonus and stock option programs have come under fire because they seem to fly in the face of the belief that executive pay aligns with his or her organization's performance. What are stock option programs, what are they designed to do, and what do managers need to know about designing appropriate ones?

**pay-for-performance programs**
Variable compensation plans that pay employees on the basis of some performance measure.

*thinking critically about* **Ethics**

You've been hired as a phone sales representative at World Adventures Travel in Austin, Texas. In this job, you help customers who have called to book vacations by finding what works best for them and their needs as you check airline flights, times, and fares and also help with rental car and hotel reservations.

Most car rental firms and hotels run contests for the sales representative who books the most cars or most hotel rooms. The contest winners receive very attractive rewards! For instance, if you book just 50 clients for one rental car company, your name is put in a drawing for $500. If you book 100 clients, the drawing is for $1,500. And if you book 200 clients, you receive an all-expenses-paid, 1-week Caribbean vacation. So the incentives are attractive enough to encourage you to "steer" customers toward one of those companies even though it might not be the best or cheapest for them. Your manager doesn't discourage participation in these programs.

Do you see anything wrong with this situation? Explain. What ethical issues do you see for (a) the employee, (b) the organization, and (c) the customer? How could an organization design performance incentive programs that encourage high levels of performance without compromising ethics?

**Stock options** are financial instruments that give employees the right to purchase shares of stock at a set price. The original idea behind stock options was to turn employees into owners and give them strong incentives to work hard to make the company successful.[91] If the company was successful, the value of the stock went up, making the stock options valuable. In other words, there was a link between performance and reward. The popularity of stock options as a motivation and compensation tool skyrocketed during the dot.com boom in the late 1990s. Because many dot.coms couldn't afford to pay employees the going market-rate salaries, stock options were offered as performance incentives. However, the shakeout among dot.com stocks in 2000 and 2001 illustrated one of the inherent risks of offering stock options. As long as the market was rising, employees were willing to give up a large salary in exchange for stock options. However, when stock prices tanked, many individuals who joined and stayed with a dot.com for the opportunity to get rich through stock options found their stock options had become worthless. And the declining stock market became a powerful demotivator.

Despite the risk of potential lost value and the widespread abuse of stock options, managers might want to consider them as part of their overall motivational program. An appropriately designed stock option program can be a powerful motivational tool for the entire workforce.[92] Exhibit 16–11 lists several recommendations for designing stock options programs.

## Learning Review

- Describe the cross-cultural challenges of motivation.
- Discuss the challenges managers face in motivating unique groups of workers.

- Describe open-book management, employee recognition, pay-for-performance, and stock option programs.

## FROM THEORY TO PRACTICE: SUGGESTIONS FOR MOTIVATING EMPLOYEES

We've covered a lot of information about motivation. If you're a manager concerned with motivating your employees, what specific recommendations can you draw from the theories and issues presented in this chapter? Although there's no simple, all-encompassing

Exhibit 16–11

**Recommendations for Designing Stock Options**

| Design Question | Choices | Recommendations |
| --- | --- | --- |
| Who receives them? | • Broad-based or restricted | • Match company growth prospects, management style, and organizational culture. |
| How many? | • Large or small percentage of employee income | • Match company growth prospects. |
| | • Many or few options in previous grants | • Know that large, previous grants may increase recipient risk aversion. |
| What terms? | • Vesting* | • Should match business cycle. |
| | • Maturity | • Terms shorter than 10 years can create stronger pay-for-performance relationships. |
| How often? | • Fixed or variable schedule | • Predictable grants may reduce incentive alignment prospects. |
| | | • Internal equity issues may result from schedules that result in a variety of exercise prices. |
| What price? | • Fair-market value | • Employees must view stock option exercise prices as feasible and believe that chosen benchmarks are appropriate. |
| | • Premium | |
| | • Discounted | |
| | • Indexed | |
| What ownership? | • Holding requirements after exercise | • Requiring recipients to hold some of their shares after exercise encourages better incentive alignment. |
| | • Ownership guidelines | • Clear general ownership guidelines can also increase incentive alignment. |

*Vesting refers to the time that must pass before a person can exercise the option.

Source: P. Brandes, R. Dharwadkar, and G.V. Lemesis, "Effective Employee Stock Option Design: Reconciling Stakeholder, Strategic, and Motivational Factors," *Academy of Management Executive*, February 2003, p. 84.

set of guidelines, the following suggestions draw on what we know about motivating employees.

**Recognize Individual Differences** Almost every contemporary motivation theory recognizes that employees aren't identical. They have different needs, attitudes, personality, and other important individual variables.

**Match People to Jobs** There's a great deal of evidence showing the motivational benefits of carefully matching people to jobs. For example, high achievers should have jobs that allow them to participate in setting moderately challenging goals and that involve autonomy and feedback. Also, keep in mind that not everybody is motivated by jobs that are high in autonomy, variety, and responsibility.

**Use Goals** The literature on goal-setting theory suggests that managers should ensure that employees have hard, specific goals and feedback on how well they're doing in achieving those goals. Should the goals be assigned by the manager or should employees participate in setting them? The answer depends on your perception of goal acceptance and the organization's culture. If you expect resistance to

**stock options**
Financial instruments that give employees the right to purchase shares of stock at a set price.

*The only requirements for a sales job at the Guitar Center, one of the fastest-growing retailers in the country, are to play music and be willing to work for minimum pay plus commission. That's one reason the chain of more than 150 stores, managed by a group of former rock and metal musicians and producers "with really big dreams," has a sales staff with almost no previous selling experience and high turnover. Motivating these employees can be a challenge for store managers like Vic Marks, who runs the Jacksonville, Florida, store. He begins each day with a "power huddle" with his troops in which he assigns sales goals and then pumps up the salespeople like a coach before a game. "We are the biggest and the baddest," he'll say. "We're about doing the right thing for our customers. This is how we win."*

goals, participation should increase acceptance. If participation is inconsistent with the culture, use assigned goals.

**Ensure That Goals Are Perceived As Attainable** Regardless of whether goals are actually attainable, employees who see goals as unattainable will reduce their effort because they'll be thinking "why bother." Managers must be sure, therefore, that employees feel confident that increased efforts *can* lead to achieving performance goals.

**Individualize Rewards** Because employees have different needs, what acts as a reinforcer for one may not for another. Managers should use their knowledge of employee differences to individualize the rewards they control, such as pay, promotions, recognition, desirable work assignments, autonomy, and participation.

*becoming* a Manager

✓ Set goals for yourself using the suggestions from goal-setting theory.

✓ Start paying attention to times when you're highly motivated and times when you're not as motivated. What accounts for the difference?

✓ When working on teams for class projects or on committees in student organizations, try different approaches to motivating others.

✓ If you're working, assess your job using the job characteristics model. How might you redesign your job to make it more motivating?

✓ As you visit various businesses, note what, if any, employee recognition programs these businesses use.

✓ Talk to practicing managers about their approaches to employee motivation. What have they found works?

Self-Assessment
Library (S.A.L.)

✓  Complete any of the following exercises from the Self-Assessment Library found on www.prenhall.com/rolls: S.A.L. #I.C.1—What Motivates Me?, S.A.L. #I.C.3—What Rewards Do I Value Most?, S.A.L. #I.C.4—What's My View on the Nature of People?, and S.A.L. #I.C.8—How Sensitive Am I to Equity Differences?

**Link Rewards to Performance** Managers need to make rewards contingent on performance. Rewarding factors other than performance will only reinforce those other factors. Important rewards such as pay increases and promotions should be given for the attainment of specific goals. Managers should also look for ways to increase the visibility of rewards, making them potentially more motivating.

**Check the System for Equity** Employees should perceive that rewards or outcomes are equal to the inputs. On a simple level, experience, ability, effort, and other obvious inputs should explain differences in pay, responsibility, and other obvious outcomes. And remember that one person's equity is another's inequity, so an ideal reward system should probably weigh inputs differently in arriving at the proper rewards for each job.

**Use Recognition** Recognize the power of recognition. In a stagnant economy where cost-cutting is widespread, using recognition is a low-cost means to reward employees. And it's a reward that most employees consider valuable.

**Show Care and Concern for Your Employees** Employees perform better for managers who care about them. Research done by the Gallup Organization with millions of employees and tens of thousands of managers consistently shows this simple truth. The best organizations create "caring" work environments.[93] When managers care about employees, performance results typically follow.

**Don't Ignore Money** It's easy to get so caught up in setting goals, creating interesting jobs, and providing opportunities for participation that you forget that money is a major reason why most people work. Thus, the allocation of performance-based wage increases, piecework bonuses, and other pay incentives is important in determining employee motivation. We're not saying that managers should focus solely on money as a motivational tool. Rather, we're simply stating the obvious—that is, if money is removed as an incentive, people aren't going to show up for work. The same can't be said for removing goals, enriched work, or participation.

# Managers Respond to a Manager's Dilemma

## Kelly Bell

District Sales Manager, Prentice Hall, Fayetteville, GA

Tom's dilemma is how he will continue to motivate employees that have proven they are already highly motivated and passionate about what they do. It's imperative that the plant continues to perform to keep from closing and relocation to China.

- Celebration—It is important to celebrate the successes.
- Recognition—Provide some special rewards for individuals who spearheaded some of the cost savings and customer services.
- Personalize the recognition—Send handwritten notes to each employee thanking them for the part they have played.
- Empower them—Employees want to be part of the solution. Allow employees to brainstorm ideas and solutions for overcoming the corporate relocation issues.
- Make them a part of the solution—Once the ideas have been identified, design a plan of implementation and then assign groups parts of the implementation plan.

## Willis A. Dibble

Executive Director, United Cerebral Palsy
of Philadelphia, PA

Tom's dilemma is one many would like to have. After living with all the practical realities of applying management theories (such as TQM), it appears his employees have woven it into the fabric of their workplace culture. They are performing above and beyond what should be reasonably expected. Situations like this should receive a response from the employer that, in kind, goes beyond expectation.

Besides the formal acknowledgment accompanying such performance (note to employee, copy to their personnel file), in the spirit of praising publicly, Tom might use any or all of the following:

- Openly acknowledge to the customer that employee dedication got the job done on time (pass on the credit).
- Provide an "award" that can be worn with a motto acknowledging the specific event (such as badge or t-shirt).
- Provide a "replacement" New Year's Eve celebration.
- Provide a special lunch onsite or an event offsite (picnic/ballgame/movie/etc.).
- Provide coupons/vouchers to stores/movies that can be used at the employee's convenience.

Any such ideas that tangibly acknowledge the employees for their specific effort should further motivate them to respond similarly in the future.

# Learning Summary

## What Is Motivation?

The process by which a person's efforts are energized, directed, and sustained toward attaining a goal

- Energy—intensity or drive
- Direction—effort channeled in a way that benefits the organization
- Persistence—sustained effort to achieve goals

## What Are the Early Theories of Motivation?

- **Maslow's hierarchy of needs**
  - Five needs: physiological, safety, social, esteem, and self-actualization
  - Person moves up hierarchy as needs are substantially satisfied
  - Substantially satisfied need no longer motivates
- **McGregor's Theory X and Theory Y**
  - Theory X—assumes people don't like to work, won't seek out responsibility, and have to be threatened and coerced to put forth effort
  - Theory Y—assumes people like to work, seek out responsibility, and will exercise self-direction
- **Herzberg's two-factor theory** (also called motivation-hygiene theory)
  - Factors associated with job satisfaction (motivators) were intrinsic
  - Factors associated with job dissatisfaction (hygiene) were extrinsic

## What Are the Contemporary Theories of Motivation?

- **Three-needs theory**—three acquired (not innate) needs
  - Need for achievement, need for affiliation, and need for power
- **Goal-setting theory**—specific goals increase performance and difficult goals, when accepted, result in higher performance than do easy goals
  - Intention to work toward a goal is a major source of job motivation
  - Specific hard goals produce higher levels of output than generalized goals
  - Goal setting (difficult goals) versus need for achievement (moderately challenging goals)
  - Participation is probably preferable to assigning goals, but not always
  - Feedback guides and motivates behavior—especially self-generated feedback
  - Contingencies in goal setting: goal commitment, self-efficacy, and national culture
- **Reinforcement theory**—behavior is a function of its consequences
  - Use positive reinforcers to reinforce desirable behaviors
  - Ignore undesirable behavior rather than punish it
- Designing motivating jobs
  - **Job enlargement**—horizontally expanding job scope: number of different tasks required in a job and the frequency with which these tasks are repeated
  - **Job enrichment**—vertically expanding job depth: degree of control employees have over their work
  - **Job characteristics model (JCM)**—identifies five primary job dimensions that can be used to design motivating jobs: skill variety, task identity, task significance, autonomy, and feedback
- **Equity theory**—focuses on how employees compare their inputs–outcomes ratios to relevant others' (referents) inputs–outcomes ratios
  - Perception of inequity will cause employee to distort own or other's inputs or outcomes, induce others to change their inputs or outcomes, or change their own inputs or outcomes
  - Procedural justice (perceived fairness of the process used to determine the distribution of rewards) has greater influence on employee satisfaction than does distributive justice (perceived fairness of amount and allocation of rewards among individuals)

- **Expectancy theory**—an individual tends to act in a certain way based on the expectation that the act will be followed by a given outcome and the attractiveness of that outcome to the individual
  - Expectancy or effort–performance linkage
  - Instrumentality or performance–reward linkage
  - Valence or attractiveness of reward

### What Current Motivational Issues Must Managers Be Aware Of?

- Cross-cultural challenges—know cultural characteristics before designing motivational program
- Motivating unique groups of workers
  - Diverse workforce—flexibility is key; use flexible work arrangements such as compressed workweek, flextime, job sharing, telecommuting
  - Professionals—job challenge, support, work itself
  - Contingent workers—opportunity to become permanent, training
  - Low-skilled, minimum-wage workers—employee recognition programs, sincere appreciation for work done
- Designing appropriate rewards programs
  - Open-book management
  - Employee recognition programs
  - Pay-for-performance programs
  - Stock option programs

# Management: By the Numbers

- Only 29 percent of employees polled believed that their performance is rewarded when they do a good job.
- Twenty-five percent of HR managers polled said that telecommuting hurts an employee's career; 30 percent said it helped; and 39 percent said it neither helped nor hurt.
- Sixty-eight percent of employees polled said that bonus payments can have a negative impact if they're not paid or if they're not large enough.
- At the top of employees' wish lists at work: a bonus or raise, which is what 48 percent of survey respondents said.
- In a survey that asked employees what they'd be willing to do in exchange for being able to leave work early every day, 6 percent said they'd take a salary cut; 47 percent said they wouldn't do anything to be able to leave early.
- Almost 57 percent of companies surveyed said they had increased the pay-for-performance compensation of their senior executives.
- Sixty-six percent of dog owners surveyed said that they would work longer hours if they could take their dogs with them to work.

- In a survey of telecommuters from 20 countries, 46 percent of the women and 52 percent of the men said they felt more productive; 44 percent of the women and 30 percent of the men said they bathed; and 11 percent of the women and 8 percent of the men said they felt guilty about not being in the office.
- Thirty-three percent of employees surveyed said that stock options were an integral part of a competitive pay package; 25 percent said they would prefer a higher salary.

*Sources:* D. Stead, "The Big Picture: Slippers and Stubble," *Business Week,* April 3, 2006, p. 13; "Cheat Sheet: Eccentric Survey Finding," *Fast Company,* April 2006, p. 37; "Corporate Governance Survey Shows Strong Commitment to Accountability," *Ethics Newsline,* www.globalethics.org/newsline, March 20, 2006; J. Yang and D. Merrill, "HR Executives Split on Telecommuting," *USA Today,* March 1, 2006, p. 1B; J. Yang and A. Lewis, "Leaving Work Early Is Attractive," *USA Today,* December 8, 2005, p. 1B; D. Haralson and B. Laird, "Workers' Views of Stock Options," *USA Today,* September 8, 2004, p. 1B; "ThermoStat: Which One of the Following Is at the Top of Your Wish List at Work?" *Training,* August 2004, p. 15; "Can't Buy Me Love," *Training,* December 2003, p. 16; and "Are Employee Reward Programs Valuable?" *Business Finance,* September 2003, p. 18.

# Thinking About Management Issues

1. Most of us have to work for a living, and a job is a central part of our lives. So why do managers have to worry so much about employee motivation issues?

2. Describe a task you have done recently for which you exerted a high level of effort. Explain your behavior using any three of the motivation approaches described in this chapter.

3. If you had to develop an incentive system for a small company that makes tortillas, which elements from which motivation approaches or theories would you use? Why? Would your choice be the same if it was a software design firm?

4. Could managers use any of the motivation theories or approaches to encourage and support workforce diversity efforts? Explain.

5. Many job design experts who have studied the changing nature of work say that people do their best work when they're motivated by a sense of purpose rather than by the pursuit of money. Do you agree? Explain your position.

6. "Too many managers today have forgotten that work should be inspiring and fun and are too out of touch with what makes people productive." How would you respond to this assertion?

7. Can an individual be too motivated? Discuss.

# Working Together: Team-Based Exercise

List five criteria (for example: pay, recognition, challenging work, friendships, status, the opportunity to do new things, the opportunity to travel, and so forth) that would be most important to you in a job. Rank them by order of importance. Break into small groups (three or four other class members) and compare your responses. What patterns, if any, did you find?

# Ethical Dilemma Exercise

When employees feel they're being treated unfairly, they may not be the most motivated workers. As an example, many employees of financially strapped U.S. airlines and auto manufacturers are unhappy that their compensation has been cut or will be frozen for several years. "We know we had to help the airline," said a US Airways flight attendant. "But we think they took more than they needed from us." This sense of inequity could dampen motivation and affect how employees work together and how they handle customers.

Employee motivation may also suffer when concerns arise about the fairness of appraisals and rewards. Consider the new pay-for-performance program covering employees in the U.S. Department of Defense and the Homeland Security department. The goal is to motivate employees by more closely linking pay increases to job performance. However, the Merit Systems Protection Board, an agency that hears personnel appeals from government employees, says the new program "demands a higher level of supervisory skill" because supervisors have considerable leeway in rewarding performance. The report also observes: "Supervisors must treat employees fairly in terms of the assignment of work, evaluation of performance, allocation of rewards—and they [supervisors] must be held accountable for their decisions." [95]

Imagine you're a manager working for Homeland Security. You oversee a dozen supervisors who, in turn, manage hundreds of employees around the United States. How can you help these supervisors implement the new pay-for-performance program so employees perceive it as fair and are motivated to improve their effort and their performance? Look back at Exhibit 16–9 as you consider your options and decide what to do next—and why.

**Option A:** Encourage supervisors to distribute rewards evenly in the first year, despite any differences in performance, to be fair as employees adjust to the new program.

**Option B:** Review goal setting with your supervisors and have them talk with employees throughout the year about goals as well as performance feedback.

**Option C:** Emphasize how the new program will allow supervisors as well as employees to meet their individual needs for development and achievement on the job.

## Case Application

### Best Buy . . . Best Job

Customer-centricity. That's the new strategic focus that Brad Anderson, CEO of Best Buy, is betting on to keep the company from becoming a retailing casualty like Woolworth or Kmart. What is customer-centricity? Simply, it's figuring out which customers are the most profitable and doing whatever it take to please them so they want to come back often and spend money. As the biggest consumer electronics retailer in the United States, Best Buy has a lot at stake. And its 100,000-plus employees will play a crucial role in this new approach, which shifts the focus from "pushing gadgets to catering to customers." What's the best way for the company to get those employees on board? Well, the way it's always treated its employees undoubtedly is a good start!

"At Best Buy, People Are the Engines That Drive Our Success." That's the up-front and central phrase on the company's Web-based career center. And to Best Buy, it's not just an empty slogan. The company has tried to create an environment in which employees, wherever they are, have numerous opportunities to learn, work, play, and achieve. One way they do that is by providing facts and figures to employees on everything from new technology to industry changes to company actions. At store meetings or on the intranet, employees can get the information they need to do their jobs and do them well. But that's not all the company does for its employees.

Like many other companies, Best Buy "struggled to meet the demands of its business—how to do things better, faster, and cheaper than its competitors—with an increasingly stressed-out workforce." Its culture had always rewarded long hours and sacrifice. For instance, one manager used a plaque to recognize the employee "who turns on the lights in the morning and turns them off at night." However, that approach was taking

its toll on employees. Instead of trying another work–life balance program, Best Buy decided to experiment with the very concept of work, which all too long had been tied to the amount of time spent at work. Thousands of Best Buy employees now work under a ROWE (results-oriented work environment), which means they work when and where they like, as long as they get the job done. Managers have had to learn to not be control freaks and hourly workers have been empowered to do their jobs the best way they know how. As ROWE has been implemented, entire departments would join at once. These work groups would find different ways to keep the flexibility from turning into chaos. For instance, one team got pagers to make sure someone was always available for emergencies. Others realized that they needed only one regular weekly or monthly staff meeting and eliminated all other unproductive ones.

Another change Best Buy has made is to its employee incentive program. Again, the CEO, Brad Anderson, initiated this change, in this case, to help the company retain its best and brightest managers and executives. He wanted to know why the company didn't have an "innovative incentive program to foster our innovative culture." Anderson was particularly interested in giving these employees incentive choices, an approach that many companies stay away from because of the associated communications and administrative burdens. But employee incentive program experts say that "providing choice is a great way to recruit and retain employees and is important for workforce management because it recognizes that employees are in different places in their lives and have different needs." After experimenting with different plans, the company introduced its incentive plan on September 30, 2005, offering participants four choices with varying levels of performance payouts. So far, as a recent survey showed, employees seem to feel good about the change.

But now it seems that employees are about to face another change . . . this time to a customer-centricity focus and are likely to see the way they work change also.

### Discussion Questions

1. Explain the advantages and disadvantages of Best Buy's different employee programs using Maslow's hierarchy of needs theory, reinforcement theory, and expectancy theory.

2. Log onto Best Buy's Web site and find the information on "Careers." Click on two job titles listed there and assess these jobs according to the job characteristics model.

3. Design an employee recognition program that might fit in with Anderson's managerial philosophy.

*Best Buy employees.*

4. Suppose that you're a store manager for Best Buy and you want to ensure that your employees are motivated to make this new customer-centricity approach succeed. What are you going to do?

*Sources:* J. Marquez, "Best Buy Offers Choice in Its Long-term Incentive Program to Keep the Best and Brightest," *Workforce Management,* April 24, 2006, pp. 42–43; M. Boyle, "Best Buy's Giant Gamble," *Fortune,* April 3, 2006, pp. 68–75; J. S. Lublin, "A Few Share the Wealth," *Wall Street Journal,* December 12, 2005, pp. B1+; J. Thotta, "Reworking Work," *Time,* July 25, 2005, pp. 50–55; and M. V. Copeland, "Best Buy's Selling Machine," *Business 2.0,* July 2004, pp. 92–102.

# Learning Outline

*Use this Learning Outline as you read and study this chapter.*

## Who Are Leaders and What Is Leadership?

- Define leaders and leadership.
- Explain why managers should be leaders.

## Early Leadership Theories

- Discuss what research has shown about leadership traits.
- Contrast the findings of the four behavioral leadership theories.
- Explain the dual nature of a leader's behavior.

## Contingency Theories of Leadership

- Explain how Fiedler's model of leadership is a contingency model.
- Contrast situational leadership theory and the leader participation model.
- Discuss how path-goal theory explains leadership.

## Contemporary Views on Leadership

- Differentiate between transactional and transformational leaders.
- Describe charismatic and visionary leadership.
- Discuss what team leadership involves.

## Leadership Issues in the Twenty-First Century

- Tell the five sources of a leader's power.
- Discuss the issues today's leaders face.
- Explain why leadership is sometimes irrelevant.

# Leadership

## A Manager's Dilemma

Judy McGrath has what many young (and even "young-thinking") people would consider a really fun job![1] As the chairman and CEO of MTV Networks (MTV), she gets to hang out with the likes of Jon Stewart, SpongeBob SquarePants, Bono, Michael Stipe, Mariah Carey, and John Legend. Founded as a music video channel in 1981, MTV now does way more than play music videos. It's actually a collection of several TV channels, some of which include Nickelodeon, VH1, Comedy Central, TVLand/Nick at Nite, and CMT. Today, MTV—a $7 billion subsidiary of Viacom—has a broad and deep reach—more than 440 million households in some 169 countries.

As a kid, McGrath loved music, and as an only child, her parents encouraged her to never be afraid to speak her opinions. Her initial career aspiration was to be a writer for *Rolling Stone* magazine—a dream job that she thought would combine her love of music and being opinionated. Although she never made it to the editorial staff of *Rolling Stone,* she was so good at her first job writing for *Mademoiselle* magazine that it led to her being hired by Robert W. Pittman, who was just launching the MTV format.

From the start, MTV was considered hip and cutting-edge. Pretty much every teenager and young adult knew about MTV. In fact, the format was so innovative that *Forbes* named MTV "product of the year" in 1981. And over the years, MTV has continued to "push the envelope" in terms of programming. For instance, in January 1990, the acoustic music series *MTV Unplugged* debuted. The first *Real World* episode aired in May 1992, starting the now-popular reality TV trend. In September 1998, MTV started its hit daily countdown show *TRL.*

But now MTV is over 25 years old and McGrath's challenge is to keep her employees focused on making sure that MTV stays bold and experimental. "McGrath is known for her skillful management of talent and the chaos that comes with a creative enterprise." One of her most important leadership skills is her ability to listen to all the people in the organization—from interns to senior managers. Says one executive, "Judy's ability to concentrate on people is intense."

Put yourself in Judy's position. What else can she do to be a good team leader, especially with her global employees?

**What would you do?**

Judy McGrath is a good example of what it takes to be a good leader in today's organizations. She has created an environment in which creativity and innovation thrive and in which employees feel like they're heard. However, it's important that she continue to nurture this culture *and* be seen as an effective leader in other ways as well. Why is leadership so important? Because the leaders in organizations make things happen. If leadership is so important, it's only natural to ask: What makes leaders different from nonleaders? What's the most appropriate style of leadership? And what can you do if you want to be seen as a leader? In this chapter, we'll try to answer these and other questions about leaders.

## WHO ARE LEADERS AND WHAT IS LEADERSHIP?

Let's begin by clarifying who leaders are and what leadership is. Our definition of a **leader** is someone who can influence others and who has managerial authority. **Leadership** is what leaders do. More specifically, it's the process of influencing a group to achieve goals.

Are all managers leaders? Because leading is one of the four management functions, yes, ideally, all managers *should* be leaders. Thus, we're going to study leaders and leadership from a managerial perspective.[2] However, even though we're looking at leaders from a managerial perspective, we're aware that groups often have informal leaders who emerge. Although these informal leaders may be able to influence others, they have not been the focus of most leadership research and are not the types of leaders we're studying in this chapter.

Leaders and leadership, like motivation, are organizational behavior topics that have been researched a lot and most of that research has been aimed at answering the question: *What is an effective leader?* We'll begin our study of leadership by looking at some early leadership theories.

## Learning Review

- Define leaders and leadership.
- Explain why managers should be leaders.

## EARLY LEADERSHIP THEORIES

People have been interested in leadership since they've started coming together in groups to accomplish goals. However, it wasn't until the early part of the twentieth century that researchers actually began to study it. These early leadership theories focused on the *leader* (trait theories) and how the *leader interacted* with his or her group members (behavioral theories).

### Trait Theories

As one of the U.S. senators from the state of Illinois, Barack Obama is catching the eyes of political analysts and the public.[3] He has been compared to popular historical leaders such as Abraham Lincoln and Martin Luther King, Jr. Many are saying that he has what it takes to be a leading political figure—maybe even President—characteristics such as self-awareness, clarity of speech, keen intellect, and an ability to relate to people. Is Obama a leader? The trait theories of leadership would answer that by focusing on his traits.

Leadership research in the 1920s and 1930s focused on leader traits—characteristics that might be used to differentiate leaders from nonleaders. ( 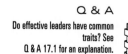 Go to www.prenhall.

**Q & A**
Do effective leaders have common traits? See Q & A 17.1 for an explanation.

com/rolls) The intent was to isolate traits that leaders possessed and nonleaders did not. Some of the traits studied included physical stature, appearance, social class, emotional stability, fluency of speech, and sociability. Despite the best efforts of researchers, it proved impossible to identify one set of traits that would *always* differentiate leaders (the person) from nonleaders. Maybe it was a bit optimistic to think there could be consistent and unique traits that would apply universally to all effective leaders, no matter whether they were in charge of Toyota Motor Corporation, the Moscow Ballet, a local chapter of Alpha Chi Omega, the country of France, Ted's Malibu Surf Shop, or Oxford University. However, later attempts to identify traits consistently associated with *leadership* (the process, not the person) were more successful. The seven traits shown to be associated with effective leadership are drive, the desire to lead, honesty and integrity, self-confidence, intelligence, job-relevant knowledge, and extraversion.[4] These traits are described briefly in Exhibit 17–1.

Researchers eventually recognized that traits alone were not sufficient for identifying effective leaders since explanations based solely on traits ignored the interactions of leaders and their group members as well as situational factors. Possessing the appropriate traits only made it more likely that an individual would be an effective leader. ( ◆ Go to www.prenhall.com/rolls) Therefore, leadership research from the late 1940s to the mid-1960s concentrated on the preferred behavioral styles that leaders demonstrated. Researchers wondered whether there was something unique in what effective leaders *did*—in other words, in their *behavior*.

**Q & A**
What about leadership experience? Does that make leaders more effective? Q & A 17.2 discusses.

## Behavioral Theories

Paul Johnston is president and general manager of Agri-Mark Inc., a successful and growing Massachusetts dairy cooperative that's known for its high-quality dairy products. Johnston is a demanding, autocratic boss who's described as "blunt, sarcastic, tactless, and tough." In contrast, Gerald Chamales, founder and chairman of Rhinotek

Exhibit 17–1

**Seven Traits Associated with Leadership**

1. *Drive.* Leaders exhibit a high effort level. They have a relatively high desire for achievement; they are ambitious; they have a lot of energy; they are tirelessly persistent in their activities; and they show initiative.

2. *Desire to lead.* Leaders have a strong desire to influence and lead others. They demonstrate the willingness to take responsibility.

3. *Honesty and integrity.* Leaders build trusting relationships between themselves and followers by being truthful or nondeceitful and by showing high consistency between word and deed.

4. *Self-confidence.* Followers look to leaders for an absence of self-doubt. Leaders, therefore, need to show self-confidence in order to convince followers of the rightness of their goals and decisions.

5. *Intelligence.* Leaders need to be intelligent enough to gather, synthesize, and interpret large amounts of information, and they need to be able to create visions, solve problems, and make correct decisions.

6. *Job-relevant knowledge.* Effective leaders have a high degree of knowledge about the company, industry, and technical matters. In-depth knowledge allows leaders to make well-informed decisions and to understand the implications of those decisions.

7. *Extraversion.* Leaders are energetic, lively people. They are sociable, assertive, and rarely silent or withdrawn.

*Sources:* S. A. Kirkpatrick and E. A. Locke, "Leadership: Do Traits Really Matter?" *Academy of Management Executive,* May 1991, pp. 48–60; T. A. Judge, J. E. Bono, R. Ilies, and M. W. Gerhardt, "Personality and Leadership: A Qualitative and Quantitative Review," *Journal of Applied Psychology,* August 2002, pp. 765–780.

**leader**
Someone who can influence others and who has managerial authority.

**leadership**
The process of influencing a group to achieve goals.

Computer Products, a California-based manufacturer of inkjet and laser cartridges, has learned to tap into his employees' passions and strengths and get the best out of them. How? By encouraging their participation and letting them figure out how best to do things.[5] Agri-Mark and Rhinotek are two successful companies whose leaders, as you can see, behave in two very different ways. What do we know about leader behavior and how can it help us in our understanding of what an effective leader is?

Researchers hoped that the **behavioral theories** approach would provide more definitive answers about the nature of leadership than did the trait theories. There are four main leader behavior studies we need to look at. (Exhibit 17–2 provides a summary of the major leader behavior dimensions and the conclusions of each of these studies.)

**University of Iowa Studies** The University of Iowa studies (conducted by Kurt Lewin and his associates) explored three leadership styles.[6] The **autocratic style** described a leader who typically tended to centralize authority, dictate work methods, make unilateral decisions, and limit employee participation. The **democratic style** described a leader who tended to involve employees in decision making, delegate authority, encourage participation in deciding work methods and goals, and use feedback as an opportunity for coaching employees. Finally, the **laissez-faire style** leader generally gave the group complete freedom to make decisions and complete the work in whatever way it saw fit. Lewin and his associates researched which style was the most effective. Their results seemed to indicate that the democratic style contributed to both good quantity and quality of work. ( ◆ Go to www.prenhall.com/rolls) Had the answer to the question of the most effective leadership style been found? Unfortunately, it wasn't that simple. Later studies of the autocratic and democratic styles showed mixed results. For instance, the democratic style sometimes produced higher performance levels than the autocratic style, but at other times, it produced

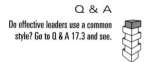

**Q & A**

Do effective leaders use a common style? Go to Q & A 17.3 and see.

Exhibit 17–2

**Behavioral Theories of Leadership**

|  | Behavioral Dimension | Conclusion |
|---|---|---|
| University of Iowa | *Democratic style:* involving subordinates, delegating authority, and encouraging participation<br>*Autocratic style:* dictating work methods, centralizing decision making, and limiting participation<br>*Laissez-faire style:* giving group freedom to make decisions and complete work | Democratic style of leadership was most effective, although later studies showed mixed results. |
| Ohio State | *Consideration:* being considerate of followers' ideas and feelings<br>*Initiating structure:* structuring work and work relationships to meet job goals | High–high leader (high in consideration and high in initiating structure) achieved high subordinate performance and satisfaction, but not in all situations. |
| University of Michigan | *Employee-oriented:* emphasized interpersonal relationships and taking care of employees' needs<br>*Production-oriented:* emphasized technical or task aspects of job | Employee-oriented leaders were associated with high group productivity and higher job satisfaction. |
| Managerial Grid | *Concern for people:* measured leader's concern for subordinates on a scale of 1 to 9 (low to high)<br>*Concern for production:* measured leader's concern for getting job done on a scale of 1 to 9 (low to high) | Leaders performed best with a 9.9 style (high concern for production and high concern for people). |

lower or equal performance levels. More consistent results were found, however, when a measure of subordinate satisfaction was used. Group members' satisfaction levels were generally higher under a democratic leader than under an autocratic one.[7] ( Go to www.prenhall.com/rolls)

Now leaders had a dilemma! Should they focus on achieving higher performance or higher member satisfaction? This recognition of the dual nature of a leader's behavior—that is, focusing on the task and focusing on the people—was also a key characteristic of the other behavioral studies.

**The Ohio State Studies** The Ohio State studies identified two important dimensions of leader behavior.[8] Beginning with a list of more than 1,000 behavioral dimensions, the researchers eventually narrowed it down to just two that accounted for most of the leadership behavior described by group members. The first was called **initiating structure**, which referred to the extent to which a leader defined and structured his or her role and the roles of group members in the search for goal attainment. It included behavior that involved attempts to organize work, work relationships, and goals. The second one was called **consideration**, which was defined as the extent to which a leader had job relationships characterized by mutual trust and respect for group members' ideas and feelings. A leader who was high in consideration helped group members with personal problems, was friendly and approachable, and treated all group members as equals. He or she showed concern for (was considerate of) his or her followers' comfort, well-being, status, and satisfaction.

Were these behavioral dimensions adequate descriptions of leader behavior? Research found that a leader who was high in both initiating structure and consideration (a **high-high leader**) achieved high group task performance and high satisfaction more frequently than one who rated low on either dimension or both. However, the high-high style didn't always yield positive results. Enough exceptions were found to indicate that perhaps situational factors needed to be integrated into leadership theory.

*Leaders are often responsible for structuring their roles and the roles of others in the organization. Anthony Bourdain, executive chef at New York's Les Halles restaurant, and his highly disciplined staff thrive on a hierarchical structure that is, in some ways, at odds with the increasingly flat structures of corporate organizations. Bourdain likens his model to the military, with a rigid chain of command and an us-versus-them psychology that fosters team effort. "Because of its very rigidity and clarity," he says, "the hierarchical system allows you to speak your mind in an environment where there's no ego allowed or needed. . . . Everyone lives and dies by the same rules."*

**behavioral theories**
Leadership theories that identified behaviors that differentiated effective leaders from ineffective leaders.

**autocratic style**
A leader who tended to centralize authority, dictate work methods, make unilateral decisions, and limit employee participation.

**democratic style**
A leader who tended to involve employees in decision making, delegate authority, encourage participation in deciding work methods and goals, and use feedback as an opportunity for coaching employees.

**laissez-faire style**
A leader who generally gave the group complete freedom to make decisions and complete the work in whatever way it saw fit.

**initiating structure**
The extent to which a leader defined and structured his or her role and the roles of group members.

**consideration**
The extent to which a leader had job relationships characterized by mutual trust and respect for group members' ideas and feelings.

**high-high leader**
A leader high in both initiating structure and consideration behaviors.

**University of Michigan Studies** Leadership studies conducted at the University of Michigan's Survey Research Center at about the same time as those being done at Ohio State had a similar research objective: Identify behavioral characteristics of leaders that were related to performance effectiveness. The Michigan group also came up with two dimensions of leadership behavior, which they labeled employee oriented and production oriented.[9] Leaders who were *employee oriented* were described as emphasizing interpersonal relationships; they took a personal interest in the needs of their followers and accepted individual differences among group members. The *production-oriented* leaders, in contrast, tended to emphasize the technical or task aspects of the job, were concerned mainly with accomplishing their group's tasks, and regarded group members as a means to that end. The conclusions of the Michigan researchers strongly favored leaders who were employee oriented as they were associated with high group productivity and high job satisfaction.

**The Managerial Grid** The behavioral dimensions from these early leadership studies provided the basis for the development of a two-dimensional grid for appraising leadership styles. This **managerial grid** used the behavioral dimensions "concern for people" and "concern for production" and evaluated a leader's use of these behaviors, ranking them on a scale from 1 (low) to 9 (high).[10] Although the grid (shown in Exhibit 17–3) had 81 potential categories into which a leader's behavioral style might fall, emphasis was placed on five styles: impoverished management (1,1), task management

Exhibit 17–3    **The Managerial Grid**

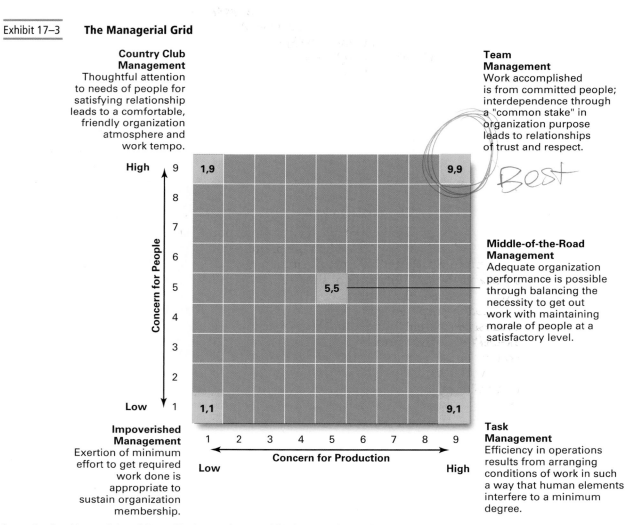

**Country Club Management**
Thoughtful attention to needs of people for satisfying relationship leads to a comfortable, friendly organization atmosphere and work tempo.

**Team Management**
Work accomplished is from committed people; interdependence through a "common stake" in organization purpose leads to relationships of trust and respect.

**Middle-of-the-Road Management**
Adequate organization performance is possible through balancing the necessity to get out work with maintaining morale of people at a satisfactory level.

**Impoverished Management**
Exertion of minimum effort to get required work done is appropriate to sustain organization membership.

**Task Management**
Efficiency in operations results from arranging conditions of work in such a way that human elements interfere to a minimum degree.

Concern for People — High 9, Low 1

Concern for Production — Low, High

(9,1), middle-of-the-road management (5,5), country club management (1,9), and team management (9,9). Of these five styles, the researchers concluded that managers performed best when using a 9,9 style. Unfortunately, the grid offered no answers to the question of what made a manager an effective leader; it only provided a framework for conceptualizing leadership style. In fact, there's been little substantive evidence to support the conclusion that a 9,9 style is most effective in all situations.[11]

Leadership researchers were discovering that predicting leadership success involved something more complex than isolating a few leader traits or preferred behaviors. They began looking at situational influences. Specifically, which leadership styles might be suitable in certain situations and what were these situations?

## Learning Review

- Discuss what research has shown about leadership traits.
- Contrast the findings of the four behavioral leadership theories.
- Explain the dual nature of a leader's behavior.

## CONTINGENCY THEORIES OF LEADERSHIP

"The corporate world is filled with stories of leaders who failed to achieve greatness because they failed to understand the context they were working in."[12] Being an effective leader requires not only an understanding of traits and behaviors, but an understanding of the situation in which the leader is attempting to lead, as well. In this section we examine four contingency theories—Fiedler, Hersey-Blanchard, leader participation, and path-goal. Each looks at defining leadership style and the situation, and attempts to answer the *if–then* contingencies (that is, *if* this is the context or situation, *then* this is the best leadership style to use).

### The Fiedler Model

The first comprehensive contingency model for leadership was developed by Fred Fiedler.[13] The **Fiedler contingency model** proposed that effective group performance depended upon the proper match between the leader's style of interacting with his or her followers and the degree to which the situation allowed the leader to control and influence. The model was based on the premise that a certain leadership style would be most effective in different types of situations. The key was to define those leadership styles and the different types of situations and then to identify the appropriate combinations of style and situation.

Fiedler proposed that a key factor in leadership success was an individual's basic leadership style, either task oriented or relationship oriented. To measure a leader's style, Fiedler developed the **least-preferred co-worker (LPC) questionnaire**. This questionnaire contained 18 pairs of contrasting adjectives—for example, pleasant–unpleasant, cold–warm, boring–interesting, and friendly–unfriendly. Respondents were asked to think of all the co-workers they had ever had and to describe that one person they *least enjoyed* working with by rating him or her on a scale of 1 to 8 (the 8 always described the

---

**managerial grid**
A grid of two leadership behaviors—concern for people and concern for production—which resulted in five different leadership styles.

**Fiedler contingency model**
A contingency theory that proposed that effective group performance depended upon the proper match between a leader's style of interacting with his or her followers and the degree to which the situation allowed the leader to control and influence.

**least-preferred co-worker (LPC) questionnaire**
A questionnaire that measured whether a leader was task or relationship oriented.

positive adjective out of the pair and the 1 always described the negative adjective out of the pair) for each of the 18 sets of adjectives. Fiedler believed that you could determine a person's basic leadership style on the basis of the responses to the LPC questionnaire.

If the leader described the least preferred co-worker in relatively positive terms (in other words, a "high" LPC score—a score of 64 or above), then the respondent was primarily interested in good personal relations with co-workers. That is, if you described the person that you least liked to work with in favorable terms, your style would be described as *relationship oriented*. In contrast, if you saw the least preferred co-worker in relatively unfavorable terms (a low LPC score—a score of 57 or below), you were primarily interested in productivity and getting the job done; thus, your style would be labeled as *task oriented*. Fiedler did acknowledge that there was a small group of people who fell in between these two extremes and who did not have a cut-and-dried leadership personality style. One other point is that Fiedler assumed that a person's leadership style was always the same (fixed) regardless of the situation. (◆ Go to www.prenhall.com/rolls) In other words, if you were a relationship-oriented leader, you'd always be one, and the same for task-oriented.

After an individual's leadership style had been assessed through the LPC, it was necessary to evaluate the situation in order to match the leader with the situation. Fiedler's research uncovered three contingency dimensions that defined the key situational factors for determining leader effectiveness. These were

- **Leader-member relations**: The degree of confidence, trust, and respect employees had for their leader; rated as either good or poor.
- **Task structure**: The degree to which job assignments were formalized and procedurized; rated as either high or low.
- **Position power**: The degree of influence a leader had over power-based activities such as hiring, firing, discipline, promotions, and salary increases; rated as either strong or weak.

Each leadership situation was evaluated in terms of these three contingency variables, which, when combined, produced eight possible situations in which a leader could find himself or herself (see the bottom of the chart in Exhibit 17–4). Each of these situations was further described in terms of its favorableness for the leader. Situations I, II, and III were classified as very favorable for the leader. Situations IV, V,

**Q & A**

Is a leader's style of leading fixed? Q & A 17.4 looks at this.

Exhibit 17–4   **Findings of the Fiedler Model**

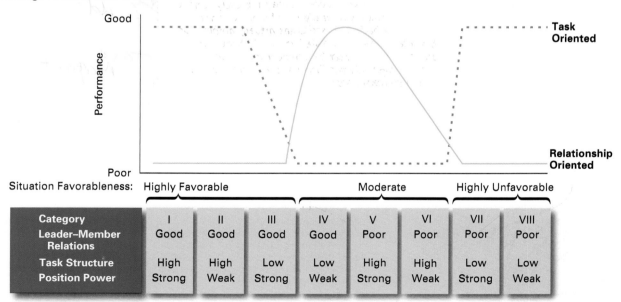

| Situation Favorableness: | Highly Favorable | | | Moderate | | | Highly Unfavorable | |
|---|---|---|---|---|---|---|---|---|
| **Category** | I | II | III | IV | V | VI | VII | VIII |
| **Leader–Member Relations** | Good | Good | Good | Good | Poor | Poor | Poor | Poor |
| **Task Structure** | High | High | Low | Low | High | High | Low | Low |
| **Position Power** | Strong | Weak | Strong | Weak | Strong | Weak | Strong | Weak |

and VI were moderately favorable for the leader. And, situations VII and VIII were described as very unfavorable for the leader.

Once Fiedler had described the leader variables and the situational variables, he was ready to define the specific contingencies for leadership effectiveness. To do so, he studied 1,200 groups where he compared relationship-oriented versus task-oriented leadership styles in each of the eight situational categories. He concluded that task-oriented leaders performed better in very favorable situations and in very unfavorable situations. (See the top of Exhibit 17–4, where performance is shown on the vertical axis and situation favorableness is shown on the horizontal axis.) On the other hand, relationship-oriented leaders performed better in moderately favorable situations.

Because Fiedler treated an individual's leadership style as fixed, there were only two ways to improve leader effectiveness. First, you could bring in a new leader whose style better fit the situation. For instance, if the group situation rated as highly unfavorable but was led by a relationship-oriented leader, the group's performance could be improved by replacing that person with a task-oriented leader. The second alternative was to change the situation to fit the leader. This could be done by restructuring tasks or increasing or decreasing the power that the leader had over factors such as salary increases, promotions, and disciplinary actions.

Reviews of the major studies undertaken to test the overall validity of Fiedler's model have shown considerable evidence to support the model.[14] However, his theory wasn't without criticisms. For instance, additional variables were probably needed to fill in some gaps in the model. Moreover, there were problems with the LPC, and the practicality of it needed to be addressed. In addition, it's probably unrealistic to assume that a person can't change his or her leadership style to fit the situation. Effective leaders can, and do, change their styles to meet the needs of a particular situation. Finally, the contingency variables were difficult for practitioners to assess.[15] Despite its shortcomings, the Fiedler model showed that effective leadership style needed to reflect situational factors.

*Effective corporate leaders can and do change their style of leading. For instance, after attending a "Corporate Athlete" program for Procter & Gamble managers, A. G. Lafley changed his leadership style. "I've learned how to manage my energy," says the company's president and CEO. "During my first year in this job, I worked every Saturday and every Sunday morning. Now I work really hard for an hour or an hour and a half. . . . I used to eat virtually nothing for breakfast. Now I have a V-8 juice, half a bagel, and a cup of yogurt. . . . I can't remember the last time I wrote a memo. I write little handwritten notes. . . . I prefer conversations."*

**leader-member relations**
One of Fiedler's situational contingencies that described the degree of confidence, trust, and respect employees had for their leader.

**task structure**
One of Fiedler's situational contingencies that described the degree to which job assignments were formalized and procedurized.

**position power**
One of Fiedler's situational contingencies that described the degree of influence a leader had over power-based activities such as hiring, firing, discipline, promotions, and salary increases.

## Hersey and Blanchard's Situational Leadership Theory

Paul Hersey and Ken Blanchard developed a leadership theory that has gained a strong following among management development specialists.[16] This model, called **situational leadership theory (SLT)**, is a contingency theory that focuses on followers' readiness. Hersey and Blanchard argue that successful leadership is achieved by selecting the right leadership style, which is contingent on the level of the followers' readiness. Before we proceed, there are two points we need to clarify: why a leadership theory focuses on the followers, and what is meant by the term *readiness*.

The emphasis on the followers in leadership effectiveness reflects the reality that it *is* the followers who accept or reject the leader. Regardless of what the leader does, effectiveness depends on the actions of his or her followers. ( 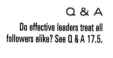 Go to www.prenhall.com/rolls) This is an important dimension that has been overlooked or underemphasized in most leadership theories. And **readiness**, as defined by Hersey and Blanchard, refers to the extent to which people have the ability and willingness to accomplish a specific task.

SLT uses the same two leadership dimensions that Fiedler identified: task and relationship behaviors. However, Hersey and Blanchard go a step further by considering each as either high or low and then combining them into four specific leadership styles described as follows:

- *Telling* (high task–low relationship): The leader defines roles and tells people what, how, when, and where to do various tasks.
- *Selling* (high task–high relationship): The leader provides both directive and supportive behavior.
- *Participating* (low task–high relationship): The leader and follower share in decision making; the main role of the leader is facilitating and communicating.
- *Delegating* (low task–low relationship): The leader provides little direction or support.

The final component in the model is the four stages of follower readiness:

- *R1:* People are both unable and unwilling to take responsibility for doing something. They're neither competent nor confident.
- *R2:* People are unable but willing to do the necessary job tasks. They're motivated but currently lack the appropriate skills.
- *R3:* People are able but unwilling to do what the leader wants.
- *R4:* People are both able and willing to do what is asked of them.

Q & A

Do effective leaders treat all followers alike? See Q & A 17.5.

*Kristen Cardwell is an infectious diseases researcher at St. Jude's Children's Research Hospital in Memphis, Tennessee. Cardwell and other medical researchers at the hospital have a high level of follower readiness. As responsible, experienced, and mature employees, they are both able and willing to complete their tasks under leadership that gives them freedom to make and implement decisions. This leader-follower relationship is consistent with Hersey and Blanchard's situational leadership theory.*

SLT essentially views the leader–follower relationship as analogous to that of a parent and a child. Just as a parent needs to relinquish control as a child becomes more mature and responsible, so, too, should leaders. As followers reach high levels of readiness, the leader responds not only by continuing to decrease control over their activities, but also by continuing to decrease relationship behavior. The SLT says if followers are *unable* and *unwilling* to do a task, the leader needs to give clear and specific directions—use the telling style; if followers are *unable* and *willing*, the leader needs to display high task orientation to compensate for the followers' lack of ability and high relationship orientation to get followers to "buy into" the leader's desires—use the selling style; if followers are *able* and *unwilling*, the leader needs to use a supportive (participative) style; and if employees are both *able* and *willing*, the leader doesn't need to do much (use the delegating style).

SLT has intuitive appeal. It acknowledges the importance of followers and builds on the logic that leaders can compensate for ability and motivational limitations in their followers. Yet research efforts to test and support the theory generally have been disappointing.[17] Why? Possible explanations include internal inconsistencies in the model itself as well as problems with research methodology. So despite its appeal and wide popularity, any enthusiastic endorsement should be done with caution.

## Leader Participation Model

Another early contingency model, developed by Victor Vroom and Phillip Yetton, was the **leader participation model**, which related leadership behavior and participation to decision making.[18] Developed in the early 1970s, the model argued that leader behavior must adjust to reflect the task structure—whether it was routine, nonroutine, or in between. Vroom and Yetton's model is what we call a *normative* one, because it provided a sequential set of rules (norms) that the leader followed in determining the form and amount of participation in decision making, as determined by the different situations.

The leader participation model has changed as research continues to provide additional insights into effective leadership style.[19] A current model reflects *how* and *with whom* decisions are made and uses variations of the same five leadership styles identified in the original model (see a description of these styles in Exhibit 17–5). It also expands upon the decision-making contingencies leaders look at in determining what leadership style would be most effective.[20] These contingencies—decision significance, importance of commitment, leader expertise, likelihood of commitment, group support, group expertise, and team competence—are either present (H for high) or absent (L for Low). Exhibit 17–6 shows a current leader participation model—the Time-Driven Model, which is short term in its orientation and concerned with making effective decisions with minimum cost. To use the model, a leader goes from left to

**Exhibit 17–5**

**Leadership Styles in the Vroom Leader Participation Model**

- *Decide:* Leader makes the decision alone and either announces or sells it to group.
- *Consult Individually:* Leader presents the problem to group members individually, gets their suggestions, and then makes the decision.
- *Consult Group:* Leader presents the problem to group members in a meeting, gets their suggestions, and then makes the decision.
- *Facilitate:* Leader presents the problem to the group in a meeting and, acting as facilitator, defines the problem and the boundaries within which a decision must be made.
- *Delegate:* Leader permits the group to make the decision within prescribed limits.

*Source:* Based on V. Vroom, "Leadership and the Decision-Making Process," *Organizational Dynamics*, vol. 28, no. 4 (2000), p. 84.

**situational leadership theory (SLT)**
A leadership contingency theory that focuses on followers' readiness.

**readiness**
The extent to which people have the ability and willingness to accomplish a specific task.

**leader participation model**
A leadership contingency model that related leadership behavior and participation in decision making.

Exhibit 17–6

**Time-Driven Model**

*Source:* Adapted from V. Vroom, "Leadership and the Decision-Making Process," *Organizational Dynamics*, vol. 28 (4), 2000, p. 87.

| Decision Significance | Importance of Commitment | Leader Expertise | Likelihood of Commitment | Group Support | Group Expertise | Team Competence | |
|---|---|---|---|---|---|---|---|
| H | H | H | H | – | – | – | Decide |
| | | | L | H | H | H | Delegate |
| | | | | | | L | Consult (Group) |
| | | | | | L | – | Consult (Group) |
| | | | | L | – | – | Consult (Group) |
| | | L | H | H | H | H | Facilitate |
| | | | | | | L | Consult (Individually) |
| | | | | | L | – | Consult (Individually) |
| | | | | L | – | – | Consult (Individually) |
| | | | L | H | H | H | Facilitate |
| | | | | | | L | Consult (Group) |
| | | | | | L | – | Consult (Group) |
| | | | | L | – | – | Consult (Group) |
| | L | H | – | – | – | – | Decide |
| | | L | H | H | H | H | Facilitate |
| | | | | | | L | Consult (Individually) |
| | | | | | L | – | Consult (Individually) |
| | | | | L | – | – | Consult (Individually) |
| L | H | – | H | – | – | – | Decide |
| | | | L | – | – | H | Delegate |
| | | | | | | L | Facilitate |
| | L | – | – | – | – | – | Decide |

right, determining whether each contingency factor is high or low. After assessing all these contingencies, the most effective leadership style is identified on the far right-hand side of the model. Another model—the Development-Driven Model—is structured the same way but emphasizes making effective decisions with maximum employee development outcomes and places no value on time.

## Path-Goal Model

Currently, one of the most respected approaches to understanding leadership is **path-goal theory**, which states that it's the leader's job to assist his or her followers in attaining their goals and to provide the direction or support needed to ensure that their goals are compatible with the overall objectives of the group or organization. Developed by Robert House, path-goal theory is a contingency model of leadership that takes key elements from the expectancy theory of motivation.[21] The term *path-goal* is derived from the belief that effective leaders clarify the path to help their followers get from where they are to the achievement of their work goals and make the journey along the path easier by reducing roadblocks and pitfalls.

House identified four leadership behaviors:

- *Directive leader:* Lets subordinates know what's expected of them, schedules work to be done, and gives specific guidance on how to accomplish tasks.
- *Supportive leader:* Is friendly and shows concern for the needs of followers.
- *Participative leader:* Consults with group members and uses their suggestions before making a decision.
- *Achievement-oriented leader:* Sets challenging goals and expects followers to perform at their highest level.

In contrast to Fiedler's view that a leader couldn't change his or her behavior, House assumed that leaders are flexible. In other words, path-goal theory assumes that the same leader can display any or all of these leadership styles depending on the situation.

As Exhibit 17–7 illustrates, path-goal theory proposes two situational or contingency variables that moderate the leadership behavior–outcome relationship: those in the *environment* that are outside the control of the follower (factors including task structure, formal authority system, and the work group) and those that are part of the personal characteristics of the *follower* (including locus of control, experience, and perceived ability). Environmental factors determine the type of leader behavior required if subordinate outcomes are to be maximized; personal characteristics of the follower determine how the environment and leader behavior are interpreted. The theory proposes that leader behavior will be ineffective when it's redundant with sources of environmental structure or incongruent with follower characteristics. For example, some predictions from path-goal theory are:

- Directive leadership leads to greater satisfaction when tasks are ambiguous or stressful than when they are highly structured and well laid out.
- Supportive leadership results in high employee performance and satisfaction when subordinates are performing structured tasks.
- Directive leadership is likely to be perceived as redundant among subordinates with high perceived ability or with considerable experience.
- The clearer and more bureaucratic the formal authority relationships, the more leaders should exhibit supportive behavior and deemphasize directive behavior.

Exhibit 17–7

**Path–Goal Theory**

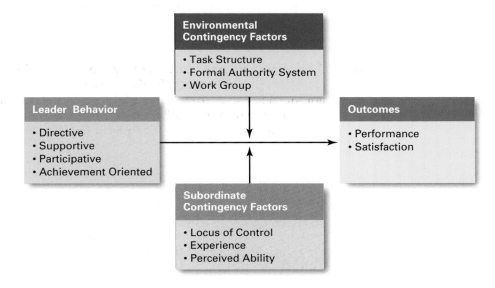

**path-goal theory**
A leadership theory that says it's the leader's job to assist his or her followers in attaining their goals and to provide the direction or support needed to ensure that their goals are compatible with the overall objectives of the group or organization.

- Directive leadership will lead to higher employee satisfaction when there is substantive conflict within a work group.
- Subordinates with an internal locus of control will be more satisfied with a participative style.
- Subordinates with an external locus of control will be more satisfied with a directive style.
- Achievement-oriented leadership will increase subordinates' expectancies that effort will lead to high performance when tasks are ambiguously structured.

**Q & A**

Okay ... the path-goal model seems logical, but how does it really work in real life? See Q & A 17.6 for an explanation.

Research on the path-goal model is generally encouraging. ( Go to www. prenhall.com/rolls) Although not every study has found support, the majority of the evidence supports the logic underlying the theory.[22] In summary, path-goal theory says that employee performance and satisfaction are likely to be positively influenced when the leader compensates for shortcomings in either the employee or the work setting. However, if the leader spends time explaining tasks that are already clear or when the employee has the ability and experience to handle them without interference, the employee is likely to see such directive behavior as redundant or even insulting.

## Learning Review

- Explain how Fiedler's model of leadership is a contingency model.
- Contrast situational leadership theory and the leadership participation model.

- Discuss how path-goal theory explains leadership.

## CONTEMPORARY VIEWS ON LEADERSHIP

What are the latest views of leadership in organizations? In this section, we want to look at three contemporary approaches to leadership including transformational–transactional leadership, charismatic–visionary leadership, and team leadership.

### Transformational–Transactional Leadership

**Q & A**

Some leaders do a good job of "looking like" leaders but don't seem to be able to lead. Are those types of leaders effective? Check out Q & A 17.7

Many early leadership theories viewed leaders as **transactional leaders**; that is, leaders that lead primarily by using social exchanges (or transactions). Transactional leaders guide or motivate followers to work toward established goals by exchanging rewards for their productivity.[23] ( Go to www.prenhall.com/rolls) But there's another type of leader who stimulates and inspires (transforms) followers to achieve extraordinary outcomes. These are **transformational leaders**, and examples include Jim Goodnight of SAS Institute and Andrea Jung of Avon. They pay attention to the concerns and developmental needs of individual followers; they change followers' awareness of issues by helping those followers look at old problems in new ways; and they are able to excite, arouse, and inspire followers to put out extra effort to achieve group goals.

Transactional and transformational leadership shouldn't be viewed as opposing approaches to getting things done.[24] Transformational leadership is built on top of transactional leadership. Transformational leadership produces levels of employee effort and performance that go beyond what would occur with a transactional approach alone. Moreover, transformational leadership is more than charisma since the transformational leader attempts to instill in followers the ability to question not only established views but those views held by the leader, as well.[25]

The evidence supporting the superiority of transformational leadership over transactional leadership is overwhelmingly impressive. For instance, studies that looked at managers in different settings, including the military and business, found that transformational leaders were evaluated as more effective, higher performers, more promotable than their transactional counterparts, and more interpersonally sensitive.[26] In addition, evidence indicates that transformational leadership is strongly correlated with lower turnover rates and higher levels of productivity, employee satisfaction, creativity, goal attainment, and follower well-being.[27]

## Charismatic–Visionary Leadership

Jeff Bezos, founder and CEO of Amazon.com, is a person who exudes energy, enthusiasm, and drive.[28] He's fun-loving (his legendary laugh has been described as a flock of Canadian geese on nitrous oxide), but has pursued his vision for Amazon with serious intensity and has demonstrated an ability to inspire his employees through the ups and downs of a rapidly growing company. Bezos is what we call a **charismatic leader**—that is, an enthusiastic, self-confident leader whose personality and actions influence people to behave in certain ways.

**Q & A**
Should every leader have charisma?
Q & A 17.8 discusses.

Several authors have attempted to identify personal characteristics of the charismatic leader.[29] The most comprehensive analysis identified five such characteristics that differentiate charismatic leaders from noncharismatic ones: they have a vision, are able to articulate that vision, are willing to take risks to achieve that vision, are sensitive to both environmental constraints and follower needs, and exhibit behaviors that are out of the ordinary.[30] ( ◆ Go to www.prenhall.com/rolls)

What can we say about the charismatic leader's effect on his or her followers? There's an increasing body of evidence that shows impressive correlations between charismatic leadership and high performance and satisfaction among followers.[31] However, a recent study of the impact of a charismatic CEO on subsequent organizational performance found no relationship.[32] Despite this, charisma is still believed to be a desirable leadership quality.

If charisma is desirable, can people learn to be charismatic leaders? Or are charismatic leaders born with their qualities? Although a small number of experts still think that charisma can't be learned, most others believe that individuals can be trained to exhibit charismatic behaviors.[33] For example, researchers have succeeded in teaching undergraduate students to "be" charismatic. How? They were taught to articulate a sweeping goal, communicate high performance expectations, exhibit confidence in the ability of subordinates to meet those expectations, and empathize with the needs of their subordinates; they learned to project a powerful, confident, and dynamic presence; and they practiced using a captivating and engaging voice tone. The researchers also trained the student leaders to use charismatic nonverbal behaviors including leaning toward the follower when communicating, maintaining direct eye contact, and having a relaxed posture and animated facial expressions. In groups with these "trained" charismatic leaders, members had higher task performance, higher task adjustment, and better adjustment to the leader and to the group than did group members who worked in groups led by noncharismatic leaders. ( ◆ Go to www.prenhall.com/rolls)

Self-Assessment
Library (S.A.L.)
Are you a charismatic leader? Try
S.A.L. #II.B.2 and see!

One last thing we should say about charismatic leadership is that it may not always be needed to achieve high levels of employee performance. It may be most appropriate when the follower's task has an ideological purpose or when the environment involves a high degree of stress and uncertainty.[34] This may explain why, when charismatic leaders surface, it's more likely to be in politics, religion, or wartime; or when a business firm is starting up or facing a survival crisis. For example, Martin Luther King Jr. used his charisma to bring about social equality through nonviolent means; and Steve Jobs achieved unwavering loyalty and commitment from Apple Computer's technical staff in the early 1980s by articulating a vision of personal computers that would dramatically change the way people lived.

---

**transactional leaders**
Leaders who lead primarily by using social exchanges (or transactions).

**transformational leaders**
Leaders who stimulate and inspire (transform) followers to achieve extraordinary outcomes.

**charismatic leader**
An enthusiastic, self-confident leader whose personality and actions influence people to behave in certain ways.

The management style of Reed Hastings, founder and CEO of Netflix, has been described as analytical, detail-oriented, and "very charismatic." The creator of two successful start-ups—Netflix and an earlier venture, Pure Software, which he sold for more than $500 million—Hastings is a hands-on manager whose engineering and computer science background is as much an influence on his style as the memory of his first job after college, teaching math in Swaziland for the Peace Corps. "Absolutely loved it," he says of that experience.

Although the term *vision* is often linked with charismatic leadership, **visionary leadership** goes beyond charisma since it's the ability to create and articulate a realistic, credible, and attractive vision of the future that improves upon the current situation.[35] This vision, if properly selected and implemented, is so energizing that it "in effect jump-starts the future by calling forth the skills, talents, and resources to make it happen."[36]

A vision should offer clear and compelling imagery that taps into people's emotions and inspires enthusiasm to pursue the organization's goals. It should be able to generate possibilities that are inspirational and unique and offer new ways of doing things that are clearly better for the organization and its members. Visions that are clearly articulated and have powerful imagery are easily grasped and accepted. For instance, Michael Dell (Dell Computer) created a vision of a business that sells and delivers a finished PC directly to a customer in less than a week. The late Mary Kay Ash's vision of women as entrepreneurs selling products that improved their self-image gave impetus to her cosmetics company, Mary Kay Cosmetics.

What skills do visionary leaders exhibit? Once the vision is identified, these leaders appear to have three qualities that are related to effectiveness in their visionary roles.[37] First is the *ability to explain the vision to others* by making the vision clear in terms of required goals and actions through clear oral and written communication. The second skill is the *ability to express the vision not just verbally but through behavior,* which requires behaving in ways that continually convey and reinforce the vision. For example, former Southwest Airlines CEO Herb Kelleher continually demonstrated his commitment to customer service. He was legendary within the company for his boundless energy and for jumping in, when needed, to help check-in passengers, load baggage, fill in for flight attendants, or do anything else to make the customers' experiences more pleasant and memorable. The third skill visionary leaders need is the *ability to extend or apply the vision to different leadership contexts.* For instance, the vision has to be as meaningful to the people in accounting as to those in customer service, to employees in Cleveland as to those in Sydney.

## Team Leadership

Because leadership is increasingly taking place within a team context and more organizations are using work teams, the role of the leader in guiding team members has become increasingly important. The role of team leader *is* different from the traditional leadership role, as J. D. Bryant, a supervisor at Texas Instruments' Forest Lane plant in Dallas, discovered.[38] One day he was contentedly overseeing a staff of 15 circuit board assemblers. The next day he was told that the company was going to use

**Q & A**

How is being a team leader different from other leadership?
See Q & A 17.9.

employee teams and he was to become a "facilitator." He said, "I'm supposed to teach the teams everything I know and then let them make their own decisions." But, confused about his new role, he admitted, "There was no clear plan on what I was supposed to do." What *is* involved in being a team leader? ( 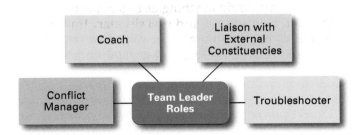 Go to www.prenhall. com/rolls)

Many leaders are not equipped to lead employee teams. As one consultant noted, "Even the most capable managers have trouble making the transition because all the command-and-control type things they were encouraged to do before are no longer appropriate. There's no reason to have any skill or sense of this."[39] This same consultant estimated that "probably 15 percent of managers are natural team leaders; another 15 percent could never lead a team because it runs counter to their personality—that is, they're unable to sublimate their dominating style for the good of the team. Then there's that huge group in the middle: Team leadership doesn't come naturally to them, but they can learn it."[40]

The challenge for many managers is learning how to become an effective team leader. They have to learn skills such as having the patience to share information, being able to trust others and to give up authority, and understanding when to intervene. And effective team leaders have mastered the difficult balancing act of knowing when to leave their teams alone and when to get involved. New team leaders may try to retain too much control at a time when team members need more autonomy, or they may abandon their teams at times when the teams need support and help.[41]

One study looking at organizations that had reorganized themselves around employee teams found certain common responsibilities of all leaders. These included coaching, facilitating, handling disciplinary problems, reviewing team and individual performance, training, and communication.[42] However, a more meaningful way to describe the team leader's job is to focus on two priorities: (1) managing the team's external boundary and (2) facilitating the team process.[43] These priorities entail four specific leadership roles (see Exhibit 17–8).

First, team leaders are *liaisons with external constituencies*. These may include upper management, other organizational work teams, customers, or suppliers. The leader represents the team to other constituencies, secures needed resources, clarifies others' expectations of the team, gathers information from the outside, and shares that information with team members.

Next, team leaders are *troubleshooters*. When the team has problems and asks for assistance, team leaders sit in on meetings and try to help resolve the problems. Troubleshooting rarely involves technical or operational issues because the team members typically know more about the tasks being done than does the team leader. The leader is most likely to contribute by asking penetrating questions, helping the team talk through problems, and getting needed resources to tackle problems.

Third, team leaders are *conflict managers*. They help identify issues such as the source of the conflict, who's involved, the issues, the resolution options available, and

**Exhibit 17–8**

**Specific Team Leadership Roles**

```
                Coach          Liaison with
                               External
                               Constituencies


  Conflict        Team Leader        Troubleshooter
  Manager           Roles
```

the advantages and disadvantages of each. By getting team members to address questions such as these, the leader minimizes the disruptive aspects of intrateam conflicts.

Finally, team leaders are *coaches*. They clarify expectations and roles, teach, offer support, and do whatever else is necessary to help team members keep their work performance high. ( Go to www.prenhall.com/rolls)

## Learning Review

- Differentiate between transactional and transformational leaders.
- Describe charismatic and visionary leadership.
- Discuss what team leadership involves.

## LEADERSHIP ISSUES IN THE TWENTY-FIRST CENTURY

It's not easy being a chief information officer (CIO) today. As the person responsible for managing a company's information technology activities, there are a lot of external and internal pressures. Technology continues to change rapidly—almost daily, it sometimes seems—and business costs continue to rise. Rob Carter, CIO of FedEx, is on the hot seat facing such challenges.[44] "He's responsible for all the computer and communication systems that keep this staggeringly complex outfit running. He has to connect 39 hubs around the world with 677 airplanes, over 90,000 vehicles, and more than 200,000 employees delivering 6 million packages a day in 220 countries. If anything goes wrong, he takes the heat." However, Carter has been an effective leader in this seemingly chaotic environment.

For most leaders, being effective in today's environment is unlikely to involve such challenging and changing circumstances. However, twenty-first-century leaders do face some important leadership issues. In this section, we're going to look at some of these issues including managing power, developing trust, providing ethical leadership, empowering employees, cross-cultural leadership, gender differences in leadership, the demise of celebrity leadership, and substitutes for leadership.

### Managing Power

Where do leaders get their power—that is, their capacity to influence work actions or decisions? ( Go to www.prenhall.com/rolls) Five sources of leader power have been identified: legitimate, coercive, reward, expert, and referent.[45]

**Legitimate power** and authority are the same. Legitimate power represents the power a leader has as a result of his or her position in the organization. People in positions of authority are also likely to have reward and coercive power, but legitimate power is broader than the power to coerce and reward.

**Coercive power** is the power that rests on the leader's ability to punish or control. Followers react to this power out of fear of the negative results that might occur if they did not comply. As a manager, you typically have some coercive power, such as being able to suspend or demote employees or to assign them work they find unpleasant or undesirable.

**Reward power** is the power to give positive benefits or rewards. These rewards can be anything that another person values. In an organizational context, that might include money, favorable performance appraisals, promotions, interesting work assignments, friendly colleagues, and preferred work shifts or sales territories.

**Expert power** is influence that's based on expertise, special skills, or knowledge. As jobs have become more specialized, managers have become increasingly dependent on staff "experts" to achieve the organization's goals. If an employee has skills, knowledge, or expertise that's critical to the operation of a work group, that person's expert power is enhanced.

Finally, **referent power** is the power that arises because of a person's desirable resources or personal traits. If I admire you and identify with you, you can exercise power over me because I want to please you. Referent power develops out of admiration

# *managing your* **Career**

## The Ins and Outs of Office Politics

*Office politics.* You've probably heard the term and probably have experienced it if you've worked in an organization. Office politics is a fact of life in organizations.[46] Since organizations are made up of individuals and groups with different values, goals, and interests, this sets up the potential for conflict over resources such as budgets, space allocations, project responsibilities, and salary adjustments. To gain control over these resources, people exert power. People want to carve out a niche from which to exert influence, to earn awards, and to advance their careers. When employees convert their power into action, we describe them as being engaged in office politics. Those with good political skills use their various sources of power effectively to get what they need and want. Although you may not like the idea of engaging in office politics, it *is* important that you know how to be politically adept. You can use the following suggestions to improve *your* political effectiveness.

1. *Frame arguments in terms of organizational goals.* Effective politicking requires camouflaging your self-interests. People whose actions appear to blatantly further their own interests at the expense of the organization are almost universally denounced, are likely to *lose* influence, and may even be expelled from the organization.
2. *Develop the right image.* Know your organization's culture; understand what the organization wants and values from its employees. Because the assessment of your performance isn't fully objective, you must pay attention to style as well as substance.
3. *Gain control of organizational resources.* The control of scarce and important organizational resources is a source of power. Knowledge and

expertise are particularly effective resources to control.

4. *Make yourself appear indispensable.* If the organization's key decision makers believe there is no ready substitute for what you bring to the organization, they are likely to go to great lengths to ensure that your desires are satisfied.
5. *Be visible.* Make your boss and those in power aware of your contributions. Routinely highlight your successes in reports, have satisfied customers express their satisfaction to your managers, be seen at company social functions, be active in your professional associations, and so forth.
6. *Develop powerful allies.* It helps to have powerful people on your side. Cultivate contacts with potentially influential people above you, at your own level, and at lower organizational levels. These allies can speak positively about your accomplishments to others and provide you with important information that might not otherwise be available.
7. *Avoid "tainted" members.* In every organization, there are individual whose status is questionable. Their performance and loyalty are suspect. Keep your distance from such individuals so that your own effectiveness isn't compromised.
8. *Support your boss.* Your immediate future is in your boss's hands. Since he or she evaluates your performance, try to do whatever is necessary to have your boss on your side. Make every effort to help your boss look good and succeed, support your boss, and find out what criteria will be used to assess your effectiveness. Don't speak negatively of your boss to others and definitely don't undermine your boss.

PRISM

Getting power in an organizational setting isn't easy. Begin practicing your skill at doing so by completing PRISM #5.

of another and a desire to be like that person. If you admire someone to the point of modeling your behavior and attitudes after him or her, that person has referent power over you.

Most effective leaders rely on several different forms of power to affect the behavior and performance of their followers. For example, Commander Geoffrey Wadley, commanding officer of one of the Australian Navy's state-of-the-art submarines, the HMAS *Sheean*, employs different types of power in managing his crew and equipment. He gives orders to the crew (legitimate), praises them (reward), and disciplines those who commit infractions (coercive). As an effective leader, he also strives to have expert power (based on his expertise and knowledge) and referent power (based on his being admired) to influence his crew.[47] (  Go to www.prenhall.com/rolls)

**legitimate power**
The power a leader has as a result of his or her position in the organization.

**coercive power**
The power a leader has because of his or her ability to punish or control.

**reward power**
The power a leader has because of his or her ability to give positive benefits or rewards.

**expert power**
Influence that's based on expertise, special skills, or knowledge.

**referent power**
Power that arises because of a person's desirable resources or personal traits.

## *thinking critically about* **Ethics**

Your boss isn't satisfied with the way one of your colleagues is handling a project and she reassigns the project to you. She tells you to work with this person to find out what he has done already and to discuss any other necessary information that he might have. She wants your project report by the end of the month. This person is pretty upset and angry over the reassignment and won't give you the information you need to even start, much less complete, the project. You won't be able to meet your deadline unless you get this information.

What type of power does your colleague appear to be using? What type of influence could you possibly use to gain his cooperation? If you were involved in this situation, what could you do to resolve it successfully, yet ethically?

## Developing Trust

**Self-Assessment Library (S.A.L.)**

Do others see you as trustworthy? Do S.A.L. #II.B.4 and see.

After reluctantly agreeing to union contract concessions they believed were necessary to keep their company from bankruptcy and accepting the fact that their paychecks would be reduced, American Airlines' employees were stunned at CEO Don Carty's after-the-fact disclosure of lucrative compensation policies and pension protections designed to retain key executives. Suddenly, Carty's pleas for "shared sacrifice" seemed insincere and false. Any trust that employees had in Carty's ability to lead the airline into the future had completely evaporated. Not long after the disclosure, Carty was forced by American's board of directors to resign.[48]

Carty's situation illustrates how fragile leader trust can be. In today's uncertain environment, an important consideration for leaders is building trust and credibility. Before we can discuss ways leaders can build trust and credibility, we have to know what trust and credibility are and why they're so important. ( Go to www.prenhall. com/rolls)

The main component of credibility is honesty. Surveys show that honesty is consistently singled out as the number-one characteristic of admired leaders. "Honesty is absolutely essential to leadership. If people are going to follow someone willingly, whether it be into battle or into the boardroom, they first want to assure themselves that the person is worthy of their trust." In addition to being honest, credible leaders are competent and inspiring.[49] They are personally able to communicate effectively their confidence and enthusiasm. Thus, followers judge a leader's **credibility** in terms of his or her honesty, competence, and ability to inspire.

Trust is closely entwined with the concept of credibility, and, in fact, the terms are often used interchangeably. **Trust** is defined as the belief in the integrity, character,

*Amy Schulman knows the benefits of trust. As a partner in the global law firm DLA Piper Rudnick Gray Cary, she works long hours and travels about half the time. "It's hard to be successful and be a control freak," she says, "because if you cling to things, you're going to be a bottleneck. Delegating to other people—appropriately delegating—is very liberating. There isn't anybody on my team I don't trust 100 percent. Remember, I've been building this team for 10 years." Schulman inspires trust in client meetings, too, with the simple technique of leaving her cell phone behind. "People get anxious when they feel they're going to be interrupted," she notes. "What a good lawyer brings to a problem, in addition to creative solutions, is a quality of attentiveness."*

and ability of a leader. Followers who trust a leader are willing to be vulnerable to the leader's actions because they are confident that their rights and interests will not be abused.[50] Research has identified five dimensions that make up the concept of trust:[51]

- *Integrity:* Honesty and truthfulness
- *Competence:* Technical and interpersonal knowledge and skills
- *Consistency:* Reliability, predictability, and good judgment in handling situations
- *Loyalty:* Willingness to protect a person, physically and emotionally
- *Openness:* Willingness to share ideas and information freely

Of these five dimensions, integrity seems to be the most critical when someone assesses another's trustworthiness.[52] However, both integrity and competence were seen in our earlier discussion of leadership traits found to be consistently associated with leadership.

Workplace changes have reinforced why such leadership qualities are so important. For instance, the trend toward empowerment (which we'll discuss later in this chapter) and self-managed work teams have reduced or eliminated many of the traditional control mechanisms used to monitor employees. If a work team is free to schedule its own work, evaluate its own performance, and even make its own hiring decisions, trust becomes critical. Employees have to trust managers to treat them fairly, and managers have to trust employees to conscientiously fulfill their responsibilities.

Also, leaders have to increasingly lead others who may not be in their immediate work group or who even may be physically separated—members of cross-functional or virtual teams, individuals who work for suppliers or customers, and perhaps even people who represent other organizations through strategic alliances. These situations don't allow leaders the luxury of falling back on their formal positions for influence. Many of these relationships, in fact, are fluid and fleeting. So the ability to quickly develop trust and sustain that trust is crucial to the success of the relationship.

Why is it important that followers trust their leaders? Research has shown that trust in leadership is significantly related to positive job outcomes including job performance, organizational citizenship behavior, job satisfaction, and organizational commitment.[53]

Given the importance of trust to effective leadership, how should leaders build trust? Exhibit 17–9 lists some suggestions, which are explained in the Skills Module on Developing Trust found on pages 627-628.[54] (  Go to www.prenhall.com/rolls)

**PRISM**

You can begin to develop your skills at developing trust. Try PRISM #4.

Exhibit 17–9

**Suggestions for Building Trust**

> *Practice openness.*
> *Be fair.*
> *Speak your feelings.*
> *Tell the truth.*
> *Show consistency.*
> *Fulfill your promises.*
> *Maintain confidences.*
> *Demonstrate competence.*

*Never promise something you can't fulfill*

**credibility**
The degree to which followers perceive someone as honest, competent, and able to inspire.

**trust**
The belief in the integrity, character, and ability of a leader.

developing budgets, scheduling workloads, controlling inventories, solving quality problems, and engaging in similar activities that until very recently were viewed exclusively as part of the manager's job.[66] For instance, at The Container Store, any employee who gets a customer request has permission to take care of it. The company's chairman Garret Boone says, "Everybody we hire, we hire as a leader. Anybody in our store can take an action that you might think of typically being a manager's action."[67]

Why are more and more companies empowering employees? One reason is the need for quick decisions by those people who are most knowledgeable about the issues—often those at lower organizational levels. If organizations are to successfully compete in a dynamic global economy, they have to be able to make decisions and implement changes quickly. Another reason is the reality that organizational downsizings left many managers with larger spans of control. In order to cope with the increased work demands, managers had to empower their people. Although empowerment is not appropriate for all circumstances, when employees have the knowledge, skills, and experience to do their jobs competently and when they seek autonomy and possess an internal locus of control, it can be beneficial.

## Cross-Cultural Leadership

One general conclusion that surfaces from leadership research is that effective leaders do not use any single style. They adjust their style to the situation. Although not mentioned explicitly, national culture is certainly an important situational variable in determining which leadership style will be most effective. What works in China isn't likely to be effective in France or Canada. For instance, one study of Asian leadership styles revealed that Asian managers preferred leaders who were competent decision makers, effective communicators, and supportive of employees.[68]

National culture affects leadership style because it influences how followers will respond. Leaders can't (and shouldn't) choose their styles randomly. They're constrained by the cultural conditions their followers have come to expect. Exhibit 17–10 provides some findings from selected examples of cross-cultural leadership studies. Since most leadership theories were developed in the United States, using U.S. subjects, they have an American bias. They emphasize follower responsibilities rather than rights; assume self-gratification rather than commitment to duty or altruistic motivation; assume centrality of work and democratic value orientation; and stress rationality rather than spirituality, religion, or superstition.[69] However, the GLOBE research program, which we first introduced in Chapter 4, is the most extensive and comprehensive

**Exhibit 17–10**

**Selected Cross-Cultural Leadership Findings**

- Korean leaders are expected to be paternalistic toward employees.
- Arab leaders who show kindness or generosity without being asked to do so are seen by other Arabs as weak.
- Japanese leaders are expected to be humble and speak frequently.
- Scandinavian and Dutch leaders who single out individuals with public praise are likely to embarrass, not energize, those individuals.
- Effective leaders in Malaysia are expected to show compassion while using more of an autocratic than a participative style.
- Effective German leaders are characterized by high performance orientation, low compassion, low self-protection, low team orientation, high autonomy, and high participation.

*Sources:* Based on J. C. Kennedy, "Leadership in Malaysia: Traditional Values, International Outlook," *Academy of Management Executive,* August 2002, pp. 15–17; F. C. Brodbeck, M. Frese, and M. Javidan, "Leadership Made in Germany: Low on Compassion, High on Performance," *Academy of Management Executive,* February 2002, pp. 16–29; M. F. Peterson and J. G. Hunt, "International Perspectives on International Leadership," *Leadership Quarterly,* Fall 1997, pp. 203–31; R. J. House and R. N. Aditya, "The Social Scientific Study of Leadership: Quo Vadis?" *Journal of Management,* vol. 23, no. 3, (1997), p. 463; and R. J. House, "Leadership in the Twenty-First Century," in A. Howard (ed.), *The Changing Nature of Work* (San Francisco: Jossey-Bass, 1995), p. 442.

cross-cultural study of leadership ever undertaken. One of the results coming from the GLOBE program is that there are some universal aspects to leadership. Specifically, a number of elements of transformational leadership appear to be associated with effective leadership regardless of what country the leader is in.[70] Which elements appear universal? Vision, foresight, providing encouragement, trustworthiness, dynamism, positiveness, and proactiveness. The results led two members of the GLOBE team to conclude that "effective business leaders in any country are expected by their subordinates to provide a powerful and proactive vision to guide the company into the future, strong motivational skills to stimulate all employees to fulfill the vision, and excellent planning skills to assist in implementing the vision."[71] Some people suggest that the universal appeal of these transformational leader characteristics is due to the pressures toward common technologies and management practices, as a result of global competitiveness and multinational influences.

## Gender Differences and Leadership

There was a time when the question "Do males and females lead differently?" could be accurately characterized as a purely academic issue—interesting, but not very relevant. That time has certainly passed! Many women now hold senior management positions, and many more around the world will continue to join the management ranks. For instance, in the United States, women held 50.3 percent of managerial, professional, and related positions in 2004—a decline from 50.5 percent in both 2003 and 2002.[72] And the percentage of female managerial and administrative workers in other selected countries is as follows: Australia (36 percent), Brazil (24 percent), Canada (35 percent), Germany, (36 percent), Japan (10 percent), Philippines (58 percent), Poland (34 percent), South Africa (27 percent), Sweden (30 percent), and United Kingdom (33 percent).[73] Misconceptions about the relationship between leadership and gender can adversely affect hiring, performance evaluation, promotion, and other human resource decisions for both men and women. For instance, evidence indicates that a "good" manager is still perceived as predominantly masculine.[74]

A warning before we proceed: This topic is controversial. If male and female styles differ, is one inferior? If there is a difference, does labeling leadership styles by gender encourage stereotyping? These are important questions and we'll address them shortly.

A number of studies focusing on gender and leadership style have been conducted in recent years. Their general conclusion is that males and females *do* use different styles. Specifically, women tend to adopt a more democratic or participative style. Women are more likely to encourage participation, share power and information, and attempt to enhance followers' self-worth. They lead through inclusion and rely on their charisma, expertise, contacts, and interpersonal skills to influence others. Women tend to use transformational leadership, motivating others by transforming their self-interest into organizational goals. Men are more likely to use a directive, command-and-control style. They rely on formal position authority for their influence. Men use transactional leadership, handing out rewards for good work and punishment for bad.[75]

There is an interesting qualifier to these findings. The tendency for female leaders to be more democratic than males declines when women are in male-dominated jobs. Apparently, group norms and male stereotypes influence women and they tend to act more autocratically.[76]

Another issue to consider is how male and female leaders are perceived in the workplace. A recent U.S. study sheds some light on this topic.[77] One major finding of this research was that men consider women to be less skilled at problem-solving, which is one of the qualities often associated with effective leadership. Another finding was that both men and women believed women to be superior to men at "take care" behaviors and men superior to women at "take charge" behaviors. Such gender-based stereotyping creates challenges both for organizations and for leaders within those organizations. Organizations need effective leaders at all levels, but they need to ensure that stereotypical perceptions don't limit who those leaders might be.[78] One company that has made a

Exhibit 17–11

**Where Female Managers Do Better: A Scorecard**

*Source:* R. Sharpe, "As Leaders, Women Rule," *BusinessWeek*, November 20, 2000, p. 75.

**Where Female Managers Do Better:**
**A Scorecard**

None of the five studies set out to find gender differences. They stumbled on them while compiling and analyzing performance evaluations.

| Skill (Each check mark denotes which group scored higher on the respective studies) | MEN | WOMEN |
|---|---|---|
| **Motivating Others** | | ✓ ✓ ✓ ✓ ✓ |
| **Fostering Communication** | | ✓ ✓ ✓ ✓* |
| **Producing High-Quality Work** | | ✓ ✓ ✓ ✓ ✓ |
| **Strategic Planning** | ✓ ✓ | ✓ ✓* |
| **Listening to Others** | | ✓ ✓ ✓ ✓ |
| **Analyzing Issues** | ✓ ✓ | ✓ ✓* |

*In one study, women's and men's scores in these categories were statistically even.
Data: Hagberg Consulting Group, Management Research Group, Lawrence A. Pfaff, Personnel Decisions International Inc., Advanced Teamware Inc.

commitment to finding effective leaders no matter the gender is Xerox.[79] Xerox is one of only nine *Fortune* 500 companies with a female CEO (Anne Mulcahy) and women hold close to one-third of top management jobs at Xerox.

Although it's interesting to see how male and female leadership styles differ, a more important question is whether they differ in effectiveness. Although some researchers have shown that males and females tend to be equally effective as leaders[80], an increasing number of studies have shown that women executives, when rated by their peers, employees, and bosses, score higher than their male counterparts on a wide variety of measures.[81] (See Exhibit 17–11 for a summary.) Why? One possible explanation is that in today's organizations, flexibility, teamwork and partnering, trust, and information sharing are rapidly replacing rigid structures, competitive individualism, control, and secrecy. In these types of workplaces, effective managers must use more social and interpersonal behaviors. They listen, motivate, and provide support to their people. They inspire and influence rather than control. And women seem to do those things better than men.[82]

Although women seem to rate highly on those leadership skills needed to succeed in today's dynamic global environment, we don't want to fall into the same trap as the early leadership researchers who tried to find the "one best leadership style" for all situations. We know that there is no one *best* style for all situations. Instead, which leadership style is effective will depend on the situation. So even if men and women differ in their leadership styles, we shouldn't assume that one is always preferable to the other.

## The Demise of Celebrity Leadership

Polls show that just 16 percent of Americans trust business executives. And the number of senior business executives who said they would not want to be a CEO doubled in just one year from 26 percent to 54 percent.[83] Business leaders seem to be losing their luster. When and how did corporate leaders go from visionary, larger-than-life heroes who were almost as popular as rock stars to being reviled outcasts?

One factor that obviously has contributed to this shift of opinion is the publicity from ongoing ethical and financial scandals at both for-profit and nonprofit organizations around the world. Another factor would be the controversy surrounding executive pay. When the public hears that the average CEO salary is 531 times the average worker's salary or when you consider that had the minimum wage increased since 1990 at the same rate as executive pay had, it would be $21.41 an hour, not $5.15, it's no wonder that the public is outraged.[84] There's further resentment when huge management salaries or benefits are given to executives when their company's performance, in fact, has declined.

In many ways, the demise of the "celebrity leader" has been brought about by arrogance, greed, and hype. But perhaps corporate leaders should never have been

*Anne Mulcahy had a long career in sales and human resources at Xerox Corp. when she was named president of the company and, a year later, its CEO. Despite being the manager who pulled Xerox out from near-bankruptcy, Mulcahy works at keeping out of the limelight, avoiding interviews and focusing her priorities on employees and customers around the world.*

anointed as celebrities or superheroes to begin with.[85] They don't have all the answers, and they definitely can't run companies all by themselves. The myth of the "savior CEO" who could single-handedly expand and enrich a corporation was just that—a myth based on the idea that having a vision and the ability to inspire others to reach that vision were what made CEOs worth the hundreds of millions of dollars they were paid. Although this celebrity leader may not be real, it doesn't mean that the CEO is irrelevant. Instead, his or her role as organizational leader needs to change.

Boards of directors need to have a more pragmatic view of what the CEO's job really is and what an appropriate salary should be. And CEOs need to get back to the basics of what it means to be a leader.[86] How? Here are some suggestions:

1. *Give people a reason to come to work.* Help them develop a passion for their work, a commitment to their colleagues, and a sense of responsibility to the organization's customers.

2. *Be loyal to the organization's people.* Southwest Airlines, for example, will do whatever it takes to keep from laying off employees because they genuinely believe that their employees are the key to the company's success. This loyalty is a two-way street. When employees feel that their organization is being loyal to them, they work harder, are more productive, and give better service to customers. If financial problems arise, CEOs should show employees they matter by cutting their own salaries and the salaries of top managers first rather than downsizing.

3. *Spend time with people who do the real work of the organization*—people down at the loading dock, or in the checkout line, or out on sales calls. These people are critical to the success of any organization.

4. Finally, *be more open and more candid about what business practices are acceptable and proper and how the unacceptable ones should be fixed.* CEOs should be prepared to take strong decisive action when something wrong is discovered. For instance, when Harvey Kraemer, former CEO of Baxter International, discovered that dialysis filters manufactured by a company Baxter had recently acquired had been involved in patients' deaths, he did something. "He took responsibility for the problem. He apologized for it. He directed his team to make sure it never happened again. He took a $189 million hit to the company's books and then recommended to his own board of directors that it reduce his bonus by 40 percent as a measure of his own responsibility for the problem."[87] Today's CEOs need to show that type of openness, integrity, and accountability.

## becoming a Manager

√ As you interact with various organizations, note the different styles used by the leaders in those organizations.

√ Think of people that you would consider effective leaders and try to determine why they're effective.

√ If you have the opportunity, take leadership development courses.

√ Practice building trust in relationships that you have with others.

√ Read books on great leaders (not just business leaders) and on leadership development topics.

**Self-Assessment Library (S.A.L.)**

√ Complete any of the following exercises from the Self-Assessment Library found on www.prenhall.com/rolls: S.A.L. #II.B.1—What's My Leadership Style?, S.A.L. #II.B.2—How Charismatic Am I?, S.A.L. #II.B.4—Do Others See Me As Trusting?, and S.A.L. #II.B.6—How Good Am I at Building and Leading a Team?

## Substitutes for Leadership

**Q & A**

What do you mean leadership may not always be important? See Q & A 17.11 for an explanation.

Despite the belief that some leadership style will always be effective regardless of the situation, leadership may not always be important! (  Go to www.prenhall.com/rolls) Research indicates that, in some situations, any behaviors a leader exhibits are irrelevant. In other words, certain individual, job, and organizational variables can act as "substitutes for leadership," negating the influence of the leader.[88]

For instance, follower characteristics such as experience, training, professional orientation, or need for independence can neutralize the effect of leadership. These characteristics can replace the employee's need for a leader's support or ability to create structure and reduce task ambiguity. Similarly, jobs that are inherently unambiguous and routine or that are intrinsically satisfying may place fewer demands on the leadership variable. Finally, such organizational characteristics as explicit formalized goals, rigid rules and procedures, or cohesive work groups can substitute for formal leadership.

## Learning Review

- Tell the five sources of a leader's power.
- Discuss the issues today's leaders face.

- Explain why leadership is sometimes irrelevant.

# Managers Respond to a Manager's Dilemma

## Rachel Mara Doyle

President and Founder, GlamourGals Foundation,
Inc., Commack, NY

Judy's ability to engage herself with all her employees and listen to what they say is great. But as her company continues to grow, she will find it necessary to be a proactive communicator. With employees around the world, focus and direction can be diluted if not clearly outlined. Judy should establish overarching values or "tenets" by which the company's employees should abide in their creative discussion. This message can and should be executed via a memo and global Web conference call. The importance of the Web conference call is to speak directly to her employees who may be thousands of miles away. Seeing her on a screen speaking with them will make them feel a part of her vision. Her employees can confidently continue MTV's overall vision of "bold and experimental entertainment" within the framework and focus Judy has given them.

# Learning Summary

## Who Are Leaders and What Is Leadership?

**Leaders:** people who can influence others and who have managerial authority

**Leadership:** process of influencing a group to achieve goals

All managers ideally should be leaders

## What Do Early Leadership Theories Tell Us?

- Trait theories tried to identify traits that would differentiate leaders from nonleaders
  - Impossible to identify one set of traits that would always differentiate leaders
  - Seven traits associated with leadership: drive, the desire to lead, honesty and integrity, self-confidence, intelligence, job-relevant knowledge, and extraversion
- Behavioral theories looked for behaviors that differentiated effective leaders from ineffective leaders
  - University of Iowa studies identified *autocratic, democratic,* and *laissez-faire* styles of leadership
  - Ohio State studies identified *consideration* and *initiating structure* behaviors
  - University of Michigan studies identified *employee-oriented* and *production-oriented* behaviors
  - Managerial Grid identified *concern for people* and *concern for production* behaviors and emphasized five styles of leadership: impoverished (1,1), task (9,1), middle-of-the-road (5,5), country club (1,9), and team (9,9)
- Effective leader behavior for all situations could not be determined

## What Do Contingency Theories of Leadership Say?

Each theory looks at defining leadership style and the situation

Each theory also answers if–then contingencies

- **Fiedler's contingency model**
  - Measured leader style using **least-preferred co-worker questionnaire**
    - Relationship oriented
    - Task oriented
    - Assumed leader's style was fixed
  - Measured three contingency dimensions
    - **Leader-member relations**
    - **Task structure**
    - **Position power**
  - Task-oriented leaders performed best in very favorable and very unfavorable situations; relationship-oriented leaders performed best in moderately favorable situations
- Hersey and Blanchard's **situational leadership theory**
  - Focused on followers' **readiness**—ability and willingness to accomplish a specific task
  - Four specific leadership styles: telling (high task–low relationship), selling (high task–high relationship), participating (low task–high relationship), and delegating (low task–low relationship)
  - Four stages of readiness: unable and unwilling (use telling style); unable but willing (use selling style); able but unwilling (use participative style); and able and willing (use delegating style)
- **Leader participation model**
  - Developed by Vroom and Yetton
  - Related leadership behavior to decision making
- **Path-goal theory** (developed by Robert House)
  - Four leadership behaviors: directive, supportive, participative, and achievement-oriented; assumes leader can and should be able to use any of these styles
  - Two situational contingency variables: environmental and follower
  - Summarized as: leader should provide direction and support as needed

## What Are the Contemporary Views on Leadership?

- **Transactional** (leaders exchange rewards for productivity) and **transformational** (leaders stimulate and inspire followers to achieve goals)
- **Charismatic** and **visionary** leaders
- Team leadership

## What Are the Major Leadership Issues Today?

- Managing power (legitimate, coercive, reward, expert, and referent)
- Developing **trust**: belief in the integrity, character, and ability of a leader
  - Five dimensions of trust: integrity, competence, consistency, loyalty, and openness
- Providing ethical leadership
- Empowering employees
- Cross-cultural leadership
- Gender differences in leadership
- Demise of celebrity leaders
- Substitutes for leadership

# Management: By the Numbers

- Thirty-two percent of women prefer a male boss, while only 23 percent prefer a female boss.
- Thirteen percent of men prefer a female boss.
- Sixty-eight percent of companies have a defined set of qualities they look for when hiring leaders.
- Seventy-seven percent of Americans surveyed said they have negative views about the country's moral climate.
- A survey of U.S. employees found that only 29 percent are actively engaged in their job.
- Eighty-nine percent of senior executives surveyed said that it's more challenging today to be a company leader than it was 5 years ago.

- Fifty-one percent of company leaders report that they have used a leadership coach or mentor.

*Sources:* L. Saad, "Morality Ratings the Worst in Five Years," *The Gallup Poll,* poll.gallup.com, May 25, 2006; J. Yang and J. Snider, "Tougher to Be a Leader," *USA Today,* March 6, 2006, p. 1B; "Leadership Needs Development," *Training,* February 2006, p. 7; S. Armour, "Do Women Compete in Unhealthy Ways at Work?" *USA Today,* December 30, 2005, pp. 1B+; "Not Very Engaged," *Springfield News-Leader,* October 17, 2005, p. 6C; and Hewitt Associates Press Release, "Companies See Limited Success in Developing Leaders," June 5, 2002.

# Thinking About Management Issues

1. What types of power are available to you? Which ones do you use most? Why?

2. Do you think that most managers in real life use a contingency approach to increase their leadership effectiveness? Discuss.

3. If you were to ask people why a given individual is a leader, they tend to describe the person in terms such as *competent, consistent, self-assured, inspiring a shared vision,* and *enthusiastic.* How do these descriptions fit in with leadership concepts presented in the chapter?

4. What kinds of campus activities could a full-time college student do that might lead to the perception that he or she is a charismatic leader? In pursuing those activities, what might the student do to enhance this perception of being charismatic?

5. Do you think trust evolves out of an individual's personal characteristics or out of specific situations? Explain.

6. Is there an ethical problem if leaders focus more on looking like a leader than actually being one? Discuss.

7. Leadership experts cite the following reasons why leaders fail: arrogant, distant, eccentric, impulsive, interpersonal insensitivity, perfectionist, volatile, argumentative, arrogant, and cautious. Why do you think these factors might lead to leadership failure? What could leaders do to avoid these?

# Chapter 18

## Learning Outline

*Use this Learning Outline as you read and study this chapter.*

### What Is Control and Why Is It Important?

- Define control.
- Contrast the three approaches to designing control systems.
- Discuss the reasons why control is important.
- Explain the planning–controlling link.

### The Control Process

- Describe the three steps in the control process.
- Explain why what is measured is more critical than how it's measured.
- Explain the three courses of action managers can take in controlling.

### Controlling for Organizational Performance

- Define organizational performance.
- Describe the most frequently used measures of organizational performance.

### Tools for Controlling Organizational Performance

- Contrast feedforward, concurrent, and feedback controls.
- Explain the types of financial and information controls managers can use.
- Describe how balanced scorecards and benchmarking are used in controlling.

### Contemporary Issues in Control

- Describe how managers may have to adjust controls for cross-cultural differences.
- Discuss the types of workplace concerns managers face and how they can address those concerns.
- Explain why control is important to customer interactions.
- Explain what corporate governance is and how it's changing.

# Foundations of Control

## A Manager's Dilemma

Behind the boom in air travel is an organization trying to ensure that domestic air traffic moves safely and efficiently. The U.S. Federal Aviation Administration (FAA) was created by Congress in 1958 to "oversee air safety, inspect airplanes, and aid airports." However, the FAA's biggest job is "running the air traffic control system, a nationwide network of navigation aids, computers and 36,000 employees who guide 34,000 aircraft carrying 2.2 million travelers from one airport to another every day." And the person in charge of making sure this all happens efficiently and effectively is Russell G. Chew, the chief operations officer of the FAA.[1]

Mr. Chew reluctantly joined the FAA in 2003, coming from American Airlines, where he managed the airline's system operations control center. However, despite his reluctance at the time, he was motivated by a sense of public service and feeling that he had a responsibility to tackle the agency's problems because not doing so would mean that his company and the other airlines might not have a viable future.

Although working for a struggling organization (an airline) trying to make a profit in a challenging industry might, in itself, seem like a tough task, Russell would soon be facing the hardest work of his career—bringing "business principles and discipline to a sprawling operations dogged by cost overruns and outdated technology." The first thing he did was to put in place "practices that are commonplace in the corporate world"—things like doing the organization's first equipment inventory and eliminating a dozen mid-level management jobs. Another thing that Russell implemented was capturing information on plane delays and cancellations and what caused the problems. The FAA had never created or used this data to help in making decisions. Now, using this information, when there's bad weather leading to long delays at airports, airplanes headed for those airports are held at their home airports to relieve pressure on the affected area.

Russell faces significant challenges from congress, the National Air Traffic Controllers Association, and the bureaucratic mentality of a government agency in his desire to continue controlling costs. However, he isn't letting up. Put yourself in Russell's shoes. What management control tools might he use to help continue improving his agency's performance?

### What would you do?

R ussell Chew's situation illustrates how important controls are to managers. Even in nonprofit organizations, like the FAA, managers want to achieve high levels of performance and one way they can do that is by searching out the best control tools to use in improving performance. Appropriate controls can help managers look for specific performance gaps and areas for improvement—areas where there needs to be better controls over work being done. No matter how thorough the planning, organizing, and leading, decisions still may be poorly implemented without a satisfactory control system in place. This chapter describes controls and how to create a well-designed organizational control system.

## WHAT IS CONTROL?

A press operator at the Denver Mint noticed a flaw—an extra up leaf or an extra down leaf—on Wisconsin state quarters being pressed at one of his five press machines. He stopped the machine and left for a meal break. When he returned, he saw the machine running and assumed that someone had changed the die in the machine. However, after a routine inspection, the machine operator realized the die had not been changed. The faulty press had likely been running for over an hour and thousands of the flawed coins were now "commingled" with unblemished quarters. As many as 50,000 of the faulty coins entered circulation, setting off a coin collector buying frenzy. In the airline industry, the amount of "mishandled baggage—lost, delayed, or stolen baggage"—increased 23 percent nationwide in one year. The cost to airlines— about $2 billion a year. The cost to passengers—untold frustration and aggravation. Errors by Pearson Educational Measurement in scanning and scoring SAT exams were discovered by test takers who challenged their scores. One college admissions director said, "The story here is not that they made a mistake in the scanning and scoring, but that they seem to have no fail-safe to alert them directly and immediately of a mistake. To depend on test takers who challenge the scores to learn about system failure is not good." For approximately 4,400 students, these errors may have affected college admission decisions. At American Airlines, an internal Web site intended only for the airline's employees was briefly available to the public and the information on there was not something the company wanted publicized. The Web site described how much revenue had increased since American tightened its excess baggage allowance in November 2005. A newsletter addressed to a ground crew at one airport said, "For the month of December 2005, we collected $264,000 in excess, overweight, and oversized bag charges. This is a 7 percent increase over December 2004!" The newsletter called the fees "an important ingredient" to success and ended with the word, "Ka-ching!" A spokesman for American called the open Web site an "oversight" in the company's security and said steps had been taken to repair it.[2] Are you beginning to see why controlling is such an important managerial function?

What is **controlling**? It's the process of monitoring, comparing, and correcting work performance. All managers should be involved in the control function even if their units are performing as planned.(  Go to www.prenhall.com/rolls) Managers can't really know whether their units are performing properly until they've evaluated what activities have been done and have compared the actual performance with the desired standard.[3] An effective control system ensures that activities are completed in ways that lead to the attainment of goals. The criterion that determines the effectiveness of a control system, then, is how well it helps employees and managers achieve their goals.[4]

Ideally, every organization would like to efficiently and effectively reach its goals. Does this mean the control systems that organizations use are identical? Probably not. Three different types of control systems have been identified and are described in Exhibit 18–1.[5] Let's look at how these are used by three different organizations— Matsushita, BP, and SAS Institute, Inc.

Q & A

If things are going as planned, why is control necessary? See Q & A 18.1

Exhibit 18–1

**Characteristics of Three Approaches to Control Systems**

| Type of Control | Characteristics |
|---|---|
| Market | Uses external market mechanisms, such as price competition and relative market share, to establish standards used in system. Typically used by organizations whose products or services are clearly specified and distinct and that face considerable marketplace competition. |
| Bureaucratic | Emphasizes organizational authority. Relies on administrative and hierarchical mechanisms, such as rules, regulations, procedures, policies, standardization of activities, well-defined job descriptions, and budgets to ensure that employees exhibit appropriate behaviors and meet performance standards. |
| Clan | Regulates employee behavior by the shared values, norms, traditions, rituals, beliefs, and other aspects of the organization's culture. Often used by organizations in which teams are common and technology is changing rapidly. |

**Market control** is an approach that emphasizes the use of external market mechanisms, such as price competition and relative market share, to establish the standards used in the control system. Using market control, a company's divisions often are turned into profit centers and evaluated by the percentage of total corporate profits each contributes. For instance, at Matsushita, the company's four divisions (audiovisual and communication networks, components and devices, home appliances, and factory automation equipment) are evaluated according to the profits each generates.

Another approach is **bureaucratic control**, which emphasizes organizational authority and relies on administrative rules, regulations, procedures, and policies. The oil company BP provides a good example of bureaucratic control. Although managers at BP's various divisions have considerable autonomy and freedom to run their units as they see fit, they're expected to adhere closely to their budgets and stay within corporate guidelines.

Under **clan control**, employee behaviors are regulated by the shared values, norms, traditions, rituals, beliefs, and other aspects of the organization's culture. Whereas bureaucratic control is based on strict hierarchical mechanisms, clan control is dependent on the individual and the group (or clan) to identify appropriate and expected behaviors and performance measures. For instance, at SAS Institute, individuals are well aware of the expectations regarding appropriate work behavior and performance standards. The organizational culture—through the shared values, norms, and stories about the company's founder, Jim Goodnight—conveys to individual employees "what is and isn't acceptable around here." Rather than relying on prescribed administrative controls, SAS employees are guided and controlled by the clan's culture.

In reality, most organizations don't rely totally on just one of these types of control systems. Instead, organizations usually emphasize either bureaucratic or clan control, and use selected market control measures. The key is having a control system that helps employees and the organization efficiently and effectively reach their goals.

**controlling**
The process of monitoring, comparing, and correcting work performance.

**market control**
An approach to control that emphasizes the use of external market mechanisms to establish the control standards.

**bureaucratic control**
An approach to control that emphasizes organizational authority and relies on administrative rules, regulations, procedures, and policies.

**clan control**
An approach to control in which employee behavior is regulated by the organization's culture.

## Managers *speak out*

**Ted V. Schaefer**

**Partner**
**PricewaterhouseCoopers**
**Denver, CO**

*Describe your job.*

I am a partner in PricewaterhouseCoopers' Denver office, and I work in the System & Process Assurance group. I provide our clients with internal control and process improvement services.

*Why are controls important to your organization?*

Controls are critical to the quality delivery of PricewaterhouseCoopers' audit, tax, and advisory services. We have many professional, regulatory, and internal controls that help to ensure that we meet our goals. Controls provide staff with a clear road map to follow for client service delivery, human resources, career development, client independence, code of conduct, and regulatory and professional rules. Our industry is based on controls that provide staff with the ability to carry out their jobs in an orderly fashion.

*What control issues do you think are particularly important to managers today?*

Continuing business scandals have raised the bar for strong internal controls. The government took a major step in regulating internal control through the enactment of Sarbanes-Oxley, which requires public companies to implement an effective internal control structure that must be externally audited. However, even if Sarbanes-Oxley wasn't law, internal controls are just good business for several reasons. Controls allow companies to manage regulatory compliance and financial and operational activities to meet business goals. They also provide for an orderly environment so management can focus their time on strategic issues. Companies with poor controls are constantly putting out fires, taking away from more important activities. Companies need to align controls with the goals of the organization and ensure they provide a cost benefit.

*What skills do you think managers need to be effective?*

Due to the fast-paced business environment, managers must be lifelong learners to maintain their edge. Soft skills like communication, creativity, and the ability to motivate and challenge employees are equally important for success. Knowing when employees need help or when to stay out of their way is a skill necessary to manage people. It is important to be a good mentor and provide career-enhancing opportunities to employees, so they can continue to grow and advance in their careers.

## WHY IS CONTROL IMPORTANT?

**Q & A**

How is controlling related to the other functions of management? Q & A 18.2 explains.

Why is control so important? Planning can be done, an organizational structure created to facilitate efficient achievement of goals, and employees motivated through effective leadership. ( Go to www.prenhall.com/rolls) Still, there's no assurance that activities are going as planned and that the goals employees and managers are working toward are, in fact, being attained. Control is important, therefore, because it's the only way managers know whether organizational goals are being met and if not, the reasons why. The value of the control function can be seen in three specific areas: planning, empowering employees, and protecting the workplace.

In Chapter 7, we described goals, which provide specific direction to employees and managers, as the foundation of planning. However, just stating goals or having employees accept goals is no guarantee that the necessary actions to accomplish those goals have been taken. As the old saying goes, "The best-laid plans often go awry." The effective manager follows up to ensure that what others are supposed to do is being done and that goals are being achieved. In reality, managing is an ongoing process. As the final step in the management process, controlling provides the critical link back to planning (Exhibit 18–2). If managers didn't control, they'd have no way of knowing whether their goals and plans were on target and what future actions to take.

**Q & A**

Can managers delegate the responsibility for controlling to employees? Go to Q & A 18.4 and find out.

The second reason controlling is important is because of employee empowerment. Many managers are reluctant to empower their employees because they fear employees will do something wrong for which the manager would be held responsible. Many managers are tempted to do things themselves and avoid empowering. But an effective control system can provide information and feedback on employee performance, thus reducing potential problems. ( Go to www.prenhall.com/rolls)

Exhibit 18–2

**The Planning–
Controlling Link**

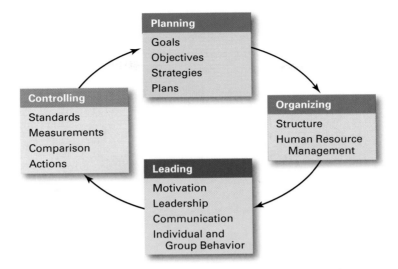

The final reason that managers control is to protect the organization and its assets.[6] Today's environment brings heightened threats from natural disasters, financial scandals, workplace violence, supply chain disruptions, security breaches, and even possible terrorist attacks. Managers must have plans in place to protect the organization's employees, facilities, data, and infrastructure. As many organizations discovered in the aftermath of catastrophes, such as 9/11 and Hurricane Katrina, having comprehensive controls and backup plans helps assure only minimal disruptions of their ongoing business operations.

## Learning Review

- Define control.
- Contrast the three approaches to designing control systems.

- Discuss the reasons why control is important.
- Explain the planning–controlling link.

## THE CONTROL PROCESS

When Maggine Fuentes joined Core Systems in Painesville, Ohio, as human resources manager, she knew that employee injury reduction was her top priority. Employee injuries were "through the roof; above the industry average." The high frequency and severity of the company's injury rates not only affected worker morale but also resulted in lost workdays and affected the bottom line.[7] Maggine needed to rely on some systematic approach, such as the control process, to turn this situation around.

The **control process** is a three-step process: measuring actual performance, comparing actual performance against a standard, and taking managerial action to correct deviations or inadequate standards (see Exhibit 18–3). The control process assumes that performance standards already exist. These standards against which performance progress is measured are the specific goals created during the planning process.

**control process**
A 3-step process including measuring actual performance, comparing actual performance against a standard, and taking managerial action.

Exhibit 18–3

**The Control Process**

## Measuring

To determine what actual performance is, a manager must acquire information about it. The first step in control, then, is measuring. Let's consider how we measure and what we measure.

**How We Measure** Four sources of information frequently used by managers to measure actual performance are personal observation, statistical reports, oral reports, and written reports. Exhibit 18–4 summarizes the advantages and drawbacks of each approach. For most managers, using a combination of approaches increases both the number of input sources and the probability of getting reliable information.

Q & A

Why is WHAT managers control more important than HOW they control? See Q & A 18.5.

**What We Measure** What we measure is probably more critical to the control process than how we measure. Why? ( ◆ Go to www.prenhall.com/rolls) Selecting the wrong criteria can create serious problems. Besides, *what* is measured often determines what people in the organization will attempt to excel at.[8] What control criteria might managers use?

   Some control criteria are appropriate for any management situation. For instance, because all managers, by definition, coordinate the work of others, criteria such as employee satisfaction or turnover and absenteeism rates can be measured. Most managers also have dollar cost budgets for their area of responsibility. Keeping costs within budget is, therefore, a fairly common control measure. Other control criteria need to recognize the diversity of activities that managers do. For instance, a production manager at a paper tablet manufacturer might use measures such as quantity of paper tablets produced per day and per labor-hour, scrap rate, or percent of rejects returned

Exhibit 18–4

**Common Sources
of Information
for Measuring Performance**

|  | Advantages | Drawbacks |
|---|---|---|
| **Personal Observations** | • Get firsthand knowledge<br>• Information isn't filtered<br>• Intensive coverage of work activities | • Subject to personal biases<br>• Time-consuming<br>• Obtrusive |
| **Statistical Reports** | • Easy to visualize<br>• Effective for showing relationships | • Provide limited information<br>• Ignore subjective factors |
| **Oral Reports** | • Fast way to get information<br>• Allow for verbal and nonverbal feedback | • Information is filtered<br>• Information can't be documented |
| **Written Reports** | • Comprehensive<br>• Formal<br>• Easy to file and retrieve | • Take more time to prepare |

by customers. On the other hand, the manager of an administrative unit in a governmental agency might use number of document pages typed per day, number of client requests completed per hour, or average time required to process paperwork. Marketing managers often use measures such as percentage of market held, average dollar per sale, number of customer visits per salesperson, or number of customer impressions per advertising medium.

Most jobs and activities can be expressed in tangible and measurable terms. However, when a performance indicator can't be stated in quantifiable terms, managers should use subjective measures. Although subjective measures have significant limitations, they're better than having no standards at all and ignoring the control function. If an activity is important, the excuse that it's difficult to measure is unacceptable.

## Comparing

The comparing step determines the degree of variation between actual performance and the standard. Although some variation in performance can be expected in all activities, it's critical to determine the acceptable **range of variation** (see Exhibit 18–5). Deviations that exceed this range become significant and need the manager's attention. In the comparison stage, managers are particularly concerned with the size and direction of the variation. An example can help make this concept clearer.

Chris Tanner is sales manager for Eastern States, a distributor of imported beers in several states on the U.S. East Coast. Chris prepares a report during the first week of each month that describes sales for the previous month, classified by brand name. Exhibit 18–6 displays both the sales goal (standard) and actual sales figures for the month of July.

Should Chris be concerned about July's sales performance? Sales were a bit higher than originally targeted, but does that mean there were no significant deviations? Even though overall performance was generally quite favorable, several brands might need closer scrutiny. However, the number of brands that deserve attention depends on what Chris believes to be *significant*. How much variation should Chris allow before corrective action is taken?

Exhibit 18–5

**Defining the Acceptable Range of Variation**

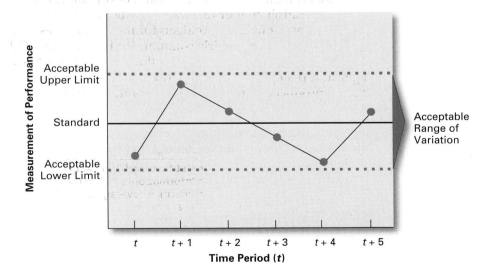

**range of variation**
The acceptable parameters of variance between actual performance and the standard.

Exhibit 18–6

**Sales Performance Figures for July, Eastern States Distributors**

| Brand | Standard | (Hundreds of Cases) Actual | Over (Under) |
|---|---|---|---|
| Heineken | 1,075 | 913 | (162) |
| Molson | 630 | 634 | 4 |
| Irish Amber | 800 | 912 | 112 |
| Victoria Bitter | 620 | 622 | 2 |
| Labatt's | 540 | 672 | 132 |
| Corona | 160 | 140 | (20) |
| Amstel Light | 225 | 220 | (5) |
| Dos Equis | 80 | 65 | (15) |
| Tecate | 170 | 286 | 116 |
| Total cases | 4,300 | 4,464 | 164 |

The deviations on several brands (Molson, Victoria Bitter, and Amstel Light) are minimal and don't need special attention. On the other hand, are the shortages for Corona and Dos Equis brands significant? That's a judgment Chris must make. However, Heineken sales were 15 percent below goal—a significant deviation that needs attention. Chris should look for a cause. In this instance, the decrease is attributed to aggressive advertising and promotion by Anheuser Busch and SABMiller. Because Heineken is Eastern States' number one selling import, it's vulnerable to such promotions. If the decline in sales of Heineken is more than a temporary slump (that is, if it happens again next month), then Chris will need to cut back on inventory stock.

*Under* stating sales can be as troublesome as *over*stating. For instance, is the surprising popularity of Tecate (up 68 percent) a one-month aberration, or is this brand becoming more popular with customers? If the brand is increasing in popularity, Chris will want to order more product to meet customer demand and not risk running short and losing customers. Again, Chris will have to interpret the information and make a decision. Our Eastern States' example illustrates that both overvariance and undervariance in any comparison of measures may require managerial attention. (  Go to www.prenhall.com/rolls)

**Q & A**

Is under-variance more serious than over-variance? Q & A 18.6 discusses this.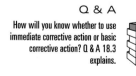

## Taking Managerial Action

The third and final step in the control process is taking managerial action. Managers can choose among three possible courses of action: They can do nothing; they can correct the actual performance; or they can revise the standards. Because "doing nothing" is fairly self-explanatory, let's look more closely at the other two.

**Correct Actual Performance** If the source of the performance variation is unsatisfactory work, the manager will want to take corrective action. Examples might include changing strategy, structure, compensation practices, or training programs; redesigning jobs; or firing employees.

A manager who decides to correct actual performance has to make another decision: Should immediate or basic corrective action be taken? **Immediate corrective action** corrects problems at once to get performance back on track. **Basic corrective action** looks at how and why performance has deviated and then proceeds to correct the source of deviation. ( Go to www.prenhall.com/rolls) It's not unusual for managers to rationalize that they don't have the time to take basic corrective action and therefore must be content to perpetually "put out fires" with immediate corrective action. Effective managers, however, analyze deviations and, when the benefits justify it, take the time to pinpoint and correct the causes of variance.

**Q & A**

How will you know whether to use immediate corrective action or basic corrective action? Q & A 18.3 explains.

To return to our Eastern States example, taking immediate corrective action on the negative variance for Heineken, Chris might contact the company's retailers and have them immediately drop the price on Heineken by 5 percent. However, taking basic corrective action would involve more in-depth analysis by Chris. After assessing how and why sales deviated, Chris might choose to increase in-store promotional efforts, increase the advertising budget for this brand, or reduce future purchases from the breweries. The action Chris takes will depend on the assessment of each brand's potential profitability.

*Among the corrective actions at the top of the list for Timberland, the outdoor clothing maker, is an ambitious reduction in green house-gas emissions from its manufacturing processes. One initiative is to look for new feed for the cows that yield boot leather for the company's footwear products, since the cows are the source of a surprisingly large amount of methane. Another is the generation of power by means of renewable resources, such as solar panels on a distribution center in Ontario, California.*

**Revise the Standard** It's possible that the variance was a result of an unrealistic standard; that is, the goal may have been too high or too low. In such instances, it's the standard that needs corrective attention, not the performance. In our example, Chris might need to raise the sales goal (standard) for Tecate to reflect its growing popularity.

Managers need to be more cautious, however, before revising a performance standard downward. If an employee, work team, or work unit falls significantly short of reaching its goal, their natural response is to shift the blame for the variance to the goal. For instance, students who make a low grade on a test often attack the grade cutoff standards as too high. Rather than accept the fact that their performance was inadequate, students often argue that the standards are unreasonable. Similarly, salespeople who fail to meet their monthly quota may attribute the failure to an unrealistic quota. It may be true that when standards are too high, it can result in a significant variation and may even contribute to demotivating those employees being measured. But keep in mind that if employees or managers don't meet the standard, the first thing they're likely to attack is the standard. If you believe that the standard is realistic, fair, and achievable, explain your position. Reaffirm to the employee, team, or unit that you expect future performance to improve, and then take the necessary corrective action to help turn that expectation into reality.

## Summary of Managerial Decisions

Exhibit 18–7 summarizes the manager's decisions in the control process. The standards evolve out of goals that are developed during the planning process. These goals then provide the basis for the control process, which is essentially a continuous flow between measuring, comparing, and taking managerial action. Depending on the results of comparing, a manager's decisions about what course of action to take might be: Do nothing, revise the standard, or correct the performance.

## Learning Review

- Describe the three steps in the control process.
- Explain why what is measured is more critical than how it's measured.

- Explain the three courses of action managers can take in controlling.

**immediate corrective action**
Corrective action that corrects problems at once to get performance back on track.

**basic corrective action**
Corrective action that looks at how and why performance deviated and then proceeds to correct the source of deviation.

Exhibit 18–7    **Managerial Decisions in the Control Process**

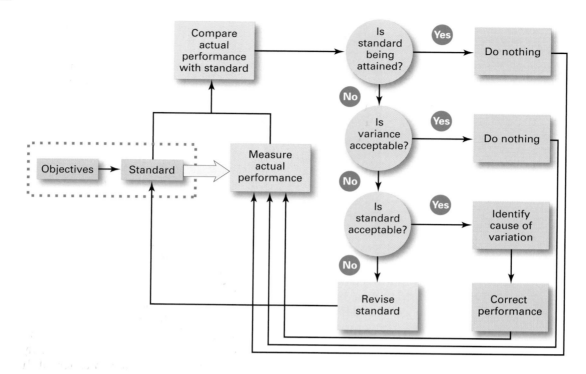

## CONTROLLING FOR ORGANIZATIONAL PERFORMANCE

Cost efficiency. How long callers are kept on hold. How satisfied callers are after they hang up. These are just a few of the important performance indicators that executives in the intensely competitive call-center service industry measure. To make good decisions, managers in the call-center industry want and need this type of information so they can manage organizational performance. Managers in all types of businesses are responsible for managing organizational performance.

### What Is Organizational Performance?

When you hear the word *performance*, what do you think of? A summer evening concert given by a local community orchestra? An Olympic athlete striving for the finish line in a close race? A Southwest Airlines ramp agent in Tulsa, Oklahoma, loading passengers as quickly and efficiently as possible in order to meet the company's 20 minute gate turnaround goal? A Web site designer at Prentice Hall Publishers creating an online learning site, such as R.O.L.L.S., that professors and students will find valuable? **Performance** is all of these. It's the end result of an activity. And whether that activity is hours of intense practice before a concert or race or whether it's carrying out job responsibilities as efficiently and effectively as possible, performance is what results from that activity.

Managers are concerned with **organizational performance**—the accumulated end results of all the organization's work activities. It's a complex but important concept. And managers need to understand the factors that contribute to high organizational performance. After all, they don't want (or intend) to manage their way to mediocre performance. They *want* their organizations, work units, or work groups to achieve high levels of performance. (   Go to www.prenhall. com/rolls)

**Q & A**

Do you know WHY managers want to control organizational performance? Check out Q & A 18.7.

## Measures of Organizational Performance

Theo Epstein, executive vice president and general manager of the Boston Red Sox, uses some unusual statistics to evaluate his baseball players' performance rather than the century-old standards like batting average, home runs, and runs batted in. These "new" performance measures include on-base percentage, pitches per plate appearance, at-bats per home run, and on-base plus slugging percentage.[9] Also, by using these statistics to predict future performance, Epstein has been able to identify some potential star players in both the major and minor leagues and sign them for a fraction of the cost of a big name player. His management team is already working on new statistics that will measure the impact of a player's defensive skills. Epstein has identified the performance measures that are most important to his organizational decisions.

Like Epstein, all managers must know what organizational performance measures will give them the information they need. The most frequently used measures include organizational productivity, organizational effectiveness, and industry rankings.

**Organizational Productivity** Productivity is the overall output of goods or services produced divided by the inputs needed to generate that output. Organizations strive to be productive. They want the most goods and services produced using the least amount of inputs. Output is measured by the sales revenue an organization receives when those goods and services are sold (selling price 3 number sold). Input is measured by the costs of acquiring and transforming the organizational resources into the outputs.

It's management's job to increase this ratio. The easiest way to do this, of course, is to raise the selling price of the outputs, but this is a risky choice in today's competitive environment and it may, in fact, decrease the total output sold. The only other viable option, then, for increasing productivity is to decrease the input part of the ratio—that is, the organization's expenses. Doing so means being more efficient in performing the organization's work activities. Thus, organizational productivity becomes a measure of how efficiently employees do their work. (  Go to www.prenhall.com/rolls)

Q & A
So is productivity related to efficiency and effectiveness? Go to Q & A 18.9 and find out.

**Organizational Effectiveness** In Chapter 1, we defined managerial effectiveness as goal attainment. Can the same interpretation apply to organizational effectiveness? Yes, it can. **Organizational effectiveness** is a measure of how appropriate organizational

Fred Eintracht is director of organizational development for Lennox International, which manufactures heating and air conditioning equipment in Texas. His firm measures intangibles like communication, leadership, and employee involvement with a "vitality metric." Says Eintracht, "Making the metrics more visible to everyone is as important as having the metric itself," and he believes that such visibility also motivates employees to reach their performance goals.

**performance**
The end result of an activity.

**organizational performance**
The accumulated end results of all the organization's work activities.

**productivity**
The overall output of goods or services produced divided by the inputs needed to generate that output.

**organizational effectiveness**
A measure of how appropriate organizational goals are and how well an organization is achieving those goals.

goals are and how well an organization is achieving those goals. It's a common performance measure used by managers.

Other descriptions of organizational effectiveness have been suggested by management researchers.[10] For instance, the systems resource model of organizational effectiveness proposes that effectiveness is measured by the organization's ability to exploit its environment in acquiring scarce and valued resources. The process model emphasizes the transformation processes of the organization and how well the organization converts inputs into desired outputs. And the multiple constituencies model says that several different effectiveness measures should be used, reflecting the different criteria of the organization's constituencies. For example, customers, advocacy groups, suppliers, and security analysts each would have their own measures of how well the organization was performing. Although each of these models is useful for measuring certain aspects of organizational effectiveness, the bottom line for managers continues to be how well the organization meets its goals. That's what guides managerial decisions in designing strategies and work activities and in coordinating the work of employees.

**Q & A**
Why would companies want to be on these rankings? Q & A 18.10 discusses this.

**Industry and Company Rankings** There's no shortage of different types of industry and company rankings. Exhibit 18–8 lists some of the more popular rankings used to measure organizational performance. ( ◆ Go to www.prenhall.com/rolls) The rankings for each list are determined by specific performance measures. For instance, *Fortune's* Top Performing Companies of the *Fortune* 500 are determined by financial results including, for example, profits, return on revenue, and return on shareholder's equity; growth in profits for 1, 5, and 10 years; and revenues per employee, revenues per dollar of assets, and revenues per dollar of equity.[11] *Fortune's* 100 Best Companies to Work For are chosen by answers given by thousands of randomly selected employees on a questionnaire called "The Great Place to Work® Trust Index®," on materials filled out by thousands of company managers including a corporate culture audit created by the Great Place to Work Institute, and on a human resources questionnaire designed by Hewitt Associates.[12] *Industry Week's* Best Managed Plants are determined by organizational accomplishments and demonstrations of superior management skills in the areas of financial performance, innovation, leadership, globalization, alliances, and partnerships, employee benefits and education, and community involvement.[13] The American Customer Satisfaction Index (ACSI) measures customer satisfaction with the quality of goods and services available to household consumers in the United States and then links the results to

## managing workforce **Diversity**

### Diversity Success Stories

U.S. companies are making progress in diversity management. Although many still have a long way to go, some companies are doing their best to make employees of all races into full and active participants in their businesses.[14] Every year, DiversityInc identifies the top 50 companies for diversity. Companies that make the list demonstrate consistent strength in the four areas the survey measures: human capital, corporate communications, supplier development, and CEO commitment. Each has made a strong commitment to diversity at every organizational level and in every aspect—from new hires to suppliers, and even to the charitable causes supported. Who are some of these diversity champions and what are they doing? Let's look at a few examples.

Verizon Communications/Wireless is number 1 on the list. More than 20 percent of the company's officers and 24 percent of middle managers are minorities. The company also has the largest number of minority franchises.

Number 3 on the list is the Coca-Cola Company, whose CEO created an external diversity advisory board and a diversity officer position. The company's career management program was changed to focus on helping minorities advance.

Finally, HBO is number 5 on the list for its community partnerships. For instance, with money it raised from special promotions, the Greater Grace Chapel in Detroit was able to purchase a van that it uses to haul elderly citizens for shopping and banking trips, medical and social appointments, and other needs.

Exhibit 18–8

**Popular Industry and Company Rankings**

| | |
|---|---|
| **Fortune (www.fortune.com)** | **Industry Week (www.industryweek.com)** |
| 100 Best Companies to Work For | |
| *Fortune* 1000 | World's Best Plants |
| *Fortune* 1000 Top Performing Companies | Technology and Innovation Awards |
| Global 500 | of the Year |
| America's Most Admired Companies | Census of Manufacturers |
| World's Most Admired Companies | 25 Fastest Growing Companies |
| America's Best Wealth Creators | *Industry Week* 1000 |
| | |
| **BusinessWeek (www.businessweek.com)** | **Customer Satisfaction Indexes** |
| Standard & Poor's 500 | American Customer Satisfaction Index— |
| Global 1000 | University of Michigan Business School |
| | Customer Satisfaction Measurement |
| **Forbes (www.forbes.com)** | Association |
| *Forbes* 500 | |
| *Forbes* International 500 | |
| 500 Top Private Companies | |
| 200 Best Small Companies | |

Q & A

What drawbacks might there be to placing high on these rankings? See Q & A 18.11.

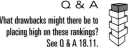

financial returns.[15] Each of the other rankings listed in Exhibit 18–8 is compiled from specific performance measures chosen by the organization doing the ranking. ( Go to www.prenhall.com/rolls)

## Learning Review

- Define organizational performance.
- Describe the most frequently used measures of organizational performance.

## TOOLS FOR CONTROLLING ORGANIZATIONAL PERFORMANCE

Managers at Applebee's Neighborhood Grill & Bar restaurant chain play by their own rules. They're applying cutting-edge ideas to a traditional industry. Rather than carefully locating restaurants so that the sales of one don't eat into another's sales, Applebee's floods an area with stores in order to gain brand recognition and market dominance. For instance, in Kansas City, where its corporate headquarters are located, the company has 10 restaurants. In contrast, Chili's, its biggest competitor, only has 5 units. Appleby's philosophy: Faster is better. Get into a neighborhood before the competition. Keep things moving by giving customers a convenient experience.[16] Given its approach to business, what kinds of tools would Applebee's managers need for monitoring and measuring performance?

At Murata Manufacturing Company of Kyoto, Japan, managers know that performance will be measured against a challenging goal set by Yasutaka Murata, the company's chairman. That goal? Thirty percent of annual sales should come from new products. Since Murata manufactures components for information-age devices such as cellular phones, personal digital assistants, and so forth, measures of new product innovation are key indicators.[17]

As these examples illustrate, managers need appropriate tools for monitoring and measuring organizational performance. Before describing some specific types of organizational performance control tools managers might use, let's look at the concept of feedforward, concurrent, and feedback control.

## Feedforward/Concurrent/Feedback Controls

Managers can implement controls *before* an activity begins, *during* the time the activity is going on, and *after* the activity has been completed. The first type is called *feedforward control*, the second is *concurrent control*, and the last is *feedback control* (see Exhibit 18–9).

**Feedforward Control** The most desirable type of control—**feedforward control**—prevents anticipated problems since it takes place before the actual activity.[18] Let's look at some examples of feedforward control.

When McDonald's opened its first restaurant in Moscow, it sent company quality control experts to help Russian farmers learn techniques for growing high-quality potatoes and bakers to learn processes for baking high-quality breads. Why? Because McDonald's strongly emphasizes product quality no matter the geographical location. They want a cheeseburger in Moscow to taste like one in Omaha. Still another example of feedforward control is the scheduled preventive maintenance programs on aircraft done by the major airlines. These are designed to detect and, it is hoped, to prevent structural damage that might lead to an accident. Another example of feedforward control can be seen at St. Joseph's Hospital in West Bend, Indiana, where a new facility was designed with identical rooms, nonslip floors, and glass walls to reduce errors in patient care and to increase employee safety.[19]

The key to feedforward controls is taking managerial action *before* a problem occurs. Feedforward controls are desirable because they allow managers to prevent problems rather than having to correct them later after the damage (such as poor quality products, lost customers, lost revenue, and so forth) has already been done. Unfortunately, these controls require timely and accurate information that often is difficult to get. As a result, managers frequently end up using the other two types of controls.

**Concurrent Control** **Concurrent control**, as its name implies, takes place while an activity is in progress. When control occurs while the work is being performed, management can correct problems before they come too costly.

The best-known form of concurrent control is direct supervision. When managers use **management by walking around**, which is a term describing when a manager is out in the work area interacting directly with employees, they're using concurrent control. For example, at National Gypsum's Apollo Beach plant in Florida, quality and production managers meet out on the floor with production associates whenever

Exhibit 18–9

**Types of Control**

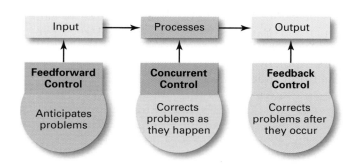

*Yun Jong-Yong, CEO of Samsung Electronics, describes how he practices an effective kind of concurrent control. "I spend much of my time visiting our domestic and overseas work sites to examine operations from the ground, receiving face-to-face reports and indicating areas for improvement. This gives me the opportunity to freely discuss matters with the person directly involved, from the top management to the junior staff of that work site. . . . I still believe that no [technological] innovation can replace the valuable information that is gathered through direct discussions."*

**Q & A**

Wouldn't MBWA be a pretty subjective way to control employees' work? Q & A 18.8 explains why it isn't.

a problem occurs. This practice has allowed the plant to achieve 99.99 percent of the wallboard shipped being perfect.[20] When a manager directly oversees the actions of employees, he or she can monitor their actions and correct problems as they occur. ( Go to www.prenhall.com/rolls) Although obviously, there's some delay between the activity and the manager's corrective response, the delay is minimal. Problems usually can be addressed before much resource waste or damage has been done. Also, technical equipment (computers, computerized machine controls, and so forth) can be programmed for concurrent controls. For instance, you may have experienced concurrent control when using a computer program such as word processing software, which alerts you to misspelled words or incorrect grammatical usage. In addition, many organizational quality programs rely on concurrent controls to inform workers if their work output is of sufficient quality to meet standards.

**Feedback Control** The most popular type of control relies on feedback. In **feedback control**, the control takes place *after* the activity is done. For instance, when the Denver Mint discovered the flawed Wisconsin quarters, it was discovered with feedback control. The damage had already occurred even though the organization corrected the problem once it was discovered.

As this example shows, the major drawback of this type of control is that by the time the manager has the information, the problems have already occurred—leading to waste or damage. But for many activities, feedback is the only viable type of control available. For instance, financial statements are an example of feedback controls. If the income statement shows that sales revenues are declining, the decline has already occurred. So at this point, the manager's only option is to try to determine why sales decreased and to correct the situation.

Feedback controls do have two advantages.[21] First, feedback provides managers with meaningful information on how effective their planning efforts were. Feedback that indicates little variance between standard and actual performance is evidence that the planning was generally on target. If the deviation is significant, a manager can use that information when formulating new plans to make them more effective. Second, feedback control can enhance employee motivation. People want information on how well they have performed and feedback control provides that information. ( Go to www.prenhall.com/rolls)

Self-Assessment Library (S.A.L.)

Do you think you would do a good job of providing feedback? Find out by doing S.A.L. #III.A.3!

---

**feedforward control**
A type of control that takes place before a work activity is done.

**concurrent control**
A type of control that takes place while a work activity is in progress.

**management by walking around**
A term used to describe when a manager is out in the work area interacting directly with employees.

**feedback control**
A type of control that takes place after a work activity is done.

# Financial Controls

Q & A

How useful can financial statements be if they only show after-the-fact results? Go to Q & A 18.12 for an explanation.

One of the primary purposes of every business firm is to earn a profit. To achieve this goal, managers need financial controls. ( Go to www.prenhall.com/rolls) Managers might, for instance, carefully analyze quarterly income statements for excessive expenses. They might also calculate several financial ratios to ensure that sufficient cash is available to pay ongoing expenses, that debt levels haven't become too high, or that assets are being used productively. Or, they might use some newer financial control tools such as EVA (economic value added) to see if the company is creating economic value.

**Traditional Financial Control Measures** Traditional financial measures managers might use include ratio analysis and budget analysis. Exhibit 18–10 summarizes some of the most popular financial ratios used in organizations. The liquidity ratios measure an organization's ability to meet its current debt obligations. Leverage ratios examine the organization's use of debt to finance its assets and whether it's able to meet the interest payments on the debt. The activity ratios assess how efficiently the firm is using its assets. Finally, the profitability ratios measure how efficiently and effectively the firm is using its assets to generate profits. These are calculated using selected information from the organization's two primary financial statements (the balance sheet and the income statement), which are then expressed as a percentage or ratio. Because you've undoubtedly studied these ratios in introductory accounting and finance courses, or will in the near future, we aren't going to elaborate on how they're calculated. Instead, we mention these ratios only briefly here to remind you

Exhibit 18–10    **Popular Financial Ratios**

| Objective | Ratio | Calculation | Meaning |
|---|---|---|---|
| Liquidity | Current ratio | $\dfrac{\text{Current assests}}{\text{Current liabilities}}$ | Tests the organization's ability to meet short-term obligations |
| | Acid test | $\dfrac{\text{Current assests less inventories}}{\text{Current liabilities}}$ | Tests liquidity more accurately when inventories turn over slowly or are difficult to sell |
| Leverage | Debt to assets | $\dfrac{\text{Total debt}}{\text{Total assets}}$ | The higher the ratio, the more leveraged the organization |
| | Times interest earned | $\dfrac{\text{Profits before interest and taxes}}{\text{Total interest charges}}$ | Measures how many times the organization is able to meet its interest expenses |
| Activity | Inventory turnover | $\dfrac{\text{Sales}}{\text{Inventory}}$ | The higher the ratio, the more efficiently inventory assets are being used |
| | Total asset turnover | $\dfrac{\text{Sales}}{\text{Total assets}}$ | The fewer assets used to achieve a given level of sales, the more efficiently management is using the organization's total assets |
| Profitability | Profit margin on sales | $\dfrac{\text{Net profit after taxes}}{\text{Total sales}}$ | Identifies the profits that various products are generating |
| | Return on investment | $\dfrac{\text{Net profit after taxes}}{\text{Total assets}}$ | Measures the efficiency of assets to generate profits |

that managers use such ratios as internal control devices for monitoring how efficiently and profitably the organization uses its assets, debt, inventories, and the like.

We discussed budgets as a planning tool in Chapter 9. When a budget is formulated, it's a planning tool because it gives direction to work activities. It indicates what activities are important and how much resources should be allocated to each activity. But budgets are also used for controlling.

Budgets provide managers with quantitative standards against which to measure and compare resource consumption. By pointing out deviations between standard and actual consumption, they become control tools. If the deviations are judged to be significant enough to require action, the manager examines what has happened and tries to uncover the reasons behind the deviations. With this information, he or she can take whatever action is necessary. For example, if you use a personal budget for monitoring and controlling your monthly expenses, you might find one month that your miscellaneous expenses were higher than you had budgeted for. At that point, you might cut back spending in another area or work extra hours to try to get more income.

**Other Financial Control Measures** In addition to the traditional financial tools, managers are using measures such as EVA (economic value added) and MVA (market value added). The fundamental concept behind these financial tools is that companies are supposed to take in capital from investors and make it worth more. When managers do that, they've created wealth. When they take in capital and make it worth less, they've destroyed wealth.

**Economic value added** is a tool for measuring corporate and divisional performance. It's calculated by taking after-tax operating profit minus the total annual cost of capital.[22] EVA is a measure of how much economic value is being created by what a company does with its assets, less any capital investments the company has made in its assets. As a performance control tool, EVA focuses managers' attention on earning a rate of return over and above the cost of capital. Companies such as Hewlett-Packard, Equifax, Boise Cascade Corporation, and even the U.S. Postal Service have integrated EVA measures into their organizations and improved their performance as a result.[23] When EVA is used as a performance measure, employees soon learn that they can improve their organization's or business unit's EVA by either using less capital or by investing capital in high-return projects.

**Market value added (MVA)** adds a market dimension since it measures the stock market's estimate of the value of a firm's past and expected capital investment projects. If the company's market value (value of all outstanding stock plus company's debt) is greater than all the capital invested in it (from shareholders, bondholders, and retained earnings), it has a positive MVA indicating that managers have created wealth. If the company's market value is less than all the capital invested in it, the MVA will be negative indicating that managers have destroyed wealth. Studies have shown that EVA is a predictor of MVA and that consecutive years of positive EVA generally lead to a high MVA.[24] (  Go to www.prenhall.com/rolls)

**Q & A**
How do EVA and MVA help managers control? See Q & A 18.13.

**The Practice of Managing Earnings** A financial practice that has come under increased scrutiny is managing earnings. When organizations "manage" earnings, they "time" income and expenses to enhance current financial performance, which gives an unrealistic picture of the organization's financial performance. For instance, many organizations have used deferred compensation programs for their top executives. Since deferred compensation programs didn't have to be counted as current expenses—although there is usually a short reference to them buried in footnotes in

---

**economic value added (EVA)**
A financial tool for measuring corporate and divisional performance, calculated by taking after-tax operating profit minus the total annual cost of capital.

**market value added (MVA)**
A financial tool for measuring the stock market's estimate of the value of a firm's past and expected investment projects.

the annual report—earnings look better in the present. The problem is they can add up to a huge future corporate liability. For example, when Jack Welch retired as chairman of General Electric, his retirement package (including, among other things, unlimited access to company jets, exclusive use of a New York City apartment, a chauffeured limousine and a leased Mercedes-Benz, personal assistant, and bodyguards for his speaking engagements and book tours) was estimated by the SEC to be worth $2.5 million in the first year alone. And at pharmaceutical company Wyeth, company executives could participate in a retirement program that allowed them to set aside, pretax, as much as 100 percent of their cash compensation. Wyeth guaranteed executives a 10 percent return on this deferred pay.[25] Needless to say, these types of earnings manipulations not only raise serious ethical questions, but create financial uncertainty. To address some of the problems that have occurred because of "managed" earnings, external controls—primarily governmental laws and regulations—have been enacted with the intent of forcing companies to clarify their financial information.

The Sarbanes–Oxley Act, passed by the U.S. Congress in 2002, requires more financial disclosure by organizations and even goes so far as to have senior managers certify the financial statements. But some companies are doing more. For instance, at Krispy Kreme Doughnuts, new details added to financial statement footnotes better explain specific loan guarantees to franchisees. The amounts had been reported only in aggregate, but now the amount of each guarantee is spelled out.[26] The American Jobs Creation Act of 2004 required companies to review all executive deferred compensation plans and to change them to fit the new requirements. And the Securities and Exchange Commission is significantly overhauling the rules governing what companies must disclose about compensation of top executives.[27]

## Balanced Scorecard

The balanced scorecard approach to performance measurement was introduced as a way to evaluate organizational performance from more than just the financial perspective.[28] The **balanced scorecard** is a performance measurement tool that looks at four areas—financial, customer, internal processes, and people/innovation/growth assets—that contribute to a company's performance. According to this approach, managers should develop goals in each of the four areas and then measure if the goals are being met. (  Go to www.prenhall.com/rolls) For instance, a company might include cash flow, quarterly sales growth, and ROI as measures for success in the financial area. Or, it might include percentage of sales coming from new products as a measure of customer goals. The intent of the balanced scorecard is to emphasize that all of these areas are important to an organization's success and that there should be a balance among them.

Although a balanced scorecard makes sense, managers still tend to focus on areas that drive their organization's success.[29] Their scorecards reflect their strategies. If those strategies center on the customer, for example, then the customer area is likely to get more attention than the other three areas. Yet, you really can't focus on measuring only one performance area because ultimately other performance areas are affected. For instance, at IBM Global Services in Houston, managers developed a scorecard around an overriding strategy of customer satisfaction. However, the other areas (financial, internal processes, and people/innovation/growth) are intended to support that central strategy. The division manager described the approach as follows, "The internal processes part of our business is directly related to responding to our customers in a timely manner, and the learning and innovation aspect is critical for us since what we're selling to our customers above all is our expertise. Of course, how successful we are with those things will affect our financial component."[30] And in Canada, the Ontario Hospital Association developed a scorecard designed to evaluate four main areas: clinical utilization and outcomes, financial performance and financial condition of the hospital, patient satisfaction, and how the hospital was investing for the future. The scorecard was purposefully designed to recognize the synergies

**Q & A**

Would you know how to create a balanced scorecard? Q & A 18.14 provides some suggestions.

among each of these measures. After hospitals were evaluated on the scorecard measures, the results were made available to patients, giving them an objective basis for choosing a hospital.[31]

## Information Controls

A computer with personal information stored electronically on up to 26.5 million military veterans, including Social Security numbers and birth dates, was stolen from the residence of a Department of Veteran Affairs employee who had taken the computer home without authorization. Although the computer was recovered eventually and the personal information was found not to have been compromised, the situation could have been disastrous for a large number of people. However, as bad as it could have been, that wasn't the largest theft of personal data. Some 40 million individuals had their personal information, which was stored electronically at data processor CardSystems, stolen.[32]

There are two ways to view information controls: (1) as a tool to help managers control other organizational activities and (2) as an organizational area that managers need to control. Let's look first at information as a control tool.

### How Is Information Used in Controlling?
Information is critical to monitoring and measuring an organization's activities and performance. Managers need the right information at the right time and in the right amount. Without information, they would find it difficult to measure, compare, and take action as part of the controlling process. Inaccurate, incomplete, excessive, or delayed information will seriously impede performance.

For instance, in measuring actual performance, managers need information about what is, in fact, happening within their area of responsibility, about what the standards are in order to be able to compare actual performance with the standard, and to help them determine acceptable ranges of variation within these comparisons. And they rely on information to help them develop appropriate courses of action if there are or are not significant deviations between actual and standard. As you can see, information is an important tool in monitoring and measuring organizational performance. Most of the information tools that managers use arise out of the organization's management information system.

Although there's no universally agreed-upon definition of a **management information system (MIS)**, we'll define it as a system used to provide management with needed information on a regular basis. In theory, this system can be manual or computer-based,

*Accurate information is so critical for monitoring performance that when Edward Zander became CEO of Motorola, one of the first things he did was change the kind of information division heads were used to reporting. At a meeting of 18 senior executives, Zander interrupted a presentation of revenue forecasts to ask, "Are these commitments?" One exec answered, "This is forecasting." Said Zander, "I'm looking for commitments. The numbers that you tell me today are your commitments for the quarter."*

**balanced scorecard**
A performance measurement tool that looks at four areas—financial, customer, internal processes, and people/innovation/growth assets—that contribute to a company's performance.

**management information system (MIS)**
A system used to provide management with needed information on a regular basis.

although all current discussions focus on computer-supported applications. The term *system* in MIS implies order, arrangement, and purpose. Further, an MIS focuses specifically on providing managers with *information*, not merely *data*. These two points are important and require elaboration.

A library provides a good analogy. Although it can contain millions of volumes, a library doesn't do users much good if they can't find what they want quickly. That's why librarians spend a great deal of time cataloging a library's collections and ensuring that materials are returned to their proper locations. Organizations today are like well-stocked libraries. There's no lack of data. There is, however, an inability to process that data so that the right information is available to the right person when he or she needs it. Likewise, a library is almost useless if it has the book you need immediately, but either you can't find it or the library takes a week to retrieve it from storage. An MIS, on the other hand, has organized data in some meaningful way and can access the information in a reasonable amount of time. **Data** are raw, unanalyzed facts, such as numbers, names or quantities. Raw unanalyzed facts are relatively useless to managers. When data are analyzed and processed, they become **information**. An MIS collects data and turns them into relevant information for managers to use.

**Controlling Information**   As critically important as an organization's information is to everything it does, managers must have comprehensive and secure controls in place to protect that information. Such controls can range from data encryption to system firewalls to data backups, and other techniques as well.[33] Problems can lurk in places that an organization might not even have considered, like search engines. Sensitive, defamatory, confidential, or embarrassing organizational information has found its way into search engine results. For instance, detailed monthly expenses and employee salaries on the National Speleological Society's Web site turned up in a Google search.[34] Laptop computers are also proving to be a weak link in an organization's data security. For instance, Boston-based mutual fund company Fidelity Investments disclosed that a stolen laptop computer had the personal information of almost 200,000 current and former Hewlett-Packard employees.[35] Even RFID (radio-frequency identification) tags, now being used by more and more organizations to track and control products, may be vulnerable to computer viruses.[36] Needless to say, whatever information controls are used must be monitored regularly to ensure that all possible precautions are in place to protect the organization's important information.

## Benchmarking of Best Practices

Managers in diverse industries from medical and educational to financial services and information technology are discovering what manufacturers have long recognized—the benefits of benchmarking. For instance, the American Medical Association is developing more than 100 standard measures of performance in an effort to improve medical care. Carlos Ghosn, CEO of Nissan, benchmarked Wal-Mart's operations in purchasing, transportation, and logistics.[37] And when the first Chrysler Sebring convertible rolled off the assembly line at DaimlerChrysler's assembly plant, the company

*thinking critically about* **Ethics**

Duplicating software for co-workers and friends is a widespread practice, but software in the United States is protected by copyright laws. Copying it is punishable by civil damages of up to $100,000 and criminal penalties including fines and imprisonment to up to five years in jail.

Is reproducing copyrighted software ever an acceptable practice? Explain. Is it wrong for employees of a business to pirate software but permissible for struggling college students who can't afford to buy their own software? As a manager, what types of ethical guidelines could you establish for software use? What if you were a manager in another country where software piracy was an accepted practice?

*SYSCO Corporation is a food-services firm, headquartered in Houston, Texas, that operates more than 120 subsidiary companies around the country. A recent innovation developed by its human resources department is the Innovation Key Metrics Benchmark System, which provides executives at all SYSCO's regional offices with scorecards showing how well their company has performed against others in the SYSCO family. A database of its business practices also lets SYSCO executives look up subsidiary companies of similar size and learn about what has made them strong in particular areas. Site visits to these benchmark firms are encouraged.*

was able to avoid $100 million in production costs because it was built using manufacturing best practices shared by Mercedes-Benz, Chrysler's German owner.[38]

We first introduced the concept of benchmarking in Chapter 9. Remember that **benchmarking** is the search for the best practices among competitors or noncompetitors that lead to their superior performance. The **benchmark** is the standard of excellence against which to measure and compare.[39] At its most fundamental level, benchmarking means learning from others.[40] As a tool for monitoring and measuring organizational performance, benchmarking can be used to help identify specific performance gaps and potential areas of improvement.[41] ( ◆ Go to www.prenhall.com/rolls) But managers shouldn't just look at external organizations for best practices. It's also important for managers to look inside their organization for best practices that can be shared.

Have you ever worked somewhere that had an employee suggestion box? When an employee had an idea about a new way of doing something—such as reducing costs, improving delivery time, and so forth—it went into the suggestion box where it usually sat until someone decided to empty the box. Businesspeople frequently joked about the suggestion box and cartoons lambasted the futility of putting ideas in the employee suggestion box.

Unfortunately, this attitude about suggestion boxes still persists in many organizations, and it shouldn't. Research shows that best practices frequently already exist within an organization but usually go unidentified and unused.[42] In today's environment, organizations striving for high performance levels can't afford to ignore such potentially valuable information. Some companies already have recognized the potential of internally benchmarking best practices as a tool for monitoring and measuring performance. For example, Toyota Motor Corporation developed a suggestion-screening system to prioritize best practices based on potential impact, benefits, and difficulty of implementation. Ameren Corporation's power plant managers used internal benchmarking to help identify performance gaps and opportunities.[43] Exhibit 18–11 provides a summary of what managers must do to implement an internal benchmarking best practices program.

**Q & A**

Benchmarking also provides information for controlling. See Q & A 18.15 for an explanation.

---

**data**
Raw, unanalyzed facts.
**information**
Processed and analyzed data.

**benchmarking**
The search for the best practices among competitors or noncompetitors that lead to their superior performance.

**benchmark**
The standard of excellence against which to measure and compare.

Exhibit 18–11

**Steps to Successfully
Implement an Internal
Benchmarking Best
Practices Program**

1. *Connect best practices to strategies and goals.* The organization's strategies and goals should dictate what types of best practices might be most valuable to others in the organization.

2. *Identify best practices throughout the organization.* Organizations must have a way to find out what practices have been successful in different work areas and units.

3. *Develop best practices reward and recognition systems.* Individuals must be given an incentive to share their knowledge. The reward system should be built into the organization's culture.

4. *Communicate best practices throughout the organization.* Once best practices have been identified, that information needs to be shared with others in the organization.

5. *Create a best practices knowledge-sharing system.* There needs to be a formal mechanism for organizational members to continue sharing their ideas and best practices.

6. *Nurture best practices on an ongoing basis.* Create an organizational culture that reinforces a "we can learn from everyone" attitude and emphasizes sharing information.

*Source:* Based on T. Leahy, "Extracting Diamonds in the Rough," *Business Finance,* August 2000, pp. 33–37.

## Learning Review

- Contrast feedforward, concurrent, and feedback controls.
- Explain the types of financial and information controls managers can use.

- Describe how balanced scorecards and benchmarking are used in controlling.

## CONTEMPORARY ISSUES IN CONTROL

The employees of Arizona-based Integrated Information Systems Inc. thought there was nothing wrong with exchanging copyrighted digital music over a dedicated office server they had set up. Like office betting on college basketball games, it was technically illegal, but harmless, or so they thought. But after the company had to pay a $1 million settlement to the Recording Industry Association of America, managers wished they had controlled the situation better.[44] After significant political and public criticism—both domestic and international—over its poorly executed response following Hurricane Katrina, American Red Cross officials are overhauling the organization's operations. Without these changes, it faced the possibility of losing its status as the only charity chartered by Congress to assist Americans when catastrophe strikes.[45]

Control is an important managerial function. What types of control issues do today's managers face? We're going to look at four: cross-cultural differences, workplace concerns, customer interactions, and corporate governance.

### Adjusting Controls for Cross-Cultural Differences

The concepts of control that we've been discussing are appropriate for an organization whose units are not geographically separated or culturally distinct. But what about global organizations? Will control systems be different, and what should managers know about adjusting controls for national differences?

Methods of controlling people and work can be quite different in different countries. The differences we see in organizational control systems of global organizations are primarily in the measurement and corrective action steps of the control process. In a global corporation, managers of foreign operations tend to be less controlled directly by the home office, if for no other reason than distance keeps managers from being able to observe work directly. Because distance creates a tendency to formalize controls, the home office of a global company often relies on extensive formal reports for control. The global company also may use information technology to control work activities. For instance, the Japanese company Seven & I Holdings Co., Ltd., owner of the 7-Eleven convenience store chain, uses automated cash registers not only to record sales and monitor inventory, but to schedule tasks for store managers and track managers' use of the built-in analytical graphs and forecasts. If managers don't use them enough, they're told to increase their activities.[46]

Technology's impact on control also can be seen when comparing technologically advanced nations with less technologically advanced countries. In countries such as the United States, Japan, Canada, Great Britain, Germany, and Australia, global managers use indirect control devices—especially computer-generated reports and analyses—in addition to standardized rules and direct supervision to ensure that work activities are going as planned. In less technologically advanced countries, managers tend to rely more on direct supervision and highly centralized decision making for control.

Also, constraints on what corrective actions managers can take may affect managers in foreign countries because laws in some countries do not allow managers the option of closing facilities, laying off employees, taking money out of the country, or bringing in a new management team from outside the country.

Finally, another challenge for global companies in collecting data for measurement and comparison is comparability. For instance, a company that manufactures apparel goods in Cambodia might produce the same products at a facility in Scotland. However, the Cambodian facility might be much more labor intensive than its Scottish counterpart (to take strategic advantage of lower labor costs in Cambodia). If the top-level executives were to control costs by, for example, calculating labor costs per unit or output per worker, the figures would not be comparable. Global managers must address these types of control challenges.

## Workplace Concerns

Today's workplace presents considerable control challenges for managers. From monitoring employees' computer usage at work to protecting the workplace against disgruntled employees or even possible terrorist attacks, managers must control the workplace to ensure that the organization's work can be carried out efficiently and effectively as planned. In this section we want to look at three main workplace concerns: workplace privacy, employee theft, and workplace violence.

**Workplace Privacy** If you work, do you think you have a right to privacy at your workplace? What can your employer find out about you and your work? You might be surprised by the answers! Employers can (and do), among other things, read your e-mail (even those marked "personal or confidential"), tap your telephone, monitor your work by computer, store and review computer files, monitor you in an employee bathroom or dressing room, and track your whereabouts in a company vehicle. And these actions aren't all that uncommon. In fact, some 26 percent of companies have fired workers for misusing the Internet; another 25 percent have terminated workers for e-mail misuse; and 6 percent have fired employees for misusing office phones.[47] Exhibit 18–12 summarizes the percentage of employers engaging in different forms of workplace monitoring.

Why do managers feel they must monitor what employees are doing? A big reason is that employees are hired to work, not to surf the Web checking stock prices, placing bets at online casinos, or shopping for presents for family or friends. Recreational on-the-job Web surfing is thought to cost billions of dollars in lost work productivity annually. In fact, a recent survey of U.S. employers said that 87 percent of employees look at non-work-related Web sites while at work and more than half engage in personal Web site surfing every day.[48] That adds up to significant costs to businesses.

Another reason that managers monitor employee e-mail and computer usage is that they don't want to risk being sued for creating a hostile workplace environment because of offensive messages or an inappropriate image displayed on a co-worker's computer

Exhibit 18–12

**Types of Workplace Monitoring**

| Workplace Computer Use | |
| --- | --- |
| Monitoring Web site connections | 76% |
| Tracking content, keystrokes, and time spent at keyboard | 36% |
| Store and review employees' computer files | 50% |
| Retain and review e-mail messages | 55% |

| Workplace Phone Use | |
| --- | --- |
| Block access to 900- and other unauthorized numbers | 57% |
| Monitor time spent on phone and track phone numbers | 51% |
| Tape phone conversations in selected jobs | 19% |
| Record and review all phone calls | 3% |
| Tape or review voice mail | 15% |

| Video Monitoring | |
| --- | --- |
| Video monitoring to counter theft, violence, and sabotage | 51% |
| Video surveillance of work performance in selected jobs | 10% |
| Video surveillance of work performance in all jobs | 6% |

| Tracking Employee Productivity and Movement (Using GPS or AGP*) | |
| --- | --- |
| Monitor cell phone | 5% |
| Track company vehicles | 8% |
| Monitor employee ID/smartcards | 8% |

| Physical Security and Access | |
| --- | --- |
| Smartcard technology | 53% |
| Fingerprint scans | 5% |
| Facial recognition | 2% |
| Iris scans | .5% |

*Global positioning system or assisted global positioning.

*Source:* American Management Association/ePolicy Institute Research, "2005 Electronic Monitoring & Surveillance Survey," American Management Association.

screen. Concern about racial or sexual harassment is one of the reasons why companies might want to monitor or keep backup copies of all e-mail. This electronic record can help establish what actually happened and can help managers react quickly.[49]

Finally, managers want to ensure that company secrets aren't being leaked.[50] In addition to typical e-mail and computer usage, companies are beginning to monitor instant messaging and even banning camera phones in the office. Although protecting intellectual property is important for all businesses, it's especially important in high-tech industries. Managers need to be certain that employees are not, even inadvertently, passing information on to others who could use that information to harm the company.

Even with the workplace monitoring organizations can do, U.S. employees have some protection through the federal Electronic Communications Privacy Act, which prohibits unauthorized interception of electronic communication. Although this law gives employees some privacy protection, it doesn't make workplace electronic monitoring illegal as employers are allowed to monitor communications for business reasons or when employees have been notified of the practice.[51] Although employees may think that it's unfair for a company to monitor their work electronically and to fire them for what they feel are minor distractions, the courts have ruled that since the computer belongs to the company, managers have a right to view everything on it.[52]

Because of the potentially serious costs and given the fact that many jobs now entail work that involves using a computer, many companies are developing and enforcing workplace monitoring policies. The responsibility for this falls on managers. It's important to develop some type of viable workplace monitoring policy. What can managers do to maintain control but do so in a way that isn't demeaning to employees? They should develop a clear and unambiguous electronic equipment and computer usage policy and

*Julian E. Montoya, founder of the Burrito King chain of restaurants, has seen his once-thriving business falter as a result of fierce competition. Employee theft was sometimes a problem as well. Montoya recalls the difficulty of monitoring the performance of all his stores at the height of expansion. One night he went to one of his restaurants unannounced, donned an apron, and went up front to cover the cash register. "The cook took me aside," Montoya remembers, "and said, 'Here's how it works: You take the order; you take the cash and don't put it in the register. At the end of the night we split it.' "*

make sure that every employee knows about it. Tell employees upfront that any and all computer or other electronic equipment use may be monitored at any time and provide clear and specific guidelines as to what constitutes acceptable use of company e-mail systems and the Web.

**Employee Theft** Would you be surprised to find out that up to 85 percent of all organizational theft and fraud is committed by employees, not outsiders?[53] And, it's a costly problem—estimated to be around $4,500 per U.S. worker each year.[54]

**Employee theft** is defined as any unauthorized taking of company property by employees for their personal use.[55] It can range from embezzlement to fraudulent filing of expense reports to removing equipment, parts, software, and office supplies from company premises. While retail businesses have long faced serious potential losses from employee theft, loose financial controls at start-ups and small companies and the ready availability of information technology have made employee stealing an escalating problem in all kinds and sizes of organizations. It's a control issue that managers need to educate themselves about and with which they must be prepared to deal.[56]

Why do employees steal? The answer depends on whom you ask.[57] Experts in various fields—industrial security, criminology, clinical psychology—all have different perspectives. The industrial security people propose that people steal because the opportunity presents itself through lax controls and favorable circumstances. Criminologists say that it's because people have financial-based pressures (such as personal financial problems) or vice-based pressures (such as gambling debts). And the clinical psychologists suggest that people steal because they can rationalize whatever they're doing as being correct and appropriate behavior ("everyone does it," "they had it coming," "this company makes enough money and they'll never miss anything this small," "I deserve this for all that I put up with," and so forth).[58] Although each of these approaches provides compelling insights into employee theft and has been instrumental in program designs to deter it, unfortunately, employees continue to steal. So what can managers do? Let's look at some suggestions for managing employee theft.

We can use the concept of feedforward, concurrent, and feedback control to identify measures for deterring or reducing employee theft.[59] Exhibit 18–13 summarizes several possible managerial actions.

**Workplace Violence** On January 30, 2006, a former employee who was once removed from a Santa Barbara, California, postal facility because of "strange behavior"

**Exhibit 18–13**

**Control Measures for Deterring or Reducing Employee Theft or Fraud**

| Feedforward | Concurrent | Feedback |
|---|---|---|
| Careful prehiring screening. | Treat employees with respect and dignity. | Make sure employees know when theft or fraud has occurred—not naming names but letting people know this is not acceptable. |
| Establish specific policies defining theft and fraud and discipline procedures. | Openly communicate the costs of stealing. | |
| Involve employees in writing policies. | Let employees know on a regular basis about their successes in preventing theft and fraud. | Use the services of professional investigators. |
| Educate and train employees about the polices. | Use video surveillance equipment if conditions warrant. | Redesign control measures. |
| Have professionals review your internal security controls. | Install "lock-out" options on computers, telephones, and e-mail. | Evaluate your organization's culture and the relationships of managers and employees. |
| | Use corporate hotlines for reporting incidences. | |
| | Set a good example. | |

*Sources:* Based on A. H. Bell and D. M. Smith, "Protecting the Company Against Theft and Fraud," *Workforce Online* (www.workforce.com), December 3, 2000; J. D. Hansen, "To Catch a Thief," *Journal of Accountancy,* March 2000, pp. 43–46; and J. Greenberg, "The Cognitive Geometry of Employee Theft," in *Dysfunctional Behavior in Organizations: Nonviolent and Deviant Behavior,* eds. S. B. Bacharach, A. O'Leary-Kelly, J. M. Collins, and R. W. Griffin (Stamford, CT: JAI Press, 1998), pp. 147–93.

came back and shot five workers to death, critically wounded another, and killed her-self. On January 26, 2005, an autoworker at a Jeep plant in Toledo, Ohio, who had met the day before with plant managers about a problem with his work, came in and killed a supervisor and wounded two other employees before killing himself. During April 2003 in Indianapolis, a manager of a Boston Market restaurant was killed by a fellow employee after the restaurant closed because the manager had refused the employee's sexual advances. In July 2003, an employee at an aircraft assembly plant in Meridian, Mississippi walked out of a mandatory class on ethics and respect in the workplace, returned with firearms and ammunition, shot 14 of his co-workers, killing five and himself.[60] Is workplace violence really an issue with which managers might have to deal? Yes. Despite these examples, the number of workplace homicides has decreased slightly.[61] However, the U.S. National Institute of Occupational Safety and Health says that each year, some 2 million American workers are victims of some form of work-place violence. In an average week, one employee is killed and at least 25 are seriously injured in violent assaults by current or former co-workers. And according to a Department of Labor survey, 58 percent of firms reported that managers received ver-bal threats from workers.[62] Exhibit 18–14 describes the results from a survey of workers and their experiences with office rage. Anger, rage, and violence in the workplace are intimidating to co-workers and adversely affect their productivity. The annual cost to

**Exhibit 18–14**

**Workplace Violence**

| | |
|---|---|
| • Witnessed yelling or other verbal abuse | 42% |
| • Yelled at co-workers themselves | 29% |
| • Cried over work-related issues | 23% |
| • Seen someone purposely damage machines or furniture | 14% |
| • Seen physical violence in the workplace | 10% |
| • Struck a co-worker | 2% |

*Source:* Integra Realty Resources, October–November Survey of Adults 18 and Over, in "Desk Rage," *BusinessWeek,* November 20, 2000, p. 12.

U.S. businesses is estimated at between $20 and $35 billion.[63] And office rage isn't a uniquely American problem. A survey of aggressive behavior in Britain's workplaces found that 18 percent of managers say they have personally experienced harassment or verbal bullying and 9 percent claim to have experienced physical attacks.[64]

What factors are believed to be contributing to workplace violence? Undoubtedly, employee stress caused by rising layoffs, declining value of retirement accounts, long hours, information overload, other daily interruptions, unrealistic deadlines, and uncaring managers play a role. Even office layout designs with small cubicles where employees work amidst the noise and commotion from those around them have been cited as contributing to the problem.[65] Other experts have described dangerously dysfunctional work environments characterized by the following as primary contributors to the problem:[66]

- Employee work driven by TNC (time, numbers, and crises).
- Rapid and unpredictable change where instability and uncertainty plague employees.
- Destructive communication style where managers communicate in an excessively aggressive, condescending, explosive, or passive-aggressive styles; excessive workplace teasing or scapegoating.
- Authoritarian leadership with a rigid, militaristic mind-set of managers versus employees; employees aren't allowed to challenge ideas, participate in decision making, or engage in team-building efforts.
- Defensive attitude where little or no performance feedback is given; only numbers count; and yelling, intimidation, or avoidance are the preferred ways of handling conflict.
- Double standards in terms of policies, procedures, and training opportunities for managers and employees.
- Unresolved grievances because there are no mechanisms or only adversarial ones in place for resolving them; dysfunctional individuals may be protected or ignored because of long-standing rules, union contract provisions, or reluctance to take care of problems.
- Emotionally troubled employees and no attempt by managers to get help for these people.
- Repetitive, boring work where there's no chance for doing something else or for new people coming in.
- Faulty or unsafe equipment or deficient training, which keeps employees from being able to work efficiently or effectively.
- Hazardous work environment in terms of temperature, air quality, repetitive motions, overcrowded spaces, noise levels, excessive overtime, and so forth. To minimize costs, no additional employees are hired when workload becomes excessive leading to potentially dangerous work expectations and conditions.
- Culture of violence where there's a history of individual violence or abuse; violent or explosive role models; or tolerance of on-the-job alcohol or drug abuse.

Reading through this list, you may feel that workplaces where you'll spend your professional life won't be anything like this. However, the competitive demands of succeeding in a 24/7 global economy put pressure on organizations and employees in many ways.

What can managers do to deter or reduce possible workplace violence? Once again, we can use the concept of feedforward, concurrent, and feedback control to identify actions that managers can take.[67] Exhibit 18–15 summarizes several suggestions.

## Controlling Customer Interactions

Every month, every local branch of Enterprise Rent-a-Car conducts telephone surveys with customers.[68] Each branch earns a ranking based on the percentage of its customers who say they were "completely satisfied" with their last Enterprise experience—a level

Exhibit 18–15

**Control Measures for Deterring or Reducing Workplace Violence**

| Feedforward | Concurrent | Feedback |
|---|---|---|
| Management commitment to functional, not dysfunctional, work environments. | MBWA (managing by walking around) to identify potential problems; observe how employees treat and interact with each other. | Communicate openly about incidences and what's being done. |
| Employee assistance programs (EAP) to help employees with serious behavioral problems. | Allow employees or work groups to "grieve" during periods of major organizational change. | Investigate incidences and take appropriate action. |
| Organizational policy that any workplace rage, aggression, or violence will not be tolerated. | Be a good role model in how you treat others. | Review company policies and change, if necessary. |
| Careful prehiring screening. | Use corporate hotlines or some mechanism for reporting and investigating incidences. | |
| Never ignore threats. Train employees about how to avoid danger if situation arises. | Use quick and decisive intervention. Get expert professional assistance if violence erupts. | |
| Clearly communicate policies to employees. | Provide necessary equipment or procedures for dealing with violent situations (cell phones, alarm systems, code names or phrases, and so forth). | |

*Sources:* Based on M. Gorkin, "Five Strategies and Structures for Reducing Workplace Violence," *Workforce Online* (www.workforce.com), December 3, 2000; "Investigating Workplace Violence: Where Do You Start?" *Workforce Online* (www.forceforce.com), December 3, 2000; "Ten Tips on Recognizing and Minimizing Violence," *Workforce Online* (www.workforce.com), December 3, 2000; and "Points to Cover in a Workplace Violence Policy," *Workforce Online* (www.workforce.com), December 3, 2000.

of satisfaction referred to as "top box." Top box performance is important to Enterprise because completely satisfied customers are far more likely to be repeat customers. And by using this service quality index measure, employees' careers and financial aspirations are linked with the organizational goal of providing consistently superior service to each and every customer. Managers at Enterprise Rent-a-Car understand the connection between employees and customers and the importance of controlling these customer interactions.

There's probably no better area to see the link between planning and controlling than in customer service. If a company proclaims customer service as one of its goals, it quickly and clearly becomes apparent whether that goal is being achieved by seeing how satisfied customers are with their service! How can managers control the interactions between the goal and the outcome when it comes to customers? The concept of a service profit chain can help (see Exhibit 18–16).

The **service profit chain** is the service sequence from employees to customers to profit.[69] According to this concept, the company's strategy and service delivery system influences how employees service customers—their attitudes, behaviors, and service capability. Service capability, in turn, enhances how productive employees are in providing service and the quality of that service. The level of employee service productivity and service quality influences customer perceptions of service value. When service value is high, it has a positive impact on customer satisfaction, which leads to customer loyalty. And customer loyalty improves organizational revenue growth and profitability.

So what does the concept of a service profit chain mean for managers? Managers who want to control customer interactions should work to create long-term and mutually beneficial relationships among the company, employees, and customers. How? By creating a work environment that not only enables employees to deliver high levels of quality service, but also makes them feel they're capable of delivering top-quality service. In such a service climate, employees are motivated to deliver superior service. These employee

Exhibit 18–16    **The Service Profit Chain**

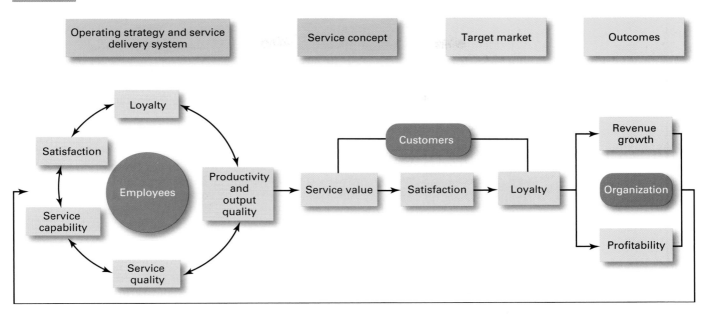

Source: Adapted and reprinted by permission of *Harvard Business Review*. An exhibit from "Putting the Service Profit Chain to Work," by J. L. Heskett, T. O. Jones, G. W. Loveman, W. E. Sasser, Jr., and L. A. Schlesinger. March–April 1994: 166. Copyright © by the President and Fellows of Harvard College. All rights reserved. See also J. L. Heskett, W. E. Sasser, and L. A. Schlesinger, *The Service Profit Chain* (New York: Free Press, 1997).

efforts to satisfy customers, coupled with the service value provided by the organization, improve customer satisfaction. And when customers receive high service value, they're loyal and come back, which ultimately improves the company's growth and profitability.

There's no better example of the service profit chain in action than Southwest Airlines. Southwest is the most consistently profitable U.S. airline (the year 2005 marked 33 straight profitable years) and its customers are fiercely loyal. This is because the company's operating strategy (hiring, training, rewards and recognition, teamwork, and so forth) is built around customer service. Employees consistently deliver outstanding service value to customers. And Southwest's customers reward the company by coming back. It's through efficiently and effectively controlling these customer interactions that companies like Southwest and Enterprise have succeeded.

## Corporate Governance

Although Andrew Fastow—Enron's former chief financial officer who pled guilty to wire and securities fraud—had an engaging and persuasive personality, that still doesn't explain why Enron's board of directors failed to raise even minimal concerns about management's questionable accounting practices. The board even allowed Fastow to set up off-balance-sheet partnerships for his own profit at the expense of Enron's shareholders.

**Corporate governance**, the system used to govern a corporation so that the interests of corporate owners are protected, failed abysmally at Enron, as it did at many companies caught in financial scandals. In the aftermath of these scandals, there have been increased calls for better corporate governance. Two areas in which corporate governance is being reformed are the role of boards of directors and financial reporting. These improvements aren't limited to U.S. corporations. The problem of corporate governance is a global one.[70] A full 75 percent of senior executives at U.S. and western European corporations expect their boards of directors to take a more active role.[71]

**service profit chain**
The service sequence from employees to customers to profit.

**corporate governance**
The system used to govern a corporation so that the interests of corporate owners are protected.

*becoming* a Manager

✓ Identify the types of controls you use in your own personal life and whether they're feedforward, concurrent, or feedback controls.

✓ When preparing for major class projects, identify some performance measures that you can use to help you determine whether or not the project is going as planned.

✓ Try to come up with some ways to improve your personal efficiency and effectiveness.

✓ ◆ Complete any of the following exercises from the Self-Assessment Library found on www.prenhall.com/rolls: S.A.L.: #II.B.5—How Good Am I at Disciplining Others?, #III.A.2—How Willing Am I to Delegate?, #I.E.2—What Time of Day Am I Most Productive?, and #II.A.3—How Good Am I at Giving Performance Feedback?

Self-Assessment
Library (S.A.L.)

**The Role of Boards of Directors** The original purpose of a board of directors was to have a group, independent from management, looking out for the interests of shareholders who, because of the corporate structure, were not involved in the day-to-day management of the organization. However, it doesn't always work that way in practice. Board members often enjoy a cozy relationship with managers in which board members "take care" of the CEO and the CEO "takes care" of the board members.

This "quid pro quo" arrangement is changing. Since the passage of the Sarbanes–Oxley Act of 2002, demands on board members of publicly traded companies in the United States have increased considerably.[72] To help boards do their job better, researchers at the Corporate Governance Center at Kennesaw State University developed 10 governance principles for U.S. public companies that have been endorsed by the Institute of Internal Auditors. (See Exhibit 18–17 for a list of these principles.)

Exhibit 18–17

**Twenty-First Century Governance Principles for U.S. Public Companies**

1. *Interaction:* Sound governance requires effective interaction among the board, management, the external auditor, and the internal auditor.

2. *Board Purpose:* The board of directors should understand that its purpose is to protect the interests of the corporation's stockholders, while considering the interests of other stakeholders (e.g., creditors, employees, etc.).

3. *Board Responsibilities:* The board's major areas of responsibility should be monitoring the CEO, overseeing the corporation's strategy, and monitoring risks and the corporation's control system. Directors should employ healthy skepticism in meeting these responsibilities.

4. *Independence:* The major stock exchanges should define an "independent" director as one who has no professional or personal ties (either current or former) to the corporation or its management other than service as a director. The vast majority of the directors should be independent in both fact and appearance so as to promote arm's-length oversight.

5. *Expertise:* The directors should possess relevant industry, company, functional area, and governance expertise. The directors should reflect a mix of backgrounds and perspectives. All directors should receive detailed orientation and continuing education to assure they achieve and maintain the necessary level of expertise.

6. *Meetings and Information:* The board should meet frequently for extended periods of time and should have access to the information and personnel it needs to perform its duties.

7. *Leadership:* The roles of Board Chair and CEO should be separate.

8. *Disclosure:* Proxy statements and other board communications should reflect board activities and transactions (e.g., insider trades) in a transparent and timely manner.

9. *Committees:* The nominating, compensation, and audit committees of the board should be composed only of independent directors.

10. *Internal Audit:* All public companies should maintain an effective, full-time internal audit function that reports directly to the audit committee.

*Source:* P. D. Lapides, D. R. Hermanson, M. S. Beasley, J. V. Carcello, F. T. DeZoort, and T. L. Neal. Corporate Governance Center, Kennesaw State University. March 26, 2002.

Exhibit 18–18

**Twenty-First Century *Financial Reporting* Principles for U.S. Public Companies**

1. *Reporting Model:* The current GAAP financial reporting model is becoming increasingly less appropriate for U.S. public companies. The industrial-age model currently used should be replaced or enhanced so that tangible and intangible resources, risks, and performance of information-age companies can be effectively and efficiently communicated to financial statement users. The new model should be developed and implemented as soon as possible.

2. *Philosophy and Culture:* Financial statements and supporting disclosures should reflect economic substance and should be prepared with the goal of maximum informativeness and transparency. A legalistic view of accounting and auditing (e.g., "can we get away with recording it this way?") is not appropriate. Management integrity and a strong control environment are critical to reliable financial reporting.

3. *Audit Committees:* The audit committee of the board of directors should be composed of independent directors with financial, auditing, company, and industry expertise. These members must have the will, authority, and resources to provide diligent oversight of the financial reporting process. The board should consider the risks of audit committee member stock/stock option holdings and should set audit committee member compensation at an appropriate level given the expanded duties and risks faced by audit committee members. The audit committee should select the external auditor, evaluate external and internal auditor performance, and approve the audit fee.

4. *Fraud:* Corporate management should face strict criminal penalties in fraudulent financial reporting cases. The Securities and Exchange Commission should be given the resources it needs to effectively combat financial statement fraud. The board, management, and auditors all should perform fraud risk assessments.

5. *Audit Firms:* Audit firms should focus primarily on providing high-quality audit and assurance services and should perform no consulting for audit clients. Audit firm personnel should be selected, evaluated, compensated, and promoted primarily based on technical competence, not on their ability to generate new business. Audit fees should reflect engagements' scope of work and risk.

6. *External Auditing Profession:* Auditors should view public accounting as a noble profession focused on the public interest, not as a competitive business. The profession should carefully consider expanding audit reports beyond the current "clean" versus modified dichotomy so as to enhance communication to financial report users.

7. *Analysts:* Analysts should not be compensated (directly or indirectly) based on the investment banking activities of their firms. Analysts should not hold stock in the companies they follow, and they should disclose any business relationships between the companies they follow and their firms.

*Source:* P. D. Lapides, D. R. Hermanson, M. S. Beasley, J. V. Carcello, F. T. DeZoort, and T. L. Neal. Corporate Governance Center, Kennesaw State University. March 26, 2002.

**Financial Reporting** In addition to expanding the role of boards of directors, the previously mentioned Sarbanes–Oxley Act also called for more disclosure and transparency of corporate financial information. In fact, senior managers in the United States are now required to certify their companies' financial results. These types of changes should lead to better information—that is, information that is more accurate and reflective of the firm's financial condition. In fulfilling their financial reporting responsibilities, managers might want to follow the principles also developed by the researchers at the Corporate Governance Center at Kennesaw State University. These seven principles are explained in Exhibit 18–18.

## Learning Review

- Describe how managers may have to adjust controls for cross-cultural differences.
- Discuss the types of workplace concerns managers face and how they can address those concerns.
- Explain why control is important to customer interactions.
- Explain what corporate governance is and how it's changing.

# Managers Respond to a Manager's Dilemma

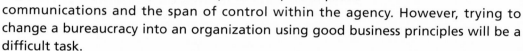

### Joseph S. Lia

Vice President, Mid-Hudson Region
MVP Health Plan
Fishkill, New York

As the chief operations officer of the FAA, Russell is off to a good start by getting a basic equipment inventory in place and also by flattening the FAA organizational structure. These steps will help to improve communications and the span of control within the agency. However, trying to change a bureaucracy into an organization using good business principles will be a difficult task.

Russell will need to use the full scope of financial controls starting out with an organizational budget, which will need to be broken down into separate budgets for each department or unit of the organization. He also will need to encourage a culture of "operating within budget" by tracking the budgets on a monthly basis and also planning throughout the year on how they can be more efficient—not an easy change for a bureaucracy.

He should also introduce the concept of organizational planning and control, which in conjunction with the financial controls can be used to initiate the planning cycle that will lead to a system of setting goals and objectives for his management team. The management team can then break down those organizational goals and objectives into more specific and objectives for all managers and supervisors to track the performance of their units throughout the year. Again, this type of cultural change won't be easy, but is necessary.

Russell will have to be a strong leader, which he appears to be, to foster a change in the environment of the organization. He will need to develop a culture of performance based on measuring key performance indicators and comparing these indicators against agreed-upon standards. The management team will need to learn that when they deviate from agree-upon standards, they may have to initiate corrective action so that they will meet their goals and objectives at the end of the year.

Finally, since the safety of the traveling public is one of the agency's primary responsibilities, it's important that Russell continue to emphasize developing standards to measure the performance of the entire air traffic control system as well as standards for tracking preventive and routine maintenance of all the aircraft under its jurisdiction.

# Learning Summary

## What Is Control and Why Is It Important?

**Controlling:** the process of monitoring, comparing, and evaluating work performance

Three types of control systems:

1. Market control—emphasizes external market mechanisms as standards
2. Bureaucratic control—emphasizes organizational authority, rules, regulations, procedures, and policies as standards
3. Clan control—uses organizational culture (shared values, norms, traditions, rituals, beliefs) as standards

Controlling is important because it:

- Provides critical link back to planning
- Provides information and feedback if employees have been empowered
- Protects organization and its assets

## What Happens in the Control Process?

- Measuring
  - How to measure? (Personal observation; and statistical, oral, and written reports)
  - What is measured? (More important choice than "how" to measure)
- Comparing—size and direction of variation between actual performance and standard—that is, the goal(s) established during planning
- Taking action
  - Do nothing
  - Correct actual performance: immediate corrective action or basic correction action
  - Revise the standard

## How Should Managers Measure Organizational Performance?

**Performance:** end result of an activity; **organizational performance:** accumulated end results of all the organization's work activities

Measures of organizational performance:

- Organizational productivity (efficiency)
- Organizational effectiveness (goal achievement)
- Industry rankings

## How Should Managers Control Organizational Performance?

- **Feedforward** (takes place before work activities), **concurrent** (takes place while work is being performed), and **feedback** (takes place after work has been completed)
- Types of organizational controls:
  - Financial
  - Traditional financial controls: ratios and budgets
  - Other financial controls: EVA, MVA, and managing earnings
  - Balanced scorecard—evaluates performance from 4 areas: financial, customers, internal processes, and people/innovation/growth assets
  - Information
  - Tool to help managers control other organizational activities
  - An organizational area that needs to be controlled
  - Benchmarking—search for best practices or benchmarks, which become standards of excellence against which to measure and compare

## What Contemporary Control Issues Do Managers Face?

* Adjusting controls for cross-cultural differences—primarily in the areas of measuring and taking corrective actions
* Workplace concerns
  * Workplace privacy
  * Employee theft
  * Workplace violence
* Controlling customer interactions
  * **Service profit chain:** service sequence from employees to customers to profit
* **Corporate governance:** the system used to govern a corporation so that the interests of corporate owners are protected
  * Role of board of directors
  * Financial reporting

# Management: By the Numbers

* Organizations lose $759 billion annually in productivity due to employees' personal Internet usage while on the job.
* Thirty-seven percent of the time spent at work is wasted because of poor management and supervision.
* Sixty-four percent of companies surveyed said their boards of directors are more actively involved in company performance evaluation.
* Fifty-five percent of employees surveyed support the use of biometric technology to record employee time and attendance.
* The top items employees steal from work include pens/pencils—60 percent; Post-it notes—40 percent; envelopes—32 percent; notepads—28 percent; and paper—28 percent.
* Sixty percent of employees surveyed said they use the Internet at work within limits and it does not decrease their productivity; 4 percent said they use the Internet more than they should but it increases their productivity.
* Seventy-five percent of finance managers say Sarbanes–Oxley has increased their workload.

* Retailers lose more than $10 billion annually from shoplifting.
* Eighty percent of board directors surveyed said that Sarbanes–Oxley needs to provide better guidance.
* Some 15 percent of the U.S. workforce is affected by workplace alcohol use.
* Employees waste 2.1 hours surfing the Internet each working day.

*Sources:* S. Levy, "The Digit," *Newsweek,* May 15, 2006, p. 18; J. Gordon, "Wasting Time on the Company Dime," *Training,* May 2006, p. 6; "What Directors Know About Their Companies: A McKinsey Survey," *The McKinsey Quarterly Online,* www.mckinseyquarterly. com, March 2006; J. Yang and J. Snider, "Many Support Biometric Technology," *USA Today,* March 30, 2006, p. 1B; J. Yang and K. Simmons, "Top Items Employees Pilfer," *USA Today,* March 29, 2006; J. Yang and M. E. Mullins, "Internet Usage's Impact on Productivity," *USA Today,* March 21, 2006, p. 1B; D. Beucke, "Sore About Sarbox," *BusinessWeek,* March 13, 2006, p. 13; D. Stuckey and S. Ward, "Stealing From Stores," *USA Today,* March 9, 2006, p. 1A; J. Yang and K. Simmons, "Improving Sarbanes–Oxley," *USA Today,* March 7, 2006, p. 1B; "Good News, Bad News from Study on Workplace Alcohol Use," *HR Powerhouse,* www.hrpowerhouse.com, March 1, 2006; and P. J. Lim, "Surf's Up for Workplace Slackers," *US News & World Report,* July 25, 2005, p. 42.

# Thinking About Management Issues

1. What would an organization have to do to change its dominant control approach from bureaucratic to clan? From clan to bureaucratic?

2. In Chapter 13 we discussed the white-water rapids view of change. Do you think it's possible to establish and maintain effective standards and controls in this type of environment? Explain.

3. How could you use the concept of control in your own personal life? Be specific. (Think in terms of feedforward, concurrent, and feedback controls as well as controls for the different areas of your life.)

4. When do electronic surveillance devices such as computers, video cameras, and telephone monitoring step over the line from "effective management controls" to "intrusions on employee rights"?

5. "Every individual employee in the organization plays a role in controlling work activities." Do you agree, or do you think control is something that only managers are responsible for? Explain.

# Working Together: Team-Based Exercise

You're a professor in the School of Accountancy at Collins State College. Several of your colleagues have expressed an interest in developing some specific controls to minimize opportunities for students to cheat on homework assignments and exams. You and some other faculty members have volunteered to write a report outlining some suggestions that might be used.

Form teams of three or four and discuss this topic. Write a bulleted list of your suggestions from the perspective of controlling possible cheating (1) before it happens, (2) while in-class exams or assignments are being completed, and (3) after it has happened. Please keep the report brief (no more than 2 pages). Be prepared to present your suggestions before the rest of the class.

# Ethical Dilemma Exercise

Pornography and offensive e-mail are two major reasons why many companies establish strict policies and monitor their employees' use of the Internet. Citing legal and ethical concerns, managers are determined to keep inappropriate images and messages out of the workplace. In fact, "if we don't make some effort to keep offensive material off our network, we could end up on the wrong end of a sexual harassment lawsuit or other legal action that could cost the company hundreds of thousands of dollars," says a small business manager. Moreover, unauthorized online activity wastes time and ties up network resources. Thus, many companies have systems to screen e-mail messages and monitor employees' Internet activities. With such systems in place, businesses such as the British retailer Harvey Nichols permit employees to surf the Web during lunch or after hours.

Having a clear policy and a monitoring system are only first steps. Employees must be made aware of the rules and see that management is serious about cleaning up any ethics violations. More firms are taking action: According to research, 26 percent of companies have fired employees for inappropriate Internet access and 25 percent have fired employees for misusing e-mail. British Telecom (BT), for example, twice sent e-mails to remind employees they could be fired for viewing online pornography. Despite the warnings, management had to fire

200 employees in an 18-month period. The company also told police about 10 employees' activities, and one has been sentenced to prison. "We took this decision for the good of BT," a spokesperson explains, "and since we have taken this action, the problem has reduced dramatically.[73]

Imagine that you are the administrative assistant for a high-ranking executive at British Telecom. One afternoon you receive an urgent phone call for your boss. You knock on his office door but get no answer, so you open the door, thinking you'll leave a note on his desk. Then you notice that your boss is watching a very graphic adult Web site on his personal laptop. As you quietly back out of the office, you wonder how to handle this situation. Review this chapter's section about workplace concerns as you consider this ethical challenge and decide which of the following options to choose—and why.

**Option A:** Say nothing but anonymously report what you saw by calling BT's ethics hotline as soon possible.

**Option B:** Go back in, interrupt your boss, and explain why you entered. Look pointedly at the laptop screen to show that you're aware of what's been going on.

**Option C:** Knock more loudly to get your boss's attention, wait a moment, and go in and deliver the message without mentioning what you saw.

# Case Application

## Blurred Vision

It's unrealistic to think that all products can be guaranteed 100 percent safe at all times in all places for all people. But as consumers we'd like to believe that manufacturers are doing whatever they can to ensure that products are as safe as possible . . . especially when it comes to products used on or in our bodies that have the potential to do serious harm or damage. And more importantly, we'd like to believe that if manufacturers discovered something potentially wrong with one of their products, that they would take immediate action to correct it. Executives at Bausch & Lomb found themselves dealing with such a scenario as problems with one of its most popular and lucrative products—a contact lens cleaner, ReNu With MoistureLoc®—became more evident.

Doctors in Hong Kong first started noticing cases of a troubling eye infection *Fusarium* keratitis in July of 2005, but were not able to make the connection specifically to Bausch & Lomb's product. Yet, in February of 2006, the company agreed to stop selling that lens cleaner in Hong Kong and Singapore. By March 2006, more than 100 people in Hong Kong, Singapore, and the United States had developed eye infections, "with some of the worst cases requiring cornea transplants," and the connection to the ReNu product was pretty evident. Health officials in Singapore said "they had established a strong statistical connection between Bausch & Lomb's ReNu With MoistureLoc cleaner and *Fusarium* eye fungus infections." But it wasn't until April 13, 2006, after some U.S. retailers independently began removing the product from shelves, that Bausch & Lomb took its first public action—a voluntary market withdrawal—asking retailers to remove the ReNu product from their shelves temporarily until it could further investigate the reports of fungal keratitis infections among contact lens wearers. In open ads in *USA Today* and regional newspapers, the company also recommended that consumers switch to another lens care solution product. Company CEO Ron Zerrella said, "For more than 150 years, Bausch & Lomb's mission has been to enhance your vision. We find ourselves in a position where the safety of one of our products manufactured at our United States plant is in question. We've done a series of exhaustive tests on the product, and a thorough inspection of the plant, and nothing has yet been found to show that *ReNu With MoistureLoc* contributed to these infections in any way. However, in the cases of infections reviewed to date, the majority of patients reported using *ReNu With MoistureLoc* manufactured at our U.S. factory. Bausch & Lomb's first priority is the health and safety of consumers. If there is a problem with our product, we'll find it and we'll fix it."

On May 15, 2006, the company explained that it had "finally, after months of sleuthing, found a link between the product and a potentially blinding eye

infection." In a release by the U.S. Food and Drug Administration, Bausch & Lomb proposed that "unique characteristics of the formulation of the ReNu With MoistureLoc product in certain unusual circumstances can increase the risk of *Fusarium* infection. Based on this scientific data, Bausch & Lomb has decided to permanently remove the ReNu With MoistureLoc product worldwide." Although the company said it moved as "rapidly as possible to understand and respond to its product's role in the outbreak," others say it did not move fast enough to avert a crisis.

## Discussion Questions

1. What role should an organization's control system play in situations like these?

2. Did Bausch & Lomb do enough? Could its control system have been more effective? How?

3. Which type of control—feedforward, concurrent, or feedback—do you think would be most important in this type of situation? Explain your choice.

4. How might immediate corrective action have been used in this situation? How about basic corrective action?

5. What role would information controls play in this situation? Financial controls? Customer interactions?

6. What could other organizations learn from this situation?

*Sources:* K. Bradsher and W. Arnold, "Asian Officials Call Bausch Slow to React," *New York Times Online,* www.nytimes.com, May 22, 2006; B. J. Feder, "From Asia to America: How Bausch's Crisis Grew," *New York Times Online,* www.nytimes.com, May 18 2006; FDA Statement, "Bausch & Lomb Global Recall of ReNu With MoistureLoc Contact Lens Cleaning Solution," www.fda.gov, May 15, 2006; P. Mintz and F. DiMeglio, "Bausch & Lomb: Crisis Management 101," *BusinessWeek Online,* www.businessweek.com, April 17, 2006; and Press Release, Bausch & Lomb, April 13, 2006.

# Learning Outline

*Use this Learning Outline as you read and study this chapter.*

## What Is Operations Management and Why Is It Important?

- Explain what operations management is.
- Contrast manufacturing and services organizations.
- Describe managers' role in improving productivity.
- Discuss the strategic role of operations management.

## Value Chain Management

- Define value chain and value chain management.
- Describe the goal of value chain management.
- Discuss the requirements for successful value chain management.
- Describe the benefits that result from value chain management.
- Explain the obstacles to value chain management.

## Current Issues in Operations Management

- Discuss technology's role in manufacturing.
- Tell some of the various quality dimensions.
- Explain ISO 9000 and Six Sigma.
- Describe mass customization and how operations management contributes to it.

# Operations and Value Chain Management

## A Manager's Dilemma

It's one of the oldest post offices in North America. Sepomex (Servicio Postal Mexicano), Mexico's state postal system, was established over four centuries ago in 1580. In August 1986, it became a semi-independent decentralized organization with the mandate to "serve as the public post office in Mexico." Carlos Rodarte is the head of regional operations for Sepomex, a job that entails many operational challenges.[1]

The Mexican postal system handles some 700 million letters a year, which may sound like a lot. But that number translates into just 7 pieces of mail per person. Compare that to Brazil, where the postal system handles 8 billion mailings a year, or 46 letters per person. It's clear that "Mexico's postal system is under-used by a skeptical public." Data collected by a Mexican polling organization found that "a shocking 29 percent of Mexicans hadn't even heard of Sepomex. Of those familiar with the mail service, 32 percent considered it to be slow and almost the same percentage preferred to use private messengers to hand-deliver documents, a common practice in Latin American cities."

Carlos is trying to improve both the efficiency and the effectiveness of the country's postal system. He oversees Pantaco, the dispatch center where most of the country's mail passes through at some point. He has made improvements there including installing a new roof to make the building look more modern, and investing in cutting-edge technology like security cameras, barcode scanners, and machines that can read and sort 70 letters per minute. In addition, Mexico's Transport and Communications Ministry provided more funds in 2005 to Sepomex, almost doubling capital outlays in 2005. These additional funds will go toward purchasing new vehicles, renovating dilapidated post offices, and making other infrastructure improvements. In addition, one of the things that Carlos does to test his "own company's efficiency" is to send postcards to himself from almost every place he travels. However, there are still operational challenges to tackle, especially in the area of quality.

Put yourself in Carlos's position. What else could he do to successfully implement a quality program?

**What would you do?**

This chapter focuses on the importance of operations management to the organization. Operations management encompasses such topics as productivity, value chain management, e-manufacturing, and quality. As the "Manager's Dilemma" points out, it's important for managers in any type of organization anywhere to have well-thought-out and well-designed operating systems, organizational control systems, and quality programs to survive in the increasingly competitive global environment. If managers have these, their organizations will be able to produce high-quality services and products at prices that meet or beat those of their competitors.

## WHAT IS OPERATIONS MANAGEMENT AND WHY IS IT IMPORTANT?

Inside Intel's factory in New Mexico, employee Trish Roughgarden is known as a "seed"—an unofficial title for technicians who transfer manufacturing know-how from one Intel facility to another.[2] Her job is to make sure that this new factory works just like an identical one that opened eight months earlier in Oregon. Then, in 2003, when a third plant opened in Ireland, several hundred other seeds copied the same techniques. The company's newest facility in Arizona also benefited from "seeding." What the seeds do is part of a major Intel strategy known as "Copy Exactly," which Intel implemented after frustrating variations between factories hurt productivity and product quality. In the intensely competitive chip-making industry, Intel knows that decisions it makes about operations management issues will determine its likelihood of success.

What is **operations management**? The term refers to the design, operation, and control of the transformation process that converts resources into finished goods and services. Exhibit 19–1 portrays, in a very simplified fashion, the fact that every organization has an operations system that creates value by transforming inputs into outputs. The system takes in inputs—people, technology, capital, equipment, materials, and information—and transforms them through various processes, procedures, work activities, and so forth into finished goods and services. (  Go to www.prenhall.com/rolls) And just as every organization produces something, every unit in an organization also produces something. Marketing, finance, research and development, human resources, and accounting convert inputs into outputs such as sales, increased market share, high rates of return on capital, new and innovative products, motivated and committed employees, and accounting reports. As a manager, you'll need to be familiar with operations management concepts regardless of the area you manage in order to achieve your goals efficiently and effectively.

Why is operations management so important to organizations and managers? There are three reasons: It encompasses both services and manufacturing, it's important in effectively and efficiently managing productivity, and it plays a strategic role in an organization's competitive success.

**Q & A**

Understanding this transformation process for a service business may not be totally clear. Check out Q & A 19.1 for an explanation.

Exhibit 19–1

**The Operations System**

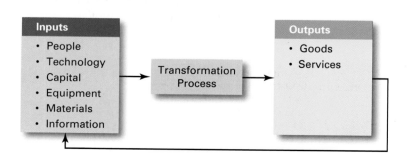

| Inputs | | Outputs |
|---|---|---|
| • People | | • Goods |
| • Technology | Transformation | • Services |
| • Capital | Process | |
| • Equipment | | |
| • Materials | | |
| • Information | | |

## Services and Manufacturing

With a menu that offers over 200 items, The Cheesecake Factory restaurants rely on a finely tuned production system. One food-service consultant says, "They've evolved with this highly complex menu combined with a highly efficient kitchen."[3]

Every organization produces something. Unfortunately, this fact is often overlooked except in obvious cases such as in the manufacturing of cars, cell phones, or lawnmowers. After all, **manufacturing organizations** produce physical goods. It's easy to see the operations management (transformation) process at work in these types of organizations because raw materials are turned into recognizable physical products. But that transformation process isn't as readily evident in **service organizations** because they produce nonphysical outputs in the form of services. For instance, hospitals provide medical and health care services that help people manage their personal health, airlines provide transportation services that move people from one location to another, a cruise line provides a vacation and entertainment service, military forces provide defense capabilities, and the list goes on and on. All these service organizations transform inputs into outputs, although the transformation process isn't as easily recognizable as that of manufacturing organizations. Take a university, for example. University administrators bring together inputs—professors, books, academic journals, technology materials, computers, classrooms, and similar resources—to transform "unenlightened" students into educated and skilled individuals.

The reason we're making this point is that the U.S. economy, and to a large extent the global economy, is dominated by the creation and sale of services. Most of the world's industrialized nations are predominantly service economies. In the United States, for instance, over 78 percent of all economic activity is services and in the European Union, it's nearly 71 percent.[4] Most industrialized countries are over 50 percent; for example, United Kingdom—73 percent; Japan—74 percent; Brazil—51 percent; Russia—60 percent; Germany—70 percent; Canada—69 percent; Australia—70 percent; and Mexico—70 percent.[5]

## Managing Productivity

One jetliner has some 4 million parts. Efficiently assembling such a finely engineered product requires intense focus. Boeing and Airbus, the two major global manufacturers have copied techniques from Toyota. However, not every technique can be copied because airlines demand more customization than do car buyers and there are significantly more rigid safety regulations for jetliners than for cars.[6] At the Evans Findings Company in East Providence, Rhode Island, which makes the tiny cutting devices on dental-floss containers, one production shift each day is run without people.[7] The company's goal is to do as much as possible with no labor. And it's not because they don't care about their employees. Instead, like many U.S. manufacturers, Evans needed to raise productivity in order to survive, especially against low-cost competitors. So they turned to "lights-out" manufacturing where machines are designed to be so reliable that they make flawless parts on their own, without people operating them.

Although most organizations don't make products that have 4 million parts and most organizations can't function without people, improving productivity has become a major goal in virtually every organization. By **productivity**, we mean the overall output of goods or services produced divided by the inputs needed to generate that output. For countries, high productivity can lead to economic growth and

**operations management**
The design, operation, and control of the transformation process that converts resources into finished goods or services.

**manufacturing organizations**
Organizations that produce physical goods.

**service organizations**
Organizations that produce nonphysical outputs in the form of services.

**productivity**
The overall output of goods or services produced divided by the inputs needed to generate that output.

*Improving productivity is a major task in operations management. At BJ's Wholesale Club, managers use high-speed wireless Internet technology, known as "wifi," to send voice messages among far-flung departments in the huge retail stores. "We looked at it more from a productivity standpoint than a cost-savings standpoint," says the firm's vice president of system services.*

**Q & A**

Is productivity an individual or an organizational measure? Q & A 19.2 explains.

development. Employees can receive higher wages and company profits can increase without causing inflation. For individual organizations, increased productivity gives them a more competitive cost structure and the ability to offer more competitive prices.( ◆ Go to www.prenhall.com/rolls)

Over the past decade, U.S. businesses have made dramatic improvements to increase their efficiency. For example, at Latex Foam International's state-of-the-art digital facility in Shelton, Connecticut, engineers can monitor all of the factory's operations. The new facility boosted capacity by 50 percent in a smaller space but with a 30 percent efficiency gain.[8] And it's not just in manufacturing that companies are pursuing productivity gains. At Pella Corporation in Iowa, the purchasing office improved productivity by reducing purchase order entry times anywhere from 50 percent to 86 percent, decreasing voucher processing by 27 percent, and eliminating 14 financial systems. Its information technology department slashed e-mail traffic in half and implemented work design improvements for heavy PC users such as call center users. The human resources department cut the time to process benefit enrollment by 156.5 days. And the finance department now takes 2 days, instead of 6 to do its end-of-month closeout.[9]

Organizations that hope to succeed globally are looking for ways to improve productivity. For example, McDonald's Corporation drastically reduced the amount of time it takes to cook its french fries—now only 65 seconds as compared to the 210 seconds it once took, saving time and other resources.[10] The Canadian Imperial Bank of Commerce, based in Toronto, automated its purchasing function, saving several million dollars annually.[11] And koda, the Czech car company owned by Germany's Volkswagen AG, improved its productivity through an intensive restructuring of its manufacturing process. The company recently produced its 5-millionth car.[12]

**Self-Assessment Library (S.A.L.)**

Do you know what time of day that you're personally most productive? Try S.A.L. #I.E.2 and find out.

Productivity is a composite of people and operations variables.( ◆ Go to www.prenhall.com/rolls) To improve productivity, managers must focus on both. The late W. Edwards Deming, best known as a quality expert, believed that managers, not workers, were the primary source of increased productivity. He outlined 14 points for improving management's productivity (see Exhibit 19–2). A close look at these suggestions reveals Deming's understanding of the interplay between people and operations. High productivity can't come solely from good "people management." The truly effective organization will maximize productivity by successfully integrating people into the overall operations system. For instance, at Simplex Nails Manufacturing in Americus, Georgia, employees were an integral part of the company's much-needed turnaround effort.[13] Some production workers were redeployed on a plant-wide clean-up and organization effort, which freed up floor space. The company's sales force was

Exhibit 19–2

**Deming's 14 Points
for Improving
Management's Productivity**

1. Plan for the long-term future.

2. Never be complacent concerning the quality of your product.

3. Establish statistical control over your production processes and require your suppliers to do so as well.

4. Deal with the best and fewest number of suppliers.

5. Find out whether your problems are confined to particular parts of the production process or stem from the overall process itself.

6. Train workers for the job that you are asking them to perform.

7. Raise the quality of your line supervisors.

8. Drive out fear.

9. Encourage departments to work closely together rather than to concentrate on departmental or divisional distinctions.

10. Do not adopt strictly numerical goals.

11. Require your workers to do quality work.

12. Train your employees to understand statistical methods.

13. Train your employees in new skills as the need arises.

14. Make top managers responsible for implementing these principles.

*Source:* W. E. Deming, "Improvement of Quality and Productivity Through Action by Management," *National Productivity Review,* Winter 1981–1982, pp. 12–22. With permission. Copyright 1981 by Executive Enterprises, Inc., 22 West 21st St., New York, NY 10010-6904. All rights reserved.

retrained and refocused to sell what customers wanted rather than what was in inventory. The results were dramatic. Inventory was reduced by more than 50 percent, the plant had 20 percent more floor space, orders were more consistent, and employee morale improved. Here's a company that recognized the important interplay between people and the operations system.

## Strategic Role of Operations Management

The era of modern manufacturing originated over 100 years ago in the United States, primarily in Detroit's automobile factories. The success that U.S. manufacturers experienced during World War II led manufacturing executives to believe that troublesome production problems had been conquered. These executives focused, instead, on improving other functional areas such as finance and marketing and gave manufacturing little attention.

However, as U.S. executives neglected production, managers in Japan, Germany, and other countries took the opportunity to develop modern, computer-based, and technologically advanced facilities that fully integrated manufacturing operations into strategic planning decisions. The competition's success realigned world manufacturing leadership. U.S. manufacturers soon discovered that foreign goods were being made not only less expensively but also with better quality. Finally, by the late 1970s, U.S. executives recognized that they were facing a true crisis and responded. They invested heavily in improving manufacturing technology, increased the corporate authority and visibility of manufacturing executives, and began incorporating existing and future production requirements into the organization's overall strategic plan. Today, successful organizations recognize the crucial role that operations management plays as part of the overall organizational strategy to establish and maintain global leadership.[14] ( Go to www.prenhall.com/rolls)

Q & A

Operations management issues are vitally important to all kinds of organizations. Why? See Q & A 19.3.

The strategic role that operations management plays in successful organizational performance can be seen clearly as more organizations move toward managing their operations from a value chain perspective, which we're going to discuss next.

## Learning Review

- Explain what operations management is.
- Contrast manufacturing and services organizations.

- Describe managers' role in improving productivity.
- Discuss the strategic role of operations management.

## VALUE CHAIN MANAGEMENT

It's 11 P.M., and you're reading a text message from your parents saying they want to buy you a computer for your birthday this year and to go ahead and order it. You log on to Dell's Web site and configure your dream machine that will serve even your most demanding computing needs for the remainder of your college years. You hit the order button and within 3 or 4 days, your dream computer is delivered to your front door, built to your exact specifications, ready to set up and use immediately to type that management assignment due tomorrow. Or consider Siemens AG's Computed Tomography manufacturing plant in Forcheim, Germany, which has established partnerships with about 30 suppliers. These suppliers are partners in the truest sense as they share responsibility with the plant for overall process performance. This arrangement has allowed Siemens to eliminate all inventory warehousing and has streamlined the number of times paper changes hands to order parts from 18 to one. At the Timken Company's plant in Canton, Ohio, electronic purchase orders are sent across the street to an adjacent "Supplier City" where many of its key suppliers have set up shop. The process takes milliseconds and costs less than 50 cents per purchase order. And when Black & Decker wanted to extend its line of handheld tools to include a glue gun, they chose to totally outsource the entire design and production to the leading glue gun manufacturer. Why? Because they understood that glue guns don't require motors, which was Black & Decker's strong point.[15]

As these examples show, closely integrated work activities among many different players are possible. How? The answer lies in value chain management. The concepts of value chain management are transforming operations management strategies and turning organizations around the world into finely tuned models of efficiency and effectiveness strategically positioned to exploit competitive opportunities as they arise.

### What Is Value Chain Management?

Every organization needs customers if it's going to survive and prosper. Even a not-for-profit organization must have "customers" who use its services or purchase its products. Customers want some type of value from the goods and services they purchase or use, and these end users decide what has value. Organizations must provide that value to attract and keep customers. **Value** is defined as the performance characteristics, features and attributes, and any other aspects of goods and services for which customers are willing to give up resources (usually money). For example, when you purchase Shakira's new CD at Best Buy, a new pair of Australian sheepskin Ugg boots online at the company's Web site, a Wendy's bacon cheeseburger at the drive-through location on campus, or a haircut from your local hair salon, you're exchanging (giving up) money in return for the value you need or desire from these products— providing music during your evening study time, keeping your feet warm *and* fashionable during winter's cold weather, alleviating the lunchtime hunger pangs quickly since your next class starts in 15 minutes, or looking professionally groomed for the job interview you've got next week. Or, using one of our earlier examples, even Siemens AG willingly exchanges money for the value of having reliable supplier relationships. (  Go to www.prenhall.com/rolls)

How *is* value provided to customers? Through transforming raw materials and other resources into some product or service that end users need or desire when,

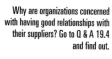

**Q & A**
Why are organizations concerned with having good relationships with their suppliers? Go to Q & A 19.4 and find out.

where, and how they want it. However, that seemingly simple act of turning varied resources into something that customers value and are willing to pay for involves a vast array of interrelated work activities performed by different participants (suppliers, manufacturers, and even customers)—that is, it involves the value chain. The **value chain** is the entire series of organizational work activities that add value at each step from raw materials to finished product. In its entirety, the value chain can encompass the supplier's suppliers to the customer's customer.[16] (  Go to www.prenhall.com/rolls)

Q & A

How does value chain management provide value? Check out Q & A 19.5.

**Value chain management** is the process of managing the sequence of activities and information along the entire product chain. In contrast to supply chain management, which is *internally* oriented and focuses on efficient flow of incoming materials (resources) to the organization, value chain management is *externally* oriented and focuses on both incoming materials and outgoing products and services. (  Go to www.prenhall.com/rolls) Although supply chain management is efficiency oriented (its goal is to reduce costs and make the organization more productive), value chain management is effectiveness oriented and aims to create the highest value for customers.[17]

Q & A

You may think that such close collaboration with outside organizations might give managers LESS control over important work activities. Q & A 19.6 discusses this.

## Goal of Value Chain Management

Who has the power in the value chain? Is it the suppliers providing needed resources and materials? After all, they have the ability to dictate prices and quality. Is it the manufacturer who assembles those resources into a valuable product or service? Their contribution in creating a product or service is quite obvious. Is it the distributor that makes sure the product or service is available where and when the customer needs it? Actually, it's none of these! In value chain management, ultimately customers are the ones with power.[18] They're the ones who define what value is and how it's created and provided. Using value chain management, managers hope to find that unique combination where customers are offered solutions that truly meet their unique needs incredibly fast and at a price that can't be matched by competitors. For example, in an effort to better anticipate customer demand and replenish customer stocks, Shell Chemical Company developed a supplier inventory management order network. The software used in this network allowed managers to track shipment status, calculate safety stock levels, and prepare resupply schedules.

With this in mind then, the goal of value chain management is to create a value chain strategy that meets and exceeds customers' needs and desires and allows for full and seamless integration among all members of the chain. A good value chain is one in which a sequence of participants work together as a team, each adding some component of value—such as faster assembly, more accurate information, better customer response and service, and so forth—to the overall process.[19] The better the collaboration among the various chain participants, the better the customer solutions. When value is created for customers and their needs and desires are satisfied, everyone along the chain benefits. For example, at automotive interior supplier Johnson Controls Inc., managing the value chain started first with improved relationships with internal suppliers, then expanded out to external suppliers and customers. As the company's experience with value chain management intensified and improved, so did its connection with its customers, which ultimately will pay off for all its value chain partners.[20]

## Requirements for Value Chain Management

Q & A

Well...if managing the value chain isn't easy, how do managers ever successfully do so? See Q & A 19.7 for suggestions.

Managing an organization from a value chain perspective isn't easy.(  Go to www.prenhall.com/rolls) Approaches to giving customers what they want that may have worked in the past are likely no longer efficient or effective. Today's dynamic

---

**value**
The performance characteristics, features and attributes, and other aspects of goods and services for which customers are willing to give up resources.

**value chain**
The entire series of organizational work activities that add value at each step from raw materials to finished product.

**value chain management**
The process of managing the sequence of activities and information along the entire product chain.

Q & A
What is a business model? Go to
Q & A 19.8 and find out.

competitive environment demands new solutions from global organizations. Understanding how and why value is determined by the marketplace has led some organizations to experiment with a new business model, a concept we introduced in Chapter 8. ( 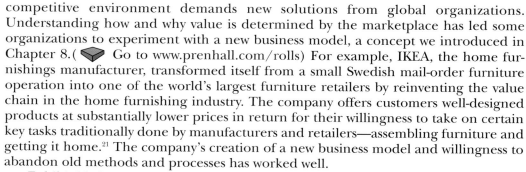 Go to www.prenhall.com/rolls) For example, IKEA, the home furnishings manufacturer, transformed itself from a small Swedish mail-order furniture operation into one of the world's largest furniture retailers by reinventing the value chain in the home furnishing industry. The company offers customers well-designed products at substantially lower prices in return for their willingness to take on certain key tasks traditionally done by manufacturers and retailers—assembling furniture and getting it home.[21] The company's creation of a new business model and willingness to abandon old methods and processes has worked well.

Exhibit 19–3 summarizes the six main requirements of successful value chain management: coordination and collaboration, technology investment, organizational processes, leadership, employees, and organizational culture and attitudes.

**Coordination and Collaboration**   For the value chain to achieve its goal of meeting and exceeding customers' needs and desires, collaborative relationships among all chain participants must exist.[22] Each partner must identify things they may not value but that customers do. And sharing information and being flexible as far as who in the value chain does what are important steps in building coordination and collaboration. This sharing of information and analysis requires more open communication among the various value chain partners. For example, Kraft Foods believes that better communication with customers and with suppliers has facilitated timely delivery of goods and services.[23]

**Technology Investment**   Successful value chain management isn't possible without a significant investment in information technology. The payoff from this investment, however, is that information technology can be used to restructure the value chain to better serve end users. For example, at American Standard's Trane facilities, a comprehensive IT strategy throughout its value chain, which extends globally, has helped it achieve significant work process improvements.[24]

**Organizational Processes**   Value chain management radically changes **organizational processes**—that is, the ways that organizational work is done. When managers decide to manage operations using value chain management, old processes are no longer appropriate. All organizational processes must be critically evaluated from beginning to end to see where value is being added. Non-value-adding activities should be eliminated. Questions such as "Where can internal knowledge be leveraged to improve the flow of material and information?" "How can we better configure our product to satisfy both customers and suppliers?" "How can the flow of material and information be improved?" and "How can we improve customer service?" should be asked for each and every process. For example, when managers at Deere and Company implemented value chain management, a thorough process evaluation revealed that work activities needed to be better synchronized and interrelationships

Exhibit 19–3

**Six Requirements
for Successful Value Chain
Management**

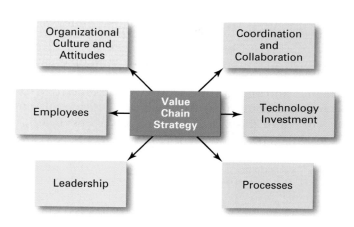

*At the HON Co. in Cedartown, Georgia, over 700 employees make steel and wooden office furniture—desks, file cabinets, bookshelves. Organizational processes are driven by a fast-paced production line that can make the job very demanding, but the company works with employees, like Steven Whatley pictured here, to make processes easier and safer as well as faster and more efficient, even installing custom-designed and ergonomic machine tools where needed.*

between multiple links in the value chain better managed. They changed numerous work processes division-wide in order to do this.[25]

We can make three important conclusions about organizational processes. First, better demand forecasting is necessary *and* possible because of closer ties with customers and suppliers. For example, in an effort to make sure that Listerine was on the store shelves when customers wanted it (known in the retail industry as *product replenishment rates*), Wal-Mart and Pfizer's Consumer Healthcare Group collaborated on improving product demand forecast information. Through their mutual efforts, the partners boosted Wal-Mart's sales of Listerine, an excellent outcome for both supplier and retailer. Customers also benefited because they were able to purchase the product when and where they wanted it.

Second, selected functions may need to be done collaboratively with other partners in the value chain. This collaboration may even extend to sharing employees. For instance, Saint-Gobain Performance Plastics places its own employees in customer sites and brings in employees of suppliers and customers to work on its premises.[26]

Finally, new measures are needed for evaluating performance of various activities along the value chain. Because the goal in value chain management is meeting and exceeding customers' needs and desires, managers need a better picture of how well this value is being created and delivered to customers. For example, when Nestlé USA implemented a value chain management approach, it redesigned its metrics system to focus on one consistent set of measurements—including, among other measures, accuracy of demand forecasts and production plans, on-time delivery, and customer-service levels—that allowed them to more quickly identify problem areas and take actions to resolve them.[27]

**Leadership** Successful value chain management isn't possible without strong and committed leadership. From top organizational levels to lower levels, managers must support, facilitate, and promote the implementation and ongoing practice of value chain management. Managers must make a serious commitment to identifying what value is, how that value can best be provided, and how successful those efforts have been. A culture where all efforts are focused on delivering superb customer value isn't possible without a serious commitment on the part of the organization's leaders.

Also, it's important that managers outline expectations for what's involved in the organization's pursuit of value chain management. Ideally, this should start with a vision or mission statement that expresses the organization's commitment to identifying, capturing, and providing the highest possible value to customers. For instance, when plumbing fixtures company, American Standard, began its pursuit

**organizational processes**
The ways that organizational work is done.

*thinking critically about* **Ethics**

What happens when one partner in the value chain wields its power like a bully? That seems to be an apt description of what some large retailers are doing in the e-commerce arena. Manufacturers are learning that the big retailers—the companies they've always depended on to sell most of their product—can be e-commerce bullies. Instead of the manufacturers using their Web sites to sell products and risk the wrath of their customers (that is, the retailers), most choose to refer potential online buyers to the "dealer nearest you." For example, Newell Rubbermaid had sold an array of its products online. However, its Web site has been stripped of its e-commerce capability. Why? Because of a letter sent by Home Depot to most of its suppliers "suggesting" that they not sell their products to consumers over the Web.

Do you consider such "bully" behavior ethical? Why or why not? Would successful value chain management even be possible given the nature of the relationships here? Explain.

of value chain management, the CEO held dozens of meetings across the United States to explain the new competitive environment and why the company needed to create better working relationships with its value chain partners in order to better serve the needs of its customers.[28]

Then, managers should clarify expectations regarding each employee's role in the value chain. But clear expectations aren't just important for internal partners. Being clear about expectations also extends to external partners. For example, managers at American Standard identified clear requirements for suppliers and were prepared to drop any that couldn't meet them. The company was so serious about its expectations that it did cut hundreds of suppliers from its plumbing, air conditioning, and automotive businesses. The upside, though, was that those suppliers that met the expectations benefited from more business and American Standard had partners willing to work with them in delivering better value to customers.

*managing* **IT**

## IT's Role in Managing the Value Chain

Because value chain management requires such intensive collaboration among partners, getting and sharing information is critical.[29] One type of IT that many value chain partners are finding particularly relevant is RFID or radio-frequency identification. In fact, Wal-Mart has been phasing in an RFID program for its suppliers who must comply by the company's deadlines.

**What Is RFID?** RFID is an automatic identification method in which information can be stored and remotely retrieved. It's similar to, but more sophisticated than, the old familiar bar code. Information is stored on and retrieved from RFID tags (sometimes called *chips*), which are like "little radio towers or transponders that send out information to a reader." An *active* RFID tag has a tiny battery in it that powers the internal circuits that store and send information at a pretty good distance. A *passive* tag has no internal power supply and must be "awakened" by a tag reader in order to send information. The whole RFID system usually requires tags, tag readers, computer servers, and software.

**What Benefits Are There to RFID?** RFID technology has several benefits. First, it has the potential to streamline the supply chain, eliminate theft and waste, and solve logistics

problems. Another benefit is that, unlike bar codes, RFID tags don't have to be in the line of sight to read. (Think about a grocery store checkout where the products have to be directly scanned by a laser.) RFID tags can be read at a distance, even through crates or other packing materials. In addition, RFID tags can be attached to each item in a shipment so that manufacturers, distributors, transportation companies, retailers, and marketers can track individual units across every step of the value chain.

**What Drawbacks Are There to RFID?** The main drawbacks of RFID technology are the cost of the chips, the lack of standardization of chips and the machines that read them, the challenge of analyzing the vast amounts of data that RFID produces, and the privacy concerns of customers.

**How Are Organizations Using RFID?** Many hospitals are experimenting with RFID in patient bracelets that hold medical information and in tracking doctors and nurses so they can be located quickly in an emergency. Law firms, libraries, and research centers are using RFID to track the movement of documents, files, and books within the company. One of the most unusual applications is probably at the University of California, where RFID tags have been inserted into cadavers used for research to prevent the illegal selling of the corpses for profit.

**Employees/Human Resources** We know from our discussions of management theories throughout this textbook that employees are the organization's most important resource. Without employees, there would be no products produced or services delivered—in fact, there would be no organized efforts in the pursuit of common goals. So not surprisingly, employees play an important role in value chain management. The three main human resource requirements for value chain management are flexible approaches to job design, an effective hiring process, and ongoing training.

Flexibility is the key to job design in a value chain management organization. Traditional functional job roles—such as marketing, sales, accounts payable, customer service, and so forth—are inadequate in a value chain management environment. Instead, jobs must be designed around work processes that create and provide value to customers. But it takes more than flexible jobs; flexible employees are needed as well.

In a value chain organization, employees may be assigned to work teams that tackle a given process and may be asked to do different things on different days depending on need. In such an environment where customer value is best delivered through collaborative relationships that may change as customer needs change and where there are no standardized processes or job descriptions, an employee's ability to be flexible is critical. Therefore, the organization's hiring process must be designed to identify those employees who have the ability to learn and adapt.

Finally, the need for flexibility also requires that there be a significant investment in continual and ongoing employee training. Whether training involves learning how to use information technology software, how to improve the flow of materials throughout the chain, how to identify activities that add value, how to make better decisions faster, or how to improve any other number of potential work activities, managers must see to it that employees have the knowledge and tools they need to do their jobs efficiently and effectively.

**Organizational Culture and Attitudes** The last requirement for value chain management is having a supportive organizational culture and attitudes. From our extensive description of value chain management, you could probably guess the type of organizational culture that's going to support its successful implementation! Those cultural attitudes include sharing, collaborating, openness, flexibility, mutual respect, and trust. And these attitudes encompass not only the internal partners in the value chain, but extend to external partners as well.

*To cope with the change that flexible jobs can bring, employees like these may participate in simulations, games, and other kinds of training to learn about and role-play other jobs within their firms. That knowledge in turn makes people more open to adapting their own roles when value chain management practices require it.*

**RFID**
An automatic identification method in which information can be stored and remotely retrieved.

## Benefits of Value Chain Management

Collaborating with external and internal partners in creating and managing a successful value chain strategy requires significant investments in time, energy, and other resources, and a serious commitment by all chain partners. Given this, why would managers ever choose to implement value chain management? A survey of manufacturers noted four primary benefits of value chain management: improved procurement, improved logistics, improved product development, and enhanced customer order management.[30]

## Obstacles to Value Chain Management

As desirable as these benefits may be, managers must deal with several obstacles in managing the value chain including organizational barriers, cultural attitudes, required capabilities, and people (see Exhibit 19–4).

**Organizational Barriers** Organizational barriers are among the most difficult obstacles to handle. These barriers include refusal or reluctance to share information, reluctance to shake up the status quo, and security issues. Without shared information, close coordination and collaboration is impossible. And the reluctance or refusal of employees to shake up the status quo can impede efforts toward value chain management and prevent its successful implementation. Finally, because value chain management relies heavily on a substantial information technology infrastructure, system security and Internet security breaches are issues that need to be addressed.

**Cultural Attitudes** Unsupportive cultural attitudes—especially trust and control—also can be obstacles to value chain management. The trust issue is a critical one, both lack of trust and too much trust. To be effective, partners in a value chain must trust each other. There must be a mutual respect for, and honesty about, each partner's activities all along the chain. When that trust doesn't exist, the partners will be reluctant to share information, capabilities, and processes. But too much trust also can be a problem. Just about any organization is vulnerable to theft of **intellectual property—** that is, proprietary information that's critical to an organization's efficient and effective functioning and competitiveness. And today's increased terrorist threats further illustrate the importance of being able to trust your value chain partners so that you don't compromise your organization's valuable assets.[31] Although value chain partners must trust each other, the potential for theft can be minimized by better understanding each other's operations and by being careful with proprietary intellectual property.

Another cultural attitude that can be an obstacle is the belief that when an organization collaborates with external and internal partners, it no longer controls its own destiny. However, this just isn't the case. Even with the intense collaboration that's so important to value chain management, organizations still control critical decisions such as what customers value, how much value they desire, and what distribution channels are important.[32]

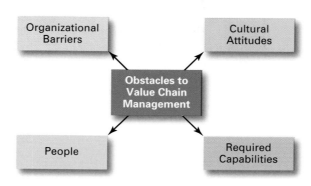

**Required Capabilities** We know from our earlier discussion of requirements for the successful implementation of value chain management that there are numerous capabilities value chain partners need. Several of these—coordination and collaboration, the ability to configure products to satisfy customers and suppliers, and the ability to educate internal and external partners—aren't easy. But they're essential to capturing and exploiting the value chain. Many of the companies we've described throughout this section endured critical, and oftentimes difficult, self-evaluations of their capabilities and processes in order to become more effective and efficient at managing their value chains.

**People** The final obstacles to successful value chain management can be an organization's members. Without their unwavering commitment to do whatever it takes, value chain management won't be successful. If employees refuse to be flexible, it's going to be difficult to make the necessary changes to meet changing situational demands. After all, it's the employees who do the work. If they're not willing to be flexible in their work—how and with whom they work—collaboration and cooperation throughout the value chain will be hard to achieve.

In addition, value chain management takes an incredible amount of time and energy by an organization's employees. Managers must motivate those high levels of effort from employees, not an easy thing to do.

Finally, a major human resource problem is the lack of experienced managers who are able to lead value chain management initiatives. Since it's still not that widespread, there aren't a lot of managers who've done it successfully. However, this hasn't prevented progressive organizations from pursuing the benefits to be gained from value chain management.

## Learning Review

- Define value chain and value chain management.
- Describe the goal of value chain management.
- Discuss the requirements for successful value chain management.

- Describe the benefits that result from value chain management.
- Explain the obstacles to value chain management.

## CURRENT ISSUES IN OPERATIONS MANAGEMENT

Rowe Furniture has an audacious goal: the 10-day sofa. It wants to "become as efficient at making furniture as Toyota is at making cars." Reaching that goal, however, requires revamping its operations management process to exploit technology *and* maintaining quality.[33] Rowe's actions illustrate three of today's most important operations management issues: technology, quality, and mass customization.

### Technology's Role in Operations Management

As we know from our previous discussion of value chain management, today's competitive marketplace has put tremendous pressure on organizations to deliver products and services that customers value in a timely manner. Smart companies are looking at ways to harness technology to improve operations management. Many fast food companies are competing to see who can deliver faster and better service to drive-through customers. With drive-through now representing a huge portion of sales, faster and

**intellectual property**
Proprietary information that's critical to an organization's efficient and effective functioning and competitiveness.

*Computer technology makes it possible for Toyota's digital engineers to simulate assembly-plant processes, troubleshoot them, and share solutions with Toyota plants everywhere, helping maintain the company's reputation for running the most efficient assembly lines in the world.*

better delivery can be a significant competitive edge. For instance, Wendy's International Inc. has added awnings to some of its menu boards and replaced some of the text with pictures. Others use confirmation screens, a technology that helped McDonald's boost accuracy by more than 11 percent. And a new technology used by two national chains tells managers how much food they need to prepare by counting vehicles in the drive-through line and factoring in demand for current promotional and popular staple items.[34]

Although an organization's production activities are being driven by the recognition that the customer is king, managers still need to be more responsive. For instance, operations managers need systems that can reveal available capacity, status of orders, and product quality while products are in the process of being manufactured, not just after the fact. To connect more closely with customers, production must be synchronized across the enterprise. To avoid bottlenecks and slowdowns, the production function must be a full partner in the entire business system.

What's making this type of extensive collaboration possible is technology. Technology is also allowing organizations to control costs particularly in the areas of predictive maintenance, remote diagnostics, and utility cost savings. For instance, how is technology affecting the equipment maintenance function—an important operations management activity? New generations of Internet-compatible equipment contain embedded Web servers that can communicate proactively—that is, if a piece of equipment breaks or reaches certain preset parameters indicating that it's about to break, it can ask for help. But technology can do more than sound an alarm or light up an indicator button. For instance, some devices have the ability to initiate e-mail or signal a pager at a supplier, the maintenance department, or contractor describing the specific problem and requesting parts and service. How much is such e-enabled maintenance control worth? It can be worth quite a lot if it prevents equipment breakdowns and subsequent production downtime.

Managers who understand the power of technology to contribute to more effective and efficient performance know that managing operations is more than the traditional view of simply producing the product. Instead, the emphasis is on working together with all the organization's business functions to find solutions to customers' business problems.

## Quality Initiatives

Quality problems are expensive. For example, even though Apple Computer has had phenomenal success with its iPod, the batteries in the first three versions died after 4 hours instead of lasting the up-to-12 hours that buyers expected. Apple's settlement with consumers is expected to cost as much as $100 million. At Schering-Plough, problems

*If this man does not look familiar, it's probably because Scott Siegel has never won an Academy Award; he owns the company that manufactures the coveted golden statuettes. Each Oscar takes more than a day to make, using the alloy britannia and an electroplated layer of copper, nickel, and silver topped with a hand-dipped finish of 24-karat gold. Quality controls at the plant are stringent. Even the smallest blemish or flaw requires the statuette to be melted down and begun anew.*

with inhalers and other pharmaceuticals were traced to chronic quality control short-comings, for which the company eventually paid a $500 million fine. And the auto industry paid $14.5 billion to cover the cost of warranty and repair work in one recent year.[35]

Many experts believe that organizations unable to produce high-quality products won't be able to compete successfully in the global marketplace. Look back at the "Manager's Dilemma." Even Carlos Rodarte of Sepomex recognizes that he has to improve the quality of his organization's service in order to be efficient and effective. (  Go to www.prenhall.com/rolls)

What is quality? When you consider a product or service to have quality, what does that mean? Does it mean that the product doesn't break or quit working—that is, that it's reliable? Does it mean that the service is delivered in a way that you intended? Does it mean that the product does what it's supposed to do? Or does quality mean something else? Exhibit 19–5 provides a description of several quality dimensions. We're going to define **quality** as the ability of a product or service to reliably do what it's supposed to do and to satisfy customer expectations.

How is quality achieved? That's an issue managers must address. A good way to look at quality initiatives is the management functions—planning, organizing and leading, and controlling—that need to take place.

**Planning for Quality** Managers must have quality improvement goals and strategies and plans formulated to achieve those goals. Goals can help focus everyone's attention toward some objective quality standard. For instance, at Peoria, Illinois–based Caterpillar, its goal is to apply quality improvement techniques to help cut costs.[36] Although this goal is specific and challenging, managers and employees are partnering together to pursue well-designed strategies to achieve the goals, and are confident they can do so.

**Organizing and Leading for Quality** Because quality improvement initiatives are carried out by organizational employees, it's important for managers to look at how they can best organize and lead them. For instance, at the Moosejaw, Saskatchewan, plant of General Cable Corporation, every employee participates in continual quality assurance training. In addition, plant manager Ray Funke believes wholeheartedly in giving employees the information they need to do their jobs better. He says, "Giving people who are running the machines the information is just paramount. You can set up your cellular structure, you can cross-train your people, you can

**Q & A**
Why is quality improvement so important? Q & A 19.9 explains.

**quality**
The ability of a product or service to reliably do what it's supposed to do and to satisfy customer expectations.

Exhibit 19–5

**Quality Dimensions of Goods and Services**

**Product Quality Dimensions**

1. Performance—Operating characteristics
2. Features—Important special characteristics
3. Flexibility—Meeting operating specifications over some period of time
4. Durability—Amount of use before performance deteriorates
5. Conformance—Match with preestablished standards
6. Serviceability—Ease and speed of repair or normal service
7. Aesthetics—How a product looks and feels
8. Perceived quality—Subjective assessment of characteristics (product image)

**Service Quality Dimensions**

1. Timeliness—Performed in promised period of time
2. Courtesy—Performed cheerfully
3. Consistency—Giving all customers similar experiences each time
4. Convenience—Accessibility to customers
5. Completeness—Fully serviced, as required
6. Accuracy—Performed correctly each time

*Sources:* Adapted from J. W. Dean, Jr., and J. R. Evans, *Total Quality: Management, Organization and Society* (St. Paul, MN: West Publishing Company, 1994); H. V. Roberts and B. F. Sergesketter, *Quality Is Personal* (New York: The Free Press, 1993); D. Garvin, *Managed Quality: The Strategic and Competitive Edge* (New York: The Free Press, 1988); and M. A. Hitt, R. D. Ireland, and R. E. Hoskisson, *Strategic Management,* 4th ed. (Cincinnati, OH: SouthWestern, 2001), p. 211.

use lean tools, but if you don't give people information to drive improvement, there's no enthusiasm." Needless to say, this company shares production data and financial performance measures with all employees.[37]

Organizations with extensive and successful quality improvement programs tend to rely on two important people approaches: cross-functional work teams and self-directed or empowered work teams. Because achieving product quality is something that all employees from upper to lower levels must participate in, it's not surprising that quality-driven organizations rely on well-trained, flexible, and empowered employees.

**Controlling for Quality** Quality improvement initiatives aren't possible without having some way to monitor and evaluate their progress. Whether it involves standards for inventory control, defect rate, raw materials procurement, or any other operations management area, controlling for quality is important. For instance, at the Northrup Grumman Corporation plant in Rolling Meadows, Illinois, several quality controls have been implemented, such as automated testing and IT that integrates product design and manufacturing and tracks process quality improvements. Also, employees are empowered to make accept/reject decisions about products throughout the manufacturing process. The plant manager explains, "This approach helps build quality into the product rather than trying to inspect quality into the product." But one of the most important things they do is "go to war" with their customers—soldiers preparing for war or in live combat situations. Again, the plant manager says, "What discriminates us is that we believe if we can understand our customer's mission as well as they do, we can help them be more effective. We don't wait for our customer to ask us to do something. We find out what our customer is trying to do and then we develop solutions."[38]

These types of quality improvement success stories aren't just limited to U.S. operations. For example, at a Delphi assembly plant in Matamoros, Mexico, employees worked hard to improve quality and made significant strides. For instance, the customer reject rate on shipped products is now 10 ppm (parts per million), down from 3,000 ppm—an improvement of almost 300 percent.[39] Quality initiatives at several

Australian companies including Alcoa of Australia, Wormald Security, and Carlton and United Breweries have led to significant quality improvements.[40]And at Valeo Klimasystemme GmbH of Bad Rodach, Germany, assembly teams build different climate-control systems for high-end German cars including the Mercedes E-Class and the BMW 5 Series. Quality initiatives by Valeo's employee teams have led to significant improvements in various quality standards.[41]

## Quality Goals

**Q & A**

Which is better: ISO certification or Six Sigma standards? Check out Q & A 19.10 and see!

To publicly demonstrate their quality commitment, many organizations worldwide have pursued challenging quality goals—the two best-known being ISO 9000 and Six Sigma. (  Go to www.prenhall.com/rolls)

**ISO 9000** ISO 9000 is a series of international quality management standards established by the International Organization for Standardization (www.iso.org), which set uniform guidelines for processes to ensure that products conform to customer requirements. These standards cover everything from contract review to product design to product delivery. The ISO 9000 standards have become the internationally recognized standard for evaluating and comparing companies in the global marketplace. In fact, this type of certification is becoming a prerequisite for doing business globally. Gaining ISO 9000 certification provides proof that a quality operations system is in place.

The latest survey of ISO 9000 certificates showed that the number of registered sites worldwide exceeded 670,000, an increase of almost 35 percent over the previous year.[42] And these certificates had been awarded in 154 countries.

**Six Sigma** Motorola popularized the use of stringent quality standards more than 30 years ago through a trademarked quality improvement program called Six Sigma.[43] Very simply, **Six Sigma** is a quality standard that establishes a goal of no more than 3.4 defects per million units or procedures. What does the name mean? Sigma is the Greek letter that statisticians use to define a standard deviation from a bell curve. The higher the sigma, the fewer the deviations from the norm—that is, the fewer the defects. At One Sigma, two-thirds of whatever is being measured falls within the curve. Two Sigma covers about 95 percent. At Six Sigma, you're about as close to defect-free as you can get.[44] It's an ambitious quality goal! Although it may be an extremely high standard to achieve, many quality-driven businesses are using it and benefiting from it. For instance, General Electric estimates that it has saved billions in costs since 1995, according to company executives.[45] Other well-known companies pursuing Six Sigma include ITT Industries, Dow Chemical, 3M Company, American Express, Sony Corporation, Nokia Corporation, and Johnson & Johnson. Although manufacturers seem to make up the bulk of Six Sigma users, service companies such as financial institutions, retailers, and health care organizations are beginning to apply it. What impact can Six Sigma have? Let's look at an example.

It used to take Wellmark Blue Cross & Blue Shield, a managed-care health care company, 65 days or more to add a new doctor to its medical plans. Now, thanks to Six Sigma, the company discovered that half the processes they used were redundant. With those unnecessary steps gone, the job now gets done in 30 days or less and with reduced staff. The company also has been able to reduce its administrative expenses by $3 million per year, an amount passed on to consumers through lower health premiums.[46]

---

**ISO 9000**
A series of international quality management standards that set uniform guidelines for processes to ensure that products conform to customer requirements.

**Six Sigma**
A quality standard that establishes a goal of no more than 3.4 defects per million parts or procedures.

*Home Depot's CEO Bob Nardelli, shown here with employees celebrating the opening of a New York City store, is a firm believer in the value of Six Sigma, not only for maintaining quality control but also for investing in the company's human capital. How important is quality control in hiring and training? Says Nardelli, "We're only as good as our worst shop assistant. You need to get together a group of people with real leadership skills and put them to work."*

**Summary**  Although it's important for managers to recognize that many positive benefits can accrue from obtaining ISO 9000 certification or Six Sigma, the key benefit comes from the quality improvement journey itself. In other words, the goal of quality certification should be having work processes and an operations system in place that enable organizations to meet customers' needs and employees to perform their jobs in a consistently high-quality way.

## Mass Customization

The term "mass customization" seems an oxymoron. However, the design-to-order concept is becoming an important operations management issue for today's managers. **Mass customization** provides consumers with a product when, where, and how they want it.[47] Companies as diverse as BMW, Ford, Levi Strauss, Wells Fargo, Mattel, and Dell Computer are adopting mass customization to maintain or attain a competitive advantage. Mass customization requires flexible manufacturing techniques and continual customer dialogue.[48] Technology plays an important role in both.

With flexible manufacturing, companies have the ability to quickly readjust assembly lines to make products to order. Using technology such as computer-controlled factory equipment, intranets, industrial robots, barcode scanners, digital printers, and logistics software, companies can manufacture, assemble, and ship customized products with customized packaging to customers in incredibly short timeframes. Dell Computer is a good example of a company that uses flexible manufacturing techniques and technology to custom-build computers to customers' specifications.

*becoming* a Manager

✓ As you interact with various businesses, think about the value chain of each.

✓ Read about quality management techniques.

✓ Think of ways that you could (1) be more productive and (2) have higher quality output.

✓ Take advantage of mass customization opportunities and assess what was positive and negative about the experience.

Self-Assessment
Library (S.A.L.)

✓  Go to www.prenhall.com/rolls and complete the following exercise from the Self-Assessment Library: S.A.L. #I.E.2—What Time of Day Am I Most Productive?

Technology also is important in the continual dialogue with customers. Using extensive databases, companies can keep track of customers' likes and dislikes. And the Internet has made it possible for companies to have ongoing dialogues with customers to learn about and respond to their exact preferences. For instance, on Amazon's Web site, customers are greeted by name and can get personalized recommendations of books and other products. The ability to customize products to a customer's desires and specifications starts an important relationship between the organization and the customer. If the customer likes the product and it provides value, he or she is more likely to be a repeat customer.

# Learning Review

- Discuss technology's role in manufacturing.
- Tell some of the various quality dimensions.
- Explain ISO 9000 and Six Sigma.

- Describe mass customization and how operations management contributes to it.

# Managers Respond to a Manager's Dilemma

## Christy Wood

Manager of Compliance, MarkWest Hydrocarbon, Inc., Englewood, CO

Although Carlos has invested in upgrades and new equipment to improve quality at Sepomex, no analysis has been performed to determine what the issues are and how they should be addressed. His first step should be to identify the customers' expectations. This, of course, means reasonable expectations of performance for a fair price. Once he understands what is required, he should then develop a detailed understanding of the process, or processes, used to handle mail. This can be done through interviews with each person responsible for a part of the process. The process should then be documented using a flowchart or other form of documentation. The next step is to develop measurements. Two types of measurements are used; one type measures the end result of the process. The other provides warning flags when the process is not working as expected and the organization could be prevented from meeting their goal. After collecting the measurement data over a period of time, Carlos can determine areas within the process that need improvement. At this point, he can identify enhancements that would result in process improvement. After implementing the changes, the process should continue to be measured to ensure the expected results. If the process performs as expected, Carlos can then replicate the process in other facilities.

**mass customization**
Providing consumers with a product when, where, and how they want it.

# Learning Summary

## What Is Operations Management and Why Is It Important?

**Operations management:** the design, operation, and control of the transformation process that converts resources into finished goods and services. It's important because:

1. It's used in both services and manufacturing organizations
   - **Manufacturing organizations** produce physical goods
   - **Service organizations** produce nonphysical outputs (services)
2. It's necessary for effectively and efficiently managing productivity
   - **Productivity:** the overall output of goods or services produced divided by the inputs needed to generate that output
3. It plays a strategic role in an organization's competitive success

*What is the goal of value chain management?*

**Value:** the performance characteristics, features and attributes, and other aspects of goods and services for which customers are willing to give up resources

**Value chain:** the entire series of work activities that add value at each step from raw materials to finished product

**Value chain management:** the process of managing the sequence of activities and information along the entire product chain

- The goal of value chain management is to create a value chain strategy that meets and exceeds customers' needs and desires and allows for full and seamless integration among all members of the value chain

## What Does Value Chain Management Require?

- Collaborative relationships among all chain participants
- Investment in technology
- Integrated organizational processes
- Strong, committed leadership
- Flexible and committed employees
- Appropriate culture and attitudes

## What Obstacles Are There to Value Chain Management?

- Organizational barriers (refusal to share information, reluctance to shake up status quo, and security issues)
- Unsupportive cultural attitudes (mistrust, too controlling, or fear of giving up control)
- Required capabilities lacking
- People (uncommitted, refusal to be flexible, unmotivated, lack of experienced managers)

## What Current Operations Management Issues Do Managers Face?

There are three important current issues:

- Technology
  - Enables extensive involvement and collaboration
  - Helps control costs
- **Quality:** the ability of a product or service to reliably do what it's supposed to do and to satisfy customer expectations
  - Quality is achieved by planning and organizing it, leading quality improvement activities, and controlling it
  - Quality goals include Six Sigma and ISO 9000
    - **ISO 9000:** a series of international quality management standards established by the International Organization for Standardization, which set uniform guidelines for processes to ensure that products conform to customer specifications

- **Six Sigma:** a quality standard that establishes a quality goal of no more than 3.4 defects per million units or procedures
- Mass customization: provides customers with a product when, where, and how they want it
  - Requires both flexible manufacturing techniques and continual customer dialogue
  - Technology plays an important role

## Management: By the Numbers

- *Industry Week's* best manufacturing plants finalists have 99.98 percent (near-perfect) delivery performance.
- One hundred percent of these best plants use just-in-time inventory systems with their suppliers.
- Almost 90 percent of these best plants use **cellular manufacturing**, which is an approach to manufacturing that uses work cells or groups of workstations to process products progressively.
- Almost 3.5 percent of sales are lost each year due to information inefficiencies in value chains.

- Almost 32 percent of manufacturing plants provide more than 20 hours of annual formal training to employees.
- More than 24 percent of manufacturing plant employees are in empowered or self-managed work teams.

*Sources:* G. Taninecz, "Long-Term Commitments," *Industry Week,* February 2004, pp. 51–54; J. Teresko, "Benefiting from Synchronized Data," *Industry Week,* November 2003, p. 12; and "Lean Manufacturing: The Why and How," *Industry Week,* October 2003, p. 76.

## Thinking About Management Issues

1. Do you think that manufacturing or service organizations have the greater need for operations management? Explain.

2. How might operations management apply to other managerial functions besides control?

3. How could you use value chain management concepts in your everyday life?

4. Which is more critical for success in organizations: continuous improvement or quality control? Support your position.

5. Choose some large organization that you're interested in studying. Research this company to find out what types of operations management strategies it is using. Focus on describing what it's doing that's unusual or effective or both.

## Working Together: Team-Based Exercise

Break into groups of four or five students. Your team's task is to assess how you believe technology will change the way your college disseminates information to students a decade from now. Specifically, what do you believe the typical college's teaching technologies will look like in the year 2015. Here are some questions to consider:

1. Will there still be a need for a college campus spanning several hundred acres?

2. Do you believe every student will be required to have a laptop for classes?

3. How, if at all, will technology change the classroom?

4. Do you believe students will be required to physically come to campus for their classes?

5. What role will distance learning and telecommuting play in classroom activities? You have 30 minutes to discuss these issues and develop your responses. Appoint someone on your team to present your team's findings to the class.

**cellular manufacturing**
An approach to manufacturing that uses work cells or groups of workstations to process products progressively.

# Ethical Dilemma Exercise

When should a company make public a quality problem that could put lives at stake? This was the situation facing Guidant Corporation, which makes implantable defibrillators to regulate patients' heartbeats. When executives learned that some units had failed because of short-circuiting, they waited to notify doctors for two reasons. First, they worried about the risks to which patients would be exposed when undergoing surgery to replace the defibrillators. Second, they initially thought the problem affected only a small number of units.

Month after month, management studied the data that flowed in and debated what to do. Finally the *New York Times* reported that Guidant had been aware of the problem for three years—without telling doctors or patients. As the Food and Drug Administration began a probe, Guidant quickly recalled more than 100,000 units, redesigned the products, and alerted doctors about the problem, by then linked to at least seven deaths. The company's reputation was damaged: A number of doctors told sales reps they had stopped implanting Guidant's devices because they questioned the company's ethics. At management's request, medical experts investigated and concluded that Guidant's products were generally reliable. They also recommended that doctors be involved in recall decisions because of the serious consequences. Now

Guidant, along with its biggest competitors, works closely with independent medical panels when assessing product safety.[49]

Imagine you're a senior product manager working for Boston Scientific, Guidant's parent company. You get a call from a sales rep who has heard about a problem with a new Guidant product. Knowing how the product works, you're certain the problem is not a matter of life and death. It's your job to recommend how the company should proceed. Review Exhibit 19–5 as you consider this ethical dilemma and choose one of the following options.

**Option A:** Recommend referring the matter to Guidant's medical panel and notifying doctors and patients later, after the cause of the problem has been pinpointed.

**Option B:** Recommend referring the matter to Guidant's medical panel and temporarily halting sales of the product until the problem has been studied in detail.

**Option C:** Recommend privately informing doctors that the problem is minor and launching an internal investigation before involving the medical panel in a larger review.

# Case Application

### Behind the Scenes When the Sun Goes Down

You've probably never really thought about the operations management activities and processes that go on behind the scenes of a major concert tour. However, Kenny Chesney's *Somewhere in the Sun* 2005 tour provides a fun—and unusual—look at efficient and effective operations management.

Like any profit-oriented business that produces a product, Chesney's tour required both people and operations variables (including equipment and inventory) to be brought together in the right numbers, at the right

places, and at the right times. Let's look behind the scenes to see how the magic happened!

Planning for the *Somewhere in the Sun* tour began a year ahead of time. Chesney and his production manager made a pen-and-paper sketch of how they envisioned the stage. Some of the design goals included big amplifiers, vertical screens, and a clean rock 'n' roll look. Once the final computer renderings were finished, it took 5 months to prepare all the components of the set—mainly lighting and sound because Chesney wanted to keep the stage set design simple. One month before the tour began, Chesney sat down with the lighting director to ensure that the lights projected the right colors and desired effects for each song.

So what did the stage set consist of? Some of the physical components included 30-foot-tall speakers, of which the main column composed of 16 speakers provided the majority of the sound coverage; interior and exterior LCD monitors that provided show performance close-ups of Chesney and the audience; 175 stage and 28 remote lights that add visual effects to the performance; and of course, computers, which were used to control all the amplifiers and lights. Although the stage equipment and inventory were impressive enough in themselves, it was the people who also had a role in making it all happen.

Shows that took place in arenas (which typically hold about 20,000 people) took a day for some 200 people to

*Country music star Kenny Chesney on tour.*

set up (stage, lighting, and sound). But it was the 3 stadium concerts that were the true test of the operational skills of the people behind the scenes. The stadiums (most of which would hold about 55,000 fans) took 5 days to set up the 50 truckloads of equipment. Even an engineer was brought in to measure the distance from the stage to different points in the stadium and then these measurements were used to determine the angle at which to hang speakers for maximum sound quality.

In March 2005, the sold-out tour began and proved to be a resounding success! It ranked as one of the top grossing tours for 2005. And the fun continues! Chesney's *The Road & The Radio Tour* is off to a fantastic start—undoubtedly with a strong dose of operations management behind the scenes as the sun goes down.

## Discussion Questions

1. Using Exhibit 19–1, describe the operations system for the *Somewhere in the Sun* tour.

2. Would quality be important to a concert tour? How might the tour manager plan, organize, lead, and control for quality? Explain.

3. How might value chain management be useful in this type of organizational setting? Explain.

4. Would productivity measures be important to a concert tour? How might productivity be measured in this type of organizational setting?

*Sources:* News Release, "Kenny Is One of the Top Grossing Tours for 2005," Kenny Chesney Web site, www.kenneychesney.com, January 5, 2006; and A. Umminger and F. Pomma, "Chesney's Stadium Concerts Super-Size Sight and Sound," *USA Today,* July 6, 2005, p. 6D.

# Part Six

# You're the Manager: Putting Ethics into Action

*As a manager, you'll often face decisions involving ethical questions. How can you learn to identify an ethical dilemma, keep stakeholders in mind, think through the alternatives, and foresee the consequences of your decisions? This unique interactive feature, positioned at the end of Parts 2, 3, 4, 5, and 6, casts you in the role of a manager dealing with hypothetical yet realistic ethical issues. To begin, read the preview paragraph below. Then log onto www.prenhall.com/rolls to consider the decisions you would make in the role of manager.*

Although product flaws are never good news, they're especially unwelcome in medical devices. As a precaution,

Boston Scientific and other manufacturers of heart devices maintain patient databases in case they must notify people about potential problems with these life-saving products. In this hypothetical scenario, you play the role of a Boston Scientific product manager. An unauthorized person— probably a dishonest employee—has just broken into Boston Scientific's patient database. Despite numerous security safeguards, you fear that names, addresses, Social Security numbers, and other personal information may have been stolen and used for fraudulent purposes. What ethical dilemmas will you face as you decide how to proceed? Log onto www.prenhall.com/rolls to put ethics into action!

# Passport

### Scenario 1

Nelson Naidoo is vice president of logistics for Diamonds International, a global exporter of high-quality colored diamonds based in Johannesburg, South Africa. Nelson oversees the company's shipping and transportation to the company's other facilities in Rio de Janeiro, New York, Lisbon, and Moscow. It's the Rio facility where Nelson is currently having a problem.

Tatiana Mercado is the logistics manager in Rio and has been employed by Diamonds International for a year. The company's top managers believe strongly in employee job training, and Tatiana has been well trained in the company's procedures for accepting and checking in new inventory. But for the last two shipments, Tatiana's paperwork has been missing some key pieces of information. Because of the dollar value involved in the product shipments, Nelson flies to Rio tomorrow to discuss the problems with Tatiana. What will be the best approach for Nelson to handle this situation? He doesn't really want to fire Tatiana as her previous job performance had been good. But how can he ensure that the problems get resolved and don't happen again?

*To answer these questions, you'll have to do some research on the countries. Go to www.prenhall.com/rolls and click on Passport. When the map appears, click on the countries you need to research. You'll find background information on the country and general information about the country's economy, population, and workforce. In addition, you'll find specific information on the country's culture and the unique qualities associated with doing business there.*

### Scenario 2

Kristen Mesicek is the product quality manager for Global One Cellular, a cell phone distributor based in San Diego, California. Global One imports cellular phone components from China and assembles them at a facility in Guadalajara, Mexico. Once assembled, the cell phones

are shipped to customers around the world. Global One's phones are known for their reliability and durability, a reputation that isn't easy to get in this intensely competitive market.

Carlos Lopez, the operations manager in Guadalajara, had alerted Kristen last week that the last 7 shipments of cell phone components from the Chinese manufacturer had serious quality problems and 15 percent of the product components had to be discarded. Because of the cost involved, Kristen knew she needed to attend to the problem immediately.

Kristen has scheduled a videoconference for tomorrow with Carlos and with the Chinese plant manager, Dai Tan, to get the problems resolved. What cross-cultural issues might Kristen run into as she attempts to get this quality control problem fixed? How can she make sure the problem is fixed and minimize the potential recurrence of the problem?

*To answer these questions, you'll have to do some research on the countries. Go to www.prenhall.com/rolls and click on Passport. When the map appears, click on the countries you need to research. You'll find background information on the country and general information about the country's economy, population, and workforce. In addition, you'll find specific information on the country's culture and the unique qualities associated with doing business there.*

### Scenario 3

From his office on the 28th floor of the UOB Plaza One in Singapore, Danny Lim was enjoying the view out his window and contemplating his upcoming trip to Italy. He had been out of school for about 5 years after graduating with a degree in operations and materials management from the University of Florida. Now with the problem he was facing, Danny wished he had paid more attention in his management classes when the topic of cross-cultural characteristics had been discussed.

As the vice president of quality assurance for 88WebCom, a telecommunications company, Danny had final responsibility for the products his company sold around the world. And over the last month, there had been some major problems with the company's personal communication devices reported to the customer service department. An assessment of the situation revealed that all these products had been manufactured in the company's facility in Genoa, Italy. Since he felt that this was something that needed to be addressed in person and not over the phone, Danny was making a trip to meet with the plant manager, Delia Moretti, to come up with an action plan. What will be the best approach for Danny to handle this situation? Whatever plan they develop will have to take into account the facility's Italian workforce and what they will be willing to do to get the quality control problem fixed. What cultural issues should Danny be aware of? How might these affect any action plan that is developed?

*To answer these questions, you'll have to do some research on the countries. Go to www.prenhall.com/rolls and click on Passport. When the map appears, click on the countries you need to research. You'll find background information on the country and general information about the country's economy, population, and workforce. In addition, you'll find specific information on the country's culture and the unique qualities associated with doing business there.*

# Continuing Case

## Starbucks—Controlling

Once managers have established goals and plans, organized and structured work activities, and developed programs to motivate and lead people to put forth effort to accomplish those goals, the manager's job is not done. Quite the opposite! Managers must now monitor work activities to make sure they're being done as planned and correct any significant deviations. This process is called *controlling*. It's the final link in the management process, and although controlling happens last in the process, that doesn't make it any less important than any of the other managerial functions. At Starbucks, managers control various functions, activities, processes, and procedures to ensure that desired performance standards are achieved at all organizational levels.

## Controlling the Coffee Experience

Why has Starbucks been so successful? Although there are many factors that have contributed to its success, one significant factor has been its ability to provide customers with a unique product of the highest quality delivered with exceptional service. Everything that each Starbucks' partner does, from top level to bottom level, contributes to the company's ability to do that efficiently and effectively. And managers need controls in place to help monitor and evaluate what's being done and how it's being done. Starbuck's managers use different types of controls to ensure that Starbucks remains, as its mission states, "the premier purveyor of the finest coffee in the world while maintaining our uncompromising principles as we grow." These controls include transactions controls, security controls, employee controls, and organizational performance controls.

A legal recruiter stops by Starbucks on her way to her office in downtown Chicago and orders her daily Caffè Mocha tall. A construction site supervisor pulls into the drive-through line at the Starbucks store in Rancho Cucamonga, California, for a cinnamon chip scone and grande Caffè Americano. It's 11 P.M. and, needing a break from studying for her next-day's management exam, a student heads to the local Starbucks for a tasty treat—a banana coconut Frappuccino® blended coffee. Now she's ready again to tackle that chapter material on managerial controls.

Every single day, an average of 636 transactions just like these happen at every Starbucks store. Worldwide, about 34 million transactions take place each week. The average sale per transaction is $4.05. These transactions between partners (employees) and customers—the exchange of products for money—are the major source of sales revenue for Starbucks. Measuring and evaluating the efficiency and effectiveness of these transactions for both walk-in customers and customers at drive-through windows is important. As Starbucks has been doing walk-in transactions for a number of years, numerous procedures and processes are in place to make those transactions go smoothly. However, as Starbucks adds more drive-through windows, the focus of the transaction is on being fast as well as on quality, a different metric than for walk-in transactions. When a customer walks into a store and orders, he can step aside while the order is being prepared; that's not possible in a drive-through line. Recognizing these limitations, the company is taking steps to improve its drive-through service. For instance, digital timers are placed where employees can easily see them to measure service times; order confirmation screens are used to help keep accuracy rates high; and additional pastry racks have been conveniently located by the drive-through windows.

Security is also an important issue for Starbucks. Keeping company assets (such as people, equipment, products, financial information, and so forth) safe and secure requires security controls. The company's written Standards of Business Conduct document states, "Starbucks is committed to providing all partners with a clean, safe and healthy work environment. To achieve this goal, we must recognize our shared responsibilities to follow all safety rules and practices, to cooperate with officials who enforce those rules and practices, to take necessary steps to protect ourselves and other partners, to attend required safety training and to report immediately all accidents, injuries and unsafe practices or conditions." When hired, each partner is provided with a Safety, Security, and Health Standards manual and trained on the requirements outlined in the manual. In addition, managers receive ongoing training about these issues and are expected to keep employees trained and up-to-date on any changes. And at any time, any partner can contact the Partner & Asset Protection department for information and advice.

One security area that has been particularly important to Starbucks has been with its gift cards, in which it does an enormous volume of business. (Review the data in the continuing case at the end of Part 3 for this information.) With these gift cards, there are lots of opportunities for an unethical employee to "steal" from the company. The company's director of compliance says that "detecting such fraud can be difficult because there is no visibility from an operations standpoint." However, Starbucks uses transactional data analysis technology to detect multiple card redemptions in a single day and has identified other "telltale" activities that pinpoint possible fraud. When the company's technology detects transaction activity outside the norm, Starbucks' corporate staff is alerted and a panel of company experts reviews the data. Investigators have found individuals at stores who confess to stealing as much as $42,000. When smaller exceptions are noted, the individuals are sent letters asking them to explain what's going on. The director of compliance says, "I view this as a gentle touch on the shoulder saying we can see what is happening." Employees who have been so "notified" often quit.

Starbucks' part-time and full-time hourly partners are the primary—and most important—source of contact between the company and the customer, and outstanding customer service is a top priority at Starbucks. The Standards of Business Conduct document states, "We strive to make every customer's experience pleasant and fulfilling, and we treat our customers as we treat one another, with respect and dignity." What kinds of employee controls does Starbucks use to ensure that this happens? Partners are trained in and are required to follow all proper procedures relating to the storage, handling, preparation, and service of Starbucks' products. In addition, partners are told to notify their managers immediately if they see anything that suggests a product may pose a danger to the health or safety of themselves or of customers. Partners also are taught the warning signs associated with possible workplace violence and how to reduce their vulnerability if faced with a potentially violent situation. In either circumstance where product or partner safety and security are threatened, store managers have been trained as far as the appropriate steps to take if such a situation occurs.

The final types of control that are important to Starbucks' managers are the organizational performance and financial controls. Starbucks uses the typical financial control measures, but also looks at growth in sales at stores open at least one year as a performance standard. One issue with which company executives are dealing is that store operating costs have increased. One contributing factor is the health care packages offered to every worker who puts in 20 hours a week. Another factor is that, as the company continues to expand, there are more employees. However, CEO Jim Donald is not too worried at this point. He says, "No problem. We could tighten this thing up at a moment's notice, but we're a growing business. Instead, the trick is basic retailing—sell more stuff at more stores." There's a fine balance the company has to achieve between keeping costs low and keeping quality

high. However, there are steps the company has taken to control costs. For instance, new thinner garbage bags will save the company half a million dollars a year.

In addition to the typical financial measures, corporate governance procedures and guidelines are an important part of Starbucks' financial controls as they are at any public corporation that's covered by Sarbanes-Oxley legislation. The company has identified guidelines for its board of directors with respect to responsibilities, processes, procedures, and expectations.

## Starbucks' Value Chain: From Bean to Cup

The steaming cup of coffee placed in a customer's hand at any Starbucks' store location starts as coffee beans (berries) plucked from fields of coffee plants. From harvest to storage to roasting to retail to cup, Starbucks understands the important role each participant in its value chain plays.

Starbucks offers a selection of coffees from around the world, and its coffee buyers personally travel to the coffee-growing regions of Latin America, Africa/Arabia, and Asia/Pacific in order to select and purchase the highest-quality *arabica* beans. Once the beans arrive at any one of the four roasting facilities (in Washington, Pennsylvania, Nevada, or Amsterdam), Starbucks' master professional roasters do their "magic" in creating the company's rich signature roast coffee, a process that's the "cumulative result of expert roasters knowing coffee and bringing balance to all of its flavor attributes." There are many potential challenges to "transforming" the raw material into the quality product and experience that customers have come to expect at Starbucks. Weather, shipping and logistics, technology, political instability, and so forth all could potentially impact what Starbucks is in business to do.

One issue of great importance to Starbucks is environmental protection. Starbucks has taken actions throughout its entire supply chain to minimize its "environmental footprint." For instance, suppliers are asked to sign a Supplier

Code of Conduct that deals with business standards and practices that "produce social, environmental, and economic benefits for the communities where Starbucks does business." Even company stores are focused on the environmental impact of their store operations. Partners at stores around the world have found innovative ways to reuse coffee grounds. For example, in Japan, a team of Starbucks partners realized that coffee grounds could be used as an ingredient to make paper. A local printing company uses this paper to print the official Starbucks Japan newsletter. In Bahrain, partners dry coffee grounds in the sun, package them, and give them to customers as fertilizer for house plants.

## Discussion Questions

1. What control criteria might be useful to a retail store manager? What control criteria might be appropriate for a barista at one of Starbucks' retail stores (walk-in only)? How about for a store that has a drive-through window?

2. What types of feedforward, concurrent, and feedback controls does Starbucks use? Are there others that might be important to use? If so, describe.

3. What "red flags" might indicate significant deviations from standard for (a) an hourly employee; (b) a store manager; (c) a district manager; (d) the executive vice president of finance; and (e) the CEO? Are there any similarities? Why or why not?

4. Would it be easy to keep costs low and quality high? Discuss.

5. Evaluate the control measures Starbucks is using with its gift cards from the standpoint of the three steps in the control process.

6. Using the company's most current financial statements, calculate the following financial ratios: current, debt to assets, inventory turnover, total asset turnover, profit margin on sales, and return on investment. What do these ratios tell managers?

7. Describe and evaluate Starbucks' operations in terms of the service profit chain illustrated in Exhibit 18–16.

8. Would you describe Starbucks' production/operations technology in its retail stores as unit, mass, or process? How about in its roasting plants? Explain. (Hint: You might need to review material in Chapter 10, as well, in order to answer this question.)

9. Describe the things Starbucks is doing to manage its value chain. Are these activities appropriate? Why or why not?

10. Can Starbucks manage the uncertainties in its value chain? If so, how? If not, why not?

11. Go to the company's Web site [www.starbucks.com] and find the information on the company's environmental activities from bean to cup. Select one of the steps in the chain (or your professor may assign one). Describe and evaluate what environmental actions it's taking. How might these affect the planning, organizing, and leading that take place in these areas?

12. Look at the company's mission and Guiding Principles. How might these affect the way Starbucks controls? How do the ways Starbucks controls contribute to the attainment or pursuit of these?

# Appendix A

# Learning Outline

*Use this Learning Outline as you read and study this appendix.*

## The Context of Entrepreneurship

- Differentiate between entrepreneurial ventures and small businesses.
- Explain why entrepreneurship is important in the United States and globally.
- Describe the four key steps in the entrepreneurial process.
- Explain what entrepreneurs do.
- Discuss why social responsibility and ethics are important considerations for entrepreneurs.

## Start-Up and Planning Issues

- Discuss how opportunities are important to entrepreneurial ventures.
- Describe each of the seven sources of potential opportunity.
- Explain why it's important for entrepreneurs to understand competitive advantage.
- List possible financing options for entrepreneurs.
- Describe the six major sections of a business plan.

## Organizing Issues

- Contrast the six different forms of legal organization.
- Describe the organizational design issues that entrepreneurs face.
- Discuss the unique human resource management issues entrepreneurs face.
- Describe what an innovation-supportive culture looks like.

## Leading Issues

- Explain what personality research shows about entrepreneurs.
- Discuss how entrepreneurs can empower employees.
- Explain how entrepreneurs can be effective at leading employee work teams.

## Controlling Issues

- Describe how entrepreneurs should plan, organize, and control growth.
- Describe the boiled frog phenomenon and why it's useful for entrepreneurs.
- Discuss the issues an entrepreneur needs to consider when deciding whether to exit the entrepreneurial venture.

# Managing Entrepreneurial Ventures

## THE CONTEXT OF ENTREPRENEURSHIP

Russell Simmons is an entrepreneur.[1] He co-founded Def Jam Records because the emerging group of New York hip-hop artists needed a record company, and the big record companies refused to take a chance on unknown artists. Def Jam was just one piece of Simmons's corporation, Rush Communications, which also included a management company; a clothing company called Phat Farm; a movie production house; television shows; a magazine; and an advertising agency. In 1999, Simmons sold his stake in Def Jam to Universal Music Group, and in 2004, he sold Phat Farm. *Inc.* magazine has named Simmons one of America's 25 Most Fascinating Entrepreneurs.

In this appendix on entrepreneurship, we're going to look at the activities engaged in by entrepreneurs like Russell Simmons. We'll start by looking at the context of entrepreneurship and then examining entrepreneurship from the perspective of the four managerial functions: planning, organizing, leading, and controlling.

### What Is Entrepreneurship?

**Entrepreneurship** is the process of starting new businesses, generally in response to opportunities. Entrepreneurs are pursuing opportunities by changing, revolutionizing, transforming, or introducing new products or services. For example, Hong Liang Lu of UTStarcom knew that less than 10 percent of the Chinese population was served by a land-line phone system and service was very poor.[2] He decided that wireless technology might be the answer. Now, his company's inexpensive cell phone service is a hit in China with more than 66 million subscribers and growing. Looking to continue his success, Lu's company is moving into other markets including Africa, Southeast Asia, India, and Panama.

Many people think that entrepreneurial ventures and small businesses are one and the same, but they're not. There are some key differences between the two. Entrepreneurs create **entrepreneurial ventures**—organizations that pursue opportunities, are characterized by innovative practices, and have growth and profitability as their main goals. On the other hand, a **small business** is one that is independently owned, operated, and financed; has fewer than 100 employees; doesn't necessarily engage in any new or innovative practices, and has relatively little impact on its industry.[3] A small business isn't necessarily entrepreneurial because it's small. To be entrepreneurial means that the business must be innovative, seeking out new opportunities. Even though entrepreneurial ventures may start small, they pursue growth. Some new small firms may grow, but many remain small businesses, by choice or by default.

### Why Is Entrepreneurship Important?

Entrepreneurship is, and continues to be, important to every industry sector in the United States and in most advanced countries.[4] Its importance in the United States can be shown in three areas: innovation, number of new start-ups, and job creation.

*Innovation.* Innovating is a process of changing, experimenting, transforming, revolutionizing, and a key aspect of entrepreneurial activity. The "creative destruction" process that characterizes innovation leads to technological changes and employment growth. Entrepreneurial firms act as "agents of change" by providing an essential source

---

**entrepreneurship**
The process of starting new businesses, generally in response to opportunities.

**entrepreneurial ventures**
Organizations that are pursuing opportunities, are characterized by innovative practices, and have growth and profitability as their main goals.

**small business**
An organization that is independently owned, operated, and financed; has fewer than 100 employees; doesn't necessarily engage in any new or innovative practices, and has relatively little impact on its industry.

of new and unique ideas that may otherwise go untapped.[5] Statistics back this up. New small organizations generate 24 times more innovations per research and development dollar spent than do *Fortune 500* organizations, and they account for more than 95 percent of new and "radical" product developments.[6] A report released by the U.S. Small Business Administration documented that patent applications by small businesses were more likely to be cited in subsequent patent applications than were patent applications of larger firms.[7] This is important because research has shown that highly-cited patents represent economically and technologically significant inventions. This is further proof of how important small business is to innovation in America.

*Number of New Start-Ups.* Because all businesses—whether they fit the definition of entrepreneurial ventures or not—were new start-ups at one point in time, the most suitable measure we have of the important role of entrepreneurship is to look at the number of new firms over a period of time. Data collected by the U.S. Small Business Administration shows that the number of new start-ups has increased every year since 2002. Estimates for 2005 showed that some 671,000 new businesses were created.[8]

*Job Creation.* We know that job creation is important to the overall long-term economic health of communities, regions, and nations. The latest figures show that, over the last decade, small businesses created between 60 and 80 percent of net new jobs.[9] Small organizations have been creating jobs at a fast pace even as many of the world's largest and well-known global corporations continued to downsize. These numbers reflect the importance of entrepreneurial firms as job creators.

*Global Entrepreneurship.* What about entrepreneurial activity outside the United States? What kind of impact has it had? An annual assessment of global entrepreneurship called the Global Entrepreneurship Monitor (GEM) studies the impact of entrepreneurial activity on economic growth in various countries. The GEM 2005 report covered 35 countries that were divided into two clusters based on GDP (gross domestic product) per capita and real GDP growth rate in 2005. (See Exhibit A–1.)

What did the researchers find? The highest levels of entrepreneurial activity tended to be in middle-income countries: Venezuela (25 percent), Thailand (20.7 percent), Jamaica (17 percent), and China (13.7 percent). High-income countries tended to have lower percentages of individuals starting a business. The GEM report concludes that "…the type, quality, and quantity of entrepreneurship contribute (in a

**Exhibit A–1**

**Global Entrepreneurship Monitor 2005—Country Clusters**

| Cluster 1: Middle-Income, High-Growth | Cluster 2: High-Income, High-Growth |
|---|---|
| Argentina | Australia |
| Brazil | Austria |
| Chile | Belgium |
| China | Canada |
| Croatia | Denmark |
| Hungary | Finland |
| Jamaica | France |
| Latvia | Germany |
| Mexico | Greece |
| Slovenia | Iceland |
| South Africa | Ireland |
| Thailand | Italy |
| Venezuela | Japan |
|  | Netherlands |
|  | New Zealand |
|  | Norway |
|  | Singapore |
|  | Spain |
|  | Sweden |
|  | Switzerland |
|  | United Kingdom |
|  | United States |

*Source:* Adapted from M. Minniti, W. D. Bygrave, and E. Autio, "Global Entrepreneurship Monitor: 2005 Executive Report," Babson College and London Business School.

way not yet quite known) to the growth and development of a country."[10] From a global perspective, therefore, we also can state that entrepreneurship plays an important role in a country's economic growth.

## The Entrepreneurial Process

What's involved in the entrepreneurial process? There are four key steps that entrepreneurs must address as they start and manage their entrepreneurial ventures.

The first is *exploring the entrepreneurial context*. The context includes the realities of today's economic, political/legal, social, and work environment. It's important to look at each of these aspects of the entrepreneurial context because they determine the "rules" of the game and which decisions and actions are likely to meet with success. Also, it's through exploring the context that entrepreneurs confront the next critically important step in the entrepreneurial process—*identifying opportunities and possible competitive advantages*. We know from our definition of entrepreneurship that the pursuit of opportunities is an important aspect.

Once entrepreneurs have explored the entrepreneurial context and identified opportunities and possible competitive advantages, they must look at the issues involved with actually bringing their entrepreneurial venture to life. Therefore, the next step in the entrepreneurial process is *starting the venture*. Included in this phase are researching the feasibility of the venture, planning the venture, organizing the venture, and launching the venture.

Finally, once the entrepreneurial venture is up and running, the last step in the entrepreneurial process is *managing the venture*, which an entrepreneur does by managing processes, managing people, and managing growth. We can explain these important steps in the entrepreneurial process by looking at what it is that entrepreneurs do.

## What Do Entrepreneurs Do?

Describing what entrepreneurs do isn't an easy or simple task! No two entrepreneurs' work activities are exactly alike. In a general sense, entrepreneurs create something new, something different. They search for change, respond to it, and exploit it.[11]

Initially, an entrepreneur is engaged in assessing the potential for the entrepreneurial venture and then dealing with start-up issues. In exploring the entrepreneurial context, entrepreneurs gather information, identify potential opportunities, and pinpoint possible competitive advantage(s). Then, armed with this information, the entrepreneur researches the venture's feasibility—uncovering business ideas, looking at competitors, and exploring financing options.

After looking at the potential of the proposed venture and assessing the likelihood of pursuing it successfully, the entrepreneur proceeds to plan the venture. This includes such activities as developing a viable organizational mission, exploring organizational culture issues, and creating a well-thought-out business plan. Once these planning issues have been resolved, the entrepreneur must look at organizing the venture, which involves choosing a legal form of business organization, addressing other legal issues such as patent or copyright searches, and coming up with an appropriate organizational design for structuring how work is going to be done.

Only after these start-up activities have been completed is the entrepreneur ready to actually launch the venture. This involves setting goals and strategies, and establishing the technology-operations methods, marketing plans, information systems, financial-accounting systems, and cash flow management systems.

Once the entrepreneurial venture is up and running, the entrepreneur's attention switches to managing it. What's involved with actually managing the entrepreneurial venture? An important activity is managing the various processes that are part of every business: making decisions, establishing action plans, analyzing external and internal environments, measuring and evaluating performance, and making needed changes. Also, the entrepreneur must perform activities associated with managing people including selecting and hiring, appraising and training, motivating, managing conflict, delegating tasks, and being an effective leader. Finally, the entrepreneur must manage the venture's growth including such activities as developing and designing growth strategies, dealing with crises, exploring various avenues for financing growth, placing a value on the venture, and perhaps even eventually exiting the venture.

## Social Responsibility and Ethics Issues Facing Entrepreneurs

As they launch and manage their ventures, entrepreneurs are faced with the often-difficult issues of social responsibility and ethics. Just how important are these issues to entrepreneurs? An overwhelming majority of respondents (95 percent) in a study of small companies believed that developing a positive reputation and relationship in communities where they do business is important for achieving business goals.[12] However, despite the importance these individuals placed on corporate citizenship, more than half lacked formal programs for connecting with their communities. In fact, some 70 percent of the respondents admitted that they failed to consider community goals in their business plans.

Yet, there are some entrepreneurs who take their social responsibilities seriously. For example, Alicia Polak used to work on Wall Street, helping companies go public. In 2004, she founded the Khayelitsha Cookie Company in Khayelitsha, South Africa, 30 minutes from Cape Town. She now employs 11 women from the impoverished community to bake cookies and brownies that are sold to high-end hotels, restaurants, and coffee houses throughout South Africa. Polak says, "My driving force in this company is that I want them [the hundreds of thousands of people living in poverty in South Africa] out of those shacks. I want to help change their lives using this company as a vehicle."[13]

Other entrepreneurs have pursued opportunities with products and services that protect the global environment. For example, Univenture Inc. of Columbus, Ohio, makes recyclable sleeves and packaging for disc media. Its products are better for the environment as compared with the traditional jewel boxes most compact disks are packaged in. Ross Youngs, founder and president/CEO says, "Our products won't break. If someone throws it away, it's because they don't want it. Hopefully they will end up in the recycle bin because our products are recyclable."[14]

Ethical considerations also play a role in decisions and actions of entrepreneurs. Entrepreneurs do need to be aware of the ethical consequences of what they do, especially in today's post-Enron climate where businesspeople are often viewed as unethical. The example they set—particularly if there are other employees—can be profoundly significant in influencing behavior.

If ethics are important, how do entrepreneurs stack up? Unfortunately, not too good! In a survey of employees from different sizes of businesses who were asked if they thought their organization was highly ethical, 20 percent of employees at companies with 99 or fewer employees disagreed.[15]

## ⌐Learning Review

- Differentiate between entrepreneurial ventures and small businesses.
- Explain why entrepreneurship is important in the United States and globally.

- Describe the four key steps in the entrepreneurial process.
- Explain what entrepreneurs do.
- Discuss why social responsibility and ethics are important considerations for entrepreneurs.

## START-UP AND PLANNING ISSUES

Although pouring a bowl of cereal may seem like a simple task, even the most awake and alert morning person has probably ended up with cereal on the floor. Philippe Meert, a product designer based in Erpe-Mere, Belgium, has come up with a better way. Meert sensed an opportunity to correct the innate design flaw of cereal boxes and developed the Cerealtop, a plastic cover that snaps onto a cereal box and channels the cereal into a bowl.[16]

The first thing that entrepreneurs like Philippe Meert must do is to identify opportunities and possible competitive advantages. Once they've done this, they're ready to start the venture by researching its feasibility and then planning for its launch. These start-up and planning issues are what we're going to look at in this section.

## Identifying Environmental Opportunities and Competitive Advantage

How important is the ability to identify environmental opportunities? Consider the following: More than 4 million baby boomers turn 50 every year. Almost 8,000 turned 60 each day in 2006. More than 57.5 million baby boomers are projected to be alive in 2030, which would put them between the ages of 66 to 84. J. Raymond Elliott, CEO of Zimmer Holdings, is well aware of that demographic trend. Why? His company, which makes orthopedic products including reconstructive implants for hips, knees, shoulders, and elbows, sees definite marketing opportunities.[17]

In 1994, when Jeff Bezos first saw that Internet usage was increasing by 2,300 percent a month, he knew that something dramatic was happening. "I hadn't seen growth that fast outside of a Petri dish," he said. Bezos was determined to be a part of it. He quit his successful career as a stock market researcher and hedge fund manager on Wall Street and pursued his vision for online retailing, now the Amazon.com Web site.[18]

What would you have done had you seen that type of number somewhere? Ignored it? Written it off as a fluke? The skyrocketing Internet usage that Bezos observed and the recognition of the baby boomer demographic by Elliott's Zimmer Holdings are prime examples of identifying environmental opportunities. Remember from our discussion in Chapter 8 that opportunities are positive trends in external environmental factors. These trends provide unique and distinct possibilities for innovating and creating value. Entrepreneurs need to be able to pinpoint these pockets of opportunities that a changing context provides. After all, "organizations do not see opportunities, individuals do."[19] And they need to do so quickly, especially in dynamic environments, before those opportunities disappear or are exploited by others.[20]

The late Peter Drucker, a well-known management author, identified seven potential sources of opportunity that entrepreneurs might look for in the external context.[21] These include the unexpected, the incongruous, the process need, industry and market structures, demographics, changes in perception, and new knowledge.

1. *The unexpected.* When situations and events are unanticipated, opportunities can be found. The event may be an unexpected success (positive news) or an unexpected failure (bad news). Either way, there can be opportunities for entrepreneurs to pursue. For instance, the dramatic increase in fuel prices has proved to be a bonanza for companies that offer solutions. For instance, Jeff Pink, CEO of EV Rental Cars, uses only hybrid vehicles. The company's utilization rate—the percentage of days a vehicle is out generating revenue—is around 90 percent.[22] The unexpected increase in fuel prices proved to be an opportunity for this entrepreneur. And for RSA Security, the unexpected opportunity came in the form of identity theft. Art Coviello's company develops software that helps make online transactions more secure. He stated, "A lot of factors are about to turn in RSA's favor, namely the need for more secure, traceable financial transactions in a world beset by online fraud and identity theft."[23]

2. *The incongruous.* When something is incongruous, there are inconsistencies and incompatibilities in the way it appears. Things "ought to be" a certain way, but aren't. When conventional wisdom about the way things should be no longer holds true, for whatever reason, there are opportunities to capture.

Entrepreneurs who are willing to "think outside the box"—that is, to think beyond the traditional and conventional approaches—may find pockets of potential profitability. Sigi Rabinowicz, founder and president of Tefron, an Israeli firm, recognized incongruities in the way that women's lingerie was made. He knew that a better way was possible. His company spent more than a decade adapting a circular hosiery knitting machine to make intimate apparel that is nearly seamless.[24] Another example of how the incongruous can be a potential source of entrepreneurial opportunity is Fred Smith, founder of FedEx, who recognized in the early 1970s the inefficiencies in the delivery of packages and documents. His approach was: Why not? Who says that overnight delivery isn't possible? Smith's recognition of the incongruous led to the creation of FedEx, now a multibillion dollar corporation.

3. *The process need.* What happens when technology doesn't immediately come up with the "big discovery" that's going to fundamentally change the very nature of some product or service? What happens is that there can be pockets of entrepreneurial opportunity in the various stages of the process as researchers and technicians continue to work for the monumental breakthrough. Because the full leap hasn't been possible, opportunities abound in the tiny steps. Take the medical products industry, for example. Although researchers haven't yet discovered a cure for cancer, there have been many successful entrepreneurial biotechnology ventures created as knowledge about a possible cure continues to grow. The "big breakthrough" hasn't yet happened, but there have been numerous entrepreneurial opportunities throughout the process of discovery.

4. *Industry and market structures.* When changes in technology change the structure of an industry and market, existing firms can become obsolete if they're not attuned to the changes or are unwilling to change. Even changes in social values and consumer tastes can shift the structures of industries and markets. These markets and industries become open targets for nimble and smart entrepreneurs. For instance, while working part-time at an auto body shop while finishing his engineering graduate degree, Joe Born wondered if the industrial paint buffer used to smooth out a car's paint job could be used to smooth out scratches on CDs. He tried it out on his favorite Clint Black CD that had been ruined and the newly-polished CD played flawlessly. After this experience, Born spent almost four years perfecting his disk repair kit invention, the SkipDr.[25] Then, there's the whole Internet area which provides several good examples of existing industries and markets being challenged by upstart entrepreneurial ventures. For instance, eBay has prospered as an online middleman between buyers and sellers. And it's not just Beanie Babies or used books being bought and sold by individuals—even businesses are getting in on the auction action. For example, Sun Microsystems lists numerous items per day on eBay, including servers that sell for more than $15,000. And the Disney Company uses the site to auction off authentic studio props from its movies. Meg Whitman, eBay's CEO, says that the company's job is connecting people, not selling them things. And connect them, they do! The online auction firm had 180 million registered users in 2006.[26]

5. *Demographics.* The characteristics of the world population are changing. These changes influence industries and markets by altering the types and quantities of products and services desired and customers' buying power. Although many of these changes are fairly predictable if you stay alert to demographic trends, others aren't as obvious. Either way, there can be significant entrepreneurial opportunities in anticipating and meeting the changing needs of the population. For example, Thay Thida was one of three partners in Khmer Internet Development Services (KIDS) in Phnom Penh, Cambodia. She and her co-founders saw the opportunities in bringing Internet service to Cambodians and profited from their entrepreneurial venture.[27]

6. *Changes in perception.* Perception is one's view of reality. When changes in perception take place, the facts do not vary, but their meanings do. Changes in perception get at the heart of people's psychographic profiles—what they value, what they believe in, and what they care about. Changes in these attitudes and values create potential market opportunities for alert entrepreneurs. For example, think about your perception of healthy foods. As our perception of whether or not certain food groups are good for us has changed, there have been product and service opportunities for entrepreneurs to recognize and capture. For example, John Mackey started Whole Foods Market in Austin, Texas, as a place for customers to purchase food and other items free of pesticides, preservatives, sweeteners, and cruelty. Now, as the world's number one natural foods chain, Mackey's entrepreneurial venture consists of about 180 stores in more than 30 U.S. states, Canada, and the United Kingdom.[28] Michael and Ellen Diamant changed the perception that baby necessities—diaper bags, bottle warmers, and bottle racks—couldn't be fashionable. Their baby gear company, Skip Hop, offers pricey products that design-conscious new parents have embraced.[29]

7. *New knowledge.* New knowledge is a significant source of entrepreneurial opportunity. Although not all knowledge-based innovations are significant, new knowledge ranks pretty high on the list of sources of entrepreneurial opportunity! It takes more than just having new knowledge, though. Entrepreneurs must be able to do something with that knowledge and to protect important proprietary information from competitors. For example, French scientists are using new knowledge about textiles to develop a wide array of innovative products to keep wearers healthy and smelling good. Neyret, the Parisian lingerie maker, innovated lingerie products woven with tiny perfume microcapsules that stay in the fabric through about 10 washings. Another French company, Francital, developed a fabric treated with chemicals to absorb perspiration and odors.[30]

Being alert to entrepreneurial opportunities is only part of an entrepreneur's initial efforts. He or she must also understand competitive advantage. As we discussed in Chapter 8, when an organization has a competitive advantage, it has something that other competitors don't; does something better than other organizations; or does something that others can't. Competitive advantage is a necessary ingredient for an entrepreneurial venture's long-term success and survival. Getting and keeping a competitive advantage is tough. However, it is something that entrepreneurs must consider as they begin researching the venture's feasibility.

## Researching the Venture's Feasibility—Generating and Evaluating Ideas

On a trip to New York, Miho Inagi got her first taste of the city's delicious bagels. After her palate-expanding experience, she had the idea of bringing bagels to Japan. Five years after her first trip to New York and a subsequent apprenticeship at a New York bagel business, Miho opened Maruichi Bagel in Tokyo. After a struggle to get the store up and running, it now has a loyal following of customers.[31]

It's important for entrepreneurs to research the venture's feasibility by generating and evaluating business ideas. Entrepreneurial ventures thrive on ideas. Generating ideas is an innovative, creative process. It's also one that will take time, not only in the beginning stages of the entrepreneurial venture, but throughout the life of the business. Where do ideas come from?

*Generating Ideas.* Studies of entrepreneurs have shown that the sources of their ideas are unique and varied. One survey found that "working in the same industry" was the major source of ideas for an entrepreneurial venture (60 percent of respondents).[32] Other sources included personal interests or hobbies, looking at familiar and unfamiliar products and services, and opportunities in external environmental sectors (technological, sociocultural, demographics, economic, or legal-political).

Exhibit A–2

**Evaluating Potential Ideas**

| *Personal Considerations:* | *Marketplace Considerations:* |
|---|---|
| • Do you have the capabilities to do what you've selected? | • Who are the potential customers for your idea: who, where, how many? |
| • Are you ready to be an entrepreneur? | • What similar or unique product features does your proposed idea have compared to what's currently on the market? |
| • Are you prepared emotionally to deal with the stresses and challenges of being an entrepreneur? | • How and where will potential customers purchase your product? |
| • Are you prepared to deal with rejection and failure? | • Have you considered pricing issues and whether the price you'll be able to charge will allow your venture to survive and prosper? |
| • Are you ready to work hard? | • Have you considered how you will need to promote and advertise your proposed entrepreneurial venture? |
| • Do you have a realistic picture of the venture's potential? | |
| • Have you educated yourself about financing issues? | |
| • Are you willing and prepared to do continual financial and other types of analyses? | |

What should entrepreneurs look for as they explore these idea sources? They should look for limitations of what's currently available, new and different approaches, advances and breakthroughs, unfilled niches, or trends and changes. For example, John C. Diebel, founder of Meade Instruments Corporation, the Irvine, California telescope maker, came up with the idea of putting computerized attachments on the company's inexpensive consumer models so that amateur astronomers could enter on a keypad the coordinates of planets or stars they wanted to see. The telescope would then automatically locate and focus on the desired planetary bodies. It took the company's engineers two years to figure out how to do it, but Meade now controls more than half the amateur astronomy market.[33]

*Evaluating Ideas.* Evaluating entrepreneurial ideas revolves around personal and marketplace considerations. Each of these assessments will provide an entrepreneur with key information about the idea's potential. Exhibit A–2 describes some questions that entrepreneurs might ask as they evaluate potential ideas.

A more structured evaluation approach that an entrepreneur might want to use is a **feasibility study**—an analysis of the various aspects of a proposed entrepreneurial venture designed to determine its feasibility. Not only is a well-prepared feasibility study an effective evaluation tool to determine whether an entrepreneurial idea is a potentially successful one, it can serve as a basis for the all-important business plan.

A feasibility study should give descriptions of the most important elements of the entrepreneurial venture and the entrepreneur's analysis of the viability of these elements. Exhibit A–3 provides an outline of a possible approach to a feasibility study. Yes, it covers a lot of territory and takes a significant amount of time, energy, and effort to prepare it. However, an entrepreneur's potential future success is worth that investment.

## Researching the Venture's Feasibility—Researching Competitors

Part of researching the venture's feasibility is looking at the competitors. As we discussed in Chapter 9, researching the competition through competitor intelligence

Exhibit A–3

**Feasibility Study**

<table>
<tr><td>**A.**</td><td>**Introduction, historical background, description of product or service:**</td></tr>
</table>

1. Brief description of proposed entrepreneurial venture
2. Brief history of the industry
3. Information about the economy and important trends
4. Current status of the product or service
5. How you intend to produce the product or service
6. Complete list of goods or services to be provided
7. Strengths and weaknesses of the business
8. Ease of entry into the industry, including competitor analysis

**B.**    **Accounting considerations:**

1. Pro forma balance sheet
2. Pro forma profit and loss statement
3. Projected cash flow analysis

**C.**    **Management considerations:**

1. Personal expertise—strengths and weaknesses
2. Proposed organizational design
3. Potential staffing requirements
4. Inventory management methods
5. Production and operations management issues
6. Equipment needs

**D.**    **Marketing considerations:**

1. Detailed product description
2. Identify target market (who, where, how many)
3. Describe place product will be distributed (location, traffic, size, channels, etc.)
4. Price determination (competition, price lists, etc.)
5. Promotion plans (role of personal selling, advertising, sales promotion, etc.)

**E.**    **Financial considerations:**

1. Start-up costs
2. Working capital requirements
3. Equity requirements
4. Loans—amounts, type, conditions
5. Breakeven analysis
6. Collateral
7. Credit references
8. Equipment and building financing—costs and methods

**F.**    **Legal considerations:**

1. Proposed business structure (type; conditions, terms, liability, responsibility; insurance needs; buyout and succession issues)
2. Contracts, licenses, and other legal documents

**G.**    **Tax considerations: sales/property/employee; federal, state, and local**

**H.**    **Appendix: charts/graphs, diagrams, layouts, resumes, etc.**

can be a powerful tool. What would entrepreneurs like to know about their potential competitors? Here are some possible questions:

What types of products or services are competitors offering?

What are the major characteristics of these products or services?

**feasibility study**
An analysis of the various aspects of a proposed entrepreneurial venture designed to determine its feasibility.

What are their products' strengths and weaknesses?

How do they handle marketing, pricing, and distributing?

What do they attempt to do differently from other competitors?

Do they appear to be successful at it? Why or why not?

What are they good at?

What competitive advantage(s) do they appear to have?

What are they not so good at?

What competitive disadvantage(s) do they appear to have?

How large and profitable are these competitors?

For instance, Ezra Dabah, CEO of The Children's Place, carefully examined the competition as he took his chain of children's clothing stores nationwide. Although he faces stiff competition from the likes of GapKids, J.C. Penney, and Gymboree, he feels that his company's approach to manufacturing and marketing will give it a competitive edge.[34]

Once an entrepreneur has this information, he or she should assess how the proposed entrepreneurial venture is going to "fit" into this competitive arena. Will the entrepreneurial venture be able to compete successfully? This type of competitor analysis becomes an important part of the feasibility study and the business plan. If, after all this analysis, the situation looks promising, the final part of researching the venture's feasibility is to look at the various financing options. This isn't the final determination of how much funding the venture will need or where this funding will come from but is simply gathering information about various financing alternatives.

## Researching the Venture's Feasibility—Researching Financing

Getting financing isn't always easy. For instance, when William Carey first proposed building a liquor distributor business in Poland, more than 20 investment banking houses in New York passed on funding his idea. Carey recalls, "They didn't know Poland, and the business was small. We were ready to give up." Then, a New York investment banking boutique agreed to fund the venture. Today, Carey's company, CEDC (Central European Distribution), has almost 2,000 employees and sales revenues of more than $500 million.[35]

Because funds likely will be needed to start the venture, an entrepreneur must research the various financing options. Possible financing options available to entrepreneurs are shown in Exhibit A–4.

## Planning the Venture—Developing a Business Plan

Planning is also important to entrepreneurial ventures. Once the venture's feasibility has been thoroughly researched, the entrepreneur then must look at planning the

**Exhibit A–4**

**Possible Financing Options**

- Entrepreneur's personal resources (personal savings, home equity, personal loans, credit cards, etc.)
- Financial institutions (banks, savings and loan institutions, government-guaranteed loan, credit unions, etc.)
- **Venture capitalists**—external equity financing provided by professionally-managed pools of investor money
- **Angel investors**—a private investor (or group of private investors) who offers financial backing to an entrepreneurial venture in return for equity in the venture
- **Initial public offering (IPO)**—the first public registration and sale of a company's stock
- National, state, and local governmental business development programs
- Unusual sources (television shows, judged competitions, etc.)

venture. The most important thing that an entrepreneur does in planning the venture is developing a **business plan**—a written document that summarizes a business opportunity and defines and articulates how the identified opportunity is to be seized and exploited.

For many would-be entrepreneurs, developing and writing a business plan seems like a daunting task. However, a good business plan is valuable. It pulls together all of the elements of the entrepreneur's vision into a single coherent document. The business plan requires careful planning and creative thinking. But if done well, it can be a convincing document that serves many functions. It serves as a blueprint and road map for operating the business. And the business plan is a "living" document, guiding organizational decisions and actions throughout the life of the business, not just in the start-up stage.

If an entrepreneur has completed a feasibility study, much of the information included in it becomes the basis for the business plan. A good business plan covers six major areas: executive summary, analysis of opportunity, analysis of the context, description of the business, financial data and projections, and supporting documentation.

*Executive summary.* The executive summary summarizes the key points that the entrepreneur wants to make about the proposed entrepreneurial venture. These might include a brief mission statement; primary goals; brief history of the entrepreneurial venture, maybe in the form of a timeline; key people involved in the venture; nature of the business; concise product or service descriptions; brief explanations of market niche, competitors, and competitive advantage; proposed strategies; and selected key financial information.

*Analysis of opportunity.* In this section of the business plan, an entrepreneur presents the details of the perceived opportunity. Essentially, this means 1. sizing up the market by describing the demographics of the target market; 2. describing and evaluating industry trends; and 3. identifying and evaluating competitors.

*Analysis of the context.* Whereas the opportunity analysis focuses on the opportunity in a specific industry and market, the context analysis takes a much broader perspective. Here, the entrepreneur describes the broad external changes and trends taking place in the economic, political-legal, technological, and global environments.

*Description of the business.* In this section, an entrepreneur describes how the entrepreneurial venture is going to be organized, launched, and managed. It includes a thorough description of the mission statement; a description of the desired organizational culture; marketing plans including overall marketing strategy, pricing, sales tactics, service-warranty policies, and advertising and promotion tactics; product development plans such as an explanation of development status, tasks, difficulties and risks, and anticipated costs; operational plans including a description of proposed geographic location, facilities and needed improvements, equipment, and work flow; human resource plans including a description of key management persons, composition of board of directors including their background experience and skills, current and future staffing needs, compensation and benefits, and training needs; and an overall schedule and timetable of events.

*Financial data and projections.* Every effective business plan contains financial data and projections. Although the calculations and interpretation may be difficult, they are absolutely critical. No business plan is complete without financial information. Financial plans should cover at least three years and contain projected income statements, pro forma cash flow analysis (monthly for the first year and quarterly for the next two), pro forma balance sheets, breakeven analysis, and cost controls. If major equipment or

**venture capitalists**
External equity financing provided by professionally managed pools of investor money.

**angel investors**
A private investor (or group of private investors) who offers financial backing to an entrepreneurial venture in return for equity in the venture.

**initial public offering (IPO)**
The first public registration and sale of a company's stock.

**business plan**
A written document that summarizes a business opportunity and defines and articulates how the identified opportunity is to be seized and exploited.

other capital purchases are expected, the items, costs, and available collateral should be listed. All financial projections and analyses should include explanatory notes, especially where the data seem contradictory or questionable.

*Supporting documentation.* This *is* an important component of an effective business plan. The entrepreneur should back up his or her descriptions with charts, graphs, tables, photographs, or other visual tools. In addition, it might be important to include information (personal and work-related) about the key participants in the entrepreneurial venture.

Just as the idea for an entrepreneurial venture takes time to germinate, so does the writing of a good business plan. It's important for the entrepreneur to put serious thought and consideration into the plan. It's not an easy thing to do. However, the resulting document should be valuable to the entrepreneur in current and future planning efforts.

## Learning Review

- Discuss how opportunities are important to entrepreneurial ventures.
- Describe each of the seven sources of potential opportunity.

- Explain why it's important for entrepreneurs to understand competitive advantage.
- List possible financing options for entrepreneurs.
- Describe the six major sections of a business plan.

## ORGANIZING ISSUES

Donald Hannon, president of Graphic Laminating Inc. in Solon, Ohio, redesigned his organization's structure by transforming it into an employee-empowered company. He wanted to drive authority down through the organization so employees were responsible for their own efforts. One way he did this was by creating employee teams to handle specific projects. Employees with less experience were teamed with veteran employees. He says, "I want to build a good team and give people the ability to succeed. Sometimes that means giving them the ability to make mistakes, and I have to keep that in perspective. The more we allow people to become better at what they do, the better they will become—and the better we all will do."[36]

Once the start-up and planning issues for the entrepreneurial venture have been addressed, the entrepreneur is ready to begin organizing the entrepreneurial venture. There are five organizing issues an entrepreneur must address: the legal forms of organization, organizational design and structure, human resource management, stimulating and making changes, and the continuing importance of innovation.

### Legal Forms of Organization

The first organizing decision that an entrepreneur must make is a critical one. It's the form of legal ownership for the venture. The two primary factors affecting this decision are taxes and legal liability. An entrepreneur wants to minimize the impact of both of these factors. The right choice can protect the entrepreneur from legal liability as well as save tax dollars, in both the short run and the long run.

What alternatives are available? There are three basic ways to organize an entrepreneurial venture: sole proprietorship, partnership, and corporation. However, when you include the variations of these basic organizational alternatives, you end up with six possible choices, each with its own tax consequences, liability issues, and pros and cons. These six choices are sole proprietorship, general partnership, limited liability partnership (LLP), C corporation, S corporation, and limited liability company (LLC). Let's briefly look at each one with their advantages and drawbacks. (Exhibit A–5 summarizes the basic information about each organizational alternative.)

Exhibit A–5 **Legal Forms of Business Organization**

| Structure | Ownership Requirements | Tax Treatment | Liability | Advantages | Drawbacks |
|---|---|---|---|---|---|
| Sole proprietorship | One owner | Income and losses "pass through" to owner and are taxed at personal rate | Unlimited personal liability | *Low start-up costs* Freedom from most regulations *Owner has direct control* All profits go to owner Easy to exit *business* | Unlimited personal liability *Personal finances at risk* Miss out on many business tax deductions *Total responsibility* May be more difficult to raise financing |
| General partnership | Two or more owners | Income and losses "pass through" to partners and are taxed at personal rate; *flexibility in profit-loss allocations to partners* | Unlimited personal liability | *Ease of formation* Pooled talent *Pooled resources* Somewhat easier access to financing *Some tax benefits* | Unlimited personal liability *Divided authority and decisions* Potential for conflict *Continuity of transfer of ownership* |
| Limited liability partnership (LLP) | Two or more owners | Income and losses "pass through" to partner and are taxed at personal rate; *flexibility in profit-loss allocations to partners* | Limited, although one partners must retain unlimited liability | *Good way to acquire capital from limited partners* | Cost and complexity of forming can be high *Limited partners cannot participate in management of business without losing liability protection* |
| C corporation | Unlimited number shareholders; *no limits on types of stock or voting arrangements* | Dividend income is taxed at corporate and personal shareholder levels; *losses and deductions are corporate* | Limited | *Limited liability* Transferable ownership *Continuous existence* Easier access to resources | Expensive to set up *Closely regulated* Double taxation *Extensive record keeping* Charter restrictions |
| S corporation | Up to 75 shareholders; *no limits on types of stock or voting arrangements* | Income and losses "pass through" to partners and are taxed at personal rate; *flexibility in profit-loss allocation to partners* | Limited | *Easy to set up* Enjoy limited liability protection and tax benefits of partnership *Can have a tax-exempt entity as a shareholder* | Must meet certain requirements *May limit future financing options* |
| Limited liability company (LLC) | Unlimited number of "members"; *flexible membership arrangements for voting rights and income* | Income and losses "pass through" to partners and are taxed at personal rate; *flexibility in profit-loss allocations to partners* | Limited | *Greater flexibility* Not constrained by regulations on C and S corporations *Taxed as partnership, not as corporation* | Cost of switching from one form to this can be high *Need legal and financial advice in forming operating agreement* |

*Sole proprietorship.* A **sole proprietorship** is a form of legal organization in which the owner maintains sole and complete control over the business and is personally liable for business debts. There are no legal requirements for establishing a sole proprietorship other than obtaining the necessary local business licenses and permits. In a sole proprietorship, income and losses "pass through" to the owner and are taxed at the owner's personal income tax rate. The biggest drawback, however, is the unlimited personal liability for any and all debts of the business.

*General partnership.* A **general partnership** is a form of legal organization in which two or more business owners share the management and risk of the business. Even though a partnership is possible without a written agreement, the potential and inevitable problems that arise in any partnership make a written partnership agreement drafted by legal counsel a highly recommended thing to do.

*Limited liability partnership (LLP).* The **limited liability partnership (LLP)** is a form of legal organization in which there are general partners and limited partners. The general partners actually operate and manage the business. They are the ones who have unlimited liability. There must be at least one general partner in an LLP. However, there can be any number of limited partners. These partners are usually passive investors, although they can make management suggestions to the general partners. They also have the right to inspect the business and make copies of business records. The limited partners are entitled to a share of the business's profits as agreed to in the partnership agreement, and their risk is limited to the amount of their investment in the LLP.

*C corporation.* Of the three basic types of ownership, the corporation (also known as a C corporation) is the most complex to form and operate. A **corporation** is a legal business entity that is separate from its owners and managers. Many entrepreneurial ventures are organized as a **closely held corporation** which, very simply, is a corporation owned by a limited number of people who do not trade the stock publicly. Whereas the sole proprietorship and partnership forms of organization do not exist separately from the entrepreneur, the corporation does. The corporation functions as a distinct legal entity and, as such, can make contracts, engage in business activities, own property, sue and be sued, and of course, pay taxes. A corporation must operate in accordance with its charter and the laws of the state in which it operates.

*S corporation.* The **S corporation** (also called a subchapter S corporation) is a specialized type of corporation that has the regular characteristics of a corporation but is unique in that the owners are taxed as a partnership as long as certain criteria are met. The S corporation has been the classic organizing approach for getting the limited liability of a corporate structure without incurring corporate tax. However, this form of legal organization must meet strict criteria. If any of these criteria are violated, a venture's S status is automatically terminated.

*Limited liability company (LLC).* The **limited liability company (LLC)** is a relatively new form of business organization that's a hybrid between a partnership and a corporation. The LLC offers the liability protection of a corporation, the tax benefits of a partnership, and fewer restrictions than an S corporation. However, the main drawback of this approach is that it's quite complex and expensive to set up. Legal and financial advice is an absolute necessity in forming the LLC's **operating agreement** which is the document that outlines the provisions governing the way the LLC will conduct business.

*Summary of legal forms of organization.* The organizing decision regarding the legal form of organization is an important one because it can have significant tax and liability consequences. Although the legal form of organization can be changed, it's not an easy thing to do. An entrepreneur needs to think carefully about what's important, especially in the areas of flexibility, taxes, and amount of personal liability in choosing the best form of organization.

## Organizational Design and Structure

The choice of an appropriate organizational structure is also an important decision when organizing an entrepreneurial venture. At some point, successful entrepreneurs find that they can't do everything alone. More people are needed. The entrepreneur must then decide on the most appropriate structural arrangement for effectively and efficiently carrying out the organization's activities. Without some suitable type of organizational structure, the entrepreneurial venture may soon find itself in a chaotic situation.

In many small firms, the organizational structure tends to evolve with very little intentional and deliberate planning by the entrepreneur. For the most part, the structure may be very simple—one person does whatever is needed. As the entrepreneurial venture grows and the entrepreneur finds it increasingly difficult to go it alone, employees are brought on board to perform certain functions or duties that the entrepreneur can't handle. These individuals tend to perform those same functions as the company grows. Then, as the entrepreneurial venture continues to grow, each of these functional areas may require managers and employees.

With the evolution to a more deliberate structure, the entrepreneur faces a whole new set of challenges. All of a sudden, he or she must share decision making and operating responsibilities. This is typically one of the most difficult things for an entrepreneur to do—letting go and allowing someone else to make decisions. *After all*, he or she reasons, *how can anyone know this business as well as I do?* Also, what might have been a fairly informal, loose, and flexible atmosphere that worked well when the organization was small may no longer be effective. Many entrepreneurs are greatly concerned about keeping that "small company" atmosphere alive even as the venture grows and evolves into a more structured arrangement. But having a structured organization doesn't necessarily mean giving up flexibility, adaptability, and freedom. In fact, the structural design may be as fluid as the entrepreneur feels comfortable with and yet still have the rigidity it needs to operate efficiently.

Organizational design decisions in entrepreneurial ventures revolve around the six key elements of organizational structure discussed in Chapter 10: work specialization, departmentalization, chain of command, span of control, amount of centralization-decentralization, and amount of formalization. Decisions about these six elements will determine whether an entrepreneur designs a more mechanistic or organic organizational structure (concepts also discussed in Chapter 10). When would each be preferable? A mechanistic structure would be preferable when cost efficiencies are critical to the venture's competitive advantage; when more control over employees' work activities is important; if the venture produces standardized products in a routine fashion; and when the external environment is relatively stable and certain. An organic structure would be most appropriate when innovation is critical to the organization's competitive advantage; for smaller organizations where rigid approaches to dividing and coordinating work aren't necessary; if the organization produces customized products in a flexible setting; and where the external environment is dynamic, complex, and uncertain.

## Human Resource Management Issues in Entrepreneurial Ventures

As an entrepreneurial venture grows, additional employees will need to be hired to perform the increased workload. As employees are brought on board, the entrepreneur faces certain human resource management (HRM) issues. Two HRM issues of particular importance to entrepreneurs are employee recruitment and employee retention.

---

**sole proprietorship**
A form of legal organization in which the owner maintains sole and complete control over the business and is personally liable for business debts.

**general partnership**
A form of legal organization in which two or more business owners share the management and risk of the business.

**limited liability partnership (LLP)**
A form of legal organization in which there are general partner(s) and limited liability partner(s).

**corporation**
A legal business entity that is separate from its owners and managers.

**closely held corporation**
A corporation owned by a limited number of people who do not trade the stock publicly.

**S corporation**
A specialized type of corporation that has the regular characteristics of a C corporation but is unique in that

the owners are taxed as a partnership as long as certain criteria are met.

**limited liability company (LLC)**
A form of legal organization that's a hybrid between a partnership and a corporation.

**operating agreement**
The document that outlines the provisions governing the way an LLC will conduct business.

*Employee recruitment.* An entrepreneur wants to ensure that the venture has the people to do the required work. Recruiting new employees is one of the biggest challenges that entrepreneurs face. In fact, the ability of small firms to successfully recruit appropriate employees is consistently rated as one of the most important factors influencing organizational success.[37]

Entrepreneurs, particularly, are looking for high-potential people who can perform multiple roles during various stages of venture growth. They look for individuals who "buy into" the venture's entrepreneurial culture—individuals who have a passion for the business.[38]Unlike their corporate counterparts who often focus on filling a job by matching a person to the job requirements, entrepreneurs look to fill in critical skills gaps. They're looking for people who are exceptionally capable and self-motivated, flexible, multi-skilled, and who can help grow the entrepreneurial venture. While corporate managers tend to focus on using traditional HRM practices and techniques, entrepreneurs are more concerned with matching characteristics of the person to the values and culture of the organization; that is, they focus on matching the person to the organization.[39]

*Employee retention.* Getting competent and qualified people into the venture is just the first step in effectively managing the human resources. An entrepreneur wants to keep the people he or she has hired and trained. Sabrina Horn, president of The Horn Group based in San Francisco, understands the importance of having good people on board and keeping them. Her public relations firm employs around 45 employees who create PR for technology firms. In this rough-and-tumble, intensely competitive industry, Sabrina knows that the loss of talented employees could harm client services. To combat this, she offers employees a wide array of desirable benefits such as raises of 6 percent or more each year, profit sharing, trust funds for employees' children, paid sabbaticals, personal development funds, and so forth. But more importantly, Sabrina recognizes that employees have a life outside the office and treats them accordingly. This type of HRM approach has kept her employees loyal and productive.[40]

A unique and important employee retention issue entrepreneurs must deal with is compensation. Whereas traditional organizations are more likely to view compensation from the perspective of monetary rewards (base pay, benefits, and incentives), smaller entrepreneurial firms are more likely to view compensation from a total rewards perspective. For these firms, compensation encompasses psychological rewards, learning opportunities, and recognition in addition to monetary rewards (base pay and incentives).[41]

## Stimulating and Making Changes

We know that the context facing entrepreneurs is one of dynamic change. Both external and internal forces (see Chapter 13) may bring about the need for making changes in the entrepreneurial venture. Entrepreneurs need to be alert to problems and opportunities that may create the need to change. In fact, of the many hats an entrepreneur wears, that of change agent may be one of the most important.[42] If changes are needed in the entrepreneurial venture, often it is the entrepreneur who first recognizes the need for change and acts as the catalyst, coach, cheerleader, and chief change consultant. Change isn't easy in any organization, but it can be particularly challenging for entrepreneurial ventures. Even if a person is comfortable with taking risks—as entrepreneurs usually are—change can be hard. That's why it's important for an entrepreneur to recognize the critical roles he or she plays in stimulating and implementing change. For instance, Jeff Fluhr, CEO of StubHub, Inc., is well aware of the important role he plays in stimulating and implementing changes. As the leading Internet player in the ticket reselling market, Fluhr has to continually look for ways to keep his company competitive. One recent change was the creation of an exclusive advertising agreement with the National Hockey League to promote StubHub.com on NHL.com.[43]

During any type of organizational change, an entrepreneur also may have to act as chief coach and cheerleader. Since organizational change of any type can be disruptive and scary, the entrepreneur must explain the change to employees and encourage change efforts by supporting employees, getting them excited about the change, building them up, and motivating them to put forth their best efforts.

Finally, the entrepreneur may have to guide the actual change process as changes in strategy, technology, products, structure, or people are implemented. In this role, the entrepreneur answers questions, makes suggestions, gets needed resources, facilitates conflict, and does whatever else is necessary to get the change(s) implemented.

## The Continuing Importance of Innovation

In today's dynamically chaotic world of global competition, organizations must continually innovate new products and services if they want to compete successfully. Innovation is a key characteristic of entrepreneurial ventures and, in fact, it's what makes the entrepreneurial venture "entrepreneurial."

What must an entrepreneur do to encourage innovation in the venture? Having an innovation-supportive culture is crucial. What does such a culture look like?[44] It's one in which employees perceive that supervisory support and organizational reward systems are consistent with a commitment to innovation. It's also important in this type of culture that employees not perceive their workload pressures are excessive or unreasonable. And research has shown that firms with cultures supportive of innovation tend to be smaller, have fewer formalized human resource practices, and less abundant resources.[45]

## Learning Review

- Contrast the six different forms of legal organization.
- Describe the organizational design issues entrepreneurs face as the venture grows.

- Discuss the unique HRM issues entrepreneurs face.
- Describe what an innovation-supportive culture looks like.

## LEADING ISSUES

The 45 employees of designer Liz Lange's company have to flexible. Many don't have job descriptions, and everyone is expected to contribute ideas and pitch in with tasks in all departments. Lange says, "The phrase 'That's not my job' doesn't belong here." In return, Lange is a supportive leader who gives her employees considerable latitude.[46]

Leading is an important function of entrepreneurs. As an entrepreneurial venture grows and people are brought on board, an entrepreneur takes on a new role—that of a leader. In this section, we want to look at what's involved with the leading function. First, we're going to look at the unique personality characteristics of entrepreneurs. Then we're going to discuss the important role entrepreneurs play in motivating employees through empowerment and leading the venture and employee teams.

## Personality Characteristics of Entrepreneurs

Think of someone you know who is an entrepreneur. Maybe it's someone you personally know or maybe it's someone like Bill Gates of Microsoft, Dineh Mohajer of Hard Candy, or Larry Ellison of Sun Microsystems. How would you describe this person's personality? One of the most researched areas of entrepreneurship has been the search to determine what—if any—psychological characteristics entrepreneurs have in common; what types of personality traits entrepreneurs have that might distinguish them from non-entrepreneurs; and what traits entrepreneurs have that might predict who will be a successful entrepreneur.

Is there a classic "entrepreneurial personality?" Although trying to pinpoint specific personality characteristics that all entrepreneurs share has the same problem as identifying the trait theories of leadership—that is, being able to identify specific personality traits that *all* entrepreneurs share—this hasn't stopped entrepreneurship researchers from listing common traits.[47] For instance, one list of personality characteristics included the following: high level of motivation, abundance of self-confidence, ability to be involved for the long term, high energy level, persistent problem solver, high degree of initiative, ability to set goals, and moderate risk-taker.[48] Another list of characteristics of "successful" entrepreneurs included high energy level, great persistence, resourcefulness, the desire and ability to be self-directed, and relatively high need for autonomy.

Another development in defining entrepreneurial personality characteristics was the proposed use of a proactive personality scale to predict an individual's likelihood of pursuing entrepreneurial ventures. What is a **proactive personality**? Very simply, it's a personality trait describing those individuals who are more prone to take actions to influence their environment—that is, they're more proactive. Obviously, an entrepreneur is likely to exhibit proactivity as he or she searches for opportunities and acts to take advantage of those opportunities.[49] Various items on the proactive personality scale were found to be good indicators of a person's likelihood of becoming an entrepreneur, including gender, education, having an entrepreneurial parent, and possessing a proactive personality. In addition, studies have shown that entrepreneurs have greater risk propensity than do managers.[50] However, this propensity is moderated by the entrepreneur's primary goal. Risk propensity is greater for entrepreneurs whose primary goal is growth versus those whose focus is on producing family income.

## Motivating Employees Through Empowerment

At Sapient Corporation (creators of Internet and software systems for e-commerce and automating back-office tasks such as billing and inventory), co-founders Jerry Greenberg and J. Stuart Moore recognized that employee motivation was vitally important to their company's ultimate success.[51] They designed their organization so individual employees are part of an industry-specific team that works on an entire project rather than on one small piece of it. Their rationale was that people often feel frustrated when they're doing a small part of a job and never get to see the whole job from start to finish. They figured people would be more productive if they got the opportunity to participate in all phases of a project.

When you're motivated to do something, don't you find yourself energized and willing to work hard at doing whatever it is you're excited about? Wouldn't it be great if all of a venture's employees were energized, excited, and willing to work hard at their jobs? Having motivated employees is an important goal for any entrepreneur, and employee empowerment is an important motivational tool entrepreneurs can use.

Although it's not easy for entrepreneurs to do, employee empowerment—giving employees the power to make decisions and take actions on their own—is an important motivational approach. Why? Because successful entrepreneurial ventures must be quick and nimble, ready to pursue opportunities and go off in new directions. Empowered employees can provide that flexibility and speed. When employees are empowered, they often display stronger work motivation, better work quality, higher job satisfaction, and lower turnover.

For example, employees at Butler International, Inc., a technology consulting services firm based in Montvale, New Jersey, work at client locations. President and CEO Ed Kopko recognized that employees had to be empowered to do their jobs if they were going to be successful.[52] Another entrepreneurial venture that found employee empowerment to be a strong motivational approach is Stryker Instruments in Kalamazoo, Michigan, a division of Stryker Corporation. Each of the company's production units is responsible for its operating budget, cost reduction goals, customer-service levels, inventory management, training, production planning and forecasting, purchasing, human resource management, safety, and problem solving. In addition, unit members work closely with marketing, sales, and R&D during new product introductions and continuous improvement projects. Says one team supervisor, "Stryker lets me do what I do best and rewards me for that privilege."[53]

Empowerment is a philosophical concept that entrepreneurs have to "buy into." This doesn't come easily. In fact, it's hard for many entrepreneurs to do. Their life is tied up in the business. They've built it from the ground up. But continuing to grow the entrepreneurial venture is eventually going to require handing over more responsibilities to employees. How can entrepreneurs empower employees? For many entrepreneurs, it's a gradual process.

Entrepreneurs can begin by using participative decision making in which employees provide input into decisions. Although getting employees to participate in decisions isn't quite taking the full plunge into employee empowerment, at least it's a way to begin tapping into the collective array of employees' talents, skills, knowledge, and abilities.

Another way to empower employees is through delegation—the process of assigning certain decisions or specific job duties to employees. (See the Building Your Skills module on Delegating in Appendix B to find out how to empower effectively.) By delegating decisions and duties, the entrepreneur is turning over the responsibility for carrying them out.

When an entrepreneur is finally comfortable with the idea of employee empowerment, fully empowering employees means redesigning their jobs so they have discretion over the way they do their work. It's allowing employees to do their work effectively and efficiently by using their creativity, imagination, knowledge, and skills.

If an entrepreneur implements employee empowerment properly—that is, with complete and total commitment to the program and with appropriate employee training—results can be impressive for the entrepreneurial venture and for the empowered employees. The business can enjoy significant productivity gains, quality improvements, more satisfied customers, increased employee motivation, and improved morale. Employees can enjoy the opportunities to do a greater variety of work that is more interesting and challenging.

In addition, employees are encouraged to take the initiative in identifying and solving problems and doing their work. For example, at Mine Safety Appliances Company in Pittsburgh, Pennsylvania, employees are empowered to change their work processes in order to meet the organization's challenging quality improvement goals. Getting to this point took an initial 40 hours of classroom instruction per employee in areas such as engineering drawing, statistical process control, quality certifications, and specific work instruction. However, the company's commitment to an empowered workforce has resulted in profitability increasing 57 percent over the last four years and 95 percent of the company's employees achieving multi-skill certifications.[54]

## The Entrepreneur as Leader

The last topic we want to discuss in this section is the role of the entrepreneur as a leader. In this role, the entrepreneur has certain leadership responsibilities in leading the venture and in leading employee work teams.

*Leading the venture.* Today's successful entrepreneur must be like the leader of a jazz ensemble known for its improvisation, innovation, and creativity. Max DePree, former head of Herman Miller, Inc., a leading office furniture manufacturer known for its innovative leadership approaches, said it best in his book, *Leadership Jazz,* "Jazz band leaders must choose the music, find the right musicians, and perform—in public. But the effect of the performance depends on so many things—the environment, the volunteers playing the band, the need for everybody to perform as individuals and as a

**proactive personality**
A personality trait that describes individuals who are more prone to take actions to influence their environments.

group, the absolute dependence of the leader on the members of the band, the need for the followers to play well….The leader of the jazz band has the beautiful opportunity to draw the best out of the other musicians. We have much to learn from jazz band leaders, for jazz, like leadership, combines the unpredictability of the future with the gifts of individuals."[55]

The way an entrepreneur leads the venture should be much like the jazz leader—drawing the best out of other individuals, even given the unpredictability of the situation. One way an entrepreneur does this is through the vision he or she creates for the organization. In fact, the driving force through the early stages of the entrepreneurial venture is often the visionary leadership of the entrepreneur. The entrepreneur's ability to articulate a coherent, inspiring, and attractive vision of the future is a key test of his or her leadership. But if an entrepreneur can do this, the results can be worthwhile. A study contrasting visionary and nonvisionary companies showed that visionary companies outperformed the nonvisionary ones by six times on standard financial criteria, and their stocks outperformed the general market by 15 times.[56]

*Leading employee work teams.* As we know from Chapter 15, many organizations—entrepreneurial and otherwise—are using employee work teams to perform organizational tasks, create new ideas, and resolve problems.

Employee work teams tend to be popular in entrepreneurial ventures. An *Industry Week* Census of Manu-facturers showed that nearly 68 percent of survey respondents used teams to varying degrees.[57] The three most common ones respondents said they used (similar to those discussed in Chapter 15) included empowered teams (teams that have the authority to plan and implement process improvements), self-directed teams (teams that are nearly autonomous and responsible for many managerial activities), and cross-functional teams (work teams composed of individuals from various specialties who work together on various tasks).

These entrepreneurs also said that developing and using teams is necessary because technology and market demands are forcing them to make their products faster, cheaper, and better. Tapping into the collective wisdom of the venture's employees and empowering them to make decisions just may be one of the best ways to adapt to change. In addition, a team culture can improve the overall workplace environment and morale.

For team efforts to work, however, entrepreneurs must shift from the traditional command-and-control style to a coach-and-collaboration style (look back at the discussion of team leadership in Chapter 17). They must recognize that individual employees can understand the business and can innovate just as effectively as they can. For example, at Marque, Inc., of Goshen, Indiana, CEO Scott Jessup recognized that he wasn't the smartest guy in the company as far as production problems, but he was smart enough to recognize that, if he wanted his company to expand its market share in manufacturing medical-emergency-squad vehicles, new levels of productivity needed to be reached. He formed a cross-functional team—bringing together people from production, quality assurance, and fabrication—that could spot production bottlenecks and other problems and then gave the team the authority to resolve the constraints.[58]

## Learning Review

- Explain what personality research shows about entrepreneurs
- Discuss how entrepreneurs can empower employees.

- Explain how entrepreneurs can be effective at leading employee work teams.

## CONTROLLING ISSUES

Philip McCaleb still gets a kick out of riding the scooters his Chicago-based company, Genuine Scooter Co., makes. However, in building his business, McCaleb has had to acknowledge his own limitations. As a self-described "idea" guy, he knew that he would need someone else to come in and ensure that the end product was *what* it was supposed to be, *where* it was supposed to be, and *when* it was supposed to be there.[59]

Entrepreneurs must look at controlling their venture's operations in order to survive and prosper in both the short run and long run. Those unique control issues that face entrepreneurs include managing growth, managing downturns, exiting the venture, and managing personal life choices and challenges.

## Managing Growth

Growth is a natural and desirable outcome for entrepreneurial ventures. Growth is what distinguishes an entrepreneurial venture. Entrepreneurial ventures pursue growth.[60] Growing slowly can be successful, but so can rapid growth.

Growing successfully doesn't occur randomly or by luck. Successfully pursuing growth typically requires an entrepreneur to manage all the challenges associated with growing. This entails planning, organizing, and controlling for growth.

*Planning for growth.* Although it may seem we've reverted back to discussing planning issues instead of controlling issues, actually controlling is closely tied to planning as we know from our discussion in Chapter 18 (see Exhibit 18–2). And the best growth strategy is a well-planned one.[61] Ideally, the decision to grow doesn't come about spontaneously, but instead is part of the venture's overall business goals and plan. Rapid growth without planning can be disastrous. Entrepreneurs need to address growth strategies as part of their business planning but shouldn't be overly rigid in that planning. The plans should be flexible enough to exploit unexpected opportunities that arise. With plans in place, the successful entrepreneur must then organize for growth.

*Organizing for growth.* The key challenges for an entrepreneur in organizing for growth include finding capital, finding people, and strengthening the organizational culture. Norbert Otto is the founder of Sport Otto, an online business based in Germany that sold almost $2 million worth of skates, skis, snowboards, and other sporting goods on eBay in 2005. As the company grows, Otto is finding that he has to be more organized.[62]

Having enough capital is a major challenge facing growing entrepreneurial ventures. The money issue never seems to go away, does it? It takes capital to expand. The processes of finding capital to fund growth are much like going through the initial financing of the venture. Hopefully, at this time the venture has a successful track record to back up the request. If it doesn't, it may be extremely difficult to acquire the necessary capital. That's why we said earlier that the best growth strategy is a planned one.

*managing* **IT**

### IT for Entrepreneurs

IT presents a number of challenges—and opportunities—for entrepreneurs. According to a survey of business owners, 53 percent cite integrating different applications and different software systems as one of the primary IT challenges. These IT tools (software and hardware) were often purchased separately as funds became available or as needs changed. However, it has created a problem because it's hard for employees to share information or to get work done when the information isn't available because it's sitting in separate and different applications or on incompatible hardware. Another similar IT challenge facing small businesses is integrating Web sites with applications software. This was noted by 47 percent of the survey respondents. The remaining IT challenges noted by the survey respondents were: outgrowing the system (45 percent); insufficient IT staff (42 percent); and outdated applications (34 percent).

Despite these challenges, there are many IT tools that can support an entrepreneur's business. One of the primary tools is e-mail marketing, which can be a great way for smaller firms to maintain contact with current and potential customers. And despite the potential integration problems, other important IT tools include all the various types of business applications software that is available. This software can make planning, organizing, leading, and controlling the entrepreneurial venture more efficient and more effective.

*Source:* R. Breeden, "Owners Want Software Programs Integrated," *Wall Street Journal,* April 4, 2006, p. A16.

Part of that planning should be how growth will be financed. For example, The Boston Beer Company, America's largest microbrewer and producer of Samuel Adams beer, grew rapidly by focusing almost exclusively on increasing its top-selling product line. However, the company was so focused on increasing market share that it had few financial controls and an inadequate financial infrastructure. During periods of growth, cash flow difficulties would force company chairman and brewmaster Jim Koch to tap into a pool of unused venture capital funding. However, when a chief financial officer joined the company, he developed a financial structure that enabled the company to manage its growth more efficiently and effectively by setting up a plan for funding growth.[63]

Another important issue that a growing entrepreneurial venture needs to address is finding people. If the venture is growing quickly, this challenge may be intensified because of time constraints. It's important to plan the numbers and types of employees needed as much as possible in order to support the increasing workload of the growing venture. It may also be necessary to provide additional training and support to employees to help them handle the increased pressures associated with the growing organization.

Finally, when a venture is growing, it's important to create a positive, growth-oriented culture that enhances the opportunities to achieve success, both organizationally and individually. This can sometimes be difficult to do, particularly when changes are rapidly happening. However, the values, attitudes, and beliefs that are established and reinforced during these times are critical to the entrepreneurial venture's continued and future success. Exhibit A–6 lists some suggestions that entrepreneurs might use to ensure that their venture's culture is one that embraces and supports a climate in which organizational growth is viewed as desirable and important. Keeping employees focused and committed to what the venture is doing is critical to the ultimate success of its growth strategies. If employees don't "buy into" the direction the entrepreneurial venture is headed, it's unlikely the growth strategies will be successful.

*Controlling for growth.* Another challenge that growing entrepreneurial ventures face is reinforcing already established organizational controls. Maintaining good financial records and financial controls over cash flow, inventory, customer data, sales orders, receivables, payables, and costs should be a priority of every entrepreneur—whether pursuing growth or not. However, it's particularly important to reinforce these controls when the entrepreneurial venture is expanding. It's all too easy to let things "get away" or to put them off when there's an unrelenting urgency to get things done. Rapid growth—or even slow growth—does not excuse the need to have effective controls in place. In fact, it's particularly important to have established procedures, protocols, and

---

**Exhibit A–6**

**Suggestions for Achieving a Supportive Growth-Oriented Culture**

- Keep the lines of communication open—inform employees about major issues.
- Establish trust by being honest, open, and forthright about the challenges and rewards of being a growing organization.
- Be a good listener—find out what employees are thinking and facing.
- Be willing to delegate duties.
- Be flexible—be willing to change your plans if necessary.
- Provide consistent and regular feedback by letting employees know the outcomes—good and bad.
- Reinforce the contributions of each person by recognizing employees' efforts.
- Continually train employees to enhance their capabilities and skills.
- Maintain the focus on the venture's mission even as it grows.
- Establish and reinforce a "we" spirit since a successful growing venture takes the coordinated efforts of all the employees.

processes and to use them. Even though mistakes and inefficiencies can never be eliminated entirely, an entrepreneur should at least ensure that every effort is being made to achieve high levels of productivity and organizational effectiveness. For example, at Green Gear Cycling, co-founder Alan Scholz recognized the importance of controlling for growth. How? By following a "Customers for Life" strategy, which meant continually monitoring customer relationships and orienting organizational work decisions around their possible impacts on customers. Through this type of strategy, Green Gear hopes to keep customers for life. That's significant because they figured that, if they could keep a customer for life, the value would range from $10,000 to $25,000 per lifetime customer.[64]

## Managing Downturns

Although organizational growth is a desirable and important goal for entrepreneurial ventures, what happens when things don't go as planned—when the growth strategies don't result in the intended outcomes and, in fact, result in a decline in performance? There are challenges, as well, in managing the downturns.

Nobody likes to fail, especially entrepreneurs. However, when an entrepreneurial venture faces times of trouble, what can be done? How can downturns be managed successfully? The first step is recognizing that a crisis is brewing.

*Recognizing crisis situations.* An entrepreneur should be alert to the warning signs of a business in trouble. Some signals of potential performance decline include inadequate or negative cash flow, excess number of employees, unnecessary and cumbersome administrative procedures, fear of conflict and taking risks, tolerance of work incompetence, lack of a clear mission or goals, and ineffective or poor communication within the organization.[65]

Another perspective on recognizing performance declines revolves around what is known as the **"boiled frog" phenomenon.**[66] The "boiled frog" is a classic psychological response experiment. In one case, a live frog that's dropped into a boiling pan of water reacts instantaneously and jumps out of the pan. But, in the second case, a live frog that's dropped into a pan of mild water that is gradually heated to the boiling point fails to react and dies. A small firm may be particularly vulnerable to the boiled frog phenomenon because the entrepreneur may not recognize the "water heating up"—that is, there is a subtly declining situation. When changes in performance are gradual, a serious response may never be triggered or may be done too late to do anything about the situation.

So what does the boiled frog phenomenon teach us? It teaches us that entrepreneurs need to be alert to signals that the venture's performance may be worsening. Don't wait until the water has reached the boiling point before you react.

*Dealing with downturns, declines, and crises.* Al-though an entrepreneur hopes to never have to deal with organizational downturns, declines, or crises, there may come a time when he or she must do just that. After all, nobody likes to think about things going bad or taking a turn for the worse. But that's exactly what the entrepreneur should do—think about it *before* it happens (remember feedforward control from Chapter 18).[67] It's important to have an up-to-date plan for covering crises. It's like mapping exit routes from your home in case of a fire. An entrepreneur wants to be prepared before an emergency hits. This plan should focus on providing specific details for controlling the most fundamental and critical aspects of running the venture—cash flow, accounts receivable, costs, and debt. Beyond having a plan for controlling the venture's critical inflows and outflows, other actions would involve identifying specific strategies for cutting costs and restructuring the venture.

**"boiled frog" phenomenon**
A perspective on recognizing performance declines that suggests watching out for subtly declining situations.

## Exiting the Venture

Getting out of an entrepreneurial venture may seem to be a strange thing for entrepreneurs to do. However, there may come a point when the entrepreneur decides it's time to move on. That decision may be based on the fact that the entrepreneur hopes to capitalize financially on the investment in the venture—called **harvesting**—or that the entrepreneur is facing serious organizational performance problems and wants to get out, or even on the entrepreneur's desire to focus on other pursuits (personal or business). The issues involved with exiting the venture include choosing a proper business valuation method and knowing what's involved in the process of selling a business.

*Business valuation methods.* Valuation techniques generally fall into three categories: 1. asset valuations, 2. earnings valuations, and 3. cash flow valuations.[68] Setting a value on a business can be a little tricky. In many cases, the entrepreneur has sacrificed much for the business and sees it as his or her "baby." Calculating the value of the baby based on objective standards such as cash flow or some multiple of net profits can sometimes be a shock. That's why it's important for an entrepreneur who wishes to exit the venture to get a comprehensive business valuation prepared by professionals.

*Other important considerations in exiting the venture.* Although the hardest part of preparing to exit a venture is valuing it, other factors also should be considered.[69] Exhibit A–7 lists these issues. The process of exiting the entrepreneurial venture should be approached as carefully as the process of launching it. If the entrepreneur is selling the venture on a positive note, he or she wants to realize the value built up in the business. If the venture is being exited because of declining performance, the entrepreneur wants to maximize the potential return.

## Managing Personal Life Choices and Challenges

Being an entrepreneur is extremely exciting and fulfilling, yet extremely demanding. There are long hours, difficult demands, and high stress. Yet, there are many rewards to being an entrepreneur as well. In this section, we want to look at how entrepreneurs can make it work—that is, how can they be successful and effectively balance the demands of their work and personal lives?[70]

Entrepreneurs are a special group. They are focused, persistent, hardworking, and intelligent. Because they put so much of themselves into launching and growing their entrepreneurial ventures, many may neglect their personal lives. Entrepreneurs often have to make sacrifices to pursue their entrepreneurial dreams. However, they can make it work. They can balance their work and personal lives. But how?

One of the most important things an entrepreneur can do is *become a good time manager.* Prioritize what needs to be done. Use a planner (daily, weekly, monthly) to help schedule priorities. Some entrepreneurs don't like taking the time to plan or prioritize, or they think it's a ridiculous waste of time. Yet identifying the important duties and distinguishing them from those that aren't so important actually makes an entrepreneur more efficient and effective. In addition, part of being a good time manager is delegating those decisions and actions the entrepreneur doesn't have to be personally involved in to trusted employees. Although it may be hard to let go of some of the

Exhibit A–7

**Issues in Exiting the Entrepreneurial Venture**

| |
|---|
| *Be prepared.* |
| Decide who will sell the business. |
| Consider the tax implications. |
| Screen potential buyers. |
| *Decide whether to tell employees before or after selling.* |

things they've always done, entrepreneurs who delegate effectively will see their personal productivity levels rise.

Another suggestion for finding that balance is to *seek professional advice* in those areas of business where it's needed. Although entrepreneurs may be reluctant to spend scarce cash, the time, energy, and potential problems saved in the long run are well worth the investment. Competent professional advisers can provide entrepreneurs with information to make more intelligent decisions. Also, it's important to *deal with conflicts* as they arise. This includes both workplace and family conflicts. If an entrepreneur doesn't deal with conflicts, negative feelings are likely to crop up and lead to communication breakdowns. When communication falls apart, vital information may get lost, and people (employees *and* family members) may start to assume the worst. It can turn into a nightmare situation that feeds upon itself. The best strategy is to deal with conflicts as they come up. Talk, discuss, argue (if you must), but an entrepreneur shouldn't avoid the conflict or pretend it doesn't exist.

Another suggestion for achieving that balance between work and personal life is to *develop a network of trusted friends and peers.* Having a group of people to talk with is a good way for an entrepreneur to think through problems and issues. The support and encouragement offered by these people can be an invaluable source of strength for an entrepreneur.

Finally, *recognize when your stress levels are too high.* Entrepreneurs *are* achievers. They like to make things happen. They thrive on working hard. Yet, too much stress can lead to significant physical and emotional problems (as we discussed in Chapter 13). Entrepreneurs have to learn when stress is overwhelming them and to do something about it. After all, what's the point of growing and building a thriving entrepreneurial venture if you're not around to enjoy it?

## Learning Review

- Describe how entrepreneurs should plan, organize, and control growth.
- Describe the boiled frog phenomenon and why it's useful for entrepreneurs.

- Discuss the issues an entrepreneur needs to consider when deciding whether to exit the entrepreneurial venture.

**harvesting**
Exiting a venture when an entrepreneur hopes to capitalize financially on the investment in the venture.

# Learning Summary

## What Is Entrepreneurship and Why Is It Important?

Entrepreneurship: the process of starting new businesses, generally in response to opportunities. It's important because:

1. Contributes to innovation
2. Reflected in the number of new start-ups
3. Contributes to job creation

## What's Involved in the Entrepreneurial Process?

- Exploring the entrepreneurial context
- Identifying opportunities and possible competitive advantages
- Starting the venture
- Managing the venture

## How Do Entrepreneurs Identify Opportunities?

Seven potential sources of opportunity include the unexpected, the incongruous, the process need, industry and market structures, demographics, changes in perception, and new knowledge

## What Factors Need to Be Considered in Determining the Venture's Feasibility?

- Generating and evaluating ideas: **feasibility study**
- Researching competitors
- Researching financing

　　Then, the entrepreneur is ready to develop a **business plan**— a written document that summarizes a business opportunity and defines and articulates how the opportunity is to be seized and exploited

## What Organizing Issues Does an Entrepreneur Face?

- The legal forms of organization: sole proprietorship, general partnership, limited liability partnership (LLP), C corporation, S corporation, and limited liability company (LLC)
- Organizational design and structure: six elements of organization design and mechanistic or organic structure
- Human resource management: employee recruitment and employee retention
- Stimulating and making changes: entrepreneur as change agent and change guide
- Continuing importance of innovation: innovative-supportive culture

## What Personality Characteristics Do Entrepreneurs Have?

Identifying specific traits common to all entrepreneurs is difficult. They tend to have high levels of motivation, abundance of self-confidence, ability to be involved for the long term, high energy level, persistent problem solver, high degree of initiative, ability to set goals, and moderate risk taker. Many have a **proactive personality**, a trait that describes individuals who are more prone to take actions to influence their environment.

## What Leading Issues Do Entrepreneurs Face?

- Empowering employees
- Leading the venture
- Leading employee work teams

## What Control Issues Do Entrepreneurs Face?

- Managing growth: planning, organizing, and controlling growth
- Managing downturns: recognizing crisis situations (**boiled frog phenomenon**) and then being able to deal with these
- Exiting the venture: when is the best time to leave?
- Managing personal life choices and challenges: managing demands and stress

# Entrepreneurship: By the Numbers

- Americans 55 and older make up one of the fastest-growing groups of self-employed workers.
- Two-thirds of new businesses survive at least two years after start-up and 44 percent survive at least four years.
- Complying with federal regulations is more costly for small business than for larger ones. It costs a business with fewer than 20 employees $7,647 per year to meet all federal regulations. For businesses with 500 or more employees, the cost is $5,282 per year.
- Seventy-nine percent of owners of smaller companies say that it is more rewarding to work in a small business than a large one.

*Sources:* J. M. Pethokoukis and E. Brandon, "Going Your Own Way," *US News & World Report,* April 3, 2006, pp. 52–55; R. Breeden, "Small vs. Big," *Wall Street Journal,* January 3, 2006, p. A23; R. Breeden, "Price of Compliance," *Wall Street Journal,* December 20, 2005, p. B8; and J. McDowell, "Small Business Continues to Drive U.S. Economy," Office of Advocacy, U.S. Small Business Administration, October 3, 2005.

# Thinking About Entrepreneurship Issues

1. What do you think would be the hardest thing about being an entrepreneur? What do you think would be the most fun thing?
2. How does the concept of social entrepreneurship (see Chapter 5) relate to entrepreneurs and entrepreneurial ventures?
3. Would a good manager be a good entrepreneur? Discuss.
4. Why do you think many entrepreneurs find it hard to step aside and let others manage their business?
5. Do you think a person can be taught to be an entrepreneur? Why or why not?
6. What do you think it means to be a successful entrepreneurial venture? How about a successful entrepreneur?

# Working Together: Team-Based Exercise

Many entrepreneurs have started numerous ventures. They'll start a business, grow it, and then sell the business—supposedly to relax on a beach somewhere. But then the entrepreneurial "itch" will take over again, and they'll start another business. You are to do some research on "serial entrepreneurs" as part of a small group (three to four students) and write a short paper on the topic. Look for the following in your research: What is a serial entrepreneur? Who are some well-known serial entrepreneurs? What special characteristics do these serial entrepreneurs have? What can other entrepreneurs learn from serial entrepreneurs?

# Case Application

### A Flickr of an Idea

It started "as a lark—a way to let people share photos as they text-messaged." Or that was what Flickr co-founders Stewart Butterfield and Caterina Fake intended. However, when they added the ability for people to tag their digital photos and others' digital photos with labels so they could be grouped and found more easily, communities began to form. And all of a sudden, the "lark" was a full-fledged business with 1.5 million users and 60 million photos.

As many entrepreneurial ventures do, Flickr started as a scrapped project. An engineer at Fake's Vancouver-based online game start-up had created a tool to share photos and save them to a Web page while playing the game. She scrapped the game because "it turned out the fun was in the photo sharing." Caterina and her programmer husband, Stewart, transformed the photo-sharing project into Flickr. It didn't take long for Web junkies to flock to it and, in less than two years, it became one of the Web's fastest-growing properties. Flickr's traffic grew 448 percent from December 2004 to December 2005. Caterina says, "Had we sat down and said 'Let's start a photo application,' we would have done all this research and done all the wrong things." Instead, Flickr exploited the social nature of photography.

What makes Flickr so appealing is the ease with which photos can be shared or sent to friends and family, linked to blogs, or donated to a virtual gallery. Friends can check out newly posted photos by searching and can add their own "notes" to photos they like. Another distinctive tool lets bloggers post photos simultaneously on their blogs and on Flickr. It also uses a tool called "tagging"—allowing a user to add a few words of text to each posted photo so a photo can be easily searched online.

In March 2005, Yahoo! purchased Flickr, both for the company itself and for what Caterina and Stewart brought to the table. An industry analyst says, "Caterina is very dynamic, smart, and energetic, and Stewart is a brilliant programmer."

### Discussion Questions

1. Describe the creation of Flickr using the seven potential sources of opportunity.
2. What competitive advantage(s) did Flickr have?
3. What issues may have arisen when a business is growing that fast?
4. Do you agree with Caterina's statement that "Had we sat down and said 'Let's start a photo application,' we would have done all this research and done all the wrong things"? Why or why not?

*Sources:* J. Graham, "Flickr of Idea on a Gaming Project Led to Photo Website," *USA Today,* February 28, 2006, p. 5B; "Best Leaders: Entrepreneurs," *BusinessWeek,* December 19, 2005, p. 66; and D. Whelan, "The Shutterbugs," *Forbes,* September 5, 2005, p. 112.

# Appendix B: Skill-Building Modules

In this section of the textbook, you will have the opportunity to learn about, practice, and reinforce specific management skills. We have included 22 skills that encompass the four functions of management: planning, organizing, leading, and controlling. (See the matrix that follows.)

For each of the skills, we provide the following:

1. A short introduction discusses some basic facts about the skill and defines it, if necessary.

2. A section called "Learning About" describes the suggested behaviors for doing that skill. These behaviors

are presented in numbered lists to illustrate the specific actions associated with that skill.

3. A section entitled "Practice" presents a short scenario designed to provide you with an opportunity to practice the behaviors associated with the skill. Your professor may have you do different things with the practice scenarios.

4. A section entitled "Reinforcement" is designed to present additional activities that you could do to practice and reinforce the behaviors associated with the skill.

## Management Skills and Management Functions Matrix

| Skill | Planning | Organizing | Leading | Controlling |
|---|---|---|---|---|
| Acquiring power | | ✓ | ✓ | |
| Active listening | | | ✓ | ✓ |
| Budgeting | ✓ | | | ✓ |
| Choosing an effective leadership style | | | ✓ | |
| Coaching | | | ✓ | |
| Creating effective teams | | ✓ | ✓ | |
| Delegating (empowerment) | | ✓ | ✓ | |
| Designing motivating jobs | | ✓ | ✓ | |
| Developing trust | | | ✓ | |
| Disciplining | | | ✓ | ✓ |
| Interviewing | | ✓ | ✓ | |
| Managing conflict | | | ✓ | ✓ |
| Managing resistance to change | | ✓ | ✓ | ✓ |
| Mentoring | | | ✓ | |
| Negotiating | | | ✓ | |
| Providing feedback | | | ✓ | ✓ |
| Reading an organization's culture | | ✓ | ✓ | |
| Running productive meetings | ✓ | ✓ | ✓ | ✓ |
| Scanning the environment | ✓ | | | ✓ |
| Setting goals | ✓ | | | ✓ |
| Solving problems creatively | ✓ | ✓ | ✓ | ✓ |
| Valuing diversity | ✓ | ✓ | ✓ | ✓ |

## ACQUIRING POWER

Power is a natural process in any group or organization, and to perform their jobs effectively, managers need to know how to acquire and use **power**—the capacity of a leader to influence work actions or decisions. We discussed the concept of power in Chapter 17 and identified five different sources of power for leaders including legitimate, coercive, reward, expert, and referent. Why is having

power important? Because power makes you less dependent on others. When a manager has power, he or she is not as dependent on others for critical resources. And if the manager-controlled resources are important, scarce, and non-substitutable, her power will increase because others will be more dependent on her for those resources.

# Learning About: Acquiring Power

You can be more effective at acquiring and using power if you use the following eight behaviors.

1. *Frame arguments in terms of organizational goals.* To be effective at acquiring power means camouflaging your self-interests. Discussions over who controls what resources should be framed in terms of the benefits that will accrue to the organization; do not point out how you will personally benefit.

2. *Develop the right image.* If you know your organization's culture, you already understand what the organization wants and values from its employees in terms of dress, associates to cultivate and those to avoid, whether to appear risk-taking or risk-aversive, the preferred leadership style, the importance placed on getting along well with others, and so forth. With this knowledge, you're equipped to project the appropriate image. Because the assessment of your performance isn't always a fully objective process, you need to pay attention to style as well as substance.

3. *Gain control of organizational resources.* Controlling organizational resources that are scarce *and* important is a source of power. Knowledge and expertise are particularly effective resources to control. They make you more valuable to the organization and, therefore, more likely to have job security, chances for advancement, and a receptive audience for your ideas.

4. *Make yourself appear indispensable.* Because we're dealing with appearances rather than objective facts, you can enhance your power by appearing to be indispensable. You don't really have to *be* indispensable as long as key people in the organization believe that you are.

5. *Be visible.* If you have a job that brings your accomplishments to the attention of others, that's great. However, if you don't have such a job, you'll want to find ways to let others in the organization know what you're doing by highlighting successes in routine reports, having satisfied customers relay their appreciation to senior executives, being seen at social functions, being active in your professional associations, and developing powerful allies who speak positively about your accomplishments. Of course, you'll want to be on the lookout for those projects that will increase your visibility.

6. *Develop powerful allies.* To get power, it helps to have powerful people on your side. Cultivate contacts with potentially influential people above you, at your own level, and at lower organizational levels. These allies often can provide you with information that's otherwise not readily available. In addition, having allies can provide you with a coalition of support if and when you need it.

7. *Avoid "tainted" members.* In almost every organization, there are fringe members whose status is questionable. Their performance and/or loyalty may be suspect. Keep your distance from such individuals.

8. *Support your boss.* Your immediate future is in the hands of your current boss. Because he or she evaluates your performance, you'll typically want to do whatever is necessary to have your boss on your side.

You should make every effort to help your boss succeed, make her look good, support her if she is under siege, and spend the time to find out the criteria she will use to assess your effectiveness. Don't undermine your boss. And don't speak negatively of her to others.

(Based on H. Mintzberg, *Power In and Around Organizations* [Upper Saddle River, NJ: Prentice Hall, 1983], p. 24; P. L. Hunsaker, *Training in Management Skills* [Upper Saddle River, NJ: Prentice Hall, 2001], pp. 339–364; G. Ferris, S. Davidson, and P. Perrewé, "Developing Political Skill at Work," *Training*, November 2005, pp. 40–45; B. Uzzi and S. Dunlap, "How to Build Your Network," *Harvard Business Review*, December 2005, pp. 53–60; and B. Brim, "The Best Way to Influence Others," *Gallup Management Journal*, February 9, 2006, http://gmj.gallup.com.)

# Practice: Acquiring Power

Read through the following scenario. Write down some notes about how you would handle the situation described. Be sure to refer to the eight behaviors described for acquiring power. Your professor will then tell you what to do next.

**SCENARIO:**

You used to be the star marketing manager for Hilton Electronics Corporation. But for the past year, you've been outpaced again and again by Conor, a new manager in the design department, who has accomplished everything expected of her and more. Meanwhile your best efforts to do your job well have been sabotaged and undercut by Leonila—your and Conor's manager. For example, prior to last year's international consumer electronics show, Leonila moved $30,000 from your budget to Conor's. Despite your best efforts, your marketing team couldn't complete all of the marketing materials normally developed to showcase your organization's new products at this important industry show. And Leonila has chipped away at your staff and budget ever since. Although you've been able to meet most of your goals with less staff and budget, Leonila has continued to slice away the resources of your group. Just last week, she eliminated two positions from your team of eight marketing specialists to make room for a new designer and some extra equipment for Conor. Leonila is clearly taking away your resources while giving Conor whatever she wants and more. You think it's time to do something, or soon you won't have any team or resources left.

# Reinforcement: Acquiring Power

The following suggestions are activities you can do to practice and reinforce the behaviors associated with acquiring power.

1. Keep a one-week journal of your behavior describing incidences when you tried to influence others around you. Assess each incident by asking: Were you successful at these attempts to influence them? Why or why not? What could you have done differently?

2. Review recent issues of a business periodical (such as *BusinessWeek, Fortune, Forbes, Fast Company, Industry Week,* or the *Wall Street Journal*). Look for articles on reorganizations, promotions, or departures from management positions. Find at least two articles where you believe power issues are involved. Relate the content of the articles to the concepts introduced in this skill module.

# ACTIVE LISTENING

The ability to be an effective listener is often taken for granted. Hearing is often confused with listening, but hearing is merely recognizing sound vibrations. Listening is making sense of what we hear and requires paying attention, interpreting, and remembering. Effective listening is active rather than passive. Active listening is hard work and requires you to "get inside" the speaker's head in order to understand the communication from his or her point of view.

## Learning About: Active Listening

We can identify eight specific behaviors that effective active listeners demonstrate. You can be more effective at active listening if you use these behaviors.

1. *Make eye contact.* Making eye contact with the speaker focuses your attention, reduces the likelihood that you'll be distracted, and encourages the speaker.

2. *Exhibit affirmative nods and appropriate facial expressions.* The effective active listener shows interest in what's being said through nonverbal signals. Affirmative nods and appropriate facial expressions that signal interest in what's being said, when added to eye contact, convey to the speaker that you're really listening.

3. *Avoid distracting actions or gestures.* The other side of showing interest is avoiding actions that suggest your mind is elsewhere. When listening, don't look at your watch, shuffle papers, play with your pencil, or engage in similar distractions.

4. *Ask questions.* The serious active listener analyzes what he or she hears and asks questions. This behavior provides clarification, ensures understanding, and assures the speaker you're really listening.

5. *Paraphrase.* Restate *in your own words* what the speaker has said. The effective active listener uses phrases such as "What I hear you saying is…" or "Do you mean…?" Paraphrasing is an excellent control device to check whether or not you're listening carefully and is also a control for accuracy of understanding.

6. *Avoid interrupting the speaker.* Let the speaker complete his or her thoughts before you try to respond. Don't try to second-guess where the speaker's thoughts are going. When the speaker is finished, you'll know it.

7. *Don't overtalk.* Most of us would rather discuss our own ideas than listen to what others say. While talking may be more fun and silence may be uncomfortable, you can't talk and listen at the same time. The good active listener recognizes this fact and doesn't overtalk.

8. *Make smooth transitions between the roles of speaker and listener.* In most work situations, you're continually shifting back and forth between the roles of speaker and listener. The effective active listener makes transitions smoothly from speaker to listener and back to speaker.

(Based on C. R. Rogers and R. E. Farson, *Active Listening* [Chicago: Industrial Relations Center of the University of Chicago, 1976]; and P. L. Hunsaker, *Training in Management Skills* [Upper Saddle River, NJ: Prentice Hall, 2001], pp. 61–62.)

## Practice: Active Listening

Read through the following scenario. Write down some notes about how you would handle the situation described. Be sure to refer to the eight behaviors described for active listening. Your professor will tell you what to do next.

### SCENARIO:

Ben Lummis has always been one of the most reliable technicians at the car stereo shop you manage. Even on days when the frantic pace stressed most other employees, Ben was calm and finished his work efficiently and effectively. You don't know much about his personal life except that he liked to read books about model railroading during his lunch break and he asked to listen to his favorite light jazz station on the shop radio for part of the day. Because his work has always been top-notch, you were happy to let him maintain his somewhat aloof attitude. But over the past month, you wish you knew Ben better. He's been averaging an absence a week, and he no longer spends his lunch break reading in the break room. When he returns from wherever he goes, he seems even more remote than before he left. You strongly suspect that something is wrong. Even his normally reliable work has changed. Several irate customers have returned with sound systems he installed improperly. At the time of these complaints, you reviewed each problem with him carefully, and each time he promised to be more careful. In addition, you've checked the company's work absence records and found that Ben has enough time saved up to take seven more sick days this year. But things don't seem to be improving. Just this week, Ben took another suspicious sick day, and another angry customer has demanded that his improperly installed system be fixed.

## Reinforcement: Active Listening

The following suggestions are activities you can do to practice and reinforce the active listening behaviors.

1. In another lecture-format class, practice active listening for one day. Then ask yourself: Was this harder for me than a normal lecture? Did it affect my note taking? Did I ask more questions? Did it improve my understanding of the lecture's content?

2. For one week, practice active listening behaviors during phone conversations that you have with others. Keep a journal of whether listening actively was easy or difficult, what distractions there were, how you dealt with those distractions, and your assessment of whether or not active listening allowed you to get more out of the conversations.

# BUDGETING

Managers do not have unlimited resources to do their jobs. Most managers will have to deal with a **budget**, a numerical plan for allocating resources to specific activities. As planning tools, they indicate what activities are important and how many resources should be allocated to each activity. However, budgets aren't just used in planning. They're also used in controlling. As control tools, budgets provide managers with quantitative standards against which to measure and compare resource consumption. By pointing out deviations between standard and actual consumption, managers can use the budget for control purposes.

## Learning About: Budgeting

You can develop your skills at budgeting if you use the following seven suggestions.

1. *Determine which work activities are going to be pursued during the coming time period.* An organization's work activities are a result of the goals that have been established. Your control over which work activities your unit will pursue during a specific time period will depend on how much control you normally exercise over the work that must be done to meet those goals. In addition, the amount of control you have often depends on your managerial level in the organization.

2. *Decide which resources will be necessary to accomplish the desired work activities; that is, those that will ensure goals are met.* Although there are different types of budgets used for allocating resources, the most common ones involve monetary resources. However, you also may have to budget time, space, material resources, human resources, capacity utilization, or units of production.

3. *Gather cost information.* You'll need accurate cost estimates of those needed resources. Old budgets may be of some help, but you'll also want to talk with your manager, colleagues, and key employees, and to use other contacts you have developed inside and outside your organization.

4. *Once you know which resources will be available to you, assign the resources as needed to accomplish the desired work activities.* In many organizations, managers are given a monthly, quarterly, or annual budget to work with. The budget will detail which resources are available during the time period. As the manager, you have to assign the resources in an efficient and effective manner to ensure that your unit goals are met.

5. *It's wise to review the budget periodically.* Don't wait until the end of the time period to monitor whether you're over or under budget.

6. *Take action if you find that you're not within your budget.* Remember that a budget also serves as a control tool. If resources are being consumed more quickly than budgeted, you may need to determine why and take corrective action.

7. *Use past experience as a guide when developing your budget for the next time period.* Although every budgeted time period will be different, it is possible to use past experience to pinpoint trends and potential problems. This knowledge can help you prepare for any circumstances that may arise.

(Based on R. N. Anthony, J. Dearden, and N. M. Bedford, *Management Control Systems*, 5th ed. [Homewood, IL: Irwin, 1984], Chapters 5–7.)

## Practice: Budgeting

Read through the following scenario and complete the assigned questions. Be sure to refer to the seven behaviors described for budgeting. Your professor will tell you what to do next.

**SCENARIO:**

You have recently been appointed as advertising manager for a new monthly health and lifestyle magazine, *Global Living for Life*, being developed by the magazine division of LifeTime Publications. You were previously an advertising manager on one of the company's established magazines. In this new position, you will report to the new magazine's publisher, Molly Tymon.

Estimates of first-year subscription sales for *Global Living for Life* are 125,000 copies. Newsstand sales should add another 5,000 copies a month to that number, but your concern is with developing advertising revenue for the magazine. You and Molly have set a goal of selling advertising space totaling $6 million during the magazine's first year. You think you can do this with a staff of 10 people. Because this is a completely new publication, there is no previous budget for your advertising group. You've been asked by Molly to submit a preliminary budget for your group.

Write up a report (no longer than two pages in length) that describes in detail how you would go about fulfilling this request by Molly. For example, where would you get budget categories? Whom would you contact? Present your best ideas for creating this budget for your department.

## Reinforcement: Budgeting

The following suggestions are activities you can do to practice and reinforce the budgeting skill behaviors.

1. Create a personal budget for the next month. Be sure to identify sources of income and planned expenditures. At the end of the month, answer the following questions:

   a. Did your budget help you plan what you could and could not do this month?

   b. Did unexpected situations arise that weren't included in the budget? How did you handle those?

   c. How is a personal budget similar to and different from a budget that a manager might be responsible for?

2. Interview three managers from different organizations. Ask them about their budgeting responsibilities and the "lessons" they've learned about budgeting.

# CHOOSING AN EFFECTIVE LEADERSHIP STYLE

Effective leaders are skillful at helping the groups they lead be successful as the group goes through various stages of development. There is no leadership style that is consistently effective. Situational factors, including follower characteristics, must be taken into consideration in the selection of an effective leadership style. The key situational factors that determine leadership effectiveness include stage of group development, task structure, position power, leader-member relations, the work group, employee characteristics, organizational culture, and national culture.

## Learning About: Choosing an Effective Leadership Style

You can choose an effective leadership style if you use the following six suggestions.

1. *Determine the stage in which your group or team is operating: forming, storming, norming, or performing.* Because each team stage involves specific and different issues and behaviors, it's important to know in which stage your team is. **Forming** is the first stage of group development during which people join a group and then help define the group's purpose, structure, and leadership. **Storming** is the second stage, characterized by intragroup conflict. **Norming** is the third stage, characterized by close relationships and cohesiveness. **Performing** is the fourth stage, when the group is fully functional.

2. *If your team is in the forming stage, there are certain leader behaviors you want to exhibit.* These include making certain that all team members are introduced to one another, answering member questions, working to establish a foundation of trust and openness, modeling the behaviors you expect from the team members, and clarifying the team's goals, procedures, and expectations.

3. *If your team is in the storming stage, there are certain leader behaviors you want to exhibit.* These behaviors include identifying sources of conflict and adopting a mediator role, encouraging a win-win philosophy, restating the team's vision and its core values and goals, encouraging open discussion, encouraging an analysis of team processes to identify ways to improve, enhancing team cohesion and commitment, and providing recognition to individual team members as well as the team.

4. *If your team is in the norming stage, there are certain leader behaviors you want to exhibit.* These include clarifying the team's goals and expectations, providing performance feedback to individual team members and the team, encouraging the team to articulate a vision for the future, and finding ways to publicly and openly communicate the team's vision.

5. *If your team is in the performing stage, there are certain leader behaviors you want to exhibit.* These behaviors include providing regular and ongoing performance feedback, fostering innovation and innovative behavior, encouraging the team to capitalize on its strengths, celebrating achievements (large and small), and providing the team whatever support it needs to continue doing its work.

6. *Monitor the group for changes in behavior and adjust your leadership style accordingly.* Because a group is not a static entity, it will go through up periods and down periods. You should adjust your leadership style to the needs of the situation. If the group appears to need more direction from you, provide it. If it appears to be functioning at a high level on its own, provide whatever support is necessary to keep it functioning at that level.

(Based on D. A. Whetten and K. S. Cameron, *Developing Management Skills*, 4th ed. [Upper Saddle River, NJ: Prentice Hall, 1998], Chapter 9.)

## Practice: Choosing an Effective Leadership Style

Read through the following scenario. Write down some notes about how you would handle the situation described. Be sure to refer to the six suggestions given for choosing an effective leadership style. Your professor will then tell you what to do.

**SCENARIO:**

You've been put in charge of a three-person team working on the implementation of a central accounting function for all training done by your *Fortune* 500 company. This project is new and your position is a new one. Two team members, Tony and Maria, used to be supervisors themselves, but due to an ongoing corporate reorganization, they now find themselves reporting to you. You feel like the only way to get them to do anything is to stay on them all the time. The other team member, Corbett, typically has very good ideas, but he's becoming quite reluctant to share them, particularly because Tony and Maria glare at him if he says anything. This situation is proving to be a real test of your leadership skills, but you've got a six-month deadline to complete this project, and one month is already over. You've got to figure out a way to lead this team to a successful completion of the project.

## Reinforcement: Choosing an Effective Leadership Style

The following suggestions are activities you can do to practice and reinforce the behaviors in choosing an effective leadership style.

1. Think of a group or team to which you currently belong or of which you have been a part. What type

of leadership style did the leader of this group appear to exhibit? Give some specific examples of the types of leadership behaviors he or she used. Evaluate the leadership style. Was it appropriate for the group? Why or why not? What would you have done differently? Why?

2. Observe a sports team (college or professional) that you consider extremely successful and one that you would consider unsuccessful. What leadership styles appear to be used in these team situations? Give

some specific examples of the types of leadership behaviors you observe. How would you evaluate the leadership style? Was it appropriate for the team? Why or why not? To what degree do you think the leadership style influenced the team's outcomes?

3. Interview three different managers about the leadership styles they use. Ask for specific examples of how they use their leadership style. Ask the managers how they chose the style they use and how they know if they need to change their style.

---

# COACHING

Effective managers are increasingly being described as *coaches* rather than as *bosses*. Just like coaches, they're expected to provide instruction, guidance, advice, and encouragement to help employees improve their job performance.

## Learning About: Coaching

There are three general skills that managers should exhibit if they are to help their employees generate performance breakthroughs. You can be more effective at coaching if you use those skills and practice the following specific behaviors associated with each.

1. *Analyze ways to improve an employee's performance and capabilities.* A coach looks for opportunities for an employee to expand his or her capabilities and improve performance. How? By using the following behaviors: Observe your employee's behavior on a daily basis. Ask questions of the employee: Why do you do a task this way? Can it be improved? What other approaches might be used? Show genuine interest in the employee as an individual, not merely as an employee. Respect his or her individuality. Listen to the employee.

2. *Create a supportive climate.* It's the coach's responsibility to reduce development barriers and to facilitate a climate that encourages personal performance improvement. How? By using the following behaviors: Create a climate that contributes to a free and open exchange of ideas. Offer help and assistance. Give guidance and advice when asked. Encourage your employees. Be positive and upbeat. Don't use threats. Focus on mistakes as learning opportunities. Ask: What did we learn from this that can help us in the future? Reduce obstacles. Express to the employee that you value his or her contribution to the unit's goals. Take personal responsibility for the outcome, but don't rob employees of their full responsibility. Validate the employees' efforts when they succeed. Point to what was missing when they fail. Never blame the employees for poor results.

3. *Influence employees to change their behavior.* The ultimate test of coaching effectiveness is whether or not an employee's performance improves. The concern is with ongoing growth and development. How can you do this? By using the following behaviors: Encourage continual improvement. Recognize and reward small

improvements and treat coaching as a way of helping employees to continually work toward improvement. Use a collaborative style by allowing employees to participate in identifying and choosing among improvement ideas. Break difficult tasks down into simpler ones. Model the qualities that you expect from your employees. If you want openness, dedication, commitment, and responsibility from your employees, you must demonstrate these qualities yourself.

(Based on "Blowing the Whistle on the Boss," *Training*, February 2005, p. 15; and C. D. Orth, H. E. Wilkinson, and R. C. Benfari, "The Managers' Role as Coach and Mentor," *Organizational Dynamics*, Spring 1987, p. 67.)

## Practice: Coaching

Read through the following scenario. Write down some notes about how you would handle the situation described. Be sure to refer to the three general coaching skills and the specific behaviors associated with each. Your professor will then tell you what to do next.

**SCENARIO:**

Store manager Ian McCormick was thrilled with Barbara Kim's work. She was simply the best assistant department manager he had ever seen. Barbara made friends with everyone who came into the store, and customers would often bring their items over to her and wait in line just for a chance to visit with her. When a department manager position opened up, Ian was glad to give Barbara the promotion. Barbara was even happier! She told Ian, "I can't tell you how much this means to me. I'll do anything to make this work."

As a department manager, Barbara was just as friendly as ever—too friendly, in fact. She seemed incapable of saying "no" to her former co-workers. She let them off nearly every time they asked, throwing the work schedule into disarray and leaving checkout lines open. Customers who were once happy about Barbara were now complaining. Transaction error rates also increased. Ian brought this to Barbara's attention several times, and each time Barbara said she would talk to the clerks about being more careful. But mistakes continued. Ian knows that Barbara has potential, but he's not sure what to do about this current situation. Something definitely needs to be done.

## Reinforcement: Coaching

The following suggestions are activities you can do to practice and reinforce the coaching behaviors.

1. Talk to several instructors about ways they deal with a student whose performance is not at the level it should be. What kinds of techniques do they use? Which, if any, of the coaching behaviors described do the instructors use?

2. Most of us are aware of coaches and what they do in an athletic team setting. Observe different coaches (on television or firsthand) and how they deal with individuals on their team. What types of behaviors do they exhibit? Based on what you see, what coaching advice could you use as a manager?

## CREATING EFFECTIVE TEAMS

What differentiates a *team* from a group is that members are committed to a common purpose, have a set of specific performance goals, and hold themselves mutually accountable for the team's results. Teams can produce outputs that are greater than the sum of their individual contributions. The primary force that makes a work group an effective team—that is, a real high-performing team—is its emphasis on performance.

### Learning About: Creating Effective Teams

Managers and team leaders have a significant impact on a team's effectiveness. As a result, they need to be able to create effective teams. You can be more effective at creating effective teams if you use the following nine behaviors.

1. *Establish a common purpose.* An effective team needs a common purpose to which all members aspire. This purpose is a vision. It's broader than any specific goal. This common purpose provides direction, momentum, and commitment for team members.

2. *Assess team strengths and weaknesses.* Team members will have different strengths and weaknesses. Knowing these strengths and weaknesses can help the team leader build upon the strengths and compensate for the weaknesses.

3. *Develop specific individual goals.* Specific individual goals help lead team members to achieve higher performance. In addition, specific goals facilitate clear communication and help maintain the focus on getting results.

4. *Get agreement on a common approach for achieving goals.* Goals are the ends a team strives to attain. Defining and agreeing upon a common approach ensure that the team is unified on the *means* for achieving those ends.

5. *Encourage acceptance of responsibility for both individual and team performance.* Successful teams make members individually and jointly accountable for the team's purpose, goals, and approach. Members understand what they are individually and jointly responsible for.

6. *Build mutual trust among members.* When there is *trust,* team members believe in the integrity, charac-

ter, and ability of each other. When trust is lacking, members are unable to depend on each other. Teams that lack trust tend to be short-lived.

7. *Maintain an appropriate mix of team member skills and personalities.* Team members come to the team with different skills and personalities. To perform effectively, teams need three types of skills. First, teams need people with technical expertise. Next, they need people with problem-solving and decision-making skills to identify problems, generate alternatives, evaluate those alternatives, and make competent choices. Finally, teams need people with good interpersonal skills.

8. *Provide needed training and resources.* Team leaders need to make sure that their teams have both the training and the resources they need to accomplish their goals.

9. *Create opportunities for small achievements.* Building an effective team takes time. Team members have to learn to think and work as a team. New teams can't be expected to hit home runs every time they come to bat, especially at the beginning. Instead, team members should be encouraged to try for small achievements at the beginning.

(Based on P. L. Hunsaker, *Training in Management Skills* [Upper Saddle River, NJ: 2001], Chapter 12.)

### Practice: Creating Effective Teams

Read through the following scenario. Write down some notes about how you would handle the situation described. Be sure to refer to the nine behaviors given for creating effective teams. Your professor will then tell you what to do next.

**SCENARIO:**

You're the leader of a five-member project team assigned the task of moving your engineering firm into the new booming area of high-speed rail construction. You and your team members have researched the field, identified specific business opportunities, negotiated alliances with equipment vendors, and evaluated high-speed rail experts and consultants from around the world. Throughout the process, Tonya, a highly qualified and respected engineer, has challenged everything you say during team meetings and in the workplace. For example, at a meeting two weeks ago, you presented the team with a list of 10 possible high-speed rail projects identified by the team and started evaluating your organization's ability to compete for them. Tonya contradicted virtually all of your comments, questioned your statistics, and was quite pessimistic about the possibility of contracts. After this latest display of displeasure, two other group members, Liam and Ahmed, came to you and complained that Tonya's actions were damaging the team's effectiveness. You originally put Tonya on the team for her unique expertise and insight. You'd like to find a way to reach her and get the team on the right track to its fullest potential.

## Reinforcement: Creating Effective Teams

The following suggestions are activities you can do to practice and reinforce the skills in creating effective teams.

1. Interview three managers at different organizations. Ask them about their experiences in managing teams. What behaviors have they found that have been successful in creating an effective team? What about those behaviors that have been unsuccessful in creating an effective team?

2. After completing a team project for one of your classes, assess the team's effectiveness by answering the following questions: Did everyone on the team know exactly why the team did what it did? Did team members have a significant amount of input into or influence on decisions that affected them? Did team members have open, honest, timely, two-way communications? Did everyone on the team know and understand the team's priorities? Did team members work together to resolve destructive conflicts? Was everyone on the team working toward accomplishing the same thing? Did team members understand the unwritten rules of how to behave within the group?

# DELEGATING

Managers get things done through other people. Because there are limits to any manager's time and knowledge, effective managers need to understand how to delegate. **Delegation** is the assignment of authority to another person to carry out specific duties. It allows an employee to make decisions. Delegation should not be confused with participation. In participative decision making, there's a sharing of authority. In delegation, an employee makes decisions on his or her own.

## Learning About: Delegating

A number of actions differentiate the effective delegator from the ineffective delegator. There are five behaviors that effective delegators will use.

1. *Clarify the assignment.* Determine *what* is to be delegated and *to whom.* You need to identify the person most capable of doing the task and then determine whether or not he or she has the time and motivation to do it. If you have a willing and able employee, it's your responsibility to provide clear information on what is being delegated, the results you expect, and any time or performance expectations you may have. Unless there's an overriding need to adhere to specific methods, you should delegate only the results expected. Get agreement on what is to be done and the results expected, but let the employee decide the best way to complete the task.

2. *Specify the employee's range of discretion.* Every situation of delegation comes with constraints. Although you're delegating the authority to perform some task or tasks to an employee, you're not delegating unlimited authority. You are delegating authority to act on certain issues within certain parameters. You need to specify what those parameters

are so that employees know—without any doubt—the range of their discretion.

3. *Allow the employee to participate.* One of the best ways to decide how much authority will be necessary to accomplish a task is to allow the employee who will be held accountable for that task to participate in that decision. Be aware, however, that allowing employees to participate can present its own set of potential problems as a result of employees' self-interests and biases in evaluating their own abilities.

4. *Inform others that delegation has occurred.* Delegation shouldn't take place behind the scenes. Not only do the manager and employee need to know specifically what has been delegated and how much authority has been given, so does anyone else who's likely to be affected by the employee's decisions and actions. This includes people inside and outside the organization. Essentially, you need to communicate what has been delegated (the task and amount of authority) and to whom.

5. *Establish feedback channels.* To delegate without establishing feedback controls invites problems. The establishment of controls to monitor the employee's performance increases the likelihood that important problems will be identified and that the task will be completed on time and to the desired specifications. Ideally, these controls should be determined at the time of the initial assignment. Agree on a specific time for the completion of the task and then set progress dates when the employee will report back on how well he or she is doing and any major problems that may have arisen. These controls can be supplemented with periodic checks to ensure that authority guidelines aren't being abused, organizational policies are being followed, proper procedures are being met, and the like.

(Based on P. L. Hunsaker, *Training in Management Skills* [Upper Saddle River, NJ: Prentice Hall, 2001], pp. 135–36 and 430–32; R. T. Noel, "What You Say to Your Employees When You Delegate," *Supervisory Management*, December 1993, p. 13; and S. Caudron, "Delegate for Results," *Industry Week*, February 6, 1995, pp. 27–30.)

## Practice: Delegating

Read through the following scenario. Write down some notes about how you would handle the situation described. Be sure to refer to the five behaviors described for delegating. Your professor will then tell you what to do next.

### SCENARIO:

Ricky Lee is the manager of the contracts group of a large regional office supply distributor. His boss, Anne Zumwalt, has asked him to prepare the department's new procedures manual by the end of the month. The manual will outline the steps followed when negotiating contracts with office products manufacturers who supply the organization's products. Because Ricky has another major proj-ect he's working on, he went to Anne and asked if it would be possible to assign the rewriting of the procedures manual to Bill Harmon, one of his employees who's worked in the contracts group for about three years. Anne said she had no problems with Ricky reassigning the project as long as Bill knew the parameters and the expectations for the completion of the project. Ricky is preparing for his meeting in the morning with Bill regarding this assignment.

## Reinforcement: Delegating

The following suggestions are activities you can do to practice and reinforce the behaviors in delegating.

1. Interview a manager regarding his or her delegation skills. What activities doesn't he or she delegate? Why?

2. Teach someone else how to delegate effectively. Be sure to identify the behaviors needed in delegating effectively as well as explain why these behaviors are important.

---

# DESIGNING MOTIVATING JOBS

As a manager, it's likely you're going to have to design or redesign jobs at some point. How will you ensure that these jobs are motivating? What can you do regarding job design that will maximize your employees' motivation and performance? The job characteristics model, which defines five core job dimensions (skill variety, task identity, task significance, autonomy, and feedback) and their relationships to employee motivation, provides a basis for designing motivating jobs.

## Learning About: Designing Motivating Jobs

The following five suggestions, based on the job characteristics model, specify the types of changes in jobs that are most likely to lead to improving the motivating potential for employees.

1. *Combine tasks.* As a manager, you should put existing specialized and divided tasks back together to form a new, larger module of work. This step will increase skill variety and task identity.

2. *Create natural work units.* You should design work tasks that form an identifiable and meaningful whole. This step will increase "ownership" of the work and will encourage employees to view their work as meaningful and important rather than as irrelevant and boring.

3. *Establish client relationships.* The client is the user of the product or service that is the basis for an employee's work. Whenever possible, you should establish direct relationships between your workers and your clients. This step increases skill variety, autonomy, and feedback for the employees.

4. *Expand jobs vertically.* Vertical expansion of a job means giving employees responsibilities and controls that were formerly the manager's. It partially closes the gap between the "doing" and "controlling" aspects of the job. This step increases employee autonomy.

5. *Open feedback channels.* By increasing feedback, employees not only learn how well they are performing their jobs but also whether their performance is improving, deteriorating, or remaining at a constant level. Ideally, this feedback should be received directly as the employee does the job, rather than from his or her manager on an occasional basis.

(Based on J. R. Hackman, "Work Design," in J. R. Hackman and J. L. Suttle (eds.), *Improving Life at Work* [Santa Monica, CA: Goodyear, 1977], pp. 132–33.)

## Practice: Designing Motivating Jobs

Read through the following scenario. Write down some notes about how you would handle the situation described. Be sure to refer to the five suggestions described for designing motivating jobs. Your professor will tell you what to do next.

### SCENARIO:

You work for Sunrise Deliveries, a freight transportation company that makes local deliveries of products for your customers. In your position, you supervise Sunrise's six delivery drivers. Each morning, your drivers drive their preloaded trucks to their destinations and wait for the products to be unloaded. There's a high turnover rate in the job. In fact, most of your drivers don't stay longer than six months. Not only is employee turnover getting expensive, it's hard to develop a quality customer service program when you've constantly got new faces. You've also heard complaints from the drivers that "all they do is drive." You know that you're going to have to do something to solve this problem.

## Reinforcement: Designing Motivating Jobs

The following suggestions are activities you can do to practice and reinforce the behaviors associated with designing motivating jobs.

1. Think of the worst job you ever had. Analyze the job according to the five dimensions identified in the job characteristics model. Redesign the job to make it more satisfying and motivating.

2. Interview two people in two different job positions on your campus. Ask them questions about their jobs using the job characteristics model as a guide. Using the information provided, list recommendations for making the jobs more motivating.

## DEVELOPING TRUST

Trust plays an important role in the manager's relationships with his or her employees. Given the importance of trust, today's managers should actively seek to develop it within their work group.

### Learning About: Developing Trust

You can be more effective at developing trust among your employees if you use the following eight suggestions.

1. *Practice openness.* Mistrust comes as much from what people don't know as from what they do. Being open with employees leads to confidence and trust. Keep people informed. Make clear the criteria you use in making decisions. Explain the rationale for your decisions. Be forthright and candid about problems. Fully disclose all relevant information.

2. *Be fair.* Before making decisions or taking action, consider how others will perceive them in terms of objectivity and fairness. Give credit where credit is due. Be objective and impartial in performance appraisals. Pay attention to equity perceptions in distributing rewards.

3. *Speak your feelings.* Managers who convey only hard facts come across as cold, distant, and unfeeling. When you share your feelings, others will see that you are real and human. They will know you for who you are, and their respect for you is likely to increase.

4. *Tell the truth.* Being trustworthy means being credible. If honesty is critical to credibility, then you must be perceived as someone who tells the truth. Employees are more tolerant of hearing something "they don't want to hear" than of finding out that their manager lied to them.

5. *Be consistent.* People want predictability. Mistrust comes from not knowing what to expect. Take the time to think about your values and beliefs and let those values and beliefs consistently guide your decisions. When you know what's important to you, your actions will follow, and you will project a consistency that earns trust.

6. *Fulfill your promises.* Trust requires that people believe that you are dependable. You need to ensure that you keep your word. Promises made must be promises kept.

7. *Maintain confidences.* You trust those whom you believe to be discreet and those on whom you can rely. If people open up to you and make themselves vulnerable by telling you something in confidence, they need to feel assured you won't discuss it with others or betray that confidence. If people perceive you as someone who leaks personal confidences or someone who can't be depended on, you've lost their trust.

8. *Demonstrate competence.* Develop the admiration and respect of others by demonstrating technical and professional ability. Pay particular attention to developing and displaying your communication, negotiation, and other interpersonal skills.

(Based on F. Bartolome, "Nobody Trusts the Boss Completely—Now What?," *Harvard Business Review*, March-April 1989, pp. 135–42; and J. K. Butler Jr., "Toward Understanding and Measuring Conditions of Trust: Evolution of a Condition of Trust Inventory," *Journal of Management*, September 1991, pp. 643–63.)

### Practice: Developing Trust

Read through the following scenario. Write down some notes about how you would handle the situation. Be sure to refer to the eight behaviors described for developing trust. Your professor will tell you what to do next.

**SCENARIO:**

Donna Romines is the shipping department manager at Tastefully Tempting, a gourmet candy company based in Phoenix. Orders for the company's candy come from around the world. Your six-member team processes these orders. Needless to say, the two months before Christmas are quite hectic. Everybody counts the days until December 24 when the phones finally stop ringing off the wall, at least for a couple of days. You and all of your team members breathe a sigh of relief as the last box of candy is sent on its way out the door.

When the company was first founded five years ago, the owners would shut down Tastefully Tempting for two weeks after Christmas. However, as the business has grown and moved into Internet sales, that practice has become too costly. There's too much business to afford that luxury. And the rush for Valentine's Day orders start pouring in the week after Christmas. Although the two-week, post-holiday, companywide shutdown has been phased out formally, some departments have found it difficult to get employees to gear up once again after the Christmas break. The employees who come to work after Christmas usually accomplish little. This year though, things have got to change. You know that the cultural "tradition" won't be easy to overcome, but your shipping team needs to be ready to tackle the orders that have piled up. After all, Tastefully Tempting's customers want their orders filled promptly and correctly!

## Reinforcement: Developing Trust

The following suggestions are activities you can do to practice and reinforce the behaviors associated with developing trust.

1. Keep a one-week log describing ways that your daily decisions and actions encouraged people to trust you or to not trust you. What things did you do that led to trust? What things did you do that may have led to distrust? How could you have changed your behavior so that the situations of distrust could have been situations of trust?

2. Review recent issues of a business periodical (such as *BusinessWeek, Fortune, Forbes, Fast Company, Industry Week,* or the *Wall Street Journal*) for articles where trust (or lack of trust) may have played a role. Find two articles and describe the situation. Explain how the person(s) involved might have used skills at developing trust to handle the situation.

# DISCIPLINING

If an employee's performance regularly isn't up to par or if an employee consistently ignores the organization's standards and regulations, the manager may have to use discipline as a way to control behavior. What exactly is **discipline**? It's an action taken by a manager to enforce the organization's expectations, standards, and rules. The most common types of discipline problems managers have to deal with include attendance (absenteeism, tardiness, abuse of sick leave), on-the-job behaviors (failure to meet performance goals or to use safety devices, disobedience, alcohol or drug abuse), and dishonesty (theft, lying to managers).

## Learning About: Disciplining

You can be more effective at disciplining employees if you use the following eight behaviors.

1. *Respond immediately.* The more quickly a disciplinary action is issued following a problem behavior, the more likely that the employee will associate the discipline with the behavior rather than with you as the disciplinarian. It's best to begin the disciplinary process as soon as you notice a violation.

2. *Provide a warning.* You have an obligation to warn an employee before initiating disciplinary action. This means that the employee must be aware of and accept the organization's rules and standards of behavior and performance. Disciplinary action is more likely to be seen as fair when employees have received a warning that a given behavior will lead to discipline and when they know what that disciplinary action will be.

3. *State the problem specifically.* Give the date, time, place, individuals involved, and any extenuating circumstances surrounding the problem behavior. Be sure to define the problem behavior in exact terms instead of just reciting company regulations. Explain why the behavior isn't acceptable by showing how it specifically affects the employee's job performance, the work unit's effectiveness, and the employee's colleagues.

4. *Allow the employee to explain his or her position.* Regardless of the facts you have, due process demands that an employee be given the opportunity to explain his or her position. From the employee's perspective, what happened? Why did it happen? What was his or her perception of the expectations, rules, regulations, and circumstances?

5. *Keep discussion impersonal.* Make sure that the discipline is directed at what the employee has done (or failed to do) and not at the employee personally.

6. *Be consistent.* Fair treatment of employees demands that disciplinary action be consistent. This doesn't mean, however, treating everyone exactly alike. Be sure to clearly justify disciplinary actions that might appear inconsistent to employees.

7. *Take progressive action.* Choose a disciplinary action that's appropriate to the problem behavior. Penalties should get progressively stronger if, or when, the problem is repeated. For example, you may start with an oral warning, then move progressively to a written warning, a suspension, and then, if the problem behavior warrants, dismissal. Keep in mind, however, that there may be some behaviors that warrant immediate dismissal, and these should be made clear to employees.

8. *Obtain agreement on change.* Disciplining should include guidance and direction for correcting the problem behavior. Let the employee state what he or she plans to do in the future to ensure that the problem won't be repeated.

(Based on A. Belohlav, *The Art of Disciplining Your Employees* [Upper Saddle River, NJ: Prentice Hall, 1985]; and R. H. Lussier, "A Discipline Model for Increasing Performance," *Supervisory Management*, August 1990, pp. 6–7.)

## Practice: Disciplining

Read through the following scenario. Write down some notes about how you would handle the disciplinary situation described. Be sure to refer to the eight behaviors suggested for effective disciplining. Your professor will then tell you what to do next.

**SCENARIO:**

You're a team leader in the customer services department at Mountain View Microbrewery. Carla is the newest member of your 10-person team, having been there only six weeks. She came to Mountain View with good recommendations from her previous job as a customer support representative at a car dealership. However, not long after joining your team, she was late in issuing an important purchasing order. When you talked to her about it, she said it was "lost." But you discovered it in her in-box where it had been properly placed. Then, just last week, she failed to make an immediate return call to an unhappy customer who could easily have been satisfied at that point. Instead, the customer worked himself into an unhappy rage and vented his unhappiness in a letter to the company's CEO. The latest incident with Carla came up just yesterday. As part of your company's continual quality improvement program, your team members prepare periodic reports on the service they provide to each customer and turn these reports over to an upper management team that evaluates them. Carla didn't meet the deadline for getting her report into this evaluation group, and you received a call from one of the team members wanting to know where this report was. Because Carla is still on probation for another six weeks, it appears that the time has come for you to talk to her about her failure to meet expected work performance goals.

## Reinforcement: Disciplining

The following suggestions are activities you can do to practice and reinforce the disciplining behaviors.

1. Talk with a manager at three different organizations. Ask them what guidance they've received from their organizations in disciplining employees. Have them describe specific employee discipline problems they've faced and how they've handled them.

2. Interview three of your current or past instructors. Ask them about their approaches to discipline. How do they handle late papers, cheating, excessive absenteeism, or other disciplinary problems?

---

# INTERVIEWING

The interview is used almost universally as part of the employee selection process. Not many of us have ever gotten a job without having gone through one or more interviews. Interviews can be valid and reliable selection tools, but they need to be structured and well organized.

## Learning About: Interviewing

You can be an effective interviewer if you use the following seven suggestions for interviewing job candidates.

1. *Review the job description and job specification.* Be sure that, prior to the interview, you have reviewed pertinent information about the job. Why? Because this will provide you with valuable information on which to assess the job candidate. Furthermore, knowing the relevant job requirements will help eliminate interview bias.

2. *Prepare a structured set of questions to ask all job applicants.* By having a set of prepared questions, you ensure that you'll get the information you want. Furthermore, by asking similar questions, you're able to better compare all candidates' answers against a common base.

3. *Before meeting a candidate, review his or her application form and resume.* By doing this, you'll be able to create a complete picture of the candidate in terms of what is represented on the resume or application and what the job requires. You can also begin to identify areas to explore during the interview. That is, areas that are not clearly defined on the resume or application but are essential to the job can be come a focal point in your discussion with the candidate.

4. *Open the interview by putting the applicant at ease and by providing a brief preview of the topics to be discussed.* Interviews are stressful for job candidates. Opening the discussion with small talk, such as the weather, can give the candidate time to adjust to the interview setting. By providing a preview of topics to come, you are giving the candidate an agenda. This helps the candidate to begin framing what he or she will say in response to your questions.

5. *Ask your questions and listen carefully to the candidate's answers.* Select follow-up questions that flow naturally from the answers given. Focus on the candidate's responses as they relate to information you need to ensure that the person meets your job requirements. If you're still uncertain, use a follow-up question to further probe for information.

6. *Close the interview by telling the applicant what is going to happen next.* Applicants are anxious about the status of your hiring decision. Be up-front with candidates regarding others who will be interviewed and the remaining steps in the hiring process. Let the person know your time frame for making a decision. In addition, tell the applicant how you will notify him or her about your decision.

7. *Write your evaluation of the applicant while the interview is still fresh in your mind.* Don't wait until the end of the day, after interviewing several people, to write your analysis of each person. Memory can (and often will) fail you! The sooner you write your impressions after an interview, the better chance you have of accurately noting what occurred in the interview and your perceptions of the candidate.

(Based on S. P. Robbins and D. A. DeCenzo, *Fundamentals of Management*, 5e, [Upper Saddle River, NJ: Prentice Hall, 2005], p. 202.)

## Practice: Interviewing

Read through the following list and do the actions. Be sure to refer to the seven suggestions for conducting effective interviews. Your professor will then tell you what to do next.

1. Break into groups of three.

2. Take up to 10 minutes to compose five challenging job interview questions that you think should be relevant in the hiring of new college graduates for a sales-management training program at Kraft Foods. Each hiree will spend 18 to 24 months as a sales representative, calling on retail grocery and restaurant accounts. After this training period, successful performers can be expected to be promoted to the position of district sales supervisor.

3. Exchange your five questions with another group.

4. Each group should allocate one of the following roles to their three members: interviewer, applicant, and observer. The person playing the applicant should rough out a brief resume of his or her background and experience and give it to the interviewer.

5. Role play a job interview. The interviewer should include, but not be limited to, the five questions provided by the other group.

6. After the interview, the observer should evaluate the interviewer's behaviors in terms of the effective interview suggestions.

## Reinforcement: Interviewing

The following suggestions are activities you can do to practice and reinforce the interviewing skill.

1. On your campus, there's probably a job and career placement service provided for graduating seniors. If possible, talk to two or three graduating seniors who have been interviewed by organizations through this campus service. Ask them to share what happened during their interviews. Then write a brief report describing what you found out, comparing the students' experiences with the suggestions for effective interviewing.

2. Interview a manager about the interview process he or she uses in hiring new employees. What types of information does the manager try to get during an interview? (Be sure that, as you interview this manager, you're using the suggestions for good interviewing! Although you're not "hiring" this person, you are looking for information, which is exactly what managers are looking for during a job interview.)

# MANAGING CONFLICT

Conflict is a natural by-product of people's interactions in organizations and can't be—nor should it be—eliminated. Conflict arises because organizational members have different goals and organizations have scarce resources. In addition, contemporary management practices such as empowerment and self-managed work teams—where people's work is interdependent and must be coordinated—create the potential for conflict. The ability to manage conflict is, therefore, one of the most important skills a manager needs. In fact, when human resource managers of *Fortune* 1000 companies were asked to rank the importance of certain management skills, managing conflict was in the top ten.

## Learning About: Managing Conflict

You can develop your skills at managing conflict if you use the following six behaviors.

1. *Assess the nature of the conflict.* The first thing you should do is assess the source of the conflict. Has the conflict arisen because of communication differences (semantic difficulties, misunderstandings, or noise in the communication channel)? Is the conflict the result of job or organizational structural differentiation such as disagreements over goals, decision alternatives, performance criteria, or resource allocations? Or is the conflict due to personal differences (individual behavioral idiosyncrasies or personal value systems)? Also, are there any positive aspects to the conflict that make it more functional than dysfunctional?

2. *Decide if this is a conflict that needs to be handled.* Some conflicts don't justify the manager's attention. Some aren't worth the effort and others may be unmanageable. Try to avoid trivial conflicts and focus on the ones that need attention.

3. *Evaluate the persons involved in the conflict.* It's important that you identify and be familiar with all individuals involved with the conflict. What interests or concerns does each person have? What's important to them? Who has power? What's at stake? What's their time frame? What are their personalities, feelings, and resources? You're likely to manage a conflict better if you're able to view the conflict situation from the perspective of the conflicting parties.

4. *Know your options for handling the conflict.* Managers can choose from five conflict management options. Here's a short description of each:

   **Avoidance:** Withdrawing from or suppressing the conflict. Most appropriate when the conflict is trivial, when emotions are running high, and time is needed for the conflicting parties to become less emotional, or when the potential disruption from a more assertive action outweighs the benefits of resolution.

   **Accommodation:** Maintaining harmonious relationships by placing others' needs and concerns above your own. Most viable when the issue under dispute isn't that important to you or when you want to "build up credits" for later issues.

**Forcing:** Satisfying one's own needs at the expense of another's. Works well when you need a quick resolution on important issues where unpopular actions must be taken and when commitment by others to your solution isn't crucial.

**Compromise:** A solution to conflict in which each party gives up something of value. Can be an optimum strategy when conflicting parties are about equal in power, when it's desirable to achieve a temporary solution to a complex issue, or when time pressures demand an expedient solution.

**Collaboration:** The ultimate win-win situation in which all parties to a conflict seek to satisfy their own interests. It's the best conflict option when time pressures are minimal, when all parties seriously want a win-win solution, and when the issue is too important to be compromised.

5. *Deal with the emotional aspects of conflict.* During conflict, emotions (anger, fear, resentment, etc.) tend to run high. Therefore, it's usually better to deal with those aspects rather than trying to settle the substantive aspects of the conflict. This typically involves three steps: treat the other person with respect by being aware of your own emotions and keeping them under control; listen to the other person's point of view and make that person feel understood; and briefly state your own views, needs, and feelings.

6. *Select the best option.* Start by looking at your own preferred conflict handling style. You can assess this using the self-assessment exercise "What's My Preferred Conflict Handling Style?" found on the Self-Assessment Library on R.O.L.L.S. [www.prenhall.com/rolls]. Then, look at your goals for resolving the conflict: What is the importance of the conflict issue? How concerned are you about maintaining long-term supportive interpersonal relations? And how quickly does the conflict need to be resolved?

All other things being equal, if the issue is critical to the organization's unit or success, collaboration is preferred. If sustaining relationships is important, the best strategies in order of preference are accommodation, collaboration, compromise, and avoidance. If it's crucial to resolve the conflict as quickly as possible, the best options are forcing, accommodation, and compromise—in that order.

Finally, knowing the source of the conflict can help you decide the best option. Communication-based conflicts that revolve around misinformation and misunderstandings are best resolved by collaboration. Conflicts based on personal differences, however, arise out of dissimilarities in values and personalities. These types of conflicts are susceptible to avoidance because the differences are often deeply rooted. However, managers who have to resolve these types of conflicts frequently rely on forcing, not so much because it's best for the parties, but because it works. Finally, structural conflicts can be resolved by choosing to use any of the conflict resolution options.

(Based on S. P. Robbins and P. L. Hunsaker, *Training in Interpersonal Skills*, 3e [Upper Saddle River, NJ: Prentice Hall, 2003], pp. 223–226;

P. L. Hunsaker, *Training in Management Skills* [Upper Saddle River, NJ: Prentice Hall, 2001]; S. Caudron, "On the Contrary: Productive Conflict Has Value," *Workforce*, February 1999, pp. 25–27; and C. Luporter, "Improving Managers' Interpersonal Skills," *Luporter Report*, January 14, 1999.)

## Practice: Managing Conflict

Read through the following scenario. Write down some notes about how you would handle the situation described. Be sure to refer to the six behaviors described for managing conflict. Your professor will tell you what to do next.

**SCENARIO:**

Shannon Walter has been the sales manager at Super Sports, a Midwestern sporting goods distributor, for four years. During that time, he has seen sales grow steadily. Now, however, he feels his accomplishments are being overshadowed by one of his own account reps, Maria Hampton.

Yesterday, at one of the quarterly organization-wide brainstorming sessions introduced recently by CEO Reid Sommers, Maria suggested that Super Sports change its focus drastically by going after a specialized market rather than being a full-line distributor. She argued that, "Right now our numbers are okay, but we sell too little of too much. I think we can do so much more by focusing on the children's market that's clamoring for new sporting goods all year round."

Shannon was quite surprised at Maria's suggestion since she had brought up the subject with him last week and, after discussing it, had concluded that it wasn't a good idea. He immediately replied, "We've talked about that idea already, Maria, and as we discussed, Good Sports has been very successful with a full product line."

"Wait a second," Reid interrupted. "This is just a brainstorming session, Shannon. Let's get all the ideas out before we rip them to shreds."

Shannon sighed. He knew Reid meant well with her open management style, but frequently felt it meant wasting a lot of time. And he was also irritated by Maria for bringing up a subject he thought they had already dealt with sufficiently in private.

His irritation increased considerably when Reid decided to explore Maria's proposal after the brainstorming session. She asked Maria to put together an analysis of why she believed a focus on children's products could potentially outperform the full line that Super Sports carried now. "What happened to Maria being my employee?" Shannon wondered. Although he feels that the proposed strategy will not be good for the company, he also gets the feeling that if he doesn't go along with it, it will only make things worse.

## Reinforcement: Managing Conflict

The following activities are suggestions you can do to practice and reinforce the behaviors associated with managing conflict.

1. Think of a recent conflict you've had with a friend, colleague, or family member. What was the source of

the conflict? How did you handle the conflict? Was the conflict resolved in a way that was consistent with your goals? The other person's goals? What other ways of handling the conflict might have been more effective?

2. Interview three managers at different organizations. Ask them about their experiences in managing conflict. What behaviors have they found that have been successful in managing conflict? What have they found that doesn't work?

# MANAGING RESISTANCE TO CHANGE

Managers play an important role in organizational change—that is, they often serve as change agents. However, managers may find that change is resisted by employees. After all, change represents ambiguity and uncertainty, or it threatens the status quo. How can this resistance to change be effectively managed?

## Learning About: Managing Resistance to Change

You can be more effective at managing resistance to change if you use the following suggestions.

1. *Assess the climate for change.* One major factor why some changes succeed and others fail is the readiness for change. Assessing the climate for change involves asking several questions. The more affirmative answers you get, the more likely it is that change efforts will succeed.

   • Is the sponsor of the change high enough in the hierarchy to have power to effectively deal with resistance?

   • Is senior management supportive of the change and committed to it?

   • Is there a strong sense of urgency from senior managers about the need for change and is this feeling shared by others in the organization?

   • Do managers have a clear vision of how the future will look after the change?

   • Are there objective measures in place to evaluate the change effort and have reward systems been explicitly designed to reinforce them?

   • Is the specific change effort consistent with other changes going on in the organization?

   • Are managers willing to sacrifice their personal self-interests for the good of the organization as a whole?

   • Do managers pride themselves on closely monitoring changes and actions by competitors?

   • Are managers and employees rewarded for taking risks, being innovative, and looking for new and better solutions?

   • Is the organizational structure flexible?

   • Does communication flow both down *and* up in the organization?

   • Has the organization successfully implemented changes in the recent past?

   • Is employee satisfaction with and trust in management high?

   • Is there a high degree of interaction and cooperation between organizational work units?

   • Are decisions made quickly and do decisions take into account a wide variety of suggestions?

2. *Choose an appropriate approach for managing the resistance to change.* There are six tactics that have been suggested for dealing with resistance to change. Each is designed to be appropriate for different conditions of resistance. These include *education and communication* (used when resistance comes from lack of information or inaccurate information), *participation* (used when resistance stems from people not having all the information they need or when they have the power to resist), *facilitation and support* (used when those with power will lose out in a change), *manipulation and cooptation* (used when any other tactic will not work or is too expensive), and *coercion* (used when speed is essential and change agents possess considerable power). Which one of these approaches will be most effective depends on the source of the resistance to the change.

3. *During the time the change is being implemented and after the change is completed, communicate with employees regarding what support you may be able to provide.* Your employees need to know that you are there to support them during change efforts. Be prepared to offer the necessary assistance to help your employees enact the change.

(Based on J. P. Kotter and L. A. Schlesinger, "Choosing Strategies for Change," *Harvard Business Review*, March-April 1979, pp. 106–14; and T. A. Stewart, "Rate Your Readiness to Change," *Fortune*, February 7, 1994, pp. 106–10.)

## Practice: Managing Resistance to Change

Read through the following scenario. Write down some notes about how you would handle the situation described. Be sure to refer to the three suggestions for managing resistance to change. Your professor will tell you what to do next.

SCENARIO:

You're the nursing supervisor at a community hospital employing both emergency room and floor nurses. Each of these teams of nurses tends to work almost exclusively with others doing the same job. In your professional reading, you've come across the concept of cross-training nursing teams and giving them more varied responsibilities, which in turn has been shown to improve patient care while lowering costs. You call the two team leaders, Sue and Scott, into your office to explain that you want the nursing teams to move to this approach. To your surprise, they're both opposed to the idea. Sue says she and the other emergency room nurses feel they're needed in the ER where they fill the most vital role in the hospital. They work special hours when needed, do whatever tasks are required, and often work in difficult and stressful circumstances. They think the floor nurses have relatively easy jobs for the pay they receive. Scott, leader of the floor nurse team, tells you that his group believes the ER nurses lack the special training and extra experience that the floor nurses bring to the hospital. The floor nurses claim they have the heaviest responsibilities and do the most exacting work. Because they have ongoing contact with patients and families, they believe they shouldn't be called away from vital floor duties to help the ER nurses complete their tasks.

## Reinforcement: Managing Resistance to Change

The following suggestions are activities you can do to practice and reinforce the behaviors associated with effectively managing resistance to change.

1. Think about changes (major and minor) that you have dealt with over the last year. Perhaps these changes involved other people and perhaps they were personal. Did you resist the change? Did others resist the change? How did you overcome your resistance or the resistance of others to the change?

2. Interview a manager at three different organizations about changes they have implemented. What was their experience in implementing the change? How did they manage resistance to the change?

---

# MENTORING

A **mentor** is someone in the organization, usually older, more experienced, and in a higher-level position, who sponsors or supports another employee (a protégé) who is in a lower-level position in the organization. A mentor can teach, guide, and encourage. Some organizations have formal mentoring programs, but even if your organization does not, mentoring should be an important skill for you to develop.

## Learning About: Mentoring

You can be more effective at mentoring if you use the following six suggestions as you mentor another person.

1. *Communicate honestly and openly with your protégé.* If your protégé is going to learn from you and benefit from your experience and knowledge, you're going to have to be open and honest as you talk about what you've done. Bring up the failures as well as the successes. Remember that mentoring is a learning process and in order for learning to take place, you're going to have to be open and honest in "telling it like it is."

2. *Encourage honest and open communication from your protégé.* You need to know as the mentor what your protégé hopes to gain from this relationship. You should encourage the protégé to ask for information and to be specific about what he or she wants to gain.

3. *Treat the relationship with the protégé as a learning opportunity.* Don't pretend to have all the answers and all the knowledge, but do share what you've learned through your experiences. And in your conversations and interactions with your protégé, you may be able to learn as much from that person as he or she does from you. So be open to listening to what your protégé is saying.

4. *Take the time to get to know your protégé.* As a mentor, you should be willing to take the time to get to know your protégé and his or her interests. If you're

not willing to spend that extra time, you should probably not embark on a mentoring relationship.

5. *Remind your protégé that there is no substitute for effective work performance.* In any job, effective work performance is absolutely essential for success. It doesn't matter how much information you provide as a mentor if the protégé isn't willing to strive for effective work performance.

6. *Know when it's time to let go.* Successful mentors know when it's time to let the protégé begin standing on his or her own. If the mentoring relationship has been effective, the protégé will be comfortable and confident in handling new and increasing work responsibilities. And just because the mentoring relationship is over doesn't mean that you never have contact with your protégé. It just means that the relationship becomes one of equals, not one of teacher and student.

(Based on H. Rothman, "The Boss as Mentor," *Nation's Business*, April 1993, pp. 66–67; J. B. Cunningham and T. Eberle, "Characteristics of the Mentoring Experience: A Qualitative Study," *Personnel Review*, June 1993, pp. 54–66; S. Crandell, "The Joys of Mentoring," *Executive Female*, March-April 1994, pp. 38–42; W. Heery, "Corporate Mentoring Can Break the Glass Ceiling," *HRFocus*, May 1994, pp. 17–18; and M. Boyle, "Most Mentoring Programs Stink—But Yours Doesn't Have to," *Training*, August 2005, pp. 12–15.)

## Practice: Mentoring

Read through the following scenario. Write down some notes about how you would handle the situation described. Be sure to refer to the six behaviors for mentoring. Your professor will then tell you what to do next.

### SCENARIO:

Lora Slovinsky has worked for your department in a software design firm longer than any of your other employees. You value her skills and commitment and you frequently ask for her judgment on difficult issues. Very often, her ideas have been better than yours and you've let her know through both praise and pay increases how much you appreciate her contributions. Recently though, you've begun to question Lora's judgment. The fundamental problem is in the distinct difference in the ways you both approach your work. Your strengths lie in getting things done on time and under budget. Although Lora is aware of these constraints, her creativity and perfectionism sometimes makes her prolong projects, continually looking for the best approaches. On her most recent assignment, Lora seemed more intent than ever on doing things her way. Despite what you felt were clear guidelines, she was two weeks late in meeting an important customer deadline. And while her product quality was high, as always, the software design was far more elaborate than what was needed at this stage of development. Looking over her work in your office, you feel more than a little frustrated and certain that you need to address matters with Lora.

## Reinforcement: Mentoring

The following suggestions are activities you can do to practice and reinforce the behaviors needed in mentoring.

1. If there are individuals on your campus who act as mentors (or advisors) to first-time students, make an appointment to talk to one of them. These mentors may be upper-division students or they may be professors or college staff employees. Ask them about their role as a mentor and the skills they think it takes to be an effective mentor. How do the skills they mention relate to the behaviors described here?

2. Athletic coaches often act as mentors to their younger assistant coaches. Interview a coach about her or his role as a mentor. What types of things do coaches do to instruct, teach, advise, and encourage their assistant coaches? Could any of these activities be transferred to an organizational setting? Explain.

## NEGOTIATING

Negotiating is another interpersonal skill that managers use. For instance, they may have to negotiate salaries for incoming employees, negotiate for resources from their managers, work out differences with associates, or resolve conflicts with subordinates. **Negotiation** is a process of bargaining in which two or more parties with different preferences must make joint decisions and come to an agreement.

## Learning About: Negotiating

You can be more effective at negotiating if you use the following six recommended behaviors.

1. *Research the individual with whom you will be negotiating.* Acquire as much information as you can about the person with whom you'll be negotiating. What are this individual's interests and goals? Understanding this person's position will help you to better understand his or her behavior, predict his or her responses to your offers, and frame solutions in terms of his or her interests.

2. *Begin with a positive overture.* Research shows that concessions tend to be reciprocated and lead to agreements. Therefore, begin bargaining with a positive overture and then reciprocate the other party's concessions.

3. *Address problems, not personalities.* Concentrate on the negotiation issues, not on the personal characteristics of the individual with whom you're negotiating. When negotiations get tough, avoid the tendency to attack this person. Remember it's that person's ideas or position that you disagree with, not him or her personally.

4. *Pay little attention to initial offers.* Treat an initial offer as merely a point of departure. Everyone must have an initial position. Such positions tend to be extreme and idealistic. Treat them as such.

5. *Emphasize win-win solutions.* If conditions are supportive, look for an integrative solution. Frame options in terms of the other party's interests and look for solutions that can allow this person, as well as yourself, to declare a victory.

6. *Create an open and trusting climate.* Skilled negotiators are better listeners, ask more questions, focus their arguments more directly, are less defensive, and have learned to avoid words or phrases that can irritate the person with whom they're negotiating (such as "generous offer," "fair price," or "reasonable arrangement"). In other words, they are better at creating the open and trusting climate that is necessary for reaching a win-win settlement.

(Based on M. H. Bazerman and M. A. Neale, *Negotiating Rationally* [New York: The Free Press, 1992]; J. A. Wall, Jr. and M. W. Blum, "Negotiations," *Journal of Management*, June 1991, pp. 278–82; L. Babcock, S. Laschever, M. Gelfand, and D. Small, "Nice Girls Don't Ask," *Harvard Business Review*, October 2003, pp. 14–15; and M. Kaplan, "How to Negotiate Anything," *Money*, May 2005, pp. 117–119.)

## Practice: Negotiating

Read through the following scenario. Write down some notes about how you would handle the situation. Be sure to refer to the six behaviors described for negotiating. Your professor will then tell you what to do next.

**SCENARIO:**

As marketing director for Done Right, a regional home repair chain, you've come up with a plan you believe has significant potential for future sales. Your plan involves a customer information service designed to help people make their homes more environmentally sensitive. Then, based upon homeowners' assessments of their homes' environmental impact, your firm will be prepared to help them deal with problems or concerns they may uncover. You're really excited about the competitive potential of this new service. You envision pamphlets, in-store appearances by environmental experts, as well as contests for consumers and school kids. After several weeks of preparations, you make your pitch to your boss, Patrick Wong. You point out how the market for environmentally sensitive products is growing and how this growing demand represents the perfect opportunity for Done Right. Patrick seems impressed by your presentation, but he's expressed one major concern. He thinks your workload is already too heavy. He doesn't see how you're going to have enough time to start this new service *and* still be able to look after all of your other assigned marketing duties.

## Reinforcement: Negotiating

The following suggestions are activities you can do to practice and reinforce the negotiating behaviors.

1. Find three people who have recently purchased new or used cars. Interview each to learn which tactics, if any, they used to get a better deal (lower price, more car features, and so forth). Write a short paper comparing your findings and relating them to the negotiating behaviors presented in this section.

2. Research current business periodicals for two examples of negotiations. The negotiations may be labor-management negotiations or negotiations over buying and selling real estate or a business. What did the article say about the negotiation process? Write down specific questions that each party to the negotiation might have had. Pretend that you were a consultant to one of the parties in the negotiation. What recommendations would you have made?

# PROVIDING FEEDBACK

Ask a manager about the feedback he or she gives employees, and you're likely to get an answer followed by a qualifier! If the feedback is positive, it's likely to be given promptly and enthusiastically. However, negative feedback is often treated very differently. Like most of us, managers don't particularly enjoy communicating bad news. They fear offending the other person or having to deal with the recipient's defensiveness. The result is that negative feedback is often avoided, delayed, or substantially distorted. However, it is important for managers to provide both positive and negative feedback.

## Learning About: Providing Feedback

You can be more effective at providing feedback if you use the following six specific suggestions.

1. *Focus on specific behaviors.* Feedback should be specific rather than general. Avoid such statements as "You have a bad attitude" or "I'm really impressed with the good job you did." They're vague and although they provide information, they don't tell the recipient enough to correct the "bad attitude" or on what basis you concluded that a "good job" had been done so the person knows what behaviors to repeat or to avoid.

2. *Keep feedback impersonal.* Feedback, particularly the negative kind, should be descriptive rather than judgmental or evaluative. No matter how upset you are, keep the feedback focused on job-related behaviors and never criticize someone personally because of an inappropriate action.

3. *Keep feedback goal oriented.* Feedback should not be given primarily to "unload" on another person. If you have to say something negative, make sure it's directed toward the recipient's goals. Ask yourself whom the feedback is supposed to help. If the answer is *you,* bite your tongue and hold the comment. Such feedback undermines your credibility and lessens the meaning and influence of future feedback.

4. *Make feedback well timed.* Feedback is most meaningful to a recipient when there's a very short interval between his or her behavior and the receipt of feedback about that behavior. Moreover, if you're particularly concerned with changing behavior, delays in providing feedback on the undesirable actions lessen the likelihood that the feedback will be effective in bringing about the desired change. Of course, making feedback prompt merely for the sake of promptness can backfire if you have insufficient information, if you're angry, or if you're otherwise emotionally upset. In such instances, "well timed" could mean "somewhat delayed."

5. *Ensure understanding.* Make sure your feedback is concise and complete so that the recipient clearly and fully understands your communication. It may help to have the recipient rephrase the content of your feedback to find out whether or not it fully captured your intended meaning.

6. *Direct negative feedback toward behavior that the recipient can control.* There's little value in reminding a person of some shortcoming over which he or she has no control. Negative feedback should be directed at behavior that the recipient can do something about. In addition, when negative feedback is given concerning something that the recipient can control, it might be a good idea to indicate specifically what can be done to improve the situation.

(Based on P. L. Hunsaker, *Training in Management Skills* [Upper Saddle River, NJ: Prentice Hall, 2001], pp. 60–61; J. M. Jackman and M. H. Strober, "Fear of Feedback," *Harvard Business Review,* April 2003, pp. 101–107; and D. D. Van Fleet, T. O. Peterson, and E. W. Van Fleet, "Closing the Performance Feedback Gap with Expert Systems," *Academy of Management Executive,* August 2005, pp. 38–53.)

## Practice: Providing Feedback

Read through the following scenario. Write down some notes about how you would handle the situation. Be sure to refer to the six behaviors described for providing feedback. Your professor will tell you what to do next.

**SCENARIO:**

Craig is an excellent employee whose expertise and productivity have always met or exceeded your expectations. But recently he's been making work difficult for other members of your advertising team. Like his co-workers, Craig researches and computes the costs of media coverage for your advertising agency's clients. The work requires laboriously leafing through several large reference books to find the correct base price and add-on charges for each radio or television station and time slot, calculating each actual cost, and compiling the results in a computerized spreadsheet. To make things more efficient and convenient, you've always allowed your team members to bring the reference books they're using to their desks while they're using them. Lately, however, Craig has been piling books around him for days and sometimes weeks at a time. The books interfere with the flow of traffic past his desk and other people have to go out of their way to retrieve the books from Craig's pile. It's time for you to have a talk with Craig.

## Reinforcement: Providing Feedback

The following suggestions are activities you can do to practice and reinforce the behaviors in providing feedback.

1. Think of three things that a friend or family member recently did well. Did you praise the person at the time? If not, why? The next time someone close to you does something well, give him or her positive feedback.

2. You have a good friend who has a mannerism (for instance, speech, body movement, style of dress, or whatever) that you think is inappropriate and detracts from the overall impression that he or she makes. Come up with a plan for talking with this person. What will you say? When will you talk with your friend? How will you handle his or her reaction?

# READING AN ORGANIZATION'S CULTURE

The ability to read an organization's culture can be a valuable skill. For instance, if you're looking for a job, you'll want to choose an employer whose culture is compatible with your values and in which you'll feel comfortable. If you can accurately assess a potential employer's culture before you make your job decision, you may be able to save yourself a lot of anxiety and reduce the likelihood of making a poor choice. Similarly, you'll undoubtedly have business transactions with numerous organizations during your professional career, such as selling a product or service, negotiating a contract, arranging a joint work project, or merely seeking out who controls certain decisions in an organization. The ability to assess another organization's culture can be a definite plus in successfully performing those pursuits.

## Learning About: Reading an Organization's Culture

You can be more effective at reading an organization's culture if you use the following behaviors. For the sake of simplicity, we're going to look at this skill from the perspective of a job applicant. We'll assume that you're interviewing for a job, although these skills can be generalized to many situations. Here's a list of things you can do to help learn about an organization's culture.

1. *Observe the physical surroundings.* Pay attention to signs, posters, pictures, photos, style of dress, length of hair, degree of openness between offices, and office furnishings and arrangements.

2. *Make note of those with whom you met.* Was it the person who would be your immediate supervisor? Or did you meet with potential colleagues, managers from other departments, or senior executives? Based on what they revealed, to what degree do people interact with others who may not be in their particular work area or at their particular organizational level?

3. *How would you characterize the style of the people you met?* Are they formal? Casual? Serious? Laid-back? Open? Not willing to provide information?

4. *Look at the organization's human resources manual.* Are formal rules and regulations printed there? If so, how detailed are these policies?

5. *Ask questions of the people with whom you meet.* The most valid and reliable information tends to come from asking the same questions of many people (to see how closely their responses align) and by talking with individuals whose jobs link them to the outside environment. Questions that will give you insights into organizational processes and practices may include:

What is the background of the founders?

What is the background of current senior managers?

What are their functional specialties?

Were they promoted from within or hired from outside?

How does the organization integrate new employees?

Is there a formal orientation program?

Are there formal employee training programs?

How does your boss define his or her job success?

How would you define fairness in terms of reward allocations?

Can you identify some people here who are on the "fast track"?

What do you think has put them on the fast track?

Can you identify someone in the organization who seems to be considered an oddball or deviant?

How has the organization responded to this person?

Can you describe a decision that someone made that was well received?

Can you describe a decision that didn't work out well?

What were the consequences for the decision maker?

Could you describe a crisis or critical event that has occurred recently in the organization?

How did top management respond?

What was learned from this experience?

(Based on D. Sacks, "Cracking Your Next Company's Culture," *Fast Company*, October 2005, pp. 85–87; and S. P. Robbins and T. A. Judge, *Organizational Behavior* 12e [Upper Saddle River, NJ: Prentice Hall, 2007], pp. 587–588.)

## Practice: Reading an Organization's Culture

Read through the following scenario. Write down some notes about how you would handle the situation. Be sure to refer to the suggested behaviors for reading an organization's culture. Your professor will tell you what to do next.

### SCENARIO:

After spending your first three years after college graduation as a freelance graphic designer, you're looking at pursuing a job as an account executive at a graphic design firm. You feel that the scope of assignments and potential for technical training far exceed what you'd be able to do on your own, and you're looking to expand your skills and meet a brand-new set of challenges. However, you want to make sure you "fit" into the organization where you're going to be spending more than eight hours every work day. What's the best way for you to find a place where you'll be happy and where your style and personality will be appreciated?

## Reinforcement: Reading an Organization's Culture

The following suggestions are activities you can do to practice and reinforce the behaviors associated with reading an organization's culture.

1. If you're taking more than one course, assess the culture of the various classes in which you're enrolled. How do the classroom cultures differ? Which culture(s) do you seem to prefer? Why?

2. Do some comparisons of the atmosphere or feeling you get from various organizations. Because of the number and wide variety that you'll find, it will probably be easiest for you to do this exercise using restaurants, retail stores, or banks. Based on the atmosphere that you observe, what type of organizational culture do you think these organizations might have? On what did you base your decision? Which type of culture do you prefer? Why? If you can, interview three employees at this organization for their descriptions of the organization's culture. Did their descriptions support your interpretation? Why or why not?

# RUNNING PRODUCTIVE MEETINGS

Each day some 25 million meetings take place in corporate America. That's a lot of meetings and according to a 2005 report by the Society for Human Resource Management, a lot of wasted time and effort. A survey of almost 1,500 employees showed that 75 percent believed that the meetings they attend could be more effective. Because managers convene and attend many meetings, knowing how to run meetings productively is an important management skill to have.

## Learning About: Running Productive Meetings

You can be more effective at running productive meetings and at making them more satisfying to meeting participants by first recognizing the basic problems with meetings and second, by using guidelines to plan and conduct the meeting.

Many meetings are unproductive because they suffer from the following basic problems:

1. the meeting is unnecessary—the topic is unimportant, not critical, or doesn't require an exchange of ideas;

2. the meeting organizer tries to accomplish too much during the meeting;

3. the meeting itself lacks clear goals and organization;

4. meeting participants don't have clearly defined roles;

5. meeting participants exhibit either too much or too little conflict and emotional expression during the meeting; and

6. nothing ever happens as a result of the meeting, leading to the widely-held belief that meetings are unproductive.

You can make meetings more productive using the following suggestions: 1. make sure a meeting is necessary and establish a clear purpose for the meeting; 2. select participants based on the purpose of the meeting; 3. prepare the participants by distributing advance information including date, starting time and ending time, location of meeting, agenda, and any pre-meeting tasks that need to be completed; 4. start the meeting on time with a short introduction that restates the purpose of the meeting and provides any necessary background information; 5. keep the meeting moving along by keeping participants focused on the agenda items and encouraging balanced participation; 6. recognize that conflict among meeting participants is natural and may even be desirable, but be prepared to manage the conflict if it gets out of hand; 7. manage unproductive behavior or dysfunctional group members by laying down any rules in the beginning, strategically seating potentially dysfunctional group members, assigning potentially dysfunctional members specific tasks such as group recorder, asking participants to speak in a specific order, interrupting monopolizers, encouraging non-talkers, and praising and encouraging those who seem to need it; 8. conclude the meeting at the specified time; 9. summarize what was discussed and assign any action items; and 10. follow up the meeting with recorded minutes from the meeting and a re-statement of any decisions and plans.

Keep in mind that these suggestions are appropriate for face-to-face meetings. However, today, many organizational meetings take place among participants who are in different geographic locations. Although these meetings require technological collaboration (such as teleconferencing, videoconferencing, or so forth), many of the same suggestions apply. The meeting coordinator is still responsible for preparing for the meeting, keeping the meeting on time and on task, and for ending the meeting and following up.

(Based on S. Armour, "Some Companies Aim to Tame Meetings," *USA Today*, July 6, 2006, p. 3B; M. E. Guffey, *Business Communication*, 5e [Mason, OH: Thomson South-Western, 2006], pp. 55–64; and M. Prospero, "Two Words You Never Hear Together: Great Meeting," *Fast Company*, June 2004, p. 38.)

## Practice: Running Productive Meetings

Read through the following scenario. Write down some notes about how you would handle the situation described. Be sure to refer to the suggestions for running productive meetings. Your professor will then tell you what to do next.

### SCENARIO:

As the director of human resources for Enterprise Bank and Trust Company, you are responsible for all issues related to the company's employees. A year ago, the CEO approved a "casual Friday" dress code policy. However, the results from a recent customer survey seem to indicate that some employees have been pushing the limits of casual dress. The CEO has asked you to head up a team of nine employees (with representatives from all organizational levels) and come up with more specific guidelines. You are to plan a meeting for the end of the month. Describe what you need to do to set up and prepare for this meeting.

During the meeting, two of the employees representing the front-line tellers and clerks have been reluctant to give their opinions. Yet, since these individuals are the ones who interact first-hand with customers, getting their opinions is important. On the other hand, the individuals representing the top executive team have been very vocal in expressing their opinions. As the meeting leader, what will you do about this situation?

After much discussion, the group comes up with several recommendations for more specific guidelines for casual Friday dress and the meeting concludes. What do you need to do now?

## Reinforcement: Running Productive Meetings

The best way to reinforce your skills at running productive meetings is to continue to do it whenever you have the opportunity to do so. At work, at school, or in student organizations to which you might belong, be involved with setting up meetings, running meetings, and following up after meetings. This type of practice will give you the experience you need for being skilled at running productive meetings.

# SCANNING THE ENVIRONMENT

Anticipating and interpreting changes that are taking place in the environment is an important skill that managers need. Information that comes from scanning the environment can be used in making decisions and taking actions. Managers at all levels of an organization need to know how to scan the environment for important information and trends.

## Learning About: Scanning the Environment

You can be more effective at scanning the environment if you use the following suggestions:

1. *Decide which type of environmental information is important to your work.* Perhaps you need to know changes in customers' needs and desires or perhaps you need to know what your competitors are doing. Once you know the type of information that you'd like to have, you can look at the best ways to get that information.

2. *Regularly read and monitor pertinent information.* There is no scarcity of information to scan, but what you need to do is read pertinent information sources. How do you know information sources are pertinent? They're pertinent if they provide you with the information that you identified as important.

3. *Incorporate the information that you get from your environmental scanning into your decisions and actions.* Unless you use the information you're getting, you're wasting your time getting it. Also, the more that you find you're using information from your environmental scanning, the more likely it is that you'll want to continue to invest time and other resources into gathering it. You'll see that this information is important to your being able to manage effectively and efficiently.

4. *Regularly review your environmental scanning activities.* If you find that you're spending too much time getting non-useful information or if you're not using the pertinent information that you've gathered, you need to make some adjustments.

5. *Encourage your subordinates to be alert to information that is important.* Your employees can be your "eyes and ears" as well. Emphasize to them the

importance of gathering and sharing information that may affect your work unit's performance.

(Based on L. M. Fuld, *Monitoring the Competition* [New York: Wiley, 1988]; E. H. Burack and N. J. Mathys, "Environmental Scanning Improves Strategic Planning," *Personnel Administrator*, 1989, pp. 82–87; and R. Subramanian, N. Fernandes, and E. Harper, "Environmental Scanning in U.S. Companies: Their Nature and Their Relationship to Performance," *Management International Review*, July 1993, pp. 271–86.)

## Practice: Scanning the Environment

Read through the following scenario. Write down some notes about how you would handle the situation described. Be sure to refer to the suggestions for scanning the environment. Your professor will then tell you what to do next.

#### SCENARIO:

You're the assistant to the president at your college. You've been asked to prepare a report outlining the external information that you think is important for her to monitor. Think of the types of information the president would need in order to do an effective job of managing the college now and over the next three years. Be as specific as you can in describing this information. Also, identify where this information could be found.

## Reinforcement: Scanning the Environment

The following suggestions are activities you can do to practice and reinforce the behaviors associated with scanning the environment.

1. Select an organization with which you're familiar, either as an employee or perhaps as a frequent customer. Assume that you're the top manager in this organization. What types of environmental scanning information do you think would be important? Where would you find this information? Now assume that you're a first-level manager in this organization. Would the types of information you'd get from environmental scanning change? Explain.

2. Assume you're a regional manager for a large bookstore chain. Using the Internet, what types of environmental and competitive information were you able to identify? For each source, what information did you find that might help you do your job better?

# SETTING GOALS

Employees should have a clear understanding of what they're attempting to accomplish. In addition, managers have the responsibility for seeing that this is done by helping employees set work goals. Setting goals is a skill every manager needs to develop.

## Learning About: Setting Goals

You can be more effective at setting goals if you use the following eight suggestions.

1. *Identify an employee's key job tasks.* Goal setting begins by defining what it is that you want your employees to accomplish. The best source for this information is each employee's job description.

2. *Establish specific and challenging goals for each key task.* Identify the level of performance expected of each employee. Specify the target toward which the employee is working.

3. *Specify the deadlines for each goal.* Putting deadlines on each goal reduces ambiguity. Deadlines, however, should not be set arbitrarily. Rather, they need to be realistic given the tasks to be completed.

4. *Allow the employee to actively participate.* When employees participate in goal setting, they're more likely to accept the goals. However, it must be sincere participation. That is, employees must perceive that you are truly seeking their input, not just going through the motions.

5. *Prioritize goals.* When you give someone more than one goal, it's important for you to rank the goals in order of importance. The purpose of prioritizing is to encourage the employee to take action and expend effort on each goal in proportion to its importance.

6. *Rate goals for difficulty and importance.* Goal setting should not encourage people to choose easy goals. Instead, goals should be rated for their difficulty and importance. When goals are rated, individuals can be given credit for trying difficult goals, even if they don't fully achieve them.

7. *Build in feedback mechanisms to assess goal progress.* Feedback lets employees know whether their level of effort is sufficient to attain the goal. Feedback should be both self-generated and supervisor generated. In either case, feedback should be frequent and recurring.

8. *Link rewards to goal attainment.* It's natural for employees to ask, "What's in it for me?" Linking rewards to the achievement of goals will help answer that question.

(Based on S. P. Robbins and D. A. DeCenzo, *Fundamentals of Management*, 5e [Upper Saddle River, NJ: Prentice Hall, 2005], p. 97.)

## Practice: Setting Goals

Read through the following scenario. Write down some notes about how you would handle the situation described. Be sure to refer to the eight suggestions for setting goals. Your professor will then tell you what to do next.

#### SCENARIO:

You worked your way through college while holding down a part-time job bagging groceries at Food Town supermarket chain. You like working in the food industry and when you graduated, you accepted a position with Food Town as a management trainee. Three years have passed, and you've gained experience in the grocery store industry and in operating a large supermarket. About a year ago, you received a promotion to store manager at one of the chain's locations. One of the things you've liked about Food Town is that it gives store managers a great deal of autonomy in running their stores. The company provided very general guidelines to its managers. The concern was with the bottom line; for the most part, how you got there was up to you. Now that you're finally a store manager, you want to establish an MBO-type program in your store. You like the idea that everyone should have clear goals to work toward and then they are evaluated against those goals.

Your store employs 90 people although, except for the managers, most work only 20 to 30 hours per week. You have six people reporting to you: an assistant manager; a week-end manager; and grocery, produce, meat, and bakery managers. The only highly skilled jobs belong to the butchers who have strict training and regulatory guidelines. Other less-skilled jobs include cashier, shelf stocker, cleanup, and grocery bagger.

Specifically describe how you would go about setting goals in your new position. Include examples of goals for the jobs of butcher, cashier, and bakery manager.

## Reinforcement: Setting Goals

The following suggestions are activities you can do to practice and reinforce the behaviors in setting goals.

1. Where do you want to be in five years? Do you have specific five-year goals? Establish three goals you want to achieve in five years. Make sure these goals are specific, challenging, and measurable.

2. Set personal and academic goals you want to achieve by the end of this college term. Prioritize and rate them for difficulty.

# SOLVING PROBLEMS CREATIVELY

In a global business environment, where changes are fast and furious, organizations desperately need creative people. The uniqueness and variety of problems that managers face demand that they be able to solve problems creatively. Creativity is a frame of mind. You need to expand your mind's capabilities—that is, open up your mind to new ideas. Every individual has the ability to improve his or her creativity, but many people simply don't try to develop that ability.

## Learning About: Solving Problems Creatively

You can be more effective at solving problems creatively if you use the following 10 suggestions.

1. *Think of yourself as creative.* Although this may be a simple suggestion, research shows that if you think you can't be creative, you won't be. Believing in your ability to be creative is the first step in becoming more creative.

2. *Pay attention to your intuition.* Every individual has a subconscious mind that works well. Sometimes answers will come to you when you least expect them. Listen to that "inner voice." In fact, most creative people will keep a notepad near their bed and write down ideas when the thoughts come to them. That way, they don't forget them.

3. *Move away from your comfort zone.* Every individual has a comfort zone in which certainty exists. But creativity and the known often do not mix. To be creative, you need to move away from the status quo and focus your mind on something new.

4. *Determine what you want to do.* This includes such things as taking time to understand a problem before beginning to try to resolve it, getting all the facts in mind, and trying to identify the most important facts.

5. *Look for ways to tackle the problem.* This can be accomplished by setting aside a block of time to focus on it; working out a plan for attacking it; establishing subgoals; imagining or actually using analogies wherever possible (for example, could you approach your problem like a fish out of water and look at what the fish does to cope? Or can you use the things you have to do to find your way when it's foggy to help you solve your problem?); using different problem-solving strategies such as verbal, visual, mathematical, theatrical (for instance, you might draw a diagram of the decision or problem to help you visualize it better or you might talk to yourself out loud about the problem telling it as you would tell a story to someone); trusting your intuition; and playing with possible ideas and approaches (for example, look at your problem from a different perspective or ask yourself what someone else, like your grandmother, might do if faced with the same situation).

6. *Look for ways to do things better.* This may involve trying consciously to be original; not worrying about looking foolish; eliminating cultural taboos (like gender stereotypes) that might influence your possible solutions; keeping an open mind; being alert to odd or puzzling facts; thinking of unconventional ways to use objects and the environment (for instance, thinking about how you could use newspaper or magazine headlines to help you be a better problem solver); discarding usual or habitual ways of doing things; and striving for objectivity by being as critical of your own ideas as you would those of someone else.

7. *Find several right answers.* Being creative means continuing to look for other solutions even when you think you have solved the problem. A better, more creative solution just might be found.

8. *Believe in finding a workable solution.* Like believing in yourself, you also need to believe in your ideas. If

9. *Brainstorm with others.* Creativity is not an isolated activity. Bouncing ideas off of others creates a synergistic effect.

10. *Turn creative ideas into action.* Coming up with creative ideas is only part of the process. Once the ideas are generated, they must be implemented. Keeping great ideas in your mind or on papers that no one will read does little to expand your creative abilities.

(Based on J. Calano and J. Salzman, "Ten Ways to Fire Up Your Creativity," *Working Woman*, July 1989, p. 94; J. V. Anderson, "Mind Mapping: A Tool for Creative Thinking," *Business Horizons*, January-February 1993, pp. 42–46; M. Loeb, "Ten Commandments for Managing Creative People," *Fortune*, January 16, 1995, pp. 135–36; M. Henricks, "Good Thinking," *Entrepreneur*, May 1996, pp. 70–73; and J. Paskin, "How to Handle a Crushing Deadline," *Money*, November 2005, p. 44A–44B.)

## Practice: Solving Problems Creatively

Read through the following scenario. Write down some notes about how you would handle the situation. Be sure to refer to the 10 suggestions for solving problems creatively. Your professor will then tell you what to do next.

### SCENARIO:

Every time the phone rings, your stomach clenches and your palms start to sweat. And it's no wonder! As sales manager for Brinkers, a machine tool parts manufacturer, you're besieged by calls from customers who are upset about late deliveries. Your boss, Carter Hererra, acts as both production manager and scheduler. Every time your sales representatives negotiate a sale, it's up to Carter to determine whether or not production can actually meet the delivery date the customer specifies. And Carter invariably says, "No problem." The good thing about this is that you make a lot of initial sales. The bad news is that production hardly ever meets the shipment dates that Carter authorizes. And he doesn't seem to be all that concerned about the aftermath of late deliveries. He says, "Our customers know they're getting outstanding quality at a great price. Just let them try to match that anywhere. It can't be done. So even if they have to wait a couple of extra days or weeks, they're still getting the best deal they can." However, the customers don't see it that way, and they let you know about their unhappiness. Then it's up to you to try to soothe the relationship. You know this problem has to be taken care of, but what possible solutions are there? After all, how are you going to keep from making your manager or the customers mad?

## Reinforcement: Solving Problems Creatively

The following suggestions are activities you can do to practice and reinforce the behaviors associated with solving problems creatively.

1. Take out a few sheets of paper. You have 20 minutes to list as many medical or health care related jobs as you can that begin with the letter *r* (for instance, radiologist, registered nurse). If you run out of listings before time is up, it's OK to quit early, but try to be as creative as you can.

2. List on a piece of paper some common terms that apply to both *water* and *finance*. How many were you able to come up with?

## VALUING DIVERSITY

"Understanding and managing people who are similar to us are challenges—but understanding and managing those *who are dissimilar from us and from each other* can be even tougher." The increasing diversity of workplaces around the world means that managers need to recognize that not all employees want the same thing nor will they act in the same manner, and thus can't be managed the same way. What is a diverse workforce? It's one that's more heterogeneous in terms of gender, race, ethnicity, age, and other characteristics that reflect differences. The ability to value diversity and help a diverse workforce achieve its maximum potential is a skill that managers increasingly will find is needed.

## Learning About: Valuing Diversity

The diversity issues an individual manager might face are many. They may include issues such as communicating with employees whose familiarity with the language may be limited; creating career development programs that fit the skills, needs, and values of a particular group; helping a diverse team cope with a conflict over goals or work assignments; or learning which rewards are valued by different groups. You can improve your handling of diversity issues by following these eight behaviors.

1. *Fully accept diversity.* Successfully valuing diversity starts with each individual accepting the principle of diversity. Accept the value of diversity for its own sake—not simply because it's the right thing to do. And it's important that you reflect your acceptance in all you say and do.

2. *Recruit broadly.* When you have job openings, work to get a diverse applicant pool. Although referrals from current employees can be a good source of applicants, they tend to produce candidates similar to the present workforce.

3. *Select fairly.* Make sure that the selection process doesn't discriminate. One suggestion is to use job-specific tests rather than general aptitude or knowledge tests. Such tests measure specific skills, not subjective characteristics.

4. *Provide orientation and training for diverse employees.* Making the transition from outsider to insider can be particularly difficult for a diverse employee.

Provide support either through a group or through a mentoring arrangement.

5. *Sensitize non-diverse employees.* Not only do you personally need to accept and value diversity, as a manager you need to encourage all your employees to do so. Many organizations do this through diversity training programs. In addition, employees can also be part of ongoing discussion groups whose members meet monthly to discuss stereotypes and ways of improving diversity relationships. And, as mentioned above, the most important thing a manager can do is show by his or her actions that diversity is valued.

6. *Strive to be flexible.* Part of valuing diversity is recognizing that different groups have different needs and values. Be flexible in accommodating employee requests.

7. *Seek to motivate individually.* Motivating employees is an important skill for any manager; motivating a diverse workforce has its own special challenges. Managers must be more in tune with the background, cultures, and values of employees.

8. *Reinforce employee differences.* Encourage individuals to embrace and value diverse views. Create traditions and ceremonies that promote diversity. Celebrate diversity by accentuating its positive aspects. However, also be prepared to deal with the challenges of diversity such as mistrust, miscommunication, lack of cohesiveness, attitudinal differences, and stress.

(Based on: C. Harvey and J. Allard, *Understanding and Managing Diversity: Readings, Cases, and Exercises,* 3e [Upper Saddle River, NJ: Prentice Hall, 2005]; P. L. Hunsaker, *Training in Management Skills* [Upper Saddle River, NJ: Prentice Hall, 2001]; and J. Greenberg, *Managing Behavior in Organizations: Science in Service to Practice,* 2e [Upper Saddle River, NJ: Prentice Hall, 1999].)

## Practice: Valuing Diversity

Read through the following scenario. Write down some notes about how you would handle the situation described. Be sure to refer to the eight behaviors described for valuing diversity. Your professor will tell you what to do next.

### SCENARIO:

Read through the descriptions of the following employees who work for the same organization. After reading each description, write a short paragraph describing what you think the goals and priorities of each employee might be. With what types of employee issues might the manager of each employee have to deal? How could these managers exhibit the value of diversity?

**Lester.** Lester is 57 years old, a college graduate, and a vice president of the firm. His two children are married, and he is a grandparent of three beautiful grandchildren. He lives in a condo with his wife who does volunteer work and is active in their church. Marvin is healthy and likes to stay active, both physically and mentally.

**Sanjyot.** Sanjyot is a 30-year-old clerical worker who came to the United States from Indonesia 10 years ago. She completed high school after moving to the United States and has begun to attend evening classes at a local community college. Sanjyot is a single parent with two children under the age of eight. Although her health is excellent, one of her children suffers from a severe learning disability.

**Yuri.** Yuri is a recent immigrant from one of the former Soviet republics. He is 42 years old and his English communication skills are quite limited. He has an engineering degree from his country but since he's not licensed to practice in the United States, he works as a parts clerk. He is unmarried and has no children but feels obligated to his relatives back in his home country. He sends much of his paycheck to them.

## Reinforcement: Valuing Diversity

The following suggestions are activities you can do to practice and reinforce the behaviors associated with valuing diversity.

1. Indicate which employees (age, gender, ethnicity, family status, and so forth) you think might be motivated by the following additional employee benefits: onsite day care, fitness center, tuition reimbursement, job sharing, English classes, having a mentor, being a mentor, performance bonus plan, more time off, flextime, enhanced retirement benefits, supervisory training, subsidized dependent care, discounts on company products, religious holidays, free candy and snacks in employee break room, onsite physician, country club membership, and onsite dry cleaning services. Looking at your responses, what are the implications for a manager?

2. Ask your friends who are part of a minority group what kinds of biases they perceive in school or at work. Think about how you, as a manager, might deal with instances of these types of biases.

3. Come up with a list of suggestions that you can personally use to improve your sensitivity to diversity issues.

# Endnotes

## Chapter 1

1. Information from company Web site, www.pressroom.ups.com, and Hoover's Online, www.hoovers.com, February 27, 2006; C. Dahlson, "Who's the Boss in 25 Key Industries and Why," *Hispanic Trends,* www.hispaniconline.com/trends, March–April 2005; and J. Erickson, "Air Authority," *Hispanic Business,* April 2004, pp. 26–30.

2. Information from Catalyst Web page, www.catalyst.org, December 1, 2005.

3. K. A. Tucker and V. Allman, "Don't Be a Cat-and-Mouse Manager," The Gallup Organization, www.brain.gallup.com, September 9, 2004.

4. "WorkUSA® 2004/2005: Effective Employees Drive Financial Results," Watson Wyatt Worldwide, Washington, DC.

5. D. J. Campbell, "The Proactive Employee: Managing Workplace Initiative," *Academy of Management Executive,* August 2000, pp. 52–66.

6. J. S. McClenahen, "Prairie Home Champion," *Industry Week,* October 2005, pp. 45–47.

7. P. Panchak, "Sustaining Lean," *Industry Week,* October 2005, pp. 48–50.

8. H. Fayol, *Industrial and General Administration* (Paris: Dunod, 1916).

9. For a comprehensive review of this question, see C. P. Hales, "What Do Managers Do? A Critical Review of the Evidence," *Journal of Management,* January 1986, pp. 88–115.

10. J. T. Straub, "Put on Your Manager's Hat," *USA Today Online,* www.usatoday.com, October 29, 2002; and H. Mintzberg, *The Nature of Managerial Work* (New York: Harper & Row, 1973).

11. H. Mintzberg and J. Gosling, "Educating Managers Beyond Borders," *Academy of Management Learning and Education,* September 2002, pp. 64–76.

12. See, for example, M. J. Martinko and W. L. Gardner, "Structured Observation of Managerial Work: A Replication and Synthesis," *Journal of Management Studies,* May 1990, pp. 330–357; A. I. Kraut, P. R. Pedigo, D. D. McKenna, and M. D. Dunnette, "The Role of the Manager: What's Really Important in Different Management Jobs," *Academy of Management Executive,* November 1989, pp. 286–293; Hales, "What Do Managers Do?"; C. M. Pavett and A. W. Lau, "Managerial Work: The Influence of Hierarchical Level and Functional Specialty," *Academy of Management Journal,* March 1983, pp. 170–177; A. W. Lau and C. M. Pavett, "The Nature of Managerial Work: A Comparison of Public and Private Sector Managers," *Group and Organization Studies,* December 1980, pp. 453–466; M. W. McCall, Jr., and C. A. Segrist, "In Pursuit of the Manager's Job: Building on Mintzberg," *Technical Report No. 14* (Greensboro, NC: Center for Creative Leadership, 1980); L. D. Alexander, "The Effect Level in the Hierarchy and Functional Area Have on the Extent Mintzberg's Roles Are Required by Managerial Jobs," *Academy of Management Proceedings* (San Francisco, 1979), pp. 186–189.

13. Pavett and Lau, "Managerial Work."

14. S. J. Carroll and D. A. Gillen, "Are the Classical Management Functions Useful in Describing Managerial Work?" *Academy of Management Review,* January 1987, p. 48.

15. S. J. Carroll and D. A. Gillen, "Are the Classical Management Functions Useful in Describing Managerial Work?" *Academy of Management Review,* January 1987, p. 48; and H. Koontz, "Commentary on the Management Theory Jungle—Nearly Two Decades Later," in H. Koontz, C. O'Donnell, and H. Weihrich (eds.), *Management: A Book of Readings,* 6th ed. (New York: McGraw-Hill, 1984).

16. R. L. Katz, "Skills of an Effective Administrator," *Harvard Business Review,* September–October 1974, pp. 90–102.

17. W. C. Symonds, S. Baker, M. Arndt, and R. D. Hof, "The Future of Work," *BusinessWeek,* March 22, 2004, pp. 50–52.

18. American Management Association Survey of Managerial Skills and Competence: March/April 2000, found on American Management Association Online, www.amanet.org, October 30, 2002.

19. C. Ansberry, "What's My Line?" *Wall Street Journal,* March 22, 2002, pp. A1+.

20. J. Fox, "A Meditation on Risk," *Fortune,* October 3, 2005, pp. 50–62.

21. F. F. Reichheld, "Lead for Loyalty," *Harvard Business Review,* July–August 2001, p. 76.

22. Cited in E. Naumann and D. W. Jackson, Jr., "One More Time: How Do You Satisfy Customers?" *Business Horizons,* May–June 1999, p. 73.

23. Data from Associated Press, "Service Sector Grows in November, But Pace Slows," *USA Today,* www.usatoday.com, December 6, 2005; and *The World Factbook 2005,* www.cia.gov/publications/factbook/index.html, December 5, 2005.

24. K. A. Eddleston, D. L. Kidder, and B. E. Litzky, "Who's the Boss? Contending with Competing Expectations from Customers and Management," *Academy of Management Executive,* November 2002, pp. 85–95.

25. See, for instance, S. D. Pugh, J. Dietz, J. W. Wiley, and S. M. Brooks, "Driving Service Effectiveness Through Employee-Customer Linkages," *Academy of Management Executive,* November 2002, pp. 73–84; Eddleston, Kidder, and Litzky, "Who's the Boss? Contending with Competing Expectations from Customers and Management"; B. A. Gutek, M. Groth, and B. Cherry, "Achieving Service Success Through Relationships and Enhanced Encounters," *Academy of Management Executive,* November 2002, pp. 132–144; W. C. Tsai, "Determinants and Consequences of Employee Displayed Positive Emotions," *Journal of*

*Management,* vol. 27 (4), 2001, pp. 497–512; S. D. Pugh, "Service with a Smile: Emotional Contagion in the Service Encounter," *Academy of Management Journal,* October 2001, pp. 1018–1027; Naumann and Jackson, Jr., "One More Time: How Do You Satisfy Customers?"; and M. D. Hartline and O. C. Ferrell, "The Management of Customer-Contact Service Employees: An Empirical Investigation," *Journal of Marketing,* October 1996, pp. 52–70.

26. R. A. Hattori and J. Wycoff, "Innovation DNA," *Training and Development,* January 2002, p. 24.

27. R. A. Hattori, "Sometimes Innovation Starts with a Relationship," found on the Innovation Network, www.thinksmart.com, March 14, 2003.

28. R. Wagner, "One Store, One Team at Best Buy," *Gallup Brain,* August 12, 2004, http://brain.gallup.com/content, November 28, 2005.

29. Q. Hardy, "Google Thinks Small," *Forbes,* November 14, 2005, pp. 198–202.

30. C. Jacobs and D. Coghlan, "Sound from Silence: On Listening in Organizational Learning," *Human Relations,* vol. 58 (1), 2005, pp. 115–138; C. E. Connelly and D. G. Gallagher, "Emerging Trends in Contingent Work Research," *Journal of Management,* vol. 30 (6), 2004, pp. 959–983; J. S. Harrison and R. E. Freeman, "Is Organizational Democracy Worth the Effort?" *Academy of Management Exectuive,* August 2004, pp. 49–53; H. G. Barkema, J. A. C. Baum, and E. A. Mannix, "Management Challenges in a New Time," *Academy of Management Journal,* October 2002, pp. 916–930; M. A. Hitt, "Transformation of Management for the New Millennium," *Organizational Dynamics,* Winter 2000, pp. 7–17; and "Workplace Trends Shifting over Time," *Springfield News Leader,* January 2, 2000.

31. J. Sandberg, "Down over Moving Up: Some New Bosses Find They Hate Their Jobs," *Wall Street Journal,* July 27, 2005, p. B1.

## Chapter 2

1. Information from company Web site, www.nike.com, February 27, 2006; and S. Holmes, "Green Foot Forward," *BusinessWeek,* November 28, 2005, p. 24.

2. C. S. George Jr., *The History of Management Thought,* 2d ed. (Upper Saddle River, NJ: Prentice Hall, 1972), p. 4.

3. Ibid., pp. 35–41.

4. F. W. Taylor, *Principles of Scientific Management* (New York: Harper, 1911), p. 44. For other information on Taylor, see R. Kanigel, *The One Best Way: Frederick Winslow Taylor and the Enigma of Efficiency* (New York: Viking, 1997); and M. Banta, *Taylored Lives: Narrative Productions in the Age of Taylor, Veblen, and Ford* (Chicago: University of Chicago Press, 1993).

5. See, for example, F. B. Gilbreth and L. M. Gilbreth, *Fatigue Study* (New York: Sturgis and Walton, 1916); and F. B. Gilbreth, *Motion Study* (New York: Van Nostrand, 1911).

6. G. Colvin, "Managing in the Info Era," *Fortune,* March 6, 2000, pp. F6–F9; and A. Harrington, "The Big Ideas," *Fortune,* November 22, 1999, pp. 152–153.

7. H. Fayol, *Industrial and General Administration* (Paris: Dunod, 1916).

8. M. Lounsbury and E. J. Carberry, "From King to Court Jester? Weber's Fall from Grace in Organizational Theory," *Organization Studies,* vol. 26 (4), 2005, pp. 501–525; and M. Weber, *The Theory of Social and Economic Organizations,* ed. T. Parsons, trans. A. M. Henderson and T. Parsons (New York: Free Press, 1947).

9. N. Zamiska, "Plane Geometry: Scientists Help Speed Boarding of Aircraft," *Wall Street Journal,* November 2, 2005, pp. A1+.

10. F. J. Roethlisberger and W. J. Dickson, *Management and the Worker* (Cambridge, MA: Harvard University Press, 1939); and E. Mayo, *The Human Problems of an Industrial Civilization* (New York: Macmillan, 1933).

11. See, for example, G. W. Yunker, "An Explanation of Positive and Negative Hawthorne Effects: Evidence from the Relay Assembly Test Room and Bank Wiring Observation Room Studies," paper presented, Academy of Management Annual Meeting, August 1993, Atlanta, Georgia; S. R. Jones, "Was There a Hawthorne Effect?" *American Sociological Review,* November 1992, pp. 451–468; S. R. G. Jones, "Worker Interdependence and Output: The Hawthorne Studies Reevaluated," *American Sociological Review,* April 1990, pp. 176–190; J. A. Sonnenfeld, "Shedding Light on the Hawthorne Studies," *Journal of Occupational Behavior,* April 1985, pp. 111–130; B. Rice, "The Hawthorne Defect: Persistence of a Flawed Theory," *Psychology Today,* February 1982, pp. 70–74; R. H. Franke and J. Kaul, "The Hawthorne Experiments: First Statistical Interpretations," *American Sociological Review,* October 1978, pp. 623–643; and A. Carey, "The Hawthorne Studies: A Radical Criticism," *American Sociological Review,* June 1967, pp. 403–416.

12. K. B. DeGreene, *Sociotechnical Systems: Factors in Analysis, Design, and Management* (Upper Saddle River, NJ: Prentice Hall, 1973), p. 13.

13. G. Colvin, "America Isn't Ready," *Fortune,* July 25, 2005, p. 72.

14. Ibid.

15. J. E. Garten, "Globalism Without Tears," *Strategy & Business,* Fourth Quarter 2002, pp. 36–45; L. L. Bierema, J. W. Bing, and T. J. Carter, "The Global Pendulum," *Training and Development,* May 2002, pp. 70–78; C. Taylor, "Whatever Happened to Globalization?" *Fast Company,* September 1999, pp. 228–236; and S. Zahra, "The Changing Rules of Global Competitiveness in the 21st Century," *Academy of Management Executive,* February 1999, pp. 36–42.

16. K. McCoy, "Former Tyco Execs Sentenced to up to 25 Years," *USA Today,* September 20, 2005, www.usatoday.com.

17. R. W. Judy and Carol D'Amico, *Workforce 2020* (Indianapolis: Hudson Institute, August 1999).

18. "Hispanics Now Top Minority," *Hispanic Business,* March 2003, p. 16.

19. P. Coy, "Old. Smart. Productive." *BusinessWeek,* June 27, 2005, pp. 78–86.

20. S. Pasha, "Corporations Woo Baby Boomers," *CNNMoney*, September 29, 2005, cnnmoney.com.

21. S. Armour, "Generation Y: They've Arrived at Work with a New Attitude," *USA Today*, November 7, 2005, pp. B1+.

22. G. Naik, L. Chang, and J. Slater, "Leveraging the Age Gap," *Wall Street Journal*, February 27, 2003, pp. B1+.

23. G. W. Loveman and J. J. Gabarro, "The Managerial Implications of Changing Work Force Demographics: A Scoping Study," *Human Resource Management*, Spring 1991, pp. 7–29.

24. "Minority Report," *BusinessWeek*, April 25, 2005, p. 11.

25. F. Johansson, "Masters of the Multicultural," *Harvard Business Review*, October 2005, pp. 18–19.

26. M. Hancock, managing editor, *Global Entrepreneurship Monitor 2004 Executive Report*, www.gemconsortium.org, December 22, 2005; and "The Third Millennium: Small Business and Entrepreneurship in the 21st Century," Office of Advocacy, U.S. Small Business Administration, accessed on U.S. Small Business Administration Web site, www.sba.gov, February 15, 2002.

27. Information for this box came from K. Fuson, "iPods Now Double as Study Aids," *USA Today*, March 15, 2006, p. 4D; P. Tyre, "Professor in Your Pocket," *Newsweek*, November 28, 2005, pp. 46–47; S. Hamm, "Motivating the Troops," *BusinessWeek*, November 21, 2005, pp. 88–103; P. Davidson, "Gadgets Rule on College Campuses," *USA Today*, March 29, 2005, pp. 1B+; and M. J. Tippins and R. S. Sohi, "IT Competency and Firm Performance: Is Organizational Learning a Missing Link?" *Strategic Management Journal*, August 2003, pp. 745–761.

28. T. J. Mullaney, "E-Biz Strikes Again," *BusinessWeek*, May 10, 2004, pp. 80–90; J. Edwards, "The New New Economy," *CFO*, January 2004, pp. 19–20; and R. D. Hof and S. Hamm, "How E-Biz Rose, Fell, and Will Rise Anew," *BusinessWeek*, May 13, 2002, pp. 64–72.

29. D. A. Menasce and V. A. F. Almeida, *Scaling for E-Business* (Upper Saddle River, NJ: Prentice Hall PTR, 2000).

30. Menasce and Almeida, *Scaling for E-Business*; M. Lewis, "Boom or Bust," *Business 2.0*, April 2000, pp. 192–205; J. Davis, "How It Works," *Business 2.0*, February 2000, pp. 112–115; and S. Alsop, "e or Be Eaten," *Fortune*, November 8, 1999, pp. 86–98.

31. R. S. Boyd, "World Choking on a Deluge of Data," *Springfield News-Leader*, February 22, 2004, p. 5A.

32. J. Gordon, "Making Knowledge Management Work," *Training*, August 2005, pp. 16–21; K. G. Smith, C. J. Collins, and K. D. Clark, "Existing Knowledge, Knowledge Creation Capability, and the Rate of New Product Introduction in High-Technology Firms," *Academy of Management Journal*, April 2005, pp. 346–357; L. Argote, "Reflections on Two Views of Managing Learning and Knowledge in Organizations," *Journal of Management Inquiry*, March 2005, pp. 43–48; J. S. Brown and P. Duguid, "Balancing Act: How to Capture Knowledge Without Killing It," *Harvard Business Review*, May–June 2000, pp. 73–80; E. C. Wenger and W. M. Snyder, "Communities of Practice: The Organizational Frontier," *Harvard Business Review*, January–February 2000, pp. 139–145; and M. T. Hansen, N. Nohria, and T. Tierney, "What's Your Strategy for Managing Knowledge?" *Harvard Business Review*, March–April 1999, pp. 106–116.

33. See, for example, J. Jusko, "Tried and True," *IW*, December 6, 1999, pp. 78–84; T. A. Stewart, "A Conversation with Joseph Juran," *Fortune*, January 11, 1999, pp. 168–170; T. C. Powell, "Total Quality Management as Competitive Advantage: A Review and Empirical Study," *Strategic Management Journal*, January 1995, pp. 15–37; J. R. Hackman and R. Wageman, "Total Quality Management: Empirical, Conceptual, and Practical Issues," *Administrative Science Quarterly*, June 1995, pp. 309–342; R. K. Reger, L. T. Gustafson, S. M. Demarie, and J. V. Mullane, "Reframing the Organization: Why Implementing Total Quality Is Easier Said Than Done," *Academy of Management Review*, July 1994, pp. 565–584; C. A. Reeves and D. A. Bednar, "Defining Quality: Alternatives and Implications," *Academy of Management Review*, July 1994, pp. 419–445; J. W. Dean Jr. and D. E. Bowen, "Management Theory and Total Quality: Improving Research and Practice Through Theory Development," *Academy of Management Review*, July 1994, pp. 392–418; A. Gabor, *The Man Who Discovered Quality* (New York: Random House, 1990); and B. Krone, "Total Quality Management: An American Odyssey," *The Bureaucrat*, Fall 1990, pp. 35–38.

## Notes for the Part 1 Continuing Case

Information from company Web site, www.starbucks.com, and Hoover's *Online*, www.hoovers.com, June 14, 2006; J. Simmons, *My Sister's a Barista: How They Made Starbucks a Home away from Home* (London: Cyan Books, 2005); A. Serwer, "Hot Starbucks to Go," *Fortune*, January 26, 2004, pp. 60–74; S. Holmes, I. M. Kunii, J. Ewing, and K. Capell, "For Starbucks, There's No Place Like Home," *BusinessWeek*, June 9, 2003, p. 48; and H. Schultz and D. Jones Yang, *Pour Your Heart into It: How Starbucks Built a Company One Cup at a Time* (New York: Hyperion, 1997).

## Chapter 3

1. Information from company Web site, www.ubisoft.com, February 24, 2006; and G. Keighley, "Massively Multinational Player," *Business 2.0*, September 2005, pp. 64–66.

2. A. Merrick, "Sears Shuffles Its Management Team," *Wall Street Journal*, September 9, 2005, p. A3.

3. S. Kirchhoff, "Manufactured Home, Travel Trailer Stocks Rise," *USA Today*, September 16, 2005, p. 5B.

4. "Why CEO Churn Is Healthy," *BusinessWeek*, November 13, 2000, p. 230; S. M. Puffer and J. B. Weintrop, "Corporate Performance and CEO Turnover: The Role of Performance Expectations," *Administrative Science Quarterly*, March 1991, pp. 1–19; C. R. Schwenk,

"Illusions of Management Control? Effects of Self-Serving Attributions on Resource Commitments and Confidence in Management," *Human Relations*, April 1990, pp. 333–347; D. C. Hambrick and S. Finkelstein, "Managerial Discretion: A Bridge Between Polar Views of Organizational Outcomes," in L. L. Cummings and B. M. Staw (eds.), *Research in Organizational Behavior*, vol. 9 (Greenwich, CT: JAI Press, 1987), pp. 369–406; J. A. Byrne, "The Limits of Power," *BusinessWeek*, October 23, 1987, pp. 33–35; J. R. Meindl and S. B. Ehrlich, "The Romance of Leadership and the Evaluation of Organizational Performance," *Academy of Management Journal*, March 1987, pp. 91–109. For insights into the symbolic view, see J. Pfeffer, "Management as Symbolic Action: The Creation and Maintenance of Organizational Paradigms," in L. L. Cummings and B. M. Staw (eds.), *Research in Organizational Behavior*, vol. 3 (Greenwich, CT: JAI Press, 1981), pp. 1–52.

5. T. M. Hout, "Are Managers Obsolete?" *Harvard Business Review*, March–April 1999, pp. 161–168; and Pfeffer, "Management as Symbolic Action."

6. "Fun and Feel-Good ROI," *Workforce*, December 2000, p. 38.

7. K. Shadur and M. A. Kienzle, "The Relationship Between Organizational Climate and Employee Perceptions of Involvement," *Group & Organization Management*, December 1999, pp. 479–503; D. R. Denison, "What Is the Difference Between Organizational Culture and Organizational Climate? A Native's Point of View on a Decade of Paradigm Wars," paper presented at Academy of Management Annual Meeting, 1993, Atlanta, GA; M. J. Hatch, "The Dynamics of Organizational Culture," *Academy of Management Review*, October 1993, pp. 657–693; and L. Smircich, "Concepts of Culture and Organizational Analysis," *Administrative Science Quarterly*, September 1983, p. 339.

8. J. A. Chatman and K. A. Jehn, "Assessing the Relationship Between Industry Characteristics and Organizational Culture: How Different Can You Be?" *Academy of Management Journal*, June 1994, pp. 522–553; and C. A. O'Reilly III, J. Chatman, and D. F. Caldwell, "People and Organizational Culture: A Profile Comparison Approach to Assessing Person–Organization Fit," *Academy of Management Journal*, September 1991, pp. 487–516.

9. A. E. M. Va Vianen, "Person–Organization Fit: The Match Between Newcomers' and Recruiters' Preferences for Organizational Cultures," *Personnel Psychology*, Spring 2000, pp. 113–149; K. Shadur and M. A. Kienzle, *Group & Organization Management*; P. Lok and J. Crawford, "The Relationship Between Commitment and Organizational Culture, Subculture, and Leadership Style," *Leadership & Organization Development Journal*, vol. 20 (6/7), 1999, pp. 365–374; C. Vandenberghe, "Organizational Culture, Person–Culture Fit, and Turnover: A Replication in the Health Care Industry," *Journal of Organizational Behavior*, March 1999, pp. 175–184; and C. Orphen, "The Effect of Organizational Cultural Norms on the Relationships Between Personnel Practices and Employee Commitment," *Journal of Psychology*, September 1993, pp. 577–579.

10. See for example, J. B. Sorensen, "The Strength of Corporate Culture and the Reliability of Firm Performance," *Administrative Science Quarterly,* vol. 47 (1), 2002, pp. 70–91; R. Goffee and G. Jones, "What Holds the Modern Company Together?" *Harvard Business Review*, November–December 1996, pp. 133–148; J. C. Collins and J. I. Porras, *Built to Last* (New York: HarperBusiness, 1994); Collins and Porras, "Building Your Company's Vision," *Harvard Business Review*, September–October 1996, pp. 65–77; J. P. Kotter and J. L. Heskett, *Corporate Culture and Performance* (New York: Free Press, 1992), pp. 15–27; G. G. Gordon and N. DiTomaso, "PredictingCorporate Performance from Organizational Culture," *Journal of Management Studies*, November 1992, pp. 793–798; and D. R. Denison, *Corporate Culture and Organizational Effectiveness* (New York: Wiley, 1990).

11. L. B. Rosenfeld, J. M. Richman, and S. K. May, "Information Adequacy, Job Satisfaction, and Organizational Culture in a Dispersed-Network Organization," *Journal of Applied Communication Research,* vol. 32, 2004, pp. 28–54; and Sorensen, pp. 70–91.

12. E. H. Schien, *Organizational Culture and Leadership* (San Francisco: Jossey-Bass, 1985), pp. 314–315.

13. Y. Chouinard, *Let My People Go Surfing* (New York: Penguin Press, 2005); and A. Lustgarten, "14 Innovators," *Fortune*, November 15, 2004, www.fortune.com.

14. This box is based on J. Sandberg, "Sometimes an Office Visit Can Feel Like a Visit to a Very Foreign Land," *Wall Street Journal,* October 20, 2005, p. B1; D. Sacks, "Scout's Honor," *Fast Company,* April 2005, p. 94; D. W. Brown, "Searching for Clues," *Black Enterprise,* November 2002, pp. 114–120; L. Bower, "Weigh Values to Decide If Working for 'Beasts' Worthwhile," *Springfield Business Journal,* November 4, 2002, p. 73; S. Shellenbarger, "How to Find Out if You're Going to Hate a New Job Before You Agree to Take It," *Wall Street Journal,* June 13, 2002, p. D1; and M. Boyle, "Just Right," *Fortune,* June 10, 2002, pp. 207–208.

15. R. Berner, "At Sears, A Great Communicator," *BusinessWeek,* October 31, 2005, pp. 50–52.

16. S. E. Ante, "The New Blue," *BusinessWeek,* March 17, 2003, p. 82.

17. P. Kafka, "Bean Counter," *Forbes,* February 28, 2005, pp. 78–80; A. Overholt, "Listening to Starbucks," *Fast Company,* July 2004, pp. 50–56; S. Gruner, "Lasting Impressions," *Inc.,* July 1998, p. 126; and B. Filipczak, "Trained by Starbucks," *Training,* June 1995, pp. 73–79.

18. S. Denning, "Telling Tales," *Harvard Business Review,* May 2004, pp. 122–129; T. Terez, "The Business of Storytelling," *Workforce,* May 2002, pp. 22–24; J. Forman, "When Stories Create an Organization's Future," *Strategy & Business,* Second Quarter 1999, pp. 6–9; C. H. Deutsch, "The Parables of Corporate Culture," *New York Times,* October 13, 1991, p. F25; and D. M. Boje, "The Storytelling Organization: A

Study of Story Performance in an Office-Supply Firm," *Administrative Science Quarterly*, March 1991, pp. 106–126.

19. E. Ransdell, "The Nike Story? Just Tell It!" *Fast Company*, January–February 2000, pp. 44–46.

20. J. Useem, "Jim McNerney Thinks He Can Turn 3M from a Good Company into a Great One—With a Little Help from His Former Employer, General Electric," *Fortune*, August 12, 2002, pp. 127–132.

21. Denning, 2004; and A. M. Pettigrew, "On Studying Organizational Cultures," *Administrative Science Quarterly*, December 1979, p. 576.

22. D. Drickhamer, "Straight to the Heart," *Industry Week*, October 2003, pp. 36–38.

23. M. Zagorski, "Here's the Drill," *Fast Company*, February 2001, p. 58.

24. A. Bryant, "The New Power Breakfast," *Newsweek*, May 15, 2000, p. 52.

25. C. Palmeri, "The Fastest Drill in the West," *BusinessWeek*, October 24, 2005, pp. 86–88.

26. This box is based on "Diversity Is Important to the Bottom Line," *HR Powerhouse*, www.hrpowerhouse.com, January 21, 2006; P. Rosinski, *Coaching Across Cultures: New Tools for Leveraging National, Corporate, and Professional Differences* (London: Nicholas Brealey Publishing, 2003); "Diversity at the Forefront," *BusinessWeek*, November 4, 2002, pp. 27–38; "Talking to Diversity Experts: Where Do We Go From Here?" *Fortune*, September 30, 2002, pp. 157–172; "Keeping Your Edge: Managing a Diverse Corporate Culture," *Fortune*, June 11, 2001, pp. S1–S18; "Diversity Today," *Fortune*, June 12, 2000, pp. S1–S24; O. C. Richard, "Racial Diversity, Business Strategy, and Firm Performance: A Resource-Based View," *Academy of Management Journal*, April 2000, pp. 164–177; A. Markels, "How One Hotel Manages Staff's Diversity," *Wall Street Journal*, November 20, 1996, pp. B1+; C. A. Deutsch, "Corporate Diversity in Practice," *New York Times*, November 20, 1996, pp. C1+; and D. A. Thomas and R. J. Ely, "Making Differences Matter: A New Paradigm for Managing Diversity," *Harvard Business Review*, September–October 1996, pp. 79–90.

27. See company's Web site, www.stlukes.co.uk; P. LaBarre, "Success: Here's the Inside Story," *Fast Company*, November 1999, pp. 128–132; and A. Law, *Creative Company: How St. Luke's Became "The Ad Agency to End All Ad Agencies"* (New York: Wiley, 1999).

28. A. Raghavan, K. Kranhold, and A. Barrionuevo, "Full Speed Ahead: How Enron Bosses Created a Culture of Pushing Limits," *Wall Street Journal*, August 26, 2002, pp. A1+.

29. J. A. Byrne et al., "How to Fix Corporate Governance," *BusinessWeek*, May 6, 2002, pp. 68–78.

30. See M. W. Dickson, D. B. Smith, M. W. Grojean, and M. Ehrhart, "An Organizational Climate Regarding Ethics: The Outcome of Leader Values and the Practices That Reflect Them," *Leadership Quarterly*, Summer 2001, pp. 197–217; L. K. Trevino, "A Cultural Perspective on Changing and Developing Organizational Ethics," in W. A. Pasmore and R. W. Woodman (eds.), *Research in Organizational Change and Development*, vol. 4 (Greenwich, CT: JAI Press, 1990); and B. Victor and J. B. Cullen, "The Organizational Bases of Ethical Work Climates," *Administrative Science Quarterly*, March 1988, pp. 101–125.

31. J. A. Byrne, "After Enron: The Ideal Corporation," *BusinessWeek*, August 26, 2002, p. 74.

32. T. Kelley and J. Littman, *The Ten Faces of Innovation: IDEO's Strategies for Defeating the Devil's Advocate and Driving Creativity Throughout Your Organization* (New York: Currency, 2005); C. Fredman, "The IDEO Difference,"*Hemispheres*, August 2002, pp. 52–57; and T. Kelley and J. Littman, *The Art of Innovation* (New York: Currency, 2001).

33. L. Tischler, "Join the Circus," *Fast Company*, July 2005, pp. 52–58; and "Cirque du Soleil: Creating a Culture of Extraordinary Creativity," available on the Innovation Network Web site, www.thinksmart.com, March 14, 2003.

34. L. Simpson, "Fostering Creativity," *Training*, December 2001, p. 56.

35. L. Gary, "Simplify and Execute: Words to Live By in Times of Turbulence," *Harvard Management Update*, January 2003, p. 12.

36. Based on S. D. Pugh, J. Dietz, J. W. Wiley, and S. M. Brooks, "Driving Service Effectiveness Through Employee–Customer Linkages," *Academy of Management Executive*, November 2002, pp. 73–84; K. A. Eddleston, D. L. Kidder, and B. E. Litzky, "Who's the Boss? Contending with Competing Expectations from Customers and Management," *Academy of Management Executive*, November 2002, pp. 85–95; B. A. Gutek, M. Groth, and B. Cherry, "Achieving Service Success Through Relationships and Enhanced Encounters," *Academy of Management Executive*, November 2002, pp. 132–144; R. C. Ford and C. P. Heaton, "Lessons from Hospitality That Can Serve Anyone," *Organizational Dynamics*, Summer 2001, pp. 30–47; L. A. Bettencourt, K. P. Gwinner, and M. L. Mueter, "A Comparison of Attitude, Personality, and Knowledge Predictors of Service-Oriented Organizational Citizenship Behaviors," *Journal of Applied Psychology*, February 2001, pp. 29–41; B. Schneider, D. E. Bowen, M. G. Ehrhart, and K. M. Holcombe, "The Climate for Service: Evolution of a Construct," in N. M. Ashkanasy, C. P. M. Wilderom, and M. F. Peterson (eds.), *Handbook of Organizational Culture and Climate* (Thousand Oaks, CA: Sage, 2000), pp. 21–36; M. D. Hartline, J. G. Maxham III, and D. O. McKee, "Corridors of Influence in the Dissemination of Customer-Oriented Strategy to Customer Contact Service Employees," *Journal of Marketing*, April 2000, pp. 35–50; M. L. Lengnick-Hall and C. A. Lengnick-Hall, "Expanding Customer Orientation in the HR Function," *Human Resource Management*, Fall 1999, pp. 201–214; M. D. Hartline and O. C.

Ferrell, "The Management of Customer-Contact Service Employees: An Empirical Investigation," *Journal of Marketing,* October 1996, pp. 52–70; and M. J. Bitner, B. H. Booms, and L. A. Mohr, "Critical Service Encounters: the Employee's Viewpoint," *Journal of Marketing,* October 1994, pp. 95–106.

37. R. A. Giacalone and C. L. Jurkiewicz (eds.), *Handbook of Workplace Spirituality and Organizational Performance* (New York: M. E. Sharp, 2003).

38. This section is based on D. Grant, "What Should a Science of Workplace Spirituality Study? The Case for a Relational Approach," *Academy of Management Proceedings Best Paper,* August 2005; C. D. Pielstick, "Teaching Spirituality Synchronicity in a Business Leadership Class," *Journal of Management Education,* February 2005, pp. 153–168; G. A. Gull and J. Doh, "The 'Transmutation' of the Organization: Toward a More Spiritual Workplace," *Journal of Management Inquiry,* June 2004, pp. 128–139; H. Ashar and M. Lane-Maher, "Success and Spirituality in the New Business Paradigm," *Journal of Management Inquiry,* June 2004, pp. 249–260; K. C. Cash and G. R. Gray, "A Framework for Accommodating Religion and Spirituality in the Workplace," *Academy of Management Executive,* August 2000, pp. 124–133; I. A. Mitroff and E. A. Denton, *A Spiritual Audit of Corporate-America: A Hard Look at Spirituality, Religion, and Values in the Workplace* (San Francisco: Jossey-Bass, 1999); J. Milliman, J. Ferguson, D. Trickett, and B. Condemi, "Spirit and Community at Southwest Airlines: An Investigation of a Spiritual Values-Based Model," *Journal of Organizational Change Management,* vol. 12 (3), 1999, pp. 221–233; E. H. Burack, "Spirituality in the Workplace," *Journal of Organizational Change Management,* vol. 12 (3), 1999, pp. 280–291; and F. Wagner-Marsh and J. Conley, "The Fourth Wave: The Spiritually-Based Firm," *Journal of Organizational Change Management,* vol. 12 (3), 1999, pp. 292–302.

39. J. Reingold, "Walking the Walk," *Fast Company,* November 2005, p. 82.

40. Cited in F. Wagner-Marsh and J. Conley, "The Fourth Wave," p. 295.

41. P. Paul, "A Holier Holiday Season," *American Demographics,* December 2001, pp. 41–45; and M. Conlin, "Religion in the Workplace: The Growing Presence of Spirituality in Corporate America," *BusinessWeek,* November 1, 1999, pp. 151–158.

42. Cited in M. Conlin, "Religion in the Workplace," p. 153.

43. C. P. Neck and J. F. Milliman, "Thought Self-Leadership: Finding Spiritual Fulfillment in Organizational Life," *Journal of Managerial Psychology,* vol. 9 (8), 1994, p. 9.

44. A. K. Miles, S. Sledge, and S. Coppage, "Linking Spirituality to Workplace Performance: A Qualitative Study of the Brazilian Candomble," *Academy of Management Proceedings Best Conference Paper,* August 2005; J. Millman, A. Czaplewski, and J. Ferguson, "An Exploratory Empirical Assessment of the Relationship Between Spirituality and Employee Work Attitudes," paper presented at the National

Academy of Management meeting, Washington, DC, August 2001; P. Leigh, "The New Spirit at Work," *Training and Development,* vol. 51 (3), 1997, p. 26; P. H. Mirvis, "Soul Work in Organizations," *Organization Science,* vol. 8 (2), 1997, p. 193; E. Brandt, "Corporate Pioneers Explore Spiritual Peace," *HRMagazine,* vol. 41 (4), 1996, p. 82; and D. W. McCormick, "Spirituality and Management," *Journal of Managerial Psychology,* vol. 9 (6), 1994, p. 5.

45. "2005 Global Water Report: A Worldview," Beverage Marketing Corporation, www.beveragemarketing.com, January 12, 2006; P. Bowers, S. Friedhoff, and S. Scully, "War on the Water Front," *Time,* December 19, 2005, p. 60; L. Conley, "Coin-Op Nation," *Fast Company,* December 2005, p. 42; and R. D. Hof, "The Power of US," *BusinessWeek,* June 20, 2005, pp. 74–82.

46. See, for instance, A. S. Hayes, "Layoffs Take Careful Planning to Avoid Losing the Suits That Are Apt to Follow," *Wall Street Journal,* November 2, 1990, p. B1.

47. A good source of information about legal/political factors in other countries is Cornell University's Legal Information Institute, which can be accessed at www.law.cornell.edu/world.

48. B. McKay, "Fit to Eat?" *Wall Street Journal,* September 23, 2002, pp. A1+.

49. F. Hansen, "Mega Shifts Remake Marketing," *Business Finance,* March 2003, p. 9.

50. J. P. Walsh, "Book Review Essay: Taking Stock of Stakeholder Management," *Academy of Management Review,* April 2005, pp. 426–438; R. E. Freeman, A. C. Wicks, and B. Parmar, "Stakeholder Theory and 'The Corporate Objective' Revisited," *Organization Science,* vol. 15, 2004, pp. 364–369; T. Donaldson and L. E. Preston, "The Stakeholder Theory of the Corporation: Concepts, Evidence, and Implications," *Academy of Management Review,* January 1995, pp. 65–91; and R. E. Freeman, *Strategic Management: A Stakeholder Approach* (Boston: Pitman/Ballinger, 1984).

51. J. S. Harrison and C. H. St. John, "Managing and Partnering with External Stakeholders," *Academy of Management Executive,* May 1996, pp. 46–60.

52. S. L. Berman, R. A. Phillips, and A. C. Wicks, "Resource Dependence, Managerial Discretion, and Stakeholder Performance," *Academy of Management Proceedings Best Conference Paper,* August 2005; A. J. Hillman and G. D. Keim, "Shareholder Value, Stakeholder Management, and Social Issues: What's the Bottom Line?" *Strategic Management Journal,* March 2001, pp. 125–139; J. S. Harrison and R. E. Freeman, "Stakeholders, Social Responsibility, and Performance: Empirical Evidence and Theoretical Perspectives," *Academy of Management Journal,* July 1999, pp. 479–487; and J. Kotter and J. Heskett, *Corporate Culture and Performance* (New York: The Free Press, 1992).

53. Harrison and St. John, 1996.

54. Situation adapted from information in "Two Admit to Securities Fraud," *Los Angeles Times,* April 25, 2006, p. C3; Alex Berenson, "Software Chief Admits

to Guilt in Fraud Case," *New York Times,* April 25, 2006, pp. A1+.

## Chapter 4

1. Information from company Web site, www.inditex. com, February 16, 2006; P. Bhatnagar, "Liz Claiborne in Kuwait?" *CNN Money.com,* cnnmoney.com, February 8, 2006; D. Rushkoff, "Back in the Box," *Fast Company,* November 2005, p. 37; P. Bhatnagar, "Will Japan Knock Off the Gap?" *CNNMoney.com,* cnnmoney.com, August 23, 2005; R. Watson, "An Evolutionary Approach to Innovation," *Fast Company,* www.fastcompany.com, August 9, 2004; M. Tchong, "Why Fast Is in Retail Fashion," *Fast Company,* www.fastcompany.com, July 26, 2004; S. Godin, "The Scarcity Shortage," *Fast Company,* December 2003, p. 121; and J. M. Folpe, "Zara Has a Made-to-Order Plan for Success," *Fortune,* cnnmoney. com, September 4, 2000.

2. G. Koretz, "Things Go Better with Multinationals— Except Jobs," *BusinessWeek,* May 2, 1994, p. 20.

3. The idea for this quiz adapted from R. M. Hodgetts and F. Luthans, *International Management,* 2d ed. (New York: McGraw-Hill, 1994).

4. Reuters Limited, *USA Today Online,* www.usatoday. com, February 21, 2006; and "Learning the Lingo," *USA Today,* January 26, 2006, p. 1A.

5. Ibid.

6. N. Adler, *International Dimensions of Organizational Behavior,* 4th ed. (Cincinnati: South-Western, 2002).

7. M. R. F. Kets De Vries and E. Florent-Treacy, "Global Leadership from A to Z: Creating High Commitment Organizations," *Organizational Dynamics,* Spring 2002, pp. 295–309; P. R. Harris and R. T. Moran, *Managing Cultural Differences,* 4th ed. (Houston: Gulf Publishing Co., 1996); R. T. Moran, P. R. Harris, and W. G. Stripp, *Developing the Global Organization: Strategies for Human Resource Professionals* (Houston: Gulf Publishing Co., 1993); Y. Wind, S. P. Douglas, and H. V. Perlmutter, "Guidelines for Developing International Marketing Strategies," *Journal of Marketing,* April 1973, pp. 14–23; and H.V. Perlmutter, "The Tortuous Evolution of the Multi-national Corporation," *Columbia Journal of World Business,* January–February 1969, pp. 9–18.

8. A. K. Gupta and V. Govindarajan, "Cultivating a Global Mind-set," *Academy of Management Executive,* February 2002, pp. 117–118.

9. *WTO Policy Issues for Parliamentarians,* document published by the World Trade Organization, available on the World Trade Organization Web site, www.wto.org, p. 1.

10. European Union official Web site, europa.eu.int; M. Champion and M. Karnitschnig, "EU Clears Talks with Turkey on Membership," *Wall Street Journal,* October 4, 2005, p. A15; and B. Mitchener, "Ten New Members to Weigh In on Future of EU," *Wall Street Journal,* April 16, 2003, p. A16.

11. G. Thomas Sims, "Uncommon Market," *Wall Street Journal,* November 1, 2005, pp. A1+.

12. "State of Practical Preparations for the Future Enlargement of the Euro Area," europa.eu.int/euro, September 2005; and H. Cooper, "The Euro: What You Need to Know," *Wall Street Journal,* January 4, 1999, pp. A5+.

13. P. Gumbel, "Euro-Division?" *Time Bonus Section,* July 2005, p. A18; N. Knox, "Leaders of Embattled EU Head to Washington," *USA Today,* June 20, 2005, p. A8; and N. Knox, "European Union Struggles with Constitution Rejection," *USA Today,* May 31, 2005, p. A10.

14. D. Beachy, "A Decade of NAFTA," *Hispanic Business,* July/August 2004, pp. 42–44.

15. E. Malkin, "Central American Trade Deal Is Being Delayed by Partners," *New York Times Online,* www.nytimes.com, March 2, 2006; J. McClenahen, "Pressures Dampening Outlook," *Industry Week,* October 2005, p. 13; and J. DeCordoba, J. Lyons, and L. Luhnow, "Despite CAFTA, U.S. Clout Wanes in Latin America," *Wall Street Journal,* July 29, 2005, p. A11.

16. J. Forero, "U.S. and Colombia Reach Trade Deal After 2 Years of Talks," *New York Times Online,* www.nytimes. com, February 28, 2006.

17. "Ministerial Declaration," Web site of the Free Trade Area of the Americas, www.ftaa-alca.org, January 23, 2006; and M. Moffett and J. D. McKinnon, "Failed Summit Casts Shadow on Global Trade Talks," *Wall Street Journal,* November 7, 2005, pp. A1+.

18. J. Epstein, "The Bell Tolls for Mercosur," *Latin Trade,* January 2002, p. 20; R. Colitt, "Rain on Mercorsur's Parade," *Latin Trade,* March 2001, pp. 42–45; and C. Sims, "Chile Will Enter a Big South American Free-Trade Bloc," *New York Times,* June 26, 1996, p. C2.

19. Information from ASEAN official Web site, www. aseansec.org.

20. "2004–2007 Strategic Plan," *Commission of the African Union,* www.africa-union.org; and D. Kraft, "Leaders Question, Praise African Union," *Springfield News-Leader,* July 10, 2002, p. 8A.

21. SAARC Official Web site, www.saarc-sec.org; and N. George, "South Asia Trade Zone in Works," *Springfield News-Leader,* January 4, 2004, p. 1E+.

22. This section is based on materials from the World Trade Organization Web site, www.wto.org.

23. These examples are taken from M. Maynard and J. W. Peters, "2 Asian Automakers Plan Ventures in 2 States Left by U.S. Carmakers," *New York Times Online,* www.nytimes.com, March 14, 2006; McDonald's Press Release, "First McDonald's Drive-Thru Opens in China," www.mcdonalds.com, December 10, 2005; L. Chang, "McDonald's Still Plans Growth in China, Despite Cuts in U.S.," *Wall Street Journal,* November 14, 2002, p. B10; C. Belton, "To Russia with Love: The Multinationals' Song," *BusinessWeek,* September 16, 2002, pp. 44–46; and P. J. Kiger, "How Deloitte Builds Global Expertise," *Workforce,* June 2002, p. 62.

24. C. A. Barlett and S. Ghoshal, *Managing Across Borders: The Transnational Solution* 2e (Boston: Harvard Business School Press, 2002); and N. J. Adler, *International Dimensions of Organizational Behavior* 4e (Cincinnati, OH: South-Western, 2002), pp. 9–11.

25. P. F. Drucker, "The Global Economy and the Nation-State," *Foreign Affairs,* September–October, 1997, pp. 159–171.

26. D. A. Aaker, *Developing Business Strategies* 5th ed. (New York: John Wiley & Sons, 1998); and J. A. Byrne et al., "Borderless Management," *BusinessWeek,* May 23, 1994, pp. 24–26.

27. G. A. Knight, S. T. Cavusgil, "A Taxonomy of Born-Global Firms," *Management International Review,* vol. 3, 2005, pp. 15–35; S. A. Zahra, "A Theory of International New Ventures: A Decade of Research," *Journal of International Business Studies,* January 2005, pp. 20–28; and B. M. Oviatt and P. P. McDougall, "Toward a Theory of International New Ventures," *Journal of International Business Studies,* January 2005, pp. 29–41.

28. B. Davis, "Migration of Skilled Jobs Abroad Unsettles Global-Economy Fans," *Wall Street Journal,* January 26, 2004, p. A1.

29. This box based on information from K. Bahadur, D. Desmet, and E. van Bommel, "Smart IT Spending: Insights from European Banks," *The McKinsey Quarterly,* www.mckinseyquarterly.com, January 2006; S. Hamm, "Motivating the Troops," *BusinessWeek,* November 21, 2005, pp. 88–103;

30. J. Teresko, "United Plastics Picks China's Silicon Valley," *Industry Week,* January 2003, p. 58.

31. I. Bremmer, "Managing Risk in an Unstable World," *Harvard Business Review,* June 2005, pp. 51–60.

32. "Companies See Little Impact from Costlier Yuan—For Now," *Wall Street Journal News Roundup,* July 22, 2005, pp. B1+.

33. "Emerging Economies Are Following the Global Trend of Disinflation," *The Economist,* October 19, 2002, p. 36.

34. Central Intelligence Agency, *The World Factbook* (Washington, DC: Potomac Books, 2005), www.cia.gov/cia/publications/factbook.

35. These examples taken from L. Khosla, "You Say Tomato," *Forbes,* May 21, 2001, p. 36; and T. Raphael, "Savvy Companies Build Bonds with Hispanic Employees," *Workforce,* September 2001, p. 19.

36. See G. Hofstede, *Culture's Consequences: International Differences in Work-Related Values,* 2nd ed. (Thousand Oaks, CA: Sage Publications, 2001), pp. 9–15.

37. This box based on information from M. Javidan, P. W. Dorfman, M. S. deLuque, and R. J. House, "In the Eye of the Beholder: Cross-Cultural Lessons in Leadership from Project GLOBE," *Academy of Management Perspective,* February 2006, pp. 67–90; and M. Javidan, G. K. Stahl, F. Brodbeck, and C. P. M. Wilderon, "Cross-Border Transfer of Knowledge: Cultural Lessons from Project GLOBE," *Academy of Management Executive,* May 2005, pp. 59–76.

38. G. Hofstede, *Culture's Consequences;* and G. Hofstede, "The Cultural Relativity of Organizational Practices and Theories," *Journal of International Business Studies,* Fall 1983, pp. 75–89.

39. Hofstede called this dimension "masculinity versus femininity," but we have changed it because of the strong sexist connotation in his choice of terms.

40. Hofstede, *Culture's Consequences,* pp. 355–358.

41. R. J. House, P. J. Hanges, M. Javidan, P. W. Dorfman, and V. Gupta, *Culture, Leadership, and Organizations: The GLOBE Study of 62 Societies* (Thousand Oaks, CA: Sage Publications), 2004.

42. These examples taken from: J. M. Olsen, Associated Press, "Toy Maker Lego Moves Production to Czech Republic," *USA Today Online,* www.usatoday.com, September 1, 2005; M. Gunther, "Cops of the Global Village," *Fortune,* June 27, 2005, pp. 158–166; J. Sapsford, "Nissan to Sell in China Minivans Made in the U.S.," *Wall Street Journal,* March 17, 2005; D. Michaels, "Sukhoi Has the World in Its Sights," *Wall Street Journal,* August 7, 2003, p. A9; and J. Slater, "GE Takes Advantage of India's Talented Research Pool," *Wall Street Journal,* March 26, 2003, p. A10.

43. D. J. Lynch, "Some Would Like to Build a Wall Around U.S. Economy," *USA Today,* March 16, 2006, p. 1B+; D. E. Sanger, "A Bush Alarm: Urging U.S. to Shun Isolationism," *New York Times Online,* www.nytimes.com, March 13, 2006; "Collapse of Port Deal Takes on New Dimension," *Ethics Newsline,* www.globalethics.org/newsline, March 13, 2006; G. Ip and N. King Jr., "Ports Deal Shows Roadblocks for Globalization," *Wall Street Journal,* March 11, 2006, pp. A1+; and M. A. Stein, "A Big Deal Overshadowed by the Politics of Ports," *New York Times Online,* www.nytimes.com, March 11, 2006.

44. D. Yergin, "Globalization Opens Door to New Dangers," *USA Today,* May 28, 2003, p. 11A; K. Lowrey Miller, "Is It Globaloney?" *Newsweek,* December 16, 2002, pp. E4–E8; L. Gomes, "Globalization Is Now a Two-Way Street—Good News for the U.S.," *Wall Street Journal,* December 9, 2002, p. B1; J. Kurlantzick and J. T. Allen, "The Trouble with Globalism," *U.S. News & World Report,* February 11, 2002, pp. 38–41; and J. Guyon, "The American Way," *Fortune,* November 26, 2001, pp. 114–120.

45. Guyon, "The American Way," p. 114.

46. Situation adapted from information in Roger Parloff, "Not Exactly Counterfeit," *Fortune,* May 1, 2006, pp. 108+; Sharon Edelson, "Cirque du Soleil Builds Brand Beyond the Ring," *WWD,* February 6, 2006, p. 22; Rachel Miller, "Licensing: Unlock the Equity Within Your Brand," *Marketing,* April 24, 2003, pp. 21+; Gabriel Kahn, "Factor Fight: A Sneaker Maker Says China Partner Became Its Rival," *Wall Street Journal,* December 19, 2002, pp. A1+.

## Chapter 5

1. Information from company Web site, www.cascadeeng.com, February 24, 2006; and J. Jusko, "The Sustainable Enterprise," *Industry Week,* July 2005, p. 12.

2. M. Friedman, "The Social Responsibility of Business Is to Increase Profits," *New York Times Magazine*, September 13, 1970, p. 33; and Friedman, *Capitalism and Freedom* (Chicago: University of Chicago Press, 1962).

3. Information from Avon's Web site, www.avoncrusade.com, February 6, 2006.

4. M. Kepp, "Best Face Forward," *Latin Trade*, June 2005, p. 25; and P. Prada and M. Rueda, "The Good-Deed Column," *Latin Trade*, May 2005, pp. 26–31.

5. "The McKinsey Global Survey of Business Executives: Business and Society," *The McKinsey Quarterly*, www.mckinseyquarterly.com, January 2006.

6. See, for example, A. B. Carroll, "The Pyramid of Corporate Social Responsibility: Toward the Moral Management of Organizational Stakeholders," *Business Horizons*, July–August 1991, pp. 39–48.

7. This section has been influenced by K. B. Boal and N. Peery, "The Cognitive Structure of Social Responsibility," *Journal of Management*, Fall–Winter 1985, pp. 71–82.

8. This section is based on J. D. Margolis and J. P. Walsh, "Misery Loves Companies: Rethinking Social Initiatives by Business," *Administrative Science Quarterly*, vol. 48 (2), 2003, pp. 268–305; K. Davis and W. C. Frederick, *Business and Society: Management, Public Policy, Ethics*, 5th ed. (New York: McGraw-Hill, 1984), pp. 28–41; and R. J. Monsen Jr., "The Social Attitudes of Management," in J. M. McGuire (ed.), *Contemporary Management: Issues and Views* (Upper Saddle River, NJ: Prentice Hall, 1974), p. 616.

9. A. B. Carroll, "A Three-Dimensional Conceptual Model of Corporate Performance," *Academy of Management Review*, October 1979, p. 499.

10. See S. P. Sethi, "A Conceptual Framework for Environmental Analysis of Social Issues and Evaluation of Business Response Patterns," *Academy of Management Review*, January 1979, pp. 68–74.

11. See, for example, D. J. Wood, "Corporate Social Performance Revisited," *Academy of Management Review*, October 1991, pp. 703–708.

12. Information from "Giving Back," found on American Express Web site, www.americanexpress.com, February 6, 2006.

13. See, for example, R. A. Buccholz, *Essentials of Public Policy for Management*, 2d ed. (Upper Saddle River, NJ: Prentice Hall, 1990).

14. "2003–04 Sustainability Report," *Aspen Skiing Company*, www.aspensnowmass.com/environment, February 6, 2006; and A. Schendler, "Where's the Green in Green Business?" *Harvard Business Review*, June 2002, p. 28.

15. Information from company Web site, www.walmartstores.com, March 16, 2006; and one of the advertisements from *USA Today*, March 6, 2006, p. 5A.

16. S. L. Wartick and P. L. Cochran, "The Evolution of the Corporate Social Performance Model," *Academy of Management Review*, October 1985, p. 763.

17. See, for instance, D. O. Neubaum and S. A. Zahra, "Institutional Ownership and Corporate Social Performance: The Moderating Effects of Investment Horizon, Activism, and Coordination," *Journal of Management*, February 2006, pp. 108–131; P. C. Godfrey, "The Relationship Between Corporate Philanthropy and Shareholder Wealth: A Risk Management Perspective," *Academy of Management Review*, October 2005, pp. 777–798; D. K. Peterson, "The Relationship Between Perceptions of Corporate Citizenship and Organizational Commitment," *Business & Society*, September 2004, pp. 296–319; B. Seifert, S. A. Morris, and B. R. Bartkus, "Having, Giving, and Getting: Slack Resources, Corporate Philanthropy, and Firm Financial Performance," *Business & Society*, June 2004, pp. 135–161; S. L. Berman et al., "Does Stakeholder Orientation Matter? The Relationship Between Stakeholder Management Models and Firm Financial Performance, *Academy of Management Journal*, October 1999, pp. 488–506; S. A. Waddock and S. B. Graves, "The Corporate Social Performance–Financial Performance Link," *Strategic Management Journal*, April 1997, pp. 303–319; D. B. Turban and D. W. Greening, "Corporate Social Performance and Organizational Attractiveness to Prospective Employees," *Academy of Management Journal*, June 1996, pp. 658–672; J. B. McGuire, A. Sundgren, and T. Schneeweis, "Corporate Social Responsibility and Firm Financial Performance," *Academy of Management Journal*, December 1988, pp. 854–872; K. Aupperle, A. B. Carroll, and J. D. Hatfield, "An Empirical Examination of the Relationship Between Corporate Social Responsibility and Profitability," *Academy of Management Journal*, June 1985, pp. 446–463; and P. Cochran and R. A. Wood, "Corporate Social Responsibility and Financial Performance," *Academy of Management Journal*, March 1984, pp. 42–56.

18. See J. Surroca and J. A. Tribo, "The Corporate Social and Financial Performance Relationship: What's the Ultimate Determinant?" *Academy of Management Best Conference Paper*, 2005; H. Wang, J. Choi, and J. Li, "Too Little or Too Much? Reexamining the Relationship Between Corporate Giving and Corporate Financial Performance," *Academy of Management Best Conference Paper*, 2005; Wood and Jones, "Stakeholder Mismatching: A Theoretical Problem in Empirical Research on Corporate Social Performance," *International Journal of Organizational Analysis*, 1995, pp. 229–267; R. Wolfe and K. Aupperle, "Introduction to Corporate Social Performance: Methods for Evaluating an Elusive Construct," pp. 265–268, in J. E. Post (ed.), *Research in Corporate Social Performance and Policy*, vol. 12, 1991; R. E. Wokutch and B. A. Spencer, "Corporate Saints and Sinners: The Effects of Philanthropic and Illegal Activity on Organizational Performance," *California Management Review*, Winter 1987, pp. 62–77; and A. A. Ullmann, "Data in Search of a Theory: A Critical Examination of the Relationships Among Social Performance, Social Disclosure, and Economic Performance of U.S. Firms," *Academy of Management Review*, July 1985, pp. 540–557.

Systems: Influences of Executive Commitment and Environmental Factors," *Academy of Management Journal*, February 1999, pp. 41–57; R. B. Morgan, "Self- and Co-Worker Perceptions of Ethics and Their Relationships to Leadership and Salary," *Academy of Management Journal*, February 1993, pp. 200–214; and B. Z. Posner and W. H. Schmidt, "Values and the American Manager: An Update," *California Management Review*, Spring 1984, pp. 202–216.

57. G. Weaver, "Ethics and Employees: Making the Connection"; V. Anand, B. E. Ashforth, and M. Joshi, "Business As Usual: The Acceptance and Perpetuation of Corruption in Organizations," *Academy of Management Executive,* May 2004, pp. 39–53; J. Weber, L. B. Kurke, and D. W. Pentico, "Why Do Employees Steal?" *Business & Society,* September 2003, pp. 359–380; V. Arnold and J. C. Lampe, "Understanding the Factors Underlying Ethical Organizations: Enabling Continuous Ethical Improvement," *Journal of Applied Business Research*, Summer 1999, pp. 1–19; R. R. Sims, "The Challenge of Ethical Behavior in Organizations," *Journal of Business Ethics*, July 1992, pp. 505–513; Victor and Cullen, "A Theory and Measure of Ethical Climate in Organizations," in Frederick and Preston (eds.), *Business Ethics*, pp. 77–97; J. B. Cullen, B. Victor, and C. Stephens, "An Ethical Weather Report: Assessing the Organization's Ethical Climate," *Organizational Dynamics*, Autumn 1989, pp. 50–62; and B. Victor and J. B. Cullen, "The Organizational Bases of Ethical Work Climates," *Administrative Science Quarterly*, March 1988, pp. 101–125.

58. T. Barnett, "Dimensions of Moral Intensity and Ethical Decision Making: An Empirical Study," *Journal of Applied Social Psychology,* May 2001, pp. 1038–1057; and T. M. Jones, "Ethical Decision Making by Individuals in Organizations: An Issue-Contingent Model," *Academy of Management Review*, April 1991, pp. 366–395.

59. Ibid., pp. 374–378.

60. J. Hyatt, "Ethics Alert: Foreign Corrupt Practices Prosecutions Doubled," *Business Ethics,* Winter 2005, p. 9.

61. L. Paine, R. Deshpande, J. D. Margolis, and K. E. Bettcher, "Up to Code: Does Your Company's Conduct Meet World-Class Standards?" *Harvard Business Review,* December 2005, pp. 122–133; G. R. Simpson, "Global Heavyweights Vow 'Zero Tolerance' for Bribes," *Wall Street Journal,* January 27, 2005, pp. A2+; A. Spicer, T. W. Dunfee, and W. J. Bailey, "Does National Context Matter in Ethical Decision Making? An Empirical Test of Integrative Social Contracts Theory," *Academy of Management Journal,* August 2004, pp. 610–620; J. White and S. Taft, "Frameworks for Teaching and Learning Business Ethics Within the Global Context: Background of Ethical Theories," *Journal of Management Education,* August 2004, pp. 463–477; J. Guyon, "CEOs on Managing Globally," *Fortune,* July 26, 2004, p. 169; A. B. Carroll, "Managing Ethically with Global Stakeholders: A Present and Future

Challenge," *Academy of Management Executive,* May 2004, pp. 114–120; and C. J. Robertson and W. F. Crittenden, "Mapping Moral Philosophies: Strategic Implications for Multinational Firms," *Strategic Management Journal,* April 2003, pp. 385–392.

62. Information from The Global Compact Web site, www.unglobalcompact.org, February 15, 2006; J. Cohen, "Socially Responsible Business Goes Global," *In Business,* March/April 2000, p. 22; and C. M. Solomon, "Put Your Ethics to a Global Test," *Personnel Journal*, January 1996, pp. 66–74.

63. "The OECD Anti-Bribery Convention: Does It Work?" www.oecd.org, February 6, 2006.

64. Enron example taken from P. M. Lencioni, "Make Your Values Mean Something," *Harvard Business Review,* July 2002, p. 113; Sears example taken from series of posters called "Sears Ethics and Business Practices: A Century of Tradition," in *Business Ethics*, May/June 1999, pp. 12–13; and B. J. Feder, "The Harder Side of Sears," *New York Times*, July 20, 1997, pp. BU1+.

65. Trevino and Youngblood, "Bad Apples in Bad Barrels," p. 384.

66. J. S. McClenahen, "UTC's Master of Principle," *Industry Week,* January 2003, pp. 30–36.

67. M. Weinstein, "Survey Says: Ethics Training Works," *Training,* November 2005, p. 15.

68. J. E. Fleming, "Codes of Ethics for Global Corporations," *Academy of Management News,* June 2005, p. 4.

69. "Global Ethics Codes Gain Importance As a Tool to Avoid Litigation and Fines," *Wall Street Journal*, August 19, 1999, p. A1; and J. Alexander, "On the Right Side," *World Business*, January/February 1997, pp. 38–41.

70. P. Richter, "Big Business Puts Ethics in Spotlight," *Los Angeles Times*, June 19, 1986, p. 29.

71. F. R. David, "An Empirical Study of Codes of Business Ethics: A Strategic Perspective," paper presented at the 48th Annual Academy of Management Conference, Anaheim, California, August 1988.

72. "Ethics Programs Aren't Stemming Employee Misconduct," *Wall Street Journal*, May 11, 2000, p. A1.

73. J. M. Stevens, H. K. Steensma, D. A. Harrison, and P. L. Cochran, "Symbolic or Substantive Document? The Influence of Ethics Codes on Financial Executives' Decisions," *Strategic Management Journal,* February 2005, pp. 181–195.

74. "Codes of Conduct," information from the Center for Ethical Business Cultures, www.cebcglobal.org, February 15, 2006; L. Paine, R. Deshpande, J. D. Margolis, and K. E. Bettcher, "Up to Code: Does Your Company's Conduct Meet World-Class Standards"; A. K. Reichert and M. S. Webb, "Corporate Support for Ethical and Environmental Policies: A Financial Management Perspective," *Journal of Business Ethics,*

May 2000; G. R. Weaver, L. K. Trevino, and P. L. Cochran, "Corporate Ethics Programs As Control Systems: Influences of Executive Commitment and Environmental Factors"; G. R. Weaver, L. K. Trevino, and P. L. Cochran, "Integrated and Decoupled Corporate Social Performance: Management Commitments, External Pressures, and Corporate Ethics Practices"; R. B. Morgan, "Self- and Co-Worker Perceptions of Ethics and Their Relationships to Leadership and Salary"; and B. Z. Posner and W. H. Schmidt, "Values and the American Manager: An Update."

75. L. Nash, "Ethics Without the Sermon," *Harvard Business Review*, November–December 1981, p. 81.

76. V. Wessler, "Integrity and Clogged Plumbing," *Straight to the Point,* newsletter of VisionPoint Corporation, Fall 2002, pp. 1–2.

77. R. M. Kidder, "The Changing Face of Business Ethics," *Ethics Newsline from the Institute for Global Ethics,* www.globalethics.org/newsline, October 24, 2005.

78. Ibid.

79. T. A. Gavin, "Ethics Education," *Internal Auditor*, April 1989, pp. 54–57.

80. L. Myyry and K. Helkama, "The Role of Value Priorities and Professional Ethics Training in Moral Sensitivity," *Journal of Moral Education,* vol. 31 (1), 2002, pp. 35–50; W. Penn and B. D. Collier, "Current Research in Moral Development As a Decision Support System," *Journal of Business Ethics*, January 1985, pp. 131–136.

81. J. A. Byrne, "After Enron: The Ideal Corporation," *BusinessWeek*, August 19, 2002, pp. 68–71; D. Rice and C. Dreilinger, "Rights and Wrongs of Ethics Training," *Training & Development Journal,* May 1990, pp. 103–109; and J. Weber, "Measuring the Impact of Teaching Ethics to Future Managers: A Review, Assessment, and Recommendations," *Journal of Business Ethics*, April 1990, pp. 182–190.

82. D. Zielinski, "The Right Direction: Can Ethics Training Save Your Company," *Training,* June 2005, pp. 27–32.

83. See, for instance, A. Wheat, "Keeping an Eye on Corporate America," *Fortune*, November 25, 2002, pp. 44–46; R. B. Schmitt, "Companies Add Ethics Training: Will It Work?" *Wall Street Journal,* November 4, 2002, pp. B1+; and P. F. Miller and W. T. Coady, "Teaching Work Ethics," *Education Digest*, February 1990, pp. 54–55.

84. G. Farrell and J. O'Donnell, "Ethics Training As Taught by Ex-Cons: Crime Doesn't Pay," *USA Today,* November 16, 2005, pp. 1B+.

85. J. Weber, "The New Ethics Enforcers," *BusinessWeek,* February 13, 2006, pp. 76–77.

86. The Ethics and Compliance Officer Association Web site, www.theecoa.org, February 17, 2006; K. Maher, "Global Companies Face Reality of Instituting Ethics Programs," *Wall Street Journal*, November 9, 2004, p. B8; and R. B. Schmitt, "Companies Add Ethics Training: Will It Work?"

87. See, for example, S. Gaines, "Handing Out Halos," *Business Ethics*, March–April 1994, pp. 20–24; L. S. Paine, "Managing for Organizational Integrity," *Harvard Business Review*, March–April 1994, pp. 106–117; W. D. Hall, *Making the Right Decision: Ethics for Managers* (New York: John Wiley & Sons, 1993); A. Stark, "What's the Matter with Business Ethics?" *Harvard Business Review*, May–June 1993, pp. 38–48; and "More Big Businesses Set Up Ethics Offices," *Wall Street Journal*, May 10, 1993, p. B1.

88. F. Norris, "At Radio Shack, Some Questions (and Now, Answers)," *New York Times,* www.nytimes.com, February 16, 2006; J. Weber, "Online Extra: Calling the Ethics Cops," *BusinessWeek Online,* www.businessweek.com, February 13, 2006; A. Horowitz, "101 Dumbest Moments in Business," *Business 2.0,* cnnmoney.com, February 1, 2006; and R. Grover, "Red-Faced at Red Robin," *BusinessWeek Online,* www.businessweek.com, October 10, 2005.

89. J. Weber, "Online Extra: Calling the Ethics Cops."

90. Associated Press, "Cheating Rampant in Workplace, Study Says"; and H. Fountain, "Of White Lies and Yellow Pads," *New York Times*, July 6, 1997, p. F7.

91. H. Oh, "Biz Majors Get an F for Honesty," *BusinessWeek,* February 6, 2006, p. 14.

92. "Students Aren't Squealers," *USA Today,* March 27, 2003, p. 1D; and J. Merritt, "You Mean Cheating Is Wrong?" *BusinessWeek,* December 9, 2002, p. 8.

93. Information for this box came from J. Christoffersen, Associated Press, "Another Trial Is Planned in Cendant Case," *Houston Chronicle,* www.chron.com, March 15, 2006; A. Meek, "Corporate Scandals Create Focus on Nonprofit Accountability," *Memphis Daily News,* www.memphisdailynews.com, March 9, 2006; M. Hayakawa, "Scandals Hurt Japanese Firms' Image in China," *The Asahi Shimbun,* www.asahi.com, February 20, 2006; R. M. Fulmer, "The Challenge of Ethical Leadership," *Organizational Dynamics,* vol. 33 (3), 2004, pp. 307–317; J. S. McClenahen, "UTC's Master of Principle," *Industry Week,* January 2003, pp. 30–33; and L. K. Trevino, M. Brown, and L. P. Hartman, "A Qualitative Investigation of Perceived Executive Ethical Leadership: Perceptions from Inside and Outside the Executive Suite," *Human Relations,* January 2003, pp. 5–37.

94. D. Lidsky, "Transparency: It's Not Just for Shrink Wrap Anymore," *Fast Company,* January 2005, p. 87.

95. J. McCafferty, "Space Invaders," *CFO,* November 2004, p. 21.

96. "Trust Busters," *CFO,* August 2002, p. 17.

97. D. Jones, "Do You Trust Your CEO?" *USA Today,* February 12, 2003, p. 7B.

98. C. E. Johnson, *Meeting the Ethical Challenges of Leadership,* 2d ed. (Thousand Oaks, CA: Sage Publications Inc., 2005); M. S. McClenahen, "Leading Execution," *Industry Week,* July 2005, pp. 49–50;

T. Thomas, J. R. Schermerhorn Jr., and J. W. Dienhart, "Strategic Leadership of Ethical Behavior in Business," *Academy of Management Executive*, May 2004, pp. 56–66; D. Seidman, "The Case for Ethical Leadership," *Academy of Management Executive*, May 2004, pp. 134–138; and C. Hymowitz, "Managers Must Respond to Employees' Concerns About Honest Business," *Wall Street Journal*, February 19, 2002, p. B1.

99. D. Hastings, "Halliburton Accuser Fights to Keep Her Job," Associated Press, *Springfield News-Leader*, August 7, 2005, pp. 1A+.

100. J. O'Donnell, "Blowing the Whistle Can Lead to Harsh Aftermath, Despite Law," *USA Today*, August 1, 2005, p. 2B; and J. O'Donnell, "Some Whistle-Blowers Don't Want Lost Jobs," *USA Today*, August 1, 2005, p. 2B.

101. W. Zellner et al., "A Hero—and a Smoking-Gun Letter," *BusinessWeek*, January 28, 2002, pp. 34–35.

102. R. Lacayo and A. Ripley, "Persons of the Year," *Time*, December 30, 2002–January 5, 2003, pp. 30–33.

103. E. Krell, "Corporate Whistleblowers: How to Stop Wrongdoing Dead in Its Tracks," *Business Finance*, September 2002, p. 20.

104. L. Grant, "Wal-Mart to Workers: Report Ethical Lapses," *USA Today*, March 30, 2005, p. 5B; and S. Armour, "More Companies Urge Workers to Blow the Whistle," *USA Today*, December 16, 2002, p. 1B.

105. J. Wiscombe, "Don't Fear Whistleblowers," *Workforce*, July 2002, pp. 26–27.

106. T. Reason, "Whistle Blowers: The Untouchables," *CFO*, March 2003, p. 18; and C. Lachnit, "Muting the Whistle-blower?" *Workforce*, September 2002, p. 18.

107. J. O'Donnell, "Blowing the Whistle Can Lead to Harsh Aftermath, Despite Law;" and D. Solomon, "For Financial Whistle-Blowers, New Shield Is an Imperfect One," *Wall Street Journal*, October 4, 2004, pp. A1+.

108. B. Dobbin, "Dealers Market Global Trade with Social Conscience," The Associated Press, *Springfield News-Leader*, February 16, 2005, p. 5B.

109. This definition based on The Schwab Foundation for Social Entrepreneurship, www.schwabfound.org, February 20, 2006; and J. G. Dees, J. Emerson, and P. Economy, *Strategic Tools for Social Entrepreneurs* (New York: John Wiley & Sons, Inc., 2002).

110. D. Bornstein, *How To Change the World: Social Entrepreneurs and the Power of New Ideas* (New York: Oxford University Press, 2004), inside cover jacket.

111. K. Greene, "Tapping Talent, Experience of Those Age 60-Plus," *Wall Street Journal*, November 29, 2005, p. B12.

112. PATH Web site, www.path.org, February 20, 2006; and C. Dahle, "Filling the Void," *Fast Company*, January/February 2006, pp. 54–57.

113. M. C. Gentile, "Social Impact Management: A Definition," a discussion paper of the Aspen Institute's Initiative for Social Innovation Through Business, available on the Aspen Institute Web site, www.aspeninstitute.org, April 12, 2003, p. 3.

114. Situation adapted from information in Juliet Eilperin, "Despite Efforts, Some Tours Do Leave Footprints," *Washington Post*, April 2, 2006, p. P1; Cynthia G. Wagner, "The Conscientious Tourist: Ethical Choices Influence Travelers' Vacation Planning," The *Futurist*, September–October 2005, pp. 14+.

## Part Two Continuing Case

A. Serwer and K. Bonamici, "Hot Starbucks to Go," *Fortune*, January 26, 2004, pp. 60–74; R. Gulati, Sarah Huffman, G. Neilson, "The Barista Principle," *Strategy and Business*, Third Quarter 2002, pp. 58–69; J. Cummings, "Legislative Grind," *Wall Street Journal*, April 12, 2005, pp. A1+; B. Horovitz, "Starbucks Nation," *USA Today*, May 29–21, 2006, pp. A1+; J. Lawless, "Historian Studies Impact of Starbucks Globally," *Marketing News*, May 15, 2006, p. 44; K. M. Butler, "Examining the Benefits of Corporate Social Responsibility," *Employee Benefit News*, May 2006, p. 16; R. Tiplady, "Can Starbucks Blend into France?" *BusinessWeek*, April 21, 2006, p. 7; A. Serwer, Interview with Howard Schultz," *Fortune* (Europe), March 20, 2006, pp. 35–36; E. Barraclough, "Starbucks and Ferrero Celebrate China Victories," *Managing Intellectual Property*, February 2006, p. 12; K. Bonamici, S. Herman, and P. Jarvis, "Decoding the Dress Code," *Fortune*, January 23, 2006, pp. 130–131; A. Lustgarten, "A Hot, Steaming Cup of Customer Awareness," *Fortune*, November 15, 2004, p. 192; W. Meyers, "Conscience in a Cup of Coffee," *US News & World Report*, October 31, 2005, pp. 48–50; M. Berglind and C. Nakata, "Cause-Related Marketing: More Buck Than Bang?" *Business Horizons*, September–October 2005, pp. 443–453; I. Mochari, "Coffee with Cream, Sugar, and Interest," *CFO*, September 2005, p. 23; C. Williamson, "Starbucks, Calvert Support Fair Trade," *Pensions & Investments*, July 11, 2005, p. 8; T. Howard, "Starbucks Takes Up Cause for Safe Drinking Water," *USA Today*, August 3, 2005, p. 5B; P. Orsi, "Selling Charity in a Bottle," *Business 2.0*, October 2005, p. 38; P. L. Green, "US Firms Widen the Net," *Global Finance*, January 2006, pp. 28–29; J. Simmons, *My Sister's A Barista: How They Made Starbucks a Home Away from Home* (London: Cyan Books, 2005); H. Schultz and D. Jones Yang, *Pour Your Heart Into It: How Starbucks Built a Company One Cup at a Time* (New York: Hyperion, 1997).

## Chapter 6

1. Information from company Web site, www.asbhawaii.com, February 24, 2006; J. Edwards, "Help Yourself," *CFO*, July 2005, pp. 58–62; M. Wells, "Have It Your Way," *Forbes*, February 14, 2005, pp. 78–86; and B. Horovitz, "It's a Do-It-Yourself World," *USA Today*, April 27, 2004, p. 1A.

2. M. Trottman, "Choices in Stormy Weather," *Wall Street Journal*, February 14, 2006, pp. B1+.

3. D. A. Garvin and M. A. Roberto, "What You Don't Know About Making Decisions," *Harvard Business Review*, September 2001, pp. 108–116.

4. W. Pounds, "The Process of Problem Finding," *Industrial Management Review*, Fall 1969, pp. 1–19.

5. R. J. Volkema, "Problem Formulation: Its Portrayal in the Texts," *Organizational Behavior Teaching Review*, vol. 11 (3), 1986–1987, pp. 113–126.

6. M. W. McCall Jr. and R. E. Kaplan, *Whatever It Takes: Decision Makers at Work* (Upper Saddle River, NJ: Prentice Hall, 1985), pp. 36–38.

7. T. A. Stewart, "Did You Ever Have to Make Up Your Mind?" *Harvard Business Review*, January 2006, p. 12; and E. Pooley, "Editor's Desk," *Fortune*, June 27, 2005, p. 16.

8. J. Pfeffer and R. I. Sutton, "Why Managing by Facts Works," *Strategy & Business*, Spring 2006, pp. 9–12.

9. See A. Langley, "In Search of Rationality: The Purposes Behind the Use of Formal Analysis in Organizations," *Administrative Science Quarterly*, December 1989, pp. 598–631; and H. A. Simon, "Rationality in Psychology and Economics," *Journal of Business*, October 1986, pp. 209–224.

10. F. A. Shull Jr., A. L. Delbecq, and L. L. Cummings, *Organizational Decision Making* (New York: McGraw-Hill, 1970), p. 151.

11. J. G. March, "Decision-Making Perspective: Decisions in Organizations and Theories of Choice," in A. H. Van de Ven and W. F. Joyce (eds.), *Perspectives on Organization Design and Behavior* (New York: Wiley-Interscience, 1981), pp. 232–233.

12. See D. R. A. Skidd, "Revisiting Bounded Rationality," *Journal of Management Inquiry*, December 1992, pp. 343–347; B. E. Kaufman, "A New Theory of Satisficing," *Journal of Behavioral Economics*, Spring 1990, pp. 35–51; and N. McK. Agnew and J. L. Brown, "Bounded Rationality: Fallible Decisions in Unbounded Decision Space," *Behavioral Science*, July 1986, pp. 148–161.

13. See, for example, G. McNamara, H. Moon, and P. Bromiley, "Banking on Commitment: Intended and Unintended Consequences of an Organization's Attempt to Attenuate Escalation of Commitment," *Academy of Management Journal*, April 2002, pp. 443–452; V. S. Rao and A. Monk, "The Effects of Individual Differences and Anonymity on Commitment to Decisions," *Journal of Social Psychology*, August 1999, pp. 496–515; C. F. Camerer and R. A. Weber, "The Econometrics and Behavioral Economics of Escalation of Commitment: A Reexamination of Staw's Theory," *Journal of Economic Behavior and Organization*, May 1999, pp. 59–82; D. R. Bobocel and J. P. Meyer, "Escalating Commitment to a Failing Course of Action: Separating the Roles of Choice and Justification," *Journal of Applied Psychology*, June 1994, pp. 360–363; and B. M. Staw, "The Escalation of Commitment to a Course of Action," *Academy of Management Review*, October 1981, pp. 577–587.

14. W. Cole, "The Stapler Wars," *Time Inside Business*, April 2005, p. A5.

15. See M. H. Bazerman and D. Chugh, "Decisions Without Blinders," *Harvard Business Review*, January 2006, pp. 88–97; C. C. Miller and R. D. Ireland, "Intuition in Strategic Decision Making: Friend or Foe in the Fast-Paced 21st Century," *Academy of Management Executive*, February 2005, pp. 19–30; E. Sadler-Smith and E. Shefy, "The Intuitive Executive: Understanding and Applying 'Gut Feel' in Decision-Making," *Academy of Management Executive*, November 2004, pp. 76–91; T. A. Stewart, "How to Think with Your Gut," *Business 2.0*, November 2002, pp. 98–104; A. L. Tesolin, "How to Develop the Habit of Intuition," *Training & Development*, March 2000, p. 76; L. A. Burke and M. K. Miller, "Taking the Mystery Out of Intuitive Decision Making," *Academy of Management Executive*, October 1999, pp. 91–99; O. Behling and N. L. Eckel, "Making Sense Out of Intuition," *The Executive*, February 1991, pp. 46–47; W. H. Agor (ed.), *Intuition in Organizations* (Newbury Park, CA: Sage Publications, 1989); and K. R. Hammond, R. M. Hamm, J. Grassia, and T. Pearson, "Direct Comparison of the Efficacy of Intuitive and Analytical Cognition in Expert Judgment," *IEEE Transactions on Systems, Man, and Cybernetics SMC-17* (1987), pp. 753–770.

16. C. C. Miller and R. D. Ireland, "Intuition in Strategic Decision Making: Friend or Foe," p. 20.

17. B. Barnes, "Trusting Gut Instincts," WB Network Stops Testing TV Pilots," *Wall Street Journal*, May 30, 2004, pp. B1+.

18. K. R. Brousseau, M. J. Driver, G. Hourihan, and R. Larsson, "The Seasoned Executive's Decision-Making Style," *Harvard Business Review*, February 2006, pp. 111–121.

19. Information for this box came from S. Caudron, "Some New Rules for the New World of Work," *Business Finance*, October 2001, p. 24; C. Kanchier, *Dare to Change Your Job and Your Life*, 2d ed. (Indianapolis, IN: Jist Publishing, 2000); and S. Hagevik, "Responsible Risk Taking," *Journal of Environmental Health*, November 1999, pp. 29+.

20. Information for this box came from D. Jones and A. Shaw, "Slowing Momentum: Why BPM Isn't Keeping Pace with Its Potential," *BPM Magazine*, February 2006, pp. 4–12; B. Violino, "IT Directions," *CFO*, January 2006, pp. 68–72; D. Weinberger, "Sorting Data to Suit Yourself," *Harvard Business Review*, March 2005, pp. 16–18; and C. Winkler, "Getting a Grip on Performance," *CFO-IT*, Winter 2004, pp. 38–48.

21. S. Holmes, "Inside the Coup at Nike," *BusinessWeek*, February 6, 2006, pp. 34–37; and M. Barbaro, "Slightly Testy Nike Divorce Came Down to Data Versus Feel," *New York Times Online*, www.nytimes.com, January 28, 2006.

22. A. J. Rowe, J. D. Boulgarides, and M. R. McGrath, *Managerial Decision Making, Modules in Management Series* (Chicago: SRA, 1984), pp. 18–22.

23. Information for this box came from N. J. Adler (ed.), *International Dimensions of Organizational Behavior*, 4th ed. (Cincinnati: South-Western College

Publishing, 2001); B. C. McDonald and D. Hutcheson, "Dealing with Diversity Is Key to Tapping Talent," *Atlanta Business Chronicle*, December 18, 1998, pp. 45A+; and P. M. Elsass and L. M. Graves, "Demographic Diversity in Decision-Making Groups: The Experience of Women and People of Color," *Academy of Management Review*, October 1997, pp. 946–973.

24. E. Teach, "Avoiding Decision Traps," *CFO*, June 2004, pp. 97–99; and D. Kahneman and A. Tversky, "Judgment Under Uncertainty: Heuristics and Biases," *Science*, vol. 185, 1974, pp. 1124–1131.

25. Information for this section taken from S. P. Robbins, *Decide & Conquer* (Upper Saddle River, NJ: Financial Times/Prentice Hall, 2004).

26. L. Margonelli, "How IKEA Designs Its Sexy Price Tags," *Business 2.0,* October 2002, p. 108.

27. P. C. Chu, E. E. Spires, and T. Sueyoshi, "Cross-Cultural Differences in Choice Behavior and Use of Decision Aids: A Comparison of Japan and the United States," *Organizational Behavior & Human Decision Processes,* vol. 77 (2), 1999, pp. 147–170.

28. Information for this box came from R. J. House, P. J. Hanges, M. Javidan, P. W. Dorfman, and V. Gupta (eds.), *Culture, Leadership, and Organizations: The GLOBE Study of 62 Societies* (Thousand Oaks, CA: Sage Publications, 2004); E. W. K. Tsang, "Superstition and Decision-Making: Contradiction or Complement?" *Academy of Management Executive,* November 2004, pp. 92–104; N. J. Adler, *International Dimensions of Organizational Behavior,* 4th ed., (Cincinnati, OH: South-Western, 2002); and G. Hofstede, *Culture's Consequences* (Thousand Oaks, California: Sage Publications, 2001).

29. S. Thurm, "Seldom-Used Executive Power: Reconsidering," *Wall Street Journal,* February 6, 2006, p. B3.

30. J. S. Hammond, R. L. Keeney, and H. Raiffa, *Smart Choices: A Practical Guide to Making Better Decisions* (Boston, MA: Harvard Business School Press, 1999), p. 4.

31. This discussion is based on E. W. Ford, W. J. Duncan, A. G. Bedeian, P. M. Ginter, M. D. Rousculp, and A. M. Adams, "Mitigating Risks, Visible Hands, Inevitable Disasters, and Soft Variables: Management Research That Matters," *Academy of Management Executive,* November 2005, pp. 24–38; K. H. Hammonds, "5 Habits of Highly Reliable Organizations: An Interview with Karl Weick," *Fast Company,* May 2002, pp. 124–128; and K. E. Weick, "Drop Your Tools: An Allegory for Organizational Studies," *Administrative Science Quarterly,* vol. 41 (2), 1996, pp. 301–313.

32. Situation adapted from information in "Pensions: Conflict-of-Interest Issues Being Probed," *Los Angeles Times,* February 4, 2006, p. C3; Jessica Marquez, "Pension Consultants Under the Microscope in Wake of Conflict-of-Interest Findings," *Workforce Management,* October 10, 2005, pp. 58+.

## Chapter 7

1. Information from Mi-Bospo's Web site, www.mibospo.org, Women's World Banking Web site, www.swwb.org, and United Nations Capital Development Fund Web site, www.uncdf.org/English/microfinance, February 27, 2006; and K. A. Dolan, "Up from the Rubble," *Forbes,* April 18, 2005, pp. 158–160.

2. Harley-Davidson *Annual Report,* 2004, p. 3; K. J. Lamiman, "Leader of the Pack: Harley-Davidson, Inc.," *Better Investing,* May 2003, pp. 42–44; and E. Eldridge, "Investors Fear Harley's Thunder Grows Faint," *USA Today,* April 8, 2003, p. 3B.

3. See, for example, F. Delmar and S. Shane, "Does Business Planning Facilitate the Development of New Ventures?" *Strategic Management Journal,* December 2003, pp. 1165–1185; R. M. Grant, "Strategic Planning in a Turbulent Environment: Evidence from the Oil Majors," *Strategic Management Journal,* June 2003, pp. 491–517; P. J. Brews and M. R. Hunt, "Learning to Plan and Planning to Learn: Resolving the Planning School/Learning School Debate," *Strategic Management Journal*, December 1999, pp. 889–913; C. C. Miller and L. B. Cardinal, "Strategic Planning and Firm Performance: A Synthesis of More Than Two Decades of Research," *Academy of Management Journal*, March 1994, pp. 1649–1685; N. Capon, J. U. Farley, and J. M. Hulbert, "Strategic Planning and Financial Performance: More Evidence," *Journal of Management Studies*, January 1994, pp. 22–38; D. K. Sinha, "The Contribution of Formal Planning to Decisions," *Strategic Management Journal*, October 1990, pp. 479–492; J. A. Pearce II, E. B. Freeman, and R. B. Robinson Jr., "The Tenuous Link Between Formal Strategic Planning and Financial Performance," *Academy of Management Review*, October 1987, pp. 658–675; L. C. Rhyne, "Contrasting Planning Systems in High, Medium, and Low Performance Companies," *Journal of Management Studies*, July 1987, pp. 363–385; and J. A. Pearce II, K. K. Robbins, and R. B. Robinson Jr., "The Impact of Grand Strategy and Planning Formality on Financial Performance," *Strategic Management Journal*, March–April 1987, pp. 125–134.

4. R. Molz, "How Leaders Use Goals," *Long Range Planning*, October 1987, p. 91.

5. C. Hymowitz, "When Meeting Targets Becomes the Strategy, CEO Is on Wrong Path," *Wall Street Journal,* March 8, 2005, p. B1.

6. Ford Report on the Business Impact of Climate Change, 2005, www.ford.com; A. Taylor III, "Getting Ford in Gear," *Fortune,* April 28, 2003, pp. 44–47; B. Morris, "Can Ford Save Ford?" *Fortune,* November 18, 2002, pp. 52–64; K. Naughton, "Ford Goes for the Green," *Newsweek,* August 7, 2000, p. 62; J. Ball, "Ford Contacts Environmentalists Behind Scenes," *Wall Street Journal*, May 15, 2000, p. B2; and B. Morris, "This Ford Is Different," *Fortune*, April 3, 2000, pp. 122–136.

7. Annual reports from Claire's Stores (2005), Nike (2005), Winnebago (2005), Deutsche Bank (2004); and EnCana Corporate Constitution (2004), www.encana.com.

8. See, for instance, C. K. Warriner, "The Problem of Organizational Purpose," *Sociological Quarterly,*

Spring 1965, pp. 139–146; and J. Pfeffer, *Organizational Design* (Arlington Heights, IL: AHM Publishing, 1978), pp. 5–12.

9. Information for this box from Special Report on America's Best Leaders, "Leading With His Life," *US News & World Report,* October 31, 2005, p. 34; R. A. Posthuma, "How Ideology, Party Status, and Risk Framing Influence Lawsuit Settlement Negotiation," *Academy of Management Proceedings,* 2005, pp. A1–A6; D. C. Hambrick, S. Finkelstein, and A. C. Mooney, "Executive Job Demands: New Insights for Explaining Strategic Decisions and Leader Behaviors," *Academy of Management Review,* July 2005, pp. 472–491; G. T. Fairhurst and R. A. Starr, *The Art of Framing: Managing the Language of Leadership* (San Francisco: Jossey-Bass, 1996); R. M. Entman, "Framing: Toward Clarification of a Fractured Paradigm," *Journal of Communication,* Autumn 1993, pp. 51–58; and A. Tversky and D. Kahneman, "The Framing of Decisions and the Psychology of Choice," *Science,* January 1981, pp. 453–458.

10. J. D. Hunger and T. L. Wheelen, *Strategic Management and Business Policy,* 10th ed. (Upper Saddle River, NJ: Prentice Hall, 2006).

11. J. L. Roberts, "Signed. Sealed. Delivered?" *Newsweek,* June 20, 2005, pp. 44–46.

12. F Hansen, "Meeting the HR Challenge," *Business Finance,* July 2003, p. 16.

13. D. Drickhamer, "Braced for the Future," *Industry Week,* October 2004, pp. 51–52.

14. P. N. Romani, "MBO by Any Other Name Is Still MBO," *Supervision,* December 1997, pp. 6–8; and A. W. Schrader and G. T. Seward, "MBO Makes Dollar Sense," *Personnel Journal,* July 1989, pp. 32–37.

15. R. Rodgers and J. E. Hunter, "Impact of Management by Objectives on Organizational Productivity," *Journal of Applied Psychology,* April 1991, pp. 322–336.

16. G. P. Latham, "The Motivational Benefits of Goal-Setting," *Academy of Management Executive,* November 2004, pp. 126–129.

17. For additional information on goals, see, for instance, P. Drucker, *The Executive in Action* (New York: HarperCollins Books, 1996), pp. 207–214; and E. A. Locke and G. P. Latham, *A Theory of Goal Setting and Task Performance* (Upper Saddle River, NJ: Prentice Hall, 1990).

18. Several of these factors were suggested by R. K. Bresser and R. C. Bishop, "Dysfunctional Effects of Formal Planning: Two Theoretical Explanations," *Academy of Management Review,* October 1983, pp. 588–599; and J. S. Armstrong, "The Value of Formal Planning for Strategic Decisions: Review of Empirical Research," *Strategic Management Journal,* July–September 1982, pp. 197–211.

19. Brews and Hunt, "Learning to Plan and Planning to Learn: Resolving the Planning School/Learning School Debate."

20. Ibid.

21. D. Clark, "Power-Hungry Computers Put Data Centers in Bind," *Wall Street Journal,* November 14, 2005, pp. A1+.

22. C. Prystay, M. Hiebert, and K. Linebaugh, "Companies Face Ethical Issues over Tamiflu," *Wall Street Journal,* January 16, 2006, pp. B1+.

23. A. Campbell, "Tailored, Not Benchmarked: A Fresh Look at Corporate Planning," *Harvard Business Review*, March–April 1999, pp. 41–50.

24. J. H. Sheridan, "Focused on Flow," *IW,* October 18, 1999, pp. 46–51.

25. H. Mintzberg, *The Rise and Fall of Strategic Planning* (New York: Free Press, 1994).

26. Ibid.

27. Ibid.

28. G. Hamel and C. K. Prahalad, *Competing for the Future* (Boston: Harvard Business School Press, 1994).

29. D. Miller, "The Architecture of Simplicity," *Academy of Management Review*, January 1993, pp. 116–138.

30. M. C. Mankins and R. Steele, "Stop Making Plans—Start Making Decisions," *Harvard Business Review,* January 2006, pp. 76–84; L. Bossidy and R. Charan, *Execution: The Discipline of Getting Things Done* (New York: Crown/Random House, 2002); and P. Roberts, "The Art of Getting Things Done," *Fast Company,* June 2000, p. 162.

31. Associated Press, "Dow Jones to Shrink 'Wall Street Journal,' Cut Some Data," *USA Today Online,* www.usatoday.com, October 12, 2005.

32. Brews and Hunt, "Learning to Plan and Planning to Learn: Resolving the Planning School/Learning School Debate."

33. Information on Wipro Limited from Hoover's Online, www.hoovers.com, March 21, 2006; R. J. Newman, "Coming and Going," *US News & World Report,* January 23, 2006, pp. 50–52; T. Atlas, "Bangalore's Big Dreams," *US News & World Report,* May 2, 2005, pp. 50–52; and K. H. Hammonds, "Smart, Determined, Ambitious, Cheap: The New Face of Global Competition," *Fast Company,* February 2003, pp. 90–97.

34. Situation adapted from information in "Moto to Pay Schools for Phones," *Crain's Chicago Business,* March 21, 2005, p. 14; Jackie Leatherman, "Are Schools' Relationships with Private Businesses Ethical? Dealing for Dollars," *The Tribune (Mesa, AZ),* January 21, 2006.

## Chapter 8

1. Information from company Web site, www.uabiz.com, February 24, 2006; and C. Salter, "Protect This House," *Fast Company,* August 2005, pp. 70–75.

2. Examples from the Associated Press, "Shake-Up at Microsoft Stresses Importance of Online Strategy,"

*New York Times Online,* www.nytimes.com, March 24, 2006; T. Howard, "Big Companies Buy Small Brands with Big Values," *USA Today,* March 22, 2006, p. 1B; and S. Rai, "Dell to Double India Workforce," *New York Times Online,* www.nytimes.com, March 21, 2006.

3. L. Tischler, "Al Jazeera's Global Mission," *Fast Company,* April 2006, pp. 42–48; D. A. Crowe, "Concrete Strategy," *Latin Trade,* March 2006, pp. 20–21; and S. Hamm, "Speed Demons," *BusinessWeek,* March 27, 2006, pp. 68–76.

4. J. W. Dean Jr. and M. P. Sharfman, "Does Decision Process Matter? A Study of Strategic Decision-Making Effectiveness," *Academy of Management Journal,* April 1996, pp. 368–396.

5. Based on A. A. Thompson Jr., A. J. Strickland III, and J. E. Gamble, *Crafting and Executing Strategy,* 14th ed. (New York: McGraw-Hill Irwin, 2005).

6. J. Magretta, "Why Business Models Matter," *Harvard Business Review,* May 2002, pp. 86–92.

7. *American Idol* Web site, www.idolonfox.com, March 24, 2006; and D. Lieberman, "*American Idol* Zooms from Hit Show to Massive Business," *USA Today,* March 30, 2005, pp. A1+.

8. H. J. Cho and V. Pucik, "Relationship Between Innovativeness, Quality, Growth, Profitability, and Market Value," *Strategic Management Journal,* June 2005, pp. 555–575; W. F. Joyce, "What Really Works," *Organizational Dynamics,* May 2005, pp. 118–129; M. A. Roberto, "Strategic Decision-Making Processes," *Group & Organization Management,* December 2004, pp. 625–658; A. Carmeli and A. Tischler, "The Relationships Between Intangible Organizational Elements and Organizational Performance," *Strategic Management Journal,* December 2004, pp. 1257–1278; D. J. Ketchen, C. C. Snow, and V. L. Street, "Improving Firm Performance by Matching Strategic Decision-Making Processes to Competitive Dynamics," *Academy of Management Executive,* November 2004, pp. 29–43; E. H. Bowman and C. E. Helfat, "Does Corporate Strategy Matter?" *Strategic Management Journal,* vol. 22, 2001, pp. 1–23; P. J. Brews and M. R. Hunt, "Learning to Plan and Planning to Learn: Resolving the Planning School-Learning School Debate," *Strategic Management Journal,* vol. 20, 1999, pp. 889–913; D. J. Ketchen Jr., J. B. Thomas, and R. R. McDaniel Jr., "Process, Content and Context; Synergistic Effects on Performance," *Journal of Management,* vol 22 (2), 1996, pp. 231–257; C. C. Miller and L. B. Cardinal, "Strategic Planning and Firm Performance: A Synthesis of More Than Two Decades of Research," *Academy of Management Journal,* December 1994, pp. 1649–1665; and N. Capon, J. U. Farley, and J. M. Hulbert, "Strategic Planning and Financial Performance: More Evidence," *Journal of Management Studies,* January 1994, pp. 105–110.

9. "A Solid Strategy Helps Companies' Growth," *Nation's Business,* October 1990, p. 10.

10. See, for example, J. A. Byrne, "Strategic Planning: It's Back!" *BusinessWeek,* August 26, 1996, pp. 46–52; S. J. Wall and S. R. Wall, "The Evolution (Not the Death) of Strategy," *Organizational Dynamics,* Autumn 1995, pp. 7–19; and H. Mintzberg, *The Rise and Fall of Strategic Planning* (New York: Free Press, 1994).

11. You can see this document at the United States Postal Service Web site at www.usps.com/strategicplanning.

12. These examples came from J. D. Miller, "Which Colleges Will Make the Grade?" *Better Investing,* April 2006, p. 49; R. J. Newman, "Can America Keep Up?" *US News & World Report,* March 27, 2006, p. 55; and W. Cole, S. Steptoe, and S. S. Dale, "The Multi-tasking Generation," *Time,* March 27, 2006, pp. 48–55.

13. S. Bowles, "What, Movies Worry?" *USA Today,* March 20, 2006, pp. 1B+; S. Waxman, "When Moviegoers Vote with Their Feet," *New York Times Online,* www.nytimes.com, March 16, 2006; R. Levine, "Can Theaters Thrive in Another Dimension?" *Business 2.0,* March 2006, p. 38; D. Leonhardt, "Change Ahead for a Theater Near You," *New York Times Online,* www.nytimes.com, February 15, 2006; A. Breznican and G. Strauss, "Where Have All the Moviegoers Gone?" *USA Today,* June 23, 2005, pp. 1B+; and R. Chittum, "The Show Before the Movie," *Wall Street Journal,* June 15, 2005, pp. B1+.

14. C. K. Prahalad and G. Hamel, "The Core Competence of the Corporation," *Harvard Business Review,* May–June 1990, pp. 79–91.

15. A. Taylor, "How Toyota Does It," *Fortune,* March 6, 2006, pp. 107–124; C. Woodyard, "Slow and Steady Drives Toyota's Growth," *USA Today,* December 21, 2005, pp. 1B+; I. M. Kunii, C. Dawson, and C. Palmeri, "Toyota Is Way Ahead of the Hybrid Pack," *BusinessWeek,* May 5, 2003, p. 48; and S. Spear and H. K. Bowen, "Decoding the DNA of the Toyota Production System," *Harvard Business Review,* September–October 1999, pp. 96–106.

16. See, for example, H. J. Cho and V. Pucik, "Relationship Between Innovativeness, Quality, Growth, Profitability, and Market Value"; W. F. Joyce, "Building the 4+2 Organization," *Organizational Dynamics,* May 2005, pp. 118–129; R. S. Kaplan and D. P. Norton, "Measuring the Strategic Readiness of Intangible Assets," *Harvard Business Review,* February 2004, pp. 52–63; C. M. Fiol, "Managing Culture as a Competitive Resource: An Identity-Based View of Sustainable Competitive Advantage," *Journal of Management,* March 1991, pp. 191–211; T. Kono, "Corporate Culture and Long-Range Planning," *Long Range Planning,* August 1990, pp. 9–19; S. Green, "Understanding Corporate Culture and Its Relation to Strategy," *International Studies of Management and Organization,* Summer 1988, pp. 6–28; C. Scholz, "Corporate Culture and Strategy—The Problem of Strategic Fit," *Long Range Planning,* August 1987, pp. 78–87; and J. B. Barney, "Organizational Culture: Can It Be a Source of Sustained Competitive Advantage?" *Academy of Management Review,* July 1986, pp. 656–665.

17. J. P. Kotter and J. L. Heskett, *Corporate Culture and Performance* (New York: Free Press, 1992).

18. K. E. Klein, "Slogans That Are the Real Thing," *BusinessWeek Online,* www.businessweek.com, August 4, 2005; and T. Mucha, "The Payoff for Trying Harder," *Business 2.0,* July 2002, pp. 84–85.

19. A. Carmeli and A. Tischler, "The Relationships Between Intangible Organizational Elements and Organizational Performance;" P. W. Roberts and G. R. Dowling, "Corporate Reputation and Sustained Financial Performance," *Strategic Management Journal,* December 2002, pp. 1077–1093; and C. J. Fombrun, "Corporate Reputations as Economic Assets," in *Handbook of Strategic Management,* edited by M. A. Hitt, R. E. Freeman, and J. S. Harrison (Malden, MA: Blackwell Publishers, 2001), pp. 289–312.

20. "Johnson & Johnson Ranks No. 1 in National Corporate Reputation Survey for Seventh Consecutive Year," Harris Interactive Press Release, www.harrisinteractive. com, December 7, 2005.

21. Information in this box from R. S. Hansen and K. Hansen, "Using a SWOT Analysis in Your Career Planning," *Quintessential Careers,* www.quintcareers. com, March 25, 2006; "Personal SWOT Analysis," *Mindtools,* www.mindtools.com, January 2006; S. Miller, "Have You Done Your SWOT Analysis Lately?" *Entreprenur,* www.entrepreneur.com, January 14, 2002; and A. Williams, "Career Planning: Build on Strengths, Strengthen Weaknesses," *The Black Collegian*, September–October 1993, pp. 78–86.

22. Information in this box from D. McGinn, "From Harvard to Las Vegas," *Newsweek,* April 18, 2005, pp. E8–E14; G. Lindsay, "Prada's High-Tech Misstep," *Business 2.0,* March 2004, pp. 72–75; G. Loveman, "Diamonds in the Data Mine," *Harvard Business Review,* May 2003, pp. 109–113; and L. Gary, "Simplify and Execute: Words to Live By in Times of Turbulence," *Harvard Management Update,* January 2003, p. 12.

23. J. W. Peters, "Auto Supplier Finds Business Is Better Elsewhere," *New York Times Online,* www.nytimes. com, February 1, 2006.

24. H. Quarls, T. Pernsteiner, and K. Rangan, "Love Your Dogs," *Strategy & Business,* Spring 2006, pp. 58–65; and P. Haspeslagh, "Portfolio Planning: Uses and Limits," *Harvard Business Review*, January–February 1982, pp. 58–73.

25. *Perspective on Experience* (Boston: Boston Consulting Group, 1970).

26. J. B. Barney, "Looking Inside for Competitive Advantage," *Academy of Management Executive,* November 1995, pp. 49–61; M. A. Peteraf, "The Cornerstones of Competitive Advantage: A Resource-Based View," *Strategic Management Journal,* March 1993, pp. 179–191; J. Barney, "Firm Resources and Sustained Competitive Advantage," *Journal of Management* vol. 17 (1), 1991, pp. 99–120; M. E. Porter, *Competitive Advantage: Creating and Sustaining*

*Superior Performance* (New York: Free Press, 1985); and Rumelt, "Towards a Strategic Theory of the Firm," in R. Lamb (ed.), *Competitive Strategic Management* (Upper Saddle River, NJ: Prentice Hall, 1984), pp. 556–570.

27. Information from Kellogg's Web site, www.kellogg. com, March 27, 2006.

28. N. A. Shepherd, "Competitive Advantage: Mapping Change and the Role of the Quality Manager of the Future," *Annual Quality Congress,* May 1998, pp. 53–60; T. C. Powell, "Total Quality Management as Competitive Advantage: A Review and Empirical Study," *Strategic Management Journal*, January 1995, pp. 15–37; and R. D. Spitzer, "TQM: The Only Source of Sustainable Competitive Advantage," *Quality Progress,* June 1993, pp. 59–64.

29. See special issue of *Academy of Management Review* devoted to TQM, July 1994, pp. 390–584; B. Voss, "Quality's Second Coming," *Journal of Business Strategy,* March–April 1994, pp. 42–46; C. A. Barclay, "Quality Strategy and TQM Policies: Empirical Evidence," *Management International Review*, Special Issue 1993, pp. 87–98; R. Krishnan, A. B. Shani, R. M. Grant, and R. Baer, "In Search of Quality Improvement Problems of Design and Implementation," *Academy of Management Executive*, November 1993, pp. 7–20; R. Jacob, "TQM: More Than a Dying Fad?" *Fortune*, October 18, 1993, pp. 66–72; and R. J. Schonenberger, "Is Strategy Strategic? Impact of Total Quality Management on Strategy," *Academy of Management Executive*, August 1992, pp. 80–87.

30. See, for example, N. Argyres and A. M. McGahan, "An Interview with Michael Porter," *Academy of Management Executive,* May 2002, pp. 43–52; A. Brandenburger, "Porter's Added Value: High Indeed!" *Academy of Management Executive,* May 2002, pp. 58–60; D. F. Jennings and J. R. Lumpkin, "Insights Between Environmental Scanning Activities and Porter's Generic Strategies: An Empirical Analysis," *Strategic Management Journal*, vol. 18 (4), 1992, pp. 791–803; I. Bamberger, "Developing Competitive Advantage in Small and Medium-Sized Firms," *Long Range Planning*, October 1989, pp. 80–88; A. I. Murray, "A Contingency View of Porter's 'Generic Strategies,'" *Academy of Management Review*, July 1988, pp. 390–400; C. W. L. Hill, "Differentiation Versus Low Cost or Differentiation and Low Cost: A Contingency Framework," *Academy of Management Review*, July 1988, pp. 401–412; M. E. Porter, "From Competitive Advantage to Corporate Strategy, *Harvard Business Review*, May–June 1987, pp. 43–59; Dess and Davis, "Porter's (1980) Generic Strategies and Performance: An Empirical Examination with American Data—Part I: Testing Porter," *Organization Studies*, vol. 1, 1986, pp. 37–55; Dess and Davis, "Porter's (1980) Generic Strategies and Performance: An Empirical Examination with American Data—Part II: Performance Implications," *Organization Studies*, vol. 3, 1986, pp. 255–261; Porter, *Competitive Advantage: Creating and Sustaining Superior Performance*; G. G. Dess and P. S. Davis, "Porter's (1980)

Generic Strategies as Determinants of Strategic Group Membership and Organizational Performance," *Academy of Management Journal*, September 1984, pp. 467–488; and M. E. Porter, *Competitive Strategy: Techniques for Analyzing Industries and Competitors* (New York: Free Press, 1980).

31. J. W. Bachmann, "Competitive Strategy: It's O.K. to Be Different," *Academy of Management Executive*, May 2002, pp. 61–65; S. Cappel, P. Wright, M. Kroll, and D. Wyld, "Competitive Strategies and Business Performance: An Empirical Study of Select Service Businesses," *International Journal of Management*, March 1992, pp. 1–11; D. Miller, "The Generic Strategy Trap," *Journal of Business Strategy*, January–February 1991, pp. 37–41; R. E. White, "Organizing to Make Business Unit Strategies Work," in H.E. Glass (ed.), *Handbook of Business Strategy*, 2d ed. (Boston: Warren Gorham and Lamont, 1991), pp. 24.1–24.14; and Hill, "Differentiation Versus Low Cost or Differentiation and Low Cost."

32. J. N. Sheth and R. S. Sisodia in "Competitive Markets and the Rule of Three," *Ivey Business Journal*, September/October 2002, pp. 1–5; and *The Rule of Three: Surviving and Thriving in Competitive Markets* (New York: Free Press, 2002).

33. R. Frost, "Local to Global: Easy as 1-2-3?" *Brand Channel*, www.brandchannel.com, March 27, 2006; and A. Paul, "Explanation of Rule of Three by Sheth and Sisodia," *12 Manage*, www.12manage.com, March 27, 2006.

34. Information from IFPI, www.ifpi.org, March 27, 2006; E. Gunderson, "Music Industry Hopes for a Solid Year," *USA Today*, March 23, 2006, p. 1D; D. Bauder, Associated Press, "Poll Shifts Blame from Downloads," *Springfield News-Leader*, February 4, 2006, p. 5C; E. Gunderson, "Ring-Tone Sales Ring Up Music Profits," *USA Today*, January 26, 2006, p. 1D; and K. Barnes, "Album Sales Slump as Downloads Rise," *USA Today*, January 6, 2006, p. 1D.

35. K. Shimizu and M. A. Hitt, "Strategic Flexibility: Organizational Preparedness to Reverse Ineffective Decisions," *Academy of Management Executive*, November 2004, p. 44.

36. Information in this box from R. D. Ireland and M. A. Hitt, "Achieving and Maintaining Strategic Competitiveness in the 21st Century: The Role of Strategic Leadership," *Academy of Management Executive*, November 2005, pp. 63–77.

37. T. Lowry, "In the Zone," *BusinessWeek*, October 17, 2005, pp. 66–77.

38. E. Kim, D. Nam, and J. L. Stimpert, "The Applicability of Porter's Generic Strategies in the Digital Age: Assumptions, Conjectures, and Suggestions," *Journal of Management*, vol. 30 (5), 2004, pp. 569–589; and G. T. Lumpkin, S. B. Droege, and G. G. Dess, "E-Commerce Strategies: Achieving Sustainable Competitive Advantage and Avoiding Pitfalls," *Organizational Dynamics*, Spring 2002, pp. 325–340.

39. Kim, Nam, and Stimpert, "The Applicability of Porter's Generic Strategies in the Digital Age: Assumptions, Conjectures, and Suggestions."

40. J. Gaffney, "Shoe Fetish," *Business 2.0*, March 2002, pp. 98–99.

41. "And the Winners Are . . . the 100 Best Companies to Work For," *Fortune*, January 11, 2006, p. 89–113; K. L. Allers, "Retail's Rebel Yell," *Fortune*, November 10, 2003, pp. 137–142; and M. Boyle, "Rapid Growth in Tough Times," *Fortune*, September 2, 2002, p. 150.

42. J. Doebele, "The Engineer," *Forbes*, January 9, 2006, pp. 122–124.

43. S. Ellison, "P&G to Unleash Dental Adult-Pet Food," *Wall Street Journal*, December 12, 2002, p. B4.

44. Situation adapted from information in Sarah McBride and Mylene Mangalindan, "Coming Attraction: Downloadable Movies from Amazon," *Wall Street Journal*, Mach 10, 2006, pp. B1+; Ethan Smith and Mylene Mangalindan, "Amazon Plans Music Service to Rival iTunes," *Wall Street Journal*, February 16, 2006, pp. B1+; "Largest Share," Book-Off financial report, www.bookoff.co.jp/ir/pdf/com_info.pdf, July 2005; Jim Frederick, "War of Words," *Time International*, February 17, 2003, p. 33; Keith Regan, "Bugging Out over Bezos' Bargain Book Bin," *E-Commerce Times*, www.ecommercetimes.com, April 17, 2002.

## Chapter 9

1. Information from organization's Web site, www.sandiegozoo.org, February 24, 2006; and T. Reason, "Budgeting in the Real World," *CFO*, July 2005, pp. 42–48.

2. J. Trotsky, "The Futurists," *US News & World Report*, April 19, 2004, pp. EE4–EE6.

3. F. Vogelstein, "Search and Destroy," *Fortune*, May 2, 2005, pp. 73–82.

4. V. K. Garg, B. A. Walters, and R. L. Priem, "Chief Executive Scanning Emphases, Environmental Dynamism, and Manufacturing Firm Performance," *Strategic Management Journal*, August 2003, pp. 725–744; C. G. Wagner, "Top 10 Reasons to Watch Trends," *The Futurist*, March–April 2002, pp. 68–69; K. Kumar, R. Subramanian, and K. Strandholm, "Competitive Strategy, Environmental Scanning and Performance: A Context Specific Analysis of Their Relationship," *International Journal of Commerce and Management*, Spring 2001, pp. 1–18; D. S. Elkenov, "Strategic Uncertainty and Environmental Scanning: The Case for Institutional Influences on Scanning Behavior," *Strategic Management Journal*, vol. 18, 1997, pp. 287–302; B. K. Boyd and J. Fulk, "Executive Scanning and Perceived Uncertainty: A Multidimensional Model," *Journal of Management*, vol. 22 (1), 1996, pp. 1–21; R. Subramanian, N. Fernandes, and E. Harper, "Environmental Scanning in U.S. Companies: Their Nature and Their Relationship to Performance," *Management International Review*, July 1993,

pp. 271–286; E. H. Burack and N. J. Mathys, "Environmental Scanning Improves Strategic Planning," *Personnel Administrator*, April 1989, pp. 82–87; L. M. Fuld, *Monitoring the Competition* (New York: John Wiley & Sons, 1988); and S. C. Jain, "Environmental Scanning in U.S. Corporations," *Long Range Planning*, April 1984, pp. 117–128.

5. J. Barnett, "Can a '50s Icon Do It Again?" *Newsweek*, March 20, 2006, p. E20; L. Grant, "Party Time: Home Events See Sales," *USA Today*, October 5, 2005, p. 4B; R. Brooks, "Sealing Their Fate," *Wall Street Journal*, February 18, 2004, pp. A1+; and T. L. Wheelen and J. D. Hunger, *Strategic Management*, 8th ed. (Upper Saddle River, NJ: Prentice Hall, 2001), pp. 52–53.

6. "Know Your Enemy," *Business 2.0*, June 2004, p. 89; K. Girard, "Snooping on a Shoestring," *Business 2.0*, May 2003, pp. 64–66; D. Kinard, "Raising Your Competitive IQ: The Payoff of Paying Attention to Potential Competitors," *Association Management*, February 2003, pp. 40–44; K. Western, "Ethical Spying," *Business Ethics*, September–October 1995, pp. 22–23; J. P. Herring, "The Role of Intelligence in Formulating Strategy," *Journal of Business Strategy*, September–October 1992, pp. 54–60; L. Fuld, "A Recipe for Business Intelligence," *Journal of Business Strategy*, January–February 1991, pp. 12–17; and B. Gilad, "The Role of Organized Competitive Intelligence in Corporate Strategy," *Columbia Journal of World Business*, Winter 1989, pp. 29–35;

7. C. Davis, "Get Smart," *Executive Edge*, October/November 1999, pp. 46–50.

8. B. Ettore, "Managing Competitive Intelligence," *Management Review*, October 1995, pp. 15–19.

9. A. Serwer, "P&G's Covert Operation," *Fortune*, September 17, 2001, pp. 42–44.

10. B. Rosner, "HR Should Get a Clue: Corporate Spying Is Real," *Workforce*, April 2001, pp. 72–75.

11. Western, "Ethical Spying."

12. W. H. Davidson, "The Role of Global Scanning in Business Planning," *Organizational Dynamics*, Winter 1991, pp. 5–16.

13. T. Smart, "Air Supply," *US News & World Report*, February 28, 2005, p. EE10.

14. "Is Supply Chain Collaboration Really Happening?" *ERI Journal*, www.eri.com, January/February 2006; L. Denend and H. Lee, "West Marine: Driving Growth Through Shipshape Supply Chain Management, A Case Study" *Stanford Graduate School of Business*, www.vics.org, April 7, 2005; N. Nix, A. G. Zacharia, R. F. Lusch, W. R. Bridges, and A. Thomas, "Keys to Effective Supply Chain Collaboration: A Special Report from the Collaborative Practices Research Program," *Neeley School of Business, Texas Christian University*, www.vics.org, November 15, 2004; Collaborative, Planning, Forecasting, and Replenishment Committee Web site, www.cpfr.org, May 20, 2003; and J. W. Verity, "Clearing the Cobwebs from the Stockroom," *BusinessWeek*, October 21, 1996, p. 140.

15. See T. Leahy, "Building Better Forecasts," *Business Finance*, December 1999, pp. 10–12; L. Lapide, "New Developments in Business Forecasting," *Journal of Business Forecasting Methods & Systems*, Summer 1999, pp. 13–14; F. Elikai and W. Hall Jr., "Managing and Improving the Forecasting Process," *Journal of Business Forecasting Methods & Systems*, Spring 1999, pp. 15–19; G. Hamel and C. K. Prahalad, "Competing for the Future," *Harvard Business Review*, July–August 1994, pp. 122–128; P. Schwartz, *The Art of the Long View* (New York: Doubleday/Currency, 1991); J. A. Fraser, "On Target," *Inc.*, April 1991, pp. 113–114; and A. B. Fisher, "Is Long-Range Planning Worth It?" *Fortune*, April 23, 1990, pp. 281–284.

16. J. Goff, "Start with Demand," *CFO*, January 2005, pp. 53–57.

17. L. Brannen, "Upfront: Global Planning Perspectives," *Business Finance*, March 2006, pp. 12+.

18. R. Durand, "Predicting a Firm's Forecasting Ability: The Roles of Organizational Illusion of Control and Organizational Attention," *Strategic Management Journal*, September 2003, pp. 821–838.

19. T. Leahy, "Turning Managers into Forecasters," *Business Finance*, August 2002, pp. 37–40; Elikai and Hall, "Managing and Improving the Forecasting Process."; M. A. Giullian, M. D. Odom, and M. W. Totaro, "Developing Essential Skills for Success in the Business World: A Look at Forecasting," *Journal of Applied Business Research*, Summer 2000, pp. 51–65; and P. N. Pant and W. H. Starbuck, "Innocents in the Forest: Forecasting and Research Methods," *Journal of Management*, June 1990, pp. 433–460.

20. T. Leahy, "Turning Managers into Forecasters."

21. J. Hope, "Use a Rolling Forecast to Spot Trends," *Harvard Business School Working Knowledge*, hbswk.hbs.edu, March 13, 2006.

22. This section is based on H. Johnson, "All in Favor Say Benchmark!" *Training*, August 2004, pp. 30–34; E. Krell, "Now Read This," *Business Finance*, May 2000, pp. 97–103; "E-Benchmarking: The Latest E-Trend," *CFO*, March 2000, p. 7; V. Prabhu, D. Yarrow, and G. Gordon-Hart, "Best Practice and Performance Within Northeast Manufacturing," *Total Quality Management*, January 2000, pp. 113–121; R. L. Ackoff, "The Trouble with Benchmarking," *Across the Board*, January 2000, p. 13; J. Martin, "Are You As Good As You Think You Are?" *Fortune*, September 30, 1996, pp. 142–152; S. Greengard, "Discover Best Practices," *Personnel Journal*, November 1995, pp. 62–73; Y. K. Shetty, "Benchmarking for Superior Performance," *Long Range Planning* 1 (April 1993), pp. 39–44; and G. H. Watson, "How Process Benchmarking Supports Corporate Strategy," *Planning Review*, January–February 1993, pp. 12–15.

23. "Newswatch," *CFO*, July 2002, p. 26.

24. Benchmarking examples from the following: S. Carey, "Racing to Improve," *Wall Street Journal,* March 24, 2006, pp. B1+; D. Waller, "NASCAR: The Army's Unlikely Adviser," *Time,* July 4, 2005, p. 19; A. Taylor III, "Double Duty," *Fortune,* March 7, 2005, p. 108; M. A. Prospero, "In Indy's Pits, It's More Than Speed," *Fast Company,* August 2004, p. 26; P. Gogoi, "Thinking Outside the Cereal Box," *BusinessWeek,* July 28, 2003, pp. 74–75; "Benchmarkers Make Strange Bedfellows," *IW,* November 15, 1993, p. 8; G. Fuchsberg, "Here's Help in Finding Corporate Role Models," *Wall Street Journal,* June 1, 1993, p. B1; and A. Tanzer, "Studying at the Feet of the Masters," *Forbes,* May 10, 1993, pp. 43–44.

25. E. Krell, "The Case Against Budgeting," *Business Finance,* July 2003, pp. 20–25; J. Hope and R. Fraser, "Who Needs Budgets?" *Harvard Business Review,* February 2003, pp. 108–115; T. Leahy, "The Top 10 Traps of Budgeting," *Business Finance,* November 2001, pp. 20–26; T. Leahy, "Necessary Evil," *Business Finance,* November 1999, pp. 41–45; J. Fanning, "Businesses Languishing in a Budget Comfort Zone?" *Management Accounting,* July/August 1999, p. 8; "Budgeting Processes: Inefficiency or Inadequate?" *Management Accounting,* February 1999, p. 5; A. Kennedy and D. Dugdale, "Getting the Most from Budgeting," *Management Accounting,* February 1999, pp. 22–24; G. J. Nolan, "The End of Traditional Budgeting," *Bank Accounting & Finance,* Summer 1998, pp. 29–36; and J. Mariotti, "Surviving the Dreaded Budget Process," *IW,* August 17, 1998, p. 150.

26. See, for example, S. Stiansen, "Breaking Even," *Success,* November 1988, p. 16.

27. S. E. Barndt and D. W. Carvey, *Essentials of Operations Management* (Upper Saddle River, NJ: Prentice Hall, 1982), p. 134.

28. E. E. Adam Jr. and R. J. Ebert, *Production and Operations Management,* 5th ed. (Upper Saddle River, NJ: Prentice Hall, 1992), p. 333.

29. See, for instance, C. Benko and F. W. McFarlan, *Connecting the Dots: Aligning Projects with Objectives in Unpredictable Times* (Boston, MA: Harvard Business School Press, 2003); M. W. Lewis, M. A. Welsh, G. E. Dehler, and S. G. Green, "Product Development Tensions: Exploring Contrasting Styles of Project Management," *Academy of Management Journal,* June 2002, pp. 546–564; C. E. Gray and E. W. Larsen, *Project Management: The Managerial Process* (Columbus, OH: McGraw-Hill Higher Education, 2000); and J. Davidson Frame, *Project Management Competence: Building Key Skills for Individuals, Teams, and Organizations* (San Francisco, CA: Jossey-Bass, 1999).

30. For more information, see Project Management Software Directory, infogoal.com/pmc/pmcswr.htm.

31. D. Zielinski, "Soft Skills, Hard Truth," *Training,* July 2005, pp. 19–23.

32. H. Collingwood, "Best Kept Secrets of the World's Best Companies: Secret 05, Bad News Folders," *Business 2.0,* April 2006, p. 84.

33. G. Colvin, "An Executive Risk Handbook," *Fortune,* October 3, 2005, pp. 69–70; A. Long and A. Weiss, "Using Scenario Planning to Manage Short-Term Uncertainty," *Outward Insights,* www.outwardinsights.com, 2005; B. Fiora, "Use Early Warning to Strengthen Scenario Planning," *Outward Insights,* www.outwardinsights.com, 2003; L. Fahey, "Scenario Learning," *Management Review,* March 2000, pp. 29–34; S. Caudron, "Frontview Mirror," *Business Finance,* December 1999, pp. 24–30; and J. R. Garber, "What if . . . ?," *Forbes,* November 2, 1998, pp. 76–79.

34. S. Caudron, "Frontview Mirror," p. 30.

35. Situation adapted from information in "Scrushy Reaches a Settlement," *Wall Street Journal,* March 11, 2006, p. B3; "Loss Doubles at HealthSouth," *New York Times,* March 30, 2006, p. C12; Carrie Mason-Draffen, "Pressure to Meet Goals Is Cause of Unethical Business Behavior, Says Study," *Newsday,* January 26, 2006; John Helyar, "The Bizarre Reign of King Richard," *Fortune,* July 7, 2002, pp. 76–86; Reed Abelson, "Scrushy Chided Staff About Profits, Tape Reveals," *New York Times,* May 22, 2003, p. C1.

## Notes for the Part 3 Continuing Case

"Coffee Penetration," *Springfield Business Journal,* June 12–18, 2006, p. 70; B. Horovitz, "Starbucks Nation," *USA Today,* May 29–31, 2006, pp. A1+; S. E. Lockyer, "Operators Aim to Build More Than Restaurants When Adding Locations," *Nation's Restaurant News,* May 22, 2006, pp. 72–74; N. Ramachandran, "Java and a Shot of Hip-Hop," *US News & World Report,* May 22, 2006, pp. EE14–EE15; The Associated Press, "Starbucks Profit Climbs 27% in Quarter," *New York Times Online,* www.nytimes.com, May 4, 2006; S. Bradbury, "Rethinking Every Rule of Reinvention," *Advertising Age,* May 1, 2006, pp. 14–16; S. Waxman, "A Small Step at Starbucks from Mocha to Movies," *New York Times Online,* www.nytimes.com, May 1, 2006; Interview with Jim Donald, *Smart Money,* May 2006, pp. 31–32; P. R. LaMonica, "Coffee and Popcorn," *CNNMoney.com,* April 28, 2006; "Industry News," *National Petroleum News,* April 2006, p. 44; K. Macarthur, "Latte Reward: Cards Add Up at Starbucks," *Advertising Age,* March 20, 2006, p. S2; B. G. Francella, "Coffee Clash," *Convenience Store News,* March 6, 2006, pp. 43–46; D. Anderson, "Starbucks, Yahoo! Make a Match," *Brandweek,* February 20, 2006, p. 23; C. J. Farley, "A Tall Skinny Latte, a Nice, Comfy Chair and Now, Kid Tunes," *Wall Street Journal,* February 14, 2006, pp. B1+; D. Anderson, "Starbucks Eyes Good Will from Times' Crosswords," *Brandweek,* February 13, 2006, p. 8; S. Thompson and K. MacArthur, "Starbucks, Kellogg Plot Cereal Killing," *Advertising Age,* February 6, 2006, pp. 1+; S. Gray and K. Kelly, "Starbucks Plans to Make Debut in Movie Business," *Wall Street Journal,* January 12, 2006, pp. A1+; "Hot Drinks in the United States: Industry Profile," *DataMonitor,* December 2005; M. Moran, "Starbucks to Shutter Torrefazione Coffee Bars," *Gourmet Retailer,* August 2005, p. 10; Interview with Jim Donald, *Fortune,* April 4, 2005, p. 30; and

A. Serwer and K. Bonamici, "Hot Starbucks to Go," *Fortune,* January 26, 2004, pp. 60–74.

**Chapter 10**

1. Information from company Web site, www.enbs. com/about; Hoover's Online, www.hoovers.com, February 24, 2006; and N. Heintz, "Why Can't We Be Friends?" *Inc.,* January 2004, pp. 31–32.

2. B. Fenwick, "Oklahoma Factory Turns Out U.S. Bombs Used in Iraq," *Planet Ark,* www.planetark.com, November 4, 2003; A. Meyer, "Peeking Inside the Nation's Bomb Factory," *KFOR TV,* www.kfor.com, February 27, 2003; G. Tuchman, "Inside America's Bomb Factory," *CNN,* cnn.usnews.com, December 5, 2002; and C. Fishman, "Boomtown, U.S.A.," *Fast Company,* June 2002, pp. 106–114.

3. T. Starner, "Room for Improvement," *IQ Magazine,* March/April 2003, pp. 36–37.

4. See, for example, R. L. Daft, *Organization Theory and Design*, 9th ed. (Mason, OH: South-Western College Publishing), 2007.

5. M. Hiestand, "Making a Stamp on Football," *USA Today,* January 25, 2005, pp. 1C+.

6. D. Drickhamer, "Moving Man," *IW,* December 2002, pp. 44–46.

7. For a discussion of authority, see W. A. Kahn and K. E. Kram, "Authority at Work: Internal Models and Their Organizational Consequences," *Academy of Management Review*, January 1994, pp. 17–50.

8. E. P. Gunn, "Who's the Boss?" *Smart Money,* April 2003, p. 121.

9. L. Hawkins, Jr., "Lost in Transmission," *Wall Street Journal,* March 8, 2006, p. A1+.

10. D. Van Fleet, "Span of Management Research and Issues," *Academy of Management Journal,* September 1983, pp. 546–552.

11. Information in this box from B. J. Avolio and S. S. Kahai, "Adding the 'E' to E-Leadership: How It May Impact Your Leadership," *Organizational Dynamics,* vol. 31 (4), 2003, pp. 325–338; C. O. Grosse, "Managing Communication Within Virtual Intercultural Teams," *Business Communication Quarterly,* December 2002, pp. 22–38; M. M. Montoya-Weiss, A. P. Massey, and M. Song, "Getting It Together: Temporal Coordination and Conflict Management in Global Virtual Teams," *Academy of Management Journal,* December 2001, pp. 1251–1262; B. J. Avolio, S. Kahai, and G. E. Dodge, "E-Leadership: Implications for Theory, Research, and Practice," *Leadership Quarterly,* Winter 2000, pp. 615–668; and W. F. Cascio, "Managing a Virtual Workplace," *Academy of Management Executive,* August 2000, pp. 473–492.

12. See, for example, J. Child, *Organization: A Guide to Problems and Practices* (London: Kaiser & Row, 1984); and H. Mintzberg, *Power In and Around Organizations* (Upper Saddle River, NJ: Prentice Hall, 1983).

13. P. Siekman, "Dig It!" *Fortune,* May 3, 2004, pp. 128[B]–[L].

14. C. Tohurst, "Companies March on the Morale of Their Workers," *Australian Financial Review*, November 13, 1998, p. SP2.

15. Information on company from Hoover's Online, www.hoovers.com, April 8, 2006; and A. Ross, "BMO's Big Bang," *Canadian Business,* January 1994, pp. 58–63.

16. E. W. Morrison, "Doing the Job Well: An Investigation of Pro-Social Rule Breaking," *Journal of Management,* February 2006, pp. 5–28.

17. Ibid.

18. D. A. Morand, "The Role of Behavioral Formality and Informality in the Enactment of Bureaucratic Versus Organic Organizations," *Academy of Management Review,* October 1995, pp. 831–872; and T. Burns and G. M. Stalker, *The Management of Innovation* (London: Tavistock, 1961).

19. J. Whalen, "Bureaucracy Buster? Glaxo Lets Scientists Choose Its New Drugs," *Wall Street Journal,* March 27, 2006, p. B1+.

20. J. Goodwin, "MoDOT Warns of Funding Drop," *Springfield News-Leader,* February 8, 2006, p. 1A.

21. A. D. Chandler Jr., *Strategy and Structure: Chapters in the History of the Industrial Enterprise* (Cambridge, MA: MIT Press, 1962).

22. See, for instance, D. Jennings and S. Seaman, "High and Low Levels of Organizational Adaptation: An Empirical Analysis of Strategy, Structure, and Performance," *Strategic Management Journal*, July 1994, pp. 459–475; D. C. Galunic and K. M. Eisenhardt, "Renewing the Strategy-Structure-Performance Paradigm," in B. M. Staw and L. L. Cummings, (eds.), *Research in Organizational Behavior*, vol. 16 (Greenwich, CT: JAI Press, 1994), pp. 215–255; R. Parthasarthy and S. P. Sethi, "Relating Strategy and Structure to Flexible Automation: A Test of Fit and Performance Implications," *Strategic Management Journal,* 14 (6), 1993, pp. 529–549; H. A. Simon, "Strategy and Organizational Evolution," *Strategic Management Journal,* January 1993, pp. 131–142; H. L. Boschken, "Strategy and Structure: Reconceiving the Relationship," *Journal of Management,* March 1990, pp. 135–150; R. E. Miles and C. C. Snow, *Organizational Strategy, Structure, and Process* (New York: McGraw-Hill, 1978); and D. Miller, "The Structural and Environmental Correlates of Business Strategy," *Strategic Management Journal*, January–February 1987, pp. 55–76.

23. See, for instance, R. Z. Gooding and J. A. Wagner III, "A Meta-Analytic Review of the Relationship Between Size and Performance: The Productivity and Efficiency of Organizations and Their Subunits," *Administrative Science Quarterly*, December 1985, pp. 462–481; D. S. Pugh, "The Aston Program of Research: Retrospect and Prospect," in A. H. Van de Ven and W. F. Joyce (eds.), *Perspectives on Organization Design and Behavior*

(New York: John Wiley, 1981), pp. 135–166; and P. M. Blau and R. A. Schoenherr, *The Structure of Organizations* (New York: Basic Books, 1971).

24. J. Woodward, *Industrial Organization: Theory and Practice* (London: Oxford University Press, 1965).

25. See, for instance, C. C. Miller, W. H. Glick, Y. D. Wang, and G. Huber, "Understanding Technology-Structure Relationships: Theory Development and Meta-Analytic Theory Testing," *Academy of Management Journal,* June 1991, pp. 370–399; J. D. Thompson, *Organizations in Action* (New York: McGraw-Hill, 1967); J. Hage and M. Aiken, "Routine Technology, Social Structure, and Organizational Goals," *Administrative Science Quarterly,* September 1969, pp. 366–377; and C. Perrow, "A Framework for the Comparative Analysis of Organizations," *American Sociological Review,* April 1967, pp. 194–208.

26. D. M. Rousseau and R. A. Cooke, "Technology and Structure: The Concrete, Abstract, and Activity Systems of Organizations," *Journal of Management,* Fall–Winter 1984, pp. 345–361; and D. Gerwin, "Relationships Between Structure and Technology," in P. C. Nystrom and W. H. Starbuck (eds.), *Handbook of Organizational Design,* vol. 2 (New York: Oxford University Press, 1981), pp. 3–38.

27. M. Yasai-Ardekani, "Structural Adaptations to Environments," *Academy of Management Review,* January 1986, pp. 9–21; P. Lawrence and J. W. Lorsch, *Organization and Environment: Managing Differentiation and Integration* (Boston: Harvard Business School, Division of Research, 1967); and F. E. Emery and E. Trist, "The Causal Texture of Organizational Environments," *Human Relations,* February 1965, pp. 21–32.

28. S. Reed, "He's Brave Enough to Shake Up Shell," *BusinessWeek,* July 18, 2005, p. 53.

29. H. Mintzberg, *Structure in Fives: Designing Effective Organizations* (Upper Saddle River, NJ: Prentice Hall, 1983), p. 157.

30. R. J. Williams, J. J. Hoffman, and B. T. Lamont, "The Influence of Top Management Team Characteristics on M-Form Implementation Time," *Journal of Managerial Issues,* Winter 1995, pp. 466–480.

31. See, for example, D. F. Twomey, "Leadership, Organizational Design, and Competitiveness for the 21st Century," *Global Competitiveness,* Annual 2002, pp. S31–S40; G. J. Castrogiovanni, "Organization Task Environments: Have They Changed Fundamentally over Time?" *Journal of Management,* vol. 28 (2), 2002, pp. 129–150; M. Hammer, "Processed Change: Michael Hammer Sees Process As 'The Clark Kent of Business Ideas'—A Concept That Has the Power to Change a Company's Organizational Design," *Journal of Business Strategy,* November–December 2001, pp. 11–15; I. I. Mitroff, R. O. Mason, and C. M. Pearson, "Radical Surgery: What Will Tomorrow's Organizations Look Like?" *Academy of Management Executive,* February 1994, pp. 11–21; T. Clancy, "Radical Surgery: A View from the Operating

Theater," *Academy of Management Executive,* February 1994, pp. 73–78; and R. E. Hoskisson, C. W. L. Hill, and H. Kim, "The Multidivisional Structure: Organizational Fossil or Source of Value?" *Journal of Management,* vol. 19 (2), 1993 pp. 269–298.

32. Q. Hardy, "Google Thinks Small," *Forbes,* November 14, 2005, pp. 198–202.

33. See, for example, D. R. Denison, S. L. Hart, and J. A. Kahn, "From Chimneys to Cross-Functional Teams: Developing and Validating a Diagnostic Model," *Academy of Management Journal,* December 1996, pp. 1005–1023; L. Grant, "New Jewel in the Crown," *U.S. News & World Report,* February 28, 1994, pp. 55–57; D. Ray and H. Bronstein, *Teaming Up: Making the Transition to a Self-Directed Team-Based Organization* (New York: McGraw Hill, 1995); J. A. Byrne, "The Horizontal Corporation," *BusinessWeek,* December 20, 1993, pp. 76–81; J. R. Katzenbach and D. K. Smith, *The Wisdom of Teams* (Boston: Harvard Business School Press, 1993); B. Dumaine, "Payoff from the New Management," *Fortune,* December 13, 1993, pp. 103–110; and H. Rothman, "The Power of Empowerment," *Nation's Business,* June 1993, pp. 49–52.

34. D. Brady, A. Carter, and S. Lacy, "Eating Too Fast at Whole Foods," *BusinessWeek,* October 24, 2005, pp. 82–84; B. Streisand, "Rhapsody in Chow," *US News & World Report,* June 20, 2005, pp. EE3–EE8; and C. Fishman, "Whole Foods Is All Teams," *Fast Company,* Greatest Hits, vol. 1, 1997, pp. 102–113.

35. Information from Skanska Web site, www.skanska.co. uk, April 9, 2006.

36. P. Kaihla, "Best-Kept Secrets of the World's Best Companies," *Business 2.0,* April 2006, p. 83; C. Taylor, "School of Bright Ideas," *Time Inside Business,* April 2005, pp. A8–A12; and B. Nussbaum, "The Power of Design," *BusinessWeek,* May 17, 2004, pp. 86–94.

37. See, for example, G. G. Dess, A. M. A. Rasheed, K. J. McLaughlin, and R. L. Priem, "The New Corporate Architecture," *Academy of Management Executive,* August 1995, pp. 7–20.

38. For additional readings on boundaryless organizations, see M. F. R. Kets de Vries, "Leadership Group Coaching in Action: The Zen of Creating High Performance Teams," *Academy of Management Executive,* February 2005, pp. 61–76; J. Child and R. G. McGrath, "Organizations Unfettered: Organizational Form in an Information-Intensive Economy," *Academy of Management Journal,* December 2001, pp. 1135–1148; M. Hammer and S. Stanton, "How Process Enterprises Really Work," *Harvard Business Review,* November–December 1999, pp. 108–118; T. Zenger and W. Hesterly, "The Disaggregation of Corporations: Selective Intervention, High-Powered Incentives, and Modular Units," *Organization Science,* 1997, vol. 8, pp. 209–222; R. Ashkenas, D. Ulrich, T. Jick, and S. Kerr, *The Boundaryless Organization: Breaking the Chains of Organizational Structure* (San Francisco: Jossey-Bass, 1997);

R. M. Hodgetts, "A Conversation with Steve Kerr," *Organizational Dynamics*, Spring 1996, pp. 68–79; and J. Gebhardt, "The Boundaryless Organization," *Sloan Management Review*, Winter 1996, pp. 117–119. For another view of boundaryless organizations, see B. Victor, "The Dark Side of the New Organizational Forms: An Editorial Essay," *Organization Science*, November 1994, pp. 479–482.

39. See, for instance, Y. Shin, "A Person-Environment Fit Model for Virtual Organizations," *Journal of Management,* December 2004, pp. 725–743; D. Lyons, "Smart and Smarter," *Forbes,* March 18, 2002, pp. 40–41; W. F. Cascio, "Managing a Virtual Workplace," *Academy of Management Executive,* August 2000, pp. 81–90; D. Pescovitz, "The Company Where Everybody's a Temp," *New York Times Magazine,* June 11, 2000, pp. 94–96; M. Sawhney and D. Parikh, "Break Your Boundaries," *Business 2.0,* May 2000, pp. 198–207; G. G. Dess, A. M. A. Rasheed, K. J. McLaughlin, and R. L. Priem, "The New Corporate Architecture"; H. Chesbrough and D. Teece, "When Is Virtual Virtuous: Organizing for Innovation," *Harvard Business Review,* January–February 1996, pp. 65–73; and W. H. Davidow and M. S. Malone, *The Virtual Corporation* (New York: Harper Collins, 1992).

40. T. Howard, "StrawberryFrog Hops to a Different Drummer," *USA Today,* October 10, 2005 p. 4B.

41. R. E. Miles, C. C. Snow, J. A. Matthews, G. Miles, and H. J. Coleman Jr., "Organizing in the Knowledge Age: Anticipating the Cellular Form," *Academy of Management Executive,* November 1997, pp. 7–24; C. Jones, W. Hesterly, and S. Borgatti, "A General Theory of Network Governance: Exchange Conditions and Social Mechanisms," *Academy of Management Review,* October 1997, pp. 911–945; R. E. Miles and C. C. Snow, "The New Network Firm: A Spherical Structure Built on Human Investment Philosophy," *Organizational Dynamics,* Spring 1995, pp. 5–18; and R. E. Miles and C. C. Snow, "Causes of Failures in Network Organizations," *California Management Review,* vol. 34 (4), 1992, pp. 53–72.

42. C. H. Fine, "Are You Modular or Integral?" *Strategy & Business,* Summer 2005, pp. 44–51; D. A. Ketchen, Jr. and G. T. M. Hult, "To Be Modular or Not to Be? Some Answers to the Question," *Academy of Management Executive,* May 2002, pp. 166–167; M. A. Schilling, "The Use of Modular Organizational Forms: An Industry-Level Analysis," *Academy of Management Journal,* December 2001, pp. 1149–1168; D. Lei, M. A. Hitt, and J. D. Goldhar, "Advanced Manufacturing Technology: Organizational Design and Strategic Flexibility," *Organization Studies,* 1996, vol. 17, pp. 501–523; R. Sanchez and J. Mahoney, "Modularity Flexibility and Knowledge Management in Product and Organization Design," *Strategic Management Journal,* 1996, vol. 17, pp. 63–76; and R. Sanchez, "Strategic Flexibility in Product Competition," *Strategic Management Journal,* vol. 16, 1995, pp. 135–159.

43. S. Reed, A. Reinhardt, and A. Sains, "Saving Ericsson," *BusinessWeek,* November 11, 2002, pp. 64–68.

44. P. Engardio, "The Future of Outsourcing," *BusinessWeek,* January 30, 2006, pp. 50–58.

45. C. E. Connelly and D. G. Gallagher, "Emerging Trends in Contingent Work Research," *Journal of Management,* November 2004, pp. 959–983.

46. Information in this box from C. Edwards, "Wherever You Go, You're On the Job," *BusinessWeek,* June 20, 2005, pp. 87–90; and S. E. Ante, "The World Wide Work Space," *BusinessWeek,* June 6, 2005, pp. 106–108.

47. P. M. Senge, *The Fifth Discipline: The Art and Practice of Learning Organizations* (New York: Doubleday, 1990).

48. A. N. K. Chen and T. M. Edgington, "Assessing Value in Organizational Knowledge Creation: Considerations for Knowledge Workers," *MIS Quarterly,* June 2005, pp. 279–309; K. G. Smith, C. J. Collins, and K. D. Clark, "Existing Knowledge, Knowledge Creation Capability, and the Rate of New Product Introduction in High-Technology Firms," *Academy of Management Journal,* April 2005, pp. 346–357; B. Marr, "How to Knowledge Management," *Financial Management,* February 2003, pp. 26–27; R. Cross, A. Parker, L. Prusak, and S. P. Borgati, "Supporting Knowledge Creation and Sharing in Social Networks," *Organizational Dynamics,* Fall, 2001, pp. 100–120; M. Schulz, "The Uncertain Relevance of Newness: Organizational Learning and Knowledge Flows," *Academy of Management Journal,* August 2001, pp. 661–681; D. Zell, "Overcoming Barriers to Work Innovations: Lessons Learned at Hewlett-Packard," *Organizational Dynamics,* Summer 2001, pp. 77–86; G. Szulanski, "Exploring Internal Stickiness: Impediments to the Transfer of Best Practice Within the Firm," *Strategic Management Journal*, Winter Special Issue, 1996, pp. 27–43; and J. M. Liedtka, "Collaborating Across Lines of Business for Competitive Advantage," *Academy of Management Executive*, April 1996, pp. 20–37;

49. N. M. Adler, *International Dimensions of Organizational Behavior,* 4th ed. (Cincinnati, OH: South-Western), 2002, p. 66.

50. P. B. Smith and M. F. Peterson, "Demographic Effects on the Use of Vertical Sources of Guidance by Managers in Widely Differing Cultural Contexts," *International Journal of Cross Cultural Management,* April 2005, pp. 5–26.

51. Situation adapted from information in Ann Pomeroy, "The Ethics Squeeze," *HR Magazine,* March 2006, pp. 48+; Cheryl Soltis, "Eagle-Eyed Employers Scour Résumés for Little White Lies," *Wall Street Journal,* March 21, 2006, p. B7; "Departing Radio Shack CEO to Get $1 Million," *MSNBC,* February 21, 2006, www.msnbc.msn.com; Floyd Norris, "Radio Shack CEO Resigns After Lying," *New York Times,* February 21, 2006, www.nytimes.com.

## Chapter 11

1. Information from Hoover's Online, www.hoovers.com, February 24, 2006; L. Calabro, "The NFL's Kim Williams," *CFO,* February 2006, pp. 36–38; and

P. R. LaMonica, "Super Bowl Ads Generate Super Hype," *CNN Money,* cnnmoney.com, February 3, 2006.

2. P. G. Clampitt, *Communicating for Managerial Effectiveness,* 3rd ed. (Thousand Oaks, CA: Sage Publications, 2005); T. Dixon, *Communication, Organization, and Performance* (Norwood, NJ: Ablex Publishing Corporation, 1996), p. 281; and L. E. Penley, E. R. Alexander, I. Edward Jernigan, and C. I. Henwood, "Communication Abilities of Managers: The Relationship to Performance," *Journal of Management,* March 1991, pp. 57–76.

3. "Electronic Invective Backfires," *Workforce,* June 2001, p. 20; and E. Wong, "A Stinging Office Memo Boomerangs," *New York Times,* April 5, 2001, pp. C1+.

4. C. O. Kursh, "The Benefits of Poor Communication," *Psychoanalytic Review,* Summer–Fall 1971, pp. 189–208.

5. News Release, IABC News, news.iabc.com, March 29, 2006.

6. W. G. Scott and T. R. Mitchell, *Organization Theory: A Structural and Behavioral Analysis* (Homewood, IL: Richard D. Irwin, 1976).

7. D. K. Berlo, *The Process of Communication* (New York: Holt, Rinehart & Winston, 1960), pp. 30–32.

8. Clampitt, *Communicating for Managerial Effectiveness.*

9. A. Warfield, "Do You Speak Body Language?" *Training & Development,* April 2001, pp. 60–61; D. Zielinski, "Body Language Myths," *Presentations,* April 2001, pp. 36–42; and "Visual Cues Speak Loudly in Workplace," *Springfield News-Leader,* January 21, 2001, p. 8B.

10. Information in this box from J. Langdon, "Differences Between Males and Females at Work," *USA Today,* www.usatoday.com, February 5, 2001; J. Manion, "He Said, She Said," *Materials Management in Health Care,* November 1998, pp. 52–62; G. Franzwa and C. Lockhart, "The Social Origins and Maintenance of Gender Communication Styles, Personality Types, and Grid-Group Theory," *Sociological Perspectives,* vol. 41 (1), 1998, pp. 185–208; and D. Tannen, *Talking from 9 to 5: Women and Men in the Workplace* (New York: Avon Books, 1995).

11. American Management Association, "E-Mail Rules, Policies, and Practices Survey," www.amanet.org, 2003; V. Murphy, "You've Got Expertise," *Forbes,* February 5, 2001, p. 134; and "Fast Fact," *Fast Company,* November 2000, p. 104.

12. Berlo, *The Process of Communication,* p. 103.

13. R. Buckman, "Why the Chinese Hate to Use Voice Mail," *Wall Street Journal,* December 1, 2005, pp. B1+.

14. A. Mehrabian, "Communication Without Words," *Psychology Today,* September 1968, pp. 53–55.

15. L. Haggerman, "Strong, Efficient Leadership Minimizes Employee Problems," *Springfield Business Journal,* December 9–15, 2002, p. 23.

16. See, for instance, S. P. Robbins and P. L. Hunsaker, *Training in InterPersonal Skills,* 4e (Upper Saddle River, NJ: Prentice Hall, 2006); M. Young and J. E. Post, "Managing to Communicate, Communicating to Manage: How Leading Companies Communicate with Employees," *Organizational Dynamics,* Summer 1993, pp. 31–43; J. A. DeVito, *The Interpersonal Communication Book,* 6th ed. (New York: HarperCollins, 1992); and A. G. Athos and J. J. Gabarro, *Interpersonal Behavior* (Upper Saddle River, NJ: Prentice Hall, 1978).

17. O. Thomas, "Best-Kept Secrets of the World's Best Companies: The Three Minute Huddle," *Business 2.0,* April 2006, p. 94.

18. A. Overholt, "Power Up the People," *Fast Company,* January 2003, p. 50.

19. J. S. Lublin, "The 'Open Inbox,'" *Wall Street Journal,* October 10, 2005, pp. B1+.

20. Cited in "Shut Up and Listen," *Money,* November 2005, p. 27.

21. See, for instance, D. Sagario and L. Ballard, "Workplace Gossip Can Threaten Your Office," *Springfield News-Leader,* September 26, 2005, p. 5B; A. Bruzzese, "What To Do About Toxic Gossip," *USA Today,* www.usatoday.com, March 14, 2001; N. B. Kurland and L. H. Pelled, "Passing the Word: Toward a Model of Gossip and Power in the Workplace," *Academy of Management Review,* April 2000, pp. 428–438; N. DiFonzo, P. Bordia, and R. L. Rosnow, "Reining in Rumors," *Organizational Dynamics,* Summer 1994, pp. 47–62; M. Noon and R. Delbridge, "News from Behind My Hand: Gossip in Organizations," *Organization Studies,* vol. 14 (1), 1993, pp. 23–26; and J. G. March and G. Sevon, "Gossip, Information and Decision Making," in J. G. March (ed.), *Decisions and Organizations* (Oxford: Blackwell, 1988), pp. 429–442.

22. "Effective Communication: A Leading Indicator of Financial Performance—2005/2006 Communication ROI Study," Watson Wyatt Worldwide, Washington, DC.

23. These examples taken from S. Kirsner, "Being There," *Fast Company,* January/February 2006, pp. 90–91; R. Breeden, "More Employees Are Using the Web at Work," *Wall Street Journal,* May 10, 2005, p. B4; C. Woodward, "Some Offices Opt for Cellphones Only," *USA Today,* January 25, 2005, p. 1B; and J. Rohwer, "Today, Tokyo. Tomorrow, the World," *Fortune,* September 18, 2000, pp. 140–152.

24. Based on E. Frauenheim, "Stop Reading This Headline and Get Back to Work," *C/Net,* www.news.com, July 13, 2005; and R. Breeden, "More Employees Are Using the Web at Work."

25. Information from Technorati, www.technorati.com, April 14, 2006.

26. Information from Wikipedia, en.wikipedia.org, April 14, 2006.

27. K. C. Laudon and J. P. Laudon, *Essentials of Management Information Systems* (Upper Saddle River, NJ: Prentice Hall, 1995), p. 234.

28. B. DeLollis, "Talking Heads Are Catching On as Web Meetings Take Off," *USA Today,* September 8, 2004, p. 1B.

29. J. Karaian, "Where Wireless Works," *CFO,* May 2003, pp. 81–83.

30. Information from JiWire.com, www.jiwire.com, April 14, 2006.

31. Information from Computer Industry Almanac, www.c-i-a.com, April 14, 2006.

32. K. Hafner, "For the Well Connected, All the World's an Office," *New York Times,* March 30, 2000, pp. D1+.

33. S. Luh, "Pulse Lunches at Asian Citibanks Feed Workers' Morale, Lower Job Turnover," *Wall Street Journal,* May 22, 2001, p. B11.

34. R. D. Hof, "Your Undivided Attention Please," *BusinessWeek,* January 19, 2004, p. 14.

35. J. Eckberg, "E-Mail: Messages Are Evidence," *Cincinnati Enquirer,* www.enquirer.com, July 27, 2004.

36. M. Conlin, "E-Mail Is So Five Minutes Ago," *BusinessWeek,* November 28, 2005, pp. 111–112.

37. J. Scanlon, "Woman of Substance," *Wired,* July 2002, p. 27.

38. H. Dolezalek, "Collaborating in Cyberspace," *Training,* April 2003, p. 33.

39. E. Wenger, R. McDermott, and W. Snyder, *Cultivating Communities of Practice: A Guide to Managing Knowledge* (Boston: Harvard Business School Press, 2002), p. 4.

40. Ibid., p. 39.

41. B. A. Gutek, M. Groth, and B. Cherry, "Achieving Service Success Through Relationship and Enhanced Encounters," *Academy of Management Executive,* November 2002, pp. 132–144.

42. R. C. Ford and C. P. Heaton, "Lessons from Hospitality That Can Serve Anyone," *Organizational Dynamics,* Summer 2001, pp. 30–47.

43. M. J. Bitner, B. H. Booms, and L. A. Mohr, "Critical Service Encounters: The Employee's Viewpoint," *Journal of Marketing,* October 1994, pp. 95–106.

44. S. D. Pugh, J. Dietz, J. W. Wiley, and S. M. Brooks, "Driving Service Effectiveness Through Employee-Customer Linkages," *Academy of Management Executive,* November 2002, pp. 73–84.

45. "Assisting Customers with Disabilities: A Summary of Policies and Guidelines Regarding the Assistance of Customers with Disabilities for the Sears Family of Companies," pamphlet from Sears, Roebuck and Company, obtained at Springfield, Missouri, Sears store, May 28, 2003.

46. J. Leo, "Language in the Dumps," *U.S. News & World Report,* July 27, 1998, p. 16; and M. L. LaGanga, "Are There Words That Neither Offend Nor Bore?" *Los Angeles Times,* May 18, 1994, pp. 11–27.

47. Situation adapted from information in Brad Stone, "I Want to See Most of the Planet Online," *Newsweek,* May 8, 2006, p. 46; "Can Bloggers Make Money?" *Wall Street Journal Online,* April 19, 2006, online.wsj.com; Thom Weidlich, "The Corporate Blog Is Catching On," *New York Times,* June 22, 2003, sec. 3, p. 12; "CNN Shuts Down Correspondent's Blog," *EuropeMedia,* March 24, 2003, www.vandusseldorp.com.

## Chapter 12

1. Information from company's Web site, www.scotiabank.com, and Hoover's *Online,* www.hoovers.com, March 3, 2006; J. Kirby, "In the Vault," *Canadian Business,* March 1–14, 2004, pp. 68–72; and R. Waugh, "Getting More Leaders Is Hard Enough, but the Job Skills Needed Are Changing, Too," *Canadian HR Reporter,* January 26, 2004, p. 18.

2. L. Bassi and D. McMurrer, "How's Your Return on People?" *Harvard Business Review,* March 2004, p. 18; J. Pfeffer, *The Human Equation* (Boston: Harvard Business School Press, 1998); C. J. Collins and K. D. Clark, "Strategic Human Resource Practices, Top Management Team Social Networks, and Firm Performance: The Role of Human Resource Practices in Creating Organizational Competitive Advantage," *Academy of Management Journal,* December 2003, pp. 740–751; J. Pfeffer, *Competitive Advantage Through People* (Boston: Harvard Business School Press, 1994); A. A. Lado and M. C. Wilson, "Human Resource Systems and Sustained Competitive Advantage," *Academy of Management Review,* October 1994, pp. 699–727; and P. M. Wright and G. C. McMahan, "Theoretical Perspectives for Strategic Human Resource Management," *Journal of Management,* vol. 18 (1), 1992, pp. 295–320.

3. "Maximizing the Return on Your Human Capital Investment: The 2005 Watson Wyatt Human Capital Index® Report," "WorkAsia 2004/2005: A Study of Employee Attitudes in Asia," and "European Human Capital Index 2002," Watson Wyatt Worldwide (Washington, D.C.).

4. See, for example, Y. Y. Kor and H. Leblebici, "How Do Interdependencies Among Human-Capital Deployment, Development, and Diversification Strategies Affect Firms' Financial Performance?" *Strategic Management Journal,* October 2005, pp. 967–985; D. E. Bowen and C. Ostroff, "Understanding HRM—Firm Performance Linkages: The Role of the 'Strength' of the HRM System," *Academy of Management Review,* April 2004, pp. 203–221; R. Batt, "Managing Customer Services: Human Resource Practices, Quit Rates, and Sales Growth," *Academy of Management Journal,* June 2002, pp. 587–597; A. S. Tsui, J. L. Pearce, L. W. Porter, and A. M. Tripoli, "Alternative Approaches to the Employee–Organization Relationship: Does Investment in Employees Pay Off?" *Academy of Management Journal,* October 1997, pp. 1089–1121; M. A. Huselid, S. E. Jackson, and R. S. Schuler, "Technical and Strategic Human Resource Management Effectiveness As Determinants of Firm Performance," *Academy of*

*Management Journal*, January 1997, pp. 171–188; J. T. Delaney and M. A. Huselid, "The Impact of Human Resource Management Practices on Perceptions of Organizational Performance," *Academy of Management Journal*, August 1996, pp. 949–969; B. Becker and B. Gerhart, "The Impact of Human Resource Management on Organizational Performance: Progress and Prospects," *Academy of Management Journal*, August 1996, pp. 779–801; M. J. Koch and R. G. McGrath, "Improving Labor Productivity: Human Resource Management Policies Do Matter," *Strategic Management Journal*, May 1996, pp. 335–354; and M. A. Huselid, "The Impact of Human Resource Management Practices on Turnover, Productivity, and Corporate Financial Performance," *Academy of Management Journal*, June 1995, pp. 635–672.

5. "Human Capital a Key to Higher Market Value," *Business Finance*, December 1999, p. 15.

6. M. Boyle, "Happy People, Happy Returns," *Fortune*, January 11, 2006, p. 100.

7. J. Visser, "Union Membership Statistics in 24 Countries," *Monthly Labor Review*, January 2006, pp. 38–49; and "Foreign Labor Trends—Mexico," U.S. Department of Labor, 2002.

8. P. Digh, "Religion in the Workplace," *HRMagazine*, December 1998, p. 88.

9. S. Armour, "Lawsuits Pin Target on Managers," *USA Today*, www.usatoday.com, October 1, 2002.

10. E. Blass, "Generation Y: They've Arrived at Work with a New Attitude," *USA Today*, November 6, 2005, pp. 1A+; K. Greene, "Bye-Bye Boomers," *Wall Street Journal*, September 20, 2005, pp. B1+; A. Fisher, "How to Battle the Coming Brain Drain," *Fortune*, March 21, 2005, pp. 121–128; and U.S. Census Bureau, www.census.gov.

11. K. Greene, "Bye-Bye Boomers."

12. "John Deere Lays the Foundation," *Training*, April 2001, p. 56.

13. J. Sullivan, "Workforce Planning: Why to Start Now," *Workforce*, September 2002, pp. 46–50.

14. N. Byrnes, "Star Search," *BusinessWeek*, October 10, 2005, pp. 68–78.

15. J. W. Boudreau and P. M. Ramstad, "Where's Your Pivotal Talent?" *Harvard Business Review*, April 2005, pp. 23–24.

16. A. S. Bargerstock and G. Swanson, "Four Ways to Build Cooperative Recruitment Alliances," *HRMagazine*, March 1991, p. 49; and T. J. Bergmann and M. S. Taylor, "College Recruitment: What Attracts Students to Organizations?" *Personnel*, May–June 1984, pp. 34–46.

17. J. R. Gordon, *Human Resource Management: A Practical Approach* (Boston: Allyn and Bacon, 1986), p. 170.

18. J. Hitt, "Are Brands Out of Hand?" *Fast Company*, November 2000, p. 52.

19. C. Lachnit, "Going for Generation Y," *Workforce*, April 2002, p. 16.

20. S. Burton and D. Warner, "The Future of Hiring—Top 5 Sources for Recruitment Today," *Workforce Vendor Directory 2002*, p. 75.

21. S. Leibs, "Online Talent Shopping," *CFO-IT*, Fall 2005, p. 25.

22. See, for example, R. W. Griffeth, P. W. Hom, L. S. Fink, and D. J. Cohen, "Comparative Tests of Multivariate Models of Recruiting Sources Effects," *Journal of Management*, vol. 23 (1), 1997, pp. 19–36; and J. P. Kirnan, J. E. Farley, and K. F. Geisinger, "The Relationship Between Recruiting Source, Applicant Quality, and Hire Performance: An Analysis by Sex, Ethnicity, and Age," *Personnel Psychology*, Summer 1989, pp. 293–308.

23. J. McGregor, "Background Checks That Never End," *BusinessWeek*, March 20, 2006, p. 40.

24. A. Fisher, "For Happier Customers, Call HR," *Fortune*, November 28, 2005, p. 272.

25. A. M. Ryan and R. E. Ployhart, "Applicants' Perceptions of Selection Procedures and Decisions: A Critical Review and Agenda for the Future," *Journal of Management*, vol. 26, (3), 2000, pp. 565–606; G. C. Thornton, *Assessment Centers in Human Resource Management* (Reading, MA: Addison-Wesley, 1992); C. Fernandez-Araoz, "Hiring Without Firing," *Harvard Business Review*, July–August, 1999, pp. 108–120; A. K. Korman, "The Prediction of Managerial Performance: A Review," *Personnel Psychology*, Summer 1986, pp. 295–322; E. E. Ghiselli, "The Validity of Aptitude Tests in Personnel Selection," *Personnel Psychology*, Winter 1973, p. 475; I. T. Robertson and R. S. Kandola, "Work Sample Tests: Validity, Adverse Impact, and Applicant Reaction," *Journal of Occupational Psychology*, vol. 55 (3), 1982, pp. 171–183; G. Grimsley and H. F. Jarrett, "The Relation of Managerial Achievement to Test Measures Obtained in the Employment Situation: Methodology and Results," *Personnel Psychology*, Spring 1973, pp. 31–48; J. J. Asher, "The Biographical Item: Can It Be Improved?" *Personnel Psychology*, Summer 1972, p. 266; and G. W. England, *Development and Use of Weighted Application Blanks*, rev. ed. (Minneapolis: Industrial Relations Center, University of Minnesota, 1971).

26. G. Flynn, "A Legal Examination of Testing," *Workforce*, June 2002, pp. 92–94; S. Randall, "An Overview of Personality Testing in the Workforce," *Workforce Online*, www.workforce.com, December 13, 2000; S. Randall, "Legal Challenges to Personality Tests," *Workforce Online*, www.workforce.com, December 13, 2000; and Gilbert Nicholson, "Tests and the Law," *Workforce*, October 2000, p. 73.

27. J. McNair, "Ford Settles Employee Suit Alleging Bias in Testing," *USA Today*, June 6, 2005, p. 6B.

28. E. White, "Walking a Mile in Another's Shoes," *Wall Street Journal*, January 16, 2006, p. B3; D. A. Waldman

and T. Korbar, "Student Assessment Center Performance in the Prediction of Early Career Success," *Academy of Management Learning and Education,* June 2004, pp. 151–167; D. J. Woehr and W. Arthur Jr., "The Construct-Related Validity of Assessment Center Ratings: A Review and Meta-Analysis of the Role of Methodological Factors," *Journal of Management,* vol. 29 (2), 2003, pp. 231–258; and P. G. W. Jansen, and B. A. M. Stoop, "The Dynamics of Assessment Center Validity: Results of a 7-Year Study," *Journal of Applied Psychology,* August 2001, pp. 741–753.

29. E. White, "Walking a Mile in Another's Shoes."

30. R. L. Dipboye, *Selection Interviews: Process Perspectives* (Cincinnati: South-Western Publishing, 1992), p. 6.

31. See, for instance, M. M. Harris, "Reconsidering the Employment Interview: A Review of Recent Literature and Suggestions for Future Research," *Personnel Psychology,* Winter 1989, pp. 691–726; and R. D. Arveny and J. E. Campion, "The Employment Interview: A Summary and Review of Recent Research," *Personnel Psychology,* Summer 1982, pp. 281–322.

32. S. Caudron, "Who Are You Really Hiring?" *Workforce,* November 2002, pp. 28–32.

33. P. Johnson, "Fibbing Applicants Filtered Out," *Springfield News Leader,* August 4, 2002, p. 6E.

34. See, for example, Y. Ganzach, A. Pazy, Y. Ohayun, and E. Brainin, "Social Exchange and Organizational Commitment: Decision-Making Training for Job Choice As an Alternative to the Realistic Job Preview," *Personnel Psychology,* Autumn 2002, pp. 613–637; B. M. Meglino, E. C. Ravlin, A. S. DeNisi, "A Meta-Analytic Examination of Realistic Job Preview Effectiveness: A Test of Three Counterintuitive Propositions," *Human Resource Management Review,* vol. 10 (4), 2000, pp. 407–434; J. A. Breaugh and M. Starke, "Research on Employee Recruitment: So Many Studies, So Many Remaining Questions," *Journal of Management,* vol. 26 (3), 2000, pp. 405–434; and S. L. Premack and J. P. Wanous, "A Meta-Analysis of Realistic Job Preview Experiments," *Journal of Applied Psychology,* November 1985, pp. 706–720.

35. M. Conlin, "You Are What You Post," *BusinessWeek,* March 27, 2006, pp. 52–53; and J. Kornblum and M. B. Marklein, "What You Say Online Could Haunt You," *USA Today,* March 8, 2006, pp. 1A+.

36. K. Gustafson, "A Better Welcome Mat," *Training,* June 2005, pp. 34–41.

37. D. G. Allen, "Do Organizational Socialization Tactics Influence Newcomer Embeddedness and Turnover?" *Journal of Management,* April 2006, pp. 237–256; C. L. Cooper, "The Changing Psychological Contract at Work: Revisiting the Job Demands-Control Model," *Occupational and Environmental Medicine,* June 2002, p. 355; D. M. Rousseau and S. A. Tijoriwala, "Assessing Psychological Contracts: Issues, Alternatives and Measures," *Journal of Organizational Behavior,* vol. 19, 1998, pp. 679–695; and S. L. Robinson, M. S. Kraatz, and D. M. Rousseau, "Changing Obligations and the Psychological Contract: A Longitudinal Study," *Academy of Management Journal,* February 1994, pp. 137–152.

38. T. Raphael, "It's All in the Cards," *Workforce,* September 2002, p. 18.

39. H. Dolezalek, "2005 Industry Report," *Training,* December 2005, pp. 14–28.

40. M. Weinstein, "Training Top 100—Suite Success: On Demand Delivers for IBM," *Training,* March 2006, pp. 18–21.

41. H. Dolezalek, "2005 Industry Report," p. 22.

42. B. Hall, "The Top Training Priorities for 2003," *Training,* February 2003, p. 40.

43. Information in this box from M. Weinstein, "Flying High: Lockheed Martin Prepares Leaders for Takeoff," *Training,* March 2006, pp. 36–38; M. Frese, S. Beimel, and S. Schoenborn, "Action Training for Charismatic Leadership: Two Evaluations of Studies of a Commercial Training Module on Inspirational Communication of a Vision," *Personnel Psychology,* vol. 56, 2003, pp. 671–697; and T. Dvir, D. Eden, and B. J. Avolio, "Impact of Transformational Leadership on Follower Development and Performance: A Field Experiment," *Academy of Management Journal,* August 2002, pp. 735–744.

44. K. Clark, "Judgment Day," *U.S. News & World Report,* January 13, 2003, pp. 31–32; E. E. Lawler III, "The Folly of Forced Ranking," *Strategy & Business,* Third Quarter 2002, pp. 28–32; K. Cross, "The Weakest Links," *Business2.Com,* June 26, 2001, pp. 36–37; J. Greenwald, "Rank and Fire," *Time,* June 18, 2001, pp. 38–39; D. Jones, "More Firms Cut Workers Ranked at Bottom to Make Way for Talent," *USA Today,* May 30, 2001, pp. B1+; and M. Boyle, "Performance Reviews: Perilous Curves Ahead," *Fortune,* May 28, 2001, pp. 187–188.

45. J. McGregor, "The Struggle to Measure Performance," *BusinessWeek,* January 9, 2006, pp. 26–28.

46. D. Jones, "Study: Thinning Herd from Bottom Helps," *USA Today,* March 14, 2005, p. 1B.

47. S. E. Cullen, P. K. Bergey, and L. Aiman-Smith, "Forced Distribution Rating Systems and the Improvement of Workforce Potential: A Baseline Simulation," *Personnel Psychology,* Spring 2005, pp. 1–32.

48. J. McGregor, "The Struggle to Measure Performance."

49. R. D. Bretz Jr., G. T. Milkovich, and W. Read, "The Current State of Performance Appraisal Research and Practice: Concerns, Directions, and Implications," *Journal of Management,* June 1992, p. 331.

50. "Is 360-Degree Feedback a Fad?" William Sternberg Consultants, 2004.

51. J. D. Glater, "Seasoning Compensation Stew," *New York Times,* March 7, 2001, pp. C1+.

52. This section based on R. I. Henderson, *Compensation Management in a Knowledge-Based World,* 9th ed. (Upper Saddle River, NJ: Prentice Hall, 2003).

53. M. P. Brown, M. C. Sturman, and M. J. Simmering, "Compensation Policy and Organizational Performance:

The Efficiency, Operational and Financial Implications of Pay Levels and Pay Structure," *Academy of Management Journal,* December 2003, pp. 752–762; J. D. Shaw, N. P. Gupta, and J. E. Delery, "Pay Dispersion and Workforce Performance: Moderating Effects of Incentives and Interdependence," *Strategic Management Journal,* June 2002, pp. 491–512; E. Montemayor, "Congruence Between Pay Policy and Competitive Strategy in High-Performing Firms," *Journal of Management,* vol. 22 (6), 1996, pp. 889–908; and L. R. Gomez-Mejia, "Structure and Process of Diversification, Compensation Strategy, and Firm Performance," *Strategic Management Journal* vol. 13, 1992, pp. 381–397.

54. R. Levering and M. Moskowitz, "The 100 Best Companies to Work For—You Get What?" *Fortune,* January 11, 2006, p. 106.

55. J. D. Shaw, N. Gupta, A. Mitra, and G. E. Ledford Jr., "Success and Survival of Skill-Based Pay Plans," *Journal of Management,* February 2005, pp. 28–49; C. Lee, K. S. Law, and P. Bobko, "The Importance of Justice Perceptions on Pay Effectiveness: A Two-Year Study of a Skill-Based Pay Plan," *Journal of Management,* vol. 26 (6), 1999, pp. 851–873; G. E. Ledford, "Paying for the Skills, Knowledge and Competencies of Knowledge Workers," *Compensation and Benefits Review,* July–August 1995, pp. 55–62; and E. E. Lawler III, G. E. Ledford Jr., and L. Chang, "Who Uses Skill-Based Pay and Why," *Compensation and Benefits Review,* March–April 1993, p. 22.

56. J. D. Shaw, N. Gupta, A. Mitra, and G. E. Ledford Jr., "Success and Survival of Skill-Based Pay Plans."

57. Information from Hewitt Associates Studies, "Hewitt Study Shows Pay-for-Performance Plans Replacing Holiday Bonuses," December 6, 2005; "Salaries Continue to Rise in Asia Pacific," Hewitt Annual Study Reports, November 23, 2005; and "Hewitt Study Shows Base Pay Increases Flat for 2006 with Variable Pay Plans Picking Up the Slack," Hewitt Associates, LLC, www.hewitt.com, August 31, 2005.

58. Information in this box from R. E. DeRouin, B. A. Fritzsche, and E. Salas, "E-Learning in Organizations," *Journal of Management,* December 2005, pp. 920–940; K. O'Leonard, *HP Case Study: Flexible Solutions for Multi-Cultural Learners* (Oakland: CA: Bersin & Associates, 2004); S. Greengard, The Dawn of Digital HR," *Business Finance,* October 2003, pp. 55–59; and J. Hoekstra, "Three in One," *Online Learning,* vol. 5, 2001, pp. 28–32.

59. D. E. Super and D. T. Hall, "Career Development: Exploration and Planning," in M. R. Rosenzweig and L. W. Porter (eds.), *Annual Review of Psychology,* vol. 29 (Palo Alto, CA: Annual Reviews, 1978), p. 334.

60. A. K. Smith, "Charting Your Own Course," *U.S. News & World Report,* November 6, 2000, pp. 56–65; S. E. Sullivan, "The Changing Nature of Careers: A Review and Research Agenda," *Journal of Management,* vol. 25 (3), 1999, pp. 457–484; D. T. Hall,

"Protean Careers of the 21st Century," *Academy of Management Executive,* November 1996, pp. 8–16; M. B. Arthur and D. M. Rousseau, "A Career Lexicon for the 21st Century," *Academy of Management Executive,* November 1996, pp. 28–39; N. Nicholson, "Career Systems in Crisis: Change and Opportunity in the Information Age," *Academy of Management Executive,* November 1996, pp. 40–51; and K. R. Brousseau, M. J. Driver, K. Enertoh, and R. Larsson, "Career Pandemonium: Realigning Organizations and Individuals," *Academy of Management Executive,* November 1996, pp. 52–66.

61. Smith, "Charting Your Own Course"; and Hall, "Protean Careers of the 21st Century."

62. M. B. Arthur and D. M. Rousseau, *The Boundaryless Career: A New Employment Principle for a New Organizational Era* (New York: Oxford University Press, 1996).

63. M. Cianni and D. Wnuck, "Individual Growth and Team Enhancement: Moving Toward a New Model of Career Development," *Academy of Management Executive,* February 1997, pp. 105–115.

64. L. S. Richman, "The New Worker Elite," *Fortune,* August 22, 1994, pp. 56–66; E. P. Cook and M. Arthur, *Career Theory Handbook* (Upper Saddle River, NJ: Prentice Hall, 1991), pp. 99–131; and D. E. Super, "A Life-Span Life Space Approach to Career Development," *Journal of Vocational Behavior,* Spring 1980, pp. 282–298.

65. D. D. Dubois, "The 7 Stages of One's Career," *Training & Development,* December 2000, pp. 45–50; A. K. Smith, "Charting Your Own Course"; A. Fisher, "Six Ways to Supercharge Your Career," *Fortune,* January 13, 1997, pp. 46–48; "10 Tips for Managing Your Career," *Personnel Journal,* October 1995, p. 106; and R. Henkoff, "Winning the New Career Game," *Fortune,* July 12, 1993, pp. 46–49.

66. J. W. Peters, "GM Lays Off Hundreds of White-Collar Employees," *New York Times Online,* March 29, 2006; The Associated Press, "Washington Mutual to Cut 2,500 Jobs," *New York Times Online,* February 16, 2006; S. Power and N. E. Boudette, "Daimler to Cut Management by 20%," *Wall Street Journal,* January 24, 2006, pp. A2+; Reuters, "Merck to Cut 7,000 Jobs, Close or Sell Five Plants," *USA Today,* November 28, 2005, p. 3B; and L. T. Cullen, "Where Did Everyone Go?" *Time,* November 18, 2002, pp. 64-66.

67. L. Uchitelle, "Retraining Laid-Off Workers, But for What?" *New York Times Online,* March 26, 2006; D. Tourish, N. Paulsen, E. Hobman, and P. Bordia, "The Downsides of Downsizing: Communication Processes and Information Needs in the Aftermath of a Workforce Reduction Strategy," *Management Communication Quarterly,* May 2004, pp. 485–516; J. Brockner, G. Spreitzer, A. Mishra, W. Hochwarter, L. Pepper, and J. Weinberg, "Perceived Control As an Antidote to the Negative Effects of Layoffs on Survivors' Organizational Commitment and Job Performance," *Administrative Science Quarterly,*

vol. 49, 2004, pp. 76–100; E. Krell, "Defusing Downsizing," *Business Finance,* December 2002, pp. 55–57; C. Hymowitz, "Getting a Lean Staff to Do 'Ghost Work' of Departed Colleagues," *Wall Street Journal,* October 22, 2002, p. B1; and S. Alleyne, "Stiff Upper Lips," *Black Enterprise,* April 2002, p. 59.

68. F. Moody, "Wonder Women in the Rude Boys' Paradise," *Fast Company,* www.fastcompany.com, April 17, 1997; and interview with Bill Gates, "Bill Gates on Rewiring the Power Structure," *Working Woman*, April 1994, p. 62.

69. R. Leger, "Linked by Differences," *Springfield News–Leader,* December 31, 1993, pp. B6+.

70. The Associated Press, "Gender Bias Lawsuit to Cost Boeing $72.5 Million," *Springfield News-Leader,* November 13, 2005; The Associated Press, "Abercrombie & Fitch to Pay $40M to Settle Bias Case," *USA Today,* November 17, 2004, p. 3B; and M. Warner, "Home Depot Goes Old School," *Business 2.0,* June 2004, p. 74.

71. Sexual Harassment Charges: FY 1992—FY 2005, *The U.S. Equal Employment Opportunity Commission,* www.eeoc.gov.

72. A. B. Fisher, "Sexual Harassment, What to Do," *Fortune,* August 23, 1993, pp. 84–88.

73. M. Velasquez, "Sexual Harassment Today: An Update—Looking Back and Looking Forward," *Diversity Training Group,* www.diversitydtg.com, 2004.

74. P. M. Buhler, "The Manager's Role in Preventing Sexual Harassment," *Supervision,* April 1999, p. 18; and "Cost of Sexual Harassment in the U.S.," *The Webb Report: A Newsletter on Sexual Harassment* (Seattle, WA: Premier Publishing, Ltd.), January 1994, pp. 4–7 and April 1994, pp. 2–5.

75. V. Di Martino, H. Hoel, and C. L. Cooper, "Preventing Violence and Harassment in the Workplace," *European Foundation for the Improvement of Living and Working Conditions,* 2003, p. 39.

76. W. Hardman and J. Heidelberg, "When Sexual Harassment Is a Foreign Affair," *Personnel Journal*, April 1996, pp. 91–97; and "U.S. Leads Way in Sex Harassment Laws, Study Says," *Evening Sun,* November 30, 1992, pp. A1+.

77. "Sexual Harassment," *The U.S. Equal Employment Opportunity Commission,* www.eeoc.gov.

78. Ibid.

79. A. R. Karr, "Companies Crack Down on the Increasing Sexual Harassment by E-Mail," *Wall Street Journal*, September 21, 1999, p. A1; and A. Fisher, "After All This Time, Why Don't People Know What Sexual Harassment Means?" *Fortune,* January 12, 1998, p. 68.

80. See T. S. Bland and S. S. Stalcup, "Managing Harassment," *Human Resource Management,* Spring 2001, pp. 51–61; K. A. Hess and D. R. M. Ehrens, "Sexual Harassment—Affirmative Defense to Employer Liability," *Benefits Quarterly*, Second Quarter 1999, p. 57; J. A. Segal, "The Catch-22s of Remedying Sexual Harassment Complaints," *HRMagazine,* October 1997, pp. 111–117; S. C. Bahls and J. E. Bahls, "Hand-Off Policy," *Entrepreneur,* July 1997, pp. 74–76; J. A. Segal, "Where Are We Now?" *HRMagazine,* October 1996, pp. 69–73; B. McAfee and D. L. Deadrick, "Teach Employees to Just Say No," *HRMagazine,* February 1996, pp. 86–89; G. D. Block, "Avoiding Liability for Sexual Harassment," *HRMagazine,* April 1995, pp. 91–97; and J. A. Segal, "Stop Making Plaintiffs' Lawyers Rich," *HRMagazine,* April 1995, pp. 31–35. Also, it should be noted here that under the Title VII and the Civil Rights Act of 1991, the maximum award that can be given, under the Federal Act, is $300,000. However, many cases are tried under state laws that permit unlimited punitive damages, such as the $7.1 million that Rena Weeks received in her trial based on California statutes.

81. S. Shellenbarger, "Supreme Court Takes on How Employers Handle Worker Harassment Complaints," *Wall Street Journal,* April 13, 2006, p. D1.

82. S. Jayson, "Workplace Romance No Longer Gets the Kiss-Off," *USA Today,* February 9, 2006, p. 9D.

83. R. Mano and Y. Gabriel, "Workplace Romances in Cold and Hot Organizational Climates: The Experience of Israel and Taiwan," *Human Relations,* January 2006, pp. 7–35; J. A. Segal, "Dangerous Liaisons," *HRMagazine,* December 2005, pp. 104–108; "Workplace Romance Can Create Unforeseen Issues for Employers," *HR Focus,* October 2005, p. 2; C. A. Pierce and H. Aguinis, "Legal Standards, Ethical Standards, and Responses to Social-Sexual Conduct at Work," *Journal of Organizational Behavior,* September 2005, pp. 727–732; and C. A. Pierce, B. J. Broberg, J. R. McClure, and H. Aguinis, "Responding to Sexual Harassment Complaints: Effects of a Dissolved Workplace Romance on Decision-Making Standards," *Organizational Behavior and Human Decision Processes,* September 2004, pp. 66–82.

84. J. A. Segal, "Dangerous Liaisons."

85. J. Miller and M. Miller, "Get A Life!" *Fortune,* November 28, 2005, pp. 108–124.

86. M. Elias, "The Family-First Generation," *USA Today,* December 13, 2004, p. 5D.

87. M. Mandel, "The Real Reasons You're Working So Hard . . . and What You Can Do About It," *BusinessWeek,* October 3, 2005, pp. 60–67.

88. C. Farrell, "The Overworked, Networked Family," *BusinessWeek,* October 3, 2005, p. 68.

89. F. Hansen, "Truths and Myths About Work/Life Balance," *Workforce,* December 2002, pp. 34–39.

90. J. H. Greenhaus and G. N. Powell, "When Work and Family Are Allies: A Theory of Work–Family Enrichment," *Academy of Management Review,* January 2006, pp. 72–92.

91. Ibid., p. 73.

92. L. B. Hammer, M. B. Neal, J. T. Newsom, K. J. Brockwood, and C. L. Colton, "A Longitudinal Study of the Effects of Dual-Earner Couples' Utilization of Family-Friendly Workplace Supports on Work and Family Outcomes," *Journal of Applied Psychology,* July 2005, pp. 799–810.

93. M. M. Arthur, "Share Price Reactions to Work–Family Initiatives: An Institutional Perspective," *Academy of Management Journal,* August 2003, pp. 497–505.

94. N. P. Rothbard, T. L. Dumas, and K. W. Phillips, "The Long Arm of the Organization: Work–Family Policies and Employee Preferences for Segmentation," paper presented at the 61st Annual Academy of Management meeting, Washington, D.C., August 2001.

95. These examples taken from A. Zimmerman, R. G. Matthews, and K. Hudson, "Can Employers Alter Hiring Policies to Cut Health Costs?" *Wall Street Journal,* October 27, 2005, pp. B1+; A. Fisher, "Helping Employees Stay Healthy," *Fortune,* August 8, 2005, p. 114; S. Armour, "Trend: You Smoke? You're Fired!" *USA Today,* May 12, 2005, p. 1A; and I. Mochari, "Belt-Tightening," *CFO Human Capital,* 2005, pp. 10–12.

96. A. Zimmerman, Matthews, and Hudson, "Can Employers Alter Hiring Policies to Cut Health Costs?"

97. L. Cornwell, The Associated Press, "Companies Tack on Fees on Insurance for Smokers," *Springfield News-Leader,* February 17, 2006, p. 5B.

98. J. Appleby, "Companies Step Up Wellness Efforts," *USA Today,* August 1, 2005, pp. 1A+.

99. J. Fox, "Good Riddance to Pensions," *CNN Money,* January 12, 2006.

100. M. Adams, "Broken Pension System in Crying Need of a Fix," *USA Today,* November 15, 2005, pp. 1B+.

101. E. Porter and M. Williams Nash, "Benefits Go the Way of Pensions," *NY Times Online,* February 9, 2006; and J. Fox, "Good Riddance to Pensions."

102. Situation adapted from information in Dick Grote, "Forced Ranking: Making Performance Management Work," *Harvard Business School Working Knowledge,* November 14, 2005, hbswk.hbs.edu/item.jhtml?id=5091&t=organizations; John Russell, "Older Goodyear Workers Who Say Age Played into Evaluations Get Day in Court," *Akron Beacon Journal,* July 3, 2003, www.ohio.com/bj; Kim Clark, "Judgment Day," *U.S. News & World Report,* January 13, 2003, pp. 31–32.

## Chapter 13

1. Information from company Web site, www.oxo.com, February 24, 2006; and C. Salter, "OXO's Favorite Mistakes," *Fast Company,* October 2005, pp. 66–67.

2. J. Zawacki, "Saving Manufacturing Jobs in the U.S.," Michigan Business Network, www.mibiz.com, January 31, 2006; J. S. McClenahen, "Waking Up to a New World," *Industry Week,* June 2003, pp. 22–26; and D. J. Klein and J. Zawacki, *It's Not Magic: The Rebirth of a Small Manufacturing Company* (East Lansing, MI: Michigan State University Press, 1999).

3. G. Nadler and W. J. Chandon, "Making Changes: The FIST Approach," *Journal of Management Inquiry,* September 2004, pp. 239–246; and C. R. Leana and B. Barry, "Stability and Change As Simultaneous Experiences in Organizational Life," *Academy of Management Review,* October 2000, pp. 753–759.

4. E. Nee, "The Hottest CEO in Tech," *Business 2.0,* June 2003, p. 86.

5. The idea for these metaphors came from J. E. Dutton, S. J. Ashford, R. M. O'Neill, and K. A. Lawrence, "Moves That Matter: Issue Selling and Organizational Change," *Academy of Management Journal,* August 2001, pp. 716–736; B. H. Kemelgor, S. D. Johnson, and S. Srinivasan, "Forces Driving Organizational Change: A Business School Perspective," *Journal of Education for Business,* January/February 2000, pp. 133–37; G. Colvin, "When It Comes to Turbulence, CEOs Could Learn a Lot from Sailors," *Fortune,* March 29, 1999, pp. 194–196; and P. B. Vaill, *Managing as a Performing Art: New Ideas for a World of Chaotic Change* (San Francisco: Jossey-Bass, 1989).

6. K. Lewin, *Field Theory in Social Science* (New York: Harper & Row, 1951).

7. D. Lieberman, "Nielsen Media Has Cool Head at the Top," *USA Today,* March 27, 2006, p. 3B.

8. G. Hamel, "Take It Higher," *Fortune,* February 5, 2001, pp. 169–170.

9. A. Sains and S. Reed, "Electrolux Cleans Up," *BusinessWeek,* February 27, 2006, pp. 42–43.

10. "Trends and Countertrends for 2006 and Beyond," Hallmark Web site, www.hallmark.com.

11. S. Crock, J. Carey, P. Magnusson, G. Smith, and O. Port, "Storming the Streets of Baghdad," *BusinessWeek,* October 21, 2002, pp. 46–47.

12. J. Jesitus, "Change Management: Energy to the People," *IW,* September 1, 1997, pp. 37, 40.

13. D. Lavin, "European Business Rushes to Automate," *Wall Street Journal,* July 23, 1997, p. A14.

14. See, for example, B. B. Bunker, B. T. Alban, and R. J. Lewicki, "Ideas in Currency and OD Practice," *The Journal of Applied Behavioral Science,* December 2004, pp. 403–422; L. E. Greiner and T. G. Cummings, "Wanted: OD More Alive Than Dead!" *Journal of Applied Behavioral Science,* December 2004, pp. 374–391; W. Nicolay, "Response to Farias and Johnson's Commentary," *Journal of Applied Behavioral Science,* September 2000, pp. 380–381; G. Farias, "Organizational Development and Change Management," *Journal of Applied Behavioral Science,* September 2000, pp. 376–379; S. Hicks, "What Is Organization Development?" *Training & Development,* August 2000, p. 65; N. A. Worren, K. Ruddle, and K. Moore, "From Organizational Development to Change Management," *Journal of Applied Behavioral Science,*

September 1999, pp. 273–286; W. L. French and C. H. Bell Jr., *Organization Development: Behavioral Science Interventions for Organization Improvement*, 6th ed. (Upper Saddle River, NJ: Prentice Hall, 1998); A. H. Church, W. W. Burke, and D. F. Van Eynde, "Values, Motives, and Interventions of Organization Development Practitioners," *Group & Organization Management*, March 1994, pp. 5–50; and T. C. Head and P. F. Sorensen, "Cultural Values and Organizational Development: A Seven-Country Study," *Leadership & Organization Development Journal*, March 1993, pp. 3–7.

15. T. White, "Supporting Change: How Communicators at Scotiabank Turned Ideas into Action," *Communication World*, April 2002, pp. 22–24.

16. M. Javidan, P. W. Dorfman, M. S. deLuque, and R. J. House, "In the Eye of the Beholder: Cross-Cultural Lessons in Leadership from Project GLOBE," *Academy of Management Perspective,* February 2006, pp. 67–90; and E. Fagenson-Eland, E. A. Ensher, and W. W. Burke, "Organization Development and Change Interventions: A Seven-Nation Comparison," *The Journal of Applied Behavioral Science,* December 2004, pp. 432–464.

17. E. Fagenson-Eland, Ensher, and Burke, "Organization Development and Change Interventions: A Seven-Nation Comparison," p. 461.

18. J. Pfeffer, "Breaking Through Excuses," *Business 2.0,* May 2005, p. 76.

19. See, for example, A. Deutschman, "Making Change: Why Is It So Hard to Change Our Ways?" *Fast Company,* May 2005, pp. 52–62; S. B. Silverman, C. E. Pogson, and A. B. Cober, "When Employees at Work Don't Get It: A Model for Enhancing Individual Employee Change in Response to Performance Feedback," *Academy of Management Executive,* May 2005, pp. 135–147; C. E. Cunningham, C. A. Woodward, H. S. Shannon, J. MacIntosh, B. Lendrum, D. Rosenbloom, and J. Brown, "Readiness for Organizational Change: A Longitudinal Study of Workplace, Psychological and Behavioral Correlates," *Journal of Occupational and Organizational Psychology*, December 2002, pp. 377–392; M. A. Korsgaard, H. J. Sapienza, and D. M. Schweiger, "Beaten Before Begun: The Role of Procedural Justice in Planning Change," *Journal of Management,* vol. 28 (4), 2002, pp. 497–516; R. Kegan and L. L. Lahey, "The Real Reason People Won't Change," *Harvard Business Review,* November 2001, pp. 85–92; S. K. Piderit, "Rethinking Resistance and Recognizing Ambivalence: A Multidimensional View of Attitudes Toward an Organizational Change," *Academy of Management Review,* October 2000, pp. 783–794; C. R. Wanberg and J. T. Banas, "Predictors and Outcomes of Openness to Changes in a Reorganizing Workplace," *Journal of Applied Psychology,* February 2000, pp. 132–142; A. A. Armenakis and A. G. Bedeian, "Organizational Change: A Review of Theory and Research in the 1990s," *Journal of Management*, vol. 25 (3), 1999, pp. 293–315; and B. M. Staw, "Counterforces to Change," in P. S. Goodman and Associates (eds.), *Change in Organizations* (San Francisco: Jossey-Bass, 1982), pp. 87–121.

20. A. Reichers, J. P. Wanous, and J. T. Austin, "Understanding and Managing Cynicism About Organizational Change," *Academy of Management Executive*, February 1997, pp. 48–57; J. Mariotti, "Troubled by Resistance to Change," *IW*, October 7, 1996, p. 30; P. Strebel, "Why Do Employees Resist Change?" *Harvard Business Review*, May–June 1996, pp. 86–92; and J. P. Kotter and L. A. Schlesinger, "Choosing Strategies for Change," *Harvard Business Review*, March–April 1979, pp. 107–109.

21. S. Oreg, "Resistance to Change: Developing an Individual Differences Measure," *Journal of Applied Psychology,* August 2003, pp. 680–693; J. A. LePine, J. A. Colquitt, and A. Erez, "Adaptability to Changing Task Contexts: Effects of General Cognitive Ability, Conscientiousness, and Openness to Experience," *Personnel Psychology,* Fall 2000, pp. 563–593; S. K. Piderit, "Rethinking Resistance and Recognizing Ambivalence: A Multidimensional View of Attitudes Toward an Organizational Change;" K. W. Mossholder, R. P. Settoon, A. A. Armenakis, S. G. Harris, "Emotion During Organizational Transformations," *Group & Organization Management*, September 2000, pp. 220–243; J. P. Wanous, A. E. Reichers, and J. T. Austin, "Cynicism About Organizational Change," *Group & Organization Management*, June 2000, pp. 132–153; L. K. Lewis, "Disseminating Information and Soliciting Input During Planned Organizational Change," *Management Communication Quarterly*, August 1999, pp. 43–75; D. Harrison, "Assess and Remove Barriers to Change," *HR Focus*, July 1999, pp. 9–10; T. A. Judge, C. J. Thoresen, V. Pucki, and T. M. Welbourne, "Managerial Coping with Organizational Change: A Dispositional Perspective," *Journal of Applied Psychology*, February 1999, pp. 107–122; R. Maurer, *Beyond the Wall of Resistance: Unconventional Strategies That Build Support for Change* (Austin: Bard Books, 1996); P. Pritchett and R. Pound, *The Employee Handbook for Organizational Change* (Dallas: Pritchett Publishing, 1994); V. D. Miller, J. R. Johnson, and J. Grau, "Antecedents to Willingness to Participate in a Planned Organizational Change," *Journal of Applied Communication Research*, February 1994, pp. 59–80; A. Sagie and M. Koslowsky, "Organizational Attitudes and Behaviors As a Function of Participation in Strategic and Tactical Change Decisions: An Application of Path-Goal Theory," *Journal of Organizational Behavior*, January 1994, pp. 37–47; J. Landau, "Organizational Change and Barriers to Innovation: A Case Study in the Italian Public Sector," *Human Relations*, December 1993, pp. 1411–1429; C. O'Connor, "Resistance: The Repercussions of Change," *Leadership & Organization Development Journal*, October 1993, pp. 30–36; K. Matejka and R. Julian, "Resistance to Change Is Natural," *Supervisory Management*, October 1993, p. 10; and Kotter and Schlesinger, "Choosing Strategies for Change," pp. 106–111.

22. Information in this box from H. Ibarra, "How to Stay Stuck in the Wrong Career," *Harvard Business Review,* December 2002, pp. 40–47; "Before Uprooting Your Career," *BusinessWeek,* October 22, 2001, p. 131; N. G. Carr, " Being Virtual: Character

and the New Economy," *Harvard Business Review*, May–June 1999, pp. 181–190; W. Kiechel III, "A Manager's Career in the New Economy," *Fortune*, April 4, 1994, pp. 68–72; C. B. Bardwell, "Career Planning & Job Search Guide 1994," *The Black Collegian*, March–April 1994, pp. 59–64; A. D. Pinkney, "Winning in the Workplace," *Essence*, March 1994, pp. 79–80; and B. Kaye, "Career Development— Anytime, Anyplace," *Training & Development*, December 1993, pp. 46–49.

23. J. Useem, "Jim McNerney Thinks He Can Turn 3M from a Good Company into a Great One—With a Little Help from His Former Employer; General Electric," *Fortune*, August 12, 2002, pp. 127–132; and C. Hymowitz, "How Leader at 3M Got His Employees to Back Big Changes," *Wall Street Journal*, April 23, 2002, p. B1.

24. See P. Anthony, *Managing Culture* (Philadelphia: Open University Press, 1994); P. Bate, *Strategies for Cultural Change* (Boston: Butterworth-Heinemann, 1994); C. G. Smith and R. P. Vecchio, "Organizational Culture and Strategic Management: Issues in the Strategic Management of Change," *Journal of Managerial Issues*, Spring 1993, pp. 53–70; D. C. Pheysey, *Organizational Cultures: Types and Transformations* (London: Routledge, 1993); J. Martin, *Cultures in Organizations: Three Perspectives* (New York: Oxford University Press, 1992); P. F. Drucker, "Don't Change Corporate Culture—Use It!" *Wall Street Journal*, March 28, 1991, p. A14; B. Dumaine, "Creating a New Company Culture," *Fortune*, January 15, 1990, pp. 127–131; and T. H. Fitzgerald, "Can Change in Organizational Culture Really Be Managed?" *Organizational Dynamics*, Autumn 1988, pp. 5–15.

25. K. Maney, "Famously Gruff Gerstner Leaves IBM a Changed Man," *USA Today*, November 11, 2002, pp. 1B+; and Louis V. Gerstner, *Who Says Elephants Can't Dance: Inside IBM's Historic Turnaround* (New York: Harper Business, 2002).

26. See, for example, D. C. Hambrick and S. Finkelstein, "Managerial Discretion: A Bridge Between Polar Views of Organizational Outcomes," in L. L. Cummings and B. M. Staw (eds.), *Research in Organizational Behavior*, vol. 9 (Greenwich, CT: JAI Press, 1987), p. 384; and R. H. Kilmann, M. J. Saxton, and R. Serpa (eds.), *Gaining Control of the Corporate Culture* (San Francisco: Jossey-Bass, 1985).

27. C. Daniels, "The Last Taboo," *Fortune*, October 28, 2002, pp. 137–144; J. Laabs, "Time-Starved Workers Rebel," *Workforce*, October 2000, pp. 26–28; M. A. Cavanaugh, W. R. Boswell, M. V. Roehling, and J. W. Boudreau, "An Empirical Examination of Self-Reported Work Stress Among U.S. Managers," *Journal of Applied Psychology*, February 2000, pp. 65–74; and M. A. Verespej, "Stressed Out," *IW*, February 21, 2000, pp. 30–34.

28. A report on Job Stress compiled by the American Institute of Stress, www.stress.org/job, 2002–2003.

29. Information in this box from C. Lindsay, "Paradoxes of Organizational Diversity: Living Within the Paradoxes," in L. R. Jauch and J. L. Wall (eds.),

*Proceedings of the 50th Academy of Management Conference*, San Francisco, 1990, pp. 374–378.

30. V. P. Sudhashree, K. Rohith, K. Shrinivas, "Issues and Concerns of Health Among Call Center Employees," *Indian Journal of Occupational Environmental Medicine*, vol. 9 (3), 2005, pp. 129–132; E. Muehlchen, "An Ounce of Prevention Goes A Long Way," Wilson Banwell, www.wilsonbanwell.com, January 2004; UnionSafe, "Stressed Employees Worked to Death," unionsafe.labor.net.au/news, August 23, 2003; O. Siu, "Occupational Stressors and Well-Being Among Chinese Employees: The Role of Organizational Commitment," *Applied Psychology: An International Review*, October 2002, pp. 527–544; O. Siu, P. E. Spector, C. L. Cooper, L. Lu, and S. Yu, "Managerial Stress in Greater China: The Direct and Moderator Effects of Coping Strategies and Work Locus of Control," *Applied Psychology: An International Review*, October 2002, pp. 608–632; A. Oswald, "New Research Reveals Dramatic Rise in Stress Levels in Europe's Workplaces," University of Warwick, www.warwick.ac.uk/news/pr, 1999; and Y. Shimizu, S. Makino, and T. Takata, "Employee Stress Status During the Past Decade [1982–1992] Based on a Nationwide Survey Conducted by the Ministry of Labour in Japan," Japan Industrial Safety and Health Association, July 1997, pp. 441–450.

31. Adapted from the UK National Work-Stress Network, www.workstress.net.

32. R. S. Schuler, "Definition and Conceptualization of Stress in Organizations," *Organizational Behavior and Human Performance*, April 1980, p. 191.

33. B. L. de Mente, "Karoshi: Death from Overwork," Asia Pacific Management Forum, www.apmforum.com, May 2002.

34. H. Benson, "Are You Working Too Hard?" *Harvard Business Review*, November 2005, pp. 53–58; B. Cryer, R. McCraty, and D. Childre, "Pull the Plug on Stress," *Harvard Business Review*, July 2003, pp. 102–107; C. Daniels, "The Last Taboo"; A. A. Brott, "New Approaches to Job Stress," *Nation's Business*, May 1994, pp. 81–82; P. Froiland, "What Cures Job Stress?" *Training*, December 1993, pp. 32–36; C. L. Cooper and S. Cartwright, "Healthy Mind, Healthy Organization— A Proactive Approach to Occupational Stress," *Human Relations*, April 1994, pp. 455–471; C. A. Heaney et al., "Industrial Relations, Worksite Stress Reduction and Employee Well-Being: A Participatory Action Research Investigation," *Journal of Organizational Behavior*, September 1993, pp. 495–510; C. D. Fisher, "Boredom at Work: A Neglected Concept," *Human Relations*, March 1993, pp. 395–417; and S. E. Jackson, "Participation in Decision Making As a Strategy for Reducing Job-Related Strain," *Journal of Applied Psychology*, February 1983, pp. 3–19.

35. D. Cole, "The Big Chill," *US News & World Report*, December 6, 2004, pp. EE2–EE5.

36. See R. S. Schuler, "Time Management: A Stress Management Technique," *Personnel Journal*, December 1979, pp. 851–55; and M. E. Haynes, *Practical Time Management: How to Make the Most*

*of Your Most Perishable Resource* (Tulsa: Penn Well Books, 1985).

37. Well Workplace 2005 Award Executive Summaries, Wellmark BlueCross BlueShield and Zimmer Holdings, Inc., available on Wellness Councils of America Web site, www.welcoa.org.

38. D. Cole, "The Big Chill."

39. P. A. McLagan, "Change Leadership Today," *T&D,* November 2002, pp. 27–31.

40. Ibid, p. 29.

41. C. Haddad, "UPS: Can It Keep Delivering?" *BusinessWeek Online Extra,* www.businessweek.com, Spring 2003.

42. Information in this box from P. Bennett, T. Demos, J. Elliott, E. Ellis, Al Fung, J. Guyon, C. Kano, J. Mero, N. D. Schwartz, and Z. Dan, "50 Most Powerful International Women," *Fortune,* November 14, 2005, pp. 157–163; "Importance of Leadership Survey," American Management Association, 2004; W. Pietersen, "The Mark Twain Dilemma: The Theory and Practice for Change Leadership," *Journal of Business Strategy,* September–October 2002, pp. 32–37; C. Hymowitz, "To Maintain Success, Managers Must Learn How to Direct Change," *Wall Street Journal,* August 13, 2002, p. B1; and J. E. Dutton, S. J. Ashford, R. M. O'Neill, and K. A. Lawrence, "Moves That Matter: Issue Selling and Organizational Change," *Academy of Management Journal,* August 2001, pp. 716–736.

43. W. Pietersen, "The Mark Twain Dilemma: The Theory and Practice for Change Leadership," p. 35.

44. P. A. McLagan, "The Change-Capable Organization," *T&D,* January 2003, pp. 50–58.

45. J. McGregor, "The World's Most Innovative Companies," *BusinessWeek,* April 24, 2006, p. 64.

46. J. E. Perry-Smith and C. E. Shalley, "The Social Side of Creativity: A Static and Dynamic Social Network Perspective," *Academy of Management Review,* January 2003, pp. 89–106; and P. K. Jagersma, "Innovate or Die: It's Not Easy, But It Is Possible to Enhance Your Organization's Ability to Innovate," *Journal of Business Strategy,* January–February 2003, pp. 25–28.

47. These definitions are based on T. M. Amabile, *Creativity in Context* (Boulder, CO: Westview Press, 1996).

48. R. W. Woodman, J. E. Sawyer, and R. W. Griffin, "Toward a Theory of Organizational Creativity," *Academy of Management Review,* April 1993, pp. 293–321.

49. T. M. Egan, "Factors Influencing Individual Creativity in the Workplace: An Examination of Quantitative Empirical Research," *Advances in Developing Human Resources,* May 2005, pp. 160–181; N. Madjar, G. R. Oldham, and M. G. Pratt, "There's No Place Like Home? The Contributions of Work and Nonwork Creativity Support to Employees' Creative Performance," *Academy of Management Journal,* August 2002, pp. 757–767; T. M. Amabile, C. N. Hadley, and S. J. Kramer, "Creativity Under the Gun," *Harvard Business Review,* August 2002, pp. 52–61; J. B. Sorensen and T. E. Stuart, "Aging, Obsolescence, and Organizational Innovation," *Administrative Science Quarterly,* March 2000, pp. 81–112; G. R. Oldham and A. Cummings, "Employee Creativity: Personal and Contextual Factors at Work," *Academy of Management Journal,* June 1996, pp. 607–634; S. D. Saleh and C. K. Wang, "The Management of Innovation: Strategy, Structure, and Organizational Climate," *IEEE Transactions on Engineering Management,* February 1993, pp. 14–22; and F. Damanpour, "Organizational Innovation: A Meta-Analysis of Effects of Determinants and Moderators," *Academy of Management Journal,* September 1991, pp. 555–590.

50. P. R. Monge, M. D. Cozzens, and N. S. Contractor, "Communication and Motivational Predictors of the Dynamics of Organizational Innovations," *Organization Science,* May 1992, pp. 250–274.

51. T. M. Amabile, C. N. Hadley, and S. J. Kramer, "Creativity Under the Gun."

52. N. Madjar, G. R. Oldham, and M. G. Pratt, "There's No Place Like Home? The Contributions of Work and Nonwork Creativity Support to Employees' Creative Performance."

53. For more information on 3M's innovation efforts, check out its Web site, www.3m.com; J. McGregor, "The World's Most Innovative Companies"; M. Loeb, "Ten Commandments for Managing Creative People with an Environment That Fosters Innovative Thinking, You Can Stumble onto a Lot of Lucky Accidents. Just Ask the CEO of 3M," *Fortune Online Extra,* January 16, 2005; and E. von Hippel, S. Thomke, and M. Sonnack, "Creating Breakthroughs at 3M," *Harvard Business Review,* September–October 1999, pp. 47–57.

54. C. Salter, "Mattel Learns to 'Throw the Bunny,'" *Fast Company,* November 2002, p. 22.

55. See, for instance, J. E. Perry-Smith, "Social Yet Creative: The Role of Social Relationships in Facilitating Individual Creativity," *Academy of Management Journal,* February 2006, pp. 85–101; C. E. Shalley, J. Zhou, and G. R. Oldham, "The Effects of Personal and Contextual Characteristics on Creativity: Where Should We Go from Here?" *Journal of Management,* vol. 30 (6), 2004, pp. 933–958; J. E. Perry-Smith and C. E. Shalley, "The Social Side of Creativity: A Static and Dynamic Social Network Perspective"; J. M. George and J. Zhou, "When Openness to Experience and Conscientiousness Are Related to Creative Behavior: An Interactional Approach," *Journal of Applied Psychology,* June 2001, pp. 513–524; G. Hamel, "Reinvent Your Company," *Fortune,* June 12, 2000, pp. 98–118; J. Zhou, "Feedback Valence, Feedback Style, Task Autonomy, and Achievement Orientation: Interactive Effects on Creative Behavior," *Journal of Applied Psychology,* vol. 83, 1998, pp. 261–276; A. deGues, "The Living Company," *Harvard Business Review,* March–April 1997, pp. 51–59; T. M. Amabile, R. Conti, H. Coon, J. Lazenby, and M. Herron, "Assessing the Work Environment for

Creativity," *Academy of Management Journal*, October 1996, pp. 1154–1184; S. G. Scott and R. A. Bruce, "Determinants of Innovative People: A Path Model of Individual Innovation in the Workplace," *Academy of Management Journal*, June 1994, pp. 580–607; G. Morgan, "Endangered Species: New Ideas," *Business Month*, April 1989, pp. 75–77; R. Moss Kanter, "When a Thousand Flowers Bloom: Structural, Collective, and Social Conditions for Innovation in Organization," in B. M. Staw and L. L. Cummings, (eds.), *Research in Organizational Behavior*, vol. 10 (Greenwich, CT: JAI Press, 1988), pp. 169–211; Amabile, *Creativity in Context;* and M. Tushman and D. Nadler, "Organizing for Innovation," *California Management Review*, Spring 1986, pp. 74–92.

56. J. McGregor, "The World's Most Innovative Companies," p. 70.

57. Ibid., p. 74.

58. J. Ramos, "Producing Change That Lasts," *Across the Board*, March 1994, pp. 29–33; T. Stjernberg and A. Philips, "Organizational Innovations in a Long-Term Perspective: Legitimacy and Souls-of-Fire As Critical Factors of Change and Viability," *Human Relations*, October 1993, pp. 1193–2023; P. A. Carrow-Moffett, "Change Agent Skills: Creating Leadership for School Renewal," *NASSP Bulletin*, April 1993, pp. 57–62; and J. M. Howell and C. A. Higgins, "Champions of Change," *Business Quarterly*, Spring 1990, pp. 31–32.

59. "Spirit Struggles to Survive the Martian Winter," NASA Web site, marsrovers.jpl.nasa.gov, April 4, 2006; The Associated Press, "Mars Rover Is Launched on Voyage to Look for Water," *USA Today*, www.usatoday.com, June 11, 2003; NASA's Web site, www.nasa.gov, June 11, 2003; and W. J. Broad, "A Tiny Rover, Built on the Cheap, Is Ready to Explore Distant Mars," *New York Times*, July 5, 1997, p. 9.

60. Situation adapted from information in "HR Director Backs Team to Stay Focused During Boots Upheaval," *Personnel Today*, March 21, 2006, p. 2; "Boots' Revamp As Group to Shut 17 Depots," *Europe Intelligence Wire*, March 15, 2006.

**Notes for the Part 4 Continuing Case**

A. Serwer and K. Bonamici, "Hot Starbucks to Go," *Fortune*, January 26, 2004, pp. 60–74; J. Cummings, "Legislative Grind," *Wall Street Journal*, April 12, 2005, pp. A1+; Interview with Jim Donald, *Smart Money*, May 2006, pp. 31–32; A. Serwer, Interview with Howard Schultz," *Fortune (Europe)*, March 20, 2006, pp. 35–36; A. Lustgarten, "A Hot, Steaming Cup of Customer Awareness," *Fortune*, November 15, 2004, p. 192; W. Meyers, "Conscience in a Cup of Coffee," *US News & World Report*, October 31, 2005, pp. 48–50; S. Gray, "Fill 'er Up— With Latte," *Wall Street Journal*, January 6, 2006, pp. A9+; S. Holmes, "A Bitter Aroma at Starbucks," *BusinessWeek*, June 6, 2005, p. 13; K. Maher and J. Adamy," Do Hot Coffee and 'Wobblies' Go Together?" *Wall Street Journal*, March 21, 2006, pp. B1+; P. Sellers, "Starbucks: The

Next Generation," *Fortune*, April 4, 2005, p. 20; J. M. Cohn, R. Khurana, and L. Reeves, "Growing Talent as if Your Business Depended It," *Harvard Business Review*, October 2005, pp. 62–70; B. Nussbaum, R. Berner, and D. Brady, "Get Creative," *BusinessWeek*, August 1, 2005, pp. 60–68; "Training Top 100," *Training*, March 2006, pp. 40–59 and p. 72; P. Kafka, "Bean Counter," *Forbes*, February 28, 2005, pp. 78–80; Beyond the Cup: Corporate Social Responsibility, Fiscal 2005 Annual Report, Starbucks Corporation.

## Chapter 14

1. Information from company Web site, www.otelecom.com, February 24, 2006; A. Allam, "Egyptian Mobile Phone Provider Treads Where Others Dare Not," *New York Times*, www.nytimes.com, February 13, 2006; S. Reed, "A Telecom King Broadens His Horizons," *BusinessWeek Online*, www.businessweek.com, December 27, 2005; and S. Reed, "Where Western Telcos Fear to Tread," *BusinessWeek*, March 21, 2005, pp. 48–49.

2. K. O'Toole, "Cold-Calling Van Horne," *Stanford Business Magazine*, www.gsb.stanford.edu, May 2005; and S. Orenstein, "Feeling Your Way to the Top," *Business 2.0*, June 2004, p. 146.

3. K. M. Kroll, "Absence-Minded," *CFO Human Capital*, 2006, pp. 12–14.

4. J. A. LePine, A. Erez, and D. E. Johnson, "The Nature and Dimensionality of Organizational Citizenship Behavior: A Critical Review and Meta-Analysis," *Journal of Applied Psychology*, February 2002, pp. 52–65; and D. W. Organ, *Organizational Citizenship Behavior: The Good Soldier Syndrome* (Lexington, MA: Lexington Books, 1988), p. 4.

5. R. Ilies, B. A. Scott, and T. A. Judge, "The Interactive Effects of Personal Traits and Experienced States on Intraindividual Patterns of Citizenship Behavior," *Academy of Management Journal*, June 2006 (in press); P. Cardona, B. S. Lawrence, and P. M. Bentler, "The Influence of Social and Work Exchange Relationships on Organizational Citizenship Behavior," *Group & Organization Management*, April 2004, pp. 219–247; M. C. Bolino and W. H. Turnley, "Going the Extra Mile: Cultivating and Managing Employee Citizenship Behavior," *Academy of Management Executive*, August 2003, pp. 60–73; M. C. Bolino, W. H. Turnley, and J. J. Bloodgood, "Citizenship Behavior and the Creation of Social Capital in Organizations," *Academy of Management Review*, October 2002, pp. 505–522; and P. M. Podsakoff, S. B. MacKenzie, J. B. Paine, and D. G. Bachrach, "Organizational Citizenship Behaviors: A Critical Review of the Theoretical and Empirical Literature and Suggestions for Future Research," *Journal of Management*, vol. 26, (3), 2000, pp. 543–548.

6. M. C. Bolino and W. H. Turnley, "The Personal Costs of Citizenship Behavior: The Relationship Between Individual Initiative and Role Overload, Job Stress, and Work-Family Conflict," *Journal of Applied Psychology*, July 2005, pp. 740–748.

E. A. Douthitt, "The Role of Justice in Team Member Satisfaction with the Leader and Attachment to the Team," *Journal of Applied Psychology*, April 2001, pp. 316–325; J. E. Mathieu, T. S. Heffner, G. F. Goodwin, E. Salas, and J. A. Cannon-Bowers, "The Influence of Shared Mental Models on Team Process and Performance," *Journal of Applied Psychology*, April 2000, pp. 273–283; G. L. Stewart and M. R. Barrick, "Team Structure and Performance: Assessing the Mediating Role of Intrateam Process and the Moderating Role of Task Type," *Academy of Management Journal*, April 2000, pp. 135–148; J. D. Shaw, M. K. Duffy, and E. M. Stark, "Interdependence and Preference for Group Work: Main and Congruence Effects on the Satisfaction and Performance of Group Members," *Journal of Management*, vol. 26 (2), 2000, pp. 259–279; M. Mattson, T. Mumford, and G. S. Sintay, "Taking Teams to Task: A Normative Model for Designing or Recalibrating Work Teams," *Academy of Management Proceedings* (CD-Rom), 1999; V. U. Druskat and S. B. Wolff, "The Link Between Emotions and Team Effectiveness: How Teams Engage Members and Build Effective Task Processes"; R. Forrester and A. B. Drexler, "A Model for Team-Based Organization Performance," *Academy of Management Executive*, August 1999, pp. 36–49; A. R. Jassawalla and H. C. Sashittal, "Building Collaborative Cross-Functional New Product Teams," *Academy of Management Executive*, August 1999, pp. 50–63; and G. R. Jones and G. M. George, "The Experience and Evolution of Trust: Implications for Cooperation and Teamwork," *Academy of Management Review*, July 1998, pp. 531–546.

45. B. L. Kirkman, C. B. Gibson, and D. L. Shapiro, "Exporting Teams: Enhancing the Implementation and Effectiveness of Work Teams in Global Affiliates," *Organizational Dynamics*, Summer 2001, pp. 12–29; J. W. Bing and C. M. Bing, "Helping Global Teams Compete," *Training & Development*, March 2001, pp. 70–71; C. G. Andrews, "Factors That Impact Multi-Cultural Team Performance," Center for the Study of Work Teams, University of North Texas, www.workteams.unt.edu/reports, November 3, 2000; P. Christopher Earley and E. Mosakowski, "Creating Hybrid Team Cultures: An Empirical Test of Transnational Team Functioning," *Academy of Management Journal*, February 2000, pp. 26–49; J. Tata, "The Cultural Context of Teams: An Integrative Model of National Culture, Work Team Characteristics, and Team Effectiveness," *Academy of Management Proceedings* (CD-Rom), 1999; D. I. Jung, K. B. Baik, and J. J. Sosik, "A Longitudinal Investigation of Group Characteristics and Work Group Performance: A Cross-Cultural Comparison," *Academy of Management Proceedings* (CD-Rom), 1999; and C. B. Gibson, "They Do What They Believe They Can? Group-Efficacy Beliefs and Group Performance Across Tasks and Cultures," *Academy of Management Proceedings* (CD-Rom), 1996.

46. R. Bond and P. B. Smith, "Culture and Conformity: A Meta-Analysis of Studies Using Asch's [1952, 1956] Line Judgment Task," *Psychological Bulletin*, January 1996, pp. 111–137.

47. I. L. Janis, *Groupthink*, 2d ed. (New York: Houghton Mifflin Company, 1982), p. 175.

48. See P. C. Earley, "East Meets West Meets Mideast: Further Explorations of Collectivistic and Individualistic Work Groups," *Academy of Management Journal*, April 1993, pp. 319–348; and P. C. Earley, "Social Loafing and Collectivism: A Comparison of the United States and the People's Republic of China," *Administrative Science Quarterly*, December 1989, pp. 565–581.

49. N. J. Adler, *International Dimensions of Organizational Behavior*, 4th ed. (Cincinnati, OH: Southwestern, 2002), p. 142.

50. Ibid., p. 144.

51. K. B. Dahlin, L. R. Weingart, and P. J. Hinds, "Team Diversity and Information Use," *Academy of Management Journal*, December 2005, pp. 1107–1123.

52. Adler, *International Dimensions of Organizational Behavior*, p. 142.

53. S. Paul, I. M. Samarah, P. Seetharaman, and P. P. Mykytyn, "An Empirical Investigation of Collaborative Conflict Management Style in Group Support System-Based Global Virtual Teams," *Journal of Management Information Systems*, Winter 2005, pp. 185–222.

54. S. Chang and P. Tharenou, "Competencies Needed for Managing a Multicultural Workgroup," *Asia Pacific Journal of Human Resources*, 42 (1), 2004, pp. 57–74; and Adler, *International Dimensions of Organizational Behavior*, p. 153.

55. C. E. Nicholls, H. W. Lane, and M. Brehm Brechu, "Taking Self-Managed Teams to Mexico," *Academy of Management Executive*, August 1999, pp. 15–27.

56. P. Balkundi and D. A. Harrison, "Ties, Leaders, and Time in Teams: Strong Inference About Network Structures' Effects on Team Viability and Performance," *Academy of Management Journal*, February 2006, pp. 49–68.

57. T. Casciaro and M. S. Lobo, "Competent Jerks, Lovable Fools, and the Formation of Social Networks," *Harvard Business Review*, June 2005, pp. 92–99.

58. Balkundi and Harrison.

59. J. McGregor, "The Office Chart That Really Counts," *BusinessWeek*, February 27, 2006, pp. 48–49.

60. Situation adapted from information in "Bluetooth Backers Agree to Boost Transfer Speed," *Los Angeles Times*, March 29, 2006, p. C2; "Bluetooth Transmission Speed Set to Increase," *Wall Street Journal*, March 29, 2006, p. 1; Lee Gomes, "Committees Are Useful and Very Efficient—Well, in the Tech World," *Wall Street Journal*, July 7, 2003, p. A9; John Swaffield, "Code Committees—Gatekeepers or Pathfinders?" *PM Engineer*, January 2003, pp. 25+.

## Chapter 16

1. Information from *Hoover's Online*, www.hoovers.com, February 24, 2006; and T. Vinas, "A Passionate People," *Industry Week*, October 2005, pp. 57–58.

2. C. Taylor, "Rallying the Troops," *Smart Money*, February 2003, pp. 105–106.

3. R. M. Steers, R. T. Mowday, and D. L. Shapiro, "The Future of Work Motivation Theory," *Academy of Management Review*, July 2004, pp. 379–387.

4. N. Ellemers, D. De Gilder, and S. A. Haslam, "Motivating Individuals and Groups at Work: A Social Identity Perspective on Leadership and Group Performance," *Academy of Management Review*, July 2004, pp. 459–478.

5. J. Krueger and E. Killham, "At Work, Feeling Good Matters," *Gallup Management Journal*, gmj.gallup.com, December 8, 2005.

6. S. L. Hwang, "For Some Employees, Great Parking Spaces Fulfill a Primal Need," *Wall Street Journal*, June 26, 2002, p. B1.

7. "Dialogue," *Academy of Management Review*, October 2000, pp. 696–701; M. L. Ambrose and C. T. Kulik, "Old Friends, New Faces: Motivation Research in the 1990s," *Journal of Management*, vol. 25 (3), 1999, pp. 231–192; A. Maslow, D. C. Stephens, and G. Heil, *Maslow on Management* (New York: John Wiley & Sons, 1998); and A. Maslow, *Motivation and Personality* (New York: McGraw-Hill, 1954).

8. See, for example, M. L. Ambrose and C. T. Kulik, "Old Friends, New Faces: Motivation Research in the 1990s"; J. Rowan, "Ascent and Descent in Maslow's Theory," *Journal of Humanistic Psychology*, Summer 1999, pp. 125–133; J. Rowan, "Maslow Amended," *Journal of Humanistic Psychology*, Winter 1998, pp. 81–92; R. M. Creech, "Employee Motivation," *Management Quarterly*, Summer 1995, pp. 33–39; E. E. Lawler III and J. L. Suttle, "A Causal Correlational Test of the Need Hierarchy Concept," *Organizational Behavior and Human Performance*, April 1972, pp. 265–287; and D. T. Hall and K. E. Nongaim, "An Examination of Maslow's Need Hierarchy in an Organizational Setting," *Organizational Behavior and Human Performance*, February 1968, pp. 12–35.

9. D. McGregor, *The Human Side of Enterprise* (New York: McGraw-Hill, 1960). For an updated description of Theories X and Y, see G. Heil, W. Bennis, and D. C. Stephens, *Douglas McGregor, Revisited: Managing the Human Side of Enterprise* (New York: Wiley, 2000).

10. J. M. O'Brien, "The Next Intel," *Wired*, July 2002, pp. 100–107.

11. M. L. Ambrose and C. T. Kulik, "Old Friends, New Faces: Motivation Research in the 1990s"; R. M. Creech, "Employee Motivation"; F. Herzberg, *The Managerial Choice: To Be Effective or to Be Human*, rev. ed. (Salt Lake City, Olympus, 1982); and F. Herzberg, B. Mausner, and B. Snyderman, *The Motivation to Work* (New York: John Wiley, 1959).

12. R. M. Steers, R. T. Mowday, and D. L. Shapiro, "The Future of Work Motivation Theory"; E. A. Locke and G. P. Latham, "What Should We Do About Motivation Theory? Six Recommendations for the Twenty-First Century," *Academy of Management*

*Review*, July 2004, pp. 388–403; and M. L. Ambrose and C. T. Kulik, "Old Friends, New Faces: Motivation Research in the 1990s."

13. M. J. Stahl, *Managerial and Technical Motivation: Assessing Needs for Achievement, Power, and Affiliation* (New York: Praeger, 1986); D. C. McClelland, *Power: The Inner Experience* (New York: Irvington, 1975); J. W. Atkinson and J. O. Raynor, *Motivation and Achievement* (Washington, DC: Winston, 1974); and D. C. McClelland, *The Achieving Society* (New York: Van Nostrand Reinhold, 1961).

14. McClelland, *The Achieving Society*.

15. McClelland, *Power*; D. C. McClelland and D. H. Burnham, "Power Is the Great Motivator," *Harvard Business Review*, March–April 1976, pp. 100–110.

16. D. Miron and D. C. McClelland, "The Impact of Achievement Motivation Training on Small Businesses," *California Management Review*, Summer 1979, pp. 13–28.

17. "McClelland: An Advocate of Power," *International Management*, July 1975, pp. 27–29.

18. A. Barrett, "Cracking the Whip at Wyeth," *BusinessWeek*, February 6, 2006, pp. 70–71.

19. M. L. Ambrose and C. T. Kulik, "Old Friends, New Faces: Motivation Research in the 1990s."

20. G. P. Latham, "The Motivational Benefits of Goal-Setting," *Academy of Management Executive*, November 2004, pp. 126–129; Y. Fried and L. H. Slowik, "Enriching Goal-Setting Theory with Time: An Integrated Approach," *Academy of Management Review*, July 2004, pp. 404–422; M. L. Ambrose and C. T. Kulik, "Old Friends, New Faces: Motivation Research in the 1990s"; E. A. Locke, "Motivation Through Conscious Goal Setting," *Applied and Preventive Psychology*, vol. 5, 1996, pp. 117–124; M. E. Tubbs, D. M. Boehne, and J. S. Dahl, "Expectancy, Valence, and Motivational Force Functions in Goal-Setting Research: An Empirical Test," *Journal of Applied Psychology*, June 1993, pp. 361–373; M. P. Collingwood, "Why Don't You Use the Research?" *Management Decision*, May 1993, pp. 48–54; M. E. Tubbs, "Commitment As a Moderator of the Goal-Performance Relation: A Case for Clearer Construct Definition," *Journal of Applied Psychology*, February 1993, pp. 86–97; E. A. Locke, "Facts and Fallacies About Goal Theory: Reply to Deci," *Psychological Science*, January 1993, pp. 63–64; A. R. Pell, "Energize Your People," *Managers Magazine*, December 1992, pp. 28–29; and J. C. Naylor and D. R. Ilgen, "Goal Setting: A Theoretical Analysis of a Motivational Technique," in B. M. Staw and L. L. Cummings (eds.), *Research in Organizational Behavior*, vol. 6 (Greenwich, CT: JAI Press, 1984), pp. 95–140.

21. J. B. Miner, *Theories of Organizational Behavior* (Hinsdale, IL: Dryden Press, 1980), p. 65.

22. S. G. Harkins and M. D. Lowe, "The Effects of Self-Set Goals on Task Performance," *Journal of Applied Social Psychology*, January 2000, pp. 1–40; T. D.

Ludwig and E. S. Geller, "Assigned Versus Participative Goal Setting and Response Generalization: Managing Injury Control Among Professional Pizza Deliverers," *Journal of Applied Psychology*, April 1997, pp. 253–261; J. George-Falvey, "Effects of Task Complexity and Learning Stage on the Relationship Between Participation in Goal Setting and Task Performance," *Academy of Management Proceedings* (on disk), 1996; and J. A. Wagner III, "Participation's Effects on Performance and Satisfaction: A Reconsideration of Research and Evidence," *Academy of Management Review*, April 1994, pp. 312–330.

23. J. M. Ivancevich and J. T. McMahon, "The Effects of Goal Setting, External Feedback, and Self-Generated Feedback on Outcome Variables: A Field Experiment," *Academy of Management Journal*, June 1982, pp. 359–372; and E. A. Locke, "Motivation Through Conscious Goal Setting."

24. J. W. Smither, M. London, and R. R. Reilly, "Does Performance Improve Following Multisource Feedback? A Theoretical Model, Meta-Analysis, and Review of Empirical Findings," *Personnel Psychology*, Spring 2005, pp. 171–203; Tubbs, "Commitment As a Moderator of the Goal-Performance Relation; J. C. Wofford, V. L. Goodwin, and S. Premack, "Meta-Analysis of the Antecedents of Personal Goal Level and of the Antecedents and Consequences of Goal Commitment," *Journal of Management*, September 1992, pp. 595–615; and J. R. Hollenbeck, C. R. Williams, and H. J. Klein, "An Empirical Examination of the Antecedents of Commitment to Difficult Goals," *Journal of Applied Psychology*, February 1989, pp. 18–23.

25. A. Bandura, *Self-Efficacy: The Exercise of Control* (New York: Freeman, 1997); and M. E. Gist, "Self-Efficacy: Implications for Organizational Behavior and Human Resource Management," *Academy of Management Review*, July 1987, pp. 472–485.

26. A. Bandura, "Cultivate Self-Efficacy for Personal and Organizational Effectiveness," in E. Locke (ed.), *Handbook of Principles of Organizational Behavior* (Malden, MA: Blackwell, 2004), pp. 120–136; A. D. Stajkovic and F. Luthans, "Self-Efficacy and Work-Related Performance: A Meta-Analysis," *Psychological Bulletin*, September 1998, pp. 240–261; M. E. Gist and T. R. Mitchell, "Self-Efficacy: A Theoretical Analysis of Its Determinants and Malleability," *Academy of Management Review*, April 1992, pp. 183–211; and E. A. Locke, E. Frederick, C. Lee, and P. Bobko, "Effect of Self-Efficacy, Goals, and Task Strategies on Task Performance," *Journal of Applied Psychology*, May 1984, pp. 241–251.

27. R. Ilies and T. A. Judge, "Goal Regulation Across Time: The Effects of Feedback and Affect," *Journal of Applied Psychology*, May 2005, pp. 453–467; and A. Bandura and D. Cervone, "Differential Engagement in Self-Reactive Influences in Cognitively-Based Motivation," *Organizational Behavior and Human Decision Processes*, August 1986, pp. 92–113.

28. See J. P. Meyer, B. Schacht-Cole, and I. R. Gellatly, "An Examination of the Cognitive Mechanisms by Which Assigned Goals Affect Task Performance and Reactions to Performance," *Journal of Applied Social Psychology*, vol. 18 (5), 1988, pp. 390–408; and J. C. Anderson and C. A. O'Reilly, "Effects of an Organizational Control System on Managerial Satisfaction and Performance," *Human Relations*, June 1981, pp. 491–501.

29. B. F. Skinner, *Beyond Freedom and Dignity* (New York: Knopf, 1972); and Skinner, *Science and Human Behavior* (New York: Free Press, 1953).

30. The same data, for instance, can be interpreted in either goal-setting or reinforcement terms, as shown in E. A. Locke, "Latham Versus Komaki: A Tale of Two Paradigms," *Journal of Applied Psychology*, February 1980, pp. 16–23. Also, see, M. O. Ambrose and C. T. Kulik, "Old Friends, New Faces: Motivation Research in the 1990s."

31. Information in this box from R. McNatt, "The Young and the Restless," *BusinessWeek*, May 22, 2000, p. 12; "On the Job," *Wall Street Journal*, April 11, 2000, p. B18; P. Kruger, "Does Your Job Work?" *Fast Company*, November 1999, pp. 181–196; and M. A. Verespej, "What Each Generation Wants," *Industry Week*, October 18, 1999, pp. 14–15.

32. See, for example, M. Campion, "Interdisciplinary Approaches to Job Design: A Constructive Replication with Extensions," *Journal of Applied Psychology*, August 1988, pp. 467–481; and R. W. Griffin, "Toward an Integrated Theory of Task Design," in L. L. Cummings and B. M. Staw (eds.), *Research in Organizational Behavior*, vol. 9 (Greenwich, CT: JAI Press, 1987), pp. 79–120.

33. K. H. Hammonds, K. Kelly, and K. Thurston, "Rethinking Work," *BusinessWeek*, October 12, 1994, pp. 75–87; W. Bridges, "The End of the Job," *Fortune*, September 19, 1994, pp. 62–74; and S. Caudron, "The De-Jobbing of America," *Industry Week*, September 5, 1994, pp. 31–36.

34. M. A. Campion and C. L. McClelland, "Follow-Up and Extension of the Interdisciplinary Costs and Benefits of Enlarged Jobs," *Journal of Applied Psychology*, June 1993, pp. 339–351; and M. L. Ambrose and C. T. Kulik, "Old Friends, New Faces: Motivation Research in the 1990s."

35. See, for example, M. L. Ambrose and C. T. Kulik, "Old Friends, New Faces: Motivation Research in the 1990s"; J. L. Cotton, *Employee Involvement* (Newbury Park, CA: Sage, 1993), pp. 141–172; R. W. Griffin, "Effects of Work Redesign on Employee Perceptions, Attitudes, and Behaviors: A Long-Term Investigation," *Academy of Management Journal*, June 1991, pp. 425–435; Miner, *Theories of Organizational Behavior*, pp. 231–266; and J. R. Hackman and G. R. Oldham, *Work Redesign* (Reading, MA: Addison-Wesley, 1980).

36. J. R. Hackman and G. R. Oldham, "Motivation Through the Design of Work: Test of a Theory," *Organizational Behavior and Human Performance*, August 1976, pp. 250–279; and J. R. Hackman and G. R. Oldham, "Development of the Job Diagnostic Survey," *Journal of Applied Psychology*, April 1975, pp. 159–170.

37. M. L. Ambrose and C. T. Kulik, "Old Friends, New Faces: Motivation Research in the 1990s"; and J. R. Hackman, "Work Design," in J. R. Hackman and J. L. Suttle (eds.), *Improving Life at Work* (Glenview, IL: Scott, Foresman, 1977), p. 129.

38. "Involve Your Customers," *Success*, October 1995, p. 28.

39. Ibid.

40. M. L. Ambrose and C. T. Kulik, "Old Friends, New Faces: Motivation Research in the 1990s"; and J. S. Adams, "Inequity in Social Exchanges," in L. Berkowitz (ed.), *Advances in Experimental Social Psychology*, vol. 2 (New York: Academic Press, 1965), pp. 267–300.

41. See, for example, J. Greenberg, "Cognitive Reevaluation of Outcomes in Response to Underpayment Inequity," *Academy of Management Journal,* March 1989, pp. 174–184; E. Walster, G. W. Walster, and W. G. Scott, *Equity: Theory and Research* (Boston: Allyn & Bacon, 1978); and P. S. Goodman and A. Friedman, "An Examination of Adams' Theory of Inequity," *Administrative Science Quarterly*, September 1971, pp. 271–288.

42. See, for example, J. E. Dittrich and M. R. Carrell, "Organizational Equity Perceptions, Employee Job Satisfaction, and Departmental Absence and Turnover Rates," *Organizational Behavior and Human Performance*, August 1979, pp. 29–40; R. G. Lord and J. A. Hohenfeld, "Longitudinal Field Assessment of Equity Effects on the Performance of Major League Baseball Players," *Journal of Applied Psychology*, February 1979, pp. 19–26; and M. R. Carrell, "A Longitudinal Field Assessment of Employee Perceptions of Equitable Treatment," *Organizational Behavior and Human Performance*, February 1978, pp. 108–118.

43. C. T. Kulik and M. L. Ambrose, "Personal and Situational Determinants of Referent Choice," *Academy of Management Review*, April 1992, pp. 212–237; R. W. Scholl, E. A. Cooper, and J. F. McKenna, "Referent Selection in Determining Equity Perception: Differential Effects on Behavioral and Attitudinal Outcomes," *Personnel Psychology*, Spring 1987, pp. 113–127; S. Ronen, "Equity Perception in Multiple Comparisons: A Field Study," *Human Relations*, April 1986, pp. 333–346; and P. S. Goodman, "An Examination of Referents Used in the Evaluation of Pay," *Organizational Behavior and Human Performance*, October 1974, pp. 170–195.

44. See, for example, J. Brockner, "Why It's So Hard to Be Fair," *Harvard Business Review,* March 2006, pp. 122–129; J. A. Colquitt, "Does the Justice of One Interact with the Justice of Many? Reactions to Procedural Justice in Teams," *Journal of Applied Psychology,* August 2004, pp. 633–646; M. A. Konovsky, "Understanding Procedural Justice and Its Impact on Business Organizations," *Journal of Management,* vol. 26 (3), 2000, pp. 489–511; D. B. McFarlin and P. D. Sweeney, "Distributive and Procedural Justice As Predictors of Satisfaction with Personal and Organizational Outcomes," *Academy of Management Journal,* August 1992, pp. 626–637; and R. C. Dailey and D. J. Kirk, "Distributive and Procedural Justice As Antecedents of Job Dissatisfaction and Intent to Turnover," *Human Relations,* March 1992, pp. 305–316.

45. G. P. Latham and C. C. Pinder, "Work Motivation Theory and Research at the Dawn of the Twenty-First Century," *Annual Review of Psychology,* vol. 56, 2005, pp. 485–516; J. Greenberg, "A Taxonomy of Organizational Justice Theories," *Academy of Management Review,* January 1987, pp. 9–22; and P. S. Goodman, "Social Comparison Process in Organizations," in B. M. Staw and G. R. Salancik (eds.), *New Directions in Organizational Behavior* (Chicago: St. Clair, 1977), pp. 97–132.

46. V. H. Vroom, *Work and Motivation* (New York: John Wiley, 1964).

47. See, for example, L. Reinharth and M. Wahba, "Expectancy Theory As a Predictor of Work Motivation, Effort Expenditure, and Job Performance," *Academy of Management Journal*, September 1975, pp. 502–537; and H. G. Heneman III and D. P. Schwab, "Evaluation of Research on Expectancy Theory Prediction of Employee Performance," *Psychological Bulletin*, July 1972, pp. 1–9.

48. See, for example, M. L. Ambrose and C. T. Kulik, "Old Friends, New Faces: Motivation Research in the 1990s"; W. Van Eerde and H. Thierry, "Vroom's Expectancy Models and Work-Related Criteria: A Meta-Analysis," *Journal of Applied Psychology,* October 1996, pp. 575–586; L. W. Porter and E. E. Lawler III, *Managerial Attitudes and Performance* (Homewood, IL: Richard D. Irwin, 1968); and V. H. Vroom, "Organizational Choice: A Study of Pre- and Postdecision Processes," *Organizational Behavior and Human Performance*, April 1966, pp. 212–225.

49. See, for instance, M. Siegall, "The Simplistic Five: An Integrative Framework for Teaching Motivation," *The Organizational Behavior Teaching Review,* vol. 12 (4), 1987–1988, pp. 141–143.

50. N. J. Adler, *International Dimensions of Organizational Behavior*, 4th ed. (Cincinnati, OH: SouthWestern, 2002), p. 174.

51. G. Hofstede, "Motivation, Leadership and Organization: Do American Theories Apply Abroad?" *Organizational Dynamics,* Summer 1980, p. 55.

52. Ibid.

53. J. K. Giacobbe-Miller, D. J. Miller, and V. I. Victorov, "A Comparison of Russian and U.S. Pay Allocation Decisions, Distributive Justice Judgments and Productivity Under Different Payment Conditions," *Personnel Psychology,* Spring 1998, pp. 137–163.

54. S. L. Mueller and L. D. Clarke, "Political-Economic Context and Sensitivity to Equity: Differences Between the United States and the Transition Economies of Central and Eastern Europe," *Academy of Management Journal,* June 1998, pp. 319–329.

55. I. Harpaz, "The Importance of Work Goals: An International Perspective," *Journal of International Business Studies,* First Quarter 1990, pp. 75–93.

56. G. E. Popp, H. J. Davis, and T. T. Herbert, "An International Study of Intrinsic Motivation Composition," *Management International Review,* January 1986, pp. 28–35.

57. R. W. Brislin, B. MacNab, R. Worthley, F. Kabigting Jr., and B. Zukis, "Evolving Perceptions of Japanese Workplace Motivation: An Employee-Manager Comparison," *International Journal of Cross-Cultural Management,* April 2005, pp. 87–104.

58. J. R. Billings and D. L. Sharpe, "Factors Influencing Flextime Usage Among Employed Married Women," *Consumer Interests Annual,* 1999, pp. 89–94; and I. Harpaz, "The Importance of Work Goals: An International Perspective," *Journal of International Business Studies*, First Quarter 1990, pp. 75–93.

59. N. Ramachandran, "New Paths at Work," *US News & World Report,* March 20, 2006, p. 47; S. Armour, "Generation Y: They've Arrived at Work with a New Attitude," *USA Today,* November 6, 2005, pp. B1+; and R. Kanfer and P. L. Ackerman, "Aging, Adult Development, and Work Motivation," *Academy of Management Review,* July 2004, pp. 440–458.

60. S. Armour, "Fewer Working Flex-Time Hours, Report Says," *USA Today,* July 24, 2005, p. 1B.

61. Ibid.

62. M. Arndt, "The Family That Flips Together . . . ," *"BusinessWeek,* April 17, 2006, p. 14.

63. M. Conlin, "The Easiest Commute of All," *BusinessWeek,* December 12, 2005, pp. 78–80.

64. Ibid.

65. T. D. Golden and J. F. Veiga, "The Impact of Extent of Telecommuting on Job Satisfaction: Resolving Inconsistent Findings," *Journal of Management,* April 2005, pp. 301–318.

66. Information in this box from D. Jones, "Ford, Fannie Mae Tops in Diversity," *USA Today,* www.usatoday.com, May 7, 2003; S. N. Mehta, "What Minority Employees Really Want," *Fortune,* July 10, 2000, pp. 180–186; K. H. Hammonds, "Difference Is Power," *Fast Company,* July 2000, pp. 258–266; "Building a Competitive Workforce: Diversity, the Bottom Line," *Forbes,* April 3, 2000, pp. 181–194; and "Diversity: Developing Tomorrow's Leadership Talent Today," *BusinessWeek,* December 20, 1999, pp. 85–100.

67. See, for instance, S. R. Barley and G. Kunda, "Contracting: A New Form of Professional Practice," *Academy of Management Perspectives,* February 2006, pp. 45–66; T. J. Allen and R. Katz, "Managing Technical Professionals and Organizations: Improving and Sustaining the Performance of Organizations, Project Teams, and Individual Contributors," *Sloan Management Review,* Summer 2002, pp. S4–S5;

G. Poole, "How to Manage Your Nerds," *Forbes ASAP*, December 1994, pp. 132–136; and M. Alpert, "The Care and Feeding of Engineers," *Fortune*, September 21, 1992, pp. 86–95.

68. R. J. Bohner Jr. and E. R. Salasko, "Beware the Legal Risks of Hiring Temps," *Workforce,* October 2002, pp. 50–57.

69. J. P. Broschak and A. Davis-Blake, "Mixing Standard Work and Nonstandard Deals: The Consequences of Heterogeneity in Employment Arrangements," *Academy of Management Journal,* April 2006, pp. 371–393; M. L. Kraimer, S. J. Wayne, R. C. Liden, and R. T. Sparrowe, "The Role of Job Security in Understanding the Relationship Between Employees' Perceptions of Temporary Workers and Employees' Performance," *Journal of Applied Psychology,* March 2005, pp. 389–398; and C. E. Connelly and D. G. Gallagher, "Emerging Trends in Contingent Work Research," *Journal of Management,* November 2004, pp. 959–983.

70. L. Landro, "To Get Doctors to Do Better, Health Plans Try Cash Bonuses," *Wall Street Journal,* September 17, 2004, pp. A1+; and C. Haddad, "FedEx: Gaining on the Ground," *BusinessWeek,* December 16, 2002, pp. 126–128.

71. K. E. Culp, "Playing Field Widens for Stack's Great Game," *Springfield News-Leader,* January 9, 2005, pp. 1A+.

72. D. Drickhamer, "Open Books to Elevate Performance," *Industry Week,* November 2002, p. 16; J. Case, "Opening the Books," *Harvard Business Review,* March–April 1997, pp. 118–127; J. P. Schuster, J. Carpenter, and M. P. Kane, *The Power of Open-Book Management* (New York: John Wiley, 1996); and J. Case, "The Open-Book Revolution," *Inc.,* June 1995, pp. 26–50.

73. B. J. Simkins, "Open Book Management—Optimizing Human Capital," *Business Horizons,* September–October 2001, pp. 5–13; and Schuster, Carpenter, and Kane, *The Power of Open-Book Management.*

74. F. Luthans and A. D. Stajkovic, "Provide Recognition for Performance Improvement," in E. A. Locke (ed.), *Principles of Organizational Behavior* (Oxford, England: Blackwell, 2000), pp. 166–180.

75. D. Drickhamer, "Best Plant Winners: Nichols Foods Ltd.," *Industry Week,* October 1, 2001, pp. 17–19.

76. *Hoover's Online,* www.hoovers.com, June 20, 2003; and M. Littman, "Best Bosses Tell All," *Working Woman,* October 2000, p. 54.

77. E. White, "Praise from Peers Goes a Long Way," *Wall Street Journal,* December 19, 2005, p. B3.

78. Ibid.

79. K. J. Dunham, "Amid Sinking Workplace Morale, Employers Turn to Recognition," *Wall Street Journal,* November 19, 2002, p. B8.

80. Cited in S. Caudron, "The Top 20 Ways to Motivate Employees," *Industry Week,* April 3, 1995, pp. 15–16. See also J. Wiscombe, "Rewards Get Results," *Workforce,* April 2002, pp. 42–48; and B. Nelson, "Try Praise," *Inc.,* September 1996, p. 115.

81. E. White, "The Best Versus the Rest," *Wall Street Journal,* January 30, 2006, pp. B1+.

82. A. M. Dickinson and K. L. Gillette, "A Comparison of the Effects of Two Individual Monetary Incentive Systems on Productivity: Piece Rate Pay Versus Base Pay Plus Incentives," *Journal of Organizational Behavior Management,* Spring 1994, pp. 3–82; C. R. Williams and L. P. Livingstone, "Another Look at the Relationship Between Performance and Voluntary Turnover," *Academy of Management Journal,* April 1994, pp. 269–298; J. R. Schuster and P. K. Zingheim, "The New Variable Pay: Key Design Issues," *Compensation and Benefits Review,* March–April 1993, pp. 27–34; and R. K. Abbott, "Performance-Based Flex: A Tool for Managing Total Compensation Costs," *Compensation and Benefits Review,* March–April 1993, pp. 18–21.

83. Hewitt Associates, LLC, "Hewitt Study Shows Base Pay Increases Flat for 2006 with Variable Pay Plans Picking Up the Slack," August 31, 2005.

84. E. Beauchesne, "Pay Bonuses Improve Productivity, Study Shows," *Vancouver Sun,* September 13, 2002, p. D5; and "More Than 20 Percent of Japanese Firms Use Pay Systems Based on Performance," *Manpower Argus,* May 1998, p. 7.

85. M. Tanikawa, "Fujitsu Decides to Backtrack on Performance-Based Pay," *New York Times,* March 22, 2001, p. W1.

86. "Do Incentive Awards Work?" *HRFocus,* October 2000, pp. 1–3; G. Sprinkle, "The Effect of Incentive Contracts on Learning and Performance," *Accounting Review,* July 2000, pp. 299–326; and H. Rheem, "Performance Management Programs," *Harvard Business Review,* September–October 1996, pp. 8–9.

87. R. D. Banker, S. Y. Lee, G. Potter, and D. Srinivasan, "Contextual Analysis of Performance Impacts on Outcome-Based Incentive Compensation," *Academy of Management Journal,* August 1996, pp. 920–948.

88. T. Reason, "Why Bonus Plans Fail," *CFO,* January 2003, p. 53; and "Has Pay for Performance Had Its Day?" *The McKinsey Quarterly,* number 4, 2002, accessed on Forbes Web site, www.forbes.com.

89. "New Study Faults High CEO Compensation Despite Poor Performance," *Ethics Newsline* (a publication of the Institute for Global Ethics), www.globalethics.org/newsline, April 10, 1006.

90. S. DeCarlo, "The Best and Worst Bosses," *Forbes,* May 8, 2006, pp. 131–144.

91. W. J. Duncan, "Stock Ownership and Work Motivation," *Organizational Dynamics,* Summer 2001, pp. 1–11.

92. P. Brandes, R. Dharwadkar, and G. V. Lemesis, "Effective Employee Stock Option Design: Reconciling Stakeholder, Strategic, and Motivational Factors," *Academy of Management Executive,* February 2003, pp. 77–95; and J. Blasi, D. Kruse, and A. Bernstein, *In the Company of Owners: The Truth About Stock Options* (New York: Basic Books, 2003).

93. K. A. Tucker and V. Allman, "Don't Be a Cat-and-Mouse Manager," *Gallup Brain,* brain.gallup.com, September 9, 2004.

94. Situation adapted from information in Stephen Barr, "A Road Map for Agencies Switching to Pay for Performance," *Washington Post,* March 28, 2006, p. D4; Stephen Barr, "Pentagon's Pay System Will Use New Terms to Rate Performance," *Washington Post,* December 6, 2005, p. B2; Wendy Zellner, "'They Took More Than They Needed from Us,'" *BusinessWeek,* June 2, 2003, p. 58.

95. Situation adapted from information in Stephen Barr, "A Road Map for Agencies Switching to Pay for Performance," *Washington Post,* March 28, 2006, p. D4; Stephen Barr, "Pentagon's Pay System Will Use New Terms to Rate Performance," *Washington Post,* December 6, 2005, p. B2; Wendy Zellner, "'They Took More Than They Needed from Us,'" *BusinessWeek,* June 2, 2003, p. 58.

## Chapter 17

1. T. Lowry, "Can MTV Stay Cool?" *BusinessWeek,* February 20, 2006, pp. 50–60; E. Gundersen, "Music Videos Changing Places," *USA Today,* August 26, 2005, pp. 1E+; and J. L. Roberts, "World Tour," *Newsweek,* June 6, 2005, pp. 34–35.

2. Most leadership research has focused on the actions and responsibilities of managers and extrapolated the results to leaders and leadership in general.

3. P. Bacon Jr. and M. Calabresi, "The Up-and-Comers," *Time Canada,* April 24, 2006, p. 28; P. Bacon Jr., "The Exquisite Dilemma of Being Obama," *Time,* February 20, 2006, pp. 24–28; A. Stephen, "10 People Who Will Change the World," *New Statesman,* October 17, 2005, pp. 18–20; "Ten to Watch," *Fortune,* September 9, 2005, p. 282; P. Bacon Jr., "Barack Obama," *Time,* April 18, 2005, pp. 60–61; and A. Ripley, D. E. Thigpen, and J. McCabe, "Obama's Ascent," *Time,* November 11, 2004, pp. 74–78.

4. See T. A. Judge, J. E. Bono, R. Ilies, and M. W. Gerhardt, "Personality and Leadership: A Qualitative and Quantitative Review," *Journal of Applied Psychology,* August 2002, pp. 765–780; and S. A. Kirkpatrick and E. A. Locke, "Leadership: Do Traits Matter?" *Academy of Management Executive,* May 1991, pp. 48–60.

5. P. C. Judge, "From Country Boys to Big Cheese," *Fast Company,* December 2001, pp. 38–40; and C. Hymowitz, "Bosses Need to Learn Whether They Inspire, Or Just Drive, Staffers," *Wall Street Journal,* August 14, 2001, p. B1.

6. Lippitt, "An Experimental Study of the Effect of Democratic and Authoritarian Group Atmospheres," *University of Iowa Studies in Child Welfare*, vol. 16, 1940, pp. 43–95; Lewin, Lippitt, and R. K. White, "Patterns of Aggressive Behavior in Experimentally Created Social Climates," *Journal of Social Psychology*, vol. 10, 1939, pp. 271–301; Lewin, "Field Theory and Experiment in Social Psychology: Concepts and Methods," *American Journal of Sociology*, vol. 44, 1939, pp. 868–896; and K. Lewin and R. Lippitt, "An Experimental Approach to the Study of Autocracy and Democracy: A Preliminary Note," *Sociometry*, vol. 1, 1938, pp. 292–300.

7. B. M. Bass, *Stogdill's Handbook of Leadership* (New York: Free Press, 1981), pp. 289–299.

8. R. M. Stogdill and A. E. Coons (eds.), *Leader Behavior: Its Description and Measurement*, Research Monograph No. 88 (Columbus: Ohio State University, Bureau of Business Research, 1951). For an updated literature review of Ohio State research, see B. M. Fisher, "Consideration and Initiating Structure and Their Relationships with Leader Effectiveness: A Meta-Analysis," in F. Hoy (ed.), *Proceedings* of the 48th Annual Academy of Management Conference, Anaheim, California, 1988, pp. 201–205; and S. Kerr, C. A. Schriesheim, C. J. Murphy, and R. M. Stogdill, "Toward a Contingency Theory of Leadership Based upon the Consideration and Initiating Structure Literature," *Organizational Behavior and Human Performance*, August 1974, pp. 62–82.

9. R. Kahn and D. Katz, "Leadership Practices in Relation to Productivity and Morale," in D. Cartwright and A. Zander (eds.), *Group Dynamics: Research and Theory*, 2d ed. (Elmsford, NY: Row, Paterson, 1960).

10. R. R. Blake and J. S. Mouton, *The Managerial Grid III* (Houston: Gulf Publishing, 1984).

11. P. C. Nystrom, "Managers and the Hi-Hi Leader Myth," *Academy of Management Journal*, June 1978, pp. 325–331; and L. L. Larson, J. G. Hunt, and R. N. Osborn, "The Great Hi-Hi Leader Behavior Myth: A Lesson from Occam's Razor," *Academy of Management Journal*, December 1976, pp. 628–641.

12. W. G. Bennis, "The Seven Ages of the Leader," *Harvard Business Review*, January 2004, p. 52.

13. F. E. Fiedler, *A Theory of Leadership Effectiveness* (New York: McGraw-Hill, 1967).

14. R. Ayman, M. M. Chemers, and F. Fiedler, "The Contingency Model of Leadership Effectiveness: Its Levels of Analysis," *Leadership Quarterly*, Summer 1995, pp. 147–167; C. A. Schriesheim, B. J. Tepper, and L. A. Tetrault, "Lease Preferred Co-Worker Score, Situational Control, and Leadership Effectiveness: A Meta-Analysis of Contingency Model Performance Predictions," *Journal of Applied Psychology*, August 1994, pp. 561–573; and L. H. Peters, D. D. Hartke, and J. T. Pholmann, "Fiedler's Contingency Theory of Leadership: An Application of the Meta-Analysis Procedures of Schmidt and Hunter," *Psychological Bulletin*, March 1985, pp. 274–285.

15. See B. Kabanoff, "A Critique of Leader Match and Its Implications for Leadership Research," *Personnel Psychology*, Winter 1981, pp. 749–764; and E. H. Schein, *Organizational Psychology*, 3rd ed. (Upper Saddle River, NJ: Prentice Hall, 1980), pp. 116–117.

16. P. Hersey and K. H. Blanchard, *Management of Organizational Behavior: Leading Human Resources*, 8th ed. (Englewood Cliffs, NJ: Prentice Hall, 2001); and P. Hersey and K. Blanchard, "So You Want to Know Your Leadership Style?" *Training and Development Journal*, February 1974, pp. 1–15.

17. See, for instance, E. G. Ralph, "Developing Managers' Effectiveness: A Model with Potential," *Journal of Management Inquiry*, June 2004, pp. 152–163; C. L. Graeff, "Evolution of Situational Leadership Theory: A Critical Review," *Leadership Quarterly*, vol. 8 (2), 1997, pp. 153–170; and C. F. Fernandez and R. P. Vecchio, "Situational Leadership Theory Revisited: A Test of an Across-Jobs Perspective," *Leadership Quarterly*, vol. 8 (1), 1997, pp. 67–84.

18. V. H. Vroom and P. W. Yetton, *Leadership and Decision-Making* (Pittsburgh: University of Pittsburgh Press, 1973).

19. V. H. Vroom and A. G. Jago, *The New Leadership: Managing Participation in Organizations* (Upper Saddle River, NJ: Prentice Hall, 1988). See especially Chapter 8.

20. V. H. Vroom, "Leadership and the Decision-Making Process," *Organizational Dynamics*, vol. 18 (4), 2000, pp. 82–94.

21. R. J. House, "Path-Goal Theory of Leadership: Lessons, Legacy, and a Reformulated Theory," *Leadership Quarterly*, Fall 1996, pp. 323–352; House and T. R. Mitchell, "Path-Goal Theory of Leadership," *Journal of Contemporary Business*, Autumn 1974, p. 86; and R. J. House, "A Path-Goal Theory of Leader Effectiveness," *Administrative Science Quarterly*, September 1971, pp. 321–338.

22. A. Sagie and M. Koslowsky, "Organizational Attitudes and Behaviors As a Function of Participation in Strategic and Tactical Change Decisions: An Application of Path-Goal Theory," *Journal of Organizational Behavior*, January 1994, pp. 37–47; and J. C. Wofford and L. Z. Liska, "Path-Goal Theories of Leadership: A Meta-Analysis," *Journal of Management*, Winter 1993, pp. 857–876.

23. B. M. Bass and R. E. Riggio, *Transformational Leadership*, 2d ed. (Mahwah, NJ: Lawrence Erlbaum Associates, Inc., 2006), p. 3.

24. J. Seltzer and B. M. Bass, "Transformational Leadership: Beyond Initiation and Consideration," *Journal of Management*, December 1990, pp. 693–703; and B. M. Bass, "Leadership: Good, Better, Best," *Organizational Dynamics*, Winter 1985, pp. 26–40.

25. B. J. Avolio and B. M. Bass, "Transformational Leadership, Charisma, and Beyond," working paper, School of Management, State University of New York, Binghamton, 1985, p. 14.

26. R. S. Rubin, D. C. Munz, and W. H. Bommer, "Leading from Within: The Effects of Emotion Recognition and Personality on Transformational Leadership Behavior," *Academy of Management Journal,* October 2005, pp. 845–858; T. A. Judge and J. E. Bono, "Five-Factor Model of Personality and Transformational Leadership," *Journal of Applied Psychology,* October 2000, pp. 751–765; B. M. Bass and B. J. Avolio, "Developing Transformational Leadership: 1992 and Beyond," *Journal of European Industrial Training*, January 1990, p. 23; and J. J. Hater and B. M. Bass, "Supervisors' Evaluation and Subordinates' Perceptions of Transformational and Transactional Leadership," *Journal of Applied Psychology*, November 1988, pp. 695–702.

27. R. F. Piccolo and J. A. Colquitt, "Transformational Leadership and Job Behaviors: The Mediating Role of Core Job Characteristics," *Academy of Management Journal,* April 2006, pp. 327–340; O. Epitropaki and R. Martin, "From Ideal to Real: A Longitudinal Study of the Role of Implicit Leadership Theories on Leader-Member Exchanges and Employee Outcomes," *Journal of Applied Psychology,* July 2005, pp. 659–676; J. E. Bono and T. A. Judge, "Self-Concordance at Work: Toward Understanding the Motivational Effects of Transformational Leaders," *Academy of Management Journal,* October 2003, pp. 554–571; T. Dvir, D. Eden, B. J. Avolio, and B. Shamir, "Impact of Transformational Leadership on Follower Development and Performance: A Field Experiment," *Academy of Management Journal,* August 2002, pp. 735–744; N. Sivasubramaniam, W. D. Murry, B. J. Avolio, and D. I. Jung, "A Longitudinal Model of the Effects of Team Leadership and Group Potency on Group Performance," *Group and Organization Management,* March 2002, pp. 66–96; J. M. Howell and B. J. Avolio, "Transformational Leadership, Transactional Leadership, Locus of Control, and Support for Innovation: Key Predictors of Consolidated-Business-Unit Performance," *Journal of Applied Psychology,* December 1993, pp. 891–911; R. T. Keller, "Transformational Leadership and the Performance of Research and Development Project Groups," *Journal of Management*, September 1992, pp. 489–501; and Bass and Avolio, "Developing Transformational Leadership."

28. F. Vogelstein, "Mighty Amazon," *Fortune,* May 26, 2003, pp. 60–74.

29. J. M. Crant and T. S. Bateman, "Charismatic Leadership Viewed from Above: The Impact of Proactive Personality," *Journal of Organizational Behavior*, February 2000, pp. 63–75; G. Yukl and J. M. Howell, "Organizational and Contextual Influences on the Emergence and Effectiveness of Charismatic Leadership," *Leadership Quarterly*, Summer 1999, pp. 257–283; and J. A. Conger and R. N. Kanungo, "Behavioral Dimensions of Charismatic Leadership," in J. A. Conger, R. N. Kanungo and Associates, *Charismatic Leadership* (San Francisco: Jossey-Bass, 1988), pp. 78–97.

30. J. A. Conger and R. N. Kanungo, *Charismatic Leadership in Organizations* (Thousand Oaks, CA: Sage, 1998).

31. K. S. Groves, "Linking Leader Skills, Follower Attitudes, and Contextual Variables via an Integrated Model of Charismatic Leadership," *Journal of Management,* April 2005, pp. 255–277; J. J. Sosik, "The Role of Personal Values in the Charismatic Leadership of Corporate Managers: A Model and Preliminary Field Study," *Leadership Quarterly,* April 2005, pp. 221–244; A. H. B. deHoogh, D. N. den Hartog, P. L. Koopman, H. Thierry, P. T. van den Berg, J. G. van der Weide, and C. P. M. Wilderom, "Leader Motives, Charismatic Leadership, and Subordinates' Work Attitudes in the Profit and Voluntary Sector," *Leadership Quarterly,* February 2005, pp. 17–38; J. M. Howell and B. Shamir, "The Role of Followers in the Charismatic Leadership Process: Relationships and Their Consequences," *Academy of Management Review,* January 2005, pp. 96–112; J. Paul, D. L. Costley, J. P. Howell, P. W. Dorfman, and D. Trafimow, "The Effects of Charismatic Leadership on Followers' Self-Concept Accessibility," *Journal of Applied Social Psychology,* September 2001, pp. 1821–1844; J. A. Conger, R. N. Kanungo, and S. T. Menon, "Charismatic Leadership and Follower Effects," *Journal of Organizational Behavior,* vol. 21, 2000, pp. 747–767; R. W. Rowden, "The Relationship Between Charismatic Leadership Behaviors and Organizational Commitment," *Leadership & Organization Development Journal*, January 2000, pp. 30–35; G. P. Shea and C. M. Howell, "Charismatic Leadership and Task Feedback: A Laboratory Study of Their Effects on Self-Efficacy," *Leadership Quarterly*, Fall 1999, pp. 375–396; S. A. Kirkpatrick and E. A. Locke, "Direct and Indirect Effects of Three Core Charismatic Leadership Components on Performance and Attitudes," *Journal of Applied Psychology*, February 1996, pp. 36–51; D. A. Waldman, B. M. Bass, and F. J. Yammarino, "Adding to Contingent-Reward Behavior: The Augmenting Effect of Charismatic Leadership," *Group & Organization Studies*, December 1990, pp. 381–394; and R. J. House, J. Woycke, and E. M. Fodor, "Charismatic and Noncharismatic Leaders: Differences in Behavior and Effectiveness," in Conger and Kanungo, *Charismatic Leadership*, pp. 103–104.

32. B. R. Agle, N. J. Nagarajan, J. A. Sonnenfeld, and D. Srinivasan, "Does CEO Charisma Matter? An Empirical Analysis of the Relationships Among Organizational Performance, Environmental Uncertainty, and Top Management Team Perceptions of CEO Charisma," *Academy of Management Journal,* February 2006, pp. 161–174.

33. R. Birchfield, "Creating Charismatic Leaders," *Management*, June 2000, pp. 30–31; S. Caudron, "Growing Charisma," *Industry Week*, May 4, 1998, pp. 54–55; and J. A. Conger and R. N. Kanungo, "Training Charismatic Leadership: A Risky and Critical Task," in Conger and Kanungo, *Charismatic Leadership*, pp. 309–323.

34. J. G. Hunt et al., "The Effects of Visionary and Crisis-Responsive Charisma on Followers: An Experimental Examination," *Leadership Quarterly*, Fall 1999, pp. 423–448; R. J. House and R. N. Aditya, "The Social

Scientific Study of Leadership: Quo Vadis?" *Journal of Management*, vol. 23 (3), 1997, pp. 316–323; and House, "A 1976 Theory of Charismatic Leadership."

35. This definition is based on J. R. Lucas, "Anatomy of a Vision Statement," *Management Review*, February 1998, pp. 22–26; N. H. Snyder and M. Graves, "Leadership and Vision," *Business Horizons*, January–February 1994, p. 1; B. Nanus, *Visionary Leadership* (New York: Free Press, 1992), p. 8; and M. Sashkin, "The Visionary Leader," in Conger and Kanungo et al., *Charismatic Leadership*, pp. 124–125.

36. Nanus, *Visionary Leadership*, p. 8.

37. Based on M. Sashkin, "The Visionary Leader," pp. 128–130; and J. R. Baum, E. A. Locke, and S. A. Kirkpatrick, "A Longitudinal Study of the Relation of Vision and Vision Communication to Venture Growth in Entrepreneurial Firms," *Journal of Applied Psychology*, February 1998, pp. 43–54.

38. S. Caminiti, "What Team Leaders Need to Know," *Fortune*, February 20, 1995, pp. 93–100.

39. Ibid., p. 93.

40. Ibid., p. 100.

41. N. Steckler and N. Fondas, "Building Team Leader Effectiveness: A Diagnostic Tool," *Organizational Dynamics*, Winter 1995, p. 20.

42. R. S. Wellins, W. C. Byham, and G. R. Dixon, *Inside Teams* (San Francisco: Jossey-Bass, 1994), p. 318.

43. Steckler and Fondas, "Building Team Leader Effectiveness," p. 21.

44. G. Colvin, "The FedEx Edge," *Fortune*, April 3, 2006, pp. 77–84.

45. See T. R. Hinkin and C. A. Schriesheim, "Development and Application of New Scales to Measure the French and Raven (1959) Bases of Social Power," *Journal of Applied Psychology*, August 1989, pp. 561–567; D. E. Frost and A. J. Stahelski, "The Systematic Measurement of French and Raven's Bases of Social Power in Workgroups," *Journal of Applied Social Psychology*, April 1988, pp. 375–389; P. M. Podsakoff and C. A. Schriesheim, "Field Studies of French and Raven's Bases of Power: Critique, Reanalysis, and Suggestions for Future Research," *Psychological Bulletin*, May 1985, pp. 387–411; R. K. Shukla, "Influence of Power Bases in Organizational Decision Making: A Contingency Model," *Decision Sciences*, July 1982, pp. 450–470; and J. R. P. French Jr. and B. Raven, "The Bases of Social Power," in D. Cartwright and A. F. Zander (eds.), *Group Dynamics: Research and Theory* (New York: Harper & Row, 1960), pp. 607–623.

46. Information in this box from S. P. Robbins and P. L. Hunsaker, *Training in InterPersonal Skills: TIPS for Managing People at Work*, 4th ed. (Upper Saddle River, NJ: 2006); S. B. Bacharach, "Politically Proactive," *Fast Company*, May 2005, p. 93; H. Mintzberg, *Power In and Around Organizations* (Upper Saddle River, NJ: Prentice Hall, 1983); J. Pfeffer, *Power in Organizations* (Marshfield, MA: Pitman,

1981); and S. A. Culbert and J. J. McDonough, *The Invisible War: Pursuing Self-Interest at Work* (New York: John Wiley, 1980).

47. See Australian Navy Web site, www.navy.gov.au.

48. W. Zellner, "What Was Don Carty Thinking?" *BusinessWeek*, May 5, 2003, p. 32; M. Adams and D. Reed, "Workers in Limbo, Morale Horrible," *USA Today*, April 25, 2003, p. 3B; D. Reed, "Carty Resigns As Two Unions Agree to New Concessions," *USA Today*, April 25, 2003, p. 1B; D. Reed, "Carty Faces Crisis," *USA Today*, April 23, 2003, p. 3B; and D. Reed, "Sorry Doesn't Sway AMR Workers," *USA Today*, April 22, 2003, p. 1B.

49. J. M. Kouzes and B. Z. Posner, *Credibility: How Leaders Gain and Lose It, and Why People Demand It* (San Francisco: Jossey-Bass, 1993), p. 14.

50. Based on G. M. Spreitzer and A. K. Mishra, "Giving Up Control Without Losing Control," *Group & Organization Management*, June 1999, pp. 155–187; R. C. Mayer, J. H. Davis, and F. D. Schoorman, "An Integrative Model of Organizational Trust," *Academy of Management Review*, July 1995, p. 712; and L. T. Hosmer, "Trust: The Connecting Link Between Organizational Theory and Philosophical Ethics," *Academy of Management Review*, April 1995, p. 393.

51. P. L. Schindler and C. C. Thomas, "The Structure of Interpersonal Trust in the Workplace," *Psychological Reports*, October 1993, pp. 563–573.

52. H. H. Tan and C. S. F. Tan, "Toward the Differentiation of Trust in Supervisor and Trust in Organization," *Genetic, Social, and General Psychology Monographs*, May 2000, pp. 241–260.

53. R. C. Mayer and M. B. Gavin, "Trust in Management and Performance: Who Minds the Shop While the Employees Watch the Boss?" *Academy of Management Journal*, October 2005, pp. 874–888; and K. T. Dirks and D. L. Ferrin, "Trust in Leadership: Meta-Analytic Findings and Implications for Research and Practice," *Journal of Applied Psychology*, August 2002, pp. 611–628.

54. This section is based on Dirks and Ferrin, "Trust in Leadership: Meta-Analytic Findings and Implications for Research and Practice"; J. K. Butler Jr. "Toward Understanding and Measuring Conditions of Trust: Evolution of a Conditions of Trust Inventory," *Journal of Management*, September 1991, pp. 643–663; and F. Bartolome, "Nobody Trusts the Boss Completely—Now What?" *Harvard Business Review*, March–April 1989, pp. 135–142.

55. R. Zemke, "The Confidence Crisis," *Training*, June 2004, pp. 22–30; J. A. Byrne, "Restoring Trust in Corporate America," *BusinessWeek*, June 24, 2002, pp. 30–35; J. Scott, "Once Bitten, Twice Shy: A World of Eroding Trust," *New York Times*, April 21, 2002, p. WK5; S. Armour, "Employees' New Motto: Trust No One," *USA Today*, February 5, 2002, p. 1B; and J. Brockner, P. A. Siegel, J. P. Daly, T. Tyler, and C. Martin, "When Trust Matters: The Moderating Effect of Outcome Favorability," *Administrative Science Quarterly*, September 1997, p. 558.

56. "Weathering the Storm: A Study of Employee Attitudes and Opinions," *WorkUSA 2002 Study*, Watson Wyatt, www.watsonwyatt.com.

57. "Fannie Mae Fined $400 Million," Reuters, *CNNMoney.com*, May 23, 2006.

58. This section is based on N. M. Tichy and A. McGill (eds.), *The Ethical Challenge: How to Build Honest Business Leaders* (New York: John Wiley & Sons, 2003); J. D. Costa, *The Ethical Imperative: Why Moral Leadership Is Good Business* (Cambridge, MA: Perseus Press, 1999); J. B. Ciulla (ed.), *Ethics: The Heart of Leadership* (New York: Praeger Publications, 1998); R. N. Kanungo and M. Mendonca, *Ethical Dimensions of Leadership* (Thousand Oaks, CA: Sage Publications, 1996); J. C. Rost, "Leadership: A Discussion About Ethics" *Business Ethics Quarterly*, January 1995, pp. 129–142; E. P. Hollander, "Ethical Challenges in the Leader-Follower Relationship," *Business Ethics Quarterly*, January 1995, pp. 55–65; and R. B. Morgan, "Self- and Co-Worker Perceptions of Ethics and Their Relationships to Leadership and Salary," *Academy of Management Journal*, February 1993, pp. 200–214.

59. "Former McKesson Chairman Indicted for Alleged Fraud," *USA Today*, www.usatoday.com, June 5, 2003; and M. Benjamin, "Risky Business," *U.S. News & World Report*, September 9, 2002, pp. 34–37.

60. J. M. Burns, *Leadership* (New York: Harper & Row, 1978).

61. J. M. Avolio, S. Kahai, and G. E. Dodge, "The Ethics of Charismatic Leadership: Submission or Liberation?" *Academy of Management Executive*, May 1992, pp. 43–55.

62. J. S. McClenahen, "UTC's Master of Principle," *Industry Week*, January 2003, pp. 30–33.

63. L. K. Trevino, M. Brown, and L. P. Hartman, "A Qualitative Investigation of Perceived Executive Ethical Leadership: Perceptions from Inside and Outside the Executive Suite," *Human Relations*, January 2003, pp. 5–37.

64. T. Vinas, "DuPont: Safety Starts at the Top," *Industry Week*, July 2002, p. 55.

65. Information in this box from J. M. Cohn, R. Khurana, and L. Reeves, "Growing Talent As if Your Business Depended on It," *Harvard Business Review*, October 2005, pp. 62–70; B. Breen, "The Clear Leader," *Fast Company*, March 2005, pp. 65–67; D. A. Ready, "How to Grow Great Leaders," *Harvard Business Review*, December 2004, pp. 92–100; D. V. Day, "Leadership Development: A Review in Context," *Leadership Quarterly*, Winter 2000, pp. 581–613.

66. P. K. Mills and G. R. Ungson, "Reassessing the Limits of Structural Empowerment: Organizational Constitution and Trust As Controls," *Academy of Management Review*, January 2003, pp. 143–153; W. Alan Rudolph and M. Sashkin, "Can Organizational Empowerment Work in Multinational Settings?" *Academy of Management Executive*, February 2002, pp. 102–115; C. Gomez and B. Rosen, "The Leader-Member Link Between Managerial Trust and Employee Empowerment," *Group & Organization Management*, March 2001, pp. 53–69; C. Robert and T. M. Probst, "Empowerment and Continuous Improvement in the United States, Mexico, Poland, and India," *Journal of Applied Psychology*, October 2000, pp. 643–658; R. C. Herrenkohl, G. T. Judson, and J. A. Heffner, "Defining and Measuring Employee Empowerment," *Journal of Applied Behavioral Science*, September 1999, p. 373; R. C. Ford and M. D. Fottler, "Empowerment: A Matter of Degree," *Academy of Management Executive*, August 1995, pp. 21–31; and W. A. Randolph, "Navigating the Journey to Empowerment," *Organizational Dynamics*, Spring 1995, pp. 19–32.

67. T. A. Stewart, "Just Think: No Permission Needed," *Fortune*, January 8, 2001, pp. 190–192.

68. F. W. Swierczek, "Leadership and Culture: Comparing Asian Managers," *Leadership & Organization Development Journal*, December 1991, pp. 3–10.

69. House, "Leadership in the Twenty-First Century," p. 443; M. F. Peterson and J. G. Hunt, "International Perspectives on International Leadership," *Leadership Quarterly*, Fall 1997, pp. 203–231; and J. R. Schermerhorn and M. H. Bond, "Cross-Cultural Leadership in Collectivism and High Power Distance Settings," *Leadership & Organization Development Journal*, vol. 18 (4/5), 1997, pp. 187–193.

70. D. E. Carl and M. Javidan, "Universality of Charismatic Leadership: A Multi-Nation Study," paper presented at the National Academy of Management Conference, Washington, DC, August 2001; and R. J. House, P. J. Hanges, S. A. Ruiz-Quintanilla, P. W. Dorfman, and Associates, "Culture Specific and Cross-Culturally Generalizable Implicit Leadership Theories: Are the Attributes of Charismatic/Transformational Leadership Universally Endorsed?" *Leadership Quarterly*, Summer 1999, pp. 219–256.

71. D. E. Carl and M. Javidan, "Universality of Charismatic Leadership," p. 29.

72. Women Administrative and Managerial Workers, United Nations Statistics Division—Demographic and Social Statistics, unstats.un.org/unsd/demographic, April 22, 2005.

73. "Women in Management," Catalyst, www.catalyst.org, April 4, 2005.

74. G. N. Powell, D. A. Butterfield, J. D. Parent, "Gender and Managerial Stereotypes: Have the Times Changed?" *Journal of Management*, vol. 28 (2), 2002, pp. 177–193.

75. See K. M. Bartol, D. C. Martin, and J. A. Kromkowski, "Leadership and the Glass Ceiling: Gender and Ethnic Influences on Leader Behaviors at Middle and Executive Managerial Levels," *Journal of Leadership & Organizational Studies*, Winter 2003, pp. 8–19; A. H. Eagly and S. J. Karau, "Role Congruity Theory of Prejudice Toward Female Leaders," *Psychological Review*, July 2002, pp. 573–598; J. Becker, R. A. Ayman,

and K. Korabik, "Discrepancies in Self/Subordinates' Perceptions of Leadership Behavior: Leader's Gender, Organizational Context, and Leader's Self-Monitoring," *Group & Organization Management*, June 2002, pp. 226–244; N. Z. Selter, "Gender Differences in Leadership: Current Social Issues and Future Organizational Implications," *Journal of Leadership Studies*, Spring 2002, pp. 88–99; J. M. Norvilitis and H. M. Reid, "Evidence for an Association Between Gender-Role Identity and a Measure of Executive Function," *Psychological Reports*, February 2002, pp. 35–45; W. H. Decker and D. M. Rotondo, "Relationships Among Gender, Type of Humor, and Perceived Leader Effectiveness," *Journal of Managerial Issues*, Winter 2001, pp. 450–465; C. L. Ridgeway, "Gender, Status, and Leadership," *Journal of Social Issues*, Winter 2001, pp. 637–655; M. Gardiner and M. Tiggemann, "Gender Differences in Leadership Style, Job Stress and Mental Health in Male- and Female-Dominated Industries," *Journal of Occupational and Organizational Psychology*, September 1999, pp. 301–315; and F. J. Yammarino, A. J. Dubinsky, L. B. Comer, and M. A. Jolson, "Women and Transformational and Contingent Reward Leadership: A Multiple-Levels-of-Analysis Perspective," *Academy of Management Journal*, February 1997, pp. 205–222.

76. Gardiner and Tiggemann, "Gender Differences in Leadership Style, Job Stress and Mental Health in Male- and Female-Dominated Industries."

77. "Women 'Take Care,' Men 'Take Charge:' Stereotyping of U.S. Business Leaders Exposed," Catalyst (New York, 2005).

78. C. Hymowitz, "Too Many Women Fall for Stereotypes of Selves, Study Says," *Wall Street Journal*, October 24, 2005, p. B1; B. Kantrowitz, "When Women Lead," *Newsweek*, October 24, 2005, pp. 46–61; and "Why Can't Women Be Leaders Too?" *Gallup Management Journal*, gmj.gallup.com, October 13, 2005.

79. D. McGinn, "In Good Company," *Newsweek*, October 24, 2005, pp. 68–69.

80. J. Guyon, "The Art of the Decision," *Fortune*, November 14, 2005, p. 144; H. Aguinis and S. K. R. Adams, "Social-Role Versus Structural Models of Gender and Influence Use in Organizations: A Strong Inference Approach," *Group & Organization Management*, December 1998, pp. 414–446; A. H. Eagly, S. J. Karau, and M. G. Makhijani, "Gender and the Effectiveness of Leaders: A Meta-Analysis," *Psychological Bulletin*, vol. 117, 1995, pp. 125–145; W. H. Decker and D. M. Rotondo, "Relationships Among Gender, Type of Humor, and Perceived Leader Effectiveness"; and J. M. Norvilitis and H. M. Reid, "Evidence for an Association Between Gender-Role Identity and a Measure of Executive Function."

81. Bartol, Martin, and Kromkowski, "Leadership and the Glass Ceiling: Gender and Ethnic Group Influences on Leader Behaviors at Middle and Executive Managerial Levels"; and R. Sharpe, "As Leaders, Women Rule," *BusinessWeek*, November 20, 2000, pp. 74–84.

82. Bartol, Martin, and Kromkowski, "Leadership and the Glass Ceiling: Gender and Ethnic Group Influences on Leader Behaviors at Middle and Executive Managerial Levels."

83. J. Useem, "From Heroes to Goats and Back Again?" *Fortune*, November 18, 2002, pp. 40–48.

84. K. Lowrey Miller, "The Quiet CEOs," *Newsweek*, December 30, 2004, pp. E10–E14.

85. A. Webber, "CEO Bashing Has Gone Too Far," *USA Today*, June 3, 2003, p. 15A; N. Minow, "Show Some Real Leadership, CEOs"; J. Useem, "From Heroes to Goats and Back Again?"; and B. Horovitz, "Scandals Grow Out of CEOs' Warped Mind-Set," *USA Today*, October 11, 2002, p. B1.

86. A. Webber, "Above-It-All CEOs Forget Workers," *USA Today*, November 11, 2002, p. 13A.

87. Ibid.

88. P. M. Podsakoff, B. P. Niehoff, S. B. MacKenzie, and M. L. Williams, "Do Substitutes for Leadership Really Substitute for Leadership? An Empirical Examination of Kerr and Jermier's Situational Leadership Model," *Organizational Behavior and Human Decision Processes*, February 1993, pp. 1–44; J. P. Howell, D. E. Bowen, P. W. Dorfman, S. Kerr, and P. M. Podsakoff, "Substitutes for Leadership: Effective Alternatives to Ineffective Leadership," *Organizational Dynamics*, Summer 1990, pp. 21–38; J. P. Howell, P. W. Dorfman, and S. Kerr, "Leadership and Substitutes for Leadership," *Journal of Applied Behavioral Science*, vol. 22 (1), 1986, pp. 29–46; and S. Kerr and J. M. Jermier, "Substitutes for Leadership: Their Meaning and Measurement," *Organizational Behavior and Human Performance*, December 1978, pp. 375–403.

89. Situation adapted from information in Alan Murray, "The CEO As Global Corporate Ambassador," *Wall Street Journal*, March 29, 2006, p. A2; Jeremy W. Peters, "Still Advertising to Gays, Ford Under Boycott Again," *New York Times*, March 15, 2006, p. C5; Jack Neff, "Wildmon Wins PR Battles, But Not His Gay-Ads War," *Advertising Age*, December 12, 2005, p. 1.

## Notes for the Part 5 Continuing Case

A. Serwer and K. Bonamici, "Hot Starbucks to Go," *Fortune*, January 26, 2004, pp. 60–74; Interview with Jim Donald, *Fortune*, April 4, 2005, p. 30; Interview with Jim Donald, *Smart Money*, May 2006, pp. 31–32; A. Serwer, "Interview with Howard Schultz," *Fortune (Europe)*, March 20, 2006, pp. 35–36; W. Meyers, "Conscience in a Cup of Coffee," *US News & World Report*, October 31, 2005, pp. 48–50; J. M. Cohn, R. Khurana, and L. Reeves, "Growing Talent As If Your Business Depended It," *Harvard Business Review*, October 2005, pp. 62–70; P. Kafka, "Bean Counter," *Forbes*, February 28, 2005, pp. 78–80; S. Gray, "Starbucks's CEO Announces Plan to Retire in March," *Wall Street Journal*, October 13, 2004, p. A6; Beyond the Cup: Corporate Social Responsibility, Fiscal 2005 Annual Report, Starbucks Corporation.

## Chapter 18

1. Information from FAA Web site, www.faa.gov, March 6, 2006; and L. Meckler, "Flight Plan," *Wall Street Journal,* January 30, 2006, pp. A1+.

2. A. Tugend, "Packing and Wondering Where Bags Will Land," *New York Times Online,* www.nytimes.com, May 27, 2006; C. Elliott, "An Airline's Inner Thoughts Get Unintended Exposure," *New York Times Online,* www.nytimes.com, April 29, 2006; K. W. Arenson, "SAT Problems Even Larger Than Reported," *New York Times Online,* www.nytimes.com, March 23, 2006; K. W. Arenson and D. B. Henriques, "Company's Errors on SAT Scores Raise New Qualms About Testing," *New York Times Online,* www.nytimes.com, March 10, 2006; and B. Hagenbaugh, "State Quarter's Extra Leaf Grew out of Lunch Break," *USA Today,* January 20, 2006, p. 1B.

3. K. A. Merchant, "The Control Function of Management," *Sloan Management Review,* Summer 1982, pp. 43–55.

4. E. Flamholtz, "Organizational Control Systems Managerial Tool," *California Management Review,* Winter 1979, p. 55.

5. W. G. Ouchi, "Markets, Bureaucracies, and Clans," *Administrative Science Quarterly,* March 1980, pp. 129–141; and Ouchi, "A Conceptual Framework for the Design of Organizational Control Mechanisms," *Management Science,* August 1979, pp. 833–838.

6. T. Vinas and J. Jusko, "5 Threats That Could Sink Your Company," *Industry Week,* September 2004, pp. 52–61; "Workplace Security: How Vulnerable Are You?" Special section in *Wall Street Journal,* September 29, 2003, pp. R1–R8; P. Magnusson, "Your Jitters Are Their Lifeblood," *BusinessWeek,* April 14, 2003, p. 41; S. Williams, Company Crisis: CEO Under Fire," *Hispanic Business,* March 2003, pp. 54–56; T. Purdum, "Preparing for the Worst," *Industry Week,* January 2003, pp. 53–55; and S. Leibs, "Lesson from 9/11: It's Not About Data," *CFO,* September 2002, pp. 31–32.

7. A. Dalton, "Rapid Recovery," *Industry Week,* March 2005, pp. 70–71.

8. S. Kerr, "On the Folly of Rewarding A, While Hoping for B," *Academy of Management Journal,* December 1975, pp. 769–783.

9. M. Starr, "State-of-the Art Stats," *Newsweek,* March 24, 2003, pp. 47–49.

10. A. M. Ristow, T. L. Amos, and G. E. Staude, "Transformational Leadership and Organizational Effectiveness in the Administration of Cricket in South Africa," *South African Journal of Business Management,* March1999, pp. 1–5.

11. "Fortune 500 Top Performers," *Fortune,* www.fortune.com, May 27, 2006.

12. R. Levering and M. Moskowitz, "100 Best Companies to Work For: How We Pick the 100 Best," *Fortune,* www.fortune.com., January 7, 2003.

13. T. Purdum, "50 Best in Manufacturing," *Industry Week,* June 2006, pp. 43–46.

14. Information in this box from DiversityInc Top 50 Companies for Diversity, June 2006, pp. 40-84; and S. M. Mehta, "What Minority Employees Really Want," *Fortune,* July 10, 2000, pp. 180–186.

15. "ACSI Methodology," American Customer Satisfaction Index, found online at www.theacsi.org/model.htm, May 27, 2006.

16. Information from company Web site, www.applebees.com, May 27, 2006; R. Barker, "Applebee's Looks Appetizing," *BusinessWeek,* September 19, 2005, p. 30; and J. Rosenfeld, "Down-Home Food, Cutting-Edge Business," *Fast Company,* April 2000, pp. 56–58.

17. P. Landers, "Japan Tech Star Sticks to Manufacturing," *Wall Street Journal,* April 24, 2000, p. A22.

18. H. Koontz and R. W. Bradspies, "Managing Through Feedforward Control," *Business Horizons,* June 1972, pp. 25–36.

19. G. Naik, "Ounce of Prevention," *Wall Street Journal,* May 8, 2006, pp. A1+.

20. J. Teresko, "Faster, Leaner, Greener," *Industry Week,* October 2005, pp. 52–53.

21. W. H. Newman, *Constructive Control: Design and Use of Control Systems* (Upper Saddle River, NJ: Prentice Hall, 1975), p. 33.

22. J. Teresko, "Driving Ongoing Profitability with EVA," *Industry Week,* August 2003, pp. 16–17; and F. Hansen, "The Value-Based Management Commitment," *Business Finance,* September 2001, pp. 2–5.

23. T. Leahy, "Capitalizing on Economic Value Added," *Business Finance,* July 2000, pp. 83–86.

24. S. Taub, "MVPs of MVA," *CFO,* July 2003, pp. 59–66; and K. Lehn and A. K. Makhija, "EVA and MVA As Performance Measures and Signals for Strategic Change," *Strategy & Leadership,* May/June 1996, pp. 34–38.

25. L. Pulliam Weston, "The Secret Pensions of Fat-Cat Executives," *MSN Money,* moneycentral.msn.com/content, May 27, 2006; M. V. Rafter, "IRS Advice to Large Companies: Hit the Books," *Workforce,* January 2005, pp. 60–61; and E. E. Schultz and T. Francis, "Buried Treasure: Well-Hidden Perk Means Big Money for Top Executives," *Wall Street Journal,* October 11, 2002, pp. A1+.

26. R. Fink, "No More Holes," *CFO,* August 2002, p. 42.

27. S. Labaton, "Spotlight on Pay Could Be a Wild Card," *New York Times Online,* www.nytimes.com, April 9, 2006; and M. Doran, "Executive Compensation Reform and the Limits of Tax Policy," *Tax Policy Center,* www.taxpolicycenter.org, November 23, 2004.

28. R. S. Kaplan and D. P. Norton, "How to Implement a New Strategy Without Disrupting Your Organization," *Harvard Business Review,* March 2006, pp. 100–109; L. Bassi and D. McMurrer, "Developing Measurement

Systems for Managing in the Knowledge Era," *Organizational Dynamics,* May 2005, pp. 185–196; G. M. J. de Koning, "Making the Balanced Scorecard Work (Part 2), *Gallup Brain,* brain.gallup.com, August 12, 2004; G. M. J. de Koning, "Making the Balanced Scorecard Work (Part 1), *Gallup Brain,* brain.gallup.com, July 8, 2004; Balanced Scorecard Collaborative, www.bscol.com, June 29, 2003; K. Graham, "Balanced Scorecard," *New Zealand Management,* March 2003, pp. 32–34; K. Ellis, "A Ticket to Ride: Balanced Scorecard," *Training,* April 2001, p. 50; and T. Leahy, "Tailoring the Balanced Scorecard," *Business Finance,* August 2000, pp. 53–56.

29. T. Leahy, "Tailoring the Balanced Scorecard."

30. Ibid.

31. Ibid.

32. D. Stout and T. Zeller Jr., "Vast Data Cache About Veterans Has Been Stolen," *New York Times Online,* www.nytimes.com, May 23, 2006.

33. J. McPartlin, "Hackers Find Backers," *CFO,* January 2006, pp. 75–77; J. Swartz, "Data Losses Push Businesses to Encrypt Backup Tapes," *USA Today,* June 13, 2005, p. 1B; J. Goff, "New Holes for Hackers," *CFO,* May 2005, pp. 64–73; B. Grow, "Hacker Hunters," *BusinessWeek,* May 30, 2005, pp. 74–82; J. Swartz, "Crooks Slither into Net's Shady Nooks and Crannies," *USA Today,* October 21, 2004, pp. 1B+; J. Swartz, "Spam Can Hurt in More Ways Than One," *USA Today,* July 7, 2004, p. 3B; and T. Reason, "Stopping the Flow," *CFO,* September 2003, pp. 97–99.

34. D. Whelan, "Google Me Not," *Forbes,* August 16, 2004, pp. 102–104.

35. J. Levitz and J. Hechinger, "Laptops Prove Weakest Link in Data Security," *Wall Street Journal,* March 24, 2006, pp. B1+.

36. J. Markoff, "Study Says Chips in ID Tags Are Vulnerable to Viruses," *New York Times Online,* www.nytimes.com, March 15, 2006.

37. R. Pear, "A.M.A. to Develop Measure of Quality of Medical Care," *New York Times Online,* www.nytimes.com, February 21, 2006; and A. Taylor III, "Double Duty," *Fortune,* March 7, 2005, pp. 104–110.

38. "Mercedes-Benz Benchmarking Saves DaimlerChrysler $100 Million," *Industry Week,* www.industryweek.com, October 27, 2000.

39. Y. F. Jarrar and M. Zairi, "Future Trends in Benchmarking for Competitive Advantage: A Global Survey," *Total Quality Management,* December 2001, pp. 906–912.

40. M. Simpson and D. Kondouli, "A Practical Approach to Benchmarking in Three Service Industries," *Total Quality Management,* July 2000, pp. S623–S630.

41. K. N. Dervitsiotis, "Benchmarking and Paradigm Shifts," *Total Quality Management,* July 2000, pp. S641–S646.

42. T. Leahy, "Extracting Diamonds in the Rough," *Business Finance,* August 2000, pp. 33–37.

43. B. Bruzina, B. Jessop, R. Plourde, B. Whitlock, and L. Rubin, "Ameren Embraces Benchmarking As a Core Business Strategy," *Power Engineering,* November 2002, pp. 121–124.

44. J. Yaukey and C. L. Romero, "Arizona Firm Pays Big for Workers' Digital Downloads," *Springfield News-Leader,* May 6, 2002, p. 6B.

45. J. R. Wilke, "Red Cross Receives New Scrutiny," *Wall Street Journal,* April 27, 2006, p. D3; S. Strom, "Red Cross Plans Changes After Hurricane Problems," *New York Times Online,* www.nytimes.com, April 12, 2006; S. Strom, "Foreign Experts Critique U.S. Red Cross on Katrina," *New York Times Online,* www.nytimes.com, April 5, 2006; and R. Carroll, Associated Press, "Head of Red Cross Admits Response Uneven," *Springfield News-Leader,* October 1, 2005, p. 3A.

46. N. Shirouzu and J. Bigness, "7-Eleven Operators Resist System to Monitor Managers," *Wall Street Journal,* June 16, 1997, p. B1.

47. AMA/ePolicy Institute, "2005 Electronic Monitoring & Surveillance Survey," *American Management Association,* www.amanet.org.

48. S. Armour, "Companies Keep an Eye on Workers' Internet Use," *USA Today,* February 21, 2006, p. 2B.

49. P-W Tam, E. White, N. Wingfield, and K. Maher, "Snooping E-Mail by Software Is Now a Workplace Norm," *Wall Street Journal,* March 9, 2005, pp. B1+; D. Hawkins, "Lawsuits Spur Rise in Employee Monitoring," *U.S. News & World Report,* August 13, 2001, p. 53; L. Guernsey, "You've Got Inappropriate Mail," *New York Times,* April 5, 2000, pp. C1+; and R. Karaim, "Setting E-Privacy Rules," *CNNfn Online,* www.cnnfn.com, December 15, 1999.

50. S. Armour, "More Companies Keep Track of Workers' E-Mail," *USA Today,* June 13, 2005, p. 4B; and E. Bott, "Are You Safe? Privacy Special Report," *PC Computing,* March 2000, pp. 87–88.

51. R. Karaim, "Setting E-Privacy Rules."

52. K. Naughton, "CyberSlacking," *Newsweek,* November 29, 1999, pp. 62–65.

53. A. M. Bell, and D. M. Smith, "Theft and Fraud May Be an Inside Job," *Workforce Online,* www.workforce.com, December 3, 2000.

54. C. C. Verschoor, "New Evidence of Benefits from Effective Ethics Systems," *Strategic Finance,* May 2003, pp. 20–21; and E. Krell, "Will Forensic Accounting Go Mainstream?" *Business Finance,* October 2002, pp. 30–34.

55. J. Greenberg, "The STEAL Motive: Managing the Social Determinants of Employee Theft," in R. Giacalone and J. Greenberg (eds.), *Antisocial Behavior in Organizations* (Newbury Park, CA: Sage, 1997), pp. 85–108.

56. B. E. Litzky, K. A. Eddleston, and D. L. Kidder, "The Good, the Bad, and the Misguided: How Managers Inadvertently Encourage Deviant Behaviors," *Academy of Management Perspective,* February 2006, pp. 91–103; "Crime Spree," *BusinessWeek,* September 9, 2002, p. 8; B. P. Niehoff and R. J. Paul, "Causes of Employee Theft and Strategies That HR Managers Can Use for Prevention," *Human Resource Management,* Spring 2000, pp. 51–64; and G. Winter, "Taking at the Office Reaches New Heights: Employee Larceny Is Bigger and Bolder," *New York Times,* July 12, 2000, pp. C1+.

57. This section is based on J. Greenberg, *Behavior in Organizations: Understanding and Managing the Human Side of Work,* 8e (Upper Saddle River, NJ: Prentice Hall, 2003), pp. 329–330.

58. A. H. Bell and D. M. Smith, "Why Some Employees Bite the Hand That Feeds Them," *Workforce Online,* www.workforce.com, December 3, 2000.

59. B. E. Litzky, et al., "The Good, the Bad, and the Misguided"; A. H. Bell and D. M. Smith, "Protecting the Company Against Theft and Fraud," *Workforce Online,* www.workforce.com, December 3, 2000; J. D. Hansen, "To Catch a Thief," *Journal of Accountancy,* March 2000, pp. 43–46; and J. Greenberg, "The Cognitive Geometry of Employee Theft," in *Dysfunctional Behavior In Organizations: Nonviolent and Deviant Behavior* (Stamford, CT: JAI Press, 1998), pp. 147–193.

60. CBS News, "Former Postal Worker Kills 5, Herself," www.cbsnews.com/stories, January 31, 2006; CBS News, "Autoworker's Grudge Turns Deadly," www.cbsnews.com/stories, January 27, 2005; D. Sharp, "Gunman Just Hated a Lot of People," *USA Today,* July 10, 2003, p. 3A; and M. Prince, "Violence in the Workplace on the Rise; Training, Zero Tolerance Can Prevent Aggression," *Business Insurance,* May 12, 2003, p. 1.

61. "Workplace Homicides Declined in 2004," Bureau of Labor Statistics, www.bls.gov, September 1, 2005.

62. J. McCafferty, "Verbal Chills," *CFO,* June 2005, p. 17; S. Armour, "Managers Not Prepared for Workplace Violence," July 15, 2004, pp. 1B+; and "Workplace Violence," OSHA Fact Sheet, U.S. Department of Labor, Occupational Safety and Health Administration, 2002.

63. "Ten Tips on Recognizing and Minimizing Violence," *Workforce Online,* www.workforce.com, December 3, 2000.

64. "Bullying Bosses Cause Work Rage Rise," *Management Issues News,* www.management-issues.com, January 28, 2003.

65. R. McNatt, "Desk Rage," *BusinessWeek,* November 27, 2000, p. 12.

66. M. Gorkin, "Key Components of a Dangerously Dysfunctional Work Environment," *Workforce Online,* www.workforce.com, December 3, 2000.

67. "Ten Tips on Recognizing and Minimizing Violence"; M. Gorkin, "Five Strategies and Structures for Reducing Workplace Violence"; "Investigating Workplace Violence: Where Do You Start?"; and "Points to Cover in a Workplace Violence Policy," all articles from *Workforce Online* www.workforce.com, December 3, 2000.

68. A. Taylor, "Enterprise Asks What Customer's Thinking and Acts," *USA Today,* May 22, 2006, p. 6B; and A. Taylor, "Driving Customer Satisfaction," *Harvard Business Review,* July 2002, pp. 24–25.

69. S. D. Pugh, J. Dietz, J. W. Wiley, and S. M. Brooks, "Driving Service Effectiveness Through Employee–Customer Linkages," *Academy of Management Executive,* November 2002, pp. 73–84.

70. T. Buck and A. Shahrim, "The Translation of Corporate Governance Changes Across National Cultures: The Case of Germany," *Journal of International Business Studies,* January 2005, pp. 42–61; and "A Revolution Where Everyone Wins: Worldwide Movement to Improve Corporate-Governance Standards," *BusinessWeek,* May 19, 2003, p. 72.

71. J. S. McClenahen, "Executives Expect More Board Input," *Industry Week,* October 2002, p. 12.

72. D. Salierno, "Boards Face Increased Responsibility," *Internal Auditor,* June 2003, pp. 14–15.

73. Situation adapted from information in Lindsey Gerdes, "You Have 20 Minutes to Surf. Go," *BusinessWeek,* December 26, 2005, p. 16; Jared Sandberg, "Monitoring of Workers Is Boss's Right But Why Not Include Top Brass?" *Wall Street Journal,* May 18, 2005, p. B1; Karl Cushing, "E-Mail Policy," *Computer Weekly,* June 24, 2003, p. 8; "Spam Leads to Lawsuit Fears, Lost Time," *InternetWeek,* www.internetweek.com, June 23, 2003.

## Chapter 19

1. Information from Sepomex Web site, www.sepomex.gob.mx, February 24, 2006; and A. Guthrie, "Going Postal," *Latin Trade,* July 2005, pp. 84–85.

2. D. Clark, "Inside Intel, It's All Copying," *Wall Street Journal,* October 28, 2002, pp. B1+.

3. D. McGinn, "Faster Food," *Newsweek,* April 19, 2004, pp. E20–E22.

4. *World Fact Book 2006,* available online at www.odci.gov/cia/publications.

5. Ibid.

6. D. Michaels and J. L. Lunsford, "Streamlined Plane Making," *Wall Street Journal,* April 1, 2005, pp. B1+.

7. T. Aeppel, "Workers Not Included," *Wall Street Journal,* November 19, 2002, pp. B1+.

8. A. Aston and M. Arndt, "The Flexible Factory," *BusinessWeek,* May 5, 2003, pp. 90–91.

9. P. Panchak, "Pella Drives Lean Throughout the Enterprise," *Industry Week,* June 2003, pp. 74–77.

10. J. Ordonez, "McDonald's to Cut the Cooking Time of Its French Fries," *Wall Street Journal,* May 19, 2000, p. B2.

11. C. Fredman, "The Devil in the Details," *Executive Edge,* April–May, 1999, pp. 36–39.

12. Information from company Web site, www.skoda-auto.com, May 30, 2006; and T. Mudd, "The Last Laugh," *Industry Week,* September 18, 2000, pp. 38–44.

13. T. Vinas, "Little Things Mean a Lot," *Industry Week,* November 2002, p. 55.

14. P. Panchak, "Shaping the Future of Manufacturing," *Industry Week,* January 2005, pp. 38–44; M. Hammer, "Deep Change: How Operational Innovation Can Transform Your Company," *Harvard Business Review,* April 2004, pp. 84–94; S. Levy, "The Connected Company," *Newsweek,* April 28, 2003, pp. 40–48; and J. Teresko, "Plant Floor Strategy," *Industry Week,* July 2002, pp. 26–32.

15. T. Laseter, K. Ramdas, and D. Swerdlow, "The Supply Side of Design and Development," *Strategy & Business,* Summer 2003, p. 23; J. Jusko, "Not All Dollars and Cents," *Industry Week,* April 2002, p. 58; and D. Drickhamer, "Medical Marvel," *Industry Week,* March 2002, pp. 47–49.

16. J. H. Sheridan, "Managing the Value Chain," *Industry Week,* September 6, 1999, pp. 1–4, available online at www.industryweek.com.

17. Ibid, p. 3.

18. J. Teresko, "Forward, March!" *Industry Week,* July 2004, pp. 43–48; D. Sharma, C. Lucier, and R. Molloy, "From Solutions to Symbiosis: Blending with Your Customers," *Strategy & Business,* Second Quarter 2002, pp. 38–48; and S. Leibs, "Getting Ready: Your Suppliers," *Industry Week,* September 6, 1999, available online at www.industryweek.com.

19. D. Bartholomew, "The Infrastructure," *Industry Week,* September 6, 1999, p. 1, available online at www.industryweek.com.

20. T. Stevens, "Integrated Product Development," *Industry Week,* June 2002, pp. 21–28.

21. R. Normann and R. Ramirez, "From Value Chain to Value Constellation," *Harvard Business Review on Managing the Value Chain* (Boston, MA: Harvard Business School Press, 2000), pp. 185–219.

22. J. Teresko, "The Tough Get Going," *Industry Week,* March 2005, pp. 25–32; D. M. Lambert and A. M. Knemeyer, "We're in This Together," *Harvard Business Review,* December 2004, pp. 114–122; and V. G. Narayanan and A. Raman, "Aligning Incentives in Supply Chains," *Harvard Business Review,* November 2004, pp. 94–102.

23. D. Drickhamer, "Looking for Value," *Industry Week,* December 2002, pp. 41–43.

24. J. Teresko, "Tying IT Assets to Process Success," *Industry Week,* September 2005, p. 21.

25. J. H. Sheridan, "Managing the Value Chain," p. 3.

26. S. Leibs, "Getting Ready: Your Customers," *Industry Week,* September 6, 1999, p. 1, available online at www.industryweek.com.

27. G. Taninecz, "Forging the Chain," *Industry Week,* May 15, 2000, pp. 40–46.

28. S. Leibs, "Getting Ready: Your Customers."

29. Information in this box from J. McPartlin, "Making Waves," *CFO-IT,* Spring 2005, pp. 32–37.

30. T. Vinas, "A Map of the World: IW Value-Chain Survey," *Industry Week,* September 2005, pp. 27–34.

31. "Top Security Threats and Management Issues Facing Corporate America: 2003 Survey of *Fortune* 1000 Companies," ASIS International and Pinkerton, available at www.asisonline.org.

32. J. H. Sheridan, "Managing the Value Chain," p. 4.

33. R. Russell and B. W. Taylor, *Operations Management,* 5e (New York: Wiley, 2005); C. Liu-Lien Tan, "U.S. Response: Speedier Delivery," *Wall Street Journal,* November 18, 2004, pp. D1+; and C. Salter, "When Couches Fly," *Fast Company,* July 2004, pp. 80–81.

34. S. Anderson, The Associated Press, "Restaurants Gear Up for Window Wars," *Springfield News-Leader,* January 27, 2006, p. 5B.

35. D. Bartholomew, "Quality Takes a Beating," *Industry Week,* March 2006, pp. 46–54; J. Carey and M. Arndt, "Making Pills the Smart Way," *BusinessWeek,* May 3, 2004, pp. 102–103; and A. Barrett, "Schering's Dr. Feelbetter?" *BusinessWeek,* June 23, 2003, pp. 55–56.

36. T. Vinas, "Six Sigma Rescue," *Industry Week,* March 2004, p. 12.

37. J. S. McClenahen, "Prairie Home Champion," *Industry Week,* October 2005, pp. 45–46.

38. T. Vinas, "Zeroing In on the Customer," *Industry Week,* October 2004, pp. 61–62.

39. W. Royal, "Spotlight Shines on Maquiladora," *Industry Week,* October 16, 2000, pp. 91–92.

40. See B. Whitford and R. Andrew (eds.), *The Pursuit of Quality* (Perth: Beaumont Publishing, 1994).

41. D. Drickhamer, "Road to Excellence," *Industry Week,* October 16, 2000, pp. 117–118.

42. *ISO Survey of Certifications 2004,* September 15, 2005, available at www.iso.org.

43. G. Hasek, "Merger Marries Quality Efforts," *Industry Week,* August 21, 2000, pp. 89–92.

44. M. Arndt, "Quality Isn't Just for Widgets," *BusinessWeek,* July 22, 2002, pp. 72–73.

45. E. White, "Rethinking the Quality-Improvement Program," *Wall Street Journal,* September 19, 2005, p. B3.

46. M. Arndt, "Quality Isn't Just for Widgets."

47. S. McMurray, "Ford's F-150: Have It Your Way," *Business 2.0,* March 2004, pp. 53–55; "Made-to-Fit Clothes Are on the Way," *USA Today,* July 2002, pp. 8–9; and L. Elliott, "Mass Customization Comes a Step Closer," *Design News,* February 18, 2002, p. 21.

48. E. Schonfeld, "The Customized, Digitized, Have-it-Your-Way Economy," *Fortune,* October 28, 1998, pp. 114–120.

49. Situation adapted from information in Barry Meier, "Heart Device Makers Plan Enhanced Safety Reviews," *New York Times,* May 16, 2006, p. C3; "Anatomy of a Flawed Company," *New York Times,* April 1, 2006, p. A14; Barry Meier, "Internal Turmoil at Device Maker As Inquiry Grew," *New York Times,* February 28, 2006, p. A1; and "When Medical Devices Fail," *New York Times,* May 1, 2006, p. A18.

**Notes for the Part 6 Continuing Case**

A. Serwer and K. Bonamici, "Hot Starbucks to Go," *Fortune,* January 26, 2004, pp. 60–74; Interview with Jim Donald, *Smart Money,* May 2006, pp. 31–32; A. Serwer, "Interview with Howard Schultz," *Fortune (Europe),* March 20, 2006, pp. 35–36; W. Meyers, "Conscience in a Cup of Coffee," *US News & World Report,* October 31, 2005, pp. 48–50; S. Gray, "Fill 'er Up—With Latte," *Wall Street Journal,* January 6, 2006, pp. A9+; P. Kafka, "Bean Counter," *Forbes,* February 28, 2005, pp. 78–80; J. Schnack, L. Adamson, S. Brull, L. Conger, P. Paulden, and J. Sutherland, "Starbucks Shells Out to Safeguard Schultz," *Institutional Investor,* January 2006, p. 11; R. Ruggless, "Starbucks Exec: Security from Employee Theft Important When Implementing Gift Card Strategies," *Nation's Restaurant News,* December 12, 2005, p. 24; R. Ruggless, "Transaction Monitoring Boosts Safety, Perks Up Coffee Chain Profits," *Nation's Restaurant News,* November 28, 2005, p. 35; Standards of Business Conduct, Starbucks Web site [www.starbucks.com].

**Appendix A**

1. S. Berfield, "Hip-Hop Nation," *BusinessWeek,* June 13, 2005, p. 12; R. Kurtz, "Russell Simmons, Rush Communications," *Inc.,* April 2004, p. 137; J. Reingold, "Rush Hour," *Fast Company,* November 2003, pp. 68–80; S. Berfield, "The CEO of Hip Hop," *BusinessWeek,* October 27, 2003, pp. 90–98; J. L. Roberts, "Beyond Definition," *Newsweek,* July 28, 2003, pp. 40–43; and C. Dugas, "Hip-hop Legend Far Surpassed Financial Goals," *USA Today,* May 15, 2003, p. 6B.

2. P. Burrows, "Ringing Off the Hook in China," *BusinessWeek,* June 9, 2003, pp. 80–82.

3. J. W. Carland, F. Hoy, W. R. Boulton, and J. C. Carland, "Differentiating Entrepreneurs from Small Business Owners: A Conceptualization," *Academy of Management Review,* Vol. 9, No. 2, 1984, pp. 354–359.

4. J. McDowell, "Small Business Continues to Drive U.S. Economy," Office of Advocacy, U.S. Small Business Administration, October 3, 2005, www.sba.gov/advo/press.

5. P. Almeida and B. Kogut, "The Exploration of Technological Diversity and Geographic Localization in Innovation: Start-Up Firms in the Semiconductor Industry," *Small Business Economics,* vol. 9, (1), 1997, pp. 21–31.

6. R. J. Arend, "Emergence of Entrepreneurs Following Exogenous Technological Change," *Strategic Management Journal,* vol. 20, (1), 1999, pp. 31–47.

7. J. McDowell, "New Study Confirms Small Businesses' Power as Innovators," Office of Advocacy, February 2003, available online at www.sba.gov/advo.

8. "Frequently Asked Questions—Advocacy Small Business Statistics and Research—2005," U.S. Small Business Administration, www.sba.gov/faqs, July 13, 2006.

9. Ibid.

10. M. Minnitti, W. D. Bygrave, and E. Autio, "Global Entrepreneurship Monitor: 2005 Executive Report," www.gemconsortium.org, p. 14.

11. P. F. Drucker, *Innovation and Entrepreneurship: Practice and Principles,* (New York: Harper & Row, 1985).

12. W. Royal, "Real Expectations," *Industry Week,* September 4, 2000, pp. 31–34.

13. "Creating a Sustainable Business Among South Africa's Poor "One Bite at a Time," *Knowledge @ Wharton,* http://knowledge.wharton.upenn.edu, July 13, 2006.

14. T. Purdum, "25 Growing Companies," *Industry Week,* November 20, 2000, p. 82.

15. C. Sandlund, "Trust is a Must," *Entrepreneur,* October 2002, pp. 70–75.

16. B. I. Koerner, "Cereal in the Bowl, Not on the Floor," *New York Times Online,* www.nytimes.com, June 18, 2006.

17. "Facts for Features," *U.S. Census Bureau Newsroom,* January 3, 2006; and M. Arndt, "Zimmer: Growing Older Gracefully," *BusinessWeek,* June 9, 2003, pp. 82–84.

18. G. B. Knight, "How Wall Street Whiz Found a Niche Selling Books on the Internet," *Wall Street Journal,* May 15, 1996, pp. A1+.

19. N. F. Krueger, Jr., "The Cognitive Infrastructure of Opportunity Emergence," *Entrepreneurship Theory and Practice,* Spring 2000, p. 6.

20. D. P. Forbes, "Managerial Determinants of Decision Speed in New Ventures," *Strategic Management Journal,* April 2005, pp. 355–366.

21. P. Drucker, *Innovation and Entrepreneurship,* (New York: Harper & Row, 1985).

22. G. Bounds, "Hybrids Fuel Agency's Fast Ride," *Wall Street Journal,* July 11, 2006, pp. B1+.

23. B. Bergstein, The Associated Press, "RSA Security Finds Future in Threat of Identity Theft," *Springfield News-Leader,* August 22, 2005, p. 5B.

24. B. McClean, "This Entrepreneur Is Changing Underwear," *Fortune*, September 18, 2000, p. 60.

25. S. Schubert, "The Ultimate Music Buff," *Business 2.0,* March 2006, p. 64.

26. Latest figures on registered users from Hoover's Online www.hoovers.com, July 13, 2006; and A. Cohen, "eBay's Bid to Conquer All," *Time*, February 5, 2001, pp. 48–51.

27. S. McFarland, "Cambodia's Internet Service Is in Kids' Hands," *Wall Street Journal*, May 15, 2000, p. A9A.

28. Information on Whole Foods Market from Hoovers Online, www.hoovers.com, July 13, 2006.

29. D. Fahmy, "Making Necessities Stylish and Getting a Higher Price," *New York Times Online,* www.nytimes.com, March 9, 2006.

30. A. Eisenberg, "What's Next: New Fabrics Can Keep Wearers Healthy and Smelling Good," *New York Times*, February 3, 2000, pp. D1+.

31. A. Morse, "An Entrepreneur Finds Tokyo Shares Her Passion for Bagels," *Wall Street Journal,* October 18, 2005, pp. B1+.

32. S. Greco, "The Start-Up Years," *Inc. 500*, October 21, 1997, p. 57.

33. T. Stevens, "Master of His Universe," *Industry Week*, January 15, 2001, pp. 76–80; and R. Grover, "Back from a Black Hole," *BusinessWeek*, May 29, 2000, p. 186.

34. E. Neuborne, "Hey, Good-Looking," *BusinessWeek*, May 29, 2000, p. 192.

35. A. Barrett, B. Turek, and C. Faivre d'Arcier, "Bottoms Up—and Profits, Too," *BusinessWeek,* September 12, 2005, pp. 80–82; and C. Hajim, "Growth in Surprising Places," *Fortune,* September 5, 2005, bonus section.

36. J. Hovey, "25 Growing Companies," *Industry Week*, November 20, 2000, p. 66.

37. I. O. Williamson, "Employer Legitimacy and Recruitment Success in Small Businesses," *Entrepreneurship Theory and Practice*, Fall 2000, pp. 27–42.

38. R. L. Heneman, J. W. Tansky, and S. M. Camp, "Human Resource Management Practices in Small and Medium-Sized Enterprises: Unanswered Questions and Future Research Perspectives," *Entrepreneurship Theory and Practice*, Fall 2000, pp. 11–26.

39. Ibid.

40. "Best Employer," *Working Woman*, May 1999, p. 54.

41. Heneman, Tansky, and Camp, "Human Resource Management Practices in Small and Medium-Sized Enterprises: Unanswered Questions and Future Research Perspectives."

42. Based on G. Fuchsberg, "Small Firms Struggle With Latest Management Trends," *Wall Street Journal*, August 26, 1993, p. B2; M. Barrier, "Re-engineering Your Company," *Nation's Business*, February 1994, pp. 16–22; J. Weiss, "Re-engineering the Small Business," *Small Business Reports*, May 1994, pp. 37–43; and K. D. Godsey, "Back on Track," *Success*, May 1997, pp. 52–54.

43. S. Stecklow, "StubHub's Ticket to Ride," *Wall Street Journal,* January 17, 2006, pp. B1+.

44. G. N. Chandler, C. Keller, and D. W. Lyon, "Unraveling the Determinants and Consequences of an Innovation-Supportive Organizational Culture," *Entrepreneurship Theory and Practice*, Fall 2000, pp. 59–76.

45. Ibid.

46. P. Gogoi, "Pregnant with Possibility," *BusinessWeek*, December 26, 2005, p. 50.

47. P. B. Robinson, D. V. Simpson, J. C. Huefner, and H. K. Hunt, "An Attitude Approach to the Prediction of Entrepreneurship," *Entrepreneurship Theory and Practice*, Summer 1991, pp. 13–31.

48. B. M. Davis, "Role of Venture Capital in the Economic Renaissance of an Area," in R. D. Hisrich (ed.), *Entrepreneurship, Intrapreneurship, and Venture Capital,* Lexington, MA: Lexington Books, 1986, pp. 107–18.

49. J. M. Crant, "The Proactive Personality Scale as Predictor of Entrepreneurial Intentions," *Journal of Small Business Management*, July 1996, pp. 42–49.

50. W. H. Stewart, "Risk Propensity Differences between Entrepreneurs and Managers: A Meta-Analytic Review," *Journal of Applied Psychology*, February 2001, pp. 145–153.

51. Information from company's Web site www.sapient.com, July 7, 2003; and S. Herrera, "People Power," *Forbes*, November 2, 1998, p. 212.

52. "Saluting the Global Awards Recipients of Arthur Andersen's Best Practices Awards 2000," *Fortune Online*, www.fortune.com, January 16, 2001.

53. T. Purdum, "Winning with Empowerment," *Industry Week*, October 16, 2000, pp. 109–110.

54. Company financial information from Hoover's Online www.hoovers.com, July 13, 2006; and P. Strozniak, "Rescue Operation," *Industry Week*, October 16, 2000, pp. 103–104.

55. M. DePree, *Leadership Jazz*, New York: Currency Doubleday, 1992, pp. 8–9.

56. J. C. Collins and J. I. Porras, *Built to Last: Successful Habits of Visionary Companies,* New York: Harper-Business, 1994.

57. P. Strozniak, "Teams at Work," *Industry Week*, September 18, 2000, pp. 47–50.

58. Ibid.

59. T. Siegel Bernard, "Scooter's Popularity Offers A Chance for Growth," *Wall Street Journal,* September 20, 2005, p. B3.

60. G. R. Merz, P. B. Weber, and V. B. Laetz, "Linking Small Business Management with Entrepreneurial Growth,"

*Journal of Small Business Management*, October 1994, pp. 48–60.

61. J. Bailey, "Growth Needs a Plan or Only Losses May Build," *Wall Street Journal,* October 29, 2002, p. B9; and L. Beresford, "Growing Up," *Entrepreneur*, July 1995, pp. 124–28.

62. R. D. Hof, "EBay's Rhine Gold," *BusinessWeek,* April 3, 2006, pp. 44–45.

63. J. Summer, "More, Please!" *Business Finance,* July 2000, pp. 57–61.

64. T. Stevens, "Pedal Pushers," *Industry Week*, July 17, 2000, pp. 46–52.

65. P. Lorange and R. T. Nelson, "How to Recognize—and Avoid—Organizational Decline," *Sloan Management Review*, Spring 1987, pp. 41–48.

66. S. D. Chowdhury and J. R. Lange, "Crisis, Decline, and Turnaround: A Test of Competing Hypotheses for Short–Term Performance Improvement in Small Firms," *Journal of Small Business Management*, October 1993, pp. 8–17.

67. C. Farrell, "How to Survive a Downturn," *BusinessWeek*, April 28, 1997, pp. ENT4-ENT6.

68. R. W. Pricer and A. C. Johnson, "The Accuracy of Valuation Methods in Predicting the Selling Price of Small Firms," *Journal of Small Business Management*, October 1997, pp. 24–35.

69. J. Bailey, "Selling the Firm and Letting Go of the Dream," *Wall Street Journal,* December 10, 2002, p. B6; P. Hernan, "Finding the Exit," *Industry Week,* July 17, 2000, pp. 55–61; D. Rodkin, "For Sale by Owner," *Entrepreneur*, January 1998, pp. 148–53; A. Livingston, "Avoiding Pitfalls When Selling a Business," *Nation's Business*, July 1998, pp. 25–26; and G. Gibbs Marullo, "Selling Your Business: A Preview of the Process," *Nation's Business*, August 1998, pp. 25–26.

70. K. Stringer, "Time Out," *Wall Street Journal,* March 27, 2002, p. R14; T. Stevens, "Striking a Balance," *Industry Week*, November 20, 2000, pp. 26–36; and S. Caudron, "Fit to Lead," *Industry Week*, July 17, 2000, pp. 63–68.

# Photo Credits

# Name Index

# Organization Index

# Glindex

organizational behavior, 36–37, 36E2-5
quantitative approach, 34–35
scientific management, 30–32
systems approach, 38, 38E2-6
**Manager** *Someone who coordinates and oversees the work of other people so that organizational goals can be accomplished,* 4, 5
becoming, 21
challenges of, dealing with, 414–415
importance of, 5, 10
nonmanagerial duties of, 5
and nonmanagerial employees, differences in, 4
skills required of, 5, 194
**Managerial grid** *A grid of two leadership behaviors—concern for people and concern for production—which resulted in five different leadership styles,* 492–493, 492E17-3
Mann Gulch fire, 176
**Manufacturing organizations** *Organizations that produce physical goods,* 565
**Market control** *An approach to control that emphasizes the use of external market mechanisms to establish the control standards* 527
**Market economy** *An economic system in which resources are primarily owned and controlled by the private sector,* 102, 103
**Mass customization** *Providing consumers with a product when, where, and how they want it,* 580–581
**Mass production** *The production of items in large batches,* 277
Material symbols, of organization's personality, 66
**Matrix structure** *An organizational structure that assigns specialists from different functional departments to work on one or more projects,* 280–281, 281E10-9
Maximax choice, 168–170
Maximin choice, 168–170
MBTI®, 399, 399E14-3
Meaning, transfer and understanding of, 292
**Means-ends chain** *An integrated network of goals in which the accomplishment of goals at one level serves as the means for achieving the goals, or ends, at the next level,* 192, 193
**Mechanistic organization** *An organizational design that's rigid and tightly controlled,* 275, 275E10-5
"Melting pot" approach, 44
**Message** *A purpose to be conveyed,* 294, 295
Microchronometer, 31
**Microfinance** *The lending of small sums to poor people who would otherwise be shut out of access to capital,* 183
**Middle managers** *Managers between the first level and the top level of the organization who manage the work of first-line managers,* 6, 7
titles of, 6
Minimax choice, 169–170
Mintzberg's role categories, 9, 10, 11E1-4, 429

Mirror manufacturing, 52–53
**Mission** *A statement of the purpose of an organization,* 195, 210–211
components of, 211, 211E8-2
Modular organization, 282
Monolingualism, 91
**Motivation** *The process by which a person's efforts are energized, directed, and sustained towards attaining a goal,* 452–453
contemporary theories of, 456–468
current issues in, 468–476
early theories of, 453–456
**Motivators** *Factors that increase job satisfaction and motivation,* 455
**Multidomestic corporation** *An international company that decentralizes management and other decisions to the local country,* 97–98, 100
**Multinational corporations (MNCs)** *A broad term that refers to any and all types of international companies that maintain operations in multiple countries,* 97–98
**Multiperson comparisons** *Appraising performance by comparing it with others' performance,* 338
Multivariable testing, 250
Mutual funds, social responsibility in, 121–122
MVA (market value added), 541

**N**

**National culture** *The values and attitudes shared by individuals from a specific country that shape their behavior and beliefs about what is important,* 103
dimensional differences in, identified by GLOBE research, 106–107, 107E4-8
dimensions of, 105
Nature resource depletion, 123
**Need for achievement (nAch)** *The drive to excel, to achieve in relation to a set of standards, and to strive to succeed,* 457, 457E16-4
**Need for affiliation (nAff)** *The desire for friendly and close interpersonal relationships,* 457, 457E16-4
**Need for power (nPow)** *The need to make others behave in a way that they would not have behaved otherwise,* 457, 457E16-4
**Network organization** *An organization that uses its own employees to do some work activities and networks of outside suppliers to provide other needed product components or work processes,* 282
**Noise** *Any disturbances that interfere with the transmission, receipt, or feedback of a message,* 294–295
**Nonmanagerial employees** *Organizational members who worked directly on a job or task and had no one reporting to them*
managerial activities of, 4–5
**Nonprogrammed decisions** *A unique decision that requires a custom-made solution,* 166, 167
*vs.* programmed decisions, 166–167, 167E6-8

**Nonverbal communication** *Communication transmitted without words,* 298
**Norming** *The third stage of group development, which is characterized by close relationships and cohesiveness,* 425
**Norms** *Standards or expectations that are accepted and shared by a group's members,* 429–430
**North American Free Trade Agreement (NAFTA)** *An agreement among the Mexican, Canadian, and U.S. governments in which barriers to trade have been eliminated,* 94, 95, 110
Nurturing *vs.* achievement, 105, 106

**O**

Objective function, 251
Office politics, 505
The Ohio State Studies, 491
**Omnipotent view of management** *The view that managers are directly responsible for an organization's success,* 58, 59
100 Most Sustainable Corporations in the World (Global 100), 125
**Open-book management** *A motivational approach in which an organization's financial statements (the "books") are shared with all employees,* 473
**Open systems** *Systems that interact with their environment,* 38, 39, 39E2-6
**Operant conditioning** *A type of learning in which desired voluntary behavior leads to a reward or prevents a punishment,* 409–410
**Operational plans** *Plans that specify the details of how the overall goals are to be achieved,* 189
**Operations management** *The design, operation, and control of the transformation process that converts resources into finished goods or services,* 564–581, 564E19-1. See also value chain management
quality initiatives, 576–579, 578E19-5
services and manufacturing, 565
strategic role of, 567
technology's role in, 575–576
**Organic organization** *An organizational design that's highly adaptive and flexible,* 275, 275E10-5
**Organization** *A deliberate arrangement of people to accomplish some specific purpose,* 17–18, 371, 371E13-8
changing concept of, 18, 18E1-10
characteristics of, 17–18, 17E1-9
**Organizational behavior (OB)** *The field of study concerned with the actions (behavior) of people at work,* 36–37, 37E2-5
advocates of, early, 36, 37E2-5
aspects of, 388E14-1
contemporary issues in, 413–415
focus of, 388–389
goals of, 389–390
Hawthorne Studies, 36–37, 391
individual behavior and, 388–389
use of today, by managers, 37
**Organizational change** *Any alteration of people, structure, or technology in an organization,* 360–366

Role conflict, 429
Romance, in the workplace, 344–345
**Rule** *An explicit statement that tells managers what they can or cannot do,* 165
Rule of three, 225–226
Rules of thumb. *See* heuristics
Rumors, 306

**S**

**Safety needs** *A person's needs for security and protection from physical and emotional harm,* 453
Sales, under/overstating, 532
Sarbanes-Oxley Act, 138, 542, 554, 555
SARS (sudden acute respiratory syndrome), 204, 308
**Satisficing** *Acceptance of solutions that are "good enough,"* 163
**Scenario** *A consistent view of what the future is likely to be,* 245–255
**Scheduling** *Detailing what activities have to be done, the order in which they are to be completed, who is to do each, and when they are to be completed,* 245–249. *See also* PERT network
Gantt charts, 246, 246E9-5
load charts, 246–247, 247E9-6
**Scientific management** *Using the scientific method to determine the "one best way" for a job to be done,* 30–32
Scientific research, 230
**Selection** *Screening job applicants to ensure that the most appropriate candidates are hired,* 328–333
decision outcomes, 329E12-6
devices for, types of, 330–332, 331E12-7, 333E12-10
hiring errors, 328–329
realistic job preview (RJP), 333, 333E12-10
validity and reliability in, 330–331
workforce diversity and, 343
Selective perception bias, 173
**Self-actualization needs** *A person's need to become what he or she is capable of becoming,* 453
**Self-efficacy** *An individual's belief that he or she is capable of performing a task,* 459
**Self-esteem** *An individual's degree of like or dislike for himself or herself,* 400–401
**Self-managed work team** *A type of work team that operates without a manager and is responsible for a complete work process or segment,* 439–440
**Self-monitoring** *An individual's ability to adjust his or her behavior to external situational factors,* 401
**Self-serving bias** *The tendency for individuals to attribute their own successes to internal factors while putting the blame for failures on external factors,* 173, 408
September 11, 2001, 90, 255, 308, 405
Service jobs, 15–16
**Service organizations** *Organizations that produce nonphysical outputs in the form of services,* 565
**Service profit chain** *The service sequence from employees to customers to profit,* 552–553, 553E18-16

*The 7 Habits of Highly Effective People* (Covey), 86
**Sexual harassment** *Any unwanted action or activity of a sexual nature that explicitly or implicitly affects an individual's employment, performance, or work environment,* 344–345, 548
**Shaping behavior** *Systematically reinforcing each successive step to move an individual closer to the desired behavior,* 411–412
Short-term orientation, 105, 106
**Short-term plans** *Plans covering 1 year or less,* 189–190
Silent or nonresponsive personality types, 410
**Simple structure** *An organizational design with low departmentalization, wide spans of control, centralized authority, and little formalization,* 278
**Single-use plan** *A one-time plan specifically designed to meet the needs of a unique situation,* 190–191
**Situational approach.** *See* contingency approach
**Situational leadership theory (SLT)** *A leadership contingency theory that focuses on followers' readiness,* 496–497, 496E17-5
**Six Sigma** *A quality standard that establishes a goal of no more than 3.4 defects per million parts or procedures,* 579, 580
**Skill-based pay** *A pay system that rewards employees for the job skills they can demonstrate,* 339–340
**Skill variety** *The degree to which a job requires a variety of activities so that an employee can use a number of different skills and talent,* 462
**Slack time** *The amount of time an individual activity can be delayed without delaying the whole project,* 247
**Social entrepreneur** *An individual or organization who seeks out opportunities to improve society by using practical, innovative, and sustainable approaches,* 142, 143
**Social impact management** *An approach to managing in which managers examine the social impacts of their decisions and actions,* 143
Social involvement, and economic performance, 120–122
Social irresponsibility and ethical lapses, managing, 139–142
**Socialization** *The process that helps employees adapt to the organization's culture,* 64, 65
**Social learning theory** *A learning theory that says people learn through observation and direct experience,* 411
**Social loafing** *The tendency for individuals to expend less effort when working collectively than when working individually,* 432
**Social needs** *A person's needs for affection, belongingness, acceptance, and friendship,* 453
**Social network structure** *The patterns of informal connections among individuals within a group,* 444

**Social obligation** *When a firm engages in social actions because of its obligation to meet certain economic and legal responsibilities,* 119, 120
**Social responsibility** *A business's intention, beyond its legal and economic obligations, to do the right things and act in ways that are good for society,* 116–120
arguments for and against, 118, 118E5-2
economic performance and, 120–121
in mutual funds, 121–122
progression, four stage model of, 117–118, 117E5-1
social obligation and, 119, 120
social responsiveness and, 119, 120, 120E5-3
views of, 116–118
**Social responsiveness** *When a firm engages in social actions in response to some popular need,* 119, 120
**Social screening** *Applying social criteria (screens) to investment decisions,* 121–122
Sociocultural conditions, 76–77
**Socioeconomic view, of social responsibility** *The view that management's social responsibility goes beyond making profits to include protecting and improving society's welfare,* 116–118
South Asian Association for Regional Cooperation (SAARC), 96, 110
Spam, 311
**Span of control** *The number of employees a manager can efficiently and effectively manage,* 270–271, 271E10-3
**Specific environment** *Those external forces that have a direct impact on managers' decisions and actions and are directly relevant to the achievement of the organization's goals,* 74–76
competitors, 75
customers, 74
pressure groups, 75–76
suppliers, 74–75
**Specific plans** *Plans that are clearly defined and that leave no room for interpretation,* 190, 190E7-3
**Stability strategy** *A corporate strategy characterized by an absence of significant change in what the organization is currently doing,* 219
Stable environment, 79
Stakeholder relationships, management of, 80–82
ethically questionable behavior and, 86
importance of, 81
steps in, 81–82
**Stakeholders** *Any constituencies in the organization's environment that are affected by the organization's decisions and actions,* 80–81
influence of, 80
types of, 81E3-12
**Standing plans** *Ongoing plans that provide guidance for activities performed repeatedly,* 190–191
Star businesses, 221